UNITED STATES ARMY IN WORLD WAR II
Kent Roberts Greenfield, General Editor

Advisory Committee
(As of 31 March 1954)

James P. Baxter	Brig. Gen. Verdi B. Barnes
President, Williams College	Army War College
John D. Hicks	Brig. Gen. Leonard J. Greeley
University of California	Industrial College of the Armed Forces
William T. Hutchinson	Brig. Gen. Elwyn D. Post
University of Chicago	Army Field Forces
S. L. A. Marshall	Col. Thomas D. Stamps
Detroit News	United States Military Academy
Charles S. Sydnor*	Col. C. E. Beauchamp
Duke University	Command and General Staff College

Charles H. Taylor
Harvard University

Office of the Chief of Military History
Maj. Gen. Albert C. Smith, Chief**

Chief Historian	Kent Roberts Greenfield
Chief, War Histories Division	Col. George G. O'Connor
Chief, Editorial and Publication Division	Lt. Col. Thomas E. Bennett
Chief, Editorial Branch	Joseph R. Friedman
Chief, Cartographic Branch	Wsevolod Aglaimoff
Chief, Photographic Branch	Maj. Arthur T. Lawry

* Deceased.
** Maj. Gen. Orlando Ward was succeeded by General Smith on 1 February 1953.

Francis A. Drexel
LIBRARY

Books For College Libraries
Third Edition

Core Collection

SAINT JOSEPH'S UNIVERSITY

UNITED STATES ARMY IN WORLD WAR II

The War Department

GLOBAL LOGISTICS
AND STRATEGY

1940–1943

by

Richard M. Leighton

and

Robert W. Coakley

MILITARY INSTRVCTION

CENTER OF MILITARY HISTORY

UNITED STATES ARMY

WASHINGTON, D.C., 1995

Library of Congress Catalog Number: 55–60001

First Printed 1955—CMH Pub 1–5

For sale by the U.S. Government Printing Office
Superintendent of Documents, Mail Stop: SSOP, Washington, D.C. 20402

. . . to Those Who Served

Foreword

The present volume, and its successor, depict a massive achievement: the performance by the Army of the task of effecting the orderly assembly, movement, and delivery of great masses of men and matériel throughout the world to meet not only American requirements but also those of the other nations fighting the Axis. The authors show how the demands of this task affected American strategy and how it reacted on the shape and mission of the Army.

These volumes present the outlook of the War Department as a whole on this task, rather than that of any one agency or command of the Army. Two other volumes in the same subseries will deal with the Army's procurement of munitions and supplies from that standpoint. The rest of the logistical story will be told in volumes on the Army Service Forces, the seven technical services, and the theaters of operations.

Logistical tasks account in large measure for the enormous administrative machinery that the Army developed in the course of the war. Its development, though not a complete surprise, exceeded all anticipations. The demand for service troops seemed insatiable and required repeated revisions of the troop basis. With this went a "proliferation of overhead" in the form of complex controls and higher headquarters that ate up officers needed for the training and leading of fighting troops, drew into the service a multitude of specialists, and confused the chain of command. The trend ran counter to the traditional American belief that the overriding mission of the Army is to fight, a conviction so deep that some commanders, like General McNair, fought to keep the Army lean and simple. In World War II they lost this fight.

Those who fear that administration is supplanting combat as the primary mission of the Army will find much to ponder in this book and its companion volumes.

A. C. SMITH
Major General, USA
Chief, Military History

Washington, D. C.
12 March 1954

The Authors

Richard M. Leighton, who received the degree of Doctor of Philosophy in History from Cornell University, has taught in Brooklyn College, the University of Cincinnati, and George Washington University. During World War II, commissioned in the Quartermaster Corps, he was assigned to the Control Division, Headquarters, Army Service Forces, as a historical officer, and wrote various studies on the organization and administration of that command.

Robert W. Coakley, who has a Ph. D. in History from the University of Virginia, has taught in that university, Tulane University, the University of Arkansas, and the Fairmont State College, West Virginia. After serving as a noncommissioned officer in Headquarters Battery, 927th Field Artillery Battalion, 102d Infantry Division, he became a member of the Historical Division of ETOUSA and USFET and wrote for that office the studies, "Organization and Command in ETO" and "Supply of the Army of Occupation."

Since 1948 the authors have been members of the Logistics Section of this Office. Dr. Leighton is chief of the section.

Preface

The great conflict of 1939–45 was not the first world war (nor even the second), nor was it the first war that drove some of its participants close to the limits of their material resources. But in the combination of these characteristics it brought forth problems, in the technical and administrative spheres, of a degree if not of a kind that was new in the history of warfare. World War II produced, in effect, a new logistics—new in that it was at once interconnected and global. Every local logistical problem was part of a larger whole; none could be settled without consideration of the impact its settlement would have on other local problems, often in a widening circle of repercussions rippling clear around to the other face of the world. As the war itself was global, the logistics of each battle or campaign often had world-wide ramifications, even though the outcome of the operation itself might be purely local in its effects. A handful of landing craft, two or three freighters, a few precious tanks used at one spot might mean a desperate lack somewhere else.

In this volume we have viewed the logistical problems of the U.S. Army in World War II from the point of view that most accentuated their interconnected and global character—the point of view of the high command and staffs in Washington. We have confined ourselves to those large problems that more or less constantly engaged the attention of the high command: transportation across oceans and continents—division of effort and resources in a coalition of sovereign, unequally endowed nations, different in their interests and outlook—co-ordination of logistical support of "joint" operations employing land, sea, and air power in varying admixtures—development of effective planning techniques for anticipating needs in men and matériel long before they emerged—organizational and administrative difficulties attendant upon mobilization and an unprecedented expansion of the nation's military power—the delicate relationships between strategy and logistics, especially in the formulation of strategic plans—the frictions of interagency co-ordination, both within the Military Establishment and between it and the civilian authorities. The most persistent theme is the chronic, pervasive competition for resources—a competition that was scarcely diminished even when the war machine began to pour out those resources with a prodigality the world had never before seen.

This approach has its disadvantages. In looking out from the center at a distant horizon, so to speak, we may have missed some of the hard and humdrum reality of logistics, as many of our readers no doubt experienced it—

ix

perhaps while driving a truck in New Guinea or, on another war front, while inventorying underwear and blankets in a North Carolina warehouse. Of such realities a Yankee friend of ours, learning one day in 1944 that he was about to be transferred from this latter war front to a more active one overseas, scribbled a few exultant verses:

> Shake, shake, oh dust of Charlotte, from my feet!
> Leave off, oh rebel twangings, from my ears;
> Unpackage me, oh package factory,
> That from your ancient war that never ends
> I may go on to this one that today
> Is real . . . .

This reaction was understandable. The "package factory" in North Carolina was unexciting enough, Heaven knows, yet it was indispensable to the "real" war that our friend yearned to see. It was, in fact, one of the realities of the Army's logistical experience that, regrettably, does not figure largely in this book.

In so broad an approach, moreover, certain topical omissions have been unavoidable in the effort to achieve, within the space at our disposal, a reasonable depth of treatment. We have made no attempt to cover the entire potpourri of activities that official usage in recent years has labeled as "logistics." Most of the subject areas here treated only lightly or not at all have been assigned to other volumes in the series—such areas as training, military procurement and manpower, the administration of the Army's establishment in the United States, the internal logistics of overseas theaters, and the detailed aspects of the various specialized commodity and service activities for which the Army's technical services were responsible. We have left to the historians of the Army Air Forces, moreover, the task of treating the logistics of air power. What remains, in general, is a central view of the logistics of ground warfare, heavily accenting supply and transportation, and bounded in space on one side by the factory and depot in the United States, on the other by the overseas port or beachhead. Chronologically, the book covers the prewar mobilization period and the first year and a half of American participation in the war, stopping on the eve of the Washington conference of May 1943. A second volume, now in preparation, will carry the story through to the end of the war.

This is a work of collaboration. Very few chapters are solely the product of one author's labors. With little visible strain upon good nature or friendship, we have freely exchanged criticism and suggestions, editing, substantive data, and even draft segments of chapters, though one or the other of us has undertaken the final writing of each chapter. The general scheme of the book is a joint product. Over all, the division of labor has shaped up approximately as follows: Chapters and sections dealing with Anglo-American strategic planning, ship construction and munitions production, allocation of merchant shipping, landing craft, the Army's supply programs and its machinery for supply and transportation, the Pearl Harbor crisis, the logistical build-up in the British Isles and the North African operation are by Leighton—Introduction, and

Chapters I (in part), II, V, VI (in part), VIII, IX, XII–XIV, XVI, XVII, XXII, XXIII, and XXV–XXVII. Those dealing with foreign aid, the logistical machinery of the joint and combined committee systems and the combined boards, Army-Navy logistical co-ordination, and the war against Japan are by Coakley—Chapters I (in part), III, IV, VI (in part), VII, X, XI, XV, XVIII–XXI, and XXIV.

Our large debt to others can only be sketchily described here. First and most grateful mention goes to Dr. Kent Roberts Greenfield, Chief Historian of the Army and conscientious literary godfather, who has patiently read and meticulously criticized the manuscript at each of its many stages, and through it all has never allowed us to forget—however little our endeavors seemed to justify the hope—that a specialized subject can be made interesting to others besides specialists. Mrs. Susan Frost Parrish not only did much of the basic research for the chapters on the Pacific war, but also made important monographic contributions to those chapters. Similarly, parts of the chapters on the North African operation are based on material prepared in draft by Dr. Mae Link. Mr. Charles Owens, coming late into this project, was yet able to do most of the work of compiling and drafting the charts and tables and to shepherd the manuscript through innumerable proofreadings. To our editor, Miss Mary Ann Bacon, and copy editor, Miss Nancy L. Easterling, for their indefatigable labor in what might be called the logistics of publishing this book, we are eternally grateful. Our statistical data have undergone the vigilant scrutiny of Messrs. Theodore E. Whiting, George R. Powell, and Joseph A. Logan of the Army Comptroller's Office; our photographs were assembled by Miss Margaret E. Tackley; our maps were prepared by Mr. Wsevolod Aglaimoff and his staff, with the exception of the three map-sketches on pages 47, 51, and 720, which were drawn by Miss Muriel Chamberlain of the Government Printing Office. Our massive index is the work of Dr. Rose C. Engelman, who we hope will never again have to undertake such a chore. The task of digging through mountains of administrative records would have been immeasurably more difficult without the cheerful assistance given by Mrs. Hazel E. Ward and other members of the staff of the Departmental Records Branch, AGO, in Alexandria; Mrs. Mary Margaret Gansz Greathouse and Miss Wava Phillips of the General Research Unit, G-3; and the personnel of the Federal Records Depot on Lawrence Avenue, N.E., Washington, D.C. The specific contributions of our colleagues in the Office of Military History, who have all had a direct or indirect influence on the book, have been shown in the footnotes and Bibliographical Note. In particular, we owe much to Mr. Maurice Matloff's special competence in the field of strategic planning. Many others have given generously of their time in reading and criticizing large sections of the manuscript; we would like especially to thank Col. Vincent J. Esposito, Dr. Benjamin H. Williams, Col. George G. O'Connor, Capt. Tracy B. Kittredge, USNR (Ret), Maj. Gen. Orlando Ward (Ret), Dr. John D. Millett, Dr. John Bowditch, Dr. Stetson Conn, Dr. Louis Morton, Lt. Gen. LeRoy Lutes (Ret), Lt. Col. Leo J.

Meyer, Maj. Gen. William M. Goodman (Ret), Brig. Gen. Frank A. Bogart, Maj. Gen. Walter A. Wood, Jr. (Ret), Maj. Gen. Richard C. Moore (Ret), Maj. Gen. Robert W. Grow (Ret), Maj. Gen. Carter B. Magruder, Brig. Gen. William E. Carraway, Col. George A. Lincoln, and Maj. Gen. George H. Olmstead. Members of the Historical Section of the British Cabinet Office have also contributed helpful comments on portions of the manuscript.

31 March 1954   RICHARD M. LEIGHTON
Washington, D. C.   ROBERT W. COAKLEY

Contents

Part Six: The Casablanca Period—Strategic Plans and Logistical Method

Tables

Charts

Maps

Illustrations

The illustrations on pages 218 and 219 are from the U.S. Maritime Commission. All others are from the Department of Defense files.

GLOBAL LOGISTICS
AND STRATEGY

1940–1943

Logistics—The Word and the Thing

Logistics is an ancient word and a still more ancient thing.[1] Like many ancient words, it has meant different things at different times, and the thing itself has been, and still is, often called by other names. Yet the several current usages of the word, in military vocabulary, seem to be of rather recent vintage, probably no earlier than 1838 when Antoine Henri Jomini erected a theory of the art of war upon the trinity—strategy, grand tactics, and logistics.[2] While the word had been used occasionally in military parlance before that time, it apparently had had no single or very specific meaning. Since then its uses have been varied, and for long periods it has fallen into almost complete disuse. Meanwhile, the thing itself (whether we define the word narrowly or broadly) has grown from the comparatively humdrum, routine activity it once was into a very complex "Big Business," embracing a considerable part, some would say the greater part, of all the business of modern war.

The Revolution in Warfare

Jomini's attempt to incorporate into a rational theory of war the miscellaneous noncombatant activities on which armies and navies had always depended in order to live and fight occurred at a time when warfare itself was about to undergo a fundamental transformation. Signs of the impending change had already appeared during the long period of almost continuous warfare in Europe from 1792 to 1815—most conspicuously, a tremendous increase in mobility and the range of movement of armies, made possible by improved roads and the growing productivity of agriculture. Jomini himself, though most impressed by the tactical symptoms

---

[1] The original derivation of the word "logistics" was Greek, from *logistikos* meaning "skilled in calculating." In Roman and Byzantine times there appears to have been a military administrative official with the title *logista*, whose duties, it is easy to imagine, must have required an intimate familiarity with *logistics*, the science of mathematical computation—a meaning still carried in most general dictionaries along with the more modern military meaning. For many centuries European warfare lacked an organized administrative science in anything like the modern sense, and most noncombatant services (as well as certain combatant ones such as siegecraft and the use of artillery) were performed for a long time by civilians. The word "logistics," as applied to military administration, did not appear until the eighteenth century. See articles on logistics in the *Enciclopedia universal ilustrada* (Barcelona, 1907–30), Vol. XXX; the *Enciclopedia italiana* (Rome, 1934), Vol. XXI; and the *Encyclopedia Americana* (New York, 1953), Vol. XVII.

[2] See Antoine Henri, Baron de Jomini, *Précis de l'art de la guerre*, 2 vols. (Paris, 1838), Vol. II, Ch. VI. Jomini mentioned, but without discussing them, two additional branches of warfare—engineering and minor tactics.

of these underlying changes, dimly perceived other more disturbing phenomena—the growing size of armies, the mounting ferocity of warfare, and the emergence of a new, more murderous technology. Jomini's attention was mainly captured by the latest improvements in artillery, particularly by a new "steam" gun that seemed to hold horrendous promise. A far more portentous phenomenon, steam-propelled rail transport, he dismissed as an instrument of peace only, although five years earlier a French general had declared in the Chamber of Deputies that the strategic use of railways would cause a revolution in military science, and across the Rhine Friedrich List was trying hard to impress the same point on his countrymen.[3] All of these developments were in fact harbingers of a revolution that was not to reach full tide until the great wars of the twentieth century, though governments and high commands began to grapple with the problems it presented from the midnineteenth century on.[4]

Like all revolutions, this one grew out of the double challenge of new demands and new opportunities. Nationalism and conscription produced huge armies; new weapons multiplied fire power. To feed the armies and unleash their fire power, military staffs had no choice but to come to terms with the new technologies of supply and movement—mass production of munitions and foodstuffs, the railroad, the steamship, the long-distance pipeline, the internal combustion engine, eventually the transport airplane. Wars came to be fought along wide fronts of continental extent; lines of communications became deep zones containing an elaborate establishment of military administration and services.

Stupendous magnitudes were involved. World War I saw an expenditure of artillery ammunition by British and French forces, during one average month, more than twice as great as that by the Union forces during the entire four years of the

[3] (1) Jomini, *Précis de l'art de la guerre*, II, 284-85. (2) Edwin A. Pratt, *The Rise of Rail Power in War and Conquest, 1833-1914* (London, 1915), Ch. I. (3) Edward Mead Earle, *Makers of Modern Strategy: Military Thought from Machiavelli to Hitler* (Princeton University Press, Princeton, N. J., 1948), pp. 148-52.

[4] Only a sampling of the literature on this subject can be given here. (1) Most of the works of Maj. Gen. John F. C. Fuller deal with the subject, primarily with reference to mechanization and armor; see especially his *The Reformation of War* (New York, E. P. Dutton & Co., Inc., 1923), and *Armament and History: A Study of the Influence of Armament on History* (New York, C. Scribner's Sons, 1945). See also: (2) Baron Colmar von der Goltz, *The Nation in Arms,* translated by Philip A. Ashworth (London, 1913), and *The Conduct of War,* translated by Joseph T. Dickman (Kansas City, Mo., 1896), Chs. I-II, VIII; (3) Jan Gottlieb Bloch, *The Future of War in Its Technical, Economic and Political Relations,* translated by R. C. Long (Boston, Ginn & Company, 1902); (4) Jean Colin, *The Transformations of War* (London, 1913), Chs. IV-V; (5) Edwin A. Pratt, *The Rise of Rail Power in War and Conquest, 1833-1914* (London, 1915); (6) Victor W. Germains, *Mechanization of War* (London, 1927), Chs. IX, XII; (7) Lowell M. Limpus, *Twentieth Century Warfare: How Modern Battles Are Won and Lost* (New York, E. P. Dutton & Co., Inc., 1910); (8) Quincy Wright, *A Study of War,* 2 vols. (Chicago, The University of Chicago Press, 1942), Ch. XII; (9) Benedict Crowell, *America's Munitions, 1917-1918* (Washington, 1919); (10) Brooks Emeny, *The Strategy of Raw Materials* (New York, The Macmillan Company, 1944); (11) Bernard Brodie, *Sea Power in the Machine Age* (Princeton, N. J., Princeton University Press, 1941); (12) James P. Baxter, III, *Scientists Against Time* (Boston, Little, Brown and Company, 1946); (13) Vannevar Bush, *Modern Arms and Free Men* (New York, Simon & Schuster, Inc., 1949); (14) John U. Nef, *War and Human Progress: An Essay on the Rise of Industrial Civilization* (Harvard University Press, Cambridge, Mass., 1950); (15) Lewis Mumford, *Technics and Civilization* (New York, Harcourt, Brace and Company, 1934); (16) Irving B. Holley, *Ideas and Weapons* (New Haven, Conn., Yale University Press, 1953); (17) George E. Turner, *Victory Rode the Rails: The Strategic Place of the Railroads in the Civil War* (Indianapolis, Ind., Bobbs-Merrill, 1953); and (18) Lt. Col. John D. Millett, "Logistics and Modern War," *Military Affairs,* Vol. IX, No. 3 (Fall 1945), pp. 193-207.

War Between the States, a conflict that itself revealed many characteristics of the new warfare. In the seven days of the Battle of the Somme in 1916, British artillery fired about 4 million rounds, roughly 1,200 times as many as the Union Army fired in the three-day Battle of Gettysburg in 1863.[5] World War II piled Pelion upon Ossa. During the first nineteen months of its participation in World War II, the U.S. Army purchased almost 950,000 trucks, nineteen times the number it had procured during the corresponding period of World War I. From Pearl Harbor to V-J Day it procured for its own and Allied forces some 84,000 tanks, 2.2 million trucks, 6.2 million rifles, 350,000 artillery pieces, .5 billion rounds of ground artillery ammunition, 41 billion rounds of small arms ammunition. It shipped overseas 127 million measurement tons of cargo, and 7.3 million troops and other passengers. The U.S. Army Air Forces dropped over two million tons of bombs on the enemy.[6]

The new juggernaut armies' voracious appetite for food, fuel, and munitions dictated a basic change in the method of supply. From the earliest times the swiftly moving, hard-hitting, self-contained force, living off the country and a lean baggage train, had been the dream of every commander. In the hands of Hannibal, Xenophon, Subotai, Gustavus, Marlborough, Napoleon, Jackson, and Sherman, such forces had performed spectacular exploits. When armies became chained to depots and their trains grew heavy and sluggish, as happened in some of the wars of the eighteenth century, warfare itself became a mere appendage of logistics in which, as Frederick the Great is said to have observed, "the masterpiece of a skillful general is to starve his enemy." In the new warfare, the possibility of self-containment

almost disappeared. Under the logistical system that emerged in the late nineteenth century, first formalized by Prussia in 1866, armies were supplied not by a train, but by a "tail"—vehicles shuttling in relays over segments of the total distance between the army and its sources of supply, thus pushing freight continuously forward as though by a series of endless conveyor belts. As an army advanced, its "tail," in order not to lose contact with the base, naturally stretched out, requiring more and more transport to keep supplies moving forward.[7]

The basic elements of this system were adopted by all large modern armies in the first half of the twentieth century. Given the necessity for continuous resupply, some system of staging was dictated in any case when freight was transshipped from one form of transportation to another—normally, at port, at railhead, and at truckhead. The principle of continuous movement of supply from rear to front was supplemented, on a large scale, by the older method of stocking supplies at convenient distribution points. Since the rate of movement over all stages of the line of supply could never be uniform because of differences in the capabilities of the means of transport and handling, backlogs of freight piled up at bottlenecks along the

---

[5] Benedict Crowell and Robert F. Wilson, *The Armies of Industry*, 2 vols. (New Haven, Conn., Yale University Press, 1921), I, 27, 29, 31.

[6] (1) *Annual Report of the Army Service Forces, 1943* (Washington, 1944), p. 271. (2) Theodore E. Whiting, Statistics, a volume in preparation for the series UNITED STATES ARMY IN WORLD WAR II, Procurement Sec, 9 Apr 52 draft. (3) *Third Report of the Commanding General of the Army Air Forces to the Secretary of War, 12 November 1945*, p. 64.

[7] (1) Brevet Lt. Col. G. C. Shaw, *Supply in Modern War* (London, 1938). (2) Goltz, *The Nation in Arms*, Pt. IV, Ch. 6, and Pt. V. (3) Henry G. Sharpe, *The Art of Subsisting Armies in War* (New York, John Wiley & Sons, 1893), Ch. III.

line, usually at transshipping points. Additional reserves had to be stocked forward of such critical bottlenecks as insecure transoceanic communication lines and ports of entry of meager capacity. Against the threat of enemy penetration and in order to utilize alternate communication lines, reserves in war theaters had to be dispersed among many magazines, both laterally and in depth. Large-scale offensive operations, in addition, demanded immense accumulations of munitions, fuel, and subsistence close behind the point of impact—requiring months and sometimes years to build up—in order to provide crushing initial force and sustained impetus.

World War I, in the western theater, with its creeping, sealed front and enormous concentration of forces in small areas, offered a natural habitat for the modified system of staged, continuous resupply. The abrupt return to mobility in 1939–45 strained the system to the limit. To supply staffs, a break-through by their own forces presented problems almost as formidable as one by the enemy, for the methodical disposition forward of depots, dumps, fuel pipelines, and transport systems could not possibly keep pace with racing armored columns, even if the capacity of supply lines to the rear could be expanded rapidly enough. Roads, rail lines, and bridges in territory abandoned by the enemy could be expected to be seriously damaged; in the absence of prepared relay and transshipping facilities, transport would have to operate in abnormally long shuttles. The mobility necessary to sustain a break-through, in consequence, could only be gained by lavish use of all forms of transportation, far beyond the amounts normally available.

Yet, short of curtailing drastically the scale of military operations, World War II brought forth no real alternative to continuous resupply. Guerrilla forces, ill armed and without regular supply lines, won amazing successes against regular troops in the Soviet Union and the Balkans, and on occasion were able to carry out large-scale operations, but only for limited periods at a time. What was likely to happen to an army cut off from its sources of resupply, even when it had substantial stocks on hand, seemed to be demonstrated by the fate of MacArthur's forces in the Philippines·in 1942, an experience that made a lasting impression on the American high command. Mountains, jungles, and vast ocean distances in the theaters of the war against Japan dictated many compromises in the lavish logistical support to which American forces were accustomed, but the solution was not found in a return to self-containment. In the end, these obstacles were overcome simply by moving up the apparatus of land, sea, and air power on so massive a scale that it was possible not merely to crush the enemy at selected points of impact but also to contain him elsewhere, to protect communication lines and bases of operations, and even to neutralize and bypass major enemy strongholds.[8] This kind of logistical support demands virtually unlimited resources in munitions, supplies, and transport. With them, and employing the staging method of resupply in combination with accumulated reserves near the front, armies can

[8] (1) For the logistical problems created by the Allied break-through in France in July 1944, see Roland G. Ruppenthal, *Logistical Support of the Armies* (Washington, 1953). (2) See also, Louis Morton's forthcoming volume on strategy, command, and logistics in the Pacific war, and, for the first Philippine campaign in particular, his *The Fall of the Philippines* (Washington, 1953). All are in the series UNITED STATES ARMY IN WORLD WAR II.

strike hard, move swiftly, and sustain their driving force, even though with diminishing returns in mobility and flexibility, and increasing risk that road, rail, or port bottlenecks may clog and result in paralysis. Without abundant resources, armies can only strive by austere living and improvisation to stretch their limited transport, using it mainly to sustain fire power, and to make mobility offset weakness in offensive strength. Austerity, improvisation, and even mobility are military virtues, not because they are ends in themselves but because they serve to extract the maximum of effective power from available resources, thus to some degree compensating for lack of abundance.

Supply and transportation were only one aspect, though unquestionably the most important one, of the new logistics. This logistics was deeply embedded in the economy of the nation. Armies drew from science and the civil professions many things besides weapons and means of transport—medicine and surgery, electric power, the telegraph, the telephone, radio and radar, the bulldozer, psychiatry, business management, propaganda, planned recreation, techniques of indoctrination. Armies became, in fact, complex communities in themselves, miniature and specialized replicas of the societies that sustained them. The traditional cleavages between the noncombatant and combatant skills, and those between military and civilian spheres of activity, became blurred. Engineers in many armies became shock troops; signal corpsmen were expected to work and fight with the most advanced units, truck drivers to man antiaircraft machine guns. In coming to terms with the new technologies of war, the military profession had to broaden and dilute its training to include dozens of skills re-

mote from combat and command. The technicians and administrators within its ranks multiplied and in many fields drew closer to the civilian community in outlook and professional qualifications than to their colleagues in the combat arms.

Even so, the military profession could not hope to master all the skills it had to exploit. In time of war the needs of sudden expansion could only be met by a wholesale influx of civilians into the military administrative establishment, and whether they donned uniform or not scarcely affected the character of their employment. Nor could the military extend very far, in relation to the immensity of the field, its administrative control and supervision over the noncombatant activities it was unable to master. In the United States the military services controlled the procurement of most of the finished munitions and a limited part of the transportation they used, but even this control was vigorously attacked during World War II and after.[9] In many other countries the power rested in civilian government agencies. In fact, from the late nineteenth century on, the pressure to expand military control over various segments of national economies usually encountered, and yielded to, the more powerful drive of the state, through its central civil agencies, to mobilize under its own aegis the nation's war-making resources.[10]

---

[9] For the attack on the military procurement power in the United States, see: (1) John D. Millett, *The Organization and Role of the Army Service Forces*, UNITED STATES ARMY IN WORLD WAR II (Washington, 1954), Ch. XIX; (2) Bureau of the Budget, *The United States at War: Development and Administration of the War Program of the Federal Government* (Washington, 1946), pp. 129–31.

[10] For a survey of the systems in various countries during World War II, see Foreign Logistical Organizations and Methods, 15 October 1947, Report of the Secretary of the Army, OCMH.

The revolution in warfare thus brought an immense growth in the range and complexity of activities supporting armies and navies. The range of professional military skills also broadened, but not nearly to the limits of the whole field that war now exploited, while military control tended to shade off into various forms of partnership with government agencies and private enterprise as it reached back into the vast expanse of services that supported a nation's military effort. What theorists had once called logistics had spread to embrace a considerable part of the economic life of the nation.

Since the end of World War II the rapid development of the air arm, the promise of transcontinental guided missiles, and above all the emergence of a whole family of weapons employing the principles of nuclear fission and fusion have enormously accelerated two very old trends in weapons—increasing destructiveness and increasing range. Whether these developments presage a new revolution in logistics it is still too early to determine. Certainly they seem likely to accentuate and continue trends already manifest. By bringing rear administrative areas, lines of communications, and even sources of supply progressively under fire, the new weapons will further enhance the necessity for dispersion of installations and channels of movement, disrupt orderly administration, interrupt the continuity, and reduce the net volume of supply—phenomena familiar to every Allied theater commander in World War II and conspicuous ones in the final collapse of Germany and Japan. On the other hand, the growing range of fire power involves a corresponding diminution of the distances over which the ingredients of fire power must be transported, to that extent sim-plifying the logistical problem; conceivably the necessity for massive overseas establishments may eventually disappear altogether. There are signs, moreover, that growing reliance on long-range weapons of tremendous per-unit destructiveness may in time actually reduce the aggregate amounts of supply requirements for all forces in the field, thus reversing one of the oldest trends of logistics. In the end, by raising the possibility that a conflict may be won or lost within the first few days or even hours, the new technology may virtually eliminate the whole problem of military supply and reduce to irrelevance most of the complex apparatus of industrial potential that for almost a century has been an indispensable requirement for sustaining, as well as for launching, a major war. Neither World War II nor the Korean conflict, however, put the newest weapons to the test. As these words are being written, armies appear to be still dependent upon an elaborate rear area administrative establishment and a massive, uninterrupted flow of food, fuel, and munitions from secure sources of supply.

Changing Conceptions of Logistics

This transformation of the environment in which logistics operated inevitably brought about an adjustment in attitudes and conceptions concerning it. The character of the adjustment was strongly colored by the doctrines of Karl von Clausewitz, whose teachings dominated European military thought during the last quarter of the nineteenth century.[11] A

[11] (1) Dallas D. Irvine, "The French Discovery of Clausewitz and Napoleon," *Journal of the American Military Institute*, Vol. IV, No. 3 (Fall, 1940), pp. 144–45. (2) Herbert Rosinski, *The German Army* (New York, Harcourt, Brace and Company, 1940), pp. 121–29.

contemporary of Jomini, Clausewitz did not even use the term "logistics." In his celebrated work *On War,* he defined the "conduct of war"—which he identified with strategy and tactics—as "the art of making use of given means in combat," and from this he sharply differentiated, as purely preparatory and contributory processes, both the creation of armed forces (mobilization, training, and so forth) and their maintenance in time of war—"subservient" services which, although they stood "in a constant reciprocal relation to the use of troops," were not yet part of "the conduct of war properly so called." Clausewitz was well aware that certain activities, notably "marches, camps and quarters" and subsistence, sometimes exerted a decisive influence on the outcome of battles and campaigns, but he dismissed them as irrelevant to his discussion.

We are at present occupied not with the concrete facts of any individual case, but with abstract theory . . . . the theory of war itself is occupied not with perfecting these means but with their use for the object of the war. It needs only the results of them, that is to say the knowledge of the principal properties of the means it has taken over.

Convinced as he was of the superiority of moral to material forces in war, Clausewitz had little interest in the "subservient" services, even though he conceded their importance. Out of the 125 chapters of *On War,* his discussion of these services occupies only half a chapter.[12]

The generation that burned incense at Clausewitz' altar did not, of course, keep this doctrine pure. A very few exaggerated and oversimplified it into a crass disparagement of all noncombatant services, which they relegated to technicians and menials as something apart from the profession of arms. Veneration of Clausewitz,

however, did not prevent his most brilliant disciples—the elder Moltke and Schlieffen, for example—from readily grasping and vigorously exploiting the potentialities of "given means" that Clausewitz could not have foreseen. The Prussian victories of 1866 and 1870–71 owed much to the railroad and the telegraph, perhaps even more to a well-greased machinery of military administration, which functioned as it did because professional soldiers did not scorn to give it their personal attention.[13] The importance of the major logistical innovation of nineteenth-century warfare, moreover, was recognized by the formation of a Railway Section in the Prussian Great General Staff, specially trained military railway troops, and a centralized military-civilian organization for co-ordinating railway operations in Prussia in time of war.[14]

More fundamentally, military organization and practice rejected the doctrine, strongly implied though not explicitly asserted by Clausewitz, that the "subservient" services could be relegated to a separate compartment from the conduct of combat operations. European armies after 1870, and ultimately the U.S. Army, placed the specific function of co-ordinating important logistical activities (as well

---

[12] Karl von Clausewitz, *On War,* translated by O. J. Matthijs Jolles (New York, Random House, Inc., 1943), pp. 61–66.

[13] (1) General Fieldmarshal Count Alfred von Schlieffen, *Cannae* (Fort Leavenworth, Kans., The Command and General Staff School Press, 1931), Chs. III–IV. (2) Pratt, *The Rise of Rail Power,* Chs. X–XII.

[14] (1) Dallas D. Irvine, "The French and Prussian Staff Systems Before 1870," *Journal of the American Military History Foundation,* Vol. II, No. 4 (Winter, 1938), pp. 193–94. (2) James D. Hittle, *The Military Staff: Its History and Development* (Harrisburg, Pa., Military Service Pub. Co., 1949), p. 66. (3) Pratt, *The Rise of Rail Power,* Chs. X–XI.

as the responsibility for general co-ordination) at the general staff level cheek by jowl with the staff sections charged with strategy and tactics.[15] "Logistics," declared a U.S. Army staff text in 1926, "cannot be separated from tactics and strategy. It is a major factor in the execution of strategic and tactical conceptions, so inextricably interwoven that it is an integral part of each"—a doctrine that harked back almost a hundred years to Jomini's observation that logistics was the province "not merely of staffs, but also of generals-in-chief."[16]

Yet the basic ingredients of the Clausewitzian view remained. In the analytical and interpretive literature on war by professional military writers since the middle of the nineteenth century, the expanding role of the noncombatant services has received only perfunctory recognition, while scarcely any of the writers have chosen to describe the actual mechanics of administration. Among professional officers of the U.S. Army, at least until recently, indifference to logistics was widespread and traditional—a striking paradox in an army that can claim some of the most spectacular advances in that field. This attitude, in the opinion of many who once shared it, can be traced back to a general military education in which, down to World War II, logistics was held in low esteem.[17] Since the end of World War II logistical subjects have been given a more prominent place in courses at the U.S. Military Academy and the Command and General Staff School as well as at the more specialized schools, and, with the broadening of opportunities for advancement in the logistical field, there has been some quickening of interest in it. But staff organization and practice, in the American as in most other armies, continue to elevate

the operations function over the administrative, and officers schooled in the mysteries of logistics are employed more as expert consultants than as active participants in the processes of strategic and tactical planning.[18]

Military thought, in short, has clung to two characteristically Clausewitzian ideas: that the primary function of the soldier is to use the tools of war in combat, not to fashion or provide them, and that material forces have not yet diminished the classic and decisive role of courage, leadership, and the arts of command. The development of warfare has subjected both these principles to considerable strain. The once clear distinction between the use and the providing of weapons has been virtually obliterated, and modern war engages more soldiers in the latter task than in the former. Courage and leadership are steadily losing the power to override heavy material odds. The Clausewitzian conception of logistics, in its pure form, is clearly unsuited to the conditions of modern warfare. It remains to be seen whether it can continue to adapt itself to a revolution in warfare still under way, or whether it will be replaced by a radically new approach.

---

[15] (1) See Hittle, *The Military Staff*, Chs. 3–6, *passim*. (2) See also, Otto L. Nelson, Jr., *National Security and the General Staff* (Washington, Infantry Journal Press, 1946). (3) FM 100-10, Field Service Regulations: Administration, any edition. (4) FM 100-5, Field Service Regulations: Operations, any edition.

[16] (1) Command, Staff and Logistics: A Tentative Text, issued by The General Service Schools, Fort Leavenworth, Kans., 1926, Sec 11, par. 12. (2) Jomini, *Précis de l'art de la guerre*, II, 150.

[17] See the testimony of Lt. Gen. LeRoy Lutes and other observers as noted below, Ch. XVI.

[18] For a statement of this doctrine, see Ray S. Cline, *Washington Command Post: The Operations Division*, UNITED STATES ARMY IN WORLD WAR II (Washington, 1951), pp. 1–7, 258–61. See also below, Chs. IX, XXIV.

The Vagaries of Usage

The revolution in warfare raised a semantic problem in connection with the term "logistics" that remains unresolved to this day. What precisely is the scope of activity embraced by logistics? The question was and is of more than academic interest, for, as one writer pointed out in 1917, when the word was only beginning to come into American military usage,

> The purpose of the definition is to establish a division of labor, and if two divisions [strategy and tactics] are properly drawn while the third is not, there will be either duplication of effort, or some functions will be overlooked entirely, with the result that certain preparations for war will not be made.[19]

In Jomini's own day logistics was thought of vaguely as military staff business in general, a "science of detail." Jomini ascribed the derivation of the word to the title of the *major généraux* (or *maréchaux*) *des logis* in French armies of the eighteenth century who, originally charged with miscellaneous administrative functions such as the arrangements for marches and quarters, had come to serve in effect as chiefs of staff to higher commanders—as did their counterparts, the *Quartiermeister*, in. Prussian armies. While Jomini clearly intended to use "logistics" in a broader sense, his discussion, in contrast to the logical clarity of most of his writing, is inconclusive and vague.[20] Tradition, nevertheless, drew from Jomini's brief disquisition the implication that he supposed logistics to cover all or almost all of the field of military activities supporting combat.

As a practical matter such a conception had little meaning for military men who had to organize and administer these activities. Such matters as transportation, supply, engineering, and medical care were continuing problems, which no commander or staff could afford to ignore, particularly under the new conditions of warfare, while others, such as legal and religious affairs, pay and allowances, and many of the details of personnel administration, were under ordinary circumstances peripheral or routine. To lump them all under a single name implied a unity that did not in fact exist. It is significant that the word "logistics," despite the enormous influence of Jomini's writings during the long middle span of the nineteenth century, remained an academic, almost archaic term throughout that century, rarely used by theorists, hardly at all by soldiers.[21] Shortly before World War I it began to creep into military service parlance in the United States, but down to World War II it seldom appeared in the working vocabulary of the average Army or Navy officer. It was used, moreover, in a rather narrow sense, meaning simply transportation and supply in the field; the noncombatant services as a whole were known, instead, by the term "administration," a usage similar to that in British service terminology.[22]

With World War II the word "logistics" in American usage came into sudden,

---

[19] George Cyrus Thorpe, *Pure Logistics: The Science of War Preparation* (Kansas City, Mo., Franklin Hudson Publishing Co., 1917), p. 16.

[20] Jomini, *Précis de l'art de la guerre*, II, 146–50.

[21] For example, see: (1) Marmont, *Esprit des institutions militaires* (Paris, 1845); (2) Ardant du Picq, *Battle Studies: Ancient and Modern Battle,* translated by Col. John N. Greely and Maj. Robert C. Cotton (New York, The Macmillan Company, 1921); (3) V. Derrécagaix, *Modern War,* 3 vols., translated by C. W. Foster (Washington, 1888); and (4) M. Alfred Rambaud, *Termes militaires français-anglais* (Paris, 1903). None of these mention the word "logistics."

[22] (1) Command, Staff and Logistics, Sec 11, par. 12. (2) FM 100-10, Field Service Regulations: Administration, 9 Dec 40.

luxuriant vogue. Every writer on military subjects began to employ it with joyous abandon, and its meaning lost what little stability it had possessed when restricted to the vocabularies of military theorists and a few bookish staff officers. Wide usage brought immediately into conflict the urge to adopt "logistics" as a convenient term covering all primarily noncombatant military activities and the inertia of habit wedded to a more limited meaning. Official Army usage of the word received a powerful impulse toward a broader definition as a result of the consolidation, during World War II, of most of the Army's supply and service activities in the United States under a single command, the Army Service Forces (Services of Supply in the period covered by this volume). That organization's final report defined "logistics," largely in terms of its own functions, to include an impressive list of activities: procurement, storage, and distribution of equipment and supplies; transport of troops and cargo; construction and maintenance of facilities; communications; care of the sick and wounded; induction, classification, assignment, welfare, and separation of personnel.[23] Many military agencies during and after the war began to adopt the label "logistics" or "logistical," though none performed so wide a range of functions as had the Army Service Forces, and soon after the end of the war the Army developed a group of type headquarters called "logistical commands," each designed to co-ordinate all the supporting services for a territorial area of specified size within a theater of operations.[24] In the Navy the word "logistics," with a somewhat longer tradition behind it, enjoyed a comparable renaissance.[25] In 1950, the Year IV of Unification, the whole process culminated when the three military services agreed on an official definition, assigning to "logistics" all activities in the military establishment involved in the handling of personnel, matériel, facilities, and services—in effect, the entire field of military administration.[26]

But official definitions, as Burke observed of the English constitution, go but a little way. Usage remains stubbornly inconsistent, conservative, and opportunist. Army field service regulations, a bible for operating personnel, did not even recognize the term "logistics" until 1949, and then in a sense more narrow than that of the official joint definitions of 1948 and 1950.[27] Among the Army's technical services, especially the Engineer, Signal, and Chemical Corps, which have a strong combat tradition, there is an ingrained resistance to any label such as "logistics" that seems to imply nonexposure to battle. None of the agencies so labeled, in any case, has functional responsibilities covering more than a portion of the field of logistics as officially defined.

To the average Army officer, at least, "logistics" is something both narrower and vaguer than the official definition of 1950, though perhaps not so narrow or vague as it was to one highly placed officer in 1943 who held that a certain committee handled "not only logistics matters but also . . . personnel, organization,

---

[23] *Logistics in World War II,* Final Report of the Army Service Forces (Washington, 1947), p. vii.

[24] James A. Huston, Time and Space, MS, 1953, Pt. 1, Ch. II, pp. 180–88, and Pt. 2, Ch. V, pp. 12–19, OCMH.

[25] Duncan S. Ballantine, *U.S. Naval Logistics in the Second World War* (Princeton, N. J., Princeton University Press, 1947), Ch. I, especially pp. 1–8, 30–31.

[26] *Dictionary of U.S. Military Terms for Joint Usage* (Washington, June 1950).

[27] FM 100-10, Field Service Regulations: Administration, Sep 49.

troop basis, requirements, production, supplies and matériel." [28] Repeated use of such locutions as "logistics and administration," "logistics and construction," and even, inexplicably, "logistics and supply" betrays a widespread uncertainty in the military profession itself as to precisely where logistics stops and something else begins. Evidently the term is still in process of rapid and healthy growth.[29] Until it matures and settles down, we must accept it, perforce, in whatever guise it appears— that is to say, with the specific shape, content, and emphases it derives from its concrete environment.

The Army's Logistical Effort, 1940–43

Such an environment was the spreading conflict that opened in September 1939, bringing to a spectacular climax the revolution in warfare whose dim beginnings Jomini had observed a century earlier. During the three years from spring 1940 to spring 1943 the U.S. Army, facing first the possibility then the actuality of participation in the war, developed a logistical system that its leaders believed best adapted to this new environment. The system was conceived and fashioned pragmatically, with little deference to traditional logistical doctrine, and it differed not only from the systems to which it was opposed but also in important respects from those of Allied forces. It can best be described by reference to the underlying factors of geography, economics, and history from which it took its distinctive form.

American Industrial Power

Inferior to the Axis powers at the outset in developed capacity to produce munitions, though outweighing them in manpower, the other nations opposing the Axis inevitably depended upon the United States to give their side industrial superiority. In any case, it was almost inevitable that this country, possessing a vast industrial potential disproportionate even to its large population, would make its greatest contribution to the Allied effort in weight of matériel rather than in weight of manpower.[30] The degree of this emphasis has been obscured by the fact that the United States at the peak of its mobilization was able to put some twelve million of its able-bodied citizens into uniform. However, almost half of these went into the "armament heavy" naval and air arms; the ground army, biggest single user of manpower, was held down to a modest size, both in relation to the entire Military Establishment and as compared to the armies that European belligerents with smaller populations were able to put in the field, in order that industry and agriculture, producing for Allied as well as the domestic economy, might have the workers they needed.[31] The high command

---

[28] Memo, Brig Gen Albert C. Wedemeyer for CofS, 5 Mar 43, sub: Orgn of Plng Agencies Subsidiary to JCS, WDCSA 334 JCS.

[29] For a recent, far from definitive, effort to fix the meaning of the word, see Rear Adm. Henry E. Eccles, USN (Ret.), "Logistics—What Is It?" *U.S. Naval Institute Proceedings*, Vol. 79, No. 6 (June 1953), pp. 645–53.

[30] From the beginning of the war through 1944 the United States produced nearly 40 percent of the combat munitions produced by the United Nations for use against the European Axis. See: (1) *World Production of Munitions at the End of the War in Europe*, WPB Doc 25 (Washington, June 15, 1945), pp. 1, 4, 13–14; (2) Raymond W. Goldsmith, "The Power of Victory, Munitions Output in World War II," *Military Affairs*, Vol. X, No. 1 (Spring, 1946), pp. 69–80; and (3) Bureau of the Budget, *The United States at War*, pp. 505–06.

[31] Approximate peak strengths of the U.S. Army and Navy at the end of World War II were 8,291,300

sought, therefore, to make weight of matériel compensate for limited numbers, stressing air and naval power, equipping all its forces on a lavish scale, and developing massive fire power. American industry not merely met these demands, but was able in addition to equip and support large Allied forces. The emphasis upon weight and quantity of matériel, sometimes at the expense of qualitative superiority over the enemy, radiated through every aspect of the Army's logistics. It was reflected above all, perhaps, in a supply system that accepted and greatly extended the modern mass army's dependence on continuous resupply. By employing myriads of ships, trucks, and other transport, performing miracles in port rehabilitation, stocking supplies in depth on a huge scale, and copying the managerial techniques of American big business, the U.S. Army was able to achieve a continuity and volume of supply— and therefore sustained offensive power—that even the Germans, who had pioneered in this field, could not equal.

---

and 3,408,300, respectively. The Army Air Forces reached a strength of 2,354,210 on 30 April 1945; the Navy's air arm numbered 437,998 on V-J Day. See: (1) Kent Roberts Greenfield, Robert R. Palmer, and Bell I. Wiley, *The Organization of Ground Combat Troops*, UNITED STATES ARMY IN WORLD WAR II (Washington, 1947), pp. 235–36; (2) Office of Naval Operations, *The U.S. Navy at War, 1941–1945* (Washington, 1946), pp. 152–317; (3) Strength of the Army Report, STM-30, 1 May 45; and (4) Archibald D. Turnbull and Clifford L. Lord, *History of U.S. Naval Aviation* (New Haven, Conn., Yale University Press, 1949), p. 322. (6) In the *World Almanac and Book of Facts for 1952* (New York, New York World-Telegram and The Sun, 1952), p. 512, peak World War II strength of all armed forces of Germany is given as 10,200,000, of Japan as 6,905,000, of Italy as 3,750,000, of the United Kingdom as 5,120,000. In the first two of these countries, at least, the ratio of ground army forces to other armed forces was considerably higher than in the United States.

Eighteen Months of Unmolested Rearmament

In December 1941, thanks to the prolonged threat of enemy aggression since spring of 1940, the U.S. Army was better prepared than ever before on the eve of a great war. It had swelled to a strength of 1,600,000 men, partially trained, partially equipped, backed by an industrial mobilization that had, by and large, completed the critical "tooling up" phase and that was ready to swing into production of munitions on an unprecedented scale. In a deeper sense, the Army had bridged the gulf between smallness and bigness, more a matter of thinking, doctrine, and method than even of physical growth. By the time the Japanese struck, the U.S. high command was thinking in terms of an army of 10 million men and 250 divisions.[32] There had been concrete experience in bigness, too. The Army's commanders had learned how to maneuver divisions, corps, and armies. Perhaps even more important, its logistical staffs had gained some notion of what was involved in moving a division with its ancillary units, guns, tanks, trucks, and other impedimenta across half a continent, and loading the whole apparatus into transports and freighters for a transoceanic voyage. The ports of embarkation and the depots behind them had had months of experience in building up overseas establishments on something like a wartime scale and in providing the continuous sustenance needed to keep them alive. The central staffs in Washington had had to keep in balance all the divergent and competitive purposes of a vast expansion program—training and equipping a mo-

---

[32] See below, Ch. V.

bilizing conscript army, providing garrisons and mobile striking forces to meet any sudden emergency, and diverting munitions to embattled anti-Axis forces in Europe and Asia. In terms of practical experience, plans, and even blueprints, the Army was ready to shoulder, with surprising ease and swiftness, the logistical burdens of a great global war.

The Ocean Gap

Under the conditions of warfare in 1940–43 the United States still could derive a large measure of security from the wide, encircling oceans. American hemisphere defense plans in 1940 and 1941 counted on exploiting to the utmost the logistical advantages conferred by a single economic-geographic center of gravity, interior lines, mutually supporting, accessible outposts, and the vast stretches of water over which an attacking enemy would have to advance. But in the event, the United States had to sacrifice these advantages in order to carry the war to the enemy. At the outset, moreover, the United States suffered a catastrophic defeat in the Philippines, largely because the Navy and Air Forces were unable to keep open the lines of communications supporting that distant outpost. During 1942 German submarines very nearly succeeded in sealing off the eastward passage of munitions and supplies across the Atlantic. The impact upon American strategic and logistical thinking was profound. The Army's planners, with Bataan and Corregidor fresh in their memories, were prone to insist upon secure and, if possible, short sea communications as a condition of any strategy. The Army became the largest user of the nation's merchant shipping. Army staffs had to become expert in

operating ships and ports, in scheduling transoceanic troop and cargo movements, in adjusting the rhythm of demand and supply to the exigencies of traffic control, convoy schedules, and the availability of bottoms. Because of the time required to move supplies from factory to overseas consumer, the Army had to order huge quantities, not actually to be used or consumed, but merely to "fill the pipeline," besides further quantities to replace the cargoes lost or to be lost at sea, and still other quantities to be stocked overseas against possible cutting of the ocean supply line. Army logistics, in short, became predominantly a logistics of overseas deployment and supply, simply because the ocean gap was the longest, most vulnerable stage on the long road from factory and training camp to battle front. After mid-1943 secure Allied command of the sea lanes, together with the mammoth output of American shipyards, was to enable the Army to take full advantage of the mobility of sea communications, making them a source of strength rather than of weakness.

Involvements of a Coalition War

That the United States fought in World War II as a member of a coalition, against a coalition, was of decisive importance in shaping the Army's logistical effort. The geographical location of the belligerents in itself dictated the world-wide extension of the conflict; the differences in their military capabilities and the disposition of their power, on both sides, went far to determine the character of American participation—the use of land, sea, and air forces, the apportionment of munitions, and the areas in which American forces operated. During 1939, 1940, and 1941, while the European war was spreading and the alignment of powers was taking shape, American strategic and logistical plans, veering to meet each shift in the fortunes of the war, ran the gamut from a last-ditch defense of the Western Hemisphere, as envisaged in the RAINBOW 4 plan of mid-1940, to the actual multifront global war into which the United States plunged in December 1941. Long before then, Army staffs had acquired through lend-lease a working familiarity with many of the practical logistical problems of a coalition war—the amounts and manifold types of military matériel required for operations in remote corners of the globe and the immense difficulties of delivering them there, the complex administrative machinery needed to apportion munitions and the use of shipping among several claimants, the baffling question of standardization of equipment design, the delicate political and psychological problems that arise even on the administrative level in such an enterprise. In December 1941 the final major shift in the power alignment brought both Japan and the United States into the war. Japan's unexpected attack and the prompt American decision to fight back from bases in the southwest as well as the central Pacific forced the United States to establish and defend a supply line across the world's broadest ocean, and in that distant theater to carry on a "triphibious" warfare under conditions that imposed tremendous logistical difficulties. It was the struggle in this theater, above all, that forced Army and Navy staffs to work out methods of co-ordinating the logistics of land, air, and sea forces operating together. To the eastward, where approved strategy dictated the major effort, the Army before the end of 1942 also became

involved in a vast program of logistical undertakings reaching half-way around the globe. Army ships and cargoes plied around the Cape of Good Hope to the Red Sea, the Persian Gulf, and beyond; Army service troops were scattered along supply routes across Africa and operating supply bases in the Near and Middle East, India, and China. Two foci of this network—the growing service establishments in the Persian Corridor and in the China-Burma-India theater—had the primary mission of forwarding munitions by rail, truck, and transport aircraft to the Soviet Union and China. All these activities extended the Army's logistical effort, in range and volume, far beyond what would have been required for the support only of its own relatively modest forces deployed overseas by spring of 1943. They were concomitants, in fact, of the Army's role in a coalition war.

In the three years of preparing for and entering World War II, the Army's logistical staffs had both to learn and to apply their craft, unlearning in the process much that they had inherited from their predecessors. It was in these three years that the Army built the logistical machine, assembled the resources, and completed the initial deployment that enabled it to carry out the great offensives of 1943–45. Its contacts with the enemy during 1942 and 1943 were essentially holding actions, limited offensives, and incidents of its overseas deployment. While the Army was gathering strength and striving to avoid premature commitments, the brunt of the enemy attack was necessarily borne by the other nations opposing the Axis and by the U.S. Navy, which began to convoy ocean shipping and had its first encounters with enemy submarines months before Pearl Harbor. This division of labor was a logical product of circumstances. British and Soviet forces were already in the field, their mobilization well advanced, and the U.S. Navy, with a strong striking force in being, was the nation's first line of defense. The Army's mobilization and deployment and, even more, the industrial mobilization needed to wage full-scale war, started from a low ebb in 1940 and would have been disrupted by an early trial of strength with Axis land and air forces. This danger, indeed, threatened more than once during 1942, while the enemy held the strategic initiative and the American public clamored for victories. When the day came for the Army finally to throw its full weight into the scale, it was prepared to exert decisive power.

PART ONE

THE NEUTRALITY PERIOD

CHAPTER I

Rearmament and Foreign Aid Before Lend-Lease

In logistics, as in other fields of military activity, the two years of neutrality preceding December 1941 were for the U.S. Army a period of learning—hard, costly, but supremely valuable. The logistical experience of this period went far beyond the routine supply problems of a tiny peacetime establishment. In three fields of activity, above all, the Army gained forward-looking experience in dealing with logistical problems, without which it could scarcely have met the challenge of full-scale war in the years following: in rearming for hemisphere defense, in providing material aid to the nations opposing the Axis, and, from late 1940 on, in planning for possible military collaboration with those nations. The conflict between rearmament and foreign aid, which emerged during the last half of 1940, foreshadowed what was to be perhaps the most fundamental problem of military policy facing the United States as a member of a coalition—how to apportion resources between its own armed forces and those of its allies.

The Peacetime Logistical Establishment

In the late summer of 1939, on the eve of the European war, the U.S. Army had a total active strength of 190,690 men (almost 20,000 under its authorized strength), of whom less than 50,000 were stationed outside the continental United States. These Regular forces could be augmented in an emergency by the partially trained National Guard (about 200,000) and an Officers' Reserve Corps of about 110,000. The Army was largely an infantry-artillery army, the Air Corps numbering only 25,722 and the organized armored units only about 1,400. Forces overseas were mainly in five garrisons—Hawaii (21,500), Panama Canal (13,500), Philippines (10,900), Puerto Rico (900), and Alaska (400). In the United States there were, on paper, four field armies, which were responsible for training the field forces and serving as a framework for mobilization. Actually these armies had no staffs and contained only four organized and seven partially organized divisions, all, of course, far below war strength.[1]

The level of equipment was even lower. At the end of 1939 the Air Corps had only 1,800 planes on hand, of which a handful were of modern types. Many of the ground

---

[1] (1) Annual *Report of the Secretary of War, 1940*, Tables C, D. (2) Annual *Report of the Secretary of War, 1939*, Table C. (3) Annual *Report of the Secretary of War, 1941*, Chart 1. (4) Ray S. Cline, *Washington Command Post: The Operations Division*, UNITED STATES ARMY IN WORLD WAR II (Washington, 1951), pp. 8–9.

army's weapons were of ancient vintage, some—such as the Springfield rifle, the 75-mm. gun, and the 3-inch antiaircraft gun—inherited from World War I. Most of these were to be replaced by modern weapons—notably the Garand semiautomatic rifle (M1) and the high-speed 105-mm. howitzer—when production permitted. Comparatively large stocks of the older weapons were on hand, more than enough to outfit the one-million-man army (augmented Protective Mobilization Plan (PMP) force) that full mobilization was expected to put in the field—for example, over 2,500,000 bolt-action rifles, 113,000 machine guns, and almost 9,000 field artillery pieces. But there were no modern tanks capable of meeting on equal terms those unleashed by the German Wehrmacht in Poland in September. Of the 329 tanks available, most were light. There were only 438 antiaircraft guns, 93 mortars, and no aircraft cannon or rocket launchers. There were only limited quantities of ammunition, even for the obsolescent weapons. Scarcely more than token numbers of the new weapons were being produced—for example, only 4,000 Garand rifles and 30 light tanks per month. In short, the state of equipment was such that in late 1939 not even a single division could have been put in the field on short notice.[2]

The logistical support of this establishment, shaped to the routine needs of peace, was meager by later standards. Service troops of all categories numbered about 38,400, or 21 percent of the whole active Army. Of this number, the four supply services accounted for 69 percent (Quartermaster Corps 31 percent, Medical Department 28 percent, Ordnance Department 8 percent, and Chemical Warfare Service 2 percent); the two supply arms 28 percent (Corps of Engineers 17 percent and Signal Corps 11 percent); and the five administrative services 3 percent (Adjutant General's Department, Inspector General's Department, Judge Advocate General's Department, Finance Department, and Corps of Chaplains). Only a little more than a quarter of this personnel belonged to the two supply arms, which trained troops to take part in combat, and only 10 percent to services (Ordnance and Chemical Warfare) that procured and serviced weapons and ammunition.[3]

In the ground army, supply and transportation operations, the major logistical functions, centered in the four supply services and the two service arms; they provided the Army's supplies and equipment, the personnel to service them, and the means to transport both troops and matériel. The Quartermaster Corps was the principal transportation agency; it designed, procured, and serviced the Army's wheeled motor vehicles, trained troops to operate them, controlled Army traffic on inland commercial carriers, and supervised Army water transportation, including the operation of the New York and San Francisco Ports of Embarkation and the Army's fleet of transports and cargo vessels. The only other service having a considerable role in transportation was

---

[2] (1) Troyer S. Anderson, Munitions for the Army: A Five Year Report on the Procurement of Munitions by the War Department, 1946, p. 5, OCMH. (2) Stetson Conn and Byron Fairchild, The Defense of the Western Hemisphere: I, The Framework of Hemisphere Defense, a volume in preparation for the series UNITED STATES ARMY IN WORLD WAR II, Ch. I, pp. 19–34.

[3] Annual *Report of the Secretary of War, 1940,* Table D.
Chemical Warfare Service, though not an "arm," trained certain units—for example, chemical mortar units, which had a combat mission.

the Corps of Engineers, which was responsible for the construction, operation, and maintenance of military railways. Apart from the Quartermaster Corps, which procured a miscellaneous assortment of supplies and equipment, each supply arm and service had responsibility for procurement, storage, and issue of a well-defined group of related commodities—for example, the Signal Corps for communications equipment, the Corps of Engineers for construction material, and the Medical Department for medical supplies and equipment.[4] In the United States the distribution of supply was decentralized regionally to the nine corps areas. Since 1932 when the four armies were created, the corps areas—originally the basic territorial organization for administration, training, and mobilization—had served primarily as "housekeeping" agencies for supply and other services for the Army in the United States.[5] (Chart 1)

The Army's logistical operations, in the years of peace, were almost wholly separate from those of the Navy, and only rudimentary machinery for interservice co-ordination existed. There was no executive mechanism. The Joint Army and Navy Board, a committee composed of the Army Chief of Staff, Deputy Chief of Staff, and Chief of the War Plans Division (WPD), and their Navy opposite numbers, served as a meeting ground for discussion of whatever problems the heads of the two services were willing to bring before it. It reported to the two service secretaries and, after July 1939, to the President as well.[6] The board was assisted by the Joint Planning Committee, consisting of six or more members equally representing the two War Plans Divisions. There were three interservice boards in 1939 concerned with promoting logistical co-ordination be-

tween the two services—the Joint Army and Navy Munitions Board (ANMB) in the fields of supply procurement and planning for industrial mobilization, the Joint Economy Board in administration and organization, and the Joint Aeronautical Board in the development of aviation.[7]

On the top level of staff supervision and planning in the War Department, there was no single agency or official responsible for the field of logistics as a whole, and only two—the Supply Division (G-4) of the War Department General Staff (WDGS), and the Office of the Assistant Secretary of War—whose responsibilities might, by a liberal interpretation of the term, be considered as exclusively logistical. G-4 was the principal logistical agency on the General Staff. It was charged with planning, policy making, and staff supervision in the fields of supply requirements, distribution, storage and issue, equipment

[4] (1) Chester Wardlow, The Transportation Corps: I, Responsibilities, Organization, and Operations, UNITED STATES ARMY IN WORLD WAR II (Washington, 1951) (hereafter cited as Wardlow, Trans I), 35–37. (2) John D. Millett, The Organization and Role of the Army Service Forces, UNITED STATES ARMY IN WORLD WAR II (Washington, 1954) (hereafter cited as Millett, ASF), Ch. I.

[5] (1) Cline, Washington Command Post, pp. 8–9. (2) Kent Roberts Greenfield, Robert R. Palmer, and Bell I. Wiley, The Organization of Ground Combat Troops, Vol. I of the subseries The Army Ground Forces in UNITED STATES ARMY IN WORLD WAR II (Washington, 1947) (hereafter cited as Greenfield, Palmer, and Wiley, AGF I), 3–4.

[6] One of the conspicuous achievements of the Joint Board in recent years had been the issuance in 1927 of Joint Action, a compendium of procedures and policies for wartime interservice co-ordination in logistical and other areas.

[7] (1) Cline, Washington Command Post, pp. 45–46. (2) Mark S. Watson, Chief of Staff: Prewar Plans and Preparations, UNITED STATES ARMY IN WORLD WAR II (Washington, 1950), pp. 79–81. (3) Civilian Production Administration, Industrial Mobilization for War: I, Program and Administration (Washington, 1947) (hereafter cited as CPA, Industrial Mobilization for War), 3–5.

CHART 1—THE PEACETIME ARMY: SEPTEMBER 1939

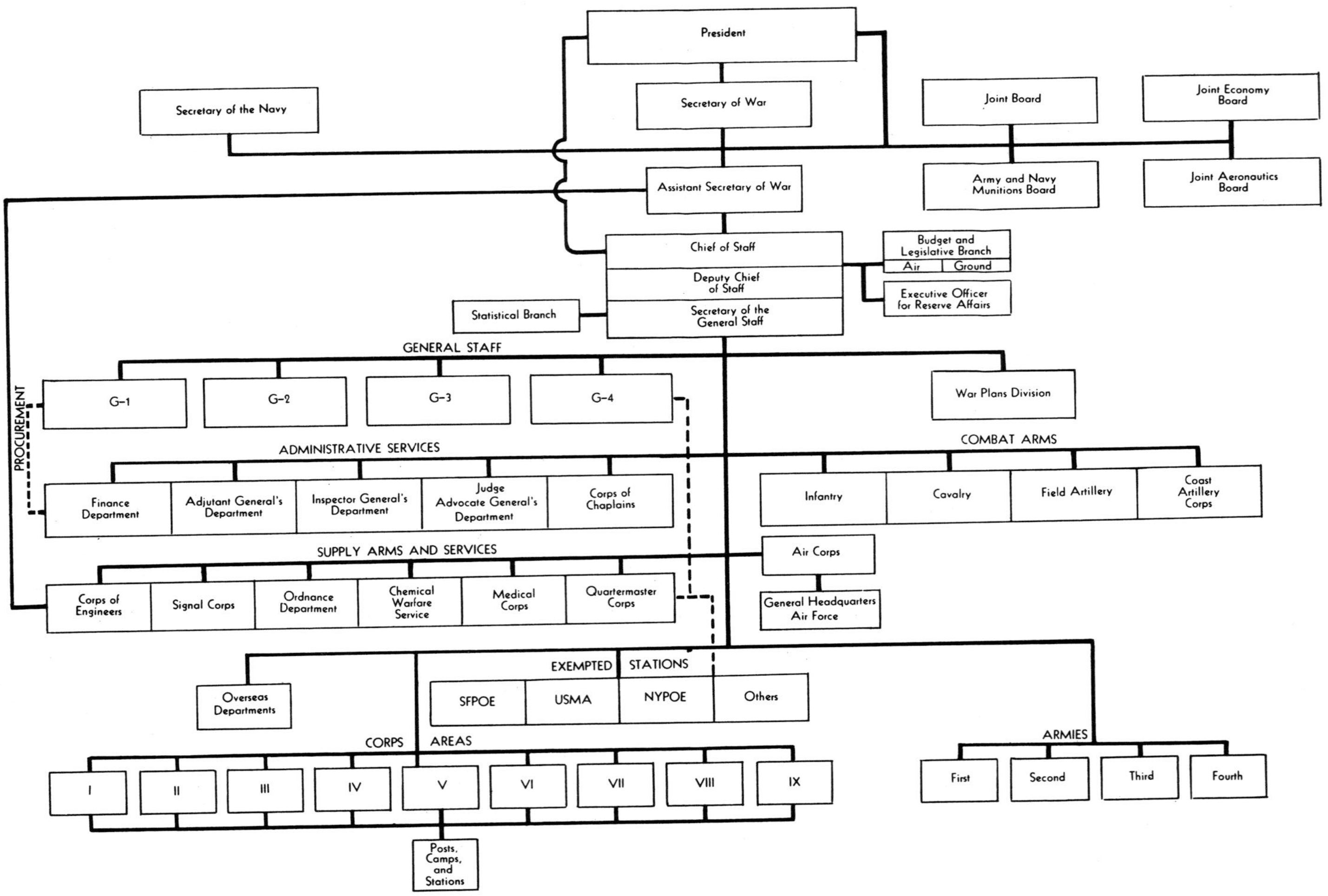

Joint Economy Board

Joint Aeronautics Board

Joint Board

Army and Navy Munitions Board

President

Secretary of War

Assistant Secretary of War

Secretary of the Navy

Budget and Legislative Branch — Air | Ground

Executive Officer for Reserve Affairs

Chief of Staff

Deputy Chief of Staff

Secretary of the General Staff

War Plans Division

Statistical Branch

GENERAL STAFF

G-1 | G-2 | G-3 | G-4

ADMINISTRATIVE SERVICES

Finance Department | Adjutant General's Department | Inspector General's Department | Judge Advocate General's Department | Corps of Chaplains

COMBAT ARMS

Infantry | Cavalry | Field Artillery | Coast Artillery Corps

Air Corps

General Headquarters Air Force

SUPPLY ARMS AND SERVICES

Corps of Engineers | Signal Corps | Ordnance Department | Chemical Warfare Service | Medical Corps | Quartermaster Corps

Overseas Departments

EXEMPTED STATIONS

SFPOE | USMA | NYPOE | Others

CORPS AREAS

I | II | III | IV | V | VI | VII | VIII | IX

Posts, Camps, and Stations

ARMIES

First | Second | Third | Fourth

PROCUREMENT

and supply allowances tables, transportation and traffic control, procurement of real estate, construction and maintenance of buildings, hospitalization, and distribution of noncombat troops.[8] Each of the other four WDGS divisions was also concerned with some aspect of logistics—G-1 (personnel) with administration, G-2 (intelligence) with logistical capabilities of foreign countries, G-3 (operations and training) with equipment allowances of tactical units and some of the training of service troops, War Plans Division with logistical capabilities in general since war planning could not safely ignore any aspect of them. Logistics similarly was a part, though not all, of the purview of the single Deputy Chief of Staff, who relieved the Chief of Staff of decisions on routine matters, generally of a budgetary, legislative, or administrative nature, and of that of the secretary of the General Staff, who co-ordinated and often initiated staff action on all kinds of matters.

The organization of the General Staff, in fact, did not recognize logistics as a well-defined field of activity requiring separate, specialized attention; lines of specialization in the General Staff cut across that field and were not too sharply drawn in any case. (*Chart 1*) General Staff officers, in American doctrine and tradition, were expected to possess a general competence and perspective enabling them to advise the Chief of Staff on broad problems of policy, not merely on the substantive and technical matters with which each, in the interests of orderly division of staff work, gained a special familiarity. For technical counsel the Chief of Staff looked rather to the chiefs of arms and services, sometimes called collectively the War Department Special Staff. And as the General Staff was not supposed to specialize, similarly it was

prohibited from "operating"—from engaging in "administrative duties for the performance of which an agency exists"—in contrast to the chiefs of arms and services, who operated as well as advised. From supervision, explicitly a WDGS function, it was, to be sure, only a short step to participation in the operations supervised, and thence to specialization. Until 1940 the General Staff did not move far in this direction, partly because of the entrenched prerogatives of the arms and services, partly because the General Staff was too small (only 232 officers in 1939, many of whom were serving in the field with troops) to descend far below its assigned sphere of plans, policy, and broad supervision.[9]

In the largest area of logistics—supply—staff supervision did not center in the General Staff but was divided between the Supply Division and the Office of the Assistant Secretary of War. This situation grew out of the National Defense Act of 1920 and the reorganization of the War Department resulting from the Harbord Board (Maj. Gen. James G. Harbord, Chairman) recommendations in 1921. The former had charged the Assistant Secretary of War with "supervision of the procurement of all military supplies" and "assurance of adequate provision," that is, advance planning, for industrial mobilization in time of war. These functions embraced the "business or industrial" aspects of supply, which the Harbord Board had sharply distinguished from the purely military aspects. In the long process of supply, the board argued, the concern of the professional Army was primarily with the de-

---

[8] AR 10-15, 18 Aug 36.
[9] (1) Cline, *Washington Command Post*, pp. 24–28. (2) Watson, *Prewar Plans and Preparations*, Ch. III. (3) Annual *Report of the Secretary of War, 1939*, Table C.

termination of requirements and specifications at the beginning, and the acceptance of finished munitions at the end; supervision of these activities belonged properly to G-4. The vast middle portion, comprising the War Department's dealings with private industry and the government agencies concerned with production of munitions, could be most effectively controlled by a civilian official, preferably a "captain of industry," though it seemed unlikely, as Secretary of War Newton D. Baker had pointed out, that the services of such a tycoon could be secured in time of peace. During the two interwar decades, at any rate, the supply arms and services—the procuring and issuing agencies—had two masters, the Assistant Secretary of War in matters of procurement, the "business" side of supply, and G-4 in matters of requirements and distribution, the "military" side.[10]

The leisurely pace and modest volume of the Army's logistical business in the years of peace did not unduly strain this structure. Yet there were ample portents of future trouble. The division between the business and military aspects of supply proved difficult to observe in practice. Both transportation and storage, occupying borderline positions, were causes of occasional contention between G-4 and the Assistant Secretary's office. It was obviously unrealistic to determine equipment specifications and requirements without reference to production capabilities; yet co-ordination between G-4, charged with the former, and the Assistant Secretary's office, charged with the latter, would surely impede the swift action demanded in an emergency. Moreover, the planning of industrial mobilization, assigned to the Assistant Secretary, was clearly part of the broader task, charged to the General Staff

in the National Defense Act, of planning for "the mobilization of the manhood of the nation and its material resources." Clear evidence that mobilization was an indivisible process was afforded in 1938, when Secretary of War Harry H. Woodring found it necessary to order the size of the planned initial force under PMP scaled down to the indicated capacity of industry.[11]

Finally, the very existence of divided authority caused uneasiness in the General Staff, which was mindful of its long struggle to control the supply and administrative bureaus. The Office of the Assistant Secretary in the late 1930's was a growing organization; by mid-1940 it numbered 181 persons at a time when the whole General Staff, including many officers in the field, comprised less than 350. As early as 1930 General Charles P. Summerall, the Chief of Staff, complained of encroachment by the Office of the Assistant Secretary of War into the domain of General Staff jurisdiction and warned, "the unity of control necessary to the efficient development of our military system no longer exists." He continued:

We, therefore, find ourselves dangerously near the status of divided authority in the War Department which prevailed in 1898 and again in 1917 . . . .

There is no doubt as to what general course affairs would take on the occurrence of a national emergency if the present situation should continue. As in 1917–18, the necessity for integrating the services of sup-

---

[10] (1) John D. Millett, "The Direction of Supply Activities in the War Department," *American Political Science Review,* XXXVIII (June 1944), 475–84. (2) Otto L. Nelson, Jr., *National Security and the General Staff* (Washington, Infantry Journal Press, 1946), Ch. VI and pp. 320–22.
[11] (1) Millett, "The Direction of Supply Activities . . . ," pp. 488–92, cited n. 10(1). (2) Annual *Report of the Secretary of War, 1938,* p. 1.

ply would early become apparent, and action analogous to that found essential during that period would be taken. In the meantime, important preparatory measures would have been neglected, and a delay and confusion that might prove fatal to the success of our arms would be inevitable.[12]

The Impulse Toward Rearmament and Foreign Aid

In the nine months following the outbreak of the war in Europe in September 1939, the United States did little either to augment her own forces or to arm those of the Western Allies with which her official and popular sympathies lay. These powers and Germany seemed to have reached a deadlock, while in the Far East Japan cautiously awaited the outcome, held in check for the present by fear of an attack by the USSR and by the threat of the U.S. Pacific Fleet. Uneasy rather than alarmed, and seeking above all to insulate the Western Hemisphere against war, the United States added less than 55,000 men to the Regular Army, bringing it to a strength of 245,413 by the end of May 1940. With this increase it was possible to organize five triangular divisions, create sufficient corps and army units to make up a full army corps and a field army, and hold large-scale maneuvers. At the same time the National Guard, its authorized level raised to 235,000, began more intensive training, and a number of Reserve officers were recalled for short tours of active duty. The Navy, meanwhile, kept its main fleet in the Pacific, and in the Atlantic instituted a "neutrality patrol" extending a few hundred miles out to sea.[13]

As for aid to the Western Allies, the Neutrality Act of November 1939 restricted the United States to the role of a disinterested purveyor of munitions to all who could buy them and carry them away. Great Britain and France purchased, accordingly, with an eye to conserving their limited fund of dollars. In the main they sought aircraft and machine tools, looking to the United States as a source of emergency and reserve supply in other respects while building up their own munitions industries. Several neutral nations also placed small orders with American manufacturers, and Finland made some purchases during her brief war with the Soviet Union during the winter of 1939-40. The total volume of orders was not large, but it did give an impetus, particularly in the field of aircraft, to the development of an American munitions industry—an impetus that the Army's own orders, filled largely by government arsenals, were wholly unable to provide.[14]

In the spring of 1940 the German mili-

---

[12] (1) Annual *Report of the Secretary of War, 1930*, pp. 108, 116. (2) Millett, "The Direction of Supply Activities . . . ," pp. 489, 493, cited n. 10(1). (3) For growing difficulties in supply organization during 1940 and 1941, see below, Ch. IX.

[13] (1) Annual *Report of the Secretary of War, 1940*, Table C. (2) Conn and Fairchild, Framework of Hemisphere Defense, Ch. I, pp. 27-41. (3) Annual *Report of the Secretary of War, 1941*, pp. 48-50.

[14] (1) W. K. Hancock and M. M. Gowing, *British War Economy* (London, His Majesty's Stationery Office, 1949), p. 106. (2) International Division, ASF, Lend-Lease as of September 30, 1945, I, MS (hereafter cited as ID, Lend-Lease), 66-72, OCMH. (3) Rpt, President's Ln Com, sub: Foreign Purch Other Than Br, 1 Jul-1 Oct 40, President's Ln Com file CC ANMB, Job A46-299. Clearance Committee files are with those of the Defense Aid Division, Office of the Under Secretary of War, and are generally catalogued with records of the International Division, ASF. (4) CPA, *Industrial Mobilization for War*, p. 4. (5) For a detailed account of Anglo-French purchasing activities during this period, see H. Duncan Hall, North American Supply, a volume in preparation for the British series HISTORY OF THE SECOND WORLD WAR, galley proof, Chs. III-IV, Hist Br, Cabinet Off, London.

tary machine burst through the defenses of the Allies, and almost overnight the threat to the countries of the Western Hemisphere took on terrifying proportions. Late in May, while the debacle in western Europe was at full tide, the military staffs prepared an emergency plan for a large-scale descent on the coast of Brazil to counter any major Axis move in that direction; the plan's name, "Pot of Gold," aptly suggests the total unreadiness of the Army and Navy to carry out any such undertaking. In the same month the planning staffs hurriedly set to work to revise plans for hemisphere defense under what seemed to be all too probable assumptions—that both France and Great Britain would be defeated (rather than merely neutral, as under earlier assumptions), that remnants of their fleets would be taken over by the victors, and that the United States and Canada would have to face the combined power of Germany, Italy, and Japan. Against such overwhelming odds, the planners concluded, the United States would be forced to fall back upon Hawaii and Alaska in the Pacific, concentrate most of her fleet in the Caribbean, and for the time being try to defend the Western Hemisphere only as far south as the bulge of South America. The completed plan, RAINBOW 4, was approved by the Joint Board on 7 June 1940 and by the President on 14 August.[15]

On 10 June, a week before France capitulated, President Franklin D. Roosevelt hopefully proclaimed at Charlottesville that the United States intended not only to rearm but also to help the nations opposing the Axis:

We will extend to the opponents of force the material resources of this nation and, at the same time, . . . harness and speed up the use of those resources in order that we ourselves in the Americas may have equipment and training equal to the task of any emergency and every defense.[16]

Two weeks later Britain was the only important "opponent of force" remaining in the field against Germany, and few doubted that she would either sue for peace or be overrun by the Wehrmacht. Army planners feared also that a Japanese invasion of Indochina was brewing, possibly to be preceded by an attack on Hawaii or the Panama Canal, and a Japanese-Soviet alliance against the United States in the Pacific seemed to the Chief of Staff, General George C. Marshall, a strong possibility. In this situation the military leaders saw no hope of carrying out both courses of action laid down by the President. They urged him to subordinate foreign aid wholly to rearmament in order to build up sufficient forces to defend the hemisphere within the limits indicated in the current RAINBOW 4 plan. They warned:

The naval and military operations necessary to assure successful Hemisphere defense call for a major effort which we are not now ready to accomplish. . . . To overcome our disadvantage in time, the concerted effort of our whole national life is required. The outstanding demands on this national effort are—first a radical speed-up of production, and second, the assembly and training of organized manpower.[17]

Into these two tasks the administration, Congress, and the armed services plunged with spectacular energy in the summer of

---

[15] (1) Conn and Fairchild, Framework of Hemisphere Defense, Ch. II, pp. 2–10. (2) Watson, *Prewar Plans and Preparations*, pp. 95–96, 104–07.

[16] U.S. Dept of State, *Peace and War: United States Foreign Policy, 1931–1941*, Pub 1853 (Washington, 1943), p. 76.

[17] (1) Memo, CNO and CofS for President, 27 Jun 40, WPD 4250-3. (2) Watson, *Prewar Plans and Preparations*, pp. 107–11.

1940. On 28 May the President had revived the Advisory Commission to the Council of National Defense of World War I, and under it, in the following months, the machinery of economic mobilization began to take form. Congress immediately raised the authorized strength of the Regular Army to 375,000 and voted funds to purchase badly needed seacoast defense equipment, aircraft, and other critical items, to expand the pilot training program, to establish ordnance munitions plants, and to conduct field maneuvers. The President's call for a 50,000-plane air force in May set the mood, if not the actual objectives, for mobilization. By the middle of September Congressional appropriations for the armed forces totaled over $8 billion, of which about three fourths was allotted to the Army. The Army also established a separate Armored Force, provided commanders and staffs for the four continental field armies, and set up in skeleton form the new General Headquarters (GHQ) which, under plans prepared soon after World War I, was intended eventually to become the command post for directing military operations in the next conflict—for the present, it merely took charge of an accelerated training program.

By the end of the summer, legislation was also enacted to authorize the manpower for a vast program of mobilization, through the induction of the National Guard, by calling up the Organized Reserve, and through Selective Service. This program contemplated the expansion of the Army to 1,400,000 men by the following July. Meanwhile, the Army laid down and the President approved a program of matériel mobilization to match the provision of military manpower—the great Munitions Program of 30 June 1940. This aimed at producing by autumn of 1941 equipment and reserves for an initial Protective Mobilization Plan force of 1,200,000 men, and by the end of 1941 equipment and reserves for 2,000,000. Within the same period the aircraft industry was to be built to a capacity of 18,000 planes a year, with a view to creating by spring of 1942 an air force of 12,000 planes and 54 combat groups. Beyond these goals, productive capacity was to be created sufficient eventually to equip and support an army of 4,000,000. Balancing this expansion of land and air power, Congress on 19 July also approved a "two-ocean Navy," of approximately double the Navy's existing strength.[18]

But the surge of American rearmament in the summer of 1940, while impressive, was not the all-out effort that the military leaders had urged. The President at the end of June rejected their more extreme proposals—longer hours and three-shift operations in munitions factories, an immediate draft, and complete mobilization—and, as a corollary, stipulated that aid to Britain must continue, though on a small scale. As General Marshall reported his decision:

. . . if . . . the British displayed an ability to withstand the German assault, and it appeared that a little help might carry them through to the first of the year, then we might find it desirable from the point of view

---

[18] (1) Annual *Report of the Secretary of War, 1941*, pp. 50–53, 60–61, Chart 3. (2) Wesley Frank Craven and James Lea Cate, eds., *Plans and Early Operations—January 1939 to August 1942*, Vol. I in THE ARMY AIR FORCES IN WORLD WAR II (Chicago, The University of Chicago Press, 1948) (hereafter cited as Craven and Cate, *AAF I*), 105. (3) Watson, *Prewar Plans and Preparations*, pp. 168–82. (4) Samuel Eliot Morison, *The Battle of the Atlantic: September 1939–May 1943* (Boston, Little, Brown and Company, 1947), pp. 27–28. (5) CPA, *Industrial Mobilization for War*, Pt. I, Chs. 2–3 and chart on p. 37.

of our defense to turn over other material that apparently would exercise an important effect on the action.[19]

The President directed further that British munitions orders were to be accepted in the United States, even though at some cost to American rearmament. This policy reflected the President's determined faith, not fully shared by the Army staff nor even by General Marshall, that American industry could produce munitions for nations fighting the Axis in ever-increasing volume without "seriously retarding" the huge rearmament program launched in June.

Events abroad soon lent some support to the President's policy. From the moment when, on 3–4 July, the British neutralized or destroyed the bulk of the French Navy, most of the danger of an early expansion of German naval power evaporated. By mid-September the repulse of the Luftwaffe's assaults upon England ended, for the time being, the menace of a German invasion and immeasurably improved the outlook for Britain's survival. American staff planners, cautiously surveying the scene toward the end of that month, estimated that Britain could probably hold out for at least another six months, thus giving the United States a year's respite, possibly longer, since the Germans would require six months to refit and man whatever remnants of the British Fleet they might capture. Aid to Britain began to appear less a course of desperation than a long-term investment in American security.[20]

Early Organization and Policy for Control of Foreign Purchases

The machinery of foreign aid had begun to take form in 1939, before the outbreak of the European war. Anticipating a flood of orders from Great Britain and France, the Assistant Secretaries of War and the Navy proposed in July 1939 that the Army and Navy Munitions Board, of which they were chairmen, should be made responsible for co-ordinating foreign purchases. The President approved, and a Clearance Committee was set up in the ANMB before the end of the year. This committee was to obtain information on all foreign orders and facilitate the placing of such orders by "friendly foreign governments" where they would promote the growth of an American arms industry, at the same time striving to prevent competition with Army or Navy procurement. U.S. designs and specifications were to be released to friendly governments if they placed firm, substantial orders and as long as release would not prejudice national defense. From the beginning, in short, an effort was made to draw from foreign aid the maximum benefit for American security.

The War and Navy Departments originally envisaged the Clearance Committee as the central organization for controlling foreign purchases, but the President in December 1939 superimposed upon it an interdepartmental liaison committee,[21] in which Treasury influence was dominant, to handle all contracts with foreign

---

[19] Informal memo, G. C. M. [Marshall] for Brig Gen George V. Strong, 24 Jun 40, WPD 4250-3.

[20] (1) Memo, ACofS WPD for CofS, 25 Sep 40, sub: Prob of Pdn of Mun in Relation to the Ability of the U.S. To Cope With Its Def Probs in the Present World Sit, WPD 4321-9. (2) Watson, *Prewar Plans and Preparations*, pp. 110–17. (3) Conn and Fairchild, Framework of Hemisphere Defense, Ch. II, pp. 17–19, 63.

[21] The liaison committee in June 1940 was given the name Interdepartmental Committee for Coordination of Foreign and Domestic Purchases. Before and after that date, however, it was known as the President's Liaison Committee.

ARMY AND NAVY MUNITIONS BOARD, JUNE 1941. *Seated left to right: Brig. Gen. Charles Hines, Brig. Gen. Harry K. Rutherford, Robert P. Patterson, James V. Forrestal, Capt. Edmund D. Almy, Capt. Anton B. Anderson; standing left to right: Maj. Gerson K. Heiss, Col. Henry S. Aurand, Comdr. Vernon H. Wheeler, Comdr. Leon B. Scott.*

governments relating to purchases of war materials in the United States. The President answered protests from the military by pointing out that over half of the foreign procurement would be of nonmilitary items. It seems more likely that the President's real reason was his desire to keep the negotiations in the hands of Henry L. Morgenthau, Jr., Secretary of the Treasury, who earlier had established a close and sympathetic relationship with Arthur B. Purvis, the Scottish-Canadian industrialist who headed the Anglo-French Purchasing Board. Morgenthau was an enthusiastic supporter of aid to the Allies while Harry Woodring, Secretary of War, was an outspoken isolationist. At all events, the Clearance Committee was reduced to a subordinate role, and the principle of civilian control over foreign aid was established. Army members of the Clearance Committee continued to carry out their earlier prescribed duties where purchases of military material were involved, acting for the Secretary of War through the President's Liaison Committee rather than for the ANMB. This action, during the period of the "phony war," consisted largely of collecting information and rendering assistance. Nearly all orders were for foreign types of munitions rather than for those standard to the

U.S. Army, and only in the case of aircraft was there any serious question of release of U.S. designs.[22]

In April and May 1940 the British and French Governments appealed frantically to the United States for all kinds of military material. The British cabinet scrapped its cautious financial approach, deciding to rely on American production to the extent of British need, rather than of British ability to pay, hoping naturally for an eventual relaxation of the American "cash and carry" restriction. In May the new Prime Minister, Winston S. Churchill, appealed directly to the President for supplies, and the Anglo-French Purchasing Board in the United States began to comb the country for facilities to produce small arms and artillery. When France fell, the British Purchasing Commission supplanted the board and took over all French contracts. The mushrooming of British orders dictated a tightening of the whole machinery of control.[23]

Congress on 28 June 1940 passed an act enabling the President to give priority to all Army and Navy orders over deliveries for private account or for export. By October 1940 a Priorities Board had been formed within the Advisory Commission to the Council of National Defense, and to it the President delegated his own powers. The ANMB assumed control of determining priorities for production of all munitions. Beginning in July 1940 foreign governments were required to file Purchase Negotiation Reports, which had to be approved by the Advisory Commission, on all proposed contracts over $150,000. When military materials were involved, the Clearance Committee screened the contracts, working through the Advisory Commission and the President's Liaison Committee.[24] The machinery provided a

means of eliminating British competition with the American defense program, and the spirit of the Congressional legislation and the inclination of the military leaders was to use it to this end. The President, however, insisted that the British program be accommodated as far as possible.

The issue of British aid during and after the crisis of May and June centered in the two questions of what could be given immediately from surplus Army stocks and what could be planned on a long-range basis from future production. These two aspects, together with their implications for the U.S. Army's rearmament program, will be treated in turn.

Use of Army Stocks To Aid Anti-Axis Nations

The Army's largest stocks of weapons, as already noted, were of obsolescent types upon which, until industry could produce

---

[22] (1) Memo, ASW and ASN for President, 30 Jul 39. (2) Memo, ANMB for Col Charles Hines, Chm CC ANMB, et al., 1 Dec 39, sub: ANMB Com for Clearance on Mun, with incl on rules and policies. (3) Ltr, President to SW, 6 Dec 39. (4) Memo, ASW and ASN for President, 9 Dec 39. (5) Memo, President for Chairmen ANMB, 14 Dec 39. (6) Memo, Hines for ASW, 22 Mar 40, sub: Present Status of CC ANMB. All in ID, Lend-Lease, Doc Suppl, I. (7) Watson, *Prewar Plans and Preparations*, p. 300. (8) For information on the work of the Clearance Committee, see its weekly reports to the Secretary of War in Rpts to ASW file, CC ANMB. (9) For an informative account of the Morgenthau-Purvis channel, see Hall, North American Supply, Ch. IV, galleys 1–4, Hist Br, Cabinet Off, London.
[23] (1) Hancock and Gowing, *British War Economy*, p. 119. (2) Edward R. Stettinius, Jr., *Lend-Lease: Weapon for Victory* (New York, The Macmillan Company, 1944), pp. 31–35. (3) Rpt 40, CC ANMB to SW et al., Rpts to ASW file, CC ANMB. (4) Winston S. Churchill, *The Second World War: Their Finest Hour* (Boston, Houghton Mifflin Company, 1949), pp. 23–25.
[24] (1) CPA, *Industrial Mobilization for War*, pp. 17–28, 50–51. (2) PL 671, 76th Cong. (3) ID, Lend-Lease, I, 72–73. (4) Ltr, Morgenthau to President, 19 Dec 40, President's Ln Com file, CC ANMB.

modern ones, the Army would have to depend for any sudden mobilization in the near future. Only in a limited sense could they be considered as "surplus." Requests from Latin American and European neutral countries in 1939 first raised the question of releases from these stocks. On 1 March 1940, in response to a request from the Swedish Government, G-4 drew up a fairly definitive list of items that the staff believed could be turned over without undue risk. The list included 100,000 Enfield rifles and 300 British-type 75-mm. guns and some obsolescent machine guns, heavy artillery, and mortars. On 12 March the Secretaries of State and War agreed that such surplus should be sold directly to neutral governments, but not to private individuals, corporations, or other potential intermediaries who might transfer the matériel to belligerent governments and thus lay the administration open to the charge of violating the neutrality laws. Under this policy sales were made to Finland, Sweden, Greenland, and several Latin American republics.[25]

It was the President himself who reversed this neutral policy in May and June 1940 over the strenuous objections of Secretary of War Woodring. At his direction, the War Department searched existing statutes for authority to turn over surplus arms to the British and came to the conclusion that it would be entirely legal to sell them to a private corporation, which could in turn sell to the British. A new surplus list was hastily prepared, obviously based more on what the British and French wanted than on what Army officials really conceived to be surplus. The President lengthened the list. The U.S. Steel Corporation assumed the role of intermediary, and on 11 June 1940 the material was transferred from the govern-

ment to the steel corporation and from the corporation to the British on the same day and for the same price—500,000 Enfield rifles with 129,140,708 rounds of ammunition, 80,583 machine guns of various types, 316 3-inch mortars, 20,000 revolvers, 25,000 Browning automatic rifles, 895 75-mm. guns with a million rounds of ammunition, and other miscellaneous items. In a few weeks this matériel was on its way to England, there to be used to arm the Home Guard and the troops who had returned from Dunkerque against the apparently inevitable German invasion. The Army also agreed, as a separate transaction, to trade ninety-three Northrop light bombers back to the manufacturer who could then deliver them as part of a British contract; the Navy took similar action on fifty Curtiss-Wright dive bombers.[26]

Both General Marshall and Admiral Harold R. Stark, Chief of Naval Operations, were convinced that no more surplus stocks could be released without endangering defense preparations. But the President's decisions on military policy at the end of June kept the door open for further releases. Also, Congress passed a law legalizing an exchange contract technique

[25] (1) Memo, ACofS G-4 for CofS, 1 Mar 40, sub: Surplus Ord Mat Available for Sale to Foreign Govts, G-4/26057-2. (2) Related papers in same file and in AG 400.703 (2-20-40). (3) Memo, Cordell Hull and Harry Woodring, no addressee, 12 Mar 40, ID, Lend-Lease, Doc Suppl, I. (4) A summary of the laws covering sales of surplus is in G-4/33184. (5) Records of surplus sales are in the AG 400.3295 series and in the Clearance Committee, ANMB files, classified by countries. The most convenient summary is a list compiled by the Clearance Committee as of 17 February 1941 (hereafter cited as CC surplus list, 17 Feb 41), in Corresp re Surplus Mat file, CC ANMB.

[26] (1) Watson, *Prewar Plans and Preparations*, pp. 309–12. (2) Stettinius, *Lend-Lease: Weapon for Victory*, pp. 26–31. (3) CC surplus list, 17 Feb 41. (4) Hall, North American Supply, Ch. V, Galley 4, Hist Br, Cabinet Off, London.

by which the Secretary of War could exchange surplus or obsolescent military equipment for newer types under production on foreign contracts. One important brake was provided, however. On 28 June 1940 Congress ruled that any military material sold or exchanged to foreign governments must be certified by the Chief of Staff as surplus to the defense needs of the United States.[27] In the months that followed General Marshall used this power judiciously, though he showed himself willing to take certain calculated risks. After June 1940 the releases of surplus equipment to Britain were grounded, at least nominally, on the principle that the equipping of the initial PMP force should not thereby be seriously retarded.

The course of this policy and the calculated risk it involved, both in June 1940 and later, may best be illustrated by the cases of rifles and light artillery. There were in government arsenals in June 1940 approximately 1,800,000 Enfield and 900,000 Springfield rifles; 240,000 Garands were in prospect by June 1942. Since two million rifles would serve four million men, there was an ample margin of safety if the possible needs of State Guards were disregarded. Some 500,000 Enfields were declared surplus and transferred to the British in June 1940, and more were released in the following months until the total reached 1,135,000 in February 1941.[28] Though these releases were made without serious deprivation to the U.S. Army during 1940 and 1941, they resulted in a serious shortage of rifles for training the vastly larger forces mobilized after Pearl Harbor.

The transfer of ammunition, without which the rifles were of no use to the British, was a more serious problem. There were only 588,000,000 rounds of rifle ammunition on hand in the United States in June 1940, and the rate of current production was pitifully small—four million rounds monthly in June and July, with a scheduled expansion to ten million monthly from August through December. Requirements for the initial PMP force were estimated by G-4 in early June at 458,000,000 rounds, an estimate that evidently ignored training needs entirely. But this figure, together with the premise that the ammunition was deteriorating in storage, provided the basis in June for releasing the 129,000,000 rounds to accompany the rifles.[29]

This amount was far from an adequate supply for the rifles released. The British were dependent on the United States for .30-caliber ammunition since their own production was entirely of .303-caliber. They requested 250,000,000 rounds from U.S. stocks in May 1940, and placed a contract with Remington Arms, but deliveries on this contract would not begin until April 1941. Army authorities at first agreed that old ammunition from stocks should be released in exact ratio as the new came off the production line—four million rounds a month in June and July, ten million per month from August through December. In August General Marshall repudiated this agreement. A review of the situation revealed that training requirements for the National Guard and Selective Service troops over the next year would be 1.6 billion rounds, and there were further needs for stocking island garrisons. Indeed, .30-caliber ammu-

---

[27] (1) PL 671, 76th Cong. (2) PL 703, 76th Cong.

[28] (1) Memo, ACofS G-4 for CofS, 5 Jun 40, sub: Surplus Ord Mat Available for Sale to Foreign Govts, G-4/26057-2. (2) CC surplus list, 17 Feb 41.

[29] Memo, ACofS G-4 for CofOrd, 6 Jun 40, sub: Exch of Deteriorated Am, with note for rcd only, G-4/16110-6.

nition promised to be the most gaping of all the deficits in meeting the PMP schedule. After the release of the first eight million rounds in June and July, Marshall refused to certify further releases in August; not until February 1941 did he agree to let the British have fifty million additional rounds, and then with the proviso that they should replace it from the May–July production on their Remington contract.[30]

This release of 188,000,000 rounds of rifle ammunition, though large in terms of current stocks and production, was a relatively small factor in the serious shortage, which continued well into 1942. The entire amount represented only eight days' combat supply for the rifles and machine guns released. The basic cause of the shortage was the delay in reaching full production. For this various factors were responsible—serious miscalculations in the development of new production facilities, labor difficulties, an untimely explosion at an important ordnance plant, to mention only a few. As a result, it was impossible to meet British, U.S. Army, Navy, and other needs.[31]

Of light artillery, the U.S. Army had on hand in the spring of 1940 4,470 75-mm. guns, including 3,450 of the French type, 700 of the British, and 320 of the American. Of these, only the French-type weapons were considered suitable for combat, and were being modernized for the purpose. In an emergency they would have to serve not only in their normal role of infantry support, but also as the only available substitute for the 37-mm. anti-tank gun. Brig. Gen. Richard C. Moore, the Deputy Chief of Staff, estimated on the basis of PMP requirements and normal wastage that there would be a shortage of 3,220 of these guns within a year after war broke out. Nevertheless, he was willing to dispose of the British-type guns. Two hundred were sold to the Finns in March, and on 4 June General Moore approved release to the British of the 395 remaining serviceable British-type guns.[32] The President, dissatisfied with this contribution, ordered the release of five hundred of the French type over the protests of the General Staff. One staff officer commented at the time that if sudden mobilization were necessary "everyone who was a party to the deal might hope to be found hanging from a lamp-post."[33] After June 1940 General Marshall approved no further transfers of artillery until the following February, when prospects for production of the new 105-mm. howitzer seemed much brighter. He also resisted pressure from both the British and the President to release Army bombers, and in agreeing early in 1941 to release of a

---

[30] (1) Ltr, Charles T. Ballantyne, Secy Gen Anglo-French Purch Bd, to Donald M. Nelson, Chm President's Ln Com, 17 Jun 40, sub: Small Arms Am, AG 400.3295 (6-17-40) (1). (2) Watson, *Prewar Plans and Preparations,* pp. 312–14. (3) Memo, unsigned, no addressee, 16 Aug 40 [sub: Br Arms and Am], Binder 4, Foreign Sale or Exch of Mun file, OCofS. (4) CC surplus list, 17 Feb 41. An additional six million rounds of .30-caliber ammunition for machine guns were transferred from naval stocks on 22 July 1940. (5) See material in AG 400.3295 (6-22-40). (6) Memo, President for SW, 4 Feb 41, and accompanying papers, in AG 400.3295 (2-4-41) (1).

[31] (1) Memo, Brig Gen Richard C. Moore, DCofS, for CofOrd, 23 Sep 40, sub: Pdn of Small Arms Am, G-4/31773. (2) For a discussion of production problems in this period, see R. Elberton Smith, Army Procurement and Economic Mobilization. (3) Harry C. Thomson and Lida Mayo, The Ordnance Department: II, Procurement and Supply. Last two are volumes in preparation for the series UNITED STATES ARMY IN WORLD WAR II.

[32] (1) Memo cited n. 28(1). (2) Memo, unsigned, no addressee, 11 Jun 40. (3) Memo, Gen Moore for CofS, 11 Jun 40, sub: Sale of 75-mm. Guns. Last two in Binder 4, Foreign Sale or Exch of Mun file, OCofS.

[33] (1) Memo for info, W. B. S. [Maj Walter Bedell Smith], no addressee, 11 Jun 40, Binder 4, Foreign Sale or Exch of Mun file, OCofS. (2) Watson, *Prewar Plans and Preparations,* p. 312.

few light tanks, he insisted that the British replace them, with interest, at a later date from output under their own contracts.[34]

Army surplus stocks released to the British nevertheless put them in a much better position to resist invasion. Similarly, the fifty over-age destroyers transferred to the British in September in exchange for Atlantic bases immeasurably strengthened the sea communications on which Britain's survival depended. To British morale the contribution was of inestimable value. Nevertheless, transfers of surplus matériel were only stopgap measures. Without assurance of continuing support from the United States in the form of modern weapons, which could only come from new production, the British could hardly hope to carry on indefinitely, much less win the war.

Anglo-American Co-ordination of Production Planning

The President's decisions at the end of June 1940 had erected a barrier against complete subordination of British arms orders to American defense needs.[35] In almost continuous discussions between American and British representatives in Washington throughout the last half of 1940, a solution was worked out on the assumption that the British aid program must be accommodated along with American rearmament. In these negotiations the War Department insisted that the British must present a broad program of requirements instead of placing individual contracts at random, that these requirements must be confined as far as possible to standard U.S. Army equipment, and that no British orders should be allowed to interfere with achievement of the goal of equipping the initial PMP force by the end of 1941.[36]

Co-ordination of aircraft production and deliveries was the most pressing problem and the one on which agreement was first reached. By the end of June 1940, after absorbing French orders, the British had contracts with American manufacturers for 10,800 airplanes, against a U.S. Army-Navy program for only 4,500. Expansion of aircraft production was going ahead far more rapidly than that of ground equipment, but was still very small in relation to the need. In conferences in mid-July 1940 it was agreed that the British should be allowed to continue to get deliveries on their existing contracts, and that the solution should be vastly increased production. Under the expanded program, contracts for 33,467 planes were to be placed for delivery by 1 April 1942. Of these, 14,375 were to be for the British and the rest for the U.S. Army and Navy. Arthur Purvis, taking what then seemed an almost unbelievably optimistic view of American production capabilities, secured an additional promise that after 1 January 1941 the British should be permitted to order an additional 3,000 planes a month if they could be produced. The British agreed to adjust their requirements, as far as possible, to planes and accessory equipment standard to the U.S. Army and Navy. In September 1940 the Army-Navy-British Purchasing Commission Joint Committee (later called the Joint

[34] (1) On planes, see Watson, *Prewar Plans and Preparations,* pp. 306–09. (2) On the tank question, see voluminous correspondence in G-4/31691-1 and AG 400.3295 (8-7-40) (1), and Staff Study 29A, Br Purch Comm file, CC ANMB.
[35] See above, pp. 29–30.
[36] (1) Memo cited n. 20(1). (2) Draft memo, G-2 for CofS, Oct 40, sub: Br Mun Reqmts for Calendar Year 1941, WPD 4340-3. (3) Watson, *Prewar Plans and Preparations,* pp. 316–18. (4) Rudolph A. Winnacker, The Office of the Secretary of War Under Henry L. Stimson, MS, Pt. I, p. 52, OCMH.

Aircraft Committee), consisting of American and British Air officers, was established to carry on a continuing consultation on aircraft standardization and adjustment of production schedules. The Joint Aircraft Committee became, in actual practice, also the body that arranged for allocation of finished planes when delivered. Under these arrangements no priority was in fact assured for the expanding U.S. Army Air Corps, and production inevitably fell behind the highly optimistic estimates. The President in November expressed a desire that planes coming off the production line be divided 50-50 with the British, but in reality no set formula was adopted.[37]

In September a similar arrangement was made for tanks, an article for which the British had placed no earlier orders. The British agreed to order American-type tanks of the medium M3 series, recently developed, if these were modified in accordance with British battle experience. By November the British had been allowed to place orders for 2,048 medium tanks with firms not then producing tanks for the U.S. Army. They also placed an experimental order for 200 light tanks, but later canceled it. Henceforth, the countries co-operated closely in developing tank-type weapons, Great Britain depending increasingly on the United States to fill its needs.[38]

For the general run of ground equipment standard to infantry divisions, however, the problem of types proved more difficult. The British used .303-caliber rifles, 25-pounders, 4.5-inch and 5.5-inch field artillery, and 40-mm. and 6-pounder (57-mm.) tank and antitank guns, while the Americans used .30-caliber rifles, 105-mm. and 155-mm. field artillery, 37-mm. and 75-mm. tank and antitank guns, and

37-mm. and 90-mm. antiaircraft artillery. Each country regarded its own types as superior and its own production program as too far advanced to permit a change. A separate program for production of British types in the United States would absorb scarce machine tools and plants and violate the principle that facilities for British aid must be capable of rapid conversion to meet American needs. In late September 1940 Sir Walter Layton of the British Ministry of Supply arrived in the United States to negotiate the whole issue. Layton presented a preliminary comprehensive statement of British requirements, the basis of which was a recently developed plan to arm fifty-five divisions by the end of 1941. The United States was asked to provide marginal quantities that British industry could not produce in time and quantities necessary to insure against loss of British capacity because of German air bombardment. This British "A" Program, as it was entitled, included one million .303-caliber rifles; 1,000 2-pounder antitank guns and 2,000 37-mm. guns; 2,250 2-pounder tank guns for tanks manufactured in Britain; 1,500 37-mm. and 1,500 75-mm. tank guns to match the British tank program in the United States; 1,600 37-mm. and 1,800 90-mm. antiaircraft guns; and 1,800 25-pounder artillery pieces and 300 4.5-inch or 5.5-inch pieces. Negotiations hung fire for several weeks because the War Department re-

---

[37] (1) Hall, North American Supply, Ch. VI, Galleys 7–8, 18–19, Hist Br, Cabinet Off, London. (2) Watson, *Prewar Plans and Preparations*, pp. 305–09. (3) Winnacker MS, Pt. I, pp. 52–53, cited n. 36(4). (4) Ltr, SW to Gen Moore, 13 Sep 40, ID, Lend-Lease, Doc Suppl, I.

[38] (1) AG ltr to WD Rep President's Ln Com, 6 Sep 40, sub: Release of Designs for Medium Tanks . . . , and accompanying papers, AG 400.3295 (8-7-40) (1). (2) Hall, North American Supply, Ch. VI, Galley 12, Ch. VII, Galley 27, Hist Br, Cabinet Off, London.

fused to consider the British types involved. To break the deadlock, Layton finally proposed in late October a solution on an entirely different basis—the British would place orders for American standard equipment for ten British divisions. This plan, subsequently known as the "B" Program, was accepted by the War Cabinet reluctantly since the British did not have any definite plans for completely equipping and maintaining ten British divisions with American equipment. Yet it offered the British a measure of participation in the developing American munitions program and promised an increase in American capacity for production of arms, a step that the British regarded as desirable as did the U.S. General Staff. They also hoped that acceptance of the Ten Division Program would open the gates for the placing of orders for their "A" Program, which they continued to regard as far more important.[39]

In November the Army's War Plans Division undertook a study to determine to what extent the British programs could be met without interfering with the delivery of equipment to an American force capable of protecting the Western Hemisphere in case of British collapse. It was assumed that full training requirements must be on hand by 30 June 1941 and full operational requirements as soon thereafter as possible. Though WPD found a wide variation in the expected degree of interference with respect to different items of equipment, the staff concluded that the British "B" program should be accepted with an adjustment of time schedules since in the end it would serve to expand production of munitions.[40] On 29 November 1940, Secretary of War Henry L. Stimson informed Sir Walter Layton that the Ten Division Program was acceptable, subject to the proviso that no final commitments could be made as to time or delivery and to certain other conditions. British orders must be placed immediately and with the approval of the appropriate supply branches of the War Department. Complicated legal and financial questions would have to be resolved, and a provision must be placed in each contract permitting its assumption by the United States if necessary for national defense.[41]

Meanwhile, the Advisory Commission and the Treasury agreed on 29 October 1940 on the principle that "henceforth the general rule would prevail . . . that orders would be entertained in this country only for items of equipment which were standard for this country."[42] In keeping with this principle, Stimson also informed Layton that while existing British orders for nonstandard equipment—.303-caliber rifles, 2-pounder guns, 4.5-inch and 5.5-inch artillery—would be allowed to stand, no additional contracts could be placed for them. No orders for ammunition for these types beyond existing contracts for .303-caliber would be permitted. For the rest of their "A" Program, the British were required to place orders for American types. In no case could any of these "A" Program orders be given priority over fulfillment of the complete American program.[43]

[39] (1) Winnacker MS, Pt. I, pp. 54–55, cited n. 36(4). (2) Memo, Arthur E. Palmer, Sp Asst to SW, for SGS, 6 Nov 40, AG 400.3295 (11-6-40). (3) CPA, *Industrial Mobilization for War*, p. 52. (4) Hall, North American Supply, Galleys 12–16, Hist Br, Cabinet Off, London.

[40] Memo, ACof S WPD for CofS, 20 Nov 40, sub: Mat Assistance for Gt Brit, WPD 4323-7.

[41] Ltr, Stimson to Layton, 29 Nov 40, Br A&B Progs file, DAD, Job A46-299.

[42] Memo cited n. 39(2).

[43] (1) Ltr cited n. 41. (2) Ltr, A. E. Palmer to William S. Knudsen, NDAC, 19 Nov 40, Br A&B Progs file, DAD.

Concurrently with the negotiations over the ground force program, the British presented an additional proposal for letting contracts for 12,000 airplanes, over and above those set up under the July agreement, and for a speed-up in delivery schedules. By the end of November this proposal had also been accepted, though with the same reservations as to time of delivery. Aircraft production schedules were projected further into the future, and automobile manufacturers were brought into the aircraft production picture.[44]

General Marshall on 10 December 1940 expressed satisfaction with both the air and the ground force programs, pointing out that the former would provide planes for 60 additional air groups in case of British collapse and the latter, equipment for 300,000 additional men for the ground forces. In the meantime, he had prescribed priorities for delivery of equipment for the Ten Division Program with the aim of safeguarding the equipping of the initial PMP force. The general policy was to be:

a. No deliveries . . . will be made prior to July 1, 1941, and no deliveries of any items . . . until the minimum training requirements of the Army of the United States (PMP and replacement centers) are filled.

b. During the period July 1–September 15, 1941, minimum training requirements of the British 10-Division program will be filled as far as practicable.

c. Following the fulfillment of the initial training requirements for the British no additional items will be furnished them until the full American requirements of the PMP and replacement centers are filled.[45]

These decisions on the Ten Division Program met all the conditions of the War Department and at the same time promised a larger measure of aid to Britain than had at first been thought possible. The principle on which they were based—

British use of U.S. standard equipment—recommended itself to Army planners since it promised to expand production. The specific arrangements, to be sure, proved to be ephemeral, but they were an important step toward systematizing planning with a view to dividing the munitions output of American industry among the forces of both nations in a manner best calculated to defeat the Axis—that is to say, toward uniting U.S. defense and foreign aid munitions requirements in a single consolidated supply program. While the British were undoubtedly disappointed both in their failure to secure acceptance of their own types for production and in the priority accorded to deliveries of ground equipment under their contracts, they had gained their major objective—a share in the vast output of munitions of which the American industrial machine would eventually be capable.

Aid to Other Nations

Virtually every independent nation in the world outside the Axis orbits made inquiries or tried to place munitions contracts in the United States in 1940. The requests of nations within the British Commonwealth of Nations and of refugee governments residing in London were largely absorbed within the British programs, but others lay outside the British sphere—notably those of Latin American nations, China, and the Netherlands In-

[44] (1) Winnacker MS, Pt. I, pp. 58–60, cited n. 36(4). (2) CPA, *Industrial Mobilization for War*, pp. 49–50.

[45] (1) Memo, SGS for ACofS WPD, 2 Dec 40, sub: Mat Assistance to Gt Brit Under Br "B" Prog, Br A&B Progs file, DAD. (2) Memo, CofS for SW, 10 Dec 40, sub: New Airplane Prog and U.S.-Type Ord Prog of Br Purch Comm, Br A&B Progs file, DAD.

dies. Under prevailing policy and strategy, aid to Britain came first. British needs, when added to those for American rearmament, so absorbed existing stocks and production facilities that scant consideration could be given these other demands.

Military aid to Latin American nations might, indeed, have been regarded as a logical part of the scheme of hemisphere defense. But while the principle was accepted in 1940, very little was done to implement it. The Pittman Resolution, passed by Congress on 15 June 1940, permitted the War Department to sell coast defense and antiaircraft material from surplus stocks to Latin American countries and to manufacture these arms for them in government arsenals and factories. Releases of surplus stocks to Latin American nations in 1940, however, were limited to a few thousand rifles to Haiti and Nicaragua, and some obsolete coast artillery to Brazil. In his decisions on military supply policy at the end of June 1940, the President stipulated that, in view of the requirements for U.S. rearmament and aid to nations fighting the Axis, only token aid to countries south of the border would be possible.[46] Some plans were made for future aid from new production. Latin American governments were invited to make their needs known, and arrangements were made to extend credit through the Export-Import Bank of Washington. The Joint Army-Navy Advisory Board on American Republics was set up to handle all Latin American munitions requests and to draft a detailed program. To equip the forces of these republics, WPD in December 1940 established a priority that would permit them to receive small quantities of U.S. standard-type weapons once the needs of the initial PMP force were met, but this program

could not be expected to get under way before early 1942. In effect, U.S. policy indicated an intention to rely largely on U.S. forces for defense of the Western Hemisphere.[47]

China and the Netherlands Indies occupied positions of vital importance in the Far East but the American policy after mid-1940 was to avoid war with Japan or, if this were not possible, to commit no more forces west of Hawaii. Aid to China received little consideration until the very end of the year. The Chinese Government, with scanty financial resources, could purchase in the United States only by borrowing. The Export-Import Bank granted China a loan of $100 million late in 1940, and the Universal Trading Corporation, the Chinese agent in this country, presented requests for an air program and for considerable quantities of ordnance either from stocks or from future production contracts. These requests coincided with the visit of Col. Claire L. Chennault,[48] American air adviser to the Chinese Government, and Maj. Gen. Mao Pang-tzo[49] to the United States to press the issue of Chinese aid. The Chinese were allowed to place some contracts with Curtiss-Wright for aircraft, and the British agreed to divert one hundred old-type P-40's from their own contract with this firm to be replaced from the Chinese contract later. The hundred P-40's became the initial equipment of the American Volunteer Group, the Flying Tigers, under Chennault, but the War Depart-

---

[46] (1) Pub Resolution 83, 76th Cong. (2) CC surplus list, 17 Feb 41. (3) Informal memo cited n. 19.
[47] Conn and Fairchild, Framework of Hemisphere Defense, Ch. IX.
[48] This was a Chinese Air Force rank. He held also the rank of captain, USA-Ret., until 9 April 1942, when he was ordered to active duty as a colonel.
[49] Often anglicized to Peter T. Mow.

ment was unable to do anything further to satisfy the Mao-Chennault requests.[50]

The position of the Netherlands Indies was the most difficult of all. Its government commanded ample financial resources and presented a well-defined program of ground, naval, and air requirements. By February 1941 it had placed contracts valued at $83 million, ranking it as the second largest foreign purchaser in this country. But its low priority gave little hope of receiving deliveries of critical items for a long time to come. The Dutch were unable even to place contracts for many of their most vital needs such as rifles and ammunition, and the Army refused to release material to them from its stocks. As Lt. Col. Edward E. Mac-Morland, Secretary of the Clearance Committee, ANMB, confessed in February 1941:

. . . the possibilities of early deliveries for the Netherlands East Indies are hopeless under present laws and priority conditions . . . they are competing with the United States and British in a market with limited immediate supplies and must wait a long time for sizeable deliveries.[51]

The Drift Toward Collaboration With Britain

By the end of 1940 the mobilization and rearmament programs were in full swing. The Army had grown mightily in numbers—from 264,118 at midyear to 619,403 at the end of the year—and its service establishment now included 149,400 troops. Since August, troops had been moving to the overseas garrisons in considerable numbers, raising the total overseas strength from 64,500 the preceding May to almost 92,000 in December; the acquisition of a fringe of new bases from Britain in the Atlantic in September foreshadowed an even greater overseas de-

ployment. Some $270 million in military construction had been initiated, largely to accommodate the flood of selectees sent to the camps for training beginning in the autumn. Federalization of the National Guard had begun. The activation of GHQ, the designation of Army commanders and staffs, and the further separation of the territorial organization for administration, supply, and "housekeeping" (the corps areas) from the tactical and training organization (GHQ and the field armies) were all important steps in launching mobilization on a large scale. The enormous increase in the business of staff control incident to this mobilization was reflected in the addition of two new deputies to the Chief of Staff's office late in 1940, one for Air Corps matters and one (General Moore) for a miscellany of largely logistical business—construction, maintenance, supply, transportation, land acquisition, and hospitalization—and problems concerning the Armored Force. The number of officers on the General Staff, including those in the field, rose from less than 350 in mid-1940 to over 550 at the end of the year.[52]

---

[50] (1) Ltr, Archie Lockhead, Universal Trading Corp., to Philip Young, Chm President's Ln Com, 8 Jan 41. (2) Memo, Maj Gen James H. Burns, U.S. Army member President's Ln Com, for Young, 28 Jan 41. Both in China (2) file, DAD. (3) For details, see Charles F. Romanus and Riley Sunderland, *Stilwell's Mission to China,* UNITED STATES ARMY IN WORLD WAR II (Washington, 1953), pp. 7–13.
[51] (1) Memo, MacMorland for G-2, 14 Feb 41, sub: Netherlands Mun Reqmts, Netherlands file, DAD. (2) Rpt cited n. 14(3). (3) Ltr, SW to Secy of State, no date, with accompanying papers, AG 400.3295 (9-4-40) (1).
[52] (1) Annual *Report of the Secretary of War, 1940,* Tables C, D. (2) Annual *Report of the Secretary of War, 1941,* Tables C, D. (3) Watson, *Prewar Plans and Preparations,* pp. 69–71. (4) Cline, *Washington Command Post,* pp. 8–11, 24. (5) Greenfield, Palmer, and Wiley, *AGF I,* pp. 6–8. (6) Anderson, Munitions for the Army, p. 15, cited n. 2(1).

But the very substantial progress a- chieved in this six-month period was largely in the necessary preparatory work of defining policy, working out procedures and organization, placing contracts, and "tooling up." The output of organized, trained, and equipped troops was not im- pressive. The influx of selectees into the Army had a disrupting and retarding effect on training; "blind leading the blind, and officers generally elsewhere," was Maj. Gen. Lesley J. McNair's dry comment after visiting one division in September.[53] Organization tables for the triangular division, the basic unit of the new army, were not completed until late in 1940. Six months of munitions produc- tion, moreover, had added relatively little to the Army's stock of weapons.[54] *(See Ap- pendix B.)* The output included no me- dium tanks, no heavy-caliber antiaircraft guns, no new standard 105-mm. howitzers (the bulk of light artillery pieces produced were 37-mm. and 75-mm. antitank guns), and almost no new heavy artillery (all ex- cept three pieces were modified older models). The production of .50-caliber ammunition had been meager. In this record can be seen at a glance the reason why foreign aid during 1940 consisted largely of releases from stocks of obsoles- cent matériel.

Both rearmament and foreign aid were falling short of meeting the needs of the situation developing abroad in the late summer and autumn of 1940. The repulse of the Luftwaffe's attack on Britain in Sep- tember, heartening though it was, scarcely diminished German power, but rather di- verted it into other channels. In the latter part of 1940 the signs pointed to an im- pending German drive to the southwest, in conjunction with Italy's effort to over- run Greece and to crush British power in the eastern Mediterranean. During Octo- ber Vichy France seemed about to col- laborate, at least passively, with Germany in this design. While an invasion of the Western Hemisphere did not yet seem im- minent, Germany probably had the strength to capture Gibraltar and push down the west coast of Africa. If she should gain the whole eastern shore of the Atlantic from the English Channel to Dakar, her aircraft and naval raiders could make a shambles of the Atlantic sea lanes, and it would be difficult to prevent Latin American countries from being drawn into her political orbit. In Septem- ber, too, Japan formally joined the Axis and made her first move into northern Indochina.[55]

Against the full-scale aggression on which Japan seemed about to embark, the U.S. Fleet, then concentrated mainly in the eastern Pacific, was the only real deterrent. It could remain there, however, only as long as the British Navy guarded the Atlantic, and because the U.S. Navy would be for some time to come the country's only real mobile defense, it could not be committed to action any- where until the nation's very existence was at stake. Under RAINBOW 4 it would attempt to hold the Alaska-Hawaii- Panama triangle. For a major effort in the Far East, the planners warned, "we are not now prepared and will not be pre- pared for several years to come."[56] To counter the threat from the east, they

[53] Personal ltr, Gen McNair to Maj Gen Walter C. Short, 23 Oct 40, GHQ 320.2/21.

[54] (1) War Production Board and Civilian Produc- tion Administration, Official Munitions Production of the United States by Months, July 1, 1940–August 31, 1945. (2) Greenfield, Palmer, and Wiley, *AGF I,* p. 36.

[55] Conn and Fairchild, Framework of Hemisphere Defense, Ch. II, pp. 58–66, and Ch. III.

[56] Memo cited n. 20(1).

thought the United States would have to move rapidly—occupying the Azores at the first indication of a German advance into Spain and Portugal, occupying ports and airfield sites in northeastern Brazil if the Germans took Gibraltar and moved into North Africa. And if the worst should befall, if the British Fleet were destroyed or surrendered, "from that very day the United States must within 3 months securely occupy all Atlantic outpost positions from Bahia [Baía] in Brazil northward to include Greenland."[57]

If this RAINBOW 4 situation should in fact develop, Army planners estimated that a minimum force of 1,400,000 troops completely trained and equipped would be needed to defend the hemisphere north of Brazil. The objectives of the munitions program were revised upward late in 1940 to provide for equipping an initial PMP force of this size, with a first augmentation of 2,800,000; the 4,000,000-man force remained a long-term goal. But there was no expectation that even the initial PMP force would be ready before April 1942. By April 1941, the staff estimated, not more than six full-strength divisions with supporting units (150,000 men) could be put in the field. Currently (September 1940) it would be possible to muster perhaps five skeleton divisions (about 55,000 men), virtually without support, only by dint of scalping other units of personnel and equipment and reducing training allowances across the board by half. The Army, in fact, could not at this time have maintained in combat any balanced force without slashing training allowances of ammunition all along the line.[58]

At the end of 1940, therefore, the survival of Britain and her fleet appeared more than ever a prerequisite to the security of the Western Hemisphere. In November both General Marshall and Admiral Stark concluded that the United States could not afford to allow Britain to lose the war. To this end, they agreed, the United States would probably have to engage eventually in large-scale land operations against Germany in Europe in conjunction with British forces. This might well mean temporarily sacrificing American interests in the Far East. General Marshall thought it imperative to "resist proposals that do not have for their immediate goal the survival of the British Empire and the defeat of Germany."[59] "The issues in the Orient," asserted the Joint Planning Committee, "will largely be decided in Europe."[60] Army and Navy leaders disagreed only as to the degree to which the armed forces (in effect, the Navy) could afford at this time to be committed to resisting Japanese aggression. Admiral Stark assumed that a vigorous defense, at least, must be undertaken, but General Marshall warned, "a serious commitment in the Pacific is just what Germany would like to see us undertake."[61]

To avoid such a commitment was the aim of the cautious course of action that

---

[57] (1) *Ibid.* (2) Memo, Gen Strong for CofS, 1 Oct 40, WPD 4175-15.

[58] (1) Memo cited n. 20(1). (2) WD ltr, 18 Feb 41, sub: Def Objectives, AG 381 (2-17-41). (3) Watson, *Prewar Plans and Preparations,* pp. 318–19. Army records for the closing months of 1940 contain numerous allusions to the revised PMP objectives, which probably were formulated in connection with RAINBOW 4. (4) For the difficulties of mounting expeditionary forces late in 1940, see below, Ch. II.

[59] Memo, CofS for CNO, 29 Nov 40, sub: Tentative Draft, Navy Bsc War Plan–RAINBOW 3, WPD 4175-15.

[60] Memo, JPC for JB, 21 Dec 40, sub: Natl Def Policy for the U.S. in Response to a 14 Dec 40 Dir From JB, JB 325, Ser 670.

[61] (1) Memo cited n. 59. (2) Memo, Adm Stark fo. SN, 12 Nov 40 (familiarly known as the Plan Dog Memo), WPD 4175-15. This is a revised version of Admiral Stark's memo of 4 November 1940 to the Secretary of the Navy, no copy of which exists in

the President in January 1941 laid down for the armed services to follow in the immediate future. The Navy was to remain on the defensive in the Pacific, based on Hawaii, without reinforcing its squadrons in far Pacific waters. In the Atlantic the Navy was to prepare to convoy shipments of munitions to Britain, a course that the President was not yet ready to risk but one that some of his advisers, notably Stimson and Secretary of the Navy Frank Knox, were already urging as the only further contribution the United States could now make to Britain's defense. The Army was to undertake no aggressive action at all for some time; "our military course," the President warned, "must be very conservative until our strength [has] developed." [62] Late in the month British and American military staff representatives began conversations in Washington looking to the more distant and hypothetical contingency of full participation by the United States in the war against the European Axis. [63]

Britain's most pressing need, in any case, was material aid, and Prime Minister Churchill in a long, eloquent message to the President on 8 December 1940, drove home this point. Even though deliveries on existing contracts would continue for some time, the dwindling of Britain's dollar resources had reached a point where the supply programs then under discussion—by now an important part of the plans for continuing the war—could not be financed. The cost of supplies actually on order for the British at the end of 1940 totaled $2.7 billion; the larger pro-

grams would cost $6.5 billion more. By the most strenuous efforts, the British could not muster more than half this sum in dollar exchange. On the American side, it appeared virtually impossible to continue aid to Britain, as heretofore, without enabling legislation. Involved legal arrangements would be necessary to finance plant expansion with mixed American and British funds, and to place contracts with the same firms under different conditions of payment. Part of the matériel for the Ten Division Program would have to be produced in government-owned or government-leased plants, and there was no legal method of transferring this matériel to the British except as surplus certified by the Chief of Staff to be nonessential to American defense. The placing of British contracts came to a virtual standstill while these issues were being threshed out, and the Ten Division Program remained, along with its allied arrangements, largely a paper proposition. [64]

The President, after mulling over these problems early in December during a cruise in the Caribbean (where Churchill's appeal reached him), returned to the United States in mid-December with the idea of lend-lease. The famous metaphor with which Roosevelt illustrated this idea in a press conference on the 17th—of the loan of a garden hose to put out a fire in a neighbor's house—actually was not par-

[62] Memo, CofS for ACofS WPD, 17 Jan 41, sub: White House Conf Thursday, January 16, 1941, WPD 4175-18.

[63] For American-British Conversations, see below, Ch. II.

[64] (1) Ltr, Churchill to President, 8 Dec 40, as quoted in Churchill, *Their Finest Hour*, pp. 558-67. (2) Memo, Maj Gen Charles M. Wesson, CofOrd, for SW, 4 Dec 40, sub: Procurement of Br "B" Prog, Br A&B Progs file, DAD. (3) CPA, *Industrial Mobilization for War*, p. 53. (4) Hall, North American Supply, Ch. VI, Galleys 26-27, Hist Br, Cabinet Off, London.

War Department files. (3) See discussion in Watson, *Prewar Plans and Preparations*, pp. 119-23. (4) Maurice Matloff and Edwin M. Snell, *Strategic Planning for Coalition Warfare: 1941-1942*, UNITED STATES ARMY IN WORLD WAR II (Washington, 1953), pp. 25-28.

ticularly apt, since relatively little of the material "lent" to Britain and other nations under lend-lease was to be returned or made good after the world conflagration was finally extinguished. If lend-lease embodied the idea of a loan at all, it was in the notion of free and continuous exchange of assistance of all kinds—goods, services, and information—that over the long haul would be of roughly equal benefit to both sides. The central idea, as the President put it in the same press conference, was to "get rid of the silly, foolish, old dollar sign"—in short, to remove all financial obstacles to the flow of American aid to nations fighting against a common enemy. A few days later, in his Fireside Chat of 29 December, Roosevelt tossed out another catchy phrase—arsenal of democracy—which, by emphasizing the primary role of the United States as a supplier of munitions, unquestionably bolstered the deep-seated hope that it would not be necessary to "send the boys overseas" as well. Nevertheless, the debate over lend-lease, in Congress and throughout the country, raged for more than two months before the lend-lease bill (HR 1776) finally became law on 11 March.[65]

At one stroke the Lend-Lease Act cleared away the legal and financial barriers that stood in the way of aid to Britain and other nations claiming American aid. It held out the promise of a single consolidated military production program financed entirely with American funds to meet both foreign and domestic military needs, something the War Department had frequently urged during 1940. It put the stamp of Congressional approval on the President's policy of dividing American resources between U.S. rearmament and anti-Axis nations abroad, and promised that aid to these nations would continue so long as they showed any ability to resist. And since Britain's claims overshadowed all others at the moment, it was a long step toward partnership with Britain in military supply, just as the staff conversations going on in Washington, while the lend-lease bill was being debated, were a step toward full military collaboration. Hemisphere defense remained the bedrock on which both lend-lease and plans for collaboration rested, but lend-lease was to be an important factor in enabling the United States to wage war as a member of a powerful and victorious coalition rather than as the sole defender of her own shores.

---

[65] (1) Winnacker MS, Pt. I, pp. 56–57, 61, cited n. 36(4). (2) Robert E. Sherwood, *Roosevelt and Hopkins: An Intimate History* (rev. ed., New York, Harper & Brothers, 1950), pp. 221–29.

CHAPTER II

War Plans and Emergency Preparations

By the end of 1940 American military leaders were convinced that American security was bound up with Britain's survival, and that for practical reasons this would require the defeat of the European Axis. American military policy, they agreed, must be decisively oriented to this end, if necessary at the expense of American interests in the Far East and at the risk of eventual direct involvement in the war. They began, therefore, to give thought to the probable terms and form of direct involvement. In the Army staff, at least, habituated to the logistics of hemisphere defense, the far-ranging expanse of Britain's imperial commitments and her long, exposed lines of communications inspired misgivings. Discussions with British military staff representatives in Washington late in the winter of 1940–41 brought the maturing ideas of the Americans on this subject squarely into conflict with British views. While agreeing that defeat of Hitler must be the primary goal of an Anglo-American partnership, the staffs tended, on each side, to approach military collaboration in terms of their own experience and plans, especially with reference to oceanic lines of communications. The British were influenced, too, by the fact that theirs was a "going" war, and their mobi-

lization and deployment well advanced, while American military power was still largely potential. Out of these differences in outlook grew a sharp disagreement as to the best methods for pursuing the common end and, more particularly, as to the role that American armed forces should play.

During the winter and spring of 1941, meanwhile, as Britain's military fortunes steadily deteriorated, the United States prepared to expand its principal contribution to Britain's war—material aid—and also moved rapidly closer to direct participation through "measures short of war" in the Atlantic. Until the end of May, moreover, the threat of a German move to the southwest into northwest and west Africa remained acute, provoking the United States in that month to actively prepare for an occupation of the Azores, a project that fell just short of being carried out. The Army thus labored under a double logistical burden during this period—equipping the rapidly expanding mass of the Army in training, and deploying garrison forces to outlying bases and territories, while concurrently preparing small, mobile, striking forces for emergency action. In both these tasks, by late spring 1941, preparations had fallen far short of what the rapidly developing situation seemed to demand, accentuating an unreadiness that appeared almost as acute as that of June 1940.

Britain's War

By the beginning of 1941 the logistical scope of Britain's war was more vast and involved than the actual localization of the fighting would indicate. The conspicuous battles were being fought in Libya and in the air over the home islands. But the effort to sustain armies in Egypt, Libya, east Africa, and elsewhere in the Near and Middle East, and to maintain naval and air power in the Mediterranean was absorbing, or was soon to absorb, half of Britain's war production, transported at enormous cost over the long route around the Cape of Good Hope or in occasional convoys forced through the Mediterranean. In all the imperial outposts from Hong Kong and Singapore to the West Indies, Britain and her Commonwealth associates had to maintain forces, meager in numbers but costly in shipping and material. On the seaways binding together the scattered parts of the Empire and Commonwealth, the deadly war against the submarine, long-range bomber, and raider went on—a war that Britain in spring of 1941 was losing.

Geography forced Britain to operate on exterior lines, around the periphery of her opponents' compact land-based power. Prime Minister Churchill wrote to the President in December 1940:

The form which this war has taken, and seems likely to hold, does not enable us to match the immense armies of Germany in any theatre where their main power can be brought to bear. We can, however, by the use of sea-power and air-power, meet the German armies in regions where only comparatively small forces can be brought into action. We must do our best to prevent the German domination of Europe from spreading into Africa and into Southern Asia. We have also to maintain in constant readiness in this island armies strong enough to make the problem of an oversea invasion insoluble. . . . Shipping, not men, is the limiting factor, and the power to transport munitions and supplies claims priority over the movement by sea of large numbers of soldiers.[1]

Even with the mobility conferred by sea power, Britain's strength in men and munitions, as well as in shipping, was inadequate to overcome the disadvantage of long and exposed lines of communications. Germany could move larger forces into the Mediterranean with far less effort than could Britain. Germany could concentrate her armies on the English Channel more rapidly than the British could ship divisions back from Egypt or from the Far East and, therefore, Britain had to keep large forces idle at home.

Britain's logistical disadvantage was not merely a matter of distance; the geographical disposition of the various parts of the Empire and Commonwealth also contributed to it. The British imperial axis stretched halfway around the globe joining two centers of gravity, the British Isles and the far eastern dominions (Australia and New Zealand). (Map 1) In between stood the Middle East and east Africa, draining military strength from both, their nearest support the Union of South Africa. A military liability, the whole area was essentially a link in the imperial lifeline, a valuable source of oil, and the dwelling place of peoples whose good will was vital to the Empire. In the summer of 1940, with the German invasion expected at any

---

[1] Ltr, Churchill to President, 8 Dec 40, as quoted in Churchill, *Their Finest Hour*, pp. 559–60.

time, Churchill had dared to weaken the home defenses in order to send to Egypt a full armored brigade along with almost half the few tanks available in England. To abandon the eastern Mediterranean, even if a line somewhat farther south and east could be held, would enable the enemy to move Romanian and Soviet oil through the Dardanelles, tap the oil fields of Iraq, capture immense stocks of matériel in Egypt, and swallow up Turkey. Far-reaching political repercussions would be felt in Iran, Afghanistan, and India. But expulsion from the Far East, British leaders thought, would be incomparably more disastrous. Australia and New Zealand contributed to the Commonwealth war effort important military forces, food for the United Kingdom and the Middle East, training facilities for British air pilots and crews, merchant shipping, and a substantial production of aircraft, munitions, and warships. Britain also drew upon the manpower and wealth of India, the tin and rubber of Malaya, and the oil of the Netherlands Indies. Churchill wrote to the prime ministers of Australia and New Zealand in August 1940 that, in the event of a Japanese invasion of those countries,

. . . we should then cut our losses in the Mediterranean and sacrifice every interest, except only the defence and feeding of this island, on which all depends, and would proceed in good time to your aid with a fleet able to give battle to any Japanese force which could be placed in Australian waters, and able to parry any invading force, or certainly cut its communications with Japan.[2]

Six months later British staff representatives in Washington asserted that loss of the Far East would mean "disintegration of the British Commonwealth and a crippling reduction in our war effort."[3]

"This island" was indeed a first charge,

but there was a limit beyond which Britain could not afford, except in the ultimate extremity, to reduce her overseas commitments. Even though costly to defend, the overseas territories and dominions made important contributions to British power, and the home islands, vulnerable to starvation as well as attack, could not survive for long if cut off from their outlying sources of nourishment. The British staff representatives declared:

We are a maritime Commonwealth; the various dominions and colonies are held together by communications and trade routes across the oceans of the world. Our population in the United Kingdom depend for existence on imported food and on the fruits of trade with the overseas dominions and colonies, with India and with foreign countries, including the vast area of China. Finally, we are trustees for the sub-continent of India, with a population more than twice that of the United States, many of them turbulent, temperamental and excitable people, who depend on us entirely for defense against external aggression and security against internal disorders.[4]

Britain was forced to compromise between her imperial obligations and the obvious desirability of drawing upon near sources of supply in the interests of shipping economy. During the first nine months of the war, only 36 percent of Britain's imports came from the accessible North Atlantic region, and even at the end of 1940, when every possible economy was being sought, almost half her imports were still coming from the more remote areas, which depended on British power to sustain their

[2] Msg, 11 Aug 40, as quoted in Churchill, *Their Finest Hour*, p. 436.
[3] (1) Note by U.K. Deleg, U.S.-Br Stf Convs, 31 Jan 41. (2) Statement by U.K. Deleg, U.S.-Br Stf Convs, 29 Jan 41. (3) Appreciation by U.K. Deleg, U.S.-Br Stf Convs, 11 Feb 41. All in Item 11, Exec 4. (4) Churchill, *Their Finest Hour*, pp. 428, 436, 446.
[4] Appreciation cited n. 3(3).

defense and on British shipping and commodities to maintain their economies.[5]

Britain's logistical position thus offered no pattern for a defensive strategy of relinquishing outposts in order to fall back upon contracting and progressively stronger defense lines toward a common center—no pattern for defense in depth. The enemy was massed at her doorstep and ranged along the flank of her major lifelines in the Atlantic and the Mediterranean, and a formidable potential enemy threatened her in the Far East. Britain's own external sources of strength were remote, and she had to accept the exorbitant logistical costs of defending them. But under the pressures the European Axis and Japan (or even the former alone) were capable of bringing to bear, the brittle and attenuated imperial structure seemed likely to break, and its defenders likely to be forced back upon its two centers of gravity, which would then no longer be able to support one another. (See Map 1.)

In the winter and spring of 1941 this catastrophe seemed neither unlikely nor too far distant. Before the end of 1940 the diminishing threat of invasion had been replaced by the equally deadly and more persistent menace of economic strangulation, which in turn presently revived the danger of invasion. Shipping losses, while declining somewhat from a peak of almost 450,000 gross tons a month during September and October, remained high through the fall and winter and in the following spring climbed even higher. In April 1941 the sinkings for the month—British, Allied, and neutral—came to 654,000 gross tons. During the last half of 1940 shipping losses had aggregated almost 2.5 million tons; during the six months following they rose to more than 2.8 million. This attrition was not alone

the work of German U-boats but also that of long-range aircraft, magnetic mines, and merchant and heavy warship raiders. (See Appendix H-1.)

Apart from sinkings, the effective capacity of shipping declined. "The convoy system, the détours, the zigzags, the great distances from which we now have to bring our imports, and the congestion of our western harbours," Churchill wrote, "have reduced by about one-third the fruitfulness of our existing tonnage."[6] In March, April, and May 1941 the Luftwaffe pounded with devastating effect at British ports, almost paralyzing the movement of goods. As a result, imports into the British Isles fell to a volume less than that needed to feed the population and to keep war industries running. From a rate of over 45 million tons per year during the first nine months of the war, they fell to an annual rate of only 30 million tons during the last few weeks of 1940. During the first quarter of 1941 the rate declined further to 28 million tons, and rose only slightly thereafter. In the year to come, Churchill warned the President at the end of 1940, the capacity to transport across the ocean would be "the crunch of the whole war."[7]

While Britain's home economy was weakening under this attrition, her armies met disaster in the Middle East. Early in

[5] (1) Ibid. (2) Hancock and Gowing, British War Economy, p. 241.

[6] Churchill, Their Finest Hour, p. 564.

[7] (1) The above figures do not include tanker imports. Loss figures vary somewhat; those given here are from Winston S. Churchill, The Second World War: The Grand Alliance (Boston, Houghton Mifflin Company, 1950), p. 782, and Churchill, Their Finest Hour, p. 714. (2) Ltr, Churchill to President, 8 Dec 40, as quoted in Churchill, Their Finest Hour, p. 560. (3) Hancock and Gowing, British War Economy, pp. 205, 242, 249-56, 263-68. (4) Frederick C. Lane, Ships for Victory: A History of Shipbuilding Under the U.S. Maritime Commission in World War II (Baltimore, Md., The Johns Hopkins Press, 1951), p. 62.

the year the forces of General Sir Archibald Wavell had virtually destroyed the Italian armies invading Egypt and had rapidly swept over Cyrenaica, and by the middle of May Italian power in east Africa was crushed. But in April the Germans overran Yugoslavia and Greece, almost destroying a sizable British expeditionary force in the process, while in Libya the recently arrived *Afrika Korps* of Generalfeldmarschall Erwin Rommel drove the British back to the Egyptian border, leaving a large imperial garrison beleaguered in Tobruk. In May came the devastating German airborne conquest of Crete, which threatened to drive the British eastern Mediterranean fleet through the Suez Canal. Against these reverses, Britain's success during May and June in overcoming local revolts and Nazi infiltration in Syria and Iraq seemed small indeed.

The Logistics of Hemisphere Defense

Britain's war was not the war for which the U.S. Army had been preparing. The logistics of hemisphere defense presented formidable problems, but they were incomparably simpler than the global logistics with which Britain had to struggle. American military power had a single center of gravity in continental North America. This central base was rich in manpower and material resources; it possessed the capacity to create and sustain powerful armed forces and also to feed its population. To the east, southeast, and west, outlying islands provided footholds for outpost defense; far to the north inhospitable land masses barred the approach of an invader. Against an aggressor operating anywhere north of Brazil the United States would have the supreme advantage, which Britain lacked, of fighting on interior lines. Against superior power, defending forces could withdraw along radial lines toward the central base, shortening their communications in the process. Only after an invader had secured substantial lodgments on the North American continent would this advantage give way to the serious problems of integrated defense created by the distribution of population and industry and by mountain barriers, among other factors. But to gain lodgments in North America, an aggressor would first require a tremendous margin of superiority.

To defend the whole Western Hemisphere was another matter. South and Central America were generally lacking in the political, economic, and military capabilities for effective resistance to a powerful aggressor. U.S. forces in South America would have to operate at the end of lines of communication longer than those of a European enemy attacking from the east, where the bulge of northeastern Brazil faces Dakar across the South Atlantic narrows. The American planning staffs were therefore anxious to establish advance bases in northeastern Brazil at the first sign of an Axis move toward west Africa. To eject a powerful aggressor from the distant southern portion of South America below the Brazilian bulge, Army planners thought, would be a task far beyond the capabilities of the initial PMP force of 1,400,000; that force, indeed, was considered "barely sufficient" to defend U.S. territory (not including the Philippines) and to provide "limited task forces" to support Latin American governments against fifth-column activities. Hemisphere defense plans (RAINBOW 1 and 4) contemplated that the region below the Brazilian bulge could be secured only in later stages of a war, after the area to the north had been firmly consolidated.[8]

In most areas, however, the logistical difficulties confronting an invader of the Western Hemisphere were more formidable than those of the defense. In the far north, terrain, climate, and economic development were unfavorable to military operations; both there and far to the south, immense distances from possible bases of operations were an added obstacle and tended on the whole to give the logistical advantage to the defense. To the west, Hawaii provided a strong naval and air base, readily accessible to logistical support from the west coast, and in turn supported Midway, which otherwise would have been dangerously exposed to attack from Japan's main base at Truk and advanced positions in the Marshall Islands.

In the last resort the United States did not have to defend the entire hemisphere in order to survive. (Map 2) A citadel defense of the area north of the Brazilian bulge could be so formidable, many military observers believed, as to deter any possible aggressor. The Joint Planning Committee even ventured the opinion (which many challenged) that the United States could "safeguard the North American continent, and probably the Western Hemisphere, whether allied with Britain or not." [9] It was not so much the logistical difficulties of hemisphere defense that made the danger of invasion real; it was rather the possibility that potential aggressors might be able to muster the necessary margin of superior power to override the meager forces defending the hemisphere despite the logistical advantages the latter would enjoy.

American policy makers had accepted the possibility of military collaboration with Britain on the premise that American security could be assured in no other way,

but hemisphere defense remained the point of departure in any consideration of participation in Britain's war. American planners naturally tended to visualize that participation as a projection of their plans for hemisphere defense and, as a corollary, to project the logistical principles on which hemisphere defense was based. Military power pushed far outward from a central base was a diminishing power, long lines of communications were costly to protect, and an enemy became progressively stronger as he was pressed back on his bases of operations. The British could not deny the validity of these principles, which their enemies had so long and so often exploited against them; they had grown accustomed, however, to making the most of such compensating advantages as the mobility inherent in sea power and a network of established overseas bases. U.S. Army planners were understandably reluctant to abandon completely the comparative security of the Western Hemisphere in order to share fully the risks and costs of Britain's global war. If American power must be projected overseas beyond hemisphere boundaries, they reasoned, let it be projected mainly into the North Atlantic area. On the Atlantic seaboard were centered most of America's heavy industry, her densest transportation net, her best ports; in the Atlantic was the bulk of her merchant shipping. A partnership of the United States, Britain, and Canada, moreover, could generate immense military power, sufficient to control the narrow span of the North Atlantic and, in

---

[8] (1) WPD study, Jan 41, title: Possible Necessity for an Army of 1,400,000 Men and One of 4,000,000 Men, Item 5, Exec 4. (2) Conn and Fairchild, Framework of Hemisphere Defense, Chs. I–II.

[9] Ltr, JPC to JB, 21 Jan 41, sub: Jt Instns for A&N Reps for Holding Stf Convs With the Br, JB 325, Ser 674.

effect, to create a single center of military and economic gravity in that area. Such a power could dominate the entire Atlantic region and perhaps eventually crush the power of Germany entrenched in Europe, despite her advantage of interior lines. *(See Map 8.)*

ABC-1 and Rainbow 5

Late in January 1941, as Britain's fortunes declined, British and American staff representatives in Washington began a series of secret meetings that became known as the ABC (American British Conversations) meetings. The discussions were concerned with "the best methods by which the armed forces of the United States and the British Commonwealth can defeat Germany and the powers allied with her, should the United States be compelled to resort to war." [10]

How the United States intended to contribute to this endeavor, if compelled to enter the war, had in general terms already been spelled out with Presidential sanction before the conference began— first and basically, secure the Western Hemisphere; then exert the principal American military effort in the Atlantic area and only "navally" in the Mediterranean; if Japan should enter the war despite all efforts to keep her out, limit American operations in the Pacific and Far East to such a scope as not to interfere with concentration in the Atlantic; hold to the defeat of the European Axis as the major goal of coalition strategy. [11]

These stipulations, particularly the first three, reflected the misgivings with which the Army representatives viewed the logistical problems of full involvement in Britain's war, and their determination that

American land and air forces should be employed primarily within a short radius of North America. In principle the stipulations did not conflict with British notions as to the bases for collaboration; the fourth one, of course, was the concept to which the British had hoped above all to bind their prospective allies. But sharp differences of opinion emerged as soon as the discussion got down to the specific questions of employment of forces and division of responsibilities. Symptomatic of these differences was the discussion of assignment of naval forces to protect the communications in the Atlantic on which overseas deployment of ground forces in that area would depend. The Americans questioned the British representatives closely regarding the trend of ship sinkings and "the probable situations that might result from the loss of the British Isles." [12] U.S. naval forces, and British too, they thought, should be concentrated to cover the northwestern approaches to the British Isles in order to eliminate the most dangerous threat to communications with North America. The British refused even to discuss the contingency that the British Isles might be conquered; the question was academic, they said, since if the islands

---

[10] (1) Statement by CNO and CofS, 27 Jan 41, WPD 4402-94. (2) The agreements reached at the ABC meetings were embodied in two reports: United States-British Staff Conversations: Report, March 27, 1941, known by the short title, ABC-1 Report, covering strategy and employment of forces; and United States-British Staff Conversations: Air Collaboration, March 29, 1941, known by the short title, ABC-2 Report, covering air policy and allocation of air matériel. Both reports are reproduced in *Pearl Harbor Attack: Hearings before the Joint Committee on the Investigation of the Pearl Harbor Attack* (hereafter cited as *Pearl Harbor Hearings*), Pt. 15, pp. 1485–1550. (3) Watson, *Prewar Plans and Preparations*, pp. 367–82.

[11] (1) Statement cited n. 10. (2) See above, Ch. I.

[12] Min. 2d mtg U.S.-Br Stf Convs, 31 Jan 41, Item 11, Exec 4.

fell "the British Army and Air Force would have ceased to exist." [13] As for naval dispositions, the British insisted on spreading their forces, however thinly, throughout the Atlantic and in other oceans as well. The current rampaging in the Atlantic of the German warship raiders *Scharnhorst, Gneisenau,* and *Hipper,* lent point to their argument. The Americans were not convinced, however, and the final agreement recorded their insistence that the center of gravity for U.S. naval operations in the Atlantic would be in the northwestern approaches to the United Kingdom, and that U.S. land forces outside the Western Hemisphere would be used mainly to support U.S. naval and air forces in areas bordering on the Atlantic. [14]

The sharpest of the disagreements growing out of the Americans' desire to limit their logistical commitments centered upon Singapore and the Far East. The British hoped to secure an American commitment to help defend Singapore. "The security of the Far Eastern position," they argued, "including Australia and New Zealand, is essential to the cohesion of the British Commonwealth and to the maintenance of its war effort. Singapore is the key to defense of these interests, and its retention must be assured." [15] If the Japanese captured the great base, they might be able to cut communications to the west; India and Burma would immediately become military liabilities; Australia and New Zealand might be isolated or even overrun. Loss of Singapore, the British concluded, "would be a disaster of the first magnitude, second only to loss of the British Isles." [16] They proposed that the U.S. Asiatic Fleet, then based in the Philippines, be heavily reinforced to the point where, in conjunction with British and Dutch naval forces, it could deter or at

least delay a Japanese onslaught on Malaya. [17]

These arguments met with an unsympathetic response. Singapore was indeed a symbol and a bastion and its loss would be felt. But loss of the Philippines would also be a severe blow to the United States. Both partners must be willing to take risks and accept losses. In a private session Brig. Gen. Sherman Miles complained that British preoccupation with the Far East was diverting attention from their central problem, the security of the United Kingdom. As the British themselves conceded, the Japanese did not need Singapore to harass shipping in the Indian Ocean while, even with Singapore, they probably would not risk large naval forces far to the west as long as the U.S. Pacific Fleet menaced their eastern flank. Moreover, the Americans felt confident that the Pacific Fleet could protect communications between Australia and New Zealand and the Western Hemisphere through the South Pacific, and even deter Japan from attempting to overrun the dominions. Even if the Asiatic Fleet were reinforced, the Americans feared it might eventually be engulfed by superior enemy forces, while the Pacific Fleet would be seriously weakened and unable to send essential reinforcements to the Atlantic. The American plan was to defend the Malay Barrier as long as possible with existing forces (including the Asiatic Fleet, which would probably retire from the Philippines at

---

[13] *Ibid.*

[14] (1) Min, 2d, 4th, 6th, 8th, and 9th mtgs U.S.-Br Stf Convs, 31 Jan, 5 Feb, 10 Feb, 15 Feb, and 17 Feb 41, Item 11, Exec 4. (2) ABC-1 Report, pars. 13(b), (f), (g), *Pearl Harbor Hearings,* Pt. 15, pp. 1491–92.

[15] Statement cited n. 3(2).

[16] Appreciation cited n. 3(3).

[17] (1) *Ibid.* (2) Statement cited n. 3(2). (3) Note cited n. 3(1).

the outbreak of hostilities); the Pacific Fleet, meanwhile, would operate against Japan's eastern flank; the Chinese, fortified by American munitions, would strike at Japan's mainland forces; and the weapon of economic blockade would be exploited to the full. In general, the Americans felt that the Far East, except Japan itself and areas to its north and east, was a British and Dutch sphere of responsibility, and that if the British were bent on holding Singapore, they should themselves send the necessary naval forces via their own secure line of communications around the Cape of Good Hope. In the end, the representatives could only agree to disagree. The British recorded their conviction that the security of Singapore was essential to the joint war effort, and their intention to strengthen their naval power in the Indian Ocean. The Americans undertook to augment their own naval power in the Atlantic and Mediterranean, thus releasing British units from those areas, but indicated that no strengthening of American forces in the Far East was contemplated.[18]

To resist further entanglements in the Far East seemed to the Army staff not only sound logistics but a logical corollary of the principle on which they and the British had agreed—that defeat of Germany must be the primary objective. An American commitment to help defend Singapore might imply an undertaking "to seek the early defeat of Japan" and acceptance of "responsibility for the safety of a large portion of the British Empire." It might lead to "employment of the final reserve of the Associated Powers in a non-decisive theater."[19] As to how Germany was finally to be defeated, the American staff had as yet no definite ideas. Admiral Stark's hints, the preceding November, of

massive land operations in Europe had aroused little enthusiasm among the Army planners, particularly his suggestion of repeating Wellington's exploits in Spain. A WPD paper prepared late in January reached the conclusion, among others similarly pessimistic, that an invasion by the historic route through the Low Countries would be dangerous folly. Army thinking, in general, was oriented toward the initial, not the later, stages of an Anglo-American partnership.[20] The British had somewhat more definite and far-reaching ideas on the subject. Germany would be defeated in the end, they thought, by small, highly mechanized armies wielding tremendous fire power. These forces would enter the Continent at various points, to the accompaniment of internal uprisings, only after the enemy had been battered to the breaking point by preliminary attacks around the perimeter of Europe, air bombardment, blockade, and subversive activity.[21]

British notions as to the form American

---

[18] (1) Min, Jt mtg of A&N secs, U.S. Stf Com, 13 Feb 41. (2) Statement by U.S. Stf Com, "The U.S. Military Position in the Far East," 19 Feb 41. Both in Item 11, Exec 4. (3) Memo, Maj Gen Stanley D. Embick, Brig Gens Leonard T. Gerow and S. Miles, and Col Joseph T. McNarney for CofS, 12 Feb 41, sub: Dispatch of U.S. Forces to Singapore, WPD 4402-3. (4) ABC-1 Report, pars. 11(b), 13(d), and Annex III, par. 35, *Pearl Harbor Hearings,* Pt. 15, pp. 1490, 1492, 1518.

[19] Statement cited n. 18(2).

[20] (1) Min, 11th mtg U.S.-Br Stf Convs, 26 Feb 41, Item 11, Exec 4. (2) Statement cited n. 18(2). (3) Memo, unsigned, for ACofS WPD, no date sub: Stf Convs With Br, Item 11b, Exec 4. (4) See above, Ch. I. (5) Watson, *Prewar Plans and Preparations,* pp. 118–20.

[21] (1) See Churchill's allusion to "superior air-power" and "the rising anger" of "Nazi-gripped populations" in his letter to Roosevelt, 8 December 1940, as quoted in Churchill, *Their Finest Hour,* p. 560. (2) See also the fully developed plan described a year later in Churchill, *The Grand Alliance,* pp. 646–51. (3) For the various British views, see the minutes of the U.S. British Staff Conversations, Item 11, Exec 4.

participation in the war might take were closely related to this strategy of attrition and peripheral attack. The "party line" laid down by Churchill was expressed in his famous exhortation, "give us the tools and we'll finish the job." "We do not need the gallant armies which are forming throughout the American Union," Churchill declared. "We do not need them this year, nor next year; nor any year that I can foresee." [22] While this assertion, made during the debate over the Lend-Lease Act, was perhaps not wholly candid, the British staff representatives in Washington admitted that they dreaded a vast American mobilization and training program that would swallow up the output of American munitions in an effort to put huge armies in the field at an early date, thus cutting off the vital flow of American weapons to British forces already fighting the enemy. In the event the United States should enter the war, the British anticipated that the still embryonic American ground forces would for some time play a minor, largely defensive role, protecting their own air and naval bases and relieving the British in quiet sectors. British forces, far more advanced in their mobilization and already disposed around the periphery of enemy power, would gradually be strengthened by troops thus released and by American air units. Only for the U.S. Navy, a powerful force in being, did the British envisage an independent role. American land and air power, in short, was to be introduced piecemeal and on a small scale (except for long-range bombing forces) into the existing pattern of the war, thereby helping to perpetuate that pattern and eventually to consummate the strategy of "closing the ring" around Germany. [23] The principal American contribution would not be armies but the weapons to equip armies.

The final ABC-1 report on the whole reflected British long-range strategic thinking—emphasizing strategic air power, support of resistance movements and neutrals, "raids and minor offensives," checking of Axis advances in North Africa, knocking Italy out of the war, capture of launching positions for an "eventual" offensive. Nowhere was there any mention of a cross-Channel invasion based on the British Isles. The implication was that the process of nibbling at the fringes of Axis power would continue for a long time, and that the enemy would be defeated in the end less by shock than by exhaustion. ABC-1 also gave assurance that the flow of material aid to Britain would continue, even if this meant reducing the size of the armed forces the United States could throw into the scale. Already, important concessions were being made to the British in the allocation of aircraft and other critical matériel. [24]

Yet the Army staff reacted strongly to the British tendency to assign American forces a complementary and subordinate role. By virtue of its immense potential power, one staff paper pointed out, the United States was destined to become the dominant partner if it should enter the anti-Axis coalition, and would "constitute the final reserve of the democracies both in manpower and munitions." That reserve should be conserved "for timely employment in a decisive theater, and not

[22] Churchill's speech of 9 Feb 41, quoted in Sherwood, *Roosevelt and Hopkins*, pp. 261–62.

[23] (1) Statement cited n. 3(2). (2) Note cited n. 3(1). (3) Min, 4th and 5th mtgs U.S.-Br Stf Convs, 5 and 6 Feb 41, Item 11, Exec 4.

The British also wanted to assign some U.S. naval units piecemeal to British naval commands in the Atlantic.

[24] (1) ABC-1 Report, pars. 12–13, *Pearl Harbor Hearings*, Pt. 15, pp. 1490–91. (2) See below, Ch. III.

dissipated by dispersion in secondary theaters." [25] "We must not make the mistake," warned another staff paper, "of merely reinforcing the British in all areas, but should throw our weight in a single direction." [26] ABC-1 laid down the rule, in fact, that the forces of each partner should operate, in the main, under their own commanders "in the areas of responsibility of their own Power"—partial insurance against the absorption of American forces anonymously into the pattern of Britain's war. [27]

This reservation was reflected in the actual dispositions of American forces contemplated under the ABC-1 agreement and the RAINBOW 5 war plan drawn up during the weeks following. The RAINBOW 5 schedules provided for a maximum overseas deployment, during the first six months following American entry into the war (M Day), of 413,900 Army troops, but of these about 236,000 were definitely assigned to tasks within the Western Hemisphere and another 109,500 to cover its approaches and to forestall threats against it. The remainder were to be sent to the British Isles, within the orbit of Anglo-American power and on the direct approaches to northwestern Europe. [28] The scheduled deployment was as follows:

Hawaii	44,000
Alaska	23,000
Panama	13,400
Caribbean bases	45,800
West coast of South America (task force)	24,000
Brazil (task force)	86,000
British Isles	68,200
Iceland (relief of British)	26,500
Transatlantic operations to forestall German move toward Dakar	83,000
	413,900

Even U.S. naval power in the Atlantic, a more mobile instrument, was to be concentrated mainly to protect the northwestern approaches to the United Kingdom, although the Navy had the further mission of assisting the British occupation of the Azores and Cape Verdes if the Axis should move in that direction. In the Pacific the main fleet was to remain based on Hawaii and, in the event of war with Japan, would raid its communications and subsequently operate against the Marshall and Caroline Islands. The Philippines, in that event, would be a beleaguered citadel far beyond the limits to which American power, for many months after the outbreak of a war in the Far East, could hope to expand. Under ABC-1 the United States was assigned primary responsibility for most of the Pacific, its sphere extending westward to include Japan but not the Philippines, Formosa, or the areas to the south; on the Atlantic side, American responsibility extended only to the mid-Atlantic, short of Iceland and the Azores. [29] (See Map 2.)

Thus, except for the build-up of U.S. strategic bomber forces in the British Isles (which was to begin as soon as the United States entered the war), the bulk of Amer-

---

[25] Draft memo, no date, atchd to memo, Gen Gerow for Col McNarney, 6 Feb 41, Item 11, Exec 4.

[26] WPD paper, no date, sub: Stf Convs With Br, Item 11b, Exec 4.

[27] (1) ABC-1 Report, pars. 9, 14(b), *Pearl Harbor Hearings,* Pt. 15, pp. 1489, 1493. (2) Draft memo cited n. 25. (3) WPD paper cited n. 26.

[28] Incl A to rpt, JPC to JB, 30 Apr 41, sub: Jt Bsc War Plan—RAINBOW 5 and Rpt of U.S.-Br Stf Convs, March 27, 1941, JB 325, Ser 642–5.

[29] (1) *Ibid.* (2) Memos, WPD for CofS, 20 and 31 May 41, sub: Analysis of Plans for Overseas Expeds, RAINBOW 5, WPD 4175-22. (3) Charts atchd to memo, WPD for CofS, 15 May 41, WPD 3493-11. (4) Papers in Item 7, Exec 4. (5) Annex III to ABC-1 Report, *Pearl Harbor Hearings,* Pt. 15, pp. 1504–35. The schedule was revised from time to time throughout 1941 and included additional small forces to be sent to Greenland and Newfoundland.

ican land and air power during the early period of participation was to be held back either inside the United States or within a safe radius of North America, with short, easily protected overseas communications. This applied not merely to the great mass of the Army still in training, but even to most of the mobile striking forces, unless these should be called into action by an enemy threat to the hemisphere. Two considerations lay behind this whole plan. The paramount reason, of course, was that the Army would not be ready for large-scale action of any kind for many months—by 1 September, the earliest date on which its commitments under ABC-1 could become effective, it could expect to put in the field, at the most, only about six divisions and six air combat groups. Secondly, the staff was determined that American land and air power should not be introduced piecemeal, as it grew, into a global war in which for a long time it could play only a subordinate role. "The building up of large land and air forces for major offensive operations against the Axis powers," stated the Army's RAINBOW 5 plan, "will be the primary immediate effort of the United States Army. The initial tasks of United States land and air forces will be limited to such operations as will not materially delay this effort." [30]

Ships for Britain

In the spring of 1941 Britain needed more tangible and immediate assistance from the United States than agreements for military collaboration that were contingent upon the United States' being forced into the war and that, as far as the Army was concerned, could not become effective before September. In December the Prime Minister had warned Roosevelt:

Unless we can establish our ability to feed this island, to import the munitions of all kinds which we need, unless we can move our armies to the various theaters where Hitler and his confederate Mussolini must be met, and maintain them there, . . . we may fall by the way, and the time needed by the United States to complete her defensive preparations may not be forthcoming. [31]

American officials from December on watched Britain's blood-letting with growing concern. Stimson recorded in his diary on the 19th, ". . . it is now very clear that England will not be able to hold out very much longer unless some defense is found." [32] The President's decisions on military policy in January were based on the assumption that Britain might hold out for six more months. Harry Hopkins, visiting in England a little later, found a general expectation that the all-out invasion would certainly come in the spring, and thought that the outcome would depend on how much material could be sent from the United States "within the next few weeks." [33] Early in April Admiral Stark concluded that the situation was "hopeless except as we take strong measures to save it." [34]

The most dramatic and far-reaching response by the United States to Britain's peril was the passage of the Lend-Lease Act in March, but apart from some badly needed shipments of food made under its authority, the benefits of lend-lease lay in the future; most of the munitions sent to the British during 1941 were bought for

---

[30] Incl A to rpt cited n. 28.

[31] Ltr, Churchill to President, 8 Dec 40, as quoted in Churchill, *Their Finest Hour*, p. 560.

[32] Stimson Diary, December 19, 1940 entry, quoted in Henry L. Stimson and McGeorge Bundy, *On Active Service in Peace and War* (New York, Harper & Brothers, 1948), p. 367.

[33] Sherwood, *Roosevelt and Hopkins*, p. 257.

[34] Ltr, Adm Stark to Adm Husband E. Kimmel, 4 Apr 41, *Pearl Harbor Hearings*, Pt. 16, p. 2161.

cash.[35] Except for munitions, Britain's most pressing need was ships. Hopkins forwarded urgent pleas on this score from England in February, and Sir Arthur Salter, who came over in March to head the British Merchant Shipping Mission, carried a new warning from the Prime Minister:

The Battle of the Atlantic has begun. The issue may well depend on the speed with which our resources to combat the menace to our communications with the western hemisphere are supplemented by those of the U.S.A. I look to you to bring this fact home to the U.S. Administration . . . .[36]

The United States could do little to meet this need. Building capacity was still in the early stages of expansion—in 1939 American yards had produced only twenty-eight ocean-going ships, in 1940 only fifty-three. Late in 1940 the British had let contracts with the Todd-Kaiser Company for sixty emergency-type freighters (precursors of the Liberty ships), but none of these could be expected off the ways until late in 1941; only five were completed before the end of the year. Of U.S. shipping already in existence, substantial transfers had been made before 1941 to British and other foreign registry, thus releasing the ships from the prohibitions of the neutrality laws in order to carry British cargoes. Early in 1941 the entire U.S. merchant fleet aggregated less than ten million gross tons, of which more than half were working in the coastal trades. Only about 3.7 million tons, on the Atlantic side, were suitable for transoceanic operation. Four fifths of the entire fleet were vessels of World War I vintage, too slow for travel in danger zones except at great risk. Finally, the domestic demands upon U.S. shipping were mounting, especially for importing

strategic materials. Between mid-1940 and the end of 1941 Britain acquired about a hundred secondhand ships from the United States, most of them before the Lend-Lease Act was passed; many of these ships had to be laid up for repairs and refitting for months afterward. Of this small tonnage, only the tankers appreciably changed the situation in 1941 by building up British oil stocks, which during the summer had fallen to the danger level. The United States also turned over to the British in 1941 considerable Axis and Danish tonnage interned in U.S. harbors and persuaded other American republics to do likewise—perhaps a million deadweight tons of shipping all told. U.S. pressure helped to secure other foreign tonnage for the British under charter.[37]

This was a small beginning. In December 1940 Churchill voiced to the President his hope that American building capacity would be expanded on the scale of the Hog Island yards of World War I. From Empire resources, producing well under 2

[35] (1) See below, Ch. III. (2) Stettinius, *Lend-Lease: Weapon for Victory,* pp. 104–05 and Chs. VIII–IX.
[36] (1) Quoted in Hancock and Gowing, *British War Economy,* p. 257. (2) Sherwood, *Roosevelt and Hopkins,* pp. 257–58.
[37] Estimates of total tonnage vary widely; the figure given in the text is from Charles H. Coleman, Shipbuilding Activities of the National Defense Advisory Commission and the Office of Production Management, July 1940 to December 1941, WPB Special Study 18. (1) On U.S. merchant fleet, see Coleman, pp. 26–28, 30ff; Lane, *Ships for Victory,* pp. 42–43; Hancock and Gowing, *British War Economy,* pp. 257–58; and memo, G-4 for WPD, 28 May 41, sub: Strategic Est of Sit, with atchd tables, G-4/33052. (2) For the British shipbuilding contracts in 1940 and transfers of U.S. shipping to Britain, see Hancock and Gowing; Coleman; and Hall, North American Supply, Ch. VI, Galley 11, Hist Br, Cabinet Off, London. Shipping transferred under lend-lease to the British Commonwealth in 1941 amounted to only 1.1 percent of all lend-lease transfers in that period. (3) For relationship of gross, net, and dead-weight tonnages, see below, App. A-1.

WAR PLANS AND EMERGENCY PREPARATIONS

million dead-weight tons (1,250,000 gross tons) per year, Britain could not hope to replace her losses, which in April 1941 reached an annual rate of almost 12 million dead-weight tons (actual losses in 1941 were about 5 million tons). During the spring, in fact, both merchant and naval construction in the United Kingdom had to be cut back in order to provide labor and facilities to reduce the mountainous backlog of damaged shipping clogging the ports. The British frankly rested their hopes on receiving a flood of American tonnage in 1942—at an annual rate of 4.5 million dead-weight tons, according to early 1941 calculations. Before the end of 1941 the British had raised their estimated requirements to 8.2 million dead-weight tons per year.[38]

Expansion of American shipbuilding capacity spurred forward during 1941 in three successive waves. The first, benefiting from the British contracts with Todd-Kaiser, began early in January with the President's order for 200 emergency-type freighters to be completed in two years; under the current Maritime Commission program, a like number of standard-type vessels was to be completed by mid-1941. The second wave of expansion followed soon after the Lend-Lease Act was passed and added more than 300 vessels, including 112 emergency-type freighters and 72 tankers, to the program. The third wave, spread over the second half of the year, involved a variety of types. By the end of the year, over 1,200 vessels (about 13 million dead-weight tons) were scheduled for delivery before the end of 1943, aiming at a peak annual production capacity of more than 7 million tons. In 1941 the results of the expansion were meager. Actual construction during the last half of the year lagged behind schedule. About 100 mer-

chant vessels of all types (1,161,000 dead-weight tons) were completed in that year, of which only 7 were Liberty ships and 53 standard freighters.[39]

This expansion was aimed largely at British needs and owed much to lend-lease funds. How much tonnage actually would be turned over to the British remained, as the President remarked, an "iffy" question. Shipping lent itself more aptly than munitions to the President's homely metaphor of the garden hose to be returned to its owner after the fire was put out. The expansion program, however, gave the British the insurance they needed. The Prime Minister told the House of Commons on 25 June:

If we can resist or deter actual invasion this autumn, we ought to be able, on the present undertaking of the United States, to come through the year 1941. . . . there is no reason why the year 1942, in which the enormous American new building comes to hand, should not present us with less anxious ordeals than those we must now endure and come through.[40]

"Ships for Britain" included not merely those the United States made available in 1941 and was prepared to build in the future but also the British tonnage that, without action by the United States, might otherwise have been lost, immobilized, or uneconomically employed. Until the Neutrality Act was repealed in No-

---

[38] (1) Ltr, Churchill to President, 8 Dec 40, as quoted in Churchill, *Their Finest Hour*, p. 564. (2) Note cited n. 3(1). (3) Memo, John J. McCloy for Gen Marshall, 11 Feb 41, Item 11c, Exec 4. (4) Churchill, *The Grand Alliance*, pp. 127, 150–55; dirs by Minister of Defence, 6 and 27 Mar 41, as quoted on pp. 123–26, 865–66. (5) For the figure 8.2 million dead-weight tons (5.5 million gross tons), see below, Ch. V.

[39] (1) Lane, *Ships for Victory*, Ch. II. (2) WPB Sp Study 18, Table on p. 5 and pp. 25–51, cited n. 37. (3) See also below, App. H-1.

[40] Churchill, *The Grand Alliance*, p. 154.

vember 1941, U.S. shipping could not enter the war zones, but in April, as the east African campaign was drawing to a close, the President declared the Red Sea open to U.S. shipping, and by midyear forty-eight American freighters were plying this route, relieving British tonnage for more dangerous service. In March the Army took the first steps toward developing facilities for ferrying aircraft across the North and South Atlantic, a project that promised eventually to release substantial amounts of shipping for other uses. The government also urged private shipyards to make their repair facilities available to British merchant ships and, in March, extended the services of private and naval yards to British warships. During the last nine months of 1941 British tonnage repairing in American ports averaged 430,-000 dead-weight tons a month.[41]

Finally, in April 1941, the President took the first decisive, though limited, step toward what would certainly be the major role of the United States in the Atlantic during the initial stages of participation in the war—the convoying of merchant shipping. Although the Navy had prepared, and the President had tentatively approved, plans for full convoying by the U.S. Navy in the eastern as well as the western Atlantic, the action he actually took late in April, after long hesitation, was cautious. He ordered the Navy to patrol the sea lanes west of a mid-Atlantic line (longitude 26° west, but including Greenland and the Azores) and to broadcast the movements of potentially hostile ships and aircraft. To implement this decision naval forces in the Atlantic were augmented, late in May, by three battleships and other units representing approximately a fourth of the strength of the Pacific Fleet. The reporting patrol, as the

President warned in a speech on 27 May, was earnest of the determination of the United States to ensure Britain's survival, above all to "deliver the goods" across the Atlantic. Extended by successive steps, it was to draw the United States by the following September into a "shooting war" with German submarines.[42]

The Logistics of Emergency Expeditionary Forces

Measures to aid Britain and plans for eventual military collaboration were not the Army's most pressing concern. For the Army, during the first half of 1941, hemisphere defense was still the first order of business. The threat of imminent aggression against the Western Hemisphere remained real until the German invasion of the Soviet Union late in June canceled it for the time being.

Since June 1940 the 1st and 3d Infantry Divisions, on the east and west coasts, respectively, had been earmarked to form the nuclei of small, mobile, striking forces that might anticipate or counter a sudden enemy move. Some effort was made during the summer and fall of 1940 to provide these forces and a few supporting units with special equipment and to give them amphibious training, with a view eventually to operating in conjunction with the Marines. Little was actually done during 1940 to give effect to these plans. Equipment could not be spared from the general

---

[41] (1) Hancock and Gowing, *British War Economy*, p. 258. (2) Sherwood, *Roosevelt and Hopkins*, pp. 228–29. (3) Stettinius, *Lend-Lease: Weapon for Victory*, p. 149 and Chs. XII–XIII. (4) Craven and Cate, *AAF I*, Ch. IX.

[42] (1) Conn and Fairchild, Framework of Hemisphere Defense, Ch. V, pp. 5–15. (2) Morison, *Battle of the Atlantic*, pp. 44–57. (3) Stimson and Bundy, *On Active Service in Peace and War*, pp. 386–87.

training program. Every Regular Army unit had to provide instructors for the flood of selectees coming into the Army. Amphibious training scarcely had reached the point where joint exercises with the better-equipped and better-trained marines (who enjoyed higher priorities) would have been profitable. Even the 1st Division, the best-trained Army unit, did not engage in amphibious maneuvers until February 1941, and then with only 10 percent of its personnel.[43]

In October 1940 American relations with Vichy France were growing tense over the question of the disposition of Vichy naval forces at Martinique and Dakar. The Army took steps to form three task forces, each of division strength, to meet any emergency in the Atlantic. Besides the 1st Infantry Division, the 30th and 44th National Guard (square) Divisions and several supporting artillery, antiaircraft, and service units, were earmarked. But only the 1st Division and a single antiaircraft regiment could be given the high priority for equipment and for exemption from contributing training cadre that alone would permit rapid progress toward readiness. Only Task Force 1, built around the 1st Division, had a mission involving landings on a hostile shore in the Caribbean area or northeastern Brazil; Task Force 2 was to support and perhaps relieve it, following a successful landing; Task Force 3 was to help in the defense of Newfoundland.[44]

Late in October 1940 the President ordered the Navy to plan an emergency descent upon Martinique, to be carried out on three days' notice; the Navy in turn asked the Army to prepare to follow up the initial Marine landing. Feeling that at least 25,000 troops would be needed for such an undertaking, the Army planners urged that it not be attempted until a strong expeditionary force, organized around the 1st Division, could be formed and amphibiously trained. Nothing came of this proposal, and the Army's contribution to the projected Martinique operation consisted of three small regimental-size task forces ("A," "B," and "C"), formed in November from the 1st Division. Only the first of these was considered fit to join the attack on Martinique; B Force was slated to land on nearby Guadeloupe, which was weakly defended; C Force soon lost even its identity.[45]

The Martinique crisis swiftly faded, but the effort to prepare the Army task forces was a chastening experience in the logistics of emergency action. Forces A and B were to have jumped off five days and ten days, respectively, after M Day (the date of the initial Navy and Marine assault), but it soon became necessary to double these intervals. Preparations involved endless time-consuming details—packing, crating, shipping, uncrating, and reissuing equipment, innumerable inspections and checkings of shortages, locating and tracing the movement of units, transfering equipment from units in training to those in the task forces, and scheduling the movement of troops and equipment to port. The staffs at all levels, from G-4 down, were unfamiliar with the mechanics of mounting a task force; even the trade jargon was strange, causing misunder-

---

[43] (1) Greenfield, Palmer, and Wiley, *AGF I*, pp. 85–86. (2) Memo, WPD for G-3, 11 Jun 40, WPD 4232-3. (3) AG ltr to CG First Army, 26 Jun 40, WPD 4161-3.

[44] (1) Papers in WPD 4161-2 and WPD 4161-3. (2) Greenfield, Palmer, and Wiley, *AGF I*, p. 85.

[45] (1) Memo, CofS for CG First Army, 20 Nov 40, sub: Exped Forces, G-4/31832. (2) Papers in AG 381 (11-12-40) and WPD 4337-1. (3) Conn and Fairchild, Framework of Hemisphere Defense, Ch. IV, pp. 2–12.

standings of such terms as combat team and M Day.[46]

Had the expedition been launched, difficulties would also have been encountered in transporting the Army forces to the scene of action. The Army was operating about this time some fifteen ocean-going vessels—eight combination troop transports, which carried some cargo, and seven freighters, some of the latter under long-term charter. Two of its transports were over thirty years old, former German internees from World War I; all were more or less makeshift converts to military use; some were so nearly unseaworthy that the Department of Commerce had raised objections to their continued operation. The small and shoddy fleet was fully occupied in late 1940 in supporting the existing overseas garrisons. To this traffic was soon to be added the new deployment of garrisons, with their burden of initial equipment, reserves, and construction material, to the fringe of bases in the Atlantic recently acquired from Great Britain in the destroyers-for-bases transaction.[47] For the Martinique operation it would therefore have been necessary to acquire shipping by short-term charter or by renting space at going commercial rates—expensive methods at a time when cost was still a dominant consideration. Even these expedients might not have sufficed. A rough survey late in the summer of 1940 revealed that in any ten-day period there were likely to be in the New York area only five to ten vessels suitable for conversion to military duty and available for charter. The movement of a single triangular division, it was then estimated, would require from ten to fourteen transports. Even minimum hasty conversion of commercial vessels for military use was a complicated and lengthy process, involving installation of

messing and sanitary facilities, additional companionways, lifesaving gear, and ventilating equipment, to mention only a few. About twelve days, on the average, were required merely to negotiate the transaction, another seventeen to complete conversion.[48] Such preparations scarcely fitted into any pattern of emergency action.

Although the Army did not have to cope with the logistical problems of actually moving an expeditionary force late in 1940, Forces A and B remained earmarked, and the preliminary arrangements for supply and movement remained in suspense. The general tension, meanwhile, continued to mount. On 16 January 1941 the President, laying down military policy for the next few months, warned the services, "we must be ready to act with what [is] available."[49] Later that month WPD tried again to broaden the base of the Army's striking power by placing two more divisions and some supporting units in top priority for equipment and ammunition, with immunity from "cadre scalping." Again the attempt had to be abandoned because of the impact it would have had upon the training and equipping of the rest of the Army. For example, in order to give the four antiaircraft regiments involved in WPD's plan full allowances of .50-caliber antiaircraft machine

[46] (1) Rcd of G-4 conf, 1 Nov 40. (2) Memo, Lt Col George W. Griner, Jr., for Lt Col Henry S. Aurand, 4 Nov 40, sub: Exped Forces. Both in G-4/31832. (3) Other papers in same file.
[47] William L. Langer and S. Everett Gleason, *The Challenge to Isolation: 1937-1940* (New York, Harper & Brothers, 1952), Ch. XXII.
[48] (1) Corresp in G-4/29717-41, G-4/29717-44, and G-4/29717-46. (2) See also, Wardlow, *Trans I*, pp. 136-39.
[49] Memo, CofS for ACofS WPD, 17 Jan 41, sub: White House Conf Thursday, January 16, 1941, WPD 4175-18.

guns, it would have been necessary to strip weapons from thirty-seven other regiments already struggling to train with 20 percent allowances; if full complements of 105-mm. howitzers had been issued to the field artillery units in WPD's list, issues to the rest of the Army would have been held up five months.[50]

Under the plan approved in February, Task Force 1, built around the favored 1st Division, was the only one of the three emergency forces with an equipment and training priority adequate to advance its state of readiness appreciably beyond that of the mass of the mobilizing Army—essentially the situation that had existed the preceding October. If emergency action were called for at any time in the near future, the three task forces would have to be issued the remainder of their equipment after M Day, under a hectic schedule in which Forces 1 and 3 were to jump off in ten days, Force 2 in thirty days. G-4, mindful of its recent difficulties in preparing the small Martinique-Guadeloupe forces, warned that this could not be done; Force 1 probably could be equipped on schedule, Force 2 possibly; but to outfit Force 3, now handicapped by a low priority, within ten days, would be quite impossible. G-4 asserted in February:

If a situation exists which warrants a plan calling for the 100 percent equipping of a force within 30 days, action should be taken to equip that force at once. . . . It is optimistic to believe that men and transferred equipment can be assembled and dispatched as a well-trained force within 10 or 30 days.[51]

Meanwhile, the growth of the Army's transport fleet progressed at a pace comparable to the slow expansion of its striking forces. In mid-December 1940 the War Department finally received authorization to acquire, under various forms of control, some seventeen additional vessels. Further funds were allotted to modernize, overhaul, and refit the existing fleet, but the actual acquisition of these vessels was strewn with setbacks. Shipowners raised their charter rates steeply in the tightening market. Vessels ran aground, failed to pass inspection, and developed mechanical defects. The owners of one chartered vessel requested, and were granted, its return for Alaskan cannery operations. Technical difficulties dragged out the process of conversion for months.[52]

The U.S. Maritime Commission, moreover, showed a growing reluctance to assign shipping permanently or for long periods to the military services, not only because the tonnage assigned would not be available for more urgent needs but also because the services were to some degree guilty of uneconomical operating practices. The Maritime Commission early in 1941 took the Army to task for its waste of cargo space on inbound voyages; inbound cargo capacity was then at a premium because of the demands of the government's large program of importing strategic raw materials. On 4 February the President issued a manifesto on utilization of merchant shipping, ordering the military services to take over only a minimum number of vessels and to operate these at full capacity and only for essential

---

[50] Memo, G-4 for WPD, 10 Feb 41, sub: Readiness of Combat Divs, G-4/32509.

[51] (1) Memo, G-4 for CofS, 28 Feb 41, sub: Orgn of Emergency Exped Forces, G-4/32550. (2) Memo, WPD for G-4, 31 Jan 41, sub: Readiness of Combat Divs, G-4/32509. (3) Memo cited n. 50. (4) WD ltr to CG First Army, 11 Feb 41, sub: Orgn of Exped Forces, WPD 4161-3. (5) Memo, G-4 for Chiefs of Svs, 27 Feb 41, same sub, G-4/32550. (6) Papers in WPD 4161-4.

[52] (1) Ltr, SW to President, 4 Dec 40, G-4/29717-41. (2) Other corresp in same file. (3) Corresp in G-4/29717-56.

military needs. "This is no time," the pronouncement severely stated, "to set up a reserve of Army or Navy transports or other ships, which, since we are at peace, could be put to civilian use." [53]

The statement seemed to imply that shipping should be pooled, an idea then widely shared among officials and ship operators, but the President gave the Maritime Commission no powers and provided no mechanism for genuine pooling. The operating practices of the military transport services remained, for practical purposes, their own business, and the military fleets continued to grow, though slowly. While the commission in May received broad powers of requisition over privately owned merchant shipping, real pooling of the nation's shipping, with effective curbs on the expansion of the military transport fleets, had to await the pressure of war. [54]

From the late winter of 1940–41 on, relations between the War Department and the Maritime Commission began to improve. In an effort to win the commission's co-operation in meeting the Army's growing need for tonnage, Army transportation officials trimmed their sails to the prevailing winds. As a general practice, purchases of new tonnage were limited to those needed for "regular and permanent servicing of Army establishments"; short-term needs were met by chartering or borrowing vessels from the Maritime Commission; cargo shipments were assigned to commercial lines wherever possible. Arrangements were even made for strategic materials to be moved in Army bottoms on return voyages to the United States—mainly crude rubber from the Netherlands Indies—arrangements that, Secretary Stimson pointedly reminded Rear Adm. Emory S. Land (Ret.), chairman of

the Maritime Commission, were "in accordance with the President's policy" of 4 February. [55]

Behind these concessions there were reservations. The arrangements for transporting strategic materials actually were financially advantageous to the Army, and were carefully hedged to preclude long-term commitments and to assure that transports could be recalled without notice under military necessity. Present policies, as an official remarked, "would be subject to revision if a major emergency should develop." [56] Meanwhile the concessions bore fruit. G-4 observed in July that the Maritime Commission was "on the whole, well satisfied with Army operation of its ships and . . . on the other hand, critical of the Navy's failure to give full employment to ships turned over to it." [57]

[53] (1) Memo, President for SW, SN, and Rear Adm Emory S. Land (Ret.), 4 Feb 41, G-4/29717-48. (2) Memo, TQMG for DCofS, 27 Jan 41, sub: Acquisition of Additional Vessels. (3) Ltr, SW to Adm Land, 8 Jan 41. (4) Memo, G-4 for CofS, 8 Jan 41, sub: Augmentation of Army Trans Sv. (5) Memo, G-4 for CofS, 3 Feb 41, sub: Additional Army Trans. Last four in G-4/29717-26.

[54] (1) Ltr, John M. Franklin to Chester C. Wardlow, Chm, Trans Advisory Group, OQMG, 24 Jan 41. Franklin was president of the U.S. Lines and a member of the Transportation Advisory Group. (2) Ltr, President to Adm Land, 10 Feb 41. Both in G-4/29717-48. (3) Wardlow, *Trans I*, pp. 136–41.

[55] (1) Ltr, SW to Adm Land, 12 Mar 41, G-4/29717-54. (2) Other corresp in same file. (3) Memos, Wardlow for Col Douglas C. Cordiner, OQMG, 6 and 19 Feb 41, G-4/29717-48. (4) Memo, G-4 for CofS, 7 Mar 41, sub: Negotiations With Maritime Comm . . ., G-4/29717-26. (5) Other corresp in same file and in G-4/29717-55.

[56] (1) Memo, 6 Feb 41, cited n. 55(3). (2) Memo for rcd atchd to G-4 disposition form to TAG for TQMG, 28 Jul 41, sub: Army Trans Sv to S America, G-4/29717-26.

[57] (1) Memo, G-4 for CofS, 9 Jul 41, sub: Utilization of Army Vessels, G-4/29717-26. (2) Other corresp in same file. (3) Memo, G-4 for CofS GHQ, 16 Oct 41, sub: Delay in Shipt of Replacements, G-4/33098. (4) Wardlow, *Trans I*, p. 141.

While during the winter and spring of 1941 the Army was thus trying to build up its capacity to transport forces overseas, its education in the logistics of joint task operations continued to lag. So uncertain were the Army staffs at all levels of the mathematics of computing shipping requirements that reserve supplies shipped to depots for certain of the task forces had piled up by late winter to about four times the total requirements as estimated by G-4. It developed further that the basic factors used by the Army for computing its shipping space requirements differed radically from the Navy's, a discrepancy that could cause untold confusion when the time came to set up shipping. Since the Army's factors were of hoary vintage (dating, some suspected, back to World War I), WPD advised G-4 in some embarrassment to come to an agreement with the Navy on the matter. Tentative shipping factors, accordingly, were worked out jointly in March.[58] Efforts to co-ordinate shipping arrangements with the Navy also promised trouble for future expeditions. G-4 found flagrant evidence of "confusion and lack of control over matters relating to overseas transportation."[59]

These experiences reflected the embryonic state of Army-Navy organization and training for joint amphibious operations. The Navy itself, responsible for all amphibious operations, was behindhand in providing transports and landing craft for its own amphibious maneuvers; in the fleet landing exercise held at Culebra Island, Puerto Rico, during the winter of 1941, the Navy had to borrow two Army transports, although no Army troops participated. The Army's role in amphibious training through 1941 was that of a poor relation. Only with the greatest difficulty was the Army able to obtain, by direct purchase, sufficient landing equipment to carry out, during the winter of 1940–41, limited exercises by the 1st Division on the east coast and by the 3d Division on the west coast. In May Admiral Stark, reviewing the Army's RAINBOW 5 plan, proposed that the two services co-ordinate their preparations for emergency expeditions, and ventured the opinion that the Army was pouring too much of its strength into static defense outpost positions; more effort should be given, he thought, to preparing mobile striking forces. This criticism touched a sensitive spot, not because of any dedication to the principle of static defense among the Army staff, but because the latter scented in the Navy proposal to reduce Army garrisons an attempt to secure for the Marine Corps an even larger share of scarce ammunition and equipment. General Marshall himself remarked, about this time, "My main battle is equipping the Marines. Whether we will have anything left after the British and Marines get theirs, I do not know."[60] His staff pointed out that the Navy, not the Army, had been laggard in promoting joint amphibious training. It was in June, in fact, that the first concrete step toward joint training was taken with the organization of the 1st Joint Training Force, consisting of the Marine 1st Division and the Army 1st Division; this subsequently developed into the Amphibious Force, Atlantic Fleet, which in 1942 organized the amphibious phases of the U.S. landings in Morocco. On the west coast, simi-

---

[58] (1) Corresp in G-4/31832, G-4/32550, and G-4/32598. (2) For the agreed factors, see below, Apps. A-2, A-3.

[59] (1) Memo, G-4 for CofS, 10 Apr 41, sub: Readiness of Vessels, G-4/31832. (2) Other corresp in same file. (3) See below, Ch. IX.

[60] Min, Gen War Council mtg, 3 Jun 41, Binder 1, SW Confs File.

ARMY-NAVY AMPHIBIOUS MANEUVERS *at New River area, North Carolina, August 1941. Light tank coming off landing craft.*

larly, the 2d Joint Training Force was created in September, consisting of the Army 3d Division and the Marine 2d Division; this later became the Amphibious Force, Pacific Fleet. Both forces were under Marine command.[61]

The first large-scale joint exercises on a divisional scale were held early in August 1941 by the Army's 1st Division and the 1st Marine Division in the New River area of the North Carolina coast, under the CARIB Plan of 21 June. Virtually every feature of the exercises was severely criticized by both Army and Navy observers. Embarkation of Army and Marine troops alike was badly snarled: because of inexperience and ignorance of officers in charge of the loading, the Army trans-

ports had to be completely reloaded before proceeding to New River, and, for lack of transports, some 1,700 marines were left behind—the climax of a process of embarkation extending over a five-week period. Troop transports proved to be inadequate in gear and facilities of all kinds. The landing was executed in daylight, with a calm sea, but an Army observer found the spectacle discouraging: men burdened with heavy packs being sub-

---
[61] (1) Jeter A. Isely and Philip A. Crowl, *The U.S. Marines and Amphibious War* (Princeton, N. J., Princeton University Press, 1951), pp. 58–63. (2) Wardlow, *Trans I*, pp. 144–46. (3) Greenfield, Palmer, and Wiley, *AGF I*, pp. 85–86. (4) Ltr, Adm Stark to CofS, 22 May 41, sub: Analysis of Plans for Overseas Expeds, RAINBOW 5 Development file, G-3 Registered Docs.

BEACHHEAD SUPPLY DUMP. *Piles of unidentifiable rations at New River Army-Navy amphibious maneuvers, August 1941.*

merged as they scrambled out of the boats; a Marine captain "so mad that he was almost weeping" because the Navy had sent his ammunition boats ashore in the first wave without protection; tanks plunging off ramps into deepening holes in the surf-covered sand. "One tank . . . disappeared into a hole and was completely submerged. The driver climbed out and stood disconsolately on the turret, looking for all the world like pictures you see of Jesus walking on the water." Shore organization was chaotic, responsibilities for unloading and other beach operations had not been fixed, and as a result both Army and Marine combat troops had to serve as stevedores although, according to one report, the Marines had assigned men

for this purpose because "from past experience they had learned that the Navy never did it." Boxes of ammunition and rations, handed from the boats to men standing in the surf, were usually saturated. Cardboard cartons of C rations, stacked on the beach, disintegrated, "and the cans of vegetable hash mingled with the cans of meat stew in a tall silver pyramid which glistened in the sunlight, but which was difficult to distribute to kitchens." Equipment rusted ashore because lubricants had been stowed deep in ships' holds.[62]

---

[62] (1) Rpt, unsigned, no date, sub: Fleet Landing Exercise, G-4/33088. (2) Isely and Crowl, *The U.S. Marines and Amphibious War,* pp. 63–65.

It was a depressing experience. "The whole procedure convinced me," commented the Army observer mentioned above, "that an effective landing is impossible unless all resistance is previously neutralized." [63] The commander in chief of the Atlantic Fleet declared a few weeks later that he considered the Atlantic Fleet Amphibious Force to be unfit for combat. Brig. Gen. Harry J. Malony, Deputy Chief of Staff, found four major failings in the exercise: lack of time for preparation, lack of experience, faulty planning, and complicated channels of command. These had undermined all aspects of the operation, but especially its logistics. The staffs planning real task force landings a few months later might have read these lessons with profit. [64]

The Abortive Azores Expedition

The Army and the Navy were in no posture, therefore, to act jointly to meet an emergency that in the spring of 1941 was drawing rapidly closer. Germany's spectacular successes in the Balkans and in Libya during April, combined with reports from Marshal Henri Pétain that the Germans were hinting at moving troops through unoccupied France and French North Africa for an attack on Gibraltar, seemed to herald a major German drive to the southwest. The crisis was precipitated when on 15 May Marshal Pétain announced his government's intention to collaborate with Germany. The United States immediately issued a sharp warning to Vichy and seized eleven French ships in American ports (including the liner *Normandie*), and on the 22d the President ordered the Army and Navy to make plans to occupy the Azores, possibly against opposition, within a month's time. [65]

For the Army staff this assignment was both unexpected and unwelcome. Plans had been prepared for action against the Azores, as for many other possible operations, but the staff had consistently advised against such an operation, arguing that the islands, if occupied, would be hard to defend against enemy air power based in France or on the Iberian Peninsula and that they were too far north to provide a useful base for countering a German move toward Dakar. Under ABC-1 all the Atlantic islands lay within the British sphere of responsibility, and the British had assigned forces to occupy the Azores and the Cape Verdes if the Germans entered Spain; the U.S. Navy undertook to give assistance in this eventuality, if needed, but the Army had not anticipated that it would be involved. The Army, in May, had perhaps forty thousand troops available for an overseas expedition, but it would have been difficult to put together a balanced expeditionary force of any size. Legislative restrictions upon the employment of certain categories of personnel outside the Western Hemisphere constituted a serious obstacle to planning for emergency action. As for shipping, the Army Transport Service had under its control about twenty-six vessels, all fully engaged in routine service. [66]

As the Army staff viewed the situation, an occupation of the Azores at that time was the least desirable of possible moves

[63] Rpt cited n. 62(1).
[64] (1) Wardlow, *Trans I*, p. 147. (2) Greenfield, Palmer, and Wiley, *AGF I*, pp. 87–88.
[65] (1) Ltr, Stark to Marshall, 23 May 41, G-4/31832. (2) Conn and Fairchild, Framework of Hemisphere Defense, Ch. V, pp. 16–26.
[66] (1) Conn and Fairchild, Framework of Hemisphere Defense, Ch. V, pp. 27–29. (2) Notes on Gen War Council mtg, 19 May 41, Binder 1, SW Confs File. (3) Notes on conf in OCofS, 16 Apr 41, Binder 10, CofS Confs File. (4) Wardlow, *Trans I*, p. 140.

in the Atlantic-Caribbean area. It would rule out the fulfillment of the Army's commitments under ABC-1 (scheduled for as early as September in the event of war) for the remainder of the year, and probably could not be mounted adequately, in any case, before mid-August. Nevertheless, it was the Azores expedition that now had to be mounted—and by the President's deadline of 22 June.[67] By the end of May it was decided to use the 1st Army and 1st Marine Divisions to form the nucleus of a new task force of about 28,000 under over-all Navy command, the Marine division commander to be in charge of the landing operation. Three of the twelve battalion landing teams were to be contributed by the Army, which also set up additional reserve forces of about 11,000—approximately 25,000 Army troops in all.[68]

Ammunition was the tightest chokepoint. Minimum allowances for the assault elements and partial allowances for the follow-up forces would have exhausted all stocks of certain critical types—for example, 3-inch antiaircraft and 37-mm. antitank—and exceeded both stocks and anticipated production to 1 October in others such as .50-caliber antiaircraft. A few types, notably 60-mm. mortar, would not be available at all for several months. The ammunition allowances requested by the Army commander had to be slashed, on the average, by half.[69]

Shipping also presented a major problem, even though it was not the principal limiting factor. This shortage, at the outset, ruled out the possibility of holding joint landing rehearsals on the coast of Puerto Rico (too far away to permit more than one round trip and final assembling of the force before the target date, 22 June); the commanders had to be content

with separate, small Army and Marine rehearsals along the U.S. east coast. For the initial movement, forty-one transports and cargo vessels were needed. The services could provide twenty-nine of these; the remaining twelve, with fourteen more to take over normal duties of the diverted military shipping, would have to be found by the Maritime Commission. Practically all the vessels used in the initial movement, moreover, would have to be retained indefinitely to bring in normal maintenance supplies and construction material for building airfields and other installations. In the time available only a few transports and cargo vessels could be rigged and armed to carry assault troops and their equipment, a circumstance that severely restricted both the number of troops and the amount of gasoline, ammunition, and reserve supplies that could be carried in the initial assault.[70]

The Navy found it necessary, against strong protests by the Army, to take over six of the Army's newest and largest troop transports. Two were peculiarly suited for use on the long transpacific run, and a third was needed in the Bermuda and Newfoundland service. Army officials argued that to use vessels such as these in a

---

[67] See below, n. 82.

[68] (1) Papers in WPD 4422-3; WPD 4422-4; WPD 4232-5; WPD 4232-10; WPD 4232-11; AG 353 (5-23-41), Sec 1; AG 370.5 (5-26-41); Exec 13; and G-4/33088. (2) See also, notes on Gen War Council mtg, 26 May 41, Binder 1, SW Confs File. (3) Gen Gerow's Diary, 29 May and 2 Jun 41 entries, Item 1, Exec 10.

[69] Memo, Maj Louis E. Cotulla for Col Francis B. Mallon, 3 Jun 41, sub: Am for Exped Force (GRAY), G-4/33088.

[70] (1) Draft ltr, SN to President, in Tab A to memo for rcd, unsigned, 26 May 41, sub: Trf of Army Trans to Navy, Tab M, Item 7, Exec 4. (2) Notes cited n. 68(2). (3) Memo, G-4 for Chiefs of Svs and CG NYPOE, 31 May 41, sub: Tng Exercise. (4) Memo, Lt Col Albert W. Waldron for Col Mallon, 4 Jun 41, sub: Lack of Co-ord . . . . Last two in G-4/33088.

combat-loaded convoy would sacrifice the advantages of their speed and capacity on normal runs. While the loss to the Army would be made up by equivalent tonnage, this involved inevitable delays and disruption of service, and there was always the danger that Hawaii and Alaska might have to be suddenly reinforced during the change-over.[71]

As it happened, the Azores expedition did not have to be launched. On 4 June the President approved the joint plan, but at the same time ordered the services to prepare another plan—one for the relief of British forces in Iceland. On the 7th, probably as a result of information pointing to the impending German invasion of the USSR, he suspended the Azores project, and the first American ground forces (marines) landed in Iceland a month later.[72] The Army's portion of the Azores force remained earmarked, as Task Force GRAY, for its original mission, and the transfer of Army transports to the Navy was carried out. The effort to mount the Azores expedition had emphasized, among other things, the strategic importance of the small military transport fleets, for on the disposition of these few specialized vessels, a tiny fraction of the total merchant marine, depended the ability of the armed forces to react promptly and effectively to an emergency. It had emphasized also the fact that, a year after the launching of the defense mobilization program, an expedition involving some twenty-five thousand miscellaneous Army troops, with only three battalion landing teams, represented a maximum effort.

To the man in the ranks, far from Washington staff offices, the logistics of task force movements seemed to be largely a matter of being moved about and waiting to be moved about. The saga of one unit

added a plaintive postscript to the history of the Azores expedition.

"In May," began the chronicle, "a secret letter was received . . . ." The unit was to be part of a task force, then forming, and was to draw its cold-weather clothing. But soon a new order came. The unit was now assigned to Task Force GRAY and was to prepare for tropical service. For the next two weeks the troops were busy packing equipment, turning in cold-weather clothing, drawing tropical clothing, and requisitioning personnel. "With all equipment packed and crated and, for the most part, loaded on trucks, the regiment waited for movement orders which never came." About 1 July the unit learned that the task force had been disbanded—three days later that it had been reconstituted.

Consequently the regiment still waited and no equipment was unpacked; only such training as could be conducted with individual equipment, or convoys, was given. Batteries disposed of day room and kitchen property, and officers and enlisted men owning automobiles generally disposed of them at a financial loss.

Presently Battery E was ordered to join another task force. This necessitated transfers of personnel from three other batteries, which meanwhile uncrated part of their equipment and began to train. But it was Battery E that waited; F and G, ordered to join a new training force, hastily repacked equipment and departed on 11 July.

---

[71] (1) Ltr, Marshall to Stark, 25 May 41, in Tab B to memo for rcd cited n. 70(1). (2) Draft ltr cited n. 70(1). (3) Memo, Col Theodore H. Dillon for Col Mallon, 23 May 41, G-4/29717-26. (4) Memo, G-4 for WPD, 24 May 41, sub: Utilization of Army Trans, G-4/29717-71. (5) Ltr cited n. 61(4).

[72] Conn and Fairchild, Framework of Hemisphere Defense, Ch. V, pp. 35–49.

Their average strength was 63 men when ordered away, and I [the station commandant] was directed by General Ord [Brig. Gen. Garesché J.] to bring them to war strength, which required the transfer of 226 men including several non-commissioned officers. As the other automatic weapons had been depleted to fill Battery E and the latter was still a part of a task force prepared for movement, the 226 filler replacements for Batteries F and G had to be taken from the 1st Battalion. . . . The above so depleted the 1st Battalion as to prevent manning much of its equipment until about 356 replacements were received on July 23d and relieved the situation somewhat. However, as it was originally understood that Batteries F and G were to return about September 1st, the above replacements were assigned according to the eventual needs of all units of the regiment. Subsequent information indicates that Batteries F and G will not rejoin until about October 15th. Finally, on September 6th a letter was received from II Army Corps to the effect that all instructions with reference to Task Force 3 [the one to which the regiment was first assigned] were rescinded.

The chronicle ended with a bleak survey of the damage:

. . . waiting for orders . . . financial loss . . . disruption of family life . . . cancellation of furloughs and leaves . . . camp improvements were given away . . . . For a period of 1½ months there was little artillery training . . . thereafter equipment sufficient for training was unpacked as required and training resumed, but always with half an idea on the possibility of having to pack up quickly in the same boxes and crates . . . .

All of which "had an adverse effect on morale, training and housekeeping."[73]

State of Readiness: Mid-1941

At midyear the Army's emergency forces were hardly formidable. In April Task Forces 2 and 3 had finally been given the equipment priorities thought necessary to bring them rapidly to a condition of readiness, but the process of actually equipping the units was still going on. Three more infantry divisions—the 2d, 3d, and 5th—were added to the emergency list early in June and assigned higher priorities for equipment. By the end of July the proliferation of task forces had brought the total to nine—two small Martinique-Guadeloupe Forces, A and B; Forces 1 through 5, GRAY (Azores), and CARIB (Army component of the 1st Joint Training Force). The versatile 1st Division was the nucleus of most of these task forces, and many smaller units also had multiple assignments. For each force supplies had been stocked, transportation tentatively arranged, and movement procedures set up. But experience indicated that any specific emergency was likely to demand a force tailored for the occasion; in effect, the Army was attempting to build a pool of units from which such forces might be formed. Accordingly, the War Department in August abolished the first five of the forces listed above and created the War Department Pool of Task Force Units, comprising seven divisions and various supporting units.[74]

But, as Brig. Gen. Leonard T. Gerow reported to General Marshall early in

---

[73] Memo, Gen Malony for WPD, 5 Nov 41, sub: Rpt of CO Camp Stewart, Ga., . . . , WPD 4161-21.

[74] The seven divisions in the pool were the 1st, 2d, 3d, 5th, 41st, and 45th Infantry and the 6th Cavalry. Task Forces 4 and 5 were earmarked tentatively for Iceland and Brazil, respectively. (1) Memo, Gen Gerow for CofS, 9 Jun 41, sub: Readiness of Combat Divs. (2) Memo, Gerow for CofS, 28 Jun 41, sub: Emergency Exped Forces. (3) WD ltr to GHQ, AAF, CG's of Armies, Corps Areas, NYPOE, Seattle POE, and Chiefs of SAS and WDGS Divs, 20 Aug 41, sub: Units for Exped Forces. All in WPD 4161-16. (4) Other papers in same file. (5) Memo, G-4 for WPD, 9 Jun 41, sub: Readiness of Combat Divs, G-4/32509. (6) Corresp in same file and in G-4/32550.

June, "the 1st Division reinforced is the only triangular division we have which even approximates readiness for combat service involving a landing on a hostile shore." [75] This was the net result of a year of effort to create mobile striking forces for emergency action. Larger forces might have been equipped for such service by pillaging units in training, but until spring of 1941 General Marshall steadily resisted the pressure to do so and yielded only partially to it even then.

As it was, equipment was spread thin. Manpower had flowed into the expanding Army more or less as planned, bringing it by the end of June to a strength of 1,455,-565—substantially the goal set in 1940—but the flow of weapons to equip it had fallen short of expectations. Production of aircraft, mortars, certain types of antiaircraft artillery and machine guns, rifles, field artillery ammunition, light tanks, and trucks showed encouraging increases, but in most other categories progress was scant. Much of this matériel, moreover, had been diverted into foreign aid. According to a G-4 estimate in midsummer, the equipping of the ground army was about "a year behind the expectations of a year ago," [76] which meant presumably that another year's production would be needed to meet the objectives laid down in summer of 1940 for mid-1941. In certain categories the troops were relatively well equipped—for example, in clothing, personal equipage, standard engineer equipment (but not special construction items for combat theaters), and motor transport (except the versatile ¼-ton jeep and 2½-ton truck). Some medical items were plentiful, but there were acute shortages of certain drugs and laboratory and dental equipment. Signal Corps material was generally scarce. Radios had to be built

into aircraft; therefore combat vehicles, to which radios could be added as accessories, had a lower priority for this equipment. Development changes in electronics presented a perennial problem, impeding standardization and mass production. Army forces in training had received their first 20 percent "go around" in most major items but not, as yet, in the newer types; by July 1942 it might be possible to outfit the initial PMP force fully with most signal items except electronics, for which the outlook was uncertain. [77]

Shortages in ordnance equipment were a serious obstacle to readiness for combat. Light, automatic antiaircraft weapons (37-mm., 40-mm., and .50-caliber) were scarcer than heavy ones (3-inch and 90-mm.), but in neither category would full allowances for the initial PMP force be completed by the end of 1942. Ground forces suffered from the preference given the Air Corps in allocation of ordinary automatic weapons which, like radios, had to be built into aircraft; substitution of .30-caliber for .50-caliber machine guns in ground units offered only partial relief. Similarly, infantry units came off second best in distribution of 37-mm. guns, since tanks had to be equipped on the production line; the antitank gun was therefore still in the 20 percent "go around" stage for the initial PMP force, and complete allowances were not expected until mid-1942. Although 60-mm. mortars were fairly plentiful, 81-mm.'s were scarce. The new M1 Garand rifle was promised, optimistically, as it proved, for all infantry, cavalry, and engineer units by the end of

---

[75] Memo cited n. 74(1).
[76] Memo, G-4 for CofS, 28 Aug 41, sub: Status of Equip, G-4/33484.
[77] (1) *Ibid.* (2) Army strength figure is from the Annual *Report of the Secretary of War, 1941,* Table A. (3) See below, App. B.

October. Distribution of field artillery was held up by modernization of the standard 75-mm. gun, which in turn was to be replaced by the newer 105-mm. howitzer when available. All the existing forces could be equipped with one or the other weapon in a few months, but to little avail since fire control instruments would not be fully available until mid-1942. Tanks were coming along well, enough to equip six armored divisions and all the PMP tank battalions by January 1942, but only if lend-lease diversions were not taken into consideration.[78]

Finally, ammunition. In the small arms category, allocations to the Navy, Air Corps, and lend-lease had stripped the ground army bare. G-4 doubted whether, for two years to come, production would be sufficient to maintain the initial PMP force in the field. Antiaircraft (other than small calibers) and field artillery ammunition was currently in shorter supply than the weapons using it, but this situation was due to be reversed the following spring. Bombs of most types could probably be supplied for any number of aircraft likely to be put into operation, but armor-piercing ammunition of all types fell far short of requirements, and there was little prospect of production catching up with the output of weapons.[79]

The British had been promised, in ABC-1, that the U.S. Army could put into the field on 1 September about six divisions (two armored) and six air combat groups. By midyear this fair vision had vanished. The favored 1st Division, with five supporting antiaircraft regiments and two brigades of field artillery, was not expected to be fully prepared for combat in all respects until October. The GHQ Air Force did not have a single unit equipped with modern combat planes; by September it might be possible to assemble a group of light bombers, two squadrons of dive bombers, and one and a half groups of pursuits, all with inadequate reserves and ground support. Either these air forces or the ground forces would have to operate virtually without small-caliber ammunition. Not until the following March could anything like the forces promised in ABC-1 be put into the field.[80]

A 1 September M Day evidently would find the Army something less than ready to meet its commitments under ABC-1 and Rainbow 5. Shipping, if fully mobilized, was not expected to present a major problem. The Navy, upon which the responsibility would fall, estimated that it could muster for military use before the end of 1941 about 384 vessels—71 transports and 313 cargo ships. Definitely scheduled moves under Rainbow 5 would impose a peak demand, a month after M Day, of fifty-nine transports and cargo vessels. If all contingent operations were carried out, including the movement of a ten-division force beginning six months after M Day, requirements for initial movement and maintenance would climb to more than 200 vessels almost a year after M Day; maintenance thereafter would keep about 177 cargo ships steadily employed. These calculations were highly theoretical and did not actually look more than a year ahead, when both new deployment and new ship construction would enter the picture; foreign aid requirements to replace Allied shipping losses and to transport lend-lease material were not considered. Perhaps the weakest feature of the calculation, as the experience of 1942 was to show, was the assumption that large ton-

---

[78] (1) Memo cited n. 76. (2) See below, Chs. III–IV.
[79] Memo cited n. 76.
[80] Memo cited n. 37(1).

Table 1—Shipping for Rainbow 5: Estimated Availability and Requirements

Availability	Transports [a]		Cargo Vessels	
	Ships	Ship Tons	Ships	Ship Tons
Ocean-going shipping in Atlantic area [b]	85	642,000	469	4,883,000
New construction expected in 1941	10	130,000	56	685,000
Total available	95	772,000	525	5,568,000
Required for essential commercial services	24	210,000	212	2,657,000
Total available for military purposes [c]	71	562,000	313	2,911,000

Requirement	Ships
Army and Navy movements on M Day [d]	56
Prescribed movements after M Day (peak at M plus 30)	59
Prescribed and contingent movements after M Day (peak at M plus 330)	202
Maintenance after full deployment [e]	177

[a] Combination transports, carrying some cargo as well as troops.

[b] The total U.S. merchant fleet at this time, according to one estimate, comprised 1,179 vessels of 7,353,000 gross tons (about 11,000,000 ship tons).

[c] Total of 384 vessels available.

[d] For regular servicing of established garrisons and movements to be launched on M Day. Initial moves to reinforce Panama, Puerto Rico, Alaska, and Hawaii, however, were not specifically included, on the assumption that they could be absorbed into the schedule. All requirements were calculated on the basis of 1,500 troops per transport and 8,750 ship tons per cargo vessel.

[e] For maintenance factors, see below, App. A-3.

Source: Memo, Gen Malony for CofS, 20 May 41, sub: Overseas Garrisons, Rainbow 5, WPD 4175-22.

nages of commercial shipping could be mobilized for military use within a few weeks or months. Taking a longer view, G-4 estimated, about this time, that nine million gross tons of new ship construction would be needed each year to carry on a Rainbow 5 war; only two million were then scheduled for 1942. From the vantage point of mid-1941, however, a Rainbow 5 war centering in the Atlantic area did not seem likely to strain unduly the shipping capabilities of the United States.[81] *(Table 1)*

It was primarily the meagerness of ready forces rather than of shipping that caused the Army staff, in late May and June, to regard with uneasiness the President's apparently adventurous intentions in the Atlantic area. During the preparations for

the Azores operation the Army staff warned that, because of the unbalanced character of available forces and the lack of combat aviation, no expedition could be sent within a thousand miles of Europe or Africa (thus ruling out the Cape Verdes but not the Azores). Moreover, any such undertaking, unless liquidated early, would probably interfere with any September operations under ABC-1; an occupation of the Azores certainly would do so, a limited expedition to Brazil only moderately. On 27 May the Army planners suggested to General Marshall two alter-

[81] (1) Memo, Gen Malony for CofS, 20 May 41, sub: Overseas Garrisons, Rainbow 5. (2) Memo, Gen Gerow for CofS, 26 May 41, sub: Analysis of Plans for Overseas Expeds. Both in WPD 4175-22. (3) Memo cited n. 37(1).

natives, of which they favored the second: either carry out the moves to Iceland and the British Isles in September as contingently scheduled, or postpone these moves for a few weeks and send a balanced force immediately to northeastern Brazil.[82]

Even though suspended early in June an Azores expedition remained very much a live alternative, other eastern Atlantic projects were being discussed, and the Iceland movement was about to begin; with about 130,000 troops already overseas, the Army had some 75,000 more scheduled for deployment; the remaining ABC-1 commitments might soon have to be faced.[83] The Army planners felt that for the present all projects looking beyond the Western Hemisphere should be abandoned. To strike at Dakar, the most effective riposte to a German move into northwest Africa, would be far beyond the Army's power for a long time; without Dakar the Canary and Cape Verde Islands could not be held, even if taken. Neither they nor Iceland nor the Azores were essential to a static defense of the Western Hemisphere. WPD thought that an immediate occupation of northeastern Brazil, which was "within present and future means," would be the most effective and feasible move to checkmate Axis designs on the hemisphere.[84]

When the President late in June, therefore, blandly suggested that the Army raise a force of "about 75,000" looking to possible action in several quarters—Iceland, the Azores, the Cape Verdes, "or elsewhere"—the reaction of the Army staff amounted almost to an outburst. Such a force would be three times the size of the late unlamented Azores task force. The President was asking the Army, in effect, to commit its best troops, virtually all its small arms ammunition, and much of its equipment to a remote area where they might be isolated by an unlucky naval reverse, leaving the country denuded of land defense. General Marshall explained to the President that there were two main obstacles to carrying out his proposal—legislative restrictions upon sending certain categories of troops outside the Western Hemisphere, and the complex of logistical and other limitations that had stood, and would long continue to stand, in the way of creating fully trained, equipped, and balanced striking forces and moving them overseas. He bluntly told the President that "he would not give his consent to the dispatch of any troops outside the United States that were not completely trained and equipped to meet a first-class enemy." [85]

[82] (1) Memo, Lt Col Lee S. Gerow for Gen Gerow, 27 May 41, WPD 4422-5. (2) Memo, G-2 GHQ for CofS GHQ, 28 May 41, GHQ 381, Sec 1. (3) Conn and Fairchild, Framework of Hemisphere Defense, Ch. V, pp. 26–35.

[83] (1) Memo, 31 May 41, cited n. 29(2). (2) Memo, Lt Col Jay W. MacKelvie for Exec Off WPD, no date, sub: Availability of Key Units, RAINBOW 5 . . . , Item 7, Exec 4. (3) Annual *Report of the Secretary of War, 1941*, Table C.

[84] Memo, Gen Gerow for CofS, 14 Jun 41, sub: Strategic Opns, Brief Analysis . . . , Tab L, Item 7, Exec 4.

[85] Gerow Diary, 19 Jun 41 entry, Item 1, Exec 10.

CHAPTER III

The Army and Early Lend-Lease Operations

After passage of the Lend-Lease Act in March 1941, supply of military materials to foreign governments became a direct responsibility of the Army and one of its principal supply activities. Lend-lease was in its conception largely a means of overcoming financial and legal barriers to the continuance of aid to the British, and this concept was clearly reflected in the manner in which needs of the British at first absorbed both the immediate and the prospective supply of munitions to be distributed under it. But gradually other nations secured recognition of their claims, and by December 1941 China, the Soviet Union, the Netherlands Indies, and the Latin American nations had taken their places beside Britain as lend-lease beneficiaries.

While funds appropriated by Congress to finance lend-lease would contribute to the ultimate expansion of munitions production, there was no magic formula that could make these funds immediately produce weapons. Industrial mobilization continued at a slow pace, and the production estimates upon which hopes of fulfilling Army and British programs rested proved too optimistic. Competition grew keener, both for the limited stocks of munitions on hand and for the ample flow expected from future production. The situation demanded a policy to govern current and projected allocations.

There was a growing conviction within the War Department that lend-lease operations should be tied to definite national objectives, but the President, with an eye on isolationist opposition in Congress, was reluctant to spell out these objectives. He had to justify lend-lease before Congress in the first instance as a measure of defense, and the first lend-lease programs were formulated only on the general assumption that aid to Britain and China would contribute to that end. The ABC-1 meetings produced a strategic concept for American participation in the war against the Axis in alliance with Britain, but the President would never specifically sanction tying lend-lease operations to this conditional agreement. Indeed ABC-1 gave no final answer to the question of whether the American contribution should be in weapons or armies. The British pressed for delay in American rearmament in favor of foreign aid, but the Army found it difficult to accept the full implications of such a policy. The President's decisions, generally favoring foreign aid, found expression in a series of specific actions rather than in any pronouncement of a general policy for the Army to follow.

The War Department sought to center

control of procurement and distribution of military lend-lease within its own organization, combining them in one consolidated supply program with similar functions performed for the U.S. Army. In its view, such a program offered the best means of rapidly expanding production of munitions and of making allocations based on strategic principles. The President preferred to keep lend-lease powers in his own hands or to rely on civilian advisers and administrators. This gave rise to a system of administration that, when combined with the immaturity of both the civilian and the military organizations involved, compounded the confusion resulting from lack of clarity in national aims.

The Administrative Problem

The Lend-Lease Act empowered the President to transfer "defense articles" and "defense information" to any foreign government whose defense he deemed vital to that of the United States. Two types of transfers were authorized—materials produced on funds especially appropriated for lend-lease purposes, and materials from government stocks.[1] The only limitations on the President's power to transfer materials procured on lend-lease funds were those inherent in the appropriations. These were made in some ten categories with a proviso that the President could make transfers between categories up to 20 percent as long as no single category was increased by more than 30 percent. There were two lend-lease appropriations in 1941, one on 27 March for $7 billion and another on 28 October for $5.985 billion.[2] Recognizing that it would take time to procure materials with lend-lease funds, Congress also authorized transfers from stocks, but carefully circumscribed the

President's powers in this regard. He could not transfer materials produced on appropriations made subsequent to the Lend-Lease Act to regular government agencies. Transfers from material produced on previous regular appropriations were limited to a valuation of $1.3 billion, and would require the approval of the Chief of Staff or Chief of Naval Operations in the case of military or naval materials.[3] Beyond these restrictions, the procedures for carrying out lend-lease were left almost entirely to the discretion of the President.

Roosevelt decided even before the act was passed that it should be administered by existing government agencies within their various spheres of responsibility. Thus, the War Department would carry the largest share of the burden, for almost all materials to be released under the "Billion Three" clause would come from Army stocks, and approximately $4 billion of the first appropriation (of $7 billion) and $2.4 billion of the second (of $5.985 billion) fell into categories for which it had primary responsibility—*viz.*, I, ordnance and ordnance stores; II, aircraft and aeronautical equipment; III, tanks and other vehicles; and V, miscellaneous military equipment. Initially, the War Department proposed direct appropriations by Congress to the Army within these categories, but this proposal was rejected and an arrangement was finally made whereby the appropriations were made to the President and allocated by him to the proper procurement agency.[4] This system, as the President ap-

---

[1] PL 11, 77th Cong (Lend-Lease Act).
[2] (1) PL 23, 77th Cong. (2) PL 282, 77th Cong.
[3] The so-called Billion Three clause, Sec 3a(2) of Lend-Lease Act.
[4] (1) Memo, Col Aurand for Maj Gen Richard C. Moore, 15 Feb 41, sub: Conf on Method of Appropriation for Lend-lease Bill, G-4/32697-1. (2) PL cited n. 1.

plied it, led to a separation of lend-lease and Army contracts for the same articles and produced a welter of complicated administrative practices.

The President did not delegate to the War Department as much authority to administer lend-lease as Secretary Stimson had evidently expected, nor did he give to his military advisers the dominant voice in determining lend-lease policy that they thought the situation demanded. Tabling a suggestion from Stimson that overall control be vested in a cabinet board on which the service departments would predominate, Roosevelt appointed Harry Hopkins, his close personal adviser, as Lend-Lease Administrator. Hopkins did not become the head of any organization or office for the purpose, and remained a sort of lend-lease minister without portfolio, wielding vast influence, but little concerned with the details of practical administration. To fill the administrative void, the President on 2 May 1941 created the Division of Defense Aid Reports (DDAR), with Maj. Gen. James H. Burns, Executive Assistant to the Under Secretary of War, as executive officer. DDAR became the President's agency for receiving foreign requests, for co-ordinating the activities of the various government agencies involved in lend-lease, and for accounting, but it was never vested with more than limited authority to approve allocation of funds or transfers of materials. Until October 1941 nearly every specific action under lend-lease required the personal approval of the President.[5]

If the President's mode of operating was the underlying cause of the administrative confusion that followed, the War Department organization compounded it. The first organization for handling lend-lease within the War Department was estab-

lished in early April 1941. As on the higher level, existing agencies were used as far as possible. The supply arms and services—Ordnance, Quartermaster, Signal, Medical, Chemical Warfare, and Engineers—together with the Air Corps, were to be the principal operating agencies for procurement and distribution of supplies, with planning, supervision, and direction of their activities divided between the Office of the Under Secretary of War in matters of procurement, and the General Staff in requirements and distribution. A Defense Aid Division was established in the Under Secretary's office as a coordinating agency, with Colonel MacMorland, former Secretary of the ANMB Clearance Committee, as its head. To perform the detailed work necessary in reviewing foreign requirements and formulating aid programs, defense aid requirements committees were also established, one for each of the supply services. The nucleus of each committee was to be a chairman and a secretariat from G-4, a representative of the Office of the Under Secretary of War (OUSW), and a representative of the foreign country concerned. The existing Joint Aircraft Committee was continued as the requirements committee for aircraft.[6]

With so many different agencies involved, the early procedures were inevi-

---

[5] (1) Ltr, Stimson to President, 13 Feb 41, with incl, sub: Lend-lease Orgn, AG 400.3295 (2-13-41) (3). (2) Sherwood, *Roosevelt and Hopkins*, p. 278. (3) EO 8751, 2 May 41. (4) The limited delegations of authority made by the President may be found in ltrs, President to SW, 18 Mar and 4 Jun 41; ltr, President to Exec Off DDAR, 26 Jul 41; and ltr, President to Edward R. Stettinius, Jr., 18 Sep 41. All in Auth File of President's Ltrs, DAD.

[6] (1) AG ltr to Chiefs of SAS and WDGS Divs, 10 Apr 41, sub: Proced Under Lend-Lease Act, AG 020.1 (3-29-41). (2) Ltr, SW to Maj Gen Henry H. Arnold, Actg DCofS, 22 Apr 41, sub: Jt Aircraft Com, ID, Lend-Lease, Doc Suppl, I.

tably cumbersome. The requirements committees worked out programs for each category of equipment on the basis of the funds appropriated, and the President made tentative allocations of funds based on these programs. Each item in the program then had to be separately requisitioned, and each requisition had to go through a tortuous chain of offices. A foreign requisition was first received by DDAR and, if for a military article, referred to the Secretary of War. The Secretary referred it to the Defense Aid Division, which then secured action by the appropriate requirements committee and approval of G-4 (and WPD if matters of strategy were involved). The results were incorporated in a staff study for the Chief of Staff, who then prepared necessary action for the Secretary of War. The Secretary sent the ultimate decision back to DDAR, which in case of approval prepared the necessary allocation or transfer letter for the signature of the President. The President's authorization had to make the return trip through channels before a directive could be issued by the Secretary of War to the appropriate supply service to take action. The same process had to be repeated when materials became available for transfer.[7] Where requisitions or transfers merely confirmed items on approved programs, the tortuous journey was largely perfunctory, but spot requisitions, program changes, and emergency demands had to go through the whole time-consuming process. The War Department was not only hamstrung by the necessity of continually referring all sorts of minutiae to the President, but muscle-bound by its own procedures.

Between April and October the War Department gradually improved the situation within its own house. The Secretary's office was eliminated from routine administration and the Defense Aid Division made responsible for initial receipt of requisitions. The numerous requirements committees were reduced to a status of informal subcommittees under one Defense Aid Supply Committee.[8] The big stumbling block remained the division of authority between G-4 and the Under Secretary's office. The Requirements and Distribution Branch, G-4, headed by Lt. Col. Henry S. Aurand (promoted to colonel on 26 June 1941), set up its own Defense Aid Section, which provided the permanent nucleus for the Defense Aid Supply Committee and did much of the work on which the Defense Aid Division had to depend for its staff studies. There were inevitable duplications of function, and inevitable delays in processing papers between the two offices. Colonel Aurand proposed as early as May that the two sections be consolidated, but Robert P. Patterson, the Under Secretary of War, refused to surrender the procurement function, and the General Staff refused to surrender the requirements function. The final solution, approved by Secretary Stimson on 1 October 1941, was ingenious. All offices engaged in lend-lease activities, including the Defense Aid Division, OUSW, the Defense Aid Section, G-4, and the home offices of lend-lease missions then being dispatched to overseas theaters, were placed together, adjacent to the office

---

[7] (1) Ltr cited n. 6(1). (2) AG ltr to Chiefs of SAS and WDGS Divs, 17 Jun 41, sub: Proced Under Lend-Lease Act, AG 020.1 (6-12-41). (3) Agenda for Def Aid Sup Com, 8 Aug 41, ID, Lend-Lease, Doc Suppl, I.

[8] (1) Ltr cited n. 7(2). (2) AG ltr to Chiefs of SAS and WDGS Divs, 10 Jul 41, sub: Change in Proced Under Lend-Lease Act, AG 020.1 (7-9-41). (3) ID, Lend-Lease, I, 113.

of the Assistant Secretary, John J. McCloy, to whom Stimson had delegated his own functions in regard to lend-lease. The lines of responsibility remained the same but Colonel Aurand was named Defense Aid Director of the War Department and hence the head of all the separate offices. The chairmanship and secretariat of the Defense Aid Supply Committee were transferred to his jurisdiction, supply arms and services were required to appoint lend-lease officers, and foreign governments were requested to name liaison officers with Aurand's office.[9]

By the end of October Aurand had converted this physical consolidation into a genuine organizational consolidation. The separate offices were made branches of the Office of the Defense Aid Director. Aurand soon made of this organization something closely resembling a general staff section charged with supply to foreign armies, though its exact relation to G-4 remained undefined. Aurand could, at least in theory, exercise authority only in the name of one of his four superiors—the Deputy Chief of Staff, Maj. Gen. Richard C. Moore, on requirements and distribution; the Under Secretary, Mr. Patterson, on procurement; the Assistant Secretary, Mr. McCloy, on policy matters relating to the Secretary's office; and the Assistant Secretary of War for Air, Robert A. Lovett, on matters pertaining to Air Forces matériel. Nevertheless, a real measure of centralization of War Department lend-lease activities had been achieved.[10] (Chart 2)

While the War Department organization was evolving, the President finally began to delegate his lend-lease powers. In August he called in Edward R. Stettinius, Jr., as special assistant on lend-lease and, on 28 October 1941, appointed him Lend-Lease Administrator, vested with all the presidential powers under the act, save those of designating countries to be aided and those of negotiating master agreements with them.[11] The Office of Lend-Lease Administration (OLLA) absorbed the organization and functions of the Division of Defense Aid Reports. The creation of OLLA offered the prospect of simplified administrative procedures, but raised the spectre of domination of military lend-lease by a civilian agency that military officials considered to be little suited for the task. Colonel Aurand and Mr. McCloy immediately began to press Stettinius for more freedom of action. They asked that OLLA allocate funds in a lump to cover programs worked out for each country within the Defense Aid Supply Committee, grant blanket authority to the Secretary of War to transfer the articles contained therein, and set up a revolving fund of sufficient size to take care of other demands that came up outside the programs. Processing individual requisitions through OLLA should no longer be required, and the War Department should have full freedom within the limits of existing legislation to make adjustments in programs, transfer funds from one category to an-

---

[9] (1) Memo, ACofS G-4 for CofS, 22 May 41, sub: Change in Proced Under Lend-Lease Act, G-4/32697, Sec 1. (2) Memo, USW for ACofS G-4, 31 May 41, same sub. (3) G-4 consideration of noncurrence. Last two in Proced Lend-lease file, DAD. (4) Memo, Col Aurand for Lt Col Stanley R. Mickelsen, 5 Sep 41, sub: Trf of DAD, AG 020.1 (2-29-41). (5) Memo, Patterson for SW, 19 Sep 41, sub: Lend-lease Proced, ID, Lend-Lease, Doc Suppl, I. (6) AG ltr to Chiefs of SAS and WDGS Divs, 1 Oct 41, sub: Change in Proced Under Lend-Lease Act, AG 020.1 (9-19-41) OD-F.

[10] (1) Memo, Aurand for all offs in ODAD, 29 Oct 41, USSR Mis 334 file, DAD, Job 11. (2) Memo, Aurand, no addressee, 1 Nov 41, sub: Def Aid Policies and Orgn, Misc Stf Studies, Proced Lend-lease file, DAD.

[11] EO 8926, 28 Oct 41.

CHART 2—ORGANIZATION FOR HANDLING MILITARY LEND-LEASE: NOVEMBER 1941

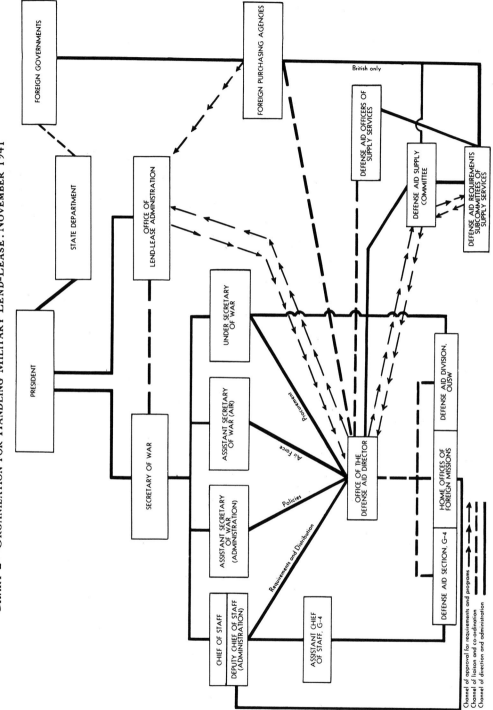

Channel of approval for requirements and programs ——→
Channel of liaison and co-ordination
Channel of direction and administration

other, make transfers under the "Billion Three" clause, and retransfer material earmarked for one country to another as the situation demanded.

Stettinius was generally co-operative and War Department fears of encroachment proved groundless, but he moved slowly and still insisted on retaining a degree of financial control within OLLA. He accepted the principle of programing and granted the Secretary of War blanket transfer authority under approved programs, but maintained most of the other restrictions on the use of funds and transfer of material. Aurand complained on the eve of Pearl Harbor that continuing control by OLLA would prevent the War Department from running a program based on military considerations.[12]

The lesson to be drawn from these administrative difficulties, War Department officials generally concluded, was that lend-lease appropriations for military articles should be consolidated with Army appropriations with a limitation only on the dollar value of lend-lease transfers. Only in this way, they thought, could the goal of a consolidated military production program with distribution on a strategic basis be achieved. A limited plan of this sort was offered to Congress as part of the Army's request for supplemental appropriations in November 1941 but was rejected in the House of Representatives. Nevertheless, this proved only a temporary setback. The temper of Congress changed rapidly after Pearl Harbor.[13]

Early Operations Under Lend-Lease

Passage of the Lend-Lease Act was closely followed by a new series of surplus releases and by the formulation of production programs for aid to Britain. In February General Marshall approved a new list made up primarily of various obsolescent types of artillery that might legitimately be considered surplus now that prospects of new production were brighter. Originally, the list was drawn up on the supposition that all materials would be turned over to the British, but since the President also wished to make some gesture of aid to Greece, and since the British themselves wanted to strengthen their influence in Turkey, the surplus was divided among the three countries by agreement with the British representatives. On 11 March 1941 the President declared defense of Great Britain and Greece vital to that of the United States; releases to Turkey were handled through the British, obviating the need for such a declaration for that country.

Shortly thereafter the German invasion of Yugoslavia added another urgent claimant. General Marshall agreed to make additional releases from U.S. stocks—some of which, 75-mm. ammunition and P-40 pursuit planes, for example, were not clearly "surplus"—and the British consented to a further division of their allotment. The lightning conquest of Yugoslavia and Greece prevented the delivery of any supplies to either country, and only Turkey got its share. The British were allowed to retain most of the remainder

---

[12] (1) Ltr, McCloy to Stettinius, 29 Oct 41, Misc Stf Studies, Proced Lend-lease file, DAD. (2) Memo, Aurand for Stettinius, 4 Dec 41, Proced Lend-lease file, DAD. (3) Min of mtgs in Aurand's off on def aid, Oct–Nov 41, Conf Memos file, DAD. (4) Ltr, Stettinius to SW, 22 Nov 41, Misc Corresp Lend-lease 3 file, DAD. (5) *Third Report to Congress on Lend-Lease Operations,* pp. 27–31. (6) ID, Lend-Lease, I, 679–80.

[13] *Hearings before the Subcommittee of the Committee on Appropriations,* HR, 77th Cong, 1st Sess, on Third Supplemental National Defense Appropriations Bill for 1942, 17–26 Nov 41, Pt. 2, pp. 1–256.

for their own hard-pressed forces in the Middle East.[14]

Meanwhile in February, while the lend-lease bill was being considered in Congress, the British presented a statement of their over-all requirements through 30 June 1942. Calculated on a very generous scale, they were regarded by the British themselves as more a hope than a reality, a measure of the expansion of American production that would eventually be needed rather than a precise program or a basis for contract action. The British used the "balance sheet" technique developed by Jean Monnet, the French industrialist associated with the British Supply Council in North America, balancing against the stated requirements their estimates of British production and presenting the deficit as the amount that must be met from American production.[15]

These requirements, when adjusted to what preliminary studies indicated would be the maximum capacity of American production, and undoubtedly to what the President thought would be politically expedient, served as the basis for the first $7 billion lend-lease appropriation.[16] They also had to serve, during March and April 1941, as a blueprint for working out expenditure programs for submission to the President. The aircraft program was formulated by the Joint Aircraft Committee largely in terms of agreements reached in 1940 and at the ABC staff meetings, adjusted of course to the actual current prospects of production. The ground force programs were at first handled by informal committees of supply services and British representatives, later giving way, as the War Department lend-lease organization became defined, to formal defense aid requirements committees. In presenting their ground force requirements, the Brit-

ish quietly dropped the Ten Division Program as a separate entity, though for some time they retained in their programs the individual articles involved. The battle of types was, to some degree, renewed, though to little avail for the British since the U.S. representatives on the requirements committees refused to budge from the basic decision of 1940 that American production for foreign aid must be of equipment capable of filling U.S. Army needs. Some British types—the Bofors 40-mm. antiaircraft gun, the 4.5-inch gun (on an American carriage), and the British 6-pounder (57-mm.)—had been accepted for full or limited use by the U.S. Army as a result of tests made early in 1941. Beyond this, the British were able to get only a small program devoted to nonstandard articles of their own types despite the emphasis they placed upon it. Of the nonstandard requirements in the British "A" Program of 1940, only those for .303-caliber rifles and ammunition were ever

---

[14] (1) Memo, Moore for CofS, 24 Feb 41, WPD 4323-21. (2) Memo, CofS for President, 11 Mar 41, AG 400.3295 (1-6-41) (1). (3) Ltr, President to SW, 11 Mar 41, AG 400.3295 (1-6-41). (4) Ltr, President to SW, 23 Mar 41, AG 400.3295 (3-11-41). (5) Related papers in last two files. (6) Memo, Marshall for Hopkins, 5 Apr 41, sub: Mun Which Can Be Delivered . . . to Yugoslavia. (7) Memo for rcd in OCofS, 7 Apr 41, sub: Mun for Yugoslavia. Last two in AG 400.3295 (4-5-41) (1). (8) For detailed material on all aspects of redistribution of this surplus, see English Lend-lease Stocks file, Case B-1, DAD; English Corresp Lend-Lease 1 and 2 files, DAD; and AG 400.3295 (3-11-41) (2).

[15] (1) Hancock and Gowing, *British War Economy*, p. 232. (2) M. M. Postan, *British War Production* (London, Her Majesty's Stationery Office and Longmans, Green and Co., 1952), p. 237. (3) Memo, Henry Morgenthau for Maj Gen Edwin M. Watson, 13 Feb 41, AG 400.3295 (2-13-41) (2). (4) Memo, Aurand for Moore, 25 Feb 41, sub: Discussion With Regard to Br Reqmts, G-4/33247.

[16] Min, informal com mtg with Br reps, 18 Mar 41, Reqmts Com Mtgs file, DAS G-4. The DAS G-4 files are with those of the DAD.

accepted in the United States either on British contracts or as a part of lend-lease. Under lend-lease they also received a sizable new commitment for Universal carriers, a British-type armored vehicle that the U.S. Army did not use. The rest of the program devoted to noncommon articles consisted of components for tanks, planes, and other finished equipment to be produced in Great Britain. Also, in accordance with the Hyde Park Declaration of 20 April 1941 establishing a common program for the United States and Canada, contracts for other British-type weapons were placed in Canada with lend-lease funds. As the lend-lease programs took shape, it appeared that the British would adapt their entire program to permit use of specific American types as substitutes or as supplementary equipment and rely on American production for supplying items that British industry was ill prepared to produce in volume. For example, they would depend very heavily on the United States for medium tanks and other combat vehicles, revolvers, and small arms ammunition of all types, and entirely for Thompson submachine guns, but would meet their own needs in their entirety for most standard items of equipment for infantry divisions, such as the Bren gun (.303-caliber) and the 25-pounder.[17]

By mid-June, the basic expenditure programs had been accepted and allocation of funds and submission of detailed requisitions were well under way. While no contracts already placed by the British could legally be absorbed under lend-lease, pending contracts were, and many others conveniently deferred in favor of lend-lease contracts for the same articles. The most important British contracts that remained were those for aircraft and medium tanks. The President exerted continual pressure to see that contracts with lend-lease funds were let as rapidly as possible. The primary consideration in the early months was to put the money to work.[18] But haste, combined with involved procedures, inevitably caused a great deal of confusion. Little consideration could be given to establishing the justification for individual British requests. Spelling out the British program in detail was a complicated matter and required adjustments at every step of the way. The British presented requisitions not only for items on the agreed programs but also for new demands and items to be financed under future appropriations. There was insufficient co-ordination among the British agencies involved in presenting these requirements. The British Supply Council in North America, embracing all British civilian agencies in Washington, presented all formal requisitions, but the British Army Staff (British Army representatives in Washington) furnished the members for the requirements committees and was responsible for justifying military requests. The British Joint Staff Mission, established

---

[17] (1) Minutes of the early defense aid committee meetings are in DAS G-4 and DAD files. The development of the committee system and the formulation of early programs are traced in these minutes and in memorandum, Aurand for ACofS G-4, 25 March 1941, sub: Recent Lend-lease Activities, G-4/32697, Sec 1. (2) AG ltr to CofOrd, 11 Mar 41, sub: Pdn for Br Reqmts, WPD 4323-23. (3) Papers in G-4/32575, G-4/31691-10, and AG 400.3295 (12-12-40) (3). (4) Hyde Park Declaration of President Roosevelt and Prime Minister Mackenzie King, 20 Apr 41, ID, Lend-Lease, Doc Suppl, I. (5) Memo, ACofS WPD for ACofS G-4, 16 Jul 41, sub: Proposed New Lend-lease Appropriations Bill, WPD 4323-38. (6) Postan, *British War Production,* p. 245.

[18] (1) Memo, SW for Exec Off DDAR, 20 Jul 41, in separate folder of DAD files. (2) Ltr, President to SW, 29 May 41. (3) Memo, Aurand for Finance Br G-4, 11 Jun 41, sub: Obligation of Funds Available to WD. Last two in G-4/32697, Sec 1. (4) Memo, USW for Marshall, 6 Jun 41, OCofS 21210-38.

after the ABC meetings, sometimes presented particularly urgent demands that might or might not duplicate requests submitted through regular channels.

In spite of confusion, all the funds in the first appropriation were rapidly earmarked or allocated and consideration of a second lend-lease appropriation began in July, largely on the basis of British requirements in the February presentation not yet financed, and requests made during the interim.[19] Again there was little time for a review of the basis of British requests. WPD admitted, when asked for a strategic justification, that it could not relate British requirements to British war strategy and concluded with a general justification sufficient at least for the moment:

So long as the maintenance of Great Britain's war effort is considered as furthering the interests of the United States, we should . . . supplement British production of equipment to the extent that such equipment can be provided without jeopardizing our own security. . . . The time lag between the placing of orders and the delivery of the equipment makes it impracticable to predict whether the equipment will actually be allocated to the British or used by our own forces . . . . Any surplus over actual Lend-Lease needs at the time the equipment is delivered cán be allocated to our own use . . . .[20]

The Injection of Chinese Demands

While the initial lend-lease programs were framed entirely for aid to Britain, demands for lend-lease soon came from the Far East also. Though there is no indication that aid to China was considered in the passage of the Lend-Lease Act, President Roosevelt had dispatched Dr. Lauchlin Currie, one of his administrative assistants, to China early in the year. Currie re-

turned on the very day lend-lease became law. Shortly thereafter Dr. T. V. Soong, Chiang Kai-shek's brother-in-law, presented to General Burns a complete statement of Chinese requirements. A corporation chartered in Delaware, China Defense Supplies, Inc. (CDS), with Soong as president but staffed largely by American businessmen, was formed as a counterpart of the British Supply Council to represent the Chinese Government in lend-lease transactions. On the American side, on 4 April Harry Hopkins assigned Lauchlin Currie "primary responsibility in developing our contacts with the Chinese Government in the administration of the Lend-Lease Bill." [21] Currie's efforts were to be largely responsible for the formulation of a sizable Chinese aid program along the lines indicated by Soong. On the basis of a preliminary War Department review of the availability of commercial materials, Currie on 6 May 1941 secured from the President an allocation of $45.1 million for transportation and construction materials, and an immediate transfer of 300 trucks originally intended for Yugoslavia. Transfer of the trucks was accompanied by the all-important declaration that the defense of China was vital to that of the United States.[22]

[19] (1) Memo, Exec Off DDAR for SW, 7 Jul 41, Misc Corresp Lend-lease 1 file, DAD. (2) Memo, ACofS G-4 for CofS, 18 Jul 41, sub: Lists of Def Articles . . . To Be Included in New Def Aid Appropriations, G-4/32697, Sec 1. (3) Related papers in same file. (4) See Lend-lease 2 file, DAS G-4.

[20] Memo cited n. 17(5).

[21] (1) Ltr, Chinese reps to Gen Burns, 31 Mar 41. (2) Ltr, Hu Shih, Chinese Ambassador, to Secy of State, 24 May 41. (3) Related papers. (4) Ltr, Hopkins to Gen Burns et al., 4 Apr 41. All in China Lend-lease file, Stf Study C-1-A, DAD.

[22] (1) Memo, Stimson for Currie, 22 Apr 41, sub: Aid Prog for China. (2) Memo, Currie for President, 23 Apr 41, sub: Preliminary Aid Prog for China. (3) Ltr, President to SW, 6 May 41. All in AG 400.3295 (4-14-41) Sec 1.

Meanwhile, the requirements committees had concluded a detailed analysis of the Soong program, and on 3 May 1941 Patterson presented the results to Currie. He urged a cautious approach in the face of Currie's pressure for speedy action. The program would cost $1,064,000,000 as opposed to the Chinese estimate of $567 million. Allocation of lend-lease funds had been based entirely on aid to the British, who would naturally expect to get the material thus financed. Even if money could be found, it would be a long time before materials could be produced under lend-lease contracts. Surplus Army stocks had been depleted by releases to Great Britain, and plans for future releases were based on continuation of this policy. Patterson also felt that shipping would act as a further limitation on the amount of aid that could be furnished China.[23]

Currie was undaunted by these difficulties, and a few days later secured reluctant approval from the War Department for an additional allocation of $50 million for selected ordnance items. By adjustments here and there, funds in other categories to an eventual total of over $200 million were similarly earmarked for China. By July 1941 aid to China had become an established policy. In plans for the second lend-lease appropriation, Chinese requirements were given a definite place beside those of Britain.[24]

Soong's March program had provided the over-all blueprint on which the Chinese aid program was based. It included (1) a thousand planes for the Chinese Air Force; (2) ground munitions for an army capable of offensive operations; (3) material for improving the transportation system from Burma; (4) material for operating arsenals manufacturing small arms

and ammunition within China. The major portion of these requirements, except those for the arsenals, fell within the War Department categories. The Chinese began to present specific requisitions on a wholesale basis, but because of their lack of knowledge of American types, the requisitions were often wholly inadequate, and bore little relation to actual need. Indeed, it soon became apparent that the Chinese were mainly interested in getting any and all material that they could secure from American sources without more than a vague idea of how it was to be moved to China or how used once there. It became the task of the War Department to work out an orderly program from the deluge of Chinese requests and to find a place for it within the existing Anglo-American structure.

Any appraisal had to take into consideration the means of access to Free China. The only route remaining open was through the port of Rangoon in Burma, over the Burmese railroad to Lashio, and thence into China over the Burma Road. This whole system in early 1941 was in condition to carry but few supplies, and any aid program for China would obviously depend upon overhauling it. Soong originally proposed not only improving the Burma Road, but constructing a Burma–Yunnan railroad to parallel it, and a new highway from British India

---

[23] Ltr, Patterson, Actg SW, to Currie, 3 May 41, with incl DAD rpt on def aid prog for China, AG 400.3295 (4-14-41) Sec 1.

[24] (1) Memo, Currie for MacMorland, DAD, 10 May 41. (2) Memo, Stimson for Currie, 16 May 41. Both in China Lend-lease file, Stf Study C-1-C, DAD. (3) Memo, Patterson for CofS, 19 Jul 41, sub: Co-ord of Chinese Def Aid, in separate folder of DAD files. (4) On policy, see Romanus and Sunderland, *Stilwell's Mission to China*, pp. 13–25.

to China. The new highway was ruled out as impractical, and efforts were concentrated on providing necessary materials for improving the Burma Road and building the subsidiary railway. Requirements for both were elaborately calculated by U.S. Army engineers, and procurement of materials began. While construction and transportation materials did not offer such procurement difficulties as guns and ammunition, it was clear that heavy material for the railroad could not be ready until late 1942 and when available would be difficult to transport.

The ultimate aim would be to equip a Chinese army and air force capable of effectively resisting the Japanese. An air force seemed to offer the best prospects of immediate results. Plans for Chennault's volunteer group were already well advanced. A training program for Chinese pilots in the United States was inaugurated. Because furnishing more planes to China would affect either the British or American program, the Joint Aircraft Committee referred Soong's aircraft requirements to the Joint Army-Navy Board for decision. Currie, in the meantime, proposed a short-term program of approximately 350 pursuits and 150 bombers and transports. The Joint Board approved in principle in July, with a statement of broad policy:

Without jeopardizing our own preparedness, to furnish material aid to China by providing aircraft . . . in quantities sufficient for effective action against Japanese military and naval forces operating in China and in neighboring countries and waters.[25]

By September a schedule had been worked out providing for delivery of 269 pursuits, 66 light bombers, 10 transports, and 70 trainers before the end of March 1942. Even these allocations, though mainly of obsolescent-type planes, brought serious objections from the British of interference with their aircraft procurement program under lend-lease.[26]

The ground force requirements presented by Soong evidently were based on a project to arm thirty Chinese divisions on a scale considered adequate for warfare in China. Though these requirements could be reasonably well defined and were not comparable to those for thirty U.S. divisions, they brought in their wake problems of type and availability that seemed virtually insoluble. Little could be done to furnish small arms or ammunition. The standard Chinese caliber was 7.92-mm., which the United States refused to produce because it would interfere with the existing .30-caliber program, and it seemed a futile gesture to offer the few thousand .30-caliber rifles still available from old stocks, since no ammunition for them could be sent.[27] For other ordnance equipment — machine guns, field artillery, and antitank and antiaircraft guns — either outlets must be found for lend-lease contracts or equipment must be released from stock. The prospects in April and May 1941 were that only driblets could be furnished to meet the Chinese thirty division program for at least a year, but the program was accepted, and by dint of scraping here and there it was found that some matériel at least could be provided to meet it. Lauchlin Currie

---

[25] JB 355, Ser 691.

[26] Ltr, Currie to SW and SN, 18 Sep 41, sub: China Def Aid Aircraft Reqmts in 1942, JB 355, Ser 727.

[27] (1) Min, mtg of Def Aid Ord Reqmts Com for consideration of items submitted by CDS, 25 Apr 41, Rpts on Confs on Lend-lease file, AMMISCA 337, Job 11. (2) Memo, Col Victor V. Taylor, DAD, for CofOrd, 10 Jul 41, sub: China Reqmts for Ord Mat, G-4/32192, Sec 1. (3) See China Rifles file, DAD.

found facilities in Canada for many substitute items of British types.[28] Thus, despite all obstacles, a sizable program of aid to China took shape on the planning boards, intensifying the competition for the limited supply of munitions available.

Inclusion of the Netherlands Indies

Other pleas for aid against the Japanese came from the Netherlands Indies. Though not yet actively in the war, these islands occupied a position of critical strategic importance in the Far East. In response to continuing Dutch complaints over their inability to get priorities for their contracts, Assistant Secretary of War Patterson agreed in March 1941 that it was generally in the interests of the United States to furnish them with adequate materials for defense, but ruled that Dutch requirements must be placed in lower priority than those of Britain, Greece, and China, "nations . . . actually engaged in warfare for the defense of democracy."[29] This priority helped very little, and Dutch wealth only made Dutch representatives prey to financial adventurers seeking to sell nonexistent rifles from government stocks.

Seeking a way out the Dutch foreign minister, on a visit to the United States in June 1941, asked for inclusion under lend-lease, with the understanding that the Dutch would continue to pay for their goods. Their most pressing needs were for small arms, antiaircraft guns, and ammunition to repel a Japanese invasion, which the Dutch believed to be imminent. The War Department undertook to review the Dutch requirements, and concluded that forty thousand Enfield rifles could be released, but that no ammunition would be available to go with them. The dilemma

was finally resolved in August by sending only twenty thousand rifles and taking seven million rounds of ammunition from stocks originally set up as a reserve for the Iceland expedition. On 21 August 1941 the President formally declared the Netherlands Indies eligible for lend-lease aid and transferred the rifles and ammunition on a cash reimbursement basis. This step insured more careful consideration of Dutch requirements and their inclusion in the framework of lend-lease priorities, but still left their specific priority low in relation to other demands.[30]

The Latin American Program

The republics of Latin America had already been established as claimants for aid in 1940, but as long as the chances for British survival seemed good their priority remained even lower than that of the Netherlands Indies. On 3 March 1941,

---

[28] (1) Memo cited n. 24(1). (2) Memo, Marshall for Hopkins, 26 Mar 41, sub: Army Equip From Pdn in Near Future Available for Trf to China, AG 400.3295 (4-14-41) Sec 1. (3) See China Tanks file, DAD. (4) Ltr, Currie to Col Taylor, DAD, 27 Aug 41. (5) Ltr, Currie to Patterson, 24 Nov 41. (6) Related papers. Last three in China Corresp Lend-lease file, DAD.

[29] (1) Ltr, Patterson to Young, Chm President's Ln Com, 25 Mar 41. (2) Ltr, Young to Marshall, 3 May 41. (3) Ltr, Marshall to Young, 7 May 41. (4) Related papers. All in AG 400.3295 (3-17-41) (1).

[30] (1) Ltr, Sumner Welles, Under Secy of State, to Marshall, 4 Jun 41. (2) Ltr, Marshall to Welles, 14 Jun 41. (3) Related papers. All in AG 400.3295 (3-17-41) (1). (4) Memo, ACofS WPD for CofS, 10 Jun 41. (5) Memo, unsigned, for ACofS G-4, 19 Aug 41. (6) Related papers. Last three in WPD 4363-6. (7) Biennial Report of the Chief of Staff of the United States Army, July 1, 1941 to June 30, 1943 to the Secretary of War, p. 94. (8) Ltr, President to SW, 21 Aug 41, AG 400.3295 (3-17-41).

Cash reimbursement lend-lease meant that the beneficiary nation would pay the U.S. Government for goods received, but the U.S. Government, not the foreign purchasing commission, would place contracts with private firms as part of the lend-lease production program.

shortly before the passage of lend-lease, the Joint Army-Navy Advisory Board on American Republics completed the draft of a Latin American arms program. By July this program had been placed in relatively permanent form. The board set up a gross allocation of $400 million for both Army and Navy materials, $300 million of which was for Army equipment, the materials to be supplied over a three-year period or longer. Each individual nation was given a specific allocation in proportion to its anticipated contribution to hemisphere defense. In view of Brazil's strategic importance and general tendency to co-operate, her needs were given first consideration and she received $100 million of the total allocation. In late April the President agreed that the Latin American republics should be declared eligible for lend-lease. No allocation was made for Latin American countries under the first lend-lease appropriation, but $150 million was earmarked in the second, $100 million of which fell into War Department categories. Master agreements were subsequently negotiated with each nation (except Argentina), obligating each to pay in cash for a certain proportion of the equipment provided, in accordance with the country's presumed ability to pay. But most of these master agreements (in effect supply protocols for the nations concerned) were not negotiated until after Pearl Harbor.

The Advisory Board on American Republics recommended that all armaments furnished the republics be in accordance with their needs for hemisphere defense as evaluated in the United States, that procurement be entirely of U.S. standard equipment and through U.S. military channels, and that it be handled in such a manner as not to interfere with procurement plans and deliveries for U.S. armed forces and for the lend-lease programs for Britain and China. Not more than $70 million in Army supplies was to be delivered before 30 June 1942. Adoption of these recommendations meant continuation of the policy of 1940 under which deliveries could be postponed indefinitely as long as other needs were deemed more pressing.[31]

Search for an Allocation Policy
February–August 1941

Programs based on foreign requirements added to the net total of munitions production. The Vinson Priorities Act of 31 May 1941 gave the President authority to accord lend-lease contracts priority equal to that for Army and Navy production.[32] The War Department, however, refused to accept the premise that the allocation of funds constituted a definite promise that munitions produced with them would always be delivered to the country designated. Rather, as indicated earlier, it desired a consolidated military production program with distribution to be based on strategic policy.

During the ABC meetings, the American and British staffs agreed that immediate steps should be taken to provide "a method of procedure which will ensure the allocation of Military Material . . . in the manner best suited to meet the demands of the Military situation."[33] But only in the case of aircraft allocations did the conference take any steps to carry out this recommendation. It was agreed that aircraft production should be accelerated,

[31] (1) Conn and Fairchild, Framework of Hemisphere Defense, Ch. IX. (2) ID, Lend-Lease, II, 1226–33.
[32] PL 89, 77th Cong.
[33] ABC-2 Report, *Pearl Harbor Hearings,* Pt. 15, p. 1543.

and that the British should receive all planes from their own production, the output of their approved 14,375-airplane and 12,000-airplane programs in the United States,[34] and all additional U.S. production resulting from new capacity until such time as the United States should enter the war. The existing 54-group U.S. Air Corps goal was accepted, as well as one of 15,000 planes for the U.S. Navy, and a 100-group force for the Army projected in case of British collapse, but it was stipulated that actual deliveries would be conditioned by the ability of the respective organization, British or American, "to absorb material usefully." This meant a practical priority for the British programs, though no definite schedule of allocations was set up.[35] As the principle was applied, allocation of planes was largely arranged by the Joint Aircraft Committee in planning production schedules. The British received all planes produced on their own and lend-lease contracts, while the U.S. Army and Navy received those on funds from military appropriations. The major source for the British continued to be planes produced on their own contracts. Only a few diversions from U.S. Army contracts were made before the introduction of the Soviet demands for aircraft. This arrangement of production priorities gave the British a definite advantage and substantially met their request that development of a U.S. air force be delayed in their favor.

No similar agreement for the allocation of ground equipment was reached during the ABC meetings. Ground munitions lent themselves far less readily to allocation on the basis of production priorities, except of course in case of noncommon articles produced specifically for a foreign country. For the great bulk of common articles

that made up both the Army and lend-lease programs, contracts were let with the same firms and administered by the same people in the supply arms and services, though they were financed with separate funds. Much of the final assembly work was done in Army arsenals, where it was impractical to separate components produced under two types of contracts.[36] Even where separation of the two types of contracts was possible, it was undesirable in the interests of both maximum production and intelligent distribution. In this situation the source of financing gradually became an administrative and accounting matter. As such it caused all sorts of procedural headaches, and while necessarily serving as the basis of long-range planning for both requirements and allocations, it could not be used to determine a time schedule of deliveries. Interpreted strictly according to source of financing, lend-lease production of munitions in 1941 was largely a matter of future promise. Immediate aid could come only from production already planned, principally production on Army contracts financed before the passage of lend-lease. The "Billion Three" clause of the Lend-Lease Act provided one means by which release of some of these materials to foreign powers could be accomplished, the juggling of contracts another. It soon became clear that any allocation policy would have to be based upon considering lend-lease and Army production of common articles as a single program, and using these devices to provide delivery to the country desired regardless of the source of financing. The

[34] See above, Ch. I.
[35] ABC-2 Report, *Pearl Harbor Hearings*, Pt. 15, pp. 1545–50.
[36] See remarks of Col Alfred B. Quinton, Jr., Ord rep at Def Aid Ord Reqmts Com mtg, 21 May 41, Mtgs May file, DAD.

"Billion Three" was the principal reliance in the beginning. And, it will be remembered, under this clause the Chief of Staff had final say on all transfers.

Under lend-lease, as earlier, General Marshall adopted the principle that foreign aid should not be allowed to interfere with the initial development plans of the Army. The formula adopted in connection with the Ten Division Program—that nothing beyond minimum training requirements for the British should be furnished before the fulfillment of American requirements for the PMP program— remained the official basis of transfers long after the Ten Division Program had been abandoned. This formula was revised in February 1941 to provide that no additional items would be furnished the British until

. . . full American requirements for certain task forces are completed. Following completion of such deliveries to Task Forces, further deliveries will be apportioned *according to the situation existing at that time.*[37]

The immediate calculation of task force requirements on a satisfactory basis did not prove feasible, however, and the policy as put into practice made the initial PMP force plus three months of maintenance the minimum American requirement. During the spring of 1941 the size of this initial force was again expanded, this time to 1,820,000 men, with a first augmentation to 3,200,000. The target date for completely equipping the first force was changed from 1 April to 30 June 1942, and the policy adopted held this goal to be sacrosanct, not to be compromised by lend-lease releases.

The requirements committees, in planning the British lend-lease programs in March, applied this yardstick to determine what proportion of British requirements could be met by releases from production on Army orders. A tentative list of such releases was prepared but no attempt was made to state when they would take place. Actual releases, meanwhile, were made on the basis of specific decisions by the Chief of Staff on a flood of requests from the British and later from the Chinese. The emergency nature of most of these requests put the utmost pressure on General Marshall to make exceptions to the above policy, and in some cases he did.[38]

The most important single instance of an exception came in response to urgent demands of the British for supplies for their forces in the Middle East. The visit of Brigadier J. F. M. Whiteley to the United States in May 1941, as representative of General Wavell, bearing tidings of the critical needs of the British in that area and a specific list of equipment desired, moved General Marshall and Secretary Stimson to decide that maximum possible support should be given to the Middle East during the next few months "even if some sacrifice of our own plans for expanding our own military strength is necessary." [39] In keeping with this decision, two hundred light tanks, twenty-four antiaircraft guns, four 155-mm. guns, a considerable amount of 155-mm. ammunition, and sizable quantities of engi-

[37] (1) Memo, Gen Moore, DCofS, for CofS, 25 Feb 41, AG 008 Lend-lease (4-15-41). Italics are the authors'. (2) On the earlier policy, see above, Ch. I.

[38] (1) Min cited n. 16. (2) Ag ltr to Chiefs of SAS, 18 Apr 41, sub: WD Lend-lease Policies and Action To Be Taken Thereunder in Immediate Future, AG 008 Lend-lease (4-15-41). (3) Action on most of these individual requests was taken in G-4, and the record is preserved in G-4 inds to DAD in G-4/31691-1 and G-4/32192.

[39] Note for rcd only accompanying disposition form, DAD for AG, 23 May 41, sub: Army Equip Available for Trf to U.K. for Middle East, AG 400.3295 (5-12-41) (2).

neer equipment were released. The rest of the requirements on the "Whiteley List" were placed on a high priority basis for production.[40]

Nevertheless, actions by the Chief of Staff on this and other special requests failed to produce any new policy on diversions from stocks or production for defense aid. As early as 7 April, 1941 a G-4 memorandum, the work of Colonel Aurand, called attention to the lack. With characteristic boldness and breadth of conception, Aurand proposed not only a formula on which releases of ground force equipment might be based but also that an Anglo-American organization be formed to allocate on a strategic basis available lend-lease supplies and to prepare a plan for a "sufficient supply effort to insure victory." Confining consideration at present to Aurand's concrete proposals for a distribution formula, his suggestion was that minimum Army requirements should be based on having on hand at all times complete equipment plus three months of maintenance for base and task forces and minimum training requirements for PMP. On this basis, Aurand thought, a time schedule of defense aid releases might be prepared. General Moore, Deputy Chief of Staff, agreed to the preparation of such a schedule but insisted that proposed releases in contravention of the February policy must still be submitted item by item to the Chief of Staff.[41]

Hardly had G-4 entered on these computations when WPD requested that the task force requirements be based on placing RAINBOW 5 in effect on 1 September 1941. Despite Aurand's protest that maintenance requirements for the RAINBOW 5 force would preclude any sizable transfers to the British before 30 June 1942, releases were suspended while the complicated

calculations on the basis of RAINBOW 5 were made. These calculations, too, were soon interrupted by a request from the President for an estimate of total quantities to be transferred under the "Billion Three" clause to 30 June 1942, broken down into monthly schedules by item, quantity, and country. The President's request made immediate determination of a distribution policy mandatory and carried the implication that such a policy must be reasonably generous.[42]

Again it was Aurand who proposed the solution.[43] He began by demonstrating that a distribution policy must include all common articles, whether financed under Army appropriations, lend-lease, or certain types of foreign contracts. He dismissed as too complicated the calculation of surplus above either Army requirements for PMP plus three months maintenance or those for RAINBOW 5. He also pointed out that such calculations had to be based on unreliable production sched-

---

[40] (1) Ltr, Arthur B. Purvis to SW and SN, 12 May 41, sub: Urgent Br Reqmts in Middle East Campaign. (2) Memo, ACofS WPD for ACofS G-4, 1 May 41, sub: Additional Br Reqmts in Middle East Campaign. (3) Note cited n. 39. (4) Ltr, Marshall to Hopkins, 26 May 41, sub: Army Equip Available for Trf to U.K. for Middle East. All in AG 400.3295 (5-12-41) (2). (5) Related papers in G-4/31691, Sec 1.

[41] (1) Memo, ACofS G-4 for DCofS, 7 Apr 41, sub: WD Lend-lease Policies and Action To Be Taken Thereunder in Immediate Future, G-4/32697. (2) Memo [signed Gen Moore], no addressee, no date, atchd to memo cited above, AG 008 Lend-lease (4-15-41).

[42] (1) Memo, ACofS G-4 for ACofS WPD, 16 May 41, sub: Release of Mil Equip, G-4/31691-1, Sec 1. (2) Min, Def Aid Ord Reqmts Com mtg, 21 May 41, Mtgs May file, DAD. (3) Memo, Gen Burns for SW, 18 Jun 41. (4) Ltr, President to SW, 24 Jun 41. Last two in G-4/32697, Sec 1.

[43] Memo, ACofS G-4 for CofS, 26 Jun 41, sub: Trf Prog of WD Under Def Aid, G-4/32697, Sec 1. Though officially proposed by Brig. Gen. Eugene Reybold, ACofS G-4, to General Marshall, it was clearly the work of Colonel Aurand.

ules and would result in transferring unbalanced quantities of equipment. He suggested instead that 20 percent of the monthly production of each type of equipment be transferred to defense aid, arguing that such a fixed ratio would provide for concurrently meeting U.S. and foreign requirements, permit lend-lease nations to obtain sufficient U.S. equipment to familiarize themselves with its use, and provide balanced quantities instead of widely varying ones of mutually essential items. Aurand chose 20 percent as the most equitable figure since he felt it would cause little delay in RAINBOW 5 schedules, though he recognized the grave danger that the figure was "subject to arbitrary revision upwards by agencies higher than the War Department."[44] Transfers of 30 percent he thought would require postponements up to three or four months in delivering certain critical items to U.S. forces. In view of the acute shortage of ammunition he suggested that transfer of 20 percent of production should not begin until October.

Aurand's proposal, presented officially to General Marshall by G-4, was concurred in for the most part by the rest of the General Staff divisions. War Plans Division, looking into the future, added the provision that after PMP requirements plus three months maintenance were met, 80 percent of monthly production should go to defense aid. General Moore recommended the solution to General Marshall as the "only practicable method by which we can comply with the directive of the President."[45] General Marshall approved on 1 July, amending the WPD addition in ink to permit 80 percent of monthly production to go to defense aid once the PMP and *one* month's combat maintenance were in the hands of U.S. troops.[46]

Applying the 80-20 formula to monthly production for the next year, G-4 drew up an "Availability List" that projected transfers through 30 June 1942. This became the basis for the report to the President (made on 18 July 1941) and for furnishing the British and Chinese with tentative schedules of what they might expect to receive during the next twelve months. Division between the two countries was based generally on the proportion of contracts financed for each under lend-lease. A monthly revision was planned to keep the Availability List in line with changing production forecasts.[47] The G-4 Availability List at least provided some basis on which both the U.S. Army and foreign governments could anticipate transfers, and the 80-20 formula firmly established the principle that American and foreign needs for munitions would be met concurrently. But the formula provided no complete solution to the problem of allocation, and did not eliminate the necessity for individual decisions by the Chief of Staff and the President. It proved impossible for G-4, with limited personnel, to keep the transfer schedules adjusted to the latest production information. Also the formula was rigid and divorced from strategic considerations. The source of financing was as poor a guide to distribution between

---

[44] *Ibid.*

[45] Memo, Gen Moore for CofS, 30 Jun 41, sub: Schedule of Items Which Can Be Trfd to Other Countries, Trfs-Policy file, DAS G-4.

[46] (1) Memo, ACofS WPD for ACofS G-4, 28 Jun 41, sub: Comments on Trf Prog of WD Under Def Aid. (2) Memo cited n. 45. (3) Memo, Col Mickelsen, Asst SGS, for ACofS G-4, 1 Jul 41, sub: Trf Prog of WD Under Def Aid. All in Trfs-Policy file, DAS G-4.

[47] (1) Memo, McCloy for Exec Off DDAR, 12 Jul 41. (2) Related papers. Both in G-4/32697, Sec 1. (3) Memos, ACofS G-4 for DAD, 26 and 28 Jul 41, subs: Items Available for Trf to Foreign Countries, G-4/31691-1, Sec 3.

claimant countries as it was to distribution between the U.S. Army and foreign aid. If any transfers were to be made to the Netherlands Indies, to Latin America, or to the USSR, they would have to come out of the allotted 20 percent, lessening the share of Britain and China. Emergency demands from all claimants were bound to arise that could not be satisfied within the formula.

Exceptions had to be made from the very start, the most important single one being tanks. The British relied heavily on American production for tanks as a result of the decisions of 1940. By the end of June 1941 General Marshall had agreed to release to them, largely for the Middle East, 20 medium tanks out of a total U.S. production of 26, and 480 light tanks out of a total production of 1,133 (based on actual production figures through the end of July 1941). Under the proposed 20 percent policy, the British would receive a far smaller proportion for the rest of the year. Quite in contrast, the British presented requests that would have virtually absorbed American tank production, and urged acceleration of the tank production program. The President on 14 July 1941 asked the War Department to review the entire tank situation and to make a special effort to expedite production, indicating at the same time that any increase "should in the main go to the British, because of their very great necessity." [48] General Marshall finally agreed that 760 light tanks out of a prospective production of 1,420 before the end of the year should go to the British under lend-lease, and that out of a total production of 1,350 mediums they should receive 537 on their own contracts and 163 under lend-lease. It appeared in July that these allocations would not seriously delay the U.S. program for six armored

divisions and fifteen separate tank battalions as part of the initial PMP force, if production schedules could be met. But the allocations proposed by Marshall were based on a production schedule that was highly optimistic in view of the fact tank priorities (A-1-d) were far lower than those of ships and planes (A-1-a), and in fact actual production soon fell in arrears. [49]

The proposal to delay ammunition transfers also created problems. Any transfers of rifles, machine guns, tanks, or planes inevitably brought in their train a demand for ammunition to make them usable in combat. For example, a delicate situation arose when a hundred P-40's, released by the British, were shipped to Chennault's American Volunteer Group. Although the British had assumed the obligation of supplying the planes with ammunition and spare parts, they were unable to do so, and the responsibility fell on the United States. General Marshall was reluctant to accept this responsibility in view of the ammunition shortage, but Lauchlin Currie appealed to Hopkins and the President, "If we don't get the ammunition over there there will be an international scandal and we might as well forget the rest of the lend-lease program for

[48] Ltr, President to SW, 14 Jul 41, Auth File of President's Ltrs, DAD.

[49] (1) Memo, ACofS G-4 for DAD, 12 Jun 41, sub: Release of Tanks to Britain, G-4/31691-1, Sec 2. (2) WPD and CPA, Official Munitions Production of the United States by Months, July 1, 1940–August 31, 1945, pp. 225–26. (3) Memo, G. C. M. [Gen Marshall], no addressee, 11 Jul 41. (4) Memo, McCloy for SW, 28 Jul 41. Last two in Misc Corresp Lend-lease 1 file, DAD. (5) Memo, unsigned, for CofS, 19 Jul 41, sub: Trf of Tanks to Britain, Misc Corresp Lend-lease 2 file, DAD. (6) Memo, SW for President, 26 Jul 41, sub: Tank Pdn, G-4/31691-1, Sec 3. (7) See also material in English Corresp Lend-lease 1 file, DAD; England Tanks, England Lend-lease Cases 3 file, DAD; and WPD 4323-34.

China." [50] The President suggested a "token amount to show them we mean business," and General Marshall finally agreed to release a million rounds of .30-caliber and five hundred thousand rounds of .50-caliber on the recommendation of WPD that these amounts could be spared with a reasonable margin of safety if prospective U.S. task forces did not exceed two divisions. [51]

While action from February to August 1941 was being based almost entirely on expediency, a movement was under way to link lend-lease allocations to over-all strategic and supply planning for ultimate victory over the Axis Powers. The need for such a link was recognized not only by Colonel Aurand (in the memorandum of 7 April 1941) but also by Under Secretary Patterson and General Malony, acting head of WPD. "This organization for defense aid," Malony warned Marshall on 12 May 1941, "is seriously deficient in that it includes no agency directly charged with . . . assuring coordination between plans for production and distribution of means and our strategic plans and policy . . . ." But while Aurand proposed an organization specifically set up for this purpose composed of representatives of the Army, Navy, Maritime Commission, and the Office of Production Management, with their British opposite numbers, and one representative from the Chinese Army, Malony thought "recommendations for the distribution of military equipment between U.S. armed services and the armed services of other countries should never be formulated by a group containing foreign representatives as an integral part." He suggested, instead, that the Joint Board would be the "most logical and qualified agency to accomplish the task." [52]

General Marshall approved Malony's

suggestion and referred it to the Joint Board in May, though not until August, and then at the behest of Harry Hopkins, was the proposal presented to the President. On 26 August Marshall sent to General Burns as a joint Army-Navy proposal a draft executive order for the President's signature designating the Joint Board as the agency "for recommending to the President general policies and priorities which shall control the distribution among the United States and friendly powers, of munitions of war produced or controlled by the United States." [53] The proposed guides to such allocation policies were to be national policy and military strategy of the United States, production possibilities both in the United States and nations to be aided, extent to which aid could be effectively utilized, and limitations imposed by transportation. [54] The President refused to sign the order, insisting that recommendations should come to him from his Army and Navy Chiefs of Staff

[50] (1) Ltr, Currie to Hopkins, 3 Jul 41, AG 400.3295 (4-14-41), Sec 1. (2) See detailed correspondence in same file for the complete story.
[51] (1) Memo, Hopkins for Gen Burns, 12 Jul 41. (2) Ltr, Philip Young to SW, 8 Aug 41. Both in AG 400.3295 (4-14-41), Sec 1. (3) Memo, ACofS WPD for DCofS, 1 Aug 41, sub: Sup of Small Arms Am for Chinese Govt, WPD 4389-5.
[52] (1) Memo, Malony for CofS, 12 May 41, sub: Co-ord of Plng and Sup. (2) For Patterson's suggestions, see memo, Patterson for SW, 18 Apr 41, sub: Ult Mun Pdn Essential to Safety of America. Both in WPD 4321-12. (3) Memo cited n. 41(1). (4) Memo, ACofS G-4 for DCofS, 28 Apr 41, sub: Draft Ltr for SW's Signature in Connection With Ult Sup Plan, JB 325, Ser 692. (5) On the Victory Program planning, which was a companion piece to the effort to establish an agency for allocations, see below, Ch. V.
[53] Memo, Marshall for JB, 14 May 41, sub: Co-ord of Plng and Sup, WPD 4321-12.
[54] (1) *Ibid.* (2) Memo, Gen Burns for Hopkins, 26 Aug 41, sub: Proposed EO, Policies and Priorities for Distrib of Mun, WPD 4576-1. (3) Admiral Stark had not finally agreed to the draft that General Marshall sent as a joint proposal. In general, their views were similar but Stark wanted to make a more pointed cor-

individually rather than through the Joint Board. The President's refusal was a reaffirmation of his determination to maintain the reins of control in his own hands and not to delegate too wide powers to the military agencies.[55] The emergence of a new claimant for aid—the Soviet Union—and the President's desire to exercise close personal supervision over the development of a Soviet aid program may well have influenced this decision.

The principal achievement of the first few months of operations under lend-lease was the development of production programs for foreign aid which, together with the Army's own program, promised a swelling flow of munitions from American factories. This flow was still only a future promise, and the immediate effect of lend-lease was to heighten the competition for the existing limited supply. Though the principle was accepted that foreign aid should not be allowed to interfere with the achievement of the minimum essential program for development of the U.S. Army, in practice the Army found itself forced to make repeated concessions to nations whose very survival was at stake. The British were favored in the establishment of priorities for production of aircraft, in the special arrangements for division of tank production, and in specific diversions of material to the Middle East; minor concessions had been made to China and the Netherlands Indies at the expense of Army projects; and the 80-20 formula represented some sacrifice of the principle that the PMP force should have a clear priority on American munitions production. With the addition of the Soviet Union to the ranks of those receiving aid, the prospect was that further concessions must follow.

relation of national objectives to ABC-1 than Marshall was willing to accept. Marshall forwarded his own draft because General Burns was pressing for immediate presentation of the matter to the President. See material in AG 400.3295 (8-19-41) and WPD 4576-1.

[55] Memo, President for CofS and CNO, 8 Sep 41, JB 355, Ser 726.

CHAPTER IV

The Broadening Pattern of Lend-Lease Operations

The Beginnings of Aid to the USSR

The German invasion of the USSR on 22 June 1941 placed the Soviet Union in the ranks, if not of the democracies, at least of those nations opposing a common fascist enemy. On 23 June Prime Minister Churchill pledged the British Government to extend the utmost possible aid to the USSR, and on the same day President Roosevelt in a press conference made a more guarded statement pledging U.S. aid. Nevertheless, in the United States the approach to a Soviet aid program had to be cautious because of widespread suspicion of the USSR. For the time being no attempt was made to include the Soviet Union under lend-lease; aid was extended through U.S. Government agencies in return for cash payments from the Amtorg Trading Corporation, the Soviet Union's commercial representatives in New York. The first action taken toward aiding the USSR consisted of review and release of certain materials that Amtorg had purchased earlier but that had been impounded in New York because the State Department would not issue export licenses. This was followed by presidential approval in July and August 1941 of two programs for Amtorg's purchases of raw materials, industrial materials, and explo-

sives to a total value of $167 million. The programs contained semifinished military materials, the export of which might well interfere with existing lend-lease and Army production programs.[1] The Soviet requests for finished munitions in July and August threatened to interfere even more, including as they did vast quantities of aircraft, tanks, artillery, and small arms.[2]

War Department officials were extremely reluctant to make the radical readjustment that meeting even a small proportion of these demands would necessitate. With little knowledge of the Soviet Union's real capabilities of resistance, the General Staff felt the best method of aiding the USSR would be to continue aid to Britain. In early August General Marshall agreed to token releases to the Soviet Union of bombs, submachine guns, and ammunition from Army stocks, but beyond these he insisted that shipments of finished mu-

---

[1] Stettinius, *Lend-Lease: Weapon for Victory*, pp. 129–36. (2) Ltr, Gen Burns to President, 23 Jul 41. (3) Memo, President for "Pa" Watson [Gen E. M.], 25 Jul 41. (4) Memo, Burns for President, 18 Aug 41. All in Papers Taken to London Conf (Col V. V. Taylor) file, DAD.

[2] See General Burns' summary of Soviet requirements as known at the end of August 1941, attached to his memorandum for the Chief of Staff, 31 August 1941, in Papers Taken to London Conf (Col Taylor) file, DAD.

ABOARD H. M. S. *PRINCE OF WALES during the Atlantic Conference, August 1941. Seated left to right: Sir Alexander G. M. Cadogan, Air Chief Marshal Wilfred R. Freeman, Prime Minister Winston S. Churchill, President Franklin D. Roosevelt (note Fala at the President's feet), Admiral of the Fleet Sir Dudley Pound, General Sir John Dill; standing left to right: W. Averell Harriman, Harry Hopkins, Admiral Ernest J. King, Admiral Ross T. McIntire, Sumner Welles, Maj. Gen. Edwin M. Watson, John A. Roosevelt, Admiral Harold R. Stark, General George C. Marshall.*

nitions to the Soviet Union would have to come out of the British allotment.[3]

Meantime, Harry Hopkins had returned from a special mission to Moscow with a firm conviction of Soviet ability to resist, and the President decided that the USSR must be given the utmost aid possible. During his interview with Marshal Joseph V. Stalin, Hopkins had suggested that a conference be held in Moscow between representatives of the USSR, Great Britain, and the United States. At the Atlantic Conference held in August off the coast of Argentia, Newfoundland, Church-

ill seconded the suggestion, the Soviet Government agreed later, and the date was set for 1 October 1941.[4] On 31 August the President informed the Secretary of

---

[3] (1) Memo, ACofS G-4 for DAD, 4 Aug 41. (2) Memo, G-4 for CofS, 8 Aug 41. Both in G-4/33388. (3) Memo, Gen Moore for CofS, 18 Aug 41. (4) Memo, McCloy for USW, 26 Aug 41, sub: Exch of Ord Mat for Russian Account. Last two in AG 400.3295 (8-14-41) Sec 1. (5) Memo, Moore for CofS, 31 Jul 41, with pencil note by Gen Marshall thereon, Russia-Gen file, DAS G-4. (6) Min of confs in OASW on sub of Soviet requests, 9 and 11 Aug 41, AG 400.3295 (8-14-41) Sec 1.

[4] (1) Sherwood, *Roosevelt and Hopkins,* pp. 321–22, 327–43, 359. (2) Papers in WPD 4557-4.

War of these developments, directing action in the following terms:

I deem it of paramount importance for the safety and security of America that all reasonable munitions help be provided for Russia, not only immediately but as long as she continues to fight the Axis powers effectively. I am convinced that substantial and comprehensive commitments of such character must be made to Russia by Great Britain and the United States at the proposed conferences.

It is obvious that early help must be given primarily from production already provided for. I desire your department working with the Navy Department to submit to me by September 10 your recommendations of distribution of expected United States production of munitions of war, as between the United States, Great Britain, Russia and other countries to be aided—by important items, quantity time schedules and approximate values, for the period from the present time until June 30, 1942 . . . .[5]

The President then outlined plans for a preliminary conference between British and American military officials in which the Soviet allocation should be decided. The War Department now had to find additional ground force matériel from scheduled production, over and above the previously agreed 20 percent, to provide for aid to the USSR, and to reopen the whole question of air allocations. A new basis for calculating minimum U.S. Army requirements was adopted, providing that base and task forces should be 100 percent equipped before 30 June 1942, but forces in training only 50 percent. By this postponement of Army objectives, and by certain curtailments in deliveries to the British, it was calculated that 152 90-mm. guns, 991 37-mm. antitank guns, 1,135 mortars, 20,000 submachine guns, 729 light and 795 medium tanks, 155,341 miles of field telegraph wire, and a few other items could be furnished the USSR.

The Air Forces proposed to send 1,200 planes of all types, to be diverted from lend-lease contracts for the British. This list became the basis of the American offer of equipment to the Soviet Union.[6]

At the conference with the British in London, which began on 15 September 1941, the Americans first had to counter a British effort to control the entire program of aid to the USSR. Lord Beaverbrook, British Minister of Supply, wanted the Americans to make an over-all allocation to the British, out of which the latter would, with American advice, make suballocations to the Russians at the conference in Moscow. The British clearly feared the effect of American aid to the Soviet Union on their own lend-lease program. They had already made commitments of 200 pursuit planes and 250 medium tanks a month to the USSR, and counted heavily on American allocations to enable them to maintain this flow. The Americans firmly rejected this approach, and finally Lord Beaverbrook agreed that the United States should make separate allocations to the Soviet Union, in addition to the British program, and that the definite offers to be made by both countries should be agreed in London before departure for Moscow.[7]

The British continued to fight for their own lend-lease allocations in subsequent conferences and subcommittee meetings. While they eventually agreed to the U.S. offers of ground munitions except in the

---

[5] Memo, President for SW, 31 Aug 41, Auth File of President's Ltrs, DAD.

[6] (1) Memo, Moore for ASW, 6 Sep 41, sub: Availability of Items on Russian List, G-4/33388. (2) Memo, SW for President, 12 Sep 41, sub: Proposed Distrib of War Mun, Russia-Gen file, DAS G-4. (3) For task forces contemplated at this time, see above, Ch. II.

[7] Min, mtg in Cabinet Bldg, London, 15 Sep 41, Min of London Conf (Col Taylor) file, DAD. Copies of these minutes are also in WPD 4557-4.

case of tanks, they appended to this agreement a statement of the additional quantities they desired from American production.[8] On tanks the conference was unable to agree without reference back to the United States. Tank production had fallen behind the optimistic schedules furnished the President in July and showed dangerous signs of bogging down at the very moment when Soviet demands, eventually stated at 1,100 monthly, injected an additional complication. In the schedules the U.S. Army representatives brought to London, the delivery of 729 light and 795 medium tanks to the Russians was predicated on cutting British allotments drastically after the first of the new year. U.S. Army plans were also curtailed to the extent that three of the six armored divisions planned and the fifteen separate tank battalions would receive only 50 percent of their tanks by the beginning of 1942, and the 6th Armored Division would not be activated until March 1942.[9] The British were stunned by the American proposal under which the USSR would get 795 medium tanks before 30 June 1942 and Britain only 611. W. Averell Harriman, the head of the American delegation, cabled Hopkins that the British had been led to expect larger numbers of tanks at the Atlantic Conference in August and that the discussion of tanks was becoming "acrimonious." Immediately after receipt of this cable, the President peremptorily directed that tank production in the United States be doubled by 30 June 1942, and that the delivery dates on the existing program be stepped up 25 percent. Hopkins cabled back to Harriman that tanks available for export would be considerably greater than the Army figures indicated, and the conference went on to agree that 500 tanks a month should comprise the combined offer to the USSR, 250 from the United Kingdom and 250 from the United States. The British would make up the deficit that would necessarily exist in the American quota until U.S. tank production reached higher rates, in return for a substantial increase in their own allotment later.

Hurried conferences in Washington produced figures that substantially met the British request for 1,500 light and 2,000 medium tanks before 30 June 1942. Ordnance prepared schedules, based on raising preference ratings from A-1-d to A-1-a, showing a total production of 5,200 medium and 3,190 light tanks by that time. Of these totals 3,994 mediums and 1,953 lights would be surplus to the revised requirements of the U.S. Armored Force. With 2,250 promised the Russians, there was still a sufficient surplus to meet British expectations. The President also informed Harriman that the commitments to the USSR could be vastly increased during the second half of 1942.[10]

The Army viewed these promises with misgivings, fearing that if production lagged British and Soviet allocations

[8] Rpt, Subcom on Alloc of Mil Mat to Russia, 16 Sep 41, Min of London Conf (Col Taylor) file, DAD. Lord Beaverbrook remarked that the British did not agree to these allocations but had to accept them.

[9] (1) Memo cited n. 6(1). (2) Memo, Col Aurand for ASW, 12 Sep 41, sub: Tank Reqmts. (3) Memo, Gen Moore, no addressee, 18 Sep 41, sub: Conf Est of Condition of U.S. Forces on Approval of Proposed Distrib of Tanks. Last two in England Tanks file, DAD.

[10] (1) Msg 4321, Harriman to Hopkins, 17 Sep 41. (2) Msg, Hopkins to American Embassy, London, for Harriman, 17 Sep 41. (3) Msg, Harriman to President, 18 Sep 41. (4) Msg, Hopkins to Harriman via Navy radio, 20 Sep 41. (5) Msg, President to Harriman, 30 Sep 41. All in Russian Cables Supersecret file, ID. (6) Memo, Lt Col William P. Scobey, JB, 19 Sep 41, sub: A-1-a Rating on Tanks. (7) Memo, Gen Moore for Adm Stark, 23 Sep 41. Last two in Misc Corresp Lend-lease 2 file, DAD. (8) Memo, Maj Gen Charles T. Harris, Jr., OCofOrd, for USW, 13 Sep 41, sub: Pdn Schedules for . . . Tanks, G-4/31691, Sec 5.

would have to be met at the expense of the U.S. armored program. The President on 25 September followed his oral orders with a modified written directive ordering that every effort be made to increase the monthly rate of tank production over the next nine months by 15 percent and that the proposed maximum rate under this schedule of fourteen hundred monthly in June 1942 be doubled during the ensuing year. Any attainment of these objectives, Ordnance reported, would be contingent upon A-1-a preference ratings for tanks, and the Navy objected violently to this advance, fearing its effects on the pace of shipbuilding. In the end it was granted on only part of the program, and the actual pace of production of tanks during October and November proved that the Army's fears were well grounded.[11]

Aircraft allocations caused a similar crisis. The Americans proposed to send the Soviet Union twelve hundred planes, largely from production the British had expected to receive. The aircraft would be of all types, including a small number of heavy bombers. The total quantity would still be insufficient to make up half of the four hundred a month the Russians requested. The British objected to giving heavy bombers to the USSR and felt the United States should compensate for Great Britain's loss of other types by increasing their allotment of heavy bombers. This struck at a very sensitive point in American military plans since General Marshall was even then trying to get heavy bombers for Hawaii and the Philippines. The only agreement reached at the conference was that the United States and Great Britain should together furnish the Soviet Union 300 fighters and 100 bombers a month, with the question of type held in abeyance. The ultimate decision came from Washington, after the depar-

ture of the mission for Moscow, and represented a considerable concession to the British. Hopkins cabled that the United States would furnish 1,800 instead of 1,200 planes over the nine-month period, made up roughly of 900 fighters (P-40 pursuits), 698 light and 72 medium bombers, and the rest of miscellaneous types. The President had decided that no heavy bombers should be sent to the USSR and increased the number of medium bombers to compensate. The increase of six hundred planes was to be taken out of the U.S. Army allocations rather than from British lend-lease. The adjustment of British allocations necessitated by this step would have to take place later.[12]

In Moscow negotiations began on 28 September 1941 and culminated on 1 October when the First (Moscow) Protocol was signed. The protocol consisted of commitments by the United States and Great Britain of materials to be made available at their "centres of production" over the nine-month period from 1 October 1941 through 30 June 1942. The two countries also promised to "give aid to the transportation of these materials to the Soviet Union."[13] The Anglo-American commitments on major items were those agreed on at London, but on other semifinished

---

[11] (1) Ltr, President to SW, 25 Sep 41, G-4/ 31691-1, Sec 6. (2) Memo cited n. 10(7). (3) Memo, CofS and CNO for ANMB, 29 Nov 41, sub: Priority of A-1-a for Medium Tank Pdn, England Tanks file, DAD.

[12] (1) Rpt, Subcom on Aircraft Mats, 17 Sep 41. (2) Min of full conf mtg, 17 Sep 41. Both in Min of London Conf (Col Taylor) file, DAD. (3) Msg, Hopkins to American Embassy, Moscow, 26 Sep 41, Russian Cables Supersecret file, ID. (4) Craven and Cate, *AAF I*, p. 134.

[13] (1) For the official text of the protocol, see U.S. Dept of State, WARTIME INTERNATIONAL AGREEMENTS, *Soviet Supply Protocols,* Pub 2759, European Ser. 22 (Washington, no date), pp. 1–12. (2) For a description of the entire conference, see Sherwood, *Roosevelt and Hopkins,* pp. 387–93.

materials and miscellaneous military equipment, decision was withheld pending further study in Washington. Most final decisions on matters left open were communicated to Stalin by the President on 31 October 1941, and on the same day Soviet representatives in Washington were furnished detailed monthly delivery schedules for the entire American commitment. In view of Stalin's remark at the conference that the war would be won by the side with the best motor transport, the most significant additional commitment was one for 5,600 trucks immediately and 10,000 monthly thereafter to the end of the protocol period.[14]

In summary, the commitments under the protocol for which the War Department would be responsible included 1,800 planes, 2,250 tanks, 152 90-mm. antiaircraft guns, 756 37-mm. antitank guns, 5,000 jeeps, 85,000 cargo trucks, 108,000 field telephones, 562,000 miles of telephone wire, and large quantities of toluol, TNT, assorted chemicals, and army cloth. As long as the USSR was not eligible for lend-lease, there were many obstacles to the transfer of any of this material. The President decided that the time had come to declare the USSR eligible for lend-lease and on 30 October cabled Stalin that he approved the commitments made in the protocol and that the Soviet Union would be granted $1 billion under lend-lease to fulfill them. On 7 November, Roosevelt formally declared the defense of the USSR vital to that of the United States.[15]

In this manner a Soviet aid program came into being, second only in size to the British program. For the War Department it posed serious problems: reconciling new demands on American production with the equipping of task forces and of troops in training, fulfilling promises already made to Britain and China, and dealing with a new and somewhat un-co-operative ally. Above all, and this was by no means a matter solely of War Department concern, it posed the problem of how to move materials made available at such sacrifice over the inadequate supply routes to the USSR.

Adjustments in Programs and Allocations September–December 1941

The introduction of the Soviet aid program produced the major complication in the developing pattern of lend-lease operations in the three months immediately preceding Pearl Harbor. The effort to fit the Soviet program into the existing structure was accompanied, however, by a general trend toward systematizing and extending lend-lease operations. Following the passage of the second lend-lease appropriation on 28 October 1941, the Office of Lend-Lease Administration placed in effect the system of programing instead of random requisitioning, and Colonel Aurand as Defense Aid Director labored indefatigably to get all foreign military requirements, except the inevitable emergency demands, placed into programs. As a result of representations by General Marshall at the Atlantic Conference, the British agreed to collate the presentation of requirements by their civilian officials in

---

[14] (1) U.S. Dept of State, *Soviet Supply Protocols*. (2) Msg, President to Stalin, through American Embassy, Moscow, via Navy radio, 31 Oct 41, Russian Info Cables file, ID. (3) Ltr, Brig Gen Sidney P. Spalding to Andrei A. Gromyko, 31 Oct 41, Russia (1) file, DAD.

[15] (1) Memo, Aurand for DCofS, 4 Oct 41, sub: Conf on Trf of Oct Quota of Articles for Russia, Russia file, DAD. (2) Sherwood, *Roosevelt and Hopkins*, pp. 396–98. (3) Stettinius, *Lend-Lease: Weapon for Victory*, pp. 142–43. (4) Ltr, President to SW, 7 Nov 41, AG 400.3295 (4-14-41) Sec 1.

Washington with military plans of their chiefs of staff. They presented in early November a comprehensive statement of their detailed requirements from American production through the end of 1942, including those intended for future financing as well as those covered by plans for the use of the second lend-lease appropriation. An attempt was made to work out a similar program for the Chinese.

A portion of Latin American demands was set up for production under the October appropriation, and Dutch requirements were programed on a cash reimbursement basis. Because plans for the British, Chinese, and Latin American programs absorbed nearly all funds available, military items on the Soviet protocol had to be set up for delivery under the "Billion Three" clause, from production originally planned for the U.S. Army. Though it took time to reduce the existing welter of requisitions to some order and to put the new system in effect, the programs represented a considerable advance over the helter-skelter manner in which lend-lease production planning had been handled earlier.[16]

The requirements programs, nevertheless, tied up as they were with the intricacies of lend-lease financing, could not meet the mushrooming demands for immediate deliveries under lend-lease. The British continued to insist that U.S. rearmament be subordinated to increased assistance. Chinese and Dutch demands greatly added to the pressures. With the addition of the Soviet protocol, demands for lend-lease threatened anew to eclipse the Army's preparedness program. The President himself seemed inclined to the view that America's contribution to the defeat of the Axis should be weapons, not armies.

Since 1940 the 54-group program of the U.S. Army Air Forces (AAF) had been subordinated to British demands. But until the Soviet program was introduced, production on AAF contracts had normally been reserved for the United States, the British receiving all planes on their own and lend-lease contracts. As has been indicated, the large Soviet requests for planes forced re-examination of the whole question. On 9 September Maj. Gen. Henry H. Arnold, Chief of the AAF, proposed that during the period to end 30 June 1942, the anti-Axis pool should receive 15 percent of the planes produced on AAF contracts. These planes plus the aircraft from lend-lease and foreign orders would account for 66 percent of American aircraft production (excluding naval aircraft). Final tentative allocations, as agreed in British-American conferences after the Soviet protocol had been formulated, went slightly further. Out of the scheduled production to the end of June 1942, the AAF was to receive 4,189 tactical planes, Great Britain 6,634, the Soviet Union 1,835, China 407, and other nations 109. This meant that approximately 68 percent of American production of tactical planes would go to the anti-Axis pool and that Britain would receive around 75 percent of this allocation. The smallness of these production figures in proportion to those set up in the ambitious plans of 1940 illustrates the extent

[16] (1) ID, Lend-Lease, II, 943. (2) Memo, Aurand for Stettinius, 31 Oct 41, sub: WD Expenditure Prog, 2d Lend-lease, Col Joseph W. Boone's file, DAD. (3) Ltr, Lt Col Jonathan L. Holman, OLLA, to Col Aurand, 5 Nov 41, Russia (2) file, DAD. (4) Memo, Aurand for E. P. Taylor, Chm Br Sup Council, 1 Dec 41, English Corresp Lend-lease 4 file, DAD. (5) Ltr, Gen Sir John Dill to Gen Marshall, 3 Sep 41, G-4/31691-1, Sec 5.

to which the problem of allocation remained one of dividing a deficiency.[17]

In the apportionment of ground equipment, the trend was in a similar direction. In calculating what could be given the USSR, it will be recalled that the Army's minimum requirements were set at 100 percent equipment for task forces and 50 percent for forces in training before 30 June 1942. On this basis a new G-4 Availability List was drawn up on 11 September supplanting that of July, this time including the Soviet Union, the Netherlands Indies, and Latin America as well as Britain and China. General Marshall indicated that this was the limit to which the Army could go, but he was forced to make further concessions, evidently as a result of pressure from the White House. On 22 September 1941, the day Marshall attended a White House conference on the general subject of delaying Army expansion,[18] he approved a new formula for allocations that clearly envisaged further retarding the pace of rearmament in favor of diverting the lion's share of American production to lend-lease at the earliest possible moment. The July formula had provided that 80 percent of U.S. munitions production should go to defense aid after 1 June 1942, when 100 percent of the equipment for the 1942 PMP (1,820,000 men) was expected to be on hand; the new formula provided that 75 percent of total production should go to defense aid after 1 March 1942, when 70 percent of the PMP equipment was expected to be on hand. Also, the percentage division of ammunition was completely abandoned and the provision substituted that ammunition should be furnished with weapons on U.S. expenditure rates, as long as no more than 50 percent of monthly production of any given type was released. Colonel Aurand's office began in October to prepare a new schedule of defense aid releases based on this formula with deliveries projected through the end of the calendar year 1942.[19]

While these calculations were being made, crises in the Middle and Far East produced new pleas for acceleration of lend-lease aid. By making heavy tank shipments to the USSR, the British left their own position in the Middle East precarious. On 6 November 1941, General Sir John Dill (promoted to field marshal on 18 November) appealed directly and personally to General Marshall for tanks to bolster British defenses in the face of a possible German attack through the Caucasus and Anatolia. General Marshall agreed that a total of 350 medium tanks should be shipped to the Middle East from November, December, and January production, the British to make repayment out of their allotments for the first quarter of 1942. The diversion represented virtually the entire remaining medium tank production earmarked for the U.S. Armored Force. While it was partially

[17] (1) Memo, Arnold for CofS, 9 Sep 41, sub: Release of Airplanes and Related Equip for Def Aid, AWPD/2, in English Corresp Lend-lease 1 file, DAD. (2) Agreement between Gen Arnold and Capt H. H. Balfour, Br Under Secy of State for Air, 22 Oct 41, WPD 4557-20. (3) Craven and Cate, AAF I, pp. 134–35.
[18] See below, Ch. V.
[19] Documentary evidence of this change in the basis for releases is strangely absent from the records covering the time it was agreed to by General Marshall. The account here is based on the memorandum, Col. Albert W. Waldron, Requirements and Distribution Branch, G-4, for Col. Stephen J. Chamberlin, Acting G-4, 17 November 1941, subject: Transfer Bases for Defense Aid, in Colonel Boone's file, DAD. Colonel Waldron says the Chief of Staff did agree to the change in September and refers to a memorandum from Colonel Aurand for Col. Raymond A. Wheeler, Acting G-4, 22 September 1941, as the basis of the policy. Aurand's memorandum could not be located.

counterbalanced by an upsurge in production of light tanks, these could only be used as substitutes in training.[20]

The second pressure for immediate deliveries came from China. Never satisfied with promises of arms in the distant future, the Chinese feared their needs would be shoved even further into the background by the growing emphasis on aid to the USSR. None of the finished munitions promised had actually been shipped by mid-October 1941, and Lauchlin Currie, pressing for acceptance of a long-term aircraft program for China, found it impossible to get any commitments from the War Department.[21] To the Chinese, their fears of neglect seemed well grounded despite rosy promises. They seized the occasion of a threatened Japanese attack on Kunming in late October to place the utmost pressure on the U.S. Government for acceleration of deliveries. Both Chiang Kai-shek and Dr. Soong appealed directly to the President. While Roosevelt indicated that he regarded the Chinese requests as urgent, General Marshall was willing to make few concessions. A strategic and intelligence survey by WPD and G-2 indicated the situation in China was not so serious as Chiang indicated. Marshall felt that strengthening the Philippines was of far greater importance in safeguarding American interests in the Far East than aid to China. He emphatically vetoed a proposal to take twenty-four 3-inch antiaircraft guns from U.S. troops and send them to the Chinese. "It would be an outrage," he told Col. Victor V. Taylor, Aurand's deputy, "for me to deny to MacArthur something that we send on a round-about uncertain voyage up into China, and I can't give any to MacArthur because I've got these regiments with only one battery, that . . . have been in now

for a year . . . ."[22] On 12 November 1941 Stimson finally informed Soong that none of his demands could be met, though all steps would be taken to "accelerate and where possible to amplify the material now scheduled for China." Roosevelt replied to Chiang in the same vein.[23]

Another pressure point in the Far East was the Netherlands Indies, feverishly preparing as fears of a Japanese invasion mounted. At the instigation of Harry Hopkins, the War Department instructed Lt. Gen. Douglas MacArthur to send a mission to Batavia to survey the needs of the Dutch Army with a view to fitting the Dutch into the lend-lease program. The mission's report, submitted to MacArthur on 23 August 1941, corroborated the previous requirements presented by the Dutch in the United States. The mission found the shortage of small arms so acute that MacArthur cabled recommending delivery of 50,000 rifles and 30 million rounds of ammunition immediately, a re-

---

[20] (1) Msg 50326, Dill to Marshall, 6 Nov 41. (2) Msg, Marshall to Dill, 7 Nov 41. Both in Misc Stf Studies, Lend-lease file, Case Lend-lease 41, DAD. (3) Ltr, President to SW, 7 Nov 41. (4) Ltr, SW to President, 12 Nov 41. (5) Related papers. Last three in AG 400.3295 (3-11-41) (1).

[21] (1) Memo, ACofS G-2 for CofS, 20 Aug 41, sub: Chinese Resistance, WPD 4389-15. (2) Ltr, SW to Currie, 29 Oct 41, and accompanying papers, WPD 4389-20.

[22] (1) Telephone Convs Col Taylor file, Bk. 1, DAD. (2) Memo, Soong for President, 31 Oct 41. (3) Memo, Hopkins for Gen Burns, 31 Oct 41. (4) Memo, Burns for Aurand, 3 Nov 41. (5) Memo, Gen Moore for CofS, 4 Nov 41, with Marshall's marginal notes. Last four in China (2) file, DAD. (6) Ltr, Soong to Stimson, 6 Nov 41, AG 400.3295 (4-14-41) Sec 1. (7) Memo, ACofS WPD for CofS, 1 Nov 41, sub: Immediate Aid to China. (8) Memo for rcd, Col Charles W. Bundy, WPD, 1 Nov 41, same sub. (9) Notes by Bundy on conf with Currie, 1 Nov 41. Last three in WPD 4389-27.

[23] (1) Ltr, Stimson to Soong, 12 Nov 41, sub: Def of Yunnan and Burma Road, AG 400.3295 (4-14-41) Sec 1. (2) Msg, President to Chiang Kai-shek, 14 Nov 41, WPD 4389-8.

quest that could not be met because of the critical shortage of ammunition. War Plans Division, while agreeing that some efforts must be made to meet Dutch needs, felt that "no significant diversions" should be made from materials allocated to Britain, the USSR, and China.[24]

The Dutch were given a small share of the pool of common articles scheduled for distribution under lend-lease in the September G-4 Availability List, and an effort was made to see that the requirements reported by the mission were scheduled for eventual delivery under either lend-lease or private contracts. But in view of the priority established, precious little could actually be furnished as the critical hour for the Netherlands Indies approached. In November 1941 the Dutch pressed for acceleration of deliveries of antiaircraft guns, light artillery, small arms, and ammunition, much as the Chinese did, but they got only minor concessions.[25]

By 25 November 1941 Colonel Aurand and his staff had completed the new defense aid allocation table with schedules projected through the end of the calendar year 1942. In the meantime, the Joint Board had concluded that the President's rejection of the proposal to make it responsible for determining policy on lend-lease allocations still left it free to take such action in the name of the Chief of Staff and of the Chief of Naval Operations separately, and on 3 November approved a recommendation by General Marshall that the board should act on "all matters of policy concerning Lend Lease distribution and diversions incident thereto."[26] This meant that WPD, in its role as the Army representative of the Joint Planning Committee, would have most of the responsibility. But WPD had long been out of touch with the situation, and it was not

until 25 November that it was even informed of the distribution policy approved by General Marshall in September.[27]

Nevertheless, in conferences with DAD and G-4 officers, WPD representatives made a belated effort to relate defense aid allocations to strategic policy and to curtail interference of defense aid deliveries with U.S. Army plans. Because of the necessity for haste, they limited themselves to considerations of transfer schedules for the month of December 1941, but stipulated that future schedules should be reviewed monthly in a similar manner. While necessarily accepting the existing basis of division between U.S. Army and defense aid, WPD objected that many allotments were inconsistent with it and would not permit meeting 70 percent of PMP requirements by 1 March 1942, and suggested that no defense aid allotments of ammunition be made until U.S. requirements for task force reserves were filled. As a basis for strategic distribution

[24] (1) Memo, Gen Burns for CofS, 31 Jul 41. (2) Msg 202, Manila to TAG, 27 Aug 41. Both in AG 400.3295 (3-17-41) (1). (3) Rpt, Mis To Inquire Into and Verify Reqmts of Netherlands Indies Govt . . . , 23 Aug 41. (4) Memo, ACofS WPD for DAD, 6 Nov 41, sub: Rpt of U.S. Army Mis on Mun Reqmts of Netherlands Indies. Last two in U.S. Army Mis to Netherlands Indies Lend-lease file, DAD. (5) Memo, Actg ACofS G-4 for CofS, 20 Sep 41, sub: Availability of Def Aid Items for Netherlands Indies, G-4/31979.

[25] (1) Three ltrs, Lt Col A. van Oosten, Netherlands Purch Comm, to Gordon Williams, OLLA, 4 Nov 41, and accompanying papers. (2) Ltr, Aurand to van Oosten, 29 Nov 41. Both in Netherlands Nov and Dec file, DAD. (3) Memo, Col Donald Wilson for Gen Gerow, 4 Nov 41. (4) Note, Bundy for Gerow, 6 Nov 41. Last two in WPD 4363-9. (5) Msg, Netherlands Purch Comm, N.Y., to Gen Marshall, 1 Dec 41. (6) Msg, Marshall to Netherlands Purch Comm, 2 Dec 41. Last two in AG 400.3295 (3-17-41) (1).

[26] Rpt, JPC to JB, 13 Oct 41, JB 355, Ser. 726.

[27] (1) Memo, ACofS WPD for CofS, 10 Nov 41, sub: Trfs, Lend-lease Prog. (2) Memo, ACofS WPD for DAD, 18 Nov 41, sub: Distrib Progs and Diversions Therefrom. (3) Memo, Aurand for WPD, 25 Nov 41, same sub. All in WPD 4418-16.

of munitions, WPD suggested adherence to the Soviet protocol and increased aid to the Soviet Union wherever possible as first priority. As a second, in the absence of other factors, there should be a distribution of 40 percent to the United Kingdom, 40 percent to the USSR, 10 percent to China, and 10 percent to others, or an even division between Great Britain and the USSR where there were no requirements from other countries. Since actual production seldom lived up to the estimated schedules, transfers should be made on a basis proportionate to monthly allotments rather than in terms of specific quantities. As an example, the tables proposed to give 265 medium tanks to Great Britain and 184 to the Soviet Union, a total of 449. Scheduled production of 75-mm. tank guns for December was only 317, and no tanks could be shipped without their guns. WPD opposed taking any tank guns from stocks or from troops and accordingly would reduce the number of tanks allocated to 317, dividing them equally between Britain and the USSR.[28]

General Moore, Deputy Chief of Staff, who with Aurand had since September done virtually all the work on defense aid allocations and transfers, rejected most of the WPD suggestions as impractical. These suggestions ignored the financial ramifications of lend-lease and the commitments made to Britain at the London Conference and later by General Marshall. These, both Moore and Aurand realized, could not be abandoned in favor of any arbitrary percentage division between countries. Moore recognized the right of the Joint Board to make any changes in the allocation tables it thought desirable, but warned that the Soviet protocol was a "three-sided agreement" that could only be changed at the political level. The building up of task force reserves could not be accepted as an absolute first priority if it interfered with meeting the protocol. Certain sacrifices in the 70 percent PMP requirement would have to be accepted in order to honor commitments already made; all these had been personally approved by himself or General Marshall. While the principle of proportionate monthly assignments was theoretically sound, there were too many practical difficulties in carrying it out. As far as medium tanks were concerned, General Marshall himself insisted his promises to Dill must be met and vetoed the WPD scheme for a 50-50 division. Minor adjustments were made to meet WPD objections, however, including reduction of defense aid allotments of ammunition.[29]

In this way the issue was settled, but the defense aid allocation table was never issued. The Japanese attack on Pearl Harbor a few days later rendered the whole discussion academic. Nevertheless, the episode serves to illustrate the extent to which plans existing on 7 December 1941 called for sacrificing the requirements of the U.S. Army to lend-lease.

Extension of Lend-Lease Activities Overseas

The formulation of lend-lease programs and the allocation of available supplies went on at first almost entirely in response to requests made in Washington by foreign representatives, and little effort was made to inquire into the basis of these requests at their source. The theory was that

---

[28] Memo, ACofS WPD for DCofS, 3 Dec 41, sub: Def Aid Alloc Table, WPD 4418-17.

[29] (1) Rcd of conf, 2 Dec 41, WPD 4418-17. (2) Memo, Gen Moore for ACofS WPD, 4 Dec 41, sub: Def Aid Alloc Table, G-4/32697. This memo was drafted by Aurand.

lend-lease supplies, in keeping with the neutral position of the United States, should be transported abroad in the ships of the beneficiary governments and then used without further aid or assistance. This theory gave way as the need was demonstrated for American supervision in the proper use and maintenance of the equipment furnished, American participation in the development of transportation and communications facilities abroad, and some evaluation of foreign munitions requirements at their source. Plans soon took shape for military lend-lease missions to perform these functions.

The most definite and pressing need for a mission was in China. Chiang Kai-shek's army lacked not only supplies but also the organization and technical competence necessary to put them to effective use. There was little knowledge of modern equipment or experience in the handling of it, either among officers of the Chinese Army or among the civilian representatives in the United States. The operation of the last remaining line of supply through Burma was characterized by maladministration, corruption, and general confusion, and hardly half of the supplies that started over the route from Rangoon ever arrived at Chungking. Both Chiang and Dr. T. V. Soong, his spokesman in the United States, sang the continual refrain that China only needed more tanks, guns, and planes to enable her to drive Japanese forces out. But among those officers in the War Department who had had experience in China there was from the beginning a fear that Chinese lend-lease would only be wasted unless carefully controlled by Americans. This fear found expression in a staff study prepared by Maj. Haydon L. Boatner of G-4, an old "China Hand," and presented by Brig. Gen. Eugene Rey-

bold to the Chief of Staff on 16 June 1941. Boatner pointed out that aid to China was being treated exactly as aid to the British, despite "critical factors entirely different." Drawing on the previous experience of the Germans and Russians in China, Boatner asserted that "any foreign loan or gift to China, to be effective, must be carefully restricted and supervised. Our Government must supervise the shipment, receipt, storage, distribution and use of all equipment sent to China." [30]

Boatner's suggestion that a military mission be sent to China to do this "supervising" was approved by General Marshall, the Joint Board, and the President, in turn, and Brig. Gen. John Magruder, a former military attaché in China, was selected by the War Department to head it. According to the letter of instructions issued Magruder on 27 August 1941, he was to "advise and assist the Chinese Government" in all phases of procurement, transport, and maintenance of materials furnished by the United States under defense aid, and in training of Chinese personnel in their use and maintenance. [31]

General Magruder divided his mission into two parts, a home office in Washing-

---

[30] (1) Memo, ACofS G-4 for CofS, 16 Jun 41, sub: Co-ord of China Def Aid Activities, G-4/32192, Sec 1. (2) Memo, Brig Gen John Magruder for CofS, 11 Aug 41, sub: Mil Mis to China, ID, Lend-Lease, Doc Suppl, I. (3) Romanus and Sunderland, *Stilwell's Mission to China,* Ch. I. The mission, headed by David G. Arnstein who went to China at the request of Harry Hopkins, revealed to American authorities, as well as to Chiang Kai-shek, the almost hopelessly disorganized conditions on the Burma Road. Arnstein's mission was not under American auspices, but reported directly to Chiang.

[31] Memo, Patterson, Actg SW, for Magruder, 27 Aug 41, sub: Instns for Mil Mis to China, Mis to China file, DAD. For a fuller consideration of the events leading to the formation of this mission, see Romanus and Sunderland, *Stilwell's Mission to China,* Ch. I.

ton and an operating group in the field. The home office was to work toward correcting the flaws in the Chinese program in the United States, co-operating with China Defense Supplies, Inc., on the presentation of requirements and the movement of supplies to China. The operating mission would review Chinese requirements at the source, advise the home office of priorities for shipment, instruct the Chinese in the use of American weapons, and take an active part in improving the supply line through Burma.[32]

In late September 1941 General Magruder departed for China, arriving in Chungking on 1 October. Improving the supply line between Rangoon and Chungking proved the most pressing problem. Magruder organized "task forces," one of which was assigned to Burma Road operations and another to the construction of the Yunnan–Burma Railway. Before the departure of the mission, plans had been made to send U.S. civilian personnel to aid in the operation of the Burma Road. Soon afterward, other plans were hastily drawn for an extensive system of repair shops, depots, and assembly plants, to be operated under American direction, mostly under contracts with the General Motors (Overseas Operations) Corporation. Working with the home office, Magruder also began in late October a series of recommendations on a practical program for regulating this flow to the capacities of both the transport system from Rangoon and the ability of the Chinese Army to absorb supplies and equipment.[33]

As the mission to China took its place in the War Department organization, consideration of overseas lend-lease representation at other points increased. The War Department already had special observers in England and the Middle East, and

Averell Harriman held a special position as the President's civilian lend-lease representative in England. The British exerted a continual pressure for direct aid in operating the line of communications in the Middle East. All these developments came to a head in September 1941. In a memorandum on the 8th, General Burns informed the Secretary of War that there should be a general plan for lend-lease representation overseas in order to assure "assistance and supervision sufficiently close to the point of use of defense aid materials to insure maximum effectiveness." [34]

Even before sending the memorandum, Burns had on 4 September told the War Department that it would be expected to set up depots and maintenance facilities in the Middle East to support the British, and preliminary plans had begun on this basis. On 13 September, the President formally directed the step:

In order to comply with the expressed needs of the British Government, it is requested that arrangements be made at the earliest practicable time for the establishment and operation of depots in the Middle East for the maintenance and supply of American aircraft and all types of ordnance furnished the British in that area. Arrangements should also be made for the necessary port, railroad and truck facilities necessary to make the supply of American material effective. . . .

---

[32] (1) Memo cited n. 29(2). (2) Memo, Magruder for CofS, 22 Aug 41, sub: Plan of Mil Mis to China, AG 400.3295 (4-14-41) Sec 1.

[33] (1) A virtually complete record of cables exchanged between the mission in Chungking and the home office in Washington is in AMMISCA IN and OUT Cables files, Bks. 1 and 2, ID. (2) For correspondence and other material on early mission activities, see AG 400.3295 (4-14-41) Sec 1; China file, DAD; and the files of the mission itself in DRB AGO, Job 11.

[34] Memo, Burns for SW, 8 Sep 41, AG 400.3295 (8-9-41) Sec 1.

The depots and transportation facilities should be established and operated under contracts executed and administered by the appropriate branch of the War Department with American companies, preferably already existing, but if not practicable, organized especially for this purpose. . . . The necessary funds will be furnished from Defense Aid appropriations. . . . The British authorities should be consulted on all details as to location, size and character of depots and transport facilities. Their needs should govern.[35]

A survey of the situation led to the decision that instead of one mission for the whole Middle East, there should be two, one for the Red Sea region with headquarters at Cairo, and one for the Persian Gulf area with headquarters somewhere in Iraq. British forces in the two areas were under separate commands with different missions—in Africa, the defeat of Italo-German forces in the desert; in Iran-Iraq, the security of the area against possible Axis attack from the north or German-inspired insurrection. Most important of all, as events proved, Iran offered possibilities as a supply route to the USSR if its port, rail, and road facilities were properly developed. Such a mission would be entirely separate from that of support of the British forces in the eastern Mediterranean area.[36]

Two missions having been decided upon, Brig. Gen. Russell L. Maxwell was chosen to head the North African mission, and Brig. Gen. Raymond A. Wheeler the Iranian. Identical letters of instructions (except for the definition of territory) were issued to them on 21 October, charging them with two interrelated functions:

(1) establishment of essential port, transportation, storage, assembly, maintenance and training facilities . . . .
(2) advice and assistance to the British and other friendly governments in obtaining ap-

propriate military defense aid . . . and to assure that the most effective and economic use is made thereof.[37]

The task assigned to Maxwell and Wheeler of organizing supply and maintenance facilities for handling lend-lease material to another nation, to operate within the supply organization of that nation, was a highly complicated one. The supply line would have to be operated by civilian personnel through contracts financed with lend-lease funds, and all materials for mission projects would have to be channeled through the complicated lend-lease machinery. Operation by military personnel was impossible, both because of the lack of an adequate number of service troops in 1941 and because the use of troops might be construed by Congress as dispatch of an expeditionary force. The selection of projects to be undertaken had to be governed by British desires, which sometimes reached the United States through several different channels and were apt to be conflicting. Even the primary purpose of the mission to Iran—support to the British or development of a supply line to the USSR—remained undetermined.

In late November the vanguards of the missions arrived in their respective areas. General Maxwell established his headquarters at Cairo on 22 November, and General Wheeler, after a visit to Wavell in New Delhi, commenced operations at Baghdad on 30 November. The operation of the two missions on a peacetime basis was therefore short lived, and little be-

[35] Memo, President for SW, 13 Sep 41, AG 400.3295 (8-9-41) Sec 1.
[36] Memo, ACofS WPD for CofS, 24 Sep 41, sub: Mil Mis in Iran, WPD 4596.
[37] Ltr, SW to Maxwell, 21 Oct 41, sub: Ltr of Instns, AG 400.3295 (8-9-41) Sec 6.

yond planning had emerged before Pearl Harbor.[38]

Though the Iranian mission was to be at least partially concerned with supply to the USSR, the War Department decided to send yet another mission directly into Soviet territory to render technical assistance to Soviet armies in the use of lend-lease material. On 5 November a letter of instructions was issued to Maj. Gen. John N. Greely as head of this military mission, with functions generally the same as those assigned Maxwell and Wheeler. This step, however, was taken without any assurance of an invitation from the USSR itself. The Lend-Lease Administration was already represented in the Soviet Union by Col. Philip R. Faymonville and Douglas Brown. While Faymonville had urged that by being tactful American representatives could effectively render much needed technical assistance, Brown warned on 4 November 1941 that all the material America could send would be welcomed but that the Soviet Government intended to use its own technicians, experts, and personnel to employ the material in its own way, and desired no additional U.S. personnel. Brown's warning proved a very accurate estimate of the situation, for the Greely mission was never to enter the USSR.[39]

The final point at which the War Department made an effort to establish military lend-lease representation was in the United Kingdom itself. On 25 September, Maj. Gen. James E. Chaney, head of the Special Army Observer Group in London, was instructed to represent the War Department on military matters pertaining to lend-lease. But Chaney was always overshadowed by Averell Harriman, the civilian lend-lease representative in England, and the lend-lease functions of the

Special Army Observer Group never amounted to very much. The channel for presentation of British requirements was always in Washington, through the British agencies there, and not in London. Chaney's function in regard to supply and maintenance of American equipment in England was limited to technical advice.[40]

The other four military missions—to China, North Africa, Iran, and the USSR—had become an established part of the lend-lease machinery by December 1941. Following the precedent of General Magruder, all established home offices in Washington, responsible to General Moore, but placed within the Office of the Defense Aid Director for co-ordination. The functions of the missions were roughly threefold—to determine the need for lend-lease materials requested by foreign countries for use in their area, to aid in forwarding material from the United States to the theater or country concerned, and to see that once the material had arrived it was properly used.[41] While the performance of all three functions was but imperfectly realized in any case, and only the second function in the case of the mis-

---

[38] (1) For a full account of the Iranian mission, see T. H. Vail Motter, *The Persian Corridor and Aid to Russia*, UNITED STATES ARMY IN WORLD WAR II (Washington, 1952), Chs. I–VII. (2) For an account of the prewar activities of the North African mission, see T. H. Vail Motter, The Story of United States Forces in the Middle East, draft MS in OCMH.

[39] (1) Ltr, Stimson to Greely, 5 Nov 41, sub: Ltr of Instns, ID, Lend-Lease, Doc Suppl, II. (2) Msg 1875, Brown to Maj Gen George H. Brett and Averell Harriman, 4 Nov 41. (3) Cf. Msg 1876, Faymonville to Hopkins, 4 Nov 41. Last two in Russian Cables Supersecret file, ID.

[40] (1) Msg 57, AGWAR to Sp Army Observer Group, 25 Sep 41. (2) Memo, Marshall for Moore, 14 Nov 41. (3) Ltr, Gen Moore to Gen Chaney, 19 Nov 41. All in AG 400.3295 (8-9-41) Sec 2.

[41] See remarks of Colonel Aurand at meeting with members of all home offices, 2 December 1941, Conf Memos file, DAD.

sion to the Soviet Union, the concept of American supervision and assistance at the receiving end of the lend-lease line was a lasting one that filled a real need.

The Halting Flow of Lend-Lease

Despite the increased generosity of allocations and the general broadening of the scope of lend-lease activities in the last part of 1941, actual deliveries lagged. Most allocations were still in terms of futures. There were many unforeseen shortfalls in production, particularly of accessory equipment necessary to make armored vehicles, planes, and other major items useful in combat. In some cases these shortfalls resulted in cancellation of allocations, but more frequently they merely produced delays in delivery. Within the supply arms and services lend-lease work was an additional burden that at times received inadequate attention. The supply services were geared to serve the U.S. Army, not foreign armies, and when questions arose they were prone to meet Army needs first. The G-4 Availability Lists did not constitute an actual directive for transfer but only a basis for planning, with the result that the struggle for material sometimes degenerated into a game of "catch-as-catch-can" between U.S. Army and defense aid requirements, a game in which the latter would "generally come out a poor second."[42] The delays were not always the fault of the services. They in turn could complain bitterly of the inadequacy of instructions they received. The British, Russians, and Chinese often did not furnish adequate information on their desires as to shipment; neither G-4 nor the Office of the Defense Aid Director kept the allocation schedules geared to the most recent production information; orders were frequently issued changing the destination of shipments already moving to port.[43]

Further delays arose from the flaws in the machinery of distribution. Packing, crating, co-ordination of spare parts, accessories, and ammunition with major items, and movement to port all created serious problems. The establishment of special defense aid depots where final assemblies and co-ordination of shipments could take place, and of a procedure for calling material forward to port, marked a first step in solving these problems, but it took time to perfect the system. In August a co-ordinating committee of all interested agencies, set up under the auspices of the Division of Defense Aid Reports, began to work on the difficult task of co-ordinating availability of supplies with shipping, but this co-ordination, too, was inevitably imperfect in the beginning. As long as only the British were concerned, the existence of a well-developed British transport organization in New York—a branch of the British Ministry of War Transport (BMWT)—considerably eased the Army's load, but for the USSR and China, transport, storage, and shipping

---

[42] Memo, Maj Robert E. Burns, OCSigO, for Maj C. H. Thompson, OUSW, 31 Oct 41, sub: Comments on Pdn Rpts and G-4 Charts, Misc Corresp Lend-lease 3 file, DAD.

[43] (1) Appraisals by the various supply services of difficulties in lend-lease operations are included in memo, Maj Thompson for Col Taylor, 5 Nov 41, sub: Memos From Various SAS on Def Aid Pdn Rpts and G-4 Proced, Misc Corresp Lend-lease 3 file, DAD. (2) Memo, Maj Paul M. Seleen, OCofOrd, for Col Aurand, 17 Oct 41, sub: Shipg Instns to Def Aid Countries, Misc Corresp Lend-lease 2 file, DAD. (3) Memo, Col Hugh C. Minton, Exec Off OCofOrd, for DAD, 8 Nov 41, sub: 37-mm. and 75-mm. Tank Gun Deliveries, England Tanks file, DAD. (4) Related papers in same file. (5) Material in English Corresp Lend-lease 3 file, DAD

arrangements had to be accomplished almost entirely by American agencies or by the BMWT. In sum, both in the process of production and in that of distribution the confusion normally attendant on the early stages of development of any supply program delayed the flow of lend-lease aid. Even the deliveries to Britain, where the situation was best, fell behind allocation schedules. Of the total war supplies of the British Commonwealth during 1941, only 11.5 percent came from the United States, and only 2.4 percent represented lend-lease transfers.[44]

Delays in shipments to Britain were less serious than to other countries. It was only after the Chinese appeal for acceleration in late October that the first munitions were shipped to China. While seven ships with cargoes of lend-lease munitions were en route to Rangoon by 8 December, an accumulation of supplies at the CBS shipping point at Newport News, Virginia, had also begun. The most serious delays of all, however, occurred in meeting the Soviet protocol.

In the protocol, the United States and Great Britain promised to aid the Soviet Union in the delivery of the material to which they were committed. Since the Soviet merchant marine was a negligible quantity, most of the shipping had to be arranged by Britain and the United States through diversion from other routes. Roosevelt instructed Admiral Land that every effort must be made to provide the necessary ships for the Soviet aid program and that only "insurmountable difficulties" should be allowed to interfere with it.[45] The number required was large in proportion to the material to be carried because of the long, roundabout routes involved. There were three alternatives: (1) across the Atlantic and North Sea and around the coast of Norway to the Arctic and White Sea ports; (2) across the Pacific to Vladivostok and over the Siberian Railway; and (3) around the coast of Africa to the Persian Gulf and thence across Iran to the Soviet border. The shortest but most dangerous route was that around Norway, involving as it did the threat of German submarines and land-based aircraft. It was doubtful, too, if Soviet ports could be kept free from ice for year-round operations. The rail connections between Murmansk and the Soviet centers to the south were already threatened by German forces, leaving only Archangel and smaller ports on the White Sea available. Supplies delivered at Vladivostok had to be carried on limited rail facilities, and the capacity of the port itself was hardly greater than that of the rails. Supplies delivered through the Persian Gulf after a long ocean voyage had to be carried across Iran for delivery at the Soviet border. Neither port facilities nor transport facilities northward were sufficiently developed to carry any appreciable load. Yet in contrast to the northern route, the southern route was relatively free from the threat of interference by German submarines and was available for year-round operation.

At the London Conference the British

[44] (1) Capt W. H. Schmidt, Jr., The Commercial Traffic Branch in the Office of The Quartermaster General, July 1940–March 1942, Monograph 6, pp. 270–343, OCT HB. (2) AG ltr to SAS and AAF, 20 Aug 41, sub: Def Aid Storage and Trans, AG 681 (8-14-41). (3) Background papers in G-4/32697-2. (4) Memo, Aurand for ACofS G-4, 16 Oct 41, sub: Def Aid Storage and Trans, Misc Corresp Lend-lease 2 file, DAD. (5) Memo, Gen Burns for SW, 15 Aug 41, sub: Forecast, Delivery, Storage, and Mvmt of Def Aid Mats, and accompanying papers, AG 400.3295 (8–15–41) (1). (6) Hancock and Growing, British War Economy, p. 373.
[45] Ltr, President to Adm Land, 19 Nov 41, Misc Corresp Lend-lease 3 file, DAD.

and Americans agreed that the northern ports offered the greatest capacity and possibilities, but could only be used for a few immediate deliveries since they would be closed by ice from mid-November until June. About 75,000 to 90,000 tons monthly could be sent to Vladivostok pending further development of port facilities and the capacity of the Siberian Railway. While the Persian Gulf could accommodate only 6,000 tons monthly for the present, American assistance in port and railway development should increase that to 60,000 tons by the spring of 1942. The conferees felt that the Persian Gulf route would eventually offer the best avenue for the flow of supplies to the USSR.[46]

The Soviet attitude at first was one of insistence on the utmost use of the northern ports. They promised to keep Archangel free from ice the year round by use of icebreakers, and asked that all war material be shipped to that point. As their desires finally crystallized, they proposed that out of 500,000 tons monthly, 270,000 should move through Archangel and the other smaller northern ports, 224,000 through Vladivostok, and the remaining 6,000 through Iran. The British and Americans soon found this program unrealistic because the Russians had vastly overestimated the capacity of Archangel as well as their ability to keep it open. The eventual estimate of American port experts in the USSR was 90,000 tons monthly, while the British placed it as low as 60,000. A group of British shipping experts was sent to Archangel to work with the Russians in improving this capacity, but the task promised to take some time.[47]

Given these port conditions and the possibility of heavy losses on the northern route, the British and Americans turned to explore the possibilities of the Pacific and Persian Gulf routes. Only civilian-type supplies could move over the Pacific route because of the complications of Russo-Japanese relations, leaving the Persian Gulf as the only alternative for shipping war materials. Planning began for the development of this route under British auspices with the aid of the American mission under General Wheeler. It seemed possible to deliver trucks and planes via Iran even before the Iranian State Railway could be improved, and a considerable number of shipments was projected for December. But little had actually been accomplished before Pearl Harbor that would make possible the use of the Persian Gulf for movement of sizable quantities of war supplies to the Soviet Union. Of the twenty-eight ships that departed the United States carrying Soviet lend-lease supplies in October and November 1941, nineteen sailed for the northern Soviet ports, eight for Vladivostok, and only one for the Persian Gulf.[48]

Obviously these limited sailings were insufficient to keep the flow of materials up to American commitments under the protocol. The sole cause did not lie in the lack of shipping or of an adequate route of entry. While the Army bent every effort to the task in response to pressure from higher authority, it found it impossible to

---

[46] Rpt, Trans Subcom, 16 Sep 41, sub: Sup Routes to Russia, B.H. (41) 5, in Min of London Conf (Col Taylor) file, DAD.

[47] (1) Msg, Kuibyshev to Dept of State [Faymonville for Hopkins], 1 Nov 41, Russian Cables Supersecret file, ID. (2) Msg, Kuibyshev to Dept of State [Faymonville for Hopkins], 20 Nov 41, Russian Info Cables file, ID.

[48] (1) Report on War Aid Furnished by the United States to the USSR, prepared by the Protocol and Area Info Stf, USSR Br, and the Div of Research and Rpts, Dept of State, November 28, 1945 (hereafter cited as Report on War Aid to USSR, 28 Nov 45). (2) See below, App. D.

furnish material in keeping with the schedules during October and November. Difficulties arose in satisfying Soviet specifications on many articles, and material had to be prepared for shipment in the greatest haste by an Army organization not yet prepared to handle large overseas movements. No sooner had the first carloads of equipment arrived at port than the air was thick with complaints from the Soviet representatives. Many items were delivered incomplete, they said, 90-mm. guns without complementary directors, locators, or height finders; tanks, mortars, and other items in defective condition or without necessary spares or ammunition. There was the utmost confusion in shipping-documents and packing-lists that identified crates, and many materials were inadequately packed for the long voyage. They refused to have the materials shipped until these defects were remedied and as a result shipments were delayed in some cases as much as a month and a half.[49] While these difficulties could be charged off to the haste with which the first shipments had to be prepared, they made a very bad impression on the Russians and accentuated their impatience with American performance. While the War Department was ready to make a valiant effort to catch up with its schedules in December, Pearl Harbor interfered with the performance. Thus the legacy of the prewar period was a gaping deficit in meeting protocol commitments, one that was to constitute one of the most formidable logistical problems of the early months of the war. Harriman stated in a conference on 24 December 1941 that Britain was 100 percent on schedule in meeting its commitments while the United States had shipped only 25 percent of scheduled quantities.[50]

It has often been said of American aid to the nations opposing the Axis in the pre-Pearl Harbor period that it was "too little and too late." Munitions actually delivered during that period in no case exercised a decisive influence on the course of the war, nor did they prevent the long series of disasters that befell the Allied Powers in early 1942. Indeed, the drain on American resources that lend-lease created contributed to the weakness of our own defenses in the Pacific in the face of the Japanese attack. While American aid undoubtedly made an important emergency contribution to the defense of the British Isles and to the British campaign in the Middle East, it would be presumptuous to say that it enabled the British to survive. Most of the American supplies that went to Britain in 1941 were produced under British contracts rather than under lend-lease. The impact of U.S. aid to the Soviet Union was as yet insignificant and played no role in the repulse of the German attack before Moscow in the fall of 1941. The Chinese had little more than promises and Chennault's 100-plane air force, and that unable to operate at full efficiency for lack of supplies. No better example of "too little and too late" could be chosen than the case of the Netherlands Indies.

In truth, the prewar period of lend-lease operations proved to be only one phase of preparation for participation in World War II, a phase to be linked with others

---

[49] (1) Ltr, K. I. Lukashev, President Amtorg, to Gen Spalding, DDAR, 28 Oct 41. (2) Ltrs, Col Holman to Col Aurand, 30 Oct and 11 Nov 41. Both in Russia file, DAD. (3) Ltr, Maj Gen Alexander C. Repin, Soviet Mil Mis, to SW, 5 Feb 42, AG 400.3295 (8-14-41) Sec 1.
[50] Memo, Lt Col Joseph W. Boone for Col Aurand, 24 Dec 41, sub: Mtg in Mr. Stettinius' Off, Col Boone's file, DAD.

such as the expansion of the U.S. Army and its planning for future eventualities. The United States could not become the "Arsenal of Democracy" until its industry had been fully mobilized for the task. In 1941 the fruits of that developing mobilization were still meager and had to be divided among too many claimants. Lend-lease planning had to deal in terms of futures, of deliveries to be made after American industry was producing munitions in a volume that would permit their distribution on a more lavish scale. But lend-lease played an important role in demonstrating the necessity for expansion of production and established the principle that U.S. production would be distributed in such a manner as to best promote victory over the Axis regardless of the nationality of the forces employed.

CHAPTER V

Widening Commitments

During the summer and autumn before Pearl Harbor, the war spread into new areas and threatened to spread into still others. In June, when Germany invaded the Soviet Union, it seemed as though the storm was moving away from the Americas. Most of the experts expected the Soviet armies to dissolve within three months, but even so this meant a welcome respite from the threat of a German invasion of the British Isles and of a German move through Spain into France's African possessions. Signs of the impending German shift to the East had led the President early in June to suspend the scheduled occupation of the Azores and to turn to the relief of British forces in Iceland—a task that did not have to be executed in one stroke against opposition, seemed more feasible logistically, and offered justification for extending U.S. naval protection over parts of the vital North Atlantic convoy routes.[1]

But the German invasion of the USSR brought the Army no relief from the growing logistical burdens of strengthening and expanding its overseas establishment, and the prospect of having to undertake risky new overseas ventures remained. In the Far East, Japan, her hands freed by the war in the Soviet Union, moved promptly into southern Indochina, gaining positions for her eventual attack on Malaya and Singapore, now definitely decided upon. U.S. policy toward Japan immediately

stiffened, and the Army presently found itself committed to an ambitious program, reversing previous war plans, of transforming the Philippines into a great bastion of American air power. On the other side of the world, the Iceland undertaking proved unexpectedly difficult,[2] and July and August brought a sudden revival of the menace of a German incursion into northwestern and western Africa via the Iberian Peninsula. President Roosevelt, meeting Prime Minister Churchill on shipboard off Argentia, Newfoundland, in August, gave an unqualified promise that American forces would occupy the Azores, by invitation from Portugal, while the British simultaneously would seize the Canary and Cape Verde Islands, the last named to be turned over subsequently to American forces. As it happened, the German drive to the southwest failed to materialize, Portugal's attitude cooled, and the planned Anglo-American moves were not carried out. Nevertheless, the American

---

[1] (1) Msg, Stimson to President, 23 Jun 41, quoted in Sherwood, *Roosevelt and Hopkins,* pp. 303–04. (2) G-2 study, 11 Jul 41, title: Data for WD Strategic Est . . . , WPD 4510. (3) Conn and Fairchild, Framework of Hemisphere Defense, Ch. II, p. 82.

[2] For details of the Iceland operation, see: (1) Stetson Conn and Byron Fairchild, The Defense of the Western Hemisphere: II; and (2) Joseph Bykofsky and Harold Larson, The Transportation Corps: III, Activities in the Oversea Commands (hereafter cited as Bykofsky and Larson, Trans III). Both are volumes in preparation for the series UNITED STATES ARMY IN WORLD WAR II.

planners continued to discuss expeditions to the Azores, the Cape Verdes, and French North and West Africa, and late in the year a major operation against Dakar was seriously considered as a prelude to a combined Anglo-American occupation of French North Africa. Meanwhile, the U.S. Navy, reinforced from the Pacific during the spring, by September was covering in effect the whole western half of the North Atlantic convoy routes, and was actually engaged in a "shooting war" against German submarines.[3]

For the U.S. Army, the spreading conflagration thus meant an increase in present burdens and a prospect of new ones in the near future. American participation in the war, while still indirect, was growing correspondingly larger through the medium of lend-lease, and moving closer to outright belligerency through measures "short of war." These trends naturally called for a more searching scrutiny than had hitherto been attempted of the problems and costs, both immediate and ultimate, involved in open participation in the war. Army planners became even more sensitive to the prospect of having soon to shoulder the tasks of a coalition war in distant theaters, tasks for which the Army was still far from prepared. Increasingly, too, they gave much thought to the role that the United States should play as a participant. Should it be one of full military collaboration, with balanced American ground, air, and naval forces employed on a grand scale, or should it be primarily one of arming the manpower of other nations, with American forces limited mainly to the air and naval arms? This was a question of high policy, which the military could not decide, but it naturally evoked emphatic professional views. The President himself more or less accidentally opened the door to a thoroughgoing discussion and presentation of these views by the staffs when he called for an estimate of the ultimate costs in munitions of defeating the Axis. The resulting "Victory Program," completed a few weeks before Pearl Harbor, rested upon assumptions that the actual course of the war was presently to demolish, but the program afforded a revealing glimpse, nevertheless, of the logistical magnitudes involved in a global coalition war.

Britain's Bid for American Intervention

During the early summer of 1941 Army planners watched with growing uneasiness as Britain, hard-pressed at sea and in Egypt and threatened by Japanese moves toward Singapore, tried strenuously to bolster its defenses everywhere. Even more strongly than in February, the staff felt "that the Battle of the Atlantic is the final, decisive battle of the war and everything has got to be concentrated on winning it."[4] There were, indeed, encouraging developments in that very quarter; British shipping losses during June, July, and August declined spectacularly, leading the British to add two million tons to their goal for 1941 imports (lowered the preceding March to thirty-one million tons). But

---

[3] (1) Conn and Fairchild, Framework of Hemisphere Defense, Ch. VI, pp. 1–24. (2) William S. Langer and S. Everett Gleason, *The Undeclared War: 1940-1941* (New York, Harper & Brothers, 1953), Chs. XVIII, XXI. (3) Matloff and Snell, *Strategic Planning: 1941-1942*, Ch. III. (4) Louis Morton, *The Fall of the Philippines*, UNITED STATES ARMY IN WORLD WAR II (Washington, 1953), Ch. III. (5) Morison, *Battle of the Atlantic*, Ch. V.

[4] Staff views on the Battle of the Atlantic as reported by Hopkins, visiting England in July, quoted in Sherwood, *Roosevelt and Hopkins*, p. 314.

American military observers seemed little impressed by this trend. "Unless the losses of British merchant ships are greatly reduced," gloomily asserted the Joint Board in September, ". . . the resistance of the United Kingdom cannot continue indefinitely, no matter what industrial effort is put forth by the United States."[5] Britain's determination to hold on every front had already necessitated diversions of American tanks and other matériel to the Middle East in May and June; it threatened further to extend American logistical commitments in the impending joint effort against the Axis. In July, moreover, the first lists of requirements from the Soviet Union were giving some indication of the immense drain this new battle front was to place upon American munitions production. The Army's immediate resources, meanwhile, were strained by its present relatively small undertakings—relief of British forces in Iceland and the garrisoning of its other bases—to which soon was to be added the build-up in the Philippines. None of these programs was to be completed by the end of the year. The one major overseas venture that the Army staff regarded as an effective countermeasure to the German threat in the South Atlantic and within its capabilities was an occupation of northeastern Brazil. To this project the President gave little encouragement, while his aggressive support of Britain in the North Atlantic seemed likely to bring on open hostilities with Germany.

At the Atlantic Conference in August, the British staff unfolded a far-reaching program of military action—last-ditch defense in Egypt and a renewed offensive in the fall; heavy reinforcements for Singapore; preventive occupation of the Atlantic islands even at the almost certain risk of a German invasion of Spain and Portugal, and subsequently an Anglo-American occupation of North Africa. As a climax, the staff now made a strong plea for early American intervention in the war.[6]

There was little discussion of this program at the conference, but the reaction of the U.S. Army staff, analyzing the program in Washington during the weeks following, was explosive. Criticisms employed such terms as "propaganda" and "groping for panaceas." Britain's strategy seemed no more than a confession of bankruptcy. It seemed to explore no new avenues of action, no new sources of power, but merely to appeal for more American munitions, shipping, and now direct military participation. Some felt the British were laggard in exploiting their own resources; one officer (Maj. Albert C. Wedemeyer) wondered why Britain did not import some of India's 390,000,000 people to England to fill the labor shortage. These and similar tail-twisting comments reflected a sense of frustration arising from present impotence. Not for two years, by current calculations, would U.S. forces be strong enough to influence the course of the war by military action. The overseas adventures on which the British expected the U.S. to embark in northwestern Africa and elsewhere would absorb shipping that could not be spared from Britain's own import program. British requirements in munitions exceeded, in some categories, the entire present and planned production of the United States. For the present, staff

---

[5] (1) JB 355, Ser 707, 11 Sep 41, title: JB Est of U.S. Over-All Pdn Reqmts. (2) Sherwood, *Roosevelt and Hopkins*, pp. 314–17. (3) Churchill, *The Grand Alliance*, App. E, Bk. I, and pp. 128–29, 828–35. (4) Hancock and Gowing, *British War Economy*, pp. 263–68, and Table 3(d), p. 205. (5) See below, App. H-1.

[6] (1) General Strategy Review by the British Chiefs of Staff, 31 Jul 41, WPD 4402-64. This paper was presented at the conference. (2) Papers on discussions of conf in Item 11b, Exec 4.

MEETING OF THE JOINT BOARD, *November 1941. Seated around the table left to right: Brig. Gen. Harold F. Loomis, Maj. Gen. Henry H. Arnold, Maj. Gen. William Bryden, General Marshall, Admiral Stark, Rear Adm. Royal E. Ingersoll, Rear Adm. John H. Towers, Rear Adm. Richmond K. Turner.*

officers argued, "we should engage Germany with the weapon in which we claim superiority . . . i.e. economic force . . . *not* land operations in Europe against the German army."[7] The Joint Board's official reply to the British proposals emphatically declared, "the weakness of our potential allies, the present inadequacy of production, the unreadiness of our forces, the lack of shipping at this time, and the two-ocean threat to our ultimate security, present a situation we are not prepared to meet as a belligerent." Early intervention would draw the United States into "a piecemeal and indecisive commitment of our forces against a superior enemy under unfavorable logistic conditions."[8]

In September, events and the President's purposes, nevertheless, seemed to be marching irresistibly toward the early participation the staff feared. It was in this month that the first attacks on American destroyers by German U-boats occurred, and the President issued his "shoot on sight" order. In response to a personal request from Churchill, moreover, the President consented to lend a sizable block of shipping, including three of the Navy's finest transports, to move two British divisions around the Cape of Good Hope. The transports sailed in November.[9]

---

[7] Staff papers on General Strategy Review by the British Chiefs of Staff, WPD 4402-64, Sec 4.

[8] Memo, JB to Sp A&N Observers, London, 25 Sep 41, JB 325, Ser 729.

[9] (1) Churchill, *The Grand Alliance*, pp. 491–95, 817–19. (2) Sherwood, *Roosevelt and Hopkins*, pp. 375–76.

Shipping: Ferrying Versus Amphibious Transport

Shipping, as the Joint Board's statement in September indicated, was one of several bottlenecks. It was probably not the crucial one, since there seemed to be enough tonnage that could be mobilized in an emergency to deploy overseas the relatively meager forces scheduled for early movement under RAINBOW 5.[10] But in the existing situation, which did not permit full mobilization of merchant shipping, the problem of overseas deployment was acute. The effort to mount the Azores expedition late in May had thrown a glaring light on the unpreparedness of the military services, even with pooled resources, to undertake any considerable overseas movement on short notice. It would evidently be necessary, as the President conceded a few weeks later, to earmark a certain amount of privately controlled tonnage for military service and keep it within a reasonable distance of the east coast ports if any of the several emergency expeditions then in view were to be carried out. No specific action was taken to do this, and as late as October G-4 complained that the rule against holding vessels for future sailings was mainly responsible for the current bog-down of movements to Iceland.[11]

Under established Army-Navy agreements for joint action, responsibility for all military ocean transport was to pass to the Navy at the outbreak of war. In December 1940 G-4 had urged that the transfer be made immediately, since an emergency situation existed, but most Army transportation officials then frankly doubted if the Navy, with more exacting standards for training crews and rigging military transports, could meet Army schedules.

The G-4 proposal was overruled. By April 1941 this feeling had changed somewhat, partly because of current labor and conversion difficulties and partly because of the greater imminence of war. Arrangements were made accordingly to progressively transfer Army-controlled transports to the Navy, the Army retaining its responsibility for loading its own cargo and the right to obtain additional shipping, if need be, from the Maritime Commission to meet its current needs.[12]

From the outset, the transfer program lagged, the Navy encountering difficulties in manning and converting the transports. The crisis of late May brought a temporary acceleration, with the transfer of six large Army transports to the Navy to mount the Azores expedition. But these ships had to be replaced almost immediately by the Maritime Commission to meet the Army's deployment needs, and during the summer and fall the transfer of Army transports and their conversion and manning by the Navy fell farther behind schedule. By 7 December only seven were actually in operation with Navy crews. During this same period the Army's own fleet, perforce, continued to grow. When war broke it numbered, all told, 140 vessels under various forms of military control, including 33 directly owned and 29 chartered ocean-going transports.[13]

---

[10] See above, Ch. II.

[11] (1) Memo, President for Adm Land, 1 Aug 41, quoted in Elliott Roosevelt, ed., *F. D. R.: His Personal Letters, 1928-1945*, II (New York, Duell, Sloan and Pearce, 1950), 1193. (2) Memo, G-4 for CofS GHQ, 16 Oct 41, sub: Delay in Shipt of Replacements, G-4/33098.

[12] Corresp in G-4/29717-51.

[13] (1) Corresp in G-4/29717-26. (2) Memo, G-4 for CofS, 23 Jun 41, sub: Relief of Navy Crews . . . , G-4/29717-51. (3) Memo, G-4 for CofS, 11 Dec 41, sub: Shipg Sit, 10a Shipg file, Plng Div ASF.

This growth reflected the steady expansion of Army deployment to established overseas bases, a ferrying operation that employed conventional shipping to discharge passengers and cargo through developed ports. The Navy was not primarily interested in this ferrying function, which it was in the process of taking over from the Army. In naval operations the characteristic transport task was the moving of complete military formations in fighting trim to a hostile shore, there to be landed against opposition in small boats and tank lighters carried on the transports. The amphibious transport, or combat loader, was a specially designed and rigged vessel.[14] Conventional vessels could be converted for the purpose, but only by an expensive and lengthy process involving heavier ballasting, provision for heavier deck-loading, extensive armament, and elaborate installations, all of which reduced cargo and passenger capacity by 15 percent or more. Amphibious transportation was essentially a branch of naval tactics; ferrying to overseas bases was a purely logistical function. Some Army officials believed that the Navy consciously subordinated the latter "to other matters considered more vital." [15]

During the summer of 1941 the Navy expanded and accelerated its conversion program. Three of the six Army transports taken over at the end of May were to be converted to combat loaders, and two others, large passenger liners, along with a third turned over by the Maritime Commission, were to be made into aircraft carriers. Ten more Army transports were earmarked for the combat-loader program during the summer. In all, twenty-seven vessels, in addition to the three carriers-to-be, were scheduled for conversion.[16]

From the Army's point of view this program involved a dangerous and unjustifiable diversion of badly needed shipping. For ferrying purposes, the tonnage would be forever lost, while the work of conversion would immobilize ships altogether for months to come. Transfer of the ten Army transports would swallow at a gulp more than half the Army's fleet, including the newest, fastest, and largest vessels. The three liners destined to become carriers were the mainstay of the Army's troop deployment plans. In August G-4 wrote:

No large movement, approaching 12,000 or more, has been contemplated without relying on at least two of these ships . . . these three vessels are essential as transportation to fulfill the missions of the RAINBOW No. 5 plan, and to accomplish other overseas movements already initiated and suspended . . . . Their conversion will deny their use for a year for any purpose. That year, because of lack of ships, may well be a critical one.[17]

Nevertheless, the Navy for the time being, after the matter had gone to the Joint Board, had its way. The Navy undertook to adjust its combat-loader schedule in part to Army plans, but offered no replacement for the three large liners. These departed in November, in fact, to ferry

---

[14] There were two types: the attack personnel transport (APA) carrying both troops and equipment, and the attack cargo transport (AKA) carrying only cargo. See below, App. A-7.

[15] (1) Memo, G-4 for WPD, 19 Nov 41, sub: Trf of Army Trans . . . . (2) Memo, G-4, no addressee, no date, sub: Conversion of Army Trans . . . . Both in G-4/29717-51. (3) Memo, G-4 for WPD, 30 Aug 41, same sub, G-4/29717-81. (4) Memo, CNO for JB, 5 Aug 41, sub: Conversion of Army Trans for Combat Loading, JB 320, Ser 715.

[16] (1) Memo cited n. 15(4). (2) Memo, G-4 for CofS, 26 Aug 41, sub: Indefinite Postponement by Navy of Conversion . . . , G-4/29717-65.

[17] (1) Memo cited n. 15(3). (2) Memo, TQMG for G-4, 13 Aug 41, sub: Army Trans Conversion, G-4/29717-81. (3) Memo, Gen Marshall for Adm Stark, 25 Sep 41, sub: Conversion . . . , OCofS 17396-56B. (4) Other corresp in G-4/29717-65 and G-4/29717-26.

British troops to the Middle East, where they remained for many months.[18]

The Army's case in this dispute was, at bottom, a plea for balance in the instruments of overseas warfare—balance between troop-carrying and cargo-carrying capacity (the latter being, at this time, more plentiful than the former), between ferrying tonnage and amphibious tonnage, between logistics and tactics. Navy spokesmen conceded that the program would "greatly restrict the ability of the Navy to transport large Army forces to overseas destinations on short notice," as movements to the Philippines were soon amply to demonstrate. But they took their stand quite simply on service prerogative: "The Navy must be left free to use and dispose of individual ships of the Navy as it deems necessary to meet its responsibilities."[19]

The whole episode contributed to a growing reluctance on the part of Army transportation officials, during the closing months of 1941, to hasten the Navy's assumption of responsibility for all overseas transportation. When WPD at the end of the year attempted to spur the transfer program, G-4 protested sharply. The Army, that official asserted, was handling the job of ocean transportation to its own satisfaction, its relations with the Maritime Commission were excellent, and "its efficiency . . . is at present far superior to that of the Navy." The competence of the latter to undertake the growing tasks of overseas transportation, G-4 pithily concluded, should be more clearly demonstrated "before the Army gives up the power to do for the need to petition."[20]

Build-up in the Philippines

The largest single additional burden placed upon military shipping during this period grew out of the decision to reinforce the Philippines and to broaden the islands' role as a bastion against Axis aggression. Late in July the President created a new Army command in the Philippines under General Douglas MacArthur—U.S. Army Forces, Far East—and plans were put in train not merely to strengthen the island defenses but also to develop there a formidable base for offensive air power. The task thus undertaken swelled before the end of the year into a major logistical operation, involving a heavy diversion of effort from the Atlantic theater.[21]

In this plan there was curiously little consideration of the enormous logistical problems involved in building up and supporting large forces in the far Pacific. The decision rested to a large degree on the confidence of the Army Air Forces, evidently infectious, that its heavy bomber, the B-17, if based in the Philippines athwart Japan's major sea communications and within range of her home islands, would be a sufficient threat to deter Japan from further aggression. This meant that both the defenses and the striking power of the base would have to be built up rapidly and, in effect, under the noses of the Japanese, before the latter were ready to take counteraction. That failing, all depended on the ability of the Army and

---

[18] (1) Memo, JPC for JB, 8 Oct 41, sub: Conversion of Tr Trans . . . , JB 320, Ser 723. (2) Memo cited n. 15(4). (3) Memo, Gen Gerow for G-4, 2 Oct 41, sub: Conversion of Tr Trans . . . , G-4/29717-65. (4) Memo, Gerow for G-4, 18 Sep 41, sub: Conversion of Army Trans . . . , G-4/29717-81.

[19] Ibid.

[20] Memo cited n. 15(1).

[21] (1) Morton, Fall of the Philippines, Chs. II–III. (2) Watson, Prewar Plans and Preparations, pp. 434–38. (3) Matloff and Snell, Strategic Planning: 1941–1942, pp. 63–75. (4) Craven and Cate, AAF I, pp. 178–93. (5) Romanus and Sunderland, Stilwell's Mission to China, pp. 23–24. (6) See above, Ch. IV.

Navy to build up reserves in the islands, before Japan struck, sufficient for a prolonged citadel defense — at least six months, according to the plan. With the enemy controlling the whole intervening region west of Midway except for the isolated outposts of Wake and Guam, and probably possessing the means to cut the approaches from the south, General MacArthur could expect little help from the outside until the Pacific Fleet, with powerful ground and air forces, could fight its way through from the Central Pacific.

Even if communications with the Netherlands Indies and Australia could be kept open, the only secure approach from the United States was along the island chain of the South Pacific, stretching in a vast arc more than five thousand miles from Honolulu. Naval officers had long advocated construction of bases in the middle and western Pacific to extend the fleet's operating range, but up to the very eve of war Congress refused to grant appropriations for this purpose. It was a commercial airline, Pan American Airways, that pioneered the first air route across the Pacific in 1935, building way-station facilities on Guam, Wake, and Midway. Thereafter its big flying boats maintained a regular service between San Francisco and Manila. Not for four years, however, could the Navy obtain sufficient funds to capitalize on Pan American's experience. The appropriation, finally granted in 1939, enabled the Navy to start a modest program of base construction, but it was prohibited even then from dredging the harbor at Guam. By April 1940 the Navy had started to improve its west coast and Hawaiian facilities and had begun construction of patrol-plane facilities at Midway, Johnston, and Palmyra. Nine months later work was under

way on the projected air base at Wake. Using this route—Midway–Wake–Port Moresby–Darwin—nine B-17's early in September 1941 successfully completed the flight from Hawaii to Luzon. This was an historic achievement, giving some promise of quick, direct delivery of the Army's principal strategic weapon to the Far East. But the Midway–Wake approach was dangerously exposed, and in early October 1941 the War Department approved an Air Forces proposal to construct a permanent air ferry route farther east and south. Small teams of Army engineers, supplemented by civilian workmen, hastily set about building airstrips on the first two bases, Christmas and Canton, while a commercial engineering firm took over construction of the runways at the remaining two stations, Fiji and New Caledonia. The Australians, meanwhile, in co-operation with General MacArthur who was responsible for the bases lying between Australia and the Philippines, were striving to complete the western lap of the route. On 6 December, the day before the Japanese attack, Lt. Gen. Walter C. Short, commander of the Hawaiian Department, notified Washington that he expected to have the chain of new bases open to ferry traffic in January.[22]

---

[22] (1) Watson, *Prewar Plans and Preparations*, Chs. XIII–XIV. (2) Samuel Eliot Morison, *The Rising Sun in the Pacific: 1931-April 1942* (Boston, Little, Brown and Company, 1948), pp. 27–40. (3) Duncan S. Ballantine, *U.S. Naval Logistics in the Second World War* (Princeton, N. J., Princeton University Press, 1947), pp. 26–29, 60–62. (4) Craven and Cate, *AAF I*, pp. 172, 177–93. (5) Matthew Josephson, *Empire of the Air: Juan Trippe and the Struggle for World Airways* (New York, Harcourt, Brace and Company, 1944), Chs. VII–VIII. (6) *Building the Navy's Bases in World War II: History of the Bureau of Yards and Docks and the Civil Engineer Corps, 1940-1946, I* (Washington, 1947), 121. (7) Hepburn Board [Adm Arthur J. Hepburn, Chairman] Report, 1 Dec 38, with atchmts, WPD 4156. The report was printed as House Document 65, 76th

These preparations looked to the future. For the immediate task of building up the defenses of the Philippines in the summer of 1941, it was possible, though risky, to ship directly across the Pacific through Japanese-controlled waters. This was a formidable job calling for a large-scale troop-ferrying and cargo-ferrying operation, massive in terms of anything undertaken since the last war. The troop movement program was smaller than that for cargo since, with the Philippine Army being mobilized, General MacArthur's primary need was not manpower but material. By mid-November, nevertheless, the War Department was planning to ship more than 20,000 troops during the following month, in addition to about 5,000 already arrived or on the way. The demand came at an unfortunate time. The Navy's conversion program was immobilizing passenger tonnage, and six large liners were about to be sent to the Indian Ocean on British service. The arrangements for shipping the 20,000 troops required the use of five privately owned liners in addition to six Army transports. When the Japanese attack halted the program on 7 December, only 8,563 troops had actually reached the Philippines since July. Over 11,000 more were en route, but only 4,400 of these got through to Australia; the remainder were turned back.[23]

Cargo movements were of larger volume. Requests from General MacArthur during August and September totaled .9 million measurement tons, and tentative schedules to transport the bulk of this material from November through March

involved some 70 separate shipments. Even more than the troop movements, these demands were beyond the capacity of the Army's transport fleet. Out of more than a million measurement tons of shipping tentatively lined up for shipments to the Philippines during the period November to March, the Army expected to provide only 150,000; the Maritime Commission would have to assemble the remainder. Scheduling shipments and assembling shipping took time; not until November did the cargo requested in August and September begin to flow across the Pacific, and the bulk of the shipments was scheduled for December and later. By November there was a backlog of more than a million tons of material in ports and depots available for MacArthur's forces. Facilities at San Francisco and Manila were heavily taxed, especially at the latter port. In September the Navy instituted convoying between Honolulu and Manila, and later schedules spaced convoys at twelve-day intervals, creating new difficulties in traffic control and scheduling.[24]

All these problems provided the first taste of build-up operations on something like a wartime scale. But the Japanese stopped the program before it got into full stride. Only seven freighters and five passenger vessels carrying small amounts of cargo reached Manila during September

---

Congress, 1st Session, January 3, 1939. (8) *Biennial Report of the Chief of Staff of the United States Army, July 1, 1939 to June 30, 1941 to the Secretary of War; and . . . July 1, 1941 to June 30, 1943.* (9) Lewis H. Brereton, *The Brereton Diaries* (New York, William Morrow and Company, 1946), pp. 19–20.

[23] (1) Msg 277, MacArthur to Marshall, 7 Sep 41, AG 320.2 (7-28-41) Orgn and Reinf for USAFFE. (2) Memo, Lt Col Frank S. Ross for G-4, 24 Sep 41, sub: Conversion . . . , G-4/29717-65. (3) Memo, G-4 for CofS, 13 Nov 41, sub: Philippine Mvmt, G-4/29717-26. (4) Rpt, no date, sub: Shipg Sit at SFPOE Following Pearl Harbor. (5) Alfred J. Bingham, Reinforcement of the Philippines, pp. 8–11. Last two in OCT HB.

[24] (1) Corresp in G-4/27573, G-4/33451, G-4/29367-120, and SWPA folder, OCT HB. (2) Bingham, Reinforcement of the Philippines, pp. 3–7, OCT HB. (3) See below, Chs. VII, XI. (4) For various weight and space measurements, see below, App. A-1.

and October. In November only five freighters and three passenger vessels arrived. Most of the schedule lay ahead, with eighteen arrivals slated for December and thirty for January. Two days before Pearl Harbor General Marshall noted that about one hundred thousand ship tons of material were on the way, with twice as much ready to move to port, and fifty-five vessels had been assigned. The *Pensacola* convoy (containing three freighters and two troopships) and four other vessels already at sea on 7 December brought their cargo through to Australia; two other cargo vessels were lost.[25]

General MacArthur faced the Japanese onslaught with his Regular Army troops and Philippine Scouts fairly well equipped, but with the Philippine Army low on most types of equipment and supplies; defense reserves, which had been set at a six-months' level for fifty thousand troops, were only about half filled. The uncompleted build-up in the Philippines left the United States with a large military investment and an equally large legacy of frustrated hopes in the Far East, both of which would be difficult to write off.[26]

Logistics for Victory

The two policies laid down by President Roosevelt in June 1940, rearmament at home and aid to the "opponents of force" abroad, by mid-1941 were exerting a growing pressure upon the still meager output of American munitions. The objectives of the former program remained within the framework of the needs of hemisphere defense. Foreign aid, even with large lend-lease appropriations in 1941 and some expansion of plant capacity under the direct impulse of foreign orders, had been kept alive on the whole by

siphoning off a part of the production intended for American forces. It lacked long-range objectives, except those that presumably lay behind the requests of the claimant nations. There was a pressing need for a policy and a program to guide both American rearmament and foreign aid and to establish a firm ratio of emphasis between them.

On 9 July the President, perhaps unwittingly, opened the door to the formulation of such a policy and program. In the opening sentence of a letter to the two service secretaries on that date he set forth what appeared to be a sweeping proposal: to explore "at once the overall production requirements required to defeat our potential enemies." In reality, as the rest of the letter conclusively showed, he merely wanted to know the amount of munitions the United States would have to produce (in addition to the production of its present and potential friends) in order "to exceed by an appropriate amount that available to our potential enemies." He was not concerned with "requirements" as the military staffs customarily used the term—that is, as a shopping list of items needed for specific operations. The letter stated:

I am not suggesting a detailed report, but one which, while general in scope, would cover the most critical items in our defense and which could then be related by the OPM into practical realities of production facilities. It seems to me we need to know our program in its entirety, even though at a later date it may be amended.[27]

---

[25] (1) Bingham, Reinforcement of the Philippines, pp. 7–11, OCT HB. (2) Brig Gen Charles C. Drake, Report of Operations, Quartermaster General, U.S. Army, in the Philippine Campaign, 1941–1942, Pt. I, p. 3, Hist Sec OQMG.

[26] Morton, *Fall of the Philippines*, Ch. III.

[27] (1) Ltr, President to SW and SN, 9 Jul 41, WPD 4494-1. (2) Watson, *Prewar Plans and Preparations*, Ch. XI.

The President was not concerned with the strategic concept or plans that might govern eventual American participation in the war, nor with the American forces that might be required. The whole tenor of the request implied, in fact, that whether or not the United States became a belligerent, it would continue to serve primarily as an arsenal for the nations actively fighting the Axis. His basic assumption, made explicit in a supplementary message a few weeks later, was that "the reservoir of munitions power available to the United States and her friends is sufficiently superior to that available to the Axis to insure defeat of the latter." [28]

To the Army staff this approach seemed unsound. "It would be unwise to assume," General Gerow wrote to Assistant Secretary McCloy, "that we can defeat Germany simply by outproducing her." Weapons must not only be produced but also brought effectively to bear against the enemy; this required trained soldiers, transport, services, expert leadership, sound plans—the whole panoply of organized military power. Wars were won, General Gerow reminded the Assistant Secretary, by "sound strategy implemented by well-trained forces which are adequately and effectively equipped." [29] The order of priority was important. Factories produced weapons; weapons helped to produce armies, navies, and air forces; these forces provided the means of implementing strategy. The requirements for victory therefore must be approached in reverse order: first, a basic strategy, from which would be derived concrete plans; second, forces essential for carrying out strategic plans; last, productive capacity sufficient to arm these forces. [30]

The Army staff, in fact, welcomed the President's instructions as a logical extension of a task it had had in hand for several weeks. This was an effort to draw up a comprehensive strategic estimate of the current situation and its probable future development, an estimate from which concrete strategic objectives and an appropriate program of action might be derived—in brief, a strategy. Leaders of industry and officials concerned with defense production had long been pressing for such objectives to provide the basis for a master plan of economic mobilization. Some officials, notably Stacy May of the Bureau of Research and Statistics, Office of Production Management, Jean Monnet of the British Supply Council, Under Secretary of War Patterson, and Colonel Aurand thought in terms of "ultimate" requirements, the total production effort that would have to be made in order to defeat the Axis. But production officials for the most part did not yet look beyond the current defense production effort, finding it difficult enough to preserve some order in the multitude of competing short-range programs. Lack of co-ordination was perhaps the more immediate problem, and an important step toward meeting it was taken in August with the creation of the Supply Priorities and Allocations Board with powers to "determine the total requirements of materials and commodities needed respectively for defense, civilian and other purposes and to establish policies for the fulfillment of such requirements . . . ." [31] Still the lack of long-range objectives stood in the way of the expansion of capacity that the growing needs of rearmament and of foreign aid

---

[28] Ltr, President to SW, 30 Aug 41, WPD 4494-1.
[29] Memo, Gerow for McCloy, 5 Aug 41, Item 7, Exec 4.
[30] Ltr, SW to President, no date [drafted by McCloy], Item 7, Exec 4.
[31] EO 8875, 28 Aug 41.

demanded; by spring of 1941 there were already threatening shortages in critical materials and machine tools.[32]

Until the President gave the word, the military staffs could hardly set their sights above the established concepts of hemisphere defense and material aid to opponents of the Axis. Indeed, until national policy and Congressional sentiment moved definitely beyond these concepts, it was doubtful whether speculations as to "ultimate" needs would provide guidance sufficiently firm to permit much expansion of production capacity. General Marshall in May had expressed doubt whether the Army could justifiably set up requirements for more than the 2,800,000-man force of the first PMP augmentation; "we will not need a 4,000,000-man army unless England collapses," he stated.[33] He feared, moreover, that a sudden increase in orders might interfere with current production and eventually produce "a pile of stuff which is not only obsolescent but blocks other things more essential."[34] In any case, if the Army was to place demands on industry beyond the present short-range goals, such increases must be rooted firmly in strategic needs. Late in May Marshall directed his staff to draw up "a more clearcut strategic estimate of our situation" that might provide a "base of departure" for an orderly expansion of production capacity.[35]

Into this endeavor the President's letter of 9 July interjected the hypothesis of "ultimate" needs, which the Army staff gladly embraced, and the concept (or at least the implication) that industrial superiority alone was a sufficient guarantee of victory, which the staff rejected. As the staff read the President's instructions, the task was to determine the total requirements for victory—strategy, forces, and munitions. This was a monumental job and the President set impossible deadlines. As a result, the mountain of material that Mr. Stimson and Mr. Knox finally delivered to the White House on 25 September, fifteen days late, was both amorphous and incomplete. It included three "ultimate" requirements compilations with their supporting strategic estimates, one each for ground forces, air forces, and the Navy; a brief report by the Joint Board, which did not succeed in smoothing over basic interservice differences on strategy; and the existing foreign aid programs, which were variously incomplete and largely uncorrelated. Information on production capacity, which the President had requested, was not a part of this "Victory Program," as it came to be called. That information had been prepared by Mr. Stimson's staff, with the help of the Office of Production Management and British experts, and submitted two days earlier in the form of a consolidated balance sheet showing stocks of war materials on hand and expected quarterly production in the United States, United Kingdom, and Canada to the end of 1942; estimates, admittedly unreliable, of Axis stocks and production capacity were prepared separately.[36]

[32] (1) Committee on Public Administration Cases, The Feasibility Dispute: Determination of War Production Objectives for 1942 and 1943, 1950 (hereafter cited as Com on Pub Admin Cases, Feasibility Dispute), pp. 17–23. (2) CPA, Industrial Mobilization for War, Pt. II, Chs. 1–3. (3) Watson, Prewar Plans and Preparations, pp. 331–35.

[33] Notes on conf, 17 May 41, Binder 15, OCofS.

[34] Notes on conf, 31 May 41, Binder 15, OCofS.

[35] (1) Notes on conf, 21 May 41, Binder 15, OCofS. (2) Memo, CofS for WPD, 21 May 41, WPD 4510 Strategic Est.

[36] (1) Ltr, SW to President, 23 Sep 41, AG 400 (9-17-41) Sec 1. (2) Ltr, SW to President, 23 Sep 41, SW Secret File 1848-a. (3) Draft ltr, SW to President, no date, Item 7, Exec 4. (4) Ltr, SW and SN to Presi-

In the nature of the situation, any solid prediction of ultimate foreign aid requirements at this time was quite impossible. The President was evidently prepared to give generously to the Soviet Union, but the planners were pessimistic as to Soviet capacity to hold out for long; aid to China would depend largely on whether the United States would have to fight a war in the Far East, a question that probably would be decided by Japanese not American action. And at bottom the long-term ratio between foreign aid and American rearmament was itself at issue in any calculation of "victory requirements."

Only in the case of the British program was a serious attempt made to draw up a "victory program" dovetailed with the American. In response to a request in August, the British presented with some misgivings a tentative list of ultimate requirements for critical items, but proposed that a staff conference be held to draw up a comprehensive Anglo-American victory program, embracing the total needs of both countries and their allies in a coalition war fought under the strategic concept of ABC-1. This project and that of aid to the USSR were the principal topics discussed by the American and British staff representatives at the London Conference of mid-September. There, the British presented their own "Victory Programme," based on estimates of forces to be employed in their areas of strategic responsibility as marked out in ABC-1. Against total requirements of critical items thus determined, they matched the expected output of Empire production; the

deficit, they proposed, should be met by the United States. The Americans accepted the British statement and agreed to integrate it into an over-all Victory Program along with Soviet and American military requirements; the whole would then be examined by American production authorities to determine how far it could be met. Adjustments, if necessary, would be discussed at a subsequent Victory Program conference of the two staffs in the light of the strategic situation.[37]

These steps were never completed. When Japan struck on 7 December, the Office of Production Management experts were still analyzing the feasibility of the whole assemblage of hypothetical victory requirements. No Victory Program conference was ever held, but the British program submitted in September at London became, to a large extent, the basis on which the American staffs after Pearl Harbor unilaterally merged British requirements into their own wartime supply programs.[38]

The Army's Victory Program

In drawing up its own victory requirements, the Army staff had ostensibly proceeded methodically along the lines suggested by General Gerow's formula—strategy determines forces determines munitions determines productive capacity. Gerow wrote Marshall in turning over the Army study:

WPD approached this problem by first determining in a general way the strategic operations necessary to achieve victory . . . .

dent, 25 Sep 41, with reqmts studies and JB rpt, AG 400 (7-9-41) Ult Pdn. (5) The assembling and coordinating of the data is described in Watson, *Prewar Plans and Preparations*, pp. 342–52. (6) Hancock and Gowing, *British War Economy*, p. 385.

[37] (1) Rpt, Plng Com, 19 Sep 41, sub: Vic Reqmts, B.H. (41) 14, Vic Prog (Col V. V. Taylor) file, DAD. (2) For the Soviet program, see above, Ch. IV.
[38] See below, Ch. XI.

ARMY WAR PLANS DIVISION, *November 1941. Around the table left to right: Col. Lee S. Gerow, Col. Charles W. Bundy, Lt. Col. Matthew B. Ridgway, Brig. Gen. H. F. Loomis, Brig. Gen. Leonard T. Gerow (Chief), Col. Robert W. Crawford, Lt. Col. Stephen H. Sherrill, Col. Thomas T. Handy, Lt. Col. Carl A. Russell.*

These possible operations were then translated into terms of major units . . . . Having the major units we were then able to compute the critical items required . . . . In order to obtain the total productive capacity required by an all-out effort, the requirements in critical items of associated powers were added to our own.[39]

The authors of the program did not in fact follow the formula very closely. The program's troop basis, purportedly designed to implement a predetermined strategy, actually had only a loose relation to it. Lt. Col. Albert C. Wedemeyer, the program's principal author, insisted at the time that the total figure—8,795,658 men—had

been arrived at after careful study of such factors as probable enemy and Allied forces, recent developments in tactics, organization and matériel, and probable theaters of operation with their terrain, climate, communications, population, and general economy. Such considerations undoubtedly were present in his mind in connection with the strategic estimates on which the staff had been working for many weeks past. But the figure 8,795,658, according to Wedemeyer's own testimony years later and as suggested in WPD's

[39] Memo, Gerow for CofS, 10 Sep 41, sub: Ult Reqmts, WPD 4494-9.

covering missive accompanying the report when it was transmitted to the Chief of Staff on 24 September, seems to have been the product of a simpler computation. The 8,800,000 men, more or less, represented the marginal manpower that supposedly would remain for the Army to draw upon through mid-1943, after the estimated needs of the sister service, industry, and agriculture had been met. Around this total, despite General Gerow's formula, Army strategists had to wrap their strategy.[40]

Whether this approach was more realistic than the one that took strategic requirements as its starting point is highly problematical. As a professional staff officer, Wedemeyer could have had no illusions as to the value of any two-year forecast of military manpower needs, above all one made at this particular time. Being less familiar with the mysteries of labor supply and demand and of population statistics, perhaps he felt more confidence in the data gathered for him by the civilian manpower experts in the other government departments. Yet the question marks and variables surrounding any estimate of the manpower resources and needs of a fully mobilized war economy two years in the future were at least as large and numerous as those that clouded similar projections of military requirements—indeed, since the magnitudes were larger the room for error was far greater. Wedemeyer, himself, showed some awareness of this by allowing a cushion of 3.5 million men in his estimates to absorb unforeseen needs in the war economy. Considering all the variables, it is remarkable that the Victory Program figure for the Army's ultimate strength exceeded by only about .5 million men the peak strength of 8.2 million actually reached in 1945. In its composition, of course, the Army in 1945 bore little resemblance to the force envisaged in 1941.[41]

The composition of the 8.8 million-man Army envisaged in the Victory Program clearly showed the influence of the assumption that it would ultimately be necessary to grapple with heavily armed German land forces on the European continent. The total of 215 divisions was amply weighted with armored (61 divisions), motorized, antitank, and antiaircraft elements, and had substantial service support. The Air Corps program, separately prepared, reflected the doctrine that strategic bombing would play an important, if not decisive, role in defeating Germany. To this extent the troop basis served a strategic concept, though there was no attempt to determine forces needed for particular theaters of operation, except through the inclusion of garrison strengths for specific overseas bases and the two task forces destined under current war plans for operations in South Amer-

---

[40] (1) Memo, Wedemeyer for CofS, 24 Sep 41, sub: Ult Reqmts of Army Ground and Air Forces. (2) Memo, Actg ACofS WPD for CofS, 24 Sep 41, same sub. Both in WPD 4494-13. (3) Statement by Wedemeyer to Mark S. Watson in 1948, summarized in Watson, *Prewar Plans and Preparations,* pp. 343–44.

The Army total included an estimated 2,000,000 for the Air Corps; Navy requirements were set at 1,250,000.

[41] (1) For a more detailed description of the Victory Program estimates, see Watson's draft chapter, "The Victory Program," marked "6 July Revision"; and a study by Guy A. Lee, Ultimate Requirements, Ground Forces, Estimate of September 1941 (Method Used). Both in Supporting Docs to Watson, *Prewar Plans and Preparations* file, OCMH. (2) The recollections of another active participant in this episode, General J. H. Burns, do not altogether bear out Wedemeyer's account. According to Burns, the WPD planners simply applied an arbitrary 8 percent factor to the total national population in order to arrive at the number of able-bodied males that would be available for military service. See interview, Burns with Mark Watson, no date, same file.

ica. The remainder of the proposed forces consisted of five armies and a number of separate corps, divisions, and other units (three of the armies were loosely designated "potential task forces"), a force of 1.2 million to defend and administer the continental United States, and a strategic reserve of about 3 million.[42]

This absence of any specific connection between estimated troop requirements and anticipated strategic employment struck the British, at the London Conference in September, as rather odd. They were accustomed to calculate their requirements theater by theater, taking into account as far as possible such factors as climate and terrain, port capacity, rail and road nets, power facilities, expected enemy strength, and expected intensity of combat—precisely the factors Wedemeyer alleged had been considered in drawing up the Army troop basis. The American representatives at the conference dissented sharply. Their estimates, Lt. Col. Charles W. Bundy stated, were "based on the necessary troops to accomplish victory, and a general estimate was founded on enemy forces without consideration of individual theaters."[43] In the words of Assistant Secretary McCloy, interpreting the view of the military staff, "the only safe assumptions concerning theaters of operations are that they may develop in any part of the globe, and that the Atlantic and European area will be the decisive theater."[44]

Theoretically, munitions requirements were derived by straight computation from the troop basis, but in a period of expanding production, fixed ultimate objectives were of dubious value except as incentives. Maximum production, practically speaking, was the goal of economic mobilization. "The plan for material," Colonel Aurand noted toward the end of

1941, "need await neither a strategic concept nor a determination of troops to accomplish this objective. It is sufficient to know that maximum production of military equipment must be obtained in this country at the earliest possible date." The real problem was to determine the proper division of emphasis among categories of munitions. It was up to the strategists, Aurand thought, to fix the desired ultimate monthly production of each item. The production authorities could then determine how many of each item could actually be produced each month, "so that the maximum use is made of the country's resources."[45] Whether maximum production would meet the need only time would reveal. War Department supply officers were inclined to believe that "the load to be placed on both industry and raw materials in the United States will tax its maximum capacity."[46]

Global Logistics and Mass Invasion

In the Victory Program the Army staff set forth, more fully than hitherto, its case for full participation in the war, as against the President's "arsenal" policy. The Pres-

---

[42] (1) "Ultimate Requirements Study: Estimate of Army Ground Forces," accompanying "War Department Strategic Estimate . . . 11 September 1941," WPD 4494-21. (2) For the Air Corps program, set forth in a paper known as AWPD/1, see Craven and Cate, *AAF I*, pp. 131–32, 146–47, 149–50, 594, 599–600.

[43] Min of conf on U.S.-Br pdn, 17 Sep 41; WPD 4494 Br Vic Prog.

[44] Draft ltr cited n. 36(3).

[45] Memo, Col Aurand for Gen Moore, 10 Nov 41, sub: Method of Properly Financing Vic Prog, WPD 4494 Vic Prog, U.S. Data.

[46] Memo, Col Mallon for Col Bundy, 17 Nov 41, sub: Method of Properly Financing Vic Prog, WPD 4494 Vic Prog, U.S. Data.

ident's letter of 9 July did not invite such a statement, and the letter's exclusive concern with productive capacity implied that victory against the Axis would be decided in the long run by industrial power, the element, by general agreement, in which the United States excelled. The staff's insistence on the "strategy-forces-munitions" formula, however, opened the door to a comprehensive exposition of the strategic method that Army leaders believed essential to victory. This method, as Secretary Stimson summarized it, involved early, if not immediate, participation "in an avowed all-out military effort" against Germany, as opposed to a strategy that would go little beyond the present policy of contributing "munitions, transport and naval help." Army and Navy leaders were united, Stimson wrote the President, in the conviction that "in default of such participation, the British and their allies cannot defeat Germany, and that the resistance of the United Kingdom cannot continue indefinitely, no matter what industrial effort is put forth by us." [47]

In this conclusion there were traces, no doubt, of both nationalism and professionalism, but the Army's view rested also on a persuasive estimate of the probable future course of the war. There was no optimism as to Soviet ability to repel the German invaders. By July 1942, the planners predicted, the Soviet Union would be "substantially impotent," with German air power pulverizing at leisure the territories not yet conquered. Germany might then dispose of British power in the Middle East, either by negotiation or by force, opening the way for a drive to the southeast or, alternatively, southwest through Spain toward Dakar. But the planners did not despair of the ultimate outcome. Germany would require a full year to restore order in her European conquests. She would be weakened by the long struggle, suffering from blockade, bombardment, and internal unrest. In the Far East, Japan would remain opportunistic and cautious. When and if she decided to strike, Army planners hoped, air power in the Philippines, armed and revived Chinese armies, and the Soviet Siberian divisions, together with modest Allied forces along the Malay Barrier, might hold her at bay until American naval power could be brought fully to bear. [48]

In this perspective, mid-1943 was a critical point. Up to that time Germany would be spending her substance in winning military victories. Thereafter, she would begin to renew her powers and, unless prevented, would eventually become invincible. The Allied Powers could not afford to wait later than mid-1943, therefore, to take the offensive. Long before then they must weaken Germany by air bombardment, blockade, and subversive activities, and engage her land forces in peripheral areas. The outcome would depend largely on the extent and rapidity of American mobilization. The industrial potential of the United States was more than ample for the task, but productive capacity took time to build—eighteen months to two years by current estimates—and time was running out.

It is mandatory that we reach an early appreciation of our stupendous task, and gain the whole-hearted support of the entire country in the production of trained men, ships, munitions and ample reserves. Otherwise, we will be confronted in the not distant

---

[47] Ltr cited n. 36(2).

[48] (1) "War Department Strategic Estimate . . . October 1941," WPD 4494-21. (2) JB 355, Ser 707, 11 Sep 41, title: JB Est of U.S. Over-All Pdn Reqmts. (3) "Ultimate Requirements Study . . . ," cited n. 42(1).

future by a Germany strongly entrenched economically, supported by newly acquired sources of vital supplies and industries, with her military forces operating on internal lines, and in a position of hegemony in Europe which will be comparatively easy to defend and maintain. . . . The urgency of speed and the desirability of employment of our present great economic and industrial advantage over our potential enemies cannot be over-emphasized.[49]

The Victory Program strategic estimate was the first really searching look at the implications of full involvement in the war. It was a bold look, accepting with fewer qualms than earlier, apparently, all the logistical costs and risks that American forces would incur in a coalition strategy modeled on the British theory of encirclement and attrition. The planners envisaged U.S. ground and air operations in several "subsidiary" theaters—Africa, the Near East, the Iberian Peninsula, Scandinavia—to establish bases "which encircle and close in on the Nazi citadel."[50] From these bases Allied air power would shatter the enemy economy, paving the way for ground and air attacks against the central land defenses. Germany would be forced to overextend and disperse her strength and use up scarce commodities such as oil. At the same time, presumably, large American forces might also be fighting in the Philippines, which the Army Staff now hoped could be successfully defended.

This venturesomeness did not necessarily indicate that Army planners had abandoned their earlier aversion to risky and expensive logistical commitments. Their aversion was amply demonstrated, even as the Victory Program estimates were reaching completion, in the staff's sharp rejoinders to the estimates of the situation that the British had recently presented at the Atlantic Conference. The

willingness of the staff to contemplate elaborate logistical commitments far from the North American continent was no more than a logical corollary of its conviction that Germany could be defeated only if the full industrial and military power of the United States were hurled against her.

How to project that power with maximum force and minimum cost—with the greatest economy of force—was to a large degree a problem of logistics with which the American staff had not yet come to grips. Speculation on the impending conflict now embraced two distinct though complementary and sequential types of land operations. One, derived from the British strategy of encirclement, involved a large number of relatively small-scale operations, co-ordinated but separate, many of them amphibious assaults on defended shores, exploiting the mobility conferred by sea power in order to keep the enemy stretched thin and off balance. The Army staff during the summer and fall of 1941 drew up outline plans of several such operations, reflecting the strong impression made by German successes in Norway, Crete, Greece, and elsewhere. The characteristic instrument of these operations was the tailor-made task force, organized, trained, and equipped to take a specific objective. Task force operations on the German model called for meticulous, detailed planning and thorough preparations; the "hot-house" training undergone by Rommel's *Afrika Korps* was a frequently cited example.[51]

The other type of operation, in many ways the antithesis of the above, was a

[49] "Ultimate Requirements Study . . . ," cited n. 42(1).

[50] *Ibid.*

[51] (1) Studies in the series WPD 4510. (2) Comments on German operations in "Ultimate Requirements Study . . . ," cited n. 42(1).

frontal assault with maximum force, upon the enemy's main positions in Europe. Such an operation would be attempted only after a long build-up and would be aimed at winning a final decision. Most of the Army staff now felt that the British underestimated the size and weight of forces that would be needed to break into and capture the German citadel. Against the extreme champions of air and naval power, moreover, ground force members of the staff stressed the "almost invariable rule that wars cannot be finally won without the use of land armies."

We must prepare to fight Germany by actually coming to grips with and defeating her ground forces and definitely breaking her will to combat . . . . Air and sea forces will make important contributions, but effective and adequate ground forces must be available to close with and destroy the enemy within his citadel.[52]

It was clear, of course, that the Allied Powers probably could not attain numerical superiority over the Axis, much less the 2-to-1 ratio that traditional doctrine demanded for an attacker. Such a ratio would have required, by current estimates, eight hundred Allied divisions in the European area alone. Army planners were thinking of superiority in weight and fire power, not numbers. Nevertheless, they envisaged massive invading forces—five million American troops to be transported "to European ports"—far larger than those contemplated in current British plans. The Army's Victory Program Troop Basis was shaped to fit this concept.[53]

Shipping costs of the Army's contemplated victory effort were calculated, in the interests of simplicity, in terms of the tonnage that would be required when the effort reached its peak, that is, for the final struggle on the European continent. It was assumed that preliminary operations would be on whatever scale shipping permitted during the period that ship construction was being expanded. In August General Reybold warned that availability of cargo shipping would determine how rapidly American munitions could be moved overseas, and thus probably fix the timing of the offensive phase of Allied strategy; current discussion of forces to be mobilized, he noted, was already running ahead of the probable capacity of shipping two years hence.[54] In September G-4 made a rough calculation of the tonnages involved in overseas deployment on the scale contemplated in the Victory Program. *(See Table 2.)* To move 5 million troops and their equipment across the Atlantic within a period of one year, G-4 estimated, would require about 6.7 million gross tons of shipping; if two years were allowed, only 3.4 million would be needed. Ten and a half million tons would be required to sustain these forces overseas. The total tonnage for a two-year build-up program would thus rise from 3.4 million at the beginning to about 10.5 million tons at the end of the period. Additional tonnages would be absorbed by maintenance of overseas garrisons, essential commercial trades, replacement of both British and American shipping losses, maintenance of the British domestic economy, and shipments of munitions to other Allied forces. The grand total, "ships for victory," came to more than 30 million tons, to carry on

[52] (1) Memo cited n. 8. (2) "Ultimate Requirements Study . . . ," cited n. 42(1).

[53] (1) "Ultimate Requirements Study . . . ," cited n. 42(1). (2) Churchill, in December, spoke of a combined Anglo-American invading force of only 1.5 million. See paper, Churchill for President, "Part I: The Atlantic Front," 16 Dec 41, as quoted in Churchill, *The Grand Alliance,* pp. 646–51.

[54] Memo, unsigned, for WPD, 5 Aug 41, sub: Over-All Pdn Reqmts, WPD 4494 Ult Mun Reqmts, Sec 1.

TABLE 2—ARMY CALCULATIONS OF SHIPPING REQUIREMENTS FOR VICTORY PROGRAM

Requirement	Gross Tons
Essential trades	3,500,000
U.S. forces overseas [a]	10,500,000
Other Allied forces overseas	3,000,000
Navy requirements [b]	600,000
British imports [c]	4,000,000
Expected U.S. losses	3,000,000
Expected British losses [d]	6,000,000
Total requirements	30,600,000
U.S. shipping on hand [e]	6,700,000
Present building program to end of 1943	10,800,000
Additional shipping required	13,100,000

[a] Excludes garrisons in outlying possessions and bases, to be maintained by the regular transport fleets. Assumed turnaround, two months.

[b] Estimated necessary augmentation of Navy's transport fleet which, under current plans, was to absorb the Army fleet also.

[c] For an estimated 15 million weight tons of annual imports.

[d] At the London Conference in September the British asked for 5.5 million gross tons of U.S. shipping by January 1943, largely to replace anticipated losses; this included .5 million tons already under contract to them in American yards. The Army planners rounded this off to 6 million.

[e] One of a number of current estimates.

Source: Table adapted from memo, Stokes for Scoll, 27 Nov 41, sub: Shipg Reqmts of Vic Prog, Plng Div Studies folder, OCT HB.

the kind of war the Army planners had in mind.[55] *(Table 2)*

Between encirclement and frontal assault, between task force operations and massive power drives, the Army staff as yet saw no clear conflict. The American planners, like the British, envisaged preparatory medium-scale operations in peripheral theaters, followed by a large-scale invasion of the Continent. The difference was in emphasis, but it promised sharper disagreement in the future. The Americans still underestimated the logistical problems of the build-up that must precede a successful invasion of Europe, and they did not foresee the extent to which the build-up would be retarded by necessary preliminary offensives around the perimeter of the European fortress and necessary holding operations in the Pacific.

Task force operations were individually costly in training, equipment, shipping, and amphibious paraphernalia. For each operation the entire process of planning, organization, special training, and mounting must be repeated. In a series of such operations there was inevitably a high incidence of haste, waste, and last-minute upsets. The details of preparations were not readily reduced to routine, standardized procedures; each operation, to a large degree, was *sui generis.*

The logistics of a large-scale invasion of

[55] (1) Memo, Col Charles P. Gross for WPD, 9 Sep 41. (2) Memo, Maj Marcus B. Stokes, Jr., for Mr. David E. Scoll, Maritime Comm, 27 Nov 41, sub: Shipg Reqmts of Vic Prog. Both in Plng Div Studies folder, OCT HB. (3) Papers in WPD 4494 Br Vic Prog, especially Annex IV to rpt cited n. 37(1). (4) JB 355, Ser 707, 11 Sep 41, title: JB Est of U.S. Over-All Pdn Reqmts, App. I, in WPD 4494 JB Ests.

Europe promised, on the whole, to be simpler, perhaps cheaper. Even if an amphibious assault should be necessary to gain entry, it would be only a small part of the whole undertaking. Once a beachhead was gained, the whole invading force could pour in with little opposition. Transportation of the invading armies would thus become a massive ferrying operation using conventional rather than amphibious shipping. Large forces organized on a large scale meant low "unit" cost, with economies gained through standardization of organization, equipment, training, and administrative procedures. Logistical plans could be stabilized far in advance. In essence, the logistics of task force operations was retail, that of large-scale invasion wholesale. The argument of economy, all things considered, favored the latter.

Yet economy gave no guarantee of success. A given situation usually dictated short-term solutions within a narrow range of choice, in defiance of long-range plans, and costly in terms of logistics. The war was to provide no clear-cut or fair test of either of the two general methods described above, and even victory was always to leave unanswered the question of whether it might have been bought at a lower cost.

America's Contribution: Weapons or Armies?

The military leaders were all ostensibly in agreement that full participation by the United States was the only means of defeating Hitler; they were not certain, even under this assumption, that the job could be done.[56] There were wide differences, however, in the meanings the staffs attached to the concept of "full participation," the lines of cleavage conforming generally to those that divided the cham-

pions of ground, air, and naval power. Between the first two groups the differences were not deep enough to preclude general agreement on the ultimate requirements for victory, and both Air Forces and Navy leaders endorsed the principle that Germany could be finally defeated only by land armies on the European continent. But the measures and means by which the Navy proposed to put this principle into effect seemed to the Army staff wholly inadequate.

The Navy's position was that,

. . . since the principal strength of the Associated Powers is at present in naval and air categories, the strategy which they should adopt should be based on the effective employment of these forces, and the employment of land forces in regions where Germany cannot exert the full power of her land armies.[57]

This view reflected the Navy's concern over the anticipated shortage of shipping. The Navy Victory Program envisaged that only a million and a half U.S. troops would be deployed overseas (excluding garrisons of outlying possessions and bases), a third of them in Latin America. Massive U.S. naval and air power, supplementing the forces of other nations, would provide the rest of the punch needed to defeat the Axis. In the opinion of the Army staff, this program took an unduly optimistic view of the capabilities of naval and air power, even on the scale the Navy proposed to muster it, and also seemed to

[56] (1) Ltr, SW to President, 3 Sep 41, SW Secret File 1848-a. (2) JB 355, Ser 707, 11 Sep 41, title: JB Est of U.S. Over-All Pdn Reqmts.

[57] (1) JB 355, Ser 707, 11 Sep 41, title: JB Est of U.S. Over-All Pdn Reqmts. (2) For a discussion of the Air Forces program, AWPD/1, see Craven and Cate, *AAF I,* pp. 131–32, 146–47; and Maj Margaret A, Bacchus, "Manpower Planning—the Victory Program," Sec II-C, Pt. I, Ch. IV of Mobilization, Procurement and Allocation of Manpower and Material Means, hist monograph, Hist Sec, JCS.

assume that British and American land armies would be able to invade and conquer Axis Europe in the face of German forces enjoying a 5-to-1 superiority.[58] Naval shipping estimates, moreover, contemplated a more generous provision for continuing normal commerce than did the Army's estimates.[59] Navy planners, in short, evidently contemplated a war calling for something less than a maximum national effort, giving full play to U.S. sea and air power, but relying heavily on foreign manpower and mobilizing only modest U.S. land armies. This program stood in sharp contrast to the Army's conception of an all-out, balanced effort culminating in a major test of strength in central Europe with U.S. land armies playing a leading role.

The inherent conflict between these two conceptions was moving toward a showdown in the autumn of 1941, for the Army's mobilization was approaching a stage where decisions would soon have to be made as to future expansion. At the end of June 1941 the Army's strength had reached 1,455,565, culminating a year of unprecedented peacetime growth, and attaining the manpower goal for the initial PMP force set forth the preceding summer. Five months later, on 7 December, the total strength had risen only to 1,643,477. The Army's primary aim during the last half of 1941 was to complete the training and equipping of this force and to develop it into an efficient fighting machine. In this respect much remained to be done. At the beginning of October only one division, five antiaircraft regiments, and two artillery brigades were considered to be ready for combat; the Air Forces were in even a worse case, with only two bombardment squadrons and three pursuit groups ready. These small, mobile, striking forces, the staff hoped, might possibly be doubled in size by the end of 1941.[60]

To have in readiness forces adequate for hemisphere defense remained the immediate goal, and one still far from realization. The forces available to the Army in October, its spokesmen admitted, were "barely sufficient to defend our military bases and outlying possessions," many of which were still well below their authorized, peacetime, garrison strengths. To oppose any serious invasion of the Western Hemisphere the Army in its present state would be "wholly inadequate." Operations in distant theaters on the scale contemplated in the Victory Program lay far beyond the immediate horizon and might be ruled out altogether by an Axis victory in Europe before the United States was ready.[61]

The United States seemed unlikely to move rapidly toward readiness for a coalition war against the Axis as long as the

---

[58] (1) JB 355, Ser 707, 11 Sep 41, title: JB Est of U.S. Over-All Pdn Reqmts. (2) Memo, CofS for CNO, 10 Sep 41, sub: U.S. Over-All Pdn Reqmts. (3) Memo, Gerow for CofS, 10 Sep 41, same sub. (4) Memo, A.C.W. [Wedemeyer] for Gerow, 9 Sep 41. Last three in WPD 4494-10.

[59] Major differences between Army and Navy shipping estimates in gross tons were:

	Army	Navy
Essential trades............	3,500,000	6,000,000
U.S. forces overseas..........	10,500,000	2,400,000
Other Allied forces overseas...	3,000,000	5,000,000
Additional shipping needed...	13,100,000	9,500,000

See memo, Stokes for Scoll, 27 Nov 41, sub: Shipg Reqmts of Vic Prog, Plng Div Studies folder, OCT HB.

[60] (1) Strength figures are from annual *Report of the Secretary of War, 1941,* Table A; and table, Returns Sec, Misc Div, AGO, in Binder 1, Secret Papers file, GHQ. (2) For training and maneuvers in late 1941, see Greenfield, Palmer, and Wiley, *AGF I,* pp. 40–55. (3)"War Department Strategic Estimate . . . October 1941," WPD 4494-21.

[61] (1) "War Department Strategic Estimate . . . October 1941," WPD 4494-21. (2) For the status of outlying bases and possessions, see Conn and Fairchild, *Framework of Hemisphere Defense,* Ch. VI, p. 32.

country remained technically at peace. Public and Congressional sentiment, in the late summer and fall of 1941, was still far from willing to abandon this status, as was evidenced by the slim one-vote margin in Congress in favor of extending Selective Service, the continuation of the prohibition against sending selectees outside the Western Hemisphere, and the apathetic public response to submarine attacks on American destroyers in September and October. General Marshall himself, perhaps in deference to this sentiment, did not put forward definite plans for immediate substantial expansion of the Army. Plans were afoot, in fact, eventually to retire all the National Guard units, and to replace all selectees and National Guard enlisted men by recruitment, measures that would certainly delay the training program and temporarily disrupt organization somewhat, even though in the long run the Army's strength would not be reduced. Current plans late in 1941 anticipated that ground forces would be expanded by about 10 percent, and General Marshall expected to prepare no more than sixteen divisions for overseas service. When Lt. Gen. Lesley J. McNair, Chief of Staff, GHQ, proposed in October a program for "mass production of trained divisions" on the assumption that the Army, as he said, had as its mission something "more than passive hemispherical defense," the General Staff rejected the plan.[62]

Thus, despite the Army staff's conviction that full participation in the war at an early date was the only effective means of meeting the long-range threat to American security, the building of American armies late in 1941 was slowing down markedly. This trend was accompanied by a definite movement to shape plans for eventual American participation along the lines suggested by the Navy's rather than the Army's Victory Program estimates—with a view to making the United States' contribution to the war, as Walter Lippmann put it in a widely discussed article, one "basically of Navy, Air and manufacturing."[63] There was strong pressure to actually reduce the size of the ground forces in order to make more matériel available for lend-lease, especially to the Soviet Union. And on 22 September, two days after Lippmann's article had appeared, General Marshall was called to the White House to defend the present and planned strength of the Army.[64]

General Marshall's defense was vigorous. He reviewed the strategic concept embodied in the Victory Program estimates (which were to be submitted three days later) and the forces there listed as necessary for defeating Germany. He declared that if the United States remained committed to that policy,

. . . then we must build toward these forces as rapidly as possible. To seize and hold the initiative we must have forces available for employment at the time and place of our own choosing, not Hitler's. Any reduction of our present forces may result in fatal delay. . . . We are already late. We must not abandon present gains and we should push on with unremitting effort. Furthermore, sudden basic changes in policy . . . are devastating to organized effort. The "long view" is essential to our interests. In other words, to shift our national objectives by the reduction of our army at the present time might well be disastrous.[65]

[62] (1) Conn and Fairchild, Framework of Hemisphere Defense, Ch. VI, pp. 29–32. (2) Watson, *Prewar Plans and Preparations*, pp. 358–66.

[63] *New York Herald Tribune*, September 20, 1941, byline Walter Lippmann.

[64] (1) Papers in Tab K, Item 7, Exec 4. (2) Memo, CofS for President, 22 Sep 41, sub: Ground Forces. (3) Related papers. Last two in WPD 4594. (4) Watson, *Prewar Plans and Preparations*, pp. 360–66.

[65] Memo cited n. 64(2).

Reviewing the Army's current plans for overseas garrisons, task forces, and forces in the United States (within the framework of the initial PMP), Marshall reached two conclusions. Any reductions in numerical strength or equipment justified in the light of the immediate situation would not yield significant amounts of matériel of the types most needed by Great Britain and the Soviet Union. Whatever "momentary encouragement" such diversions might give the USSR and Britain "would be far outweighed by the positive indications it would give to the German government that they need not fear an eventual onslaught of ground forces."[66]

Marshall's general impression, on leaving the White House, was that the President at least did not intend to reduce the Army.[67] No further action to that end, in fact, was taken before Pearl Harbor, but until then the Victory Program remained a hypothesis without real influence on either American mobilization or foreign aid. Since midyear, moreover, plans for dividing munitions production between the U.S. Army and foreign claimants had moved steadily toward an early effectuation of the "arsenal" theory of American participation. Under the policy laid down on 22 September, the bulk of the output of American munitions was to have been allotted, beginning in March 1942, to foreign "opponents of force." Even though its minimum training allowances of equipment were expected to be only 70 percent

complete by March 1942, the Army's mobilization, in effect, would then have come abruptly to a halt. Thenceforth, the Army would have shifted over to something like a stand-by status, slowly filling its equipment shortages and perfecting its preparations to protect the hemisphere against an invader. How much of this policy might have survived if the United States had been drawn into a purely European war, instead of a two-front global one, can only be conjectured. Even though aloof, Japan would doubtless have remained a threat, pinning down a large segment of both American and British strength; one and a half million American soldiers, it is safe to say, would hardly have sufficed to secure U.S. positions in the Pacific and also to play an effective role in Europe. On the other hand, the menace of the European Axis alone might not have aroused the United States to mobilize its manpower and resources, particularly the former, on the scale that, in the event, marked this country's participation in the war. On the eve of Pearl Harbor the prospects were that America's contribution to the war would be in weapons, not armies.[68]

---

[66] *Ibid.*

[67] Memo, CofS for Col Robert W. Crawford, 22 Sep 41, WPD 4594.

[68] (1) See above, Ch. IV. (2) In his account of the developments summarized in the foregoing four paragraphs, Watson, *Prewar Plans and Preparations*, pp. 358–66, erroneously infers that steps were actually taken to reduce the ground establishment. See also, Langer and Gleason, *The Undeclared War: 1940–1941*, p. 735.

PART TWO

CRISIS

CHAPTER VI

Pearl Harbor and Early Deployment

The disadvantage imposed upon the United States by Japan's sudden attack in December 1941 went far beyond the actual losses then inflicted. To replace these, from the immense fund of military power ultimately generated by the United States, was a comparatively simple matter. But the attack, in its immediate impact, was temporarily crippling and helped the enemy to gain positions from which he could be dislodged only at massive cost over nearly four years of war. The most fundamental gain for Japan and her European partners was the loss of equilibrium suffered by the United States. U.S. national policy had accepted in advance the disadvantage of conceding to the enemy the first blow, and had counted on the compensatory effect of extensive mobilization beforehand while potential allies held potential enemies at bay. To the achievements of prewar mobilization the United States in the long run owed her salvation, but they did little to mitigate the shock of the enemy's first blow. Germany, not Japan, had been expected until very late in 1941 to strike that blow, and the daring attack on Pearl Harbor, the main U.S. base in the Pacific, in conjunction with the anticipated offensive of the Japanese to the south, had scarcely been foreseen at all. The United States thus found its lines of communications in the Pacific jeopardized beyond its worst expectations, while those in the Atlantic and the Caribbean soon proved dangerously vulnerable. The logistics of initial military action, as anticipated in prewar plans, was thus thrown off balance; virtually every previously planned movement of forces had to be modified or abandoned. Beyond this initial impact, the Japanese attack disrupted the timetable of American strategy and, for upwards of seven months, threw the weight of the Army's effort in a direction markedly different from that planned. The basic eastward orientation of strategy remained a long-range goal, but the actual development of the military situation held out little assurance that it could be put into effect. As a consequence, the whole program of logistical preparations supporting that strategy was in some measure disrupted. National policy, in short, by yielding the initiative to the enemy, laid a heavy burden upon the logistical staffs in December 1941.

Throughout the U.S. military structure the shock of war was violent. There was a vast surge of activity, both confused and purposeful, a fever of organization and reorganization, and, most visibly of course, an unprecedented expansion. In the Joint Chiefs of Staff (JCS) system, created during the early months of 1942, the Army and Navy fashioned the nucleus of a committee machinery for co-ordinating the planning and direction of American military operations, and also established the principle of unified command for all military operations employing both Army and Navy forces. The service departments themselves found it necessary to make internal structural adjustments. On the Army side the reorganization, accomplished in March 1942, was far reaching, creating among other things new machinery for logistical planning and direction. and centering control of the Army's vast logistical operations in the United States in a new command, the Services of Supply (SOS).[1]

Pearl Harbor plunged the United States into a coalition war. Toward the end of December 1941 Prime Minister Churchill arrived in Washington accompanied by his principal civilian and military planners. At the ARCADIA Conference, which followed, the Anglo-American alliance was cemented and an effort was made to formulate a broad strategy and to create an organization to guide the common endeavor. The organization that emerged was the Combined Chiefs of Staff (CCS) system, generally paralleling the JCS committee system and designed to coordinate Allied strategy and the allocation of munitions, shipping, and other resources.[2] In the realm of strategy, the ARCADIA Conference confirmed the tentative agreements reached at the ABC meetings of February–March 1941 that the principal effort of the Anglo-American coalition should be concentrated on defeating Germany. In the Pacific the Allies agreed to remain on the defensive and try to hold Japan to limited gains. But as Japan, during the winter and spring of 1942, relentlessly continued to exploit the advantages of surprise and of her opponents' unreadiness, the Allied high command found itself driven to using its meager resources piecemeal in a desperate effort to avert catastrophic losses in the Pacific. Until the situation could be stabilized somewhat in this quarter, no long-range strategic plan could remain firm, and the effort to mobilize and deploy forces against the European Axis came almost to a standstill.

The Impact of Pearl Harbor

The Japanese attack caught the U.S. Army about three months short of completing what had been planned as the most intensive phase of its rearmament—roughly definable as the three-quarters arming of the initial Protective Mobilization Plan force (increased to 1.8 million men the preceding summer). Production of munitions had made great strides during the second half of 1941, but generally had fallen short of expectations. Only moderate increases over the output of the preceding six months had been made, for example, in heavy field artillery pieces and ammunition, small arms ammunition, and trucks; antiaircraft artillery production had actually declined.[3] A hasty survey soon after Pearl Harbor indicated that by the end of March 1942 a more or less balanced force of sixteen divisions—about half the initial PMP force—could be put in the field by various expedients and, in addition, overseas garrisons could be outfitted at war strength, with most of their basic equipment but with very slim allowances of certain key

---

[1] See below, Chs. VIII–IX.
[2] See below, Chs. IX–X.
[3] See below, App. B.

items, above all, ammunition. By spreading matériel even more thinly, the entire initial PMP force might be equipped in some fashion within the same time. Yet these deficiencies, for forces that might soon have to face a powerful enemy overseas, could scarcely be regarded as other than crippling.

One bottleneck created another. The 3-inch self-propelled antitank gun, which would be in critical supply for months, could be replaced in an emergency by the 75-mm. gun; but ammunition for the latter was short, and in all types of artillery, fire control equipment was even shorter. This last shortage was expected to prevent arming the initial PMP force with heavy antiaircraft weapons until some time in 1943. Enough medium tanks were in prospect for the armored forces, but 75-mm. tank guns remained a choke point.

Ammunition was the immediate and pervasive shortage—especially .50-caliber and 37-mm. armor-piercing ammunition, without which tanks could not operate, and without which there could be no defense against tanks. Production of .50-caliber was not expected to improve until midyear, 37-mm. and 75-mm. somewhat earlier. Ammunition stocks for 60-mm. and 81-mm. mortars were practically nonexistent in the United States, and the production outlook was not hopeful.

Any precise estimate of preparedness in terms of divisions ready for combat was difficult to make. For lack of ammunition in major categories, only a single division and a single antiaircraft regiment could be made available on a full war footing for overseas service, although three divisions were reasonably well equipped and five were more or less well trained. Supply, in general, would catch up with the progress of training by February 1942, permitting eight divisions, trained and equipped with bare essentials, to take the field, but still only two of these divisions would have enough ammunition to risk combat. Two months later, supply and training would again be out of balance, with sixteen divisions trained but only thirteen adequately equipped and supplied with ammunition for full-scale operations. Even these estimates of availability of forces in the near future, Brig. Gen. Brehon B. Somervell, the new G-4, warned, were "on the optimistic side."[4] They presupposed an immediate acceleration of production and an overriding priority for U.S. forces over other claimants—in other words, an immediate cessation of lend-lease deliveries.

Even if more divisions had been ready for combat, most of them would have had to remain in the United States. As of 10 December, troop transports available in port were sufficient to move about 14,000 on the west coast and 5,700 on the east coast. By April, monthly embarkations of perhaps 46,000 across the Atlantic, 31,000 or less across the Pacific, might be undertaken.[5] The shortage of shipping, together with the shortage of ready divisions, predetermined the form that overseas deployment was to take during the next few weeks—a piecemeal movement of miscellaneous small units, mainly of supporting combat and service types.

It was not easy, immediately after 7 December 1941, to decide how the available small forces could be most effectively

[4] Memo, G-4 for DCofS, 21 Dec 41, sub: Equip for Combat Units, with atchd papers, Item 14, Exec 4.

[5] (1) Memo, Gross for Somervell, 10 Dec 41, sub: Shipg Sit As It Affects the Army, Plng Div Studies folder, OCT HB. (2) For an analysis of the shipping shortage in all its aspects, see below, Ch. VIII. (3) See also the markedly different estimate made later in December, p. 153.

disposed to meet the immediate threat. RAINBOW 5, the only war plan now applicable, was still in effect, but each scheduled movement had to be considered on its merits, and the worsening situation in the Pacific was soon to invalidate the whole schedule. On the west coast aircraft factories were almost defenseless against air raids, and during the jittery mid-December period there were numerous reports of actual enemy task forces hovering off the coast from Alaska to the Panama Canal. In Hawaii, those naval installations that were somehow passed over by the Japanese attack lay open to a second onslaught which, if it came, would have to be met by ground forces with very little air and naval support. General Short, the commander in Hawaii, was clamoring for troops, planes, bombs, and ammunition. The Panama Canal, hardly more strongly fortified than Hawaii had been, seemed a logical next objective for Japan, since the Pacific Fleet was crippled. Alaska, while less inviting, was even more vulnerable. And to the distant Philippines, soon to be cut off from help, General Marshall on 7 December sent assurance of "every possible assistance within our power," thus adding another large commitment to the Army's already overwhelming burdens.[6]

At the emergency meetings of the Joint Board on 8 and 9 December, Army and Navy leaders agreed, however, that immediate reinforcement of the Philippines was probably out of the question. The Navy placed the primary emphasis on reinforcing Hawaii. Admiral Stark urged immediate shipment of all available antiaircraft artillery there, even at the cost of denuding continental installations, and spoke of reinforcements on the scale of 100,000 troops and 500,000 gross tons of shipping. But the Navy admitted at the

same time that, with the Pacific Fleet immobilized, it could guarantee neither adequate naval protection for Hawaii nor coverage for the movement of troops and material across the Pacific. General Marshall questioned the wisdom of risking everything on defending Hawaii, which might be isolated in any case, while available equipment and ammunition were inadequate even for the defense of west coast installations and the Canal.[7]

During December, therefore, though placing major emphasis on deployment to Hawaii, the Army also moved substantial reinforcements and material to Panama, the west coast, Alaska, and the North Atlantic bases, including Iceland. Troop movements to Hawaii and Panama accounted for the great bulk of overseas deployment during December, while the cargo movements to these points were well over half the total shipped from the United States. Reinforcement of the Canal was virtually completed by the end of January, by which time some sixteen thousand troops together with bombers, pursuit planes, and air-warning equipment had been sent there. Other bases in the Caribbean and Alaska received a steady flow of troops and material through the winter and early spring.[8]

The shipments to Hawaii were made in an atmosphere of extreme urgency. Responding promptly to General Short's pleas, the War Department by the morn-

---

[6] (1) Msg 736, Marshall to MacArthur, 7 Dec 41, WPD 4544-20. (2) Matloff and Snell, *Strategic Planning: 1941-1942*, pp. 78–96. (3) For the state of Hawaii's defenses before and after 7 December, see Watson, *Prewar Plans and Preparations*, pp. 474–75.

[7] (1) Memo, CNO for CofS, 11 Dec 41, sub: Dangerous Strategic Sit in Pac Ocean, Item 4, Exec 10. (2) Memo, CofS for CNO, 12 Dec 41, sub: Def of Oahu, WPD 4544-29.

[8] (1) See below, App. E. (2) For deployment of air forces, see Craven and Cate, *AAF I,* Ch. VII.

ing of 12 December had set up seven thousand troops and most of the material requested on highest priority for shipment by the earliest transport available, and arrangements were made to fly out twenty-seven heavy bombers. On that day there were five freighters and eleven troop transports in San Francisco Harbor, including five transports that had returned safely since the 7th. Two, possibly three, of the transports were earmarked to carry the troops, due to sail in convoy about the 16th or 17th. About half the bulk cargo, it appeared, could also be dispatched at an early date.[9]

At San Francisco the Army port authorities estimated that, by strenuous efforts, the two fastest transports—*Matsonia* and *Monterey*—could be loaded with troops, pursuit aircraft, and some small arms ammunition in time to sail on the night of the 13th. To Somervell and Marshall it seemed worth the risk to waive convoy and let the transports make a dash to Honolulu without escort. Orders were given to push the loading and the matter was put to the Navy, which proved unalterably opposed to unescorted convoys and, at least in the eyes of General Somervell and General Gerow, seemed remarkably unconcerned about the Army's desire for speed. Tempers were frayed, and sharp words were exchanged, but the Navy refused to yield. Three fast transports—*Matsonia, Monterey* and *Lurline*—sailed on the 16th, under convoy as the Navy had insisted. Not until the end of January were troopships allowed to sail the Central Pacific without escort.[10]

On 17 December two more troop transports—*Bliss* and *Garfield*—left San Francisco for Hawaii with troops, planes, and other supplies. On the 27th, after the Chief of Staff had approved further rein-

forcements of one division, two antiaircraft regiments, and about ten thousand service troops, another large troop and cargo convoy sailed for Hawaii, the last of the year. By the end of December total shipments of material to Hawaii amounted to 77,756 measurement tons; troop reinforcements totaled about 15,000.[11]

Meanwhile, second thoughts were being given to Hawaii's position and to the possibilities of a Japanese landing on the U.S. west coast. The danger, on the whole, seemed to be waning. Even on the 15th, General Short had acknowledged that few of the reports of enemy parachutists, air reconnaissance, mysterious flares, suddenly surfacing submarines, and the like could be verified. Short thought there was little indication of an enemy intent to attempt a landing. On the 24th the Anglo-American Chiefs of Staff in Washington, discussing the possibility of an enemy attack on the U.S. west coast, concluded that while sporadic naval and air attacks,

---

[9] (1) Msg, CG HD to TAG, 14 Dec 41, G-4/33822. (2) Msg, CG HD to CofS, 8 Dec 41, AG 381 (11-27-41) Far Eastern Sit, Sec 1. (3) Memo, Exec Off G-4 for Br Chiefs, 10 Dec 41, sub: Proposed Reinf for Hawaii, Convoys folder, OCT HB. (4) Rpt, no date, sub: Shipg Sit at SFPOE Following Pearl Harbor, OCT HB.

[10] (1) Disposition form, WPD to G-4, 11 Dec 41, sub: Reinf for Hawaii. (2) Msg, G-4 to CG SFPOE, 11 Dec 41. (3) Disposition form, G-4 to CG HD, 18 Dec 41, sub: Units and Cargo To Be Shipped on *Matsonia, Monterey,* and *Lurline.* All in G-4/33822. (4) Memo, G-4 for CofS, 12 Dec 41, sub: Lack of Effort of Navy To Speed Up Dispatch of 21-Knot Convoy to COPPER [Territory of Hawaii], Convoys folder, OCT HB. (5) Corresp in WPD 4622-12; WPD 4622-39; and WPD 3444-14.

[11] (1) Memo, G-4 for DCofS, 16 Dec 41, sub: Water Mvmts to COPPER and "X," G-4/33817. (2) See Ship Charts and Logs, Atlantic and Pac folders, G-4/33700. (3) Rpt cited n. 9(4). (4) Memo, G-4 for CofS, 24 Dec 41, sub: Shipts to COPPER and "X,".G-4/33822. (5) Matloff and Snell, Strategic Planning for Coalition Warfare: 1941–1942, original draft chapter, "Reaction to Pearl Harbor," pp. 28–30, OCMH. (6) See below, App. E.

THE TROOP TRANSPORT SS *MONTEREY at San Francisco, January 1942.*

or even a hit-and-run raid involving landings, were within Japan's capabilities, any large amphibious operations in the eastern Pacific were unlikely. The most telling argument was the obvious southward focus of Japanese operations toward the Malay Archipelago; it seemed less and less probable, during the last days of 1941, that the admittedly weak defenses of Hawaii would soon be tested. The decisions on grand strategy reached by the Allied leaders at the end of the year, while stressing the vital role of the Alaska-Hawaii-Panama triangle to hemisphere defense, pointed out also that a major Japanese invasion of the United States was unlikely in any event.[12]

Independently of these discussions, the War Department had first lengthened the schedule of shipments to Hawaii and then, on the 24th, assigned to movements later than the 27 December convoy a priority lower than that for Australia and the Philippines. By the end of December the crisis atmosphere surrounding shipments to Hawaii had disappeared, and the focus of strategy had shifted away from the Central Pacific to the main theater far to the

---

[12] (1) Msgs, CG HD to TAG, 15, 18, and 19 Dec 41, AG 381 (11-27-41) Far Eastern Sit, Sec 1. (2) Annex 2, Probable Maximum Scale of Enemy Attack on West Coast of North America, to min, ABC-4 JCCSs-1, 24 Dec 41. (3) ABC-4/CS-1, Memo, U.S. and Br CsofS, 31 Dec 41, title: American-Br Grand Strategy.

west and to the intervening lines of communications.[13]

The Far East and the Pacific Line of Communications

The determination of the President and General Marshall that everything possible must be done to help General MacArthur's forces, however forlorn the hope, set in train a series of steps that rapidly reversed the Joint Board's initial decision (largely Navy-inspired) to write off the Philippines and concentrate all available strength for the defense of the Central Pacific. On 15 December General Marshall renewed his assurances of support to MacArthur and two days later approved a plan submitted by his new staff adviser on Far Eastern matters, Brig. Gen. Dwight D. Eisenhower, for establishing a base in Australia to support the Philippines.[14]

Meanwhile, a convoy of seven ships, carrying troops, ammunition, crated aircraft, and other material and escorted by the cruiser *Pensacola,* had been at sea Manila-bound since early in December. On the 8th the Joint Board, at the Navy's urging, ordered the convoy to return to Honolulu. But on the next day, the President having intervened, the Joint Board reversed itself and directed the convoy to proceed to Brisbane, Australia. Brig. Gen. Julian F. Barnes, senior officer aboard the convoy, was ordered to place himself and his forty-five hundred troops at General MacArthur's disposal and to make every effort to get the convoy's cargo, especially the aircraft, to the Philippines. Four other cargo vessels, also at sea on the 7th, were diverted to Australia.[15]

"Task Force, South Pacific," as Barnes entitled his command, made its uneasy way to Brisbane where it arrived safely on the 22d. Before its arrival the base, of which the task force was to be the nucleus, was placed under the command of Maj. Gen. George H. Brett, senior American Air officer in the Far East. By the 22d, the earlier emphasis upon forwarding fighter aircraft and supplies at once to the Philippines was yielding under the pressure of Japanese conquests to a broader plan for a substantial base capable of supporting extended air operations. On the 24th the War Department informed General Douglas MacArthur that, in view of the probable impossibility of staging fighter aircraft to Luzon and the impending loss of airfields there, its aim was to develop "a strong United States air power in the Far East based on Australia."[16]

An almost necessary corollary to this program was that American air power would be fitted into the scheme of Allied resistance to Japan then being hastily organized. Of the nine air combat groups allocated to the southwestern Pacific during the last week of December, three were assigned to help in the defense of the Netherlands Indies. At the end of December the Australian-British-Dutch-American (ABDA) Command, under General Wavell, was created, and in it were placed

---

[13] (1) Memos, Exec Off G-4 for Br Chiefs, 25 and 26 Dec 41, subs: Reinf for COPPER, G-4/33822. (2) Matloff and Snell, *Strategic Planning: 1941-1942,* pp. 78–87.

[14] (1) Msg 787, Marshall to MacArthur, 15 Dec 41, WPD 4544-31. (2) Memo, WPD for CofS, 17 Dec 41, sub: Plan for Australian Base, WPD 4628-1.

[15] (1) Matloff and Snell, *Strategic Planning: 1941-1942,* pp. 78–96. (2) Elizabeth Bingham and Richard M. Leighton, Development of the United States Supply Base in Australia, ASF hist monograph, OCMH.

[16] (1) Msg, Marshall to MacArthur, 24 Dec 41, WPD 3633-27. (2) For movement of the *Pensacola* convoy, see draft of Samuel Milner, Victory in Papua, a volume in preparation for the series UNITED STATES ARMY IN WORLD WAR II, Ch. I; Morton, *Fall of the Philippines,* Ch. V; and Bingham and Leighton monograph cited n. 15(2).

all Allied forces operating in the Netherlands Indies, Malaya, Burma, and, at least formally, the Philippines. The U.S. supply base in Australia, now U.S. Army Forces in Australia (USAFIA), was not included in the ABDA Command, but its supply mission was broadened to include support of operations in the ABDA area as well as in the Philippines.[17]

The program of building "overwhelming air power," as the purpose was described to General MacArthur at the beginning of January, faced terrific obstacles from the beginning.[18] The Air Forces hoped to deliver heavy bombers to the Far East via Cairo at the rate of three a day beginning about 5 January, but fighter aircraft, ground crews, and material needed to operate an air force had to move by ship in driblets across the Pacific. The flow began with the diversion to Australia of one of the three transports (*Polk*) scheduled to sail in the second convoy to Hawaii. This ship, two freighters, and a tanker departed before the end of the year, carrying aircraft, ammunition, gasoline, subsistence, vehicles, and other cargo. In all some 230 pursuit planes, besides the 17 in the *Pensacola* convoy, were shipped to Australia between 7 December and the end of the year. Innumerable obstacles stood in the way of getting these airplanes into action and forwarding supplies to either the Philippines or Netherlands Indies. A basic step had been taken with the decision to establish an Australian base, and from late December on its development began to profit by the shift from the initial emphasis upon reinforcing Hawaii and Panama.[19]

It was an inescapable corollary of this decision that the long island chain of communications through the South Pacific to the subcontinent must also be secured.

The Japanese attack caught the United States in the early stages of developing air ferry routes between Hawaii and the Philippines. In the critical area between Hawaii and Australia the total American assets consisted of embryonic air stations at Midway and Wake; engineer detachments constructing airfields on Christmas and Canton Islands; incomplete naval air facilities at Palmyra and Johnston Islands; a minor fueling and communications center, then in process of expansion, at Pago Pago Harbor in Samoa; and Guam, the "Gibraltar of the Pacific," devoid of facilities. With the possible exception of Midway, none of these American bases had anything remotely resembling an adequate defense force. Outside the American orbit, a single company of Australians garrisoned New Caledonia. The entire Fijis group, 250 islands, was defended by less than eight thousand New Zealand troops with only twenty-two planes.[20]

[17] (1) Matloff and Snell, *Strategic Planning: 1941-1942*, Ch. VI and pp. 170–71. (2) Memo, WPD for TAG, 12 Jan 42, sub: Instns to Maj Gen Lewis H. Brereton . . . , WPD 4628-20. (3) See below, Ch. VII.
General MacArthur, under special arrangements, continued to report directly to Washington.
[18] Msg, Marshall to MacArthur, 2 Jan 42, Msg 5 file, Case 17, WPD.
[19] (1) For air operations in the Far East during December and January, see Craven and Cate, *AAF I*, Chs. VI, X–XII. (2) Matloff and Snell, *Strategic Planning: 1941-1942*, pp. 78–96. (3) Memo, unsigned, for CofS, 17 Dec 41, CofS WDGS Mar–Jun 42 folder, Hq ASF. (4) Memo, A-4 for G-4, 27 Dec 41, sub: Summary of Aircraft, G-4/33861. (5) Other corresp in same file. (6) Memo, Gross for Somervell, 25 Dec 41, sub: Sailing of Trans . . . , G-4/33817. (7) Establishing a Supply Base in Australia, draft MS, OCT HB.
[20] (1) Morison, *Rising Sun*, pp. 184, 228, 250, 258. (2) ABC-4/8, Rpt, JPC to CsofS, 10 Jan 42, title: Def of Island Bases Between Hawaii and Australia. (3) Msg, Short to Arnold, 12 Dec 41, AG 381 (11-27-41) Far Eastern Sit, Gen. (4) Memo, Asst Exec Off G-4 for Br Chiefs, 1 Jan 42, G-4/33822.

Guam fell on 11 December, Wake on the 23d; Midway was attacked by a Japanese task force; the enemy came within striking distance of Canton and Palmyra; Johnston and Samoa were shelled by submarines. In the few days immediately following the outbreak of hostilities, the War Department had grave doubts as to the feasibility of attempting to hold the Central Pacific at all, and until the end of December only passing attention was given to reinforcing and developing the island chain. General Short did what little he could to bolster the defenses of Canton and Christmas from the slender resources of the Hawaiian Department. With the shift of emphasis to the far Pacific at the end of December, the line of communications gained a new strategic and logistical importance. In the grand strategy laid down at the ARCADIA Conference on 31 December, the security of the main air and sea routes in the Pacific was listed as an essential part of the 1942 program. Shortly thereafter the Anglo-American planners, in a report approved near the end of the conference, assigned to the United States responsibility for defense of Palmyra, Christmas, Canton, American Samoa, and Bora Bora—tne last a small island in the Society group, which lay to the southeast of the principal chain and which was under Free French control. New Zealand was to provide most of the garrison for the Fijis, supplemented by air units and supplies from the United States and Britain. New Caledonia was held to be within the Australian sphere of responsibility, but since Australia could not for many months spare troops to reinforce the single ill-equipped company occupying the island, the United States was also to undertake to strengthen this garrison immediately.[21]

These requirements placed new demands upon the slender pool of available troop units, supplies, and shipping. Even before the planners reported, the War Department had set up shipments to reinforce the garrisons on Christmas and Canton, and a task force of about four thousand troops was being prepared to establish a naval fueling station on Bora Bora. An AAF pursuit squadron was dispatched to the Fijis, and a much larger task force was under preparation for New Caledonia. Meanwhile, the Navy went ahead with plans to reinforce Palmyra, Johnston, and American Samoa.[22]

Plans and Deployment in the Atlantic

Despite the dangerous situation in the Pacific, the President and General Marshall still considered the aims of RAINBOW 5 in the Atlantic valid. The first post-M-Day movements overseas, under RAINBOW 5, were to have taken place mainly in the North Atlantic, with the aim of securing sea communications with the United Kingdom and relieving British forces for service in more active theaters. Before the Prime Minister and the British military chiefs arrived in Washington on the 22d for the ARCADIA meetings, the Army was already setting up forces to relieve the British in Northern Ireland and others to relieve the U.S. Marine brigade in Iceland. These decisions were confirmed during the first meeting between the President and the Prime Minister on the 23d. Movement of forces to England and Scotland, it was understood, would have to be de-

[21] (1) Min, ABC-4 JCCSs-7, 31 Dec 41. (2) ABC-4/CS-1 cited n. 12(3). (3) ABC-4/8 cited n. 20(2). (4) Morison, *Rising Sun*, p. 259. (5) Msg, CG HD to TAG, 12 Dec 41, AG 381 (11-27-41) Far Eastern Sit, Sec 1. (6) Related corresp in same file.
[22] Matloff and Snell, *Strategic Planning: 1941-1942*, pp. 114-19.

layed. As for the various South Atlantic moves contemplated during 1941, the American planners were now more dubious. The British raised the question, on the 24th at the first meeting of the military leaders, of occupying the Azores and the Canaries (for which latter project they already had a small force and shipping ready), and neutralizing the Cape Verdes. Admiral Ernest J. King's comment was, "we cannot do all these things," [23] and the matter was left for further study. The Americans were also fearful of the possible consequences of sending forces to Brazil, where the political situation was touchy. Definite steps were already in progress, however, to occupy Curaçao and Aruba, as provided under RAINBOW 5.[24]

The British had a more daring undertaking in view—the Allied occupation of northwest Africa (GYMNAST)—which Churchill had put forward the summer preceding. The Prime Minister renewed his proposal at the White House conference on 23 December. For the entry into Algeria the British had a force of fifty-five thousand troops, with shipping, ready to move in the event the Eighth Army succeeded in pushing Rommel back to the Tunisian border. If that happened, the French authorities in North Africa might be persuaded to invite an Allied occupation. Churchill wanted the Americans to undertake the occupation of French Morocco, landing in the Casablanca area, while the British moved into Algeria and Tunisia. The whole plan, it was emphasized, hinged on a friendly reception by the French.[25]

Most of the American planners were cool to this scheme, despite the interest it obviously awakened in the President. One WPD officer, Col. Matthew B. Ridgway, pointed to the "difficulties of troop move-

ment and logistical support by sea," in view of the shipping shortage and the nearness of German forces to the target area.[26] Available U.S. forces were absolutely unprepared, from the standpoint of training and equipment, to undertake an amphibious operation against a hostile shore. Some of the American planners, moreover, challenged the British estimate of the strategic value of North Africa to the Allies, regarding it rather as a "subsidiary" area peripheral to the main theater, which even if captured would contribute only indirectly to the defeat of Germany. The Army did have plans and preparations afoot for an expedition against Dakar to occupy French West Africa, and Maj. Gen. Joseph W. Stilwell was ordered to Washington immediately after Pearl Harbor to take charge of the planning. This operation, conceived with a view to securing the Atlantic sea lanes, was eventually abandoned.[27]

Most of the argument over GYMNAST seemed academic, before the end of December 1941, in the face of the shipping shortage. A subcommittee set up by the British-American planners, with General

[23] Min, ABC-4 JCCSs-1, 24 Dec 41.

[24] (1) Notes, SW, sub: Memo of Decisions at White House, Sunday December 21, 1941, WDCSA 381 (12-21-41). (2) Notes, G. C. M. [Marshall], 23 Dec 41, sub: Notes on Mtg at White House With President and Br Prime Minister Presiding, WPD 4402-136. (3) Min cited n. 23. (4) Matloff and Snell, *Strategic Planning: 1941-1942*, Ch. V. (5) Watson, *Prewar Plans and Preparations*, pp. 491–92.

[25] (1) Paper, Churchill for President, "Part I: The Atlantic Front," 16 Dec 41, as quoted in Churchill, *The Grand Alliance*, pp. 646–51. (2) Notes cited n. 24(2).

[26] Memo, Ridgway for Marshall, 23 Dec 41, Tab Misc, Bk. 1, Exec 8.

[27] (1) Memo, Gen Embick, no addressee, no date, sub: Notes on Est of Br CsofS, separate folder, Item 13, Exec 4. (2) Notes cited n. 24(2). (3) Draft study, no date, title: Decline of the SUPER-GYMNAST Concept, OPD Hist Unit File.

Somervell and Col. Charles P. Gross representing the Army, presented an array of figures on the 26th that pointed inescapably to the conclusion that if GYMNAST were attempted, no other major movements could be carried out in the Atlantic until spring, at least. The limitation was in troop-carrying shipping. Somervell's staff had to reckon on a number of movements already ordered or in progress—to Hawaii and Panama, Australia, Alaska, Curaçao and Aruba, and Iceland. Beyond these undertakings and the maintenance of other existing garrisons, there was enough American troop shipping in the Atlantic to lift a total of about 25,000 troops by mid-January, 43,000 by 1 February, 58,000 by 1 March, and 83,000 by 1 April. A smaller capacity was available in the Pacific, but could not be transferred to the Atlantic in so short a period. These figures stood for something like a maximum effort. Losses were estimated at a low level; transfers to Britain and assignment of more ships to lend-lease during the three months in question were ruled out. A number of the regular services, currently operating, would be interrupted. No help could be expected from the British, who would be hard pressed to mount their own part of the undertaking.[28]

The planners, meanwhile, had gone ahead and studied some of the other logistical problems involved. A mass of more or less fragmentary information, dating back to the 1941 plans, offered little encouragement. The Atlantic coast line of North Africa for most of its length, the prevailing weather, the ground swell, and the tide were all unfavorable for amphibious landings. Limited port facilities and road and rail communications indicated that the main landing on the Atlantic coast would have to be made at Casablanca, with smaller ones at Fedala, Safi, Rabat, and Port-Lyautey. Casablanca was a large modern port, but hardly sufficient alone to permit a rapid build-up of forces ashore. The target area was hemmed in by the Atlas Mountains on the east and El Rif mountains to the north. From Casablanca the railroad, with a highway closely parallelling it, stretched with very few branch lines for over fourteen hundred miles to Tunis, exposed most of the way to attack from the north. At the end of December the American planners decided that much larger forces than the British had contemplated would be required, and on 4 January the Joint Planning Committee conceded that "it will be impracticable in the near future to capture French North Africa if important resistance is encountered."[29] On New Year's Day, meanwhile, the President and the Prime Minister had approved the measures already in train to carry out the relief of British forces in Northern Ireland and, eventually, both the U.S. Marines and the British in Iceland. On the 4th, following the planners' report on GYMNAST, they confirmed this decision. The first North Atlantic movements were set up for the 15th—about 14,000 troops for Northern Ireland (MAGNET) and 6,000 for Iceland (INDIGO).[30]

---

[28] Memo, Subcom for Allied JPC, 26 Dec 41, sub: U.S. Shipg Capacity To Carry Trs Overseas, G-4/29717-116.

[29] Memo, Rear Adm Richmond K. Turner for Adms Stark and King, 4 Jan 42, sub: Status of Work Before CsofS and JPC, with JCCSs-7 in ABC 337 ARCADIA (12-24-41), 2.

[30] (1) ABC-4/2, Rpt, JPC to CsofS, 25 Dec 41, title: NW Africa Project, Item 13, Exec 4. (2) WPD study, no date, title: Occupation of NW Africa, WPD 4510. (3) Conf at White House, 1630, 26 Dec 41. (4) Rcd, mtg at White House, 1830, 1 Jan 42. Last two in WDCSA 334 Mtgs and Confs (1-28-42). (5) Memo, CofS, no addressee, 1 Jan 42, sub: Initial Atlantic Tr Mvmt, WDCSA 381, 1. (6) Jt A&N Dir for MAGNET-INDIGO Mvmt, 4 Jan 42, G-4/33180. (7) Matloff and Snell, *Strategic Planning: 1941-1942*, Ch. V.

GYMNAST remained on the books. It was understood that the loading of the MAGNET-INDIGO convoy could be halted at any time up to 13 January, if circumstances called for immediate execution of the North African expedition. Churchill was anxiously waiting for news of victories in Libya that never came; during the last few days of December, in fact, Rommel had struck back with disconcerting force. Meanwhile, the Prime Minister was as eager as the Americans to get on with the North Atlantic movements, which were tied in intricately with others extending around the world to the Far East. These were more pressing for the moment than GYMNAST, and Churchill had no desire to hold back "real ships from real jobs." He and the President "could talk about the matter again in a few days." [31]

The Search for Shipping for the Far East

Atlantic deployment and the orderly strengthening of Pacific defenses were both disrupted in the middle of January by the march of events in the Far East. During the first week of the new year the Japanese drove swiftly down the last hundred miles of the Malay Peninsula toward Singapore and on 7 January crushed British imperial forces along the Sungei Slim River, the last defensible barrier before the naval base. Since Japanese aircraft had sunk the British capital ships *Prince of Wales* and *Repulse* on 10 December, Allied naval forces could only harass without seriously impeding the flow of enemy troops and material by sea. These events menaced the entire Allied strategy of a prolonged holding action against Japan. On 11 January Admiral Stark urged upon his colleagues the need for "subordinating everything in the immedi-

ate future to the necessity for getting reinforcements quickly" to the Far East, even if the movements to Northern Ireland and Iceland had to be curtailed. [32]

General Marshall immediately pointed out that it was not a question of diverting troops, but one of finding ships. Two convoys had been set up to sail to Australia in January, and despite serious altercations with the Navy over escorts and allotment of troopships, the first convoy sailed as scheduled on the 12th—three troop transports carrying about seventy-five hundred Air Corps and supporting service troops, fifty pursuit planes, and a quantity of assorted ammunition, bombs, and maintenance supplies. Other material was to follow on freighters sailing individually without escort. A smaller convoy was scheduled for the end of the month. But hopes of shipping additional pursuit planes and medium bombers with the mid-January convoy on the Navy's two converted seatrains had been dashed when one was held up for repairs and the Navy claimed the other for its own use. As for troop space, the large luxury liners that the British had already offered would not be available during January. [33] The program

---

[31] (1) Notes on conf at White House, 4 Jan 42, WDCSA 334 Mtgs and Confs (1-28-42). (2) Churchill, *The Grand Alliance*, pp. 684–85.

[32] (1) Min, ABC-4 JCCSs-9, 11 Jan 42. (2) Matloff and Snell, *Strategic Planning: 1941-1942*, Ch. IV.

[33] (1) Memo, Gross for Somervell, 26 Dec 41, sub: Conf With Navy *re* Vessels to "X." (2) Memo, Gross for CG SFPOE, 31 Dec 41, sub: Vessels To Accompany Convoy to "X." Both in G-4/33861. (3) Memo, Gross for Somervell, 2 Jan 42, Pac folder, OCT HB. (4) Rpt cited n. 9(4). (5) Memo, WPD (Navy) for Ship Mvmts Div (Navy), 23 Dec 41, sub: Employment of Kitty Hawk and Hammondsport, G-4/33822.

There were five seatrains (large vessels able to transport whole trains of railroad cars and locomotives); three were still in commercial service. The Army made arrangements late in January to use the latter, and in February the Maritime Commission launched a program to construct fifty of this type of

for building "overwhelming air power" in the Southwest Pacific, as it stood, would require three months. The immediate necessity, as General Marshall pointed out, was to speed up the program—"to accelerate three months' movement into one month, several weeks into two weeks."[34] There was also the necessity for immediately strengthening the island approaches to Australia. On 10 January the British-American planners, in their report on the South Pacific island bases, pointed out that the Japanese were then in a position to strike at New Caledonia and the Fijis at almost any time. From these positions the enemy would be able to cut the flow of troops and material to Australia.[35]

The Army moved rapidly, during early January, to accelerate troop movements as a countermeasure to this threat. Ten thousand men—antiaircraft and service units—were added to the 6,000 Air Corps troops already scheduled for dispatch to Australia. A task force (POPPY Force), consisting of a heavily augmented infantry brigade of 16,000 combat and supporting service troops, was formed to occupy New Caledonia. Five thousand Air Corps and engineer troops for Australia were to form part of the same movement, and 10,000 additional Air Corps troops were set up for later shipment. To explore the possibilities of finding shipping for these movements, the Allied Chiefs of Staff once again called in the shipping experts—General Somervell and his British opposite number, Brigadier Vernon M. C. Napier.[36]

Their report, of which Somervell and his staff were the principal authors, was ready by the 12th. The situation with regard to troop shipping was clear enough and offered little room for choice. Some British troopers, including two or perhaps three of the largest liners, were expected to be available in February, as were several other liners then operating commercially in South American waters. The U.S. Navy's block of combat loaders was then engaged in amphibious training on the Atlantic coast, and hitherto had been considered sacrosanct as far as troop ferrying was concerned. The only sizable pool of shipping otherwise available for the January movement was the MAGNET-INDIGO flotilla, then loading at New York. Somervell offered three plans. One, which could be put into effect by 1 February, contemplated using the Navy's combat loaders and two liners from the South American run. The second would use the liner *Queen Mary* and four of the South American vessels about the middle of February. Since neither of these would meet the time schedule desired, Somervell proposed, as the third alternative, to use most of the MAGNET-INDIGO fleet, along with one other transport, to move 21,800 troops about 20 January. With the remnant of that fleet, along with the British liner *Straithaird*, about 6,500 troops could still be shipped to Northern Ireland and Iceland in the same month. The one serious objection, apart from the reduction in North Atlantic deployment, was that unloading and reloading the shipping would involve much confusion at New York.[37]

Cargo shipping presented a more difficult problem. Distance and the primitive

vessel; these were later converted into passenger vessels. See correspondence in G-4/33822, G-4/29717-26, and G-4/29717-133 files; and Lane, *Ships for Victory*, pp. 145, 618.

[34] Min cited n. 32(1).

[35] (1) *Ibid.* (2) ABC-4/8 cited n. 20(2).

[36] (1) Min cited n. 32(1). (2) Matloff and Snell, *Strategic Planning: 1941-1942*, pp. 114-19.

[37] Memo, G-4 for CofS, 12 Jan 42, sub: Shipg Capabilities To Reinf ABDA Area, G-4/29717-115.

nature of local facilities at most of the Pacific bases made it necessary for troops to take with them abnormally large reserves of supplies and equipment—a heavy drain on cargo space. The shortage of cargo shipping was for the moment more acute than that of troop transport. For movements already scheduled, the Army faced a shortage of twenty-six cargo vessels. Lend-lease shipments, particularly to the USSR and the Middle East, promised to cause a heavy drain on the pool of cargo shipping, as did also imports of raw materials into the United States. Sinkings, as yet unmatched by new construction, had leaped upward with the entrance of the United States into war. (*See Appendix H.*) A few days before Somervell submitted his report, the Maritime Commission announced that the limit had been reached, for the present, in allocations of cargo shipping for military undertakings. This announcement, Somervell warned, meant a probable shortage of one hundred thousand tons of cargo shipping for the original MAGNET-INDIGO convoy, which therefore would not be available for use in the Pacific.[38]

Somervell thought the estimated twenty cargo vessels, one tanker, and special carriers for medium bombers needed to support the POPPY Force movement should be taken from other programs—British lend-lease, strategic materials imports, Soviet aid, the South American services. "The ships are in being. It is assumed that their use to support this endeavor will transcend all other calls and that the President will so direct." [39] Somervell urged further that all other overseas movements be suspended, for the present, except for about 9,000 troops a month to Northern Ireland and the same number to Hawaii. This would make it possible to maintain a steady stream of about 12,000 a month to the Far East.

On the 12th the Allied Chiefs of Staff, with scant discussion, approved the plan to divert most of the MAGNET-INDIGO convoy to the Far East, and reduced the cargo shipping problem to two alternatives (or a combination of the two) —either lend-lease shipments of tanks, vehicles, and aircraft to the Middle East, or Soviet aid would have to be cut. Their own recommendation was that shipments to the Middle East should not be interrupted. The problem was taken up to the White House that same afternoon.[40]

Besides the President and Mr. Churchill, the military chiefs, Lord Beaverbrook, and Harry Hopkins were present. As General Marshall posed the problem, the proposed movement would mean reducing shipments to the USSR over the next four months by 30 percent. The President's first reaction was that "the plan sounded good," but Churchill interjected that the Russians "would undoubtedly be disappointed," and there was some discussion of eliminating the New Caledonia portion of the convoy. At this point Hopkins broke in with the blunt observation that the 30 percent reduction amounted to only seven freighters which, he thought, surely could be found somewhere; it should not be necessary to "hold up General Marshall's plan on this account." This idea took hold and in the end the President ap-

---

[38] (1) Memo, G-4 for CofS, 12 Jan 42, sub: Capacity of Shipg for War Effort Overseas in Early 1942, G-4/29717-116. (2) Related papers in same file and in Shipg 1941–43 folder, Hq ASF.

[39] Memo cited n. 37.

[40] (1) Min, ABC-4 JCCSs-10, 12 Jan 42. (2) Secretary Stimson also wrote the President urging that both Soviet aid and Middle East lend-lease be cut in order to support movements to the Far East. See memo, SW for President, 12 Jan 42, sub: Alloc of Shipg To Reinf Far East, G-4/29717-115.

proved the plan with the remark that, for Soviet requirements, "we will make Beaverbrook and Hopkins find ships." [41]

The MAGNET-INDIGO shipping accordingly was unloaded, and the great POPPY Force convoy sailed from New York late on 22 January—seven vessels carrying about 20,500 troops (including 4,000 service troops bound for Australia) and two months' assorted supplies. A long voyage and an uncertain destination lay ahead. Marshall commented almost three weeks later, "we have constantly in mind the possibility of the New Caledonia force being so badly needed in ABDA or Australia that it might never reach its projected destination." [42]

POPPY Force was the largest movement yet attempted, and its arrangements were complicated. The two-day postponement of the original sailing date resulted from the decision to combine the movement, in order to save escorts, with that of the small Bora Bora force sailing from Charleston a few days later. The heavy organizational impedimenta and much other material were shipped later in unescorted freighters sailing at intervals from the west coast. All ships were routed first to Australia, where they were to await their equipment, unload material (especially aircraft) for forces in Australia, and reload with a view to rapid debarkation and possibly early action in New Caledonia. [43]

These arrangements were sharply criticized. The Navy and even some Army officers were outraged by a distribution of cargo which, even if only one vessel were sunk, would leave some units without any equipment. The President, in Admiral King's presence, demanded from General Marshall an explanation of why the convoy had not been combat loaded directly to New Caledonia, and Brigadier Napier,

the British shipping expert, was unhappy about sending troops into a combat area without their heavy equipment. But under the circumstances, the Army had had little choice. Shortage of cargo shipping and lack of time dictated maximum economy in stowage and use of all available vessels, fast or slow, thus ruling out a single combat-loaded, troop-and-cargo convoy; the New York convoy was out loaded, in fact, between 17 and 23 January, at the same time that the Navy's Atlantic amphibious force, back from maneuvers, was disembarking—a scrambled operation. In any case, the Army did not possess sufficient combat loaders, and there was no time for conversion. A further consideration was the immediate need for aircraft in Australia. In short, the arrangements aimed, as General Marshall explained, at utilizing "to the utmost the available capacity of shipping . . . at the sacrifice of speed"; they seemed "the best way out of a difficult situation." [44]

Though Soviet lend-lease shipments fell

[41] (1) Min of conf at White House, 12 Jan 42, quoted in Sherwood, *Roosevelt and Hopkins,* pp. 460–66. (2) Memo, CofS for WPD, G-3, and G-4, 13 Jan 42, G-4/33983.

[42] (1) Memo, Marshall for Dill, 11 Feb 42, WPD 3718-25. (2) The largest vessel in the convoy was the *Kungsholm,* a recently purchased Swedish liner. See report, NYPOE Statistical Summary, in OCT HB.

[43] (1) Memo, G-4 for CofS, 18 Feb 42, sub: Moving of Trs Directly to New Caledonia, G-4/33888. (2) Related papers in same file. (3) Memo, Gross for CG's NYPOE and SFPOE, 15 Jan 42, sub: Shipt of Equip and Sups Accompanying Mvmt to "X," G-4/33861. (4) See also, Pac folder, OCT HB. (5) Harold Larson, Water Transportation for the U.S. Army 1939–1942, Monograph 5, p. 184, OCT HB. (6) For the Bora Bora movement, see below, Ch. VII.

[44] (1) Memo, Marshall for King, 20 Jan 42, sub: Loading of Trans, OCofS 21359-32. (2) Memo, Marshall for President, 23 Feb 42, OCofS 21381-7. (3) Memo, Lt Col Carter B. Magruder for Br Chiefs G-4, 14 Jan 42, sub: Shipt 6814, Pac folder, OCT HB. (4) Min cited n. 40(1). (5) Study, no date, title: Early Orgn and Activities of Hq USAFIA, OCT HB.

behind schedule in January and February, this could not be laid directly at the door of the POPPY convoy. The burden of providing its cargo shipping seems to have been distributed so widely over time and other programs that it became imperceptible. Indeed, as Admiral Land and Maj. Gen. Brehon B. Somervell admitted, the estimated 30 percent reduction in Soviet lend-lease was suspect to begin with; no man could weigh with precision all the variables that went into that elusive abstraction, "available shipping." [45]

In the plans for February movements to Australia, the large British liners played a prominent part. In the second week of January London tentatively promised the "monsters" *Queen Elizabeth* and *Aquitania* for February sailings from the west coast and the *Queen Mary* for a run early in the month to the Far East from the Atlantic coast via the Cape of Good Hope and the Indian Ocean. The "lesser monsters"— *Mauretania, Île de France,* and *Nieuw Amsterdam*—which the British had been using to ferry troops between South Africa and the Middle East, were to be retained to move Australian and New Zealand divisions back to the Far East. The whole transaction was part of an intricate arrangement by which several British troopers were to be diverted to the U.S. east coast, on their return trip from the Indian Ocean, to transport American troops across the North Atlantic to Northern Ireland and Iceland.[46]

These plans went awry. Delayed for repairs, the *Queen Mary* finally sailed from Boston on 18 February with a full complement of troops on the long eastward voyage to Australia. The *Aquitania* and *Queen Elizabeth* were also held up for repairs and neither sailed in February. The *Aquitania* was later assigned to the Honolulu run be-

cause her unusually deep draft made the anchorages at Australian and intermediate ports hazardous. She left San Francisco on her first trip on 10 March. *Queen Elizabeth* did not reach San Francisco until the middle of March, whence she sailed on the 19th for Sydney. The loss of the two "monsters" for South Pacific movements during February was partially made up by other vessels, temporarily diverted from the Hawaii run. The giant *Normandie,* in New York since late in 1941 being fitted for troop duty, caught fire there on 9 February and was irreparably damaged—a serious loss to Allied overseas deployment during World War II. Troop movements to Australia declined from 25,000 in January to 20,000 in February, but cargo shipments rose from 115,000 to 212,000 measurement tons during the same period, reflecting delayed shipments of equipment and supplies supporting the January troop movements.[47]

Change of Pace in the Atlantic

After a wild scramble of unloading and reloading and shuffling of troop units, the rump MAGNET-INDIGO convoy sailed from

---

[45] (1) See above, n. 41. (2) See also below, Ch. XIX.
[46] (1) See British file, Mvmts Div, OCT HB. (2) See also, Wardlow, *Trans I,* Ch. VI.
The term "monsters" was used loosely, usually with reference to the *Queens,* the *Normandie,* and the *Aquitania;* "lesser monsters" appears less frequently in the records. Gradually both terms lost currency, possibly because British officials in London requested they not be used.
[47] (1) See British file, and *Queen Mary* and *Normandie* folders, OCT HB. (2) Rpt cited n. 9(4). (3) Memo, G-4 for WPD, 5 Feb 42, sub: Shipg Capabilities in Pac, G-4/33992. (4) Roland W. Charles, *Troopships of World War II* (Washington, Army Transportation Assn, 1947). (5) Rpt cited n. 42(2). (6) See below, App. E.

New York on 15 January—four ships crammed with some seven thousand troops. The Northern Ireland contingent amounted to only a quarter of that originally planned, while the Iceland contingent, a little less than three thousand, left the Marine brigade still unrelieved.[48] For a time it looked as though the flow of deployment across the North Atlantic might be resumed in February with full force, using the *Queen Mary*, the old coal-burner *George Washington* (recently in British service but returned as unfit), and other British transports returning from the Indian Ocean. The principal movement was scheduled for about 10 February. But London decided that the *Queen Mary* could not be risked at this time in the dangerous North Atlantic waters, and the old *George Washington* could not be coaxed out of dry dock. Considerable troop capacity remained, but cargo shipping became the main bottleneck. On 25 January the Joint Planning Committee concluded, on the basis of the decision that lend-lease and the nonmilitary programs could not be touched, that the 10 February convoy would have to be abandoned. The newly organized Combined Chiefs of Staff faced the question of whether North Atlantic deployment should be allowed to lapse until the cargo shipping sent to the Far East returned late in May. Once again the heads of state had to render a decision. The President and Mr. Churchill decided on 27 January that the Navy's fleet of combat loaders and specially rigged cargo vessels, hitherto reserved for amphibious training for a possible North African operation, should be used for a single voyage across the North Atlantic. Delayed by difficulties in finding British escort vessels, the convoy of Navy ships and three Army transports left New York

on the night of 18–19 February carrying about fourteen thousand troops.[49]

Throughout the late winter and the spring the cargo shipping shortage remained the most acute problem in North Atlantic deployment. Movement of cargo was further impeded, during January and February, by port congestion at Reykjavík, Iceland. Routing the contingents bound for Iceland raised problems of escorting and added a sizable lap to each transatlantic voyage. Beginning in March cargo shipments to Iceland began to rise as harbor congestion was broken, but the movement of troops to both Iceland and Northern Ireland in March and most of April virtually lapsed. Except for a small shipment of about 4,000 troops to Iceland early in April, no large movement across the North Atlantic occurred until the last day of that month when 19,000 troops embarked.[50]

GYMNAST, meanwhile, remained on the shelf. In mid-January the British Eighth Army's offensive was losing momentum and Rommel receiving reinforcements. On the 14th the Allied chiefs definitely placed the North African operation in a priority below MAGNET and INDIGO and approved a revised version of GYMNAST to be executed whenever the means and opportunity presented. D Day was tentatively set for 25 May, the earliest date that

---

[48] (1) See NYPOE folder, and British file, OCT HB. (2) Papers in Shipg 1941–43, ACofS G-4, and ACofS OPD folders, Hq ASF. (3) Papers in G-4/33940 and G-4/33180. (4) Rpt cited n. 42(2).

[49] (1) Paper, U.S. JPS to CPS, 25 Jan 42, sub: Mvmt of U.S. Trs to N Ireland, with CPS 4 in ABC 370.5 N Ireland (1-22-42). (2) Min, 2d mtg CCS, 27 Jan 42. (3) Rpt cited n. 42(2). (4) See also above, n. 48.

[50] (1) Rpt cited n. 42(2). (2) Corresp in G-4/33180. (3) See also below, Ch. XII.

The last marines left Iceland on 9 March.

EN ROUTE TO NORTHERN IRELAND, *February 1942.*

some 230,000 measurement tons of cargo shipping could return from the far Pacific. An earlier launching date might be managed, if a favorable opportunity should suddenly offer itself, by using the Navy's amphibious shipping. This would be risky since only about 12,000 troops could be moved in these vessels and seven months would be consumed in shuttling less than 100,000 troops to North Africa. Nor would this remedy the shortage of cargo shipping, which could only be found by robbing other undertakings. The decision to use the amphibious shipping for North Atlantic movements in February eliminated all possibility of launching GYMNAST until April, in any case. Late in February, finally, a new study by Somervell indi-

cated that by June the Army's current deployment schedule would completely absorb the cargo shipping available for military use. For the Army to mount GYMNAST with its own resources would mean suspending North Atlantic movements altogether and reducing the reinforcement of the southwestern Pacific and Hawaii to a trickle. There was more shipping to be had, of course; the British and the U.S. Navy held some, and large tonnages were still tied up in commercial services. Fundamental preliminary decisions were required—on strategy, long-range deployment, and allocation of shipping—and in the end the President would probably have to make them. Until then, "planning for a movement such as Super-

QUONSET HUTS IN NORTHERN IRELAND *and newly arrived troops.*

Gymnast must necessarily be nebulous."[51]

Somervell's study provided the clinching arguments that led the chiefs to conclude that GYMNAST would not be "a practical possibility during 1942." On 3 March plans for the operation were formally relegated to an "academic" basis; training and planning continued, but actual resources would now be available for other ventures.[52]

Pressure of Scarcity in Hawaii

Troop deployment to the Central Pacific in January and February 1942 was confined to movement of the garrisons for Christmas and Canton and small reinforcements for Hawaii, a total of about forty-five hundred troops. Though the flow of material was substantially greater than in December, it fell far below the expectations of Lt. Gen. Delos C. Emmons, who

[51] (1) Memo, G-4 for WPD, 14 Feb 42, sub: Shipg for SUPER-GYMNAST, G-4/34025. This was circulated as CPS 2/3, 21 Feb 42. (2) SUPER-GYMNAST—code name given the plan for an Anglo-American invasion of French North Africa, combining U.S. and British plans and often used interchangeably with GYMNAST. (3) Min cited n. 41(1). (4) Memo, Gross for Somervell, 13 Jan 42, sub: Ability To Execute SUPER-GYMNAST, Plng Div Studies folder, OCT HB. (5) ABC-4/2A, Rpt, JPC to CsofS, 13 Jan 42, title: Opn SUPER-GYMNAST. (6) Memo, Somervell for CofS, 13 Jan 42, sub: Shipg Criticism of Jt Rpt to CsofS on SUPER-GYMNAST, G-4/32697-19. (7) Matloff and Snell, *Strategic Planning: 1941-1942*, Ch. V.

[52] (1) CCS 5/2, 3 Mar 42, title: SUPER-GYMNAST. (2) Min, 9th mtg CCS, 3 Mar 42. (3) See also, Craven and Cate, *AAF I*, p. 614.

had relieved General Short as commander of the Hawaiian Department on 17 December.[53] Emmons had seen his department superseded on the priority list first by Australia and then by the ferry islands. On 15 January he sent a bitter message to the War Department in which he complained that shipping was standing idle on the Pacific west coast, awaiting assignment of naval escorts, while thousands of tons of critically needed materials were piled on docks and in warehouses at San Francisco and Los Angeles. His convoys, he declared, were being retarded by slow ships, and valuable cargo space was being wasted by loading low-priority supplies (including a shipment of beer) at the expense of badly needed items.

General Marshall in reply pointed out that there were not enough fast ships to go around, and that slow ones would have to be employed whenever and wherever possible, especially on the short Honolulu run. He denied that there were empty freighters on the west coast. Frequency of shipments, he pointed out, depended in the last analysis upon intertheater priorities and on the Navy's escort policy, both matters over which the War Department could not exercise exclusive control. The order in which items had been shipped had been determined by Emmons' own priorities. Marshall reminded Emmons pointedly of the over-all shortage of shipping and told him his supply agencies must "confine their requests to bare necessities exploiting local resources and facilities to the utmost."[54]

General Emmons' discontent was not allayed. His requests in January included a quantity of sulfanilamide greater than the total capacity of U.S. industry, over thirty-seven thousand of the new Garand rifles to arm the civilian population, and

enough rocket guns (a weapon still under development) to defend fifteen airfields. He approached the Matson Navigation Co. directly in an effort to obtain more ships. Finally, near the end of February, he poured out his troubles to a Mr. William H. Husted, a representative of the War Production Board (WPB) then in Honolulu investigating scrap iron shipments. Husted was so impressed that he sent a long report, sharply critical of the War Department, to his own superiors, which Emmons supplemented by a personal letter to Donald M. Nelson, chairman of the WPB. Emmons gave a copy of Husted's report to Assistant Secretary of War McCloy, who visited the islands in March. Mr. Harold L. Ickes, Secretary of the Interior, meanwhile learned of the report's contents, and passed on to James V. Forrestal, Under Secretary of the Navy, some of Husted's allegations of Army-Navy friction in Hawaii. Thus, before the War Department could act, the matter had become more or less public property within government circles.[55]

The gist of Husted's charges was that the Army supply system had "broken down completely" in Hawaii. Gasoline stocks had fallen to eighteen days' supply; the cement shortage was so acute that

[53] (1) Control Division, ASF, Statistical Review, World War II (Washington, 1946). (2) See also above, Ch. V.
[54] (1) Msg, CofS to CG HD, 16 Jan 42, AG 381 (11-27-41) Far Eastern Sit, Sec 1. General Somervell's draft was more blunt; see Central Pac 1942–44 folder, Hq ASF. (2) Msg, Emmons to TAG, 15 Jan 42, AG 381 (11-27-41) Far Eastern Sit, Sec 1.
[55] (1) Corresp in G-4/33822. (2) Memo, G-4 for CofEngrs, 2 Mar 42. (3) Memo, G-4 for CG HD, 24 Feb 42, sub: Contl of Shipts From W Coast to Hawaii. Last two in G-4/33817. (4) Rpt, Husted to Mr. E. A. Locke, Jr., 4 Mar 42, sub: Honolulu and Critical Shortages, filed with most of the related corresp in Hawaiian Sup Sit envelope, Plng Div ASF.

seventy-three freighters, plying continuously for three months, would be needed to remedy it; aircraft spare parts were almost exhausted; ammunition stocks were too small "for even a half-hearted defense of the islands"; there were no gas masks for children under five years of age. Husted repeated the complaint about slow ships, pointed to the tanker shortage, and mentioned such chronic problems as inefficient loading, shipment of low-priority material, and lack of discharge facilities and labor in Honolulu. "Additional shipping," the report declared, "should and *must* be assigned to the Honolulu route," if necessary by diverting it from the Atlantic. Husted also charged that the Army and Navy, below the top levels, were at loggerheads, refusing to co-ordinate such matters as the supply of oil and aviation gasoline. There seemed to be, he thought, "a woeful lack of understanding that this is a real war." [56]

A special feature of Hawaii's supply problem was the prominence of civilian interests, both organized and unorganized. General Emmons, as military governor, controlled the civilian as well as the military economy. Beneath the tight clamp of Hawaii's low strategic priorities, the more powerful of these interests—notably the large construction, power, and shipping firms known as the "Big Five"—had already sought to bring pressure to bear through unofficial channels. With these interests, the military administration of the islands had close ties. [57] Both Emmons and Husted emphasized the interdependence of military and civilian needs in Hawaii. Husted urged that the local electrical, acetylene gas, and railroad facilities be secured against attack at all costs, and pointed out the detrimental effects that gasoline rationing and breakdowns in air-

mail service would have upon civilian morale.

The climax of Husted's report was his accusation that the War Department had shown no understanding of the problem and that "there has been no attempt to rectify an obviously bad situation." Husted based his charge presumably on information received from Emmons and his staff, and Emmons himself remarked shortly afterward in a letter to Lt. Gen. Brehon B. Somervell, "I think the report speaks for itself." [58] He hastened to assure General Marshall, on the other hand, that "we need lots of things, but understand the situation." [59] Subsequently he complained that Husted had misrepresented him, and he explicitly disavowed the charges of non-co-operation with the Navy. [60] At all events, even before Husted's report burst over the War Department, supply shipments to Hawaii had begun to mount in volume. During March three large convoys to Honolulu moved over 200,000 measurement tons, consisting entirely of material Emmons had requisitioned earlier. In March and early April, moreover, as the *Aquitania* was put on the Hawaii run, the 27th Division was sent out to bolster the defenses there. On the other hand, for lack of new priorities, the bulk of some

---

[56] Rpt cited n. 55(4).

[57] Husted was a friend of Alexander Budge, president of the firm of Castle and Cooke, of Honolulu, who is mentioned as representing General Emmons at San Francisco in efforts to secure priorities for essential materials. See letter, Emmons to D. M. Nelson, 24 Feb 42, in Hawaiian Sup Sit envelope, Plng Div ASF; and other papers in same file.

[58] Ltr, Emmons to Somervell, 21 Mar 42, Hawaiian Sup Sit envelope, Plng Div ASF.

[59] Memo, Emmons for CofS, 9 Mar 42, WDCSA 520 (3-5-42).

[60] U.S. Army Forces, Middle Pacific and Predecessor Commands, WD hist monograph, Vol. IV, Pt. 2, pp. 1023–24, OCMH.

115,000 measurement tons of engineer materials that had been piled on the docks at San Francisco since early January remained unshipped. A few additional tankers were assigned to the Central Pacific area, but no important changes were made in the existing distribution of dry cargo shipping.[61]

Emmons' "out of the ordinary" procedure (as Judge Patterson dryly called it), in taking his case directly to the War Production Board, went largely unreprimanded.[62] The Chief of Staff admonished him mildly for his "direct action" and requested him to "please have your people keep within channels"[63]—language that represented considerable toning-down of a stronger message drafted for him by Somervell. What caused more concern was the evident failure of the Hawaiian commander to appreciate or accept the larger exigencies that had relegated his theater to a secondary strategic role. On the matter of shipping, for example, Somervell pointed out to Emmons that neither the Husted report nor his own communications showed any awareness of the "priorities between overseas theaters and departments prescribed by the President, and limitations of shipping to meet overall requirements throughout the world."[64] Judge Patterson commented bluntly that the report "ignores completely these conflicting demands for shipping."[65]

By this time, however, "localitis" had become a recognized and well-nigh universal malady among theater commanders. From Australia, Lt. Gen. George H. Brett had already added his voice to MacArthur's in calling for a reversal of the whole ARCADIA strategy in order to pour enough troops and war matériel into the Australia-New Zealand area to permit a sustained offensive. Theater commanders themselves sometimes had to cope with a

similar attitude among their own subordinates. The Army commander on Canton Island somewhat later appealed to Under Secretary of the Navy Forrestal to rectify "the cramped thinking of our supply and operations, both in the War Department and in the Hawaiian Department" with a view to building up Canton to "an installation and armament comparable to Midway." Like Emmons before him, this officer was convinced that the needed material was actually available in abundance, "right in Oahu, if they would only see the right people and look around a bit." Above all, he felt that his post was a pivot of the war effort, "the most important link in the chain of air communication and ferry routes on the entire supply line from Oahu to Australia. . . ."[66]

A myopic view of the broader needs of global strategy was only to be expected, perhaps, in a local commander at any level from theater down. Recognizing in the abstract that other war areas also had pressing needs, each commander naturally felt that his own were more real and

[61] (1) *Ibid.* (2) Ltr, Somervell to Emmons, 4 Apr 42, with tabs. (3) Memo, Brig Gen LeRoy Lutes for Gen Somervell, 10 Mar 42, sub: Gasoline Sup, Hawaii. Last two in Hawaiian Sup Sit envelope, Plng Div ASF.
[62] Memo, USW for WPD, 5 Mar 42, with Husted rpt incl, Hawaiian Sup Sit envelope, Plng Div ASF.
[63] Memo, CofS for CG HD, 5 Mar 42, OCofS 520 (3-5-42). A draft copy, corrected in Marshall's hand, is in Hawaiian Sup Sit envelope, Plng Div ASF.
[64] Ltr, Somervell to Emmons, 12 Mar 42, Hawaiian Sup Sit envelope, Plng Div ASF.
[65] Memo cited n. 62.
[66] (1) Ltr, Lt Col Robert A. Ellsworth to USN, 28 Aug 42, OPD 381 Canton Island, 3. This officer requested his addressee to "please treat this as a very personal and confidential letter." In an earlier visit to Canton, Forrestal had talked to the commander and asked him to write a letter. Ellsworth was eventually transferred to another command. (2) Corresp in OPD 472.91 (9-16-42); and OPD 210.31 PTO, 18. (3) Msg, CG USAFIA to WD, 11 Mar 42, OPD 381 Australia, 19.

urgent, and found it difficult to appreciate a strategy that did not accord them the highest priority. Nor was the phenomenon altogether to be deplored, since men usually achieve more when they believe firmly in the transcendant importance of what they do. But while recognizing this, the War Department expected overseas commanders, even if they were not convinced of the wisdom of approved strategy, to exercise judgment and moderation in pressing their requirements. In the middle of March the War Department laid down for all theaters a general policy of economy in materials and shipping. "Shortage of shipping requires that you reduce drastically the amount of construction required in your command. Resurvey your needs, reduce them to the minimum, and report changes in your requirements." [67]

Three months after Pearl Harbor the Army's deployment was flowing mainly into the theaters of the Japanese war, concentrating particularly on the effort to build a base in Australia and to secure the line of communications leading to it. The establishment of American land and air power in the Atlantic region, assigned highest priority in RAINBOW 5, was running a poor second. This shift in emphasis had not been an immediate result of the Japanese onslaught in early December. For three weeks following Pearl Harbor the U.S. high command had sought to compromise between the measures immediately necessary to bolster American defenses on the west coast and along the Alaska-Hawaii-Panama triangle, and the North Atlantic deployment scheduled in RAINBOW 5. And with the arrival of Churchill and his entourage in Washington toward the end of December, planning began to look hopefully toward an early stabilization of the situation in the Far East that would permit heavier American deployment in the North Atlantic and perhaps an Anglo-American descent upon North Africa.

It was the rapid march of Japanese arms toward Singapore and the Netherlands Indies and the growing isolation of the Philippines that, beginning in January, brought a sharp shift in emphasis to Australia and the intervening island chain. In contrast to December when almost no troops and only 13 percent of cargo shipments went to this area, during the three months January through March it absorbed over 50 percent of total troop deployment and 33 percent of cargo shipments. Because of the tremendous distances and other logistical difficulties involved, this shift had an impact on movements to other areas that was out of all proportion to the number of troops and the cargo tonnages actually sent to the South and Southwest Pacific. Movements to the Caribbean and to Alaska, employing small coastal vessels to a large extent, were little affected, and cargo shipments to Hawaii, for all General Emmons' complaints, continued in an expanding volume through March. However, the flow of troops to Hawaii, until the sailing of the 27th Division late in March, shriveled to almost nothing. And in the North Atlantic, where large movements had been looked for, deployment of both troops and cargo was an insignificant part of the total outflow during this period—only 12 percent of all troop and 9 percent of all cargo shipments. What had been discussed as the opening move in the Anglo-American counteroffensive against the European Axis, the occupation of North Africa, now had to be shelved indefinitely.

---

[67] (1) Msg, WD to Theater Comdrs, 17 Mar 42, WDCSA 520. (2) See also below, Ch. XXIII.

CHAPTER VII

Improvisation in the Pacific

The United States had plunged into a war in what was, for the Army, a new, strange, and distant theater. Since mid-1941 planning for this theater had been curiously back-handed, resting on the premise that defenses in the Far East could be built to such impressive strength before Japan was ready to strike that she would not attempt to overcome them. Supply planning and operations, geared to this hope, had all been directed toward a rapid build-up of equipment and supplies in the Philippines, and little thought had been given to the problem of continuous logistical support from the United States to forces in the Far East. The Japanese attack in December 1941 entirely upset these calculations. As long as the Japanese retained the initiative, both American strategy in the Pacific and its logistical support were necessarily shaped by short-term considerations. Supply plans and operations had to dispense with methodical calculations—the logisticians' stock-in-trade—and it proved impossible to develop a stable pattern of supply organization until after the initial force of the Japanese drive had waned.

The most pressing need in the Pacific was for bases that could be held against the initial Japanese onslaught and eventually used to mount counteroffensives. The first effort to develop such bases stemmed from the immediate need to forward supplies to the Philippines and the Netherlands Indies. This effort failed but it did determine the direction of logistical effort in the Pacific. With the collapse of Allied defenses, first in the Indies and then in the Philippines, the embryonic American bases in Australia and the chain of islands in the South Pacific leading to them became the natural line of defense and communications, one that had to be strengthened and held if the far Pacific were not to be abandoned altogether.

The Australian Base

The decision in Washington in mid-December 1941 to establish a supply base in Australia grew out of the determination not to abandon the Philippines. In General Eisenhower's plan of 17 December, Australia was to serve as the rear base for logistical support of the Philippine battle front.[1] In the days following, the General Staff hastily worked out the details of the Australian project. Plan "X," completed by G-4 on 20 December, set forth in general terms the intended method of building up supplies in Australia and the Philippines. The plan established sixty days of supply as the tentative objective for accumulation of stocks of all items, including ammunition, in both areas. Material and equipment required to build up these reserves were to be shipped to Australia, without requisition, as rapidly as available shipping and supplies permitted. To relieve pressure on scarce shipping, General

---

[1] See above, Ch. VI.

Brett was ordered to exploit Australian resources to the fullest extent. Tentative arrangements were made with the Navy for forwarding critical items to MacArthur from Australia, under the assumption that Darwin, Australia's northernmost port, could be converted in short order into a major air and sea transshipment point. Reinforcements and supplies were to be landed at Brisbane, sent overland to Darwin, and thence forwarded to the Philippines via air and blockade runners. Other shipments would be sent directly from San Francisco and Panama into Darwin.[2]

Plan "X" was carried to the theater by Col. Stephen J. Chamberlin, slated to become chief of staff to General Brett, and the first of a series of War Department emissaries. Chamberlin did not get to Australia until 9 January 1942, by which time Plan "X" had been completely outdated by the march of events in the Philippines. Late in December MacArthur withdrew his forces to the Bataan Peninsula and sent his few remaining B-17 bombers to Australia under his air commander, Maj. Gen. Lewis H. Brereton. At this point the War Department determined to attempt to build up overwhelming air power in the Far East, based no longer on the Philippines but on Australia, with advance operating bases in the Netherlands Indies. Instructions to Brett in late December and early January stressed the immediate need to prepare a base establishment in Australia—airfields, air depots, and maintenance facilities. The Far East Air Force under Brereton was specifically exempted from Brett's command, but Brett was given the major responsibility for supporting it. The War Department was thus placing upon Brett's command a double logistical burden—the continuing effort to supply the Philip-

pines, as stressed in Plan "X," and the task of building up a base establishment to support air power disposed in depth.[3]

For either mission, let alone both, the logistical difficulties were staggering. When Brett arrived in Australia on 29 December 1941 his command, designated U.S. Army Forces in Australia, consisted of about four thousand U.S. troops, mostly artillerymen unversed in supply operations, who had arrived on the *Pensacola* convoy. Sizable reinforcements from the United States would not begin to reach Australia until late in January. With this handful of troops Brett had to begin the immense task of developing a supply line across a sparsely populated and generally undeveloped continent of nearly three million square miles. Australia's ports, industry, agriculture, and population were concentrated in a narrow strip of land extending southward along the coast from Brisbane (midway up the eastern seaboard) around to Perth and Fremantle in the southwestern corner of the continent. Five million of its seven million people were settled in the coastal fringe between Brisbane and Adelaide (midway to Perth), the majority of them crowded into the southeastern tip of the country. The thin rim of seaboard settlement enclosed a vast wasteland sprawled over the central portion of Australia. Communications were

---

[2] (1) Ltr, TAG to CG U.S. Forces in Australia, 20 Dec 41, sub: G-4 Admin Order—Plan "X," AG 381 (12-20-41) MSC-D-M. (2) Rpt, JPC to JB, 21 Dec 41, sub: Agreement on Orgn and Consolidation of A&N Support . . . in Pac, Netherlands E Indies, and Australia, JB 325, Ser 738.

[3] (1) See above, Ch. VI. (2) Msg, TAG to Mil Attaché Australia for Brett, 2 Jan 42, AG 381 (11-27-41). (3) Col Julian F. Barnes, Report of Organization and Activities of U.S. Forces in Australia, December 7, 1941 to June 30, 1942, photostat, Pt. II, p. 34, OCMH. (4) Msgs exchanged between Marshall and MacArthur, Msg 3-5 files, WPD. (5) Matloff and Snell, *Strategic Planning: 1941-1942*, Ch. IV.

poor and generally concentrated along the coasts, an inviting target for attack. Rail lines were few, mostly single track, and of five different gauges, requiring frequent transshipment. For lack of modern equipment, manual labor had to be used to transfer freight, with an average delay of about twenty-four hours at each transshipment point. A single railroad wound around the coastline from Perth to Cairns, on the east coast north of Townsville; north-south communication consisted of two lines, one stretching three hundred miles into the interior south from Darwin and the other one thousand miles north from Adelaide, the two being connected by a six-hundred-mile stretch of gravel road. More than half of Australia's motor roads could not be used for military transport and the best of them were concentrated, with the bulk of the nation's other economic facilities, in the southeast.[4]

Air operations in the Netherlands Indies and Philippines would have to be based upon the undeveloped areas in the north. Townsville, on the east coast about eight hundred miles north of Brisbane, and Darwin, in the north, had been chosen as termini of the air ferry route on which work had begun late in 1941, but little had been done to develop these areas. Darwin was an isolated outpost in Australia's desolate back country, its facilities primitive. Water there was very scarce and would have to be impounded to meet the needs of a military base; there was shelter for only seven hundred men and little labor for construction work. Darwin's air base was in an embryonic stage, and the good natural harbor had few docking facilities. Practically all the supplies, equipment, and construction material, together with the troops required to set up and defend the base, would have to

be brought in by water. Water routes were long, and coastwise movements were subject to the continuous threat of enemy attack. At Darwin there would inevitably be delays in unloading material.[5]

With the best will in the world, Australia simply did not have resources for the tremendous effort required. Australian manpower, scant to begin with, had already been drained for her military forces and war industries. Her continental defenses were at rock bottom, the best of her troops and the bulk of her military equipment having been sent overseas. Her economy was already stretched tight by the demands of two years of war and was scarcely sufficient to meet her own requirements. While a large part of the basic U.S. Army ration, items of clothing, and the like could be obtained locally, only a brief survey was needed to convince Americans in Australia that the great bulk of military supplies—including construction equipment and construction labor—would have to come from the United States.[6]

During the last days of December 1941 Brett, accompanied by Brereton, made a rapid survey of Australia's resources. Mindful of War Department orders to establish bases in Australia adequate to support air power in depth, Brett decided

---

[4] (1) James R. Masterson, U.S. Army Transportation in the Southwest Pacific Area, 1941–1947, monograph, pp. 656–59, 687–97, OCMH. (2) Sumner Welles, ed., *An Intelligent American's Guide to the Peace* (New York, Dryden Press, 1945), pp. 146–50. (3) Msg 9, Brett to TAG, 5 Jan 42, Msg 5 file, Case 303, WPD. (4) Msg 36, Brett to TAG, 2 Jan 42, Msg 5 file, Case 148, WPD. (5) Msg 143, Maj Gen Julian F. Barnes to AGWAR, 31 Jan 42, Pac folder, OCT HB.

[5] (1) Msgs cited n. 4(3) and n. 4(4). (2) Msg, Brett to TAG, 3 Jan 42, Msg 5 file, Case 386, WPD.

[6] (1) Ltr, Brig Gen Stephen J. Chamberlin to Gen Somervell, 26 Feb 42, Logis File, OCMH. (2) Barnes rpt, Incl 19, cited n. 3(3). (3) Milner, Victory in Papua, Chs. I–II.

that the country must be transformed into a "second England." "I am firmly convinced," he reported to Marshall on 2 January, "that it is essential to have a stable establishment in Australia prior to large-scale tactical operations."[7] At conferences with the Australian authorities and with General Wavell at Melbourne in early January, he outlined a plan for a series of bases along the Brisbane-Townsville-Darwin line in support of air operations in the Netherlands Indies. The Americans, he asserted, were prepared to build from the ground up, if necessary, and in defiance of logistical obstacles.[8]

In a steady stream of cables to the War Department early in January, Brett listed his needs: for his staff, a group of experienced air supply officers; for defense of his northern bases, four regiments and four battalions of antiaircraft troops, two air-warning service organizations, and 180 barrage balloons with operating personnel; for aircraft maintenance, two completely equipped mobile air depots; for base construction, three separate engineer battalions, one general service regiment, three engineer aviation companies, and a long list of supplies including one hundred thousand tons of asphalt, thirty asphalt-producing plants, crushing plants, compressors, jack hammers, screening plants for gravel, explosives, landing mat; for transportation, rail and rolling stock, trucks, gasoline storage tanks, and operating personnel.[9]

Brett's plans to build a "second England" were not unreasonable in view of the instructions he had received, but when his lists began to roll in, War Department officials were dismayed. No shipping was in sight to move such quantities of men and material, even if all planned moves in the Atlantic were abandoned. In separate messages originating in G-4 and WPD, Brett was ordered to apply the brakes. WPD told him he must restrict his requirements to those "absolutely necessary for effective air and anti-air operations of the immediate future;"[10] G-4 warned that construction must be limited to "pioneer," "theater of operations" types, employing the "more primitive facilities and methods" available in the theater.[11]

Clearly, there was an enormous disparity between the War Department's announced aims and actual logistical capabilities in the southwestern Pacific. The General Staff had no choice but to insist on improvisation and short-term supply plans, but almost coincident with its veto of Brett's plan, the War Department, responding to new and urgent appeals from MacArthur, renewed pressure on USAFIA to bend every effort to break through the blockade of the Philippines. Taken aback by the obvious disparity between what he was asked to do and the means with which he was expected to do it, Brett could only quote his earlier instructions and reiterate his requests.[12]

[7] Msg cited n. 4(4).

[8] Barnes rpt, Incls 11a, 13a, and 13b, cited n. 3(3).

[9] (1) Msgs cited n. 4(3) and n. 5(2). (2) Msg, Brett to TAG, 3 Jan 42, Msg 5 file, Case 151, WPD. (3) Msg, Brett to TAG, 6 Jan 42, Msg 5 file, Case 351, WPD. (4) Msg 5, Brett to TAG, 7 Jan 42, Msg 5 file, Case 359, WPD. (5) Msg 6, Brett to TAG, 7 Jan 42, Msg 5 file, Case 258, WPD. (6) Msg 17, Brett to TAG, 9 Jan 42, Msg 5 file, Case 498, WPD. (7) See summaries of msg cited n. 4(4); Msg 8, Brett to TAG, 4 Jan 42; and msg, Brett to TAG, 8 Jan 42, in G-4/33861.

[10] Memo, ACofS WPD for TAG, 8 Jan 42, sub: Personnel and Sup Policy in Australia, Msg 5 file, Case 418, WPD.

[11] Memo, ACofS G-4 for CofS, 8 Jan 42, sub: Gen Brett's Requests for Construction Equip and Mats, G-4/33861-2.

[12] (1) Msgs in AG 381 (11-27-41) Far Eastern Sit, Sec 1, and in G-4/33861. (2) Msg, Brett to AGWAR, 14 Jan 42, Msg 6 file, Case 771, WPD.

Meanwhile, the Australian base had assumed a new importance in relation to General Wavell's ABDA Command. Only northern Australia was included in the territorial boundaries of the ABDA Command, but Australia was visualized as the base through which men and materials from the United States would be fed into the fighting zone, in the same manner that India would serve as the base for men and materials coming from Britain and the Middle East. General Brett relinquished his Australian command to become deputy to Wavell and Intendant-General of ABDA Command, which post gave him general supervision over all rear area administration and supply. Brereton was assigned command of all U.S. air operations in the ABDA area. Command of USAFIA fell temporarily to Maj. Gen. Julian F. Barnes, commanding officer of the troops that had arrived in the *Pensacola* convoy. Because of the growing isolation of the Philippines, USAFIA was withdrawn from MacArthur's command and made an appendage of the ABDA Command, though its supply responsibilities for MacArthur's forces remained the same. Thus USAFIA, despite its slender resources, had to assume responsibilities for supply support of American forces stretching from the Philippines to Java and Australia.

The War Department wanted to place the whole command under Brereton, whose air operations it was charged with supporting; there were not enough senior U.S. officers in the area to permit separate tactical and logistical commands under an over-all American commander. For a few hectic days in January, Brereton held the USAFIA command and, on another flying visit to Australia, shook up the organization there. Brereton was dissatisfied both with the conglomeration of responsibilities

now thrust upon him, and with Barnes' efforts to push supply shipments through to the Philippines and Java. At Brereton's behest, Wavell made representations to Washington that he (Brereton) could not properly handle air operations in the Indies and also direct a logistical establishment three thousand miles to the rear. General Marshall accordingly relieved the latter of the unwelcome burden of USAFIA. The luckless Barnes was restored to that command and lectured on his mission to "provide timely and effective logistical support" to Brereton, now once again commanding American air forces in the ABDA area; "his calls upon you," Marshall told him, "must be answered promptly and effectively." [13]

Probing the Japanese Blockade

The Japanese, meanwhile, were rapidly closing the avenues to the Philippines and overrunning the weak defenses in the Netherlands Indies. The first American surface shipments from Australia to the Netherlands Indies were those aboard the *Bloemfontein* (one of the *Pensacola* convoy ships), which sailed to Surabaja at the end of December with a few hundred artillerymen and some old British 75's. Through January and February desperate efforts were made to ship material, including airplanes, to Java, as well as to fly planes to that area. In the great enemy air raid on Darwin on 19 February, most of the available cargo shipping was wiped out, and

---

[13] (1) Msg, Marshall to CG USAFIA, 27 Jan 42, WPD 4628-5. (2) Msg, Marshall to CG USAFIA, 30 Jan 42, WPD 4628-25. (3) Msg, Wavell to Marshall, 16 Jan 42, WPD 4369-19. (4) Delaying and Containing Action, monograph, pp. 1–8, OPD Hist Unit File. (5) Incl 18, msg, Marshall to CG USAFIA, 18 Jan 42, to Barnes rpt cited n. 3(3). (6) Brereton, *The Brereton Diaries*, pp. 76–83. (7) See also corresp in WPD 4628-20 and WPD 4628-25.

Java was sealed off from further surface shipments from Australia; on 27 February thirty-two P-40's went down when the old seaplane tender *Langley* was sunk; many other aircraft were lost, before they could get into action, while being flown north from Australia; still others were purposely destroyed during the evacuation of Java to prevent their capture. On the last day of February General Brett radioed the War Department that he considered further shipments to Java "unwarranted wastage." Ten days later, with the capture of Bandung, resistance in the Netherlands Indies came to an end.[14]

In the Philippines the debacle was more prolonged. Following his withdrawal to Bataan, General MacArthur declared himself "professionally certain" that the enemy blockade could be easily pierced. He recommended using numerous small vessels and submarines, arguing that his requirements, though urgent, were modest. The War Department, which wanted to retain the large ships for transoceanic runs, was agreeable to the use of small vessels; in any case, the Americans no longer possessed discharge facilities for large ships on Luzon. On 18 January Col. Patrick J. Hurley was sent to the southwestern Pacific as General Marshall's personal representative to infuse more energy into the search for small craft in Australia and the Netherlands Indies. Meanwhile, USAFIA headquarters dispatched Col. John N. Robinson, who had commanded the troops on the *Holbrook*, with six assistants to comb Java, Sumatra, and Celebes for food and coastal vessels. Other officers, armed with War Department authority to expend practically unlimited funds, were directed to "organize blockade running on a broad front."[15]

Small craft, fast and with sufficient fuel capacity, were hard to obtain. Masters and crews usually refused to risk death or capture, despite the offer of large bonuses. Precious time was lost in negotiations between Washington and London over alleged duplication in assignment of shipping. Only three vessels succeeded in breaking through the blockade, reaching Mindanao and Cebu during February and March, respectively, with about 10,000 tons of rations, 4,000,000 rounds of small arms ammunition, 8,000 rounds of 81-mm. mortar shell, and a quantity of medical, signal, and engineer supplies. Only a small fraction of these supplies reached the beleaguered forces on Luzon. An attempt was made, despite misgivings on the part of Admiral Thomas C. Hart and General Wavell, to run supplies through by submarine; about ten of these craft sailed from various points between early January and the surrender of Corregidor in May, and at least five actually reached "The Rock." Only three, however, were able to discharge cargo.

By the beginning of March the blockade of the southern approaches to the Philippines had become so tight that both Hurley and Brett thought the effort to pierce it should be abandoned. General MacArthur had already concluded, and urged upon the War Department, that the whole approach up to now had been wrong. Direction of the effort, he declared on 22 February, should be centralized in Washington and "re-energized," rather

---

[14] (1) Bingham and Leighton, Development of the United States Supply Base in Australia, ASF hist monograph, pp. 94–98, OCMH. (2) Blockade Running to the Philippines, MS, pp. 28–29, OCT HB. (3) Matloff and Snell, *Strategic Planning: 1941-1942*, pp. 131–36. (4) Craven and Cate, *AAF I*, pp. 391–98.

[15] (1) Bingham and Leighton monograph, pp. 100–101, cited n. 14(1). (2) MS cited n. 14(2). (3) Corresp in G-4/33861 and AG 381 (11-27-41) Far Eastern Sit, Sec 1. (4) Morton, *Fall of the Philippines*, Ch. XXII.

than being relegated to USAFIA where it was being handled, he charged, "as a subsidiary effort."[16] The resources in Australia and the Netherlands Indies, in any case, were insufficient for the task. Many shipments, MacArthur thought, should be routed along the westward passage from Honolulu. Asserting that the enemy's coverage of the approaches was still thin, MacArthur evidently envisaged an uninterrupted stream of vessels probing the approaches to the Philippines along several routes. Many ships might be lost, but many, he felt, would get through.

There had been no lack of energy in the War Department's attack upon the problem. Since mid-January it had been working on a project to fit seven old destroyers, converted into banana carriers, for the westward voyage. In response to MacArthur's message of 22 February the War Department notified him that three of the converted destroyers, each of about fifteen hundred tons cargo capacity, were being loaded identically with food, medical supplies, ammunition, and other items and would be sent to Mindanao within three weeks; the first was leaving almost immediately. But time and circumstances whittled down this plan. There were delays in arming the vessels, in providing Army gun crews (the Navy had none available), in assembling cargoes, in working out routings. The first vessel sailed from New Orleans on 2 March, and two more at approximately one-week intervals. Only one got as far as Honolulu before the surrender of Corregidor. In mid-April General MacArthur, then in Australia, acknowledged that with the enemy in possession of both the Cavite and Bataan shores of Manila Bay it was useless to send more blockade runners to Corregidor. The dreary game thus dragged to an end.

In mid-March General Eisenhower, now head of the Operations Division (OPD), had jotted a notation, "For many weeks—it seems years—I've been searching everywhere to find any feasible way of giving real help to the P. I. . . . . I'll go on trying, but daily the situation grows more desperate."[17]

Emergence of the Southwest Pacific Area Command

By the end of February both the Philippines and the ABDA Command were effectively beyond the reach of logistical support. With the fall of Java imminent, Wavell closed his headquarters there on 23 February and Brett returned to Australia to assume command of USAFIA. Allied forces in the Far East were split, driven westward into India and southeastward into Australia and the tip of New Guinea. With the collapse of ABDA Command and the War Department's futile intervention to "re-energize" blockade running to the Philippines, the supply task of the Australian base shrank to more manageable proportions. Beginning in mid-January 1942, the War Department had begun to adjust its supply plans to place major emphasis on building a permanent base in Australia. This, in reality, had been the predominant concern of the staff of USAFIA almost from the beginning.

On 10 January G-4 directed the release and redistribution of depot stocks that had been accumulating since the preceding summer for shipment to the Philippines. Shipments were to be limited, for a time, to such essential items as ammunition, food, and critical medical supplies that

[16] Msg 344, MacArthur to Marshall, 22 Feb 42, G-4/33817.
[17] (1) Notations by Eisenhower, 13 Mar 42 entry Item 3, OPD Hist Unit File. (2) See above, n. 15.

could be transported by air as well as by sea, and to additional critical supplies (up to a hypothetical thirty-day level) that would be useful in Australia if transshipment to MacArthur should prove impossible. This move to place supply of the Philippines in a special category was confirmed in a new supply plan for Australia that had taken shape by early February. Reserves to be held in Australia for the Philippines were definitely restricted to thirty days' supply, with the qualification that the Commanding General, USAFIA, was authorized to request from the War Department such additional supplies as he was able to push through to them. For Australia, on the other hand, supply levels were set at ninety days for ground force materials and five months for air force supply. Procedures were made more detailed and restrictive than in the December directive (Plan "X"), and a trend toward orderly supply methods was evident. In addition to its other responsibilities, USAFIA was assigned the obligation of supplying POPPY Force until its commander, Brig. Gen. Alexander M. Patch, could organize a base port in New Caledonia.[18]

In order to systematize local procurement, USAFIA was ordered on 3 February to establish a General Purchasing Board that would consolidate all procurement in Australia for the U.S. Army and Navy, on the pattern of the board created in France during World War I. Brig. Gen. James C. Roop, who had been executive officer of the older board, was sent to the theater as General Purchasing Agent and chairman of the General Purchasing Board. The board was to consist of the senior officer of each supply arm and service of USAFIA, a representative of the Navy supply corps, and such other members as the Commanding General, USAFIA, wished to appoint. General Roop and the board were charged with supervision of all local procurement in the Australian area by both the Army and Navy, and with making all necessary arrangements with the local governments.[19]

Simultaneously, another War Department emissary, Brig. Gen. Arthur R. Wilson, was sent out to serve as Barnes' chief quartermaster and to infuse vigor into all supply activities in Australia, including local procurement. General Marshall's letter to USAFIA on 6 February outlining Wilson's mission still placed heavy emphasis on forwarding supplies to the Philippines and Netherlands Indies.[20] But Wilson, bringing with him the February supply plan, did not arrive until March, by which time events had made this aspect of his mission almost obsolete. With the collapse of ABDA Command, the British and United States Governments had turned to a reconsideration of Pacific organization and strategy, and the overriding concern now was for the safety of Australia itself.

On 23 January the Japanese had taken Rabaul on New Britain Island, thus uncovering Port Moresby, the weakly held Australian base in southern Papua across the Torres Strait, which in turn controlled the approaches to the continent across the Coral Sea. Invasion seemed imminent, and Australian defenses were weak. Two divisions of the Australian Imperial Forces had already been hastily withdrawn from

---

[18] (1) Memo, Exec Off G-4 for Br Chiefs, 10 Jan 42, sub: Shipts for Forces in Philippines, G-4/33861. (2) AG ltr to CG USAFIA and Chiefs of SAS, 2 Feb 42, sub: Sup of USAFIA Area (1-31-42).

[19] TAG ltr to CG USAFIA, 3 Feb 42, sub: Estab of a Gen Purch Bd in Australia, AG 334.8 Australia, Gen Purch Bd (1-30-42) MSC-D-M.

[20] (1) Ltr, CofS to CG USAFIA, 6 Feb 42, G-4/33861. (2) Related papers in same file.

the Middle East and were en route to Australia; the Australian Government demanded the return of a third. The United States, on the other hand, was in the best position geographically and otherwise to provide reinforcements, and on 14 February General Marshall decided to send the 41st Division to Australia along with supporting service troops. The quest for shipping again had to be taken to the White House, via the versatile Mr. Hopkins, who contrived to have the request for additional vessels, beyond the pooled resources of the Army and Navy, put to Admiral Land at the White House level. The first phase of the movement got under way on 3 March with the sailing from New York of a large convoy of five troopships, carrying about 13,500 men; the rest of the 41st Division and support troops sailed from San Francisco in March and April. Meantime, in a message to Prime Minister John Curtin on 20 February, the President, in an effort to persuade the Australian Government to permit the diversion to Burma of the two Australian divisions en route from the Middle East, assured Curtin that the United States would reinforce the Australian position with all possible speed. In effect, Roosevelt accepted the defense of Australia as an American responsibility.[21]

In early March Churchill appealed to the President to send an additional American division to Australia and one to New Zealand in order to permit retention of one Australian and one New Zealand division in the Middle East. The President agreed, and on 25 March the 32d Division, which had been awaiting shipment to Northern Ireland, was hastily withdrawn from the MAGNET Force and put under orders for movement to Australia in April. The 37th Division was scheduled

for shipment to New Zealand in May. With the allocation of these ground forces to the theater, War Department deployment policy entered a new phase. Instead of only air units and essential service troops, the aim was now to build a balanced air and ground force for the defense of Australia. The Australian base had become the anchor of the American line of defense in the Pacific.[22]

The shift in deployment was accompanied by a dramatic change in command arrangements. General MacArthur, on orders from the President, left the Philippines and made his way to Australia, arriving at Darwin on 17 March 1942. The announcement was made on that day that he would become supreme commander of all Allied forces in Australia and the Philippines. A few days later the United States and Great Britain agreed on a general division of strategic responsibility and exercise of command for Allied forces throughout the world. The plan established three broad strategic areas—the Pacific, the Middle East-Indian Ocean, and the European-Atlantic. The conduct of the war in the Pacific would become the primary responsibility of the U.S. Joint Chiefs of Staff, the British Chiefs of Staff were to be similarly responsible for the Middle East-Indian Ocean region, and the European-

---

[21] (1) Memo, Marshall for Eisenhower, 14 Feb 42. (2) Memo for rcd, Brig Gen Robert W. Crawford, 14 Feb 42. Both in WPD 4360-65. (3) Memo, G-4 for CofS, 14 Feb 42, sub: Trans for Reinf to "X," G-4/29717-116. (4) Matloff and Snell, *Strategic Planning: 1941-1942*, Chs. VI–VII. (5) Rpt, NYPOE Statistical Summary, OCT HB.

[22] (1) Milner, Victory in Papua, Chs. I–II. (2) Matloff and Snell, *Strategic Planning: 1941-1942*, Ch. VII. (3) Memo, ACofS OPD for TAG, 10 Mar 42, sub: Est of Sit, Anzac Area, OPD 381 Australia, Case 9. (4) As a part of the general effort to strengthen the British position in the Middle East, the President also promised shipping to transport two British divisions to that area. See below, Chs. XIV, XVIII.

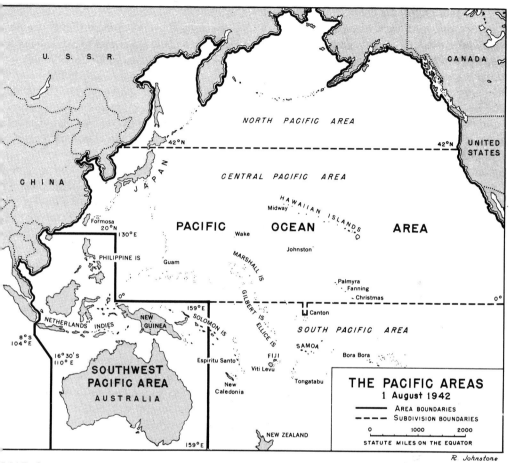

THE PACIFIC AREAS
1 August 1942
——— AREA BOUNDARIES
- - - SUBDIVISION BOUNDARIES
0   1000   2000
STATUTE MILES ON THE EQUATOR

R. Johnstone

MAP 3

Atlantic would be a combined responsibil-
ty. The Combined Chiefs would continue
o determine grand strategy for all areas.

In the Pacific, the U.S. Joint Chiefs es-
ablished two main theaters, the South-
vest Pacific Area (SWPA) and the Pacific
Ocean Area, the former to be under Gen-
ral MacArthur's command, the latter
inder Admiral Chester W. Nimitz. Aus-
ralia, the Philippines, New Guinea, the
3ismarck Archipelago, the Solomon
slands, and all of the Netherlands Indies,
xcept Sumatra, were included within

SWPA. The rest of the Pacific, with the
exception of a relatively small area in the
southeastern part for which no command
was established, fell within the Pacific
Ocean Area. This area was further divided
into North, Central, and South Pacific
subareas, the first two to be directly controlled by Admiral Nimitz and the third
by a deputy of his own choosing.[23] (Map 3)

—————————————
[23] (1) Milner, Victory in Papua, Ch. II. (2) Matloff
and Snell, Strategic Planning: 1941-1942, Ch. VII. (3)
CCS 57/2, 24 Mar 42, title: Strategic Responsibility
of U.S. and U.K.

After the approval of the Australian Government had been obtained, General MacArthur on 18 April announced the structure of his new command. All forces under his control were organized into five subordinate commands: Allied air forces under General Brett; Allied land forces under the Australian General Sir Thomas Blamey; Allied naval forces under Rear Adm. Herbert F. Leary; USAFIA, once again, under General Barnes; and U.S. Forces in the Philippines under Lt. Gen. Jonathan M. Wainwright. While supply and administration remained divided along national lines, operational control of all ground, air, and naval units whether American, Australian, or Dutch came under the Allied commander. For all American forces, USAFIA served as a supply and service agency as well as an administrative headquarters for the transmission of policy directives; in supply matters it was the channel of communication to the War Department.[24]

Soon after his arrival, General MacArthur won the Australian Chiefs of Staff to his view that the best hope of saving the dominion lay in concentrating such resources as were available on the defense of Port Moresby and undertaking limited offensive action in New Guinea at the earliest practicable date. This policy made it clear that development of the base establishment would have to be focused on northeastern Australia and carried north into Papua. This shortened the line of communications from the well-developed ports of southeastern Australia, and made Townsville rather than Darwin the focal point in the undeveloped north. USAFIA at last had a supply mission of manageable proportions and reasonable clarity.[25]

By this time, too, the base in Australia was acquiring some flesh and sinew. There were 34,000 American troops in Australia by the middle of March and 23,000 more en route. Supply operations were becoming more systematic. With more staff personnel available, seven base sections were organized under USAFIA and began to operate with some smoothness. General Wilson had taken over the functions of chief quartermaster, the General Purchasing Board under General Roop was in operation, and an Allied Supply Council had been set up. A survey of local resources indicated that most of the subsistence for American troops could be procured in Australia, as could a considerable quantity of clothing, construction materials, and other supplies. Shipments of supplies from the United States were also now arriving in quantity, and the build-up of reserve stocks was well under way. Brig. Gen. Stephen J. Chamberlin reported to General Somervell at the end of February that materials were coming so fast "we are having trouble taking care of them."[26]

The build-up in Australia represented in fact the major logistical effort of the U.S. Army during the first quarter of 1942, absorbing approximately half of the troops and a third of the cargo shipped overseas by the Army during that period. After March 1942 the proportion fell rap-

---

[24] (1) Delaying and Containing Action, pp. 32–34, cited n. 13(4). (2) Ltr, CINCSWPA to TAG, 26 May 42, sub: Sup Orgn and Proced, SWPA Sup folder, Plng Div ASF, Job A44-140. (3) Msg, USAFFE to AGWAR, 20 Apr 42, ABC 323.31 POA (1-29-42), 2.
[25] Milner, Victory in Papua, Ch. II.
[26] (1) Ltr cited n. 6(1). (2) Barnes rpt, Pt. I, pp. 38–44, and Pt. VI, cited n. 3(3). (3) Matloff and Snell, Strategic Planning: 1941-1942, Ch. VII. (4) Contl Div, ASF, Statistical Review, World War II. (5) Msg 758, Brett to TAG, 19 Mar 42. (6) Memo, Gen Wilson for CG USAFIA, 12 Jun 42, sub: Suggested Rpt to WD. Last two in SWPA Sup folder, Plng Div ASF, Job A44-140. (7) For lend-lease and reciprocal aid arrangements, see below, Ch. XVIII.

idly, as the United States and Britain held to their initial decision to concentrate first on the war against Germany. Within the Pacific itself, much of the emphasis shifted to the island chain and once again to Hawaii. MacArthur had to accept a lower priority in troops, materials, and shipping. Troop shipments to Australia dropped abruptly in May, cargo shipments in June.[27] The early build-up made possible the development of a base in Australia adequate for the defense of the continent, but hardly equal to the demands even the most limited Allied counteroffensive would impose. The fundamental logistical problems of vast distances, scanty transportation and communication facilities, and scarce and inefficient labor remained. There was no real solution to these problems in sight as long as the strategic emphasis on other areas precluded further heavy concentration of American military resources in Australia.

Manning the Island Line

Like the base in Australia, the American defense and communications line along the Pacific islands west of Hawaii was an outgrowth of circumstances rather than of plan. In the command structure set up in March 1942, the entire Pacific Ocean Area was made a naval responsibility, but the Army had to garrison most of the island bases and provide the long-range bomber support that the Navy considered essential to fleet operations. Interservice co-operation in logistics was therefore a central problem from the start.

The first phase of deployment to the island chain got under way in January with the movement of POPPY Force to New Caledonia, the establishment of the refueling station at Bora Bora, and the rein-

forcement of existing naval and air-ferry-route bases.[28] In February the Navy launched a second phase with the recommendation that joint task forces should be sent to occupy two new bases, Tongatabu, one of the Tonga (Friendly) Islands, and Efate in the New Hebrides archipelago. The two islands sat astride the undefended approaches to Samoa, Fiji, and New Caledonia. In conjunction with its current plans to dispatch a Marine force to establish supplementary air bases in the Samoan Islands, the Navy conceived of this as a three-way move to strengthen the southwestern portion of the route where a strong Japanese attack was considered most likely. The Army staff viewed the plan with some misgivings as it was concerned over growing evidence that the Navy wished to establish bases on many small islands, a program they thought would be entirely too costly in manpower, shipping, and above all in long-range bombers. Nevertheless, General Marshall finally agreed on 2 March to send Army garrisons to Tongatabu and Efate, and the movements were set up later in the month.

Efate was occupied during March by a holding force of Marine and Army troops drawn, respectively, from Hawaii and Maj. Gen. Alexander M. Patch's force on New Caledonia. The Tongatabu force, the main Efate force, and the Marine force for Samoa were sent during April from the States. About the same time, at Admiral Nimitz' request, the Hawaiian Department dispatched a small garrison to relieve New Zealand troops guarding the cable station on Fanning Island, an atoll between Palmyra and Christmas. Further down the chain and later in the spring a

[27] (1) Contl Div, ASF, *Statistical Review, World War II.* (2) See below, App. E.
[28] See above, Ch. VI.

small force, detached from the New Caledonia garrison, occupied Espiritu Santo on the recommendation of the commanding general on Efate who felt that the northern flank of his base was dangerously exposed.[29]

The third and final stage of the initial effort to secure the island chain was carried out in May 1942 when the 37th Division was sent to the Fijis, where weakness in ground troops had left a vulnerable link in the line of communications. This, along with the move of the 32d Division to Australia, was part of the effort to enable the British to retain dominion troops in the Middle East. The Navy undertook to establish important naval facilities on Viti Levu, the principal island of the Fiji group, and about the same time began to develop a major supply and fleet base at Auckland, New Zealand.[30]

Deployment of the Army contingents to the island bases followed two main patterns—movements the War Department and its field agencies handled alone, and those they shared with the Navy. Broadly speaking, the former applied to the reinforcement of the original Army ferry bases: Christmas, Canton, Fiji, and New Caledonia. Conversely, the Navy took full responsibility for reinforcing the "line" islands in which it had a prior interest: Samoa, Palmyra, and Johnston. In the category of joint deployment were the balanced task forces sent to occupy the flanking bases—Bora Bora, Tongatabu, and Efate. In the case of the joint task forces, the Army still furnished the bulk of the manpower, approximately 7,200 of the 8,200 men for Tongatabu and 4,900 of the 6,500 for Efate. On each of the three islands, the joint command of the garrison was entrusted to an Army officer. Unlike POPPY Force, where the troops sailed with only their personal equipment, the other expeditions were all combat-loaded task forces and provided the Army with its first experience in this type of movement.

These movements to the South Pacific were characterized by an inordinate amount of confusion and waste motion arising out of the haste with which each was conceived and executed, the inexperience of both Army and Navy supply personnel, and the lack of established channels of co-ordination between the two services. There was haste and waste at both ends of each movement—in the process of mounting the expedition in the United States and in the debarkation and setting up at the destination. Had the Japanese been in a position to attack, they might well have disrupted any one of these task forces before it was in a posture for defense. The assembling and loading of troops and supplies were badly managed; delays occurred in finding suitable vessels and outfitting them; scrambled loading of supplies produced confusion and delay in unloading at the destination. In no case was it possible to provide a genuinely balanced task force; each expedition was composed of miscellaneous combat units hastily assembled from different points and without much service support. On arrival the combat troops had to perform unfamiliar service functions for themselves, a burden especially onerous at Bora Bora, Tongatabu, and Efate, where neither port facilities nor civilian labor of any sort was

---

[29] (1) Matloff and Snell, *Strategic Planning: 1941-1942*, Ch. VII. (2) Ballantine, *Naval Logistics*, pp. 71-72. (3) *Building the Navy's Bases*, II, 193-94. (4) OPD Diary, 10 and 13 Apr 42 entries, OPD Hist Unit File. (5) Ltr, CG HD to CofS, 18 Apr 42, Pac folder, Logis File, OCMH.

[30] (1) Delaying and Containing Action, pp. 46-47, cited n. 13(4). (2) Jt A&N Plan for Relief of New Zealand and the Fiji Islands, 13 May 42, OPD 381 Fiji, Sec 1, Case 3.

available. There was scant knowledge of the geography, climate, terrain, or economic development of the islands to be occupied, with the result that many obstacles encountered in unloading and establishing base forces were not anticipated in the planning. In truth, there was no real logistical plan for any of the moves; each was largely a process of trial and error. The Bora Bora expedition, a capsule containing most of the ingredients of this experience, may profitably be examined in some detail.

Bobcat: Case History in Joint Task Force Logistics

The joint task force sent out to Bora Bora had the mission of establishing and defending a fueling station to serve shipping from the west coast and the Panama Canal to Australia. The expedition was given the code name BOBCAT. Following the decision on 30 December 1941 to undertake the project, and after securing the President's approval, the Navy requested the Army to provide a garrison of some four thousand troops. After two days of deliberation the War Department agreed to "make available . . . whatever troops and material Admiral King decided would be necessary." [31] Immediately, the Army and Navy war plans divisions began to work out the details.

By 5 January General Gerow, acting head of WPD, was able to submit to General Marshall a list of services and equipment the Navy was prepared to supply, together with his specific recommendations for the composition of the Army garrison. Three days later a joint plan was completed. Under it the Army's contribution was to be chiefly manpower and the Navy's base facilities. Specifically, the Army became responsible for supplying all subsistence ashore as well as for defense of the island, the Navy for moving the task force overseas and providing shore construction at its destination. The strength of the force was set at 4,400. Troops numbering 3,900 made up the defense garrison, whose main components were an antiaircraft regiment, and a reinforced infantry regiment less two battalions; the remaining 500 were naval personnel, many of whom were to be withdrawn from the island when the base was completed. The plan assigned local unity of command to the Army commander, Col. Charles D. Y. Ostrom, under General Emmons, commanding general of the Hawaiian Department. Charleston was assigned as the port of embarkation and the expedition was scheduled to leave in about two weeks' time. [32]

The core of the planned base was a tank farm for storage of fuel. In addition, there were to be a small seaplane base, harbor installations, unloading facilities, coastal defenses, a water distillation system, storage, refrigeration, and other accessory facilities. Most of the material for these installations was provided by the Navy, largely from reserve stocks at the Quonset naval depot in Rhode Island. [33] The Army, for its part, was concerned mainly with outfitting the defense garrison and assembling its maintenance supplies. Insofar as possible, shortages in organizational equip-

---

[31] (1) Memo, SW for CofS, 1 Jan 42. (2) Memo, COMINCH for CNO, 1 Jan 42. Both in WPD 4571-21. (3) Memo for rcd, Col Lee S. Gerow, 3 Jan 42, WPD 4571-22. (4) Ballantine, *Naval Logistics*, p. 67.

[32] (1) Memo, WPD for CofS, 5 Jan 42, sub: Bora Bora Def Force. (2) Memo, WPD for TAG, 17 Jan 42, sub: Ltr of Instn to Col Ostrom. Both in WPD 4571-24. (3) *Building the Navy's Bases*, II, 191.

[33] (1) *Building the Navy's Bases*, II, 191. (2) Ballantine, *Naval Logistics*, pp. 63–67. (3) Memo, cited n. 32(1).

ment were filled locally by transferring needed items to troops earmarked for BOBCAT from other units in the same corps areas; the supply arms and services were held responsible for making up the remaining deficits and were charged also with moving maintenance supplies for the garrison into the port area. For the initial movement to Bora Bora, the War Department set two months (sixty days) as the general level of maintenance, doubling it, however, in the case of rations (Class I) and gasoline (Class III). Ammunition maintenance to accompany the force was determined in terms of units of fire, seven for antiaircraft weapons and five for all others.[34]

Army troops and cargo all were scheduled to be loaded at Charleston. Naval personnel and equipment were to be picked up and redistributed in stages starting at Quonset, where specialists and most of the base materials were to be taken on. At Norfolk additional Navy cargo was to be loaded, a step that involved partial unloading and reloading. Final redistribution and loading would take place at Charleston.[35] But the original plans were soon submerged in a series of complications.

The first setback came when the Navy, charged with all transportation arrangements, ran into difficulties in obtaining adequate shipping for the force. Six vessels were required for the movement. The Navy could provide only three and on short notice had to turn to the Maritime Commission for the remaining ships. These had to be armed. It was discovered, besides, that one of the ships was damaged and could not make the journey. The *Arthur Middleton* was hastily substituted and promptly turned out to be a major problem in herself. Before she left New York her master reported to the Third Na-

val District that she was unstable and required fifteen hundred tons of ballast to compensate for the weight of her newly installed armament. Navy officials insisted that "the ship was all right," and the *Middleton* set out for Charleston with a 12-degree list.[36] At Charleston the Navy yard already had its hands full with unanticipated repairs on the *President Tyler*, one of the troopships assigned to the expedition. In the blunt words of the BOBCAT naval commander, Comdr. Carl H. Sanders, "The *Tyler* was a mess and still is. I understand that she was condemned as a passenger vessel and for the past seven years has been used as a freighter. At the time the Navy took her over nothing had been done to outfit her properly and the Yard worked on her continuously up to the time of sailing to correct deficiencies."[37]

The scheduled departure date, at first set by the Navy for 15 January, was postponed to the 25th (in the plan of 8 January), although the Army logistical staff, until the middle of the month, was under the impression it would be the 27th. Then, on the 15th, Admiral King suggested that the POPPY and BOBCAT movements be combined in order to economize on escort vessels. POPPY Force was due to leave New

---

[34] (1) Memo, G-4 for CSigO, CofEngrs, and SG, 8 Jan 42, G-4/33793. (2) Control Division, ASF, Movement of U.S. Army Troops and Supplies to South Pacific Theater of Operations, MS, p. 64, OCMH. (3) Ltr, CofTrans Br G-4 to CG SFPOE, 7 Mar 42, CPOE folder, OCT HB.

[35] (1) Memo, G-4 for TAG, 10 Jan 42, Logis File, OCMH. (2) Memo to those concerned, 10 Jan 42, sub: Info for Those Concerned With Loading of Vessels for BOBCAT, and atchd memo for rcd, WPD 4571-24. (3) *Building the Navy's Bases*, II, 197. (4) Ltr, Comdr SE Pac Force to COMINCH, 21 Mar 42, sub: Advance Bases—Loading of Store Ships and Trans, for, Bora Bora folder, Logis File, OCMH.

[36] Ltr, Comdr Carl H. Sanders to Capt Bertram J. Rodgers, OCNO, 3 Feb 42, CPOE folder, OCT HB.

[37] (1) *Ibid.* (2) Ballantine, *Naval Logistics*, p. 68. (3) *Building the Navy's Bases*, II, 197.

York for Australia on 20 January. General Marshall was willing to compromise. If the Navy would sail BOBCAT two days ahead of schedule, on the 23rd, he would direct the POPPY convoy to meet BOBCAT off the South Carolina coast on that date. This arrangement, the Army calculated, would cost the Australian movement four days of delay—one lost in waiting off Charleston (the trip from New York required two days) and the other three because of reduction of speed to match that of the slower Bora Bora convoy.[38]

Admiral King accepted this proposal and the POPPY flotilla duly cleared New York Harbor late on the 22d. On the night of the 24th, just as POPPY Force was due off Charleston, the War Department received word from the port commander there, Lt. Col. James E. Slack, that the Navy could not make ready two of the BOBCAT vessels, *Middleton* and *Hamul,* until afternoon of the following day. Charleston Navy yard was working around the clock to complete the two-day job of reballasting the *Middleton,* which should have been done at New York. Since an additional thirty-six hours had to be allowed for loading the two ships, there was no prospect of getting them out of Charleston until early morning of the 27th.[39]

This was news of the utmost gravity. Each day's delay in moving POPPY Force to the Far East added to the possibility of disaster. By acceding to the Navy's wish to combine POPPY with the slower BOBCAT convoy, the War Department had accepted a loss of several days in sailing time. The whole movement now had to be postponed until the 27th. This development, General Somervell declared indignantly to General Marshall, should be viewed " in the light of Admiral King's longhand memorandum to you to the effect that there

would be no further delays in this movement. All ships are being furnished by the Navy and all delays are attributable to the Navy." [40]

But the War Department could scarcely claim to be wholly blameless in the muddle at Charleston, where confusion prevailed at the Army port of embarkation no less than at the Navy base. Inefficient and inadequate dock labor at the Army base seriously hampered joint loading operations. Commander Sanders found that the bosses of the Army's stevedoring crews were "the only ones who knew anything about loading" and that naval personnel who were finally pressed into helping with the loading "did it twice as fast as the stevedores." [41] At a critical moment, moreover, the antiaircraft regiment, fourteen hundred strong, arrived at the port with its equipment uncrated despite specific instructions to the contrary. The I Corps headquarters, in sending the movement orders, had left out the clause pertaining to this aspect of the movement. The consequence was a scramble at the port to find labor and packing materials, and loading was held up for two days. There were other problems. Army and Navy shipments alike arrived so poorly marked as to defy identification. Loading plans turned out to be unsuited to the ships actually used. Small detachments of troops coming from distant posts required additional

[38] (1) Memo, Adm King for CofS, 15 Jan 42, sub: Convoys to BOBCAT and Australia, with atchd notes, Col Gross for Gen Somervell and Gross for Col Ross, G-4/29717-115. (2) Memo, WPD for G-4, 13 Jan 42, no sub, CPOE folder, OCT HB. (3) Memo, G-4 for CSigO, CofEngrs, and SG, 14 Jan 42, G-4/33793.
[39] (1) Memo, G-4 for CofS, 24 Jan 42, G-4/29717-114. (2) Ltr cited n. 36. (3) Ballantine, *Naval Logistics,* pp. 68–69. (4) Memo, CofS for President, 23 Feb 42, Pac folder, OCT HB.
[40] (1) Memo cited n. 39(1).
[41] Ltr cited n. 36.

clothing and individual equipment that port stocks were inadequate to supply. Advance detachments sent to the port to assist the port quartermaster in handling the supplies for their units proved to be more of a hindrance than a help, being generally ignorant of precise needs and of supply procedures. Conditions at Charleston seem, in general, to have been the product of many failures, large and small, on the part of both services. Each was handicapped by haste, inexperience, and many shortages. At the port, the first point where their earlier separate arrangements were merged into a single effort, it became clear that because BOBCAT was a joint operation, neither service could escape the consequences of the other's failures.[42]

On the 25th the *Hamul* and the luckless *Middleton* tied up at the Army base for loading. The following day, on the eve of sailing, the crowning blow fell when, without warning, some eight hundred tons of Navy cargo, which Colonel Slack was totally unprepared to handle, began to arrive at the Army wharf for loading on the two vessels. The commandant of the Navy yard, for his part, had had no advance notice of the total Navy cargo scheduled for Bora Bora, and when the unexpected shipment appeared, he could only send it on to Colonel Slack since by that time the other BOBCAT vessels at the Navy yard had been fully loaded. To make matters worse, the eight hundred tons included pontoons, heavy tractors with bulldozer attachments, vehicles, and other matériel—the very type that should have been distributed carefully among the vessels with a view to being immediately available when the convoy arrived at Bora Bora. Furthermore, the new shipment contained many heavy lifts, which added greatly to the difficulty of getting the cargo aboard in a hurry. Colonel Slack estimated that "three heavy tractors alone required eighteen gang-hours of loading time."[43] The inevitable happened. Although the *Hamul* cleared the Army pier on schedule in the early morning of the 27th, the *Middleton* was delayed nine hours past sailing time. All hands, Army and Navy, had worked without break to get her away on schedule but the deadline could not be met. Finally, in midafternoon of the 27th, the BOBCAT vessels sailed.[44]

Commander Sanders foresaw that there would be a price to pay for haphazard loading when the convoy discharged at Bora Bora, and his apprehensions were more than justified. Trouble began the moment the convoy arrived at Bora Bora on 17 February. The first problem, according to Rear Adm. John F. Shafroth who escorted the convoy, arose from the fact that "the ships could not be unloaded without the floating equipment and the floating equipment could not be assembled without unloading."

The pontoon barges which were the principal means by which the cargo could be moved from ship to shore were stored in various holds and often deep in these holds. . . . Not only were pontoons not stored near the top of the holds but in some cases were discovered in holds of ships on which pontoons were not known to be loaded.[45]

---

[42] (1) Memo, TQMG for G-4, 26 Jan 42, CPOE folder, OCT HB. (2) Ballantine, *Naval Logistics*, p. 68. (3) Charleston had been a subport of New York until 8 January when it became a port of embarkation. See CPOE folder, OCT HB. (4) Memo, Asst Exec Off G-4 for ACofS G-4, 29 Jan 42, sub: Tr Mvmt Ordered to Overseas Garrisons, G-4/33098.

[43] Ltr, Col Slack to G-4, 28 Jan 42, G-4/33793.

[44] (1) Loose paper headed "Diary," 28 Jan 42, in CPOE folder, OCT HB. By 24 January the number of vessels had been reduced from six to five—three freighters and two transports—the number that actually sailed. (2) See also, memo cited n. 35(2).

[45] Ltr cited n. 35(4).

'our thirty-ton tank lighters stowed on
eck saved the day. Within twenty-four
.ours of the arrival these were in the
vater and operating, most of them at re-
.uced speed because of engine trouble. In
he next eight days the four fifty-ton barges
.radually were put into service, but at the
nd of three weeks the two one-hundred-
)n barges still had not been uncovered.[46]

This was merely the prelude. Tie rods
nd accessories for assembling the pontoon
·arges had been buried beneath other
.argo in loading; the first few craft had
o be assembled by welding. Weight-
andling equipment (slings and cargo nets
n the supply ships) had not been pro-
ided. Three weeks went by before the
rst crane could be located and unloaded.
'op-loaded materials that were not needed
mmediately had to be strung out for two
uiles along the beach. Poorly marked sup-
·lies proved even more of a problem at
;ora Bora than at Charleston; identifica-
.on was possible only by breaking into
·acking boxes and crates. Tractors and
·ucks needed for unloading the lighters
nd barges at the beach were fairly acces-
.ble, but this advantage was offset by the
ıct that neither of the two small coral
ındings was wide enough to admit more
1an one truck at a time or substantial
nough to support a heavy load. Under
hese conditions the thirty-ton lighters
·roved doubly useful, for they could come
lose in on sloping sections of the beach.
.ven after both equipment for lightering
.argo ashore and vehicles for moving it in-
and became available, the work still
.ragged because the small boats and
ghters were too few to maintain a steady
ow of material from ship to shore.
.dmiral Shafroth pointed out:

In unloading a number of ships, four 50-
)n lighters are far more valuable than two

100-ton lighters . . . at BOBCAT it was often
necessary to stop work on board ship due to
the necessity of waiting for a lighter to be unloaded at the beach and similarly to stop
work at beach heads to await the loading of
a lighter at some cargo ship.[47]

All told, fifty-two days were required to
discharge the convoy and an additional
supply ship. Hasty loading, together with
inadequate attention to landing facilities
in the plans for the expedition, had made
the BOBCAT Force a sitting duck for any
Japanese attack during the critical first
seven weeks of the occupation. Fortunately, none came.

To the military planners, Bora Bora was
an unknown speck of land—one of many,
in fact, for which the Army and Navy in
early 1942 had suddenly to prepare detailed operational plans. The Occidental
world in general had little exact knowledge of most of the Pacific areas beyond
Hawaii; more than one of the operational
plans rested upon data gathered in the
eighteenth or nineteenth century and
never since revised, nor was there time to
explore thoroughly the knowledge that
did exist. The Bora Bora expedition had
been preceded by a naval survey ship,
which provided the force with some hy-
drographic data. But the plans for the
land installations were based on a map
drawn up by French navigators a hundred years earlier. The only topographical
information available to the Washington
planning staffs came from a naval air pilot
who had been on the island in 1936. After
the convoy had sailed the Army staff,
searching for an interpreter, more or less

---

[46] (1) Ltr, Comdr SE Pac Force to SN, 18 Feb 42,
OPD 045.44 (3-5-42). (2) Ltr cited n. 35(4).

[47] (1) Ltr cited n. 35(4). (2) Ltr, Brig Gen Charles
D. Y. Ostrom to CofS, 26 Apr 42, OPD 381 Bora
Bora, Case 1. (3) *Building the Navy's Bases*, II, 199. (4)
Ballantine, *Naval Logistics*, pp. 68–69.

accidentally ran across a young Army Reserve officer who as a graduate student had been in the Orient and on Bora Bora during the preceding summer engaged in research for a thesis on Japanese colonization. 2d Lt. Walter H. Pleiss was immediately flown to Balboa where he joined the task force as it passed through the Canal. Even he, however, was scarcely qualified to warn Colonel Ostrom in detail of the technical difficulties that lay ahead.[48]

Once ashore, the expedition encountered conditions for which it was quite unprepared. The planners had assumed the existence of a water supply; there was none. Since the dry season was close at hand, Brig. Gen. Charles D. Y. Ostrom had to assign part of his force for six weeks to building dams and laying thirteen miles of pipeline. To avoid a repetition of the earlier chaos in unloading, landing facilities had to be developed to handle future shipments from the mainland. Bora Bora's one road, encircling the island along the coast, was vital to defense; immense labor was required to put it into shape to support military traffic, for it was a single-lane road built of coral and sand on a spongy base. For this task there were no graders and only one rock crusher. The seven-ton prime movers, provided to tow assembled heavy radar equipment, were too heavy for the flimsy road; bridges and culverts were broken down and the bed damaged, and the heavy trucks finally had to be barred from use in order to keep lighter traffic moving. Meanwhile, the few troops that could be spared had begun to construct defense installations. Heavy guns for the seacoast batteries had to be hauled one to two thousand feet up 45-degree slopes to get them into position. Many items of needed construction equipment

had either been omitted from the allowance tables prepared for the force, or simply left on the Charleston docks. Before it could be moved inland, much of the construction material had to be sorted out from disordered heaps along two miles of beach. It was early April before work could be started on the tank farm. The planners had assumed that tanks for the naval fuel depot would be installed on "a coastal flat" bordering the harbor. At no point, it developed, did the flats extend more than 50 to 150 yards in from the coast before rising abruptly toward lofty peaks in the center of the island. Level stretches inland were rare. To install the tanks so that fuel lines would reach harbor moorings, the naval construction detachment was forced to blast shelves from solid rock on the steep hillsides. Even with seven hundred Army troops helping the Seabees to build tanks for the farm, it was early June before the first eight tanks were complete.[49]

The time and labor poured into the various unanticipated preliminary tasks, and into overcoming other obstacles to planned construction, seriously delayed putting the base into operation and con-

---

[48] (1) Morison, *Rising Sun*, pp. 262, 266. (2) Ballantine, *Naval Logistics*, p. 69. (3) *Building the Navy's Bases*, II, 192. (4) Nelson L. Drummond, History of the U.S. Army Forces in the South Pacific Area During World War II from 30 March 1942 to 1 August 1944, MS, Pt. IV, p. 757, unnumbered note, OCMH. (5) WDGS Info Memo 2, 8 Jan 42, in G-4 Rpts, Bora Bora, SOPA folder, Plng Div ASF. (6) Memo, Capt Rodgers for Adm Turner, 30 Jan 42. (7) Memo, WPD for Turner, 2 Feb 42. Last two in WPD 4571-34. (8) For an account of the Pleiss episode, see Cline, *Washington Command Post*, pp. 81–82.

[49] (1) Ballantine, *Naval Logistics*, pp. 69–70. (2) *Building the Navy's Bases*, II, 192, 199–201. (3) Ltr cited n. 47(2). (4) Ltr, Comdr SE Pac Force to COMINCH, 21 Mar 42, sub: Advance Bases—Motorized Equip for, Bora Bora folder, Logis File, OCMH. (5) Memo, Adm Turner for Gen Gerow, 4 Jan 42, G-4/33943.

tructing its defense installations. These delays were heaped upon those already incurred at the outset in unloading. Equally serious, from the point of view of the force's commander, was the necessity for diverting combat troops from their normal functions to labor alongside the service personnel on virtually every project. The characteristic dilemma of force commanders in overseas operations, especially those in the Pacific, had made its appearance: commanders understandably desired maximum fighting power, but the shipping shortage limited the numerical strength of the expeditions and therefore a large number of the troops, whether combat or service, had to be used for construction and administration in primitive regions. As a result, it was a common phenomenon in 1942 that commanders, who in setting up their task forces had insisted upon a high proportion of combat to service troops, clamored for more service troops as soon as they encountered the practical problems of getting a base into operation.

No single remedy was available to prevent recurrences of BOBCAT's logistical ailments. The expedition was the first venture in small-scale task force logistics under wartime pressures—as General Ostrom said, "a step into the unknown." [50] The slow accumulation of experience in time would help to smooth the process of mounting and loading these small task forces, but the difficulties presented by each were in large measure unique. After BOBCAT the Chief of Transportation did, however, direct his Washington organization to see to it that vessels sailing on such expeditions were of suitable type and possessed adequate cargo-handling gear, together with winchmen and other personnel; that each force was provided with sufficient small boats and lighters for the unloading operation; that a competent officer was on hand to assist task force commanders in assembling material and arranging loading priorities. But the remedy for hasty planning, the basic source of the difficulties, lay in early basic decisions, and this was beyond the jurisdiction of the logistical agencies. Army port commanders were told that the Office of the Chief of Transportation would "make every effort to insure that sufficient time elapses between issuing orders and sailing dates to permit assembly of cargo and troops in an orderly manner." [51] The effort was to be made, but in 1942 usually in vain.

Many of the mistakes of the Bora Bora task force were repeated in the occupation of Efate and Tongatabu. The forces sent to the Fijis and Australia about the same time did not encounter the same kind of difficulties as those going to the less developed islands, but even in Australia port facilities and labor were far from ample, and the handling of troop and supply movements to that area was often attended by waste and confusion. Logistical methods in general were in a state of upheaval, and as long as the military situation precluded an orderly sequence of planning and action, overseas deployment inevitably moved by jerks and jolts. The experience of BOBCAT and the other small task forces sent to the South Pacific in the early part of 1942 was to be repeated later in the year on a larger scale in the descent on North Africa.

[50] Ltr cited n. 47(2).
[51] Memo, Col Frank S. Ross for CG's POE's and CofWater Br OCT, 12 Apr 42, sub: Orgn and Trans of Task Forces, Bora Bora folder, Logis File, OCMH.

*The Army's Administrative Problem
in the Pacific Islands*

The piecemeal progress of occupation and the division of responsibilities between the Army and Navy for the Pacific islands from Hawaii to New Zealand did not favor the rapid establishment of a satisfactory system of command, administration, and flow of supplies. The islands were in the Central and South Pacific subareas of the Pacific Ocean Area, which was under naval command, but it was some time before the subarea commands began to function. In any case, the Navy exercised only operational control; administration and supply remained divided between the two services. At the bases garrisoned by the Marine Corps—Samoa, Palmyra and Johnston—the Navy controlled all activities, but at the others—Christmas, Canton, Bora Bora, New Caledonia, the Fijis, Tongatabu, Efate, Espiritu Santo, and Fanning—Army forces were predominant and the Army therefore had the greater administrative burden.

Theoretically at least, command and logistical arrangements for the islands under Navy control were centralized under Admiral Nimitz' headquarters at Pearl Harbor. Administration of the Army bases was shared by the War Department, the San Francisco port, the Hawaiian Department, and, to a limited extent, USAFIA. Since General Emmons' Hawaiian command was the only mature Army establishment in the entire Pacific, the War Department originally assigned to him a large part of the responsibility for the island bases. But Emmons' responsibilities for the bases were assigned piecemeal and as the specific need arose, and they varied both in nature and extent. New Caledonia, where the largest garri-

son was stationed, was beyond effective administrative range of the Hawaiian Department. The War Department retained direct control of POPPY Force, dividing supply responsibility between USAFIA and the San Francisco port. It was typical of the general muddle that Emmons retained responsibility for construction of airfields at Plaines des Gaiacs outside Nouméa in New Caledonia. By the terms of the War Department's overseas supply directive of 22 January 1942, Christmas, Canton, Bora Bora, and Fiji were assigned to the Hawaiian Department for supply, though Emmons was empowered to authorize base commanders to requisition directly on the San Francisco port. The commanders of the joint task forces sent to Tongatabu and Efate were ordered to report directly to the War Department, and the San Francisco port was made responsible for supply of the Army forces involved.[52]

There was logic in the assignment to Emmons of supply responsibility for Christmas and Canton, for these two islands lay on the shipping routes from Hawaii. But Bora Bora and the Fijis, as Emmons soon recognized, could be supplied far more easily by direct shipments from San Francisco. After the activation of the Pacific Ocean Area and its subareas, moreover, Emmons' responsibilities in the South Pacific became anomalous, since his relation to Nimitz in that area remained undefined. In April the Navy announced the formation of the South

[52] (1) TAG ltr to Gen Patch, no date, sub: Def of New Caledonia, G-4/33888. (2) TAG ltr, 22 Jan 42, sub: Sup of Overseas Depts, Theaters, and Separate Bases, AG 400 (1-17-42). (3) See below, Ch. XIII. (4) Jt Bsc Pian for the Occupation and Def of Tongatabu, 12 Mar 42, OPD 381 Tongatabu, Case 1. (5) Jt Bsc Plan for the Occupation and Def of Efate, New Hebrides, 20 Mar 42, OPD 381 Efate, Case 8.

Pacific Area Command under Vice Adm. Robert L. Ghormley. It was clearly time for the Army to take some similar step to provide an administrative structure for its own scattered bases lying within Ghormley's jurisdiction.

Emmons became increasingly disturbed and late in May recommended that an Army command be set up for the South Pacific island bases "to coordinate their operations, supply and maintenance." [53] Emmons thought this command should bear the same relationship to his Hawaiian Department that Ghormley's command bore to that of Admiral Nimitz, but the War Department waited until after Admiral Ghormley had formally assumed command of the South Pacific Area on 19 June before moving to clarify Army command and supply responsibilities in the area—and then it only partially followed Emmons' suggestions. The first step was a new supply plan for the South Pacific on 25 June, freeing Emmons of most of his logistical responsibilities there. Only Christmas, Canton, and Fanning remained wholly dependent upon Hawaii for supply (Canton alone was in the South Pacific Area); Hawaii was also made responsible for certain administrative services at Bora Bora and Fiji, and for airfield construction along the alternate ferry route. For the rest, all Army forces in the South Pacific were placed directly under the War Department for administration, and were to be supplied either by local procurement in New Zealand and Australia or by San Francisco. [54]

This measure was followed on 7 July by the establishment of a separate Army command, the U.S. Army Forces in the South Pacific Area (USAFISPA). Maj. Gen. Millard F. Harmon, Chief of the Air Staff, was appointed commanding general

under a directive that made him directly responsible to the War Department for administration, supply, and training of all Army forces in that area. Harmon was to serve under Ghormley and exercise no operational control over Army troops in the theater, but he was to assist the naval commander in planning and executing such operations as involved Army forces. With Harmon's appointment, the separation of the Army commands in the South Pacific from those in the Central Pacific and Australia was complete. [55]

Joint Versus Parallel Supply

The clarification of supply and administrative responsibilities within the Army's own organization was but one facet of the problem of logistical organization in the Pacific. In this area of joint operations, supply of Army forces was intertwined with the supply of Navy forces. Both services had to recognize the necessity for some measure of logistical co-ordination. The first rudimentary steps toward such co-ordination were taken in the separate agreements incorporated in the basic plans for establishment of forces at Bora Bora, Tangatabu, Efate, Fiji, and Samoa. Generally speaking, these agreements made the Navy responsible at each base for providing fuel, and the Army for rations (except in the Samoan group where

---

[53] Ltr, CG HD to CofS, 20 May 42, sub: Army Comd in S Pac Area, OPD 334 PTO, Sec 1, Case 18.

[54] (1) TAG ltr to CG's U.S. Army Forces in Efate, Fiji, New Caledonia, Tongatabu, and Espiritu Santo, 25 Jun 42, sub: Sup of USAFISPA, AG 400 (6-22-42). (2) Msg, Marshall to Emmons, 4 Jul 42, CM-OUT 1179. (CM-IN and CM-OUT numbers used in the footnotes of this volume refer to numbers appearing on copies of those messages in General Marshall's In and Out Logs, filed in the Staff Communications Office, Office of the Chief of Staff, U.S. Army.)

[55] Ltr, CofS to Gen Harmon, 7 Jul 42, sub: Ltr of Instn to CG USAFISPA, OPD 384 PTO, Case 18.

the Navy had sole responsibility); each service supplied its own distinctive individual and organization equipment. These agreements were tentative and loose, however, and there were no basic plans at all for New Caledonia and Espiritu Santo.[56]

Progress toward a more integrated system of joint logistics was slow, halting, and the subject of acrimonious dispute between the two services. At the meeting of the Joint Chiefs of Staff on 6 April 1942, Admiral King and Admiral Turner, Chief of the Navy War Plans Division, opened the question by pointing out that supply to New Zealand, where the Navy was planning to establish its major base in the South Pacific, was linked with that of American troops in Australia. They suggested somewhat vaguely a South Pacific service force for sending supplies to both areas. Nevertheless, the Joint Chiefs, in directing the Joint Staff Planners (JPS) to study the matter, excluded SWPA from their purview as far as joint supply from the mainland was concerned. The planners were instructed merely to investigate and make recommendations on the composition of a joint Army and Navy service force for the South Pacific Area and the possibilities of local procurement in both Australia and New Zealand as a means of reducing shipping requirements from the United States, and to recommend whether General MacArthur should be responsible for supplying any troops outside his area.[57]

The Joint Planners appointed a subcommittee composed of Brig. Gen. LeRoy Lutes, Director of Operations in the new Services of Supply, with three other SOS staff officers and three Navy supply experts, to study the problem. Specifically, it seemed necessary to (1) organize local procurement in New Zealand with machinery for co-ordination with SWPA, (2)

make shipping available in Australia, Hawaii, and on the west coast for distributing supplies to the island bases, and (3) determine whether a joint supply system was desirable (outside the area of local procurement), and, if so, how it was to be set up.[58]

On the first point, it was readily agreed that a joint purchasing board should be established in New Zealand, that competition between it and the similar agency (General Purchasing Board) in Australia must be prevented, and that to extract the most benefit from local resources, the two purchasing boards should co-operate in obtaining supplies from Australia for U.S. forces stationed in New Zealand and the island bases. The question of shipping, it was agreed, turned upon information that would have to be obtained from theater commanders. The committee decided to ask General MacArthur for an estimate of the shipping available to him that could be used for servicing Army and Navy garrisons in the South Pacific, and to question both Emmons and Nimitz as to procurement of subsistence stores in Australia and New Zealand for the South Pacific Area, availability of spare ship tonnage in Hawaii and San Francisco, and the possible advantage of "joint Army-Navy use of shipping from Hawaii to the island bases."[59]

---

[56] (1) Jt A&N Plan cited n. 30(2). (2) Jt Bsc Plan cited n. 52(4). (3) Jt Bsc Plan cited n. 52(5).

[57] (1) Min, 9th mtg JCS, 6 Apr 42. (2) JPS 21/4/D, 7 Apr 42, title: JPS Dir, Jt A&N Sv Force for the S Pac Area.

[58] (1) Memo, Secy JPS for Lutes et al., 10 Apr 42, sub: Subcom, Appointment of, with incl, Unified Sup: Army-Navy 1942-43 folder, Lutes File. (2) Min, 11th mtg JPS, 8 Apr 42. (3) JPS 21/9, 25 Apr 42, title: JPS Subcom Rpt, Jt A&N Sv Force for Pac Theater. (4) Min, 2d and 3d mtgs JPS Subcom on Sup Sv for Pac Theater, 15 and 20 Apr 42.

[59] (1) Min, 2d mtg, cited n. 58(4). (2) Memo, Lutes for Somervell, 15 Apr 42, Lutes File.

Nimitz' reply to these queries brought the question of a joint supply system to a head. He suggested that supply of the South Pacific should be handled entirely as a joint enterprise. He proposed the establishment of a "joint supply service at Auckland staffed with Navy, Marine and Army personnel," [60] to be under the naval commander of that area, and to form part of the Service Squadron, South Pacific, the Navy's supply agency in the new theater. The proposed joint staff would have responsibility for supplying to outlying islands such stores as could be obtained locally. Shipping and storage facilities would be used jointly and purchases made under joint arrangements. Interservice co-ordination was also necessary, Nimitz thought, in supply from the mainland. He recommended the establishment of a "like office with joint personnel in the Service Force Subordinate Command at San Francisco . . . but with existing storage and procurement agencies to be used." [61] All shipping and supply arrangements for the South Pacific would be handled by this office on a joint basis. [62]

General Emmons, writing independently from Hawaii on 19 April, expressed generally similar views. He felt that transportation in the Pacific Ocean Area should be pooled, with priorities on shipments determined by Admiral Nimitz as senior tactical commander. "In my judgment," he wrote, "it is just as necessary to have logistical unity of command as tactical unity of command." [63] Emmons wanted to know the War Department's attitude before making any recommendations to Admiral Nimitz. In replying to Emmons, General Somervell adroitly used certain of Emmons' earlier references to an improved supply situation in Hawaii as arguments against joint supply:

You will admit, I am sure, that you owe that [the improved supply situation] to the direct logistical support of the Army and that we were better able to serve you because we controlled both the supply facilities and the transportation necessary. . . . when you consider our greater strength in the Pacific, in Hawaii, in Australia, in Alaska, in many of the smaller islands, and our incomparably larger supply set-up, it is inevitable that the operations so undertaken would necessarily become joint in character with all the frictions, inefficiencies and divided responsibilites that flow therefrom. We have so dominant an interest; we have so clear a responsibility in the supply of our large forces; we must definitely control the means. [64]

From this position, the Army members of the subcommittee refused to budge, and in the end they carried their point. The first report of the subcommittee on 25 April recommended that "shipping out of West Coast ports continue to be co-ordinated under the principle of mutual cooperation as at present." [65] The Joint Planners returned the report for restudy, but the impasse could not be broken. The champions of joint supply had to be content with an agreement to set up joint machinery for local procurement in the South Pacific. The Joint Chiefs agreed on 11 May that the Navy's announcement that a joint purchasing staff would be formed in New Zealand satisfied their original di-

---

[60] See below, n. 61.

[61] Msg 3528, CG HD to CG SOS, 21 Apr 42, ABC 400 POA (4-4-42). This is Emmons' paraphrase of Nimitz' message. No copy of Nimitz' original message could be found in War Department files.

[62] (1) Ibid. (2) Min, 3d mtg, cited n. 58(4). (3) Ballantine, *Naval Logistics*, pp. 96–98.

[63] Min, 3d mtg, cited n. 58(4).

[64] Ltr, Somervell to Emmons, 28 Apr 42, Gross Day File, Apr–Jun 42, Case 39, OCT HB. The letter was drafted by Brig. Gen. Charles P. Gross, Chief of Transportation.

[65] JPS 21/9 cited n. 58(3).

rective to the Joint Planners.[66]

Later in the year Somervell and Lutes were to give vigorous support to an even more comprehensive scheme of joint logistics than that under consideration in April 1942. The reasons for their earlier stand are not difficult to discern. In Nimitz' April plan the Navy would hold the reins of control. Somervell and his advisers were dubious of the ability of the Navy's logistical organization, which seemed to them laggard in adjusting itself to wartime tasks, to cope with operations on the scale demanded in the Pacific, and they feared Army interests would suffer. The SOS, moreover, especially its Transportation Service (not yet risen to the eminence of a corps), was itself troubled by growing pains and feeling its way toward an orderly system of overseas supply; participation at this time in a new interservice mechanism would raise new and unwelcome problems.[67]

The subcommittee made several more positive suggestions for economies in shipping, emphasizing cross-procurement and co-ordinated exploitation of local resources between the Southwest and South Pacific Areas. The committee was convinced that these methods would produce savings of at least 10 to 15 percent in mainland supply to the South Pacific. Since most of the logistical support must still come from the United States, the committee also turned its attention to economies in utilization of ships. It urged that all vessels assigned to the long Pacific run should carry full cargoes for the greatest possible proportion of the round trip, and that large vessels should be released, as far as possible, from time-consuming "milk-runs" involved in distribution to line bases. Full shiploads should be delivered directly to the bases from the west

coast and Australia whenever possible. Admiral Ghormley was to report on the possibility of shipment to centrally located distribution points from which further distribution could be carried out in small vessels. To expedite supply to the island chain, the South Pacific Area and SWPA commanders were to make full use of space in ships returning to the United States.[68]

With the delineation of both the Army and Navy command and administrative systems in the South Pacific, steps were taken to put the recommendations into effect. On the day he formally assumed command, 19 June 1942, Admiral Ghormley activated the Joint Purchasing Board for the South Pacific, composed of three officers representing the Army, Navy, and Marine Corps, respectively, with the Army member, Col. Lawrence Westbrook, serving as president. The board soon assumed control of all procurement from sources other than the United States. In the Army's supply plan for the South Pacific of 25 June, Army commanders at Pacific bases were instructed to inform the board of any supplies available on their islands and in turn to requisition on the board for whatever supplies it could furnish. The board in turn would inform the San Francisco port of all supplies obtainable through local procurement, and San Francisco would ship the balance of supplies to whatever port the South Pacific

---

[66] (1) Min, 15th mtg JPS, 29 Apr 42, Item 4. (2) JCS 50, 6 May 42, title: Jt A&N Sv Force for the S Pac Area. (3) OPD notes on 14th mtg JCS, 11 May 42, ABC 400 (4-4-42). (4) Memo, Secy JCS for Gen Lutes *et al.*, 13 May 42, Unified Sup: Army-Navy 1942–43 folder, Case 14a, Lutes File.

[67] (1) For the decentralized system of logistical organization in the Navy at this time, see Ballantine, *Naval Logistics*, pp. 38–93. (2) See also below, Chs. XV, XXIV.

[68] JPS 21/9 cited n. 58(3).

Area commander designated. Ghormley's headquarters was to be responsible for all transshipment and for distribution of locally procured supplies.[69]

As a final step the Army and Navy in July, spurred by the imminent prospects of a campaign in the South Pacific, turned to codify in a single plan the various arrangements that had been generally agreed upon for logistical support of the South Pacific. On 15 July an agreement was reached between General Somervell and Vice Adm. Frederick J. Horne, Admiral King's deputy and senior naval supply officer, entitled "Joint Logistical Plan for the Support of United States Bases in the South Pacific Area." The existing division of responsibility for items in common use was confirmed and extended to New Caledonia and Espiritu Santo. The Army was to assume responsibility for supplying to shore-based personnel in South Pacific bases (except the Samoan group) such rations as could not be procured through the Joint Purchasing Board. In turn, the Navy undertook to provide all gasoline and oil including that for aircraft, and to supply all items available from local resources through the Joint Purchasing Board—clothing, equipment, and construction and miscellaneous materials as well as rations. Each service, after determining which items could be satisfied from local sources by the Joint Purchasing Board, was to process requisitions for the remainder of its needs directly to its own mainland sources—for the Army the San Francisco port, for the Navy the Commander, Service Force Subordinate Command, Pacific Fleet, and the Commandant, Twelfth Naval District. As far as practicable shipment of supplies from the United States was to be made in shipload lots by each service directly to

the bases. Where redistribution was necessary, control was vested in Admiral Ghormley, who was to control all ships assigned to the theater, designate the port or ports to which supplies for redistribution were to be delivered, and distribute within the theater supplies shipped for redistribution and those procured locally.[70]

The plan thus left the logistical systems of the two services intact and separate insofar as supply from the United States was concerned. On the other hand, it clarified respective responsibilities and provided for a measure of joint action within the theater. The failure to achieve greater integration reflected the lack of appreciation by either service of the impelling necessity for it.

"Logistics is still, and for a long time will be, in a muddle," General Harmon wrote in August from the South Pacific.[71] The same might have been said of the Southwest Pacific, though in less measure, for the logistical system there, owing to the early clarification of command responsibilities and stabilization of the military situation, had had longer to become settled. In the South Pacific the initial phase of manning the island chain was largely completed in May, but when the first offensive in the Pacific, the Guadalcanal Campaign, was launched the following

[69] (1) TAG ltr cited n. 54(1). (2) Ltr, Comdr S Pac Area to atchd distrib list, 19 Jun 42, sub: Jt Purch Bd of the S Pac Area. (3) Ltr, President Jt Purch Bd to CG SOS, 19 Jul 42, sub: Rpt on Orgn and Opn of Jt Purch Bd, S Pac Area, with App. B. Last two in U.S. Jt Purch Bd, S Pac Area, Wellington, New Zealand: Rpt on Orgn and Opn of Jt Purch Bd, S Pac Area folder, Plng Div ASF, Job A44-140.

[70] Jt Logis Plan for the Support of U.S. Bases in the S Pac Area, 15 Jul 42, 370.2 Jt A&N Opns and Rpt folder, Plng Div ASF, Job A44-140.

[71] Ltr, Gen Harmon to Brig Gen St. Clair Streett, 27 Aug 42, quoted in Drummond MS, Pt. I, Ch. 3, n. 25, cited n. 48(4).

August, the whole South Pacific Area administrative structure was still in the formative stage. Admiral Ghormley set up his command in June. General Harmon arrived in New Caledonia late in July to establish the Army headquarters, but it was not adequately staffed and scarcely functioned at all until September; no services of supply was created until late in October. July saw the emergence of the Army's supply plan and the Joint Logistical Plan for the South Pacific. Neither was definitive, and the scarcity of supply personnel, both Army and Navy, was a failing no paper arrangement could overcome. The Joint Logistical Plan, moreover, ratified the existing duality of separate Army and Navy supply systems, postponing a settlement of this issue until later in the year when, as the Guadalcanal Campaign reached an acute stage, it could no longer be evaded. Nevertheless, the logistical arrangements of July created a framework within which an effective supply and administrative system could take shape, and the Joint Logistical Plan, as a naval historian has remarked, "provided at least a cornerstone in the development of joint maintenance and supply procedure in the Pacific." [72]

---

[72] Ballantine, *Naval Logistics*, p. 100.

PART THREE

THE EMERGENCE OF POLICY
AND METHOD

CHAPTER VIII

Strategy, Production Goals, and Shipping

In the midst of a more or less continuous emergency in the Pacific and a mounting shipping crisis in the Atlantic and Caribbean, the military leaders and staffs had also to attempt to make plans for the more distant future—specifically to formulate a strategy for taking the offensive and defeating the enemy, and to develop programs for mobilizing the forces, munitions, and shipping needed to carry out that strategy.

The Victory Program—Morning After

Allied political and military leaders meeting in Washington soon after Pearl Harbor to formulate a coalition strategy took as their point of departure the principle already enunciated in ABC-1, that the defeat of Germany should be the first and major goal of Allied strategy, and that operations in other theaters must not be allowed to retard its attainment. Beyond this, agreement was more difficult. The British brought to the conference the plan of action they had set forth the preceding summer. This strategy looked to an eventual return to the European continent in force, possibly in the summer of 1943, with numerous landings around its perimeter. Churchill envisaged the invading armies, strong in armor but relatively

modest in numbers, serving as spearheads behind which the peoples of Europe would rise and smite their German conquerors. U.S. Army planners still took a dim view of this program, foreseeing that it would involve a long series of costly preliminary operations merely in order to gain positions for penetrating the Continent simultaneously from several directions. The main effort, they felt, should be concentrated upon one point of the enemy's defenses, and delivered with maximum force in conjunction with a Soviet offensive from the East.[1]

The American planners as yet had no positive counterplan to offer, and the whole question of how to defeat Germany seemed to lie in the dim future. For months to come, the staff pointed out, Britain would be hard pressed merely to hold her own at home and in the Middle and Far East. The United States, a staff paper stated late in December,

. . . can only inadequately defend its coasts against air raids, hold Hawaii, the Panama

---

[1] (1) Paper, Churchill for President, "Part III: The Campaign of 1943," 18 Dec 41, as quoted in Churchill, *The Grand Alliance*, pp. 655–58. (2) Memo, Br CsofS, 22 Dec 41, sub: Br-American Strategy, ABC 337 Arcadia (12-24-41), 2. (3) WPD paper, 21 Dec 41, sub: Notes on Agenda Proposed by Gt Brit, Folder-Bk. 2, Exec 4. (4) Matloff and Snell, *Strategic Planning: 1941–1942*, Ch. V. (5) See above, Chs. II, V.

Canal and other existing bases, gradually complete the relief of the British in Iceland, reinforce the Philippines or Dutch East Indies, occupy Natal, and possibly occupy some other base not seriously defended by Axis forces or sympathisers (Cape Verdes or Azores). It will be practicable and may be necessary to send some armored or infantry divisions to the British Isles in the winter or spring. . . . The shortage of U.S. flag shipping . . . precludes the possibility of executing more than one, or at most two, of these operations concurrently.[2]

In short, it looked to the planners as though Allied military action for some time to come would have to be shaped from day to day, more or less as the enemy called the tune.

The "grand strategy" upon which the Allied leaders agreed, therefore, after about a week's discussion at the end of December, was not very explicit, and it reflected British ideas more than American. Action in 1942, under the circumstances, could only be tentatively projected, and was mainly of a defensive character or preparatory to later offensives; the descent on North Africa, the major operation in the Atlantic envisaged for 1942, was already fading from view as a practical possibility. The year 1943, it was hoped, might see the way clear for "a return to the Continent, across the Mediterranean, from Turkey into the Balkans, or by landings in Western Europe." Meanwhile, it would be well to "be ready to take advantage of any opening . . . to conduct limited land offensives" in 1942, or in other ways to further the aim of "closing and tightening the ring around Germany."[3]

To the mobilization of forces and munitions for ultimate victory, therefore, the strategic planners could offer little guidance. General Gerow, who had laid down the "strategy-forces-munitions" formula

for the Victory Program in July 1941, admitted late in December, "the forces that the Associated Powers now estimate as necessary to achieve victory and for which productive capacity must be provided, may not be adequate or appropriate. No one can predict the situation that will develop while the enemy retains the strategic initiative."[4]

Current notions of the size of forces that would be needed to win the war therefore tended to reflect little more specific than a sense of urgency. A new Victory Program Troop Basis, circulated late in December, set new goals, for long-range supply planning, of more than four million men by the end of 1942 and more than ten million by mid-1944. These figures were higher than the objectives for actual expansion of the Army, which in late December 1941 contemplated 3.6 million troops (ground and air) under arms by the end of 1942, with seventy-one divisions organized, though many of these would be understrength and in the early stages of training. Mobilization plans did not at this juncture look ahead to 1943, though it was widely assumed that the Army would then double its 1942 strength.[5]

Meanwhile, the civilian production experts, who had been examining the feasibility of the original Victory Program objectives, submitted their findings to the

[2] WPD paper, sub: Immediate Mil Measures, part of WPD paper cited n. 1(3).

[3] (1) ABC-4/CS-1, memo, U.S. and Br CsofS, 31 Dec 41, title: American-Br Grand Strategy. (2) For the decline of the GYMNAST plan, see above, Ch. VI.

[4] Memo, Gerow for Marshall, no date, sub: Vic Prog, WPD 4494 Vic Prog, U.S. Data.

[5] (1) Corresp in WPD 4494 series, especially WPD 4494-23, WPD 4494-26, and WPD 4494 Vic Prog, U.S. Data; and G-4/33473. (2) Memo, Ray S. Cline for Col William A. Walker, 24 Jan 47, sub: Info Concerning Tr Basis, Stf Action Corresp folder, OPD Hist Unit File. (3) See also, Greenfield, Palmer, and Wiley, *AGF I*, pp. 198ff.

military authorities a few days after Pearl Harbor. Statisticians of the Office of Production Management estimated that the entire bill, at current prices and including the program financed to date, would come to $150 billion. About $20 billion had already been spent, and the experts calculated that industry could absorb $45 billion in 1942 and $60 to $65 billion in 1943. At this rate the program would be only three-quarters completed by the end of September 1943, the remainder some time the following spring. Other estimates were more conservative. Mr. William S. Knudsen thought that no more than $38 billion could be disbursed in 1942, $57 billion in 1943. Within these limits, moreover, the civilian production experts believed that the goals for certain items, such as small arms ammunition, Garand rifles, 155-mm. guns, and several types of trucks, were "out of line" and would have to be lowered. No one believed that all seventy-one divisions could be fully or even half equipped in 1942; a great deal would depend on how much matériel went to lend-lease. But the experts seemed reasonably confident that the 3.6 million-man Army could be equipped in some fashion by the end of 1942.[6]

Army supply officers were inclined to be skeptical of these predictions. "If this is all that can be done," remarked Colonel Aurand at one point with reference to the more cautious estimates of Mr. Knudsen and the Supply Priorities and Allocations Board, "we might as well give up."[7] But there was, in general, little impulse from within the military organization at this time to raise the sights of industrial mobilization. The staffs were immersed, during December, in a vast amount of pick-and-shovel work. New financial estimates were being rushed through for Congressional

action so that production might be accelerated. New requirements were being drawn up to close the gap between the $27 billion in production that current schedules, when projected, indicated for 1942, and the $40 to $45 billion in capacity that the civilian experts said would be available. The Victory Program itself had to be revised in greater detail to include the vast amounts of clothing, equipage, and other easy-to-produce items omitted from the original estimates. Beyond this, military supply men, from long experience, feared to tamper with production schedules already established and in operation—the machine might then have to be slowed down before it could be speeded up.[8]

Production Goals and the Problem of Balance

The impulse that lifted industrial mobilization out of the prison of peacetime conceptions of national productive capacity came from outside the Military Establishment. For more than a year Purvis, Monnet, and their associates in the British missions in the United States had labored to jar American officials into awareness of the huge quantities of munitions needed to win the war, as well as of the vast potentialities of American industry for producing them. In the last days of December Lord Beaverbrook, the British Minister of Sup-

---

[6] (1) Memo, Donald Nelson for SW, 11 Dec 41, G-4/33473. (2) Other corresp in same file. (3) Notes to accompany tabulation, "Major Combat Units That Can Be Equipped by Specific Dates," 21 Dec 41, Item 14, Exec 4. (4) CPA, *Industrial Mobilization for War,* pp. 273–74.

[7] Memo, Col Aurand for Gen Moore, 11 Dec 41, sub: All-Out Mun Prog, U.K. Vic Prog folder, DAD.

[8] (1) Memo, SW for Donald Nelson, 16 Dec 41, sub: Vic Prog, G-4/33473. (2) WD paper, 21 Dec 41, sub: Estd Pdn, WPD 4494-22 to WPD 4494-36 Vic Prog, Sec. 2. (3) Corresp in WPD 4494 Vic Prog, U.S. Data. (4) Memo, unsigned, no addressee, 25 Dec 41, sub: Sup for 1942, Misc Corresp Lend-lease 4 file, DAD.

ply, who was in Washington as part of the Prime Minister's entourage, pressed these arguments directly upon the President.[9] His efforts evidently were successful. The President wrote Stimson on 3 January that victory depended in the last analysis upon "our overwhelming mastery in the munitions of war," to achieve which "the concept of our industrial capacity must be completely overhauled." America's allies, already "extended to the utmost," could not arm their own large armies. "We must not only provide munitions for our own fighting forces but vast quantities to be used against the enemy in every appropriate theater of war, wherever that may be."[10] He directed forthwith that the war effort be geared to a new set of production goals, expressed significantly not in dollars but in quantities of a few major items— 60,000 airplanes in 1942 and 125,000 in 1943; 45,000 tanks in 1942 and 75,000 in 1943; 20,000 antiaircraft guns in 1942 and 35,000 in 1943; half a million machine guns in 1942 and as many in 1943; 8,000,000 dead-weight tons of merchant shipping in 1942 and 10,000,000 in 1943. These goals were blazoned forth three days later in the President's state-of-the-union message to Congress. "This production of ours . . . must be raised far above present levels . . . . We must raise our sights all along the production line. Let no man say it cannot be done. It must be done—and we have undertaken to do it."[11]

The response to the President's January production objectives, both among the production authorities and in the Military Establishment, was less than enthusiastic. The goals had no anchor either in feasibility or in need; they flew in the face of both the production authorities' notions of what could be produced and the military chiefs'

claim to the right to determine what should be produced. Estimates of probable cost varied, but they ranged upward from a figure of $52 billion for 1942 production alone. Mr. Nelson's advisers did indeed revise their estimates of production capacity upward to close the gap, but the President's program, when translated into detailed programs of military supply, showed a tendency to climb even higher. The Army's War Munitions Program of 11 February, precursor of the Army Supply Programs, piled up requirements estimated at $62 to $63 billion through 1943, bringing the estimated total of all war needs to $62.6 billion for 1942 and $110 for 1943. During the spring and summer individual portions of the program rose and fell in estimated valuations, but the total war production program, until autumn, climbed steadily, particularly in such categories as naval-vessel and merchant-vessel construction. The production authorities resisted this trend, but on the whole without marked success, despite a ruling from the President early in April setting a ceiling of $45 billion for 1942 and $75 billion for 1943. The revisions resulting from this rule failed to bring production goals down to the limits established, and the President himself, on 1 May, called for new quantitative goals, some of which were in excess of those announced in January.[12]

---

[9] (1) Note, Beaverbrook to President, as quoted in Churchill, *The Grand Alliance*, p. 689. (2) See also above, Chs. I, III.

[10] Memo, President for SW, 3 Jan 42, WPD 4494 Vic Prog, U.S. Data.

[11] (1) Address, President to Cong, 6 Jan 42, 77th Cong, 2d Sess, HR Doc 501, pp. 3–4. (2) CPA *Industrial Mobilization for War*, pp. 277–78. (3) Churchill, *The Grand Alliance*, pp. 688–91. (4) Hancock and Gowing, *British War Economy*, pp. 387–88, 398.

[12] (1) CPA, *Industrial Mobilization for War*, pp. 273–85. (2) For the development of the Army Supply Program, see below, Ch. XII.

At the outset the military services were determined to translate the President's major-item goals into a balanced program for all items of munitions. General Somervell, comparing the President's January goals with the amounts of the corresponding items already incorporated in the Army's supplemental estimates for 1942, concluded optimistically, "the items in the President's directive are indices of balanced production contemplated by time objectives established before its receipt. In other words, the accomplishment of the President's directive for 1942 can be accomplished by the production of a balanced equipment program." Even with respect to the still unformulated program for 1943, Somervell was confident that a balanced program "on the scale indicated in the President's directive" could be achieved.[13] What this meant in terms of total objectives the mammoth War Munitions Program of 11 February soon demonstrated. Its size, indeed, caused some uneasiness even in the services. Admiral King feared the impact of a huge expansion program upon production during the next few months. "What we need most and need urgently," he warned, "is the maximum output of plants that are now producing . . . . It is literally a case of 'first things first.'" But he, too, insisted upon balance. "It is of little use to go all out on tanks unless there are ships to ferry them, trained and equipped troops to man them, aircraft to cooperate with them, antiaircraft guns and field artillery to protect them."[14]

The civilian production officials threw up their hands in horror at the Army's 11 February program, and took their case to the President. His goals for airplanes, tanks, antiaircraft and antitank guns, and merchant shipping could be achieved, they said, but not in conjunction with the multitude of ancillary items that the services wanted to procure on a like scale. A choice must be made: either the announced objectives in major items, or a balanced program pitched at a lower level. The services accordingly were directed to revise their requirements downward, but in balance.[15] Thereafter the trend of Army requirements, in the supply programs of 1942, was downward.

On the dangers of imbalance, as on those of sin, almost everyone could agree. But "balance" meant something different to each of the claimants. The result was bitter contention within the Military Establishment, and between the military and civilian authorities, over the priorities structure that would govern the division of the national product. Long before Pearl Harbor, the lack of a firm policy and of effective machinery to decide among the competing claimants had resulted in overloading the top-priority ratings and depreciating the lower ones. In the flood of orders and new programs of early 1942 the situation quickly got out of hand. The Army and Navy Munitions Board reported late in February that, out of total war expenditures scheduled or in prospect for 1942 (about $56 billion at this juncture), over $31 billion, or almost 56 percent, was in the top-priority band. The Combined Chiefs of Staff considered the problem, but their jurisdiction over what seemed to be a distinctly American prob-

---

[13] (1) Memo, Somervell for CofS, 7 Jan 42, sub: Effect of President's Dir of 3 Jan, WPD 4494 Vic Prog, U.S. Data. (2) CPA, *Industrial Mobilization for War*, pp. 273–74.
[14] Memo, Adm King for SN, 19 Feb 42, sub: Priority of Pdn of Mat, WPD 4494-22 to WPD 4494-36 Vic Prog, Sec 2.
[15] (1) CPA, *Industrial Mobilization for War*, pp. 275–76, 283. (2) See below, Ch. XII.

lem was a matter of dispute. Not until a combined board for production and resources was established in June was the priorities question to receive any serious consideration at the combined level. In the interim, what and how much to produce became a problem for the U.S. military agencies to work out with the civilian production authorities.[16]

Within the military staffs there was general agreement that production programs should be shaped to serve strategic objectives. A "balanced" program would be one that provided adequate amounts of the various categories of munitions in time to execute an approved strategy. The basis of an Army supply program, General Somervell asserted late in January,

. . . should consist of the strategical concept for the prosecution of the war, the general policy and detailed plans for the supply of Army-type munitions to the United Nations, and the plans for the mobilization, training and utilization of the Army, to consist not only of the long-range plan but also of detailed plans for the immediate future.

It is realized that the basis . . . cannot be stated with exactitude, that broad assumptions . . . must be made, and that the statement is subject to constant change. Nevertheless . . . these factors are the impulse behind the entire Army Supply Program from the formulation of the program through allocation of facilities and raw materials, the placing of orders, production and delivery.

It might be argued that such a statement would be so full of uncertainties that it would not be worth attempting. This is not, however, the case. Under any conditions, plans must be made and actions taken . . . . Without such a statement, those responsible for various phases of supply are forced to make their own uncoordinated assumptions and guesses.[17]

The fundamental difficulty, as Somervell hinted, was that there was no approved strategy sufficiently explicit to provide a

basis for concrete programs of requirements, production schedules, and priorities. ARCADIA had produced only a concept, a "grand strategy"; the specific course of action best calculated to give effect to this strategic concept, assuming that the development of events so permitted, was a subject of lively debate on the upper staff levels and between the military and political leaders, and the advocates of each major arm of warfare naturally tended to bestow the label "balanced," like an accolade, only on programs and priorities that supported their own favored strategy. One brief, for example, evidently prepared by an Air officer, stated first the general proposition, "The national industry must be so coordinated that production meets the requirements of grand strategy, rather than the reverse," and from this proceeded to the conclusion, "Allocation of production must be predicated on the creation of the air forces set forth in the Victory Program in the shortest practicable time, *and balancing of all other requirements in relation thereto.*"[18]

Late in February the Joint Planners were directed to "review the strategical situation, to include probable . . . operations in order of priority, and determine the critical items of material such as merchant and combat vessels, tanks, aircraft, antiaircraft equipment, guns, etc., which

[16] (1) Papers in CCS 400.3 (2-17-42) Pt. 1. (2) Min, sp mtg JB, 20 Feb 42. (3) JPS 2/3/D, 22 Feb 42, title: JPS Dir, Priorities in Pdn of Mun Based on Strategical Considerations. (4) Memo, ANMB for CCS [American Sec], 26 Feb 42, sub: Resume of Priorities Sit . . . , JB 355, Ser 745. Last three in CCS 400.17 (2-20-42) Sec 1. (5) For efforts to set up a combined requirements program, see below, Ch. XI.
[17] Memo, Gen Somervell for Gen Moore, 22 Jan 42, sub: Army Supply Program, CofS WDGS 1941–42 folder, Hq ASF.
[18] Paper, unsigned, 6 Jan 42, sub: Vic Prog, WPD 4494 Vic Prog, U.S. Data. Italics are the authors'.

must be produced to implement these operations." [19] However, the Joint U.S. Strategic Committee (JUSSC), to which the task was assigned, found that it could only go in circles without the basic strategic decisions, which "control the projected development and deployment of fighting forces, which in turn control the needs of the fighting forces for war materials." [20] The committee was beset by representations from competing interests—Lt. Gen. Henry H. Arnold, for example, wanted a new priority list topped by "aircraft complete, with munitions," [21] and Admiral King complained that naval shipbuilding was being subordinated. The JUSSC finally recommended nine separate categories of war material for assignment to highest priority. These, representing a composite of all the competing claims, in effect sought to ensure material support for all the divergent strategies clamoring for favor.

On 1 May the President, worried by lagging production, announced a new set of objectives for 1942. Those for aircraft, antiaircraft guns, tanks, and artillery remained generally at the levels set in January. Machine guns were reduced from 500,000 to 400,000, certain adjustments were made in antiaircraft and antitank weapons, and "tanks" now included self-propelled artillery and other "tank-type" weapons. For merchant shipping the objectives, already raised in February, were confirmed at nine million dead-weight tons. The formidable naval program, omitted in January, was now included. Perhaps the most significant addition was "complementary equipment required for a decisive land and air offensive involving amphibious landing operations"—an important concession to balance. The President even mentioned "complementary weapons for the supporting troops required," and noted that "every effort must be made" to produce equipment for training additional forces, for lend-lease, and for "other needed items." Nevertheless, at the end he warned, "a balance in these latter items must not be attained at the expense of the specific items which I have enumerated herein." [22]

The President also declined to tie production objectives to any specific strategy. April had seen a sudden lifting of the mists that had obscured future coalition action, when General Marshall and Harry Hopkins succeeded at London in winning British acceptance to the plan for invading Europe the following spring. The decision seemed to presage a long-range course of action that could be charted in detail to provide a firm guide for mobilization and production planning alike, and it was reflected in the President's reference to "complementary weapons" for "decisive" amphibious operations. But he also appended a prophetic note to the Joint Chiefs: "We cannot foretell the critical period in our war effort, and maximum production of major items of military equipment must be obtained without delay." [23]

In the same vein the President approved, on 1 May, the recommendations of the Joint Chiefs on production priorities, which followed in the main those sub-

---

[19] Min cited n. 16(2).

[20] JPS 20, 23 Mar 42, title: Priorities in Pdn of Mun Based on Strategical Considerations, CCS 400.17 (2-20-42) Sec 1.

[21] Memo, CG AAF for USW, 17 Mar 42, sub: Priorities for Pdn of Mun Based on Strategical Considerations, CCS 400.17 (2-20-42) Sec 1.

[22] Ltr, President to Donald Nelson, 1 May 42, incl with memo, President for JCS, 1 May 42, sub: Recommendations to JCS for Priority of Pdn of War Mun, CCS 400.17 (2-20-42) Sec 1.

[23] (1) *Ibid.* (2) See below, Chs. XIV, XVI.

mitted by the JUSSC.[24] On 20 May these recommendations were translated into a new draft directive on priorities by the Army and Navy Munitions Board. The directive superimposed upon the existing structure of priorities an emergency rating band, AAA, and four other bands, AA-1 through AA-4. To the latter were assigned the existing military programs with necessary plant expansion and raw materials. Bands AA-1 and AA-2 were intended to comprise a balanced program of the most urgently needed munitions; the lower two covered less urgent military production and construction. Into AA-1 went roughly half the military programs, including half of the President's "must" items. All the nonmilitary programs, including lend-lease and the whole field of civilian requirements, were relegated by implication to the existing and now downgraded priority categories. Inexplicably, part of the vital merchant shipping program was placed in a rating that would virtually preclude its accomplishment. The directive immediately became the focus of a prolonged dispute between the services and WPB, which continued even after the directive, in revised form, was approved by Mr. Nelson and the President early in June. In the revision the Maritime Commission program was given a more favored status, and later two new rating bands, AA-2X and AA-5, were added for urgent nonmilitary items.[25]

By midyear the output of munitions, at any rate, was prodigious by all previous standards. During the first six months of 1942 more than twice the amount of munitions was produced for the Army as during the six months preceding—almost a million hand and shoulder weapons, 235,000 machine guns, 16,100 pieces of artillery, 7,329 tanks, 285,600 trucks,

3,222,000,000 rounds of small arms ammunition, 32,925,000 rounds of artillery ammunition, 212,000 tons of aircraft bombs, and 18,060 aircraft, to mention a few major categories. Monthly production rate had at least doubled in practically all categories since the end of 1941, in small arms and artillery ammunition it had tripled, and in aircraft bombs and artillery pieces it had quadrupled. Production of self-propelled weapons, at 650 a month, represented a surge in output from almost zero at the end of 1941. With this achievement, American industry was already well on the way to making 1942 the year of greatest expansion of production in American history.[26]

Shipping: Capacity To Deploy Versus Capacity To Support

Capacity to deploy and support forces overseas during the first half of 1942 lagged far behind the production of munitions and of trained and equipped forces ready for deployment. In the crisis immediately following Pearl Harbor, the greatest limitation upon the outward movement of troops was the shortage of troop-carrying tonnage. There were in December 1941 upwards of 130 ocean-going passenger vessels flying the American flag and suitable for military use, including the military transport fleets. Another dozen new transports were expected during 1942. On the other hand, the Navy was holding some twenty potential troopers for conversion into light cruisers, aircraft carriers, and other auxiliaries, and six of its largest transports, engaged in trooping for the

---

[24] (1) Memo cited n. 22. (2) JCS 30, 5 Apr 42, title: Priorities in Pdn of Mun Based on Strategical Considerations. (3) Memo, JCS for President, 10 Apr 42, CCS 400.17 (2-20-42) Sec 1.
[25] CPA, *Industrial Mobilization for War*, pp. 295–302.
[26] See below, App. B.

British in the Indian Ocean, could not return for many weeks. An indeterminate number of vessels probably would have to be kept in normal commercial services, at least for some time. Most of the conventional transports in the military fleets would be needed to reinforce existing overseas garrisons, and a block of about twenty-five combat loaders had to be reserved for possible amphibious expeditions. There would be losses. Estimates of the net total of tonnage that could be counted on for ferrying troops in any new overseas ventures in 1942 ranged between 40 and 50 transports, with a capacity of 60,000 to 70,000 troops on a single trip. In terms of deployment to the nearest possible theater of action, the European, this meant average monthly embarkations of about 30,000, or about 350,000 by the end of the year. This could hardly be called a maximum effort, however. As Army planners were at pains to point out, the Navy might give up its earmarked auxiliaries, and amphibious shipping might be used for ferrying. Various economies were possible—air transport, slashing equipment allowances, double bunking and shift sleeping on transports, curtailing commercial services. If all means were employed, perhaps as many as 850,000 to 900,000 troops could be shipped across the Atlantic in 1942.[27]

Before the end of December the Army forced the issue of the Navy's conversion program, a subject of dispute since the preceding summer. Three large transports, to be converted into aircraft carriers, were the heart of this program—*Mount Vernon, Wakefield,* and *West Point,* all three currently in the Indian Ocean in British service. There was also a new liner recently purchased from Sweden, the *Kungsholm.* In the aggregate these vessels represented a carrying capacity of twenty-two thousand troops. These and other conversions in progress and planned would hold up construction of about twenty-five new troop transports. When the Maritime Commission suggested substituting tankers for the vessels to be converted, the Navy decided to convert both tankers and transports. On 22 December General Marshall, in a "Dear Betty" letter, conveyed the protests of his staff to Admiral Stark, while Admiral Land approached the President. On the 27th, at the President's order, conversion of the four big transports was canceled and the other projects were modified. Early in January the British were granted another voyage of the *Wakefield* and *West Point,* but four other transports in Eastern waters were ordered to return.[28]

Somervell was thus able to report on 10 January that available passenger tonnage, excluding Navy combat loaders but including the giant *Normandie,* then being refitted, had a total capacity of 159,000 troops. (Soon thereafter the *Normandie* was put out of action by a fire.) Meanwhile the British had agreed to turn over for American use, beginning in February, the "monsters"—*Queen Mary, Queen Elizabeth,* and *Aquitania*—the first two with a capacity then conservatively rated at 6,000 each, the last at 4,500. Several smaller British

---

[27] (1) G-4 study, 10 Dec 41, title: Analysis of Passenger Shipg. (2) Memo, Gross for Somervell, 2 Dec 41, sub: Maximum Overseas Mvmt. (3) Memo, Gross for Somervell, 10 Dec 41, sub: Shipg Sit As It Affects the Army. All in Plng Div Studies folder, OCT HB. (4) Memo, Gross for Somervell, 21 Dec 41, sub: Est of Shipg Available for U.S. Overseas Effort 1942–43, G-4/29717-116.

[28] (1) Memo, Gross for CofS, 22 Dec 41, sub: Effect of Conversion . . . , G-4/33473. (2) Memo, Marshall for Stark, 22 Dec 41, G-429717-81. Admiral Stark had carried the nickname "Betty" ever since his first year at the Naval Academy. (3) Memo, Somervell for CofS, 7 Jan 42, sub: Br Request To Retain Six U.S. Trans, G-4/29717-111.

THE LINER *NORMANDIE* BURNING *at dockside, North River, New York, 9 February 1942.*

transports were also to be made available to the Army.[29]

Britain had far more shipping than the United States, both troop-carrying and cargo, though her capacity to build was limited. Early in March the Prime Minister appealed to the President to "double or treble the American man-lift by the summer of 1943." [30] British troop-carrying capacity then stood at about 280,000, and there seemed little prospect of augmenting it. Moreover, since the bulk of it was servicing the Indian Ocean area, the long return voyage of empty transports around the Cape kept a large proportion of this capacity out of use for extended periods. The President, on the advice of Army

shipping officials, turned a deaf ear to Churchill's request. American troop-carrying capacity in being was now estimated at about 130,000. To this it was expected another 75,000 in conversions and new construction would be added by June 1943, an additional 100,000 by the end of 1943, and 95,000 more by mid-1944—bringing the total, by that time, to 400,000. This program, Colonel Gross insisted, "cannot be advanced; it may only be ex-

[29] (1) Memo, Somervell for CofS, 19 Jan 42, sub: Maximum Tr Mvmt and Forces Overseas . . . , G-4/29717-116. (2) See also above, Ch. VI.

[30] Msg, Former Naval Person [Churchill] to President Roosevelt, 5 Mar 42, as quoted in Winston S. Churchill, *The Second World War: The Hinge of Fate* (Boston, Houghton Mifflin Company, 1950), p. 193.

tended."[31] In April, however, the Army reversed its stand to the extent of agreeing to the construction of fifty new C-4 transports, in place of the same number of seatrains, contracted for in February, which the Navy feared would be too vulnerable to attack. By May the estimated combined capacity of the British and American transport fleets had risen to about half a million.[32]

Cargo shipping from the outset presented the greater problem. Army calculations soon after Pearl Harbor showed about 1.6 million gross tons potentially available to support new deployment, beyond routine and already scheduled uses. Even with 4 million gross tons of new construction scheduled for 1942, and under optimistic assumptions as to the requirements for lend-lease shipments and for replacement of British and U.S. shipping losses, the 1.6 million tons was expected to dwindle to 1.4 million by the end of 1942. Moreover, as the troop population overseas grew, maintenance requirements would mount. Progressively larger tonnages of cargo shipping would have to be assigned, first to build up and then to maintain existing garrisons and bases yet to be established. This shipping would not be available for supporting the deployment of forces for offensive operations. Capacity to deploy offensively, as Colonel Gross epigrammatically put it, was "a diminishing function."[33] Not until 1943, after the overseas defensive and logistical establishment was complete, could new shipbuilding under the building programs current in December 1941 be expected to increase the capacity for offensive deployment. On 3 January 1942 the President raised the 1942 shipbuilding program from 6 million to 8 million dead-weight tons, and the 1943 program from 8 million

to 10 million. The Maritime Commission, with some misgivings, thought there was a fair chance of meeting these goals, but there were also new demands for cargo shipping in prospect. The President's new production goals for munitions meant increased imports of raw materials, and much of the expanded munitions output was evidently intended by the President to be transported to the Allies in American cargo ships, at the expense of supplying U.S. forces overseas.[34]

Tremendous tonnages of cargo shipping, moreover, were needed to complement a relatively small amount of troop-carrying tonnage in the deployment and support of forces overseas. The troop transports becoming available for Army deployment early in 1942 were mostly new, large, and fast. One speedy liner, for example one of the *Queens*, could, by conservative reckoning, move eighteen thousand troops in three trips across the Atlantic in seventy-two days—the time required for a slow convoy of freighters, carrying these same troops' equipment and supplies, to make a single round trip. Even with larger programs of cargo shipbuilding, the expansion of troop-carrying capacity, both accom-

---

[31] Memo, Gross for Somervell, 6 Mar 42, sub: Reply to Mr. Churchill's Cablegram . . . , Army Trans Sv folder, OCT HB.

[32] (1) Msg, Former Naval Person to President Roosevelt, 5 Mar 42, as quoted in Churchill, *Hinge of Fate*, pp. 191–94. Part of the President's reply, dated 8 March, is quoted on p. 196. (2) Min, 5th and 10th mtgs CCS, 17 Feb and 7 Mar 42. (3) Lane, *Ships for Victory*, p. 618. (4) CMT 5/3, 8 May 42, title: Availability of United Nations Shipg for Mil Trans, Chart D and appended notes, ABC 570 (2-14-42) Sec 1.

[33] Memo cited n. 27(4).

[34] Lane, *Ships for Victory*, pp. 138–39.

On the eve of Pearl Harbor about 5 million dead-weight tons (3.3 million gross tons) of new merchant shipping were scheduled for construction in 1942, and 7 million dead-weight tons (4.7 million gross tons) in 1943. By the end of December 1941 these figures had risen to 6 and 8 million tons, respectively.

TABLE 3—ESTIMATED CAPACITY OF CARGO SHIPPING TO SUPPORT OFFENSIVE
DEPLOYMENT: DECEMBER 1941 [a]

Date	Number of Troops			
	Emphasis on Offensive Deploy-ment to Europe		Emphasis on Offensive Deploy-ment to the Far East	
	Total Overseas	European Area	Total Overseas	Far East Area
1 January 1942	([b])	535,000	([b])	357,000
30 June 1942	([b])	437,000	([b])	291,000
31 December 1942	914,000	459,000	761,000	306,000
31 December 1943	1,717,000	1,262,000	1,296,000	841,000

[a] These figures are broad and rather hasty estimates of the number of troops that might be supported overseas by the cargo shipping expected to be available on each of the dates given. The estimates are unrealistic and theoretical in several respects. They assume, for example, that the task of holding the enemy on the front not chosen for offensive deployment could be performed by whatever base and garrison forces were assigned to that area, and in the case of the January 1942 figures they make no allowance for the time that would be required to deploy these forces overseas.

The primary significance of the estimates, in the present context, is to illustrate the "diminishing function" of shipping capacity to deploy during a period when overseas bases and lines of communications were also being developed and shipbuilding had not yet reached its peak—that is, according to the expectations of the estimate, during most of 1942. Thus it appeared that it would be possible to deploy forces overseas for offensive operations, either against Germany or against Japan, in larger numbers immediately—while the defensive establishment overseas was still undermanned—than could be deployed six or nine months later. By the end of 1942, the maintenance costs of the overseas establishment could be expected to level off, and the full effect of new ship construction (by then expanded to maximum capacity) would be felt thereafter in a steadily expanding capacity to deploy and maintain forces overseas. As can be seen, the estimate contemplated a defensive and logistical establishment overseas of some 455,000 troops, to be completed before the end of 1942. Note the effect of greater distance in limiting the volume of deployment to the Far East, as compared with that to the European area.

Maintenance requirements were estimated at .9 gross tons (about 2.25 measurement tons) per man per month; turnaround to the European area was taken as two months, to the Far East as three months. Compare these assumptions with others shown below in Appendixes A-2, A-3, and A-6.

[b] Not stated in source.

Source: Based on memo, Gross for Somervell, 21 Dec 41, sub: Est of Shipg Available for U.S. Overseas Effort 1942–43, G-4/29717-116.

plished and in prospect in mid-January, indicated that for a long time to come cargo shipping would probably be the chief limitation upon overseas deployment.[35] *(Tables 3 and 4)*

The Drain of Ship Losses

Sinkings during the winter and spring increased the imbalance between troop and cargo shipping. During the first ten weeks of the year, a period of intensified activity by German submarines, Allied losses of dry cargo shipping reached an annual rate of over 10 million dead-weight tons. In March alone the toll was some

788,000 tons. In June it was 936,000 tons. Tanker losses were even more alarming, reaching an all-time peak of 375,000 tons in March and leading the U.S. Government to withdraw all its tankers from the Atlantic coastal traffic. The Navy, responsible for antisubmarine defense, faced this peril with totally inadequate resources. Late in December 1941 it had only twenty assorted surface vessels and about a hundred aircraft in the critical area covered

[35] (1) Memo, Somervell for CofS, 12 Jan 42, sub: Capacity of Shipg for War Effort Overseas Early 1942, G-4/29717-116. (2) During the summer following, the *Queens* actually carried as many as fifteen thousand troops on a single trip. See below, Ch. XIV.

TABLE 4—CAPACITY TO DEPLOY VERSUS CAPACITY TO SUPPORT: JANUARY 1942

Assumption	Capacity To Transport		Capacity To Support	
	Minimum	Maximum	Minimum	Maximum
Pacific deployment restricted to Hawaii..............	797, 500	1, 312, 300	396, 000	594, 000
Substantial deployment to Far East.................	576, 400	975, 700	297, 000	456, 500

These estimates reflected the current crisis in the Far East (see above, Ch. VI). Under both assumptions deployment was oriented mainly to the Pacific.

All figures represent troops. First two columns represent troop-carrying capacity; last two columns represent number of troops that could be sustained overseas by cargo shipping.

Under "Capacity To Transport," "maximum" figures are based on assumption that Navy combat loaders, Navy chartered transports, and the six Navy transports in the Indian Ocean would be available; "minimum" figures exclude these vessels.

Under "Capacity To Support," "maximum" figures are based on assumption that some additional British tonnage in the North Atlantic, and additional Navy cargo vessels in both oceans, would be available; "minimum" figures exclude this shipping.

Source: Based on memo, Somervell for CofS, 12 Jan 42, sub: Capacity of Shipg for War Effort Overseas Early 1942, G-4/29717-116.

by the North Atlantic Naval Coastal Frontier (later the Eastern Sea Frontier) available for independent action against submarines; most of the vessels were unable to meet a submarine on equal terms, and none of the planes could maintain long-range patrol. The Army Air Forces was able to put perhaps a hundred aircraft of somewhat longer range into the battle. During the winter and spring these meager forces, only gradually augmented, attempted unsuccessfully to combat the growing number and widening range of enemy attacks on shipping throughout the western Atlantic, Gulf, and Caribbean areas. Apart from the inadequacy of forces, antisubmarine measures were hampered by divided responsibility between the Army and Navy, a problem that remained the subject of prolonged interservice controversy throughout 1942 and was never wholly resolved.[36]

The Navy held firmly to the belief that convoying was the only real answer to the submarine menace. Hampered by a severe shortage of escort vessels, it put heavy pressure on the Army to reduce the number of special convoys and to rely on regular,

widely spaced movements. Army officials, on the contrary, wanted flexible arrangements, permitting emergency movements (like those to Hawaii immediately after Pearl Harbor), without escort when the situation demanded, and they argued that the Navy's rigid standards regarding size and speed of convoyed vessels would drastically curtail the amount of usable shipping. In the late winter the dispute became bitter. "This sort of thing cannot go on," Admiral King protested in March; "we simply have not the means to escort multifarious expeditions."[37] Late in January the Navy agreed to permit freighters in

[36] For these and subsequent figures on ship losses, see: (1) Memo, Somervell for Marshall, 17 Jun 42, sub: Submarine Sinkings of Combined Merchant Fleet, Gross Day File, OCT HB; (2) Churchill, *Hinge of Fate*, p. 199 and table on p. 879; (3) Hancock and Gowing, *British War Economy*, p. 416; (4) Memo, Lt Col A. S. Palmerlee for Chester Wardlow, 14 Dec 43, sub: Shipg Losses, Shipg 1941-43 folder, Hq ASF; (5) Min, 12th mtg CCS, 17 Mar 42; and (6) CCS 39/1, 14 Mar 42, title: Relation of Merchant Shipg Losses to Prosecution of War. (7) See below, App. H.

For Army-Navy antisubmarine operations and controversy, see Craven and Cate, *AAF I*, Ch. 15, and Morison, *Battle of the Atlantic, passim.*

[37] (1) Memo, Adm King for CofS, 23 Mar 42, Convoys folder, OCT HB. (2) Other corresp in same file.

the Pacific to shift for themselves if too slow to accompany troop convoys, and on 9 February a comprehensive convoy schedule and policy was issued. Troop convoys were to run every forty days from New York to Iceland and the United Kingdom and from Boston to Newfoundland and Greenland; sailings to Bermuda, the Caribbean bases, South America, Australia, and the Pacific ferry islands were to be spaced at intervals of thirty days; sailings to Hawaii, six days. Cargo sailings were to be unescorted unless fast enough to accompany troop convoys. Troop transports, even if escorted, must have a speed of at least fifteen knots (slightly less later). Fast vessels could go without protection, except from the air, in coastal waters. The Navy required one month's advance notice on each convoy. Late in April American cargo shipments to the United Kingdom were merged with British convoys out of Halifax, and in May the Navy, with the help of borrowed British trawlers, instituted coastal convoys in the Atlantic.[38]

Despite these measures the toll of sinkings rose steadily through the spring and into the summer. In terms of percentages of the total Allied dry cargo fleet, losses rose from 1.7 percent in January to 2.5 percent in May. Tanker losses averaged 3.5 percent of the monthly tanker tonnage in use, and totaled more than two million dead-weight tons for the six-month period, about four fifths of the amount lost during the entire twenty-seven months of war before Pearl Harbor. During the first six months of 1942 losses of United Nations shipping were almost as heavy as during the whole of 1941 and exceeded new construction and other gains by almost 2.8 million dead-weight tons. While the United States was able by May to balance its own current losses by new ships, Allied replacements continued to lag behind

losses until the following August. Another year passed before building could overcome cumulative losses. "This problem," General Marshall wrote the President gloomily in June 1942, "is with us daily and hourly."[39] If sinkings continued at current rates, American forces would eventually be immobilized in the Western Hemisphere. In June the Navy urged that the whole ship construction program be revised to produce more escorts, at the expense of merchant tonnage, arguing that there was little use in building ships that the enemy would promptly sink; such action, in modified form, was to be taken later in the year. But despite the bleak outlook, General Marshall felt that strategy and industrial mobilization must be based on the assumption "that present losses by submarine will be overcome, ... Under no circumstances should the government be placed in the position where its military effort overseas will be curtailed by lack of equipment and supplies."[40]

Army Allocations and New Construction

After mid-January General Somervell pressed for a definite allocation of shipping to the Army sufficient to support a substantial deployment. Specifically, he urged either an immediate allocation of two hundred freighters with a monthly al-

---

[38] (1) Memo, CofS for G-4, 27 Jan 42, sub: Notification of Army Convoys, OCofS 21345-15. (2) Memo, G-4 for CofS, 29 Jan 42, same sub, G-4/29717-89. (3) Memo, Adm King for CofS, 30 Jan 42, Overseas Tr Mvmts 1940–42 folder, OCT HB. (4) See also, Wardlow, *Trans I*, Ch. VI. (5) Draft study, May 1945, title: Hist of Convoy and Routing, signed by Rear Adm M. K. Metcalf, U.S. Navy (Ret.), prepared in the Off of Naval Hist. (6) Hancock and Gowing, *British War Economy*, pp. 413–16. (7) See below, App. A-8.
[39] Memo, CofS for President, 10 Jun 42, CofS WDGS 1941–42 folder, Hq ASF.
[40] (1) *Ibid.* (2) Memo, Navy members MAC(G) for MAB, 4 Jun 42, sub: Balanced Building Prog of Cargo and Combat Shipg, incl to CPS 33/D, 9 Jun 42, in ABC 570 (2-14-42) Sec 2.

lotment thereafter of ten new vessels, or a monthly allotment of eighteen new ships without a large block allocation. If this were done, Somervell's staff calculated, about .8 million troops could be supported overseas by the end of 1942, mainly in the Atlantic area. This would permit an offensive deployment, over and above garrison forces, of about .6 million. If the main effort were made in the Far East, as now seemed likely, only about 480,000 troops could be deployed offensively. With its present small available tonnage of about 110 freighters, the Army could not support more than 90,000 additional troops overseas during 1942. "Such an effort," Somervell wrote to Admiral Land, "on its face fails to meet the military situation." [41]

Foreign aid was a heavy drain upon American cargo shipping, and promised to become even more demanding. Four days after Pearl Harbor Somervell warned the Chief of Staff that the Victory Program plans for American participation in the war were incompatible with the "arsenal of democracy" theory; shipping "might in time permit fulfillment of one program, or parts of both, but not both." [42] Lend-lease was then employing about 180 U.S. cargo vessels, including 100 in the Red Sea service, and Army officials eyed them covetously. Somervell was at pains to point out, in connection with his January and February ship allocation proposals, that if the foreign aid services, especially Soviet lend-lease, were "thoroughly emasculated" by the end of 1942, U.S. forces overseas might be built up to 350,000 with a main effort in the Far East, or to 1,100,000 if concentrated chiefly in the Atlantic area. [43]

Actually, Somervell's proposals did not aim at "emasculating" lend-lease services. He proposed to allow about eight new freighters for lend-lease movements each month over and above the 180 already in service. Britain's shipping problem, moreover, was reaching a stage where it could not be ignored. Her cargo fleet was bearing the brunt of the intensified German submarine campaign in the Atlantic, some of the American vessels assigned to carry British imports had been withdrawn, and shipments to the Soviet Union and British forces overseas created a mounting drain. By March imports to the British Isles were running at an annual rate of less than 22 million tons, in contrast to more than 30 million the preceding year and estimated minimum requirements of 26 million for 1942. Such a volume could not be achieved, Churchill warned Roosevelt early in March, "without very substantial additions to our shipping resources." [44]

It was already evident in January and February that the President was determined to expand rather than contract the foreign aid programs. "Under demands far more tempered than these," remarked Colonel Gross pessimistically in mid-January with reference to the new programs

---

[41] (1) Memo, cited n. 29(1). (2) Paper, 29 Jan 42, sub: Capabilities of Shipg Now Under Army Contl. (3) Memo, Lt Col Marcus B. Stokes for Rear Adm Sherwoode A. Taffinder, 5 Mar 42, sub: Est of Army Shipg Reqmts. Last two in Plng Div Studies folder, OCT HB. (4) Ltr, Somervell to Adm Land, 31 Jan 42, G-4/29717-116.

[42] Memo, Somervell for CofS, 11 Dec 41, sub: Shipg Sit, 10a Shipg file, Plng Div ASF.

[43] (1) Memo, Somervell for Gross, 13 Jan 42, Plng Div Studies folder, OCT HB. (2) Memo cited n. 29(1).

[44] (1) Msg, Former Naval Person to President Roosevelt, 4 Mar 42, as quoted in Churchill, *Hinge of Fate*, pp. 189–91. (2) Br Merchant Shipg Mis paper, 5 Feb 42, sub: Merchant Shipg in 1942, WPD 4494 Vic Prog, U.S. Data. (3) Note, Churchill to Hopkins, 10 Jan 42, MS Index to the Hopkins Papers, Bk. V, Orgn of the WSA, p. 2, Item 11. (4) Hancock and Gowing, *British War Economy*, pp. 353–57, 416–26. By strenuous efforts, British imports were brought up to 12.2 million tons by midyear.

then under discussion, "no further U.S. military overseas expeditions may be considered or undertaken."[45] Some three million tons of U.S. shipping already in British service in that month remained there, and a considerable tonnage completed under earlier contracts in the United States was transferred. Through pooling arrangements made early in the year, American freighters sailing to the British Isles often carried mixed cargoes of lend-lease and U.S. military matériel. Soviet lend-lease shipments in 1942 employed American and British bottoms in approximately equal proportions.[46]

Only two avenues remained open, therefore, to provide more cargo tonnage for Army troop deployment—ruthless economy in "nonessential" uses, and further augmentation of construction programs. Somervell advocated both. His proposals of January and February involved elimination of several commercial services and reduction of others in the Western Hemisphere and to Africa. But new construction offered the only real solution. The six hundred thousand troops that it seemed likely might be deployed overseas in 1942 were only a third of the number that were expected to be trained and equipped by the end of that year. By the end of 1943 there would be at least 3.6 million troops ready for overseas service, by current indications, but under present building programs less than a million troops could be sent and maintained overseas during 1943. Evidently the Army faced a huge unemployment problem at home unless more tonnage were provided. Somervell shared the doubts of Maritime Commission officials as to the feasibility of further increases in construction in 1942, but he along with many others believed that the 1943 program could be augmented by 50 percent. With 15 million tons of new construction in 1943, forces overseas could be raised to 2,260,000. It would be fatal to accept a deployment of only 1,500,000 or 1,800,000 as "the measure of the whole productive capacity of the country and its military might, ... An all-out effort in this field [ship construction]," he urged Marshall to tell the President, "must precede an all-out military effort. The maximum possibilities in this regard should be determined, attained, and the Army advised of what it can expect."[47]

The Army's hopes for a definite allocation of tonnage, preferably in a large block, did not materialize. With the creation of the War Shipping Administration (WSA) in February and the *modus operandi* worked out between it and the military services in May and June, U.S. merchant shipping was pooled under the tight control of WSA, and shipping other than what the services already controlled was assigned for use generally on a single voyage basis.[48] In the field of ship construction, action came suddenly and dramatically. On 18 February General Marshall sent to the President, with little change, Somervell's strongly worded plan

---

[45] Memo, Gross for Somervell, 19 Jan 42, sub: Def Aid Trfs and Trf Schedules, Plng Div Studies folder, OCT HB.

[46] (1) Hancock and Gowing, *British War Economy*, pp. 353–57, 426–27. This mentions $195 million in shipping transferred under lend-lease. (2) Churchill, *Hinge of Fate*, p. 199. (3) For Soviet aid, see below, Chs. XX–XXI. (4) For British imports, see below, Ch. XXVI.

[47] (1) Draft memo, Marshall for President, no date, Shipg 1941–43 folder, Hq ASF. This draft is evidently a paraphrase of memo, Somervell for Rear Adm Howard L. Vickery and Stacy May, 13 Feb 42, sub: Increase in 1943 Ship Construction Prog, G-4/29717-152. (2) Memo, Gens Somervell and Burns for Hopkins, 22 Feb 42, sub: Alloc of U.S. Shipg for 1942, G-4/29717-116. (3) Memo, Col Stokes for Col Gross, 3 Feb 42, sub: Overseas Effort in 1942, Plng Div Studies folder, OCT HB.

[48] See below, Ch. IX.

for an augmented program. The next day the President summoned Admiral Land to his bedroom and told him to build 9 million dead-weight tons of shipping in 1942 and 15 million in 1943, 24 million tons in all. Exactly a week before this, Land had warned, "the shipbuilding cup is full to overflowing." [49] His belief was not now changed, but orders were orders. Telephoning the news to his colleague, Rear Adm. Howard L. Vickery, who agreed that 9 million tons was more than could be produced in 1942, Land reported, ". . . all I said was we would try." [50]

Three months later the picture had changed. In terms of expansion of yard capacity and the acquisition of the know how, which could come only from actual experience in mass production, the shipbuilding industry had farther to go in 1942 than the munitions industry, since economic mobilization before 1942 had concentrated more on producing weapons than on producing ships. However, cargo ship construction, even more than that of many items of munitions, lent itself to standardization and mass production, and the basic task of designing had largely been completed during the prewar emergency period. By spring 1942 shipyards that had begun to build in 1941 had learned their craft so well that they were smashing records every week, finishing ships in 60 to 70 days, against a schedule based on 105 days. Deliveries rose from 26 in March and 36 in April to 57 in May and 67 in June. On Maritime Day, 22 May, Admiral Vickery publicly announced that American shipyards by the end of 1943 might be able to turn out, as their two-year total, not 24 million but 28 million dead-weight tons. Late in May and early in June some of the new capacity was already being absorbed by new

orders for tank landing ships (LST's) and "baby flattop" escort carriers. Even with the addition of these types, Admiral Vickery estimated in the middle of June that the commission could produce 27.4 million tons of merchant shipping by the end of 1943, 3.4 million more than the President's goal. [51]

If the expanding shipbuilding capacity was to be used, more steel would have to be fed into the yards, probably at the expense of other users. At a conference on 23 June, the President made remarks about "scraping the bottom of the barrel." Admiral Land, one of those present, interpreted this to mean that the goal of 24 million tons was again to be raised, but during the next two weeks the Navy and other users of steel pressed their claims upon the production authorities, and on 9 July Admiral Land learned from Donald Nelson that the President had once more set the limit for shipbuilding by the end of 1943 at 24 million tons, of which slightly more than 8 million was to be completed in 1942. Here, for the moment, the matter rested. [52]

The spectacular logistical achievements of these first six months of war were on the level of operations and performance—in

[49] Lane, *Ships for Victory*, p. 143.

[50] *Ibid.*, p. 144.

Admiral Land, who in 1938 had succeeded Joseph P. Kennedy as chairman of the Maritime Commission, had been retired from active service since 1937. Another naval officer, Comdr. Howard L. Vickery, became a commissioner in 1940 on Land's recommendation, and by special act of Congress was permitted to remain on the active list. The five-man commission contained a third retired naval officer, Capt. Edward Macauley, who became a commissioner in 1941. By another special act of Congress, Land was promoted in July 1944 to vice admiral; Vickery became rear admiral in January 1942 and vice admiral in October 1944. See Lane, *Ships for Victory*, pp. 12–15, 459.

[51] *Ibid.*, pp. 173–81.

[52] *Ibid.*, pp. 183ff.

the immense outpouring of war materials, and, in the spring, the attainment of mass production of cargo shipping. Expansion, training, and equipping of the Army were also advancing on an impressive scale. But in the most basic realm of logistical planning—the determination of long-range needs and the formulation of programs, schedules, and priorities for meeting them—the absence of a settled and concrete strategy, unavoidable as long as the momentum of the enemy's initial attacks continued, created a virtually insoluble problem. Approved military requirements, at least in the upper half of the priorities scale, were now in some sort of "balance," and the now standardized military supply programs purported to list item by item the long-range needs of a specific troop basis which, in theory, was designed to implement an agreed strategy. After mid-1942, however, the only concrete strategy for a long time was a series of limited operations planned at short-range or extemporized. The troop basis provided a pool of armed manpower from which forces were drawn to execute these operations, the scope and character of which were inevitably shaped by its limitations. Production programs were aimed, indeed, at the listed ultimate requirements of the troop basis, but month-to-month schedules were shaped by a multitude of factors totally unrelated to ultimate goals—shortages of materials, facilities, and labor, and the immense inertia of administration.

At the beginning of the year Colonel Aurand had observed:

It should not be necessary . . . to have to first set up a troop basis to establish the relative numbers to be produced each month of the various items . . . . This can be based upon the general view of the war, the theaters in which the war will be fought, and the

necessities for U.S. production to supply the equipment in these theaters . . . . After all, the immediate requirements, regardless of what they are, can be met only from the production which is now under way . . . . Month by month requirements at the moment are entirely dependent upon production schedules.[53]

In June month-by-month requirements apparently were still dependent on current production, and the ultimate goal, to all practical intents, was still what it had been when the Victory Program was formulated—maximum production. Particularly was this true in the field of merchant shipping, where capacity (as limited by shortages of materials) fell far short of indicated demand. The striving for an unspecified and largely unknown maximum was, in fact, the dominant motif in the whole field of logistics. Colonel Aurand, with some ironical exaggeration, noted its many ramifications—in Congressional authorizations, "more than could possibly be produced"; in planned facilities expansion, "beyond shipping possibilities and availability of raw materials"; in foreign aid programs, "more than they could possibly transport"; in planned overseas reserves, "more than would ever be used."[54] All of which, he thought, was probably necessary. Unspent funds could be returned to Treasury, what could not be produced in nine months could be produced in twelve, a "bank" of cargo was essential to efficient utilization of shipping, and excess reserves, after all, were better than "too little and too late."[55]

---

[53] Memo, Aurand for Somervell, 24 Jan 42, sub: Army Supply Program, MAB Orgn file, DAD.

[54] Memo, Brig Gen Henry S. Aurand for Brig Gen Lucius D. Clay, 18 Jun 42, sub: Basis for Present Progs, ID 334 MAB, I.

[55] Ibid.

For a judgment similar to Aurand's, made after the war, see Logistics in World War II, Final Report of the Army Service Forces (Washington, 1948), p. 57.

CHAPTER IX

The Machinery of Logistical Co-ordination and Administration

During the immediate post-Pearl Harbor period a great heaving and shifting in the structure of co-ordination and administration was under way. From it emerged, by mid-1942, a basic organizational pattern that was to endure with little important change throughout the remainder of the war.

On the international level, the ARCADIA Conference in December 1941 and January 1942 created the fundamental Anglo-American structure for the direction of strategy and control of the resources needed to execute it. The Combined Chiefs of Staff, composed of the chief military advisers (or their representatives) of the two heads of state, Roosevelt and Churchill, stood at the top of the military pyramid; the combined Munitions Assignments Boards in Washington and London, operating under the CCS, controlled the assignment of military equipment. Other combined boards for shipping, raw materials, production, and food were set up during the first six months of 1942. These stood outside the military committee system and reported directly to the President and the Prime Minister.[1]

At the same time, the national machinery for control of the American war economy, which had come into being during the emergency period, was undergoing reorganization and expansion. In January the new War Production Board took over the general direction of industrial mobilization, with full authority under the President's war powers to lay down "policies, plans, procedures, and methods" for all government agencies engaged in "war procurement and production."[2] On 12 March its chairman, Donald Nelson, reached an agreement with General Somervell that confirmed to the Army its traditional function of determining its own requirements, translating these into terms of raw materials, facilities, labor, and components, and procuring end-items directly from private industry. This agreement, hailed by Nelson as "the Magna Carta of our operation,"[3] actually left many jurisdictional

---

[1] For a discussion of the combined boards, see below, Ch. X. The British Chiefs of Staff were represented in the CCS in Washington by a permanent committee, the British Joint Staff Mission. Periodically, special conferences were held that the British Chiefs, and sometimes the heads of state, attended in person.

[2] CPA, *Industrial Mobilization for War*, p. 208.

[3] *Ibid.*, p. 215.

boundaries unsettled, and above all failed to provide a formula for dividing the national product between military and civilian needs. The conflict over this basic issue and a multitude of related disputes was to continue throughout the war.

Logistics in the Military Committee System

The CCS, which began to function in January 1942, had as its central task the "formulation of policies and plans" for "the strategic conduct of the war,"[5] and the U.S. Joint Chiefs of Staff (consisting of the military chiefs of the Army, Army Air Forces, and Navy) by February were serving similarly as the top-level co-ordinating committee for all U.S. forces. The Joint Board, made up of the Army and Navy chiefs, remained nominally in existence throughout the war. There was no central executive machinery, either combined or joint, however, to put into effect the decisions of the high command. The CCS ordinarily named either the British or the U.S. Joint Chiefs of Staff to act as its executive agent, and the U.S. Joint Chiefs of Staff in turn employed the established machinery of its service departments.

On the American side, the Army planners soon after Pearl Harbor proposed the creation of a supreme U.S. military commander, responsible to the President as Commander in Chief, and a joint general staff. Essentially the same plan had been advanced the summer before by the Navy's General Board, but by February 1942 Navy opinion had hardened against it and the scheme was dropped. When Admiral William D. Leahy was appointed a few months later as the President's personal chief of staff and assumed the chairmanship of the JCS, many believed he was destined to become supreme commander,

supplying the pinnacle that the structure still lacked. This step was never taken. When the Joint Chiefs disagreed, they could only appeal to the President.[6]

The joint committee system, as it rather haphazardly developed in 1942, was essentially a loose collection of planning and information-gathering committees and boards. Increasingly, but by no means uniformly, the JCS dealt with them through the Joint Staff Planners and the principal working committee of the JPS, the Joint U.S. Strategic Committee. The CCS similarly dealt through the Combined Staff Planners (CPS). The JPS served generally as a clearinghouse for the bulk of JCS business and, more specifically, as the central planning committee for the JCS. Planning at this level was not specialized; "strategic" plans were the end product of a process of weighing all sorts of pertinent information, logistical and other, that funneled into the JPS and JCS. Both the JCS and the CCS themselves dealt directly and continuously with logistical matters, formulating programs of requirements and assignments and, not infrequently, making final decisions on allocations of shipping for specific troop and cargo movements and of critical equipment for specific operations. The JPS and JUSSC drew the information they needed for strategic planning from the more specialized joint committees and from the technical staffs

---

[4] (1) *Ibid.*, Pt. III. (2) Millett, *ASF*. (3) R. Elberton Smith, Army Procurement and Economic Mobilization.

[5] ABC-4/CS-4, 14 Jan 42, title: Post-Arcadia Collaboration.

[6] (1) Cline, *Washington Command Post*, pp. 46, 98–104. (2) Min, JB mtgs, 28 Jan and 16 Mar 42. (3) Papers in WPD 4532-2; JB 325, Ser 742; ABC 370.26 Unity of Comd (3-16-42), 1-A. (4) Ray S. Cline and Maurice Matloff, "Development of War Department Views on Unification," *Military Affairs*, Vol. XIII, No. 2 (Summer 1949), pp. 65–74.

f the Army and Navy. There was no sep-
rate joint agency assigned the task of
naking logistical plans or of appraising
he logistical feasibility of proposed opera-
ons. In a limited sense the Joint Military
Transportation Committee (JMTC) did
erform this function in the critical field of
hipping; the JMTC consisted of two
rmy and two Navy members, making up
he American half of the corresponding
Combined Military Transportation Com-
nittee (CMTC). But the conclusions of
he JMTC, like those of the other commit-
es, usually went into the hopper of the
PS to be weighed along with other perti-
ent considerations in strategic planning.
Neither the JPS nor the JUSSC contained,
n the Army side, experts in the general,
r in any particular, field of logistics.[7]

The theory underlying these arrange-
nents was that strategic planning and
irection, if it were to be aggressive and
naginative, must not become shackled to
he judgments of experts or technicians as
o what could or could not be done. This
vas the danger, the Joint Planners feared,
n any attempt to create a separate logis-
cal planning committee to advise the JCS
irectly. In any given situation, they held,
he range of alternatives was broader and
nore flexible than any statistical computa-
on of available troops, matériel, and ship-
ing would indicate. Strategic planners
ad to consult the logistical experts, much
s they consulted the intelligence experts,
n order to obtain factual data bearing on
he situation. From these data they should
draw their own conclusions, weighing in
he balance not merely logistical limita-
ions but also the state of organization and
raining, the enemy's capabilities, the pres-
ure of strategic necessity, and other perti-
ent factors.

Such was the theory. By the logistical

experts themselves it was accepted only
with reservations, if at all. Until the invasion of North Africa, however, plans and
preparations for assembling an invasion
force in the British Isles constituted the
only major military undertaking involving
forces of all services, both British and
American, and for this operation special
committees were set up in Washington and
London to handle detailed day-to-day
preparations and much of the joint and
service staff long-range logistical planning.
On many matters during 1942 and later,
the military chiefs reached agreement
through informal discussion, the information and counsel by which they formed
their views flowing up to them through
their own service staffs, bypassing the committees altogether. The system of logistical
co-ordination under the joint and combined committees did not face the acid test
until the North Africa undertaking, and
then it very nearly broke down.[8]

Allocation and Employment of U.S. Merchant Shipping

Merchant shipping was perhaps the
principal ready resource, other than the
Navy, that the United States at the beginning of 1942 could contribute to the Allied
cause, but the co-ordinating machinery
developed before Pearl Harbor was palpa-
bly inadequate for the task of making
shipping immediately available for war

---

[7] (1) Cline, *Washington Command Post*, pp. 101–04,
124. (2) Wardlow, *Trans I*, Ch. V. The two Army
members of the JMTC were Generals Somervell and
Gross; Admiral Land, chairman of the Maritime
Commission and War Shipping Administrator, often
attended. (3) For the role of the CPS and the unsuc-
cessful efforts to make the Munitions Assignments
Board and the Combined Production and Resources
Board interallied agencies for determining requirements for production, see below, Ch. XI.

[8] See below, Chs. XIV–XVI.

uses and husbanding its employment. On the day following Pearl Harbor the President set up under his immediate supervision a Strategic Shipping Board "to establish policies for and plan the allocation of"—but not to operate—merchant shipping.[9] The board, composed of the Maritime Commission chairman, the two military chiefs, and Harry Hopkins, was not markedly successful. Its members had other heavy responsibilities, disagreement could be resolved only by appeal to the President, and administration had to be delegated to existing agencies. A meeting of minds—the board's presumed objective—could be achieved as readily through the normal process of direct communication between the members. It was symptomatic of the board's impotence that the sharp dispute between the Army and Navy during December 1941 over use of shipyards for Navy conversion did not even come before it and was settled by presidential decision.[10]

The first move to remedy the situation, a Navy proposal to create a cabinet-level "Office of Shipping Coordination" to take over both allocation and operation of all merchant shipping, was not to the Army's liking. Somervell and Gross, while agreeing in principle that "there must be some agency endowed with absolute powers over the allocation of shipping and the establishment of priorities,"[11] objected immediately to giving up the Army's transport fleet and ports of embarkation; they also sensed danger in the creation of a new cabinet officer who, in shipping matters, might challenge the influence of the Secretary of War.[12] Army shipping officials also had no desire to diminish the powers of the Maritime Commission, with which they enjoyed smooth working relations. Through the commission, they could rea-

sonably hope to fill the Army's rapidly growing shipping needs, while still retaining the Army's existing fleet. A cabinet-level superagency, possibly dominated by the Navy, would endanger both expectations. The Navy had proposed, in fact, that it should clear all Army requests for shipping. This scheme the Army rejected out of hand, and at the first meeting of the Strategic Shipping Board General Marshall advanced the principle that the Maritime Commission should be recognized as the agency "most capable in sea transportation, as is the Navy in sea combat."[13] This was followed shortly by an Army proposal that, "with the direct and full assistance of the Maritime Commission," the Army should be given control of all shipping needed to meet its deployment requirements.[14]

In response to the Navy's scheme, the Army offered a counterplan for a "Central Shipping Administration" that in effect would give the Shipping Board a chairman (Admiral Land) and replace its exalted

---

[9] Ltr, President to SW, 8 Dec 41, Shipg 1941–43 folder, Hq ASF.

[10] (1) Ltr, Hopkins to President, 8 Dec 41, MS Index to the Hopkins Papers, Bk. V, Orgn of the WSA, p. 1, Item 2. (2) Memo, Gross for CofS, 26 Dec 41, sub: Strategic Shipg Bd, Independent Action by the Navy, G-4/29717-26. (3) Duncan S. Ballantine, Shipping in Naval Logistics: The History of the Naval Transportation Service, Monograph 5 in U.S. NAVAL ADMINISTRATION IN WORLD WAR II, pp. 42–47, Naval Hist Div OCNO.

[11] Memo, CofS for Adm Stark, 31 Dec 41, sub: EO Estab Central Shipg Admin, G-4/33920.

[12] Memo, Somervell for CofS, 28 Dec 41, sub: Adm Turner's Proposed JB Action . . . , G-4/33920.

[13] Memo, Somervell for CofS, 14 Dec 41, with incl, Agenda for 1st Mtg Strategic Shipg Bd, G-4/33813-1.

[14] (1) Memo, Gross for Gerow, 23 Dec 41, sub: Overseas Trans for Army . . . . (2) Memo, CofS for Adm Stark, 24 Dec 41, sub: Sea Trans. Both in G-4/29717-26. (3) JB paper, 27 Dec 41, sub: Proposed Solution of Prob of Alloc and Contl of U.S. Merchant Shipg, G-4/33920. (4) Ballantine, Shipping in Naval Logistics, p. 46, cited n. 10(3).

membership by a board of directors consisting of the War Department G-4, his Navy opposite number, and a representative of the Office of Production Management. The two services would continue to operate their fleets, the Maritime Commission the remaining pool of merchant shipping. The administrator would allocate shipping under the supervision of a board of directors and, most significantly, in all military movements he was "to comply with the joint decisions of the Secretary of War and the Secretary of the Navy as regards their requirements." [15] This scheme, modified to meet Navy objections, had to run the gantlet of critics in the Maritime Commission, the Bureau of the Budget, the White House, and even Mr. Churchill, who feared British needs would not get a proper hearing.[16]

What emerged from all this discussion was the President's executive order of 7 February creating the War Shipping Administration as the ship operating agency of the Maritime Commission, headed by Admiral Land in the dual capacity of Chairman, Maritime Commission, and War Shipping Administrator. The new agency's powers were clearly shaped by the feeling, as Hopkins put it, that "there are so many interests involved other than Stimson and Knox, that Jerry [Admiral Land] should be made responsible for the whole business." [17] Admiral Land was to be responsible directly to the President, with authority covering not only allocation but also "operation, purchase, charter, requisition and use" of noncombatant ocean shipping other than that in the military transport fleets, which was exempted at General Somervell's insistence.[18] The restrictions, written in the Army-Navy plan, upon the administrator's powers to allocate shipping for military purposes had

been greatly watered down in the executive order; he was now held merely to "comply with strategic military requirements." [19] This vague proviso, which ran counter to the strong representations of General Somervell during preliminary discussions, was inserted at the last moment at the insistence of Hopkins and Admiral Land, with the acquiescence of the Navy, but without Somervell's knowledge. As Maritime Commission chairman, Admiral Land of course remained responsible for ship construction. He thus became, in truth, a "shipping czar" as well as a "ship construction czar," as his colleague Admiral Vickery put it, with authority that fell only a little short of the "absolute powers" to which Somervell and Gross, perhaps disingenuously, had earlier agreed in principle.[20]

The executive order of 7 February, stating explicitly that the Army should control its own transports and be allocated shipping directly by WSA, at least seemed to settle the question of whether there was to be one military shipping agency or two. The Navy evidently had assumed that this provision was only temporary, an assump-

[15] Memo, with draft charter atchd, cited n. 11.
[16] (1) Ltr, SW and SN to Hopkins, 13 Jan 42, MS Index to the Hopkins Papers, Bk. V, Orgn of the WSA, p. 3, Item 13. (2) Ltr, SN to White House for Hopkins, 13 Jan 42, sub: EO Estab Central Shipg Admin, WSA folder, OCT HB. (3) Memo, Somervell for SW, 28 Jan 42, G-4/33813-1. (4) Memo, Adm Vickery for Hopkins, 12 Jan 42, MS Index to the Hopkins Papers, Bk. V, Orgn of the WSA, p. 3, Item 12. (5) Note, Churchill to Hopkins, 10 Jan 42, MS Index to the Hopkins Papers, Bk. V, Orgn of the WSA, p. 2, Item 11.
[17] Msg, Hopkins to President, 22 Jan 42, paraphrased in MS Index to the Hopkins Papers, Bk. V, Orgn of the WSA, p. 3, Item 13.
[18] EO 9054, 7 Feb 42.
[19] Ibid.
[20] (1) Memo cited n. 16(4). (2) Papers in Shipg 1941–43 folder, Hq ASF. (3) Ballantine, Shipping in Naval Logistics, pp. 47–51, cited n. 10(3).

REAR ADM. EMORY S. LAND,
Maritime Commission chairman and War Shipping Administrator.

tion that goes far to explain its acquiescence in the vast powers conferred upon the administrator. In the last week of February Admiral Stark abruptly raised the issue, proposing not only to take over the Army's transports during the next two months but also to serve as the sole agency for consolidating military shipping requirements and presenting them to WSA. General Marshall promptly and brusquely rejected the suggestion. Present arrangements, he asserted, were "most satisfactory to the Army" and promised a "much better use of our shipping . . . than has ever obtained in the past." As far as the Army was concerned, the issue had been "disposed of."[21]

Two questions remained outstanding.

One concerned control of loading and unloading cargo vessels allocated to the Army by WSA. Among Army transportation officials it was basic doctrine that these operations, along with the flow of military cargo into and through the port, must be under military control in the interests of efficient traffic management as well as of timely and adequate supply. WSA, for its part, felt it was essential to co-ordinate the movement of military with that of non-military supplies and was especially insistent upon reducing the waste of shipping space that inevitably resulted from separate handling and loading of military and nonmilitary cargo. The other question had to do with the method of allocation. The Army, like the Navy, expected to obtain block allocations permanently or for extended periods, an expectation apparently formed during the discussions by the Strategic Shipping Board in December. In January and February Somervell sought from the Maritime Commission such long-term allocations, but it quickly became apparent that the WSA would not countenance this method of allocation, which violated the pooling principle.[22]

Both issues—control of loading and method of allocation—came to a head in June. On the 13th an agreement was signed by General Somervell, for the War Department, and Lewis W. Douglas, for WSA, that represented a concession by

---

[21] (1) Memo, CofS for CNO, 27 Feb 42. (2) Memo, CNO for CofS, 26 Feb 42. (3) Related papers. All in Army Trans Sv folder, OCT HB. (4) Ballantine, Shipping in Naval Logistics, pp. 55–57, cited n. 10(3).

[22] (1) Ltr, Traffic Dir WSA to Navy Trans Sv, 25 Feb 42. (2) Disposition form, G-4 to CG USAFIA, 28 Feb 42. This refers to an agreement that cargo vessels returning from overseas should be made available to WSA if not needed for military use. Both in G-4/ 33861. (3) See also Ballantine, *Naval Logistics*, pp. 88–90; and (4) Ballantine, Shipping in Naval Logistics, pp. 46, 57, cited n. 10(3). (5) See above, Ch. VIII.

WSA on the first issue and by the Army on the second. Under the agreement all cargo vessels assigned to the Army were to be loaded by the Army, but they were to be assigned only for the outward lap of a single voyage, reverting to WSA control after their Army cargo was discharged. On each side, however, the concession was qualified. The Army was to rely upon WSA for additional terminal facilities and labor under WSA terms of use. Idle facilities were not to be reserved for future use. Cargo was to be interchanged between vessels, whenever possible, to secure tight stowage. WSA recognized that troop transports were usually needed on an assignment longer than cargo vessels; later, transports came to be assigned normally for the round trip. Freighters, too, could be retained in a theater "as the military necessity demands." [23]

This "treaty" at least cleared the air and defined the issues. It concluded, significantly, with mutual assurances that neither signatory had designs upon the rightful jurisdiction of the other. But before the end of the year its basic provisions were again to be a subject of dispute. [24]

The Army's Logistical Organization During the Emergency Period

The prewar logistical structure of the Army had managed to carry its share of the growing burden of mobilization during the emergency period, but there was a mounting conviction on the higher levels that fundamental alterations would be required to meet the impact of war. [25] Logistical business, in the broad sense, made up the bulk of the enormous and growing volume of administration with which the General Staff daily had to deal, and which by the end of 1941 had transformed each

LEWIS W. DOUGLAS, *Deputy Administrator, War Shipping Administration.*

of its divisions into a large operating organization, immersed in details of supervision

[23] (1) Memo Covering the Interdepartmental Relationship Between the Army and WSA To Form a Basis for Full and Complete Cooperation in Connection With the Purchase, Charter, Use, and Opn of Vessels and Terminal Facilities, 13 Jun 42, Shipg 1941–43 folder, Hq ASF. (2) A similar agreement was reached between the Navy and WSA in letters dated 7 April and 7 May. See Ballantine, *Naval Logistics*, p. 89, and Wardlow, *Trans I*, Ch. VI.

Lewis W. Douglas had become a deputy administrator (there were two other deputies) of WSA, and in effect the head of that organization, under Admiral Land, in May 1942. Douglas was president of the Mutual Life Insurance Company and a former Director of the Bureau of the Budget; he was also a good friend of the President, who approved his appointment and promised to back him in what promised to be an exposed position in the "Battle of Washington." See Lane, *Ships for Victory*, p. 755.

[24] See below, Ch. XXII.

[25] For the prewar logistical organization of the Army, see above, Ch. I and Chart 1.

CHART 3—THE ARMY ON THE EVE OF PEARL HARBOR

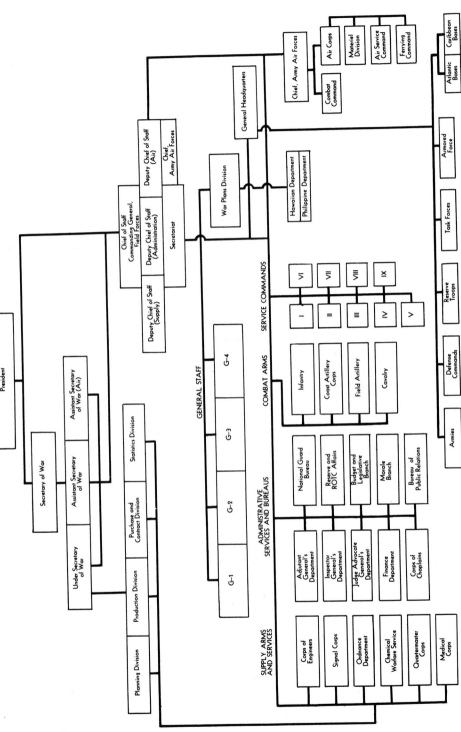

to the detriment of its policy-making and planning functions. G-4 became, next to G-2 and its affiliated intelligence services, the largest of the General Staff divisions, with an officer personnel at the beginning of March 1942 numbering upwards of two hundred.[26] *(Chart 3)* The Chief of Staff himself, despite the interposition of three deputies, a secretariat, and the five assistant chiefs, was similarly swamped as a consequence of the large number of subordinate headquarters permitted direct access to him.

Logistics was involved also in the fundamental conflicts of authority that emerged in 1941 between the General Staff and GHQ. By late winter of 1941–42 GHQ had been assigned, over and above its basic training task, command of all the Atlantic and Caribbean bases and the two theaters of operations (Western and Northeastern) activated in the United States immediately after Pearl Harbor, as well as a variety of new planning responsibilities. The War Plans Division, even more definitely, was moving toward the command post role that the Harbord Board had intended for GHQ, having been given command of the important outposts of Hawaii and the Philippines and having become the staff division upon which General Marshall relied most in directing current operations. These converging lines of development brought GHQ to a point where it needed a measure of authority in the field of logistics that the General Staff was unwilling to surrender to it. Under the first enlargement of its responsibilities in July 1941, GHQ was promised direct control of "such credits in supplies, ammunition and equipment as may, from time to time, be specifically allotted to it by the War Department."[27] As GHQ officers interpreted it, this meant block allotments of means with

full control over their use and administration, but GHQ never succeeded in securing such an arrangement. The corps areas, under G-4 supervision since their separation from army commands in mid-1940, controlled the flow of routine supply to bases and departments overseas, while G-4 exercised staff supervision directly over the movement of troops and overseas supply generally. The Chief of Engineers, under G-4's supervision, was responsible for overseas construction and the supply of construction materials. The Air Service Command provided technical items of Air Corps supplies. Thus, in the case of the Newfoundland Base Command, cited by General McNair as "an interesting example of superior command,"[28] real control of the means necessary to effective command was exercised through at least five separate channels (of which three were for logistical matters) bypassing GHQ, the headquarters theoretically in command of the base; the final word in allocation of personnel and material actually lay with WPD. GHQ's real function amounted to no more, as General McNair described it, than "such inspection and coordination as is practicable under the circumstances."[29]

WPD readily conceded, in principle, that "control of supply is an essential ele-

[26] (1) At the end of 1941 G-4 was reported to have about 150 officers and 130 civilians. See Nelson, *National Security and the General Staff*, p. 322. (2) The figure of two hundred officers is from Supply Division G-4, War Department General Staff, MS history, OCMH. (3) See also min, WD Gen Council mtg, 19 May 42. (4) Cline, *Washington Command Post*, p. 54.

[27] WD ltr, 3 Jul 41, sub: Enlargement of the Functions of GHQ, AG 320.2 (6-19-41) MC-E-M.

[28] Memo, CofS for ACofS WPD, 2 Sep 41, sub: Functions, Responsibility, and Auth of GHQ Orgn, GHQ 320.2/1.

[29] (1) Greenfield, Palmer, and Wiley, *AGF I*, pp. 6–9, 17–20, 22–23, 132, 136–37, 147; quote is from p. 133. (2) Cline, *Washington Command Post*, pp. 63–65. (3) WD ltr cited n. 27.

ment of command," but insisted that the shortage of munitions and shipping dictated "rigid control" over supply by the War Department.[30] G-4's stand in the matter was not wholly unequivocal, but generally followed this line. When the question of GHQ's authority over the "Carib" training force was raised in July 1941, G-4 insisted that existing channels of supply through Second Corps Area, and of transportation through The Quartermaster General and ports of embarkation, be maintained. The following January General Somervell, who had become G-4 at the end of November 1941, took the uncompromising stand that GHQ should exercise "no direct control over supplies or troop movements in the Zone of Interior," including those destined for overseas. GHQ, he asserted, "does not have an organization empowered or prepared to implement a supply plan for military operations. The War Department is set up for this purpose."[31]

It was under this principle that the logistical phases of Army deployment were directed during the first three months following Pearl Harbor. GHQ submitted theater plans to G-4 for analysis as to logistical feasibility; G-4, after obtaining a tentative order of priority for the various plans, proceeded to initiate procurement and "other advanced logistical arrangements."[32] In supply GHQ assumed control only from the time that troops and material left the port of embarkation, merely observing the process up to that point. Otherwise, GHQ's supply functions were limited to recommending priorities for supply among and within theaters, inspecting supply conditions and recommending to G-4 levels of reserves to be maintained overseas. Implementation of plans and recommendations was the task

of the established machinery supervised by G-4.[33]

Somervell's memorandum outlining these functions bore a significant penciled comment by his recently appointed executive officer, General Lutes: ". . . the attached will definitely limit GHQ powers and enable you to have the final word on supply." The Defense Aid Director, Colonel Aurand, had remarked two months earlier on "the crying need for reorganization of the War Department to put all supply in the hands of one man."[34] Toward this end Somervell's efforts, in January 1942, were unmistakably directed. The division of supply responsibilities between G-4 and the Office of the Under Secretary of War—with G-4 controlling requirements and distribution and the OUSW controlling procurement—was one that many observers still believed to be feasible, notably the management firm of Booz, Frey, Allen and Hamilton, which surveyed the OUSW late in 1941. But jurisdictional lines, during the expansion of 1940 and 1941, became badly blurred, as the staffs in G-4 and the OUSW grappled more and more with similar or identical problems of requirements and availability. Moreover, as the pressure on production mounted, G-4's task of expediting supply

---

[30] Memo, WPD for CofS, Aug 41, sub: Functions and Auth of GHQ, incl with memo, McNair for DCofS, 11 Aug 41, same sub, GHQ 320.2/4.

[31] (1) Memo, G-4 for WPD, 24 Jan 42, sub: Co-ord Between WPD, G-4, GHQ, and Theater Comdrs. (2) Memo, G-4 for CofS, 18 Jan 42, same sub. Both in G-4/34015. (3) Greenfield, Palmer, and Wiley, *AGF I*, pp. 142, 147. (4) Memo, G-4 for WPD, 5 Aug 41, sub: Activation of Alaskan and Caribbean Def Comds, G-4/33366.

[32] Memo cited n. 31(2).

[33] *Ibid.* Somervell here notes the Chief of Staff's approval of these definitions of responsibility on 21 January.

[34] Memo, Aurand for Moore, 24 Nov 41, sub: Necessity for Immediate Action . . . , Misc Corresp Lend-lease 3 file, DAD.

depended more and more upon the meeting of current production schedules, over which G-4 had no jurisdiction. Finally, the expansion of the OUSW, unfettered by any traditional inhibition against "operating," had far outpaced that of G-4; at the end of 1941 that organization numbered some twelve hundred persons.[35]

One of Somervell's first steps, after becoming G-4, was to call in his and Mr. Stimson's friend, Goldthwaite H. Dorr, a prominent New York attorney and Assistant Director of Munitions in World War I, to examine the whole problem of supply organization in the War Department. Dorr and a small committee began to work quietly in January, at the same time that, probably unknown to Somervell, plans for a wholesale decentralization of the War Department's operating and supervisory functions were maturing. The coincidence was ironical, for Dorr's and Somervell's explorations at the outset were aimed at consolidating in the General Staff the direction of all supply, including the procurement functions of the OUSW, somewhat as it had been concentrated during World War I under Maj. Gen. George W. Goethals in the Purchase, Storage, and Traffic Division. It was not difficult to merge the two lines of planning, when the drift of the broader reorganization project was revealed early in February, for the latter envisaged the creation of a single supply and service command for the continental United States.[36] To its commander, as readily as to an assistant chief of staff in the General Staff, could be assigned the "final word in supply."[37]

Logistics in the War Department Reorganization of March 1942

On 28 February the President signed the executive order creating "a ground force . . . an air force . . . and a service of supply command," under the Chief of Staff.[38] In the reorganized War Department, which officially came into existence on 9 March, a streamlined General Staff was restricted to the provision of "such broad basic plans" as would enable the various commands, including the three mentioned above, "to prepare and execute detailed programs."[39] The Army Ground Forces (AGF) was created and, under General McNair's command, took over the training tasks of GHQ, which was now abolished. The Army Air Forces, which had been created in July 1941, continued with little change in status. Under the Services of Supply, General Somervell's new command, was centralized control of supply and administration for the entire Army in the United States, with certain specific exceptions, principally relating to the Air Forces. Somervell's headquarters took over a number of important functions formerly assigned to the General Staff, as well as the anomalous organization charged with the administration of military lend-lease. To the Services of Supply were now subordinated most of the logistical agencies that had formerly reported directly to the General Staff: the supply and administrative services, with their regional establishments; various separate installations formerly "exempted" from higher control lower than the General

---

[35] Nelson, *National Security and the General Staff*, p. 321.

[36] (1) For details, see Millett, *ASF*, Chs. I–II. (2) See also, Millett, "The Direction of Supply Activities in the War Department," *American Political Science Review*, XXXVIII (June 1944), 492–94.

[37] Penciled comment by Lutes on memo cited n. 31(2).

[38] EO 9082, 28 Feb 42.

[39] (1) WD Circular 59, 2 Mar 42. (2) Ltr, CG SOS to Chiefs of SAS, *et al.*, 9 Mar 42, sub: Initial Dir for the Orgn of SOS, Hq ASF.

Staff, such as the ports of embarkation, holding and reconsignment points, regulating stations, proving grounds, procurement offices, and general depots; and the regional administrative machinery of the nine corps areas (renamed service commands in July), which now included most of the training installations of the supply and administrative services, induction and reception centers, alien and prisoner of war camps, dispensaries and general hospitals, repair shops, and the station complements and housekeeping facilities at ground force installations.[40] *(Chart 4)*

General Somervell, commander of the SOS, reported now to two masters—the Chief of Staff with respect to supply requirements and distribution, and the Under Secretary with respect to procurement. But inasmuch as most of the existing personnel of both the OUSW and the G-4 were transferred bodily to Somervell's staff, the two former co-ordinating offices were left with only a vague and, as experience speedily proved, nominal policy-making and planning role. G-4 found it impossible, with the eight to a dozen officers assigned to it, to exercise even policy supervision over logistical activities. The SOS rapidly moved into the vacuum to become a policy-making and planning as well as a supervisory and operating organization, and its forceful commander retained the responsibility, which he had held as G-4, of advising General Marshall directly in matters of supply. "We occupy a middle position," a G-4 officer wrote bitterly about a year after the reorganization, "between General Somervell as the Army representative in joint and international supply deals and General Somervell as the Commanding General of the Army Service Forces, a theoretical subordinate."[41] General McNair, a disapproving observer

of the trend, later told Somervell bluntly, "G-4 is the proper adviser of the Chief of Staff in logistics policies, even though such is not the case today due to the force of your personality."[42]

But the "final word on supply," which the reorganization of March 1942 snatched away from G-4 and the OUSW, was not bestowed upon the Services of Supply, powerful though Somervell's voice remained in high councils. War Plans Division (shortly renamed Operations Division and known as OPD) became, under the reorganization, the central command post that GHQ had never been allowed to be. Its functions included not only war planning but also "strategic direction of military forces in the theater of war,"[43] and it was organized as a separate general staff within the General Staff, equipped to command and operate as well as to plan. In general, the three great zone of interior commands were supposed to provide trained forces, equipment, and supplies in the United States, and the means to transport them overseas; G-1, G-3, and G-4 to formulate Army-wide policies primarily in the United States (that is, those affecting all three major commands) in the fields of personnel, unit organization, and sup-

[40] (1) *Ibid.* (2) *Annual Report of the Army Service Forces, 1943* (Washington, 1944), Ch. XIX. (3) Millett, *ASF,* Ch. III. (4) See other accounts in Greenfield, Palmer, and Wiley, *AGF I,* pp. 143–56; Watson, *Prewar Plans and Preparations,* Ch. IX; Cline, *Washington Command Post,* Ch. VI; and Nelson, *National Security and the General Staff,* Ch. VIII.
[41] Memo, Lt Col James McCormack, Jr., for Brig Gen Raymond G. Moses, 16 Apr 43, sub: Reorgn of the WD, G-4/020.
The SOS was renamed Army Service Forces in March 1943.
[42] (1) Memo, McNair for Somervell, 24 Jun 43, sub: Your Proposed Reorgn of Sv Activities, AGF 1943–44 folder, Hq ASF. (2) See Cline, *Washington Command Post,* pp. 114–15.
[43] WD Circular 59, 2 Mar 42.

CHART 4—THE REORGANIZED ARMY: SEPTEMBER 1942

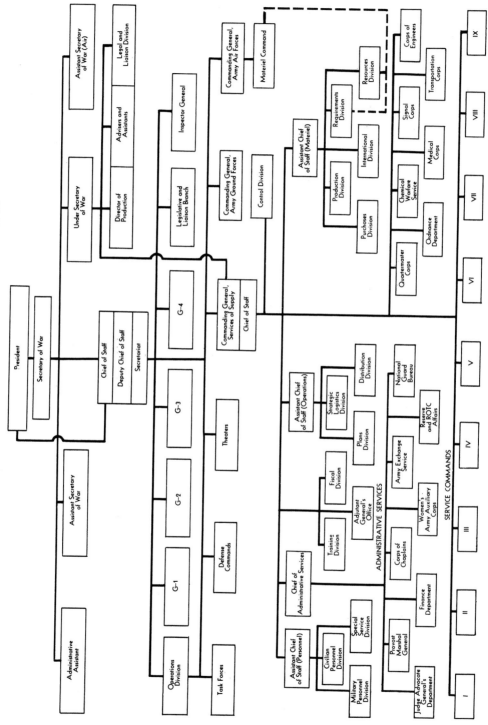

ply; OPD to direct operations overseas.[44] In practice, there were few matters, in logistics or any other field, in which OPD did not claim an interest and assert final jurisdiction, since all military activities in the zone of interior were oriented directly or indirectly to the support of overseas operations. And since OPD was not restricted, as were G–1, G–3, and G–4, to planning and policy making, it quickly built up a sizable staff of specialists in various fields to interpret the stream of technical information that daily poured into the division both from overseas theaters and from other zone of interior agencies. By mid-1942 two branches of OPD's organization, Theater Group and Logistics Group, were dealing directly and continuously with logistical matters. The former, through its theater sections, each organized as a miniature general staff, monitored the flow of messages between the War Department and overseas commanders and served as an operational control center for directing overseas operations. The Theater Group also included a Troop Movements Section, which supervised the preparation of movement orders by the three major commands and co-ordinated the flow of troops overseas. The Logistics Group, at first called Resources and Requirements, concerned itself with logistical problems in the large, rather than theater by theater, and placed special emphasis upon the balancing of requirements against assets. It was this group that, among other tasks, prepared and maintained the Victory Program Troop Basis. Necessarily, officers in the Logistics Group depended on the SOS and other sources for detailed logistical data, but they had access to the latest strategic plans, a source denied the planning staff of SOS. Through the Logistics Group, OPD became the Army's highest logistical planning and co-ordinating agency in the sense that it brought detailed knowledge and informed judgment of logistical limitations to bear in the final stages of strategic planning and decision.[45]

The Services of Supply, by contrast, was the Army's central operating and co-ordinating agency for supply in the United States and to the overseas theaters (except for material peculiar to the Air Forces). In the procurement field and in those phases of distribution that did not impinge immediately upon overseas operations, such as the management of the depot system and the supply of posts and installations in the United States, the co-ordinating function of the SOS reached upward to the policy-making level. In another dimension, wherever logistical operations could be reduced to routine procedures and automatic controls, the authority of the SOS was comparatively little subject to review or co-ordination from above. It was in logistical planning, the movement of troops to overseas theaters, and certain phases of overseas supply, activities that had a crucial bearing on military operations and, throughout 1942 at least, continued to demand a high degree of supervision, that the SOS found its information, judgments, and operations more or less constantly under scrutiny by OPD. Sometimes the scrutiny descended to routine, even humdrum questions. "Too many matters," wrote General Lutes, Somervell's Assistant Chief of Staff for Operations, in September 1942, "that are of primary interest to the SOS are being handled in the Operations Division. . . .

_____

[44] Cline, Washington Command Post, pp. 93–95.

[45] Ibid., pp. 123–31. See also Cline's draft MS, Ch. XVII, p. 632, in Supporting Docs to Cline, Washington Command Post file, OCMH.

Unless we are careful . . . we may find a great many supply matters bottlenecked in the Operations Division. Overseas commanders may not understand this and not realize that the delays are due to the General Staff."[46] Several months later the same officer complained of the "gradual tendency by the General Staff to tighten the rein of supervision over all the planning and operational procedures of Headquarters, ASF."[47]

From the point of view of the SOS, this supervision was senseless and wasteful in a structure created expressly for the purpose of lessening the administrative burdens of the General Staff. The patience of the SOS commander, never Job-like, occasionally broke under OPD interference in routine logistical business. On one occasion he wrote acidly to General Handy, the chief of OPD:

The officers who handled the matter in your office knew nothing of the situation. . . . The exchange of wires has now dragged on for over a month. In my opinion this is an inexcusable waste of time and I am sure that inefficiency will result in the event that junior officers in OPD continue to interfere in matters of supply.[48]

Understandably, this kind of irascibility caused annoyance in OPD, particularly when it was accompanied by strictures against the alleged incompetence of OPD in logistical planning. In this area the two staffs jostled repeatedly, and no really satisfactory *modus operandi* was ever found.

Supply and Transportation in the SOS

The initial organization of SOS headquarters reflected the dependence of distribution upon current production. These two functions were combined under a single Director of Procurement and Distribution; a Deputy Chief of Staff for Require-ments and Resources was responsible for "requirements, programs, resources and procurement planning,"[49] including the administration of defense aid, which was a function of distribution as well as of requirements. Both these officials were part of the commanding general's immediate office staff. The supply arms and services, with a new Transportation Division (later Service, and still later Corps) and a General Depot Service, were initially designated the "operating divisions" of the SOS.[50]

But the key agency of the SOS in co-ordinating its support of overseas operations was its Operations Division, a staff section not under the Director of Procurement and Distribution. This division was charged somewhat ambiguously with co-ordinating plans and instructions on "projected and current operations" involving two or more agencies of the SOS, with respect to troop and supply movements and "supply matters in connection with specific tactical or strategic operations, or other War Department activities."[51] Its role at first was rather narrowly defined. According to Col. Clinton F. Robinson, one of the "founding fathers" of the SOS:

The primary functions of the Operations Division are those concerned with purely military operations. Its chief duty should be the working out of the necessary supply arrangements with the War Plans Division and the Ground and Air Forces for specific mili-

---

[46] Memo, Lutes for Dir Plng Div SOS, 12 Sep 42, Misc Notes, Lutes File.

[47] Memo, Maj Gen LeRoy Lutes for Maj Gen Wilhelm D. Styer, 30 Mar 43, Misc Notes, Lutes File.

[48] Memo, Gen Somervell for Maj Gen Thomas T. Handy, 24 Feb 43, ACofS OPD 1942–44 folder, Hq ASF.

[49] Ltr cited n. 39(2).

[50] (1) *Ibid.* (2) *Report of the Chief of Transportation, ASF, World War II* (Washington, 30 Nov 45), pp. 17–18.

[51] Ltr cited n. 39(2).

tary operations. . . . The Operations Division is concerned with current and short-range military operations both within the zone of the interior and movements overseas.[52]

But from the outset the chief of the SOS Operations Division, General Lutes, whom Somervell had brought into G-4 only in January as his executive officer, interpreted his responsibilities broadly and forcefully. One of the primary areas was distribution, which Somervell on the eve of the reorganization had offered to place under Lutes' immediate supervision. Lutes had demurred, arguing that without transportation, already assigned a separate staff status, his direct control of distribution would be ineffective. But he had made it clear that he intended to co-ordinate both functions, even though the Distribution Branch was placed under the Director of Procurement and Distribution, who, unlike Lutes, was part of Somervell's immediate office. The weeks following the reorganization witnessed the anomaly of papers issuing from Distribution Branch over Lutes' signature instead of Col. Charles D. Young's, the Director of Procurement and Distribution. Finally, in July, Lutes was raised to the status of Assistant Chief of Staff for Operations, on a par with the Assistant Chiefs for Personnel and Materiel, created at the same time. Lutes' organization now included a Distribution Division and a Plans Division, with the "operations" function centered in his own office (the Operations Division had been eliminated). This was an important change, recognizing for the first time the cleavage between the requirements-procurement function, now consolidated under Brig. Gen. Lucius D. Clay, Assistant Chief of Staff for Materiel, and the distribution-logistical planning function.[53]

One of the "operations" that it seemed

might logically be performed for the Army as a whole by the Operations Division of the SOS was that of co-ordinating troop and accompanying supply movements. For this purpose Lutes' initial organization contained a Troop and Supply Movements Subsection, predecessor of the later Movements Branch. In prereorganization conferences SOS representatives had gained the impression that agreement had been reached on a procedure whereby the SOS, which was involved in all troop movements through its supply and transportation functions, would issue general directives for all movements, while AGF and AAF might issue supplementary orders as they saw fit, "if they do not conflict with SOS directives."[54] Theoretically, this procedure would combine in SOS the functions formerly performed in G-3, which had prepared the command portions of the basic order (including designation of units tables of organization, and strength breakdown), and in G-4, which had prepared the paragraph relating to supplies, equipment, and transportation.[55]

The first movement carried out under the new procedure, that of the Tongatabu task force ordered by the Joint Chiefs on 12 March, showed what the procedure meant in practice. Army Ground Forces, given full responsibility for setting up the Army portion of the joint force, and pos-

---

[52] Memo, Robinson for Styer, 19 Mar 42, Misc Notes, Lutes File.

[53] (1) Memo, Lutes for Somervell, 6 Mar 42, Misc Notes, Lutes File. (2) Memo cited n. 52. (3) SOS GO 24, 20 Jul 42. The Office of the Deputy Chief of Staff for Requirements and Resources was abolished. (4) See also, History of the Planning Division, Army Service Forces, MS, I, 8, OCMH.

[54] Memo, Lutes for Somervell, 7 Mar 42, sub: Summary of Opns, Misc Notes, Lutes File.

[55] (1) History of the Planning Division, ASF, MS, I, 34, 36, 136, OCMH. (2) Troop Movements in World War II, 31 Oct 45, MS, p. 6, OCMH.

KEY FIGURES OF THE SERVICES OF SUPPLY, *March 1942. Top left, Lt. Gen. LeRoy Lutes (then Brig. Gen.); top right, General Brehon B. Somervell (then Lt. Gen.); bottom left, Maj. Gen. Charles P. Gross (then Brig. Gen.); bottom right, Maj. Gen. Lucius D. Clay (then Brig. Gen.).*

sessing all the former G-3 officers who knew the technique of writing movement orders, issued the basic order for virtually all the Army ground elements, both combat and service; SOS issued an order for a single finance detachment, together with implementing instructions to corps areas, supply services, and ports to carry out supply and transportation arrangements for the entire force; the AAF staff, floundering in an unfamiliar task with inexperienced personnel, got out an order for the movement of air units and for the supply of items of peculiar interest to the Air Forces. Obviously, decentralization under the reorganization had complicated an already involved procedure.

On the day that the SOS movement order was published, 16 March, General Lutes took the problem to Col. William K. Harrison, Jr., one of the OPD officers who had fathered the War Department reorganization. AGF was now insistent that it must write movement orders for its own units, excepting only those portions relating to marking, transportation, and bulk supplies. Besides writing complete orders for its own units, SOS claimed the right to prepare all instructions concerning transportation and supply, including the provisions for supplies and equipment accompanying the troops, since the process of actually providing this material was the responsibility of SOS agencies. AAF was uncertain, but on the whole inclined to go along with the SOS view. The three commands agreed that the command portions of the orders should properly be prepared by each command for its own units. Maj. Gen. Joseph T. McNarney, the Deputy Chief of Staff, was prevailed upon to accept OPD's proposed solution—to centralize the co-ordinating and supervisory function once again in the General Staff, this time

in OPD, where at the beginning of April a small troop movements section was set up within the Theater Group.

On 20 March, while the staffs were still struggling with the Tongatabu movement, OPD issued a directive assigning to itself the "initiation, supervision and co-ordination" of movement orders.[56] For each movement OPD issued a single basic order; the three major commands then co-ordinated their efforts in preparing a single implementing order, each writing so much of it "as pertains to their respective activities."[57] The final draft was submitted to OPD for approval and publication. The procedure was further centralized by the requirement that all movement orders must be cleared with the Deputy Chief of Staff. Insofar as this procedure provided for the drafting of separate supply arrangements by each major command, however, it became almost immediately a fiction. AAF accepted the supply and transportation provisions for its units as drafted by the SOS staff. AGF continued to prepare for its units the provisions applying to material accompanying the movement, but it became a routine procedure for OPD to use the provisions for supply as well as transportation drafted by the SOS. In this respect, as in many others, the SOS Operations staff performed the Army-wide services given up by G-4 in the reorganization.[58]

General Lutes also exploited vigorously

---

[56] Memo, TAG for WPD, 20 Mar 42, sub: Responsibility and Proced for Preparation of Overseas Mvmt Order, OPD 370.5 Changes of Station, 12.

[57] Ibid.

[58] (1) Memo, Exec Off for ACofS WPD, 22 Mar 42, sub: Mvmt Orders, OPD 370.5 Changes of Station, 193. (2) Min, WD Gen Council mtg, 31 Mar 42. (3) Troop Movements in World War II, 31 Oct 45, MS, pp. 3-7, OCMH. (4) History of the Planning Division, ASF, MS, I, 136-37, OCMH. (5) Cline, *Washington Command Post*, pp. 125-27.

what he called "the general follow-up of the functioning of the supply system,"[59] and under a "maintain-close-liaison" clause in the initial SOS directive, he established virtually complete control over the "foreign relations" of SOS and the supply services with the other two major commands and the General Staff in the field of supply. In particular, he successfully asserted the prerogative of co-ordinating "all supply matters and supply information" between SOS and OPD.[60]

Lutes at first visualized his office as a G-4 for the SOS, having the function of "co-ordinating and supervising the operations . . . affecting principally the field forces and the War Department General Staff."[61] Presently, however, he perceived a happier analogy—with OPD. This was suggested by the rapid extension of the function of logistical planning by the SOS staff. Under the original concept of the SOS, long-range planning was dispersed among several agencies—Requirements, Resources, and the operating divisions (supply services).[62] These continued, of course, to plan, but Lutes' planning staff soon became the dominant planning agency of the SOS. The Distribution Division, after it was added to Lutes' organization, became by contrast essentially an operating or executive staff. His Plans Division, despite its name, consisted in July 1942 of branches not only for general plans, but also for mobilization, movements, storage and shipping, and hospitalization and evacuation, all of which, except the first, were concerned far more with supervision than with planning. The General Plans Branch, nucleus of the later Planning Division, was organized on the OPD pattern, with a theater section broken down by geographical areas and a "supply strategy" section, which evolved

later in the year into the Strategic Logistics Division, a small staff specializing in long-range logistical studies. Lutes wrote somewhat later:

Experience has shown . . . that a co-ordinating agency is needed in the staff of Hqs ASF to correlate supply planning in its relation to strategic plans and current operations. . . . The agency best organized to accomplish this co-ordination is believed to be the Planning Division, ASF. Further, it is believed that the Director of Operations, ASF, should have the same staff relationship to the entire staff of the Commanding General, ASF, in regard to overseas matters as the Assistant Chief of Staff for Operations, WDGS, has in relation to the other staff officers of the General Staff. The Director of Operations, ASF, should be charged with the strategic employment of the supplies, in consonance with the approved strategic plans, and charged with all ASF matters affecting overseas operations.[63]

"Operations" in the SOS, in short, just as on the General Staff, were closely linked with the planning function, and both were oriented heavily toward overseas operations. In some respects at least, General Lutes' organization became the OPD of SOS.[64]

---

[59] Memo, Lutes for CofS SOS, 21 Apr 42, Misc Notes, Lutes File.

[60] (1) Memo, Dir of Opns SOS for OPD, 20 Apr 42, Misc Notes, Lutes File. (2) Ltr cited n. 39(2). (3) Plng Div SOS Diary, 11 May and 10 Jun 42 entries, Plng Div ASF. This diary was a day-to-day account of the Planning Division's work and appeared under various of the designations of the division's antecedents, such as the Planning Branch, Operations Division, and the General Plans Branch, Plans Division. For simplification, it will be cited hereafter as Plng Div SOS Diary. (4) Memo, Dir of Opns SOS for TQMG and CofOrd, 20 May 42, 400 Sup Gen folder, Plng Div ASF.

[61] Memo cited n. 53(1).

[62] (1) Memo, Lutes for Somervell, 17 May 42, Misc Notes, Lutes File. (2) Memo cited n. 52.

[63] Memo, Lutes for Somervell, 27 Jul 43, Misc Notes, Lutes File.

[64] History of the Planning Division, ASF, MS, I, 8–13, 32–40, OCMH.

The most powerful challenge to that role came from the autonomous organization of transportation. In March 1942 the Chief of Transportation, General Gross, took over the functions of the former Transportation Branch in G-4 and the Transportation Division of the Office of The Quartermaster General, including procurement of floating equipment, command of ports of embarkation and holding and reconsignment points, and training of port headquarters and port battalions. The following September General Gross assumed responsibility for operation and maintenance of military railways from the Chief of Engineers, and similar functions pertaining to utility railroads from the Quartermaster Corps. In November the Transportation Corps took over from the Engineer Corps the design, procurement, storage, and issue of all railway equipment, the training of railway troops, and the entire Military Railway Service.[65] Control of transportation, in short, was centralized under the Chief of Transportation much as control of supply centered in the Assistant Chief of Operations, SOS. General Gross, while a line officer as chief of a supply service, also served in a staff capacity as Somervell's transportation adviser.

General Lutes' earlier confidence that he could effectively co-ordinate supply and transportation without directly controlling both functions was soon shaken. They were "intimately connected operations," as he had noted, but their organizational compartmentation made it difficult to bring them together at the numerous points where co-ordination was needed in the complicated process of arranging troop and supply movements.[66] Lutes' counterpart in the transportation organization was Gross' Director of Operations, Brig. Gen.

Robert H. Wylie, who, like Lutes, co-ordinated the activities of operating divisions and field installations and handled most of his chief's external relations with other SOS staff agencies, the Navy, civilian transportation agencies, private carriers, and the General Staff, including OPD. Most of these channels paralleled those by which Lutes' organization co-ordinated supply operations.[67] Exchange of information between the central transportation and supply organizations in SOS was not always free or continuous. One SOS staff officer once recorded, "It appears, although it cannot be proved, that subordinate agencies in Transportation have either been directed to withhold information from this office or have taken this attitude from their superiors."[68] In March 1943 Lutes registered a complaint with the Chief of Transportation.

It frequently happens that the Plans Division of this office becomes involved in detailed planning with . . . [OPD, Assistant Chief of Staff for Materiel in SOS, service commanders, AGF, and AAF]; troops are designated for overseas operations; equipment is started to the home stations . . . only to find that a change in the shipping plans has been made directly between OPD and the Office of the Chief of Transportation.

---

[65] *Report of the Chief of Transportation, ASF, World War II*, p. 18.

Procurement of motor vehicles, however, remained with the Ordnance Department, and training of truck companies was performed mainly by the Ground and Air Forces.

Gross was promoted to brigadier general on 11 March 1942 and to major general on 9 August 1942.

[66] Memo cited n. 53(1).

[67] (1) Wardlow, *Trans I*, Ch. III. (2) Memo, Lutes for Dir of Plng Div, 3 Sep 42, Misc Notes, Lutes File.

Lutes was promoted to the rank of major general on 25 October 1942.

[68] "For record" to memo, Col Frank A. Heileman for CofTrans, 4 Feb 43, sub: Sup Sit . . . , 18 Shipg file, II, Case 53, Plng Div ASF.

He requested testily that his office be informed immediately of "each and every change" in shipping arrangements.[69]

The fundamental difficulty, however, was functional, arising from the fact that supply and transportation to some degree had conflicting purposes. Success in supply was measured in terms of timely delivery of desired amounts and items of material; success in transportation, in terms of efficient traffic management and economy in use of transport. Normally, the two purposes worked to a common end, but during 1942 the converging pressures for effective supply and for economy in the use of shipping brought them often into conflict. The conflict came to a head in the question of control over the ports of embarkation.

The Contest for Control of the Ports

The prewar primary port, or port of embarkation, was almost purely a transportation agency, a funnel and transshipping point for troops and material moving overseas. While each of the three primary ports being used by the Army on the eve of Pearl Harbor (New York, San Francisco, and New Orleans) was the site of a general depot that served both overseas bases and neighboring installations, the port itself had no co-ordinating responsibility in overseas supply and no operating supply functions except in serving its own personnel and troops moving through it. The administrative and functional core of the prewar port was the Army Transport Service, headed by a Quartermaster officer with the title of superintendent, who was charged with supervision and control of all water transportation. The War Department's supervision of port operations in the years of peace was not close, but The

Quartermaster General, to whom the superintendent of the Transport Service at each port was in practice answerable, successfully resisted efforts by port commanders themselves, by the corps areas, and by other supply services to encroach upon this jurisdiction. On 17 December 1941 all ports of embarkation and general depots located at them were placed under the Chief of the Transportation Branch, G-4, and the following March they passed to the Chief of Transportation in SOS. Wartime transportation operations at the ports were thus brought under central control from the beginning. Under the immense burden of traffic moving overseas after December 1941, the importance of the ports as transshipping agencies was enhanced, and central control was tightened. Movements of Army troops and freight, including military lend-lease to and through the ports, were carefully regulated by the Chief of Transportation's office in Washington, and in March 1942 a Transportation Control Committee was established, which eventually represented the military services, the British Ministry of War Transport, the Office of Defense Transportation, and the War Shipping Administration, for co-ordinating all portbound freight movements.[70]

---

[69] Memo, Lutes for Gross, 26 Mar 43, Misc Notes, Lutes File.

[70] (1) A primary port was headquarters of a line of Army transports, and when located at a general depot both were under the same commandant. The three primary ports were also ports of embarkation. A subport was administratively subordinate to a primary port. See AR 270-5, 30 Nov 40, and AR 30-1110, 1 Apr 40. (2) WD ltr, 17 Dec 41, sub: Orders Affecting Mvmt of Trs . . . , AG 612 (12-16-41). (3) Larson, Water Transportation for the U.S. Army 1939–1942, Monograph 5, OCT HB. (4) Schmidt, The Commercial Traffic Branch in the Office of The Quartermaster General, July 1940–March 1942, OCT HB Monograph 6, OCMH. (5) Wardlow, *Trans I*, pp. 39–41, 95–110, 373. (6) Chester Wardlow, The Trans-

PREPARING TO BOARD A TROOPSHIP, *San Francisco Port of Embarkation, September 1942.*

In March 1942, when the new overseas supply plan issued in January went into effect, the Army ports also became regional centers for the routine administration of overseas supply. Each port became, in effect, the agent to which one or more overseas bases sent their supply requisitions, on which they relied to maintain a regular flow of automatic supply shipments, and to which they looked, in gen-

eral, to handle their routine supply needs. The theaters and bases that a port served in this capacity were not always those for which troop movements and many emergency cargo shipments originating at the port were destined. *(See Appendix G.)* Upon the old role of the port as transshipping agency, in short, an altogether new one was superimposed, and the administrative autonomy conferred upon the port in performing its new functions contrasted sharply with its subordination to central authority in transportation matters.[71]

portation Corps: II, Movements, Training, and Supply, a volume in preparation for the series UNITED STATES ARMY IN WORLD WAR II (hereafter cited as Wardlow, Trans II), Ch. IV. (7) Rpt, Jun 42, sub: Study of Governmental Contl of Trans Facilities, Contl Div ASF.

[71] See below, Ch. XIII.

LOADING SHIPS, NEW YORK PORT, 1943

The ports were slow in developing an organization to handle their new duties. Only a broad injunction to do so was contained in the overseas supply plan itself, and the Chief of Transportation left the matter generally to the discretion of the port commanders. Before the war the limited supply functions of the ports had usually devolved upon the port quartermaster, who had miscellaneous duties including the control of rail and highway movements into the port. An overseas supply division was established at San Francisco early in 1942, but apparently did not begin to function effectively until midyear. Not until July was a separate overseas supply division established at New York, largely under the prompting of General Lutes and headed by Brig. Gen. William M. Goodman, Lutes' nominee and a former assistant executive in G-4 under Somervell. The New York Overseas Supply Division became the prototype for overseas supply organizations at the other ports. While the overseas supply divisions were of course subordinate to the port commanders, they looked to Lutes' office in Washington for their policy direction in overseas supply and gradually assumed a role commensurate with the port's autonomous supply function, enforcing War Department policy and co-ordinating the port's relations with interior depots, supply services, SOS headquarters, and overseas commanders. General Goodman, himself, later became the New York port commander's deputy.[72]

Following a visit to the New York port in July 1942, General Lutes wrote to Somervell, "The trip has convinced me that similar visits must be made to check supply matters at other ports. To date more stress has been placed at ports on purely transportation matters."[73] Ports tended to be dilatory in following up requisitions sent to depots and not filled; port transportation agencies failed to properly "marry up" parts of assemblies, for example sending artillery shells and propelling charges overseas in separate shipments. The chief complaint was against unbalanced loading. After mid-1942 the ports and the Transportation Corps came under increasingly heavy pressure from the War Shipping Administration to economize on shipping by more efficient scheduling and loading. This pressure had its effect. Much filler cargo, especially subsistence and ammunition, was shipped overseas with little regard for need, and sometimes at the expense of more critical matériel, in order that ships might sail loaded "full and down." Ammunition and ration stocks in North Africa early in 1943 rose to embarrassingly high levels, and perishables began to deteriorate.

Supply and transportation, in short, were working at cross-purposes. The issue came to a head late in February 1943 when Lutes learned that the New York port had failed to carry out earlier instructions from his office to discontinue automatic supply of ammunition to North Africa as soon as theater reports showed sufficient stocks on hand. "The time has come," Lutes wrote Somervell on the 24th,

". . . when shipments must be loaded according to military necessity. The principal shortages overseas at present are organizational equipment and items that do not and cannot completely fill the ships." Two days later he proposed a solution. "It has been difficult," he bluntly told Somervell, "for this office to regulate overseas supply with complete control resting in the ports of embarkation."[74] His own organization, he added pointedly, contained a new Stock Control Branch responsible for regulating supply stockages. Lutes recommended that either the port overseas supply organization be turned over outright to his control, leaving the Transportation Corps to operate solely as a shipping agency, or "the Chief of Transportation look to this office for instructions relative to overseas supply, and . . . conform strictly to such instructions. The Chief of Transportation," he concluded, "has fought rightly to retain control of military shipping, but there is no advantage in such control from a military standpoint unless ships are loaded accordingly. Commercial loading and shipping

---

[72] (1) Wardlow, Trans II, Ch. V. (2) Transcript of Port Comdrs' Conf, Boston, Aug–Sep 43. (3) Harold Larson, Role of the Transportation Corps in Oversea Supply, Monograph 27, pp. 18–19, 148–51. (4) San Francisco Port of Embarkation 1941–1942, hist rcd, pp. 169–71. Last three in OCT HB. (5) Richard M. Leighton, Overseas Supply Policies and Procedures, ASF hist monograph, pp. 76–82, OCMH. (6) Interview, author with Gen Lutes, 28 Feb 48, Logis File, OCMH.

[73] Memo, Lutes for Somervell, 17 Jul 42, Misc Notes, Lutes File.

The following account of the controversy over the ports is largely based on correspondence in the possession of General Lutes (referred to elsewhere in this volume as Lutes File) and is related in detail in Leighton, Overseas Supply Policies and Procedures, pp. 83–111, OCMH.

[74] (1) Memo, Lutes for Somervell, 24 Feb 43. (2) Memo, Lutes for Somervell, 26 Feb 43.

procedures do not effect balanced supply stocks in overseas military bases." [75]

Gross agreed in principle to the second alternative. "As Chief of a Corps having line as well as staff functions," he wrote Maj. Gen. Wilhelm D. Styer, Somervell's Chief of Staff,

. . . I stand ready and willing to obey, and to see that all elements under my command obey, all directives of the Assistant Chief of Staff for Operations on overseas supply and other matters under his jurisdiction. . . . but strongly urge that no action be taken which would completely sever the present direct lines of command.[76]

Under existing arrangements, in fact, the supply staffs of the SOS were already permitted to deal directly with the overseas supply divisions at the ports. But Lutes had hoped that the overseas supply divisions "would dominate the shipping or Army Transport Service personnel in the ports in order to effect intelligent overseas supply." [77] Instead, transportation had dominated supply and was likely to continue to dominate it as long as the shipping shortage remained acute.

General Gross made a counterproposal—to establish within his own organization an overseas division to co-ordinate all matters concerning overseas supply and transportation operations. Lutes objected on the ground that

. . overseas supply is not listed as one of the major functions of the Transportation Corps. . . at no place . . . is the Chief of Transportation charged with such functions as would require him to establish an overseas supply staff in Washington to perform other than administrative duties pertaining to the transportation of supplies.[78]

Also, Lutes feared that the proposed new agency would prevent the direct contacts between his own office and the port over-seas supply organizations, which he considered indispensable. On the other hand, it was difficult to deny the right of the Chief of Transportation to set up an office to co-ordinate the supply activities of the ports, as long as they remained under his jurisdiction. A possible escape from the dilemma, suggested by a member of Lutes' staff, would be to place the ports under a new "neutral" staff agency responsible for overseas supply and transportation and reporting directly to the Commanding General, Army Service Forces (ASF).

General Lutes, understandably, was not taken by this suggestion and it went no further. The ideal solution, from his point of view, would be to place the port overseas supply organizations directly under his control, thus keeping the Transportation Corps "out of the supply business." [79] General Styer, whom Somervell assigned to mediate the quarrel, was inclined to agree. By April, however, most of the conditions about which Lutes had complained seemed to be already on the wane. "Marrying up" of assemblies, for example, was being transferred from ports to depots and holding and reconsignment points where it could be performed by specialists. Routine procedures in transportation and supply were tightened up, and General Gross bore down on his own staff to keep the supply agencies informed. Lutes admitted in April that matters were improving.

General Styer recommended, therefore, that "no radical change in organization for handling overseas supply" be

---

[75] Memo cited n. 74(2).
[76] Memo, Gross for Styer, 1 Apr 43, quoted in Larson, Role of the Transportation Corps in Oversea Supply, p. 163, OCT HB.
[77] Memo, Gen Lutes for Lt Gen John L. De Witt, 18 Apr 43.
[78] Memo, Lutes for Gross, 10 Apr 43.
[79] Memo cited n. 77.

made.[80] An exchange of memoranda between Lutes and Gross late in April provided that Lutes' office would deal with the Chief of Transportation on general matters of overseas supply policy, while on routine matters the supply staff would communicate directly with the port overseas supply divisions; on questions falling into intermediate categories, communications would be sent directly to the headquarters concerned, with notification copies to other interested agencies. General Gross' proposed overseas division never materialized as such. Thus, the dispute was settled within the existing organizational framework, and the duality of supply and transportation was reaffirmed. "As a staff officer for transportation," General Styer explained, "General Gross has the same duties and responsibilities and the same relationship with the Commanding General, ASF, in transportation matters that the Assistant Chief of Staff for Operations has in regard to supply matters." They would have to work together, he observed, "like a pair of Siamese twins."[81]

The Limits of Port Autonomy

The development of the ports during 1942 as autonomous administrative units in the system of overseas supply was carefully guided by the War Department and the SOS to avoid an extreme of decentralization that might have made each port the simple advocate and agent of its assigned theaters in the fierce competition for supply support. This middle path was not easy to follow. There were pressures, dating back to the interwar years, for a larger measure of autonomy, particularly on the distant west coast. In January 1941 Brig. Gen. John C. H. Lee, then commander of the San Francisco port, had

proposed that all the shipping and storage facilities in the San Francisco, Seattle, and Los Angeles areas be consolidated under his command, as "Commander, Pacific Ports of Embarkation"; this regional command would serve all troops on the west coast and all garrisons in the Pacific. Lee's successor, Col. Frederick Gilbreath, proposed a similar consolidation "in case of a major national effort involving a large expeditionary force"[82] to the Pacific, and Colonel Aurand, while still in G-4, recommended a grouping of all ports under two regional coastal commands, one for the west coast, the other combining the Atlantic and Gulf coasts.[83]

In the crisis following Pearl Harbor the whole future role of the ports came under review. Transfer of the Army's shipping responsibilities to the Navy seemed now to be postponed indefinitely. Army ports were being swamped by an unprecedented volume of troop and cargo movements. The overseas supply system was being revamped. On the west coast, the Navy's field organization was giving an impressive demonstration of aggressive and efficient local initiative. In chartering shipping and expediting supply movements, Army officials found themselves hampered by their subordination to a distant headquarters while the Navy could operate with relative freedom.[84] To the men on the spot, and even more to the commanders overseas whose fate hung on their efforts, the situation seemed to demand a great

---

[80] Memo, Styer for Somervell, 16 Apr 43.
[81] Ibid.
[82] Memo, CG SFPOE for G-4, 15 Jan 41, G-4, 32464.
[83] (1) San Francisco Port of Embarkation 1941–1942, p. 23, OCT HB. (2) Memo, Chief of Reqmt and Distrib Br for G-4, 7 Mar 41, sub: Things That Won't Wait, Plng folder, OCT HB.
[84] For the impact of this situation upon the Hawaiian Department, see above, Ch. VI.

national effort to make available to the west coast the reinforcements and supplies that were needed, together with greater freedom for the Army organization there to exploit local resources and facilities.

Some of this feeling emerged in a proposal made in mid-January 1942 by General Emmons, commander of the Hawaiian Department, for the creation of a Pacific coast communications zone, bringing together all the Army's west coast supply and transportation activities. The Pacific theaters would look to this communications zone for all their material requirements, including supplies for the civilian population, and would present their requirements through representatives on the zone commander's staff. The latter, in turn, would have "complete authority to act" for the War Department under a general directive, and in addition would be given access to the "alphabetical agencies" of the government for production, resources, and shipping through representatives on his staff, who would be "clothed with the necessary authority." [85]

General Marshall's reply, which was sent at once, concentrated on the immediate issue from which Emmons' proposal had sprung—the shipping shortage—and rejected the plan with little further comment. Nevertheless, the point Marshall made with reference to allocation of shipping could be applied equally to the other critical resources that Emmons' plan vaguely implied should be placed at the disposal of the proposed new command. "Our own and allied shipping is fully considered," Marshall wrote, "in every operation undertaken, and allocations are made on the basis of urgency, which can only be determined in joint [interallied] conferences. Many movements to the Pacific have and will continue to be made

from the Atlantic coast." [86] The zone commander, in Emmons' plan, would probably have been allowed to charter local shipping, as the Navy was doing, and would have enjoyed administrative contacts and channels for tapping regional resources on behalf of the Pacific theaters that were denied to other theaters and field agencies. The west coast region embraced a considerable part of the national economy, and it was far from Washington. A single autonomous logistical command dominating so important an area might well have become a powerful sectional influence in economic mobilization; in any case, the scheme pointed toward a geographical compartmentation inimical to flexible administration on a nationwide basis. Almost certainly such a command would have exerted its influence to promote a westward, as against the already approved eastward, orientation of strategy. With relation to the theaters it was to serve, the proposed command would not, of course, be a communications zone at all in the usual sense, but a full-fledged intermediate logistical "theater"; Emmons nominated Lt. Gen. John L. DeWitt to command it, evidently having in mind that it would be merged with the Western Defense Command. In a limited sense, the plan foreshadowed the intermediate role Emmons' own command in the Hawaiian Islands was later to play in the Pacific war.

The kind of autonomy envisaged in Emmons' plan stood out in sharp contrast to that in the War Department's overseas

---

[85] Msg 1709, CG HD to TAG, 15 Jan 42, AG 381 (11-27-41) Sec 1.

[86] Msg 1013, CofS to CG HD, 16 Jan 42, AG 381 (11-27-41) Sec 1.

Emmons was rebuked by the War Department somewhat later for chartering shipping directly from the Matson Navigation Company. See above, Ch. VI.

supply plan published a week later. In the War Department's plan, the autonomy of the port of embarkation was circumscribed—though unfettered within its assigned sphere. The port was not an allocating agency; in servicing requisitions it acted merely as the administrative agent of the War Department. It employed the means assigned to it—shipping and depot credits; it could not exploit the resources in its environs. After the rejection of General Emmons' proposal, the transportation activities of the ports continued to be subordinated to central control from Washington, and when Maj. Gen. Frederick Gilbreath in spring of 1943 renewed his recommendation for consolidation of west coast ports under one command, General Gross again rejected the idea.[87]

In the sphere of overseas supply, however, the autonomy already gained created pressure for further extension. In September 1942, in connection with an attempted revamping of supply reporting, General Somervell put forward a proposal that in all matters of supply the port commander should be considered the agent for his assigned theaters and bases. To the port would go all supply communications from overseas, those on which the port was not empowered to act being forwarded immediately to higher headquarters with recommendations. The port would be authorized to require from overseas bases all reports and information needed to execute its supply responsibility. But both OPD and G-4 turned their faces against the proposal, being unwilling to abandon the direct channels by which overseas commanders communicated with the General Staff on all nonroutine matters.

Late the following winter the regional principle once more reared its head, again in the sphere of supply, when Brig. Gen.

Clinton F. Robinson, Somervell's chief adviser on organization and management and probably the author of the "agent" idea, suggested the formation of an Atlantic coast service command, possibly to be followed later by similar organizations on the other coasts. General Lutes enthusiastically endorsed the idea, seeing in it a solution to his troubles in maintaining the ascendancy of supply over transportation in port operations, but General Gross' resolute hostility settled the matter. In 1943 certain ports on the east coast were sometimes brought under the control of another port, usually New York, for specific supply movements to areas in the latter's sphere of responsibility, and the actual burden of outflowing traffic on both east and west coasts was concentrated less heavily than in 1942 on the two major ports, New York and San Francisco.

Actually, there was no really strong tendency toward regionalism. The Army's sources of supply in the United States (unlike the Navy's) were spread too widely and too far back from the coasts to make feasible a regional scheme of administrative decentralization to coastal areas. Army transportation, dependent upon the nation's highly interdependent rail system, lent itself even less readily to area compartmentation, while the fierce competition for transportation facilities made real decentralization on any basis impracticable. As transshipping agencies, therefore, the ports continued to function as cogs in a nationwide transportation system that was tightly and centrally co-ordinated. As administrative centers for overseas supply, the ports enjoyed a real if limited autonomy, but their jurisdiction had no regional

[87] Memo, CofTrans for CG SFPOE, 19 Apr 43, SPTT 323.94 SF file, OCT.

character except in the sense that the theaters they served constituted geographical areas.[88]

The Theater Segment of the Pipeline

The administrative sphere of the port of embarkation did not extend beyond the harbor's mouth. Getting troops and material safely across the ocean gap was the Navy's job, and at the port of destination the theater's rear area organization took charge. The organization of the segment of the supply pipeline lying beyond the theater port of entry, like all matters of theater administration, was regarded as the theater commander's business under the prevailing American military doctrine, which gave a field commander free rein in the choice of methods for carrying out his assigned mission.[89]

This autonomy had certain disadvantages in overseas supply. As master of his own house, the theater commander could be urged, but only with difficulty required, to institute an effective system of stock control, to keep accurate records of the movement and status of supply, to determine his requirements on a realistic basis, or, in general, to maintain minimum standards of supply control. The overseas theater, moreover, was not a homogeneous segment of the pipeline, and its administration was not easily divorced from that of the lines of communications lying to the rear. In a large theater the ports of entry might be only the first of several transshipment and storage points, and the staging of supply forward might lead only gradually into the retail, dispersed system of distribution that in general characterized the theater segment of the pipeline.[90]

Under field service regulations the rear areas of a theater were ordinarily organized as a communications zone—an autonomous theater-within-a-theater that might comprise the greater part of the theater's geographical area. The communications zone commander, responsible directly to the theater commander for forwarding troops and supplies to the combat zone, also relieved the latter of the administrative burden involved in the vast complex of rear area activities necessary to the functioning of large armies.[91] This geographical division of responsibilities opened the door to a wide duplication of functions between the theater and the communications zone staffs, on the theory that most logistical functions had "theater-wide" as well as purely rear area aspects. In an effort to reduce this duplication and free his staff of administrative responsibilities, General John J. Pershing in 1918 had replaced his Line of Communication, as the rear area organization of the American Expeditionary Forces was called, by a "Services of Supply"—or, as its author, Brig. Gen. Johnson Hagood, called it, a "Services of the Rear." To this SOS were assigned, despite this latter title, most of the administrative and technical activities, not merely rear area services, supporting the U.S. armies in France. In supply, the theater staff continued to supervise only the determination of destinations and re-

---

[88] (1) Memo, Lutes for Somervell, 24 Mar 43, Misc Notes, Lutes File. (2) Wardlow, *Trans I*, Ch. IV. (3) See above, pp. 233–38, and below, pp. 327–28. (4) For a discussion of wartime rail operations and the traffic control system, see Joseph R. Rose, *American Wartime Transportation* (New York, The Thomas Y. Crowell Company, 1953), Chs. I, IV.

[89] (1) FM 101-5, Staff Officers' Field Manual, Aug 40, par. 1. (2) For the effect of Pearl Harbor in bringing about a closer direction of overseas operations by the high command in Washington, see Cline, *Washington Command Post*, Chs. V–VI.

[90] See below, Ch. XIII.

[91] FM 100-10, Field Service Regulations: Administration, 1940, Ch. 2, Sec V.

quirements, and the SOS commander was authorized to deal directly with Washington on supply matters. War Department officials, indeed, felt that the tie should be closer, and Secretary Baker proposed in July 1918 that the SOS be placed directly under War Department control. General Pershing emphatically rejected the proposal, appealing to the doctrine of "unity of command and responsibility." [92]

The precedent of 1918 lent support to two important principles: first, that a theater's rear area organization, even though most of its business was carried on far behind the combat zone, was the proper agency to handle most theater-wide administration as well, and second, that it must be permitted free and direct access to War Department logistical agencies on most matters. Both principles tended to enhance its administrative autonomy vis-à-vis the theater. The influence of the experience of 1918 was clearly evident, not only in the creation of a central Services of Supply in the War Department in March 1942, but also in the establishment during that year of several rear area organizations overseas bearing the SOS label and more or less closely resembling the original 1918 SOS—in the Central, Southwest, and South Pacific, North Africa, the Middle East, India, and the British Isles. In none of these experiments did the jurisdictional issue raised by Secretary Baker in 1918 reappear in precisely its original form since the War Department had no inclination to assume direct command over widely scattered and remote areas overseas. But in each theater the SOS or the communications zone usually was permitted to deal directly with the War Department Services of Supply on a variety of more or less routine administrative matters that comprised the bulk of the theater's logistical business

with the zone of interior. [93] In general, however, the jurisdiction of rear area organizations over theater-wide activities remained limited, and most theaters maintained large administrative staffs at theater headquarters.

In only one theater, the European, did the War Department clearly attempt to dictate the form of the rear area organization. [94] General Somervell believed, and persuaded General Marshall, that the theater SOS should parallel in its structure that of the War Department SOS, in order to permit direct dealings between "opposite numbers" of the two staffs. Marshall also accepted Somervell's recommendation of Maj. Gen. John C. H. Lee as commanding general of the theater SOS, and before his departure for England late in May 1942, Lee was thoroughly briefed by Somervell's staff and by General Harbord, former commander of the SOS in France in 1918. The plan of organization was drafted in April and May by Somervell's staff.

This scheme grouped the heads of the supply and administrative services in the theater's SOS headquarters, leaving the

[92] (1) Ltr, Pershing to Secy Baker, 6 Jul 18, quoted in John J. Pershing, My Experiences in the World War (New York, Frederick A. Stokes Company, 1931, 2 vols.), I, 190. (2) For details on the Services of Supply of 1918, see ibid., I, 109, 180–91, 321, 348, II, 55, 108, 140, 204; and General Johnson Hagood, The Services of Supply: A Memoir of the Great War (Boston, Houghton Mifflin Company, 1927). (3) Millett, "The Direction of Supply Activities in the War Department," American Political Science Review, XXXVIII (April 1944), 260–65.
[93] For a general discussion of theater supply organization, see Logistics in World War II, Ch. 7.
[94] For details, see Roland G. Ruppenthal, Logistical Support of the Armies, UNITED STATES ARMY IN WORLD WAR II (Washington, 1953), Ch. I; and Robert W. Coakley, Organization and Command in the European Theater of Operations, Vol. II, Pt. II of Administrative and Logistical History of the European Theater of Operations, MS, OCMH.

theater commander's own headquarters to be organized "along the general pattern of a command post." [95] It was bitterly attacked in the theater. The burden of the criticism was that the services, being theater-wide in function, could not be supervised by a headquarters that was merely co-ordinate with the major tactical commands reporting directly to the theater commander. Lee was forced to accept a compromise, which endured with only minor changes for the next year and a half. The SOS remained in control of supply services, but administrative services for the most part were assigned to theater headquarters. Lee's authority was so defined as not to interfere with "inherent command responsibilities of other force commanders." [96] Policy-making authority in general remained at the theater level. On the other hand, Maj. Gen. Dwight D. Eisenhower, the new theater commander, assigned the SOS broad responsibilities in supply planning and authorized direct communication with the War Department in supply and administrative matters. No serious effort was made by the War Department to restore the organization it had originally sponsored. The new one had the sanction of the theater commander, and few were inclined to challenge his right to work out his own administrative arrangements, particularly since these still conformed to the general pattern laid down by the War Department. [97]

Somervell's plan for a logistical organization in the European theater closely paralleling his own in the United States was thus defeated. Lee's own headquarters eventually assumed the traditional "G" structure, deviating markedly from the scheme of functional staff divisions that Somervell had adopted. But Somervell undoubtedly looked beyond mere organizational parallelism. From April to July 1942 there was every reason to expect that the European theater would soon overshadow all the other war zones, and that the British Isles, like France in 1918, would become the great entrepôt of American military power overseas—in effect an extension of the base of supply in the United States. In 1942, to be sure, the whole European theater, as far as the land war was concerned, was essentially a "services of the rear," engaged in the primarily logistical business of developing a base and assembling an invasion force. In these circumstances it was natural for the theater commander to maintain close control over his logistical organization, but as early as June 1942 officers in OPD foresaw that the theater commander, after the invasion began, might find himself relegated to the role of maintaining base areas and forwarding troops and supplies—to the role, in fact, of an SOS commander. [98] Evidently, if he were to direct the invasion, he would have to shift the burden of rear area administration to others. This would probably involve an organizational arrangement similar to the one Pershing had adopted in 1918. Perhaps it might lead eventually to the union proposed by Secretary Baker between the logistical agencies on both sides of the Atlantic.

[95] (1) Ltr, Marshall to CG USAFBI, 14 May 42, sub: Orgn of SOS, BOLERO 1942 folder, Lutes File. Several drafts of this letter are in same file; these and other papers indicate that the organization was drafted in Lutes' Plans Branch. (2) See also, min of SOS stf confs, 7 and 14 May 42, Contl Div ASF.

[96] Ltr cited n. 95(1).

[97] (1) See above, n. 95. (2) Ltr, Gen Lutes to Brig Gen Thomas B. Larkin, 24 Feb 42, BOLERO 1942 folder, Lutes File. (3) Corresp in OPD 320.2 Gt Brit, 52.

[98] Memo, Col John E. Hull for ACofS OPD, 6 Jun 42, sub: System of Comd for ROUNDUP, OPD 381 BOLERO, 12.

In the multitheater war that developed after mid-1942, such a solution was hardly practicable. But while rear area administration, in the European and other theaters, continued to be subject to theater control, that control was tempered in every theater by a large degree of decentralization leaning far toward regional autonomy. A theater's rear area organization was tied by the character of its functions to the central base of operations and line of communications behind it as well as to the combat zone in front. Efficient performance of those functions depended in large measure upon the smoothness, continuity, and directness of its administrative contacts with the logistical agencies farther to the rear.

Secession of the Air Forces

Long before March 1942 the movement of the Army Air Forces toward separate status had resulted in the development of a separate logistical establishment that duplicated at many points the facilities for supplying and servicing the ground forces. This duality was perpetuated by the War Department reorganization on the general principle that supplies and services peculiar to the Air Forces should be provided within the AAF establishment. After March 1942, indeed, the AAF steadily broadened its jurisdiction in such fields as storage, communications, and housekeeping and utilities functions at AAF installations.[99]

In overseas supply it was intended in the reorganization of March 1942 that the ports would serve as channels for supply of air as well as ground forces. Port commanders forwarded requests for "technical" (that is, peculiar) items of AAF supply, without action, to the Air Service Command at Wright and Patterson Fields, or to designated Air depots. The AAF determined how much and what kinds of material should be stocked at SOS depots for its troops, and AAF items were not stocked at the ports at all. Technical Air Forces supplies were stored at Air depots. Items of common use were supplied by the ports under uniform procedures for air and ground forces alike. AAF freight and troop movements through the ports were subject to port control, and air traffic to and from overseas theaters was co-ordinated by the Chief of Transportation until July 1942, when it was taken over by the AAF. AAF liaison officers were stationed at each port, and the Air Staff determined supply policies for its own forces overseas.[100]

These arrangements recognized supply of air and ground forces as distinct in many respects, but still capable of being handled under a single administrative system. The aspirations of the AAF to separate status were well understood in G-4 and the SOS, and a determined effort was made to accommodate the overseas supply system to its needs. But it became evident in pre-reorganization conferences that the ground and air commands had diametrically opposite notions as to the kind of services desired from the SOS. The former intended to utilize these to the utmost, while the Air Staff was determined to develop a supply system paralleling that of the ground forces.[101] Almost immediately, Air

---

[99] See Millett, *ASF*, Chs. I–II, IX, XI.

[100] (1) WD ltrs, 22 Jan and 28 Apr 42, sub: Sup of Overseas Depts, Theaters, and Separate Bases, AG 400 (1-17-42). (2) *Report of the Chief of Transportation, ASF, World War II*, p. 18. (3) Min, WD Gen Council mtg, 30 Jun 42.

[101] (1) Memo cited n. 54. (2) 1st Ind, Hq SOS to Hq AAF, 25 Jul 42, in Notes, Air Force Sup, Logis File, OCMH.

commanders overseas began to send requisitions for technical items directly to Wright Field, and late in June the AAF proposed that this practice be legalized. SOS representatives objected, urging the advantages of funneling all supply requests through the ports. They pointed out that the AAF enjoyed virtually complete control over the supply of its forces and argued that "as long as they are part of the Army and the Army transports their supplies, . . . the focal point for requests and water shipment must be the port commander." [102] But with the Air Forces evidently bent on developing a separate supply system, these arguments availed little. An SOS officer remarked, "I don't believe there is anything we can do about it." [103]

The desired changes were incorporated, accordingly, in the October revision of the overseas supply plan. Commanders overseas were directed to send straight to Wright Field at Dayton their requisitions not only for technical supplies but also for all regularly issued equipment procured by the AAF. Later amendments broadened the exempted categories still further. Reports on status of AAF supply overseas similarly were routed directly to the Air Service Command. [104] The autonomy thus gained was steadily extended in late 1942 and 1943. Air commanders overseas, General Lutes observed in March 1943, "have become accustomed to requisition on Dayton for everything," including clothing and other items of common use. [105] The SOS also found it increasingly difficult to co-ordinate the movement of AAF troops overseas with that of ground units. Lutes wrote Somervell in March 1943:

We are not permitted to check Air Force units under orders for overseas. We call on the Air Forces for lists of shortages in order to assist them in equipping their troops, but we

have great difficulty in obtaining such lists within the time limits. It has been the usual custom for Air Force units to arrive at staging areas with considerable shortages in individual equipment. Time frequently does not permit us to complete their equipment. [106]

Ground troops moving overseas received showdown inspections at their home stations, with SOS field agents initiating immediate action to fill shortages. "We have offered this service to the Air Forces," Lutes stated, "but have been turned down." [107] On occasion, AAF supplies were even moved into port without notification to the port commander, in violation of a cardinal principle of traffic control established immediately after Pearl Harbor. [108]

From time to time the SOS made proposals for merging the two systems at various points in order to check the growing duplication of facilities. In November 1942, for example, the Chief of Transportation suggested that the AAF use his system of intransit depots behind the ports; requisitions for Air Forces supplies would be edited at the ports and AAF supply records maintained there by a special staff of Air officers; the AAF was offered "necessary safeguards to insure that the Commanding General, AAF is at all times in

---

[102] 1st Ind cited n. 101(2).
[103] (1) Pencil note on 1st Ind cited n. 101. (2) For the background of Air Corps aspirations, see Watson, *Prewar Plans and Preparations*, Ch. IX, and Craven and Cate, *AAF I*, pp. 152–55.
[104] WD Memo W700-8-42, 10 Oct 42, sub: Sup of Overseas Depts, Theaters, and Separate Bases, and Change 1, 12 May 43.
[105] Memo, Lutes for Somervell, 4 Mar 43, Misc Notes, Lutes File.
[106] *Ibid.*
[107] Memo, Lutes for DCofS, 9 Mar 43, Misc Notes, Lutes File.
[108] (1) Memo, Lutes for ACofS Opns AAF, 31 Dec 42, Misc Notes, Lutes File. (2) See also ltr. Gross to WSA, 17 Oct 42, WSA folder, OCT HB.

control of the movement of these supplies . . . ." [109] In a similar vein General Lutes wrote to AAF headquarters:

We have a very simple overseas supply system which to date has operated with reasonable success—not perfectly, but in step with the shipping facilities available. If you could see your way clear to have your requirements for overseas shipments which are not to be forwarded by air screened through the Overseas Supply Divisions of our ports, it would greatly simplify coordination, and I believe would be of better assistance to you in the long run. [110]

But these and similar proposals faced into the prevailing winds, which were carrying Army organization toward separation, not unification, of air and ground logistics. [111]

The organizational upheaval that followed the entrance of the United States into the war had three main features: centralization of co-ordinating responsibilities at the pinnacle and upper levels of the structure, decentralization of supervisory and operating functions, and consolidation of these functions at intermediate rather than lower levels. The same pattern has often been followed by complex modern societies under the impact of war. In the system of logistical management that emerged after Pearl Harbor, the largest, most powerful concentration of authority at the intermediate level was General Somervell's Services of Supply, a large new constellation in the organizational firmament. Into it were gathered in March 1942 almost all the War Department's executive functions in the logistical sphere, and, in addition, a miscellaneous assortment of administrative functions that have only rarely borne the label "logistical." The union of all these disparate activities under one command was not altogether happy, and centrifugal forces soon came into

play; before the end of 1942 the flight of jurisdiction to the Army Air Forces, a more homogeneous organizational entity, was well under way. Within the SOS, internal stresses appeared, such as the conflicts of purpose and method between the representatives of supply and transportation. But, despite its heterogeneous composition, General Somervell's command was from the first an aggressive and expansive organization. It clashed with the War Shipping Administration in the effort to gain more control over merchant shipping, and waged bitter jurisdictional disputes—outside the province of this study—with the War Production Board and other civilian agencies. The SOS also had a natural tendency to attempt to project the interests and functions that it represented into the upper levels of planning and co-ordination, demanding for them a form of organizational representation at those levels that would ensure their consideration as a distinct and independent factor in strategy and policy. Hence the sharp conflicts between Somervell's planning staff and OPD, and the virtual elimination (which proved temporary) of G–4 as a potent influence in logistical planning. Toward the end of 1942 the pressure of the logistical "interest" in the upper realms of planning was to pose a challenge to the organization of the Joint and Combined Committee systems and to the concept of the subordinate role of logistics in strategic planning upon which that organization was based. [112]

---

[109] Paper, 20 Nov 42, sub: Proced for Shipt of Air Force Sups Overseas, POE Gen Overseas Sup folder, OCT HB.

[110] Memo cited n. 108(1).

[111] For efforts to unify naval and ground logistics, see below, Ch. XXIV.

[112] See below, Ch. XXIV.

CHAPTER X

Lend-Lease as an Instrument of Coalition Warfare

Momentarily, the reaction to Pearl Harbor left the future of lend-lease in doubt. In an emergency action to assure that its own needs would be met, the Army on the night of 7 December 1941 stopped the movement of all supplies to foreign governments. Axis propagandists trumpeted the claim that American entrance into the war meant the end of American supply aid, and even the British showed alarm at the course events were taking. But the doubt was soon dispelled by an announcement by the President that U.S. entry into the war would mean an increase, not a stoppage or decrease, in lend-lease supplies. The Army continued during December to give first priority to its own needs, but the existing schedules of lend-lease releases were reviewed and many shipments resumed. By the end of the year it was clearly established that lend-lease would continue; what remained to be determined was the extent to which the supply of Allied nations would be affected by that of the U.S. Army, now that the latter was engaged in active hostilities.[1]

Lend-lease in 1941 had been an instrument of economic warfare, based on the theory that the United States could, solely by furnishing supplies, enable other powers to defeat the Axis. Pearl Harbor put an end to this illusion. There was no longer any question about the need for large American armed forces to defeat the Axis, but the United States also remained the principal reservoir of industrial production for the entire coalition to which it now belonged, and the need for American munitions by the other Allied armed forces continued as acute as before. Lend-lease had now to be transformed into an instrument of coalition warfare, and some means had to be found for allocating the growing output of American munitions to the forces, including our own, that could use them most effectively to win the war, regardless of nationality.

The Munitions Assignments Board and the Common Pool

During 1941 the prevailing military thought had been that American resources should be allocated entirely by Ameri-

---

[1] (1) Memo, Col V. V. Taylor for CofEngrs, 8 Dec 41, sub: Suspension of Def Aid Shipts, Misc Corresp Lend-lease 4 file, DAD. (2) Telephone Convs Col Taylor file, Bk. 1, DAD. (3) Memo, Col Aurand for Gen Moore, 18 Dec 41, sub: Review of Trf Schedules, Col Boone's file, Item 79, DAD. (4) Memo, Stettinius for Hopkins, 8 Dec 41, MS Index to the Hopkins Papers, Bk. VII, Lend-lease in Opn (1941), p. 4, Item 48. (5) Ltr, Stettinius to Hopkins, 9 Dec 41, MS Index to the Hopkins Papers, Bk. V, FDR and HLH Actions Post-Dec 7, p. 2, Item 6. (6) Cable, Harriman to Hopkins, 11 Dec 41, MS Index to the Hopkins Papers, Bk. V, FDR and HLH Actions Post-Dec 7, p. 2, Item 7. (7) Memo, DAD for Chiefs of SAS, 3 Jan 42, Misc Corresp Lend-lease 1 file, DAD.

cans.[2] After the rejection of the Marshall-Stark proposal of August 1941 to place allocation of military materials under the Joint Board, the question of a suitable organization remained in abeyance until November when Harry Hopkins proposed formation of a Strategic Munitions Board to be composed of himself, the Chief of Staff, and the Chief of Naval Operations. The President acted on this suggestion immediately after Pearl Harbor, assigning to the new board the functions of establishing programs for the allocation of munitions to the United States and defense aid countries and of preparing a production program "to achieve sure and final victory."[3] The composition of the board was to be entirely American, conforming to the prevailing conception. It was also to be directly responsible to the President, indicating continuance of Roosevelt's close personal supervision over distribution of munitions.

The Strategic Munitions Board never became more than a paper organization. It never held a formal meeting, and, so far as is known, played no part either in the preparation of munitions allocation programs or in that of the Victory Program. General Marshall delegated his functions as a member to his deputy for supply, General Moore. General Moore, acting either in his capacity as a member of the board or as a representative of the Chief of Staff, and with the advice of G-4 and WPD, made item-by-item decisions on release schedules prepared by the Defense Aid Director, Colonel Aurand—continuing the practice in effect since October 1941.[4]

The Strategic Munitions Board had been conceived while the United States was still at peace and was not suited to the needs of a coalition war to be fought in close collaboration with Great Britain. Discussions at the ARCADIA Conference indicated that this collaboration would include supply as well as strategic planning, and, in view of Britain's dependence on American production, continuance of munitions allocations on a unilateral basis was soon ruled out. This was undoubtedly the most important reason why the Strategic Munitions Board never functioned.

The partnership with the British was already well advanced. There had been staff conversations and an exchange of staff missions before the United States entered the war. On the supply side the British participated in the work of the Defense Aid Supply Committee and the Joint Aircraft Committee, the bodies charged with determination of the ground and air force lend-lease programs, respectively. A combined Victory Program was on the planning boards, and the Consolidated Balance Sheet provided for mutual exchange of production information. On the supposition that America would meet a considerable proportion of British military supply requirements, Britain had gone ahead to place a far higher proportion of its available manpower in the armed services than would otherwise have been possible. American strategy, as far as it had been developed, was predicated on the existence of these British forces to be armed with American matériel. In daily contacts and mutual experience in dealing through

---

[2] See above, Ch. III.

[3] (1) Memo, President for SW, 8 Dec 41, Auth File of President's Ltrs, DAD. (2) Memo, Gen Burns for Hopkins, 24 Nov 41, MS Index to the Hopkins Papers, Bk. V, Orgn of WSA, p. 1, Item 2. (3) On the Strategic Shipping Board created at the same time, see above, Ch. IX.

[4] (1) Memo, Aurand for CofS, 13 Jan 42, sub: Def Aid Trfs and Trf Schedules, Misc Stf Studies, Lend-lease 2A file, DAD. (2) 1st Ind, Aurand to ACofS G-4, 19 Dec 41, G-4/32697.

a committee system, a practical partnership was already being welded. It remained for the ARCADIA Conference to formalize this partnership with permanent arrangements for the combined direction of a combined war effort.

The British were in a far better position to take the lead in the development of combined machinery, since their own national organizations for direction of the war effort had already crystallized during two years of war, while the Americans were only beginning to fashion theirs. The British came to ARCADIA with a plan already drawn up for a system of combined organizations—a combined strategic planning organization for all the services (the CCS committee system); a combined supply board to deal with production, the allocation of raw materials, and so forth; a combined committee to deal with the allocation of military matériel; a combined shipping committee; and other combined bodies as the situation might dictate.[5] The Americans, with no definite plan of their own, perforce accepted British leadership. But while they recognized the soundness of the British proposals, they feared that the British, with superior experience and more mature institutions of war direction, might gain an undue predominance in combined bodies. Consequently, they received the British plan with a certain wariness.

This wariness was evident in the American approach to the problem of allocating munitions. The first discussions of allocations took place between members of the British and American staffs particularly concerned with supply. Very early in the conference a combined military supply committee was informally set up, first designated as the Joint Planning Committee, later as the Joint Supply Committee. The

committee soon assumed many of the functions of the Strategic Munitions Board. While it had no specific powers to take action, it provided a forum for discussion and for agreements that could be carried out by the respective British and American members acting within the framework of their own national organizations.[6] Since its own existence was limited to the period of the ARCADIA Conference, it was almost inevitable that the committee should give some attention to the question of a permanent combined organization to carry on its work. The immediate issue that brought the problem to the committee's attention was the submission of parallel demands by the Dutch East Indies to London and Washington. At the meeting of 7 January, Lt. Gen. George N. Macready of the British Joint Staff Mission reported that "pursuant to a high level decision," all allocations to the Netherlands Government would be determined in London. This, he said, would be part of a larger scheme for the division of the United Nations into protégés of either the United States or Great Britain. The British group would include all European refugee governments, all parts of the British Empire, Egypt, and Turkey; the American group, the Latin American nations, China, and Iceland. Allocations in Washington to the United Kingdom would include, in addition to her own needs, requirements of the nations for which she

---

[5] (1) Hancock and Gowing, *British War Economy*, pp. 389–93. (2) On the organizational development on the American side, see above, Ch. IX.

[6] Min, Jt Plng Com mtg, 24 Dec 41, and Jt Sup Com mtgs, 2, 7, and 12 Jan 42, ID, Lend-Lease, Doc Suppl, II. Regular attendants for the U.S. were General Moore, Colonel Aurand, and Capt. Paul Hendren, USN; for the British, Lt. Gen. George N. Macready and Brigadier Donald Campion. This committee functioned only for the duration of the ARCADIA Conference.

assumed supply responsibility. Soviet allocations would continue to be based on the joint protocol.

This proposal of the British took the Americans by surprise, for they had heard of no such high-level decision. In reality there had been none. After a long discussion in which the Americans indicated only a general agreement on the principle of combined allocations, the matter was tabled, but after the meeting General Macready drew up a memorandum stating his conception of bulk allocations.[7] The basic principle Macready put forward was that equipment must be allocated according to the military situation and not "according to the origin of the order which produces it." A careful reading of his memorandum revealed, however, that he proposed a combined allocation committee in Washington to make bulk allocations to the British and their protégés out of American production, but a War Office, purely British, allocation committee in London to divide up these bulk allocations, as well as British production, among the Empire countries and the British protégés.

Macready's memorandum received a thorough review by War Department and lend-lease officials. Nearly everyone agreed that equipment must be allocated in accordance with military need, but all showed some suspicion of the British protégé arrangement, and the War Department spokesmen in particular thought that the pooling arrangement must extend to British stocks as well as American. In his formal reply to Macready General Moore followed this line, expressing agreement on the proposition that there should be combined committees to make allocations on strategic principles but insisting that there must be U.S. representation on the London committee as well as British representation on the one in Washington. Nevertheless, Moore raised no explicit objection to the division of the world into protégé nations, and though this acceptance of the British theory carried no official weight, the British later acted on the supposition that it did.[8]

A final decision could only be made at a higher level, in the conferences of the British and American Chiefs of Staff with the Prime Minister and the President. Toward the very end of the ARCADIA Conference, in the meeting on 13 January 1942, the British Chiefs proposed their scheme for continuing collaboration. On the supply side, they suggested that the newly formed CCS should "settle the broad programme of requirements based on strategic policy," and "from time to time issue general directives laying down policy to govern the distribution of available weapons of war." To give effect to these directives, combined allocation committees should be formed to make allocations between the United States and the British Commonwealth, "each caring for the needs of Allies for whom it has accepted responsibility."[9] The U.S. Chiefs were cautious in committing themselves, insisting that they were not yet prepared to enter into details, but they accepted the general principle of CCS authority over broad requirements programs and policy

---

[7] Memo, Gen Macready for Brig L. C. Hollis, 7 Jan 42, sub: Alloc of Finished Mil Equip to Allies, English Corresp Lend-lease 1 file, DAD.

[8] (1) For a digest of various views, see MS Index to the Hopkins Papers, Bk. V, Estab of Jt Bds Dec–Feb 42, pp. 3–7, Item 13. (2) Ltr, Moore to Macready, 12 Jan 42, English Corresp Lend-lease 1 file, DAD. Moore's letter was evidently drafted by Colonel Aurand.

[9] Annex 1, memo, Br CsofS, 8 Jan 42, title: Post-ARCADIA Collaboration, to min, ABC-4 JCCSs-11, 13 Jan 42.

for strategic allocation, and a minute was drafted for submission to the President and Prime Minister, reading:

We, the combined US-British Chiefs of Staff are agreed in principle that finished war equipment shall be allocated in accordance with strategic needs. We accordingly submit that an appropriate body should be set up under the authority of the CCS, in Washington, and a corresponding body in London, for the purpose of giving effect to this principle.[10]

In the meeting of the military chiefs it was clearly recognized that the allocation agencies, of whatever composition, should be responsible to and under the authority of the CCS. Meanwhile Lord Beaverbrook, head of the British Ministry of Supply, had been urging a different scheme, presumably with the support of Churchill. The British Ministry of Supply was generally responsible for all procurement in England and for allocation of raw materials and facilities. The British military did not enter into the picture. Lord Beaverbrook proposed that an American counterpart of the British ministry be set up under Harry Hopkins, directly responsible to the President. A combined agency representing the two, with Hopkins as chairman, would then constitute a high command for supply independent of and on a level with the CCS. Such an agency would include within its purview long-range plans for allocation of military equipment.[11]

Though President Roosevelt evidently was not ready to accept Beaverbrook's scheme *in toto*, his ideas about organization for allocation of munitions were clearly influenced by it. On the evening of 14 January 1942 the matter came up for final decision in the last formal session of ARCADIA at the White House. Before the

arrival of the rest of the conferees, General Marshall had a brief meeting with the President and Hopkins. Roosevelt read Marshall a proposal for a munitions assignments board that would be responsible directly to the President and the Prime Minister and would have broad powers. The board was to be divided into two parts, one in Washington with Hopkins as chairman, the other in London with Beaverbrook as chairman. This confirmed Marshall's worst fears, and when asked for an opinion he informed the President that unless the proposed munitions assignments board were made responsible to the CCS "he could not continue to assume the responsibilities of Chief of Staff."[12] No military organization, he thought, could assume responsibility for operations if supplies essential to their conduct were not placed under its control. The issue of civilian versus military control of munitions allocations, the overtones of which had been heard all through 1941, thus came to a sudden and dramatic crisis. The President turned to ask Hopkins his opinion, and Hopkins, evidently much to the surprise of both the President and his Chief of Staff, gave his wholehearted support to Marshall. Hopkins' attitude evidently decided the President, for when the rest of the British and American representatives arrived he presented the matter to them much as Marshall had outlined it. It was evidently a disappointment to Churchill and Beaverbrook, who raised numerous objections. Hopkins pointed out to them that the way was open for an appeal to the President and Prime Minister if political matters were involved, and Churchill finally agreed to try the system "for a

[10] Min, ABC-4 JCCSs-11, 13 Jan 42.
[11] Sherwood, *Roosevelt and Hopkins*, p. 470.
[12] *Ibid.*, p. 471–72; quote is from p. 472.

month." The President closed the discussion by saying, "We will call it a preliminary agreement and try it out that way." [13] So the issue was decided, and the preliminary agreement never came up for reconsideration. The Munitions Assignments Boards, Washington and London, responsible to the CCS in Washington, became the agencies that were to control allocation of finished munitions throughout the war. A joint public announcement of their formation was made by the President and Prime Minister on 26 January 1942, prefaced by a statement of the theory behind their operations: "The entire munitions resources of the United States and Great Britain will be deemed to be in a common pool, about which the fullest information will be interchanged." [14]

The establishment of the Munitions Assignments Boards was a logical corollary, on the supply side, of the principle of combined strategic direction of the war effort by the CCS. Some machinery was necessary to assure a continuing relationship between allocation of supplies and agreed strategy, and the assignments boards were to serve that purpose admirably. What the abstract principle of the common pool of munitions would mean in practice remained yet to be determined. Since the United States would ultimately put far more into the pool than Britain, it was inevitable that the British should become the proponents of the pooling theory and that the Americans should view it with misgivings. The actual principles under which allocations would be made had necessarily to be worked out after manifold differences in the British and American approaches were resolved. For this reason the decision to limit the scope of the Munitions Assignments Boards

solely to military materials proved a wise one. Within these limits Anglo-American co-operation was to prove possible, but it turned out to be not so feasible when extended to the broader area of over-all production planning, along the lines that Beaverbrook had evidently intended.

As to the relationship of other nations to the London and Washington boards, the Roosevelt-Churchill announcement said: "Members of the Board will confer with representatives of the USSR, China and such others of the United Nations as are necessary to attain common purposes and provide for the most effective utilization of the joint resources of the United Nations." [15] In truth the boards were, like the CCS, instruments of Anglo-American policy, and the other United Nations were left on the periphery. Of the various Allies, only China ever raised the issue of membership on the Washington board, and it was refused on the basis that only nations with a disposable surplus should be represented. [16] Undoubtedly this was only a half truth. The real reason was that neither the British nor the Americans wanted to create an unwieldy body where conflicts of many varying interests would make action impossible. Of all the other United Nations only the USSR really had the great-power status that entitled her to consideration, and by virtue of the protocol, which made allocations to her subject to arrange-

---

[13] (1) *Ibid.*, p. 472. (2) Notes on informal confs held during visit of Br CsofS in Washington, conf at White House, 14 Jan 42, WDCSA 334.

[14] Jt Declaration, President and Churchill, 26 Jan 42, ID, Lend-Lease, Doc Suppl, II.

[15] *Ibid.*

[16] (1) OPD Diary, 24 Apr 42 entry, OPD Hist Unit File. (2) Memo, Aurand for McCloy, 27 Apr 42, sub: Mtg of 28 Apr *re* China Proced, China Lend-lease 2 file, DAD.

ments transcending the powers of the boards, the USSR occupied a unique position. The Russians preferred to keep their relations on this plane.

As for the other nations, the British clung to their scheme of bulk allocations and protégés. The United States never formally accepted this procedure. Hopkins informed General Burns shortly after the formation of the Washington board: "I think it should be clearly understood that the memorandum prepared by Mac-Cready . . . and gone over by General Moore does not necessarily have to be our bible." [17] Yet during the first year of the Washington board's operations, it followed this system in practice to a considerable degree, for it conformed generally to the manner in which allocations had been handled during 1941 and to the division of strategic responsibility between the two countries as agreed afterward.

Organization of the MAB and Its Committees

The announcement by the President and Prime Minister laid down only the very broad outlines for the munitions assignments machinery. The details were left to the CCS and the two governments concerned. The CCS issued a charter for the Munitions Assignments Board in Washington (MAB) on 4 February 1942, assigning it functions as follows:

2. Working in close collaboration with the corresponding London organization the Board will maintain full information of the entire munitions resources of Great Britain and the United States and translate such resources into terms of combat forces and their material reserves. It will . . . keep the estimate up-to-date in the light of war developments and also of variations in production achievements and prospects . . . in order that the CCS may be fully informed and rec-

ommend the measures necessary to keep planned requirements programs in line with:
    a. strategic policy;
    b. changing operational conditions in their effect on war material; and
    c. the realities of production.
3. Under such strategic policies, directives and priorities as have been approved, and in accordance with agreements with the corresponding London organization, the Board will be responsible for making assignments of the stocks and production of finished war material to the United States and Great Britain and to others of the United Nations. [18]

The membership of the MAB, with Harry Hopkins as chairman, consisted of representatives of the U.S. Ground Forces, Air Forces, and Navy, with their British opposite numbers. The U.S. representatives at first were General Moore, Admiral William H. Standley, and General Harmon; the British, Lt. Gen. H. C. B. Wemyss, Admiral Sir Charles J. C. Little, and Air Marshal Douglas C. S. Evill. [19] A permanent staff and a secretariat were formed on a combined basis with General Burns as executive officer. The staff was at first divided into four parts, Army, Navy, Air, and Statistical, but other sections were added later as necessary for efficient operations. This staff, under the direction of General Burns, was responsible for preparation for meetings, examination of proposed assignments, execution of the decisions of the board, liaison with appropriate civilian agencies, and maintenance of nec-

---

[17] Memo, Hopkins for Burns, 12 Feb 42, MS Index to the Hopkins Papers, Bk. V, Estab of Jt Bds Dec–Feb 42, p. 11, Item 18 (b).

[18] CCS 19/1, 4 Feb 42, title: Order Estab MAB.
    Hereafter MAB will refer only to the Munitions Assignments Board in Washington. The London Munitions Assignments Board will be abbreviated LMAB.

[19] CCS 19/1 cited n. 18. Admiral Joseph M. Reeves replaced Admiral Standley as the U.S. naval member on 11 February 1942.

essary statistics on combined requirements and resources.[20]

In order to utilize the detailed information at the command of the individual services, the board directed the formation of three committees, a Munitions Assignments Committee (Navy) for naval materials, a Munitions Assignments Committee (Air) for air materials, and a Munitions Assignments Committee (Ground) for ground materials (MAC(N), MAC(A), and MAC(G)). The board stipulated that these three main committees should have British membership, but left their detailed composition to the service departments concerned. Accordingly, the War Department organized the Air and Ground Committees. As originally organized, Brig. Gen. Henry S. Aurand, Defense Aid Director, was chairman of the MAC(G), with membership from WPD and the British Army Staff; General Harmon, Chief of the Air Staff, was chairman of the MAC(A), with membership from the AAF and RAF.[21] In practice the three committees did all the detailed work of preparing assignment schedules, working frequently through subcommittees of their own. The MAB acted largely as a court of appeals when agreements could not be reached in the committees, and as a policy-determining body, subject always to further appeal to the CCS in case of dissent. Nevertheless, all assignments had to be formally approved by the board before they became effective.

The London Munitions Assignments Board (LMAB) was organized in the same general manner.[22] Its allocations included, in addition to British production, material assigned to the British by the Washington board and critical items of Empire production. In contrast to the policy in Washington where the MAB assigned all mili-

tary items right down to single rifles for test purposes, the British classified equipment as assignable and nonassignable, subjecting only critical items to the assignments procedure. Items not in short supply were merely allocated by War Office agencies. The committees of the London board were also allowed to make final assignments where there was no dissent, and the LMAB met only on occasions where a dissent required its decision rather than regularly as did the board in Washington. Since American bids against British production were never of large proportions, the combined aspects of the LMAB's operations were never so important as those of the Washington board. It concerned itself primarily with allocations to the nations of the British Empire, those assumed to be within the British sphere of responsibility, various agencies of the British Government, and theaters of operations in British areas of responsibility—all matters that, during 1942, the Americans were satisfied to leave under British control. The LMAB also acted as the parent board for certain Empire assignments committees set up in Australia and India during the progress of the war.[23]

A special word needs to be added about Canada. It was tentatively agreed that

[20] Tab D, Orgn of Stf of MAB, to memo, Aurand for CofS, 11 Feb 42, sub: Dir for MAB, ID 020, ID Orgn and Functions.
[21] (1) Ltr, Hopkins to SW, 9 Feb 42. (2) Ltr, SW to Hopkins, 19 Feb 42. Both in Orgn MAB file, DAD. Brig. Gen. R. W. Crawford of WPD and Brig. Donald Campion of the British Army Staff were the original members of MAC(G).
[22] The charter of LMAB is War Cabinet Paper LMAB (42) 1, 25 Mar 42, sub: LMAB, ID, Lend-Lease, Doc Suppl, II.
Col. Erle M. Wilson was the first U.S. executive of the LMAB but was succeeded later by Maj. Gen. James K. Crain.
[23] See ID, Lend-Lease, I, 166–76.

Canadian production should fall under the jurisdiction of the Washington board. But in practice only the part of it that had been contracted for by the U.S. Government through the agency of War Supplies Limited, a subsidiary corporation of the Canadian Department of Munitions and Supply, was ever so assigned. The Canadians soon established a Munitions Assignments Committee of their own in Ottawa, with representation from both the United Kingdom and the United States. The Canadian committee was more useful as a link between the civilian Department of Munitions and Supply and the Canadian armed forces than as an agency for making allocations on a strategic basis. An American observer noted in October 1942 that needs of the Canadian armed forces got top priority and that for the rest the committee made assignments in keeping with contractual obligations rather than strategic considerations. The Canadian committee was not, except perhaps in theory, under the authority of either of the other boards or of the CCS.[24] *(Chart 5)*

Other Combined Boards: A Summary View

The machinery for munitions assignments was but one part of the combined Anglo-American organization for supply collaboration. The President and Prime Minister on 26 January 1942 also announced the formation of a Combined Raw Materials Board and a Combined Shipping Adjustment Board (CSAB). The raw materials board was to make plans for development, expansion, and use of raw materials of the two nations, and to make recommendations to the various agencies of the British and American Governments for execution of such plans. The shipping board would "adjust and concert in one harmonious policy the work of the British Ministry of War Transport and the shipping authorities of the United States Government."[25] In principle, American and British shipping would be pooled, but in practice the pool would be divided into two parts in keeping with the geographical situation, one part to be administered in London, the other in Washington, each under the control of the national authorities concerned. The CSAB would recommend the interchanges necessary for the most effective utilization of shipping from both pools.[26]

The British had envisaged a combined organization for production planning as the real hub of the whole system of combined boards, but no such organization was set up at ARCADIA, evidently because the Americans had not yet developed their own national organization. But since this gap in the combined machinery was recognized on both sides, the President and Prime Minister on 9 June 1942 announced the establishment of a Combined Production and Resources Board (CPRB) composed of Donald Nelson, chairman of WPB, and Sir Oliver Lyttelton, British Minister of Production. The CPRB was assigned the broad function of combining the production programs of the United States and United Kingdom into a single integrated program, adjusted to strategic requirements of the war as indicated by the CCS and to all relevant production factors. On the same day a Combined Food Board was added to "obtain a

[24] (1) *Ibid.*, I, 185–92. (2) Memo, Maj William S. Gaud for Actg Dir ID, 18 Oct 42, sub: Asgmt of Canadian Pdn Allocated in Ottawa to War Sups Limited, ID, Lend-Lease, Doc Suppl, III.
[25] Jt Declaration cited n. 14.
[26] *Ibid.*

CHART 5—COMBINED ASSIGNMENTS MACHINERY: 1942

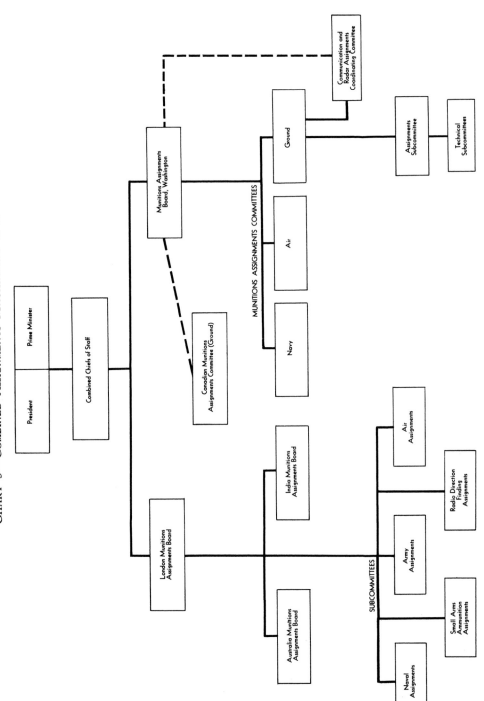

planned and expeditious utilization of the food resources of the United Nations." [27]

These two boards completed the setup of combined agencies, and with their addition the structure came to resemble closely the blueprint the British had brought to Washington in December 1941. Boards for raw materials, resources and production, food, munitions assignments, and shipping covered virtually the entire war effort. Nevertheless, the civilian combined boards were never to play the role in directing the war effort that the British had hoped they would. The Americans, with far greater resources at their disposal, proved reluctant to place too many powers in their hands. The British, for their part, too frequently looked on the boards as mechanisms for increasing the flow of American aid. Only the Munitions Assignments Boards, responsible to the CCS, had express powers to make allocations of the materials under their jurisdiction. The other combined boards had no express powers of their own; they were responsible to the President and Prime Minister directly, and could only make recommendations to be acted on by the agencies of the governments concerned. Their powers derived in the end largely from the fact that membership of each board normally consisted of only two persons, the heads of the respective British and American agencies concerned, or their deputies. The boards thus served mainly to give a formal institutional status to the consultation and collaboration between British and American officials on the economic front that was continuous throughout the war. The Combined Raw Materials Board was the only one that had any measure of success in fulfilling the functions assigned it as a board. The others, after an ambitious start in 1942, gradually declined in

power and prestige. Yet, despite their failure as genuine international bodies, they gave at least a semblance of reality to the common pool as applied to the total resources of the United States and the British Commonwealth of Nations. [28]

The Principle of Reciprocal Aid

As far as the common pool was a reality, lend-lease served as the mechanism whereby allied nations could draw on American resources without money payments; its obverse, reverse lend-lease or reciprocal aid, served as an equally convenient instrument by which the United States could draw on the resources of Great Britain and other allies. While supplies and services received by the United States under reciprocal aid were never comparable in volume to lend-lease aid given, they frequently involved greater sacrifices from nations far less rich. They were of vital importance in effecting economies in shipping for the support of American forces overseas.

The provision in the Lend-Lease Act that benefits to accrue to the United States might be "payment or repayment in kind or property, or any other direct or indirect benefit the President deems satisfactory,"

---

[27] *Report to the 78th Congress on Lend-Lease Operations From the Passage of the Act, March 11, 1941, to December 31, 1942,* submitted by Edward R. Stettinius, App. VIII.

[28] (1) For an analysis of the work of the civilian combined boards from the American point of view, see S. McKee Rosen, *The Combined Boards of World War II* (New York, Columbia University Press, 1951). (2) For a British view of the boards, see H. Duncan Hall and C. C. Wrigley, Studies of Overseas Supply, a volume in preparation for the British series HISTORY OF THE SECOND WORLD WAR, first draft, Chs. V–VI. This draft is located in the Historical Branch, Cabinet Office, London.

furnished the legal basis for reciprocal aid.[29] The President authorized receipt of supplies under this clause in May 1941, but application before Pearl Harbor was limited. The British furnished special equipment for defense of the Panama Canal, and installations and supplies were taken over from them when American forces occupied bases in Iceland and the Caribbean. The principle also served as a convenient means by which components produced on British contracts in the United States could be used interchangeably with American components in production of tanks, planes, and other munitions.[30]

After Pearl Harbor, as American troops moved overseas to Australia, New Zealand, the Pacific islands, and England, reciprocal aid soon became a matter of much greater importance. In England it was at first largely a matter of taking over British installations and using British transportation and other services. Meanwhile, in Australia and New Zealand, a much broader application of reciprocal aid was taking shape with American troops drawing on local resources for most of their food and much of their clothing and other expendable supplies. This Australian pattern was soon extended to the British Isles as the number of American troops there was increased. As early as 31 January 1942, the War Department issued instructions to overseas commanders to receive "supplies, equipment or facilities" under reverse lend-lease,[31] but this directive was limited in scope and framed to apply largely to the taking over of facilities in England that were evacuated by British troops. Basing its action on the developing pattern in the Pacific, the War Department issued more positive instructions in June and July 1942, authorizing

theater commanders to make arrangements under reciprocal aid for "any services, facilities, supplies or equipment" that in their discretion could reasonably be made available by the local government concerned.[32]

To systematize these overseas procurement activities, the War Department authorized the establishment of a General Purchasing Board in Australia in February 1942, and one in England in May.[33] These organizations, particularly the Australian, became the models for those to be organized in other theaters. As far as possible, local procurement in overseas areas was centralized in the hands of the general purchasing organizations and conducted by agencies of the government concerned. Reciprocal aid became largely a theater matter, the War Department's role being confined to general co-ordination, over-all record keeping, and establishment of general policies and procedures. But since overseas procurement had to be fitted into general requirements planning, procedures were established in late 1942 for quarterly forecasts from each

---

[29] Sec 3b.

[30] (1) International Division, ASF, History of Reciprocal Aid, 9 May 1941–31 December 1945, MS, p. 4, OCMH. (2) Ltr, President to SW, 9 May 41, ID, History of Reciprocal Aid, Doc Suppl, OCMH. (3) Ltr, C. E. I. Jones, Br Purch Comm, to Capt C. H. Dyson, DAD, 14 Nov 41, English Corresp Lend-lease 2 file, DAD. (4) Related papers in same file and in English Corresp Lend-lease 4 file, DAD.

[31] TAG ltr to all comds, 31 Jan 42, sub: Trf of Property From Foreign Govts to U.S. Army Forces in Overseas Theaters and Separate Bases, AG 400.3295 (1-21-42).

[32] (1) TAG ltr to maj comds and mil mis's, 22 Jun 42, sub: Trf of Property From Foreign Govts to U.S. Army Forces in Overseas Theaters and Separate Bases, AG 400.3295 (1-21-42). (2) Backing papers in same file and in G-4/33940 and G-4/32697-21. (3) Msg, AGWAR to all overseas comds, 14 Jul 42, Reciprocal Aid Dirs file, ID. (4) See below, Ch. XVIII.

[33] See above, Ch. VII.

theater of prospective reciprocal aid trans-fers.[34]

While reciprocal aid was at first based largely on informal arrangements, these were soon ratified by formal diplomatic agreements. The Master Lend-Lease Agreements signed with each of the lend-lease beneficiaries contained the pledge that each would "contribute to the defense of the United States . . . and . . . pro-vide such articles, services, facilities or information as it may be in a position to supply."[35] More specific reciprocal aid agreements were signed with the United Kingdom (to include her colonial empire), Australia, New Zealand, and the Free French on 3 September 1942.[36] While the United States could never complain about the implementation of these reciprocal aid agreements in the United Kingdom itself, or in Australia and New Zealand, there were difficulties in various parts of the British colonial empire where officials did not understand them as well. There were also difficulties about valuation since the United States insisted on a strict account-ing and the British maintained it would require too much time and manpower. These, however, were matters of detail. In general, by September 1942 when the final agreements were signed, reciprocal aid had already become the corollary of lend-lease as an instrument of supply col-laboration among the various United Nations.

Adjustment of Lend-Lease Procedure to Combined Arrangements

The decision on the common pool of munitions represented the attainment of the goal the War Department had set up in 1941—a consolidated production pro-gram for the United States and foreign aid

with distribution on the basis of strategic necessity. The old lend-lease procedure had to be adapted to this new arrange-ment. It involved a new system of appro-priations, a redefinition of relations be-tween the War Department and the Office of Lend-Lease Administration, and a con-solidation of control of lend-lease require-ments for Army materials within the War Department and of allocations under the new combined agencies. It marked a sep-aration of military lend-lease from its civilian counterpart, the former now com-ing under direct control of the War De-partment and the CCS, the latter remain-ing under OLLA.

Before 7 December 1941 the War Department had suggested a solution to the appropriations problem—consolida-tion of Army and lend-lease funds with only a dollar value limitation on transfers under lend-lease. This solution, rejected by the House of Representatives in No-vember 1941, was accepted with little dis-sent after Pearl Harbor. The Third Sup-plemental National Defense Appropria-tions Act, Fiscal Year 1942, was passed on 26 December 1941 and provided that materials to the value of $2 billion could be furnished out of Army stocks for lend-

---

[34] ID, History of Reciprocal Aid, pp. 7–10, 19–22, OCMH.

[35] In all, thirty-five nations entered into formal Master Lend-Lease Agreements with the United States. The agreement with the United Kingdom (which included her colonial empire) was signed 23 February 1942, that with China, 2 June 1942, and with the USSR, 11 June 1942. For the text of the agreement with the United Kingdom (substantially the same as that for all the others with the exception of certain special clauses in those with the Latin American republics), see ID, Lend-Lease, Doc Suppl, II. For discussion, see ID, Lend-Lease, I, 49–55.

[36] ID, History of Reciprocal Aid, Doc Suppl, OCMH. No separate lend-lease agreements were made with Australia and New Zealand, but they ac-cepted the principles of the U.K. Master Agreement.

lease. It established a precedent, and, until the end of the war, funds for both U.S. Army and lend-lease items to be procured by the War Department were packaged together with dollar value limitations on lend-lease transfers. A similar system of appropriations was adopted for the Navy Department and the Maritime Commission. The over-all limitation on dollar values for War Department articles reached a total of $32,170,000,000 by the end of the war, far in excess of the value of goods actually transferred.[37] Little more need be said of these financial arrangements beyond the fact that appropriations for civilian lend-lease continued to be made as before and administered by OLLA. The appropriations made to the War Department were entirely adequate and served the desired purpose, making possible a consolidated production program from which allocations were made by the Munitions Assignments Board.

Beyond the announcement of the formation of the Munitions Assignments Board by the President, and the financial arrangements set up by Congress, there was no further action by either to place the new system in operation. Exact adjustments between the War Department and OLLA had to be worked out on an administrative basis. OLLA retained the only powers the President had delegated to authorize transfer and export, and proved somewhat reluctant to restrict its activities solely to civilian materials. For some time OLLA officials continued to negotiate with foreign representatives on military requirements and to needle the War Department in various ways. But, after protracted negotiations, the Lend-Lease Administration on 9 April 1942 finally delegated to the Secretary of War authority to authorize transfer and export

of military lend-lease material, "subject to the policies and directives of the President or the Combined Munitions Assignments Board." [38]

This delegation of powers formally put the new arrangements into effect. In addition to production under lend-lease and War Department appropriations, materials under foreign contracts were also brought into the consolidated production pool as far as possible by changing financing to a lend-lease basis. While this took time and involved difficult financial and legal complications, it meant that the single munitions production program under unified direction had at last become a reality.[39]

The Office of Lend-Lease Administration remained the central agency for lend-lease accounting, for laying down broad policy outside the strategic sphere, and for planning lend-lease programs in support of the civilian economy of beneficiary nations. For military lend-lease, OLLA's functions were reduced to those of a legal or accounting nature.[40] There naturally remained many areas in which the military and civilian agencies had mutual interests, and jurisdiction was difficult to define. It was not always possible to completely separate military and civilian supply. Many items, such as trucks and railroad equipment, were of a dual nature.

---

[37] ID, Lend-Lease, I, 538–41.

[38] (1) Memo, Aurand for McCloy, 30 Jan 42, sub: Clarification of Status of WD With Respect to OLLA, Orgn MAB file, DAD. (2) Ltr, McCloy to Stettinius, 31 Jan 42, Proced 1 file, DAD. (3) Ltr, Thomas B. McCabe, Deputy Lend-Lease Admin, to SW, 9 Apr 42, ID 400.318, I.

[39] (1) Ltr, Morgenthau to Stimson, 20 Mar 42. (2) Ltr, Stimson to Morgenthau, 3 Apr 42. Both in MAC(G) Misc Corresp file, ID.

[40] The problems of lend-lease accounting are treated at some length in ID, Lend-Lease, I, 667–759. Pertinent documents are mainly in the Misc Corresp Lend-lease DAD and ID 008 series.

Machine tools, while not strictly speaking a military item, had always been procured by the Ordnance Department. Agreements had to be reached as to who should make budget estimates and procure these doubtful items. After considerable controversy, these matters were generally settled through the Procurement Policy Board of WPB. Sometimes, as in the case of medical supplies, the War Department continued to act as a procurement agency for OLLA under the old requisition system.[41] In overseas areas, OLLA maintained representatives concerned with lend-lease and reciprocal aid matters and, except in Australia, the theater commanders' control over them was never so complete as the War Department desired. Despite these overlapping areas, the broad principle of division of lend-lease into military and civilian segments under different lines of control was established. Henceforth, foreign requirements for military articles would be presented directly to the War Department and consolidated with the Army's requirements program; assignments of military material would be made exclusively by the authority of the MAB.

Readjustments in War Department Organization and Procedure

New procedures for military lend-lease aimed at making contact between the War Department and foreign representatives "as direct and simple as possible" were announced on 2 March 1942.[42] Requirements for common articles—those standard to the U.S. Army—were to be submitted to the Defense Aid Director for inclusion in the Army Supply Program (ASP), but acceptance would carry no guarantee of delivery to the nation for which the requirement was established.

Assignments of finished articles, when produced, would be made by the Munitions Assignments Committee (Air or Ground) subject to approval by the MAB. Requirements for noncommon articles— those produced to foreign specifications— were to be submitted to the Defense Aid Supply Committee in the case of ground munitions and to the Joint Aircraft Committee in that of air materials, for determination as to feasibility of procurement. If procurement were ruled feasible, transfer to the requesting nation would normally be automatic as the materials came off the production line.[43]

The Office of the Defense Aid Director under General Aurand continued to be the administrative center for War Department lend-lease activities and the point of contact for foreign representatives. It furnished the chairman and secretariat for both the MAC(G) and the Defense Aid Supply Committee, collected and consolidated international aid requirements, issued the necessary directives for procurement, transfer, and shipment, and exercised co-ordination over the lend-lease activities of the various supply services and the home offices of the lend-lease missions overseas.[44] Yet the independent status of the Office of the Defense Aid Director and its diffuse lines of responsibility were better adapted to the method of operations of 1941 than to the new conception of a consolidated supply program.

[41] See long, involved correspondence in the Misc Corresp Lend-lease (1942) DAD and ID 008 Requisitions series.

[42] Ltr, ASW to Morris Wilson, Chm Br Sup Council in N America, 2 Mar 42, ID, Lend-Lease, Doc Suppl, II.

[43] Ibid.

[44] (1) On the evolution of this lend-lease machinery during 1941, see above, Ch. III. (2) Memo, Aurand for McCloy, 5 Feb 42, sub: Orgn and Functions of ODAD, ID 020 (321) ID Orgn.

General Somervell from the time he became G-4 in early December 1941 felt that co-ordination of military lend-lease operations by a separate War Department agency posed a constant threat to U.S. Army interests. "The whole trouble with Defense Aid in the beginning," he wrote some time later, was that "it was an entirely separate and uncoordinated outfit without any knowledge of, or interest in, the supply problem as a whole." [45] When the War Department reorganization was finally accomplished in March 1942, General Aurand's office was one of the many scattered supply agencies brought into Somervell's sprawling SOS empire. While Aurand had long been a proponent of consolidation of supply responsibility within the War Department along the very lines the reorganization took, he played little part in the direct chain of events leading to it, and the net effect was to reduce the prestige and importance of the office of which he was the head. [46] The realignment of lend-lease organization and procedure that followed was a matter of fitting them into what Somervell conceived to be their proper place within the new machinery for military supply.

The Office of the Defense Aid Director was incorporated into the SOS on 9 March 1942 with no change in its organization or functions except that matters pertaining to lend-lease of air materials were turned over to the Army Air Forces. It was redesignated the International Division on 9 April 1942 and continued under that name for the rest of the war. Two studies were made of the division's activities during the summer of 1942 by the Control Division of Headquarters, SOS, and by October it had been generally integrated into the SOS organization. [47] It was the contention of General Aurand, who remained head of the International Division until mid-July 1942, and of his principal subordinates, that the division must be kept intact and on a high level within the War Department in order to preserve the principle of centralization of lend-lease activities and to avoid giving any impression to our allies that lend-lease had ceased to be important. On leaving the division, Aurand went so far as to suggest that it should be returned to the general supervision of the Assistant Secretary of War. Somervell dismissed this as a case of special pleading. He placed the International Division under General Clay, Assistant Chief of Staff for Materiel, some two steps lower in the echelons of the War Department than it had been as an independent agency. The functions of the division as defined in early September 1942, however, differed little from those set forth in the initial directive establishing the organization of the SOS. [48]

Nevertheless, integration into the SOS inevitably brought closer control over both lend-lease requirements and assignments by those responsible for supply of the U.S. Army. Long-range requirements for both the Army and lend-lease were consolidated in the Army Supply Program, formulated and administered by the Requirements Division, SOS. From

[45] Memo, Somervell for Clay, 27 Jul 42, Hq ASF folder, ID.
[46] See memo, Aurand for Somervell, 24 Jan 42, sub: Army Supply Program, MAB Orgn file, DAD.
[47] (1) SOS GO 4, 9 Apr 42. (2) Cont Div rpts in ID 020 (321) ID Orgn.
[48] (1) Memo, Aurand for Clay, 18 Jun 42, sub: Place of ID in Orgn. (2) Memo, unsigned, for Lt Col John B. Franks, Actg Dir ID, no date. (3) Related papers. All in ID 020 (321) ID Orgn. (4) Memo, Aurand for Somervell, 18 Jul 42, sub: Rpt at Time of Leaving ID, Hq ASF folder, ID. (5) Memo cited n. 45. (6) Services of Supply Organization Manual, 30 Sep 42, ASF files. (7) Cf. par. 9i of ltr, CG SOS to Chiefs of SAS et al., 9 Mar 42, sub: Initial Dir for the Orgn of SOS, Hq ASF, with memo, Dir ID for all br and sec chiefs, 12 Sep 42, ID 020, ID Orgn and Functions.

the start, Somervell and Clay sought to limit lend-lease procurement to articles approved in the ASP and to reduce non-program demands to a minimum. In the small but troublesome area of noncommon items, which at first were not included in the ASP, the Defense Aid Supply Committee had formal authority. But by early 1942 this committee had stopped holding regular meetings, and its work was largely performed by Aurand's office in consultation with subcommittees in supply services, each normally composed of one British and one American representative. Somervell found these subcommittees too free in their use of raw materials and moved to place them under stricter control. The Defense Aid Supply Committee was reconstituted as the International Supply Committee (ISC), and its formal approval was required before procurement of any item not listed in the ASP could be undertaken. The British retained membership on the new committee and General Aurand continued as chairman, but the voting members on the American side came from Clay's office, from the Production Division, SOS, and from OPD. Foreign requests for special procurement encountered a very "tough" attitude in the new ISC, against which Aurand's protests were in vain.[49]

The powers of the International Supply Committee were broadened to include cognizance of nonprogram requirements for common items and revisions of the lend-lease part of the ASP. At least in theory, it became responsible for all international aid requirements. In September 1942 the clear distinction between common and noncommon item procedures was considerably modified. All requisitions for noncommon items previously approved by the ISC were incorporated in a separate section of the September revision of the ASP (Section VI). Since bids for these items were frequently received from several different lend-lease nations, they were subjected to assignment by MAC(G) and automatic transfer was stopped except in cases where the ISC specifically stipulated it in approving procurement.[50]

On the assignments side, the SOS took the position that, except in exceptional circumstances, allocations of finished equipment should never exceed accepted requirements. A Requirements Division, SOS, member was added to MAC(G) in April, and General Somervell himself became a member of the MAB in August. The chairman and secretariat for MAC(G) came from the International Division and, working with subcommittees in the supply services, collected the basic data on which the recommendations of MAC(G) to the board were made. The chairman of MAC(G) acted as sponsor for the bids of all nations, except those of the British, before the committee. Since the MAB in 95 percent of the cases followed these recommendations, the extent to which the SOS was therefore able to determine assignments on an administrative basis is apparent, once the International Division was made a truly integrated part of its organization.[51] Nevertheless, it must be kept in mind that the basic principle on which assignments were made was that of strate-

[49] (1) Memo, Aurand for Somervell, 8 Mar 42, sub: Mtg With Def Aid Sup Com and Subcom Members, 10 Mar 42, MAB Orgn file, DAD. (2) Memo, Aurand for Somervell, 23 Apr 42, sub: International Supply Committee, ID, Lend-Lease, Doc Suppl, II. (3) Memo, Aurand for Chiefs of Sup Svs, 19 May 42, sub: Procurement of Lend-lease Spot Items, Misc Corresp Lend-lease 5 file, DAD. (4) Memo cited n. 48 (4). (5) Memo cited n. 45.

[50] (1) Rpt, Contl Div SOS, 20 Aug 42, sub: Proced Rpt on ID, ID 020 (321) ID Orgn. (2) Memo, Col John B. Franks for br chiefs ID, 10 Sep 42, sub: Proced ISC MAC(G), ID 008 Lend-lease, I. (3) Min 933, 52d mtg MAC(G), 1 Oct 42.

[51] Rpt cited n. 50 (1).

gic necessity and that the governing policies emanated from the MAB, the CCS, and the political heads of state in Great Britain and the United States. Even on the American side of MAC(G), the OPD member exerted a powerful influence whenever critical items or strategic policies were concerned. Also, the British were represented at every step in the assignments process and retained the right of appeal to the MAB and CCS.

The supply services remained the actual operating agencies, responsible for the procurement and distribution of lend-lease materials. Neither General Aurand nor the Control Division was happy about the supply services' general organization for and handling of lend-lease. Most of their inadequacy, Aurand thought, could be traced to the fact that the international supply officers in the services were on too low an echelon and frequently could not give their full time to lend-lease. Combined with what Aurand characterized as "a human desire to equip our own forces in preference to those of foreigners," this circumstance resulted in the "failure of the supply services to take proper interest and assign sufficient personnel to their Lend-Lease activities." [52] To remedy this situation, General Clay had the International Division prepare instructions clearly defining the services' responsibilities for procurement, transfer, and movement. In addition, each supply service was ordered to set up an international aid branch or division to devote its full time to lend-lease activities. Thereafter improvement in the handling of lend-lease at the operating level was rapid. [53]

By mid-October 1942 the SOS procedures for handling procurement, transfer, and export of War Department lend-lease materials had taken a sufficiently final

form to permit codification. Long-range requirements, whether for common or noncommon items, would be presented to the International Division sixty days before the semiannual revision of the ASP. The International Aid Branch of the service concerned would screen each request for need, suitability of the item, availability of materials, availability of production facilities, and possibility of substitution of a standard item if the request was for a noncommon one. On the basis of the review in the supply service, the ISC would then make a final recommendation to the Requirements Division, SOS. If approved, it would be placed in the ASP; if disapproved, the foreign representative would have the right of appeal to the Munitions Assignments Board or the Combined Production and Resources Board. In the case of interim requirements the procedure would be the same, except that the ISC would also include a recommendation for priority. Procedure for assignment would be as before, by bids on MAC(G), with final transfer dependent upon approval by the MAB. If approved by the MAB, the International Division would issue a transfer directive to be executed by the supply service concerned. When the material actually became available from production, the supply service would issue a notice of availability to the beneficiary government. [54] *(Chart 6)*

---

[52] Memo cited n. 48 (4).

[53] (1) Rpt cited n. 50 (1). (2) Note, Clay to Franks, 20 Aug 42, ID 020 (321) ID Orgn. (3) Memo, Franks for Chiefs of Sup Svs, 8 Sep 42, sub: Responsibilities of Chiefs of Sup Svs for Accomplishing Aid to United Nations, ID, Lend-Lease, Doc Suppl, III. (4) For Numerous other detailed directives, see ID 020 (321) ID Orgn.

[54] Memo, TAG for Chiefs of Sup Svs, 14 Oct 42, sub: Authorization To Procure, Trf, and Export WD Lend-lease Mats Other Than AAF Mats, ID 020, ID Orgn and Functions.

CHART 6—ORGANIZATION AND PROCEDURES FOR HANDLING LEND-LEASE (GROUND MATÉRIEL): OCTOBER 1942

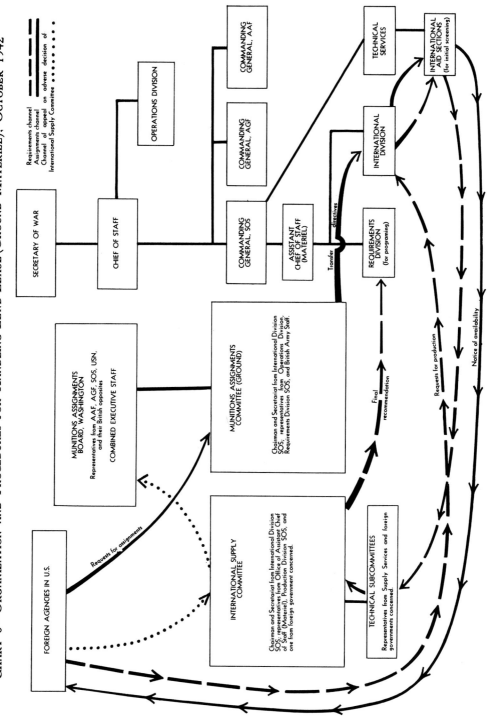

On the surface, these new operating procedures only represented refinements of those announced in March, but there were certain intangible changes resulting from the fact that lend-lease was placed under new management and integrated into an organization for the supply of the Army. General Aurand left the International Division in July to become part of the executive staff of the newly formed Combined Production and Resources Board, and with his departure the initiative in War Department lend-lease affairs passed to Generals Somervell and Clay. Aurand had been the ablest defender of the lend-lease principle within the War Department and was a far more convinced advocate of the common pool theory than either Somervell or Clay. They recognized the importance of lend-lease as an instrument of coalition warfare as well as Aurand, but their experience and orientation was toward supplying the U.S. Army first, and they tended to subordinate lend-lease to this end. They preferred direct action within the confines of the SOS staff to the involved deliberations of combined committees. In sum, the new management adopted a more national outlook, aimed at preventing foreign raids on the U.S. supply pool. Possession of the administrative machinery for War Department lend-lease operations enabled the SOS staff to make that outlook felt in decisions rendered at a high level on the distribution of American-made munitions.[55]

The area in which the British felt the impact of the new arrangements most severely was in the procurement of non-common items. The British noncommon program, as it had taken shape by mid-1942, included essential components for manufacture of finished munitions in Brit-ain, ammunition for British-type weapons, tank transporters and other heavy vehicles, and miscellaneous signal, engineer, transportation, and quartermaster materials peculiar to the British Army. While of vital importance to the British in maintaining their own war production and supplying marginal requirements of the Commonwealth's armies, the noncommon program was inevitably a nuisance to an organization concerned with planning an orderly military procurement program that would take full advantage of American mass production methods. Production of bits and pieces on spot requisitions and small orders for noncommon stores threatened to absorb vital raw materials or facilities out of all proportion to their actual volume. From March 1942 onward the British were forced to fight continually in the International Supply Committee to keep their noncommon program from being completely submerged. From the British point of view, the scope of the International Supply Committee was far too narrow, for, unlike the Joint Aircraft Committee, it confined itself to consideration of specific lend-lease requests and did not have any authority over the competing demands of the U.S. Army for raw materials and industrial facilities. This was in keeping with Somervell's outspoken philosophy that the British should have no part in shaping the American production program. The main premise on which the International Supply Committee acted was that requirements for procurement of noncommon articles should not be allowed

---

[55] The differences in points of view are clearly reflected in the long memorandum written by Aurand on the occasion of his departure from the International Division and in Somervell's and Clay's comments thereon. Memo cited n. 48 (4).

to interfere with the program for American standard equipment.[56]

Storage and Shipment of Lend-Lease Materials

In the distributive phase, the simple separation of lend-lease into its military and civilian components was no longer possible. When tanks, guns, and ammunition arrived at port they had to be shipped in the same vessels, as a part of the same shipping program, as foodstuffs, raw materials, and other supplies destined to bolster civilian economies abroad. While military lend-lease had a higher dollar value, and was made up of more highly specialized items, it represented only 20 percent of the bulk of lend-lease shipments. Shipping was either furnished by the foreign government concerned, or arranged for through the War Shipping Administration out of the Allied pool. WSA exercised over-all supervision over the whole lend-lease shipping program, working closely with the British Ministry of War Transport. The Army's direct responsibility was confined to making supplies available and delivering them to port in condition for immediate overseas shipment.

In exercising this responsibility, the Army used generally the same facilities and procedures for storage and internal movement of lend-lease materials as it did for its own supplies. It was only necessary to physically segregate lend-lease and give it special marking and packing. The Transportation Corps controlled rail movement of both types of material into the port area. When immediate movement to port was impossible, lend-lease was stored in general and branch depots under the supply services. It was moved into intransit storage in holding and reconsignment points under Transportation Corps control when necessary to prevent clogging of port areas. The main difference between movements of lend-lease and of Army material lay in that the former was called forward to port by and consigned to representatives of a foreign government instead of the Army port organization. However, Transportation Corps port agencies, initially established in 1941 under the Quartermaster Commercial Traffic Branch, were charged with doing whatever was necessary to expedite the loading and dispatching of military lend-lease shipments.[57] There were innumerable snarls in the handling of military lend-lease movements in the period following Pearl Harbor. The Army's supply organization was undergoing radical changes, and the simultaneous increase in both Army and lend-lease shipments was more than the Army could handle efficiently. Record keeping and documentation of lend-lease shipments were extremely confused and usually no one could tell the exact whereabouts of material in the pipeline. Though technical inspections were supposedly performed all along the line, material arrived in port improperly packed, with related items unassembled, or defective in one way or another. Lacking clear-cut jurisdiction over materials once they arrived in

---

[56] For an admirable statement of the British point of view, see Hall and Wrigley, Studies in Overseas Supply, first draft, Ch. III, pp. 237–77, Hist Br, Cabinet Off, London.

[57] (1) TAG ltr to Chiefs of Sup Svs, 11 May 42, sub: Trans and Storage of Lend-lease Sups, AG 486.1 (5-6-42). (2) Sec on trans in rpt, 19 May 42, sub: ID Orgn and Functions, ID 020, ID Orgn and Functions. (3) Schmidt, The Commercial Traffic Branch in the Office of The Quartermaster General, July 1940–March 1942; OCT HB Monograph 6, pp. 343ff, OCMH. (4) On the general functioning of the system of movements to port, see Wardlow, Trans II, Ch. IV.

port, the Transportation Corps port agencies were hampered in remedying these defects. There were so many agencies and individuals within and without the SOS involved in lend-lease shipments that a constant procession of co-ordinating committees, liaison arrangements, informal agreements, and an excessive use of the long distance telephone were required to keep them moving.[58]

As a part of the whole SOS effort to streamline international aid procedures during the summer of 1942, the supply services were charged with a close follow-up of each shipment from the time a transfer directive was issued until the material was loaded aboard ship. Reporting procedures were simplified and co-ordinated with those of the Lend-Lease Administration. A directive was also issued whereby all War Department-procured lend-lease except air materials would be consigned to Army port agencies and retained under their control until turned over at shipside to the foreign government. Only in this way, the SOS believed, could the control over movements in the port area be complete, proper technical inspections and assembly operations be performed, and accurate records be insured.[59] But the directive had to be revoked almost immediately on protest from the British and WSA. Under the Bland Act of March 1942 WSA had been granted control over all foreign water-borne commerce, and in November 1942 it asserted that authority by prescribing that all lend-lease freight for export should be consigned to its forwarding corporations set up at each port. A final settlement on procedure along these lines was agreed upon between the SOS and WSA in December. WSA forwarding corporations were made entirely responsible

for calling lend-lease material forward to port and handling it once it arrived there. Nevertheless, the Transportation Corps retained its responsibility for controlling all rail movements into port, and the port agencies were charged with maintaining proper liaison with forwarding corporations for follow-up of shipments, return of documents, and performance of last-minute inspections and assemblies. Procedures for reporting inventories at various stages of movement were immensely complicated by divided responsibilities. SOS would have infinitely preferred the simpler system of Army control in the port area, but there was no evading the authority of WSA in this instance. The cumbersome "water-borne export procedure" remained basically the same throughout the rest of the war.[60]

While the great bulk of lend-lease shipments was made under this system, another was devised for those cases where it was necessary or desirable for the Army to retain control even after the material arrived in the theater. This was the so-called Commanding General Shipment. Materials shipped under this arrangement were consigned to the U.S. com-

---

[58] (1) Min, SOS stf conf, 26 Jun 42, Contl Div ASF. (2) Papers in ID 008 Shipts, I.

[59] (1) Memo, CG SOS for Chiefs of Sup Svs, 9 Sep 42, sub: Doc of Lend-lease Shipts of Mat to Foreign Govts. (2) Draft ltr, evidently prepared in ID for dispatch by ASW to Lewis Douglas, WSA, no date. Both in ID 008 Shipts, I. (3) Dirs, Hq SOS to Sup Svs, 9–11 Sep 42, ID, Lend-Lease, Doc Suppl, III.

[60] (1) PL 498, 77th Cong (Bland Act). (2) WSA Dir 4, 5 Nov 42. (3) WSA Opns Regulation 23. (4) WSA Forwarding Regulation 1. Last three in ID, Lend-Lease, Doc Suppl, IV. (5) Memo, CG SOS for Chiefs of Sup Svs, 4 Dec 42, sub: Proced for Shipt of WD Lend-lease Mat for Water-Borne Export, ID 008 Shipts, II. (6) For a detailed treatment of operations under this and later modified water-borne export procedures, see ID, Lend-Lease, I, 574–97.

manding general in the area involved for delivery to the intended foreign beneficiary. This method was used principally in deliveries to China, the French in North Africa, and the Brazilian Expeditionary Force in Italy. Commanding General Shipments were consigned to and called forward by the regular Army port organization, in virtually the same manner as those for U.S. troops overseas.[61]

Thus emerged in the months following Pearl Harbor an elaborate system for the allocation and distribution of American munitions to other nations engaged in the common struggle—a system that made military lend-lease supply an effective part of the logistics of coalition warfare. The capstone of the structure was the Munitions Assignments Board, an Anglo-American body that provided a link between the allocation of munitions and the strategic policies of the CCS. The consolidation of the U.S. Army and lend-lease production programs under military control eliminated most of the administrative confusion of 1941 and created a single production pool out of which MAB could make allocations on a strategic basis. At the operational level, the old lend-lease machinery of the War Department was revamped and fitted into the new Army supply organization, the Services of Supply, establishing a close correlation between Army and lend-lease distribution. And even as the organization was taking shape, the principles under which it was to operate were also emerging.

---

[61] (1) See detailed discussion in ID, Lend-Lease, I, 605–16. (2) See also below, Chs. XVIII–XIX.

CHAPTER XI

The Anglo-American Munitions Pool

Determination of a Basis of Assignments

Winston Churchill came to Washington in December 1941 fearing that American insistence on training and equipping a large ground and air army would upset British plans, which since 1940 had been based on the expectation of a continuing flow of American munitions.[1] The agreements reached at ARCADIA went far to dissipate these fears, but the issue remained a fundamental source of conflict in the combined effort to establish a basis for allocation of material. The British, with most of their troops already trained and deployed in areas immediately threatened (the British Isles, Australia, New Zealand, Malaya, Burma, India, the Middle East, and Africa), insisted that the principle of assignments in consonance with strategy could be properly applied only by giving first priority to existing theaters of operations. In view of the critical situation in which the British found themselves, actual delivery of material in 1942 seemed to them of more vital importance than promises of an American army to fight beside them in 1943 or 1944. The American staff, though willing to make some concessions to the British, felt that its own program of preparing a vast army for future operations should constitute a first charge against American production. The lack of any specific combined plan of action for 1942 made resolution of these conflicting points of view doubly difficult.

Immediately following Pearl Harbor, while allocations were still largely a matter for unilateral determination by the General Staff, priorities were generally given to U.S. forces to the "extent necessary to meet their immediate probable consumption of munitions and build up and maintain reserves."[2] Numerous transfers of critical items scheduled for Great Britain, the USSR, and other countries were canceled, and the distribution schedules prepared before Pearl Harbor were abandoned in favor of short-term, almost day-by-day, allocations. The need to bolster continental U.S. defenses, to prepare emergency task forces, and to speed up the tempo of training made such a policy almost mandatory, but the overriding priority for U.S. forces could not continue indefinitely if the common pool was to have any semblance of reality. The President gave every indication that he would insist on generous allocations of munitions

[1] Churchill, *The Grand Alliance*, p. 642.
[2] Agenda for 1st mtg of Strategic Mun Bd, 10 De[c] 41, Col Boone's file, DAD. Though the board neve[r] met, this agenda in fact contained the principles o[n] which allocations were made during the first tw[o] months after Pearl Harbor.

for lend-lease. Recognizing this, the General Staff during January wrestled with the problem of determining some new basis for allocations. General Aurand, as Defense Aid Director, suggested a return to the percentage division formula in force before Pearl Harbor; General Somervell, as G-4, that allocations be governed by the availability of shipping to transport them. In truth, as General Moore pointed out in rejecting Aurand's solution, policy could hardly be fixed as long as neither the scope of the American effort overseas nor a combined plan of action for 1942 had been determined.[3]

At the end of January the problem passed from the surveillance of the General Staff alone to that of the combined agencies—the CCS and the Munitions Assignments Board. The MAB at its first meeting, 31 January 1942, adopted an approach that was completely in harmony with the common pool concept. Assignments, the board decided, should be based on combined Anglo-American plans for combat forces in the various theaters and for forces in training, balanced against combined munitions resources and planned production. The board, however, was in no position to establish priorities among theaters and national forces or between theaters and forces in training, since it had received no strategic guidance on these matters from the CCS. The board's program therefore remained only a long-range goal. For the present, it ruled, assignments would continue to be based on "existing transfer schedules of United States stocks and production."[4]

Following this line, the Munitions Assignments Committee (Ground) in its early actions continued to give priority to U.S. troop needs. A British protest was inevitable and was not long in coming. At the MAC(G) meeting of 21 February 1942 the War Plans Division member, Brig. Gen. Robert W. Crawford, insisted that minimum U.S. requirements for arming seventy-one divisions before the end of 1942 must be met before any critical items could be assigned to other countries. The British member, Brigadier Donald Campion, dissented emphatically, arguing that to fix such prior charges cut across the whole principle of assignment in accordance with need. MAC(G) was unable to proceed with March assignments, and General Aurand, its chairman, requested guidance from the MAB. The MAB, in turn, asked for a strategic directive from the CCS.[5]

The British representatives on the CCS came up almost immediately with a full-blown proposal centering around the principle that "the provision of full equipment for existing units available in or about to proceed to an active theater of war, or to one immediately threatened, is . . . the first charge on available assets, in such order or priority as may be assigned the various theaters."[6] They suggested equal

---

[3] (1) Memo, Aurand for CofS, 13 Jan 42, sub: Def Aid Trfs and Trf Schedules, Misc Stf Studies, Lend-lease 2A file, DAD. (2) Memo, Moore for CofS, 13 Jan 42, same sub. (3) Memo, Gross for Somervell, 19 Jan 42, same sub. (4) Memo, Somervell for Gross, 13 Jan 42. Last three in Plng Div Studies folder, OCT HB.

[4] Tab E, Preliminary Asgmts Dir by MAB, to memo, Aurand for CofS, 11 Feb 42, sub: Dir for MAB, ID 020, ID Orgn and Functions.

[5] (1) Min 32, 4th mtg MAC(G), 21 Feb 42. (2) Tab A to min cited above (1), memo, Aurand for Exec Off MAB through Moore, 21 Feb 42, sub: Basis for Asgmts. (3) Tab E to min cited above (1), 1st Ind, Moore to Exec Off MAB, and 2d Ind, Exec Off MAB to CCS, to Aurand memo. (4) Min 33, 5th mtg MAC(G), 23 Feb 42. At this meeting the British agreed to accept an interim requirement for equipping thirty-five U.S. divisions by 30 June 1942 in order that March assignments might proceed.

[6] CCS 50, memo by Br reps on CCS, 26 Feb 42, title: Asgmt of Mun.

scales of equipment, ammunition, and reserves for forces of all the United Nations in the same theater, and proportional scales of equipment and ammunition for training. They thought the CCS should indicate the relative priority of theaters, and draw up an order of battle outlining combat forces under its operational direction in all theaters as they were and as it was intended they should be on 30 June and 31 December 1942.

General Aurand thought the British approach sound, but there were strong objections within WPD. These objections, as noted privately, were, first, that the United States could not accept British standards of training, and, second, that fulfillment of requirements for forces in active theaters or about to proceed there would "consume all production for some time to come and there will be nothing left for the needs of large forces that must be developed if we are going to win the war."[7] General Marshall took something of a middle ground and ended by charging Aurand with the preparation of a statement as to the form in which allocations should be made by MAC(G). Aurand's draft followed generally along the lines of the British proposal as to the form of directive required, but was sufficiently indefinite on the question of specific priorities between theaters and training to permit General Eisenhower, the new head of WPD, to accept it.[8]

The CCS, on considering the British paper and the suggestions made by Aurand and after further consultation with the MAB on the precise nature and scope of the guidance required, entrusted the drafting of an assignments directive to the Combined Staff Planners. The CPS was unable to provide the precise and detailed sort of directive the MAB desired

but did reach agreement on a broad set of principles, and a draft assignments directive was presented to the CCS on 24 March 1942 (CCS 50/2).[9] The staff planners proposed that allocations by the assignments boards in Washington and London should be made from combined production to ground and air forces in theaters, about to proceed to theaters, and in training, according to the following principles:

14. Amounts of munitions assigned to theaters should be based on the size of forces actively engaged and the existing state of their equipment; the probable period of active operations; and the probable character of the operations.

15. Although it is impossible to give absolute priorities to the extent of entirely denying equipment and supplies to units in lower priorities, it is believed that the following general objectives should serve as a guide in the allocation of munitions:

(a) 100% equipment, reserves and maintenance, including ammunition for training: (1) for fully trained units in active theaters of war, (2) for those units which can be dispatched thereto in three months' time, and (3) for those units allocated for defense of vital installations against hostile raids in inactive theaters. Original supply, reserves, and maintenance levels will differ for differ-

[7] OPD notes on agenda for 9th mtg CCS, 3 Mar 42, ABC 400 (2-17-42) Sec 1.

[8] (1) Memo, Aurand for Moore, 2 Mar 42, sub: Conf With CofS re Basis for Asgmt to United Nations. (2) Memo, Aurand for CofS, 2 Mar 42, sub: Method of Making Asgmts to United Nations. (3) Memo, Eisenhower for CofS, 3 Mar 42, sub: Method of Allocating Mun to United Nations. All in MAB Orgn file, DAD.

[9] Steps leading to the directive may be traced in the following: (1) Min, 9th mtg CCS, 3 Mar 42. (2) MBW 3/1, memo by MAB for CCS, 10 Mar 42, title: Nature and Form of Strategic Dir To Govern Asgmts Proceed. (3) Min, 12th mtg CCS, 17 Mar 42, Item 1. (4) Min, 9th mtg CPS, 19 Mar 42, Item 1; 10th mtg, 20 Mar 42; 11th mtg, 23 Mar 42, Item 1. (5) CCS 50/2, 24 Mar 42, title: Dir for Asgmt of Mun.

MBW (Munitions Assignments Board in Washington) is an alternate abbreviation for MAB.

ent categories and locations of forces. These figures will be established by appropriate authority.

(b) 100% of equipment and training ammunition for units in training except for those items of which there is a shortage. Of these latter a minimum of 50% will be provided. If the available supply of munitions is insufficient, proportionate cuts in (a) and (b) should be made.

16. In order to eliminate inequalities between different arms and different theaters of war,

(a) Approximately equal scales of equipment, ammunition and reserves should be established for United States and British forces in the same theater.

(b) Approximately equal scales of equipment and ammunition for training should be established.

Priorities for the various theaters were established. The Middle East, India-Burma-Ceylon, Australia, and, for air operations, the United Kingdom were classified as priority "A" for continuous major operations; New Zealand and the Pacific islands on the lines of communications from the United States, priority "A" for major operations for two months; Hawaii and the United Kingdom for land operations, priority "B" for major operations for two months; Africa, Alaska, Iceland and Greenland, the United States and Canada, South America, and the Caribbean, "C" priority, as subject only to airborne or sea-borne raids. Appendixes were to be prepared showing the proposed disposition of American and British forces in each theater as of 30 June and 31 December 1942.

CCS 50/2 also recognized certain assignments problems not clearly related to theaters under control of the CCS. These were Latin America, China, the USSR, Turkey, and the Free French. Allocations to Latin America were to be limited to items that would not hamper operations

or training of the United States and British Commonwealth. The Moscow Protocol would remain the basis of assignments to the Soviet Union but should be reexamined, revised, and extended as soon as possible, "based upon giving maximum aid to Russia within the transportation capabilities to the ultimate destination, provided essential United States and British operations will not be unduly handicapped." Allocations to China should be limited to those that could be delivered to Chinese troops and effectively used by them. Limited amounts of munitions would be allocated to Turkey "as a means of influencing her to oppose Germany." Munitions for the Free French forces in Africa and the Middle East would be provided from British allocations; for French forces in the Pacific, from U.S. allocations.[10]

The Combined Chiefs gave final approval to these proposals on the day they were presented, rejecting at the same time General Marshall's request for a special directive to cover April assignments, giving priority to the equipping of certain U.S. divisions. Shortly afterward the Combined Staff Planners began work on the appendixes showing prospective deployment. These were completed and approved by the CCS on 28 April.[11]

Though the British got in CCS 50/2 the form of directive they initially had asked for, the principles of assignment there established only partially reflected their views. The spirit of compromise was evident throughout. The WPD staff had to abandon its claim for first priority on

---

[10] CCS 50/2, 24 Mar 42, title: Dir for Asgmt of Mun.

[11] (1) Min, 13th mtg CCS, 24 Mar 42, Item 17; 17th mtg, 28 Apr 42, Item 5. (2) Ltr, Gen Marshall to Field Marshal Dill, 24 Mar 42, ABC 400 (2-17-42) Sec 1.

minimum requirements for building an
American army, but in turn the British
had to accept the 50 percent requirement
for troops in training on an equal priority
with theater needs. A British proposal to
set minimum training requirements at
33⅓ percent was firmly rejected.[12] On the
other hand, troops were to be entitled
to full equipment only three months before departure for a theater, instead of six
months as WPD had asked. Also, the
British gained their point in the stipulation of approximately equal scales of
equipment for training and for various
national forces in the same theater.

The concessions made to the British in
the assignments directive itself were more
than balanced by the amount of latitude
left in interpretation. CCS 50/2 was from
the first only a general guide, not a
"bible." There were no exclusive priorities, and the actual scales of supply to be
used for both theaters and training were
left for determination by national authorities. The provision for "equal scales" was
therefore virtually a dead letter from the
start. The appendixes showing deployment were not drawn up on the basis of
any specific combined plan of action and,
at least on the American side, were regarded as only educated guesses. The approach to allocation was pragmatic rather
than doctrinaire, and the assignment of
critical items each month often brought
forth the same conflict of views that was
evident in the shaping of the initial directive. The importance of the assignments
directive lay not in the specific theater
priorities laid down, for these were bound
to vary in the fluctuating strategic situation of 1942, but in the definite confirmation by CCS action that the principle of
strategic need and not national interest
would be the guide for assignments by the

MAB. National interest, of course, could
not be completely ruled out, and certainly
the American members of MAC(G) and
the MAB managed in one way or another
under the directive to assure a certain continuing priority for U.S. Army needs.
Nevertheless, they always had to base
their actions on strategic grounds.

It was originally expected that the theater priorities set forth in CCS 50/2 would
be revised periodically in the light of shifts
in combined strategy. Only one such revision ever took place. On 10 June 1942
the CCS gave an "A" priority to forces assigned to operations on the continent of
Europe (BOLERO) in consonance with the
plan developed in April for a cross-Channel invasion in 1942 or 1943. In practice
the Americans generally gave to BOLERO
preparations a status above that of the
British priority "A" theaters in India and
the Middle East. Although the BOLERO
strategy was short-lived, the United States
meantime had been augmenting its forces
in the Pacific beyond original plans. The
first counteroffensives against the Japanese were launched on Guadalcanal and
New Guinea in August. Simultaneously,
preparations were begun for the invasion
of North Africa and by November the
U.S. Army was heavily engaged on two
fronts. While the British were able during
the first half of 1942 to get what they considered a fair share of American equipment in the general famine, during the
latter part of the year they found it increasingly harder to make their claims
stand up against American requirements
for forces actively engaged. The fact remains, nevertheless, that the most urgent
British requests were met and neither of
the most vital fronts, the Middle East

<hr>

[12] Memo, Col Thomas T. Handy for Jt Sec CCS, 21
Mar 42, ABC 400 (2-17-42) Sec 1.

and the United Kingdom, suffered inordinately for lack of American equipment. At the same time, the Americans were able to proceed with equipping their own Army and to give adequate support for its first campaigns. The relative flexibility of CCS 50/2 thus proved a definite advantage, enabling the assignments machinery to meet the pragmatic tests of the first year of American participation in the war.[13]

The Basis of Aircraft Allocations

The provisions of CCS 50/2 were never related in more than a general sense to the allocation of aircraft. At the ARCADIA Conference General Arnold negotiated with Air Chief Marshal Sir Charles Portal an agreement on air allocations for 1942 that remained the basis of assignments by MAC(A) until mid-July. Though the AAF could now count on a vastly expanded production of aircraft, Arnold insisted that the United States had so stripped itself of air materials for the defense of Great Britain during 1941 that the schedules agreed on before Pearl Harbor for delivery to the British must be curtailed. The Arnold-Portal Agreement effected a reduction, but not to the extent that Arnold desired, and he continued to insist that if allocations to Britain and the USSR were not further reduced it would be impossible to provide enough planes for the planned expansion of the AAF to 115 groups.[14]

The Arnold-Portal Agreement preceded the creation of the MAB, but was accepted by that body in early March for production planning purposes and became the tentative guide to aircraft assignments. The appendixes of CCS 50/2 contained deployment schedules for air as

AMERICAN AND BRITISH AIR CHIEFS, *Lt. Gen. Henry H. Arnold and Air Chief Marshal Sir Charles Portal.*

well as ground units, but it was a measure of the dubious validity of these schedules that the CCS ruled that the Arnold-Portal Agreement should continue to govern as-

---

[13] (1) CCS 50/3, 10 Jun 42, title: Amendment to Dir for Asgmt of Mun. (2) Min, 24th mtg CCS, 10 Jun 42, Item 7. (3) Memo, Aurand for Somervell, 18 Jul 42, sub: Rpt at Time of Leaving ID, Hq ASF folder, ID. (4) Hall and Wrigley, Studies in Overseas Supply, first draft, Ch. IV, pp. 282–92, Hist Br, Cabinet Off, London. (5) On BOLERO planning, see below, Ch. XIV. (6) On Pacific operations, see below, Ch. XV. (7) On the invasion of North Africa, see below, Chs. XVI–XVII.

[14] (1) Craven and Cate, *AAF I,* pp. 248–49. Under the Arnold-Portal Agreement the British, during 1942, were to receive from American production 589 heavy bombers, 1,744 medium bombers, 2,745 light bombers, 4,050 pursuits, 402 observation planes, and 852 transports. (2) Memo, AAF for OPD, 23 Mar 42, sub: Reduction in Commitment of All Types of Planes to the Br, OPD 452.1, Case 36. (3) For pre-Pearl Harbor schedules, see above, Ch. IV.

signments until a new agreement could be negotiated. Negotiations to this end were already in progress. In early April Arnold presented to the President his case for a reduction in the commitments of planes to the British. The decision at approximately the same time to concentrate resources on an early invasion of the Continent heightened the need for a ruling, for the Americans would need a large air force to carry out their part of such an operation, and the composition of that air force would also be an issue. The CCS appointed a special committee to study the problem but it could make no final determination of the matter until the President's disposition was known.[15]

The President's decision came in a message to Churchill on 19 May 1942:

> Today it is evident that under current arrangements the U. S. is going to have increasing trained air personnel in excess of air combat planes in sight for them to use. We are therefore anxious that every appropriate American-made aircraft be manned and fought by our own crews. Existing schedules of aircraft allocations do not permit us to do this. . . . My thought is that the CCS, with your approval and mine, would determine the strength of aircraft to be maintained in the respective theaters of war. I think the maximum number of planes possible should be maintained in combat and the minimum number consistent with security be held in reserve and in operational training units, and that American pilots and crews be assigned to man American-made planes far more greatly than at present on the combat fronts.[16]

This decision meant that the main American air contribution in the future would take the form of air units manned by Americans rather than planes for British pilots to fly. A new schedule of allocations was worked out after the horse trading so typical of Anglo-American negotiations of this sort and was approved by the CCS on 2 July 1942. The schedule, signed by General Arnold, Air Vice Marshal J. C. Slessor (representing Portal), and Rear Adm. John H. Towers, USN, and known as the Arnold-Slessor-Towers Agreement,[17] stipulated not only the numbers and types of aircraft to be turned over to the British during the rest of the year but also the size and composition of U.S. combat air forces to be established in the Middle East, India, and the United Kingdom. The agreement gave the AAF the prospect of far more planes for its own expansion. At the same time, the establishment of an American air force in the Middle East, coming as it did at a critical juncture in British affairs there, at least partially compensated the British for the reduction in aircraft deliveries.[18]

The Arnold-Slessor-Towers Agreement was to be followed by a series of similar pacts negotiated periodically throughout the rest of the war. These, rather than CCS 50/2, were to serve as the basis for assignment of aircraft by MAC(A) and MAB. Nevertheless, the principle on which these agreements were based was a similar one to that of CCS 50/2, since theater deployment of British and U.S. air forces was the criterion for determining the respective needs of each nation. However, the superior mobility of air units made it possible to determine this deploy-

---

[15] (1) Distribution of Air Materiel to the Allies 1939–1944: Control, Procedures and Policies, AAF Reference Hist 6, MS, p. 56, Air University Hist Ln Off, Washington, D.C. (2) Ltr, SW to President, 12 Apr 42, WDCSA 452.1. (3) Min, 15th mtg CCS, 7 Apr 42; 17th mtg, 28 Apr 42, Item 5. (4) Matloff and Snell, *Strategic Planning: 1941–1942*, Ch. IX. (5) Craven and Cate, *AAF I*, pp. 250, 554–56.

[16] Msg 147, President to Former Naval Person [Churchill], 19 May 42, ABC 400 (2-17-42) Sec 1.

[17] Also sometimes known as the Arnold-Portal-Towers Agreement.

[18] (1) Craven and Cate, *AAF I*, pp. 566–70. (2) On the Middle East crisis, see below, Ch. XVIII.

ment without the same regard for national composition as was the case with ground components. The air agreements provided a stable base of calculation on which both the AAF and the RAF could plan their future development. The President's decision of May 1942 assured the AAF of the larger role its commander thought it should play, and made it possible for the American air staff to accept the principle of theater deployment as a basis for aircraft allocations without fear that it would result in emphasizing expansion of British air forces at the expense of its own.

The Relation of Requirements to Assignments

The air agreements established for the rest of 1942 a close relationship between production planning and allocations, a relationship that both the British and Americans had to recognize as vitally necessary for other types of equipment as well. Even though lend-lease had been consolidated with U.S. military requirements into one grand munitions program for American industry, that program had to be framed in terms of the requirements of the individual forces and nations to be supplied. Allocations had to be closely related to these requirements, for unless assignments in the end closely approximated the total requirements of each claimant, no stable plans for development or deployment of either American or British forces were possible. The division of manpower between the military services and industry in Britain and America alike depended upon prior calculations of the equipment to be available. To a large degree the execution of any agreed strategy also depended upon it. On this funda-

mental principle the British and Americans could easily agree. But it was not so easy to resolve divergent views on the means of applying it.

By the logic of circumstances, it was the British who took the lead in urging a combined requirements program based on combined strategy as determined by the CCS. They had long calculated military requirements in terms of specific numbers and types of troops in specific theaters of war. Their position in 1942 was that the Americans should do likewise and that the combined order of battle for the entire war should determine combined production requirements. These combined strategic requirements would form the basis not only for adjustments in production programs in both countries but also for allocations by the Munitions Assignments Boards. This approach offered certain obvious advantages for the British, for it would assure them CCS approval for their requirements against American production. While the British thought that in the immediate crisis in early 1942 assignments should be made in keeping with short-term operational needs, for the long pull they wanted more definite assurances of the kind and quantity of American aid they could expect.

Meantime, the U.S. supply planners found it necessary to calculate their requirements solely in terms of the over-all size and type of military forces to be armed. British requirements against American production were included initially in terms of the deficits the British had presented in their Victory Program of 1941, deficits they could not meet from sources available to them—a generous enough basis to start with, since these requirements were generally inflated ones. However, the initial Army Supply Program, in which these requirements found expression, proved well beyond the capacity of American industry and had to be scaled downward in successive revisions during 1942.[19] The British soon learned that acceptance of a requirement, even when scaled down, did not necessarily mean that an assignment would be made to fulfill it when there were competing American demands. The British plan for combined strategic requirements as a guide to adjustments of both production plans and allocation of matériel was one phase of their general endeavor to secure recognition for their needs and a stable basis for calculating the amount of American aid they might expect in the light of ever-shifting production plans.

The method of procedure the MAB proposed to adopt was generally along the lines of the British plan. It will be recalled that in addition to its allocation function, the MAB was also charged by the CCS with maintaining information on combined munitions resources and translating them into terms of combat forces as a guide for the CCS in keeping requirements programs in line with both strategy and the realities of production. The MAB first started to follow this directive liter-ally, converting production forecasts into terms of troop units, but soon found it impractical and adopted the opposite (and older) method of determining first the troop requirements and then matching them with production schedules. The MAB proposed to determine these troop requirements in terms of deployment and training schedules, but was handicapped at first by inadequate information on prospective deployments. The first studies undertaken were therefore of a series of critical items, limited to requirements against U.S. production as determined

from the Army Supply Program. After the preparation of the appendixes of CCS 50/2, the Combined Staff Planners directed the MAB to broaden its scope to include combined requirements and resources of both the United States and United Kingdom during 1942, and to base its studies on these deployment schedules. Its conclusions would then serve as a basis both for production planning and for allocations.[20] The MAB under this plan would extend its studies to include 1943 and 1944, once a combined strategy could be determined upon which an order of battle for these years could be based. The board regarded CCS 50/2 as only a temporary guide and expected that a new directive for allocations would be prepared in terms of this combined strategic planning for ultimate victory.

For a brief period during the spring and summer of 1942 it appeared that the British and MAB plan would come to fruition. The British agreed, in conferences in London in April 1942, to the American plan for concentration of forces for early invasion of Europe as the major Allied effort. In the latter stages of the conference, the British proposed to General Marshall that

---

[19] (1) On 1941 Victory Program planning, see above, Ch. V. (2) On development of the Army Supply Program, see below, Ch. XII. (3) On inclusion of British requirements in ASP, see ID, Lend-Lease, II, 947–50, and Doc Suppl, II. (4) Memo, Gen Aurand for Brig Campion, 6 Jun 42, Col Boone's file, Item 380, DAD. (5) Memo, Gen Moore for ACofS WPD, 7 Jan 42, sub: Former Vic Prog, Vic Prog 1 file, DAD. (6) Ltr, Col Handy to Brig G. K. Bourne, Br Army Stf, 7 Mar 42, ABC 400 (2-17-42) Sec 1.

[20] (1) CCS 19/1, 4 Feb 42, title: Order Estab MAB. (2) MBW 34, 5 Nov 42, title: Rpt on Par. 2 of Order of 4 Feb 42 Estab MAB. (3) Min, 15th mtg CPS, 23 Apr 42, Item 4. (4) Memo, MAB, no addressee, no date, sub: Check of Critical Items To Gauge Relation Between Resources and Reqmts, Incl 4 to agenda for 14th mtg MAB, 6 May 42.

in the light of this strategy each country should prepare an order of battle for all areas around which a combined production program could be set up. Early in June the British formally presented their order of battle for 1 April 1943 to the Combined Staff Planners, urging action on the proposal. Citing the fact that there could be for any given date "only one order of battle whether it be for planning, for production or for munitions assignment," they urged replacement of the appendixes of CCS 50/2 by the deployments now presented and an early decision on comparable deployments for 1 April 1944.[21] The American staff planners agreed generally but declined to accept the British deployments until they had been reviewed by the Combined Staff Planners.[22]

A more potent pressure for action was not long in coming. The presentation of the British plan coincided with a visit to Washington by Sir Oliver Lyttelton, British Minister of Production, to confer with Donald Nelson, chairman of WPB, on combined production problems. Out of these conversations emerged the Combined Production and Resources Board. Formed on 9 June 1942, the CPRB was charged with combining the production programs of the United States and United Kingdom into a single integrated whole, adjusted to the strategic requirements of the war as indicated by the CCS on the one side and production realities on the other. Nelson and Lyttelton, who formed the board, were soon pointing out that existing production plans were based on requirements drawn up independently in the two countries and that they would not necessarily assure the provision of essential equipment to carry out operations scheduled by the CCS. In a resolution adopted at its first meeting, the CPRB asked that the CCS direct the appropriate service authorities to furnish a statement of combined requirements of arms and munitions necessary by the terminal dates 31 December 1942 and 31 December 1943 in order to execute strategic plans for the years 1943 and 1944, respectively. The CPRB would then put these strategic requirements to the test of feasibility.[23]

The CCS accepted the suggestion without much objection, indeed with a certain enthusiasm. It adopted the CPRB report on 2 July 1942 with only minor amendments and instructed the MAB to secure the combined requirements from the services concerned. A special committee, headed by Brigadier J. M. Younger of the British Joint Staff Mission, was appointed to investigate differences in maintenance and reserve scales of ammunition used by the American and British Armies. At this stage there was no indication that the American staff seriously questioned the idea of combined requirements planning on the basis of theater deployment.[24]

The preparation of strategic requirements as the CPRB requested depended upon agreement on combined deployments for 1943 and 1944. As long as the plan for early invasion of Europe remained the prevailing conception of strategy, this seemed feasible. The Combined

---

[21] (1) Br paper, 1 Jun 42, sub: Pdn Reqmts of United Nations, ABC 400 (2-17-42) Sec 2. (2) For a discussion of the April 1942 London conference, see below, Ch. XIV.

[22] (1) Min, 18th mtg CPS, 5 Jun 42, Item 1. (2) For strategic developments, see Matloff and Snell, *Strategic Planning: 1941-1942*, Ch. VIII.

[23] (1) On the founding of the CPRB, see above, Ch. X. (2) CCS 82, rpt by CPRB, 18 Jun 42, title: Pdn Policy.

[24] (1) Min, 26th mtg CCS, 18 Jun 42; 30th mtg, 2 Jul 42, Item 1. (2) Min, 21st mtg JCS, 23 Jun 42, Item 11. (3) CCS 82/1, rpt by Sp Com Appointed To Consider CCS 82, 27 Jun 42, title: Pdn Policy.

Staff Planners in mid-July were able to present a combined order of battle for 1 April 1943 (CCS 91), which the CCS agreed to accept for purposes of production planning. But almost simultaneously, the whole concept of strategy was changed, much to the chagrin of the American staff, by a decision to undertake the invasion of North Africa in the fall of 1942 (Operation TORCH), thus leaving strategic planning for 1943 and 1944 in an uncertain state. The CCS proved unable to arrive at any final decision that could serve as a guide for drawing up an order of battle for 1944. That for 1943 (CCS 91) proved hardly more reliable than had been the appendixes of CCS 50/2, since the Americans found it necessary to commit larger forces to the Pacific than originally planned. With this change in the situation, the American planners began to cool perceptibly toward the British proposal for a program of strategic requirements.[25]

Meanwhile the CPRB, under increasing British influence, pressed the CCS for their 1943 program. The CPRB prescribed a deadline of 1 September 1942, and in a report to the President in early August emphasized the fact that unless it received such a statement by that date, it would be impossible for the CPRB to frame production programs for 1943 intelligently. The President wrote Donald Nelson that he would "make sure these strategic requirements are in your hands at an early date," and Nelson forwarded this comment to the CCS.[26]

This pressure served only to crystallize the opposition of American staff officers. With no agreed strategy in prospect, they viewed the September deadline as impossible of attainment. Quite apart from this fact, they had also come to regard the whole proposal as one that would favor the British at the expense of equipping an American army. When the MAB on 24 July finally presented its balance sheet for combined requirements and resources of critical items for 1942 (based on CCS 91), it revealed to the American planners the vastly higher maintenance and reserve factors used by the British in calculating their theater requirements. For example, the British added to their initial requirements for tanks 76.5 percent for reserve and 68.3 percent for maintenance in contrast to a 21 percent reserve factor used for U.S. armored forces. There was an obvious implication that if these British theater requirements were accepted for production planning, they must also be accepted for assignments, thus allowing the British to accumulate vast reserves while the U.S. Army struggled to get enough equipment to make its expansion possible. "The comparison of US and UK requirements and resources," wrote a perturbed OPD officer, "infers [sic] that US production be turned over to the British and the US Army take the remainder."[27] When the balance sheet was considered by the Combined Staff Planners, the OPD member saw to it that it was returned to the MAB for reconciliation of the British and American scales. MAB referred the matter to the ground committee which, after well over three months of debate, was unable to produce more than a complete statement of the differences. Meanwhile, the deliberations of the Younger committee on scales of

---

[25] (1) CCS 91, 14 Jul 42, title: Strategic Policy and Deployment of U.S. and Br Forces. (2) Min, 31st mtg CCS, 16 Jul 42; 37th mtg, 27 Aug 42. (3) For strategic developments, see Matloff and Snell, *Strategic Planning: 1941-1942*, Chs. XII–XIII.
[26] CCS 102, 24 Aug 42, title: Pdn Policy for 1943.
[27] OPD notes on 28th mtg CPS, 7 Aug 42, ABC 400 (2-17-42) Sec 2.

ammunition resulted in the same sort of deadlock.[28]

These difficulties over the scale on which requirements should be calculated combined with the lack of an agreed strategy to lead OPD, SOS, and the executive staff of the MAB to the same conclusions— that the existing Army Supply Program was the only practical basis for American production planning and that the only British requirements to be accepted should be those included therein. General Somervell by mid-August was even questioning the role the CPRB was assuming, arguing that its consideration should not extend to "the types and quantities of munitions to be utilized in any theater"— decisions "military in character" that "must rest with the military authority."[29] With the CPRB deadline already past, the JCS on 4 September officially proposed that each country furnish its existing requirements program, the British program based on theater deployment, the American on total forces that could be transported to and maintained in transoceanic theaters and total forces required for hemisphere defense, training, or use as strategic reserves. There was little the British members of the CCS could do but accept. The MAB had in fact on 3 September already furnished the CPRB with existing requirements programs in pursuance of an informal agreement reached between the two boards.[30]

Though the British won the concession that a continuing effort should be made to develop a program of combined requirements, the U.S. staff was ready to abandon the project entirely. The CPRB, in its second report to the President on 22 September 1942, implied that the requirements furnished earlier were not based on strategy and again called on the CCS to

remedy the situation. On 4 October Churchill himself cabled Roosevelt suggesting that the adjustment of the President's January production goals to production realities—a necessity now that these goals had served their initial purpose of raising the sights—was a task to be accomplished by the CPRB on the basis of the strategic plans of the CCS. This time the President turned to the JCS for advice, and his reply to Churchill, drafted in the main by General Somervell, was a polite rebuff. It recited coldly the steps being taken in the United States to bring the production program in line with realities and ended with the statement that the CPRB "rather than questioning specific requirements items," should restrict itself to an analysis of the total United States and British requirements already presented, in order to determine the feasibility of procurement.[31]

---

[28] (1) *Ibid.* (2) Min, 28th mtg CPS, 7 Aug 42. (3) MBW 19/1, 29 Jul 42, title: Comparison of Combined Reqmts and Resources. (4) MBW 19/2, 10 Aug 42, title: Combined Resources and Reqmts as of 31 Dec 42. (5) MBW 19/3, 28 Nov 42, title: Combined Resources and Reqmts. (6) MBW 19/4, 11 Dec 42, same title. (7) CCS 117, Interim Rpt of Sp Com, 6 Oct 42, title: Study of Am.

[29] (1) Memo, Gen Somervell for Gen Burns, Exec Off MAB, 15 Aug 42, sub: Relationship of WD to MAB and CPRB, MAB folder, Hq ASF. (2) OPD notes cited n. 27. (3) Memo, Brig Gen William F. Tompkins for Exec Off MAB, 25 Aug 42, sub: Combined Reqmts, CCS 400.17 (7-6-42).

[30] (1) Min, 31st mtg JCS, 1 Sep 42. (2) Min, 39th mtg CCS, 4 Sep 42, Item 3. (3) CCS 82/2, 4 Sep 42, title: Combined Pdn Reqmts. (4) MBW 25/2, 3 Sep 42, title: Pdn Policy for 1943. (5) MBW 26, 25 Aug 42, title: Form of 1943 Reqmts.

[31] (1) Draft msg, President to Churchill, sent on 12 Oct 42. (2) Msg 156, Churchill to President, 4 Oct 42. Both in CCS 400.17 (7-6-42) Sec 2. (3) CCS 102/1, 25 Sep 42, title: Pdn Policy for 1943, with incl, memo, CPRB for CCS, transmitting 2d rpt of CPRB to President, 22 Sep 42. (4) Memo, Exec Off MAB for Secy CCS, 28 Sep 42, sub: 2d Progress Rpt to President by CPRB, Annex I to MBW 25/4, 28 Sep 42, title: Pdn Policy for 1943.

This message ended for all practical purposes the effort to arrive at a combined requirements program based on strategic deployments. On 16 October 1942 the CCS, with considerable reluctance on the part of the British members, agreed to inform the CPRB that the requirements submitted in September should be accepted as a basis of planning, and that these requirements would be adjusted from time to time to changing strategy.[32] The net result was to firmly establish the principle that production requirements on U.S. industry and priorities thereon would be handled as American problems by American agencies, and requirements on British production on a similar national basis in Britain. The effort of the CPRB to draw up a combined production program was completely thwarted, and the board itself gradually declined in importance. It is apparent that one of the major reasons for this was the distrust with which the U.S. military authorities, particularly General Somervell, had come to regard it. They were well aware that the British civilians on the CPRB had much broader authority in their own country than Donald Nelson had in the United States, and they feared that the British would dominate the board's actions. "It has been difficult," Somervell informed the Chief of Staff on one occasion, "to prevent the combined committees having to do with production and transportation from becoming dominated by the British viewpoint."[33]

Similarly, fear of over-allocations to the British dictated much of the American opposition to the combined strategic requirements program. Both OPD and SOS regarded the British demands against American production as likely to be too great if their theater requirements program were

accepted as a basis of assignments. They thought it would be easier to deal with the British in direct negotiations and in the MAB on individual issues than to accept the blanket commitments involved in any combined strategic requirements program prepared in advance. "Had we gone on a theater basis," wrote Brig. Gen. Patrick H. Tansey, head of OPD's Logistics Group, in 1945, "we would have found an undue portion of our supplies being transferred to the British to be piled up in such logistical vacuums as India."[34] These American fears combined with the inherent difficulty of arriving at valid estimates of future deployment to spell the demise of combined requirements planning and allocations based on them. As a corollary, the effort to arrive at equal scales of equipment for training and for British and American forces in the same theater also lapsed and these scales were left for determination by the respective national authorities.

The Weeks-Somervell Agreement

The failure of combined requirements planning left the British without any firm basis on which to anticipate allocations for the following year. Their experience with the munitions assignments machinery, meantime, had been generally disappointing. MAC(G) was never able to make firm assignments for more than a month in advance. The acceptance of British requirements in the Army Supply Program gave no assurance of ultimate assignment as

[32] Min, 44th mtg CCS, 16 Oct 42, Item 4.
[33] Memo, Somervell for CofS, no date, sub: Orgn of Combined Bds, WDCSA 334 (1942–43).
[34] (1) Memo, prepared by Tansey, no addressee, no date, sub: Alloc of Mun for Logis Support of Global Strategy, ABC 400 (2-17-42) Sec 6. (2) For a brief statement of the British position, see Hancock and Gowing, *British War Economy*, pp. 397, 399.

long as production schedules were uncertain and as long as elaborate strategic justification was required where there were competing bids. In fact, during the whole of 1942 the British were allocated only about 50 percent of their requirements for that year as accepted in the September 1942 version of the Army Supply Program. Even considering that many of their requirements were inflated, this performance was disappointing. Moreover, allocations, in terms of proportion of American production, declined during the last half of the year. Deliveries of components and other items on the noncommon list were even further behind schedule. Then, as Roosevelt informed Churchill in his October message, the adjustment of requirements to the realities of production was already under way in the United States, and it promised to result in further curtailment of British lend-lease expectancies. The War Production Board in September 1942 found the military requirements program for 1943 (including lend-lease), as determined by the War and Navy Departments, too great for the productive capacity of the country. The brunt of the consequent reduction fell on ground force equipment and was reflected in the 12 November 1942 revision of the Army Supply Program. In this adjustment, British requirements had to be sacrificed on at least a similar scale to American (by approximately 25 percent). By October 1942 the British had reached a crisis of their own in allocating the last reserves of manpower available, and felt they could proceed no further without more specific assurances as to the scope of future American aid. For this reason, the War Cabinet sent to the United States a mission headed by Sir Oliver Lyttelton to reach definite agreements on the whole range of matters affecting the common war effort—production, allocation of munitions, and shipping.[35]

During the visit of the Lyttelton mission General Somervell, as anxious as the British to place their lend-lease program on some definitely predictable basis, negotiated with Lt. Gen. Sir Ronald M. Weeks an agreement on ground equipment that scaled down British requirements by approximately 25 percent, but in turn gave a definite promise that the reduced requirements would be met by actual assignments. It was agreed:

(a) that the British requirements on the United States shall be the minimum necessary to cover the deficit which cannot be supplied from production under British control, and it is understood that these requirements as now stated do not exceed the British capacity to man or operate as far as their own troops and allies for whom they are responsible are concerned.

(b) that the acceptance of British requirements in the 1943 American Programme of Supply and Procurement shall carry an equal obligation to produce and make available to both forces the quantities involved in accordance with an agreed schedule for the twelve calendar months of 1943, and in the event of failure to meet the schedules, the quantities will be scaled down in proportion to the requirement accepted.

(c) that no departure will be made from this understanding, unless in the event of a major unforeseen change in the strategical situation, and then by agreement between the two parties.[36]

The agreement itself listed allocations of most major items, constituting about 60

[35] (1) Hancock and Gowing, *British War Economy*, p. 400. (2) Hall and Wrigley, Studies in Overseas Supply, first draft, Ch. IV, pp. 286–321, Hist Br, Cabinet Off, London. (3) For a discussion of the "feasibility" crisis in U.S. production planning, see below, Ch. XXII.

[36] Weeks-Somervell Agreement, incl in ltr, J. Eaton Griffith, Jt Secy London Mis, to Somervell, 19 Nov 42, ID, Lend-Lease, Doc Suppl, III.

percent of the British ground army requirements on the United States for 1943. The Americans were to make every effort to accept the other British requirements not agreed upon in detail. The minimum flow of components and complementary items necessary to maintain the British production program was also to be continued, and an earlier agreement on a special pool of raw materials to meet spot item requests was confirmed.[37]

The Weeks-Somervell Agreement was part of a whole pattern of Anglo-American accords reached during the visit of the Lyttelton mission, including a new agreement for the allocation of aircraft and one on shipping for the British Import Program.[38] The whole principle of the Weeks-Somervell Agreement was that the Army Supply Program, now geared to a realistic appraisal of U.S. productive capacity, should form the basis for both requirements and assignments of ground munitions from American production. Under this principle, allocations would be related to strategic or operational needs only insofar as the respective national requirements programs reflected them. This was in contravention of the theory on which the MAB had been proceeding. When the agreement was presented to that body, the U.S. Navy member, Admiral Joseph M. Reeves, leveled a sharp attack upon it, charging that the War Department was assuming the functions of the MAB when it made firm commitments in advance for assignment to the British. "The War Department," Reeves said, "undertakes to do this without consideration of the directives, strategic needs and strategic policies as may be issued by the Combined Chiefs of Staff, and without reference to the Combined Munitions Assignments Board."[39]

Reeves struck at a vulnerable point. If the Weeks-Somervell Agreement were accepted without qualification, the freedom of action of the MAB would be measurably reduced. Yet there had to be some foundation for long-term calculations. The allocation of aircraft had been determined from the beginning by very similar agreements, and despite Admiral Reeves' denial, naval allocations were in large measure determined by prearranged production plans. The President had already indicated to Churchill his general agreement. The MAB finally decided to approve, subject to the reservation that "assignments can be made only by the Munitions Assignments Board and that such assignments must be in conformity with the directives of the Combined Chiefs of Staff."[40]

What then remained of the principles of the common pool and of CCS 50/2? An OPD officer suggested at one point that CCS 50/2 be explicitly repealed in favor of a definite theory of assignments on the basis of requirements in the ASP.[41] The objections raised by Admiral Reeves seem to have ended consideration of this move, and CCS 50/2 remained on the books. Its

[37] On the special pool of raw materials and the procedure for noncommon items, see: (1) MBW 21, 3 Aug 42, title: Proced for Non-Programed Items; and (2) Ltr, Gen Clay to James S. Knowlson, Deputy Chm CPRB, 2 Dec 42, ID 092.2, Treaties and Agreements, I.
[38] (1) See ltr, President to Churchill, 30 Nov 42, ABC 400 (11-19-42). (2) On the shipping question, see below, Ch. XXVI.
[39] Memo, Reeves for MAB, 10 Jan 43, sub: Agreement . . . Regarding Procurement of Br Reqmts in U.S. and Subsequent Asgmt to U.K., Annex I to min, 48th mtg MAB, 10 Jan 43.
[40] (1) Min, 48th mtg MAB, 10 Jan 43, and atchd addendum. (2) See also, memo, Col Franks for CG SOS, 12 Jan 43, sub: . . . Items for Consideration at 49th Mtg of MAB, ID 334 MAC(G), I.
[41] OPD notes on 46th mtg JCS, 15 Dec 42, ABC 400 (2-17-42) Sec 4.

general principles were sometimes to be invoked, even though its specific theater priorities had long been outdated. It was never to be revised, a fact that in itself indicated its principles continued to have only a very general application. Nevertheless, the MAB reservation prevented the Weeks-Somervell Agreement from assuming the status of a definite protocol. And OPD was able during 1943 to secure tacit acceptance within the munitions assignment machinery of a new theory that *employments*—active combat use of troops—and not *deployments* should govern allocations. In accordance with this theory the British still were required during 1943 and afterward to give complete operational justification for their assignments even where the requirement had been accepted. The decisions rendered at the international conferences at Casablanca and afterward served as amendments to CCS 50/2 in providing guidance on employments and strategic priorities.[42]

The Weeks-Somervell Agreement definitely sealed the fate of combined long-range requirements planning on a strategic basis and, taken in conjunction with the air agreements, substituted the principle of periodic bilateral negotiations. After the Casablanca Conference in January 1943, the CCS instructed the Combined Staff Planners to draw up tentative deployment schedules for planning purposes, but these were never used as a basis for calculating combined requirements. As far as the MAB was concerned, the net effect was to reduce its requirements function to the nominal one of preparing statistical studies on individual items and maintaining a general balance sheet on combined production. Useful as these studies were in pointing out necessary adjustments in production that might be made by national authorities, they were only advisory in nature and but a weak substitute for the genuine combined requirements planning the MAB had set as its initial goal.[43]

As for the common pool, its fate may well be summarized in the words of an International Division study in mid-1943:

It is commonly said that . . . the resources of the two nations have been placed in a common pool. While unobjectionable as a metaphor, it is a mistake to construe this statement as being literally correct. For, whereas the two countries are engaged in a common enterprise and the resources of each are pooled in the sense that requests for munitions may be filed against each on behalf of any lend-lease country, the resources of the United States are applied primarily to equipping United States Forces, and the resources of the United Kingdom are applied primarily to equipping British Forces. Furthermore, the control of production facilities within each country remains in the hands of that country, as does the power to determine what and how much those facilities shall produce.[44]

Application of Assignments Theories: The Work of the MAC(G)

The broad theories of assignment found application in the detailed work of the assignments committees. Of these, the Munitions Assignments Committee (Ground) is of greatest interest in this volume, and a brief summary of its policies and practices is necessary to an understanding of the assignments process. The MAC(G) handled

---

[42] (1) ID, Study on International Aid for Joint Staff Planners, (mimeographed) Jun 43, pp. 2–13, ID. (2) Memo, Col Albert C. Wedemeyer for Gen Handy, ACofS OPD, 27 Nov 42, OPD 400 U.K., Case 40.

[43] (1) Min, 70th mtg CCS, 5 Feb 43, Item 9. (2) MBW 43, 19 Jan 43, title: Proposed 1943 Prog Under Par. 2 of CCS 19/1. (3) Min 4, 50th mtg MAB, 21 Jan 43. (4) Min 4, 52d mtg MAB, 3 Feb 43. (5) Hancock and Gowing, *British War Economy*, p. 397.

[44] ID, Study on International Aid for Joint Staff Planners, p. 3, cited n. 42.

a vast range of equipment from medium tanks and tractors to picks and shovels. While MAC(A) assigned all equipment peculiar to the air forces, MAC(G) handled those materials that were in common use by ground and air forces. A special Radar and Communications Coordinating Committee, with Army, Navy, Air Forces, and British representatives, was set up to assign radar and related equipment. The radar committee, though in a sense independent, reported its recommended assignments to the MAB through the ground committee.[45] The main ground committee soon found that with only the assistance of its secretariat it could not render informed decisions on transfer schedules for the thousands of items under its control. Subcommittees soon began to mushroom. The first was an assignments subcommittee charged with preparing the monthly assignments schedules. This was followed by subcommittees for explosives, tanks, tractors, trucks, signal equipment, amphibious vehicles, chemical warfare equipment, medical equipment, engineer equipment, diesel engines, and quartermaster and transportation stores. In addition, special stockpile arrangements were made for handling the manifold small items procured by the Medical and Engineer services. All these subcommittees contained British representation and reported through the Assignments Subcommittee to MAC(G). Normally, only matters upon which the subcommittees could not agree received detailed consideration in the main ground committee. In turn, only when the MAC(G) could not agree were assignments referred to the MAB. Thus, a neat and logical hierarchy of assignments committees evolved, providing for Anglo-American consultation from the lowest to the highest level, with a

system of appeals similar to that of a judicial system.[46]

During 1941 the various schedules for defense aid deliveries had been projected for a year in advance but during 1942 this proved impossible. MAC(G) at first tried to make firm assignments for one month in advance and tentative assignments for the next two, but when the first American requirements for BOLERO were presented in May, the tentative assignments were dropped. At the insistence of the British, who contended they needed this much advance notice in order to plan the utilization of shipping and equipment, the tentative assignments were resumed in August. A plan for making assignments firm by quarterly periods was thoroughly studied by the committee at this time, but finally rejected. Nevertheless, efforts were made to assign certain large and bulky materials such as tractors and tanks by quarters.[47]

Assignments were made on the basis of estimates of the next month's production. If production either fell short of or exceeded estimates, adjustment had to be made. In order to provide for these adjustments on an equitable basis, MAC(G) adopted the method, already in use by the air committee, known as the block system. A "block" for a given item was normally set at an estimated week's production. As a convenient example, say that a week's estimated production of .30-caliber am-

---

[45] Min 606, 39th mtg MAC(G), 15 Jul 42; Min 660, 41st mtg, 30 Jul 42; Min 811, 45th mtg, 27 Aug 42; Min 849, 47th mtg, 2 Sep 42; Min 885, 48th mtg, 10 Sep 42; and Min 909, 49th mtg, 17 Sep 42.

[46] (1) Min 582, 37th mtg MAC(G), 9 Jul 42; and Min 1858, 89th mtg, 15 Apr 43. (2) For Engineer and Medical common stockpiles, see ID, Lend-Lease, I, 484–94, 524–25.

[47] (1) Min 749, 43d mtg MAC(G), 13 Aug 42; and Min 806, 45th mtg, 27 Aug 42, with Tab K. (2) See also, ID, Lend-Lease, I, 231–33.

munition was 100 million rounds. Each country interested was then assigned a certain quantity from each block in a certain order of priority. The first 20 million rounds might go to the United States, then 30 million to the United Kingdom, next 20 million to the USSR, and finally 30 million to the United States. If the first block, instead of being produced in a week, took ten days, everyone would share alike in the effects of the delay. If it were produced in five days, everyone would share in the accelerated production. When some emergency demand had to be met, wedges could be inserted between blocks. Suppose after the first block had been delivered, China had an urgent demand for .30-caliber ammunition and MAC(G) made the assignment. It would be inserted as a wedge before deliveries on the second block were begun.[48]

The block system could not be applied to all types of equipment, nor did it serve as a complete solution where it was. There was an inevitable tendency for operating divisions to give priority to special needs of U.S. forces, regardless of the transfer directives issued by the International Division. The division's efforts to put an end to this practice were never completely successful so long as demand exceeded supply.[49]

In connection with his agreement with General Weeks in November 1942, General Somervell worked out with British General Macready an adaptation of the block system to long-range assignments scheduling. Estimated yearly production of each article would be divided into a number of blocks, normally between 75 and 125. Each block would then be divided into subblocks for the United Kingdom, United States, the USSR, and China. The smaller countries for whom the United States was responsible would be included in the U.S. block, the dominions, colonies, and other countries in the British sphere in the United Kingdom block. In general, the size of each subblock would be determined by the proportion of the requirement of that nation to the total 1943 Army Supply Program. To provide a means whereby paramount operational needs of one country might be met, provision was made for exchange of subblocks or insertion of wedges. Under the new system of assignments, these adjustments would be the principal means by which MAC(G) would maintain a continuing relationship between assignments and operational plans.[50] The ground committee worked out the details, and this ingenious system was put into effect in February 1943. In practice it soon proved too rigid since strategic need continued to be the criterion for action, and MAC(G) reverted to its older practice of making firm assignments for one month and tentative assignments for two, within the over-all limitations of requirements accepted for each country in the Army Supply Program.

Whatever the theories of allocation, assignment by MAC(G), both before and after the Weeks-Somervell Agreement,

---

[48] (1) Min 82, 9th mtg MAC(G), 12 Mar 42. (2) Min 1(e)(iix), 8th mtg MAB, 25 Mar 42. (3) Ltr, Lt Col Willet J. Baird to P. I. Molchanov, Soviet Purch Comm, 28 May 42, ID 400.318 USSR Mis File.

[49] (1) Memo, ID for CofOrd, 24 Aug 42, ID 400.318, I. (2) Memo, Col Franks for ACofS for Materiel, 4 Sep 42, sub: Compliance of OCofOrd With Trf Dirs of MAC(G), ID 400.318 U.K., I. (3) Memo, Secy for Chm MAC(G), 2 Nov 42, tab to agenda for 57th mtg MAC(G), 5 Nov 42. (4) Min 1156, 57th mtg MAC(G), 5 Nov 42.

[50] (1) Ltr, Macready to Somervell, 27 Nov 42. (2) Ltr, Somervell to Macready, 28 Nov 42. Both in ID, Lend-Lease, Doc Suppl, III. (3) Memo, CG SOS for Chiefs of Sup Svs, 3 Mar 43, sub: Institution of a Block System of Asgmts, ID, Lend-Lease, Doc Suppl, V.

was an item-by-item problem. The factors influencing each decision were many and varied, and normally there were compromises at any and all of the various levels. Early in 1942 a relatively arbitrary decision was rendered that for the rest of the year all .30-caliber rifles should be allotted to the U.S. Army, while the British would receive all rifle production from a special .303-caliber line. The allocation of tractors, a type of equipment in critically short supply for both military and civilian purposes, had to be arranged by a permanent tractor committee, which planned production schedules and recommended allocations on a quarterly basis. A British request in midsummer 1942 for an increased allotment of 40-mm. antiaircraft Bofors guns to protect their cities against low-flying German aircraft ran the whole gantlet of committees and subcommittees before a typical compromise decision was rendered by the MAB.[51] Space does not permit consideration in detail of these and the manifold other individual assignments problems. A brief sketch of the allocations of tanks, the most important single item of ground equipment, will have to serve as an illustration of the problems and the way the assignments machinery met them.

A long lead time was required for tank production planning, making it necessary to tie allocations closely to production plans. The British were most dependent upon American production for tanks, their requirements making up almost half the entire American tank program. In March 1942, at the invitation of the War Department, the British sent a group of tank experts to Washington to meet with a U.S. tank committee in an effort to formulate a tank program for the next two years. The combined conference was charged with reduction of tank designs to

the fewest compatible with tactical requirements, determination of combat vehicle requirements for all theaters of operations, and adjustments in production necessary to meet these requirements. The Americans had already agreed among themselves that the principal item of tank production in the United States should be the M4 medium tank series (popularly designated the General Sherman), with a subsidiary production of light tanks. The British accepted this decision since the Sherman met their requirement for a "cruiser" tank to fulfill the mobile role in armored divisions. However, they also had large requirements for an "assault" tank—heavier and less mobile than the cruiser though armed with the same guns—which they thought necessary for use in support of infantry or in attack on fortified positions. The Americans agreed to develop experimental models of an assault tank, though their own doctrine recognized no need for the type. Since all parties agreed that strategy had not yet developed far enough to permit formulation of tank requirements on a theater basis, they were computed solely in bulk for the years 1942 and 1943. Lip service was paid to the President's tank production goals, but only by including therein all the various sorts of armored combat vehicles that used either the light or medium tank chassis.[52]

[51] (1) Min 211, 18th mtg MAC(G), 9 Apr 42. (2) Background papers in English Corresp Lend-lease 2 file; Misc Corresp Lend-lease 3 file; and Col Boone's file, DAD. (3) For a summary of the tractor problem, see ID, Lend-Lease, I, 458–67. (4) MBW 22, 11 Aug 42, title: Bofors Guns, Equip, and Am. (5) Memo, Gen Clay for Subcom MAB, 26 Aug 42, sub: Ground Com Case 29, AG 400.3295 (4-5-41) (1). (6) Min 2b, 30th mtg MAB, 26 Aug 42; Min 9b, 31st mtg, 2 Sep 42.

[52] (1) Findings and Final Minutes of the Joint British Tank Mission and U.S. Tank Committee, 30 Mar 42, Mis's Sec, Ord Hist files. (2) Memo, unsigned, no addressee, 13 Jan 42, sub: Decisions Taken and Ob-

TABLE 5—PROPOSED TANK PROGRAMS: 1942–43

Type of Tank and Year	Presidential Objective	Requirements Program, 1942			
		Total	United Kingdom	United States	Other
1942					
Total...........................	44, 500	24, 588	9, 277	6, 634	8, 677
Light...........................	19, 500	10, 588	3, 500	2, 534	4, 554
Medium........................	25, 000	14, 000	5, 777	4, 100	4, 123
Assault.........................	0	0	0	0	0
1943					
Total...........................	70, 000	51, 622	24, 743	24, 334	12, 545
Light...........................	20, 000	17, 044	1, 750	9, 734	6, 450
Medium........................	50, 000	35, 178	14, 493	14, 600	6, 085
Assault.........................	0	8, 500	8, 500	0	0

There were also U.S. requirements for 115 heavy tanks in 1942 and combined requirements for 770 aero tanks in each year. The presidential objective included 500 heavy tanks in 1942 and 5,000 in 1943. For simplicity's sake the table omits other sorts of combat vehicles, which made total figures match those of the presidential objective.

Source: Findings and Final Minutes of the Joint British Tank Mission and U.S. Tank Committee, 30 Mar 42, Mis's Sec, Ord Hist files.

These production planning estimates never became a satisfactory basis for allocations. The tank schedules agreed upon after the London and Moscow Conferences in 1941 were revamped by MAC(G) in February and extended to the end of June 1942. But the actual process of assignments became a month-by-month struggle over the newest and best types, the British basing their claims on their needs for the Middle East, and the Americans insisting on training their forces with the types they were expected to use in combat. It was not until July, and then at the behest of the British, that MAC(G) made any attempt to convert the tank conference plans into allocation schedules. The newly formed tank subcommittee then worked out schedules for the rest of the year in terms of the conference's production plans, and they were approved by MAB as "firm to the end of 1942." [53]

As early as October the "firm" plans began to crumble. For lack of priorities,

servations Made in Conf With . . . . (3) Memo, Aurand for Moore, 15 Jan 42, sub: Unsigned Memo Dated 13 Jan 42 . . . . Last two in G-4/31691-1. (4) Memo, ASW for Gen Moore, 16 Jan 42. (5) Memo, Somervell for Moore, 16 Jan 42. Last two in Gen Stf (1) 1941–42 folder, Hq ASF. (6) TAG ltr to Aurand, 6 Mar 42, sub: U.S. Tank Com, AG 334 U.S. Tank Com (3-6-42). (7) For light, medium, and assault tanks as approved at the conference, see Table 5.

[53] (1) Min 668, 41st mtg MAC(G), 30 Jul 42. (2) Min 163, 13th mtg MAC(G), 26 Mar 42; Min 183, 14th mtg, 30 Mar 42; Min 186, 15th mtg, 2 Apr 42; Min 264, 22d mtg, 24 Apr 42; Min 518, 35th mtg, 22 Jun 42; Min 533, 36th mtg, 2 Jul 42; Min 570, 37th mtg, 9 Jul 42. (3) Min 37, 7th mtg MAC(G), 26 Feb 42, with Tabs A and B; Min 40, 8th mtg, 9 Mar 42. (4) Agenda for 10th mtg MAC(G), 16 Mar 42. (5) Memo, Lt Col George H. Olmstead for CofOrd, 14 Aug 42, sub: Distrib of Light and Medium Tanks . . . , ID 470.8, I.

tank production had to be cut back considerably from agreed schedules for the last quarter of the year. The British accepted a cut in their light tank deliveries without protest and the principle of a proportionate reduction in medium tanks as well, but bitterly protested a decision of the MAC(G) to cut their assignments of the M4A2 type, which they considered the most suitable for desert warfare. The issue was finally settled by a compromise by which a number of M4A2 tanks destined for the USSR were diverted to the British, there being no means of immediately shipping them to Russia. The net result of all these shifting schedules, however, was that the British during 1942 got considerably fewer tanks than they had expected after the March conference, both in numbers and in terms of proportion of American production. Out of a total medium production of 12,936 (March forecast, 14,000) they received 4,526 (March forecast, 5,777), and out of a total light production of 10,947 (March forecast, 10,588) they received 2,331 (March forecast, 3,500).[54]

The downward revision of tank production schedules for 1943 had graver implications and created the only serious crisis of the Weeks-Somervell negotiations. At a second tank conference, held in London in August 1942, the British agreed to drop their requirements for 8,500 assault tanks, but asked that this figure be added to their 1943 requirements for mediums to make a total of 22,993. When General Weeks got to Washington in November he found that General Somervell was not ready to accept even half that figure. The President's goal of 50,000, Somervell calculated, would have to be reduced to 35,500. U.S. requirements were lowered to 9,000, the Soviet figure set at 4,500, other lend-lease at 2,000, self-propelled vehicles using the

medium tank chassis at 10,000, leaving 10,000 as the maximum figure for the British. General Weeks protested violently that 12,000 was the absolute rock bottom the British could consider, and asked that the production goal be set at 40,000. He hinted broadly in a letter to Somervell that he would ask Lyttelton to take the matter up with higher authorities. Incensed, Somervell, who insisted Weeks was asking the impossible, pointed out that the British, from their own and American production, were asking for double the number of tanks required by American forces. Through Harry Hopkins he appealed to the President to support the position taken by the War Department. There is no record of any decision by the President, except that in a letter to Churchill he suggested that both countries were underrating the need for medium tanks. The Weeks-Somervell Agreement stated both the British and the American positions, and stipulated that a review of the raw material situation should take place on 1 April 1943 with a view to determining if the goal of 40,000 could be met. In the interim, actual production would be assigned at a ratio of ten medium tanks for the British to nine for the Americans. Before April, a reduction in Soviet requirements made it possible to accept the British figure of 12,000 medium tanks

---

[54] (1) Min 1022, 53d mtg MAC(G), 8 Oct 42. (2) Memo, Chm MAC(G) for Exec Off MAB, 3 Nov 42, sub: Readjustment of 4th Quarter 1942 Asgmt Medium Tanks, MAB folder, Hq ASF. (3) Min 3a, 40th mtg MAB, 4 Nov 42; Min 5a, 41st mtg, 11 Nov 42. (4) Min 1184, 58th mtg MAC(G), 12 Nov 42; Min 1244, 63d mtg, 26 Nov 42; Min 1273, 64th mtg, 7 Dec 42. (5) See tables in Hist of Lend-lease Tanks 11 Mar 41–31 Dec 44 file, ID. (6) For production figures, see below, App. B. (7) See also below, Ch. XXI, for the tank problem re the Soviet Union.

for 1943 without any change in production plans.[55]

The Adjustment of Assignments and Shipping

In framing CCS 50/2, the planners deliberately chose to recognize strategic need as the basis for assignments rather than the availability of shipping as General Somervell had suggested in January 1942. This decision reflected a general agreement that shipping should not be allowed to dictate strategic requirements, but must rather be treated as one of the several governing factors determining their feasibility. The adjustment of assignments to shipping was left as a matter for the MAB and its committees to work out without any specific directive from the CCS. Since shipping allocations and arrangements were made by other agencies, neither the Army nor the MAB could control the volume of shipping available, nor, on occasions, even accurately estimate what it would be. They had therefore to proceed from the other end to adjust the rate of assignments to the availability of shipping on a short-term basis and to devise means to prevent accumulations of unshipped assignments.

The Army took the position that either goods should be shipped by the nation to whom they were assigned in a reasonable length of time or they should be repossessed for American use or assignment to some other lend-lease claimant. This policy was aimed not so much at increasing the Army's stocks as at keeping the ports clear, insuring an effort by foreign governments to expedite shipment, and providing a guide for future assignments in terms of ability to float.[56] The first policy promulgated by the War Department in January

uary 1942 provided for optional repossession by the U.S. Army of goods awaiting transport for more than thirty days. This system produced little more than confusion since the supply services did not at first understand it and were in no position to make the reports required; the time limit of thirty days proved too short in view of a shipping cycle that averaged forty-five to fifty days. Experience with the 30-Day Rule led General Aurand and General Somervell to recommend to MAB a 45-day time limit, with mandatory rather than optional repossession at the end of that period.[57]

In June a special committee of MAB decided on a more flexible policy and one more favorable to lend-lease recipients. Material held for forty-five days was to be reported for possible repossession, but the MAB would render an individual decision after reviewing the circumstances in each case. Under the procedure finally set up, the various supply services made biweekly

[55] (1) United States Technical Mission, Joint Report and Findings, 26 Aug 42, Mis's Sec, Ord Hist files. (2) Memo, Somervell for Hopkins, 11 Nov 42, Harry L. Hopkins folder, Hq ASF. (3) Ltr, Weeks to Somervell, 11 Nov 42. (4) Ltr, Somervell to Weeks, 12 Nov 42. (5) Ltr, Somervell to Gen Sir Walter Venning, Dir-Gen Br Ministry of Sup Mis, 26 Feb 43. Last three in Br folder, Hq ASF. (6) Min 1439, 69th mtg MAC(G), 7 Jan 43. (7) Ltr, Venning to Somervell, 18 Mar 43, ID 470.8 U.K., I. (8) On reduction in Soviet requirements, see below, Ch. XXI.
[56] Memo, Gen Clay for CG SOS, 19 Oct 42, sub: Opn of 45-Day Rule, ID 319.1 Rpts Storage, I.
[57] (1) Memo, USW for Chiefs of SAS, 3 Jan 42, sub: Trf of Def Articles to Foreign Govts, ID, Lend-Lease, Doc Suppl, II. (2) TAG ltr to Chiefs of SAS, 27 Feb 42, same sub, AG 681 (2-19-42). (3) Backing papers in Misc Stf Studies, Case Lend-lease 10A, DAD. (4) Memo, Aurand for all DAD offs, 24 Feb 42, sub: One Month's Accumulation of Sups. (5) Memo, Maj William W. Goodman, Chief of Progress Sec DAD, for Aurand, 5 Jun 42, sub: Unshipped Items Held Thirty Days or Longer. Last two in ID 319.1 Rpts Storage, I. (6) Min 372, 29th mtg MAC(G), 18 May 42; Min 378, 30th mtg, 21 May 42. (7) Min 5, 18th mtg MAB, 3 Jun 42.

reports to MAC(G) of material made available to foreign governments and not shipped within forty-five days of the notice of availability. MAC(G) then made recommendations to MAB for repossession, reassignment, or extension of the time for shipping, and the MAB, as in the case of the original assignments, rendered the final decision.[58] The 45-Day Rule was put into effect just at a time when congestion at the ports was becoming dangerous, and there can be no doubt that it played an important part in clearing up the situation. Yet it was the general application of pressure under the rule and not its literal interpretation or efficient operation that accomplished this result. The first reports rendered by the supply services were so flagrantly inaccurate that MAC(G) refused to make any positive recommendations on them. It was not until after the procedures had been streamlined within the SOS and special subcommittees set up within MAC(G) that reporting became sufficiently accurate to permit intelligent action.[59]

Even with improved reporting, there were other aspects of administration of the 45-Day Rule that made it a cumbersome method of accomplishing the purpose for which it was intended. Repossession of noncommon items seldom served any useful purpose, for they were usually designed and manufactured for one specific nation and could not serve another. Even on common items, material for lend-lease had to be physically segregated and given special markings and packing. Repossession then necessitated repacking, remarking, and sometimes transshipment all the way across the country to a new port of exit. Since, in accordance with MAB policy, assignments were usually made to replace any material repossessed, the

whole process took on a certain air of futility.[60] This situation led inevitably to leniency in the enforcement of the rule. The supply services usually gave a very liberal interpretation to the date of availability, from which the forty-five days were to be calculated, and excluded from the reports material about to be shipped even though it had been held too long. Processing through the munitions assignments machinery delayed the actual act of repossession to an average of from sixty-six to seventy-three days rather than the prescribed forty-five. The ground committee and the board granted frequent extensions of time where the circumstances seemed to justify it. Actual repossessions in the end were limited. On the other hand, the effect of the pressure exerted by the rule is exemplified by the gradual decrease in the number of items reported. At the end of October 1942 the SOS informed the MAB that the 45-Day Rule was fulfilling its fundamental purposes of effectively clearing ports and storage areas, diverting needed materials from storage to use, and assisting in establishing levels for assignment.[61]

The British did not share this satisfaction and looked on the rule with some misgivings. It was not always possible to provide shipping within the time limit prescribed, even when the requirement for a

[58] (1) Min 5, 19th mtg MAB, 10 Jun 42. (2) Min 462, 34th mtg MAC(G), 15 Jun 42; ltr, Aurand to Chiefs of Sup Svs, 10 Jun 42, sub: Reporting of Lend-lease Mat Not Floated for 45 Days, Tab B to min; and see also Tabs C and E to min. (3) Min 556, 36th mtg MAC(G), 2 Jul 42. (4) ID, Lend-Lease, I, 645–57.
[59] (1) See above, Ch. X. (2) ID, Lend-Lease, I, 647–48. (3) Min 514, 35th mtg MAC(G), 22 Jun 42. (4) Min, Hq ASF stf conf mtg, 26 Jun 42.
[60] (1) ID, Lend-Lease, I, 647–49, 659–61. (2) 1st Ind, MAB to MAC(G), 11 Jun 42, Tab E to min, 34th mtg MAC(G), 15 Jun 42.
[61] MBW 9/2, 31 Oct 42, title: Repossession of Equip Awaiting Shipt for More Than 45 Days.

British theater was a most urgent one. There were particular difficulties in floating very heavy equipment—large trucks, tank transporters, locomotives, tractors, tanks, and heavy engineer equipment—and it was in these very categories that the British were most dependent upon American production. They were engaged in supplying theaters in widely scattered parts of the globe—India, Africa, Australia, and the Middle East as well as the United Kingdom itself—and they preferred to ship directly from the United States to these outlying theaters rather than to transship via the British Isles. Sailings to some of these points were infrequent and it was exceedingly difficult to operate within the limits of the 45-Day Rule. Even though the Americans were lenient in its interpretation, there would always be cases where they might use the rule to repossess particularly critical items that both countries needed badly. Brigadier Campion in August proposed that the purposes behind the rule could be better achieved by regulation of assignments than by repossession. He suggested establishment of allowable cushions for each item, consisting of an estimated thirty days' to forty-five days' assignment. When unshipped material exceeded this cushion, then the next month's assignments should be curbed in proportion. These adjustments would be made on a short-term basis, with the long-term assignments to balance long-term requirements. There was a good deal of logic in the British proposal, but the Americans rejected it, evidently because the 45-Day Rule was just becoming effective and to institute a new system would produce administrative confusion. In connection with the Weeks-Somervell Agreement and the block system of assignments, General Macready again proposed that the 45-Day Rule be abolished and shipping adjustments made by the exchange of subblocks, but again the Americans would not agree.[62]

Nevertheless, the Americans did apply the cushion policy to motor vehicles, always the most serious backlog because of the large amount of space required for their shipment. Despite intensive efforts to promote economy in the shipment of motor vehicles, the unshipped backlog mounted constantly during the spring and summer of 1942. Consequently, when it became necessary in August to reduce lend-lease vehicular requirements in the Army Supply Program, General Clay moved to do so by using as a criterion the proven ability of the countries concerned to ship them. It was to implement this principle in making assignments that MAC(G) in September established allowable "cushions" or unshipped backlogs for each type of motor vehicle consisting of a normal one and a half months' assignment. By regulating the rate of assignment, this unshipped backlog was subsequently kept fairly constant. The British asked for a ninety-day cushion for all vehicles of five tons and over, but the MAB allowed it only for the very heaviest types—20-ton and 40-ton tank transporters.[63]

---

[62] (1) Memo, Br rep MAC(G) for Chm, 31 Jul 42, sub: 45 Day Rule, Tab 19 to agenda for 42d mtg MAC(G), 6 Aug 42. (2) Min 717, 42d mtg MAC(G), 6 Aug 42; Min 776, 44th mtg, 20 Aug 42. (3) Ltr cited n. 50(1).

[63] (1) Min 787, 44th mtg MAC(G), 20 Aug 42; Min 803, 45th mtg, 27 Aug 42; Min 1022, 53d mtg, 8 Oct 42; Min 1057, 54th mtg, 15 Oct 42. (2) Min 2b, 39th mtg MAB, 28 Oct 42. (3) Memo, Col Franks for Gen Clay, 29 Aug 42, sub: Wheeled Vehicle Pdn Reqmts for International Aid, ID 451.01, I. (4) Memo, Secy for Chm MAC(G), 29 Sep 42, sub: Repossession of Motor Vehicle Backlog, Tab B to min, 52d mtg MAC(G), 1 Oct 42. (5) Rpt of Subcom on Vehicles to 54th mtg MAC(G), 15 Oct 42.

British troubles in shipping heavy equipment led to other special exceptions. Locomotives and related rail transportation stores were exempted entirely from operation of the rule. In December 1942 the Americans moved aggressively to repossess quantities of road construction machinery assigned to the British for west Africa in order to meet needs for the Alcan Highway and the Persian Gulf. The resulting controversy was finally settled by an MAB compromise establishing a rule that the repossession date for heavy engineering equipment should be ninety days rather than forty-five where there was no other demand for the item, where it was manufactured to meet exceptional needs, or where, as in the case of west Africa, sailings were infrequent.[64]

A further exception to the 45-Day Rule was made on 1 May 1943 for ammunition. A "credit balance system" was established for ammunition under which it was not physically segregated on assignment but only when called forward to port for shipment. Issues were made by Ordnance depots against credits established by assignment. This system eliminated the necessity for repossession since ammunition remained under U.S. Army control until shipping was available, and it also eliminated a great deal of crosshauling and transshipment.[65] It was the most practical method of all for handling lend-lease transfers and adjusting them to shipping, but unfortunately it could only be applied to such bulk items as ammunition.

In no aspect of its operations did the Anglo-American machinery for allocations find that its decisions could be cut too closely to a pattern. Allocations had to be made on a short-term basis and guided by many varied factors, of which strategic need and shipping availability were usually the most important. Long-range requirements planning based on strategic plans never became the guide to assignments, both because of difficulties in resolving American and British views and because of the inherent difficulty in determining such requirements. Even bilateral agreements had to be adjusted to changing strategic conditions and production realities. Yet by the end of 1942, if the ideal theories of the early part of the year looking toward allocation of Anglo-American resources as a genuine common pool had proven inapplicable, still the assignments process as it evolved represented as practicable a version of pooling as could be devised as long as divergent national interests existed and each nation wished to maintain a certain measure of control over the disposition of its own resources. Granted that the British did not get as great a proportion of American production during 1942 as they had hoped, still most of their urgent strategic requirements were satisfied and munitions withheld played their part in preparing the U.S. Army for the great campaigns of the next two years.

[64] (1) Min 1290, 64th mtg MAC(G), 7 Dec 42; Min 1536, 75th mtg, 5 Feb 43. (2) Min 2a, 45th mtg MAB, 9 Dec 42; Min 4, 48th mtg, 10 Jan 43. (3) Memo, Col Franks for CG SOS, 8 Dec 42, sub: . . . Items for Consideration at 45th Mtg MAB, ID 334 MAC(G), I.
[65] ID, Lend-Lease, I, 438–43, 650–51.

CHAPTER XII

The Army's System of Requirements and Controlled Distribution

Two of the main ingredients that logistics contributes to the support of an army's operations are the weapons, equipment, and supplies used by forces at home and abroad, and the technical and administrative services that keep equipment operating and armies functioning. To the mechanisms by which the U.S. Army attempted to meet its requirements in matériel and service personnel in 1942, this chapter and the one that follows are devoted. The present chapter deals with the development of the system of formulating matériel requirements and the policies for controlling distribution of the scarcer categories of matériel within the Army. In the next, the focus shifts more explicitly to the methods and means of supporting military operations overseas.

The Army Supply Program

The emergence of a standardized, comprehensive Army Supply Program coincided roughly with that of the Army's new logistical organization.[1] General Somervell who, first as G-4 and then as chief of the Services of Supply, was in a position to influence the development of the program, set forth his ideas on the subject late in January 1942 while Goldthwaite Dorr's informal committee was making its study of War Department supply organization. The existing "expenditure programs," since August 1940 the basic periodic statement of the Army's supply requirements, were limited mainly to equipment, omitting such important categories of supply as construction materials, subsistence, fuel, and spare parts. Army-type matériel procured for the Navy and lend-lease was also omitted. The expenditure programs, finally, were short-range projections, tied to specific appropriations, and they indicated only terminal not intermediate objectives—that is, they did not schedule requirements. Somervell wanted to bring together in one program, drawn up in G-4, all the requirements for which the Army was responsible, and to make that program serve as a directive to the procuring agencies, as a basis for planning, and as a vehicle for defending appropriations before Congress.[2]

[1] See above, Ch. IX.
[2] (1) Memo, G-4 for DCofS, 22 Jan 42, sub: Army Supply Program, CofS WDGS 1941–42 folder, Hq ASF. (2) Goldthwaite H. Dorr, Memorandum Notes on the Activities of an Informal Group in Connection With Supply Reorganization in the War Department, January–May 1942, *circa* 1 Mar 46, pp. 7–8, OCMH. (3) S. M. Frank, The Determination of Army Supply Requirements, MS (hereafter cited as Frank, Army Supply Requirements), pp. 1–15 and Doc 8, OCMH. (4) Hq ASF, Background of the Army Supply Program (1944), pp. 11–14 and Chart 6B, Sp Reference Collection 102, DRB AGO.

The huge War Munitions Program of 11 February was not what Somervell had in mind; produced in haste, it set forth only ultimate objectives and omitted Army-produced Navy requirements and stocks on hand. But the immense labor of formulating the detailed long-range compilation described in Somervell's memorandum to General Moore was already in train. After the War Department reorganization of 9 March, the Requirements Division of the new Services of Supply took over the task of formulating the Army Supply Program. Its first emission, Section III covering miscellaneous and expendable supplies, appeared on 17 March; Section I, the most important, covering ground equipment, on 6 April, and Section II, air equipment, on 9 April, both exclusive of aircraft; Section V, construction materials, on 11 April; Section IV, air force supplies, on 4 July; and Section VI, miscellaneous noncommon items for lend-lease, on 1 September.[3]

At the outset, an important decision had to be made as to the proper basis for computing requirements for U.S. Army forces. War material would be used mainly and would be most needed in the theaters of war. To many, it seemed logical that requirements should be calculated primarily on the basis of the estimated needs of forces expected to be employed in the various theaters, with additional allowances for forces to be retained in line of communication areas and in the zone of interior, for replacement of losses, and for continuous resupply of expendable items. Since the preceding September, however, the American planners had consistently rejected this method, which the British favored, as a basis for determining interallied requirements, primarily because it would have favored British forces, already

extensively deployed overseas, at the expense of the training needs of American forces at home.[4]

To determine requirements by theater would also raise the obvious question of whether deployment and operations could in fact be planned one or two years in advance in sufficient detail for the purpose—or whether, indeed, they could be planned at all so far ahead. American planners doubted this. Under British pressure in March and April 1942 the American planners drew up projected deployment tables for U.S. troops to accompany the directive issued by the CCS late in March to govern munitions assignments.[5] OPD's comment somewhat later on these tables was that "these data do not represent in any sense U.S. Army requirements, nor do they represent firm requirements for any particular theater except as of this date and hour."[6] From the beginning of 1942 OPD issued a Weekly Status Map showing current and projected numerical strengths in each theater, and during the spring began to put out in addition an overseas troop basis showing Army units overseas by location and destination, and lists of units earmarked for movement overseas. All these projections were highly unstable, although for line of communication bases and inactive areas OPD could sometimes provide the supply staffs with

[3] (1) Frank, Army Supply Requirements, pp. 22–32 and Docs 20, 33. (2) The six sections were later reduced to four by combining the ground force sections (I and III) and the air force sections (II and IV) into one section each; Section VI then became III, and V became IV. See *Annual Report of the Army Service Forces, 1943*, p. 16. (3) For the War Munitions Program of 11 February, see above, Ch. VIII.

[4] See above, Chs. V, XI.

[5] CCS 50/2, 24 Mar 42, title: Dir for Asgmt of Mun, with apps. For discussion, see above, Ch. XI.

[6] Memo, OPD for Chm MAB, 12 Jun 42, sub: Reqmts for U.S. Theaters . . . , ID 334 MAB, I.

fairly stable figures on projected garrison strengths five or six months ahead. Predictions of forces to be in major theaters more than a few weeks ahead were only guesswork.[7] Referring to the overseas troop basis, an OPD officer irritably told an SOS representative "only a gullible person would take this publication seriously."[8] Supply planners were left in an unhappy dilemma for, as an SOS diary plaintively noted, "no further basis for supply planning for overseas theaters has been furnished by OPD."[9]

Instructions issued to the supply services in September 1942 for the computation of supply requirements included a provision to cover the needs of "task forces and special operational plans . . . wherever advanced planning permits."[10] But advanced planning, until late in 1943, did not so permit. A large part of these special requirements was for equipment and supplies of irregular issue (Class IV), primarily construction material, which could not be based on numbers of troops or types of units. Late in 1942 the first steps were taken toward formulating "operational projects" for certain theaters—plans for specific logistical undertakings, usually involving construction, with lists of equipment and material that would be needed if and when they were carried out. The operational project system did not embrace a significant proportion of total supply requirements until late in 1943; during 1942 the supply services either made "general estimates" of this type of requirements or no provision at all.[11] Some of the supply programs of 1942 did, however, include special provisions for specific items, such as cold weather clothing that would be needed only in particular areas, requirements being based on rough estimates of the number of troops to be so outfitted. Late in 1942 a substantial shift of emphasis in artillery procurement resulted from the General Staff's conclusion that lighter types would be more effective in jungle warfare.[12]

From spring of 1942 on General Somervell's planning staff also began, largely without guidance from the strategists, to explore the requirements of hypothetical future overseas operations in order to have ready-made bills of particulars to present if and when these operations should be undertaken. In August 1942 Somervell set up an office in his headquarters to handle this more or less speculative logistical planning—or "strategic logistics," as it was labeled—which, according to a later report, was "believed to be logical and in consonance with plans under consideration by the Joint and Combined Chiefs of Staff."[13] But these excursions in long-range planning by an agency the General Staff regarded as "operating" not "staff" were viewed with scant favor on levels higher than the SOS.

---

[7] (1) Cline, *Washington Command Post*, pp. 87, 129. (2) 1st Ind, Hq SOS for TQMG, 7 Apr 42, to memo, TQMG for CG SOS, 18 Mar 42, sub: Strength, Overseas Bases, QM 400 PC-WP.

[8] Plng Br SOS Diary, 25 Apr 42 entry, Plng Div ASF.

[9] *Ibid.*

[10] SOS Admin Memo 38, 16 Sep 42, sub: Proced for Determination and Admin of ASP, in Frank, Army Supply Requirements, Doc 26.

[11] (1) Memo, USW, for Chiefs of SAS, 5 Feb 42, sub: Equip Sec of ASP, WPD 4321-12. (2) G-4 off memo, Exec Off for named offs, 7 Apr 42, G-4/400. (3) History of the Planning Division, ASF, MS, Vol. I, Ch. XIII, OCMH.

[12] (1) Frank, Army Supply Requirements, Doc 39. (2) *Annual Report of the Army Service Forces, 1943*, pp. 20–21.

[13] (1) *Logistics in World War II*, p. 59. (2) History of the Planning Division, ASF, Vol. I, p. 11; Vol. II, Ch. XVI, OCMH. (3) Memo, Somervell for Lutes, 15 May 42, Misc Notes, Lutes File. (4) See above, Ch. IX.

In general, supply programs in 1942 and 1943 excluded theater requirements as such. They were submerged in total estimated needs of forces set forth without indication of their destined employment in the Victory Program Troop Basis. There were those who continued to regard this method as unrealistic, among them General Lutes who declared in September 1942, when shortages of equipment were creating a crisis in training and the equipping of task forces:

A requirements program based purely on an over-all troop basis will not meet war requirements. All the probable theater plans should have been used to build up a list of both ordinary and special requirements for each theater in order of priority, and a program of production and procurement initiated for that purpose, even if it appeared beyond the capacity of industry.[14]

Others, including Colonel Aurand, rejected both troop basis and theater plans as an avenue for determining total requirements. Aurand urged, instead, the establishing of desired proportions among the various types of munitions based on "the general view of the war [and] the theaters in which the war will be fought," and concentration, within these proportions, upon achieving a maximum monthly output.[15] But the weight of opinion among SOS staff officers, including Brig. Gen. Walter A. Wood, Jr., the director of Requirements Division, was that the over-all troop basis offered the most durable foundation on which to build a system of requirements. This was also Somervell's view. "Requirements cannot be measured or determined," he asserted, "by theaters of operation. It is the availability of trained and equipped troops, with ample over-all reserves, which will enable us to take the initiative."[16]

The Method of Calculating Requirements

Calculations based on a single troop basis were simpler than those based on a complex of overlapping and unstable theater plans, theater troop bases, special projects, and deployment schedules, but the process was intricate enough to absorb the full attention of a large staff in SOS headquarters and in each supply service. To calculate initial allowances of equipment was relatively simple, involving merely the multiplication of prescribed allowances of each item to each soldier or troop unit type by the total number of soldiers or of units of each type in the troop basis. Far more complex, uncertain, and arbitrary was the calculation of quantities of equipment needed for replacing losses and for filling the supply pipeline, and quantities of expendable material needed for continuous resupply.[17]

The calculation of maintenance requirements involved the use of a "maintenance factor," a percentage figure representing, for each item of equipment, the average rate per month at which it would have to be replaced after it had been put in the hands of its users, under all the hazards of deterioration, loss, destruction,

---

[14] Memo, Lutes for Somervell, 30 Sep 42, Misc Notes, Lutes File.

[15] Memo, Aurand for Somervell, 24 Jan 42, sub: Army Supply Program, MAB Orgn file, DAD.

[16] (1) Memo, Somervell for Burns, 15 Aug 42, sub: Relationship of WD to MAB and CPRB, MAB folder, Hq ASF. (2) Ltr, Gen Wood to Maj Gen Orlando Ward, 9 Sep 52, OCMH.

[17] During 1942 and most of 1943 the term "maintenance" was used to mean replacement of losses. It also was used throughout the war to refer to the care and repair of equipment. In a more general sense it referred to the continuous supply of expendable articles such as ammunition and fuel, as well as replacement of equipment; but "maintenance factor" was used only in connection with the latter. Late in 1943 the term "replacement" was officially adopted to designate the resupply of complete items in this sense.

and damage beyond repair. Most items had two maintenance factors, one (usually quite low) for use in the zone of interior, and one for use overseas. The theater maintenance factor, if applied to the total quantity of an item actually in a theater, would give the additional quantity that would have to be provided to replace losses there during an average month of use—for example, if an artillery piece had a maintenance factor of 3 percent and there were a hundred in the theater, three new pieces would have to be supplied each month. Actually in Army Supply Program calculations the theater maintenance factor was applied rather to the total initial issue of each item for the whole troop basis, and the resulting figure was multiplied by a given number of months, estimated as necessary to provide sufficient maintenance quantities to support all the forces expected to be overseas during the period of a year. Thus, in the above example (assuming a total initial issue of ten thousand and a prescribed three months of maintenance), nine hundred pieces would be provided in the Army Supply Program to make good expected losses in overseas theaters over a period of a year. A similar procedure was followed in computing zone of interior maintenance. The prescribed number of months in each case, it can be seen, was only an arithmetical expedient; the same results could have been produced by computing twelve months of maintenance for the forces expected actually to be in overseas theaters or in the zone of interior.

Closely related to the maintenance factor was the "day of supply," representing the average daily consumption of various expendable items of supply. For ammunition it was expressed in terms of rounds fired per weapon per day, as a general average for all theaters of operations; ammunition allowances for training in the United States were computed as a fixed number of rounds per year for a given number of troops, representing, of course, a far lower rate of expenditure than the theater day of supply. Food requirements were computed as multiples of the ration, the average quantity consumed by a single soldier in a single day. Fuel requirements were based on the estimated average daily consumption of each vehicle.[18] In the Army Supply Program the day of supply thus represented multiples of rounds, rations, and other units of measure.

Beyond the amounts of equipment and supplies that the Army needed to keep operating, additional amounts had to be produced to fill the pipeline. In order that there might be a pair of boots at hand to issue to a soldier overseas as soon as his old pair wore out, there must be boots at all times in theater depots, boots in transit, and boots in depots in the United States. These additional pipeline allowances were provided for in requirements computations during 1942 and part of 1943 by a "distribution factor," expressed as a percentage of total initial requirements.[19]

---

[18] The term, "day of supply," in the present context, was used for purposes of procurement requirements and referred to supplies only. The same term and the term "month of supply" were also used in a broader sense in distribution calculations referring to both supplies and equipment. Thus, thirty days of supply stocked in a depot might include quantities of all types of material sufficient to replace equipment losses and to maintain continuous resupply of the forces dependent upon the depot for that period of time. See below, App. F.

[19] (1) Contl Div, SOS, Instruction Manual for Computation of Section 1 of the Army Supply Program, January 1943, Reqmts folder, Logis File, OCMH. (2) Report of the War Department Procurement Review Board, 31 Aug 43 (hereafter cited as Report of WD Procurement Review Board), pp. 18–21, in WD, Levels of Supply and Supply Procedures, 1 Jan 44, Vol. I, Plng Div ASF, Job A47-192.

Thus, the entire "life span" of a rifle or a bullet or a K ration, from the time it emerged from a factory to its "death" through expenditure, loss, or wear, was anticipated in the calculation of requirements by two sets of factors—"pipeline" (distribution) factors, covering movement through the channels of supply, and "use" (maintenance and day of supply) factors, covering the periods of actual service. Pipeline factors, during 1942 and part of 1943, were a kind of insurance designed to set production at sufficiently high levels to pour munitions into the empty distribution system in greater volume than they were being spewed forth and expended at the other end. In time the pipeline would become full, and each bullet or replacement rifle needed in the combat zone could be drawn from stocks close at hand, which in turn could be replenished from stocks farther to the rear. When this stage was reached, the rate of flow through the pipeline would approximately match the rate of expenditure, and procurement for the pipeline could safely be stopped. With a full and flowing pipeline, sudden losses or increased expenditure could be absorbed for a time by accumulated reserves; if the trend persisted, production could again be expanded. In 1942, however, large segments of the pipeline were void, most theater stocks were at low levels, and the "leakage" of ship sinkings along the ocean gap, where supplies could not be stocked at all, threatened to dry up the flow altogether. For many a needed item, troops overseas had to reach back all the way to a factory in the United States.

Both pipeline and use factors, in most instances, were established separately for individual items or groups of items. Ammunition for each weapon had its own day of supply, with a percentage breakdown by types (armor-piercing, tracer, and so forth); the day of supply for fuel and food, on the other hand, was less differentiated. Maintenance factors were established for many individual items of equipment, though they tended to be identical for broad classes. Distribution factors, generally for classes rather than individual items, ranged from 5 to 90 percent in the supply programs of 1942 and early 1943.[20]

The factors were not differentiated horizontally, as they were vertically. Separate factors were employed for use in the zone of interior and the theaters, but otherwise each pipeline and use factor represented a weighted average of the probabilities covering all the demands that might have to be met throughout the entire process of distribution or use. Ideally, each weighted average should have been arrived at through scientific study of a wide range of experience data together with careful analysis of probable future conditions, but the uncertainty of strategic plans in 1942 ruled out systematic study of the specific conditions of climate, terrain, and intensity of action to which material might be subjected in future campaigns. As for the lessons of past experience, technical analysis in 1941 and 1942 of the performance of material in the field only nibbled at the edge of the problem. Theater commanders were lax or sporadic in reporting on the performance of matériel under combat conditions and were inclined generally to overemphasize

[20] Report of the War Department Special Committee for Restudy of Reserves, 13 Nov 43, p. 56, in WD, Levels of Supply and Supply Procedures, I, cited n. 19(2).
For authorized levels of supply and content of the unit of fire and day of supply of ammunition, see below, App. F.

data based on short periods of combat, when attrition was heavy, in recommending weighted average use factors. Until late in 1943 ammunition expenditure tables used in the field (except those for antiaircraft ammunition) were based on "such statistics as are available from World War [I] sources."[21] In the day of supply tables used for procurement planning, certain changes had been made before 1942—for example, increases for small arms ammunition to reflect wider use of automatic weapons—but for the most part the tables continued to reflect the experience of World War I.

Pipeline factors were similarly uncertain. The time normally required to move war material through certain portions of the pipeline could be measured and averaged with fair precision—for example, fifteen days in transit time in the United States, forty-five days for movement to the theater. But the rate of movement through the theater distribution system was less predictable, and only arbitrary allowances could be made for abnormal losses and delays and disruption of communications by enemy action. For ship sinkings, in fact, a separate allowance of about 2.5 percent was made during 1942, over and above the separate distribution factors. And in the last analysis pipeline factors necessarily reflected the inaccuracy of use factors, since these had to be employed in computing the actual quantities to be stocked in theater and zone of interior depots and to be kept moving between storage points, even though the total requirements set up in the supply program for distribution purposes were computed as flat percentages of initial allowances.[22]

As official instructions early in 1943 admitted, pipeline and use factors were no more than "reasonable assumptions."

Experience data are not yet available in quantities sufficient to permit the actuarial determination of these factors . . . Both maintenance and distribution factors represent the resultant of a number of variable factors which can neither be determined nor predicted in advance. The relative effect of each variable upon the overall factors is continually shifting.[23]

It was the task of the supply services, under the supervision of SOS Requirements Division, both to determine pipeline and use factors for the items of supply each procured and to keep these factors under continuous study. The results were not encouraging. A special board reviewing the methods of determining requirements in the summer of 1943 pointed out that, after a year and a half of war, distribution factors were still set arbitrarily, and maintenance and day of supply factors, which "were originally assumptions and still are," were no more than "knowledgeful estimates and educated guesses."[24]

Development of the Army Supply Program in 1942

During 1942 the Army Supply Program, as expected, proved to be highly unstable. The troop basis, to which it was tied, was in a state of flux. In May the President authorized an increase of 750,-000 men for the current year, primarily to meet the demands of the European invasion plan; by November another 650,-000 had been added, largely recognizing

[21] FM 101-10, Staff Officers' Field Manual: Organizational, Technical and Logistical Data, Jun 41, par. 93. This manual was revised for instructional purposes in November 1942, and was revised and republished in October 1943.
[22] (1) Report of WD Procurement Review Board, pp. 17-21, 33-44. (2) Rpt, pp. 45-63, cited n. 20.
[23] Instruction Manual cited n. 19.
[24] Report of WD Procurement Review Board, pp. 46-49; first quote from p. 48, second from p. 46.

overdrafts already made, and bringing the ceiling for 1942 to about 5 million. Some of these increases were advance drafts on the 1943 troop basis. In November 1942 the 1943 ceiling was fixed at about 8.2 million, including officer strength, or 7.5 million enlisted men, far below the 8.9 million contemplated by the Victory Program early in the year. Within these numerical fluctuations the internal composition of the troop basis changed frequently and radically, abandoning the earlier emphasis on armor and building up combat and service support, while reducing the planned total of divisions and expanding air power generally at the expense of ground combat forces. At the end of 1942 the troop basis envisaged a ground army of only one hundred divisions, instead of the two hundred or more in earlier plans; the original goal of sixty-seven armored divisions had dwindled to twenty. In mid-1942 the chief of OPD confessed:

> We cannot figure now what troops we will need six months from now, or where we will have to use them. . . . no one should get the impression that we could set up a theoretical troop basis and stick to it for any length of time. . . . the desire of everyone to have some fixed goal to operate toward [is natural] but in this war it [is] impossible to establish any fixed troop basis.[25]

It had been intended that the whole Army Supply Program would be recomputed annually, but during the first four months of 1942 four sections had to be revised completely to keep pace with changes in the troop basis and allowance tables and to reflect limitations in raw materials (such as rubber) and plant facilities. In September quarterly revisions were directed. In ground army requirements, the most important interim changes were the revisions of the ground equipment program on 29 May and 1 September.[26]

The generally downward trend of the ground Army's requirements in supply programs during 1942 owed something to successive eliminations of "cushions" that had padded the program against unforeseen contingencies. Requirements for some initial-issue equipment were reduced across the board, though not below what was considered a safe level for the number of troops expected actually to be under arms. Thus, in the 6 April revision of the equipment program, essential items (readily procurable or replaceable by substitutes) to be issued in 1943 only were computed on the basis of the 6 million troops expected to be under arms, rather than the more theoretical Victory Program goal of 8.9 million. In the 1 September program a similar basis was used, but the number of expected activations by then had risen. Some potential fat was removed in the form of allowances for maintenance and for resupply of expendable items. The cuts in initial issues mentioned above automatically brought about proportionate reductions in total allowances for maintenance. Beyond this, allowances for combat (theater) maintenance, based originally on highly inflated deployment estimates, were successively reduced, first by using more realistic estimates of terminal overseas strength, and later by using estimated average overseas strengths for each year. In the case of miscellaneous and expendable supplies, an effort was made to estimate the forces to be deployed to various climatic areas in order to eliminate such obvious anomalies as procure-

---

[25] (1) Min, WD Gen Council mtg, 31 Jul 42. (2 Greenfield, Palmer, and Wiley, *AGF I*, pp. 198–217 and table "Ground Forces in the Army, Decembe 1941–April 1945." (3) Report of WD Procuremen Review Board, p. 8.

[26] (1) Frank, Army Supply Requirements, Doc 4! (2) CPA, *Industrial Mobilization for War*, p. 274.

ment of skis and mittens for troops serving in tropical climes.[27]

This method of reducing over-all requirements was employed, on the whole, with caution during 1942. Maintenance requirements in the 1 September program, while using average overseas strengths, based these in turn on a projected terminal overseas strength for 1943 of 3 million at a time when no more than 2.6 million, at the outside, seemed likely to be deployed. Somervell, defending these estimates, argued that a radical shift in the military situation, such as an Allied collapse in the Middle East or USSR, would have the effect of concentrating American overseas operations in less distant theaters, thus permitting a larger deployment. "We would be remiss in our planning," he advised the Chief of Staff, "if we did not have available adequate and appropriate forces, and the required munitions to take advantage of every reasonable contingency."[28] The Army Supply Program, by early autumn, had shrunk considerably from the massive proportions of the February War Munitions Program. Substantial cuts had been made in capital allowances. In the 1 September program initial issues of critical items other than rifles had been slashed by 50 percent for units in training in 1942, thus conforming to current distribution policy. A similar reduction was later applied to units to be activated in 1943. Unit tables of equipment allowances had been streamlined to a certain extent, especially in motor transport, reducing supply requirements. Perhaps the largest single reduction resulted from the radical curtailment of armored components in the troop basis; an armored division was estimated to require roughly five times as much matériel as an infantry division. Despite these economies, the ef-

fort to provide for "every reasonable contingency" had produced a supply program which in September was still far from austere. For the ground army this was fortunate, for it was to bear the brunt of the major cuts in war supply programs ordered in November.[29]

The Distribution of Scarce Material

Competition for scarce items of material began long before they issued from production and continued throughout the process of distribution. The first assignment of a scarce item was often not the last. In emergencies, such as that in Egypt in summer of 1942, equipment might be snatched from American units and shipped overseas to arm other Allied forces, and lend-lease equipment already transferred to one country might be diverted to other recipients. Within the Army in the States, equipment often passed through many hands. Indeed, the basic problem of distribution within the Army for a year and a half after Pearl Harbor was one of redistribution. Under pressing shortages the mounting of a task force or even the sending of a unit overseas often was possible only by taking equipment from other units, regardless of the impact upon their training.

The scarcer items of equipment and supplies, before and after Pearl Harbor, were distributed under an elaborate mechanism of central controls and prior-

---

[27] Frank, Army Supply Requirements, Docs 22, 23, 31, 32, 38–42, 44, 49.

[28] Memo, Somervell for CofS, 22 Sep 42, sub: JPS Dir, JPS 57/1/D, CofS WDGS 1942 folder, Hq ASF.

[29] (1) Frank, Army Supply Requirements, Docs cited n. 27. (2) *Annual Report of the Army Service Forces, 1943*, p. 19. (3) For the supply cutbacks of November 1942, see below, Ch. XXII. (4) For tank programs in 1942, see above, Ch. XI. (5) For reductions in equipment allowances, see below, Ch. XXIII.

ities. The most critical items were classified as "controlled," a term circularly defined as "important items which are distributed direct to organizations by the War Department according to approved priorities." Controlled-item lists were drawn up by each supply service and consolidated first by the War Department and, after March 1942, by the SOS. Growing abundance tended to shorten the lists, technological advance to lengthen them, and shifts of procurement responsibility from one service to another involved much reshuffling of items. During 1942 some of the lists dwindled, notably those for Quartermaster and Chemical Warfare items, but the general trend until spring of 1943 was to add more controlled items. The total list rose from about 400 early in 1942 to almost 800 in spring of 1943; thereafter it shrank, until in mid-1945 it numbered 130.[30]

"Credit" items, a less critical category, were distributed in fixed amounts to corps area depots, where quotas were established to the credit of units and installations in the corps areas and drawn upon by requisition, usually for a fixed period of time. This system was essentially a quota system, designed to ensure equitable distribution; the controlled-item system aimed rather at distribution according to urgency, under priorities that usually were highly inequitable from the standpoint of those who did not benefit by them. The credit system lingered on during the war period, and the credit method, in a broader sense, was used in a variety of ways—for example, in allotments placed at the disposal of the Army Air Forces by the Chief of Ordnance for certain weapons of common use. On occasion credit items were even placed under priorities, but the main trend, especially from

1943 on, was to transfer controlled items to the credit list, thus decentralizing distribution controls.[31]

On the eve of Pearl Harbor distribution policy for controlled items recognized two broad categories of recipients in the Army—units entitled to full authorized allowances (Group A), and units that were to be issued controlled items in order of priority in three successive installments, bringing them in turn up to 20, 50, and finally 100 percent of authorized allowances (Group B). Interpreted literally, this policy would have left little or no scarce equipment for units below the upper brackets of Group A; actual distribution during 1941 was governed by ad hoc considerations. As a general rule, initial issues of controlled equipment were made automatically; replacement was by requisition.[32]

Immediately after Pearl Harbor priorities were rearranged to give preference (a) to troops about to go overseas, together with forces in the Philippines; (b) to those air combat forces, with accompanying services, for which aircraft were immediately available; (c) to Hawaii and Panama; (d) to antiaircraft defenses in the United States; (e) to Atlantic and Caribbean garrisons; and (f) to west coast forces, including those in Alaska. Units going overseas and the air combat and

[30] (1) WD ltr, 30 Dec 40, sub: Current Sup Policy and Proced, AG 475 (12-27-40). (2) Distrib Div, ASF, History of Supply in the Zone of Interior, MS, 1946, pp. 2–8, OCMH. (3) Contl Div, ASF, Rpt 97, Distribution of Controlled Items of Equipment, Mar 43.
[31] (1) WD ltr, 25 Apr 42, sub: Credit Items of Equip, AG 381 (4-23-42). (2) WD ltr cited n. 30(1). Another category, "supervised" items, included certain equipment numbered serially, overlapping the other two categories; subordinate commanders were responsible for certain procedures in their distribution and use.
[32] WD ltr, 24 Sep 41, sub: Distrib of Controlled Items, AG 400 (9-13-41).

antiaircraft forces were to be equipped with controlled items from current production and, if necessary, by transferring equipment from units in Group B. Early in February Group B was broken into two categories, B and C, the latter providing a pool from which most equipment transfers were to be made. The general policy in making transfers was to draw on units in a widening circle from the unit being equipped, exploiting first the lower priority units in the corps area where the beneficiary unit was stationed, as recommended by the army commander, and then low priority units in other corps area. On the west coast the commanding general of the Western Defense Command (which included the Ninth Corps Area) was authorized to make transfers at discretion among all units under his command, but even his units were subject to the overriding priority of troops shipping out from San Francisco. Remaining forces in Group A were to be equipped as far as possible from stock or current production.[33]

During December and January the effort to arm troop transports on the Pacific coast and to equip troops sailing from Pacific coast ports seriously depleted the defenses in that area. General De Witt, the army commander there, warned the War Department at the end of December that he was being obliged to strip his own troops of ammunition, rifles, machine guns, and artillery pieces.

I am obeying my orders literally and I will not let the troops [sailing for overseas] go without this equipment, if it takes every gun I have, but you must remember that I have both an internal and an external threat here. . . . this situation has gotten to the point now where I must have my replacement materiel . . . in order that I may have something effective with which to carry out my mission.[34]

Early in January he wrote that his antiaircraft units had only enough small-caliber ammunition for about six to eight minutes' firing. When he telephoned the War Department a few days later, General Moore told him that "it's just a desperate situation."[35]

As late as mid-March the forces on the west coast had received little replacement matériel, but by then the area seemed in no immediate danger. Early in February the Western Defense Command had been dropped to a C-8 priority for distribution of controlled items. Henceforth the sharpest competition for scarce matériel was between forces going or already overseas and those in training in the United States. Throughout 1942 the War Department was torn between two conflicting urges: to concentrate upon equipping forces for early shipment overseas, or to spread equipment more thinly in an effort to build up as rapidly as possible reserves for future offensives.

The priority structure necessarily favored troops being sent overseas, as the more urgent demand, although the shortage of shipping and the slow pace of training, in addition to lack of equipment, placed limitations upon the number of troops that could be deployed. On the presumption (not always warranted) that any unit already overseas was reasonably well outfitted, overseas theaters and bases

[33] (1) WD ltr, 22 Dec 41, sub: Distrib of Controlled Items of Equip. (2) WD ltr to CG Western Def Comd, 22 Dec 41, same sub. (3) WD ltr, 12 Dec 41, same sub. All in AG 400 (12-17-41). (4) WD ltr, 4 Feb 42, same sub, AG 400 (2-1-42).
[34] Telephone msg, Gen De Witt to Gen Malony, 30 Dec 41, G-4/33819.
[35] (1) Telephone msg, Gen De Witt to Gen Moore, 7 Jan 42, Telephone Convs 1942 folder, G-4. (2) Corresp in G-4/33819 and G-4/31793. (3) Memo, Somervell for CofS, 4 Feb 42, sub: Shortages of Rifles, CofS WDGS 1941-42 folder, Hq ASF.

were placed in a lower priority for shipments of controlled material than troops being sent or about to be sent there. Early in 1942 the troops in the Philippines were the only forces overseas in an A-2 priority, the one assigned to units sent overseas. In June all overseas forces were placed in an A-6 priority, arranged generally to give active areas precedence over inactive ones; in November, following the landings in North Africa, the former category was elevated to an A-2-*b* category, immediately below that for troops moving overseas. The precedence given troops moving to a theater over troops already there caused difficulties. Except when special arrangements were made to the contrary, units that sailed without all their authorized equipment—and there were many such in 1942—might wait for it for weeks or months after arriving overseas while troops following them arrived fully equipped. "It appears to me," noted an SOS staff officer in May 1942, "that it is silly to equip units going overseas with 100 per cent of controlled items when there are other units actually in the area ready to fight, with less . . . ."[36] But not until early in 1943 were overseas theaters and bases given a higher priority than outbound units.[37]

Troops in training and newly activated were spread over the remainder of the priority structure in 1942, below the relatively small number of units about to go overseas and those already overseas. In the competition for ammunition, training received short shrift. Peacetime allowances of ammunition for training were larger in the U.S. Army than in any other army in the world, but in the crisis following Pearl Harbor they were cut to the bone. No .50-caliber ammunition at all was allotted to ground forces in training;

"absolutely essential" Air Corps training claimed all that could be spared from the forces overseas. Caliber .30 ammunition was reduced to 40 percent of prescribed allowances. Artillery officers, their normal allowances reduced by a third, were directed in the spring to "fire a simulated problem each day . . . using a matchbox, sandtable, some sort of terrain board, or any other expedient . . . ."[38] Many further cuts were made during 1942. Ammunition was also doled out to departing task forces and overseas theaters and bases in quantities smaller than their commanders thought safe, but sometimes in excess of actual needs. In spring of 1943, while General McNair was pleading for sufficient ammunition to allow ground troops to qualify in firing their individual weapons, almost a billion and a half rounds of small arms ammunition were piled in depots and dumps in North Africa.[39]

Motor vehicles, being particularly essential to training, were authorized for all units, in the initial issue, up to 50 percent of allowances, and ground combat troops were supposed to receive full allowances in the sixth month of training (normally

---

[36] Note for rcd only, with memo, Dir of Opns SOS for Chiefs of Svs, 11 May 42, sub: Controlled Items of Equip in Overseas Bases, 400.3 Distrib of Sups and Equip folder, Plng Div ASF, Job A44-140.

[37] (1) WD ltrs, 4 Feb, 8 Mar, 23 Apr, 27 Jun, and 9 Nov 42, sub: Distrib of Controlled Items of Equip with priority lists, AG 400 series. (2) WD ltr, 14 Feb 43, same sub, AG 400 (2-9-43). (3) For supply of forces overseas and forces moving overseas, see below, Ch. XIII.

[38] Robert R. Palmer, Bell I. Wiley, and William R. Keast, *The Procurement and Training of Ground Combat Troops*, Vol. II of the subseries The Army Ground Forces in UNITED STATES ARMY IN WORLD WAR II (Washington, 1948) (hereafter cited as Palmer, Wiley, and Keast, *AGF II*), p. 555.

[39] (1) Ltr, Gen Marshall to Sir John Dill, no date, OPD 400 Sups and Equip, 1. (2) Palmer, Wiley, and Keast, *AGF II,* pp. 464–65. (3) For overseas supply of ammunition, see below, Ch. XIII.

the beginning of advanced unit training). Even more favorable provisions were made, in the second half of 1942, for air force and antiaircraft units. It was further hoped that pools of new vehicles of standard, general-purpose types could be built up in overseas theaters; departing units would take with them only their administrative and special vehicles. Equipment that the units turned in could be used again for training, and old-model vehicles could eventually be relegated exclusively to administrative uses in the United States. Throughout 1942, however, training continued to depend on used, old-model, and substitute types. Much of the supply of new vehicles went to outfit task forces (which took their vehicles with them), and into foreign aid. Substantial numbers were shipped crated to the British Isles for U.S. forces there.[40]

To newly activated units most controlled equipment was initially issued up to 20 percent of authorized allowances, and a second issue was intended to bring the level up to 50 percent; both issues were made in the established priorities. But prevailing shortages postponed the second issue to many units for months, and units far down on the priority list often received only part of their initial training issue. In February 1942, in order to give the most important combat units a start in life and to protect them from being stripped bare by transfers to departing troops, newly activated infantry divisions were designated as "training" divisions and given an A-9 priority to receive half their authorized allowances of controlled equipment. A-9 stood near the bottom of the A Group, below units going overseas, garrisons overseas, and most of the combat forces in the States, but training divisions took precedence, for their 50 percent al-

lowances, over a long list of service units and a few combat units in the A Group, not to mention the large number of older units in B and C Groups. For their remaining allowances of controlled equipment the new training divisions took only a very low C priority, below the nine other divisions in C Group. They were, however, expressly shielded from transfers for the benefit of all other categories of units except those scheduled for immediate departure overseas, and they were less exposed even to this risk than a mass of less favored B and C units.[41]

These arrangements were modified from time to time in subsequent months, but training divisions continued to enjoy a favored status. Even with favored treatment, however, none of the divisions activated during the spring and summer received full training allowances on schedule or for many weeks afterward. As General Lutes observed in August, "The original conception of training divisions no longer exists. It might be said there are no training divisions or that all divisions are training divisions."[42]

---

[40] (1) WD ltr, 6 Jun 42, sub: Sup and Distrib of Automotive Vehicles, AG 400 (6-5-42). (2) WD ltr, 9 Aug 42, same sub, AG 400 (8-7-42). (3) WD Memo W850-19-42, 27 Nov 42, same sub. (4) WD ltr, 27 Jun 42, sub: Distrib of Controlled Items of Equip, AG 400 (6-16-42). (5) WD ltr, 9 Nov 42, same sub, AG 400 (11-5-42).

[41] (1) WD ltr cited n. 33(4). (2) WD ltr, 19 Feb 42, sub: Distrib of Controlled Items of Equip to Tng Divs, and amendment of 1 Mar 42, AG 400 (2-16-42). (3) Memo, G-4 for G-3, 13 Feb 42, sub: Minimum Tng Allowances of Critical Items. (4) Note for rcd only, with memo, G-4 for TAG, 1 Feb 42, sub: Distrib of Controlled Items of Equip. Last two in G-4/31793.

[42] (1) Memo, Lutes for G-3, 18 Aug 42, sub: Policy Governing Distrib of Controlled Items. (2) See also, memo, Lutes for G-3, 24 Aug 42, same sub. Both in AG 400 (8-10-42) Sec 1. (3) WD ltr, 23 Apr 42, sub: Distrib of Controlled Items of Equip, AG 400 (4-8-42). (4) WD ltr cited n. 40(4).

Moreover, the favoring of new divisions with respect to scarce equipment merely shifted the burden elsewhere—to the older divisions in training and to the growing number of nondivisional units. Stripping units in training, General Marshall wrote near the end of March, "will wreck the morale of the troops involved and undermine public confidence."[43] AGF staff officers, making field inspections during the summer, sent in gloomy reports of the losing struggle to carry out realistic training with meager equipment. Units in the 26th Division, supposedly well advanced in training, had twenty-nine of their forty-five authorized antitank (37-mm.) guns at the end of March; seven more were taken away to equip a division moving overseas. The 101st Cavalry Regiment, with only 3 of an authorized 28 antitank guns on hand, had to give up even these 3, in addition to 39 of its 73 .30-caliber machine guns (138 authorized), and 7 of its 41 .50-caliber machine guns (124 authorized).[44]

Nondivisional units, especially service units, were hit much harder. Even more dependent than infantry divisions upon equipment for training in their special functions, nondivisional units stood below them in every priority subgroup. Signal communications troops could learn little of their technical functions without radio sets and telephone switchboards, and maintenance units could scarcely gain practical experience without equipment to service. One Signal Corps unit reported in the summer of 1942 that "equipment received consists largely of many items which cannot be used for training purposes without the receipt of key items such as telephones, switchboards, etc."[45] Service units generally were far worse off than combat units with respect to basic weapons; a Quartermaster battalion late in

1942 had only 284 rifles for 1,113 men. General Lutes warned G-3 in August:

All units require some equipment for training. The insistence that "training" divisions receive 50 per cent of controlled items of equipment . . . often precludes nondivisional units from receiving any of the common items. The training of these nondivisional units is of equal importance but is jeopardized in order that divisions may be given the presently prescribed 50 per cent.[46]

In effect, the policy for distributing scarce equipment was to treat the mass of units of all types in training as a large pool from which to equip units and task forces going overseas, with mitigating provisions designed to shield air force units and certain ground combat units, particularly newly activated divisions, from being stripped. It was not an easy policy to enforce. Effective control depended on centralization of responsibility, which was inimical to speed of operation and to administrative efficiency. Authority to order transfers of controlled equipment among units in the United States rested with the three major commands and the defense commands; the SOS administered the process and it alone could delegate transfer responsibility within its own establishment. All transfers were supposed to be reported immediately to the appropriate supply services, which kept the records of

[43] Ltr cited n. 39(1).

[44] (1) Palmer, Wiley, and Keast, *AGF II,* p. 456. (2) Memo, Dir of Opns SOS for CofOrd, 13 Apr 42, sub: Replacement of Controlled Items, 400.3 Distrib of Sups and Equip folder, Plng Div ASF, Job A44-140.

[45] Palmer, Wiley, and Keast, *AGF II,* pp. 555–57; quote is from p. 556.

[46] (1) Memo cited n. 42(1). (2) Memo cited n. 42(2). (3) Memo, G-3 for G-4, 13 Mar 42, sub: Distrib of Controlled Items, WDGCT 400 (3-13-42). This directed SOS to issue controlled items to units in each group and subgroup in the order of AAF, AGF, SOS. (4) See also, WD ltrs cited n. 40(4), n. 42(3), and WD ltr, 8 Mar 42, cited n. 37(1).

controlled items (transfers of air matériel were reported to the Air Service Command). General Staff approval, besides, was required for any transfers from units in Groups A or B. Various additional restrictions were also placed on transfers of certain categories, such as tanks, antiaircraft weapons, Garand rifles, carbines, and motor vehicles.

But, in preparing troop units for movement overseas, the three major commands and the defense commands from the end of June onward were permitted, in the interests of speed, to delegate transfer authority along with other preparatory processes to their field commands. In practice, moreover, most transfers of controlled equipment in the latter half of 1942 were made to units going overseas, and therefore by field agencies exercising delegated authority, usually under the heavy pressure of imminent departure dates.[47] In these circumstances it was difficult for SOS to supervise effectively the distribution of controlled items. Both Air and Ground Forces repeatedly sought to have transfer authority delegated more broadly for purposes other than overseas movement, and there were numerous deviations from prescribed procedures. Commanders of ground units, senior in rank to the post commander, sometimes used their seniority to force the latter to transfer to them equipment already earmarked for another unit. AGF staff officers sometimes negotiated directly with a supply service, bypassing SOS headquarters, in an effort to obtain arsenal or depot stocks instead of robbing their own units.[48]

In November 1942 the prohibiting of delegation of authority was relaxed. Almost immediately the chiefs of the supply services began to complain that field agencies of AGF and AAF were either not reporting transfers, or reporting them so late that issues of controlled items were duplicated and control was lost. Early in January 1943, accordingly, the three major commands and the defense commands were again enjoined from delegating transfer authority, except as prescribed in current procedures for equipping units going overseas. The old difficulties immediately reappeared. An SOS staff report in March stated ". . . authority to transfer . . . is being usurped or delegated and the transfers are not reported."[49]

The Equipment Crisis and the Emergency Pool

During the summer and fall of 1942 the equipment problem became critical. First the flow of troops to the British Isles and then the mounting of the North African task forces, coincident with heavier deployment to the Pacific, stripped the Army of available trained units and in the process brought a hurly-burly of equipment

---

[47] (1) WD ltr, 2 Apr 42, sub: Current Sup Policy and Proced, AG 475 (4-1-42). (2) WD ltr, 10 Jun 42, same sub, AG 475 (6-7-42). (3) WD ltr, 8 Mar 42, cited n. 37(1). (4) WD ltrs cited n. 40(4), n. 40(5), and n. 42(3). (5) For troop movement procedures, see below, Ch. XIII.

[48] (1) Memo, Dir of Opns SOS for Chiefs of Svs, 1 May 42, sub: Trf of Controlled Items. (2) Memo, Dir of Opns SOS for Distrib Sec, 22 Jun 42, sub: Ord Sup. Both in 400.3 Distrib of Sups and Equip folder, Plng Div ASF, Job A44-140. (3) 1st Ind, Hq SOS to CG AAF, 20 Oct 42, 400 Sup Gen folder, Plng Div ASF, Job A44-140. (4) Memo, Hq SOS for Chiefs of Svs, Corps Area Comdrs, CofTrans Sv, 20 Jul 42, sub: Sup Deficits and Responsibilities, Notes on Tr Mvmts, Logis File, OCMH. (5) 1st Ind, Hq SOS to CG AGF, 7 Oct 42, Misc Notes, Lutes File.

[49] (1) Rpt cited n. 30(3). (2) WD ltrs cited n. 37(2) and n. 40(5). (3) WD ltr, 8 Jan 43, sub: Distrib of Controlled Items of Equip, AG 400 (1-6-43). (4) Memo, ACofS Opns SOS for G-3, 30 Dec 42, same sub. (5) Memo, ACofS Opns ASF for G-4, 12 Apr 43, sub: Trf of Controlled Items. Last two in 400.3 Distrib of Sups and Equip folder, Plng Div ASF, Job A44-140.

and personnel transfers that crippled many of the units remaining. During the last three months of 1942 activations of ground combat units, partly in consequence of the depletion of equipment available for training, had to be slowed almost to a halt. "For the first time," General Lutes wrote to Somervell in September, "we are unable to equip newly activated units with several items of training equipment." [50]

The crisis had been building up for some time. Back in January The Inspector General, disturbed by the confusion attending outbound troop movements, had advanced an obviously desirable solution—formation of a pool of units ready for emergency deployment. He recommended, in addition, procedures to ensure activation of a unit at least two months before sending it overseas, and issuance of movement orders at least forty-five days before sailing. This was easier said than done. Somervell "heartily endorsed" his recommendations as an ideal, but saw no way to avoid last-minute transfers as long as equipment was short and plans were changed from day to day. General Gerow reminded the Chief of Staff that the pool of equipped units formed the preceding August was still in existence, though depleted; it had not been kept up to strength, since otherwise "too many units would be in the 100 percent equipment group and some units in lower priority would be denied their training equipment." [51] In subsequent months it proved difficult to maintain a pool of any size. At the end of May General McNair was complaining of being called on "almost daily" to prepare units for task forces. The effort to keep the pool of equipped units (Group A) even to the absolutely minimum requirements brought the results Gerow had feared in

February. The 4 February priority list contained forty-four ground units to be fully equipped within a month; that of 8 March listed eighty. By the end of April the list approached three hundred, not counting several subcategories labeled simply "to be announced." Even larger numbers were being assigned for full equipment within two months, and from June onward a three-months category was added, which covered, in effect, units that might be sent overseas four months or more in the future. [52]

The earmarking of units for early overseas shipment had outdistanced even the rising flood of actual deployment. An OPD officer asserted in June:

The existing system is not unsound but has gone overboard because the supply of equipment, personnel and shipping cannot keep pace with the earmarking of units for service in theaters . . . . OPD does not expect AGF and SOS to earmark units long in advance of shipping available for movement. If the present system ties up equipment at the expense of training, the high priority groups should be diminished either by purging the list of all not expected to move in less than 90 days, or by eliminating the practice of earmarking entirely. [53]

In part the proliferation of earmarked

[50] (1) Memo cited n. 14. (2) Greenfield, Palmer, and Wiley, *AGF I*, pp. 208–09. (3) See also below, Ch. XVI.
[51] (1) Memo, Gerow for CofS, 13 Feb 42, sub: Overseas Mvmt. (2) Memo, TIG for CofS, 28 Jan 42, same sub. (3) Memo, Somervell for CofS, 4 Feb 42. All in WPD 4161-27. (4) Memo, Somervell for CofS, 2 Feb 42, G-4/33889.
[52] (1) Memo, Maj Harvey H. Fischer for ACofS OPD, 25 May 42, sub: Priority for Dirs . . . , OPD 370.5, 160. (2) Memo cited n. 46(3). (3) Memo, OPD for G-3, 25 Jun 42, sub: Policy Governing Distrib of Controlled Items, OPD 400 Sups and Equip, 35.
[53] Memo, Resources and Reqmts Sec Opns Group for ACofS OPD, 1 Jun 42, sub: Priority for Asgmt of Personnel and Distrib of Controlled Items . . . , OPD 370.5, 160.

units could be laid at the door of OPD itself, whose seven theater sections requisitioned units separately and with little co-ordination. In part, it was a consequence of the understandable desire of the major commands, responsible for providing troops at a moment's notice, to take out insurance in the form of a substantial backlog of at least partially ready units. But there was no insurance against the abrupt nomination for imminent departure of units far down on the priority list, a practice that became increasingly common during the hectic summer and early fall of 1942. In a similar category was the repeated demand to activate on short notice, especially during the mounting of TORCH, special units not provided in the troop basis. The repeated plundering of the equipment of low-priority units for these and more orthodox purposes had the effect of freezing them in a low-equipment status. A case study made by SOS during the summer revealed that a representative group of units had made only insignificant progress over a thirty-day period in receiving certain important items of equipment, and that units in the higher priority subgroups often were in worse state than those standing below them.[54]

Actual deployment was governed largely by availability of shipping. General Lutes argued that the pool of ready units should be limited to the number for which shipping would be available for three months to come, instead of including all the units for which a requirement was indicated during that period. Below this group, distribution of available equipment should be co-ordinated closely with the process of training in order to ensure continuous replenishment of the top priorities as they were depleted by shipment overseas.

The equipping of units must be governed by availability of equipment. Certain units for which a definite mission exists should be fully equipped as soon as possible (Group A). Other units should be given priorities based on anticipated time needs for task forces and availability of equipment. Units should normally be activated in the lowest position in the lowest group, and progress to the higher group priority as training increases and makes them suitable for field operations. By proper anticipation . . . there should always be a well-balanced group of units in Group A to meet requirements . . . .

The occasional selection of low-priority units for early shipment, Lutes thought, "must be recognized as an indication of faulty planning, and as such must be employed only in the face of an unforeseen emergency."[55] He recommended three priority groups, the first two to comprise units for which shipping was available within three and within six months, respectively. Controlled equipment would be issued to the three groups, respectively, up to 100 percent, 50 percent, and 25 percent of authorized allowances, and no new activations would be permitted unless the initial 25 percent issue could be made. Lutes thought that this initial issue should go to newly activated divisional and nondivisional units alike, and that the policy of favoring new divisions should cease. In effect the first priority group would constitute a balanced striking force of ground divisions, with adequate combat, service, and air support, kept up to strength by the orderly admission of units from lower groups.[56]

[54] (1) Memo, ACofS Materiel for ACofS Opns SOS, 14 Oct 42, AG 400 (8-10-42) Sec 1. (2) See also, Cline, *Washington Command Post,* pp. 183–86. (3) See below, Ch. XVI.

[55] Memo cited n. 42(2).

[56] (1) *Ibid.* (2) Memo cited n. 42(1). (3) Memo, Somervell for OPD, 23 Aug 42, Misc Notes, Lutes File. Lutes made a similar proposal in June.

A balanced pool of fully trained, fully equipped troops was, as OPD wrote Somervell, "the ultimate aim of every army." But with the enemy holding the initiative, OPD argued, it had been impossible up to now to create such a pool:

The basic strategy of a nation forced into hostilities while unprepared must be to contain the enemy with the means at hand until a striking force of sufficient size and capabilities has been assembled to seize the initiative and launch a decisive offensive. Attainment of this objective is best served by rapid mobilization to the extent of manpower resources and training facilities, and equipping of such mobilized units in an orderly progressive manner.

The whole mass of units in Groups A and B constituted a pool of sorts, which OPD hoped some day would develop into the desired striking force, "to be employed in a major effort in one theater." But OPD saw no need at the moment for the kind of pool from which could be produced on short notice several "completely integrated task forces," and was unwilling to build up the equipment of B units for this purpose at the expense of minimum training needs of newer units.[57]

OPD evidently was awaiting the outcome of current discussions of the 1943 troop basis. By October it was apparent that the strategy for 1943, in default of a massive land invasion of Europe, would seek partial compensation through an air offensive against Germany at the expense of ground operations. About the same time the Joint Chiefs bowed to the judgment of the production experts that military supply programs would have to be cut. The necessary reductions were made principally in the weapons of large-scale ground warfare. It was clear, moreover, that the shipping expected to be available would not permit the deployment overseas of

forces on the scale earlier planned. "Since . . . it appears," G-3 wrote late in October, "that early employment of a mass Army, which must be transported by water, is not practicable, it follows that the trend must be toward light, easily transportable units."[58] The signs pointed, in short, to a strategy of task force operations in 1943—"scatterization," as Army planners labeled it—involving a piecemeal deployment that the existing amorphous, heterogeneous pool of semiprepared troop units was ill suited to support.

The development of a settled distribution policy based upon the pooling principle, to support the new strategy, consumed the last three months of 1942. In October the War Department officially sanctioned the concept of a "reserve of fully equipped units to meet task force requirements," and OPD informally laid down for G-3 a policy of limiting the number of earmarked units to the capacity of shipping for three months in advance.[59] But the major commands continued to seek insurance against badly co-ordinated deployment by building up large reserves of equipped and nearly equipped units, necessarily at the expense of troops in early stages of training and of new activations. It was necessary, in fact, to defer activations of many ground combat units during the last three months of 1942. In November, contrary to General Lutes' proposal for equal equipment allowances to new

---

[57] (1) Memo, OPD for CG SOS, 1 Sep 42, sub: Equip of Units, OPD 320.2 (6-26-42). (2) For the OPD scheme similar to Lutes' proposal, see draft memo, OPD for CG AGF, 7 Jun 42, OPD 370.5, 160.

[58] (1) Memo, WD for AGF and SOS, 25 Oct 42, sub: Tr Basis 1943, WDGCT 320.2 Gen (10-25-42). (2) Greenfield, Palmer, and Wiley, *AGF I,* pp. 288–89. (3) See below, Ch. XXII.

[59] Memo, G-3 for CG AGF, 30 Oct 42, sub: Priority List for Distrib of Controlled Items . . . , with atchd note for rcd only, AG 400 (8-10-42) Sec 1.

divisional and nondivisional units, the War Department confirmed the established initial 50 percent allowance of controlled items for new divisions (of all types), and also ordered initial full allowances of credit items (which now included rifles); new nondivisional units still had to get along with an initial 20 percent allowance, though this was now prescribed as an irreducible minimum.[60]

By November there was, of course, more equipment available, but its actual distribution through the Army, because of the disorderly course of deployment, had deviated more and more from the established priority groupings. An increasing number of units, elevated suddenly from the depths to top priority for movement and as suddenly degraded, found themselves with assortments of new and old equipment that added up to aggregate allowances in excess of what their existing priorities entitled them to. The transfers of equipment attendant upon this process often had not been reported, and the disparity between central supply service records of controlled equipment and actual distribution in the field widened. The major commands were ordered in November to straighten out this situation by ransacking their cupboards and redistributing all excess equipment in accordance with the authorized allowances in each priority group. For this purpose, as mentioned earlier, delegation of the transfer authority was authorized. By the end of the year there seemed a reasonable likelihood that troops in training would soon have their authorized training allowances and that new units would receive full allowances of controlled items within six months of activation.[61]

It was decided, finally, to form a small pool of equipped units to meet emergency demands only. In the priority scale, it was placed at first immediately below units under a three-month alert for overseas movement; later it was shifted to a position below the group earmarked for shipment within four to six months. The pool was also limited in size by availability of equipment, in consideration of minimum training needs. It comprised, in effect, a balanced group of units in an advanced stage of training and with almost full allowances of equipment. When ordered overseas, earmarked units moved immediately into the priority for early movement (A-2) without passing through the pool, and any unit placed in the A-2 priority, whether taken from the pool or from the earmarked groups, was immediately issued the remainder of its equipment. All Group A units, by definition, were moving toward, or had already reached, a 100 percent equipment status. Group B units, authorized to receive 50 percent of full allowances, were those at least six months old or sufficiently well trained to move into the pool or one of the earmarked categories. Group C, with 20 percent allowances (except for new divisions, authorized 50 percent), included all other units.[62]

These arrangements, in some sort, provided the pool General Lutes seemed to have had in mind the preceding summer and fall, but there was still no provision for

[60] (1) Greenfield, Palmer, and Wiley, *AGF I*, pp. 208–09. (2) WD ltr cited n. 40(5), and subsequent ltrs, 14 Feb and 1 Jun 43, same sub, AG 400 series.

[61] (1) WD ltr cited n. 40(5). (2) Disposition form, OPD to G-3, 21 Dec 42, sub: Proper Priority List of Type Units . . . , OPD 400 Sups and Equip, 47. (3) Memo, Lutes for Somervell, 28 Dec 42, Misc Notes, Lutes File. (4) Rpt cited n. 30(3).

[62] (1) Memo, G-3 for maj comds, 18 Jan 43, WDGCT 475 (1-18-43). (2) WD ltr, 5 Jan 43, sub: Orgn, Tng, and Equipg of Units for Overseas Sv, AG 320.2 (1-2-43). (3) WD ltrs cited n. 37(2), and WD ltr, 1 Jun 43, cited n. 60(2). (4) Palmer, Wiley, and Keast, *AGF II*, pp. 582–87. (5) *Annual Report of the Army Service Forces, 1943*, p. 101.

relating the earmarking of units to visible capacity to move them overseas. OPD retained the option of being realistic or unrealistic, as it saw fit, in setting up the "six months' list" of troops it expected to deploy overseas. During the late winter and spring of 1943, in fact, deployment planning virtually lost touch with the estimated limitations of shipping, and deployment schedules, caught between the two, began to fluctuate in a manner reminiscent of the preceding September. Before the end of February General Lutes was complaining that OPD's changes in the list of earmarked units had "already reached such proportions as to practically nullify its value." [63]

Before the winter was out, moreover, a new crisis was looming in the training program. Ground forces were still not receiving authorized equipment and ammunition for training. On 1 March 1943 General McNair wrote Marshall that current and proposed restrictions upon equipping troops in training and providing them with ammunition threatened disaster.

Training cannot progress beyond a certain fixed point if it is based on too many assumptions, improvisations, and part-time use of equipment. . . . It is unsound to permit allocations of equipment which may operate to place our troops in combat in the same theater of operations with other allied forces who have more and better U.S. equipment than do our own forces. [64]

He recommended that all units should receive 50 percent of their authorized controlled items on activation, to be brought up to full allowances within six months for divisions and within four months for nondivisional units. [65]

Except for OPD, the Assistant Chiefs of Staff concerned in the matter—G-1, G-3, and G-4—lined up solidly behind General

McNair. "There can be no sounder judgment," G-4 declared, "than that of General McNair, whose long-considered recommendation herewith is taken at face value." [66] Army Service Forces (formerly SOS) was also sensitive to the needs of training, especially for its own nondivisional units, which were among the most starved for equipment; on the other hand, larger training allowances would interfere with its plans, then hatching, to ship large amounts of material in bulk to the British Isles. OPD took its stand on the rather theoretical argument that the Army Supply Program had set up requirements sufficient to provide every unit with full allowances within six months of its activation, and that the Munitions Assignments Board assigned munitions "on the basis of operational needs, giving full weight to all U.S. requirements, including those in the Army Supply Program." [67] Staff supporters of General McNair's proposal, an OPD officer noted irritably, "are not familiar with the operation of the JCS and CCS and Munitions Assignments Board. They likewise appear to be unfamiliar with the Army Supply Program." [68] All of which, as General Moses (G-4) retorted with some acerbity, was hardly to the point.

Regardless of the provisions of the Army Supply Program, and of pertinent CCS and

[63] (1) Memo, Lutes for Dir of Tng SOS, 30 Feb 43, Misc Notes, Lutes File. (2) For troop movement procedure, see below, Ch. XIII. (3) For early 1943 deployment, see below, Ch. XXVI.
[64] Memo, CG AGF for CofS, 1 Mar 43, sub: Vic Prog Tr Basis, OPD 400 (3-1-43) Case 2.
[65] Memo, CG AGF for CofS, 6 Apr 43, sub: Equip for AGF, OPD 475 Equipg of Trs, 25.
[66] Memo, G-4 for CofS, 7 Apr 43, sub: Equip for AGF, OPD 475 Equipg of Trs, 25.
[67] Memo, OPD for G-4, 14 Apr 43, sub: Equip for AGF, OPD 475 Equipg of Trs, 25.
[68] Note for rcd, with memo cited n. 67.

JCS papers, the AGF are not receiving sufficient equipment to meet minimum training requirements as determined by General McNair. . . . The basic question of the present discussion is whether the War Department will actively encourage the assignment of a greater percentage of manufactured material to AGF.[69]

This OPD was not prepared to do beyond a certain point, "consistent with other needs." The shortage in critical items for training was caused partly by lagging production, partly by unanticipated operational demands overseas. Output was expected to reach its peak in mid-1943. If production schedules were not met, OPD stated, all claimants would have to share the deficit proportionately. Ammunition allowances for training had, in fact, been increased somewhat since 1 March. "It is believed," OPD wrote reassuringly, while rejecting General McNair's proposal, ". . . that as the rate of production increases and requirements in overseas theaters become more stabilized, AGF will receive a greater share of current production . . . the situation, while at present somewhat somber, is continually improving."[70] The strategic planners, their eyes fixed on the impending offensives in the Mediterranean and the Pacific, were more concerned at this time with equipping units for combat and with finding shipping to move them overseas; the training problem received only secondary consideration. Two weeks before McNair's proposal was rejected, in fact, OPD had obtained from ASF a rough estimate that eighteen divisions with supporting troops could be equipped for overseas service in 1943 provided, among other things, that equipment could be withdrawn from units in training. In May ASF launched its program of stockpiling material in the British Isles for a 1944 invasion—a program that seriously threatened to cut into training allowances in the United States. Despite rising production, the War Department finally decided in June to reduce the 1943 Troop Basis, mainly by cuts in ground combat units from 7.5 million to 7 million enlisted men, thus curtailing somewhat the long-range demand for equipment for new units.[71]

In its requirements and distribution policies during 1942 the Army faced the basic problems, which conditioned its strategy and its logistics generally, of attempting to meet the demands of the immediate military situation while at the same time mobilizing large forces for later offensives. The Army's system of determining and programing requirements was an attempt primarily to meet the needs of the mobilizing reserves in the United States, in preparation for the big battles expected in 1943 and 1944, and only secondarily to provide for the relatively small forces that had to be deployed against the enemy in 1942. There was logic in this since other Allied forces were sustaining the principal weight of enemy power in all theaters except the Pacific, where the American Navy was performing a similar service. The Army's great role was to come later, and a large part of the burden

---

[69] (1) Memo, G-4 for OPD, 17 Apr 43, sub: Equip for AGF, OPD 475 Equipg of Trs, 25. (2) Greenfield, Palmer, and Wiley, *AGF I*, pp. 220–21.

[70] Memo, OPD for G-4, 22 Apr 43, sub: Equip for AGF, OPD 475 Equipg of Trs, 25.

[71] (1) Memo, ACofS Opns ASF for OPD, 6 Apr 43, sub: Equipg of Units 1943, OPD 475 Equipg of Trs, 23. (2) Memo, ACofS Opns ASF for OPD, 17 Apr 43, sub: Estd Dates of Completion of Equip for Divs, OPD 475 Equipg of Trs, 27. (3) Greenfield, Palmer, and Wiley, *AGF I*, pp. 220–27. (4) Richard M. Leighton, The Problem of Troop and Cargo Flow in Preparing the European Invasion, ASF hist monograph, Ch. III, OCMH.

of equipping forces for early deployment fell, in any case, upon current production, existing stocks, and material already in the hands of units in training. But there were those who thought, by late 1942, that the requirements system was partly to blame for the shortage of troop units ready for overseas service, in that it had failed to anticipate the specific types of equipment needed and also to spur industry to an adequate over-all volume of output. The emphasis in the requirements system upon the distant and the general need, as opposed to the immediate and the specific one, involved a method of calculation that led unavoidably to overestimates in some categories and underestimates in others. As a corollary, it virtually dictated a policy of liberality in the realm of allowances for unforeseeable contingencies. This tendency to padding by late 1942 ran head on into the production authorities' estimates of the future limits of national productivity, and the failure to make allowances in the supply programs for specific conditions of operation was to cause trouble in 1943 and 1944.

Distribution policy in 1942, by an equal logic, focused upon the immediate rather than the long-range need. Priorities and transfer policy heavily favored troops going or soon to go overseas and troops in overseas theaters and bases, rather than those in training. Under this system, the drain of equipment and ammunition to forces that had to be sent overseas threatened constantly to cripple the advancing training of the mass of troops in the United States. Equipping support-type units, especially service units, was seriously retarded by a policy, which many considered shortsighted, of favoring divisional units. In the late summer and autumn of 1942 the whole system of priorities, aimed at keeping the equipment program and the training program abreast of one another, almost broke down under the impact of sudden changes in strategic plans and the disruption of deployment schedules. Generally speaking, the erratic course of strategy and operations in 1942 created difficulties in the equipping of troops that were far beyond the power of any distribution policy to overcome. In the face of those difficulties, the system of controlled distribution did succeed, not always but during most of 1942, in producing equipped troop units up to the capacity of shipping to transport them overseas. This result was accomplished by decelerating new activations during the last few months of 1942 and by a consistent skimping on allowances of equipment and ammunition for troops in training. As late as spring of 1943, when production was approaching peak levels, General McNair considered this skimping an invitation to disaster.

CHAPTER XIII

The Support of Overseas Operations

The Army's requirements and distribution policies were both oriented to the support of overseas operations, the former in a long-term, the latter in a short-term sense. To supply the overseas theaters and the troops about to be sent to them was perhaps the largest single task of the Army's logistical organization. The procedural mechanisms developed in 1942 to perform this task are the primary subject of the present chapter. A closely related and scarcely less formidable task—training service troops to support overseas operations—was a matter of unending concern to logisticians even though it has not always been considered to belong to the sphere of logistics. While the problem of service troops cannot be treated in full in this volume, brief attention is here given to the difficulties encountered in developing an adequate service troop basis within the framework of the Army's allotted manpower.

The System of Overseas Supply

Along with other important features of the Army's wartime logistical system, the general pattern of wartime overseas supply policies, procedures, and organization was worked out by the G-4 staff before the end of January 1942. General instructions were published on the 22d, effective 1 March. The salient feature of the system there outlined was the decentralization of the administration of most overseas supply on a geographical basis to the ports of embarkation, each of which was to serve certain specified theaters and bases. To the War Department were left, in general, control of the distribution of scarce matériel, allocation of shipping, co-ordination of supply with strategic needs (for example, determining intertheater priorities), and matters of general policy. After the reorganization of March 1942, SOS and AAF took over practically all the work of central administration and supervision, and the War Department's role was largely confined to setting levels of supply, determining intertheater priorities, and allocating shipping to overseas commands. SOS now dealt directly with WSA for single-voyage allocations of shipping, designated ports of embarkation to serve particular theaters and bases, prescribed port reserves and credits in depots behind the ports, assigned shipping to the ports as needed, regulated policy for handling supply requisitions, directed replacement of shipments lost at sea, and, outside the special jurisdiction of the AAF, shared with the General Staff the co-ordination and supervision of the distribution of most types of scarce matériel to overseas forces.[1]

The principal category of controlled supply to overseas commands was a selected list of scarce items (similar to but not identical with the controlled items list, and including ammunition), of which overseas commanders each month reported the quantities on hand. This, the Materiel Status Report, was submitted directly to the War Department, there to be consolidated by the Statistical Branch into a single compilation. The individual reports were also extracted to the supply services for audit and action, subject to review and co-ordination by SOS headquarters. Air force matériel was handled under separate procedures and AAF control. In the supply services, the extracted reports were collated with records of supply shipments and authorized allowances to provide a basis for supplying the listed items; actual shipments were made, in the case of replacement items on the controlled list, on receipt of the overseas commanders' requisitions, which the ports forwarded without action to the supply services. Most items of scarce equipment shipped to forces overseas fell into this category; the relatively few items of initial issue that had to be sent to troops already overseas were shipped automatically.[2]

Ammunition (Class V supply), the scarcest of the scarce categories and a substantial part of all overseas requirements, was not supplied by requisition (although requisitions were often submitted), but under a system of allocations based on priorities, shipments being made automatically within limits of immediate availability. Allowances of ammunition to overseas commands during most of 1942 were stated in terms of "units of fire," a

primarily tactical unit of measure reflecting average expenditures in combat among all the overseas theaters. Allowances were computed, therefore, on the basis of "active" weapons in each overseas command—that is, weapons in the hands of troops, not in storage or in the pipeline.[3]

As late as June 1942 the official hope was that ammunition soon could be supplied automatically as a credit item, within the administrative sphere of the ports.

---

[1] (1) WD ltr, 22 Jan 42, sub: Sup of Overseas Depts, Theaters, and Separate Bases, AG 400 (1-17-42), and revision, 28 Apr 42. (2) WD ltr, 2 Apr 42, sub: Current Sup Policy and Proced, AG 475 (4-1-42). (3) WD ltr, 10 Jun 42, same sub, AG 475 (6-7-42). (4) The general plan of overseas supply seems to have been mainly the work of General Lutes and officers in the Supply Branch of G-4, while reflecting some of the ideas of The Quartermaster General, Maj. Gen. Edmund B. Gregory. See memo, G-4 for CofS, 17 Jan 42, sub: Sup of Overseas Depts, Theaters, and Separate Bases, G-4/33889; memo, Lutes for ACofS G-4, 15 Jan 42, sub: Overseas Sup Opns, G-4/33889; memo, G-4 for TQMG, 16 Jan 42, sub: Sup of Trs in Australia and Pac Islands, G-4/33861; memo, CofTrans Br for CofSup Br G-4, 8 Jan 42, Overseas Sup folder, OCT HB; and Lt Gen LeRoy Lutes, "Supply Reorganization for World War II," Antiaircraft Journal (March–April 1952), pp. 5–6. (5) For overseas territorial responsibilities of each port of embarkation, see below, App. G.

[2] (1) WD ltr, 6 Mar 42, sub: Monthly Materiel Status Rpt, Overseas Comds, AG 400 (2-28-42). (2) Related corresp in G-4/34224, G-4/33825, and G-4/31796.

[3] (1) WD ltrs cited n. 1(1). (2) WD Memo W700-8-42, 10 Oct 42, sub: Sup of Overseas Depts, Theaters, and Separate Bases. (3) WD ltr, 6 Aug 42, sub: Authorized Allowance of Weapons and Ord Vehicles and . . . Am, AG 400 (8-2-42). (4) WD ltr to CG USAFIA, 13 Feb 42, sub: Sup of USAFIA, G-4/33861. (5) Related corresp in same file. (6) FM 101-10, Staff Officers' Field Manual: Organizational, Technical and Logistical Data, pars. 90, 92. (7) In the case of armored vehicles, the individual vehicle rather than the weapons mounted on it was the basis of calculation. The unit of fire was broken down into percentages for each type of ammunition (for example, armor-piercing, high-explosive). See FM 100-10, Field Service Regulations: Administration, Ch. I. (8) See also below, App. F-2.

But this hope was not realized. The authorized levels of ammunition reserves assigned to each overseas command in July 1942 were theoretically minimum levels, but for most areas they remained distant goals. North Africa, by early 1943, had become a conspicuous exception; there a policy of largely unregulated automatic shipments resulted in a huge accumulation of ammunition before the flow was finally reduced—almost a billion and a half rounds of small arms types alone— an extravagance that was partly responsible, of course, for the prevailing shortages elsewhere. Because of this shortage, it was difficult if not impossible during 1942 to relate the supply of ammunition to estimated or projected needs. An SOS official wrote in June:

There will never be enough to meet the demand of all theaters, if theater commanders are authorized to submit requests based upon projected expenditures. . . . If ammunition is supplied on actual reports of expenditures, the time lag between the actual expenditure and the delivery of replacement ammunition will be so great that the supply . . . might be reduced to dangerously low levels.[4]

Except for the important item of ammunition, relatively little of the supply of overseas forces was placed under central controls. In the 22 January general instructions, administration of the bulk of overseas supply was decentralized to the ports. Two large classes of this supply, moreover—food (Class I) and fuel (Class III)—were exempted even from the requisitioning procedure and were shipped automatically by the ports on the basis of predetermined allowances. Spare parts, for a time, were also shipped automatically to certain theaters. For these categories of supply the demand was fairly constant and could be anticipated with

reasonable accuracy if the number of consuming units (soldiers, trucks, and so forth) were known and the conditions of use were not too abnormal. Clothing, weapons, vehicles, and other items for which allowances to individuals or troop units were fixed in standard tables (Class II), and items for which there were no fixed allowances (Class IV) such as machinery and construction materials and equipment were shipped in response to requisitions from overseas commanders.[5]

Petroleum fuels and lubricants (Class III supply) were not notably scarce items, despite the loss of the wells and refineries of the Netherlands Indies; the pinch was felt rather in the means of transporting and, occasionally, of storing and packaging the products. Certain controls were placed upon their use and distribution, therefore, aimed primarily at making the most effective use of transportation, especially ocean shipping. Upwards of half of the Army's tonnage shipped to forces overseas consisted of petroleum products.[6] Other factors helped to place the supply of petroleum products in a special category. Sources of supply were widely dispersed

---

[4] (1) Memo, Dir of Procurement and Distrib Div SOS for G-4, 12 Jun 42, sub: Sup of Overseas Depts, Theaters, and Separate Bases. (2) Memo, G-4 for CG's SOS and AAF, 27 May 42, same sub. Both in G-4/400. (3) Ltr, SOS, 24 May 42, sub: Handling of Requisitions at POE's, SPX 400 (5-21-42). (4) WD ltrs cited n. 1(2) and n. 1(3). (5) Report of WD Procurement Review Board, p. 36. (6) History of the Planning Division, ASF, II, 191, OCMH. (7) Col. Creswell G. Blakeney, ed., *Logistical History of NATOUSA-MTOUSA, 11 August 1942 to 30 November 1945* (Naples, Italy, 1946), pp. 89–91.

[5] (1) WD ltr cited n. 1(1). (2) WD memo cited n. 3(2).

[6] (1) Erna Risch, *Fuels for Global Conflict*, QMC Hist Study 9 (rev. ed., Washington, 1952), pp. 1, 43. The following account is based largely on this study. (2) For an account of the problem of distributing petroleum products within the United States, see Rose, *American Wartime Transportation*, Ch. VIII.

geographically and under several national jurisdictions, with a consequent need for international pooling and co-ordination of distribution, particularly among overseas theaters. The petroleum industry was perhaps the most highly integrated in the world, controlling its products directly or indirectly from source to consumer. The Army (except for the Air Forces, which contracted independently) bought most of its oil and related products under consolidated contracts made by the Treasury and the Navy; posts, depots, and supply services all purchased directly under these arrangements. Few of the Army's procuring agencies understood clearly where their responsibilities began and ended. An officer in Somervell's headquarters, trying to survey the system in March 1943, questioned ten different individuals in one service without finding out "how or where petroleum products are purchased." [7]

During 1942 and early 1943 responsibility for co-ordinating the Army's purchases of petroleum products was gradually centered in the Office of The Quartermaster General.[8] On the interservice level, the Army-Navy Petroleum Board (ANPB), established in July 1942 with limited authority to co-ordinate requirements and information, became by mid-1943 the central U.S. agency under the JCS for co-ordinating the distribution and use of petroleum products. Automatic supply by the ports of embarkation operated within the framework of allocations to each theater as determined by the ANPB. By early 1943 several theaters had area petroleum officers who served on the theater staffs but also reported to the ANPB. In other theaters supply of petroleum products was administered under earlier Army-Navy agreements; the Navy had full responsibility, for example, in the

South Pacific. In still other areas, such as the British Isles and the Middle East, American forces were served by the British through reciprocal aid. Local procurement, finally, was employed by Army forces in a few areas including Hawaii and Alaska.[9]

Very little control was exercised over spare parts supply in the early months of the war. Some spare parts were shipped overseas with every cargo of vehicles, and additional parts later, on the basis of scanty records of the number of vehicles overseas. On 24 May 1942 the resupply of automotive spare parts to all theaters became automatic. This effort to be generous in supplying the forces overseas seems to have produced adverse effects at home; The Inspector General reported in July that lack of spare parts was accounting for from two thirds to three fourths of the disabilities among vehicles in the United States.[10] By August, procurement had been planned to provide two years' supply of replacement parts for each noncombatant type of vehicle within six months after its delivery, though combat vehicles were given a lower life expectancy. Units in the United States obtained replacement parts in exchange for worn ones by requisitioning on the next highest echelon or level of maintenance if the needed parts were not available at its own installation. Spare

---

[7] Contl Div, ASF, Rpt 94, Purchasing Responsibility for Petroleum Products, Mar 43.

[8] (1) WD Circular 317, 17 Sep 42. (2) WD Procurement Regulation, Revision 12, 3 Mar 43.

[9] (1) Ltr, Vice CNO and CG SOS, 20 Jul 42, sub: ANPB, Orgn of, and atchd dir, 14 Jul 42, sub: Creation of the ANPB . . . , ANPB Dirs, Job A51-60, DRB AGO. (2) See also, Risch, *Fuels for Global Conflict*, Chs. III–IV.

[10] (1) Min, WD Gen Council mtg, 21 Jul 42. (2) Disposition form, G-4 to CG USAFIA, 5 Mar 42, sub: Automatic Shipt of Spare Parts . . . , G-4/33861. (3) SOS ltr cited n. 4(3).

parts maintenance and repair operations overseas similarly were organized in echelons representing successively more elaborate operations, but with greater dependence upon mobile maintenance units, which operated close to the combat areas. Spare parts were assembled in standard but divisible lots (usually for a hundred vehicles) sufficient for a year's maintenance. Parts having an average mortality of less than one per hundred vehicles were boxed and shipped separately. For most of the standard types of vehicles of recent model (procured by the Ordnance Department after August 1942) spare parts were supplied automatically only to overseas areas specifically designated—notably the Southwest Pacific and, somewhat later, the Persian Gulf Service Command. Forces in North Africa were supplied spare parts, and virtually everything else, automatically during the first few months of the campaign. The main burden of control was placed upon the port, which was expected to maintain a running record of vehicles in each theater and with each task force. Theater commanders, in turn, were expected to indicate to the port when automatic supply (if in force) proved either inadequate or superabundant to their needs.[11]

The overseas supply system was designed for economy and fluidity, in operations involving huge magnitudes—thousands of ocean miles, hundreds of thousands of troops, millions of separate items, and millions of tons of freight. Automatic supply was fluid, but patently uneconomical; it used precious shipping space for cargo not urgently needed and led to the accumulation of unbalanced stocks overseas. But during the first year it was the only way to maintain a regular flow of supplies to new bases, which lacked time or personnel for

paper work. Automatic supply kept these bases alive and enabled them to build up reserves. In the system as a whole, however, it was an incidental and temporary feature. Fundamentally, economy and fluidity were pursued by the same methods that had long been employed in large-scale private business: organization was decentralized, administrative procedures were standardized and made routine, operations were wholesale. Each of the ports of embarkation was the administrative center for supplying one or more overseas theaters or bases. Channels of administration ran from the theater to the port and thence directly to sources of supply, the depots backing up the port, bypassing Washington altogether; the flow of supply followed the same channel in reverse. Procedures were generalized and standardized for broad classes of material, thus reducing improvisation and waste motion. What the system lost in control, it gained in administrative economy.

Even more fundamentally, the system rested upon the principle of wholesale operations. In its broadest sense, this was an effort to free the flow of supply from the erratic pace of day-to-day demand, in order to gain flexibility in the use of transport, storage, and handling facilities. As far as possible, requirements were consolidated and material was shipped and stored in bulk, primarily to fill the long-range cumulative demand rather than the interim specific need. Such a system could justify itself in wartime, of course, only to the extent that it succeeded, in fact, in meeting this interim specific need as it

---

[11] (1) WD Memo W850-5-42, 24 Aug 42, sub: Automotive Parts Policy, and changes of 8 Sep 42. (2) WD ltr, 11 Jun 42, same sub, AG 451.9 (6-4-42). (3) Blakeney, *Logistical History of NATOUSA-MTOUSA*, pp. 265–66.

arose. To do so required careful long-range planning, based on close study of trends in past and current demand and painstaking analysis of the factors that might influence future demand. And since long-range planning, at best, could produce only educated estimates, the system depended also upon the amassing of reserves to cushion the impact of unforeseen demands. In theory, these reserves were stocked at intervals along the lines of communications as well as in the United States so that forces overseas might be supplied from sources near at hand, and these, in turn, might be replenished from sources farther to the rear. This was the modern version of the system of staged supply perfected by the Prussian Army in the 1860's, but adapted to global lines of communications over both oceanic and overland routes.

Wholesale supply could not, however, adequately serve the fluctuating and urgent needs of the battle front, which demanded retail and often emergency methods. In the overseas theaters, which lay beyond the jurisdiction of the system administered by the ports of embarkation, wholesale methods merged into retail, armies in the field provisioning themselves at need from the reservoir of depots behind them, while the reservoir in turn was replenished and kept at a safe level by an even flow of supply, through wholesale methods, across the oceans. Reserves thus tended to be massed in rear areas of overseas theaters rather than being distributed evenly through the pipeline. Economy demanded, in any case, that the number of transshipment stages be kept at a minimum. Stocks scattered along the oceanic lines of communications therefore were relatively few and small, serving to sustain garrisons at these points and to reprovision and refuel passing ships and aircraft. With

the shifting of routes and of the foci of military operations, the growing security of the sea lanes, and the forward movement of fighting fronts, many stockage points along the way, or in what had once been forward areas, were bypassed and allowed to stagnate. The "full and flowing pipeline" was never, in strict fact, altogether full—above all during 1942—and only in the intervals between stockage points could it be said to flow. The phrase did, however, suggest an important underlying purpose during 1942 and early 1943—to amass sufficient reserves at key points along the pipeline, particularly in overseas theaters, so that during the period of expanding deployment the process of supplying forces overseas from theater stocks, and of replenishing those stocks, would become part of a generally continuous forward movement. It was a system of calculated oversupply, which laid claim to long-term economy through administrative efficiency, elimination of improvisation, and the forestalling of war's greatest waste, that resulting from defeat on the field of battle.

Procedural Problems in Overseas Supply

The two basic functions of the port in routine overseas supply were to initiate and co-ordinate the filling of requisitions received from overseas, and to take the necessary action incident to forwarding automatic shipments. Action on a requisition at the port normally fell into three stages: (1) editing, an examination to detect obvious errors or omissions, and to check for conformity with authorized allowances as stated in the requisition or as indicated by port records; (2) extraction, forwarding the individual requests listed in the requisition to their appropriate sources of supply, usually either the port's own reserves or filler depots backing up the port; and (3) follow-up, checking the progress of filling the requisition at the depots. The port acted only on requisitions of a routine character; those involving controlled or status report items or otherwise out of the ordinary were referred to the headquarters of the supply services concerned or to SOS headquarters.[12] (Chart 7)

Effective supply action by the ports, both on requisitions and on automatic supply, called above all for up-to-date, pertinent information. Requests could not be accepted at face value since overseas commanders had a tendency to ask for whatever they thought the traffic would bear (in one widely publicized instance, a four years' supply of laundry soap). Overseas commanders were supposed to keep the port informed of shortages and surpluses in subsistence and fuel, quantities of supplies procured locally, storage space available in the theater, priorities desired in shipping supplies, and ports of entry to be used. Authorized levels of reserves for each overseas command were published periodically by the War Department, and the bases of issue could be found in standard allowance tables, expenditure tables, and established use factors. The chief difficulty was encountered in determining the strength and composition of the forces supplied. From the General Staff (OPD and G-3) the ports were supposed to receive for each overseas command a troop basis, revised quarterly, and a monthly troop list showing troops present at and en route to the base. Actually, both strength figures and troop bases appeared at irregular intervals in 1942, were usually many weeks out of date, and were late in reaching the ports. Further, they included no projection of strength to cover the weeks or months that would elapse before shipments actually reached the base. Fluctuating troop movement schedules in 1942 gave little help.[13]

The ports thus had to depend mainly on their own records of troop movements and such information as they could glean from the overseas bases. Both sources were uncertain. There were no procedures in 1942 for notifying a port of troops moved to its assigned bases through other ports, still less of the later peregrinations of troop units within and among overseas theaters. Discrepancies between actual strength at a base and the official or estimated figures at the port often mounted to thousands of men. Requisitions were often computed on projected rather than actual strength, inviting duplication by later requisitions. In July 1942 the War Department ordered that each requisition indicate actual troop strength, together with quantities of requested items on hand, the period covered, and "any other information necessary to indicate clearly the need and basis thereof."[14] But in August it was still necessary explicitly to prohibit the practice of requi-

---

[12] (1) OCT Circular 82, 19 Nov 42. (2) Leighton, Overseas Supply Policies and Procedures, pp. 51–54, OCMH. (3) Larson, Role of the Transportation Corps in Oversea Supply, pp. 105–07, OCT HB.

[13] (1) AG ltr, 2 Oct 43, sub: Editing of Overseas Requisitions for Laundry and Dry Cleaning Sups, SPX 438 (9-28-43). (2) Memo, OCT for Port Comdrs, 14 Aug 42, sub: Proper Editing of Requisitions . . . , SPTSP 400.212-BF, OCT. (3) WD ltrs cited n. 1(1). (4) Transcript of Overseas Sup Conf, Washington, 22 Jul 42, 10:45 A.M. to 12:00 noon, pp. 13–14, 1:15 to 2:00 P.M., p. 1 and passim, Logis File, OCMH. (5) Memo, G-4 for G-3, 4 Feb 42, sub: Overseas Tr Bases, G-4/33889. (6) Related corresp in same file and in AG 400 (1-17-42) Sec 1. (7) History of the Planning Division, ASF, II, 210–11. OCMH. (8) For use factors, see above, Ch. XII. (9) For levels of supply, see below, this chapter.

[14] WD ltr, 19 Jul 42, sub: Level of Sup for Overseas Depts . . . , AG 400 (7-11-42).

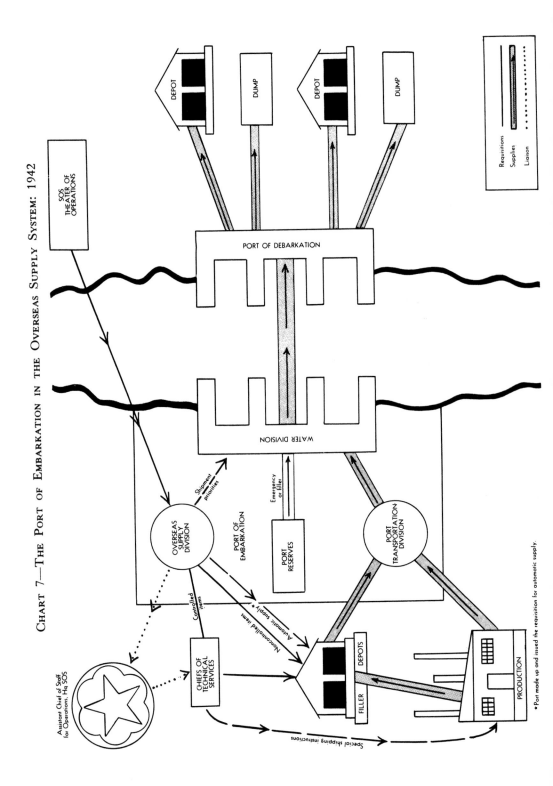

CHART 7—THE PORT OF EMBARKATION IN THE OVERSEAS SUPPLY SYSTEM: 1942

sitioning on projected strength.[15] Overseas commanders were also laggard or forgetful in notifying the ports of desired shipping priorities, with the result that they sometimes received less urgent items ahead of more urgent ones.

In both the centralized and the decentralized systems, the determination of supply status was the very heart of the process. Effective supply control, in any continuous sense, depended upon the ability of the supplying agencies to ascertain with reasonable accuracy not merely what the overseas base was entitled to receive, but what it already had on hand. Part of the difficulty of doing so was inherent in the dynamism of the supply process, which made it virtually impossible to capture, in time to be useful, a "still" picture of status based on information collected over a period of time from various points along the pipeline. This difficulty was aggravated by the inevitable sluggishness of a complicated administrative process.

Few reporting requirements were placed upon overseas commanders in the overseas supply plan of January 1942. The new Materiel Status Report, instituted in March 1942, was the most detailed and useful report, but it covered only a fraction of the items supplied. An older monthly report, submitted by the base directly to G-4, was too general in content to be useful and by the time it reached the port it was usually obsolete. Late in January 1942 the War Department turned down a request by The Quartermaster General to require a monthly report on the status of subsistence from each base. After July requisitions were supposed to contain status information as part of the justification for the items requested, but this information, when given, was difficult to

interpret because of the absence of clear definitions of the several stages of the pipeline through which supplies passed (when was an item en route?), and duplication of reporting often occurred when supplies moved from one stage to another. Quantities in the hands of troops were so difficult to determine that many bases omitted this information altogether.[16] In any case, the prolonged labor involved in piecing together the fragmentary data in many requisitions over an extended period of time in order to assemble a complete status picture, and the absence of rhythm in the flow of this information, vitiated the usefulness of any such status analysis as an instrument of supply control.

The Materiel Status Report had been originally designed by the G-4 staff to show quantities authorized (by the overseas commander's reckoning) as well as quantities on hand, and would thus have served as a requisition. This feature was abandoned on the assumption that successive reports would overlap in coverage, because of the lag in shipments, and that changes in troop strength at the base would make it impossible to correlate successive reports of shortages. There was also some concern over the security risk involved in a single consolidated status report. But the decision in March 1942 to make the report merely a control device rather than a requisitioning instrument

---

[15] (1) WD Memo, W-35-1-42, 21 Aug 42. (2) Transcript of Overseas Sup Conf, Washington, 22 Jul 42, 2 to 3 P.M., pp. 8-10, Logis File, OCMH. (3) WD memo cited n. 3(2). (4) History of the Planning Division, ASF, Vol. II, Ch. XII.

[16] (1) Disposition form, G-4 to TQMG, 29 Jan 42, sub: Rpt on Subsistence From Overseas Stations, G-4/33889. (2) WD ltr cited n. 14. (3) WD ltr, 28 Apr 42, cited n. 1(1). (4) Transcript of Overseas Sup Conf, Washington, 22 Jul 42, 2 to 3 P.M., pp. 8-9, Logis File, OCMH.

only caused confusion. Some overseas commanders evidently assumed that replacements as well as initial issues of controlled items would be supplied automatically. The New Orleans port commander wrote in June of a "long discussion" among officers of the Panama Canal Department on this vexing question, "each citing various War Department letters for authority." [17] One disillusioned critic declared that the Materiel Status Report was not satisfactory

. . . either to the overseas base, the General Staff or the various chiefs of the arms and services. There is a definite lack of pertinent information in each case. There is too much work involved. There is too much loss of time. There is no common denominator or starting point from which all parties can base their values and decisions. The result is the already experienced confusion, long-winded explanations and wasted but precious time. [18]

The salient defect seemed to be the failure to bring the port, which alone had an up-to-date picture of shipments actually cleared for overseas, into the process of compiling the status report. Moreover, the overseas commander, required to justify his requisitions, lacked most of the basic information needed to tabulate his authorized requirements. Only a quarter of this information, according to one estimate, was contained in literature and data that might be available in a field headquarters. In general, the status report system lacked provisions for a co-ordinated stream of pertinent data from various sources, flowing under a rigorous schedule into the central agencies, and showing the complete status of supply at a given base at a given time. "This masterpiece supply picture," the above-noted critic observed, "must be painted by the specialists of each part." [19]

In the realm of decentralized supply, the SOS steadily enlarged the status re-

porting responsibilities of the ports. By July each port was submitting to the Office of the Chief of Transportation a monthly automatic supply report, and was expected to maintain a "running record" of supply status for all classes at the bases that it served. [20] In effect, the ports were asked to obtain from the bases by request or hearsay information the War Department was unwilling to require in formal reports. One port supply officer, asked how overseas commanders reported their levels of supply, replied tersely, "They don't report"—and then unburdened himself at some length:

I'll tell you what I've been doing down in Charleston on that. I try to get hold of every supply officer who comes through the port and sit down with him and tell him some of the things that will be beneficial to us back in Charleston in keeping that supply level up. I have even gone so far as to dictate a memorandum on some of the things. . . . I give him a copy . . . and if he will let us know some of the things we ask for in that memorandum then we will be better guided. . . . In other words, when these fellows get over there [overseas] they shouldn't go to sleep. They should realize that somebody back here has to serve them, and they have to know something in order to really, honest and

[17] (1) 1st Ind, CG New Orleans POE for CG SOS, 9 Jun 42, to SPX 400 (5-23-42). (2) Memo, Lutes for Gross, 11 May 42. Both in Notes on Controlled Items, Logis File, OCMH. (3) Corresp in G-4/34224. (4) Ltr cited n. 4(3).
[18] Memo, CofCWS for Statistics Br WDGS, 7 Aug 42, sub: Monthly Materiel Status Rpt Outline, CWS 320.2/53 (8-7-42).
[19] Ibid.
[20] (1) Memo, CofTrans for Port Comdrs, 1 Apr 42, sub: Level of Automatic Sup at Overseas Bases, SPRVC 400.212, Overseas Bases-B. (2) Mimeographed digest of Overseas Sup Conf, Washington, 22 Jul 42, p. 12, Logis File, OCMH. (3) Memo, Lutes for Somervell, 17 Jul 42, Misc Notes, Lutes File. (4) 2d Ind, ACofS Opns SOS for CofTrans, 30 Jul 42, SPOPP 400, Sup-Overseas. (5) WD Memo cited n. 3(2).

truly, serve them. Now they just don't give us enough information.[21]

The complaint was unanimous. In July there was extended discussion of a proposed periodic status report, to be submitted by bases to ports, covering all classes of supply. The Boston port had already devised a fairly simple standard form, showing days of supply on hand for each class and subclass of supplies, which could be transmitted by radio. But itemized reports could not be sent by radio, and, in any case, required so long to prepare and transmit that they became obsolete before they could be received and used. Ports often had to make their own calculations of subsistence stocks overseas based on an earlier strength report, dropping off the appropriate quantities from day to day, a method which progressively multiplied error. Experience showed in general that whatever reports were obtained from overseas, under conditions prevailing in 1942, were irregular, stereotyped, and inaccurate. "You end up," one SOS staff officer dryly remarked, "with a bunch of piffy statements that mean nothing."[22]

The SOS supply staff had hoped from the beginning to integrate the controls for scarce items with the decentralized system of overseas supply centering in the ports. To this end SOS proposed, in September 1942, a comprehensive system of status reporting for all types of supply, including scarce items, centering in the ports but depending necessarily on regular reports from overseas bases and co-ordinated by SOS headquarters. It was the aim of the scheme to synchronize and schedule the flow of information from all segments of the pipeline into the ports, with definite assignments of status reporting responsibilities at each stage of movement through the pipeline. All this data would be consolidated in SOS headquarters, providing each month a complete picture of supply status for the entire pipeline.[23]

Opposition to the plan focused on the enlarged role proposed for the port of embarkation in overseas supply. It was inadvisable, G-4 thought, "to order overseas commanders to comply with all requests of commanders of ports for . . . reports." Port commanders could request the information; overseas commanders would "undoubtedly furnish it unless not practicable to do so"—which, as experience had shown, was a very large "unless."[24] General Staff officers felt, too, that subordinate headquarters (SOS and the ports) should not be interposed in the direct channel of communication between overseas commanders and the General Staff on nonroutine matters. General MacArthur's request for large amounts of special jungle equipment, which was submitted about this time directly to OPD and mainly handled there, was a case in point. Under the proposed procedure this matter would have come first to SOS through the port and, if interpreted in SOS as routine or technical, might have been processed on that level. G-4 thought that the existing Materiel Status Report, with a few changes, would serve its purpose.[25]

---

[21] Transcript of Overseas Sup Conf, Washington, 22 Jul 42, 2 to 3 P.M., pp. 8–10; quote is from p. 9, Logis File, OCMH.

[22] (1) *Ibid.*, pp. 10, 13–14. (2) Port and Field AG Div OCT Diary, 13 Jul 42 entry, OCT HB; see also, 2 Oct 42 entry.

[23] (1) Draft dir, no date, sub: Materiel Status Rpts and Level of Sup Rpts from POE's, OPD 400 Sups and Equip, 97. (2) Related corresp in same file and in G-4/100.

[24] Memo, G-4 for Col C. F. Robinson, 8 Oct 42, G-4/400.

[25] Corresp in G-4/400.

In the end only the report on controlled items was put into effect, and only on a trial basis. Port commanders were made responsible for preparing it as best they could, without being permitted to "require" reports from overseas. The picture of pipeline status was completed by the supply services, which added to the report the quantities of material ready for shipment at depots; they also were given responsibility for computing authorized allowances for troops at each base. Shipments of controlled items (if for replacement) continued to be made in response to requisitions. The older Materiel Status Report, submitted to the War Department not the ports, remained the official basis for determining allotments of scarce material within which shipments should be made—an imperfect instrument, which some commands neglected to submit at all and which, at best, reached the War Department late and the supply agencies even later.[26] The ports continued to prepare monthly reports on the automatic noncontrolled classes of supply and to maintain running status records on all classes, based on whatever information they could cajole from overseas commanders. The latter continued often to find it "not practicable" to provide the information.[27]

If overseas commanders seemed to harassed port officials to be the villains of the piece, the fault was in circumstances beyond the control of either. None of the overseas bases in 1942 was in a position to organize an effective system of supply control. Except in the United Kingdom, the physical facilities for efficient storage and distribution hardly existed, and even there lack of service personnel and the enormous disruption caused by the North African operation threw base develop-

ment months behind schedule. One squadron commander in England complained, for example, that he had only two spare machine gun barrels on hand; it later developed, after more had been requisitioned from the States, that there were four hundred spare barrels in a warehouse twenty-five miles away. Duplication of supply occurred on a huge scale when the North African expedition was mounted because hundreds of thousands of tons of matériel had been "lost" in depots in the United Kingdom. This kind of extravagance could be supported, though not without strain, in the limited operations of late 1942; projected on a larger scale, it might well become prohibitive.[28]

Supply Versus Transportation

With its functions split between supply and transportation, the port lived a double life involving some conflict in purpose.[29] The overseas supply function was a novelty superimposed upon an organization struggling with the unprecedented volume of wartime traffic; the transportation function, though logically subsidiary to and part of the supply function, was already a vested interest and a going op-

[26] (1) Ltr, SOS, 15 Oct 42, sub: Materiel Status Rpts . . . , SPX 400 (10-15-42). (2) WD memo cited n. 3(2). (3) Ltr, SOS to Chiefs of SAS and CofTrans, 5 Nov 42, sub: Materiel Status Rpts, SPX 400 (11-3-42). (4) Memo, Stock Contl Div ASF for Gen Lutes, 11 Apr 43, sub: Comments for Conf With Gen Lee, Conf With Gen Lee April 1943 folder, Lutes File. (5) Memo, Capt Cross for Exec Off G-4, 11 Dec 42, G-4/400. This memo notes the lack of status reports from CBI theater. (6) See below, Ch. XXIII.
[27] Memo, CofTrans for Port Comdrs, 28 Jan 43, sub: Prompt Submission of Rpts . . . , POE Gen Overseas Sup folder, OCT HB.
[28] (1) Memo, Gen Lutes for Maj Gen Richard J. Marshall, 24 Nov 42, Misc Notes, Lutes File. (2) See also below, Ch. XVI.
[29] See above, Ch. IX.

eration. To a port transportation officer, the most pressing problem was traffic management—control of the mass of freight and people pouring through the narrow funnel of the port. The greatest danger was that rail, road, and water transport, handling equipment, and storage capacity might be glutted or overburdened and movement thus paralyzed. When the emergency struck the ports after Pearl Harbor, heroic efforts were required to avert the kind of congestion that in the winter of 1917–18 had backed up over 44,000 freight cars behind the Atlantic ports as far west as Pittsburgh and Buffalo. The volume of outgoing freight handled by all the ports in December 1941 was more than 284,000 measurement tons; in January it rose to almost 480,000 tons; in February to more than 630,000 tons. Out of this experience grew the effective system of rail traffic control that successfully carried the vast burden of troop and supply movements throughout the war.[30] To avert congestion, transportation officials insisted that freight cars, trucks, and ships must be loaded with maximum economy of space, material stored in or near the port must not be allowed to clog movement, shipments must not be called forward to the port, or to any other transshipment point, until the way was clear for them to move smoothly through. In short, the full, co-ordinated capacity of the entire pipeline to move traffic must be utilized.

But whereas efficient transportation, under wartime conditions, thus emphasized the movement of freight and personnel in the mass, efficient supply demanded the delivery of specific items to specific destinations at specific times. A shipload of war material delivered safely overseas was half wasted if half the cargo consisted of filler items not needed immediately, while urgently needed tanks and signal equipment (bulky in relation to weight) had been loaded, in the interests of saving cargo space, on a later vessel. As General Lutes wrathfully protested in February 1943, "this business of just pushing on subsistence and ammunition and stuff that [is] not needed overseas as filler cargo, as has been done in the last eight months, [has got] to stop . . . ."[31] From the point of view of supply, efficiency in transportation was not an end in itself, but had to be measured in terms of effective supply.

The conflict of purpose between the supply and transportation functions of the port under wartime stresses became evident even before the ports had assumed their new role in overseas supply. In the traffic crisis following Pearl Harbor, the great depots at San Francisco and New Orleans (the one at New York had been discontinued the preceding spring) immediately became an obstacle to the free flow of supply overseas because of the cross traffic they generated in supplying units and installations in the United States. Both general depots were discontinued early in 1942. Under the new overseas supply system the ports were intended to serve only to a limited degree as sources of supply, by keeping on hand "minimum" reserves for emergency needs of overseas bases, and to fill last-minute shortages of troops moving overseas. It proved difficult in 1942 to keep these reserves down to manageable size, port com-

---

[30] (1) Benedict Crowell and Robert Forrest Wilson, *The Road to France,* I (New Haven, Conn., Yale University Press, 1921), 115. (2) Wardlow, *Trans I,* Ch. IV, and Trans II, Ch. IV. (3) Rose, *American Wartime Transportation,* Ch. IV.
[31] (1) Telephone conv, Gen Lutes and Gen Goodman, 24 Feb 43, Stock Contl 1943 folder, Lutes File. (2) See also above, Ch. IX.

manders showing a disposition to build up reservoirs for any and all purposes. By midyear SOS officials were concerned over the growth of port reserves and the increasing tendency to use them simply as depots. Port representatives were lectured on the subject at a conference in Washington in July 1942. Port reserves were there defined as "the minimum amount of supplies essential to give elasticity to the overseas supply plan, and only incidentally to fill shortages of units going overseas." [32] The reserves should have no particular relation to the size of an overseas garrison, since no port had space or facilities to serve as a filler depot, but should be confined to selected items in quantities sufficient for emergency shipments. After midyear the emergency function of port reserves began to fade. Procedures developed during the summer and autumn for replacement of shipments lost at sea, for example, speeded up the process of initiating replacement action from normal sources of supply. Concurrently, reserves were being amassed at overseas bases to provide cushions against interruptions to supply. By October 1942, in policy if not invariably in practice, the function of port reserves was to fill minor last-minute shortages and to provide filler cargo in order to permit vessels to sail fully loaded on schedule. [33]

Co-ordination of supply action with the physical movement of shipments from depots to overseas bases during 1942 was rather loose. Since scheduling hinged mainly on the uncertain availability of shipping, it was usually expedient to set up shipments in depots in advance, as requisitions arrived, and to draw upon these shipments to provide cargo when convoys or individual vessels were ready. It was not until late in the year that the

New York port, facing the problem of scheduling the flow of maintenance supplies to North Africa over a period of several months to come, began to work out procedures to co-ordinate the processing of requisitions (including those prepared by the port for automatic shipments) with the expected flow of shipments into and through the ports. Only gradually was this system extended to the other ports. [34]

Effective co-ordination of movement depended upon a system of notification by which each agency along the route learned in advance that a shipment was ready or en route, and thus could prepare to handle it. For movements from depots to ports, notification procedures were crystallized early in 1942 as part of the Transportation Corps' general traffic control system, and except for a few spectacular breakdowns in the movement of the North African and some of the smaller task forces, the system worked smoothly throughout 1942. Far less systematized were the procedures for notifying an overseas base of action taken on its requisitions, particularly after a shipment had started on its journey from the depot. Availability notices, originating at the depot when it received an extract requisition, were supposed to be forwarded to the port, and then by the port to the base;

[32] Transcript of Overseas Sup Conf, Washington, 22 Jul 42, 9:30 to 10:30 A.M., p. 9. See also, mimeographed digest of the conference, p. 4. Both in Logis File, OCMH.

[33] (1) Alvin P. Stauffer, *Quartermaster Depot Storage and Distribution Operations,* QMC Hist Study 18 (Washington, 1948), pp. 47–54. (2) Wardlow, *Trans I,* p. 107. (3) WD ltr, 22 Jan 42, cited n. 1(1). (4) Larson, Role of the Transportation Corps in Oversea Supply, pp. 43–46, 55–66, OCT HB. (5) Corresp in Misc File folder, Plng Div ASF, Job A44-140.

[34] (1) Larson study cited n. 33(4). (2) Wardlow, Trans II, Ch. V, contains a more detailed discussion of the problems of moving cargo overseas summarized in this section.

shipping lists similarly were supposed to be sent ahead of the shipment itself. Omission of these notifications was a common complaint. The principal notification instrument was the cargo manifest, which was prepared at the port while loading was in progress and was supposed to be dispatched by air mail immediately after the ship's departure. Distances in the Pacific, bad weather in the Atlantic, and human frailty everywhere undermined the procedure. A message from the Southwest Pacific in mid-1942 commented that if the manifest ever should reach the theater ahead of the ship, it would be "one of the outstanding improvements" in overseas supply procedures.[35] The loading cable, transmitted immediately after the ship's departure, was too brief to give much specific information on the contents or stowage of the cargo; even it, moreover, was often held up for days by administrative delays in transmission and might be garbled in decoding. All these delays meant trouble for the people at the overseas base who had to make preparations to handle, store, and move incoming cargo. Finally, in the endless stream of transmitted data the incidence of error and misunderstanding was high. The SOS staff in Great Britain reported the following harrowing experience early in 1943:

The British had vague information that the *Standard* had 8 P-38s on board. We cabled New York on 23 February enquiring . . . . At the time . . . the vessel was due in 8 days. New York's reply, received on 26 February, stated that 8 P-38s were on board . . . . We checked the Bill of Lading number and found that the P-38s New York was talking about had to do with the previous voyage of this vessel. We cabled again on 27 February . . . . On 3 March, the day the vessel arrived, we received New York's reply—no P-38s on board . . . . In other words, it took us 8 days to settle the question

while in the meantime [we] . . . had to make the necessary arrangements just in case the vessel did have planes onboard.

The frequent result of delays, errors, and the inertia of a large administrative machine was that, as a typical complaint from the ETO noted, "the first indication this headquarters had that cargo was aboard for our account was when the vessel arrived at Liverpool."[36]

Supply and traffic control merged in the problem of identifying shipments. For purposes of supply and movement, a shipment was identified by its address, its priority, its contents, and the requisition or other request to which it responded. With knowledge of only the first two points, transportation agencies along the route could speed the shipment forward, and the port authorities ordinarily did not even have to know the ultimate destination, but merely the theater port of entry. Knowledge of contents was not essential to the physical handling of freight, except to the extent that certain types required special treatment (for example, ammunition, perishable foods, gasoline). At the overseas port, the problem became more complex. Theoretically, it was possible to handle incoming cargo there as it was handled at the port of embarkation—in bulk—segregating matériel only by broad classes (indicated in outside markings) for shipment to theater depots, from which it

---

[35] Memo, CG SWPA for CG SOS, 25 Jul 42, AG 400 (7-25-42).

[36] (1) Memo, OCT ETOUSA for OCT WD, 9 Mar 43, sub: Late Arrival of Cargo Loading Cables . . . , OCT 565.2 ETO. (2) Corresp in Misc File folder, Plng Div ASF, Job A44-140. (3) Leighton, Overseas Supply Policies and Procedures, pp. 57–61, OCMH. (4) Wardlow, *Trans I,* pp. 85–86.

From late 1942 on, cargo security officers accompanied vessels carrying Army cargo to insure delivery of loading lists and to convey other information bearing on unloading.

would ultimately be distributed retail to its users. SOS consistently favored this method, since wholesale distribution of matériel outward from the United States was one of the pillars of the overseas supply system.

Unfortunately, wholesale supply from the United States presupposed a mature and well-equipped machinery of wholesale-retail distribution overseas, which in 1942 no theater possessed. The theater's principal concern was to deliver incoming cargo to its users as rapidly as possible. Usually this meant that shipments had to be identified at or near the port of entry so that they could immediately be shipped to a depot or supply point accessible to the troops for whom they were destined. Delay at the port of entry not only postponed delivery but also threatened congestion and invited enemy attack. To the theater supply organization anonymous cargo was of little more use than no cargo at all. Lacking a claimant and clogging movement, it was likely to be shunted out of the main stream of traffic to wait for weeks or months until its full identity, including its contents and destined users, could be determined.

During 1942 the whole emphasis in identification mechanisms was upon the needs of traffic control and movement. The marking procedures that were developed during the first half of the year prescribed symbols to indicate merely the geographical area of destination (for example, POPPY for New Caledonia) or the troop movement that the shipment accompanied, the supply service and class to which the material belonged, and in some cases priority markings. Distinctive geometrical patterns on organizational impedimenta sometimes were used to designate units, colors to identify supply services. In addition to outer markings, packing lists attached to each box or crate, bills of lading, shipping tickets, and manifests all included more or less specific information as to contents. These various papers accompanied shipments for all or part of the journey, and copies of some, as already noted, were sent ahead to facilitate preparations for handling. Documentation, in general, was not standardized in form and was haphazard in execution—packing lists, for example, were often prepared in pencil by the packers themselves. During 1942 the Transportation Corps concentrated its efforts mainly on improving the manifest, making it more detailed, standardizing nomenclature and format, and expediting transmission.[37]

The problem of identification specifically for purposes of supply was little recognized in 1942. Under the instructions issued in July, requisitions were supposed to show markings desired by the theater, with special symbols for "each unit, installation, area or project," to permit routing to final destination. Apart from the enormous burden that this procedure placed upon depots in the United States in marking thousands of packages to a dozen different overseas areas, each employing separate marking codes, it took no account of changes in destination that might occur during the long interval between preparation of a requisition and arrival of the shipment overseas. In the United Kingdom, indeed, the port of

<hr/>

[37] (1) WD ltrs, 3 Jan and 24 Feb 42, subs: Uniform Marking of Sup and Equip. (2) WD ltrs, 6 Jun and 26 Jul 42, subs: Requisitioning and Marking of Sups for Overseas Shipt. Both in AG 400.161 series. (3) Related corresp in same file. (4) Harold Larson, Handling Army Cargo in the Second World War, Monograph 19, Sec 14, OCT HB. (5) Leighton, The Problem of Troop and Cargo Flow in Preparing the European Invasion, pp. 56–57, OCMH.

entry was not selected until a vessel approached British waters. It was in this theater, where in the summer of 1942 the tide of inflowing cargo was largest and most concentrated, that the problem of identifying cargo shipments reached crisis proportions. Col. Frank S. Ross, the theater transportation chief, noted one arriving ship in which 30 percent of the cargo had no marking whatever, and 25 percent of the remainder lacked an address and had only a general marking to show the class of supplies. The whole identification system, he wrote to Washington, needed "a revision of ideas" from the embarkation end.

If we seem impatient at times because this baggage and equipment is not marked and sailing cables do not arrive, please remember that the few days that are being saved in New York in priming a ship are more than lost here in unscrambling the mess. . . . all the warehouses and some of the piers here are completely destroyed, [so] that we must load from shipside to train and thence to depot destinations. . . . Either the method must be found to spend time on it, or our efforts here will collapse.[38]

Marking and documentation, the two facets of the identification problem, remained distinct and un-co-ordinated systems during 1942, designed primarily for control of the movement of shipments as traffic, not for supplying the item wanted when and where it was wanted. Not until the following year was the basic principle of marking—use of short symbols—to be applied also to documents, both those accompanying shipments and those making up the paper work of supply (requisitions, notices of availability, and so forth). Only when the symbol in a marking or a shipping paper could be identified with the same symbol in a requisition would it be possible, at any stage along the route

traveled by a shipment, to identify the items in the shipment as those listed in a particular requisition many weeks or months earlier (and not similar items in another requisition which perhaps had already been supplied). With such identification the transaction initiated by the requisition in question could be closed, and the cycle from demand to delivery made complete.

Filling the Pipeline

In overseas supply, as in war production, the real objectives in 1942 were rather vaguely or arbitrarily defined maxima, not calculated requirements. The gap between the existing, though rising, scale of effort and the point at which it would be safe to allow that effort to level off was so wide that its precise dimensions, for the moment, did not much matter. The aim was to fill the pipeline—to amass sufficient stocks in the distribution system, especially in its overseas segments, to provide reasonable insurance for outposts and line-of-communication bases against temporary interruptions of supply, and further to support operations of a limited offensive character. Any quantitative definition of these objectives was bound to be somewhat arbitrary in view of the unstable military situation and the short-range character of strategic plans. The necessity of scattering reserves along thousands of miles of communications and in static zones far from the areas in which they could ever be used in offensive operations was an unavoidable feature of the defensive logistics of 1942, the cost of security against an enemy who held the initiative and could strike at many points.

[38] (1) Ltr, Col Ross to Col Wylie, 28 Jul 42, ETO Admin 341A Trans-Gen, DRB AGO. (2) For subsequent developments, see below, Ch. XXIII.

Authorized levels of supply for each theater or base represented more or less arbitrary estimates of the amounts, expressed in terms of days of supply (except ammunition, which was set in terms of units of fire), that would be required to sustain each base during an interruption to the regular flow of supply.[39] According to General Marshall, consideration of "shipping turnaround, security of lines of communications, and the character and extent of operations anticipated" all entered into the calculation.[40] The 180-day level authorized for Greenland, for example, had an obvious relation to the fact that the stations there were inaccessible for part of the year and so far off the beaten track that frequent calls by supply ships would be uneconomical. In the case of the distant outposts in China and India, the inordinate length of the supply route and the small size of forces there were the determining factors in the high levels authorized. By contrast the Pacific bases, while also distant and even more liable to be cut off by enemy action, were strongly manned and were serviced by a large block of shipping, and their strategic importance obviously demanded a regular flow of supply while their aggregate strength made a high reserve level impracticable. Most of the garrisons in the Western Hemisphere were sufficiently accessible to warrant low levels.[41]

In many ways it was the small, not necessarily the most distant, bases that suffered most in the competition for supplies and shipping. At Canton, for example, subsistence stocks early in May 1942 fell to two weeks' supply. The Japanese drive into the South and Central Pacific in the spring threatened a supply crisis, leading the War Department to raise the reserve levels of the South Pacific bases to 120 days of supply. Local procurement in Australia and New Zealand eventually became a mainstay for bases near the southern end of the island chain.[42]

In the North Atlantic communication lines were shorter but less shipping was available for the small bases. The Newfoundland garrison could obtain solid fuel locally, but depended upon the Navy and a small commercial line for shipments of perishable subsistence, and upon the Navy for gasoline and oil. Although authorized reserve levels were raised in April from sixty to ninety days, shipments barely met current needs. Nonperishable food stocks dwindled to about forty days' supply by the end of March and rose only slightly during the next three months. There were hardly any fresh vegetables or fruit; motor parts requisitioned in April 1941 did not arrive until June 1942; the garrison received quantities of snow shoes and skis,

---

[39] For theater and base levels of supply, see below, App. F-1.

Before 1942 overseas reserves of ammunition, like other matériel, had been prescribed in days of supply; the change was made early in 1942 in the interests of convenience since task forces, which went overseas with ammunition allowances prescribed as units of fire, often became the nuclei of theaters of operations, and the authorized reserves of a theater then became the aggregate of the reserves prescribed for the task forces sent to it. The day of supply, unlike the unit of fire, was intended to reflect average expenditures of expendable items of supply (other than ammunition) and average mortality of replaceable equipment over any long period of operations in an overseas theater not merely in combat. See above, n. 3.

[40] Ltr, Marshall to Dill, no date, OPD 400 Sups and Equip, 1.

[41] Memo, OPD for CG SOS, 11 Jun 42, sub: Sup Levels in Overseas Bases, OPD 400 Sups and Equip 1, 14.

[42] (1) Memo, CG SOS for CofTrans, 28 May 42 SPOPS 400 Overseas, Lutes File. (2) Memo, Somervell for Gross, 19 Jan 42, ACofS G-4 1941-44 folder Hq ASF. (3) Memo cited n. 41. (4) Memo, OPD for CG SOS, 19 Jun 42, sub: Sp Reserves in Oversea Theaters . . . , Opd 381.4. (5) See above, Ch. VII and below, Ch. XV.

for which they had no use, but could not obtain subcaliber artillery bores for training. Considerable administrative confusion resulted from the division of supply responsibility between the Army and Navy and between the Boston and New York ports.[43]

The small base that lacked local resources was often in a sad plight. "Nothing is available locally," wrote the Greenland base commander, "except drinking water, and sand and rocks for construction."[44] On Ascension Island there were "no local resources of any kind" and "even water must be distilled from sea water."[45] The food shortage at this base became serious in July 1942, and was only relieved by timely shipments. The Greenland troops fared somewhat better, mainly because large stocks had been accumulated before December 1941. But on the tiny island of Antigua, in the West Indies, there was an almost complete lack of natural resources or man-made facilities surplus to the needs of a poverty-stricken population. A little fresh fruit was all the island afforded in the way of food, and shipments from the mainland or from nearby Puerto Rico were extremely irregular. Stocks of canned goods, in February 1942, fell to fifteen days' supply, perishable to five days'.[46] For small bases such as this, in the backwash of overseas deployment, the authorized level of reserves meant little as long as shipments fell so far short of reaching it. While enemy submarines were terrorizing the Caribbean in the spring of 1942, the bases there were in real danger of starvation.

Iceland was better served. As in Newfoundland, the Navy was responsible for supplying liquid fuels and perishable subsistence, and did so to the apparent satisfaction of the local Army commander.

Local procurement was of modest proportions, but mutton, fish, fresh milk, and cheese purchased from the inhabitants supplemented Army diet. While the authorized level of 120 days of supply was not reached during the first half of the year, the only shortages that caused concern were in rations, small arms ammunition, and automotive spare parts, and these occurred only occasionally. Army dissatisfaction, in fact, focused primarily on the beer ration, a chronic source of interservice and interallied friction. In July the Army base commander commented, "supply of this base has been entirely satisfactory."[47]

There was some modification in 1942 in the stated purpose of reserves. Many garrisons during 1942 were forced to eat into their reserves continually, using them as operating supplies rather than holding them for emergencies, and for practical purposes the authorized level served as an ultimate or maximum objective. In May 1942 SOS informed port and overseas commanders that these levels were to be regarded as minimum reserves, to be drawn upon only in emergencies. The

[43] See corresp in AG 400 (1-17-42)(2) Sec 2.

[44] 1st Ind, Hq APO 858 N.Y. [Greenland] to TAG, 18 Jul 42, AG 400 (1-17-42)(2) Sec 2.

[45] (1) 1st Ind, Hq COMPOS Force 8012, APO 877 N.Y. [Ascension] to TAG, 7 Sep 42, AG 400 (1-17-42)(2) Sec 2. (2) Memo, QM Hq APO 877 N.Y. for TQMG, 25 Jun 42, sub: Rpt on QM Activities and Opns at AGATE [Ascension], Logis File, OCMH.

[46] (1) See document dated 17 February 1942, which is evidently a reply to a GHQ questionnaire and refers to the supply of Antigua, in AG 400 (1-17-42)(2) Sec 1. (2) Min, WD Gen Council mtg, 2 Jun 42. (3) Corresp in Overseas Sup folder and Convoys folder, OCT HB.

[47] (1) Memo, U.S. Army Forces Iceland to AG, 30 Jul 42, sub: Sup of Overseas Bases . . . , AG 400 (1-17-42)(2) Sec 2. (2) Harold H. Dunham, Transportation of the U.S. Forces in the Occupation of Iceland, 1941-1944, Monograph 14, pp. 64ff, OCT HB. (3) Memo, G-4 for CG Field Forces, 19 Feb 42, G-4/33889.

logical corollary was to establish a maximum level as well, lest a high-priority theater amass large stocks at the expense of others. General Gross, the Chief of Transportation, resisted this move on the ground that a ceiling might prevent port commanders from taking advantage of cargo space as and when it became available, but both minimum and maximum levels were embodied in the revised instructions issued in July.[48]

Under the new policy the quantity of supplies authorized over and above the minimum level — called the operating level—was to serve as a cushion, sustaining the base during intervals between regular shipments. For regularly issued equipment (Class II), this extra quantity was not to exceed three months' normal maintenance needs. The level to which subsistence and fuel (Classes I and III) reserves might be allowed to rise above minimum levels was to be settled by agreement between port and base; operating levels were not authorized for Class IV material and ammunition. In practice, maximum levels were seldom reached. Quantities above the minimum level, in fact, were not reserves at all, in the sense of stocks set aside and not used. A base with a minimum authorized level of 90 days and a maximum of 180 would normally have on hand its 90 days' minimum reserves, while additional quantities, up to 90 more days of supply, would be moving through the pipeline as far back as the port of embarkation.[49]

The minimum level remained, and was often called, an emergency reserve, although there were wide differences in the kind of emergency each base might have to face. The most serious interruption to supply likely to occur would come about as a result of the sinking of a ship. Never-

theless, the danger of blockade and isolation, after the experience of Bataan and Corregidor, was much in the minds of supply planners. A six-months' reserve of concentrated emergency rations was accordingly authorized in the spring for all the Pacific island bases except Hawaii and Australia, for which a somewhat similar provision had been made earlier, and also for the garrison recently sent to Ascension Island. In June a similar plan provided a three-months' emergency reserve of essential medical items.[50]

Equipping Outbound Troops

The Army's experience in moving troops overseas before December 1941 proved more useful in many respects than its experience in overseas supply. Prewar overseas supply had never produced a procedural system adapted to large-scale operations. By contrast prewar troop movements, while small in scope, had made Army transportation and supply people familiar with the problems of haste and emergency, and had produced a procedural pattern for equipping and trans-

---

[48] (1) Memo, Dir of Opns SOS for overseas comdr et al., 5 May 42, sub: Level of Sup for Overseas Dept . . . , Levels of Sup folder, Logis File, OCMH. (2) Related corresp in same file. (3) WD ltr, 11 May 42 same sub, AG 400 (5-5-42). (4) WD ltr cited n. 14 (5) Memo cited n. 41. (6) Memo, CofTrans for Dir of Opns SOS, 9 Jun 42, SPTSP 400.212 file, OCT. (7) History of the Planning Division, ASF, Vol. II, Ch. XI, and Apps. 11-A, 11-B, OCMH.

[49] (1) See WD ltr cited n. 14. (2) For authorize levels of overseas theaters, see below, App. F-1.

[50] (1) Memo, Dir of Opns SOS for TQMG, 30 May 42, sub: Reserve of Emergency Rations, Opns SO 1942–43 folder, Hq ASF. (2) Memo, Lutes for Somervell, 8 May 42, Misc Notes, Lutes File. (3) Ltr, CG SOS to CINCSWPA, no date, sub: Comments of Rpt . . . by Gen A. R. Wilson . . . , Pt. 2, Incl Study for Gen Lutes on Pac Area folder, Plng Div ASF.

porting the individual troop unit, the common denominator of overseas deployment.[51]

The movement of three small forces to Bermuda and Caribbean bases in September 1941 foreshadowed many later difficulties. "Failure by planning agencies to allow sufficient time between announcement of the decision . . . and the effective date of embarkation" was, according to G-4, the basic source of confusion.

At least two weeks are necessary in the case of troops completely equipped, while one month is the absolute minimum for those organizations in which shortages exist. Sufficient time must be allowed to issue supply orders, to gain control of equipment, to overhaul or check the equipment, to properly crate the items for overseas shipment and to move the articles to the port of embarkation.[52]

The stocks at Charleston, the port from which the Bermuda and Caribbean forces sailed, were insufficient to fill shortages that should have been filled earlier, and efforts to draw equipment from neighboring stations met evasions or outright refusals from commandants who, unwilling to deplete their own troops, demanded orders from Washington. Though destined for tropical stations, troops arrived at port with full allowances of winter clothing. Unit commanders failed to send ahead representatives to oversee final processing, and "many officers with the forces were totally ignorant of many details prescribed for accomplishment before leaving home stations."[53] Equipment shipped to port was improperly marked and flimsily crated; administrative records were in chaos.

In October and November 1941 The Inspector General conducted extended investigations of movement operations on both east and west coasts. Curiously enough, virtually all the reforms he recommended turned out to be already standard procedure. Evidently the deficiencies were not in the system but in its operation. New instructions published on 6 December 1941 accordingly made no important changes, but all the operating rules were presently consolidated into a set of standard procedures to be appended as "Inclosure No. 1" to each troop movement order.[54]

Under these procedures units moving overseas were equipped in two stages—at the home station and at the staging area and port. During the first stage the corps area (for air force units, the Chief of the AAF) had the primary responsibility for supply (except for controlled items) and also assumed command of the alerted unit. In the second stage, the unit passed to the port commander's control, and supply responsibility rested with the supply services and the port. When first alerted, the unit drew equipment as far as possible from stocks at the station and nearby depots, then from other depots or units in the corps area. Remaining shortages were reported by corps area inspectors to the appropriate supply services. The services were then responsible for filling the shortages from their depots, or drawing equip-

---

[51] See above, Chs. II, V.

[52] Memo, Col Aurand for Col R. A. Wheeler, 23 Sep 41, sub: Sup of Units Departing . . . , G-4/33098.

[53] Ltr, Col J. E. Slack to G-4, 19 Sep 41, sub: MAROON [Trinidad], CERISE [Antigua], VERMILION [Bermuda] Forces, G-4/33098-2.

[54] (1) Memo, TIG for CofS, 2 Dec 41, sub: Sup and Mvmt of Units . . . , G-4/33098. (2) WD ltr, 6 Dec 41, same sub, AG 370.5 (12-3-41). (3) Memo, G-4 for G-3, 6 Dec 41, sub: Revision of Policy Concerning Tr Mvmts, G-4/33378. (4) The first "Inclosure No. 1" appeared on 9 January, for a shipment through New Orleans. See AG 370.5 (1-9-42).

CHART 8—PROCEDURE FOR EQUIPPING A TYPICAL UNIT FOR OVERSEAS MOVEMENT: DECEMBER 1941

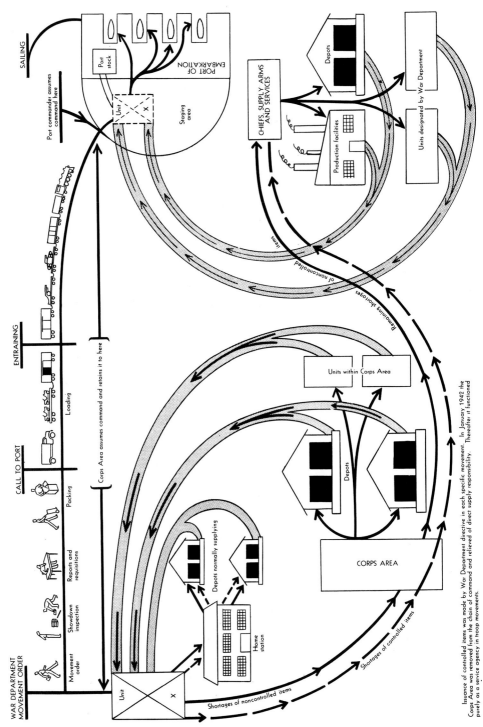

Issuance of controlled items was made by War Department directive in each specific movement. In January 1942 the Corps Area was removed from the chain of command and relieved of direct supply responsibility. Thereafter it functioned purely as a service agency in troop movements.

ment from units under their control or from units designated by the using arms and services. Shipments were made to the home station, if time permitted, or to the port of embarkation. Items that failed to arrive at port in time were supplied from port stocks if available. *(Chart 8)*

The basic weakness of this procedure, which had been apparent in the movements of late 1941, was that the corps area commander, responsible for the first stage of outfitting alerted units, lacked the authority necessary to transfer equipment from other units in the area, most of which were under the control of the field army commander. The latter naturally lacked driving incentives to take precious equipment from his own units for the benefit of units no longer under his control, and his subordinates, in turn, "failed to respond fully," as an inspecting officer cautiously observed.[55] Corps area commanders themselves appeared reluctant to press the matter. In January and February 1942, accordingly, the army commander was brought back into the supply process and made responsible for inspections to determine shortages, supervising the submission of requisitions to post supply officers and the reporting of shortages to corps area headquarters, designating units under his command that were to be required to give up equipment, and reporting remaining shortages to the supply services. In February, as a logical corollary, the corps area commander also lost his command authority over units being prepared for overseas movement; these now remained under the army or other field commander until they moved to port. As far as the home-station phase of preparation was concerned, supply and command responsibility were unified. The corps area supply system remained at the disposal of

alerted units, but post supply officers, under procedures instituted in the spring, sent requisitions directly to depots instead of through corps area headquarters; the corps area was to "progressively withdraw from the channel of supply insofar as direct supply to troops [was] concerned."[56]

After the general reorganization of 9 March 1942, over-all command of troops in the United States was lodged in the Army Ground Forces, Army Air Forces, the Services of Supply, and defense commands. To fill their equipment shortages before departure from the home station, units looked first, as before, to the normal supply machinery of the station and the depots that fed it, which, for ground combat and service troops, was administered by SOS agencies; for AAF troops, supply was centralized in that command (except for certain common categories of supply), with its own regional organization. After local sources had been exploited, if time permitted, the major command drew upon other depots and transferred equipment from other units under its command. Ordinarily, however, there was not even time for neighboring depots to make all shipments to the station before the troops departed for port, at which time the major command relinquished control of the unit to transportation agencies of the SOS. Supply responsibility then passed to the supply services, which undertook to fill

---

[55] (1) Memo, Inspector Gen for G-4, 17 Nov 41, sub: Recommendations in Connection With Sup and Mvmt . . . , G-4/33098. (2) Related corresp in same file. (3) WD ltr, 23 Dec 41, sub: Current Sup Policy and Proced, AG 475 (12-20-41).

[56] (1) WD ltr, 20 Jan 42, sub: Direct System of Sup . . . , AG 475 (1-16-42). Direct supply became effective on 30 April 1942. (2) Incl No. 1 cited n. 54(4). (3) WD ltr, 12 Feb 42, sub: Sup and Mvmt of Units Ordered Overseas, AG 370.5 (2-11-42). (4) WD ltr, 25 Feb 42, same sub, AG 370.5 (2-24-42).

remaining shortages by direct shipment to the port.[57] *(Chart 9)*

Equipping units that were hurrying to catch a boat involved more than a delivery service administered by a distant headquarters. The success of the operation depended at bottom upon prompt and intelligent determination of needs and execution of the prescribed administrative action by the supply officers of the moving units. Station supply officers and the corps area organization were permitted to offer only advice and service. War Department and SOS instructions emphasized repeatedly the need for closer supervision by tactical commanders of the process of equipping their troops. Unit supply officers were often ignorant of the rudiments of supply procedure. General Somervell, during an inspection, ran across an Air Corps officer who had never heard of a table of basic allowances and an AAF unit that did not even have a supply officer. One group of departing Air Corps officers, "not as well instructed in supply matters as they might be," arrived at New York, spent the night at the Waldorf-Astoria, and sent the bill the next morning to the port commander.[58]

The "professional" supply personnel, with less excuse for ignorance, were not always better informed, especially at the station level. Those who knew their procedures did not always temper their knowledge with judgment and a desire to help. At the first conference of service commanders in July 1942, Somervell thundered in pungent language against ritual and red tape:

. . . if anyone in any of these depots sends a requisition back because the fifth copy is a little faint or because some clerk forgot to put in a comma on the second copy, I want you to light on that bird like a ton of bricks. . . .

I do not mean that you should permit people to do sloppy work in preparing requisitions, but we must not stop the movement of supplies because someone in any of the depots does not get things in in quintuplicate Thursday morning at 7:42. . . . When somebody is supposed to have supplies, I want them to get the supplies, and we will worry about the red tape afterwards. Nobody will ever get into trouble by doing this.[59]

The SOS looked to its regional administrative organization in the service commands, now free of direct supply responsibilities, to police the process of equipping troops moving overseas. This was purely a service function, not implemented by command authority nor even by supervisory responsibility in the usual sense, and the helpful advice that service command officers thus offered in the line of duty was not always welcomed by troop commanders who shared the combat soldier's ancient suspicion of interference by an "administrative" headquarters. Nevertheless, service commanders were instructed, as Somervell put it, "to be as nosey as can be all the time, and to step in at any time, any place, to help anybody. Even the Air Forces, go in and help them." [60]

Almost invariably troops arrived in the port area without their full complement of equipment. Unit commanders themselves

[57] (1) Incl No. 1, 22 Mar 42, and revisions, 7 May and 18 Jun 42, AG 370.5. (2) WD ltr cited n. 1(2) (3) Wardlow, Trans II, Ch. II.

[58] (1) Memo, Somervell for Lutes, 17 May 42, Opns SOS 1942–43 folder, Hq ASF. (2) Min, conf of CG's Sv Comds, Chicago, 30 Jul 42, 2d Sess, p. 72, Contl Div ASF. (3) Memo for rcd atchd to memo, unsigned, no addressee, 19 Jan 42, AG 400 (1-17-42) Sec 1. (4) Ltr, AAF, 25 May 42, sub: Equip for Units Destined for Overseas, AG 400 (1-17-42) Sec 2. (5) Mimeographed digest of Overseas Sup Conf, Washington, 22 Jul 42, *passim*, Logis File, OCMH.

[59] Min, p. 72, cited n. 58(2).

[60] *Ibid.*, pp. 51, 61, 63–64, 72–73; quote is from p 72.

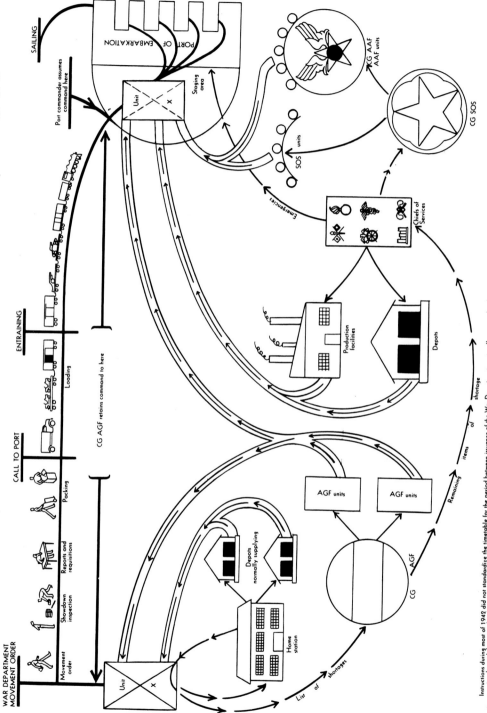

CHART 9—PROCEDURE FOR EQUIPPING A TYPICAL AGF UNIT FOR OVERSEAS MOVEMENT: MID–1942

Instructions during most of 1942 did not standardize the timetable for the period between issuance of the War Department movement order and the time of sailing. The "call to port," designating the date by which troops and freight were expected to arrive at port, was issued by the port commander through command channels, and information copies were sent directly to all concerned. Actual arrangements for transportation to the staging area or port of embarkation were made through the local station transportation officer.

were inclined to regard the port as a cornucopia from which they could obtain whatever they needed. "Don't worry about that, you will get it at the port," was the reassuring comment often heard during show-down inspections at home stations.[61] The administrative burden thus placed upon the port was aggravated by the frequent failure of unit supply officers to bring along their reports of earlier equipment inspections and of supply services to notify the port of action already taken and shipments en route to the port. There seemed to be a widespread feeling, too, that "you can repair it at the port." Late in spring of 1942 troops were still arriving at New York with 13 percent of their vehicles needing repair.[62] Similar difficulties occurred in the staging areas, which were widely used in troop movements in 1942 to avoid the confusion that had resulted the preceding autumn when troops were moved without a pause directly to the ports. When movement schedules permitted, some of the final inspections and other processing were performed in these staging areas, and stocks of selected items were established for the purpose at some of the principal ones. Sometimes troops were held in the areas for weeks or months as a result of changes in movement plans, while equipment, training, and morale deteriorated. The necessity to continue training in these instances led to jurisdictional wrangles between SOS, whose port commanders controlled the staging areas and the troops in them, and the other two major commands, especially AGF, which desired more effective control over the training of their own units. SOS successfully defended its jurisdiction, but AGF and AAF were given authority to supervise the training of their units while in staging areas.[63]

In troop movements as in overseas supply, therefore, it was difficult to curb the growth of the ports' burdens as sources of supply, and in 1942 the supply stocks that they had to maintain to handle the burden tended to increase. In July and from time to time later, as already noted, SOS tried to draw the line against further increases, but as long as deployment itself remained disorderly and ill planned, as it did throughout that year, troops continued to arrive in ports and staging areas with large gaps in their equipment that had to be filled from stocks immediately available. The primary function of the port in troop movements was to move, not to supply, outbound troops, and the Transportation Corps' procedures were directed mainly to that end by ensuring that supply shipments from the depots moved promptly but smoothly, that none were shipped to a home station after troops had started for port, and that the port received adequate advance notification of troop and freight shipments. Through the release system, from early 1942 on, the ports were able to protect themselves against being deluged by port-bound traffic.[64]

All other considerations were subordi-

[61] Memo, Port QM [of unnamed port] for CG [of unnamed port], 6 Aug 42, Misc Notes, Lutes File.

[62] (1) Note, unsigned, no addressee, *circa* May 1942, in 400 Sup Gen folder, Plng Div ASF, Job A-44-140. (2) Memo for rcd, 18 Jan 42, sub: Equipg of Trs, AG 400 (1-17-42) Sec 1. (3) WD ltr, 23 Jan 42, sub: Preparation of Automotive Equip . . . , AG 370.5 (1-22-42).(4) Memo, unsigned, for br chiefs of Opns Div SOS, 21 May 42, Misc Notes, Lutes File.

[63] (1) Palmer, Wiley, and Keast, *AGF II*, pp. 573-77. (2) Wardlow, Trans II, Ch. II. (3) Chester Wardlow, Expansion of Army Transportation Facilities in the Zone of the Interior, 1941-1944, Monograph 8, Oct HB. (4) Larson, Water Transportation for the U.S. Army, 1939-1942, OCT HB. (5) Corresp in OPD 370.5 Changes of Station, 39.

[64] Corresp in Overseas Shipts folder and Overseas Tr Mvmts 1940-42 folder, OCT HB, and in G-4/33889.

nated, in troop movements, to the necessity of meeting the scheduled sailing date. One of the very few movements during 1942 in which sufficient time was allowed to complete preparations before this date was that of the 1st Infantry Division to the United Kingdom early in August—the SOS was informally alerted to expect this move almost three months earlier, and another month elapsed before movement orders were actually issued on 19 June. Most movements were carried out in frantic haste. The wild scramble caused at the New York port during the first week of January 1942 by the last-minute diversion of the North Atlantic convoy to the Far East was the most spectacular of many outloading crises. On one occasion in May OPD first notified SOS headquarters at 5 P.M. of a movement that was to begin three hours later. In the case of the 32d Division, alerted in December 1941 for movement to Iceland, there was indeed a lapse of many weeks before it finally sailed in April. But in the interim the division's destination was changed twice; on both occasions it was hurriedly made ready for departure and then kept in a state of suspense while its equipment and morale deteriorated and its strength was depleted by transfers to other units. Finally, after its sailing to England had been postponed to July and its equipment priority reduced to C-2, the division, then at its home station in Massachusetts, was notified by telephone that it was to sail in three weeks from San Francisco for Australia. Within that time SOS had to re-equip the force and move it across the country. The task was accomplished by attaching to the division a special group of SOS officers who supervised equipment inspections and telephoned shortage lists directly to the supply services in Washington.[65]

In an effort to allow time for advance preparation, OPD began in the spring of 1942 to issue through G-3 a list of units tentatively expected to be deployed within the next three months. Some units were named specifically; others were listed by type only, leaving the major commands to designate specific units. To the limited degree permitted by equipment shortages and the prevailing policy of spreading equipment thin over many units in training, this three-month projection enabled the major commands to set up a pool of earmarked units ready to move. During 1942, however, the erratic shifting of units from low priorities to high and back again left little room for procedures aiming at an orderly and progressive equipping of units in co-ordination with their training schedules. As early as September 1941 a G-4 observer had urged, after watching the movements through Charleston, that the embarkation date in the future should "be fixed on the basis of readiness of troops," and the Chief of Staff had actually enunciated a policy that troops going overseas should be completely equipped before departure.[66] But after Pearl Harbor, the time of departure necessarily was fixed by considerations of strategic need and availability of shipping, not readiness. Beginning in March, the General Staff began to call for informal status reports from the major commands showing readiness of units alerted for movement, but these were con-

[65] (1) John D. Millett, Overseas Movement of the 1st Infantry Division and the 1st Armored Division, MS, 1943, OCMH. (2) Min, WD Gen Council mtg, 27 May 42. (3) Min, p. 54, cited n. 58(2). (4) Palmer, Wiley, and Keast, *AGF II*, pp. 572–73. (5) Corresp in OPD 370.5 Changes of Station, 93; OPD 400 Sups and Equip, 9; and G-4/33889. (6) See above, Chs. VI–VII, and below, Chs. XVI–XVII.

[66] (1) Memo cited n. 52. (2) Memo, G-3 for CG's maj comds, 19 Apr 42, sub: Units Scheduled for Mvmt . . . , OPD 370.5 Changes of Station, 24.

cerned with training and general efficiency rather than equipment. Even after status reporting was formalized in July, the required information scarcely indicated in any specific way how much of the unit's equipment would be lacking when it sailed. As a general policy, troops were not kept from sailing for lack of equipment. To that lack, however, sometimes could be traced deficiencies in training that caused many units to be judged unfit for overseas service.[67]

Rare, indeed, was the unit that sailed with all its authorized equipment, and delayed shipments from depots commonly straggled into port for months after the troops had departed. The equipment of one antiaircraft regiment that went overseas in summer of 1942 was loaded haphazardly on fifty-five separate vessels calling at several different ports. Overseas commanders naturally clamored for shipment of troops and equipment of each unit in such a manner that they would arrive together, or nearly so. They also pleaded for loading and routing that would ensure that cargo could be readily unloaded without rearrangement at several successive ports of discharge, in order to reduce the delay in "marrying up" troops and equipment.[68]

What overseas commanders desired was largely beyond the reach of procedural improvements. Except in combat-loaded convoys, rarely used in movements from the United States, it was usually not feasible for all of a unit's equipment to be loaded in the same vessels with the troops, and often not even in accompanying vessels. Availability of escorts and shipping and general considerations of scheduling all bore upon the problem. Minimum essential housekeeping items ordinarily were stowed on the transports or on vessels

in attendance; of the two barracks bags allotted to each soldier in 1942, one went with him, but the other all too frequently was buried in the hold of a later ship and never caught up with him. Most cargo had to be loaded in freighters too slow to keep up with troop transports; some of the latter, such as the *Queens,* could not even accommodate all the troops' personal baggage. In many cases troopers and freighters sailed independently from different ports — for example, the POPPY Force convoy of January 1942. In shipments to the United Kingdom the port of entry was not assigned until the vessel was approaching the British Isles. Even when departures were synchronous, cargo vessels could not keep up with troop transports except when both sailed in the same convoy; on the long overseas runs, freighters might fall weeks behind the troop transports. Crossing the North Atlantic, the speedy *Queens* could make two round trips in little more time than a cargo convoy required to make a single one-way trip. Movement orders were rarely issued early enough to permit the shipment of cargo in advance of troops. Indeed, even for simultaneous departure it was often necessary to take equipment from troops up to a month before sailing. Once a unit sailed without some of its equipment, the shipping shortage usually forced the the-

[67] (1) Memo, Exec Off for ACofS WPD, 22 Mar 42, sub: Mvmt Orders, OPD 370.5 Changes of Station, 171. (2) Memo, OPD for maj comds, 1 Jul 42, sub: Status Rpts, OPD 370.5 Changes of Station, 184. (3) Memo, TIG for DCofS, 10 Apr 43, sub: Readiness of Units for Mvmt Overseas, Sv Trs 1942–43, 62a folder, Lutes File.

[68] (1) Memo, Deputy Chief of Mvmts Div OCT for Col Noble M. Coe, 5 Jun 42, sub: Shortages of Equip, Overseas Tr Mvmts 1940–42 folder, OCT HB. (2) Memo, Lutes for CofTrans, 26 Sep 42, sub: Difficulties in Shipg Sups Overseas, Overseas Shipts folder, OCT HB.

ater staff to make an unhappy choice of receiving equipment left behind or equipment of units sailing later. Exigencies of traffic control in the flow of shipments from depots to ports and the compelling need to economize on cargo space were additional factors standing in the way of a synchronized movement of troops and equipment overseas. The Chief of Transportation found it necessary late in 1942 to emphasize as "a fundamental of movements" that organizational equipment should be shipped with troops or as soon thereafter as possible, but the backlogs of equipment at east coast ports were still so large early in 1943 that SOS ordered this matériel moved back to the depots.[69]

Fundamentally, synchronization of the flow of troops and cargo was not feasible because, considered as transportable commodities, people and freight presented different problems of handling and movement. On the whole, it was easier and required less time to transport the former than the latter. Movement of freight was further retarded by the effort to bring together troops and their equipment at three points—the home station, the port of embarkation, and the overseas port of entry—an effort that many believed unnecessary. The essential object of troop deployment was to bring military manpower as an effective force into striking range of the enemy. Fully equipped and trained forces had to be assembled in a theater for deployment in the combat zone, but this did not necessarily require an earlier union of troops and equipment. One field commander admitted:

Organizational commanders will always recommend that supplies should accompany the troop units in the same transports. . . . My personal opinion is that the main object is to use to the maximum shipping space, and

it is not mandatory that equipment and supplies go on the same transport as the troops unless it is known that these troops will be engaged immediately upon debarkation. . . . The getting together of troops with their equipment after their arrival is not an insurmountable task.

The logical drift of this line of reasoning was toward shipping equipment and supplies in advance of troops, to be stored in bulk in the theater and reissued to the troops after their arrival.[70]

Several practical difficulties stood in the way of such a policy in 1942. Until a unit was alerted it needed what equipment it had for training. The process of inspections, analysis of shortages, and submission of requisitions had to be completed. Shortages of matériel in 1942 ruled out any general program of shipping new equipment in advance and leaving the old behind, when units sailed, to be used by other units still in training. Theater commanders in general preferred to have initial equipment shipped "force marked"— for specific units—rather than in bulk since they objected to the additional burden of storage and distribution in the theater. Unit commanders counted equipment in the hand or on the way better than equipment buried in a theater depot. The War Department, for its part, was wary of investing war matériel in theater reserves for future offensives that might never be undertaken. Advance shipment

---

[69] (1) 3d Ind, OCT to NYPOE, 11 Dec 42, OCT 370.5 England. (2) Memo, CG SOS for CG USAFIME, 30 Dec 42, Misc Notes, Lutes File. (3) Corresp in Overseas Shipts folder and Overseas Tr Mvmts 1940–42 folder, OCT HB. (4) SOS Memo S270-1-42, 8 Dec 42. (5) SOS Memo S700-1-43, 2 Jan 43. Last two refer to the cancellation of back orders and clearance of backlogs.

[70] Memo, Dir of Opns SOS for Chief of Sup Br, 17 Jul 42, Policy File SWPA folder, Plng Div ASF, Job A46-371. Quotation by Gen. A. R. Wilson.

in bulk, therefore, was seldom attempted in 1942 and then only on a modest scale. Throughout that year, as a result, equipping troops for overseas movement remained largely a hand-to-mouth process.[71]

Service Troops and the Troop Basis

The authors of the Victory Program in the summer of 1941 provided generously in their estimates of service support for the armies they expected some day to defeat Germany on the European continent. Going beyond even the 33 percent that service troops had comprised in the U.S. armies in France in 1918, the planners set up percentages up to 46 percent in those parts of the Victory Program Troop Basis where service components were specified. Ground service elements not organic to combat units averaged about 36 percent in the task force pool; services were 46 percent of the planned air forces. Even higher percentages, presumably, were to be expected in the one-million-odd troops envisaged for administrative overhead and garrison duties in the United States. However, plans for actual mobilization, in late 1941 and early 1942, followed a different course. By mid-April 1942 planned services not organic to ground combat units stood at only 18 percent of the total ground strength in the 1942 War Department Troop Basis. In part this figure reflected a deliberate intent to push the activation of ground divisions ahead of that of nondivisional units, since the former required approximately twice as long to train. It reflected also an understandable desire to produce fighting strength as rapidly as possible, and to dispense with "luxuries."[72]

But meanwhile, the immediate emergency was demolishing plans and programs for orderly mobilization of the Army at home in anticipation of eventual mass employment overseas. Base garrisons had to be filled, new bases established, and task forces rushed to threatened areas. The crisis demanded immediate deployment to remote, undeveloped areas in the Pacific on a scale far beyond that anticipated. Every commander discovered when he arrived at his destination that he needed more service troops than he had brought along. Even in the highly developed economic environment of the British Isles, American commanders were disappointed in their expectations that most of the facilities and services needed to maintain a military establishment would be available on the spot. During the late winter and spring of 1942, as a consequence, service units had to be activated well in excess of mobilization schedules and before long exceeded the total service troop provisions of the 1942 Troop Basis. By May overdrafts upon the troop basis, mainly for service units, had reached 250,000.[73]

In January and again in March General Somervell unsuccessfully sought a larger authorization for services in the troop basis. In April the approval of the cross-Channel invasion plan, looking to an immediate build-up of base facilities in the British Isles, focused General Staff at-

---

[71] (1) Palmer, Wiley, and Keast, *AGF II,* pp. 457, 572. (2) For advance shipment to the United Kingdom in 1942, see below, Ch. XIV.

[72] (1) "Ultimate Requirements Study: Estimate of Army Ground Forces," accompanying "War Department Strategic Estimate . . . , 11 September 1941," WPD 4494-21. (2) Memo, Lutes for OPD, 17 Apr 42, sub: Reqmts of Sv Units . . . , Sv Units 1942–43, 2a folder, Lutes File. (3) Greenfield, Palmer, and Wiley, *AGF I,* p. 199.

[73] (1) Min cited n. 65(2). (2) Greenfield, Palmer, and Wiley, *AGF I,* p. 203. (3) See above, Ch. VII, and below, Chs. XIV–XV, XVII.

tention upon the problem. SOS presented estimates in April calling for an addition of nearly 335,000 service troops to the 1942 Troop Basis. Early in May the General Staff approved a reduced estimate of 236,000, and the President in the same month permitted an augmentation of 750,000 men for the entire 1942 Troop Basis, to cover these and other troop needs.[74]

Priceless time had been lost. The units authorized in May still had to be activated and trained. During the summer, moreover, the flow of fillers to newly activated units was retarded when the President instituted furloughs for new inductees. The Air Forces had first call on available manpower, both as to quality and as to quantity; ground units of all types, combat and service alike, were pinched, and the General Staff for the time being resisted proposals to decelerate activations in any one branch to provide manpower for others.[75] Service troops, even more than combat troops, suffered from the shortage of equipment. During the summer the General Staff, on the whole, adhered to a policy of spreading critical equipment thinly over a large number of units in various stages of training, refusing alike to pool equipment in a small, balanced force of units ready for early movement overseas, or to raise the 20 percent initial allowance of critical equipment to which new nondivisional service units were restricted.[76]

After midyear, demands for service units multiplied. Two big projects for line-of-communication development—in the Persian Corridor and in western Canada and Alaska—had not been anticipated when the 1942 Troop Basis was drawn up. These and the expanding logistical activities in certain other areas, such as the Middle East and along the African ferry route, called for service troops on a scale and of a character quite different from normal rear area support in most overseas theaters—engineer, railway, port, and truck units, many of regimental size or larger. In midsummer came the sudden decision to invade North Africa, which meant opening up a new overland line of communications of continental dimensions; it quickly became apparent that the pool of service units originally intended for the United Kingdom was inadequate in size and composition for this task. At the same time, the base development program in England continued, though at a diminished pace. At the end of the year the European theater commander was accepting partially trained units in order to keep that program alive, an expedient to which other bases, notably the Persian Gulf Service Command, were also driven. In the near and far Pacific the clamor for more service troops, particularly for port battalions, grew louder as the tempo of build-up mounted. Lt. Gen. Joseph W. Stilwell's needs in India, still largely unmet because of lack of shipping and the low priority of his theater, became steadily more insistent.

The zone of interior commands were quite unprepared to meet the flooding demands for service units, which included both standard and "odd ball" types.

[74] (1) Min, WD Gen Council mtgs, 21 Apr, 19 May, and 27 May 42. (2) Memo, SGS for CG SOS, 19 May 42, OPD 320.2 BOLERO, 8. (3) Memo, Somervell for CofS, 14 Sep 42, sub: Sv Units, Sv Units 1942–43, 3a folder, Lutes File.

[75] (1) Memo cited n. 74(3). (2) Memo, OPD for CG SOS, 2 Jul 42, sub: Tr Basis, OPD 320.2 (6-26-42). (3) Min, WD Gen Council mtg, 30 Jun 42. (4) Paper, no date, sub: Chronology of Steps To Correct Deficiency in Sv Units, Sv Units 1942–43, 3a folder, Lutes File. (5) Greenfield, Palmer, and Wiley, *AGF I*, pp. 206–08.

[76] See above, Ch. XII.

"Trained non-divisional service units," Brig. Gen. John E. Hull wrote Lt. Gen. Dwight D. Eisenhower in mid-July, "are not available . . . . The state of training and discipline of many of the service units now going and set up for departure in the near future is entirely unsatisfactory. . . . I don't see any relief in the immediate future . . . ."[77] The service troop program authorized in May, Somervell commented bitterly in September in the midst of the confusion of mounting the North African operation, had been "completely hamstrung."[78]

SOS became the principal advocate before the General Staff for overseas commanders requesting service troops, partly because it had the responsibility for activating and training most types of service units, partly because of the close personal and official relations that Somervell and Lutes maintained with SOS commanders overseas. For its own operations the AAF, of course, was an equally ardent and generally successful advocate of more generous service support; the ratio of service troops to total AAF strength ran consistently higher than the corresponding ratio in the ground forces. General McNair, the AGF commander, felt the existing proportion in the Army as a whole was too high rather than too low. "It appears," he wrote in September, "that overall production of services to combat forces is grossly excessive; and some definite measures to control the dissipation of manpower to these non-combatant functions must be instituted at once."[79] General McNair's views had many champions on the General Staff, but it was difficult to resist the pressures growing out of the peculiar conditions of warfare in 1942 and out of the American way of life in general. As G-3 admitted, "unless we will be satisfied with

an Army like the Japanese, wherein every soldier can carry a week's supply of rice, it will not be possible to greatly reduce the size of the services."[80]

Late in the summer it became evident that a deceleration of scheduled activations was the only practicable means of relieving the manpower shortage, and during the last four months of the year the activation of ground combat units was slowed almost to a stop while existing AGF units were being brought up to strength. In the AAF and SOS activations continued at a rapid rate.[81]

At the end of the year the service troop situation overseas showed marked improvement, and in the States SOS staff officers felt that the General Staff was finally, if belatedly, awake to the problem. Service troop strength in the Army had grown rapidly in recent months, benefiting by the speed-up in inductions approved by the President in September. The relative weight of service elements in the Army had grown even more. Service troops of all categories—numbering more than 1,800,000—now comprised 34.4 per-

[77] Ltr, Hull to Eisenhower, 17 Jul 42, OPD 320.2 ETO, 6.

[78] (1) Memo cited n. 74(3). (2) Memo for file, unsigned, 19 Sep 42, sub: Activation and Tng of Sv Units, Sv Units 1942-43 folder, Case 4, Lutes File. (3) Memo, Lutes for Somervell, 1 Sep 42, Misc Notes, Lutes File. (4) Cline, *Washington Command Post*, pp. 184-86. (5) Memo, Chief of Mobilization Br for Gen Lutes, 30 Nov 42, sub: Sv Units, Sv Trs 1942-43 folder, Case 17, Lutes File.

[79] (1) Ltr, CG AGF to TAG, 30 Sep 42, sub: Tr Basis, AGF 320.2/4, Tr Basis 1943, DRB AGO. (2) Ltr, Lutes to CG SOS S Pac Area, 5 Jan 43, SPAC 1942-43-mid-1944 folder, Case 25, Lutes File. (3) Ltr, Lutes to CG SOS S Pac Area, 11 Jan 43, SPAC 1942-43-mid-1944 folder, Case 33, Lutes File.

[80] Min cited n. 65(2) and n. 75(3).

[81] (1) Memo, Lutes for Somervell, 24 Sep 42, Misc Notes, Lutes File. (2) Greenfield, Palmer, and Wiley, *AGF I*, pp. 208-09. (3) Min, WD Gen Council mtg, 31 Jul 42. (4) Gen Plans Br SOS Diary, 28 Jul 42 entry, Plng Div ASF.

cent of the Army's total strength, in contrast to only 26.3 a year earlier. Prospects were that these gains would be kept during the coming year, even though the total strength of the Army was now not expected to rise above 7,500,000 enlisted men. SOS had been assured that additional service units, if needed, could be formed from the pool of unallotted strength (500,000) in the new troop basis, and had been given authority to alter the distribution of service-type units. Ground service personnel in the planned Army, including 150,000 in the Women's Army Auxiliary Corps and some 172,000 in combat-zone service units, comprised 35 percent of the then allotted manpower; in the entire Troop Basis of 7.5 million, ground service personnel of rear area types only comprised 27.6 percent.[82]

There was some quiet crowing in SOS headquarters over this achievement. General Styer reminded his chief that it was a result of "much hard work on the part of General Lutes during the last two months,"[83] and Lutes himself reported that, in view of the promising outlook, "further recommendations to the Chief of Staff are unnecessary at this time."[84] To which Somervell penciled the comment, "Excellent."[85] But the battle went on. Overseas commanders, during the winter and spring of 1943, continued to ask for more service units than the three zone of interior commands could produce under the General Staff's cautious activation policy and with the meager allowances of equipment given to service units for training. And by mid-1943 ASF once more was urging the addition of more service units to the troop basis.[86]

The course of events in 1942 that forced the War Department to provide a far more elaborate service establishment than initially planned also subjected the developing machinery of overseas supply and deployment to unanticipated strains. American ground forces were not massed in a single theater, either against the European or the Asiatic enemy, but were dispersed along lines of communications, in distant outposts, and in quiet areas; the points of actual contact with the enemy were relatively few. Most of the areas where troops were stationed were anchors and fueling points along supply routes, not reservoirs. Supplies flowed outward, perforce, along the many paths marked out by a wide deployment.

It was difficult to support this pattern of deployment by a system designed to compress the flow of supply into few rather than many channels, to extend the radius of wholesale operations, and to pour war material into overseas reservoirs for retail distribution forward. The haste with which most of the important deployments of 1942 were ordered and carried out virtually defied any orderly procedures for equipping outbound troops. The system was best adapted, in the last analysis, to a strategy of concentrated effort in one theater, a long build-up followed by massive land campaigns. For a few weeks during the spring of 1942 strategic plans moved

[82] (1) Corresp in Tr Basis 1943 folder and Sv Trs 1942–43 folder, Lutes File. (2) Memo, G-3 for SOS, 21 Nov 42, sub: Sv Trs' Tr Basis 1944 and Beyond, WDGCT 320.2 Gen (11-14-42). (3) Greenfield, Palmer, and Wiley, AGF I, pp. 208–10, 214–17, and tables on pp. 203, 210. (4) See below, App. I.
[83] Memo, Styer for Somervell, 4 Dec 42, Sv Trs 1942–43 folder, Case 23, Lutes File.
[84] Memo, Lutes for Somervell, 4 Dec 42, sub: Sv Units, Tr Basis 1943, Plan for folder, Lutes File.
[85] Memo cited n. 83.
[86] Corresp in Tr Basis 1943 folder and Sv Trs 1942–43 folder, Lutes File.

in this direction and the build-up of troops and material in the British Isles for a cross-Channel invasion actually got under way. With the suspension of invasion plans in the summer and the mounting of limited offensives in the Pacific and North Africa, the logistical system faced tasks for which it had not been designed. The forces in North Africa were supplied for several months by abnormal procedures and largely uncontrolled automatic shipments. In the mounting volume of supply to the Pacific, the essentially retail shipments to the small ferry bases remained through 1942 a considerable proportion of the whole, and supply to Alaska was an almost purely retail system of direct shipments to individual garrisons. It seemed likely that strategy for some time to come might consist of small-scale and medium-scale task force operations in several theaters, launched on short notice, variable in their requirements, and sustained in part directly from the United States rather than from overseas reserves. Such a trend would shift the whole emphasis in logistical support to retail operations and to a degree of improvisation and short-range planning that would virtually preclude systematic scheduling of supply on a large scale.

Nonetheless, the experience of 1942 and early 1943 was not wholly foreign to the system's design. The supply of any small base in a quiet area, to the extent that current demand was stable and ultimate objectives fixed, permitted a regular flow of supply under routine administration, thus foreshadowing in miniature the system for supplying a great invasion base. At a few points—Australia, New Caledonia, Espiritu Santo, Hawaii, the British Isles, North Africa—the building of supply reservoirs to support later offensives got under way, and even the limited operations of late 1942 in the Pacific and in North Africa gave a foretaste of the huge demands later campaigns would place upon the supply system. The flow of supply to the reservoir areas, after a period of initial confusion, was beginning by spring of 1943 to assume something of the routine, wholesale character, as well as the volume, to which the system was adapted, and the channels of supply to these areas tended increasingly to dominate the general pattern. *(Map 4)*

PART FOUR

BUILD-UP AND EARLY OFFENSIVES

CHAPTER XIV

Build-up in the British Isles— First Phase

At the end of February 1942 the lately proclaimed Allied strategy of concentrating all efforts first on defeating Germany had an air of unreality. The ramshackle Allied front along the Malay Barrier had collapsed, and the drain of U.S. troops, aircraft, and shipping to the far Pacific left very little for action in the Atlantic. Early in March Operation GYMNAST, the proposed Anglo-American occupation of French North Africa, was relegated to the "academic" category by the Combined Chiefs of Staff. Britain's hold on the Bay of Bengal seemed almost lost and India open to invasion; in the Middle East she faced the necessity of replacing the Australian and New Zealand divisions that those dominions were preparing to recall to face the threat of Japanese invasion. By the end of January General Sir Claude J. E. Auchinleck's promising offensive in Libya had ended in retreat and the loss of most of Cyrenaica. In an effort to avert collapse in the Middle and Far East, Churchill planned to send out almost three hundred thousand troops from the home islands from February through May. For necessary American help in transporting these troops, he was willing to accept a long postponement of the planned build-up of

U.S. forces in Northern Ireland. Meanwhile, before the end of February, the American military leaders were preparing to send further substantial reinforcements to the Central and Southwest Pacific and to the island chain connecting them. There seemed little prospect of an early "closing and tightening the ring" about Germany.[1]

Middle-of-the-Road Strategy

To General Marshall and some of his staff, this drift of strategic emphasis away from the western theater of war seemed dangerous. Unless Germany were soon attacked in force, the Soviet armies might succumb and Germany might make herself invulnerable on the European continent. Whatever might be lost in the Southwest Pacific in 1942, some members of the staff argued, the war itself was not likely to be lost there, while it could well be lost in Europe. The danger seemed the greater in January and February as the

[1] (1) CCS 5/2, 3 Mar 42, title: SUPER-GYMNAST. (2) Matloff and Snell, *Strategic Planning: 1941–1942*, Chs. VI–VII. (3) See above, Ch. VI. (4) Msg, Former Naval Person [Churchill] to President Roosevelt, 4 Mar 42, as quoted in Churchill, *Hinge of Fate*, pp. 189–91.

Soviet winter offensive came to an inconclusive halt and Soviet armies in the Crimea met serious reverses. Late in January Eisenhower noted:

> We've got to go to Europe and fight—and we've got to quit wasting resources all over the world—and still worse—wasting time. If we're to keep Russia in, save the Middle East, India and Burma; we've got to begin slugging with air at West Europe; to be followed by a land attack as soon *as possible*.[2]

The basic issue of American strategy, as it finally emerged from discussions in the joint planning committees by early March, was presented in the form of three alternatives: (a) hold in the Pacific at whatever cost to offensive operations in Europe; (b) accept risks, possibly even collapse, in the Southwest Pacific in order to concentrate forces for an attack on Europe from bases in England; or (c) provide a reasonable minimum of forces for defense in the South and Southwest Pacific while beginning to concentrate in the British Isles for an early offensive against Germany. What differentiated the third, or "middle-of-the-road," alternative, the position of General Eisenhower and most of the WPD staff, from the second—supported by the Air Staff—was evidently its moderately optimistic view that the far Pacific could be held without interfering with a substantial concentration in the European theater. Eisenhower himself considered that retention of the Southwest Pacific was only a "desirable" not a "necessary" objective.[3] Only a few of the Army planners held that "the effective defense of the Western Pacific . . . would jeopardize the success of the offensive against Germany" — the view expressed by one (probably the AAF) member of the Joint U.S. Strategic Committee.[4] The majority view was supported by estimates that the forces yet to be transported to the Pacific would be essentially the same whether the intention were to hold the existing line or to withdraw to the Central Pacific.[5]

On 16 March the Joint Chiefs agreed to recommend the third course to the President. Events demonstrated that this choice represented only a qualified endorsement of the principle of immediate concentration in the western European theater. The decision was qualified by the assumption that in the last resort the Middle East and India, and possibly even China, must be held at all costs, and it was weakened by the allotment to the Central, South, and Southwest Pacific of approximately half the Army forces slated to be sent outside the Western Hemisphere during 1942. In deciding, therefore, to propose to the British a combined effort to re-enter the European continent in 1942, the Joint Chiefs were registering their hope, but not their determination, that the other two principal theaters of war—Middle East and Pacific—would not absorb more strength than had already been allotted to them.[6]

Since the preceding autumn the conception of a large-scale invasion of the northwestern part of the Continent from bases in the British Isles had been taking form. The arguments favoring both the general strategy of concentration against

[2] (1) Notations by Eisenhower, 22 Jan 42 entry, Item 3, OPD Hist Unit File. (2) Memo, WPD for CofS, 28 Feb 42, sub: Strategic Conceptions and Their Application to the SWPA, Envelope 35, Exec 4.

[3] Memo cited n. 2(2).

[4] JPS 2/2/A (formerly JPS 12/1/A), 18 Feb 42, title: Review of the Strategic Sit in the Japanese Theater of War.

[5] (1) JPS 2/6, rpt by JUSSC, 6 Mar 42, title: Strategic Deployment of Land, Sea, and Air Forces of U.S. After revision, this paper was approved as JCS 23, 14 Mar 42, same title. (2) Matloff and Snell, *Strategic Planning: 1941-1942*, pp. 159ff.

[6] Matloff and Snell, *Strategic Planning: 1941-1942*, pp. 161ff.

Germany and the specific strategy of an invasion across the English Channel leaned heavily on logistical considerations, above all on the factor of shipping. Because of the vast distances in the Pacific, only a fraction—a half or a third—of the forces that could be deployed against western Europe could be supported, with the same amount of shipping, in operations against Japan. As Eisenhower argued, to concentrate first against Germany would actually conform to the strategic maxim that the weaker of two enemies should be attacked first, since Japan was relatively stronger than the European Axis in terms of the power that the Allies could bring to bear against her. The only alternatives to attacking Germany over water approaches—from the northwest or from the south—were to rely exclusively on air bombardment or to send large forces to the Eastern Front; the logistical difficulties of this latter course were even greater than those of operations in the far Pacific.

Man and nature, finally, had given the British Isles resources and facilities needed to build an adequate base for a land invasion of the Continent and for the strategic air bombardment that would precede it—raw materials, manpower, industry, transportation—and these were located adjacent to the direct approaches to the heart of German power. The British Isles and the eastern portions of the North American continent, together constituting the military-economic center of gravity of the western anti-Axis coalition, were closer to northwestern Europe than to any other worthwhile strategic objective—a fact American planners had dimly perceived back in spring of 1941. *(See Map 8.)* Nowhere else was it possible within a given time to assemble so large an invasion force in so advantageous a position for an amphibious assault as in the British Isles. An invasion based on the British Isles would not have to be weakened, as would one in any other quarter, by diversion of large forces to garrison the British Isles against a possible German attack across the Channel. The most powerful blow that could be struck at Germany, in short, was one based on the British Isles.[7]

The crucial questions were, would such a blow be strong enough? and could it be struck soon enough? Germany could muster great power in northwestern Europe. If the Allies could not strike before the Soviet armies had been crippled, the chances of a successful invasion would fade to almost nothing. Eisenhower thought it essential "to engage from the middle of May onward, an increasing portion of the German Air Force, and by late summer an increasing amount of his ground forces." [8] The JUSSC estimated that in order to create a "material diversion" of German strength from the Eastern Front the Allies would have to hurl a ground army of 600,000 troops, with 6,500 planes, against northwestern Europe by September at the latest. Nor could the flow of material aid to the Soviet Union be allowed to dwindle. The planners recommended that "maximum quantities" be delivered in 1942, and before the end of March, while the invasion plan was still unsettled, the President brusquely ordered that lagging deliveries be speeded up to meet earlier commitments.[9] The need for

---

[7] (1) These arguments are summed up in memo cited n. 2(2); and memo, Eisenhower for CofS, 25 Mar 42, sub: Critical Points in the Development of a Co-ord Viewpoint as to Maj Tasks of the War, OPD 381 BOLERO, 6. (2) See also above, Ch. II.

[8] Memo cited n. 2(2).

[9] (1) JPS 2/6 cited n. 5(1). (2) For aid to the USSR, see below, Ch. XX.

haste and the need for strength pulled in opposite directions.

The Changing Outlook in Shipping

The planners had come far from the optimism of midsummer 1941 when, assuming that the Soviet Union would probably be crushed, they had nevertheless believed that the United States, with modest help from Britain, would be able to beat Germany on her own ground in 1943 and 1944. One reason for the somber outlook in 1942 was the grim shipping situation. Concluded the JUSSC early in March:

> Availability of shipping controls all decisions concerning overseas movement in 1942. . . . Shipping must be used in a manner which will contribute most to effective results against the Axis in 1942, as during this year the United Nations will constantly be on the verge of ultimate defeat.[10]

The committee expected losses in 1942 to offset additions from new construction and from diversions of merchant shipping to military use; it urged that an effective pooling system be instituted, that nonmilitary uses be reduced to a minimum, and even that noncombatants be evacuated from the United Kingdom.

In studying the alternative courses of action in the Pacific—to hold or to abandon the far Pacific—the committee had decided that the effect on the scale of effort in the European theater would not be markedly different in either case. If the present line in the Pacific were held, it seemed possible to send to the European theater about 100,000 troops by July, 300,000 by October, and 435,000 by the end of the year. If the far Pacific were given up—presumably a difficult and gradual process—each of these figures

might be increased by about 60,000. Evidently the British would have to assume the main burden of any attack across the Channel in late summer or fall of 1942. Nevertheless, the committee thought that U.S. forces would be sufficient to "assist effectively" in such a venture, since the first increments would be strongly reinforced in the weeks following the assault.[11]

Almost immediately these estimates had to be re-examined. On 4 and 5 March the British Prime Minister sent urgent messages to President Roosevelt describing the deterioration of Britain's position in troop-carrying and cargo shipping, and the necessity of rebuilding the forces on the Levant-Caspian front. He requested specifically a loan of shipping to move about forty thousand troops with their equipment around the Cape (leaving the United Kingdom in April and May), and an allotment of two more American divisions to the Anzac area in the hope of persuading Australia and New Zealand not to recall the two divisions then in the Near East. Churchill was willing to defer for some time further American reinforcements for Northern Ireland, beyond those that could be transported across the Atlantic by the shipping to be sent over for the Cape voyage. The President's immediate decision to grant this request meant that, just as in January and the preceding autumn, a large block of shipping would be sent to distant waters from which it could not return for many months. Only about 40,000 troops, instead of 100,000, could be sent across the North Atlantic in American shipping before July, and direct move-

---

[10] JPS 2/5, 6 Mar 42, title: Strategic Deployment of Land, Sea, and Air Forces of U.S.

[11] JPS 2/6 cited n. 5(1).
The 11,700 troops already in Northern Ireland were not included in these totals.

ments to Iceland would have to be elimi-nated. The pre-October build-up in Eng-land, according to preliminary estimates, would be reduced to 180,000 instead of 300,000. In addition, about thirty-six freighters would have to be withdrawn from the lend-lease service to the Red Sea area.[12]

The long-range effects were less easily evaluated. Since shipping in lend-lease services was to provide the freight trans-port needed for the Pacific and Middle East reinforcements, cargo shipping would not become the limiting factor in overseas deployment until the latter part of the year. On the other hand, the appalling upsurge in ship losses during March un-dermined all estimates of future transport capabilities, and withdrawals from com-mercial services were difficult to predict. The planners found that, in general, it was "very difficult to arrive at precise answers" as to cargo shipping availability during the latter half of 1942.[13] As for troop ship-ping, certain "potentialities" had been omitted from the earlier estimates. *Aqui-tania* and *Queen Mary,* which were to be sent around the Cape, might be used on their return voyage, perhaps with other British transports as well, to move U.S. troops to the British Isles. Less promising possibilities were the use of Navy combat loaders for Pacific runs (releasing other shipping for the Atlantic), acquisition of Axis vessels interned in South America, and piecemeal movements of small de-tachments of troops on freighters. From all these facts, the JUSSC concluded that the earlier estimates of possible build-up in the British Isles—300,000 by October, 435,000 by the end of the year—might be "equalled or possibly improved."[14] The Joint Chiefs accordingly recommended on 16 March that, if the British concurred, the assem-

bling of troops and material in the British Isles for a continental invasion should be-gin at once.[15]

Late in March, as planning for the in-vasion build-up went into high gear, the transportation staff of the SOS came up with new and disturbing predictions. In view of the high rate of losses and the pre-sumed necessity of completing scheduled deployment to other theaters, it now ap-peared that cargo shipping would support only about 255,000 troops in the British Isles by the end of 1942; none would be available for this purpose until August, and very little until September. The Com-bined Staff Planners, studying the data, reached the pessimistic conclusion that for a mid-September assault only one infantry and half an armored division from the United States could be ready in the Brit-ish Isles, even if air force deployment were held down to a level that the committee judged insufficient to give decisive superi-ority. There were other limitations. To mount the assault itself would require a "virtual cessation" of imports into Eng-land during the assembly and mounting period, and its subsequent support would make severe inroads upon Britain's econ-

---

[12] (1) Msgs, Former Naval Person to President Roosevelt, 4 and 5 Mar 42, as quoted in Churchill, *Hinge of Fate,* pp. 189–94, and summary of Presi-dent's reply, pp. 195–96. (2) Matloff and Snell, *Strate-gic Planning: 1941-1942,* pp. 162–64. (3) App. II to JCS 23 cited n. 5(1). (4) See shipping study, 27 Mar 42, title: Plan "A," Plng Div Studies folder, OCT HB. (5) See also below, Ch. XX.

[13] App. II cited n. 12(3).

[14] *Ibid.*

[15] (1) Min, 5th mtg JCS, 16 Mar 42. (2) For dis-cussion of shipping losses, see min, 12th mtg CCS, 17 Mar 42. (3) CCS 39/1, 14 Mar 42, title: Relation of Merchant Shipg Losses to Prosecution of War. (4) JPS 16/1, 25 Mar 42, title: Appreciation of U.S. Mil Shipg Sit. (5) See above, Ch. VIII, and below, App. H-1.

omy.[16] Available landing craft would support a landing only about a fifth as strong as the committee believed necessary. Projecting the estimates into 1943, the committee judged an operation in the spring of 1943 to be barely feasible, provided the Soviet Union were still containing the bulk of the German Army and the use of cargo shipping in other theaters and for civilian needs were ruthlessly curtailed. Even so, the American contribution would be small, primarily air forces, with only about five ground divisions. The CPS unequivocally ruled out a 1942 assault, asserting it would not be possible to land ground forces on the Continent "with sufficient support to give reasonable assurance that they could be maintained."[17]

The new assessment of shipping capabilities came at a critical juncture in planning. On 25 March General Marshall had secured the President's approval to put the plan in shape for discussion with the British, and during the next few days arrangements were made for Marshall and Hopkins to take it to London instead of working through the combined machinery in Washington. On the 25th, also, General Eisenhower had presented a study elaborating on the thesis developed in his memorandum of 28 February. Up to this point the drift of thinking among the American planners was on the whole in the direction of a 1942 invasion, although there had been some discussion of a more cautious plan presented by the British for an operation in 1943, to be undertaken only in the event of a serious deterioration of German power in the West. Estimates of forces that might be available were reassuring. By mid-August 1942 a force of six infantry, three armored, and two motorized divisions, trained and equipped, could be mustered; by the following April, at least eighteen and probably twenty-one

infantry divisions, two of them trained and equipped for amphibious operations, besides six armored divisions, five motorized divisions, and one airborne division. The Air Forces estimated that over 700 combat aircraft could be made available by mid-September and 3,300 by the following April. But on 27 March Col. John E. Hull of WPD received from Lt. Col. Marcus B. Stokes of General Gross' staff a succinct statement of the limitations imposed by shipping. Only about 105,000 troops—equivalent perhaps to three and one-half infantry or two armored divisions with supporting ground elements, but without air forces—could be moved to England by mid-September, and only 400,000 could be moved and supported by April 1943, including the troops already in or on the way to Northern Ireland. For the program as a whole, cargo shipping was the limiting factor. If the movement of the million or more American troops that WPD had estimated as necessary for an invasion were to depend on American shipping alone, Stokes estimated it could not be completed until September 1943.[18]

---

[16] (1) CPS 26/1, 3 Apr 42, title: Offensive Opns in Europe. (2) Shipping data are from the chart "Shipping Capabilities in 1942," 1 April 1942, which was prepared by the Transportation Division, SOS, and appended as Annex D to CPS 26/1. The troop carrying estimates corresponded roughly with the earlier ones of the JUSSC. Cargo shipping estimates assumed that fourteen cargo vessels a month, over and above the eighteen already requested by the War Department, would be made available for Army use. See above, Ch. VIII.

[17] CPS 26/1 cited n. 16(1).

[18] (1) Memo, Col Thomas D. Davis for Col Hull, 27 Mar 42, sub: Availability of Certain Maj Units. (2) Memo, G-4 for WPD, 27 Mar 42, sub: Estd Dates by Which Certain Divs Will Be Equipped. (3) Memo, Stokes for Hull, 27 Mar 42, sub: Shipg Ests. All in ABC 381 BOLERO (3-16-42) Sec 4, Folder 2. For comparison, Stokes showed the far greater limitations upon deployment to the Near and Middle East. (4) Stimson and Bundy, *On Active Service in Peace and War*, pp. 416–19. (5) Sherwood, *Roosevelt and Hopkins*, p. 521.

Colonel Stokes did not rest his estimate for a September 1942 operation, as he did that for a 1943 operation, upon the recently calculated limitations of cargo shipping, which indicated that not even 105,000 troops could be supported by mid-September. Cargo shipping limitations, by their nature, could be expected to come into play gradually. In the early stages of a build-up program, cargo shipping would be required mainly to move the equipment of deploying forces; any given body of troops could live for a month or two, if necessary, on the maintenance supplies they brought with them. The wide discrepancy between Stokes' estimate and the earlier ones relating to a 1942 operation seems to have resulted from two new assumptions: first, that the build-up in the British Isles could begin only after the garrisoning of other theaters and bases had been largely completed, that is, in July and August; and second, that any British assistance in troop transport could not be provided before September. The earlier estimates had not considered the problem of timing at all, but merely matched estimated aggregate capacity against aggregate demands.

The new shipping estimates, at any rate, gave a decisive turn to planning. As late as 28 March WPD was inclined to accept the earlier figures, based primarily on aggregate troop carrying capacity, which envisaged placing almost 450,000 troops in the British Isles by the end of 1942. However, the outline plan drawn up by the WPD staff and approved by the President on 1 April focused, in the main, upon a 1943 invasion. It envisaged combined forces of 48 divisions and 5,800 combat planes, of which the United States would provide about 30 divisions and 3,250 combat planes. This would involve a build-up, by 1 April 1943, of about a million American

troops in the British Isles. In the course of these preparations it might become necessary in the autumn of 1942 to launch an emergency attack across the Channel in an effort to avert a collapse on the Eastern Front or to take advantage of an unexpected weakening of German strength in the West. Such an attack would have to be launched with whatever forces were available, and on the basis of the Stokes estimates, it was candidly described in the outline plan as a "sacrifice in the common good." [19] Except in this contingency, aid to the Soviet Union in 1942 would depend on a continuing flow of munitions and limited military assistance, for example by sending air forces to the Middle East. As for the main operation, the outline plan, pointing again to the Stokes estimates that only about four hundred thousand troops could be moved and supported by April 1943 with American shipping, suggested that British troop transports might be made available after the situation was stabilized in the eastern theaters, and that more cargo shipping would have to be diverted from other uses early in 1943. For either a 1942 or a 1943 operation, construction of landing craft would have to be greatly accelerated. In order to meet an April 1943 jump-off date, an immediate

[19] (1) One copy of the outline plan, or the Marshall Memorandum as it was called, is filed as memo, CofS for President, no date, sub: Basis for Preparation of the Atchd Outline Plan . . . , BOLERO folder, Lutes File. For others, see Matloff and Snell, *Strategic Planning: 1941-1942*, pp. 184-86. That the outline plan used the estimates in the Stokes memorandum seems fairly evident. Stokes, in turn, evidently had used the same data as the 1 April 1942 chart, "Shipping Capabilities in 1942," though its conclusions were not the same, particularly on the matter of cargo shipping limitations in 1942. The estimates of divisions to be shipped to the United Kingdom by autumn of 1942 are roughly reconcilable in Stokes' memorandum, CPS 26/1, and in the Marshall Memorandum, except that the latter includes some air forces as well as three and one-half ground divisions. (2) Notes on 9th mtg JPS, 28 Mar 42, ABC 570 (2-14-42) Sec 1.

decision was imperative so that the complex logistical preparations—base construction in the United Kingdom, procurement programs, troop and matériel deployment—might get under way. Shipping and landing craft loomed as the bottlenecks.[20]

The London Staff Conversations

In the second week of April 1942 General Marshall and Harry Hopkins went to London to sell this project to the British. To Churchill, the plan offered insurance against the danger that the Americans might turn their backs upon Europe to prosecute the Pacific war. British agreement upon the main cross-Channel operation in 1943 (ROUNDUP) with its preparatory build-up (BOLERO) therefore was quick and even enthusiastic. The British did express misgivings, however, and asked pointed questions regarding the 1942 emergency operation (SLEDGEHAMMER). They also registered an emphatic reservation indicating that Britain's precarious position in the Middle East must be held whatever the cost.[21]

Qualified agreement, with underlying doubts and reservations, was all that could be accomplished at this time. The situation was such that decision had to precede, not follow, the study, maneuvers, testing of equipment, and actual experience in amphibious warfare that would indicate whether the plan were feasible. On the crucial question of landing craft, for example, planning and production were in such a state of confusion during April that Marshall could give no concrete answers to British questions, and no one on the small staff he took to London was technically competent to discuss the problem. On shipping, the other bottleneck, there

was more discussion but little was settled. The Americans wanted to know, above all, whether the British could handle the 60 percent of the total build-up program for which American shipping appeared to be lacking. The British indicated that the *Queens* could be made available for trooping across the Atlantic after the peak of deployment to the Middle East had been passed, possibly as early as the coming July. By April 1943 these giant vessels might be able to carry some 250,000 American troops to the British Isles, and another 100,000 might be added from January 1943 on by additional transports taken from the Middle East convoys. But beyond this the British were unwilling to commit themselves. Apart from the claim of the Middle East upon their shipping, they also had their eyes upon the lagging relief of Iceland by American forces and the movement of Canadian troops and RAF trainees across the North Atlantic.[22]

The British also undertook tentatively to provide half the cargo tonnage needed for the program by cutting into their convoys to the Indian Ocean and into their domestic imports. They intimated, however, that the Americans had set their tonnage requirements rather high. They thought the equipment allowances of U.S. troops, especially of vehicles, and American standards of subsistence and maintenance were "fat," and suggested possible shipping economies by disassembling and crating vehicles and by using British

---

[20] *Ibid.*

[21] (1) Matloff and Snell, *Strategic Planning: 1941–1942,* pp. 187–90. (2) Gordon A. Harrison, *Cross-Channel Attack,* UNITED STATES ARMY IN WORLD WAR II (Washington, 1951), pp. 16–19. (3) Churchill, *Hinge of Fate,* pp. 317–20.

[22] (1) Min, 3d mtg U.S.-Br Planners, London, 12 Apr 42. (2) Notes prepared by Home Force Logis Stf, 13 Apr 42. Both in ABC 381 BOLERO (3-16-42) Sec 5.

equipment. The American response to these suggestions was cool.[23]

The British were willing, in short, to provide substantial assistance in shipping to supplement American resources, but they were not prepared at this time to underwrite the whole BOLERO program. The program could now get under way, but its completion, as far as the British were concerned, would depend on the course of events in the Middle East.

Unfortunately, the shipping tentatively promised by the British would become available, for the most part, too late to help SLEDGEHAMMER. The British response to this feature of the American plan was noticeably lukewarm; far from being an emergency operation to save the Soviet Union from collapse, SLEDGEHAMMER appeared to the British as one that must inevitably result in catastrophe unless the USSR were so far from collapse as to prevent the Germans from reacting vigorously to it. General Marshall was in the uncomfortable position of attempting to justify a venture to which the Americans could contribute very little; his only defense of the mid-September launching date, which the British and some of the Americans thought would probably be too late, was that few if any American ground forces would be in the British Isles before that date. The reason there would be so few was the determination that the BOLERO program should not be allowed to interfere with the planned build-up of forces in other theaters and along lines of communications. It was scarcely surprising that the British made similar reservations regarding the areas in which they had a primary interest.[24]

But SLEDGEHAMMER and ROUNDUP could not be kept in separate compartments. Delay in inaugurating the build-up of American forces would certainly wreck a prologue operation in September 1942, but almost as thoroughly it would ruin the "main show" seven months later. The central logistical problem of BOLERO-SLEDGEHAMMER-ROUNDUP was one of timing and scheduling. The British administrative staffs were already pointing out that if the build-up were concentrated in the last two or three months before the attack, the ports in Britain might not be able to handle the incoming traffic, let alone the additional problem—hardly mentioned at the conference—of outloading for the assault. The inflow of material, if not of troops, must begin at the earliest possible moment.[25] But the problem of scheduling seems to have attracted little attention in the conference discussions. The plan that Marshall brought to London itself alluded to the need for more cargo shipping only as a problem to be met in 1943. Colonel Hull observed that American units sent over during 1942 might have to leave behind much of their equipment, and both he and Marshall evidently accepted as unavoidable the postponement of the movement of the bulk of the cargo until the first few months of 1943, although they also admitted the necessity of completing the construction of airfields, depots, and cantonments, all requiring materials and equipment from the United States, before the end of 1942.[26]

---

[23] (1) Br stf paper, no date, sub: Note on Cargo Shipg Involved in Projected American Move. (2) Min, Br CofS mtg, attended by Gen Marshall, 14 Apr 42. Both in ABC 381 BOLERO (3-16-42) Sec 4, Folder 2. (3) Min cited n. 22(1).

[24] Harrison, Cross-Channel Attack, pp. 17–18.

[25] Paper cited n. 23(1).

[26] For the statement of Colonel Hull, see min cited n. 22(1). The Stokes estimate, possibly because of lack of information, had explicitly left British port capacity out of consideration.

There was no assurance, when Marshall and his staff left London, that the problem of timing and scheduling could be solved. The simultaneous build-up for two operations, moreover, created some conflict in emphasis. SLEDGEHAMMER's overriding need was for a heavy flow of combat troops during the coming spring and summer, while for ROUNDUP an even flow of cargo over the whole period was essential in order to avoid congestion at the end of the program. But for either operation, it was obviously desirable and probably essential that the build-up begin immediately.

The Flow of Troops

Fortunately the movement of troops and material across the North Atlantic, begun before Pearl Harbor, had not been halted but only slowed by the crisis in the Middle and Far East. By early March about 11,000 of a projected force of 105,-000 had reached Northern Ireland, and Army forces in Iceland, after the arrival of the late February shipment, amounted to almost 15,000; the last U.S. marines left Iceland on 9 March, though a sizable British garrison remained.[27]

The diversion of more American shipping into the Pacific and around the Cape, as a result of Churchill's request early in March, cut into planned movements both to Northern Ireland and to Iceland. Although direct shipments to Iceland had been ruled out at first, the remainder of the 5th Division was shipped in two small contingents during April under a complicated shuttle arrangement by which some of the British garrison was also transshipped to Ireland. These movements were a by-product of the larger movement to Northern Ireland, planned in two installments for late April and early May in the flotilla that was subsequently to carry two British divisions around the Cape. The first convoy, a large one including the British liner *Aquitania,* temporarily diverted from the Pacific, sailed from New York on 30 April with some nineteen thousand troops, including the second Iceland contingent and part of the 34th Infantry Division.[28]

Moving the 1st Armored Division to Northern Ireland proved more difficult. This was the Army's first experience in moving a unit of this type overseas. The division's impedimenta, including its reserve and replacement vehicles and maintenance supplies, came to more than 200,-000 ship tons, most of it bulky cargo. The first Iceland contingent early in April had taken some of the immediately available freighters, and space requirements turned out to have been underestimated. In an effort to avoid separating troops from their equipment, the move was scheduled in two installaments; the first echelon, nine thousand troops on the *Queen Mary,* sailed on 11 May, the remainder in two smaller transports on the 31st—the latter sailing being noteworthy as the first experiment with double loading on troop transports (rotation of passengers between sleeping and recreation quarters). Splitting the troop movement did not prevent some dis-

[27] (1) Administrative and Logistical History of the European Theater of Operations: The Predecessor Commands, Vol. I, MS, OCMH. (2) WPD Weekly Status Map, 12 Mar 42, OPD Hist Unit File. (3) See above, Ch. VI.

[28] (1) Rpt, NYPOE Statistical Summary, OCT HB. (2) Corresp in 370.5 England folder Br file, and in Iceland Misc folder, OCT HB. (3) Min, 12th, 13th, and 14th mtgs CCS, 17, 24, and 31 Mar 42. (4) CCS 58/2, rpt by CMTC, 24 Mar 42, title: Relief of Br Trs in Iceland. (5) Msg, WPD to CG USAFBI, 28 Mar 42, OPD 320.2 Gt Brit, 3. (6) Shipping study cited n. 12(4). (7) Msg, CG SOS to USFOR, 12 Apr 42, ABC 381 BOLERO (3-16-42) Sec 1.

persal of the cargo movement. All the division's tanks were carried across in two trips, on 30 April and 13 June, by the seatrain *Texas*. The remainder of the tonnage was spread over several shipments, some in the 30 April convoy, others during May. As late as 24 March, OPD had laid down the law to the transportation staffs that "troops would go overseas only when their full equipment could go with or before them."[29] Six weeks later, under pressure to accelerate troop movements to Northern Ireland, OPD informed the SOS that the remainder of the 1st Armored Division must be shipped as soon as transports were available, "even though its equipment must go later."[30] The whole experience was a foretaste of the difficulty of synchronizing the flow of troops and cargo in a long-range deployment program.[31]

Following approval of BOLERO-ROUNDUP in April, planning of the deployment program began immediately. Two combined committees were set up at the end of the month to co-ordinate the process, one in London to arrange for reception and maintenance of incoming American forces, one in Washington to schedule movements and set shipping requirements. The BOLERO Combined Committees found themselves face to face with the threat of later congestion, which only immediate measures could avert. SOS officials had already pointed out to OPD that if, as shipping estimates seemed to indicate, only 250,000 troops could be supported in the British Isles by the end of the year, then it would presumably be necessary somehow to ship the remaining 750,000, with equipment and supplies, during the first three months of 1943. British port capacity for handling incoming American forces had been given as

about 100,000 troops per month. Obviously it would be necessary to speed up the movement during the summer and fall, placing the center of gravity of the whole program "somewhere in the middle of the summer."[32]

Until the middle of May there seemed little prospect of doing so. Movements already scheduled to Northern Ireland and England, which the Combined Chiefs directed to be hastened, would bring the total force in the British Isles by July to about 51,000. Shipping in sight for July could carry only 5,000 to 5,500; British transports would not be available until August, when some 50,000 troops were tentatively scheduled to move. On both sides of the Atlantic the planning staffs

---

[29] Plng Div SOS Diary, 25 Mar 42 entry, Plng Div ASF.

[30] *Ibid.*, 6 May 42 entry.

[31] (1) *Ibid.*, 19, 26, 28 Mar; 13, 27 Apr; 1 and 2 May 42 entries. (2) Millett, Overseas Movement of the 1st Infantry Division and the 1st Armored Division, OCMH. (3) Corresp in Iceland Misc folder, OCT HB. (4) Rpt cited n. 28(1). (5) WSA Allocation Chart atchd to CMT 5/3, 8 May 42, title: Availability of United Nations Shipg for Mil Trans, ABC 570 (2-14-42) Sec 1. (6) Memo, Eisenhower for CofS, 24 Apr 42, Misc: Memos for CofS folder, Misc Exec Off file, OPD Hist Unit File. (7) For ship tonnage requirements of an armored division in late 1942 and summer 1943, see below, Apps. A-4, A-5.

[32] (1) Min, 1st mtg BCC(W), 29 Apr 42, ABC 381 BOLERO (3-16-42) Sec 1. (2) Diary, 15 Apr 42 entry, cited n. 29. (3) Msg Blue 31, BCC(W) to BCC(L), 30 Apr 42, ABC 381 BOLERO (3-16-42) Sec 4, Folder 2. (4) The BOLERO Combined Committee in Washington (BCC(W)) was headed by Col Hull of OPD, and consisted in addition of one AAF officer, two Navy officers, and one representative of each of the three British services. Eight U.S. Army assistants were also named, including one from G-4 (Col. Shiras A. Blair) and one from SOS (Lt. Col. C. B. Magruder). Both the BCC(W) and the BCC(L) (BOLERO Combined Committee in London) reported to the CPS. See memo, JCS for OPD and ACofS Plans, Navy Dept, 6 May 42, ABC 381 BOLERO (3-16-42) Sec 1. See also, min, 13th mtg JPS, 22 Apr 42; min, 17th mtg CCS, 28 Apr 42; and memo, OPD for U.S. Secy CCS, 27 Apr 42, sub: U.S. Army Membership . . . , OPD 381 BOLERO, 8.

began to talk of over-all reductions in the program. The Washington BOLERO Combined Committee anticipated other difficulties—competition between service troops and combat troops for transport during the summer, shortages of escorts, delays in "marrying up" troops and equipment. And congestion in the fall and winter would offer splendid targets to the Luftwaffe, freed from the Eastern Front by bad weather. The commitee could only suggest economies in shipping through rerouting and consolidation of movements, and postponement of the relief of the British in Iceland until after August. These measures, which the CCS forthwith approved, were only palliatives; the simple need was for more shipping.[33]

In the third week of May the British authorities, apparently deciding that no more shipping would be forthcoming from the Americans and that administrative economies would not close the gap, came to the rescue with offers to divert troop shipping from the Middle East convoys during the two lean months of June and July. For June, they offered about 13,000 more spaces (in addition to the *Queen Elizabeth*, already scheduled); for July, 15,000. These transports were to be available thereafter on a six-week cycle, supplemented after November by capacity for 10,000 more. The *Queens* would operate on a four-week turnaround from August on. *Aquitania*, then en route to the Indian Ocean, would be available for a BOLERO voyage in September, and for each trip on the triangular United States-United Kingdom-Indian Ocean run she would be replaced in theNorth Atlantic by equivalent capacity in smaller British transports. On paper, the 105,000 U.S. troops earlier set as the maximum possibility for 1 September had now risen above 150,000, and it looked as though 850,000 to 900,000 might be in position by the following April. So hopeful was the outlook that Sir John Dill asked the Combined Chiefs to resume the Iceland program, and General Marshall began to talk of sending another armored division to the United Kingdom in time for an autumn operation.[34]

June, the month in which the BOLERO program was expected to really get under way, brought instead a series of crises that left the program virtually in suspense. The first large BOLERO contingent, some 11,000 troops, primarily Air Forces, sailed on the *Queen Elizabeth* on the 4th, and on the 11th about 900 parachutists and service troops departed on a British transport, *Rampura*. These movements occurred during the Midway crisis, which at the insistence of General Marshall was not allowed to interfere seriously with BOLERO move-

---

[33] (1) Min, 1st and 2d mtgs BCC(W), 29 and 30 Apr 42, ABC 381 BOLERO (3-16-42) Sec 1; 4th and 5th mtgs, 9 and 11 May 42, ABC 381 BOLERO (3-16-42) Sec 4, Folder 2. (2) Rpt by BCC(W), 9 May 42, sub: Shipg for BOLERO, same file. (3) Rpt by BCC(W), 13 May 42, same sub, same file. This was CPS 26/3 and was approved as CCS 72, 16 May 42. (4) Other corresp in same files. (5) Extracts from two memos, DQMG(L) [Deputy Quartermaster General, London], no addressee, 1 May 42, ABC 381 BOLERO (3-16-42) Sec 4, Folder 3. (6) CMT 5/3 cited n. 31(5). (7) Min, 19th mtg CCS, 12 May 42. (8) Memo, Magruder for Hull, 14 May 42, sub: Priority of Shipt, BOLERO, BOLERO 1942 Shipg folder, Lutes File. (9) Diary, 1 May 42 entry, cited n. 29.

[34] (1) Min, 6th and 8th mtgs BCC(W), 20 May and 1 Jun 42. (2) Ltr, Col Hull to Brig Gen Charles L. Bolté, 19 May 42. (3) Msg Pink 6, BCC(L) to BCC(W), 19 May 42. All in ABC 381 BOLERO (3-16-42) Sec 4, Folder 2. (4) Memo, Hull for ACofS OPD, 21 May 42, sub: Tr Mvmt Schedules for BOLERO and NABOB [N Ireland]. (5) Memo, Col Hull for Brig Gen Thomas T. Handy, 18 May 42, no sub. Last two in ABC 381 BOLERO (3-16-42) Sec 1. (6) Note, unsigned, for Br Army Stf, Washington, *circa* 19 May 42, sub: Personnel Shipg, BOLERO folder, OCT HB. (7) See also, Relief folder, OCT HB. (8) Memo, OPD for CG USAFBI, 17 May 42, sub: Overseas Tr Mvmts for Br Isles, OPD 370.5 Gt Brit.

THE *QUEEN ELIZABETH,* ONE OF THE "MONSTERS"

ments. In the last half of June Lt. Gen. Sir Bernard L. Montgomery's Eighth Army was driven back to El Alamein, leaving a large garrison to surrender to the Germans at Tobruk. German armies meanwhile were driving into the Caucasus. It seemed likely that the British troopers on which BOLERO deployment largely depended would be diverted to rush British reinforcements to Egypt. For a time, indeed, it looked as though American ground forces also would be sent to the threatened area. Prime Minister Churchill, in Washington at the height of the crisis, asked for American help, and General Marshall offered to send the 2d Armored Division. To do so would at least be more economical in shipping than to ship British troops to Egypt and replace them by additional American

troop shipments to the United Kingdom. Cross-Channel invasion preparations seemed likely to suffer in either case.[35]

By this time the British were challenging the whole BOLERO-ROUNDUP plan, objecting particularly to its SLEDGEHAMMER feature, which they regarded more than ever as a forlorn hope. While the debate over this issue went on during June and July, the projected movement of the 2d Armored Division to Egypt was held in abeyance, and American aid for the time

---

[35] (1) Rpt cited n. 28(1). (2) Craven and Cate, *AAF I*, pp. 639–42. (3) Matloff and Snell, *Strategic Planning: 1941-1942*, Ch. XI. (4) CPS 26/4, 7 Jun 42, title: BOLERO Embarkation Schedule, approved as CCS 72/1, 10 Jun 42, same title. (5) CCS 84, 25 Jun 42, title: U.S. Reinfs for Middle East. (6) Min, 27th–29th mtgs CCS, 19, 20, and 25 Jun 42.

being was limited to shipments of tanks and self-propelled artillery and to substantial air reinforcement. About four thousand AAF personnel, the ground echelon of three air groups, sailed for Suez on 16 July on the *Pasteur,* a British transport. During July General Marshall, in an effort to convince the British that SLEDGE-HAMMER was at least as feasible as any alternative operation, used the considerable troop tonnage that then became available to hurry the movement of ground combat troops to the British Isles. The impetus of this movement carried over into August and September, even after the SLEDGE-HAMMER plan had been scrapped. The Air Forces build-up, meanwhile, was not neglected. By the end of August almost thirty thousand troops of the Eighth Air Force, comprising four heavy bomber groups, four pursuit groups, two troop carrier groups, and various other elements, were moved to the British Isles.[36]

This emphasis in BOLERO deployment upon ground combat and air units reduced the flow of service troops during July and August, stunting the growth of the base establishment on which invasion plans depended, and reversing the intention of the planners who in April had placed service troops in a priority above ground combat troops. SOS officials had at that time foreseen the inevitable conflict between base development and preparations for an emergency assault in 1942—similar to the conflict that had appeared in Australia early in the year—but the planners had argued that SLEDGEHAMMER, if mounted, would be mainly a British enterprise. The first detailed plan, at the end of May, for the American establishment in the United Kingdom provided for a Services of Supply complement of 277,000, approximately 27 percent of the total

projected strength. This figure excluded service elements that were to operate in combat zones and the service troops of the Eighth Air Force, which together would have brought the entire service establishment up to about 48 percent of the whole. Though placed in a high priority, service troop movements were scheduled opportunistically and without fixed objectives for the summer months. Competition among the various claims was fierce—construction of airdromes, depots, and cantonments, operation of depots and ports, maintenance of communications, repair and salvage of equipment, operation of utilities, assembling of motor vehicles, and performance of sundry administrative tasks. Some of the claims dropped out under pressure of time and shipping space; many units requested were not provided in the Troop Basis or were activated too late to be adequately trained. The chief conflict during the summer was between engineer aviation battalions and engineer general service regiments, the two basic types of construction units. Shipments of these two types of units remained in fair balance during the summer and made up the majority of service troops deployed, outrunning earlier expectations. Port battalions, depot and maintenance units, and most other types except Ordnance units, which were sent over in considerable numbers on the eve of the North Africa operation, were largely crowded out by the movement of engineer troops.

---

[36] (1) For AAF build-up, see Hq ETOUSA Statistical Summary 7, 7 Sep 42, OCMH; and Eighth Air Force Station Lists and Strength Rpts, 31 Aug 42, U.S. Air Force Hist Div Archives, Air University, Maxwell Air Force Base, Ala. (2) Msg, Marshall to Eisenhower, 16 Jul 42, Item 9, Exec 5. (3) Msg 549, London to AGWAR, 22 Jul 42, NATOUSA TORCH Plng folder, OCT HB.

By the end of July the SOS establishment in the United Kingdom amounted to 27 percent of the total American strength there, a considerably higher proportion than that contemplated by tentative movement schedules in May. By the end of September, however, the slump in service troop movements had reduced the ratio to about 21 percent.[37]

By the end of July the American forces in the British Isles had reached a total of 82,000. August schedules called for 108,-000 more, but actual shipments fell somewhat short of this figure. By the end of August something over 170,000 troops were in or on their way to the British Isles. This was a spectacular achievement by contrast with the 105,000 predicted four months earlier, but it left unsolved the long-range traffic problem that had then been foreseen. The British estimated their capacity to handle incoming American troops at an absolute maximum of 120,000 a month, probably less during the winter months and certainly less while outloading movements were under way during the weeks immediately preceding the invasion. Incoming American troop shipments had to be synchronized with numerous other movements, inbound and outbound, particularly the large outbound monthly Middle East (WS) convoys, averaging 50,000 troops, and the biweekly inbound Canadian (NA) convoys. The monthly BOLERO (AT) convoys, out of New York, normally joined the NA convoys, which sailed from Halifax. The *Queens,* scheduled to sail on a four-week cycle a few days apart beginning in August, were "tied to the moon," being obliged to choose the dark week of each month for navigating in British waters.[38] Late in May U.S. naval authorities had sought British acquiescence to a scheme to sail the AT convoys

at three-week intervals. The British objected on the grounds that such a schedule would conflict with the movement of the *Queens* and the NA convoys, swamping their ports with American, Canadian, and RAF troops. They suggested, instead, combining the AT and NA convoys on a fortnightly cycle, handling the *Queens* and the WS convoys during the intervals between these arrivals. This plan had to be given up for lack of escorts. As an alternative, the Washington BOLERO Committee proposed alternate fortnightly and four-week intervals for the combined convoys, but this would produce an uneven distribution of the port workload, and still pose a stiff escort requirement. Since the Navy insisted that there was absolutely "no expectation of being able to furnish an additional escort group by November," it was finally decided to follow a staggered two-week and four-week cycle for a time, eliminating alternate NA convoys; in November the problem would be re-examined.[39] "We must face the fact," the committee concluded, "that after November, either the rate of acceptance through the ports and railroads must be raised, or a solution to the escort problem must be found to permit a fortnightly convoy cycle, or the

---

[37] (1) For details, see Ruppenthal, *Logistical Support of the Armies,* Ch. II. See also above, Ch. XIII. (2) Tentative mvmt schedules for May 1942, BOLERO 1942 folder, Lutes File. (3) Related corresp in same file. (4) Other corresp in ABC 381 BOLERO (3-16-42); OPD 320.2 Gt Brit; OPD 320.2 ETO; OPD 370.5 Changes of Station; OPD 370.5 BOLERO; and min, WD Gen Council mtgs; and Diary cited n. 29.

[38] (1) Msg Black 20, BCC(W) to BCC(L), 24 Jul 42, ABC 381 BOLERO (3-16-42) Sec 4, Folder 3. (2) Hq ETOUSA Statistical Summary 2, 7 Aug 42, DRB AGO. (3) Memo, Lutes for Somervell, 10 May 42, sub: BOLERO, BOLERO 1942 folder, Lutes File. (4) See below, Apps. A-8, E-1.

[39] Min, 12th mtg BCC(W), 17 Jun 42, ABC 381 BOLERO (3-16-42) Sec 4, Folder 3.

flow of U.S. troops will fall short of the present program."[40]

The Flow of Cargo

More complex than the problem of moving troops to the British Isles was that of moving their matériel. For the remainder of 1942, at least, cargo shipping seemed likely to be scarcer than troop transport. Not until the following year, the British were told at London in April, was the building of cargo ships expected to "come level" with capacity to move troops. With the depredations of German submarines in the Atlantic becoming more deadly, the Combined Military Transportation Committee reported during the first week of May a current deficit of three million dead-weight tons of Allied cargo shipping and predicted four million by the end of the year. The Combined Chiefs, the committee concluded, would have to choose between reducing projected military requirements or imposing further deprivation upon the civilian populations of the Allied countries and reducing the flow of aid to the Soviet Union. At the April London conference the Americans talked of holding back troop movements during 1942 in order to reduce the need for maintenance shipments, and G-4 later echoed this suggestion.[41]

At the first meeting of the Washington BOLERO Combined Committee, Col. Llewelyn Wansbrough-Jones, the British shipping representative, expressed different views. The program, he insisted, must be launched immediately with whatever means were at hand, "regardless of the order of arrival of troops and equipment."[42] About this time, OPD was bowing to the necessity, in connection with the movement of the 1st Armored Division to

Northern Ireland, of abandoning the ancient doctrine that troops and equipment must move together. In the SOS the staffs working up tentative schedules of BOLERO movements found confirmation of their fears that the flow of cargo, if synchronized with the then expected flow of troops which swelled to a peak toward the end of the year, threatened to create serious congestion in the receiving ports from August on.[43]

War Shipping Administration, meanwhile, was searching its cupboards for additional cargo lift. By the beginning of May its officials had hopes that, by reshuffling various commercial trades (the process of sweating them down to meet war needs was still far from complete) and with the aid of new construction, only now beginning to boom, enough cargo shipping might be found to meet stated BOLERO requirements during the coming few months—and perhaps even some additional in July—to "take the curse off" the heavy August–September–October schedule, as General Gross put it.[44] Almost at the same time, BOLERO received a windfall

---

[40] (1) Msg Black 13, BCC(W) to BCC(L), 17 Jun 42. (2) Memo, Col Llewelyn Wansbrough-Jones for BCC(W), 7 Aug 42. Both in ABC 381 BOLERO (3-16-42) Sec 4, Folder 3. (3) Msg Black 8, BCC(W) to BCC(L), 29 May 42. (4) Msg, Br War Off to Br Army Stf, Washington, 27 May 42. Last two in ABC 381 BOLERO (3-16-42) Sec 4, Folder 2.
The *Queens* were to follow the old four-week cycle, carrying U.S. troops and Canadian personnel who would have gone on the eliminated Halifax convoy; some of the U.S. troops were to be accommodated on the Halifax convoys. See corresp in BOLERO folder and Relief folder, OCT HB.
[41] (1) CMT 5/3 cited n. 31(5). (2) Memo, G-4 for Lutes, 30 Apr 42, sub: Force BOLERO, BOLERO 1942 folder, Lutes File.
[42] Min cited n. 32(1).
[43] (1) Memo cited n. 38(3). (2) Penned note, Gross to Lewis Douglas, 1 May 42, with atchd tables and chart, Army Reqmts folder, WSA Douglas File.
[44] Note cited n. 43(2).

in the form of a substantial block of tonnage released from the northern convoys to the USSR, which the British found themselves obliged to curtail at the end of April because of attendant losses in escorting ships. On 22 May Lewis Douglas of WSA conferred with Somervell and SOS staff officers in Somervell's quarters at Fort Myer on the eve of the latter's departure for England to survey preparations for the impending flow of invasion troops and matériel. The Army's stated requirements for BOLERO during June, July, and August then stood, respectively, at 14, 25, and 67 sailings (of the average Liberty-type 11,000-ton freighter). Seventy-six of these 106 vessels, Douglas assured Somervell, could surely be provided and another 100 (a more miscellaneous lot, on the average somewhat smaller than the standard Liberty) probably would be available between 15 July and 15 August. Could not some of them, Somervell asked, be ready by the beginning of July? Douglas thought they might. Much depended, he warned, on whether the ships could be armed and degaussed in time, substitutes found for certain withdrawals from commercial trades, sufficient convoy escorts provided, and, above all, the rising trend of ship losses curbed. Moreover, the Army would have to guarantee cargo to fill ships when they were made available. Gross and Lutes promised that no ship would lack for cargo.[45]

On paper, there was thus a surplus of cargo shipping for June–July–August—ranging (as troop movement schedules fluctuated) from seventy to one hundred sailings, with a capacity that might exceed a million ship tons. How real this surplus would prove to be no one could yet tell. The ships could not be put on the shelf until the Army was ready to use them.

WSA could only hope to schedule worldwide movements of the shipping under its control in such a way that sufficient vessels would "present" at east coast ports to meet the accelerated BOLERO program. Ship sinkings were a growing incubus. Somervell himself had enough doubts on the matter to lead him, as soon as he reached England, to ask Lord Leathers, head of the British Ministry of War Transport, for a loan of fifty cargo vessels for BOLERO shipments in July and August, with the understanding that equivalent tonnage was to be turned back to British service in October and November. He stressed that the additional shipping was needed for advance cargo movements during the long daylight hours of the summer. Leathers, who had hoped the Americans would be able to get along without help until September, cautiously promised to do his best, stipulating, as Douglas had done, that there must be assurance of ample cargo to fill the ships. The paper surplus of cargo shipping now began to take on mountainous proportions.[46]

---

[45] (1) CMT 18, rpt by CMTC to BCC(W), 9 May 42, title: Shipg for BOLERO. (2) Min, 4th mtg BCC(W), 9 May 42. Both in ABC 381 BOLERO (3-16-42) Sec 4, Folder 2. (3) Memo, Douglas for Land, 13 May 42. (4) Notes on conf in Somervell's quarters, 22 May 42. Last two in Army Reqmts folder, WSA Douglas File. (5) WSA chart cited n. 31(5). (6) See below, Ch. XX.

[46] (1) Paper, unsigned, no date, sub: BOLERO Plan, BOLERO 1942 folder, Lutes File, (2) Memo, Magruder for Lutes, 20 Jun 42, sub: Cargo for Jun–Aug, Shipg folder, Lutes File. (3) Min, 10th and 11th mtgs BCC(W), 6 and 10 Jun 42, ABC 381 BOLERO (3-16-42) Sec 4, Folder 3. (4) Diary, 10 Jun 42 entry, cited n. 29. (5) Msg, Sir Arthur Salter to BMWT, 25 May 42, Br Merchant Shipg Mis folder, WSA Douglas File. (6) Memo, Somervell for Douglas, 19 Jun 42, Army Reqmts folder, WSA Douglas File. (7) Memo cited n. 45(3).
Lord Leathers later insisted he never "promised" to provide the ships. See msg, Harriman to Land, 1 Jul 42, Army Reqmts folder, WSA Douglas File.

CRATED 2½-TON TRUCKS. *Twin-unit packs, England, 1943.*

To find cargo for this expected surplus of shipping posed a formidable problem for the SOS staff. If the Army was to make good on the assurance given Douglas on 22 May, it would be necessary to assemble near the ports a large bank of freight, over and above the equipment and supplies that would accompany scheduled troop movements, and to replenish it as rapidly as it was depleted. For a time it seemed likely that almost two thirds of the expected surplus could be filled by construction materials, mainly lumber. By mid-June, however, General Lee's initial requests for this material had been drastically scaled down, partly on the basis of meeting his requirements by imports from the Soviet Union. Vehicles offered a more promising source of advance shipments during the summer. Estimates of the total number required varied widely, from as low as 160,000 to as high as 250,000. The British hoped at first that at least two thirds of the vehicles for American forces could be shipped over completely disassembled and crated (CKD). This did not prove practicable, however, since assembly plants and mechanics would have had to be sent over in advance, and the shortage of British labor was an obstacle. In the summer of 1942 the SOS concentrated its efforts on variant methods, notably the single-unit and twin-unit packs (SUP and TUP), the latter of which proved eventually to be the most satisfactory. TUP shipments, by late summer, were saving about two thirds of the space needed for fully erected vehicles. Under the program worked out in May, about 48,000 vehicles were to be shipped during the next four months, 80 percent of them boxed. The plan was to pool vehicles in the theater, the troops leaving their old ones behind in the States. It was hoped that some 400,000 ship tons of cargo could be provided from this source alone.[47]

This program lagged in its early stages. During June the SOS staff worked desperately to line up the mountains of cargo that would be needed to fill the great tonnages of American and British shipping expected soon to appear in east coast ports. All sorts of oddments were scraped together and earmarked for shipment—ammunition, subsistence, gasoline containers, lumber and other construction materials, clothing and equipage, even a chemical impregnating plant and prefabricated barracks—some of which the theater did not want. By the end of the month WSA was complaining that the Army was loading ships with "any kind of cargo, merely to satisfy the ambition . . . that no ship had been held up because of lack of cargo." [48] Even when there was freight available in the depots, it was sometimes difficult to get enough, of types suitable for balanced loads, to the port in time to meet scheduled sailings. WSA officials wanted the Army to keep freight of assorted types banked in the ports themselves; Army officials insisted that freight must be kept out of the ports until it was ready for loading in order to avoid congestion.[49]

The only large source of cargo still untapped was equipment in the hands of troops. In the second week of June SOS requested authority to ship the organiza-

tion equipment of the 1st Division (then earmarked for late July sailing) one month in advance, and a week later proposed to the Army Ground Forces that advance shipment be adopted as a regular procedure during the next three months. The plan was to withdraw enough equipment from BOLERO divisions to fill available cargo space during June, July, and August; several alternatives, involving from four to eight divisions, were suggested. Depending on the number of divisions affected, the troops would be without their equipment from six weeks to four months.[50]

General McNair did not like the plan, but his opposition was not uncompromising. He raised the orthodox objections—undermining of training and morale, deterioration of material in storage, difficulties of reissue, the danger of sending troops overseas unequipped. On the other hand,

---

[47] (1) Diary, 13, 22, 26 May, 5–9, and 11 Jun 42 entries, cited n. 29. (2) Msg Pink 5, BCC(L) to BCC(W), 15 May 42, ABC 381 BOLERO (3-16-42) Sec 4, Folder 2. (3) Msg Pink 11, BCC(L) to BCC(W), 22 Jul 42, ABC 381 BOLERO (3-16-42) Sec 4, Folder 3. (4) Memo, Lutes for Somervell, 22 May 42, BOLERO 1942 folder, Lutes File. (5) Memo, Somervell for Marshall, 24 Sep 42, CofS WDGS 1942 (2) folder, Hq ASF. (6) Memo, Somervell for Marshall, 20 Oct 42, CofS WDGS 1942 (3A) folder, Hq ASF. (7) Other corresp in same files and in Shipg 1941–43 folder and Opns SOS 1942–43 folder, Hq ASF. (8) Larson, Handling Army Cargo in the Second World War, Ch. VIII, OCT HB. (9) See above, Ch. XIII, and below, Ch. XXIII.

[48] Douglas' notes on conf, 1 Jul 42, Army Reqmts folder, WSA Douglas File.

[49] (1) Diary entries cited n. 47(1). (2) Memo, Mvmts Div for Water Div OCT, 11 Jun 42, sub: Cargo for BOLERO, OCT 563.5 Mvmt BOLERO. (3) Related corresp in same file. (4) Memo, Somervell for CG SOS ETOUSA, 11 Jun 42, BOLERO 1942 folder, Lutes File.

[50] (1) Diary, 26 May, 2, 6, and 8 Jun 42 entries, cited n. 29. (2) Corresp in OPD 370.5 BOLERO, 13. Only the AGF reply of 15 June 1942 is filed here; the original plan itself has not been found. The first use of the ambiguous term "preshipment," widely used in 1943, appears to be in the 15 June AGF memorandum.

if cargo space must be filled, there were good arguments for shipping over the equipment of troops who would soon be in the theater anyway. After some hesitation, General McNair chose the alternative that involved eight divisions, in order to spread the withdrawals as thinly as possible. On 22 June OPD notified him that equipment could be taken from BOLERO units no earlier than a month before embarkation, thus ensuring that, if the troops sailed on schedule, they would probably arrive in the theater about the same time as their equipment. The 1st and 45th Infantry Divisions were nominated forthwith to inaugurate the program.[51]

But by mid-June the prospective surplus of cargo shipping, which these measures were designed to put to use, was already evaporating. Rival claimants made some inroads. One of these was the ferry route the Air Forces had been developing since 1941 to stage short-range aircraft across the North Atlantic from Labrador via Greenland and Iceland. Plans to expand this route during the spring and summer of 1942 to a capacity of one thousand planes a month involved estimated cargo shipments up to half a million ship tons, not to mention the immobilization of some of the shipping while unloading at primitively equipped ferry bases. The Combined Military Transportation Committee warned that to carry out the project as planned would "necessitate a material contraction of the BOLERO program at a time when all circumstances indicate it should be intensified."[52] In consequence, the ferry route project was drastically curtailed late in June. Nevertheless, it cost BOLERO fourteen small freighters during the summer months.[53]

In July and August, in addition, shipments to Iceland took a small amount of cargo shipping, although most of the heavy equipment for the relieving forces was deferred. On 13 July six vessels sailed for Egypt with some three hundred tanks and one hundred self-propelled guns, hastily snatched from the 2d Armored Division to help the Eighth Army in its final stand before Alexandria. One vessel was sunk a few days out, but was replaced in record time by a second shipment of tanks on the seatrain *Texas,* which sailed on the 29th and actually overtook the convoy. Several other ships were required for the equipment and supplies of the three air groups dispatched to the Middle East in July. All these shipments, on the long Cape route, were equivalent to several times the same amount of tonnage that might otherwise have been available to BOLERO.[54]

[51] (1) Corresp in OPD 370.5 BOLERO, 13. (2) Notes on BOLERO Plan, 16 Jun 42. (3) Memo, Plng Br SOS for Lutes, 24 Jun 42, sub: Sup and Equip for BOLERO. (4) Memo, Somervell for Lutes, 14 Jun 42. Last three in BOLERO 1942 folder, Lutes File. (5) Memo, Plng Div OCT for Lutes, 14 Jun 42, sub: Shipg for BOLERO Cargo Jun–Aug, OCT 563.5 Mvmt BOLERO. (6) Min, WD Gen Council mtg, 16 Jun 42. (7) Msg, WD to CG USAFBI, 17 Jun 42, sub: Sup and Equip for Engr Regts, OPD 520.

[52] (1) CMT 21/1, 6 Jun 42, title: Shipg Implications of Proposed N Atlantic Ferry Route Project, ABC 381 BOLERO (3-16-42) Sec 4, Folder 3. (2) Related corresp in same file and in ABC 381 BOLERO (3-16-42) Sec 4, Folder 2.

[53] (1) Corresp in N Air Ferry Route folder, OCT HB. (2) Memo, Eisenhower for Somervell, 11 May 42, Item 4, Exec 1. (3) Msg, Marshall to Eisenhower, 12 Jul 42, ABC 381 (6-24-42). This states that 100,000 tons of shipping were diverted from BOLERO. (4) Diary, Mar, Apr, and 10 Jun 42 entries, cited n. 29. (5) Min, 17th and 20th mtgs JCS, 1 and 15 Jun 42. (6) Samuel Milner, "Establishing the BOLERO Ferry Route," *Military Affairs,* Vol. XI, No. 4 (Winter 1947), pp. 213–22. (7) Craven and Cate, *AAF I,* pp. 313ff, 640–45.

[54] (1) Min, 10th mtg BCC(W), 6 Jun 42, ABC 381 BOLERO (3-16-42) Sec 4, Folder 3. (2) Rpt cited n. 28(1). (3) Memo, Gross for Somervell, 11 Jul 42, sub: Loading and Sailing of Convoy to Egypt, Gross Day File, OCT HB. (4) See Vessel Name file, *Fairport*

Aside from specific diversions, the crisis in the Middle East virtually suspended British participation in the BOLERO program. In July only about a dozen of the promised fifty freighters came forward, and in August this source dried up altogether. Meanwhile, the deadly drain of sinkings continued. By mid-June thirteen out of seventy-five vessels tentatively earmarked for BOLERO for the following month had been lost. Administrative attrition eliminated others: schedules went awry, vessels were delayed, loadings failed to meet expectations. Even when there was ample cargo behind the ports, the Army sometimes failed to bring forward enough of the right kind at the right time, and early in July even had to reject five or six presenters. Sailings, as a result of all these causes, fell far behind schedule. In June there were only twenty-four departures under the program, though twice that number had been lined up as late as the 6th. July sailings came to forty-nine, but ten of these, though charged to BOLERO, were diverted to the North Atlantic ferry route and other destinations. By the end of July the backlog of BOLERO cargo of all kinds was six times the quantity that visible shipping could move, and SOS had to call back some shipments that had been sent to port.[55]

As the surplus of shipping evaporated, recriminations filled the air. Performance, Somervell wrote bitterly to Admiral Land early in August, had fallen "woefully"

short of the original goal; WSA, he charged, had failed "to make available cargo ships for the Army at the rate it indicated as possible and in accordance with a schedule to which it gave its assent."[56] Douglas drafted for Land's signature two replies, one stiffly polite, the other heavily sarcastic ("Oh shucks! Why did you write that nice appreciative letter . . ."), pointing out that WSA presenters for BOLERO had actually far exceeded the Army's original stated requirements of 22 May and, despite heavy losses at sea, had fallen only moderately behind the schedules that the Army, at WSA's urging, had later set up.[57] He reviewed the Army's past sins of incomplete and unbalanced loadings of BOLERO ships. At this very time, moreover, the volume of cargo shipments to the United Kingdom was surging upward, and by the end of the month the total number of sailings reached ninety. But even this performance fell far short of expectations, and at the end of July the whole outlook was changed by the decision to undertake the North African expedition. In preparation for the new venture a few small vessels from the BOLERO pool were immediately taken up for conversion to combat loaders, but the most

---

[55] (1) Memo, Ralph Keating for Douglas, 11 Jun 42. (2) Msg, John S. Maclay for Douglas, 13 Jul 42. Both in Army Reqmts folder, WSA Douglas File. (3) Douglas' notes cited n. 48. (4) Memo, Douglas for Hopkins, 19 Jun 42, Hopkins folder, WSA Douglas File. (5) Memo, Capt Conklin for Col Walter A. Wood, Jr., 1 Jul 42, BOLERO Reqmts folder, Plng Div ASF, Job A47-147. (6) Msg, WD to USFOR, 24 Jun 42, CM-OUT 6099. (7) Msg Black 21, BCC(W) to BCC(L), 31 Jul 42, ABC 381 BOLERO (3-16-42) Sec 4, Folder 3. (8) Diary, 19 Jun and 27 Jul 42 entries, cited n. 29. (9) Memo, Marshall for King, 19 Jun 42, OPD 560, 34.

[56] (1) Ltr, Somervell to Land, 5 Aug 42, Shipg 1941–43 folder, Hq ASF. (2) Related corresp in Wylie WSA file and Gross WSA file, OCT HB.

[57] Douglas' draft replies are in Army Reqmts folder, WSA Douglas File.

---

folder, OCT HB. (5) Ltr, Sir John Dill to Somervell, 18 Jul 42. (6) Ltr, Somervell to Dill, 18 Jul 42. Last two in Shipg 1941–43 folder, Hq ASF. (7) Memo, Somervell for Marshall, 25 Jun 42, CofS WDGS 1941–42 folder, Hq ASF. (8) CCS 87, 28 Jun 42, title: Interim Rpt by CMTC on Proposed AAF Deployment to Middle East. (9) Related papers in ABC 570 (2-14-42) Sec 2. (10) Craven and Cate, *AAF I*, pp. 566–70.

serious impact upon BOLERO movements resulted from the temporary immobilization of much of the cargo awaiting shipment. Two weeks after Somervell's stinging complaint to Admiral Land over WSA's failure to provide ships, Douglas received an embarrassed telephone call from Gross: "Well, we're finally in a position where we have to reject ships." For lack of ready cargo, Gross confessed, berthing for BOLERO loading would have to be suspended until military plans were clarified. Douglas replied graciously that he "understood thoroughly" and that "there could be no cloud of criticism cast over the Army." [58]

The BOLERO program in 1942 thus fell short of the original conception of a massive stockpiling operation designed to take full advantage of the summer months and of an expected surplus of cargo shipping, largely in advance of the deployment of the invasion force itself. During June, July, and August some 1,300,000 ship tons of Army cargo were moved to the British Isles, the bulk of it (773,000 tons) during the final month. Very little of this material was actually shipped ahead of the troops who were to use it. Almost all the units sailing after the "preshipment" directive of 22 June—the 1st Division, for example—were accompanied by, or preceded their equipment. Some of the cargo shipped in August was backlog belonging to Eighth Air Force units which had sailed early in June. Vehicles were the only item of organizational equipment advance-shipped in sizable numbers. Even this program languished in June and July, and a determined effort to get back on schedule in August was only partially successful. During the seven weeks from mid-July to mid-September, about 32,000 vehicles were shipped to England—over 11,000

during the last week of the period, and all but about 2,300 boxed. Shipments of ammunition, general supplies, subsistence, spare parts, and medical and post exchange supplies—mostly filler cargo—went somewhat beyond the needs of forces in the theater, but for lack of the hoped-for surplus of cargo shipping, advance shipment of organizational equipment, though sanctioned as a policy, remained in 1942 largely an abortive experiment that was not to bear fruit until 1943. [59]

The extent of the shortfall in these three months could not then, and cannot now, be measured with any precision. Estimates of the total amount of BOLERO cargo to be moved by April 1943 varied widely, from less than ten to more than fifteen million ship tons. But it was clear, at all events, that the summer's effort had sliced off only a thin piece of the total requirement. Had the program been continued with its original objectives, a disproportionately large amount of material would have remained to be shipped during the final seven months before April 1943, requiring a volume of flow that the ports and inland transportation facilities of the United Kingdom in all probability could not have handled—certainly far in excess of the 1,200,000 ship tons the British in June had set as the ceiling for average monthly in-

---

[58] (1) Telephone conv, Gross with Douglas, Army Reqmts folder, WSA Douglas File. (2) For the impact of TORCH preparations, see below, Ch. XVII.

[59] (1) For cargo shipment figures, see below, App. E-2. (2) Diary, 27 Jul 42 entry, cited n. 29. (3) Corresp in OCT 563.5 Mvmt BOLERO. (4) Vehicle figures are from chart, "Shipment of Advance Cargo to the United Kingdom," 10 Sep 42, BOLERO folder, Logis File, OCMH. (5) See Hq ETOUSA Statistical Summary 4, 17 Aug 42, and 7, 7 Sep 42, DRB AGO. These sources show incoming shipments of vehicles as follows: May, 2,286; June, 2,765; July, 3,486; August, 13,905; total, 22,442. (6) See also, rpt, p. 35, cited n. 28(1). (7) For shipment of 1st Division equipment, see below, Ch. XVI.

take of BOLERO cargo during the autumn and winter months.[60]

To carry through the program might also have called for more cargo shipping than the two countries could have mustered for the purpose. The amount needed could not be estimated with even approximate accuracy. BOLERO cargo, being predominantly of bulky (measurement) types, would have to be mixed in with the predominantly dense (weight) cargo Britain imported to maintain her war economy, in order to avoid the huge cumulative waste of shipping space that would result from unbalanced loading in a program of this size. During the summer of 1942 most vessels carrying Army shipments to the United Kingdom were "floored" with lend-lease steel. WSA hoped to carry this kind of pooling much further in the months to come, when American shipping would have to shoulder an increasingly heavy share of the British import program, but the rough estimates of BOLERO cargo requirements, based on rule-of-thumb per capita tonnage formulas, gave no inkling of the proportions of weight and measurement cargo involved. When the shipping authorities of the two countries examined the problem late in July, therefore, they would not even venture a guess as to the probable shipping requirements for BOLERO. They did agree, however, that even on an optimistically low reckoning of BOLERO cargo requirements, the prospects of finding enough Allied shipping to move the cargo, along with Britain's minimum import needs, were exceedingly dim.[61]

By late summer of 1942 the BOLERO program thus seemed about to run into two major pipeline bottlenecks—the capacity of the United Kingdom to absorb the flow of material, and the capacity of

Allied shipping to transport material across the Atlantic. The former limitation had not yet been felt, since even the heavy volume of August shipments was far below the intake capacity of British ports, but it was causing anxiety on both sides of the Atlantic. In September the effort to mount the North African task forces was to reveal the dangerous inadequacy of the American depot system in the ETO. As for shipping, the reports of the Combined Shipping Adjustment Boards to the President and Prime Minister at the beginning of August, resulting from their study of the BOLERO shipping problem, led directly to the decision in October to expand the American shipbuilding program. From the gloomy outlook for BOLERO the American civilian shipping authorities drew the conclusion—one the British, out of their long and unhappy experience in supporting the costly administrative "tails" of their own armies in distant theaters, had reached much earlier—that drastic economies must be sought in two directions: (1) by contriving a leaner, less elaborately accoutered invasion force and supporting establishment that would not require so much transatlantic shipping, and (2) by improving the techniques of packing,

---

[60] (1) For early estimates of cargo requirements, see memo, Magruder for Lutes, 10 Jun 42, sub: Cargo for BOLERO, OCT 563.5 BOLERO; memo cited n. 38(3); papers, no dates, subs: Total BOLERO Cargo, Opns SOS 1942–43 folder, Hq ASF; and tables and charts, 28 Apr 42, prepared by Plng Div OCT, Army Reqmts folder, WSA Douglas File. (2) For British estimates, see papers in ABC 381 BOLERO (3-16-42) Sec 4, Folders 2 and 3. (3) For ETOUSA estimate late in July, see papers in LWD [Lewis W. Douglas] Misc London Papers Jul–Aug 42 folder, WSA Douglas File.

[61] (1) Msg, Harriman and Douglas to President, 2 Aug 42, with atchd rpt by CSAB. (2) Min, mtgs of Br War Cabinet and U.S. reps, 25 and 31 Jul 42. Both in LWD Misc London Papers Jul–Aug 42 folder, WSA Douglas File.

loading, and stowing cargo and the programing and scheduling of ship movements, in order to squeeze the maximum
performance from available cargo tonnage. The Prime Minister, late in that
month, aghast at American equipment
scales that provided one vehicle for every
six soldiers in the planned invasion force,
suggested to General Marshall that his
planners start from an arbitrary figure of
one hundred thousand vehicles, weed out
all nonessential types, and "see what is the
best army that can be built up on them"
in nine months.[62] The idea found little
favor among the SOS staff, but in mounting the North African task forces two
months later it proved necessary to do, in
effect, what Churchill had suggested.[63]

One promising method of circumvent-
ing the shipping shortage was already
being pursued with some success—the use
of local resources in the United Kingdom
to support the American forces there. A
rough estimate made in November rated
the savings in shipping space brought
about through British construction of
housing and depots for U.S. forces at over
1.5 million ship tons, not counting the existing structures turned over for American
use. English coal consumed by American
troops amounted to about 15,000 long
tons a month. British-produced foodstuffs
were an important supplement to American rations. By the end of 1942 it was
estimated that locally procured supplies
other than construction materials, between May and November, were the
equivalent of 1.2 million ship tons. In these
figures can be seen some of the immense
advantages the British Isles offered as an
invasion base.[64]

By the end of August, the question of
the success or failure of the three-month-
old BOLERO program already seemed
academic, for SLEDGEHAMMER had been
abandoned and a spring 1943 ROUNDUP
was, to the American planners at least, a
possibility hardly worth reckoning on.
Viewed as a hypothesis, it already seemed
likely that a cross-Channel invasion in
1943 would have to be postponed at least
until summer of 1943.

Landing Craft: The Elusive Bottleneck

Shipping limited the build-up of invasion forces, landing craft the strength of
the assault. Both limitations were difficult
to assess at long-range, especially landing
craft. The methods and tools of amphibious warfare were new—the experts could
not even agree on what was needed and
persistently went astray in their prediction
of what could be produced.

At the beginning of 1942 the available
amphibious forces of the United States
consisted of the 3d Infantry and 2d Marine Divisions on the west coast and the
1st Infantry and 1st Marine Divisions on
the east coast. One regiment of the 2d
Marine Division was in Iceland and another was sent to Samoa in January. The
west coast forces were almost completely

---

[62] Msg, Churchill toMarshall, 1 Aug 42, LWD Misc
London Papers Jul–Aug 42 folder, WSA Douglas File.

[63] (1) See n. 61. (2) Note by Minister of War Trans,
no date, sub: U.K. Imports and BOLERO Mvmts,
LWD Misc London Papers Jul–Aug 42 folder, WSA
Douglas File. (3) For the expanded shipbuilding pro-
gram and ship economies, see below, Ch. XXII. (4)
For other economy programs, see below, Ch. XXIII.
(5) For the North African operation, see below, Ch.
XVI.

[64] For reciprocal aid in the United Kingdom, see:
(1) *Report to the 78th Congress on Lend-Lease Operations . . . March 11, 1941 to December 31, 1942*, pp. 50–
51; and (2) Ruppenthal, *Logistical Support of the Armies*,
Ch. VI.

lacking in amphibious transport; those on the east coast were somewhat better off. Neither force was adequately equipped with landing craft. There were in the United States, on 1 January, 875 landing craft and 53 amphibian tractors. Another 1,243 craft and 907 amphibian tractors were scheduled for production. All the craft were under fifty feet in length, many of the tank lighters were unseaworthy, and none could carry a medium tank. As yet the United States had no large landing ships, though a few had been ordered by the British. During January the President authorized construction of 300 tank landing ships and 300 tank landing craft (predecessors of the LST and the LCT(5), respectively), to be completed in 1944. Some 1,150 small craft also were ordered by the Navy in January and February, most of them for the British, but they, too, were to be delivered in 1944. In general, until the end of March, landing craft production was not regarded as urgent, although Churchill had stressed the need back in August 1941 at the Atlantic Conference.[65]

As discussion of future cross-Channel operations became more pointed during March, attention centered rather suddenly upon the landing craft question. The Joint Planners on the 23d rated equipment for amphibious landing operations among the three decisively limiting categories of war material, and recommended a specific program of production for 1942. Acting independently, the President on 4 April directed certain increases in production with scheduled deliveries by the following September. Priorities were raised and production schedules accelerated.[66]

On the 8th General Marshall arrived in London to win British approval for the cross-Channel invasion project. In the outline plan, landing craft requirements for the major operation were estimated roundly at 7,000. Most estimates ran higher. Later in the month General McNarney remarked that 20,000 would be a more realistic goal. The OPD staff had already settled on a conservative estimate of 8,100. The British did not examine the figures closely at this time, however, and during the London conference Marshall received an optimistic message from Washington to the effect that all requirements could be met by April 1943 and perhaps a third of them by September 1942. The War Department had already ordered about 2,300 craft from the Navy, mostly small personnel and vehicle carriers, for the autumn operation, and the Navy had let contracts in mid-April to cover this order; delivery was promised in time to allow two months for shipment across the Atlantic. All the Army estimates in April, as Eisenhower admitted, were hasty and impressionistic; no allowances were made for reserves or training, and there was no knowledge on

[65] (1) Col A. T. Mason, Special Monograph on Amphibious Warfare, Ch. II "Domestic Affairs—1942," Sec IID, Pt. III of Hist of JCS (mimeographed), JCS Hist Sec. (2) See below, App. A-7.

[66] (1) JPS 20, 23 Mar 42, title: Priorities in Pdn of Mun Based on Strategical Considerations. (2) JCS 30, 5 Apr 42, same title. (3) Related corresp in CCS 400.17 (2-20-42) Sec 1. (4) Accounts of the precise directive given by the President at the White House meeting on 4 April differ. See George E. Mowry, Landing Craft and the War Production Board, WPD Sp Study 11, p. 6; Donald M. Nelson, *Arsenal of Democracy* (New York, Harcourt, Brace and Company, 1946), p. 253; *Third Annual Report of the Special Committee Investigating the National Defense Program*, Senate, 78th Cong, 2d Sess, 3 Mar 44, Senate Rpt 10, Pt. 16, p. 157; and min, 15th mtg CCS, 7 Apr 42. (5) Mason, Special Monograph on Amphibious Warfare, p. 55, cited n. 65(1).

the American side of what the British could produce. As far as SLEDGEHAMMER was concerned, it would be executed, if at all, as Eisenhower remarked, "with whatever personnel and equipment is actually available at the time." [67]

During the latter part of April the Navy was re-examining its own needs for landing craft in amphibious operations in the Pacific and elsewhere. These approached the four-thousand mark which, according to a CPS subcommittee estimate on 2 May, would squeeze out the Army's SLEDGEHAMMER order altogether and most of the requirements for ROUNDUP. By leaving out all allowances for Army training, losses, or spare engines, the subcommittee estimated that about half the requirements for SLEDGEHAMMER could be met. The British might be able to make up this deficit, the subcommittee concluded, but for ROUNDUP, even with British resources, there would be about two thousand craft lacking. One bottleneck was in the manufacture of engines. The subcommittee also foresaw difficulties in providing crews. A few days later, in fact, the Corps of Engineers was assigned responsibility for training Army crews, primarily for shore-to-shore operations, leaving the Navy to specialize in its traditional function of ship-to-shore operations. Apart from heaping a new burden upon Navy procurement, the Army's cross-Channel needs were also disruptive because of their heavy proportion of vehicle and tank carriers; in the Navy's program the emphasis was upon personnel carriers. [68]

Meanwhile, the British experts had been growing uneasy over the American landing craft program. At the London conversations in mid-April one of them, Captain Hughes-Hallett, had remarked on the difficulties of transporting small craft across the Atlantic and on their unsuitability for an assault across the English Channel. It was not until early in May, however, that British forebodings became emphatic—which was unfortunate, since by that time the American procurement program was well under way and large numbers of the small craft were scheduled for early delivery. The matter was brought before the President on 5 May. After some preliminary explanation of the various types of craft for his benefit, the British representatives set forth in detail the objections to the three principal small types (50-foot WM boats, 36-foot personnel carriers, and 36-foot vehicle carriers). In a Channel crossing, they pointed out, many of these craft would break down or swamp, and the troops that got across would be in no physical condition to fight. The British did not believe, moreover, that the operation could be executed with small boats landing from combat loaders. Evidently these views were new to some of the professionals present as well as to the

---

[67] (1) Memo, Eisenhower for Somervell, 10 Apr 42, sub: Landing Craft To Be Available 15 Sep 42. . . . (2) Memo, Eisenhower for CG SOS, 2 Apr 42, sub: Landing Craft for Cross-Channel Opns. Both in OPD 560, Case 5. (3) CPS 26/1, App. C, cited n. 16(1). (4) Min, Wd Gen Council mtg, 29 Apr 42. (5) Msg, McNarney to Marshall, 13 Apr 42, CM-OUT 2240. (6) CPS 29/1, 2 May 42, title: Study for Landing Craft Progs. (7) Memo, Somervell for Gross, 5 Apr 42, OCT 560.

[68] (1) CPS 29/1 cited n. 67(6). (2) Blanche D. Coll and Herbert H. Rosenthal, The Corps of Engineers: Troops and Equipment, a volume in preparation for the series UNITED STATES ARMY IN WORLD WAR II (hereafter cited as Coll and Rosenthal, Engr I), draft chapter "One New Mission: The Engineer Amphibian Command." (3) Memo, Handy for Eisenhower, 2 Apr 42, sub: Landing Craft for Cross-Channel Mvmt, OPD 560, 3. (4) Memo, 25 Mar 42, cited n. 7(1). (5) Paper, circa late Mar 42, sub: Small Boat Sup, ABC 370 (1-28-42).

AMPHIBIOUS TRAINING IN MOCK LCV

President; General Somervell remarked that the Navy had assured him the small boats were suitable.[69]

The President, at any rate, seemed to be convinced. At his direction and under close British guidance a new program of requirements was drawn up that shifted the emphasis to the larger types of craft, including a substantial number of ocean-going vessels. The first list, based on recommendations from the combined planners in London, set ROUNDUP requirements at about 1,950 craft, including 200 ocean-going tank landing ships (ATL's) and 570 tank landing craft (YTL's and similar types of large lighters). Before the end of the month the list had been more than doubled by additions to the smaller types and allowances for losses and training. Early in June ROUNDUP requirements of both British and U.S. types stood at

---

[69] (1) Min cited n. 22(1). (2) Paper by Capt Hughes-Hallett, 16 Apr 42, sub: Landing Craft Required To Carry Out Marshall's Plan, ABC 381 BOLERO (3-16-42) Sec 4, Folder 2. (3) Memo, Chief of Water Div OCT for Gross, 29 Apr 42, sub: Landing Craft, OCT 560. (4) Memo, Gen Gross for Brig Gen Walter Bedell Smith, 5 May 42, sub: Min of Conf at White House . . . , Gross Day File, OCT HB. (5) Mason, Special Monograph on Amphibious Warfare, p. 61, cited n. 65(1).

about 4,100 craft, of which almost 2,900 were to be produced in the United States. A few weeks later General Eisenhower added another 100 tank landing ships and 200 large lighters to the list of initial requirements, and another 30 of each as reserves to be available each month following the assault.[70]

As requirements mounted, prospects of meeting them dwindled. The landing craft program, particularly when the new requirements for ocean-going vessels were added, competed directly with naval and merchant ship construction and indirectly with many other programs for materials, components (such as propulsion units), facilities, and labor. Antisubmarine and escort vessels were the most threatened, and Admiral King told the Combined Chiefs in June that the building of two heavy carriers and some cruisers was also being delayed. For the first six months of 1942 landing craft production did not stand high on the Navy's priority list; not until July was it placed in the top group. From late spring onward the Army's training program began to compete for craft, and the Navy's requirements for its own amphibious forces kept pace with the lengthening list of craft needed for ROUND-UP. Training of crews threatened at times to be even more of a bottleneck than production of craft. The British had undertaken to provide crews for any 1942 operation, while those for 1943 were to be divided between the two countries. But in June, as the British construction program was augmented, doubts were raised whether British crews could meet the 1942 commitment. There was some discussion of possible substitutes for landing craft in the immediate post-assault phases, and a number of American coastal excursion vessels actually attempted the Atlantic

crossing during the summer—several were lost.[71]

It was still possible to predict, in June that ROUNDUP requirements would be met; the Navy was so predicting, but Army officials were skeptical. Production was lagging seriously, and schedules had to be cut back in July. For SLEDGEHAM-MER the prospects were dim indeed. Little could be done to accelerate delivery schedules up to early or mid-July, the deadline for meeting a September target date. Actual deliveries, in fact, lagged far behind them. On 12 May General Somervell and Admiral Horne had reported to the President that some 1,850 landing

<hr>

[70] (1) See CCS 78, 7 Jun 42, title: Landing Craft and related papers in CCS 561 (4-10-42) Sec 1. (Principal items were 200 LST's, 300 LCT(L)'s, 340 LCT(5)'s, 750 LCM(3)'s, 707 LCP(L)'s, 400 LCV's 400 small (28-foot) boats, 286 LCT(1-4)'s, and 425 LCA's. For description of types, see below, App. A-7. (2) Memo, Adms King and Land, Vice Adm J. W. S Dorling, Royal Navy, and Gen Somervell for President, 12 May 42, sub: Landing Craft for BOLERO Opn, Gross Day File, OCT HB. (3) Memo, Ma Howard W. Quinn for CG SOS, 4 Jun 42, sub: Status of Landing Craft, OCT 560 England. (4) Memo Somervell for CofS, 16 Jul 42, sub: Landing Craft OCT 560 Mvmt BOLERO. (5) Msg 553, London to AGWAR, 22 Jul 42. CCS 561 (4-10-42) Sec 1.

[71] (1) For priority and production problems, see WPB Sp Study 11, Ch. II and table on p. 74, cited n. 66(4). This study, however, altogether misses the purpose of the higher priorities assigned in July by assuming that they were aimed at the requirements of the North African operation instead of SLEDGEHAMMER The decision to invade North Africa was not made of course, until the very end of July, and landing craft requirements for this operation were much smaller than those for the cross-Channel attack. See below Ch. XVI. (2) For Army amphibious training, see Col and Rosenthal, Engr I. (3) Memo cited n. 70(2). (4) Memo, Marshall for Somervell and Eisenhower, 16 May 42, OPD 381 BOLERO, 10. (5) Corresp in BOLERO 1942 Amphibious folder and BOLERO 1942 folder Lutes File. (6) Min, mtg of Sp Com on Landing Craft 6 May 42, ABC 381 BOLERO (3-16-42) Sec 4, Folder 2. (7) Corresp related to the CPS 29 series in CCS 561 (4-10-42) Sec 1. (8) For the excursion-boat experiment, see Mason, Special Monograph on Amphibious Warfare, p. 70, cited n. 65(1).

THREE TYPES OF LANDING CRAFT, *summer 1942. LCM(3) (top); LCP(L) (center); LCV (bottom).*

TABLE 6—ESTIMATES OF U.S. LANDING CRAFT TO BE AVAILABLE FOR SLEDGEHAMMER: APRIL–JUNE 1942

Plans	Total	LCP(L)	LCV	LCM(3)
April statement of Army requirements........................	2, 203	503	1, 200	500
Information submitted to Chief of Staff, 13 April.............	2, 698	466	1, 066	1, 166
Information submitted to the President, 14 May..............	1, 200	400	400	400
CPS 20/6, 3 June..	1, 331	403	513	415
CCS 78, 7 June..	846	481	305	60
CCS 78/1, 24 June........	396	288	52	56

Source: Mason, Special Monograph on Amphibious Warfare, Ch. II "Domestic Affairs—1942," Sec IID, Pt. III of Hist of the JCS (mimeographed), p. 72, JCS Hist Sec.

craft would definitely be ready in the United Kingdom for an autumn operation; 1,200 of these were to come from the United States, and the British contribution was to include four big landing ships (LST's) and 150 large lighters (LCT's). This program immediately began to limp. By the end of May only 110 of the two smallest types had been shipped to the theater, against 271 scheduled; most of the 110 had been taken from used and obsolete stocks. Some new craft, moreover, had to be allotted to the Engineer Amphibian Command for training. A disheartening setback was the discovery late in May that the Navy's 50-foot tank lighter (Bureau of Ships model) was unseaworthy; 415 of these craft scheduled for June and July delivery thus evaporated.[72] Up to 29 June, 238 craft—all of them the three small types listed in Table 6— had been shipped or were on the way to the United Kingdom; a month later this figure had been not quite doubled. Actually, few of the craft shipped in July could have been in position for a September operation. In August shipments shot belatedly upward: 627 craft had been loaded out by the 15th, and 267 more were in the pipeline.[73] But in mid-July General Hull wrote

to Eisenhower, then in London, that all the craft available and en route (including many too far back in the pipeline to be available in September) could land less than 16,000 troops and 1,100 tanks and vehicles; two months earlier the estimate had been 21,000 troops and 3,300 tanks and vehicles. Army logistical officials felt the Navy had let them down and chafed in the unaccustomed role of purchaser from another military agency. Somervell wrote Eisenhower in July:

The Navy's efforts . . . have been disappointing. This is just another indication of how difficult it is to force an issue when you have no control over the means of carrying it out. There is no lack of good will on their part, apparently, though there was much indecision in the beginning. They say that they have the best people they have on the job, and no doubt are doing all they can, according to their own lights, to get the job completed.[74]

---

[72] Memo cited n. 70(2).

The fading of hope for meeting the U.S. quota for SLEDGEHAMMER is shown in Table 6.

[73] (1) Corresp in OCT 560 England, especially rpts by Maj Quinn and Capt F. M. Warren. (2) WPB Sp Study, pp. 8–9, cited n. 66(4).

[74] (1) Ltr, Somervell to Eisenhower, 19 Jul 42, ETO (6) 1942–43 folder, Hq ASF. (2) Ltr, Hull to Eisenhower, 15 Jul 42, with tab, OPD 320.2 ETO, 6. (3) Memo cited n. 71(4).

The Demise of Sledgehammer

For more than four months after the Joint Chiefs endorsed it in the middle of March, the strategy of concentration in the British Isles and "holding" elsewhere traveled a rocky road. As General Marshall remarked following the London conference, "everyone agrees . . . in principle, but many if not most hold reservations regarding this or that." [75] The reservations fell into three major categories. The first included prior claims to which BOLERO was necessarily subordinated. Of these, the security of the Middle East was the most important. Most of the shipping for lack of which the BOLERO program lagged so disastrously during the summer was in the Middle East—ships that the British had hoped to divert from that theater and others that had to be sent there. In the same category was the commitment, insisted upon by the President, that the flow of aid to the Soviet Union must not dwindle; only the prohibitive costs of forcing the convoys through to the northern Soviet ports kept the scale of this effort low from May onward and prevented it from interfering with the BOLERO program more than it did. Shipping employed in the British import program also constituted a pool that was practically untouchable for military purposes.

A second category of reservations related to the war against Japan. From each of the many fronts, all undermanned, along which this war was being fought, came a steady stream of demands for stronger support. Each posed a threat to the concentration of effort and resources upon which BOLERO depended for success. The issue was brought to a climax early in May by the threat of new Japanese drives into the South, Central, and North Pacific. Unlike General MacArthur, who had persistently urged a complete reversal of strategy, Admiral King even now did not contest the long-range priority of the war against Germany over that against Japan. He was unwilling, however, to take "calculated" risks in the Pacific, now above all, to the extent that General Marshall felt was necessary. He declared:

The mounting of BOLERO must not be permitted to interfere with our vital needs in the Pacific. I am convinced that the Japanese are not going to allow us to "hold" but are going to drive and drive hard. . . . Important as the mounting of BOLERO may be, the Pacific problem is no less so, and is certainly the more urgent—it must be faced now. . . . We must not permit diversion of our forces . . . to the extent that we find ourselves unable to fulfill our obligation to implement our basic strategic plan in the Pacific theatre, which is to hold what we have against any attack that the Japanese are capable of launching against us.

This last sentence threatened what General Marshall feared most, that BOLERO would be starved to death as a "residuary legatee" of the war against Japan. [76] The question was settled, for the time being, by the President's assurance on 6 May that "I do not want BOLERO slowed down." [77] The Japanese drives during the next few weeks were met and countered by a redistribution of forces within the limits that General Marshall considered safe.

In May the President also made clear his determination that American forces, including ground troops, must engage in

---

[75] Msg, Marshall to McNarney, 13 Apr 42, CM-IN 3457.

[76] Memo, King for JCS, 4 May 42, sub: JCS 48—Def of Island Bases in Pac, OPD 381 Gen, 62.

[77] (1) Memo, FDR [Franklin D. Roosevelt] for Marshall, 6 May 42, filed with JCS 48 in ABC 381 Pac Bases (1-22-42), 2. (2) See also below, Ch. XV.

active operations in the European area during 1942. In June Mr. Churchill brought into the open his and his military advisers' conviction that to attempt a cross-Channel attack in 1942 would result in disaster without commensurate profit. The effect of these twin pressures was to force Marshall and his staff to defend SLEDGEHAMMER, not as a forlorn hope to be undertaken with the means available because no other operation was possible, but as the most feasible and profitable of several alternative medium-scale operations that would meet the need for "action in 1942."

On that basis SLEDGEHAMMER was very hard to defend. The weakness of the American contribution to the operation was not so much in the size of the forces that could be ready to help the British— General Marshall was able in June to promise with reasonable assurance a total of four divisions—as in the amount and types of technical apparatus. For a cross-Channel attack in September the United States could provide only a handful of small personnel and vehicle carriers, unmanned, unarmored, many of obsolete design—hardly suited to ferrying troops and armor across many miles of the most treacherous body of water in Europe. The British had made these points in detail early in May and by the end of that month their experts were convinced that with the equipment at hand the operation was not feasible. Vice Adm. Lord Louis Mountbatten, who headed the British amphibious warfare organization, visited Washington at the beginning of June to tell the President that "no landing that we could carry out" would draw off any German forces from the USSR to reinforce the twenty-five divisions Germany already had in the West.[78] If the attack were postponed

until later in the year, the larger types of landing craft would still not be available, and the attacking forces might find themselves at the beginning of the stormy season pinned on a narrow beach without a port to supply them. The American defense rested mainly on the expectation of overwhelming air power; landing forces were to serve as bait to lure the Luftwaffe into battles of attrition. Whether the Germans would in fact so react and whether the results would justify hopes were, of course, matters of opinion. In any case the implied prospect that the landing forces, even if the air effort were successful, might have to be evacuated was one before which the British understandably quailed. On 8 June the Prime Minister, and shortly thereafter the War Cabinet, ruled out a "tip-and-run" attack in any form; no lodgment on the Continent must be attempted in 1942 unless German demoralization in the East and other conditions offered a good chance that it would be permanent. Soviet victories, rather than imminent Soviet collapse, had thus become the chief prerequisite for SLEDGE-HAMMER.[79]

In July the prospects both of troop build-up and of landing craft deliveries in the United Kingdom were even gloomier. The British administrative staffs, moreover, had produced estimates indicating that the autumn operation could not be mounted without seriously disrupting preparations for ROUNDUP. Landing forces would have to be sustained and reinforced,

---

[78] (1) Conv, Mountbatten with President and Hopkins, quoted in Sherwood, *Roosevelt and Hopkins*, p. 582. (2) Memo, CofS for President, 23 Jun 42, OPD 381 Gen, 62.

[79] (1) OPD draft memo, CofS for President, no date, Item 53, Exec 10. (2) Memo, Prime Minister to Gen [Maj Gen Sir Hastings L.] Ismay, 8 Jun 42, as quoted in Churchill, *Hinge of Fate*, pp. 346–48.

at an estimated cost of 950,000 tons of shipping a year; even a "tip-and-run" would tie up 250,000 tons for some time. Diversion of coastal shipping for the operation would throw an additional load on internal transportation and require the use of ocean-going shipping at an eventual cost to the import program of almost half a million tons. Predicted shipping losses in the assault came to 50 percent. If a major operation developed, "indefinite and much greater liabilities upon shipping resources will be entailed." [80] While the operation was in progress, amphibious training of other forces would have to be suspended. In an effort to secure and hold a bridgehead, as Churchill wrote the President, "the possibility of mounting a large-scale operation in 1943 would be marred, if not ruined." [81] These new limitations, as far as the British were concerned, finished off SLEDGEHAMMER, and on 8 July Churchill so informed the President. [82]

When General Marshall and Hopkins went to London later in the month to try to persuade the British to change their minds, they thus had to defend a patently unsound operation without appealing to the two arguments by which it had originally been justified—that it might be the only way, with meager available resources, to help the Russians in an emergency, and that it could be mounted in stride, at the last moment, without hindering the larger effort in 1943. The President's instructions explicitly ruled that the main issue was to decide upon some positive action for 1942, to be undertaken regardless of the course of events on the Soviet front; what had once been regarded as the best argument for SLEDGEHAMMER, that it would strike near the heart of German power, was now turned against it as involving great risks not balanced by possible gains. As for the

second argument, the Americans evidently accepted British estimates that a cross-Channel attack in 1942 would delay the invasion the following spring, since they now suggested a July instead of an April launching date. They also tried to meet another British objection by transforming SLEDGEHAMMER from a possible "tip-and-run" into a "toehold" operation, aimed at seizing and holding the point of the Cotentin peninsula with the port of Cherbourg; the British found this almost as unattractive as the earlier schemes. After a brief debate, the Americans yielded and notified the President on 23 July of their failure. The President was not surprised. [83]

The British rejection of SLEDGEHAMMER pointed up the question of alternatives. Marshall and King now feared that the British, when the time came, might also back down on crossing the Channel in 1943, particularly if by that time other operations were under way in the Mediterranean and/or Norway. Whatever alternative was chosen for 1942, the American military chiefs were convinced, would seriously weaken and postpone any cross-Channel invasion in 1943. On 10 July General Marshall had proposed, as an alternative to further dilution of effort in the European theater, that the United States should shift its main effort immediately to the Pacific where the effort would at least be a concentrated one against a weaker enemy. How much weaker the effort would be, however, was roughly in-

---

[80] Memo, Br CsofS for War Cabinet, 2 Jul 42, sub: Future Opns, ABC 381 (7-25-42) 4-B, 19.

[81] Telegram, Former Naval Person to President Roosevelt, 8 Jul 42, as quoted in Churchill, *Hinge of Fate*, pp. 434–35.

[82] Msg, War Cabinet to Jt Stf Mis, 8 Jul 42, Item 9, Exec 5.

[83] (1) Sherwood, *Roosevelt and Hopkins*, pp. 606–10. (2) Harrison, *Cross-Channel Attack*, pp. 28–31. (3) Matloff and Snell, *Strategic Planning: 1941-1942*, Ch. XII.

dicated during the next few days as the logistical staffs hastily assembled the pertinent data. Time would be lost in transferring shipping to the Pacific. Some forces would have to be sent to Iceland and the British Isles in any event. Allowing for these, perhaps 40,000 troops a month could be sent to the Pacific, as against currently planned shipments of 100,000 and more to the British Isles. But because of the long turnaround, cargo shipping would be inadequate to support even a deployment of 40,000 a month. Behind the shipping-turnaround bottleneck, troops would pile up in the United States where, the staffs estimated, additional accommodations might have to be built for 400,000 troops. This information was instructive and depressing, but the whole question immediately became academic for on the 14th the President, with a hint of displeasure, rejected the Japan-first alternative.[84]

The choice for action in 1942 was thus limited to the orbit of the war against the European Axis. Churchill was nursing a plan for invading northern or western Norway, and the Combined Chiefs briefly considered landing at various points from the North Sea coast to and including the Iberian Peninsula. None of these projects aroused much enthusiasm among the military staffs, since they were considered to involve either less profit or greater risks than a cross-Channel attack. For American forces, with the latter alternative ruled out, the practical options narrowed down to operations in support of the British in the eastern Mediterranean area, either frontally from the east or against Rommel's back door in the west. The former seemed to the staffs to be the most feasible course. The shipping route around the Cape, while long, was organized and well-worn, and at the far terminus troops and

material could be disembarked at ports served by adequate facilities and in friendly hands. Rear area services and other features of a "going" theater were already in existence. On the other hand, military collaboration by multinational forces in a single theater raised complex administrative problems, and there was some doubt as to whether a large number of additional troops could be supported in the area. The military chiefs and their staffs, however, almost unanimously favored this course over opening a new front in northwest Africa "with all the increase of overheads and escort and transportation problems" that it involved, as Admiral King said, and particularly with the possibility of landings over hostile beaches.[85]

Political expediency overrode logistical considerations. There were many ways of meeting the President's insistence upon action in 1942, but it was no secret that he wanted above all to send an American army into French North Africa. Such a venture would satisfy Churchill's purposes and Britain's interests generally better than assigning American forces a large role in the Middle East. "It would be much to our advantage," the British Chiefs of Staff reported, "to get a footing in North Africa cheaply in the same way as the

---

[84] (1) Memo, Marshall, King, and Arnold for President, 12 Jul 42, sub: Pac Opns, OPD 381 Gen, 73. (2) Memo, Somervell for CofS, 14 Jul 42, sub: Opns in the Pac, Case 11, Item 1, Exec 5. (3) Matloff and Snell, *Strategic Planning: 1941-1942*, Ch. XII.

[85] (1) Min, 28th mtg CCS, 20 Jun 42. (2) OPD study, no date, title: Effect on BOLERO and ROUNDUP of Diverting Forces To Execute GYMNAST or To Reinf the Middle East, Data Prepared by OPD folder, Item 6, Exec 1. (3) OPD study, no date, title: Reinf of the Middle East, same file. (4) Memo, President for Hopkins, Marshall, and King, 16 Jul 42, sub: Instns for London Conf, WDCSA 381, 1.

The distance from the U.S. to Suez via the Cape was roughly three times the distance to Casablanca. *(See Map 8.)*

Germans got Norway cheaply by getting there first." [86] Churchill therefore brought all his persuasive arts to bear on the President, who indeed needed no convincing but who alone could overrule his military advisers' objections. Landings in French North Africa, Churchill insisted, would be a better "second front" in 1942 than SLEDGEHAMMER ever could have been. "This second front consists of a main body holding the enemy pinned opposite 'Sledgehammer' [that is, the English Channel] and a wide flanking movement called 'Torch' [as GYMNAST was rechristened on the 24th]." [87] Churchill's own pet Norway project would have added a left flank attack to this pattern. TORCH, Churchill argued, would be cheap, it was the only way to strike at Hitler in 1942, it was the best way to help the Russians, and it would not interrupt preparations for the main invasion in 1943, to which a flanking movement in the south would be an effective prelude. "Here," he exclaimed, "is the true second front of 1942 . . . . the safest and most fruitful stroke that can be delivered this autumn." [88]

Churchill's exuberant rhetoric masked a riddle. If TORCH were to relieve German pressure on the USSR, it must be a big operation; if it were to avoid doing "mortal injury" to ROUNDUP, it must be a small one. In one breath Churchill called TORCH a "true second front"; in the next he spoke of taking from BOLERO only six American divisions (which might "surely" be soon replaced), although his own military staffs had already decided that a U.S. attack on Casablanca would be no second front and that there must be additional landings farther east, even beyond Algiers. [89] Field Marshal Dill warned Churchill before the President's representatives reached London that, in American opinion, a North African operation would take naval forces from the Pacific, create a new and expensive line of communications, and "build up into such a large commitment as to destroy any possibility of 'Round-up' in 1943." [90] And when, after two days of fruitless debate at London, it was evident that SLEDGEHAMMER was dead, Marshall and King insisted on writing into the CCS agreement the consensus that ". . . a commitment to this operation [TORCH] renders ROUND-UP in all probability impracticable of successful execution in 1943. . . ." [91]

---

[86] Digest of min, Br CsofS mtg at Chequers, 18 Jul 42, as quoted in Churchill, *Hinge of Fate*, p. 444.

[87] Msg, Former Naval Person to President Roosevelt, 27 Jul 42, as quoted in Churchill, *Hinge of Fate*, p. 448.

[88] Telegram, Former Naval Person to President Roosevelt, 8 Jul 42, as quoted in Churchill, *Hinge of Fate*, p. 434; msg, Prime Minister to Dill, 12 Jul 42, p. 438; msg, Dill to Prime Minister, 15 Jul 42, pp. 439–40; Prime Minister's Notes for Mtg on 20 Jul 42, pp. 445–46.

[89] Telegram, 8 Jul 42, and msg, 12 Jul 42, cited n. 88.

[90] Msg, 15 Jul 42, cited n. 88.

[91] (1) Memo, U.S. CsofS for Br CsofS, 24 Jul 42, filed with CCS 94, 24 Jul 42, title: Opns in 1942–43, in ABC 381 (7-25-42) Sec 1. (2) Digest of min cited n. 86.

CHAPTER XV

Turning Point in the Pacific

Strategy and Logistics in the Pacific War

With the decision, made in April 1942, to concentrate resources in the British Isles for an early invasion of northwestern Europe, Army planners sought to limit commitments to the Pacific to those absolutely necessary for a defensive strategy, but the dangers of allowing the Japanese to extend and consolidate their conquests could not be ignored. Even after his rebuff in May, General MacArthur continued to ask for a greater concentration of resources in the Southwest Pacific, stressing the disastrous consequences that would result from a Japanese lodgment on the continent of Australia. Admiral King, for all his agreement with the Atlantic-first strategy, did not think it should be permitted to interfere with building defenses in the Pacific capable of withstanding any Japanese assault, or with undertaking limited counteroffensives to keep the Japanese off balance. King continually pressed Marshall for larger numbers of long-range bombers and additional Army air bases along the island chain between Hawaii and Australia, steps that both General Marshall and General Arnold opposed as involving unnecessary diversions of planes, troops, and shipping from the war against Germany. Their solution was to anchor a strong mobile force of bombers at each end of the chain—in Hawaii and Australia—

to cover the intervening area. The July decision to abandon SLEDGEHAMMER and undertake the invasion of North Africa as the major effort in the Atlantic in 1942 gave added strength to the pressures from MacArthur and the Navy, and the opportunity that presented itself for a limited counteroffensive in the Pacific soon gave them almost irresistible force.

During the spring of 1942 the Japanese, after establishing a major base at Rabaul on New Britain island, moved south into the Solomons and New Guinea. From Lae and Salamaua on the northern coast of New Guinea they threatened the main Australian base at Port Moresby, the key to MacArthur's defense of Australia. In June they began to build airfields on Tulagi and Guadalcanal at the southeastern tip of the Solomons, posing an even more serious threat to the Allied positions in New Caledonia and the Fijis. Meantime, early in June, U.S. military forces gained their first decisive victory in the Pacific war at the Battle of Midway, repulsing the Japanese move to gain control of the Central Pacific. Japanese losses, particularly of aircraft carriers, went far toward restoring the balance of naval power in the Pacific. The Midway victory opened the way for a limited offensive to counter the Japanese threat to Australia and the line of communications. After some controversy over command arrangements, General Marshall and Admiral King issued a joint directive on 2 July 1942 calling for such an offensive to be mounted at once with the ultimate object of seizing the New Britain-New Ireland-New Guinea area. The directive laid down three major phases or tasks. Task One was the seizure of the Santa Cruz Islands, Tulagi, and "adjacent positions"; Task Two, the conquest of the remainder of the Solomons and of the northwest coast of New Guinea; Task Three, the final assault on Rabaul and the surrounding area. Execution of Task One was to be under the command of a naval officer designated by Admiral Nimitz as commander in the South Pacific, with MacArthur providing naval and air support from forces under his command in Australia. As Task One neared completion, command was to pass to MacArthur, who would carry out Tasks Two and Three with South Pacific forces playing a supporting role.

This decision laid down the basic course of Pacific strategy for 1942. It was made, at least on the Army side, without any calculation of what the ultimate cost would be in terms of additional commitments of men and material to the Pacific war front. Indeed, both MacArthur and Admiral Ghormley, Nimitz' choice for the South Pacific command, were put off without any assurances of further support when they asked that initiation of Task One be delayed until sufficient resources were on hand to execute Tasks Two and Three. By its very nature, the plan for a Pacific offensive was bound to generate demands for additional commitments of manpower and materials, demands of an emergency nature that the Army staff in Washington could hardly resist, however much they might wish to follow the principle of concentration on the Atlantic front.

The Navy chose Guadalcanal and Tulagi as the objectives for this first American offensive in the Pacific, and the attack was launched on 7 August 1942. The forces that landed on Guadalcanal soon met with determined opposition and their hold on a small perimeter on the island was to remain tenuous for three months. In the Southwest Pacific, meanwhile, the Japanese forced MacArthur's hand by seizing Buna on the Papuan coast opposite Port Moresby and by sending expeditions over the Owen Stanley Range toward Port Moresby. To counter this threat, MacArthur dispatched additional Australian forces to New Guinea and soon committed the U.S. 32d Division there. Thus began, also in August, the Papua Campaign, a defensive-offensive operation aimed at breaking the Japanese hold on Buna as a prelude to further advances along the north coast of New Guinea. In this first limited step toward the execution of Task Two, the going proved as difficult as on Guadalcanal.[1]

The Guadalcanal and Papua operations were necessarily mounted and supported from bases within the theaters, and largely with the limited resources already there. As the difficulties of climate and terrain became evident and the stubborn character of Japanese resistance manifested itself, it became apparent that the operations could not be pushed through to victory without additional support from the United States. Urgent appeals from the commanders of the South and Southwest Pacific Areas for such support were soon arriving in Washington. At the same

---

[1] (1) Matloff and Snell, *Strategic Planning: 1941-1942*, Chs. VII–XIII, *passim.* (2) John Miller, jr., *Guadalcanal: The First Offensive*, UNITED STATES ARMY IN WORLD WAR II (Washington, 1949), pp. 1–21, 59–71. (3) Milner, Victory in Papua, Chs. V–VIII.

time, there were demands for more forces for Alaska and Hawaii, where the possibility of Japanese attacks remained strong. Even skeptical visitors from Washington, when they saw the difficulties under which all the Pacific commands were operating, usually supported these demands. As a consequence, concessions to the war in the Pacific were continuous, and they completed the jettisoning of the principle of concentration that the diversions to the Middle East and the TORCH decision had begun. The concessions resulted from spot decisions to meet pressing needs; there was little time for careful calculation of strategic goals in relation to logistical capabilities.

The Pacific war presented logistical problems differing in many respects from those of the war in Europe and the Mediterranean. The distance from San Francisco to Brisbane was 7,200 nautical miles, and to Nouméa in New Caledonia 6,400, as against only 3,500 from New York to either Liverpool or Casablanca. Distance was a heavy liability, only partially offset by the relative absence of the submarine menace in the Pacific. In July, when a shift of the major effort to the Pacific was being considered, Marshall and King estimated that shipping that could transport 100,000 troops to the British Isles would move only 40,000 to Australia, while a larger amount of cargo shipping would be needed to support the latter deployment than the former.[2]

Distances between points within the South and Southwest Pacific theaters were almost as formidable, and at the end of the long voyage to the far Pacific there were no well-developed ports or bases within striking distance of the areas where operations had to be conducted. The large ports of Melbourne, Sydney, and Brisbane on the east coast of Australia, and Auckland and Wellington in New Zealand could handle a considerable traffic in large ocean-going ships, but Brisbane was 1,100 miles from New Guinea, and Auckland 1,500 from Guadalcanal. Townsville, a port 900 miles north of Brisbane but with far less ample facilities, had to be developed as the principal transshipment point from Australia to New Guinea. Similarly Nouméa, a port with an excellent harbor but very limited docking facilities, had to serve as the main forward base in the South Pacific Area—and Nouméa was still 900 miles from Guadalcanal.[3]

Movement over these distances within the Pacific theaters depended almost entirely on water transport, not on overland facilities as in Europe and Africa. Even in Australia, coastwise shipping played a more important role in local distribution than rail or truck transport. The South Pacific Area consisted entirely of island bases that could be supplied only by water. In both the South and the Southwest Pacific all supply to forward points had to be by vessels, save for the small proportion carried by air transport. Long water distances and paucity of internal transport facilities made it difficult to distribute supplies from any central point within either theater; direct shipments from the United States to each base or port often represented the most efficient method of supply.

The development of water supply lines in the South-Southwest Pacific area imposed an enormous demand for vessels of all sorts; the need for storage, base, port, and transportation facilities imposed an

[2] See above, Ch. XIV.
[3] Bykofsky and Larson, Trans III, Chs. VII–VIII.

equally heavy demand for construction materials and labor. Both were far beyond the limited availability of local resources. In Australia and New Zealand, materials and manpower were available but they were inadequate; on most of the South Pacific islands local labor was either totally lacking or hopelessly unskilled, and the only material readily available was coral for paving roads and airfield runways.

To distance and lack of facilities were added the difficulties arising from climate and terrain. Even on bases where climate was relatively pleasant, troops had few recreational facilities and were isolated for long periods. In the Solomons, New Guinea, and the islands of the Bismarck Archipelago, areas of active operations, the tropical heat was all but unbearable, the rainfall torrential. Coral beaches gave way in the interior to dense jungle foliage, high mountains, and swollen rivers. Malaria and other tropical diseases flourished. The toll in men and materials was terrific. Losses from disease and exhaustion, often exceeding battle casualties, imposed a heavy demand for replacements. Supplies and equipment designed for use in temperate areas deteriorated rapidly; metal corroded, wood and fabric rotted, radios would not work, trucks broke down, tanks and heavy artillery bogged down in mud, sand, or jungle undergrowth. Operations in the Pacific required less heavy equipment than those in Europe and Africa, but they also demanded special types designed for jungle warfare, special kinds of packing, more frequent replacement, more abundant maintenance facilities, larger numbers of service troops.[4]

Finally, there was the man-made problem of divided administrative responsibilities. With two commands conducting what were undeniably separate parts of the same campaign, it was more difficult than it would otherwise have been to avoid duplication of facilities and supply. In the South Pacific theater, where Army and Navy forces were inextricably intermingled, the two services operated parallel supply lines; there were joint arrangements only for exploitation of local resources, and a rule-of-thumb division of responsibility for the provision of certain types of supplies. Even these arrangements, agreed on in Washington, were slow to take shape in the theater because of delay in the arrival of headquarters and service personnel.[5] Separate supply lines for two theaters and two services inevitably caused waste and duplication of effort in an area where facilities and resources were scarce.

The first offensives in the Pacific were launched with but an imperfect realization even in the theaters themselves, and much less in Washington, of the limitations imposed by logistics. Both in New Guinea and on Guadalcanal, logistical support was inadequate at the outset; disaster was only averted by a narrow margin. The experience gained in these two campaigns made it clear that forward movement in the Pacific could not be sustained on a shoestring. A build-up for future operations was well under way before the campaigns were over, but it was limited by a general shortage of troop and cargo shipping under a strategy that subordinated the needs of the war in the Pacific to those of the war in Europe.

---

[4] On the factors of climate and geography and their influence on Guadalcanal and New Guinea, see Miller, *Guadalcanal: The First Offensive*, pp. 24–25, 306–18, and Milner, *Victory in Papua*, Chs. VI, VIII, XI.

[5] See above, Ch. VI.

Deployment and the Shipping Shortage

The first four months of 1942 saw the heaviest deployment of the year to Australia, New Caledonia, and the Fijis. During the next two months emphasis shifted to strengthening defensive positions in Hawaii and Alaska. By early June 1942, when the Battle of Midway was fought, OPD considered that forces essential for a strategic defensive in the Pacific, under the BOLERO strategy, were in position. Despite the American victory at Midway, however, the Japanese moved unopposed into Attu and Kiska in the Aleutians. Maj. Gen. Robert C. Richardson, Jr., dispatched by General Marshall on a tour of inspection, reported a need for additional forces at all bases, particularly in Hawaii. Garrisons in the island chain were still weak, service troops were needed in Australia, air power throughout the Pacific was inadequate. Admiral King continued to press for a stronger air force in the South Pacific, General MacArthur for a general increase in forces in SWPA.

General Marshall made some concessions. Alaskan defenses were moderately strengthened; the 40th Division was dispatched to Hawaii with antiaircraft and other elements, bringing the total number of forces in that area to four divisions; the 37th Division in the Fijis was brought up to full strength; miscellaneous forces were allotted to the South Pacific; and service troops were promised for Australia. But the War Department refused to commit additional air groups, consenting only to bring those already in the Pacific to full strength. In July the total forces there were already stronger, by a considerable margin, than those envisaged three months earlier, and OPD sought again to hold the line against further deployment.[6]

The shift in Allied strategy in the European war late in July opened the door to a more aggressive course in the Pacific, and early in August the limited offensive in the Solomons began. Tentative deployment plans now envisaged about a one-third increase in the strength contemplated in April—specifically, the addition of fifteen air groups and one ground division. General Marshall's planners still wanted to hold back, asserting at first that there had been no final decision on TORCH, and later arguing that the movement of these forces to the Pacific must await the outcome of the North Africa venture. Marshall resisted Admiral King's urgent pleas through the first week in August. Then, having received General MacArthur's plan for Task Two on 8 August, he proposed to King that plans be made to carry it out immediately following Task One. A few days after the landings on Guadalcanal the Japanese almost wiped out the covering naval forces. King told Marshall on the 20th that Admiral Ghormley could not possibly spare any forces for Task Two, and he forwarded an urgent request from both Admiral Ghormley and General Harmon for reinforcements for the South Pacific Area.[7]

_____

[6] (1) Approved deployment for 1942, set forth on 14 March 1942 in JCS 23, was subsequently modified to allow for the deployment of the 32d and 37th Divisions to the Pacific. There were 237,000 men allotted to the South and Southwest Pacific during 1942 in the 14 March tables; 252,000 were in those theaters or en route by the end of July. See Matloff and Snell, *Strategic Planning: 1941-1942*, Chs. VII, XI, XIII. (2) Contl Div, ASF, *Statistical Review, World War II*. (3) Pacific: June 1942-January 1943, monograph, pp. 54–57, 118–32, OPD Hist Unit File. (4) On General Richardson's trip, his recommendations, and action thereon, see OPD 333 (Gen Richardson's Trip).

[7] (1) CCS 94, 24 Jul 42, title: Opns in 1942–43. (2) Matloff and Snell, *Strategic Planning: 1941-1942*, Chs. XII–XIII.

At Marshall's order, General Somervell investigated the possibilities of meeting this request. His study revealed that 20,000 troops might be shipped to the South Pacific theater only if the Navy furnished troop lift for 13,000 and some of the cargo shipping; even then, certain scheduled movements to Australia would have to be sacrificed. Accordingly the proposed balanced force, set by AGF at 26,000, was cut to 20,000, and the Navy promised its share of the shipping. The reinforcements—43d Division with supporting elements—sailed in September and October. An additional bomber group, meanwhile, had been allotted to Hawaii, and Admiral Nimitz was given more freedom in moving planes from Hawaii to the South Pacific.[8]

These decisions represented a calculated risk: the more threatened of the two main areas was strengthened at the expense of the less threatened. MacArthur was told that he must expect a sharp cutback in troop movements scheduled for his theater, at the very time that he was predicting a major Japanese move against New Guinea and warning that disaster would follow if he were not reinforced.[9] It was clear in any case that Tasks Two and Three would have to wait. In October the War Department began to allocate forces to SWPA that would give MacArthur an amphibious force of his own but few of these troops could be shipped until the Guadalcanal crisis had abated. During September, October, and November 36,000 troops and 310,000 measurement tons of cargo were shipped from the United States to the South Pacific, while only 8,300 troops and 157,000 tons of cargo went to the Southwest Pacific. In the same period 25,000 troops and 330,000 tons of cargo were shipped to Hawaii, and

16,000 troops and 547,000 tons of cargo to Alaska. While movements over these shorter runs were proportionately less costly in shipping than those to the more remote areas, the need to continue building up Pacific defenses closer to home nonetheless cut deeply into the support of even limited offensives in the far Pacific areas. Marshall and Arnold were determined, moreover, not to throw in all their uncommitted air power; the fifteen groups earmarked for the Pacific late in July were held back in strategic reserve.[10]

In October the effort to tip the precarious balance in the South Pacific reached a climax. Ghormley and Harmon decided to shift the Americal Division from New Caledonia to Guadalcanal, where the marines were being depleted by climate, disease, battle weariness, and battle casualties. The 43d Division, originally destined for New Zealand, had to be sent to New Caledonia to replace the Americal, and the War Department decided to send the 25th Division from Hawaii to either the South or the Southwest Pacific. Most of the 43d Division was transshipped from New Zealand, but the

---

[8] (1) Memo, CG SOS for CofS, no date, sub: Shipg Capacity for Reinf of S Central Pac, OPD 370.5 PTO, Case 9. (2) Related corresp in same file. (3) Memo, AGF for CofS, 22 Aug 42, sub: Additional Forces S Pac Theater, OPD 370.5, Case 14. (4) Memo, CNO for CofS, 27 Aug 42, sub: Trans of Thirteen Thousand Army Trs, OPD 381 PTO, Case 84. (5) Matloff and Snell, *Strategic Planning: 1941-1942*, pp. 298-306.

[9] (1) Msg, MacArthur to CofS, 30 Aug 42, CM-IN 11408. (2) Msg, Marshall to MacArthur, 28 Aug 42, CM-OUT 8981.

[10] (1) Contl Div, ASF, *Statistical Review, World War II*. (2) Bykofsky and Larson, Trans III, Ch. X. (3) For disposition of the fifteen air groups, see Matloff and Snell, *Strategic Planning: 1941-1942*, Ch. XIII. (4) See below, App. E.

The tonnages shipped to Alaska were mostly construction materials for the Alcan Highway and for garrison facilities at the scattered bases in the Alaska area.

THE BEACHED TRANSPORT SS *PRESIDENT COOLIDGE, October 1942.*

first regimental combat team and a harbor defense unit were shipped on the *President Coolidge* late in September directly to Nouméa and thence to Espiritu Santo, primarily to protect the new airfield from which the forces on Guadalcanal received their bomber support. Off Espiritu Santo the *Coolidge* ran into an American mine field and sank. Personnel losses were slight, but all equipment was lost. Six 155-mm. howitzers were hastily removed from a vessel at Nouméa en route to Australia; remaining losses were made up from reserves of the 43d and Americal Divisions, which in turn had to be replenished from the United States, at additional cost in cargo shipping. The untimely sinking of the *Coolidge* also delayed the movement of the 25th Division from Hawaii.[11]

---

[11] (1) Miller, *Guadalcanal: The First Offensive*, pp. 103–42, 212–17. (2) Wesley Frank Craven and James Lea Cate, eds., *The Pacific: Guadalcanal to Saipan— August 1942 to July 1944,* Vol. IV in THE ARMY AIR FORCES IN WORLD WAR II (Chicago, The University of Chicago Press, 1950) (hereafter cited as Craven and Cate, *AAF IV*), pp. 28–29, 37–56. (3) Pacific: June 1942–January 1943, pp. 195–201, OPD Hist Unit File. (4) Memo, Col Carl D. Silverthorne for Gens Handy and Streett, 5 Oct 42, sub: Mvmt of 43d Div, OPD 370.5 New Zealand (3-5-42). (5) Memo, OPD for CofS, 29 Oct 42, sub: Delay in Mvmt of 25th Div, 7a Tr Unit File SWPA Prior to 1 Jan 43 folder, Plng Div ASF. (6) Rpt by Lt Gen Millard F. Harmon, *circa* Jun 44, sub: The Army in the S Pacific, p. 4, OCMH.

SURVIVORS COMING ASHORE *at Espiritu Santo. Note* SS President Coolidge *at upper left.*

Late in October, when the Japanese made their final great effort to crush the American forces on Guadalcanal, the President asked the Joint Chiefs to commit all available weapons and resources to the fight. General Marshall in reply pointed out that there were already sufficient forces in the area and that the main problem was "to distribute and maintain them by transport in critical combat areas." [12] The shortage of cargo shipping in the Pacific, for both services, was estimated at twenty-five ships a month during the next three months; this shortage was strangling the flow of maintenance supplies and backlogged equipment to forces already in or on their way to the scene of action. About the same time War Shipping Administration officials were warning of the general shrinkage of merchant shipping and the drying up of the commercial trades as sources for further accretions to the military pool. In their opinion it would not be possible to sustain the current operations in the Pacific along with the larger undertakings in the Atlantic, except by diversions from lend-lease services or from support of the Middle East and India. The

[12] Memo, CofS for President, 26 Oct 42, sub: Memo for President, OPD 381 PTO, Sec 3, Case 107.

Army and Navy, WSA noted, were asking for forty-nine more ships in the Pacific in November than in October, creating a prospective deficit of forty-six. While many of these requirements were for small ships on the Alaska run, the deficit for the remaining three principal areas, as calculated on 5 November, was twenty-nine standard cargo vessels.[13]

On 26 October the President, in a characteristic move, ordered WSA to find twenty additional ships for the South and Southwest Pacific without taking them from either the Soviet aid program or TORCH. Since there was not time to shift vessels from the Atlantic, WSA asked the Joint Chiefs to indicate the military services in the Pacific to be cut. At the suggestion of Somervell and Gross, the Joint Planners presented a plan to divert three large ships from the Alaskan service, three from Panama, and six from those scheduled to carry lend-lease supplies from the west coast to India and the Middle East. WSA then pointed out that these last diversions would require action by the CCS, particularly in view of British allotments of shipping for TORCH, and the JCS had to agree. But suddenly in mid-November WSA announced that of the total requirement of eighty-seven ships for the Army and Navy, it would be able to make eighty-four available.[14]

Just how this magic was accomplished is not clear from the records. There seemed little prospect that it could be repeated. In December Somervell foresaw a deficit of over two million tons of cargo shipping to meet Army and Navy needs in the Pacific through June 1943.[15]

This impending shortage was measured in the light of mushrooming troop movement schedules. The pressure of the need for service troops could no longer be with-

stood. Combat and disease, and the formation of skeleton units in the theaters had created a heavy and unforeseen demand for filler replacements. After the great air and naval victory off Guadalcanal in early November, the American position there was secure, but the tedious and expensive business of reducing Japanese forces on the island still lay ahead. Vice Adm. William F. Halsey, Jr., decided to turn these operations over to the Army as soon as a second Army division could be brought in, and the 25th Division, which sailed from Hawaii in December, was diverted directly to Guadalcanal. This diversion permitted withdrawal of the 1st Marine Division to Australia where, after rehabilitation, it was to provide MacArthur with the nucleus for an amphibious force for Tasks Two and Three. By the end of December MacArthur had also been promised three engineer amphibian brigades, a parachute regiment, and a jungle combat team. While there was no expectation of sending more divisions to either the South or Southwest Pacific in the immediate future, the growing backlog of replacements, service troops, specialized combat units, and miscellaneous other troops was sufficient to occupy all troop shipping for a long time to come.

[13] Memo, Land and Douglas for President, 27 Oct 42, sub: Reqmts for Additional Tonnage, Shipg 1941-43 folder, Hq ASF. The deficit for Hawaii, the South Pacific, and SWPA is shown here as nineteen, but JPS calculated it on 5 November as twenty-nine. See JCS 143/1, 5 Nov 42, title: Alloc of Twenty Additional Ships for Use in SWPA.
[14] (1) JCS 143, 29 Oct 42, title: Alloc of Twenty Additional Ships for Use in SWPA. (2) JCS 143/1 cited n. 13. (3) JCS 143/2, 16 Nov 42, same title. (4) JCS 143/3, 17 Nov 42, same title. (5) Memo, Gross for Somervell, no date, sub: Additional Ships . . . , ABC 570 (2-14-42) Sec 3. (6) Min, 42d mtg JCS, 17 Nov 42.
[15] Memo, Somervell for CofS, 7 Dec 42, sub: Trans Reqmts Pac Theater, OPD 570, Case 17.

When Navy requirements were added to those of the Army, a definite shortage loomed ahead. As calculated on 3 December by the Joint Staff Planners, the deficit would be 28,300 troop spaces in December, 900 in January, and 10,900 in February.[16]

To meet this deficit, Admiral King ordered several Navy combat loaders (with a total carrying capacity of six thousand) to the South Pacific run and proposed to remove three Navy transports—West Point, Monticello, and Hermitage, each with troop capacity in excess of six thousand—from the Atlantic to the Pacific. The West Point was then on the way to the Persian Gulf, but the other two transports had been in the first TORCH convoy and the Army counted on them for future ones. General Somervell vigorously protested that if all these vessels were diverted to the Pacific, it would be impossible to maintain the build-up in North Africa as planned. It seemed unlikely, moreover, that cargo shipping would be available to support the additional troop movements.[17]

The matter was threshed out in the councils of the JCS. It was decided to send the Hermitage to the Pacific, but to keep the West Point in the Middle East service. The question narrowed to the employment of the Monticello, and on 9 December the Joint Planners decided that the North African convoy was the more urgent requirement. The Joint Chiefs meanwhile had given their approval to the launching of a limited offensive in Burma in March 1943, for which General Stilwell had presented requests for service troops to be in the theater before that date. To meet these requirements, to which the JCS accorded a priority second only to TORCH, the Monticello was the only suitable transport

available and consequently had to be held during December to sail for India in January.[18]

This process of robbing Peter to pay Paul left the shipping shortage still weighing heavily on the build-up of forces in the Pacific. The pressure of unsatisfied needs for supplies and labor grew stronger. As exemplified by the Monticello affair, the Navy on its side was becoming more determined to speed its own deployment to the Pacific, deployment on a scale that led both the Army and the WSA to question the validity of naval shipping requirements. On all sides economy in the use of and the demands upon shipping became a major concern and an issue in interservice rivalry. At Somervell's insistence, the Navy's combat loaders, previously assigned to voyages by the Navy without specific reference to the JCS, were definitely placed in the pool of troop shipping under joint control. An effort was begun to determine joint shipping requirements on an over-all basis, so as to permit the JCS to make allocations strictly in the light of strategic priorities. In the matter of economy the Navy, having made certain reductions in recreation facilities, pointedly called them to the attention of the Army. Somervell outspokenly criti-

---

[16] (1) Miller, Guadalcanal: The First Offensive, pp. 177–89. (2) Matloff and Snell, Strategic Planning: 1941-1942, Ch. XVI. (3) JPS 92/D, 3 Dec 42, title, Trans Reqmts to the End of Feb 43.

[17] (1) Memo cited n. 15. (2) Memo, CG SOS for CofS, 26 Nov 42, sub: Asgmt of Navy Trans, ABC 570 (2-14-42) Sec 4.

[18] (1) Ltr, King to Marshall, 3 Dec 42, sub: Employment of Monticello. (2) Memo, CG SOS for JCS, 14 Dec 42, sub: Trans Reqmts to the End of Feb 43. Both in ABC 570 (2-14-42) Sec 4. (3) JPS 92/D cited n. 16(3). (4) JPS 92/1, 9 Dec 42, title: Trans Reqmts to the End of Feb 43. (5) Min, 49th mtg JPS, 9 Dec 42, Item 13. (6) JCS 158/1, 14 Dec 42, title: Trans Reqmts to the End of Feb 43. (7) Min, 46th mtg JCS, 15 Dec 42, Item 2. (8) See below, Ch. XIX.

cized the Navy's construction program in the Pacific as excessive and its standards as extravagant, and specifically attacked the project to build a naval base at Nouméa instead of using existing facilities at Brisbane. The Joint Chiefs ordered both Halsey and MacArthur to exploit local procurement to the limit. In the meantime, as a result of acute shipping congestion at Nouméa in New Caledonia, both the Army and the Navy were forced to review their logistical systems for support of Pacific operations with a view to better coordination. Even in the aggregate, all these measures promised only to alleviate a shortage predetermined by the subordination of the Pacific war in the general strategy and by distances that precluded short-term adjustments between the Atlantic and Pacific pools of shipping.[19]

The Crisis at Nouméa

The meagerness of facilities for discharging cargo in the far Pacific aggravated the shipping shortage. At a time when the movement of cargo was being pushed to the limit, it was difficult to avoid congestion and immobilization at the end of the line. During 1942 congestion did not reach serious proportions in the Southwest Pacific since the well-developed ports of Brisbane and Sydney continued to be the principal receiving points for supplies. But in the South Pacific it became the central logistical problem, mounting to a crisis in the fall of 1942 that dramatized, as nothing else probably could have done so effectively, the need for advance planning and interservice coordination in the handling of Pacific logistics.

North of New Zealand there were few port facilities in the South Pacific capable of handling ocean-going ships. Suva and

Lautoka in the Fijis, and Nouméa, New Caledonia's principal port, had piers and docks capable of handling their leisurely peacetime commerce, but hardly equal to the burdens imposed on them by the military emergency. Espiritu Santo and Efate, the bases closest to Guadalcanal, offered nothing more than protected anchorages from which cargo had to be lightered ashore. Storage and inland communication facilities were almost entirely lacking on all the South Pacific islands. While a limited amount of native labor was available in the Fijis, there was virtually none on most of the other islands, including New Caledonia. The assault on Guadalcanal was undertaken with little advance planning by either the Army or the Navy for development of bases for logistical support of the campaign that followed. The theater command itself was organized in such impromptu fashion just before the assault that there was no time for the development of a proper SOS organization. Each force in the area had been sent out with defense of an island base as its fundamental mission. The Army's supply plans as well as the joint logistical plan of July 1942 were drawn largely in terms of maintaining island garrisons. In each task force there was a heavy preponderance of combat troops with insufficient service troops to support them. Faced with a combination of lack of facilities and lack of labor, each island command was hard put to it to carry the supply load even for these garrison forces. When it became necessary for the commands to handle the vastly greater

---

[19] (1) Min, 52d mtg JPS, 30 Dec 42, Item 4. (2) JCS 194 series, title: Trans Reqmts Pac Theater. (3) Msg 4409, AGWAR to CINCSWPA, 7 Dec 42, AG 400.3295 (9-1-42) (3) Sec 1. (4) Ltr, SN to SW, 5 Dec 42, ABC 570 (2-14-42) Sec 4. (5) For efforts to adjust long-range deployment plans to shipping, see below, Chs. XXII, XXVI. (6) For efforts at economy and co-ordination, see below, Chs. XXIII–XXIV.

burden of supplies for the Guadalcanal Campaign, they were swamped.

The heaviest load fell on New Caledonia. Nouméa rapidly became the principal point for receipt and transshipment of supplies to Guadalcanal, Espiritu Santo, and Efate. There were only a few berths in the harbor, and these had to be shared with the commercial exports of the French Nickel Company, necessary for the maintenance of the island's economy. Neither the Army nor the Navy had appreciably expanded these facilities before the avalanche of shipping incident to the Guadalcanal operation descended on Nouméa in August and September. General Patch's warnings, as early as April, about the lack of port troops, inadequate discharge and storage facilities, and poor roads had gone largely unheeded in Washington. The only port troops sent to the South Pacific in early 1942 went to New Zealand. Patch was authorized to activate a port company from his own presonnel, but by mid-September it numbered only seventy-three men.[20]

Given these conditions, a tie-up of ships awaiting discharge at Nouméa was almost inevitable. On 23 September 1942 Patch radioed that there were eighty-six ships at anchor in Nouméa Harbor; congestion continued during the next few months, reaching its highest point during November and December when the Americal Division had to be outloaded to Guadalcanal, the 43d Division and New Zealand troops disembarked with their equipment, and various supplies handled for the 25th Division, which moved directly from Hawaii to Guadalcanal. At the end of November, ninety-one ships were reported in the harbor, though these, as in September, evidently included naval vessels that did not have to be discharged.[21]

Though the lack of facilities and personnel lay at the root of the congestion at Nouméa, the relative immaturity of both Army and Navy logistical agencies in the South Pacific Area and lack of co-ordination between them made it far more difficult to manage. Army and Navy organizations on the west coast, acting independently, forwarded supplies to the South Pacific in answer to separate requests from their respective area commanders, to the extent that shipping was available for the purpose and without much consideration for discharge capacity. On arrival at Nouméa the ships were unloaded by the services separately, with no effective co-ordination of discharge activities or control of harbor traffic. There was an inevitable tendency on the part of both the Army and the Navy to unload supplies only as needed and to use the vessels in the harbor as floating warehouses, leaving partially unloaded vessels to lie idle. Lack of any over-all plan for construction of facilities led to duplication both in shipments of material from the United States and in the use of resources available in the theater. The situation at Nouméa was paralleled at Espiritu Santo and Efate,

---

[20] (1) See above, Ch. VII. (2) Bykofsky and Larson, Trans III, Ch. VIII. (3) Ltr, CG Poppy Force to CofS, 17 Apr 42, OPD 381 New Caledonia, Case 5. (4) Ltr, CG Task Force 6814 to CofS, 17 Apr 42, sub: Poppy Task Force Stf, OPD 320.2 New Caledonia, Case 12. (5) Memo, ACofS Opns SOS for OPD WDGS, 5 Jun 42, sub: Rpt on New Caledonia From Gen Patch to Gen Marshall, OPD 381 New Caledonia, Case 30. (6) Msg, New Caledonia to AGWAR, 23 Sep 42, CM-IN 10038. (7) Memo, Lutes for Somervell, 9 Oct 42, sub: Nouméa Harbor, SPAC 1942–43–mid-1944 folder, Lutes File.

[21] (1) Bykofsky and Larson, Trans III, Ch. VIII. (2) Msg cited n. 20(6). (3) On the actual number of ships requiring discharge, see Brig. Gen. Raymond E. S. Williamson's figure of thirty-seven in mid-November discussed below, p. 402. The actual amount of congestion at Nouméa seems to have been exaggerated at times, and figures are not always reconcilable. See Ballantine, *Naval Logistics*, p. 123, in which he states that at one time a hundred vessels were at Nouméa awaiting discharge.

DOCK AT NOUMÉA, *December 1942.*

where congestion on a smaller scale began to appear as these bases increased in importance. At Guadalcanal there was no joint system for calling forward cargo from rear bases.[22]

The War Department became alarmed at the indications from General Patch in late September that congestion was becoming serious at Nouméa, and this concern mounted as the situation developed. Beyond the consideration that such a concentration of shipping presented an ideal target for the Japanese, the waste of shipping involved in such long turnarounds to the Pacific could hardly be tolerated. As an immediate palliative, Patch was authorized to bring his provisional port company to full strength and use combat troops to the utmost extent possible to un-

load ships. The Navy proposed to send six hundred longshoremen by air to arrive at Nouméa early in November.

In October SOS turned to attack the problem on a broader basis. General Somervell dispatched General Lutes on a tour of Pacific bases with instructions to investigate the congestion at Nouméa and to recommend suitable bases and a suitable supply system for Army and Navy operations. Lutes was quick to recognize the need for an adequate Army SOS with vastly increased numbers of service personnel and was instrumental in getting

[22] (1) See Bykofsky and Larson, Trans III, Ch. VIII. (2) Memo cited n. 20(7). (3) Memo, Lutes for CG SOS, 12 Nov 42, sub: Recommendations for a Jt SOS in the Pac Theater. (4) Memo, Lutes for Somervell, no date. Last two in Unified Sup: Army-Navy 1942–43 folder, Lutes File.

AERIAL VIEW OF NOUMÉA, *January 1943. Note limited berthing space.*

such a command organized under Brig. Gen. Robert G. Breene. Beyond this he was appalled by the waste and confusion attendant on the operation of separate Army and Navy supply lines, and was soon convinced that any real cure for the logistical ailments of the South Pacific theater could only be found in closer interservice co-ordination. In a series of conferences with Army and Navy theater officials, he urged the formation of a joint logistical staff that would prepare joint theater requirements, determine priorities for movement to and within the theater, schedule unloading of ships, and institute close co-ordination in all logistical activity. On his return to San Francisco he similarly urged on Army and Navy port officials the need for joint scheduling of shipments in accordance with priorities established by theater authorities. Back in Washington he presented a plan for complete unification of the Army-Navy supply lines to and within the Pacific Ocean Area.[23]

In the meantime Lewis Douglas of WSA, concerned about the long turn-

[23] (1) Msg, AGWAR to CG New Caledonia, 26 Sep 42, CM-OUT 8879. (2) Msg, CG New Caledonia to AGWAR, 28 Sep 42, CM-IN 12406. (3) Memo, ACofS OPD for CG SOS, 7 Oct 42, sub: QM Co New Caledonia, with accompanying memo for rcd, OPD 320.2 New Caledonia, Case 39. (4) Memo, Somervell for Lutes, 11 Oct 42, Misc Notes, Lutes File. (5) For Lutes' recommendations on a unified supply service, see memo cited n. 22(3) and below, Ch. XXIV. (6) For Lutes' personal description of his trip, see Lt. Gen. LeRoy Lutes, "Supply: World War II," *Antiaircraft Journal,* Vol. LXXXXV No. 4 (July–August 1952), pp. 2–7, and No. 5 (September–October 1952), 2–8.

arounds, had secured the services of Frazer A. Bailey, an executive of the Matson Navigation Company in San Francisco, to work with the Army and Navy toward more efficient use of cargo shipping in the Pacific. After surveying the situation, Bailey came to conclusions not significantly different from those that Lutes had formed. He urged advance scheduling of shipments by the Army and Navy port authorities working together, carefully calculated in accordance with discharge facilities at the end of the line. Bailey's proposals came at a time when Lewis Douglas was essaying, on a broader front, to bring ship loading and scheduling by the Army and Navy under closer control by WSA. As far as the Pacific was concerned, the upshot was the formation in San Francisco of an Army-Navy-WSA committee, later known as the Joint Army-Navy-WSA Ship Operations Committee, to work out a combined loading schedule for Army, Navy, and lend-lease shipments to Pacific destinations. The committee began to function in January 1943 and was at least partially successful in introducing a larger measure of cargo pooling and more closely integrated schedules better geared to the ability of Nouméa and other Pacific ports to unload supplies.[24]

Meantime Admiral William F. Halsey, Jr., who had assumed command of the South Pacific Area in October, was moving energetically, in co-operation with General Harmon, to bring about unified operations at the working level in the South Pacific and to clear up the congestion at Nouméa. While he partially followed the lines Lutes had suggested, he did not go the full distance and set up a joint logistical staff. He chose rather to place definite responsibilities in the hands of each service and to rely on interservice

boards or informal working arrangements to provide for joint priorities. The growing efficiency of the Army SOS under General Breene made Halsey's task easier. On 16 November he requested this Army SOS to take over responsibility for all discharge and loading activities at Nouméa. On 31 December he placed in its hands responsibility for co-ordinating the forward movement of supplies to Guadalcanal, working with the advice of a priorities board composed of Army, Navy, and Marine Corps representatives. A newly created service command in New Caledonia under Brig. Gen. Raymond E. S. Williamson assumed control at Nouméa on 20 November. At that time, Williamson reported, there were 37 ships with 88,000 tons of cargo in the harbor requiring discharge. During the month following, some 52 additional ships arrived for total or partial discharge. By using the port company (now at full strength), combat troops, Navy longshoremen, and native labor, by bringing in experienced civilian and military port personnel from New Zealand and the Fijis, and by gaining authority for exclusive use of the French Nickel Company's dock for three months, Williamson was able to accomplish the discharge of sixty ships during his first month of command, leaving a continuing backlog of twenty-nine. Wharves, docks, yards, fields, and hillsides were used for open storage of cargoes brought ashore. In January an additional dock was completed, construction of another begun. While a considerable backlog continued until April, cargo discharged increased from 47,808 short

---

[24] (1) Ltrs, Bailey to Douglas, 14 Jan, 6 Feb, and 8 Mar 43, SWPA folder, WSA Douglas File. (2) Memo, Land and Douglas for President, 18 Jan 43, WSA Dir 12-18-42 folder, WSA Douglas File. (3) On the broader issues involved, see below, Ch. XXII.

tons in November to 138,085 in December and 213,982 in January. By the end of April 1943 the crisis at Nouméa had been "definitely solved," and the development of the port had reached a point where it was capable of supporting a major campaign.[25]

While it lasted, the Nouméa crisis highlighted the central problem of logistical operations in both the South and the Southwest Pacific—the lack of adequate ports and bases in advance areas for handling and transshipping supplies. The measures taken to solve it—improvement in theater SOS organization, provision of larger numbers of service troops, better interservice co-ordination in scheduling discharge of cargo and in development and use of supply facilities, closer scheduling of cargo sailings from mainland ports adjusted to discharge capacity in the South Pacific—promised to prevent any repetition of the worst features of the Nouméa confusion in the future. But the lessons of Nouméa still provided no easy answer to the problem of preventing ship congestion as new advances were made up the Solomons ladder or farther away from the Australian base in the Southwest Pacific. Granted the best system of co-ordination, commanders would inevitably continue, in the early stages of a campaign, to call forward more supplies than could be unloaded over inadequate facilities. Even as congestion at Nouméa was clearing up, it was reappearing farther up the line—by January 1943 at Espiritu Santo, by April at Guadalcanal.

In view of this situation many naval officers frankly defended the use of ships as floating depots, arguing that it would prove less expensive in both materials and shipping than building port facilities at each successive base. Army spokesmen, in Washington at least, insisted on the use of shore facilities, and WSA was unalterably opposed to lengthy retention of ships in any theater. The provision of some sort of mobile port facilities would obviously go far to solve the problem, and the Nouméa crisis gave impetus to the search for suitable equipment of this sort. The most practical suggestion was that large barges should be used as floating warehouses and towed from place to place by tugs as the tactical situation demanded. There was some experimentation during late 1942 with concrete barges but unfortunately they proved impractical for the purpose. Shortly after his assignment by Douglas to the Pacific problem, Frazer Bailey began to push enthusiastically a project for using covered steel or wooden barges of two or three thousand tons capacity. This promising idea was tentatively endorsed by both Army and Navy commanders. It turned out, however, that there were insufficient barges of a type suitable for towing to the South Pacific that could be diverted from essential trades along the rivers and coasts of the United States. The shortage of steel prevented approval of any extensive program of additional construction of large, covered barges, and in any case the tugs needed to tow them were also in short supply. While the barges sent proved useful, for other purposes as well as for floating storage, the adoption of the mobile port scheme on the scale Bailey suggested never proved possible. The problem of ship congestion resulting from lack

---

[25] (1) Bykofsky and Larson, Trans III, Ch. VIII. (2) Memo, Gen Williamson for CG SOS S Pac Area, 19 Dec 42, sub: Congestion of Shipg in Port of Nouméa. (3) Memo, Williamson for CofTrans, 15 Feb 43, sub: Trans Sv Hist Rcd. Last two in S Pac Area New Caledonia folder, OCT HB. (4) Ltrs, Breene to Lutes, 3 and 9 Jan, 4 Feb, and 19 Apr 43, SPAC 1942–43–mid-1944 folder, Lutes File.

of port and base facilities was to last as long as the Pacific theaters themselves.[26]

Problems of Cargo Shipment

Difficulties in the several stages of handling supplies—packing and marking, loading and discharge—further lessened efficiency in the use of Pacific shipping. While most of the difficulties were by no means peculiar to the Pacific, distance, climate, and lack of facilities there combined with the need for retail distribution from the United States to make them doubly troublesome. Composite loading for the various different bases offered tempting economies in the use of shipping space. Yet in the theater these economies often seemed false because they produced so much confusion in unloading and distribution. In early 1942, particularly, too little attention was given in loading to the order of discharge. Supplies for New Caledonia were frequently stowed below those intended for Australia; supplies for Sydney, Brisbane, and Townsville were jumbled together. Because of distance and poor roads, equipment unloaded at Sydney for a unit stationed near Townsville could not be delivered for weeks. The theaters insisted on unit loading and the SOS complied whenever practicable, but the tight shipping situation precluded its use as normal practice during 1942. Some improvement resulted from better exchange of information between the theaters and the San Francisco port, and from development of theater facilities for storage and distribution. Block stowage, whereby supplies for a single port were stowed in a single hatch, proved the best solution whenever composite loading still had to be practiced, but it was not until 1943 that it came into general use.

The theaters complained of marking and packing practices ill suited to the long Pacific voyage and humid climate, and of discharge and handling facilities at the end of the line. Markings on packages did not show contents and destination; many packages were too large and heavy to be handled by the limited equipment available at small island bases such as Bora Bora or by native carriers in New Guinea; light and flimsy packages loaded beneath heavy ones were crushed; paper bags containing cereals, flour, and sugar tore and their contents spilled; cardboard cartons containing rations disintegrated when exposed to heavy moisture; paper labels on cans disappeared leaving their contents a mystery to the recipients; exposed parts of equipment and machinery corroded and rusted when not heavily sprayed with cosmoline.[27] Shipment of unassembled ve-

[26] (1) Bykofsky and Larson, Trans III, Ch. VIII. (2) Ltr, Lutes to Harmon, 24 Nov 42. (3) Memo, Styer for Lutes, 25 Nov 42. (4) Memo, Lutes for Styer, 25 Nov 42. (5) Ltr, Harmon to Lutes, 15 Dec 42. (6) Ltr, Lutes to Breene, 5 Jan 43. (7) Ltrs, Breene to Lutes, 4 and 16 Feb, 7 and 19 Apr 43. Last six in SPAC 1942–43–mid-1944 folder, Lutes File. (8) Ltrs, Bailey to Douglas, 6 and 11 Feb, 8 Mar, and 13 Apr 43. (9) Ltr, Adm Horne to Douglas, 27 Feb 43. (10) Memos, Capt Edmond J. Moran, Manager Barge and Towboat Svs WSA, for Douglas, 7 May and 29 Jun 43. (11) Ltr, Adm Land to Hugh Fulton, Chief Counsel of Senate Sp Com Investigating Natl Def Prog, 30 Jul 43. Last four in SWPA and Barge Probs folder, WSA Douglas File. (12) Memo, Lt Cols A. W. Parry and R. G. Lehnau for Gen Robinson, 12 May 43, sub: Rpt on Inspection Trip, SWPA and S Pac Area, 16 Mar to 4 May 43, in 12a Gen SWPA folder, Plng Div ASF, Job A45-124. (13) For justification of the Navy's use of ships as depots, see remarks of Comdr. Selden B. Spangler at Conf of Base Maintenance Div and War Plans Offs of Bureaus and Offs Concerned, 30 Apr 43, ABC 045.93 (3-12-42).

[27] (1) Masterson, U.S. Army Transportation in the Southwest Pacific Area (hereafter cited as Masterson, Transportation in SWPA), pp. 267–89, OCMH. (2) Bykofsky and Larson, Trans III, Ch. VIII. (3) TAG ltr to all overseas comds, 15 Jun 42, sub: Sup of Overseas Bases [a G-4 questionnaire on supply] and replies

SORTING DAMAGED RATIONS, *New Caledonia, April 1942.*

hicles to the South Pacific bases also caused trouble. Only in New Caledonia was it possible to perform even the simple assemblies involved in the single and twin unit packs, and only limited numbers of vehicles for the other islands could be handled in New Caledonia. Many of the vehicles shipped directly from the United States for the 25th Division had to be sent all the way to Wellington, New Zealand, for assembly and then transshipment to

Guadalcanal. Delays in assembly and faulty assembly by untrained personnel combined with an acute shortage of spare parts and of maintenance personnel to keep large numbers of vehicles constantly deadlined.[28]

These defects in the handling of cargo shipments were the subject of endless communications between the Pacific theaters and the SOS in Washington. By early 1943 there was a marked improvement.

thereto from Pac, AG 400 (8-10-42) Sec 13. (4) Ltr, Lt Col Joseph H. Burgheim to Col Cordiner, 29 Apr 42, Sup S Pac Theater folder, Plng Div ASF. (5) Rpt by Col Frank A. Henning, 1 Aug 42, sub: Sup Opns in Australia . . . , 1-A-1 Jt Sup Prog (SWPA and S Pac Area) IV folder, Plng Div ASF.

[28] (1) Ltr, Maj Gen Robert G. Breene to Gen Lutes, 11 May 43, SPAC 1942–43–mid-1944 folder, Lutes File. (2) Memo, Gen Plans Br Plng Div SOS for Chief of Mvmts Br, 12 Dec 42, sub: Shipt of Vehicles on Wheels to S Pac Theater, 451 Vehicles Misc 1942–43 folder, Plng Div ASF.

Wooden containers replaced paper and fiber, marking and packing improved, cargo manifests were forwarded early by air mail, block stowage and unit loading were more generally practiced. As supply levels within the theaters were built up and theater distribution facilities improved, the need for retail distribution from the United States diminished.

The General Depot at Nouméa

Australia, for all its limited facilities, still provided a central base for supply operations that was totally lacking in the South Pacific. It was possible by the fall of 1942 to establish in Australia a system of depots for stocking theater reserves and a system of central supply accounting that Somervell and Lutes held up as a model for other theaters to emulate. Requisitions could thus be based on knowledge of the total resources at the theater's disposal. In the South Pacific, even after the establishment of a theater command, there were no central depots, and requisitioning on the United States by, and shipment to, each separate base continued. It was well into 1943 before Maj. Gen. Robert G. Breene, SOS commander for the South Pacific, could establish even a semblance of central supply accounting. Since consumption rates varied from base to base and troop bases were not always stable, reserve stocks at each base frequently became unbalanced. Inflexible adherence in the United States to tables of equipment often precluded furnishing vital items to small organizations on isolated islands lacking access to base facilities.[29]

Although a reasonable level of stockage had been achieved by autumn in individual island depots, there was no central reserve of supplies and no provision for prompt replacement of sudden heavy losses or meeting of emergency demands.

The invasion of Guadalcanal imposed an almost immediate strain on reserve stocks in New Caledonia. General Patch in August furnished on short notice over twenty thousand tons of supplies for Marine forces moving against Guadalcanal. He also had to provide supplies for the new bases at Efate and Espiritu Santo. "Everyone robs Poppy," General Harmon wrote OPD on 20 August 1942, and he recommended that a small general depot be established at Nouméa as a "reservoir from which emergency and unanticipated demands could be filled."[30] Harmon's recommendation received sympathetic consideration in Washington, but it was evident that such an establishment would require additional personnel and materials to build and man the depots, and little shipping was in sight to transport them. OPD also raised the question of co-ordination with the Navy in setting up strategic reserves in the South Pacific. While these matters were under discussion in Washington, stocks in New Caledonia were again depleted to re-equip the combat team that lost its equipment in the sinking of the *President Coolidge*.[31]

[29] (1) Ltr, Lutes to Breene, 2 Apr 43. (2) Ltrs, Breene to Lutes, 11 May and 29 Jun 43. Both in SPAC 1942–43–mid-1944 folder, Lutes File. (3) Drummond, History of the U.S. Army Forces in the South Pacific Area During World War II From 30 March 1942 to 1 August 1944, p. 507, OCMH. (4) Memo, Col Leonard H. Rodieck and Lt Col Edward H. McDaniel for ACofS OPD, 24 Nov 42, sub: Visit . . . to S and SW Pac Theater Bases, OPD 333.1 PTO, Sec 1.
[30] (1) Ltr, Harmon to Handy, 20 Aug 42, OPD 381 PTO, Case 91. (2) Rpt, p. 20, cited n. 11(6).
[31] (1) Disposition form, Actg ACofS OPD for CG SOS, 22 Aug 42, sub: Estab of WHITE POPPY [Nouméa] Gen Depot, OPD 400 PTO, Case 9. (2) Draft msg, Hq SOS to New Caledonia, 23 Aug 42 with accompanying memo for rcd, New Caledonia Gen folder, Plng Div ASF, Job A45-124. (3) Ltr ACofS OPD to CG USAFISPA, 12 Sep 42, with atchd OPD memo for rcd, OPD 381 PTO, Case 100. (4) Ltr, CG USAFISPA to ACofS OPD, 22 Oct 42, OPD 381 PTO, Case 109.

During his visit to the South Pacific, General Lutes recommended the establishment of supply reserves in both New Caledonia and the Fijis since the Japanese fleet was then at large and Lutes felt that an alternate base should be ready in case of an attack on New Caledonia. The defeat of the Japanese Fleet by Halsey's forces in early November removed this danger, but the need for a system for stocking reserves in the South Pacific remained. In November Harmon forwarded to Washington a plan for a supply system embracing a base depot in New Zealand, intermediate depots in New Caledonia and the Fijis, and an advance depot on Espiritu Santo. Both Harmon and Lutes thought the 30 days' supply proposed for the intermediate depots should be a strategic reserve over and above the 120-day level authorized for the theater. OPD refused to accept the plan. The establishment of a general depot on New Caledonia was finally authorized in March 1943, but with the provision that it must be stocked within existing theater supply levels. The rest of the plan for a depot system was dropped since it appeared that direct shipments from the United States to each base would offer greater economy in shipping.[32]

Landing Craft and Intratheater Transport

As the shape of warfare in the Pacific unfolded, it revealed an imperative need for all forms of water transport—landing craft for assault on hostile shores, ocean-going vessels for movement of supplies from rear to forward bases, and small craft of various sorts for short hauls along the coast and between islands. Lacking developed ports, each island base also required, in addition to barges, its complement of other types of small vessels and floating equipment. In the South Pacific, except for coastwise traffic and port operations, these matters were a Navy responsibility, and the Navy was in a better position to meet needs for landing craft and small vessels as they arose. In SWPA the shortage was so acute that it posed a limitation on all operations.

The Papua Campaign was not, nor could it have been, an amphibious operation. The first American troops of the 32d Division were sent by ship and air to Port Moresby, and from there one battalion made the tortuous trek across the Owen Stanley Range to the north coast of Papua. This trek, which took about five weeks, proved that it would be impractical to move a large force over the mountain trail and the Americans thereafter resorted to air transport. In the attack on Buna, supplies to the forces in combat moved mainly by jeep, native carrier, and airdrop. MacArthur cabled the War Department on 17 October 1942:

I am greatly hampered by the total lack of light shipping, landing boats and barges which I have previously requested. In their absence I am moving overland by air. Supply is the controlling factor and must be accomplished by native carrier and by air. Improvised landing fields have been and are being prepared. . . . Supply difficulties are incredible and limit speed of movement and size of forces and are of course multiplied by

---

[32] (1) Msg, New Caledonia to AGWAR, 27 Oct 42, CM-IN 11427. (2) Msg 14794, COMGENSOPAC [CG S Pac] to AGWAR, 3 Nov 42. (3) Memo, Lutes for Dir Plans Div SOS, 15 Jan 43, sub: Reserve Sups—S Pac. (4) Memo, Gen Lutes for Col Charles E. Dissinger, Plans Div, 20 Mar 43. Last three in SPAC 1942–43–mid-1944 folder, Lutes File. (5) Lutes, "Supply: World War II," *Antiaircraft Journal*, Vol. LXXXXV, No. 4 (July–August 1952), p. 5. (6) Memo, Lutes for OPD, 20 Apr 43, sub: Advance Depots—S Pac Theater, 13b Day File-S Pac Area-Prior to 1 Oct 43 folder, Plng Div ASF. (7) Drummond, History of the U.S. Army Forces in the South Pacific Area . . . , pp. 513–14, 686–92, OCMH.

lack of shipping and shortage of transport planes.[33]

An observer noted in December 1942 that there was "every reason to believe that Buna could have been taken during November if one of our units could have put a minimum of one combat team afloat."[34]

MacArthur had asked in July for sufficient landing craft to train and equip two American divisions and one Australian division, but was told he must rely on craft locally available and those the South Pacific Amphibious Force could loan him. The planners in Washington, engrossed in the shortage of landing craft for SLEDGE-HAMMER and ROUNDUP, were unable to divert any even for MacArthur's training needs. The Navy did promise to make some available from the South Pacific Area for training purposes, but few serviceable craft from this source had arrived in Australia by mid-December.[35]

The dwindling of BOLERO and the increase in production of landing craft altered this outlook. In setting up tentative long-range allocations of landing craft in September and October 1942, the JCS agreed to provide SWPA with a substantial number of all types, the first increment, consisting of 284 36-foot craft and 172 50-foot LCM(3)'s, in a priority just under that of the TORCH operation and the South Pacific Amphibious Force. At the same time the War Department decided to send MacArthur one Engineer amphibian brigade, an organization designed to move one infantry division in shore-to-shore landing operations, using primarily the 36-foot and 50-foot boats. Originally five of these brigades had been planned for use in Europe, and three were hastily organized in mid-1942. Only one (the 1st) had been sent to England before the North African venture placed the emphasis, for

the moment, upon ship-to-shore operations under naval control. As the Navy proposed to take over all amphibious training and operations, OPD first ruled that no more brigades should be committed to SWPA until the first one had been tested. MacArthur insisted that the shore-to-shore techniques of these brigades were better suited to SWPA than the ship-to-shore methods of the Navy, and Colonel Arthur G. Trudeau of the Engineer Amphibian Command, after a visit to Australia and New Guinea, corroborated this view. The necessity for flanking movements along the coast, the shallow and constricted waters in which operations would have to be conducted, and the usefulness of small craft in lightering supplies and equipment all argued for the use of the brigades. OPD accordingly decided, late in December 1942, that the 3d Engineer Amphibian Brigade should be earmarked for SWPA and a fourth brigade activated to be shipped there when trained. When in February 1943 General Marshall and Admiral King arrived at a general agreement that the Navy should take over amphibious training and operations, the three amphibian brigades for SWPA were excepted from the arrangement.[36]

---

[33] (1) See msg, CINCSWPA to AGWAR, 17 Oct 42, CM-IN 07247. The undecipherable part of this message was repeated in msg, CINCSWPA to AGWAR, 18 Oct 42, CM-IN 07523. (2) See also, Milner, Victory in Papua, Chs. VIII, XI.

[34] Memo, Col Arthur G. Trudeau, Engr Amphibian Comd, for ACofS OPD, 14 Dec 42, OPD 333.1 PTO, Case 3.

[35] (1) Msg, CINCSWPA to AGWAR, 6 Jul 42, CM-IN 2049. (2) Msg, AGWAR to CINCSWPA, 7 Jul 42, CM-OUT 1772. (3) Msg, CINCSWPA to AGWAR, 11 Jul 42, CM-IN 3720. (4) Msg, AGWAR to CINCSWPA, 15 Jul 42, CM-OUT 4145. (5) Memo cited n. 34.

[36] (1) Memo, OPD for CG SOS, 12 Sep 42, sub: Landing Craft, 5d Cl IV Amphibious-SWPA folder, Plng Div ASF, Job A45-124. (2) Memo cited n. 34.

The first elements of the 2d Engineer Amphibian Brigade departed the United States for Australia in December 1942, the rest early in 1943. The 3d and 4th Brigades were scheduled for shipment during the spring and summer of 1943. As of 4 January 1943, 1,380 LCVP's and 172 LCM(3)'s had been allocated for their use and, in addition, 30 105-foot LCT(5)'s were scheduled to go to MacArthur's command.[37] To ease the shipping problem, a base shop battalion was dispatched to Australia in late November 1942 to assemble the 36-foot craft in the theater. All these measures promised eventual relief of the shortage of landing craft and amphibious personnel in MacArthur's command, but there was an inevitable time lag in fulfillment of plans. Again as of 4 January 1943, only 66 LCVP's, 10 LCM(3)'s and 3 LCT(5)'s had actually been shipped, and the base shop battalion had yet to establish itself in Australia and to perfect the techniques of assembly.[38]

At an early date MacArthur had also requested large vessels to move troops and supplies from one port to another in Australia and from Australia to New Guinea. Again he was told that he must rely on local resources. These were meager enough, for all available Australian vessels were being used for domestic needs. MacArthur's main resources during the New Guinea Campaign consisted of twenty-one

Dutch vessels that had escaped capture after the fall of the Netherlands Indies, three vessels of Chinese registry, and one of Siamese. These he supplemented, despite vigorous protests from WSA, by retaining Liberty ships arriving in the theater from the States. Meanwhile, he continued to press Washington for a larger allotment of shipping.

In addition to large vessels, there was a pressing need in SWPA for a wide variety of small ships and craft, ranging from native canoes to vessels of nearly one thousand gross tons. In 1942 ocean-going vessels could not proceed along the north coast of New Guinea beyond Milne Bay. Cargo and personnel had to be transshipped at Port Moresby or Milne Bay to a miscellaneous collection of trawlers, schooners, luggers, and ketches, largely procured from Australian sources. To supplement these, a program of construction under reverse lend-lease was begun in Australia in September 1942. These measures, too, fell short of the need, and MacArthur had to place requirements on the United States for additional small vessels.

Procurement of both large and small vessels in the United States was slow. They were not a normal item of Army supply. A procurement program for small vessels was inaugurated early in 1943, but the

---

(3) Pacific: June 1942–January 1943, pp. 292–310, OPD Hist Unit File. (4) Coll and Rosenthal, Engr I, draft ch. "The Engineer Amphibian Command," OCMH. (5) Masterson, Transportation in SWPA, pp. 416–17. (6) Msg, CINCSWPA to AGWAR, 20 Nov 42, CM-IN 8583. (7) Msg, AGWAR to CINCSWPA, 24 Nov 42, CM-OUT 7727. (8) Msg, CINCSWPA to AGWAR, 2 Mar 43, CM-IN 747. (9) Memo, CofS for CNO, 16 Feb 43, sub: A&N Amphibious Boat Crews. (10) Memo of agreement, CofS, COMINCH, and CNO, 8 Mar 43. Last two in OPD 353 Amphibious Force, Case 123.

[37] The requirements for each of the three brigades were set at 540 LCVP's, 503 LCM(3)'s, and 40 LCC's or LCS(S)'s, a total of 1620 LCVP's, 1509 LCM(3)'s and 120 LCC's or LCS(S)'s. The allocations were therefore only a partial fulfillment of these requirements. The LCT(5)'s were in addition to the table of organization requirements for the brigades. See below, App. A-7.

[38] (1) Memo, Chief of SW Pac Theater Sec OPD for ACofS OPD, 4 Jan 43, sub: Rpt of Inspection of Pac Areas by Col Trudeau, OPD 333.1 PTO, Case 3. (2) Coll and Rosenthal, Engr I, draft ch. "The Engineer Amphibian Command," OCMH. (3) Corresp in 5d Cl IV Amphibious-SWPA folder, Plng Div ASF, Job A45-124.

placing of orders was late and there were few deliveries before midyear. Meanwhile, the only large vessels available were steamers diverted from commercial trades on the Great Lakes. Though old and constantly in need of repair, they were made to serve. Gradually, from January 1943 onward, the local fleet at MacArthur's disposal grew, but never to the point where it was not necessary to retain transpacific shipping in the theater.[39]

The Army also had under development amphibious vehicles that promised at least a partial solution to the small boat problem. In July 1942 SOS announced that an amphibian jeep, an amphibian trailer, and an amphibian 2½-ton truck (the DUKW) were under production, each capable of a "small amount of rough water operation."[40] None of these vehicles arrived in the theaters, however, until early 1943. After trials the performance of the DUKW was generally acclaimed, and it promised to be of great assistance in facilitating discharge at ports having inadequate facilities, or over coral beaches. Unfortunately, the Pacific theaters had to compete with other theaters and Allied forces for output, which continued in 1943 to be limited.[41]

Air transport was a main prop of the Papuan operations, but transport planes were one of the scarcest commodities in the whole catalogue of supply, demanded by every theater commander, by the British, and by the Russians. Early in 1942, seventy-eight transport planes were allocated to MacArthur's command but in mid-September, when the air transport of troops to the northern coast of New Guinea began, there were only forty-one in the theater and fifteen of these were being cannibalized to provide spare parts for the others. OPD agreed to provide two addi-

tional troop carrier squadrons. One (thirteen C-47's) reached Australia in October, but the other was detained by General Harmon for a month in the South Pacific to provide air transport between New Caledonia and Guadalcanal. The situation improved somewhat with the arrival of the second squadron in November, and OPD promised that two more squadrons would be sent to SWPA in early 1943. There were continuing limitations on air transport, however, in terms both of transports available and of landing fields from which to fly them. Any solution to the transportation problem in the Southwest Pacific would require larger quantities of all the various forms of equipment.[42] The shortage of intratheater transport combined with that of transpacific shipping and of theater base and port facilities to place definite limitations on the pace of Pacific operations.

Equipment for Jungle Warfare

Jungle warfare had been only vaguely foreseen in the Army's prewar plans and very little special equipment was designed for it. American troops fought the campaigns of most of 1942 with standard equipment and weapons. But by mid-1942, the staff in Washington was turning its attention to the development of jungle

[39] (1) Masterson, Transportation in SWPA, pp. 317–80, contains a full treatment of the vessel problem in MacArthur's command. (2) Bykofsky and Larson, Trans III, Ch. VIII. (3) Memo cited n. 34.

[40] Ltr, ACofS Opns to CG S Pac Area, 10 Jul 42, sub: Sp Reqmts for Amphibious Vehicles, 451.94 Amphibian Vehicles folder, Plng Div ASF.

[41] (1) Masterson, Transportation in SWPA, pp. 412–16. (2) Ltr, 19 Apr 43, cited n. 25(4). (3) Msg, AGWAR to CINCSWPA, 5 Jun 43, CM-OUT 2283. (4) Memo cited n. 26(12).

[42] (1) Craven and Cate, AAF IV, p. 114. (2) Msg, CINCSWPA to AGWAR, 17 Sep 42, CM-IN 7298. (3) Memo cited n. 26(12).

equipment, jungle training, and special types of units. By July 1942 a jungle kit had been developed that, with certain later modifications, satisfactorily met the needs of the individual jungle soldier. This kit consisted of one pair of jungle boots, two pairs of cushion-sole socks, a one-piece jungle uniform, camouflaged helmet liner and helmet band, a flotation bladder, machete and sheath, knit shirt, mosquito repellent gloves, light jungle pack, eight waterproof bags, jungle hammock, waterproof clothing bag, single-cell flashlight, jungle medical kit, and waterproof matchbox with compass. On 24 July 1942 OPD directed the SOS to procure 150,000 of these kits, the first 30,000 to go to the AGF for training in the United States, the second 30,000 to the Caribbean Defense Command for training jungle units in Panama and the West Indies, then 60,000 to SWPA and 30,000 to the South Pacific.[43]

In mid-August, General MacArthur submitted a long and detailed requisition for equipment needed to prepare three divisions for warfare in New Guinea. The list was based on the theory that organizational as well as individual equipment should be light, most of the items requested being patterned on equipment then being used by the Japanese. MacArthur wanted to convert his infantry cannon companies to the use of 60-mm. mortars, his 105-mm. howitzer battalions to 81-mm. mortars and 75-mm. pack howitzers. He also asked for folding bicycles, saddles, bridles, pack harnesses, light machine guns, light tractors, and other miscellaneous articles; throughout the emphasis was on light construction and manual mobility. In keeping with his stated troop basis, he increased the requirement for the jungle kits from the 60,000 allotted him to 116,000.[44] This

special requisition was given a high priority by MacArthur, and SOS agencies made strenuous efforts to meet it by immediate shipments. Some of the materials reached SWPA in time to be used in the later stages of the Buna operations. In the Army Ground Forces, meanwhile, there was considerable discussion about and planning for the development of specialized light divisions for both jungle and mountain warfare.

Experience both on New Guinea and Guadalcanal soon revealed, however, that standard heavy equipment was more effective than believed earlier, and it proved to be far superior to Japanese matériel. In the end, virtually no changes were made in tables of organization and equipment for troops in the Pacific. Some of the lighter types of equipment proved useful, but the theory of specially equipped light divisions for jungle warfare was discarded. The jungle kits, on the other hand, proved their worth. General Harmon in November 1942 raised his requirement for them from the 30,000 originally allotted to 80,000. Some time passed before either his or MacArthur's increased requirements could be met, the rate of availability varying with individual items. Shipments were still incomplete in March 1943.[45]

---

[43] (1) Min, WD Gen Council mtgs, Jun 42, especially 21 Jun. (2) Memo, ACofS OPD for CG SOS, 24 Jul 42, sub: Procurement of Jungle Clothing and Equip, 420 Clothing and Equip (Jungle and Arctic) folder, Plng Div ASF.

[44] (1) Msg C-275, CINCSWPA to AGWAR, 16 Aug 42, paraphrase copy in 3c Cl II Sups-Jungle Equip-SWPA Only folder, Plng Div ASF. (2) History of the Planning Division, ASF, III, 134, OCMH.

[45] (1) See material in 3c Cl II Sups-Jungle Equip-SWPA Only folder, Plng Div ASF. (2) History of the Planning Division, ASF, III, 138, OCMH. (3) Greenfield, Palmer, and Wiley, AGF I, pp. 339–50. (4) Msg, New Caledonia to AGWAR, 28 Nov 42, CM-IN 12106.

Apart from individual jungle kits, the special needs of the Pacific war narrowed to the question of finding standard types that would stand up under tropical conditions, and to providing larger quantities of other types of supplies for which the need in the Pacific was abnormally high. In the latter classification fell antimalarial supplies and other medical and hospital supplies and facilities. There was also a heavy demand for construction materials, which, if not greater than that of other theaters, at least imposed a heavier demand on shipping over the long distances involved. All these special needs and problems combined to add to the lag between demand and supply that characterized the war in the Pacific in 1942 and 1943.

Service Troops

Of all the overseas theaters, those in the Pacific needed service troops most, and in none was the scarcity more severe. Ignorance of the primitive conditions to be encountered, the natural desire of theater and task force commanders to squeeze the maximum of fighting strength into the shipping space allotted them, and the shortage of trained service units all conspired to keep the deployment of service troops far below requirements.

In Australia the situation was far better than on the South Pacific islands. General Brett was not behindhand in asking for service troops, and in answer to his requests a fair proportion of such units were included in the early troop build-up in Australia. But the War Department took the view that Australian labor should be used as far as possible, and Marshall gave General Wilson instructions to this effect when the latter left in February on his mission to organize supply activities in Australia. Wilson's experience in the theater did not shake his adherence to this view, and it was one of the issues on which he clashed with General Barnes, commander of USAFIA. For Barnes, as well as most other American supply officers and observers in Australia, was dissatisfied with Australian labor and found it particularly irksome to rely on it for port operations. The majority of Australian longshoremen were over forty-five years of age, jealous of the privileges won through union organization, and evidently not ardently enthusiastic in their support of the war effort. The Australian Government, at least in the eyes of many U.S. Army observers, gave in to every demand of the longshoremen because of its dependence upon organized labor for political support. American forces had also to rely heavily on services provided by the Australian Army, and General Richardson, when he visited Australia in July, voiced sharp dissatisfaction with the situation, pointing to the heavy losses of supplies handled by Australian Army agencies.[46]

In mid-July Richardson's reports and strong requests from General MacArthur for additional service units brought the problem to a head. There were then approximately 43,000 ground tactical troops in Australia, with 28,000 ground service troops to support them; in the air forces the balance was about the same. Though this was a high ratio of service support compared to that currently contemplated for the European theater, OPD conceded

---

[46] (1) Memo, Richardson for CofS, 17 Jul 42, sub: Mis to Pac Bases and Australia, OPD 333 (Gen Richardson's Trip) Case 21. (2) Memo, unsigned, no addressee, 9 Jul 42, sub: Australia, Vol. V, Item 1, Exec 2. (3) Masterson, Transportation in SWPA, pp. 481-85, 497-514. (4) Rpt, Gen Wilson to CG USAFIA, 30 May 42, sub: Plans and Projects . . . , SWPA Sup folder, Plng Div ASF, Job A44-140.

that MacArthur's additional stated requirements from July through November—about 16,750 ground and 12,900 air service troops over and above scheduled shipments of 9,000—were defensible. But the limited pool of service units in the United States was otherwise committed, mostly for BOLERO.[47]

With the dwindling of BOLERO, some of MacArthur's requests were approved, but unfortunately the shipping requirements for moving the 43d Division to the South Pacific Area, arising in September, led to curtailment of troop movements to Australia. Forced to choose, MacArthur gave priority to filler replacements, and the service troops were presently pushed even lower on the scale by amphibious and other special combat units. The vexing dependence on Australian civilian labor and military services continued; port work in Australia was handled almost entirely by Australians. Even so, American forces in Australia were better served than those who pushed into New Guinea where, as in the South Pacific, native labor could perform only the simplest and most routine tasks. "At nearly every place visited," reported two Transportation Corps observers in May 1943, "the general complaint of officers was the lack of service personnel."[48]

In the South Pacific, an area where service troops were probably more essential and needed in larger numbers than in any other theater, the ratio of service support at the end of 1942 was shockingly low—only 14,500 service troops to about 92,000 air and ground combat troops.[49] During his October survey of the South Pacific bases, one of General Lutes' principal recommendations was the shipment of additional service units to each base. With certain modifications OPD approved, but though this action promised some relief, many of the units were not immediately available, and some could not be shipped until April 1943.

The South Pacific, like the Southwest Pacific, faced steadily increasing needs in the face of a shortage of shipping. The forward movement into the Russell Islands and the prospect of further advances in the Solomons meant that a base would have to be established on Guadalcanal. Anticipating this development, General Harmon late in November 1942 requested additional service units for Guadalcanal. He was granted only one port battalion; for the rest, OPD insisted that he must move units forward from the rear.[50] General Breene could only protest:

I respectfully submit the opinion that the Operations Division fails completely to understand our problem if they refuse to send Service Units to Cactus [Guadalcanal]. It is, of course, true that the rear areas can be stripped of the meagre service units now available in order to take care of the Cactus problem, but the work in the rear areas must continue. If service troops are not available the work must necessarily be done by combat troops. . . . local labor is almost non-exist-

[47] Memo, Handy for CofS, 27 Jul 42, sub: Comments and Recommendations on Gen Richardson's Rpt on Australia, OPD 333 (Gen Richardson's Trip) Case 19.

[48] (1) Memo cited n. 26(12). (2) Memo, OPD for CINCSWPA, 10 Aug 42, sub: Additional Units Authorized for U.S. Forces in Australia, OPD 320.2 Australia, Case 53. (3) Pacific, June 1942–January 1943, pp. 192–94, 319–21, OPD Hist Unit File. (4) Masterson, Transportation in SWPA, pp. 478–513.

[49] Army Forces in S and Central Pac, 29 Dec 42, Tab, SYMBOL: Casablanca Bks., Vol. II, Exec 6.

[50] (1) Memo, OPD for CG SOS, 21 Nov 42, sub: Additional Sv Trs for S Pac Area, and subsequent memos, 4, 9, 10, 17, 27 Dec, same sub, OPD 320.2 PTO, Cases 83 and 91. (2) Ltr cited n. 26(2). (3) Msgs, New Caledonia to AGWAR, 30 Nov 42, CM-IN 12737; 13 Dec 42, CM-IN 5661; 22 Dec 42, CM-IN 9453; 15 Jan 43, CM-IN 6934; and 5 Feb 43, CM-IN 3611.

ent. . . . even though we are furnished combat troops to carry out service functions, combat troops will not take a real interest in their service job.[51]

The Pacific Outlook at the End of 1942

By early December 1942 it appeared that, despite all difficulties, the Guadalcanal and Papua Campaigns would soon be brought to a successful conclusion. On 1 December General Marshall suggested to Admiral King that the time had come to proceed with Tasks Two and Three in accordance with the July directive and proposed that command of further operations pass to General MacArthur. Again the Navy demurred, this time citing Admiral Nimitz' view that first the Solomons area must be better secured and air power, troop strength, and supporting bases built up there. Nimitz proposed that the next campaign be up the Solomons ladder, probably against New Georgia where the Japanese were beginning to build an airfield, and that the operations should remain under the direction of Admiral Halsey. General Marshall countered by pointing out that the total Allied forces in the South and Southwest Pacific possessed a comfortable superiority over the Japanese. He contended that if all these forces were brought under the unified strategic command of General MacArthur, they would be able to accomplish the objectives set up in July. The Navy planners argued that the Pacific Fleet must retain its strategic flexibility to counter any threat arising in the whole area between the west coast and Australia. They would accept MacArthur's command over operations of their South Pacific forces only if Admiral Nimitz were given over-all strategic direction of the entire Pacific. In the

end the only agreement reached was on the necessity of initiating further operations toward Rabaul; the details of strategy and command remained in abeyance.[52]

Nevertheless, at the suggestion of Admiral King, General MacArthur furnished his outline plan for the advance against Rabaul, and OPD, in preparation for the Casablanca Conference, prepared its own plan on the assumption that Allied operations in the South and Southwest Pacific would be under a single command. Both plans envisaged an advance up the two legs of the inverted V, of which Rabaul was the apex.[53]

There was no real attempt to work out the logistical implications of these outline plans. While MacArthur stressed the fact that additional resources would be necessary, OPD planners were blandly optimistic, indicating that troops, aircraft, supplies, and shipping would be available for the operations. They did take brief notice of the shortage of shipping, indicating that there would not be enough assault vessels if "separate commanders [were] . . . to conduct simultaneous operations in the South and Southwest Pacific areas," and that priorities would have to be adjusted, at the expense of other operations, if merchant shipping were to be made available.[54] They also pointed to the still unsatisfied demand for small vessels as a possible cause of delay. For the most part, however, OPD planners glossed over the welter of logistical difficulties standing in

---

[51] Ltr, 4 Feb 43, cited n. 25(4).

[52] Matloff and Snell, *Strategic Planning: 1941-1942*, pp. 367–70.

[53] (1) Msg, CINCSWPA to AGWAR, 10 Jan 43, CM-IN 4574. (2) Outline Strategic Plan, title: Allied Offensive To Seize and Occupy the Rabaul Area, Tab F-9, SYMBOL: Casablanca Bks., Vol. I, Exec 6.

[54] Outline cited n. 53(2).

the way of an early resumption of the offensive, and paid little heed to the clear warnings of Nimitz and MacArthur that the reduction of Rabaul would require large additional air and ground forces. Logistical difficulties and insufficient air power had been primarily responsible for the failure to complete Task One and launch Tasks Two and Three in 1942, and the remedy for the logistical shortcomings revealed at each stage of operations had been late in coming and usually inadequate. The complications resulting from separate Army and Navy channels had yet to be ironed out. Everything pointed to the necessity for a pause in early 1943 before any further large-scale offensive in the Solomons-New Guinea-Bismarck Archipelago area could be resumed.

In addition to the proposed advance on Rabaul, Army planners at the end of 1942 were also giving more serious attention to the northern Pacific. While the northern route had generally been ruled out as a major line of advance toward Japan, there was a strong disposition to eliminate the Japanese threat to Alaska arising from their possession of Kiska and Attu. General De Witt, commander of the Western Defense Command, continually urged such an operation. In August 1942 Adak was occupied and subsequently built up as an advanced base from which Attu and Kiska could be brought under heavy attack. But both OPD and General Marshall regarded the troops committed to Alaska (eighty-five thousand) as excessive and were reluctant to divert the amphibious forces needed for the assault. Nonetheless, the discovery that the Japanese had made a reconnaissance of Amchitka led to American occupation of that island in January 1943, and in preparation for

the Casablanca Conference an outline plan was drawn up for the occupation of Kiska. Calculations indicated that a task force of twenty-five thousand men, built around one amphibiously trained division, would be required. No extraordinary logistical difficulties were anticipated beyond the additional strain on shipping, but OPD had no enthusiasm for this project, which would mean additional dispersion of effort.[55]

Down to the end of 1942 the Army had given little consideration to reviving the prewar plan for an advance from Hawaii through the Gilberts and Marshalls and toward the Philippines; its plans were generally drawn in terms of an advance upward from the Southwest Pacific, with Truk as the next objective after the capture of Rabaul. In Navy planning, however, the Central Pacific occupied an important place, and at Casablanca Admiral King was to offer the Central Pacific route as an alternative or supplement to the Southwest Pacific line. From the logistical point of view, this approach had certain attractions since it involved shorter lines of communication and the use of the well-developed bases on Hawaii for launching the initial drive.

The outlook at the end of 1942 was thus for a continuation of the limited offensives in the Pacific with a view to wearing down and dispersing Japanese forces and to gaining bases for a final assault against Japan once the war against Germany had been won. It appeared likely that these advances would be from several directions, with all the problems incident to divided theater commands. On the logis-

---

[55] Matloff and Snell, *Strategic Planning: 1941-1942,* Ch. XVI.

tical side, the campaigns of 1942 had provided valuable lessons—the problems involved in warfare in the Pacific had been brought into proper focus and the way pointed toward their solution. Despite the optimism of Army planners, there was every prospect that the scarcity of resources would continue to delay advances during 1943 unless Pacific operations were given a higher priority. Nevertheless, the hard-won victories on Guadalcanal and New Guinea without question represented a genuine turning point. By early 1943 plans for the Pacific were being framed entirely in terms of offensive and not defensive strategy, a marked change from the situation that had characterized most of the first year of the war. This change in the strategic picture foretold a period in which logistics could in turn be based on solid advance planning rather than improvisation.

CHAPTER XVI

The Descent on North Africa

With the grudging American acceptance of the North Africa invasion project at the end of July 1942, British strategic views won a notable victory. As Churchill later put it in one of his cadenced passages, " 'Sledgehammer' fell by the wayside, and 'Gymnast' came into its own." [1] Anglo-American strategy turned again upon the path that had been optimistically charted and then abandoned the preceding December and January during the first wartime meetings of the leaders and staffs after Pearl Harbor. There now remained the task of reaching agreement on the scope and timing of the new GYMNAST—now called TORCH—a task that was to consume six tedious weeks while preparations to mount the operation floundered in uncertainty. [2]

The Essay Contest

The point at issue in this "transatlantic essay contest," as one contemporary called it, was whether the operation's center of gravity should be in the west, with the principal landings on the Atlantic coast, or inside the Mediterranean. [3] The former conception was held by the American staffs in Washington, the latter by the British and to some degree also by Eisenhower's staff in London. American plans for GYMNAST, as late as July, had ruled out inside landings altogether, aiming at occupying French Morocco, funneling all the forces through Casablanca and a few satel-

lite ports, and allowing about three months to consolidate holdings in the west before driving eastward. The impelling consideration was the belief that because of the dangers of a hostile Spanish reaction, a German move through Spain, or, at the very least, passive opposition by the North African French, it was imperative first to secure the approaches to the Strait of Gibraltar and overland communications to the east against the possibility that the Strait passage might be closed. There was also an underlying reluctance on the part of Marshall and his advisers to commit a large part of Allied strength to operations deep in the Mediterranean. [4]

The British conception was much bolder. They saw the whole operation as

---

[1] Churchill, *Hinge of Fate,* p. 447.

[2] (1) Discussion of strategic planning for TORCH in this chapter, unless otherwise indicated, is based on Matloff and Snell, *Strategic Planning: 1941-1942,* Chs. XII–XIV. (2) See above, Chs. VI, XIV. (3) See also George F. Howe, Operations in Northwest Africa: 1942–1943, a volume in preparation for the series UNITED STATES ARMY IN WORLD WAR II. (4) Wesley Frank Craven and James Lea Cate, eds., *Europe: TORCH to POINT BLANK—August 1942 to December 1943,* Vol. II in THE ARMY AIR FORCES IN WORLD WAR II (Chicago, The University of Chicago Press, 1949) (hereafter cited as Craven and Cate, *AAF II*).

[3] Capt. Harry C. Butcher, *My Three Years With Eisenhower* (New York, Simon and Schuster, 1946), p. 83.

[4] (1) OPD plng studies in Item 53, Exec 10, and Item 6, Exec 1. (2) Memo, Chief of Plng Div OCT for G-4, 1 Jul 42, sub: Shipg Available for Sp Project, NATOUSA Convoy Info folder, OCT HB.

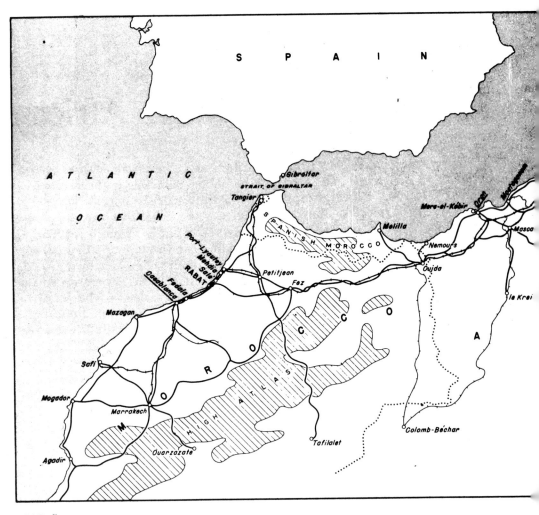

MAP 5

a major effort, in conjunction with the Eighth Army offensive from the east, to crush the enemy in a pincers and destroy his power in North Africa. To accomplish this, they held it imperative to strike early with at least the appearance of overwhelming force before the plan leaked out and while German forces, especially air forces, were pinned down in the Soviet Union, and then to gain Tunisia before German reinforcements could be rushed across the Sicilian narrows. If the Germans got to Tunisia first, they could build up strength more rapidly over their short lines of communications than could the Allies over longer lines. "The whole conception of TORCH," the British Chiefs of Staff declared on 11 August, "may stand or fall on this question of early Allied occupation of Tunisia."[5]

The more conservative views of the Washington planners aroused bewilder-

[5] Memo, Br CsofS for Eisenhower, 11 Aug 42, WDCSA TORCH, 1.

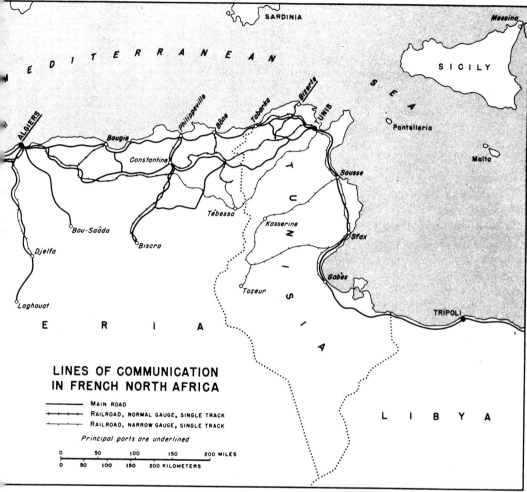

LINES OF COMMUNICATION
IN FRENCH NORTH AFRICA

——————— MAIN ROAD
+–+–+–+ RAILROAD, NORMAL GAUGE, SINGLE TRACK
—+—+—+— RAILROAD, NARROW GAUGE, SINGLE TRACK

Principal ports are underlined

R. Johnstone

ment and impatience among the British. Casablanca, they argued, was a second-rate objective that would fall automatically if the inside landings were successful, and that, if gained at the expense of lodgments in Algeria and Tunisia, would impress neither friends nor neutrals, still less enemies. Of all possible nuts, moreover, the British felt that Casablanca would be the hardest to crack because of surf conditions, which made landings impracticable four days out of every five, and because of the hostile attitude of the French authorities there. Weather and tide offered more opportunities inside the Mediterranean, giving commanders more leeway in other respects—in choosing a dark moon, for example—and as far as local attitudes were concerned, Algiers seemed the "softest and most paying spot."[6] (*Map 5*) While recognizing the value of secure communications, the Brit-

[6] Ltr, Prime Minister to Harry Hopkins, 4 Sep 42, as quoted in Churchill, *Hinge of Fate*, p. 539.

ish argued that the best way to cow the Spaniards, who held the key to the Strait, was to make a strong show of force in the Mediterranean and to "get on shore and get some ports." [7] The Spaniards, the British were confident, would resist a German incursion under those circumstances, but an Allied reverse at Casablanca would almost certainly tempt them to attack Gibraltar and let the Germans in. As Churchill summed up, a strong effort against Casablanca would

. . . be made at the expense of the landings inside, and if there is resistance inside *a fortiori* there will be resistance on the Atlantic shore, with this difference—that you can overcome the resistance inside and cannot overcome it outside unless the surf is favourable, which is four to one against. In short, the place to determine French action is inside, and if it is determined there in a favourable sense there will be no difficulty in occupying Casablanca by agreement later.[8]

"The first victory we have to win is to avoid a battle; the second if we cannot avoid it, to win it." [9]

Throughout August Eisenhower and his staff in London tried vainly to reconcile the conflicting views of the British leaders and of his superiors in Washington. The primary obstacles to combining the two conceptions in a single plan were the inadequacy of naval protection (surface and air) for ocean communications and the landings, and of assault shipping. Follow-up convoys must be at sea while the assaults were in progress; land-based air support could only be based on the single airfield at Gibraltar, directly under Spanish guns. Suspension of the northern convoys to the USSR in July released British naval units for service in the Mediterranean, but an attempt to reinforce and provision Malta during the second week of August purchased meager success at

heavy cost—one carrier sunk and another damaged. In the Pacific, American naval power was pinned down by the Guadalcanal operation launched on 7 August. In the desperate naval battles of that month a carrier and several cruisers were sunk, and in September and October a second carrier and other warships went down. Admiral King could make no definite commitments during August and September to shift naval units to the Atlantic to support TORCH.[10] Eisenhower thus could not count on sufficient naval power to support three strong and widely separated landings. His first outline plan, submitted on 9 August, provided for both inside and outside landings "approximately simultaneous" but with the latter postponed if necessary a few days after the former, and the easternmost landings very weak. His second outline plan (21 August) abandoned the Casablanca landings altogether and centered on securing a lodgment at Oran, from which twin drives would be launched into Tunisia (supporting landings farther east) and southwest across the mountains into French Morocco. But the complicated convoy arrangements necessary to bring in, within a few days, assault forces, armored striking forces, service and air forces, and material for all finally defied solution. In Washington the plan was regarded as too risky, particularly in view of the fate of the recent British Malta convoy.[11]

---

[7] *Ibid.*, p. 541.

[8] *Ibid.*

[9] Telegram, Former Naval Person to President Roosevelt, 26 Aug 42, as quoted in Churchill, *Hinge of Fate*, p. 528.

[10] (1) Churchill, *Hinge of Fate*, pp. 505–06, 533. (2) Craven and Cate, *AAF II*, p. 31. (3) See above, Ch. XV.

[11] (1) Draft Outline Plan (Partial) Opn TORCH, Hq ETOUSA, 9 Aug 42, ABC 381 (7-25-42), 4-A. (2) Outline Plan Opn TORCH, Hq ETOUSA, Norfolk

Assault shipping governed the timing of the attack and the size of the attacking forces. Most of the Navy's assault transports were in the Pacific, and there were not enough, in any case, to meet requirements for twelve regimental combat teams in three landings, estimated at from thirty to thirty-six attack troop transports (APA's) and nine to twelve attack cargo transports (AKA's). The British contribution was uncertain, possibly enough for four combat teams in the easternmost landings. To convert conventional vessels for the purpose, the Navy estimated that almost fourteen weeks would be needed— to make structural alterations, install equipment, train crews, rehearse the troops, load, and arrive at destination. On 2 August the Navy gave its opinion that 7 November was the earliest possible assault date. Some ten small vessels had already been taken off the BOLERO run and conversion work had started.[12]

On 4 August the British planners abruptly reversed their own previous calculations and set a provisional target date of 7 October (when the moon was favorable), which they admitted could be met only by "superhuman efforts." [13] To do this they were willing to skimp on training and rehearsals. The American staffs were not, but the President sided with the British and on 12 August directed Marshall to try again for a 7 October landing, even if this meant reducing the assault forces by two thirds. About the same time Eisenhower also bowed to the pressure for an

early attack, and the first drafts of his second outline plan of 21 August reduced the whole scale of the assault and placed all landings inside the Mediterranean. This would require the contingent from the United States to depart late in September, rendezvous near Gibraltar with the British and American forces from the United Kingdom, and make the principal attack at Oran. As already noted, this plan involved convoy arrangements that could not be contrived. It also seemed impossible to have the Oran contingent's assault shipping ready in time. Admiral King did not believe that even a 15 October assault date could be met. The 24th, he thought, was much more likely.[14]

It was further doubtful whether Eisenhower's American units in the United Kingdom could be equipped and rehearsed in time. The 1st Division, his only amphibiously trained American division there, still lacked most of its heavy equipment, which depots in the States had been unable to forward when the division sailed early in August. A little later a freighter carrying most of the artillery ran aground in Halifax Harbor, and only part of the cargo could be reloaded and shipped in a British convoy on the 19th, reaching England at the end of the month. The staffs

---

Group, 21 Aug 42. Original copy issued in London is Tab 35, Item 1, Exec 5, also circulated as Incl B to CCS 103, 25 Aug 42, title: Opn TORCH. (3) Memo, Marshall for President, 20 Aug 42, sub: TORCH Opn, OPD 381 TORCH, 2. (4) Memo, Marshall for President, 24 Aug 42, same sub, Item 1, Exec 5. (5) Msg 3318, AGWAR to USFOR, 14 Aug 42, Item 9, Exec 5. (6) Corresp in ABC 381 (7-25-42), 4-B.

[12] (1) Memo, Handy for CofS, 2 Aug 42, sub: TORCH, ABC 381 (7-25-42), 4-B. (2) Papers in GYMNAST folder, Item 6, Exec 1. (3) Min, 34th mtg CCS, 30 Jul 42. (4) Msg 2818, Marshall to Eisenhower, 31 Jul 42, Item 9, Exec 5. (5) Papers in BOLERO folder, OCT HB. (6) Plng Div SOS Diary, 31 Jul 42 entry, Plng Div ASF. This source indicates fourteen BOLERO vessels actually made available for conversion. Estimates of assault transport requirements varied.

[13] Msg 236, Br CsofS to Jt Stf Mis, 4 Aug 42, Item 2a, Exec 5.

[14] (1) Msg 237, Br CsofS to Jt Stf Mis, 4 Aug 42, Item 2a, Exec 5. (2) Msg, King to Marshall, 22 Aug 42, sub: Sp Opns, Item 1, Exec 5. (3) Memo, Gen Streett for CofS, 18 Aug 42, ABC 381 (7-25-42), 4-B, 69.

allowed ten days to get equipment to the troops after its arrival, a week or so for rehearsal, and then another ten days for outloading troops and equipment. Eisenhower's staff considered equipping the 1st Division with the old-style howitzers of the 34th Division (part of which was also earmarked for TORCH), or with British 25-pounders; otherwise, it would be necessary to train two regimental combat teams of the 34th to spearhead the Algiers attack. It developed that there was not time to rehearse two combat teams with landing craft and to recondition the craft for use in the assault, nor were there enough craft in England for both purposes. Still hoping for a 15 October assault, Eisenhower put one combat team of the 34th into training and alerted one team of the 1st—just in case. Meanwhile, the 1st Division's tardy equipment slowly trickled in. As late as 19 September, by which time the entire division was slated for the assault, none of the field artillery had yet reached the troops, though some was on the way, and only fractional allowances of machine guns, mortars, special vehicles, and signal equipment were on hand.[15] Back in the States, it seemed unlikely that the 2d Armored Division, stripped of its tanks in July to supply the British Eighth Army, and the tank battalions attached to the 3d and 9th Infantry Divisions could receive their new Sherman (M4) tanks before 17 September, in time for training. The 3d Armored, if used, would have to go with old-model Grants (M3); the 1st Armored, already in Northern Ireland, was in the same situation. For ammunition, forces in the United States would have to draw on BOLERO stocks and borrow from the Navy and the British. And in August the transporting of tanks in an amphibious assault was a problem still not solved; the first LST's were not expected until October or November.[16]

The 21 August outline plan pleased no one, not even its authors. Brig. Gen. James H. Doolittle was reported to have said, in a mood of exhilarated pessimism, that "the man who can put it over is a miracle man."[17] Even the British Chiefs, on the 24th, finally conceded that a November landing date might be acceptable if stronger assaults might thereby be mounted. But now the U.S. Chiefs wanted to reorient the whole operation to the westward, and so proposed on the 25th.[18]

Churchill, who had returned to London from Cairo and Moscow only the day before, immediately exploded into action. "The whole pith of the operation will be lost," he cabled to Roosevelt, "if we do not take Algiers as well as Oran on the first day."[19] Upon Eisenhower he urged ad-

[15] (1) Msg 1160, USFOR to AGWAR, 14 Aug 42. (2) Msg 1229, USFOR to AGWAR, 17 Aug 42. (3) Msg 1291, USFOR to AGWAR, 19 Aug 42. All in Item 9, Exec 5. (4) Ltr, Eisenhower to Marshall, 17 Aug 42, ABC 381 (7-25-42), 4-B, 54. (5) Memo, CofS for President, 20 Aug 42, sub: TORCH Opn, OPD 381 TORCH, 2. (6) Msg, Gross to CG ETOUSA, 19 Aug 42, OCT 370.5 England. (7) Atchmts to memo, Magruder for Lutes, 3 Oct 42, sub: Status of Equip for 1st Div, U.K. Plans folder, Logis File, OCMH. (8) Diary, 22 and 26 Sep 42 entries, cited n. 12(6). (9) Memo, Adcock for Gen Larkin, 22 Sep 42, 18 Shipg file, I, Case 29, Plng Div ASF, Job A46-371.
[16] (1) Memo, unsigned, no addressee, no date, sub: Memo on Projected Opns, ABC 381 (7-25-42), 71. (2) Memo, unsigned, no addressee, no date, sub: Date of TORCH Landings Opns, ABC 381 (7-25-42), 72. (3) Memo, Chief of Distrib Div for ACofS Opns SOS, 2 Aug 42, sub: Equip for Task Force. (4) Notes on conf, 10 Aug 42. Last two in TORCH folder, Task Force tab, Lutes File.
[17] Msg 1417, Handy to WD, 22 Aug 42, ABC 381 (7-25-42) 4-B, 52.
[18] (1) Ltr, Eisenhower to CCS, 23 Aug 42, Incl C to CCS 103 cited n. 11(2). (2) Msg 1465, USFOR to AGWAR, 24 Aug 42, ABC 381 (7-25-42), 4-B.
[19] Msg, Former Naval Person to President Roosevelt, 27 Aug 42, as quoted in Churchill, *Hinge of Fate*, p. 530.

ditional assaults at Bône and Philippeville, along with a feint at Casablanca. The operation, he declared, must be launched "along the broadest possible front" by mid-October at the very latest; outloading must be accelerated somehow, naval forces and combat loaders found somewhere—"nothing matters but success." [20]

This is an absolutely different kind of operation from the Dieppe business or any variants of "Sledgehammer." There we were up against German efficiency and the steel-bound, fortified coasts of France. In "Torch" we have to face at the worst weak, divided opposition and an enormous choice of striking-points at which to land. Risks and difficulties will be doubled by delay and will far outstrip any increase of our forces. Careful planning in every detail, safety first in every calculation, far-seeing provisions for a long-term campaign, to meet every conceivable adverse contingency, however admirable in theory, will ruin the enterprise in fact. [21]

Eisenhower thought Churchill was about to jump in a plane and fly to Washington. [22]

The President, too, was ready to intervene, but for different reasons. In the last week of August he received intelligence from North Africa that convinced him British participation in the initial landings would be a fatal provocation to local sentiment. He approved main landings, therefore, at Casablanca and Oran by purely American forces, with the British to follow through at Algiers a week later, after the Americans had made political arrangements. Like Churchill, the President was impatient of technical and administrative obstacles. His plan would leave no assault shipping for the British descent on Algiers, which might encounter resistance, nor naval protection for the British convoys that must be at sea in the interim. And he, too, wanted an early assault—"in no event later than October 30." His solution was characteristically bland: "I think we should re-examine our resources and strip everything to the bone to make the third landing possible." [23]

This implied commitment evidently broke the bottleneck. When the American naval contribution was listed a few days later it was clear, as Churchill wrote the President, that "you too have skinned yourselves to the bone." With naval protection assured, Churchill was all the more insistent on simultaneous landings. The British had managed to scrape together assault shipping for about thirty thousand troops. After a few days of bargaining on the top level, the Americans agreed to reduce the Oran and the Casablanca forces, releasing assault shipping for ten thousand troops for Algiers. About half of this was to be sent from the United States in advance, carrying a full regimental combat team (the 39th) from the 9th Division, in time to join the Algiers contingent. It was thus possible to plan for simultaneous initial attacks:

(1) Casablanca (Western Task Force), 29,-000 U.S. troops from the United States;
(2) Oran (Center Task Force), 25,000 U.S. troops from the United Kingdom;
(3) Algiers (Eastern Task Force), 10,000 U.S. troops from the United Kingdom as a spearhead, to be closely followed by larger British forces.

The British were to provide the assault shipping for the Oran force and half the

---

[20] Msg 1511, London to AGWAR, 26 Aug 42, ABC 318 (7-25-42), 4-B.
[21] Telegram cited n. 9.
[22] Msg 1559, London to AGWAR, 27 Aug 42, in untitled folder, Misc TORCH File, DRB AGO.
[23] (1) Msg, President to Churchill, 30 Aug 42, Item 1, Exec 5. (2) Memo, Marshall for Eisenhower, 28 Aug 42. (3) Msg, 1624, Eisenhower to Marshall, 29 Aug 42. Last two in Item 9, Exec 5. (4) William L. Langer, Our Vichy Gamble (New York, Alfred A. Knopf, 1947), p. 309.

Algiers force, or almost half the entire attack.[24]

With this agreement on 5 September, the long debate over the scope and orientation of TORCH came to an end. Timing still remained to be settled, though by this time an early assault was no longer possible. Since late August Eisenhower's American staff had been wrestling with the task of training and equipping about half the entire initial echelon of the TORCH force, instead of only one or two combat teams. Readiness of these forces became the limiting factor in setting the date of the attack. Equipment for the 1st Division was still arriving in driblets, and the troops began to train with British 25-pounders; on 4 September Eisenhower cabled that one combat team of the division might get no final amphibious training whatever. The promise of a combat team from the United States relieved this situation somewhat. Yet the assault date continued to recede. On the 8th Eisenhower gave the Prime Minister his latest estimate—8 November—a miraculously accurate prediction, in the light of the problems yet to be surmounted.[25]

Birth of a Task Force

During the six weeks of the "essay contest" the Army administrative staffs clung grimly to the tail of the whipsawing outline plan in an effort to keep preparations and detailed planning moving in the right direction. Preparations got under way, in fact, while the status of SLEDGEHAMMER was still in doubt. On 22 July the SOS was busy rearranging shipping schedules and movement orders to send more combat troops to the United Kingdom for that operation. On the 27th came the news that SLEDGEHAMMER was dead and orders to

dust off the GYMNAST plans and draw up a service troop basis. But more than a week later SOS planners still could not get a definite commitment that TORCH was "on." "We are busy, as are you, no doubt," Somervell wrote wryly to Eisenhower about this time, "in changing horses in mid-stream. We have changed the old nags so often that we are getting a little bit used to it even if their tramping around does muddy up the water a good deal."[26]

The principal task of the War Department and the SOS was to prepare the Western Task Force, which was to be commanded by Maj. Gen. George S. Patton, Jr. The force was to sail from the United States and make the Casablanca attack. For a week and a half after 27 July the administrative staffs, lacking definite information, made their own guesses and did what they could. Studies of the harbor facilities, internal transport, and resources in North Africa were initiated, the old GYMNAST plans were reviewed with reference to requirements for special equipment, and procurement on some of it was ordered. Ten small vessels were taken up for conversion. On 5 August Lt. Col. Car-

---

[24] (1) Msg 144, Prime Minister to President, 5 Sep 42, Item 1, Exec 5. (2) Other corresp, 31 Aug–5 Sep 42, in same file; in Misc TORCH File, DRB AGO; and in ABC 381 (7-25-42), 4-B. (3) Churchill, *Hinge of Fate,* Bk. II, Ch. 7. (4) For reference to conversion of British shipping, see paper, 27 Aug 42, sub: Implications of TORCH on Other Shipg Commitments, TORCH Jul–Sep 42 folder, OCT HB. (5) AFHQ (G-3) Outline Plan C (Provisional) for Operation TORCH, 5 Sep 42, ABC 381 (7-25-42), 4-A. (6) For conventional shipping arrangements, see below, Ch. XVII.

[25] (1) Corresp cited n. 24(2). (2) For setting of final date, see Churchill, *Hinge of Fate,* pp. 543, 545. (3) Corresp on 1st Div equip in OCT 565.2 England.

[26] (1) Ltr, Somervell to Eisenhower, 6 Aug 42. (2) Ltr, Eisenhower to Somervell, 27 Jul 42. Both in ETO (6) 1942–43 folder, Hq ASF. (3) Msg, Gross to Somervell, 22 Jul 42, Item 9, Exec 5. (4) Diary, 27 Jul 42 entry, cited n. 12(6).

ter B. Magruder, one of General Lutes' principal staff officers, told OPD that two points must be determined immediately if work was to go forward: the troop basis for the whole operation, especially for the Western Task Force, and the troop basis for U.S. forces to be kept in the British Isles. The SOS also wanted to be informed of requirements for special equipment, the sailing date and detailed composition of the first contingent of the Western Task Force, and priorities as between units to be sent to the British Isles and to North Africa. OPD was sympathetic but had little information to offer. Forces in the British Isles would probably be held to the size of the old MAGNET Force; anywhere from six to twelve American divisions might be used in TORCH—assuredly the 1st Infantry and 1st Armored then in the United Kingdom, probably the three divisions now receiving amphibious training in the United States (3d and 9th Infantry and 2d Armored), perhaps also the 45th and 36th and the 3d Armored. 2d Armored could be equipped immediately. For the present the three amphibious divisions would be considered the nucleus of the Western Task Force, though General Patton wanted "fast moving, hard hitting" units with plenty of armor.[27] SOS could also go ahead and earmark a list of about sixty thousand service troops, drawn up by the supply services. OPD also turned over a list of ground combat and supporting units representing its own guess as to the form the task force might take. But all planning was in suspense; TORCH had not even been formally approved.[28]

On this basis SOS went ahead. On 6 and 7 August orders went out to supply services to start equipping a balanced ground force of about 250,000. The order listed twenty specific units, including

seven divisions and several antiaircraft units. The three amphibious divisions and the antiaircraft units were to be equipped by 5 September, the remainder by 5 October. A long list of special equipment was appended. This equipment directive was not formally sanctioned by the General Staff, but it alerted the services to the magnitude of the task and set preparations in train. As units were earmarked and equipped, they formed a pool from which the task force could be formed. The original list of twenty grew rapidly. By the 20th it numbered 233 units, mainly service types, of which the supply services by that date had specifically designated 198. By then a sizable pool was in being and well on its way to being equipped and brought up to strength.[29]

But planning, meanwhile, had gone off on another tangent. The Casablanca landings seemed likely to be scrapped and the Western Task Force to be sent instead to Oran in two widely spaced echelons with different missions. Until 22 August Washington had only fragmentary knowl-

---

[27] Ltr, Patton to OPD, 3 Aug 42, sub: Notes on W Task Force, Item 1, Exec 5.

[28] (1) Diary of a Certain Plan, 25 Jul–5 Aug 42 entries. (2) Chronology of a Certain Plan, 25 Jul–5 Aug 42 entries. Both are extracts and amplifications of the diaries maintained in the Planning Branch, SOS, during the TORCH period, and are in Plng Div ASF files. (3) Trans studies in TORCH Jul–Sep 42 folder, OCT HB. (4) Memo for rcd, Col Magruder, 5 Aug 42, sub: TORCH, Policy file, I, 9, Plng Div ASF, Job A46-183. (5) Msg 995, Eisenhower to Marshall, 8 Aug 42, Item 9, Exec 5.

[29] (1) Memo, Gen Lutes for Chiefs of Sup Svs, 7 Aug 42, sub: Distrib of Equip, Task Force A, Sup, Gen folder, Plng Div ASF, Job A46-371. (2) Diary, 6 and 7 Aug 42 entries, cited n. 28(1). (3) Memo, OPD for SOS and AGF, 8 Aug 42, sub: Priority on Equipg. . . , OPD 320.2 BOLERO, 19. (4) Chronology, 6–20 Aug 42 entries, cited n. 28(2). (5) Papers in OPD 370.5 Task Force. (6) History of the Planning Division, ASF, I, 85–86, OCMH. (7) William C. Frierson, Preparations for "Torch," MS, p. 43, OCMH.

edge of this plan, on which the London staff had begun to work as early as the 13th. General Patton flew over from London with a version that had already changed before he landed. Maj. Gen. Thomas T. Handy flew the reverse course in order to send back a firsthand report to OPD. SOS planners received a brief of the new tactical plan on the 17th, but it was too tentative to be disseminated. Protested General Styer (Somervell's chief of staff) on the 21st:

Confusion still obtains as to requirements for supply and shipping for our Atlantic operations in the new major theater and in the U.K. No dates and no strengths have yet been made firm. . . . The supply and shipping implications of these plans . . . are so involved that it is imperative that the Commanding General SOS be given *definite* instructions regarding the support expected from the SOS for each of these plans. These decisions must be clearcut and remain firm to enable the Commander of the SOS to proceed with plans and arrangements for supply and shipping, and to take action in response to requests for the release of shipping to our allies.[30]

No reply came, and the uncertainty deepened. On the 25th SOS headquarters learned that the date of the attack seemed likely to be postponed until November. Next day, the current tactical plan once more had to be scrapped. On the 31st a diary recorded, "no decisions reference assembly of units can be made pending final decision as to mission of the force."[31]

During the last few days of the month the mists began to clear. On the 29th the SOS received a new troop basis for the Western Task Force, minus the air components. On 2–3 September the ground force came officially into being when OPD finally issued a list of units in the first echelon to be prepared for overseas serv-

ice. This echelon—the initial assault forces and the increments immediately following—was built around the three amphibious divisions (3d and 9th Infantry, 2d Armored), with reinforcing tank destroyer and tank units, additional artillery, strong combat engineer elements (including some amphibian engineers), and a long list of supporting ground combat and service units. The second echelon was built around the 3d Armored Division, the third around the 45th and 36th Infantry and 4th Motorized Divisions. Readiness dates for the three echelons were 10 September, 20 September, and 10 October, respectively. Detailed instructions for special equipment followed.[32] On 9 September the AAF issued its own troop basis.

The attack was now a little more than two months distant. The Western Task Force was taking shape. The planners were on the point of settling the central questions of scope and timing. But the administrative staffs awaited decisions on a multitude of smaller questions, or pressed forward blindly without them. On 4 September the score of "known versus unknown" was tallied somewhat as follows:

1. Units of first echelon of Western Task Force tentatively designated. But mission of force not yet settled definitely.

[30] Memo, Styer for CofS, 21 Aug 42, sub: Need for Early Definition of Forces . . . , CofS WDGS (2) 1942 folder, Hq ASF.

[31] (1) Diary, 17, 20–26, and 31 Aug 42 entries, cited n. 28(1). (2) Chronology, 14 Aug 42 entry, cited n. 28(2).

[32] (1) Diary, 30 Aug and 2 Sep 42 entries, cited n. 28(1). (2) Memo, unsigned, for CG's AGF, SOS, and Task Force "A," 3 Sep 42, sub: Creation of a Task Force, OPD 320.2 ETO. (3) Memo, unsigned, for CG's AGF, SOS, and Task Force "A," 2 Sep 42, sub: Preparation of Units for Overseas Sv, OPD 370.5 Task Force. Similar memo for AAF units, 9 September 1942. The designation "Task Force A" created some confusion, since Eisenhower at first labeled the other two forces "A" and "B" (Eastern and Center, respectively).

2. Total strength of each echelon not determined.

3. Number of echelons not decided.

4. Interval between echelons tentatively decided: forty days (turnaround).

5. Ultimate strength of Western Task Force not decided. The pool of 250,000 "was never expected to be more than a pool from which units would be taken when a definite troop basis was set up."

6.–9. Designation, strength, and movement schedules of units to compose U.S. forces in the United Kingdom and to remain there not yet known.[33]

Inside Versus Outside

In September the organization, assembling, and equipping of the task forces on both sides of the Atlantic went forward along parallel lines. Preparation of the American forces in the British Isles, however, depended to an increasing and unforeseen extent upon assistance from the United States. Eisenhower now had to organize and equip the Oran force and half the spearhead of the Algiers force from American troops and material in the British Isles, and the effort to do so speedily revealed the full degree to which the build-up during the summer had fallen short of expectations. Like the British, Eisenhower had always favored throwing the weight of the attack to the east; the compromise of 5 September, by contrast, provided a strong force in the west at the expense of those in the center and east. Eisenhower was naturally unwilling, therefore, to allow his inside forces to be further weakened for lack of adequate resources on hand in the United Kingdom. Many of the additional supporting troops and much of the material and shipping he needed had to be sent from the United States in desperate haste during September and early October in order to arrive in time for the departure of the early convoys from England. Inevitably, the Western Task Force had to foot most of the bill. General Somervell warned on 17 September that the demands of the forces in the United Kingdom threatened to "destroy Patton's force by attrition."[34]

During most of August it was assumed that Patton's force would include some of the service troops already in England, and that the unbalanced American forces in the United Kingdom would have to be supported to some extent by British service troops. It was expected, too, that some Air Forces units from the United Kingdom would be added to the Western Task Force. All told, the planned air and service contingent from the United Kingdom for Patton's force numbered from 6,000 to 7,000 troops. In the United States, by mid-August, the SOS was already scraping the bottom of the barrel for trained service units to fill the Western Task Force pool. A sizable number crowded into staging areas near New York, a backwash from General Marshall's efforts in July to speed the movement of combat troops to the United Kingdom. The equipment of many of these service units had already been sent over. Was their importance to TORCH sufficient to offset the cost of re-equipping them? After a long delay OPD on 18 August decided that it was, except for those units, immediately needed in England, that would pick up their equipment there. About half of the units whose equipment had gone ahead were assigned to the TORCH pool, along with practically all those in staging areas whose equipment

---

[33] Memo, Gen Plans Br SOS for Lutes, 4 Sep 42, sub: Need for Early Def of Forces . . . , TORCH folder, Def of Forces tab, Lutes File.

[34] Memo, Somervell for CofS, 17 Sep 42, CofS WDGS (2) 1942 folder, Hq ASF.

had not. By the 20th the staging areas were cleared for later reception of the task force.[35]

The reorientation of the outline plan late in August upset the arrangements for augmenting Patton's force from U.S. troops in the United Kingdom. The shoe was now on the other foot. Eisenhower reported that in order to mount the Oran and Algiers assaults he would have to improvise many supporting units, use all those earmarked for Patton's force, and even draw upon the TORCH pool forming in the United States. On 1 September his specific requirements began to come in—a few hospital and other miscellaneous units, numerically small but with elaborate equipment, which were needed immediately, and a long list of additional units and maintenance supplies, to be sent later. The first group of units was to sail combat loaded to the British Isles, arriving three and a half weeks before D Day (D minus 24), with a cargo vessel loaded with maintenance supplies. The second group was to go in conventional shipping directly to the Mediterranean about D plus 17. During the next two weeks numerous additions to both lists came in.[36]

Transportation officials in Washington were thunderstruck by this request for two additional convoys, and declared flatly that the shipping was not available. Many of the units requested for the later convoy had been earmarked for Patton's force and could not soon be duplicated; there were actually more units of several of these types already in England than in the States. Moreover, the combat-loaded transport requested for the first contingent could ill be spared since Patton's assault shipping was already to be depleted in order to send the 39th Regimental Combat Team to join the U.S. forces in England later in the month. Even with the vessel requested, it appeared that only 27,000 of the Western Task Force could be sent in assault shipping; without it, an additional battalion combat team would be crowded out. Patton's staff had already relegated to follow-up shipping all service troops except Engineer shore units and some communications personnel.[37]

The decision as to distribution of service and supporting troops between the western and inside forces was, of course, Eisenhower's to make, as General Marshall hastened to assure him. But the request for service troops, under analysis, looked suspiciously like a lever to obtain more shipping. The theater had directed that the combat loader with the small first increment of service troops be left unfilled for "topping off" with cargo in England. Embarrassed, OPD told transportation officials on the one hand that "a firm negative reply is being made,"[38] while on the other it asked Eisenhower apologet-

---

[35] (1) Memo cited n. 12(1). (2) Memo, Marshall and King for President, 4 Aug 42, sub: TORCH. (3) Msg, Eisenhower to WD, 13 Aug 42. Last two in ABC 381 (7-25-42), 4-B. (4) Memo, unsigned, for Gen Patton, no date, sub: Tentative Plng Data, with list of sv units atchd, ABC 381 (7-25-42). 4-A. (5) Diary, 7, 15, 17, 18, and 20 Aug 42 entries, cited n. 28(1). (6) Ltr, Eisenhower to Marshall, 9 Aug 42, Item 1, Exec 5. (7) Draft msg, OPD to London, 31 Aug 42, Opd 370.5 Gt Brit. (8) Chronology, 14 Aug 42 entry, cited n. 28(2). (9) Frierson, Preparations for "Torch," p. 17, OCMH.

[36] (1) Msg 1487, Eisenhower to WD, 25 Aug 42, Item 9, Exec 5. (2) Msg cited n. 23(3). (3) Diary, 29, 30 Aug, and 2 Sep 42 entries, cited n. 28(1). (4) Msg 1705, Eisenhower to WD, 1 Sep 42, OCT 320.2-565.14 England. Subsequent amendments in Msgs 1727, 1789, 1815, and 1953.

[37] (1) Msg R-452, WD to CG ETOUSA, 5 Sep 42, Item 1, Exec 5. (2) Memo, Col Carter B. Magruder for Gen Lutes, 25 Sep 42, sub: Action on Cables . . . , TORCH folder, Radiograms tab, Lutes File.

[38] Pencil notation on msg cited n. 36(4).

ically ("have no doubts as to our appreciation of your difficulties") to allow the service troops to be sent in a conventional vessel.[39] To this plea the theater assented, provided the first contingent of service troops reached England in time to accompany one of the initial convoys sailing for North Africa on 18 and 22 October. New urgent requests came in during the days following. By mid-September the list of special troops desired from the United States for the inside forces on D Day or shortly after included over three thousand Air Forces personnel and a growing assortment of service units in addition to the combat-loaded 39th Regimental Combat Team sailing late in September. If the troops could not be shipped to England combat loaded, the theater stipulated, they and their equipment must be sent early enough for equipment to be unloaded and reloaded in the early TORCH convoys, or loaded in fast ships that, with only partial reloading, could accompany the early convoys.[40]

Even more unsettling were the theater's demands for additional supplies and equipment. On 8 September came Message 1949, a massive document whose itemized portion ran to fourteen double-spaced legal-length pages. Only fifteen to twenty days of maintenance supplies at combat rates, the message stated, were immediately available in the United Kingdom for the 102,000-odd American troops of the Eastern and Center Forces; forty-five days of maintenance (at least two items of each type of equipment) and ten units of fire for these forces must be shipped from the States. In addition, initial allowances and sixty days of maintenance were requested for a long list of miscellaneous items, ranging from goggles to barber chairs. The grand total—344,-000 ship tons—for Message 1949 broke down into the following groups:

To reach United Kingdom by 26 September
90,000 ship tons—controlled items of equipment and supplies
To reach United Kingdom by 20 October
90,000 ship tons—motor vehicle gasoline and oil
40,000 ship tons—maintenance equipment
40,000 ship tons—construction and miscellaneous materials
To reach Mediterranean by D plus 26
84,000 ship tons—aviation materials, motor vehicle gasoline and oil

All the early requirements (for September and October) were to be set up in balanced loads, in the proportion of 10 percent for the Eastern Force and 90 for the Center Force, with high priority items on top. The vessels must be of types suitable for inclusion in the United Kingdom (KM) convoys to North Africa, since there would be no time to unload and reload into other ships.[41]

In effect, the theater wanted a mobile and readily divisible floating depot, comprising huge quantities of material and large tonnages of shipping. The message was a clear confession, moreover, that hundreds of thousands of tons of material already shipped to the United Kingdom for American forces were buried too deeply in British warehouses to be retrieved in time for the impending operations. SOS officials in Washington found the situation difficult to understand or to extenuate. "We have sunk a large quantity of sup-

[39] Msg, Marshall to Eisenhower, 9 Sep 42, Item 9, Exec 5.
[40] (1) Msg 2044, Eisenhower to WD, 10 Sep 42. (2) Msg 2288, Eisenhower to WD, 16 Sep 42. (3) Msg R-571, WD to Eisenhower, 9 Sep 42. All in Item 9, Exec 5.
[41] Msg 1949, London to AGWAR, 8 Sep 42, TORCH folder, Radiograms tab, Lutes File.

plies in the U.K.," wrote General Lutes to General Lee,

. . . and these supplies, together with those furnished for Lend Lease purposes, and those lost by submarine sinkings, are putting the staff on this side in an embarrassing position. . . . It is regrettable that we do not have a tremendous stockpile of all types of supplies and equipment—that would be ideal. But we do not.

He urged that Lee's staff "swarm on the British ports and depots and find out where these people have put our supplies and equipment." [42]

Even if General Lee's staff had been large enough to "swarm" on the British, the problem could not have been solved by such measures. During the summer the theater SOS there had been unable to cope with the flood of material that began to pour across the Atlantic. British warehouses were makeshift and space inadequate; both British and American depot personnel were untrained; differences in supply procedure, techniques, and nomenclature made co-operation difficult. Cargo had to be discharged and cleared rapidly from the docks to avoid congestion and was usually moved directly to a depot where, owing to traffic conditions in the United Kingdom, it had to remain; temporary sorting sheds near the ports began to be used only late in the summer. Proper routing thus depended mainly on accurate identification of contents and destination at the ports, which was virtually impossible under the system of marking and documentation in use during 1942. Many of the misroutings that caused shipments to stray from their intended paths and become anonymous collections of unidentifiable boxes in warehouses somewhere in England could be traced back to unintelligible or incomplete marking on crates and boxes, tardy transmission of manifests and other shipping papers, and the inadequacy of data given in those papers. The "marrying up" of troops and their initial equipment was especially difficult because of the long interval that usually elapsed between the arrival of the one and the other. [43]

Compliance with Message 1949 was no easy matter. The list was admittedly "indicative rather than definite," and a long exchange of messages was required to clarify numerous details. [44] Many units in the accompanying troop list were inexactly designated; substitute equipment was requested without specifying for which units. The theater pleaded that "time is now so critically important that we cannot always be accurate with respect to these details." [45] Little or no effort had been made to eliminate items already ordered; many of the controlled items, in fact, were already moving through the pipeline. In the absence of specific data for computing maintenance allowances, the theater requested that these merely be estimated broadly and shipped in bulk. Lack of time made the requirement of balanced loads virtually impossible to meet, especially for the ninety thousand tons of controlled items needed by late September. The effective shipping deadline was 12 September, only four days after Message 1949 was dispatched. But the ambiguities of the message with respect to controlled items were not cleared up until the 13th, and General Lutes

---

[42] Memo, Lutes for Lee, 12 Sep 42, Misc Notes, Lutes File.

[43] (1) For details, see Ruppenthal, *Logistical Support of the Armies*, Ch. II. (2) Irving Cheslaw, Quartermaster Operations in the War Against Germany, a volume in preparation for the series UNITED STATES ARMY IN WORLD WAR II, draft ch., "The Quartermaster Establishment in the United Kingdom." (3) See also above, Chs. XIII–XIV.

[44] Msg cited n. 41.

[45] *Ibid.*

TABLE 7—TENTATIVE CONVOY SCHEDULE FOR WESTERN TASK FORCE: 17 SEPTEMBER 1942

Date	Composition of Convoy	Convoy
D Day	31,000 combat-loaded troops (12 APA's, 10 XAPA's, 6 AKA's, 1 seatrain)	UGF-1
D plus 5	32,000 convoy-loaded troops (10 troop ships, 10 fast cargo ships)	UGF-2ᵃ
D plus 20	Slow cargo convoy carrying remainder of equipment for 24,000 troops and 60 days of supply for 55,000 troops (25 cargo vessels)	UGS-2
D plus 40	Fast convoy: 30,000 troops, convoy-loaded (16 or 17 troop ships)	UGF-3
D plus 45	Slow cargo convoy, carrying equipment for 30,000 troops and 30 days of supply for 55,000 troops (32 cargo vessels)	UGS-3
D plus 65	Fast convoy (34,000 troops, 19 troop ships)	UGF-4
D plus 70	Slow cargo convoy, equipment for 34,000 troops and 30 days of supply for 85,000 troops (39 cargo vessels)	UGS-4
D plus 90	Fast convoy (36,000 troops, 10 troop ships)	UGF-5
D plus 95	Slow cargo convoy, equipment for 36,000 troops and 30 days of supply for 119,000 troops (44 cargo vessels)	UGS-5

ᵃ Represents a telescoping of the first slow cargo convoy and the first post-D-Day troop convoy in an earlier tentative schedule; hence the omission of UGS-1.

Source: Schedule atchd to memo, Magruder for Lutes, 17 Sep 42, sub: Mtg Concerning Trans for Certain Opn, 18 Shipg file, I, Case 12, Plng Div ASF. A similar schedule, dated 9 September, is in TORCH folder, Shipg tab, Lutes File.

feared that even if some of the material reached the theater by the 26th, it would be necessary to sort it out by service categories in England before distributing to troops. Primarily for this reason, it was decided not to use any of Patton's fast cargo vessels for these shipments.[46]

In mid-September these proliferating demands for early troop and cargo shipments ran head on into belatedly hardening convoy arrangements, which reflected not the limitations of available shipping, matériel, and trained units, but the even tighter one of the Navy's capacity to escort. The discarded 21 August outline plan, hinging on swift capture and exploitation of a bridgehead at Oran, had foundered on the dual problem of port and escort capacity. All the versions of the planned Oran operation had involved more convoys in a short time, or larger single convoys, than the Navy could escort, and a heavier influx of cargo than the port of Oran could probably accommodate. The staffs estimated that a month or more would be needed to discharge the initial troop convoys, put the harbor into

operation, and empty the first cargo convoy.[47]

With the collapse of the eastward-oriented plan at the end of August, convoy planning came to a halt as the staffs awaited final decisions on the scope and timing of the operation. Not until the 17th of September did Patton's staff complete a tentative schedule, in co-ordination with the Navy, for the movement of the Western Task Force, under the new conception of the operation.[48] (Table 7) The schedule

[46] (1) Memo cited n. 42. (2) Memo, Brig Gen Everett S. Hughes for Brig Gen Mark W. Clark, 14 Sep 42, sub: Est of Sup and Admin Aspects of Proposed Opn, USFET AG 400 Sups and Equip, Vol. V, DRB AGO. (3) Memo, Lutes for OPD, 15 Sep 42, sub: Sups for ETO Contingent for Sp Opn, TORCH folder, Sups for ETO tab, Lutes File. (4) Related corresp in same file. (5) Other corresp in 18 Shipg file, I, Cases 11 and 16, Plng Div ASF; and S.O. folder, OCT HB.

[47] (1) Notes, 20 Aug 42, sub: Opn of One Port, TORCH Jul–Sep 42 folder, OCT HB. (2) Related papers in same file and in NATOUSA TORCH Plng folder, OCT HB. (3) Annex IV to Outline Plan cited n. 11(2). (4) Diary, 23 Aug 42 entry, cited n. 28(1). (5) Memo cited n. 11(3). (6) Msg cited n. 36(1). (7) Msg 1535, Eisenhower to WD, 27 Aug 42, Item 9, Exec 5.

[48] For convoys, see below, App. A-8.

had been drawn to Navy specifications: a limit of 20 vessels in fast convoys following the first, 35 to 40 vessels in slow convoys; a normal twenty-five-day interval between convoys of each type, starting with the UG-3 convoys, which had to await the return of the escorts of the assault convoys. The timing of the D plus 20 convoy reflected a hopeful estimate of the interval needed to clear the harbor and discharge the cargo vessels of the D plus 5 convoy.[49]

On the same day that Patton's convoy schedule was transmitted to the theater, Eisenhower's latest outline plan was brought over from London; with it came a convoy annex for the United Kingdom–North Africa movements, which Somervell immediately branded as "completely irreconcilable" both with Patton's schedule and with the capabilities for meeting the theater's recent demands for early shipments.[50] It would clearly be impossible to send Eisenhower's second contingent of service troops directly to Oran on D plus 17, as requested, or in any other convoy before D plus 40. Only a few of his service units would be ready to sail late in September with the 39th Regimental Combat Team and no additional convoy could be provided. The remaining units, therefore, must wait for the D plus 40 convoy unless the theater wanted them to be sent to England late in October in British transports. Their equipment could be shipped to England, or directly to Casablanca in the D plus 20 convoy and then shuttled over to Oran. No cargo could be shipped to the inside forces in the D plus 5 fast convoy, except by further excisions from Patton's already depleted cargo shipping.[51]

As for the Message 1949 requirements, it appeared that about 175,000 tons of the first two categories could be transported in thirteen or fourteen slow and three fast

freighters diverted from regular North Atlantic convoys scheduled to run between 17 September and early October; to ship the remainder would cut into Patton's convoys. But the convoy schedule that arrived from London on the 17th indicated that Oran harbor could accommodate only twenty-five cargo vessels at one time, and twenty of these spaces were already assigned to early convoys from the United Kingdom. Evidently only five of the sixteen or seventeen vessels from the States could be discharged soon after the assault; the remainder might have to be held back for weeks. It was extremely doubtful, in any case, whether the shipments could be set up and loaded in time for the theater's deadlines. To SOS officials it seemed the obvious course to postpone the sailing of most of the first sixteen vessels and, rather than route them first to England, to send them with Patton's later convoys to North Africa, starting with the D plus 45 convoy.[52]

However, OPD decided on the 20th to try to comply with the theater's wishes, the

---

[49] (1) Msg R-892, AGWAR to USFOR, 17 Sep 42, Item 9, Exec 5. (2) Memo, Plng Div OCT for Gen Wilson, 12 Sep 42, sub: Size of the Force Capable of Being Supplied Through Atlantic Ports . . . , TORCH Jul–Sep 42 folder, OCT HB.

[50] Memo, Somervell for Marshall, 17 Mar 42, CofS WDGS (2) 1942 folder, Hq ASF.

[51] (1) Memo cited n. 34. (2) Msg cited n. 49(1). (3) Memo for file, unsigned, 23 Sep 42, sub: Shipg Plan . . . , TORCH folder, Shipg tab, Lutes File. (4) Msg 2447, Eisenhower to WD, 19 Sep 42, 18 Shipg file, I, Case 21, Plng Div ASF. (5) Memo, Lutes for Gross, 21 Sep 42, sub: Sups for ETO . . . , 18 Shipg file, I, Case 23, Plng Div ASF.

[52] (1) Memo cited n. 46(3). (2) Memo, Lutes for Dir of Distrib Div, 16 Sep 42, sub: Sups for ETO Contingent for Sp Opn, TORCH folder, Sups for ETO tab, Lutes File. (3) Memo, Magruder for Hull, 18 Sep 42, sub: Shipts From U.S. to "E" Force, TORCH folder, Shipg tab, Lutes File. (4) Memo, Lutes for CofTrans, 18 Sep 42, sub: Sups for ETO Contingent for Sp Opn, 18 Shipg file, I, Case 14, Plng Div ASF. (5) Diary, 19 Sep 42 entry, cited n. 28(1).

real aim of which was to have a large number of ready-loaded vessels of various sizes, speeds, and cargoes from which to make up the first few convoys from the British Isles. Loading was pushed at full speed— thirteen slow freighters to sail about 25 September, three fast ones about 5 October—although the theater was warned that "anything approaching complete accomplishment" of the schedule was very unlikely.[53] Anticipating that many high-priority items (in the first 175,000 tons) would not reach port in time, SOS ordered the next 84,000 tons to port to fill holes.[54]

Scarcely had the message notifying the theater of these arrangements been put on the wires than another request arrived from London. Since no more space was available in Patton's D plus 5 fast convoy, the theater now wanted five shiploads of material to be sent in *fast* vessels to arrive in the United Kingdom no later than 21 October, for inclusion in the first separate cargo convoy (KMS-2), which was to sail for Oran on the 24th. "Every day's delay after 21 October will cause a corresponding delay in D Day."[55] Would it not be possible, in fact, to persuade the Navy to send a special convoy directly to Oran, regardless of the risk?[56]

The Navy was not to be persuaded, and SOS set about revising its loadings. The five shiploads requested evidently overlapped the "1949" requirements, but to an indeterminate degree. How much and where they overlapped, the theater itself could not say until it received, in turn, full information on shipments already on the way. A new schedule was drawn up: three slow freighters to sail as soon as possible after 25 September; two groups of four vessels, each carrying an identical assortment of gasoline, oil, bombs, ammunition, air technical items, and maintenance

equipment, to sail in the regular 1 October convoy; six balanced loads of maintenance items to sail separately soon after 1 October. The five shiploads for KMS-2 could be chosen from the two groups of four sailing about the 1st; the Navy had promised they would arrive by the 20th.[57]

The message sent on 22 September so informing the theater crossed one from London requesting that all sixteen freighters be sent as earlier scheduled, that is, all but three to sail by 25 September, now only three days away. It was also directed that an additional 4,000 tons of ammunition be loaded in one of the three fast freighters, along with some new signal and engineer equipment and a squad of railroad mechanics equipped with hand tools. This meant reloading some 4,000 tons of ammunition requested earlier. From the message SOS officials also gleaned confirmation of their earlier prediction that all but five shiploads were to be discharged in the British Isles for warehousing or reloading; in any case they could not be shipped to Africa for weeks or months.[58]

All this shifting of gears and of direction

[53] Msg R-1002, WD to USFOR, 20 Sep 42, 18 Shipg file, I, Case 19, Plng Div ASF.

[54] (1) *Ibid.* (2) Memo, Magruder for Lutes, 18 Sep 42, sub: Shipts From U.S. to "E" Force, 18 Shipg file, I, Case 15, Plng Div ASF.

[55] Msg cited n. 51(4). This message crossed the War Department's R-1002 of the 20th.

[56] Diary, 21 and 22 Sep 42 entries, cited n. 28(1).

[57] (1) Memo, Hull for Handy, 20 Sep 42, sub: Mvmt of Sups for Sp Opn, 18 Shipg file, I, Case 22, Plng Div ASF. (2) Memo cited n. 51(5). (3) Msg 2489, London to AGWAR, 21 Sep 42. (4) Msg R-1023, WD to USFOR, 21 Sep 42. (5) Msg R-1050, WD to USFOR, 21 Sep 42. (6) Msg R-1080, WD to USFOR, 22 Sep 42. Last four in TORCH Radiograms, Logis File, OCMH.

[58] (1) Msg 2592, London to AGWAR, 22 Sep 42, 18 Shipg file, I, Case 28, Plng Div ASF. (2) Diary, 24–26 Sep 42 entries, cited n. 28(1). (3) Memo, Col Magruder for Gen Larkin, 25 Sep 42, Policy file, I, 16, Plng Div ASF, Job A46-183.

produced the inevitable results. The first shipments of controlled items were held up two days because port and technical service officials waited for each other to call shipments to port; many items could not be assembled in time, especially air force material. On 25 September the 39th Regimental Combat Team with a few service troops sailed from New York as scheduled. But the three slow freighters carrying the first installment of "1949" requirements did not sail until 1 October, missing their deadline by almost a week. They alone, of all the seventeen, were fully loaded. On the same day the first group of four freighters with balanced loads also departed, but the ships were only about three-quarters full. Two days later the second group of four ships sailed, only two-thirds loaded. Two fast freighters departed on the 8th without escort, one carrying a balanced load, the other an additional four thousand tons of ammunition along with gasoline, oil, and several radio towers. During the next week four more vessels got off with balanced cargoes, and two additional ships were reserved to sail with UGS-2 to Casablanca and be shuttled over to Oran. [59]

In UGS-2, due to reach North Africa about D plus 20, a large block of space had been assigned, by the end of September, to the inside forces. Meanwhile the stream of new requests and changes in loading requirements from London continued, making the loading of UGS-2 largely a repetition of the strenuous experience of the "1949" shipments. Less than a month before the convoy's scheduled departure date (8 November), SOS in desperation registered a protest. No more changes in UGS-2, the theater was notified, could be made, "except for urgent strategic reasons," and all requirements for

UGS-3 should be in, if possible, by 20 October—positively by 1 November. [60] Would the theater in future set a deadline for requirements forty-five days, and for unavoidable changes thirty days, before sailing date? The theater agreed to call a halt to changes in UGS-2, but made no promises for future convoys. UGS-2 sailed on 13 November, five days later than scheduled—thirty-three vessels, of which eight freighters and two tankers were destined for Oran. [61]

The results of all this turmoil were disappointing. Frantic eleventh-hour efforts, sparked by Message 1949, to re-equip the initial echelons of the inside forces were only partly successful. Four vessels, besides the five squeezed into KMS-2, were assigned to early KM convoys that reached the theater within two and a half weeks after D Day. The remaining eight had to be discharged in the United Kingdom and their cargoes added to an already mountainous backlog awaiting later convoys. That backlog, even before the first

[59] (1) Msg cited n. 57(6). (2) Msg 2924, USFOR to AGWAR, 30 Sep 42. (3) Msg R-1610, WD to USFOR, 6 Oct 42. Last two in TORCH Radiograms Logis File, OCMH. (4) Corresp in S.O. folder, OCT HB. (5) Memo, Gross for Somervell, 2 Oct 42, sub Cargo Ships for Sp Opn, 18 Shipg file, I, Case 41, Plng Div ASF. (6) Msg 3400, USFOR to WD, 11 Oct 42 18 Shipg file, I, Case 52, Plng Div ASF..(7) Draft msg Somervell to CG ETO, 2 Oct 42. (8) Msg 2994, London to AGWAR, 1 Oct 42. Last two in OCT 565.3 England. (9) Memo, Gross for Somervell, 3 Oct 42 sub: Cargo for Sp Shipt, NATOUSA TORCH Plng folder, OCT HB. (10) Papers in TORCH Jul–Sep 4 folder, OCT HB. (11) Msg 3587, London to AGWAR, 14 Oct 42, OCT 565.3-900 England.
[60] Msg R-1898, WD to USFOR, 13 Oct 42, TORCH Radiograms, Logis File, OCMH.
[61] (1) Msg 3715, London to AGWAR, 17 Oct 42 TORCH Radiograms, Logis File, OCMH. (2) Memo Contl Div OCT for Somervell, 14 Nov 42, sub: Shi Activity in NW Africa, OCT 563.51-565.3 Afric 1941–42. (3) Memo, Wylie for Gross, 14 Nov 42, sub Convoys for N and NW African Ports, TORCH Sep Nov 42 folder, OCT HB.

convoys departed, represented material reordered several times over, replacing not only what had been buried in British warehouses, but also items actually on the way from the United States that the theater staff feared to count upon because specific notification had not reached them. "We have shipped all items at least twice and most items three times," protested the SOS in mid-October. "These items are all extremely critical, and we cannot continue to duplicate and triplicate shipments." [62] By that time the effort had been shown to be largely wasted, for the navies were unable to escort, or the North African ports to receive, more than a fraction of the material awaiting shipment. [63]

"We should have paid more attention," General Eisenhower later admitted, "to red tape and paper work." [64]

Cutting the Foot To Fit the Shoe

Between the 17th and 24th of September Eisenhower's staff in England had been working to straighten out the convoy tangle. On the 25th Maj. Gen. Mark W. Clark, Eisenhower's deputy, arrived in Washington accompanied by Brig. Gen. Thomas B. Larkin, G-4 of the Center Force. On their heels came a long explanatory message from Eisenhower with a new convoy schedule. This schedule was shaped by two sets of limitations: the estimated capacity of the North African ports to accommodate vessels in protected anchorages, and the size of the convoys the two navies were prepared to escort. (Table 8)

These two limitations virtually coincided. Two cargo convoys (UGS and KMS) arriving in North Africa waters at about the same time would bring one hundred vessels for which an estimated ninety-three anchorages would be available. Moreover, two naval tankers would

accompany each KMS convoy, and six each UGS convoy (including four to service British naval forces); for these, alongside berths would not be needed. [65] (Table 9) The build-up of forces in North Africa thus seemed likely to be retarded by escort and port limitations in combination, and the limited accommodations of the ports left very little margin for redistributing shipping among the three task forces. The theater proposed that, beginning with UGS-2, fifteen vessels be allotted from each slow convoy from the States to support the inside forces, besides the four tankers for the Royal Navy. The residue—twenty-six vessels—coincided neatly with the estimated capacity of the Atlantic ports, all of which might be used for supplying the forces ashore if the two U.S. Navy tankers (usually considered as fleet auxiliaries) were not included in the forty-five vessels allotted to UGS convoys. Similarly, with the fifteen to be shuttled over from each UGS convoy, the fifty-three vessels of the concurrent KMS convoy (deducting two naval tankers) would also fill inside ports to capacity. Eisenhower asked for a command decision on these arrangements.

[62] Msg R-1971, WD to USFOR, 15 Oct 42, Torch Radiograms, Logis File, OCMH.

[63] (1) Msg cited n. 61(1). (2) Msg R-2220, WD to USFOR, 21 Oct 42, NATOUSA Torch Plng folder, OCT HB. (3) Diary, 21 Oct 42 entry, cited n. 28(1).

[64] Dwight D. Eisenhower, Crusade in Europe (New York, Doubleday & Company, Inc., 1948), p. 85.

[65] In addition, each KMS convoy would have three Navy supply vessels and two "white" (gasoline) tankers for Army forces; each UGS convoy would have a single "white" tanker; the UGF convoys would have four "black" (oil) tankers for the two navies. Supplies for U.S. Navy forces ashore were carried with Army cargo. See: (1) Msg 2809, London to AGWAR, 27 Sep 42, and (2) Msg 2816, London to AGWAR, 27 Sep 42, both in Torch Radiograms, Logis File, OCMH; (3) memo, Lutes for OPD, 3 Oct 42, sub: Convoy Schedule for Sp Opn, 18 Shipg file, I, Case 44, Plng Div ASF.

TABLE 8—ANTICIPATED PORT AND CONVOY LIMITATIONS FOR SLOW CONVOYS TO NORTH
AFRICA: SEPTEMBER 1942

Ports [a]	Anchorages
Total available immediately...	73
Total available by D plus 15...	93
Eastern..	37
Early objectives: Algiers (18) and Bougie (4)...	22
To be captured by D plus 15: Philippeville (3) and Bône (12)...........................	15
Center..	30
Early objectives: Oran and Mers el Kebir..	25
To be captured by D plus 15: Mostaganem (2) and Nemours (3)...........................	5
Western: Casablanca (19), Safi (6), Fedala (1 tanker)...................................	26

Convoys (after first 2 weeks)	Interval	Ships [b]
Fast troop from United Kingdom (KMF)...	([c])	25
Slow cargo from United Kingdom (KMS)...	14 days..	55
Fast troop and cargo from United States (UGF)...	([c])	20
Slow cargo from United States (UGS)...	25 days..	45

[a] Allowances made in port estimates for berthing of naval escorts, harbor craft, coastal or French shipping, and ships not completely discharged. At Casablanca shallow anchorages were available but were required for escort destroyers. See also tables 12 and 22.

[b] Includes all ships in convoy except escorts and other combat vessels.

[c] Not yet determined exactly, but some degree of synchronization with the corresponding slow cargo convoys was assumed. See table 9.

Source: (1) Msg 2809, London to AGWAR, 27 Sep 42, and (2) Msg 2816, London to AGWAR, 27 Sep 42, both in TORCH Radiograms, Logis File, OCMH.

With little hesitation the War Department approved. Among the SOS staff, however, there was some hope that the accommodation capacity of the Atlantic ports might be increased after the first month or two, and that the Navy might be persuaded to relax the restriction on the size of convoys. In informal conversations late in September, Navy staff officers indicated that if the Army were willing to accept the risk, the Navy would go along. On 2 October General Clark cabled from London the theater's agreement to raising the UGS convoy limit to fifty-five vessels as soon as port capacity permitted.[66] But on the next day came the Navy's official verdict: forty-five ships was the limit. Even convoys of this size were considered dangerous, and the Navy doubted whether port capacity could be expanded in any case. Later in October the Navy also refused to escort fast troop and cargo convoys

[66] (1) Memo, Capt Warren, OCT, for Capt Thomas, USN, 28 Sep 42, sub: Sp Opn, 18 Shipg file, I, Case 34, Plng Div ASF. (2) Diary, 26 and 28 Sep 42 entries, cited n. 28(1). (3) Memo, Lutes for Somervell, 28 Sep 42, sub: Conf With Gen Clark, TORCH folder, Conf tab, Lutes File. (4) Memo, Lutes for Hull, 29 Sep 42, sub: Sp Opn, Policy file, Plng Div ASF. (5) Msg 3022, London to AGWAR, 2 Oct 42, TORCH Radiograms, Logis File, OCMH. (6) Memo cited n. 65(3).

TABLE 9—EISENHOWER'S PROPOSED CONVOY SCHEDULE: 27 SEPTEMBER 1942 [a]

Convoy	Sailing Date	Eastern Task Force				Center Task Force				Western Task Force			
		Arrive Algiers	Troops		Cargo[b] Ships	Arrive Oran	Troops		Cargo[b] Ships	Arrive Casablanca	Troops		Cargo[b] Ships
			Number	Ships			Number	Ships			Number	Ships	
KMS-1	D−17	D Day	(c)	0	15	D Day	(c)	0	27	....	....	....	....
KMF-1	D−13	D Day	32,000	15	0	D Day	39,000	20	0	....	....	....	....
UGF-1	....	....	....	....	....	....	....	....	....	D Day	35,000	(d)	(d)
KMS-2	D−15	D+4	0	0	22	D+3	0	0	22	....	....	....	....
KMF-2	D−7	D+4	30,000	12	0	D+3	21,000	8	0	....	....	....	....
UGF-2	D−4	....	....	....	....	....	....	....	....	D+6	31,000	10	10
KMF-3	D+5	D+14	50,000	17	0	D+13	12,000	4	0	....	....	....	....
KMS-3	D−1	D+18	0	0	36	D+17	0	0	14	....	....	....	....
UGS-2	D Day	....	....	....	....	D+22	0	0	e 10	D+20	0	0	24
KMF-4	D+19	D+28	40,000	17	0	D+27	31,000	13	0	....	....	....	....
KMS-4	D+15	D+32	0	0	35	D+31	0	0	13	....	....	....	....
UGF-3	D+25	....	....	....	....	D+41	f0	f0	f0	D+40	31,000	17	0
KMF-5	D+33	D+42	0	0	0	D+41	(g)	(g)	0	....	....	....	....
KMS-5	D+29	D+45	0	0	35	D+45	0	0	13	....	....	....	....
UGS-3	D+25	....	....	....	....	D+47	0	0	e 13	D+45	0	0	24

[a] This table should be studied in conjunction with table 8. The KM-1 and KM-2 convoys and the UGF-1 and UGF-2 convoys were planned and scheduled to meet immediate needs of the assault forces. Beginning with KMF-3, the convoys were to move on the regular build-up and maintenance schedule shown in table 8. It will be noted that the numbers of ships in regular slow convoys shown here do not tally with the combined limitations imposed by escort and port accommodation capacity shown in table 8. This is primarily because the number assigned to each task force does not include oil tankers, colliers, and other vessels assigned for naval service and supply, for which no destination is shown. From 5 to 7 such vessels were to be assigned to each KMS and 6 to each UGS convoy.

[b] Each regular KMS convoy was to include two gasoline tankers assigned, respectively, to the Eastern and Center Task Forces, and each regular UGS convoy was to include a gasoline tanker assigned to the Western Task Force (included in the figures shown).

[c] Included in KMF-1.

[d] Combat-loaded vessels; number not determined.

[e] Five additional spaces in UGS-2 and two in UGS-3 to be held in command reserve.

[f] As stated in source. Probably the number of vessels for Center ports had not yet been determined.

[g] Not determined.

Source: Msg 2816, London to AGWAR, 27 Sep 42, TORCH Radiograms, Logis File, OCMH.

of twenty-five vessels (by including up to a total of nine freighters and tankers). The ceilings remained at twenty, including no more than sixteen troop transports.[67]

The process of paring down tonnages to fit these limitations had already begun. The theater had decided to aim at building up only forty-five days of reserve supplies and ten units of fire. Even before sending his message of 27 September, Eisenhower's commanders had also slashed initial allowances in the inside assault forces. No 2½-ton trucks were to be taken at all, and only about 25 percent of allow-ances in many other types; the theater reported on 14 October that all types of organizational vehicles accompanying the

[67] (1) Msg R-1546, WD to USFOR, 3 Oct 42. (2) Msg 3333, London to AGWAR, 9 Oct 42. Both in TORCH Radiograms, Logis File, OCMH. (3) Diary, 4 and 19 Oct 42 entries, cited n. 28(1). (4) Memo, OPD for CG SOS, 5 Oct 42, sub: Convoy Schedule for Sp Opns, 18 Shipg file, I, Case 46, Plng Div ASF. (5) Memo, Col Heileman for Gen Hull, 13 Oct 42, sub: Convoys for W and Center Task Forces, 18 Shipg file, I, Case 54, Plng Div ASF. (6) Memo, Rear Adm Charles M. Cooke, Jr., for OPD, 20 Oct 42, same sub. (7) Memo, Heileman for Overseas Sup Div NYPOE, 20 Oct 42, sub: Convoy Schedules and Markings. Last two in 18 Shipg file, I, Case 59, Plng Div ASF.

inside forces had been reduced by half. These reductions left a backlog of vehicles that the follow-up convoys could not hope to absorb for many months.[68]

Meanwhile, the Western Task Force was being equipped on a lavish scale. The planned maintenance reserves for the Western Task Force were ninety days of supply and twenty units of fire—twice those of the inside forces. No effort was made by the task force staff to measure these mounting tonnages. As early as 4 September Col. Carter B. Magruder warned OPD: "It appears that the force, as now set up, is too large for cargo clearance capacity."[69] This warning went unheeded. The only curb placed on the amassing of material was the stipulation that the task force commander must vouch for the essentiality of new items.[70]

On 17 September representatives of SOS headquarters, the task force, Transportation Corps, the Navy, and other agencies compared notes on the mounting tonnages. It was all too clear that the force had far outgrown its transport; tonnages would have to be slashed. A few days later it was learned that the burden of supporting all three task forces after convoy UGS-2 would fall upon the United States. The staffs began to tabulate cargo requirements and to determine where cuts could be made. "If the foot must be carved to fit the shoe," commented an Air Forces officer, "total tonnage can be reduced approximately fifty per cent. Such reduction will eliminate reserves and all allowances for losses en route. If a ship is lost the airplanes sit on the ground. This must be a command decision."[71]

By the 28th the gap between space available and space desired could be estimated with fair accuracy. Lutes presented the problem to General Clark, who was still in Washington. Lutes started with the assumption that a three-month level of reserves for Patton's force was "out of the question," particularly since the inside forces, which would have to fight the Germans, were to get only half that allowance.[72] With the twenty-five cargo vessels allotted in each slow convoy to the Western Task Force and what little cargo space was available in fast convoys, something less than 1.5 million ship tons could be moved to the theater in three months (through D plus 95). Estimated requirements were about 2.4 million tons. The deficit, 927,000 tons, was equivalent to 84 shiploads. To absorb it, cargo convoys would have to be expanded to 66 vessels each, and port accommodation capacity in Morocco to 46 vessels. Otherwise, tonnages must be cut. The alternatives were to send the whole Western Task Force with its matériel reduced by about half, or to send a smaller force (reduced from 167,000 to about 100,000) fully equipped and mobile. Lutes recommended the latter.[73]

General Clark elected instead to have a large force, sacrificing mobility and fire power, on the ground that the mission of the Western Task Force would be primar-

[68] (1) Diary, 26 Sep 42 entry, cited n. 28(1). (2) Msg cited n. 59(11). (3) Memo cited n. 58(3). (4) Memo, Lutes for Clark, 28 Sep 42, sub: Maintenance of U.S. Trs in Center and E Task Forces, 18 Shipg file, I, Case 35, Plng Div ASF.

[69] Diary, 4 Sep 42 entry, cited n. 28(1).

[70] (1) Diary, 2 and 3 Oct 42 entries, cited n. 28(1). (2) Frierson, Preparations for "Torch," p. 45, OCMH.

[71] (1) Memo, Hq AAF for Magruder, 17 Sep 42, 18 Shipg file, I, Case 13, Plng Div ASF. (2) Corresp in 18 Shipg file, I, Cases 7 and 17, Plng Div ASF. (3) Diary, 17 and 21 Sep 42 entries, cited n. 28(1). (4) See memo, Magruder for Lutes, 17 Sep 42, sub: Mtg Concerning Trans for Certain Opn, 18 Shipg file, I, Case 12, Plng Div ASF. (5) See also, App. B of Frierson, Preparations for "Torch," OCMH.

[72] Memo cited n. 68(4).

[73] Ibid.

ily to establish and defend communications. General Patton, who apparently had not been consulted, accepted this portentous decision without protest.[74]

Launching the Western Task Force

The crowded eight weeks of wrestling with last-minute needs of the inside task forces saw the assembling, equipping, and outloading of the Western Task Force. It had early been decided, at the suggestion of SOS, to concentrate the force before sailing, but for lack of suitable staging areas near Hampton Roads (the port that was to handle the outloading of the combat-loaded elements) it proved impossible to assemble the whole force in one place. More distant military reservations had to be used—Fort Bragg in North Carolina, and Camps A. P. Hill and Pickett in Virginia, for most of the ground troops of the combat-loaded echelon; Langley Field, Virginia, for the air forces; Fort Meade, Maryland, for miscellaneous special units. Fort Dix and Camp Kilmer in New Jersey, Indiantown Gap, Pennsylvania, Fort Devens, Massachusetts, and other staging areas and reservations behind New York were used for the post-D-Day contingents, as well as for the 39th Regimental Combat Team, which sailed late in September. Instructions on 2 September ordered the first echelon, comprising the 3d and 9th Infantry and the 2d Armored Divisions with their supporting units, to be ready to move to concentration areas by the 10th; the 3d Armored with more units was to be ready by the 20th; the 45th Infantry and the 4th Motorized by 10 October. Air Forces units received their readiness orders on 9 September, with deadline dates of 5 and 10 October and 10 November. By 25 September the concentration of the first echelon was substantially complete.[75]

Equipping the force took longer, much longer. Special equipment was authorized piecemeal and more or less at the whim of troop commanders, and the task force staff fell far behind in notifying units of what had been authorized. Redesignation of special units and constitution of new ones immensely complicated the task. In equipping Air Forces units, SOS encountered particular difficulty. The instructions of 9 September had merely specified units; on the 13th SOS still was without information as to their locations or equipment tables. Officers on the task force air staff reported they were "still organizing." Two days later the information was requested again. The air staff was in a frenzy of activity; eighteen officers were laboring to turn out the data, which was promised within a few days. SOS suggested it be furnished piecemeal if necessary, and at three-day intervals thereafter repeated the request. On the 23d a list was received, but proved to be incomplete. Another promise—but at eight o'clock that evening no further word had been received. OPD was asked to apply pressure. Two days later, the air staff assured SOS that the AAF base service organizations had practically finished filling unit shortages, and SOS need concern itself only with mainte-

[74] (1) Memo cited n. 66(3). (2) Diary, 28 Sep 42 entry, cited n. 28(1). (3) Memo, Magruder for Lutes, 6 Oct 42, sub: Maintenance Reserve Task Force "A," Policy file, I, 20, Plng Div ASF. The decision included reduction of reserves to forty-five days and ten units of fire.

[75] (1) Diary, 25, 27 Aug, and 12 Sep 42 entries, cited n. 28(1). (2) See Concentration Task Force "A" folder, Logis File, OCMH. (3) History of the North African Task Force, Vol. IV, Sec 1, of History of the Mobilization Division, ASF, in Plng Div ASF. (4) Memo, OPD for AGF and SOS, 2 Sep 42, sub: Preparation of Units for Overseas Sv, and subsequent dirs in OPD 370.5, Sec 1.

nance supplies. At the same time the tardy station list was finally received, but by this time it was obsolete since many units were moving to concentration areas; shipments would have to be sent there and to the port. It developed, moreover, that the units were far from complete; AAF base services began to call on SOS for help. Equipment tables still had not come in. Fortunately, most units of the air contingent of the task force were scheduled to move in D plus 5 and later convoys.[76]

Field commanders were determined that American ground troops, in their first encounter with the enemy in Europe, should have the best equipment that the country could give them, and plenty of it. The 2d Armored Division was to be equipped with the new streamlined Sherman (M4) medium tank, which had a lower silhouette and greater gun elevation than the Grant M3, as well as a 360-degree traverse. The new light tanks had heavier front armor and greater speed than the older models, and an additional engine. Some of the tank destroyer units were equipped with a new 3-inch gun motor carriage (M10), which outclassed the old 75-mm. self-propelled gun generally. Some of the antiaircraft units were issued the new multiple gun mounts, combining a Bofors 40-mm. gun and two .50-caliber water-cooled machine guns on one mount. High-speed tractors were assigned as additional equipment for the 155-mm. howitzer regiments. The wheeled 105-mm. howitzer was to be replaced in armored divisions, as far as possible, by the M7 motor carriage, a full-tracked vehicle with a medium tank chassis armed with a .50-caliber machine gun as well. Some antiaircraft regiments were to receive additional 6-ton trucks as prime movers. Caliber .50 machine guns were to be installed,

as rapidly as possible, on 2½-ton and larger trucks. Certain quartermaster units were authorized additional weapons carriers. Officers and most noncoms were issued submachine guns instead of pistols. A special list of additional equipment for the two infantry divisions in the first echelon ran to eighty items, including rubber boats, waders, loud-speaker sets, outboard motors, mine detectors, hand cars, magnifying glasses, lighting plants, tractors with detachable angle dozers, "traction devices" for truck units, portable air compressors, flag kits, cotton sash cord rope (16,000 feet per division), hardware cloth, vehicle slings, black basketball shoes, and amphibious tractors. The most spectacular new item was the rocket launcher, nicknamed the "bazooka," which so impressed General Patton in perfunctory tests shortly before the force sailed that he insisted it be issued to his troops, even though there was no time for training.[77]

An impressive array of impedimenta was marshalled to minister to the comfort and health of the individual soldier. Over and above standard allowances, there were extra issues of wool blankets, wool gloves, cotton shirts, shoes, socks, and cotton drawers; troops were provided with sun and dust goggles, dust respirators, neck cloths, hip boots, bed sacks, mosquito bars, head nets, mosquito gloves, cook stoves, pioneer tool sets, water-saving and water-purifying devices, watch compasses, bicycles, refrigerators, alarm clocks, and

[76] (1) Diary, 7-8, 13-15, 23, 25-26 Sep, 2 and 3 Oct 42 entries, cited n. 28(1). (2) History of the North African Task Force, p. 4, cited n. 75(3). (3) Corresp in OPD 370.5 Task Force, Sec 1; and OPD 320.2 Task Force, Case 11.

[77] (1) See various equipment directives in OPD 370.5 Task Force. (2) Frierson, Preparations for "Torch," pp. 43-45 and App. D, OCMH. (3) Corresp in Task Force A Sup Gen folder, Plng Div ASF, Job A46-371.

stepladders. For insect control and sanitation in an underdeveloped country and in a hot climate, there were provided insect repellent (750,000 bottles), fumigation vaults, methyl bromide, and chloroform. Every soldier packed his personal belongings in two water-repellent barracks bags, one of which was to be accessible throughout the voyage. Officers were allowed 175 pounds of equipment, including musette bag, hand baggage, bedroll, and trunk locker; general officers had an additional trunk locker or wardrobe trunk. Each individual received two sets of antigas impregnated clothing, with impregnite and protective ointment, besides his gas mask. The task force also carried huge tonnages of construction and fortification equipment and materials, equipment to repair and operate docks and railroads, well-digging machinery, rolling stock, locomotives, bulldozers, tractors, cement, asphalt, gasoline and oil pipeline, storage tanks, beach and airfield landing mats, elaborate radio, radar, and telephonic equipment, and thousands of miles of wire. Troops carried with them packages of tea, rice, lump sugar, cotton cloth, and other articles for gifts or barter.[78]

This proliferation of material for a lengthening and changing list of units made it impossible to outfit the force in an orderly manner. Colonel Magruder pleaded with OPD on 19 September to halt the stream of changes and additions. At least fifty changes had been made since the 2d of the month, and six more had come in between eight and nine o'clock that morning. Could not special requests be made at one time, and should not requests for equipment still being developed be discouraged? But the task force had the bit in its teeth, and no one on the General Staff seemed inclined to rein it in.[79]

Loading was an end product. It suffered from every mistake and breakdown that occurred before troops and material reached the port, and it inherited the penalties of every prior delay, which pushed loading closer to a usually immutable sailing date. Depending more than any earlier operation on careful planning and scheduling, it was more likely than any to be a product of haste and improvisation. Loading plans were supposed to be worked out by the task force staff in close conjunction with the port officials who would have to execute them. They involved consideration of sailing schedules, troop and freight movement schedules, troop commanders' desires as to distribution of units and material among transports, tonnage and cubage computations of cargo to be loaded, detailed specifications of the cargo capacity (weight and volume) of the transports, the peculiar layout and structure of each vessel, details of the storage and loading facilities of the port, requirements for special handling. On 6 September SOS officials were pressing OPD for this basic information. OPD, for obvious reasons, was unable to give it. Convoy schedules had not yet crystallized. Units had yet to be assigned to specific convoys, to subtask forces, and to specific transports. Commanders had not yet specified which items should accompany each unit, subtask force, and echelon.[80]

During most of September, as already described, the accumulation of tonnages for which no shipping space was in prospect went steadily on. On the 18th the task force produced a detailed list of units

[78] (1) Equip dirs cited n. 77(1). (2) *Annual Report of the Army Service Forces, 1943*, Ch. I.

[79] Diary, 19 Sep 42 entry, cited n. 28(1).

[80] Memo, Somervell for Handy, 6 Sep 42, sub: Sp Opn, 18 Shipg file, I, Case 7, Plng Div ASF.

and material for the first two fast convoys and some of the material for the first slow convoy (scheduled to leave respectively on 25 October and 1 and 6 November). Then, on 28 September, General Clark made his decision to slash tonnages by 50 percent.

This decision undid much of the work already done. Supplies were waiting at the depots, but the task force staff and commanders now had to decide anew how much each unit could take. Lutes warned that every day's delay in loading arrangements after 30 September would cause a corresponding delay in the sailing date. Movement orders issued on the 29th did indicate the breakdown of the assault force into twenty-eight contingents, one for each transport, permitting the forwarding of some shipments. But unit assignments to the subtask forces ("X," "Y," and "Z," one for each area to be assaulted) were not released until 2 October, and unit commanders arriving at the port did not know them. Shipments of ammunition were also held up until publication of weapon lists on the same day. Even thereafter, movement orders, vessel assignments, and weapons lists proved no more stable than the troop and equipment lists that had preceded them. Combat team commanders were prone to shift vessel assignments after reaching port; this required reassignment of equipment, which in turn unsettled the distribution of ammunition. Every elimination or addition of a weapon also dictated modification in ammunition shipments to port. As late as 10 October the Navy was clamoring for final vessel assignments.[81]

A fundamental anomaly in the whole situation was the circumstance that the process of issuing equipment and shipping it to port was going on at the same time that necessary reductions in bulk and weight were being made. "It is a great waste of effort and equipment," Lutes pointed out to OPD, "to issue to units full T/BA [Tables of Basic Allowances] equipment, plus many increases, and then to have those units sail overseas leaving behind half their T/BA and most of the increases . . . ," especially since there was no likelihood of shipping any of the backlog during the next three months.[82] Lutes suggested that no equipment changes be permitted after 12 October for units whose matériel was to be shipped in the first three convoys, and that for later convoys changes should be cut off one month before sailing date. He also suggested that reductions at home stations and staging areas be based on a rough formula aimed at a net 50 percent cut while retaining essential items—for example, a flat 75 percent cut in vehicles that could be crated. Also, why should not every requested change in allowances involving an increase in weight and volume be accompanied by a recommendation for withdrawing an equivalent tonnage?[83]

These suggestions, for the present, went unheeded. Meanwhile, OPD continued to approve requests for new and additional equipment, shipments continued to pour into port from the depots, swelling the very piles of material that had to be reduced, change succeeded change in hundreds of equipment tables, and commanders made the necessary eliminations helter-skelter up to the moment of departure. On

---

[81] (1) Memo, Lutes for CG Task Force A, 28 Sep 42, sub: Loading of Task Force A, 18 Shipg file, I, Case 36, Plng Div ASF. (2) Memo cited n. 66(3). (3) Frierson, Preparations for "Torch," p. 92, OCMH.

[82] Memo, Lutes for OPD, 9 Oct 42, Policy file, I, 25, Plng Div ASF.

[83] (1) Ibid. (2) Memo, Lutes for OPD, 6 Oct 42, Policy file, I, 22, Plng Div ASF.

9 October, only two weeks before sailing date, Lutes wrote grimly to OPD, "No indication of a slackening in the stream of changes and additions in troops and equipment for Task Force A appears as the date of sailing of the first convoy approaches. Requests approved by your office in the past week number twenty-four."[84]

Despite all the confusion, matériel for the D-Day convoy was at least coming in. On 8 October General Lutes, perusing reports on freight movements into Hampton Roads, felt reasonably confident. "Although the Task Force staff delayed us seriously by failing to submit loading plans on time," he noted, ". . . we will get everything into port marked okay."[85] On 29 September Brig. Gen. John R. Kilpatrick, port commander at Hampton Roads, had called forward cargo for vessels of "Y" Force, comprising more than half (fifteen vessels) of the whole assault force. Loading plans still were not available and four of the transports were not even present. The port commander decided, nevertheless, to go ahead, flooring each ship with rations, gasoline, and other bottom cargo; the combat load could be built on this foundation. Most matériel, other than ammunition, rations, and gasoline, was delivered on arrival at the port to central warehouses in Newport News, forming a pool from which cargo could be drawn for each transport. Field rations and ammunition (other than the reserves loaded as bottom cargo) had to be routed directly to the piers for issue to troops and loading into vehicles. Most vehicle fuel tanks were filled (up to the prescribed 90 percent) at staging areas. Facilities in the area were divided between Army and Navy; loading at the Newport News pier was handled by the Army, loading at the

Navy pier and the Air Forces pier (both near Norfolk) by the Navy; at the Army Base pier near Norfolk the services operated jointly under the general direction of the Navy. These arrangements were all completed by 30 September. This deadline at least had been met.[86]

Loading was a scrambled operation. Freight called forward on 29 September deluged the port, much of it unidentifiable. Shipping papers arrived a day or more late and many freight cars were marked for the wrong destination within the port area or lacked a specific marking altogether. Since different railroads served different piers some errant freight cars had either to be lightered across the bay or sent many miles around by rail. At one point, crews of searchers had to comb through 690 cars standing on sidings at Richmond looking for certain items, while loading was suspended. Lack of a holding

---

[84] (1) Memo cited n. 82. (2) Memo cited n. 83(2). (3) Memo cited n. 74(3). (4) Memo, Magruder for Heileman, 12 Oct 42, Policy file, I, 20, Plng Div ASF. (5) History of the North African Task Force, Incls 29–31, cited n. 75(3). (6) Lt. Col. Frank A. Bogart (one of Lutes' staff officers) interrogated a year after the event, had no recollection of any action taken on the SOS proposals. See Frierson, Preparations for "Torch," p. 49, OCMH.

[85] (1) Handwritten note on memo, unsigned, for Dir of Distrib Div, 8 Oct 42, sub: Status of Equip Arriving at HRPOE, TORCH folder, Shipg tab, Lutes File. (2) For general treatments of the loading of Convoy UGF-1, see Frierson, Preparations for "Torch," OCMH; Harold H. Dunham, U.S. Army Transportation and the Conquest of North Africa, 1942–1943, Monograph 9. OCT HB; History of the North African Task Force, cited n. 75(3); Hist Rpt 1, HRPOE, OCT HB; Maj. William Reginald Wheeler, ed., The Road to Victory (New Haven, Conn., Yale University Press, 1946); and Comdr. Walter Karig, USNR, Lt. Earl Burton, and Lt. Stephen L. Freeland, Battle Report: The Atlantic War (New York, Rinehart and Company, Inc., 1946).

[86] (1) Hist Rpt 1, cited n. 85(2). (2) Frierson, Preparations for "Torch," pp. 92–96, 102, OCMH. (3) Ltr, Gen Kilpatrick to Rear Adm Trevor W. Leutze, 30 Sep 42, TORCH folder, Shipg tab, Lutes File.

and reconsignment point near the port was a serious handicap. An elaborate scheme of marking, devised to route ammunition to specific piers and ships, broke down. Wrote the port commander:

The ammunition that should have gone into bottom stowage did not arrive first. Then when units were changed from one ship to another, or from one group of ships to another, we had to rejuggle our ammunition. . . . A car would be marked 4948 J-1. That indicated the unit and the ship of the group, but if that particular unit or a portion of the unit had been transferred to a different ship, it left us hanging in the air.

All matériel, he thought, should have been shipped to port in bulk, "Thereby, complete cargo would be unloaded at the port, and be kept in open stock . . . and we could call upon it to load specific ships at specific times. That would mean that the task force might make last-minute changes without upsetting us in the least." [87]

Perhaps the most difficult requirement to meet in the loading period was that for final rehearsal in unloading and landing. General Lutes had warned the task force staff that the practice loading must begin no later than 1 October, in order to meet the scheduled departure date of the 20th. On 28 September he gave up hope. "A practice loading," he noted, "has ceased to be a possibility." [88] But he was wrong. Navy, port, and task force officers, meeting at Norfolk on the 30th, decided to make the attempt. Since berth capacity was insufficient to load the entire force simultaneously, Force "Y" could be partially loaded and moved down to Solomons Island for rehearsal while Force "X" and Force "Z" were loading. Then Force "Y" could return to complete its loading. Wires crossed at the outset when port loading agencies, ignorant of the

change in plan, stowed the wrong cargo in deep holds. Many corners had to be cut, at the expense of realism—ammunition was not unloaded, owing to risk of damage, and dummy cases could not be provided in time; unloading five-gallon gasoline cans was also omitted as too risky. The rehearsal amounted to an exercise in loading and unloading vehicles and other bulky items. As such, it was an efficient performance, and went off according to schedule.

Last-minute emergencies were numerous. Six transports floored with B rations by the Navy at New York had to be unloaded and reloaded at Hampton Roads. The transport *Lee*, completely loaded, developed engine trouble on the eve of departure; she was discharged, and her replacement, *Calvert*, loaded, all in the space of thirty-five hours. *Calvert* had not even had a shakedown cruise, and lacked amphibious equipment. This meant that the crew of the *Lee* had to take over, and the new transport had to be rigged with the *Lee's* equipment. Cargo had to be completely discharged from the *Lee* before it could be loaded into the *Calvert*, in order to preserve its arrangements. Another problem child of the flotilla was the ancient *Contessa*, a shallow-draft Honduras-registered fruit ship of 5,500 tons, drafted after intensive search to haul aviation gasoline and ammunition up the shallow Oued Sebou to Port-Lyautey, whose adjoining airfield was one of the initial objectives. At Hampton Roads, the *Contessa's* ailing engines broke down and her nondescript crew scattered to the winds.

[87] Hist Rpt 1, cited n. 85(2).
[88] (1) Memo cited n. 81(1). (2) Diary, 21–23 Sep 42 entries, cited n. 28(1). (3) Memo, Lutes for CG Task Force A, 22 Sep 42, sub: Loading of Task Force A, TORCH folder, Shipg tab, Lutes File.

But the engine was repaired, and a local naval brig raided to fill the ship's complement. On the 26th, three days late, *Contessa* left port without escort in pursuit of the convoy.[89]

On the morning of the 23d the assault forces bound· for Mehdia and Safi left port. At dawn the following day the Fedala force sailed, and the covering naval contingent set out from the Maine coast. Air force elements started from Bermuda on the 25th, and the entire force rendezvoused next day. All told, there were 33,700 officers and men besides Navy crews and some miscellaneous personnel. The convoy was joined at sea by the seatrain *New Jersey* (rechristened *Lakehurst* by the Navy), loaded at New York with 169 guns, vehicles, and tanks. With this addition, and including the tardy *Contessa* (containing only 738 tons of gasoline and bombs), the whole force carried 96,670 ship tons of cargo; this included 728 tanks and other tracked vehicles, 2,266 wheeled vehicles, and 254 guns.[90]

A few days before the convoy sailed, Somervell sent Eisenhower a short note:

This is just to let you know that we have been giving everything we have to outfitting your organization, both here and in England. I know that Patton feels pretty well satisfied with what we have been able to do for him here and hope your boys over there feel the same way. We have not only been making every effort to meet your demands, but also to do everything on our own hook that we could to further the gigantic undertaking that you have ahead of you.

God knows, Ike, we wish you the best of luck and outstanding success. The country needs one badly, and if anyone can give it to them I am sure you can.[91]

The Pay-Off and Its Lessons

The North African landings were attended by almost miraculous good fortune. The assault convoys successfully evaded enemy submarines, and those carrying the inside forces steamed unmolested through the Strait; deception measures had persuaded the enemy that the great movements of shipping, concentration of aircraft at Gibraltar, and other preparations were aimed at reinforcing Malta or attacking Dakar. The attack on Algiers met little resistance; at Oran the troops found the going harder, but by the 10th both areas had been secured. The only disasters in the Mediterranean were minor, resulting from attempts at both Oran and Algiers to force a way directly into the harbors against point-blank fire.[92]

In the west, the plan involved three landings—at Safi, Port-Lyautey, and Fedala (near Casablanca). Here, too, the attackers were lucky. The sea, following bad weather for two days, was calm on the morning of the 8th, the calmest, according to an elderly local Frenchman, in sixty-eight years. No enemy subs appeared. Caught by surprise, the French were slow and halfhearted in defense. Vice Adm. François Michelier, in command at Casablanca, used his naval forces skilfully, but they were overwhelmed. Little resistance was encountered on the beaches at Fedala and Safi, except from a few recalcitrant

---

[89] (1) Hist Rpt 1, cited n. 85(2). (2) Karig, Burton, and Freeland, *Battle Report: The Atlantic War*, p. 179. (3) Frierson, Preparations for "Torch," p. 94, OCMH. (4) Craven and Cate, *AAF II*, pp. 58, 75. (5) Wheeler, *Road to Victory*,·p. 78.

[90] (1) Karig, Burton, and Freeland, *Battle Report: The Atlantic War*, pp. 178ff. (2) Tonnage figures from Plng Div OCT chart, 17 Feb 43, Convoy Info NATOUSA folder, OCT HB. (3) NYPOE rpt, no date, sub: Embarkation of Task Force A, OCT HB.

[91] Ltr, Somervell to Eisenhower, 20 Oct 42, ETO (6) 1942–43 folder, Hq ASF.

[92] Eisenhower, *Crusade in Europe*, Ch. VI.

Submarines, concentrated south of the Azores to cover Dakar, mauled a homeward-bound British convoy.

THE "MARACAIBO" H.M.S. *MISOA, October 1942. This was one of the three converted shallow-draft oilers used as tank landing ships at Oran. Note bridge sections from ship to shore.*

coastal batteries; a company of Senegalese east of Fedala surrendered after firing a few rounds. At Port-Lyautey, to the north, three or four thousand Moroccan Tirailleurs, French Legionnaires, and naval troops fought resolutely, but by the 11th resistance had ended and an armistice was concluded. The invaders suffered their heaviest loss on the 11th and 12th when four transports—*Hewes, Scott, Bliss,* and *Rutledge*— were torpedoed outside Casablanca Harbor. Another transport, *Electra,* was attacked on the 15th while en route from Port-Lyautey to Casablanca; she was beached and eventually repaired. Nine tenths of the cargo of the *Hewes* went down with her, but most of the other cargoes had already been discharged or were salvaged.[93]

As a ship-to-shore operation, TORCH relied mainly on small 36-foot carriers of personnel and vehicles (LCP's and LCV's) and 50-foot tank lighters (LCM(3)'s) carried on the transports. No difficulty was anticipated or encountered in finding adequate numbers since production was in full tide by summer; substantial numbers had been delivered in the British Isles by the end of August. But many of the small craft used in TORCH were obsolescent, unstandardized, and plagued by "bugs." Exercises indicated that bow ramps were well-nigh indispensable; the

[93] (1) Rpt, Gen A. R. Wilson, 12 Dec 42, sub: Rpt on Opns in N Africa, 20 Gen file, I, 47, Plng Div ASF, Job A46-371. (2) Samuel Eliot Morison, *Operations in North African Waters: October 1942-June 1943* (Boston, Little, Brown and Company, 1950), Chs. III–VII.

SEATRAIN USS *LAKEHURST in North Africa, November 1942. This vessel, originally designed to carry whole trains on tracks, was used in the* Torch *operation to transport tanks and assault guns.*

later Higgins carriers had them, but the older Eureka model did not. Ramp-lowering mechanisms were sluggish and awkward, and despite British warnings none of the boats was armored against either frontal or cross fire. The LCV was too narrow, by an inch or two, to accommodate some of the Army's new ¾-ton trucks.[94]

The larger tank lighters (YTL's and LCT's) of one hundred feet and over did not figure prominently in plans for the assault, and only a few were actually used (none at Casablanca).[95] The new ocean-going landing vessels were not yet available. September saw the first large personnel carriers (LCI(L)'s) emerge from production; the first tank landing ships (LST's) came in October. For lack of

LST's Patton's assault plan required the early capture of Safi, a small port far south of Casablanca with a quay long enough and with sufficient draft alongside to berth the seatrain *Lakehurst* with its

[94] (1) Corresp in OCT 370.5 Mvmt BOLERO, especially rpts by Capt Warren. (2) Ltr cited n. 26(2). (3) Memo, Lutes for CofEngrs, 18 Jun 42, BOLERO 1942 folder, Lutes File. (4) Msg 2559, London to AGWAR, 22 Sep 42, TORCH Radiograms, Logis File, OCMH. (5) Msg 1491, London to AGWAR, 25 Aug 42, OCT 370.5 Mvmt BOLERO. (6) Msg, WD to USFOR, 23 Nov 42, 18 Shipg file, I, Case 85, Plng Div ASF.

[95] (1) Mowry, Landing Craft and the War Production Board, WPB Sp Study 11, p. 10. Only 2 LCT's were produced in the U.S. in June and July, 45 in August, 156 in September. (2) In July the British had about 90 of their own types in the United Kingdom. See Landing Craft tab to ltr, Hull to Eisenhower, 15 July 42, OPD 320.2 ETO, 6. (3) Corresp in OCT 370.5 Mvmt BOLERO, and OCT 560 Mvmt BOLERO.

fifty-nine tanks and assault guns. For the Oran attack, the British converted three shallow-draft oilers, designed for use on Lake Maracaibo, Venezuela; these, after being beached, discharged light tanks through doors in the bow over long bridge sections pushed out to shore. The "Maracaibos" were not quite large enough to take the old medium tanks (Grants) of the 1st Armored Division (Combat Command B) and new Shermans did not arrive in time for training; the Grants were shipped to Africa later.[96]

Amphibian vehicles and tractors, including the 2½-ton amphibian truck (DUKW) of later fame, were going into large-scale production on the eve of TORCH. In June Brig. Gen. Theodore H. Dillon, Deputy Chief of Transportation, wrote glowingly to the European theater of new trucks, ranging from ¼-ton "jeeps" up to 6-ton monsters, which could move from land to water and back to land without pause and allegedly possessed the same overland capabilities as ordinary trucks. With them, he averred, "we could take your stuff direct from shipside at Irish Sea ports overland and cross water to ROUNDUP with one operation."[97] The vehicles actually never quite measured up to this description, and in any event, large-scale production was too late for TORCH. The tracked Roebling "Alligator" (LVT, unarmored), available in larger numbers, had performed well in the Guadalcanal landings in August, but not enough were ready for the North Africa operation.[98]

The French in North Africa obligingly failed to exploit the attackers' weakness in amphibious equipment. In the west, Safi was captured at the outset, and *Lakehurst* discharged her tanks and guns in three days; by then the commodious facilities at Casablanca were available. In the Mediterranean the "Maracaibos"

were a complete success, both in the assault and later in ferrying tanks from Oran to Philippeville. Some of the large LCT's, after sailing without cargo to Gibraltar, were also used effectively in ferrying along the North African coast. Unfortunately, the mortality in small craft was startlingly high. Six hundred and twenty-nine small craft were used in the western landings; 216, or more than 34 percent, were reported lost or disabled, most of them at Fedala. Center Force lost only 45 craft out of 223, but at Algiers virtually the entire flotilla of 100 craft was wiped out. This slaughter was primarily a result of inept handling by inexperienced personnel, though darkness, a falling tide, and defective construction and equipment played their part. Compasses were universally condemned as worthless; ramp fastenings broke loose; craft broke up in moderate seas; engines were drowned by spray for lack of canopies; trucks would not load into narrow craft. Hostile machine gun fire, had it materialized, would have caused terrific casualties

---

[96] (1) Morison, *Operations in North African Waters*, pp. 137, 234, 269, and 269 n. 38. The LCI(L), or landing craft, infantry, large (as distinguished from the British 105-foot LCI(S)) was really an ocean-going vessel, 158 feet long. (2) WPB Sp Study 11, App. C, Table I, cited n. 95(1). October and November production of LCI's was 25 and 59, respectively; November production of LST's was 18. (3) Memo, unsigned, for Col Magruder, 2 Feb 43, sub: Notes on Talk by Maj Gen Lunsford E. Oliver, 20 Gen file, I, 72, Plng Div ASF, Job A46-371. (4) Msg 2678, London to AGWAR, 24 Sep 42, TORCH Radiograms, Logis File, OCMH.

[97] Ltr, Dillon to Ross, 17 Jun 42, OCT 370.5 Mvmt BOLERO.

[98] (1) Corresp in 451.94 Amphibious Vehicles folder, Plng Div ASF. (2) Memo, Gen Plans Br SOS for Lutes, 20 Aug 42, sub: Roebling Alligators, same file. (3) Plng Div SOS Diary, 31 Jul and 2 Sep 42 entries, Plng Div ASF. (4) Miller, *Guadalcanal: The First Offensive*, pp. 57, 75. (5) Production figures are from WPB and CPA, *Official Munitions Production of the United States by Months, July 1, 1940–August 31, 1945.*

among personnel in the unarmored craft.[99] The lack of amphibious vehicles was keenly felt, especially in clearing the beach. Despite light opposition at the shoreline, the advance on Casablanca was held up for hours until the clogged beaches could be partially cleared. Amphibian trucks and tractors could have moved supplies without a halt to dumps farther inland; they would have been useful, too, in pulling stranded boats back into the water.[100]

The beach phase in the western landings fortunately was brief, and the Moroccan ports were in better condition when captured than the invaders had a right to expect. Eight berths at Casablanca were turned over immediately to the Americans, three more at Safi, and one at Fedala. A week later, however, the twelve berths were still the only ones usable, out of the twenty-six counted upon, since efforts were concentrated on repairing the more extensive damage in the Center Force ports. By strenuous efforts, in little more than a week twenty-two out of the thirty berths hoped for at Oran and adjacent ports had been put to work. In the eastern area the situation was even better, with thirty-four out of thirty-seven berths usable.[101]

Unloading was a chaotic experience, particularly at Casablanca. At the Phosphate Pier on the 18th (when the second convoy arrived),

. . . it was as though some gigantic overhead scoop full of supplies had suddenly emptied its contents. Apparently nothing had been hauled away and nothing had been stacked. One box was simply dumped on top of another. On the other dock we could see boxes, crates, ammunition, and gasoline drums piled and scattered from one end to another . . . .[102]

In part, this situation was a result of the pell-mell loading of the vessels. The ships of the first two convoys had been loaded reasonably full, but haste had caused near chaos. Thousands of barracks bags were strewn helter-skelter about the transports. Grenades were found lying about loose. Much of the ammunition stowed between decks for immediate use was not of the types needed, while there was plenty of small arms ammunition deep in the hold out of reach. Organizations and individuals alike had smuggled aboard "all manner of unauthorized and excess equipment," while many important items, such as fire control instruments, had been left behind.[103] Vehicles had been used as catchalls for miscellaneous baggage.

Even more, the chaos on the docks resulted from inadequate planning for dis-

[99] (1) Hq SOS, Lessons Learned From Recent Amphibious Operations in North Africa, 12 Feb 43, App. G-1, copy in App. K of Frierson, Preparations for "Torch," OCMH. (2) Memo, Gross for Somervell, 12 Dec 42, sub: U.S. Landing Craft Losses in N Africa, OCT 370.5 Mvmt BOLERO. (3) Morison, *Operations in North African Waters*, pp. 59-61, 79-81, 201-02, 234, 268-69. (4) Rpt, pp. 8-9, cited n. 93(1). (5) Ltr, Kilpatrick to Gross, 28 Nov 42, copy in Frierson, Preparations for "Torch," App. H, OCMH. (6) Changes were made late in 1942 in 36-foot craft to accommodate trucks; the new Borg-Warner amphibious vehicle in 1943 was wide enough to hold a ¾-ton truck. See memo, Reqmts Div for ACofS Opns SOS, 1 Jan 43, sub: Gen Wilson's "Rpt of Opns in N Africa," 20 Gen file, I, 47, Plng Div ASF.

[100] (1) Rpt, pp. 8-9, cited n. 93(1). (2) Memo cited n. 99(6).

[101] (1) Morison, *Operations in North African Waters*, pp. 131, 157-59, 174. (2) Msg 5028, Eisenhower to WD, 18 Nov 42, OCT 565.3-900 England. (3) Memo cited n. 61(3). (4) Msg R-3041, Marshall to Eisenhower, 11 Nov 42, Item 9, Exec 5. (5) Diary, 14, 16, and 19 Nov 42 entries, cited n. 28(1). (6) Chronology, 11, 14, and 19 Nov 42 entries, cited n. 28(2). (7) Memo, Lt Col Charles F. Tank for CofS W Task Force, 27 Nov 42, NATOUSA Misc Info folder, OCT HB.

[102] History, 6th Port, Transportation Corps, 18 Apr 43, Vol. I, OCT HB.

[103] (1) Extracts from interview by HRPOE officer with transport captains, December 1942, copy in Frierson, Preparations for "Torch," App. H, OCMH. (2) Rpt, p. 35, cited n. 93(1). (3) Lessons Learned . . . in North Africa, cited n. 99(1).

AERIAL VIEWS OF CASABLANCA

charge operations. These normally would have been taken over soon after the landings by the task force services of supply, leaving the G-4 staff to attend to direct support of combat forces. But the assault convoy brought in neither G-4 nor SOS. Col. Walter J. Muller, the G-4, arrived with some of his staff on the second convoy; General Wilson, the SOS commander designate, with two assistants, "hitched" a ride in the assault convoy, courtesy of the Navy, and during the first few days ashore acted as observer only. In his perhaps prejudiced view, the dock congestion at Fedala and Casablanca was largely a result of the absence of "a few experts to take hold of the situation . . . no plan or provision was made for the orderly handling of anything, with resulting delay in the unloading of the ships."[104] It was not until early January that the Atlantic Base Section, under General Wilson, took over port operations. Moreover, until the arrival of the 6th Port with the second convoy there were no trained service troops to attack the congestion. Though Navy crews and some of the Army combat troops worked to the point of exhaustion, there was a general lack of drive and organization. The problem was not entirely one of lack of manpower. Transport captains later complained that Army details "wandered away and would not stick to their jobs . . . ."[105] Natives and soldiers loitered together among heaped-up crates on the pier. Groups wandered about in search of their assigned places. Truck drivers waiting in line to load up refused to pitch in and help. Natives looted happily among unguarded supplies. "Combat troops," General Wilson later admitted, "cannot be used for loading supplies unless they are properly supervised and unless they have previously done so in

maneuvers."[106] In an infantry regiment, he pointed out, there were some four hundred cooks, mechanics, clerks, and other noncombatant personnel who should normally be available to work on beaches and docks. "Fancy special service units" and administrative overhead, he thought, were not needed.[107] SOS headquarters later urged task force commanders to resist the pressure of "hobbyists" for specialized units, and to work their regular administrative personnel to the utmost, but emphasized that certain types of service troops were indispensable in an amphibious operation—especially port units and amphibian engineers.[108]

With more equipment, cargo might have been moved more rapidly and smoothly. Landing boats and towed life rafts were hardly adequate to discharge tens of thousands of tons of cargo. Amphibian vehicles would have been a godsend in the initial stage before transports could be moved up to the piers and lighters became available. Transports lacked sufficient heavy lifting gear, slings for wheeled vehicles, special bomb-lifting gear, roller-conveyors in the hold, and other items. Lack of salvage equipment delayed the removal of sunken hulks. No planking was available to pave the interlaced rail tracks on the Phosphate Pier so that trucks could drive to shipside.[109]

The tonnage slash of late September

[104] Rpt, pp. 26–27, cited n. 93(1).

[105] Hist Rpt 1, cited n. 85(2).

[106] Rpt, p. 27, cited n. 93(1).

[107] *Ibid.*, p. 26.

[108] (1) *Ibid.*, pp. 24–27. (2) Ltr cited n. 99(5). (3) Lessons Learned . . . in North Africa, Annex B, cited n. 99(1). (4) OCT memo, 18 Feb 43, sub: Opns in N Africa, copy in Frierson, Preparations for "Torch," App. L, OCMH. (5) See also, Bykofsky and Larson, Trans III, Ch. III.

[109] (1) Memo cited n. 108(4). (2) Msg 282, Eisenhower to WD, 11 Nov 42, Item 9, Exec 5. (3) Memo cited n. 101(7).

accounted for some of the deficiencies, especially the most serious one—trucks to clear away the piled-up cargo. Most of the cargo vehicles brought with the force were commandeered for troops operating forward, and local charcoal burners and horse-drawn wagons had to be used. Jeeps and ½-ton trucks, which had replaced heavier vehicles to save tonnage, proved poor substitutes. Not enough trucks, moreover, were equipped with winches—evidently because the task force staff had not requested them. The second fast convoy, arriving on the 18th, brought more trucks and other equipment and more port troops, but it also brought more cargo to be discharged while that from the first convoy still cluttered the docks. After the arrival of the all-cargo convoy on 1 December things went better; the convoy's twenty-five vessels were discharged in less than three weeks and the daily rate of discharge rose from less than 1,700 ship tons in November to 3,700 tons during December.[110]

The western landings, finally, drove home some hard lessons in packing, crating, and marking cargo. Cardboard cartons disintegrated here, as they had in maneuvers in 1941, and metal-strapped wooden crates, inexpertly and hastily packed at the depots, broke under rough handling. Neither cardboard nor wood offered much protection against theft. Hasty packing of organizational equipment by troops at home stations proved to be "uniformly bad."[111] Some material had been packed in cases too heavy to be manhandled or even lifted by available gear—artillery ammunition in 360-pound boxes, landing mat in bundles as heavy as 5,000 pounds. Color markings of the supply services were hard to discern in dark or half-light.[112]

The commanders and staffs of the U.S.

forces invading North Africa found no solution to the oldest problem of logistics—how to give the soldier the weapons, food, and protection he needed without immobilizing him. Despite slashes in tonnage, each soldier brought into the theater a small mountain of impedimenta. Into two barracks bags, bedroll, and pack, he crammed three pairs of shoes, woolen and cotton uniforms, antigas impregnated clothing, two bed sacks, blankets, underclothing, toilet articles, a raincoat, a mosquito bar, a mess kit, an entrenching tool, and whatever other articles he thought he might find useful and was willing to carry. Even though he carried only one barracks bag, little effort had been made to control its weight; some were reported to weigh as much as 180 pounds, and contained, as one observer later put it, "everything from a dozen pianos to several field safes."[113] The barracks bag, besides, was awkward, flimsy, and something less than water repellent. This forthright official wrote:

I am convinced that drastic action is now in order to rid the American Soldier of this contraption and provide him with a container which is more compact and built with a material that will take it. . . . I realize that the great American Public may not like

---

[110] (1) Bykofsky and Larson, Trans III, Ch. III. (2) Rpt, p. 30, cited n. 93(1). (3) Lessons Learned . . . in North Africa, cited n. 99(1). (4) Memo, Lutes for Somervell, 30 Jan 43, sub: Rpt of Gen Wilson . . . , 20 Gen file, I, 66, Plng Div ASF. (5) Memo cited n. 99(6). (6) Discharge rates based on rpt, sub: Opn of the 6th Port, Casablanca, in ASF Monthly Progress Report, Transportation, 30 Sep 43, Sec 3.
[111] Lessons Learned . . . in North Africa, Annex E-1, cited n. 99(1).
[112] (1) Memo cited n. 108(4). (2) Rpt, p. 33, cited n. 93(1).
By early 1943 the metal strap industry had launched an educational campaign in plants and depots to improve strapping operations.
[113] Memo, Col Ross for Col Thomas H. Ramsey, QMC, 4 Jan 43, sub: Barracks Bags, Hist Rcds OCT AFHQ NATOUSA, Vol. I, Tab AK, OCT HB.

BURDENED SOLDIERS DEBARKING *at Phosphate Pier, Casablanca.*

the idea of their sons going to war without a complete wardrobe akin to the one which Gary Cooper might have in Hollywood, but I also know he can't wrestle it around in North Africa and ever have it with him.[114]

On one occasion twenty-five railway cars were requested solely to move forward the barracks bags of a single regimental combat team.

In addition to his pack and barracks bag, the soldier carried ashore helmet, weapons, loaded cartridge belt, canteen, emergency rations, life belt, grenades, and the inevitable gas mask, perhaps the most detested single piece of equipment since the days of the Roman Legion. Obviously the soldier could not carry more than a fraction of all this into action; most of the residue was relegated to the trucks, but a substantial portion invariably was abandoned—on the beach, by the roadside, in the fields. As the war went on, more and

more items, particularly clothing, were distributed in bulk up to comparatively near the front, and there issued as needed. But in the North Africa landings, as the SOS admitted, "the individual officer and soldier was woefully overloaded." [115]

Most of the logistical difficulties of the North African landings could be traced to the confusion of indecision, late decisions, and later changes in decisions that had turned the whole process of preparation into a feat of improvisation. The consequences of hasty planning and inadequate preparation were cumulative. Behind the difficulties of unloading and supply ashore

---

[114] *Ibid.*

[115] (1) Lessons Learned . . . in North Africa, Annex C-2, cited n. 99(1). (2) Rpt, pp. 28, 39, cited n. 93(1). (3) Morison, *Operations in North African Waters,* p. 83. (4) Memo cited n. 108(4). (5) Memo cited n. 96(3). (6) Memo cited n. 110(4). (7) Col. S. L. A. Marshall, *The Soldier's Load and the Mobility of the Nation* (Washington, The Combat Forces Press, 1950)

TABLE 10—TIMETABLE FOR PREPARING A TASK FORCE: IDEAL SCHEDULE COMPARED WITH TORCH PREPARATIONS

Proposed Date	Prescribed Action	TORCH
S—360.............	Initiation of plans and procurement for special equipment and special troop units	S—90 (25 Jul 42)
S—180.............	Final decision on operation, including launching date	S—84 (31 Jul 42)ª (launching date not settled)
S—180.............	Major troop units earmarked	S—79 (5 Aug 42) a few units named
S—160.............	General outline plan	S—48 (5 Sep 42) launching date not yet settled ª
S—150.............	Completed troop basis	Changes up to last moment
S—140.............	Instructions on equipping troops and completing personnel	S—77 (7 Aug 42) first instructions
S—100.............	Convoy schedules and composition	S—26 (27 Sep 42) numerous changes later
S—90.............	Movement orders	S—24 (29 Sep 42) first orders
S—70.............	Loading plans completed	Changes up to last moment
S—60.............	Concentration completed	S—28 (25 Sep 42)
S—50.............	Equipping of troops completed	Continued to last moment
S—50 to S—40....	Maneuver or practice loading	S—10 to S—1 (13–22 Oct 42)
S—35.............	Replacement of unserviceable equipment	Continued to last moment
S—30.............	Equipment and supplies available to port	(ᵇ)
S—25............,.	Equipment and supplies to start to port	S—25 (29 Sep 42)
S—15.............	All equipment and supplies at port	(ᵇ)
S—15.............	Troops arrive in staging area	(ᵇ)
S.................	Sailing	23–25 Oct 42

ª On 8 September General Eisenhower estimated the launching date as 8 November.
ᵇ No equivalent date.

Source: Table in Hist Mat, Mediterranean Campaigns folder, Plng Div ASF.

lay the defects of loading; behind these, the defects of assembling and equipping the force; behind these, the indecision and delays in completing outline and tactical plans. At the root of all was the sudden reversal of the SLEDGEHAMMER-ROUNDUP preparations and the late decision to undertake a venture of altogether different scope. At every stage the staffs lacked that most precious commodity in war, time— time to design, produce, and deliver equipment, time to assemble and outfit shipping, time to train and equip troops, time to concentrate and load the assault convoys. They lacked time, above all, to plan and arrange in advance the innumerable interlocking details of what was to be done and when, under this or that assumption. Some idea of the gap between the TORCH timetable and what the logistical staffs regarded as a reasonable schedule—"the time actually required to do an adequate job" [116]—can be gained by comparing the TORCH experience with a theoretical timetable drawn up in 1943 by the SOS planning staff as a guide to the higher staffs in plans for future task forces. *(Table 10)*

[116] Paper by Col Patterson, no date, sub: The N African Opn, Hist Mat, Mediterranean Campaigns folder, Plng Div ASF.

"There was," General Lutes noted years later, "a sad reason for this"—neglect of logistics in the Army's schools.[117] His opinion was shared by virtually every logistical staff officer who took part in TORCH. A member of Lutes' staff observed:

Nothing taught in any of our schools prior to the war gave a true conception of the need for time in launching a major operation. A few days were generally considered sufficient to move an Army in position, to bring up the ammunition and to launch the Army into attack, but all the logistics that precede such an operation were unknown or at least not taught.[118]

Future staff officers, according to Lutes, "preferred to study strategy and tactics. . . . The hard factual studies in logistics were boresome and did not hold out the glamor comparable to playing the tactical games."[119] SOS staff officers during the preparations for TORCH found the task force staff to be "tactics-conscious almost to the exclusion of other considerations."[120] The strategic and tactical planners, ignoring logistical limitations, made decisions that had to be unmade as soon as the limitations became evident, but often too late for preparations to be unmade. General Marshall admitted that in the London discussions of July 1942, "the logistic situation had been given only cursory examination."[121] Preparations for TORCH, as a result, offered an object lesson in disorderly planning and brilliant improvisation.

Early in December, when hopes of early victory were beginning to fade, Eisenhower still believed that the risks taken had been justified. But the operations up to that time, he confessed, "have violated every recognized principle of war, are in conflict with all operational and logistical methods laid down in textbooks, and will be condemned in their entirety by all Leavenworth and War College classes for the next twenty-five years."[122] Logisticians were not inclined to quarrel with either the judgment or the confession; they merely argued that with firm decisions at the outset they could have mounted a stronger and more economical operation. On all sides, the overriding sensation was one of relief and amazement over successes which, General Patton told his troops, seemed to be a result of "the intervention of Divine Providence manifested in many ways."[123]

---

[117] Lt. Gen. LeRoy Lutes, "Supply: World War II—The Flight to Europe in 1942," *Antiaircraft Journal* (May–June 1952), p. 11.

[118] Paper cited n. 116.

[119] Article cited n. 117.

[120] Lessons Learned . . . in North Africa, cited n. 99(1).

[121] Min, 38th mtg CCS, 28 Aug 42.

[122] Ltr, Eisenhower to Handy, 7 Dec 42, Item 1, Exec 5.

[123] Rpt, p. 28, cited n. 93(1).

CHAPTER XVII

Follow-up in North Africa

The President had declared at the beginning of August that the North African undertaking was now "our principal objective, and the assembling of means to carry it out should take precedence over other operations." [1] To the U.S. military chiefs, who had accepted TORCH only with misgivings, the degree of precedence was important. Feeling strongly that the new undertaking was a diversion from the main effort against Germany, they were unwilling to allow it and the complementary British offensive westward from Egypt to inherit the entire legacy of the waning BOLERO program. At the end of July they had stipulated that fifteen air groups and enough shipping to move a division be earmarked for the Pacific. Throughout the autumn, too, the Americans resisted British pressure to continue shipments to the British Isles on a large scale without regard to balance in the forces there. They insisted, as indeed the British did also, that a cross-Channel invasion was still the final and overriding goal. For the present and through the remaining months of 1942, the American chiefs felt that their current and growing commitments in North Africa, and even more the precarious situation in the South and Southwest Pacific, made it impossible to continue to amass forces and material in the United Kingdom on the scale desired by the British. They suspected that British pressure to do so was designed to forestall diversions of U.S. forces to the Pacific. Striving to maintain a balance in commitments, Marshall and Arnold were able to hold back as a strategic reserve the fifteen air groups earmarked for the Pacific, but the additional division (the 43d) went out to the South Pacific, and various other limited measures were taken to strengthen positions all along the line from Hawaii to Australia. [2]

American reluctance to go all out in prosecuting the new Mediterranean strategy did not extend to the point of denying North African operations the shipping and other resources that were needed. It showed itself rather in a steady resistance to long-range commitments that might predetermine the specific character of the Europe-first strategy, and jeopardize American positions in the war against Japan. It was not lack of shipping but of naval power, together with administrative confusion and inefficient utilization of shipping and other resources, that primarily limited the logistical support of TORCH during the three months following the landings. From February 1943 onward, as the climax of the North African campaign

---

[1] Memo, Gen Smith for JCS, 1 Aug 42, sub: Notes for White House Conf, ABC 381 (7-25-42), 3-B, 79.

[2] (1) Msg 835, Eisenhower to Marshall, 2 Aug 42. (2) Msg 2913, Marshall to Eisenhower, 3 Aug 42. (3) Msg 873, Eisenhower to Marshall, 4 Aug 42. All in Item 9, Exec 5. (4) Matloff and Snell, *Strategic Planning: 1941-1942*, Chs. XII–XIV. (5) See above, Ch. XV.

approached, the limitations were slowly overcome. Concurrently, from September 1942 through April 1943, the flow of American troops and matériel to the British Isles languished and dwindled almost to nothing, a victim not of TORCH alone but of a strategy that spread resources more thinly than before to support both the Pacific and the European war.

Torch and the Atlantic Pool of Shipping

The divergence of British and American views emerged most concretely, perhaps, in the discussion of strategic shipping priorities early in August 1942, the Americans rejecting British-proposed priorities that placed TORCH at the top and omitted the Pacific altogether. In the final compromise, it was necessary to group in a single top priority not merely TORCH but also the Middle East, the Pacific, and shipments to the Soviet Union via the southern route—practically all the major competing claimants on shipping. TORCH was to have prior claim on shipping in the Atlantic only during the period when it was being mounted; thereafter, a separate decision would have to be made whenever the question arose.[3]

The actual assignment of shipping to the North African operations was governed less by these priorities than by the practical necessity of using the shipping readily available in the Atlantic. TORCH replaced BOLERO as the principal competitor of the Middle East for tonnage from the Anglo-American pool; the tonnage assembled or earmarked for BOLERO became, in fact, a pool from which the converging operations in North Africa and the new program of Soviet aid through the Persian Corridor drew sustenance.

Even before the advent of TORCH, plans for sending nine air combat groups (under the Arnold-Slessor-Towers Agreement of June) to help the British in the Middle East promised to take a substantial slice of shipping out of the BOLERO pool. In addition, some technicians were to be sent to U.S. missions in the Middle East. The total deployment was not large—about 30,000 men and 380,000 ship tons of cargo, spread over a period of seven months—but the length of the voyage magnified manyfold the cost in shipping removed from North Atlantic services. The shipping staffs calculated that BOLERO movements would lose almost a million ship tons. The British proposed, at the beginning of August, to assign for the purpose three fast transports—*Aquitania, Mauretania,* and *Pasteur* (the last named had carried the first increment in July)—in order to release escorts and smaller transports for TORCH. While these arrangements were being discussed, the President, worried by pessimistic reports on the Middle East situation from Col. Bonner F. Fellers, U.S. military attaché at Cairo, ordered the Joint Chiefs to examine the possibilities of further increasing U.S. air strength there. Almost simultaneously General Brereton, commanding U.S. air forces in the area, also asked for reinforcements and acceleration of the movements already planned.[4]

Reinforcements, in view of the impending needs of TORCH, seemed to be out of

---

[3] (1) Min, 36th mtg CCS, 13 Aug 42. (2) CCS 100/1, title: Gen Order for Priority of Shipg Mvmts.

Air forces for Britain and China were placed in second priority; relief of Iceland third; BOLERO ground forces fourth; India and China fifth; aid to Soviet Union via Murmansk (if decided upon) sixth.

[4] (1) See CCS 87 series and related papers in ABC 570 (2-14-42) Sec 2. (2) Craven and Cate, *AAF II,* pp. 22–24. (3) Matloff and Snell, *Strategic Planning: 1941-1942,* Ch. XIII.

the question. Acceleration was a problem of logistics, the choke-points being naval escorts and troop transports. If deployment to the Middle East were to be speeded up, the fast, roomy *Queens* were the only available transports that could sail unescorted, but to use the *Queens* would cripple the already weakened BOLERO program, which would also have to depend largely on unescorted troop movements while the North Africa operation was in progress. For each trip that the two *Queens* made around the Cape, BOLERO would lose 70,000 to 80,000 troops, enough to halt the program altogether. The Combined Chiefs of Staff decided, on 13 August, not to accelerate the Middle East movements. BOLERO had a short reprieve.[5]

Almost simultaneously with this decision, the British raised the question of a comprehensive allocation of shipping in the Atlantic area to support TORCH, the impending offensive by the Eighth Army in Egypt, and their existing services within the operating radius of Atlantic tonnage. They proposed to divide equally the troop-carrying burden of the initial TORCH movements—including the first two fast convoys from the United States and the first three from the United Kingdom—each country to contribute space for 25,-000 troops in assault shipping and for 66,000 troops in convoy-loaded shipping. In the build-up phase, approximately four months, the American contribution would average about 55,000 spaces a month, as against about 30,000 for the British. This arrangement actually placed a heavier burden upon Britain than her planned contribution of troops to the operation would warrant. *(Table 11)* The British hoped to restore 35,000 spaces to their Middle East convoys after the initial TORCH convoys returned, and to soften

the impact upon Middle East movements still further by assigning one of the *Queens* in October to make a triangular run from the States to England and thence around the Cape, carrying 10,000 British troops on the latter lap. This would keep the vessel away from the North Atlantic during November and December at least, with a further cost to BOLERO of perhaps 30,000 troops. The British proposed another triangular run for one of the *Queens* in January. All these arrangements, it was estimated, would reduce the flow of American troops to Britain from September through the following March to 100,000 or 120,-000, while permitting completion of the relief of the Iceland garrison by early September 1942.[6]

In cargo shipping the British placed their total requirements for TORCH and other military services within the range of Atlantic shipping at 230 vessels per month, which figure they hoped, through various economies, to compress to 185. About a hundred bottoms were available to meet this requirement. Ten more might be released if the northern convoys to the USSR, as expected, were suspended; perhaps another fifty might be squeezed out of the domestic import program and the Middle East military services. Elaborate schedules had been worked out to cushion the impact on these programs. Much of the shipping currently working around

---

[5] (1) CCS 87/4, rpt by CMTC, 9 Aug 42, title: Shipg Implications of Proposed Air Forces Deployment. (2) Min cited n. 3(1).

Later the U.S. Navy transport *West Point* was assigned to the Middle East.

[6] (1) Memo 359, Br Jt Stf Mis for Br CsofS, 19 Aug 42, Item 2a, Exec 5. (2) Memo, Styer for CofS, 21 Aug 42, sub: Need for Early Definition of Forces . . . , CofS WDGS. (2) 1942 folder, Hq ASF. (3) Pencil notes, 27 Aug 42, sub: Data From Col Wansbrough-Jones. (4) Paper, 27 Aug 42, sub: Implications of TORCH on Other Shipg Commitments. Last two in TORCH Jul–Sep 42 folder, OCT HB.

TABLE 11—PROPOSED DIVISION OF TROOP AND TROOP-CARRYING CONTRIBUTION IN TORCH

Item	United States		Britain	
	Shipping	Troops	Shipping	Troops
Initial movements—total..........................	91,000	96,000	91,000	86,000
From United States:				
Combat loaded............................	25,000	25,000	0	0
Convoy loaded............................	41,000	41,000	0	0
From United Kingdom:				
Combat loaded............................	0	25,000	a 25,000	0
Convoy loaded............................	b 25,000	5,000	c 66,000	86,000
Build-up (per month)—total.....................	55,000	57,500	30,000	27,500
From United States...........................	30,000	30,000	0	0
From United Kingdom........................	25,000	27,500	30,000	27,500

a To be provided in part by converting troopers, with resulting loss of 10,000 capacity from Middle East run.
b To be taken from BOLERO.
c Capacity for 10,000 from BOLERO; 56,000 from Middle East run.

Source: (1) Memo 359, Br Jt Stf Mis for Br CsofS, 19 Aug 42, Item 2a, Exec 5. (2) Memo, Styer for CofS, 21 Aug 42, sub: Need for Early Definition of Forces . . . , CofS WDGS (2) 1942 folder, Hq ASF.

the Cape, carrying military cargoes outbound and civilian imports inbound, was to be placed instead on a triangular routing to feed the forces in North Africa and bring imports from North America to the United Kingdom. Even this arrangement would mean a loss of about 325,000 tons of imports during the remainder of 1942, over and above another 300,000 tons to be lost by suspending, for lack of escorts, the trade convoys to and from Gibraltar and Freetown, and still more from anticipated sinkings in unescorted sailings elsewhere. The curtailment of the outward flow of military cargo around the Cape, moreover, could be accepted only as a temporary measure. The remaining twenty-five vessels needed would be taken, under the British proposal, from American tonnage on the BOLERO run, but the loss might be made good if the northern convoys to the Soviet Union were suspended. The Americans would also provide their own shipping for the convoys sailing directly from the States to North Africa, and to this end the British suggested that BOLERO cargo shipments be reduced to about twenty-five sailings per month, a level roughly commensurate with the anticipated flow of troops.[7]

General Eisenhower strongly endorsed the whole plan. All the personnel shipping requested, he pointed out, and much of the cargo shipping would actually be used to transport American troops and their equipment and supplies from the United Kingdom. It would be illogical, he thought, to ask the British to cut more deeply into their Middle East operations, which complemented TORCH, in order to

---

[7] Ibid.

spare BOLERO, which was in a low priority and would have to suffer anyway for lack of escorts. Nevertheless, Eisenhower's recommendation that the British proposal be met "as far as it does not conflict with our own needs" struck sparks from SOS officials in Washington, already irritable over the uncertainty of TORCH plans.[8] "Our needs," General Gross acidly observed, "have not been and are not now defined." To him it seemed that the British wanted "all available shipping in the Atlantic, mainly in the interest of the Middle East," except for the "small amount" allotted to the North Africa operation.[9]

For the present, long-term arrangements for dividing the shipping burden of TORCH were postponed. Three small troop transports and nine freighters were retained from BOLERO arrivals in British ports as a first installment on the American contribution to the early TORCH convoys. In September, cancellation of the next northern convoy (PQ-19) eased the situation somewhat (though the ships with high-priority cargo were held for weeks without being unloaded), and piecemeal cargo shipments from the United States in response to Eisenhower's emergency requests began to swell the shipping pool immediately available in Britain for TORCH. By mid-October some thirty-one American vessels in all were on hand for the first three KMS convoys. With the first sailing dates now imminent, the British again sought a definite division of shipping responsibility. Of the 140 vessels forming the first three KMS convoys, 60 were required solely for the needs of American forces sailing from Great Britain; the British requested, "on the basis of each country carrying its own cargo," that the 29 vessels they had already contributed of these 60 be made good by American allocations to British import services.[10] For each subsequent KMS convoy (about fifty cargo vessels) running at fortnightly intervals, they asked the Americans to contribute thirteen vessels. The latter contribution would be roughly equivalent to twenty-eight ships per month, as opposed to the twenty-five requested in August. Eisenhower again supported the British proposal since, as he said, "U.S. requirements from the U.K. will approximate that number of ships until the backlog is cleared up."[11] As before, Army transportation officials expressed misgivings, but the War Shipping Administration, with certain reservations regarding replacement of the first twenty-nine vessels, acquiesced in the scheme.[12]

The agreement envisaged national contributions of dry cargo shipping along the following lines:[13]

[8] Msg 1355, Eisenhower to WD, 20 Aug 42, Item 9, Exec 5.
[9] (1) Memo cited n. 6(2). (2) Memo, Maclay for Douglas, 14 Aug 42, Br Merchant Shipg Mis Misc folder, WSA Douglas File.
[10] Memo, Salter for Douglas, 21 Oct 42, Army Reqmts folder, WSA Douglas File.
[11] Msg 3587, London to AGWAR, 14 Oct 42, OCT 565.3-900 England.
[12] (1) Msg, Salter to Sir C. Hurcomb, 20 Aug 42. (2) Memo, Douglas for Gross, 26 Aug 42. Both in Br Merchant Shipg Mis Misc folder, WSA Douglas File. (3) Msg, Lee to Somervell, 29 Aug 42, OCT 370.5 England. (4) Msg cited n. 11. (5) Msg R-2000, WD to USFOR, 16 Oct 42, TORCH Radiograms, Logis File, OCMH. (6) Memo cited n. 10. (7) Memo, Douglas for Salter, 29 Oct 42, Reading File folder, WSA Douglas File. (8) See above, Ch. XVI, and below, Ch. XXI.
[13] Table compiled from: (1) memo cited n. 10; (2) memo cited n. 12(7); (3) msg cited n. 11; and (4) msg cited n. 12(5).
In the ships in initial convoys entry, U.S. figure excludes 29 ships, provided by the British, to be made up by U.S. allocations to British imports. The 109 British ships included the above 29.
Average sailings per month figures are based on 14-day intervals between KM convoys; 25-day intervals between UG convoys.
The figures on ships continuously engaged are based on a two-month turnaround for KM convoys, three-month turnaround for UG convoys, applied to average monthly sailings.

	United States	British
Ships in initial convoys		
KM	31	109
UG	34	0
Total	65	109
Build-up (four months)		
Average sailings per month		
KM	28	80
UG	54	0
Total	82	80
Ships continuously engaged		
KM	56	160
UG	162	0
Total	218	160

The actual division of effort, as the North African campaign developed, deviated somewhat from this pattern. Additional American vessels had to be added to the British convoys, additional UG convoys were squeezed into the schedule, and the growing volume of shipping retained in the theater for various reasons in effect greatly lengthened the average turnaround. On the other hand, the intervals between sailings of UG convoys proved to be longer than the planned twenty-five days, and no UG convoy sailed with its full complement of vessels. One dreaded contingency happily did not have to be met—the mounting of an emergency landing in the Tangier-Ceuta area to counter an enemy attempt to close the Strait; this would have diverted some twelve transports and twenty-two freighters. British troop carriers bore the main burden of deployment from Britain to North Africa, but a few American troopers were used for single voyages on this run. At the end of 1942, however, much of the American troop-carrying tonnage available for movements to North Africa was diverted elsewhere. The *Monticello* was

sent to the Indian Ocean, the *Hermitage* to the Southwest Pacific. Another transport, the *West Point*, originally assigned to TORCH, was put into the Middle East service even before the initial convoys sailed. The Navy also shifted back to the Pacific its combat loaders used in the TORCH assault.[14]

In all this shuffling of tonnage can be discerned an effective pooling of British and American controlled shipping. British troop transports carried most of the American forces to North Africa, and without the *Queens* BOLERO would have dwindled to nothing before the end of 1942. American transports moved some British troops to North Africa, and even more around the Cape. British cargo tonnage carried the main burden in the initial TORCH convoys and shared equally in the build-up. American cargo tonnage during the latter part of 1942 was plying regularly in various British services—the Red Sea, the Indian Ocean, the eastern Mediterranean, and the North Atlantic. Lend-lease steel bulked large in the cargo of freighters carrying U.S. Army matériel to Britain. Both BOLERO and the Murmansk convoys were closely co-ordinated joint undertakings. In the assignment of vessels, despite administration divided along national lines, national registry was a far less important consideration than size, capacity, speed, and availability, related to the task in hand. The enormous

---

[14] (1) For the planned Tangier-Ceuta operation, see CMT 30 series on provision of cargo space for special operation, in TORCH Sep–Nov 42 folder, OCT HB. (2) Corresp in same file. (3) Memo, Gross for Somervell, 5 Nov 42, sub: Cargo Ships for N Reserve Force, NATOUSA TORCH Plng folder, OCT HB. (4) Corresp in Army Reqmts folder, WSA Douglas File. (5) For assignment of Navy transports, see JCS 158 and JPS 92 series in ABC 570 (21-1-42) Sec 4, and other correspondence in same file and in OPD 570, Case 17. (6) See above, Ch. XV, and below, Chs. XIX–XXI.

advantages both partners derived from these arrangements are self-evident. Without them, to cite only one example, it would have been necessary to set aside and hold idle the large block of shipping that might have been needed, but in fact never was, for an emergency landing at Tangier. Instead, the planners could rely on being able to assemble the necessary tonnage on short notice from vessels of various national registry arriving regularly in British ports.

But because shipping and to some degree even cargo were pooled, it is virtually impossible to calculate the exact contribution of shipping each country made to the North African undertaking. It seems clear, however, that Britain's share of the burden was heavier, in relation to her capacity to shoulder it, than was that of the United States. The American outlay, to be sure, was larger, but Britain's contribution was taken from a shrinking merchant marine and from services that kept alive her forces already overseas and her war economy at home. These services had already been sweated down and their efficiency tightened to a point that left relatively little margin for further economies. American merchant shipping, by contrast, was an expanding asset, with construction marching well ahead of losses, and small amounts of fatty tissue were still left in some of the commercial trades. In the belief of American shipping officials, there was even more fat in some of the military maintenance services—the Caribbean, Hawaii, and Alaska, for example—and vast potential economies to be gained by pooling military and lend-lease cargo. Only one American military program—BOLERO—was seriously curtailed by the diversion of shipping and escorts to the North African convoys. The

Murmansk convoys also were temporarily suspended, primarily because of the demands of TORCH for naval escorts. The support of operations in the Pacific and the Far East and the flow of shipments to the Persian Gulf actually profited in the redistribution of shipping attendant upon postponement of the great offensive against Germany.

In the last analysis, it was Britain's absolute dependence upon shipping to maintain her very existence that spelled the fundamental difference between her contribution and that of the United States to the North African undertaking. By late 1942 the inroads upon Britain's domestic economy caused by the dwindling of her imports had become so serious, in the view of high American as well as British officials, as to dictate a comprehensive long-term redistribution of combined shipping resources in order to keep the flow of imports from falling below the danger level. This settlement was being negotiated in Washington even as the first convoys were standing off the North African coast, although its effects did not begin to be felt for another four months.[15]

Administrative Arrangements for Support of Torch

The forces in North Africa could be supplied only as rapidly and abundantly as convoy restrictions permitted. Those restrictions set fixed limits to the amounts that could be shipped directly to the theater from each of the two sources of supply, the United States and Great Britain. The division of transport capacity between the two sources, moreover, was distinctly uneven, since 45-ship convoys

---

[15] See below, Chs. XXV–XXVI.

sailing every two weeks from the United Kingdom could move considerably more cargo than 45-ship convoys at 25-day intervals from the United States.

In the War Department it was generally assumed until the second week in September that maintenance responsibility for the forces in North Africa would be divided roughly along these lines for some time to come—Patton's force to be supported from the United States, the American components of the inside task forces from the stocks accumulated in Britain. Then came Message 1949, indicating that the theater supply organization could lay hands on only about two to three weeks of supply for the forces there. Startled, SOS cabled an inquiry: Was the "floating depot" only a first installment? On the 23d the theater replied. The inside forces would have to be sustained from the States beginning with the second cargo convoy (UGS-3) arriving at Oran about D plus 46. "1949" shipments would cover the bulk of maintenance requirements for the first month and a half, and some of these, as already noted, were to be shipped in UGS-2. In effect, maintenance from the United States had already started.[16]

The mathematics of this arrangement were baffling. No one knew at this point precisely how many troops would have to be sustained one and a half months after the landings, when the United States was to assume formal responsibility. According to the schedule for U.S. convoys, about 97,000 troops of the Western Task Force would be in the theater by D plus 40, and about 160,000 by the end of the third month. Schedules for the inside forces trailed off into question marks at the end of the first six weeks; General Larkin estimated that American troops in those forces would then total about 114,000,

with no further augmentation definitely anticipated for the following six weeks at least. The total strength, British and American, of the Center and Eastern Forces was expected to be 267,000. It appeared therefore that the small, widely spaced American convoys were to be called on to support a growing troop population, starting at 200,000 or more on D plus 40, while the larger, more frequent U.K. convoys were to support only a fixed strength of 150,000—that is, only three quarters as many troops with twice as many ships.[17]

Vehicles presented a special problem. The cut in tonnage for the inside forces, like that for Patton's force, was mainly in vehicles, of which a large backlog was to be left in Britain. These vehicles, being on wheels, made bulky cargo; there was an additional backlog of some three months' supply of cased replacement vehicles. Under convoy restrictions the flow of vehicles from the United Kingdom to North Africa after the assault would be slow in relation to the troop build-up; the backlog was expected to mount at the rate of ten thousand vehicles a month for the Center Force alone. The situation was not without irony. In Britain there was a plethora of vehicles, but very little other cargo at

---

[16] (1) See above, Ch. XVI. (2) Msg R-829, WD to USFOR, 16 Sep 42, with atchd memo for rcd, Policy file, I, 15, Plng Div ASF, Job A46-183. (3) Msg 2605, London to AGWAR, 23 Sep 42. (4) Msg 2816, London to AGWAR, 27 Sep 42. Last two in TORCH Radiograms, Logis File, OCMH. (5) British forces would be supplied from their own sources; the SOS settled this point when Clark and Larkin were in Washington a few days later. See memo, Magruder for Larkin, 25 Sep 42, Policy file, I, 16, Plng Div ASF, Job A46-183.

[17] (1) See above, Ch. XVI. (2) Msg R-1702, WD to USFOR, 8 Oct 42, TORCH Radiograms, Logis File, OCMH. (3) Memo, Lutes for Clark, 28 Sep 42, sub: Maintenance of U.S. Trs in Center and E Task Forces, 18 Shipg file, I, Case 35, Plng Div ASF.

hand; the vehicles, being "balloon" cargo, had to be shipped largely as topping to other cargo, even though the latter was hard to find. Hence the difficulty, for example, of working the "1949" shipments into the convoys sailing from the United Kingdom—"each time a U.S.-loaded ship replaces a U.K.-loaded ship in a KMS convoy, the number of motor vehicles in the convoy is reduced." [18] Hence also, the necessity of partially discharging some of the vessels from the States in order to fill out the loads of other vessels carrying vehicles. Even though swamped with vehicles, Eisenhower was forced, because of restrictions on the KMS convoys, to look to convoys from the States to sustain the flow of replacement vehicles to the inside forces. Replacement vehicles would arrive in North Africa, in fact, before some of the vehicles they were intended to replace. The staff in the United Kingdom, unable to determine in advance how many of which types of vehicles would be shipped in each KMS convoy, made the arbitrary assumption, as a basis for replacement shipments from the States, that all troop units in North Africa were to have received full initial equipment within a month and a half after D Day—even though at least three months would elapse before all of it could arrive on the scheduled convoys. This was one of the minor paradoxes of the logistics of TORCH. [19]

General Patton's staff was slow to recognize the implications of its own backlog problems. Shortly before the departure of UGF-1, the staff was still busily requesting increases in initial allowances, and wanted in addition to earmark a large reserve of fourteen thousand tanks, half-tracks, and wheeled vehicles to be shipped later as replacements. But space limitations bore equally upon equipment shipped as re-

placements and equipment shipped as delayed initial allowances; even at the standard rate of replacement, it would take seven months to ship the initial equipment left behind by the assault forces. The staff was persuaded to give up its earmarked reserve. It was necessary also to explain to the staff, which wanted a full ninety days of maintenance supplies with troops in each fast convoy, that there would be room for little more than fifteen days of supply if half the limited space in the fast convoys were given to organizational equipment; more supplies would mean less equipment. On cargo convoys, arriving about five days after each troop convoy, would be loaded 50 percent or more of the organizational equipment of the troops in the preceding fast convoy, and a month's supply of material of all kinds for the entire American troop population in the theater. A month's supply every twenty-five days would build up reserve stocks, but very slowly, toward the prescribed forty-five day level. [20]

Coal presented a special problem. The War Department had some hopes that all American forces might be supplied from the ample resources in the British Isles, but late in September Eisenhower reported that the British would be unable to export any coal to North Africa and expected the United States to assume the burden. The

[18] Msg 2924, USFOR to AGWAR, 30 Sep 42, TORCH Radiograms, Logis File, OCMH.

[19] (1) Msg R-1252, WD to USFOR, 26 Sep 42, Item 9, Exec 5. (2) Msg 2897, USFOR to AGWAR, 29 Sep 42, TORCH Radiograms, Logis File, OCMH. (3) Msg cited n. 11. (4) Memo, Gross for Somervell, 3 Oct 42, sub: Cargo for Sp Shipt, NATOUSA TORCH Plng folder, OCT HB.

[20] (1) Corresp in OPD 400 Task Force, 44. (2) Min of conf, Magruder and task force reps, 20 Oct 42, Policy file, I, 31, Plng Div ASF. (3) Memo, DCofS Opn, SOS for Chiefs of Svs, 29 Oct 42, sub: Maintenance of U.S. Army Forces Engaged in Sp Opn, Hist Mat Mediterranean Campaigns folder, Plng Div ASF.

pinch, as usual, was primarily in convoyed shipping, though in Britain shortages of labor and machinery also curtailed supply. Every collier added to a convoy meant one less freighter; if shipped in freighters, coal squeezed out other cargo and had to be packed in bags, which were also in short supply. General Clark's visit to Washington resulted in an agreement that only enough coal would be shipped at the outset to operate railroads and a few other facilities near the ports; shipments from the United States would be for the Western Force only, amounting to about 7,000 tons (in bags) in each slow convoy. Under this formula (despite further requests from the theater on behalf of the inside forces) coal shipments began in UGS-2, with about five thousand long tons for the Western Force. Convoys from Great Britain moved considerably larger tonnages for the inside forces. Civilian needs posed a much greater problem, which was postponed for later consideration.[21]

As far as possible, the Western Task Force staff was relieved of administrative responsibility in maintaining the flow of supply. Over the passenger composition of troop convoys, of course, the SOS exercised no control. The troop commander in each convoy could requisition on the port for whatever he desired, within space limits; the port overseas supply officer tried merely to see to it that space limitations were fully understood. But the thirty days of maintenance that each cargo convoy normally carried was set up by the supply services near the ports, to be called forward and loaded automatically by the port without requisitions from the task force; "that thirty days," Colonel Magruder told the staff before their departure, "is not your business."[22] Equipment left behind by the troops reverted to the sup-

ply services, to be worked into later convoys whenever space became available. The task force staff was asked to leave a general priority list to govern shipments, and was warned that "hurry up" requisitions for this or that item would only cause confusion without creating additional space. For urgent special needs, radiograms could be sent directly to SOS headquarters; other correspondence went to the responsible port, New York. G-4 status reports were to be sent back to the War Department on each returning slow convoy, instead of at the usual three-month intervals. Until the prescribed reserve level of forty-five days was reached, supply of the Western Force was thus to be largely automatic. The SOS hoped thereby to ride out the period of emergency supply when routine procedures inevitably went by the board. One of the final requests to the task force staff was to "have an officer of some ability review all supply radios so as to avoid duplication and confusion."[23] The SOS wanted no repetition of the nightmare of Message 1949.

During October the general administrative pattern for supporting all the forces in North Africa began to emerge. Eisenhower evidently hoped that after the initial phase of operations supply could be pooled at the source, enabling him to draw at will upon either British or American

---

[21] (1) Msg 2870, London to AGWAR, 26 Sep 42. (2) Msg 3240, London to AGWAR, 7 Oct 42. (3) Msg 3333, London to AGWAR, 9 Oct 42. All in TORCH Radiograms, Logis File, OCMH. (4) Msg 2735, London to AGWAR, 26 Sep 42, Item 9, Exec 5. (5) Msg cited n. 17(2). (6) Other msgs in same files. (7) Diary of a Certain Plan, 28 Sep, 8 Oct 42 entries, and *passim;* Plng Div ASF. (8) Risch, *Fuels for Global Conflict,* Ch. VIII. (9) For civilian supply arrangements, see below, Ch. XVIII. (10) For coal shipments, see Table 14.

[22] Min cited n. 20(2).

[23] Memo cited n. 20(3).

sources, and to use British or American shipping, regardless of the nationality of the forces to be supplied. "Only by some such system of co-ordination can full economy be secured in long and short range production, in shipping and in the provision of the immediate needs of the operations." [24] But a committee assigned by the Combined Chiefs of Staff to study the problem carefully steered clear of any pooling arrangement beyond those already in effect for shipping and assignment of finished munitions. Eisenhower was assured that Washington and London would keep alternative sources of supply "under constant review" and co-ordinate the employment of shipping. In the theater the Allied commander could build up common stockpiles and distribute matériel among his forces "as the urgency of the situation demands." But supply and requisitioning channels were to be kept distinct, and any interchange between sources of supply would be confined to "special cases" "as determined by both countries." [25] As one draft of the official communication to Eisenhower put it, "you need not concern yourself with the actual source of supply." [26]

The theater's proposed supply plan, completed late in October, accordingly drew clear lines separating the administration and supply of national forces, with the exception that the small American contingent with the Eastern Force was to draw its supply for the present through the British First Army. Two features of the plan immediately became a subject of controversy. Requisitions for the U.S. Western and Center Forces were to be routed to London, there screened by the theater SOS, and then forwarded to Washington. Reserves in North Africa were to

be built up as rapidly as possible to ninety days of supply and twelve units of fire, and an additional sixty days of supply and three units of fire were to be established in the United Kingdom for American forces in North Africa. [27]

These provisions were aimed at the difficulties arising from distance, double lines and sources of supply, and the unbalanced distribution of shipping resulting from convoy restrictions. It seemed likely that the forces in North Africa could be served for some time more directly and continuously from the United Kingdom than from the States. Communications (by radio, air, and sea) to the north would be shorter and simpler than those to the west; emergency needs could be met more promptly in London than in Washington. Barring a change in the U.S. Navy's escort policy, the convoys from Britain would continue to provide the largest supply pipeline into the new theater. The proposed stockpile in Great Britain would provide balanced cargo to utilize this capacity fully, and flexibility in meeting unexpected needs. Admittedly, these arrangements would involve wasteful double handling and double hauling, and would commit large stocks of American supplies to the British Isles, a theater that at the moment had an uncertain future in Allied strategy. When

---

[24] Msg NAF 6, Eisenhower to CCS, 9 Oct 42, ABC 381 (7-25-42) Sec 2.
[25] CCS 103/10, 19 Oct 42, title: Method of Sup—Sp Opn, Incl B.
[26] (1) CPS 48, 15 Oct 42, title: Sup Dir to Comdr ETO. (2) See related corresp in ABC 381 (7-25-42) Sec 2. (3) See also, memo, OPD for SOS and AAF 22 Oct 42, sub: Sup of Trs of Sp Opn, OPD 400 Task Force. (4) See above, Ch. XI.
[27] (1) Msg 4132, London to AGWAR, 27 Oct 42, Policy file, I, 29, Plng Div ASF. (2) Msg R-2095, WD to USFOR, 18 Oct 42, Policy file, I, 34, Plng Div ASF.

conditions became more stable, it was expected that American forces would be supplied entirely and directly from the States. As for the high level of reserves proposed for North Africa, the theater submitted it as a goal without a time limit.[28]

The plan, in short, was interim not final. Precisely for this reason, it was disliked in Washington, where Somervell and his staff wanted to place supply to the new theater on a routine basis as soon as possible. To send requisitions to be screened in London, they thought, was merely a device "to keep the SOS ETO busy."[29] Efficient supply demanded direct and simple channels of communication and a direct flow of shipments. Why could not Eisenhower give his task force commanders appropriate instructions as to priorities, and allow them to requisition directly on the New York port? The separate TORCH reserve, finally, was anathema. General Lutes declared it would result in

. . . a confused and confounded supply system. We would find TORCH supplied with subsistence sold to the British through Lend Lease. Also, procurement of other supplies for TORCH would be made in the U.K. when such supplies were readily obtainable from the U.S. Moreover, it would be uneconomical to unload, distribute to warehouses, store and then reship to Africa.[30]

Somervell tried to persuade the theater to draw upon the British for part of the needs of the Center Force, and to accept a very limited reserve stock for TORCH in the United Kingdom, sufficient to utilize space in the KMS convoys. But Eisenhower decided in mid-November that his TORCH reserve in the United Kingdom must be sufficiently large and balanced to meet emergency needs of all his American forces. He demanded with some asperity that his desires be met.[31]

In substance they were met. After further acrimonious correspondence, a provisional arrangement was made early in December to govern the flow of supply until the full burden could be shifted to the United States. This provided in the British Isles a month's reserve for American forces in North Africa (based on actual, not future strength) consisting of subsistence, clothing, and other expendable supplies, packaged lubricants, organizational equipment, and two units of fire. Patton's force was to send its requisitions to and be supported directly by the New York port. The American contingent in the Eastern Force would be fed by convoys from the United Kingdom, drawing upon American supplies there. Center Force would be supplied from the United States up to the capacity of the UGS convoys, which would have to be supplemented by an estimated five shiploads a month from the TORCH reserve in Great Britain. Any TORCH shipments sent from the States to the United Kingdom were to join KMS convoys without unloading. Center Force requisitions would be sent through Allied headquarters to the European theater headquarters in London, which in turn would requisition on New York for what could not be provided in the United Kingdom. The simpler and more direct procedures desired by SOS had to await the general stabilization of logistical arrange-

---

[28] (1) Msg 4404, London to AGWAR, 2 Nov 42. (2) Msg 5020, London to AGWAR, 18 Nov 42. Both in TORCH Radiograms, Logis File, OCMH.

[29] Pencil notation on msg cited n. 27(1).

[30] Ltr, Lutes to Goodman, 20 Mar 42, Misc Notes, Lutes File.

[31] (1) Corresp, 30 Oct–4 Nov 42, in Policy file, I, 34, 38, 41, and 42. (2) Msg cited n. 28(2).

ments, which began the following February.[32]

The Convoy Bottleneck

It was abundantly clear, long before the assault convoys sailed, that the Navy's current convoy restrictions, rather than port or overland transport capacity in the theater, would govern the rate of build-up and maintenance in North Africa. Even the limitations upon accommodations in North African ports, as revealed in September, did not alter this fact since only more frequent convoys were needed to fill berths and anchorages as rapidly as vessels could be discharged. Studies made by the SOS staff in September and October (Table 12) indicated that the theater would be able to absorb through its western ports and to move across the Atlas Mountains enough cargo to sustain about 440,000 troops—far more than the 250,000 that might be supported by UGS convoys running at twenty-five-day intervals to Moroccan harbors, which could accommodate only twenty-seven to twenty-eight vessels at a time. If the Strait were kept open and the Oran-area ports should thus be available to receive the residue of the forty-five-ship UGS convoys that could not be accommodated in the west, enough cargo could be brought into the two groups of ports to support about 400,000 U.S. troops. But this number was far less than the intake capacity of those ports; those in the Oran area alone were estimated to have facilities to discharge seventy-five cargo ships a month, enough to support almost 600,000 troops. These calculations lay behind the strenuous efforts made by the SOS in September and October to persuade the Navy to escort larger or more frequent convoys.[33]

The experience of the first few weeks following the assault bore out these expectations. Despite the chaos on the docks of Casablanca, all but two ships with partial loads of less than two thousand tons were discharged by the time the first slow convoy arrived on 1 December. Thereafter, as order was restored and more men and trucks arrived, efficiency improved, and cargo moved more rapidly. In most cases, docks were cleared two days or more before the arrival of incoming convoys.[34] It was not inadequate port capacity, either in the west or inside the Mediterranean, but lack of rolling stock, locomotives, and motor transport, and the mire of Algerian and Tunisian roads near the front that were primarily responsible for the bog-down in Tunisia in December. True, the capacity of the ports to handle continuously the tonnages needed for large-scale operations had not yet been tested, and the deficiencies of eastern Algerian and Tunisian roads and railroads revealed in December were an ill omen for the future. (See Map 4.) In the back of all the planners' minds, moreover, lurked a grim picture of the logistical feats that would be demanded if the enemy should cut the passage of the Strait; the studies in September and October, addressed to this unpleasant possibility, had arrived at the indicated capacities for overland movement only on the assumption of heroic efforts, myriad transport equipment and personnel, and no enemy interference with

[32] (1) Memo, Maj Gen Walter Bedell Smith for TAG, 4 Dec 42, sub: Sup Plan for U.S. Forces in TORCH, copy in Frierson, Preparations for "Torch," App. F, OCMH. (2) Diary, 4 Dec 42 entry, cited n. 21(7).

[33] (1) Ibid. (2) See above, Ch. XVI.

[34] (1) Msg, Patton to WD, 3 Dec 42, OCT 563.51-565.3 Africa 1941–42. (2) Msg R–4249, WD to Algiers, 12 Dec 42, OCT 565.3-900 England. (3) Other corresp in same files. (4) See Table 13.

TABLE 12—ESTIMATED CAPACITY TO SUPPORT FORCES IN NORTH AFRICA THROUGH MOROCCO: SEPTEMBER–OCTOBER 1942 [a]

ESTIMATED INTAKE CAPACITY OF PORTS

Port	Total Troops Supported [b]	Total Ship Tons Discharged Monthly [c]	Ships Discharged Per Month			Accommodations for Military Shipping
			Total	At Berth	By Lighter	
All ports [d]	443,000	616,000	56	44	12	16
Casablanca		495,000	45	36	9	12
Safi		99,000	9	6	3	2
Fedala		[e] 22,000	[f] 2	[f] 2	0	2

ESTIMATED CAPACITY FOR OVERLAND SUPPLY—CASABLANCA TO ORAN [g]

Type of Transportation	Troops Supported [h]	Capacity in Short Tons	
		Per month	Per day
Total capacity	350,000	228,000	7,600
By rail, with existing equipment (5 trains daily)	69,000	45,000	1,500
By road, using 8,000 2½-ton trucks and trailers [i]	281,000	183,000	6,100
Additional overland capacity needed to equal port intake capacity (443,000 troops) [j]	93,000	60,000	2,000

[a] For different approaches to the same problem, and divergent estimates, see tables 8 and 22.
[b] Estimated at 1.4 ship tons per man per month.
[c] Estimated at 11,000 ship tons per vessel.
[d] The smaller ports—Rabat-Salé, Mazagan, Port-Lyautey, Agadir, and Mogador—had only shallow anchorages and no berths.
[e] Estimated sufficient to meet requirements of entire force in petroleum products.
[f] Small tankers.
[g] Since these studies were concerned primarily with the hypothesis that the Strait might be closed by the enemy, the question of overland capacity beyond Oran was not examined, but note that it is here assumed that all troops would be east of the Atlas Mountains. For studies based on the contrary assumption, see table 22.
[h] At .65 short tons per man per month (1.4 ship tons).
[i] This would require approximately 14 reinforced truck regiments.
[j] This would require running about 7 additional trains daily, for which additional railroad equipment would have to be imported.

Source: (1) Memo, Plng Div OCT for Gen Wilson, 12 Sep 42, sub: Size of Force Capable of Being Supplied Through Atlantic Ports . . . , and (2) Memo, Plng Div OCT for Strategic Logis Div SOS, 25 Sep 42, sub: Port Personnel Reqmts for Sp Opns, both in Torch Jul–Sep 42 folder, OCT HB; (3) Rpt by Strategic Logis Div SOS, 16 Oct 42, sub: Logis Implications of Opns of Sp Task Force, and (4) Rpt by Strategic Logis Div SOS, 5 Oct 42, sub: Ability for Sustained Supply of Special Operation and Operations in the Southwest Pacific, both in Plng Div ASF files.

movements over the long rail-and-road defile from Casablanca to Oran. But in November, immediately after the landings, hopes ran high, and planners bandied about target strength figures (for American forces in North Africa) of 500,000, 600,000, and higher. The implied assumption, in short, was that convoy restrictions sooner or later would have to be lifted.[35]

The convoys from the United States to Casablanca (most of them sailing from New York) were scheduled in pairs—one fast and one slow—departing about the same time. *(See Table 13.)* With few exceptions, the launching of each provided its own variation on the themes of haste and waste, though not on the epic scale of the assault convoys, and the process did not become reasonably orderly until the following spring. One basic cause of this persistent administrative confusion was the circumstance that the loading of each cargo convoy was whipsawed by every change in the troop composition of its parent troop convoy. Particularly in the UG-3 and UG-4 convoys, which sailed early in December and January, respectively, the theater's late requests for reassignment to Center Force of troop spaces earlier assigned to Patton's forces met fierce resistance from the latter's headquarters, resulting in a chain of piecemeal changes in the convoy's troop lists that threw the whole outloading process into a turmoil. At least nine major changes were made in the UGF-4 troop list during December, creating chaos in equipment shortage lists and in the routing of shipments. A multitude of minor items that ordinarily would have been supplied at home stations had to be sent from depots directly to port.

Changes which deleted units at a late date resulted in maintenance supplies being shipped which were not required. Changes which added units resulted in a complete recheck of maintenance being furnished to insure that sufficient equipment was en route. Many last-minute shipments were required.[36]

One late substitution replaced three tank destroyer battalions, conveniently located near the east coast and ready to move, by three others only half equipped, which had to be called up from a camp in Texas.[37]

The loading of the cargo convoys was further disrupted by late urgent requests for changes in their cargoes. Special shipments of salvage equipment were called for to clear the cluttered harbors, signal equipment to meet a crisis in communications. One request at the end of December for twenty thousand ship tons of Ordnance matériel to replace losses in the 1st Armored Division made it necessary to displace all but about 30 percent of the organizational equipment of Center Force troops sailing in UGF-4. A few days later came further requests for a total of 241 medium tanks to replace old-model tanks in the British 6th Armored Division; these squeezed out most of the remaining organizational equipment, and two fast freighters had to be taken from the Western Task Force allotment in the convoy to move the matériel over to Center ports. Field commanders needed 75-mm. self-propelled guns immediately to replace the 37-mm. antitank weapons, which had failed to stop new German tanks, and almost a hundred were set up for UGS-4. The Air Forces reversed a decision of weeks earlier not to

---

[35] (1) Eisenhower, *Crusade in Europe*, p. 124. (2) Memo, Gen Handy for SW, 10 Nov 42, sub: Trs in NW Africa, Item 2a, Exec 5. (3) Rpt by Strategic Logis Div SOS, 16 Oct 42, sub: Logis Implications of Opns of Sp Task Force, p. 1. (4) Rpt by Strategic Logis Div SOS, 10 Nov 42, sub: Jt Pool of Mil Sups (Sp Opn), p. 10. Last two in Plng Div ASF.
[36] Memo, Lutes for Styer, 9 Jan 43, Misc Notes, Lutes File.
[37] (1) Corresp in TORCH Radiograms, Logis File, OCMH; Item 9, Exec 5; and 18 Shipg file, I, Plng Div ASF. (2) Diary, Nov–Dec 42 entries, cited n. 21(7). (3) Chronology of a Certain Plan, Nov–Dec 42 entries, Plng Div ASF. (4) Summary Convoy UG-3 and UG-4 in History, 6th Port, Transportation Corps, 18 Apr 43, Vol. I, OCT HB. (5) See Table 13.

send aviation gasoline; at least there was no difficulty in accommodating the additional tanker, since by this time it was fairly certain that neither UG-4 convoy would have its full complement of vessels, because of late changes. On 1 January an eleventh-hour message unexpectedly canceled the huge tank order; the next day the order was restored.[38]

This train of confusion took its toll, and bad luck exacted an additional price. The two UG-3 convoys were delayed five days by successive changes in vessel assignments, engine trouble, and the late arrival of three transports, and this delay retarded the whole subsequent convoy schedule. The Navy expelled two vessels from UGS-3 because they could not muster the prescribed ten-knot speed; another vessel was damaged in collision, another fouled her anchor, another developed engine trouble. In all five ships had to turn back. A few days after sailing came news that storms had scattered part of the convoy. Two more vessels, finally, were lost within sight of their goal—one aground a few hundred yards from Casablanca Harbor, the other blown up nine miles from Oran. UGF-3 had better luck, but one transport, the *George Goethals*, with 2,000 troops aboard, broke down only 150 miles out of New York. "They say," later wrote an OPD officer, "the Captain never saw the vessel until 24 hours before it sailed and he took it out under written protest that it was not seaworthy."[39]

In the UG-4 convoys, the backing and filling over tanks and other changes forced port officials to request successive postponements, and resulted in a sloppy job of stowage that later drew complaints from the theater. Before the convoy sailed, General Lutes protested that SOS could not be held responsible "if this piecemeal system

of orders and changes of orders continues. It is realized that General Eisenhower is engaged with the enemy . . . , but there is a limit beyond which this headquarters cannot be helpful."[40] Early in January bad weather held up lightering in New York Harbor, and the convoys, with many ships only partially loaded, did not get away until 13–14 January—eight days late. Three vessels had to be left behind, two of them stuck in the mud. Four of the ships that sailed were lost, three of them victims of enemy submarines.[41]

The confusion of November, December, and January in connection with the outloading of the follow-up convoys represented to some degree a breakdown of the administrative mechanism OPD had set up to control this logistical operation. Following the departure of most of Patton's staff late in October, a rear echelon was installed in the Munitions Building near the OPD offices to look after Western Task Force interests. OPD itself kept one or two officers in New York to supervise the loading of troops and equipment, and from November on one of these officers was designated to represent Center Force. OPD also imposed direct and close surveillance upon the whole movement of troops and matériel to the theater, seeking to coordinate the competing demands of the task forces according to the policies of the theater commander, as OPD understood

---

[38] Diary, Nov–Dec 42 and Jan 43 entries, cited n. 21(7).

[39] Memo, Brig Gen Carl A. Russell for Gen Handy, 6 Jan 43, sub: Delay of Sailing Date for UGF-4 and UGS-4, Item 2, Exec 5.

[40] Memo cited n. 36.

[41] (1) Diary, Dec 42, Jan, and 2 Feb 43 entries, cited n. 21(7). (2) Chronology, Dec 42, Jan, and 2 Feb 43 entries, cited n. 37(3). (3) Corresp in OPD 045.43 Convoys Naval. (4) Memo, Hull for Styer, 30 Jan 43, 18 Shipg file, II, Plng Div ASF. (5) Corresp *re* UG-3 and UG-4 in 18 Shipg file, I and II, Plng Div ASF.

them, and within the limits of available means.[42]

This direct supervision raised jurisdictional problems. Some of the orders of the OPD representatives at the port changing priorities and vessel assignments conflicted with port officials' understanding of the theater's desires. SOS challenged one order to set aside three shiploads of food for the civilian population, since "the only known authority for [them] is a statement in a speech by the President," and in the end OPD reversed the order.[43] OPD also clashed with the Transportation Corps when the latter argued that certain orders contravened CCS shipping assignments; SOS took the position, on behalf of Transportation, that in such cases the latter could accept only "minor" not "major" revisions of troop movements—unless, of course, OPD could establish its right "to modify CCS directives."[44] So large an issue was not really involved, although the practical problems of implementing JCS and CCS directives had to be worked out later in a different context. The episode was merely a by-product of more or less improvised administrative arrangements and the friction usually produced in times of stress by the appearance, in the flesh, of supervisors from a higher echelon with whom the people on the operating level normally deal only by correspondence. Port officials became nervous—as one observer noted, "they spend more time looking over their shoulder than in looking ahead."[45] Late in December, after Patton's rear echelon had departed, supervision of the UG-4 outloading was assigned to a small staff from the 4th Motorized Division (then scheduled for early sailing). The senior officer, Brig. Gen. Fay B. Prickett, arrived late, when the confusion at the port was at its height, but after living through that ex-

perience he felt his presence had been beneficial. He also echoed the complaints of SOS officials regarding "the present hit or miss loading system with its consequent loss of time and cargo space," which had its roots, he pointed out, in unsettled loading plans and repeated changes.[46]

Widening the Bottleneck

With the arrival of UGS-4 in North African ports early in February 1943, the convoys from the United States had transported some 1,254,000 ship tons of dry cargo to the theater. This was roughly 363,000 less than earlier estimates of the amounts that should have been moved by slow convoys alone in that time. Successive delays in sailings had lengthened the planned twenty-five-day convoy cycle to one nearer thirty days. Ships had dropped out of convoy and a few had been lost; many ships had sailed not fully loaded. Unanticipated demands, moreover—signal and salvage equipment, tanks for British forces, supplies for the civilian population, arms for French troops—had crowded out organizational equipment and maintenance for U.S. forces.[47]

---

[42] Corresp in OPD 370.5 Task Force, 65, 100, 108; OPD 320.2 Task Force, 14, 73, 81; and OPD 400 Task Force, 83, 128, 144, 158, 165.

[43] Chronology, 20 Nov 42 entry, cited n. 37(3).

[44] Chronology, 26 Nov 42 entry, cited n. 37(3).

[45] Memo, Col Claude B. Ferenbaugh for Gen Handy, 15 Jan 43, sub: Informal Comments of Gen Prickett . . . , 18 Shipg file, II, Case 28, Plng Div ASF.

[46] (1) Ibid. (2) Chronology, 11, 20, 26 Nov, and 21 Dec 42 entries, cited n. 37(3).

[47] (1) See Table 13. (2) Rpt cited n. 35(3). (3) Diary, 25 and 30 Dec 42 entries, cited n. 21(7).

The expectation figure is based on an average of thirty dry cargo vessels handled each month in western ports, nineteen in center ports; 539,000 ship tons per month, 1,617,000 for three months.

In December SOS had proposed a solution—to drop every other troop convoy. This would restore balance to the flow of troops and cargo, making it possible to ship full allowances of equipment about the same time that the troops sailed, and also to clear up the backlog. Even with fewer troop convoys, SOS calculated, the use of large transports exclusively (feasible with a longer convoy interval) would permit about forty thousand troops to be sent with each convoy, enough to move all high-priority units to the theater by June; escorts would be employed more economically and some smaller transports could be diverted to other theaters. The theater staff proposed to go even further by replacing alternate troop convoys by fast cargo convoys. But SOS pointed out that fast freighters were needed on longer runs and that a full convoy of them, loaded with mixed cargo, could probably not be discharged in the five-day interval between arrival of slow and fast convoys. Both schemes went by the board, along with others, because of difficulties of timing and escorting.[48]

In December the question of larger convoys was also raised. General Eisenhower requested that the UGS convoys be enlarged to accommodate a few French ships loaded with equipment for French troops and supplies for the civilian population of North Africa, with a view to ensuring the continued co-operation of the French authorities in North Africa. The Navy was persuaded to add three vessels to each slow convoy, and later waived the requirement that they must be French vessels. Under continuing political pressure, Eisenhower in January allotted 25,000 tons per convoy for French rearmament matériel and 30,000 tons for civilian supplies. While the lend-lease ton-

nage actually carried in UGS-4 and succeeding convoys did not always come up to these levels and some of the civilian supplies were sandwiched in as filler cargo, the three-ship enlargement authorized for the slow convoys provided little or no space for Army cargo. It was, however, the prelude to further enlargements in the spring.[49]

Additional convoys could serve the same purpose. Early in December the British, to whom the first new tank landing ships (LST's) were assigned, agreed to turn over from eight to twelve of them to move cargo from the United States to North Africa, and the U.S. Navy undertook to escort a separate convoy inserted between UG-3 and UG-4. A month passed, however, before arrangements were completed, and the convoy was scheduled for 15 January, to follow UG-4. Loading the LST's presented unusual difficulties, owing to the novelty of their use as cargo carriers and to difficulties of assembling suitable cargo in time for sailing. Some of the engines, too, were defective. Escort vessels were ready on 15 January, but the LST's were not. Late in the month the Navy issued an ultimatum, and on 27 January the ten LST's limped out only partly loaded. Five promptly turned back because of engine trouble, and the others put in at Bermuda. Not until late in March did the first LST's from the States finally reach the theater. Other LST's and

---

[48] (1) Diary, 30 Dec 42 and 10 Jan 43 entries, cited n. 21(7). (2) Min of conf at Hotel St. George . . . , 25 Jan 43, 20 Gen file, Plng Div ASF, Job A46-371. (3) Msg for Br Admiralty, 31 Jan 43, 18 Shipg file, II, Case 72, Plng Div ASF.

[49] (1) Corresp in Exec 8, Vol. II, and in OPD 370.5 Africa, 86. (2) 1700 Report, 27 Dec 42, OPD Current Group files, DRB AGO. (3) Diary, 12 Nov 42, 5, 27, and 28 Feb 43 entries, cited n. 21(7). (4) See OPD 045.43 (4-8-42) Convoys Naval, Sec 1. (5) For French rearmament, see below, Ch. XVIII.

CONVOY OF LCI'S CROSSING THE ATLANTIC

some LCI's, destined for use in the impending attack on Sicily, began to move across the Atlantic in larger numbers about this time, some independently, some accompanying the slow convoys.[50]

The most dramatic move to open the convoy bottleneck came in February. Since early December the shortage of vehicles in the theater had increasingly hampered Allied operations. The railroad from Oran eastward was a poor thing, but supplies moved over it in greater volume than could be hauled from railhead to the front. When the Allied chiefs met at Casablanca in January, Eisenhower painted for them a cheerless picture, with little hope for a break-through in Tunisia; on the 16th it was decided to abandon plans for an American attack to the southeast. On the 25th Eisenhower told Marshall,

Somervell, and British staff officers in a meeting at the Hotel St. George in Algiers that his need for vehicles was desperate, and that he was considering replacing the troop transports in the next fast convoy by fast freighters in order to bring in additional trucks.[51]

[50] (1) Memo, Wansbrough-Jones for Wylie, 22 Oct 42, OCT 320.2-563.14 England. (2) Memo, Capt Warren for Opns OCT, 31 Oct 42, sub: Use of LST as Cargo Carrier, OCT 370.5 Mvmt BOLERO. (3) Diary, 8 Dec 42 and 2 Jan 43 entries, cited n. 21(7). (4) Memo, Lutes for Gross, 7 Jan 43, sub: Cargo for LST, 18 Shipg file, II, Case 19, Plng Div ASF. (5) Other corresp in 18 Shipg file, I, Plng Div ASF. (6) Memo, Gross for Styer, 30 Jan 43, sub: Rpt on Convoy LST, OPD 045.43 Sec 1. (7) Related corresp in same file. (8) Memo, Ferenbaugh for CG SOS, 25 Jan 43, sub: LST Convoy . . . . (9) Memo, Handy for COMINCH, 25 Jan 43, sub: Landing Craft to N Africa. Last two in 18 Shipg file, V, Plng Div ASF.

[51] (1) Ltr, Eisenhower to Handy, 7 Dec 42, Item 1, Exec 5. (2) Min, 57th–58th mtgs CCS, 15–16 Jan 43. (3) Min cited n. 48(2).

By this time, actually, vehicles were arriving in considerable numbers. More than 4,500 had come in UGS-3 at the end of December, and 5,300 were on the way in UGS-4. In UGF-4, moreover, were technicians and equipment for assembling crated (TUP) vehicles, capable of putting on the road 3,000 trucks per month. But to Somervell the situation presented a challenge. Eisenhower needed trucks, on wheels, in a hurry, and SOS could prove its ability to deliver in an emergency. Somervell declared that if the Navy could find escorts, he would have a special convoy ready to sail in three weeks. Admiral King promised to produce the escorts, and Somervell immediately cabled his instructions to Washington—5,000 2½-ton trucks (1,500 on wheels), 400 1½-ton trucks (200 on wheels), 72 big tank transporters, 2,000 trailers for the trucks, and some rolling stock, all to be loaded and ready by 15 February, along with certain service units. Nothing must be allowed to stand in the way.[52]

In Washington the huge SOS organization swung into action. Here was something fixed and tangible to grapple with— a specific order, unencumbered by fluctuating troop lists or uncertain priorities, with a deadline too imminent, probably, for last-minute changes. Two days after Somervell's message arrived, General Styer cabled back that the job could be done—"if you want the Pentagon Building shipped, we would like to allow more time."[53] Twenty ships were lined up, to sail from New York, Baltimore, and Hampton Roads. The service troops, it was decided, would be divided between UGF-5 and UGF-6, rather than risking passage via the slow special convoy, which would reach the theater less than two weeks ahead of UGF-6 anyway. There

were a few additions to Somervell's original order. General Arnold asked for eighty P-38's, some special vehicles and ammunition; the Navy added a tankerload of diesel fuel; 20,000 tons of lendlease filler cargo were also added; at a late hour passage was arranged for three small V-mail detachments. The operation went off like a charm. Some of the usual procedural bottlenecks were bypassed altogether: depots shipped to the port without clearance, and cargo was loaded as it arrived without priorities, any residue being held for UGS-6. By the 9th it was clear that all ships would be fully loaded; by the 11th all cargo was in port at Hampton Roads and Baltimore, practically all at New York. When the convoy sailed, as scheduled, on the 15th, it carried 6,800 vehicles. Two vessels, added to the original twenty, immediately became casualties, one because of engine trouble, the other fouled in her own antitorpedo net just outside Hampton Roads, but they joined UGS-6 the following month. There were no other mishaps.[54]

It was a brilliant performance. Its success resulted in part, obviously, from the circumstance that the convoy was not tied to a corresponding troop convoy with a fluctuating troop list and loading priorities. But UGS-5½ was no walkover. It was set up, loaded, and dispatched, from start

[52] (1) Min cited n. 48(2). (2) Diary, 4 Dec 42. 27 Jan 43 entries, and *passim*, cited n. 21(7). (3) Msg 7428, AGWAR to Styer [from Somervell, signed Eisenhower], 26 Jan 43, Hist Mat, Mediterranean Campaigns folder, Plng Div ASF. (4) See Table 14.
[53] Msg, CofS SOS to Somervell, 29 Jan 43, copy in History of the Planning Division, ASF, App. 4A, OCMH.
[54] (1) Diary, 27 Jan–11 Feb 43 entries, cited n. 21(7). (2) Memo, Dissinger for Lutes, 28 Jan 43, sub: Additional Convoy, 18 Shipg file, V, Plng Div ASF. (3) Memo, Col Normal H. Vissering for CG NYPOE, 28 Jan 43, sub: Sp Convoy . . . , 18 Shipg file, II, Plng Div ASF.

Draft of radiogram to General Somervell

Commanding General
Services of Supply
USAFME
Cairo, Egypt

CONCERNING YOUR TWO IMPORTANT COMMUNICATIONS REGARDING GENERAL GRAY AND
and our teletype communication with you

SPECIAL CONVOY, PARENTHESIS ~~FOR~~ CRAWFORD FROM STYER ~~TO BE DELIVERED TO~~ FOR
TO

SOMERVELL ~~AND~~ PARENTHESIS GENERAL GRAY ~~WAS~~ *with* SELECTED DETACHMENT OF ~~FOURTEEN~~ *ELEVEN*

WILL PROCEED BY AIR THIRTYFIRST JANUARY COMMA REMAINDER OF DETACHMENT WILL

FOLLOW BY AIR ABOUT ONE WEEK PERIOD OIL MAN FOR LARKIN BEING PROCURED

AND WILL BE DISPATCHED WITHOUT DELAY PERIOD THREE COASTER TANKERS OF ONE
each

THOUSAND TON CAPACITY ARE BEING PROCURED FOR NORTH AFRICA PERIOD PROGRESS IS

BEING MADE ON ARRANGEMENTS FOR SPECIAL CONVOY PERIOD I SAW ADMIRAL HORNE

AND HE WILL PROVIDE ESCORTS PERIOD WSA HAS NOMINATED TWENTY VESSELS WHICH ARE

BEING ASSEMBLED BETWEEN NOW AND DEPARTURE TIME PERIOD IT IS EXPECTED THAT
OR SUITABLE SUBSTITUTE FOR A FEW ITEMS

ALL EQUIPMENT LISTED WILL BE AVAILABLE PERIOD FOR REASONS OF SAFETY AND
MAJORITY OF

EARLIER ARRIVAL ~~OF PART OF THEM~~ TROOPS LISTED WILL BE DISPATCHED ON UG FIVE

PERIOD WE EXPECT TO MEET DATE AND WILL NOT LET YOU

~~AND UG SIX~~ DOWN ~~PERIOD~~ *However* IF YOU WANT PENTAGON BUILDING SHIPPED

PLEASE ALLOW MORE TIME PERIOD ABOVE HAS BEEN

REPEATED TO IKE END

CC: Gen. Clay
"
"

THE BALL IS ROLLING AND TIME IS TIGHT BUT

DRAFT OF "PENTAGON" CABLE, *Styer to Somervell, concerning the special North African convoy, UGS-5½.*

to finish, in three weeks, with operations spread over three ports and while other convoys, including the UG-5's which sailed the week before, were also being prepared. General Eisenhower was impressed.

This shipment [he wrote later] immeasurably improved our transport and supply situation and had a profound effect in all later operations. It was accomplished under circumstances that should give pause to those people who picture the War and Navy Departments as a mass of entangling red tape. . . . The trucks began arriving in Africa in less than three weeks after I made my initial request [an exaggeration, as shown above]. . . . The tremendous value of this shipment appeared in our increased ability to . . . transfer troops rapidly from one portion of the front to another.[55]

By various expedients, during the second three months of the build-up in North Africa, the convoy bottleneck was thus widened though not broken. Following the successful experiment of UGS-5½, another special convoy, UGS-6½, was dispatched in March carrying more French rearmament cargo, and a third, UGS-7½, sailed in April. Others followed. The Navy in December had reduced the minimum speed limit for slow convoys, thus permitting more flexibility in selection of vessels, and sundry cargo vessels and LST's were added to the regular convoys. Late in the winter, fast tankers began to carry bulk gasoline and oil on unescorted runs to North Africa directly from the Caribbean. These "Oil Torch" (OT) runs made room in regular convoys for more cargo vessels. Finally, starting in April, the Navy raised the ceiling for slow convoys from forty-five to sixty vessels.[56]

From early February through early May (UGS-4 through UGS-7½), the con-

voys brought in some 1,958,000 ship tons of dry cargo from the United States, almost three fifths again as much as in the preceding three-month period. With the arrival of UGS-7½, about 410,000 American troops were being supported in the theater, a month later the number had risen to slightly over 500,000. By that time, too, most of the troops were being equipped at full allowances, the backlog had been substantially cleared up, and an elaborately accoutered army was being prepared in North Africa for the descent on Sicily.[57]

On the whole, performance had borne out the September and October estimates of the logistical staffs. Six months after the landings convoys from the United States were sustaining forces of approximately the size anticipated. Advance estimates had been based on the assumption that convoy restrictions would continue in force. Instead, they had been relaxed, but only late in the period, and the flow of cargo over the whole period had been retarded by partial loadings, delays, losses, and withdrawals. Very few convoys sailed with a full complement of vessels. Moreover, even at the end of six months the inflow of cargo remained well within port capacity. In the west this was largely because the Strait, contrary to the planners'

---

[55] (1) Eisenhower, *Crusade in Europe*, pp. 148–49. In the third sentence quoted, Eisenhower may have had in mind the trucks on UGS-4, which arrived in the theater on 4 February. (2) Diary, 13 Feb 43 entry, cited n. 21(7).

[56] (1) Diary, 11 Feb 43 entry, cited n. 21(7). (2) Morison, *Battle of the Atlantic*, pp. 353–54. (3) Corresp in OPD 045.43 (4-8-42) Convoys Naval, Sec 1; OPD 370.5 Africa, 86; and Exec 8, Vol. II. (4) For UGS-6½, see below, Chs. XVIII, XXVI. (5) See below, App. A-8.

[57] (1) See Tables 13, 14. (2) Diary, 5 and 6 Mar 43 entries, cited n. 21(7).

ALLIED CONVOY PASSING GIBRALTAR

fears, had remained open; the bulk of incoming tonnages was therefore moved around to the inside ports, especially after March, and the capacity of Algiers and the small ports to the east was greatly expanded. In the west, the second three months saw an actual diminution of cargo intake—from about 455,000 to 327,000 ship tons.[58]

The Beginning of Routine Support

From early 1943 on logistical support of the forces in North Africa became more stable, its methods more routine. One of the most positive signs of this trend was the discontinuance of automatic supply. The original intention had been to close off automatic shipments after convoy UGS-5. In January General Lutes raised the issue with the General Staff, pointing out that the steady flow of stereotyped

maintenance shipments and overship ments of filler cargo had piled up large surpluses of ammunition, fuel, and food in North Africa, especially in Morocco, while the troops still lacked organizational equipment. The shift to requisition supply was made in April, with UGS-7. Unregulated shipments of all the categories except subsistence ceased, and later in the spring the North African and other theaters came under new status report and requisition procedures.[59]

Efforts were also made in late winter and spring to introduce order and system into the loading of UG convoys. Two

[58] See apps. of History, 6th Port, cited n. 37(4).
[59] (1) Diary, 3, 5, 9, 15, 17, 19, and 27 Feb 43 entries, cited n. 21(7). (2) Memo, Lutes for OPD, 20 Jan 43, sub: Visit to N Africa . . . , 20 Gen file, I, 61, Plng Div ASF. (3) Corresp in 18 Shipg file, II, Case 61, Plng Div ASF; and 20 Gen file, I, 84, Plng Div ASF. (4) See below, Ch. XXIII.

things were needed above all else—an early troop list and an embargo on changes for at least the final month before sailing. OPD had enshrined these rules in official policy the summer before, during the early BOLERO movements, and had protested repeatedly to the theater against their violation, but to no avail. General Lutes and Colonel Magruder, author of the unenforced policy, thought that the most effective solution would be

. . . to convince the theater commander that the reduction in cargo transported, because of inefficiency in loading resulting from last-minute changes, is more damaging than would be the postponement of urgently desired troop units or cargo.[60]

In mid-December OPD had tried, with no success, to persuade Eisenhower to send a small staff back to the States to coordinate the follow-up movements on the spot, where it could scarcely have failed to see the difficulties the War Department faced. Later in the winter OPD sent one of its officers, Col. Voris H. Connor, to the theater to make another effort. Connor tried earnestly to persuade the theater staff to send back each month a revised priority list of troop units desired during the coming six months, so that convoys could be made up without last-minute exchanges of messages. In the theater the problem was regarded in a different light. In effect the theater staff wanted to be able to select what it needed, at the latest possible moment before a convoy sailed, from a pool of ready units, matériel and shipping set up in advance in the States. It saw no possibility of freezing its requirements and priorities six months, or even one month, in advance.[61]

In essence, the staffs on each side wanted the same thing: for themselves a wide range of alternatives and no fixed

decisions up to the last moment, for the other side fixed plans and decisions well in advance. Under the circumstances neither side could have what it wanted. Procedures worked out in late winter and spring provided that the theater would submit each month a list or catalogue of troops that probably would be needed during the following six months, along with a priority list projected two months ahead—but both subject to change. This was an improvement, but it remained at the mercy of the military situation overseas as long as the theater itself did not possess a reservoir of troops and matériel upon which it could draw to meet the fluctuating demands of that situation.[62]

As the restrictions on size and frequency of convoys from the United States began to be relaxed in January and February, the temporary logic of the circuitous routing of part of the flow of supply through the United Kingdom also became weaker. In February use of the KMS convoys from Britain to supply American forces was discontinued as a normal procedure, though authorized as an exceptional one, and the small TORCH reserve in Britain was liquidated.[63]

---

[60] Memo cited n. 59(2).

[61] (1) Corresp in OPD 370.5 Africa, 85; and OPD 370.5 Task Force, 146, 148, 151. (2) Diary, 30 Dec 42 entry, cited n. 21(7). (3) Memo cited n. 59(2).

[62] (1) Msg 2345, FREEDOM [Algiers] to WD, 22 Feb 43. (2) Msg, NYPOE to FREEDOM, 25 Feb 43. Both in 18 Shipg file, II, Case 75, Plng Div ASF. (3) Diary, 30 Dec 42 and 2 Feb 43 entries, cited n. 21(7). (4) Msg, Marshall to Eisenhower, 9 Feb 43, CM-OUT 3050. (5) Msg, Marshall to Eisenhower, 18 Apr 43, CM-OUT 7888. (6) Msg, Marshall to Eisenhower, 26 Apr 43, CM-OUT 10758. (7) Msg, Eisenhower to Marshall, 16 Apr 43, CM-IN 9818. (8) Msg, Eisenhower to Marshall, 25 Apr 43, CM-IN 15147.

[63] (1) Msg 2122, WD to CG NATOUSA, 11 Feb 43, Policy file, I, 64, Plng Div ASF. (2) Msg, WD to CG ETOUSA, 13 Feb 43, Policy file, I, 65, Plng Div ASF. (3) Diary, 15 and 26 Feb 43 entries, cited n. 21(7).

An adequate service establishment, one of the essentials of stable logistics in a theater, developed slowly in North Africa. At the time of the landings no SOS for the entire theater-to-be had yet been created, and that of the Western Task Force existed only in skeleton form. General Wilson, commander designate of the Western Force's SOS, thought that the planned service force—about sixty thousand troops, some 22 percent of Patton's whole force—was inadequate, and that current movement schedules would not build it up rapidly enough. Yet in October and succeeding months the calls of the inside forces for troop space in the convoys took precedence generally over the needs of the Western Task Force. At the end of October General Marshall wrote Eisenhower that TORCH had exhausted the pool of available service units and was cutting into permanent zone of interior overhead; he urged the theater commander to build his service establishment as far as possible on native labor. Of this expedient most commanders, including General Wilson, took a dim view, and their experience following the landings strengthened their distaste. Eisenhower wrote in December that the native laborers deserted at the first bomb, and General Wilson's pungent report that same month dilated on their laziness and thievery. In January he again complained at length of the lack of service troops in the western sector (where he now commanded the Atlantic Base Section). The other sectors were little better off. In the entire area, American forces of almost 180,000 were supported by only 2,500 service troops along the line of communications. Not until March did substantial numbers begin to arrive. Late that month there were some 63,000 service troops in the theater, along with about the same number of air forces and 171,000 ground forces.[64]

There were other indications that the period of emergency supply was coming to an end. Theater supply requirements began to include items typical of settled occupancy—oil and gasoline pipeline, construction materials, timber, and a growing volume of civilian supplies. Air Forces planning staffs began to produce grandiose projects for developing North Africa into a great base for air power; there was talk of constructing 80 base airfields and 240 satellite fields—all of which, SOS as usual had to point out, involved far more matériel than there would be shipping to transport. And as the great battle for Tunisia drew near, SOS already was looking beyond: In February, General Lutes' staff began to draw up the first detailed supply plans for the invasion of Sicily.[65]

The Dwindling of Bolero

Far down on the priority list, the BOLERO program languished during the last four months of 1942 since the resources earlier assembled to support it were drained off into other undertakings. In the first four months of 1943 it almost expired.[66]

---

[64] (1) Corresp in OPD 320.2 Task Force, Sec 2. (2) Msg R-2593, Marshall to Eisenhower, 30 Oct 42, Item 9, Exec 5. (3) Msg, Eisenhower to Marshall, 31 Oct 42, CM-IN 4301. (4) Ltr cited n. 51(1). (5) Rpt Gen Wilson, 12 Dec 42, sub: Rpt on Opns in N Africa, 20 Gen file, I, 47, Plng Div ASF. (6) Memo, Wilson for Somervell, 20 Jan 43, copy in Frierson, Preparations for "Torch," pp. 149–56, OCMH. (7) SYMBOL: Casablanca Bk., Dec 42–Jan 43, Vol. II, ETO Tab A, and N African Theater of Opns, Tab A, TRIDENT Revision [7 Apr 43], in Exec 6. (8) For the general problem of service troops, see above, Ch. XIII.

[65] Diary, 17 Dec 42 and 26 Feb 43 entries, and *passim,* cited n. 21(7).

[66] For detailed discussion, see Ruppenthal, *Logistical Support of the Armies*, Chs. II–III.

In August 1942 the immediate impact of preparations for TORCH upon BOLERO was slight. Scheduled troop movements to the British Isles during August were reduced by about 20,000 by the withdrawal of a few small transports for conversion to combat loaders. Even so, more than 102,000 troops sailed to the United Kingdom in that month. August cargo shipments, more than double those of the month before, were somewhat less than scheduled but still very large, and the reduction reflected a shortage of immediately available cargo, not shipping. With most of the ready or near-ready divisions earmarked for TORCH, advance shipments of equipment to the British Isles were halted before they had well begun. WSA complained in mid-August that vessels were lying idle on Army berth in New York for lack of BOLERO cargo to load.[67]

No one believed that movements could continue at this rate. If they could not, the still accredited BOLERO build-up objectives were pure fiction and could cause serious imbalance in whatever limited flow of supply might be maintained. The Second BOLERO Key Plan, issued by the theater at the end of July, had set up an ultimate troop basis of 1,147,000. "We have received some enormous requests from the U.K.," noted General Lutes early in August, "which in the light of our present information appear to be unreasonable and will probably be considerably reduced."[68] In the effort to fill space, all kinds of cargo were being shipped to the United Kingdom more or less haphazardly, and certain types seemed to be piling up to excessive heights. There was reportedly enough frozen beef in England to feed American forces there for almost a year and a half. Throughout August the SOS tried vainly to obtain a decision as to

what size and kind of force should govern supply planning and shipments. "OPD will do nothing," Colonel Magruder gloomily noted in the staff diary on the 17th, "except radio General Eisenhower for his recommendations."[69] Late in the month a single division, the 29th, was placed under orders for September or October shipment; movement of the 45th was suspended. General Eisenhower, immersed in the planning of TORCH, could give little attention to the problem. OPD, in consequence, could offer importunate SOS officials nothing more than guesses, scarcely educated, as to what strength BOLERO forces might attain.[70]

SOS thus had to be content with the cloudy image in its own crystal ball. Some of its early forecasts were made simply by subtracting from the original troop basis of one million the strength of American forces expected to be sent to North Africa—which latter in early August was a low figure. More realistic calculations produced totals ranging from two hundred

---

[67] (1) Diary, 31 Jul, 5–7, and 11 Aug 42 entries, cited n. 21(7). (2) Memo, Lutes for Styer, 27 Aug 42, sub: Items To Take Up With Lee, ETO folder, Hq ASF. (3) Rpt by WSA and BMWT, 17 Aug 42, OCT 565.2 England. (4) Memo, Mvmts Div for Opns OCT, 14 Aug 42, sub: BOLERO Cargo, OCT 370.5 Mvmt BOLERO. (5) Memo, Marshall and King for President, 4 Aug 42, sub: TORCH, ABC 381 (7-25-42), 4-B. (6) Memo, unsigned, no addressee, 21 Aug 42, sub: Conv, Douglas With Franklin, WSA folder, OCT HB. (7) For troop and cargo movement figures, see below, App. E. (8) See also above, Ch. XIV.
[68] Ltr, Lutes to Larkin, 5 Aug 42, Misc Notes, Lutes File.
[69] Diary, 17 Aug 42 entry, cited n. 21(7).
[70] (1) Memo, Lutes for Overseas Sup Off NYPOE, 8 Aug 42. (2) Memo, Lutes for Styer, 18 Aug 42. Both in Misc Notes, Lutes File. (3) Diary, 25 Aug 42 entry, cited n. 21(7). (4) Plng Div SOS Diary, 20 Aug 42 entry, Plng Div ASF. (5) Msg, Eisenhower to WD, 13 Aug 42, ABC 381 (7-25-42), 4-B. (6) Msg 1127, Eisenhower to WD, 13 Aug 42, Item 5, Exec 5. (7) Msg 1380, Eisenhower to WD, 21 Aug 42, TORCH folder, Radiograms tab, Lutes File.

thousand to five hundred thousand, to be reached by April 1943—based on such considerations as the capacity of the two *Queens,* which seemed likely to be the sole remaining BOLERO carriers. On 18 August General Lutes asked for a command decision to govern supply action, and on the 21st SOS formally protested to the Chief of Staff concerning the unsettled state of logistical requirements for all Atlantic undertakings. On the 22d, no action being forthcoming, Lutes made his own decision. Supply services and the New York port were directed to ship to the European theater on the basis of a minimum level of ninety days of supply, and up to double that amount, for three hundred thousand troops. All previous requisitions based on larger strength were canceled. This arrangement the War Department and General Eisenhower accepted for the present.[71]

This was only a stopgap. Early in September General Marshall accepted OPD's recommendation that the flow of troops to the United Kingdom be adjusted to an interim target of 150,000 ground troops, forming a balanced force, with an additional air component of 95,000 and about 60,000 service troops. This total of 305,000, the OPD staff estimated, could be reached the following April by using the two *Queens* on the North Atlantic run, assuming that there were 160,000 troops not needed for TORCH remaining in the British Isles. But the theater, when asked for recommendations on the basis of a balanced ground force of 150,000, argued that larger numbers of air and service forces would be needed to prepare for future operations and to compensate, through air bombardment, for the postponement of action against Germany on the ground in western Europe. In October the War Department accepted the theater's proposed interim

troop basis of 427,000—150,000 ground, 172,000 air, 105,000 service.[72]

SOS planners felt little confidence that these objectives would remain fixed, even though OPD assured them they would, "unless the present strategic concept materially changes."[73] That "unless" was, of course, the root of the whole question. Procurement was continued, therefore, on the basis of the original BOLERO requirements, though under a low priority, and Somervell in October urged, though without success, an expanded cross-Channel operation in 1943. He foresaw that, without such a decision, the requirements of TORCH and other current undertakings were likely to snowball far beyond present proportions.[74]

The British tried hard to keep the BOLERO program alive. Early in September they submitted schedules involving regular unescorted sailings of the *Queens* and occasional runs by smaller fast transports; the *Queen Elizabeth* would be di-

---

[71] (1) Memo, Maj Richard L. Jewett, OCT, for Gen Hull, 1 Aug 42, sub: Effect of TORCH Opn on BOLERO, TORCH Jul–Sep 42 folder, OCT HB. (2) Diary, 17 and 24 Aug 42 entries, cited n. 21(7). (3) Memo for rcd, Col Magruder, 5 Aug 42, sub: TORCH, Policy file, I, 9. Plng Div ASF, Job A46-183. (4) Memo cited n.70(2). (5) Memo cited n. 6(2). (6) Memo, Opns SOS for Chiefs of Svs, 22 Aug 42, sub: Shpts to U.K., Misc file, Plng Div ASF, Job A46-183.

[72] (1) Matloff and Snell, *Strategic Planning: 1941-1942,* Ch. XIV. (2) Memo, OPD for CofS, 27 Aug 42, sub: 5440 Shipts of Tr Units, ABC 381 (7-25-42), 4-B. (3) Memo, Lt Col E. H. Qualls, OPD, for Gen Hull, 7 Sep 42. sub: BOLERO Com Mtg, ABC 381 BOLERO (3-16-42), 4. (4) Memo, Handy for CG SOS, 13 Oct 42, sub: Forces for Br Isles, OPD 320.2 Gt Brit. (5) Msg, Marshall to USFOR, 8 Nov 42, CM-OUT 2704.

[73] Memo cited n. 72(4).

[74] (1) Memo, Somervell for CofS, 5 Oct 42, ACofS OPD 1942–44 folder, Hq ASF. (2) Memo, Lutes for Clay, 20 Sep 42, Opns SOS folder, Hq ASF. (3) Memo, Lutes for Chiefs of Svs, 26 Sep 42, sub: Shipts to American Forces in U.K., BOLERO 1942 folder, Lutes File.

verted for one, perhaps two triangular voyages to the Indian Ocean. The British were also willing to step up the cycle of the *Queens* on the Atlantic run from four weeks to three, allowing them to dock in the Clyde River at any time except within four days before and after the full moon. This schedule would move about 105,000 American troops across the Atlantic by the following April, as well as 75,000 Canadians, bringing U.S. forces in the British Isles, after the TORCH contingent was withdrawn, to about 265,000. Even for this modest program there were not enough uncommitted troops ready in the United States to fill the available spaces. The Army, as Marshall put it, had had to "scalp" eight or nine other divisions and to gather up practically all the remaining service and auxiliary units fit for action in order to form the North Africa task forces. The drain on equipment in the hands of troops and on ammunition stocks had also been severe. The 29th Division, which sailed for the United Kingdom early in the autumn, was almost literally the only major ground unit available.[75]

When Colonel Wansbrough-Jones asked General Hull early in September, in a meeting of the BOLERO Combined Committee, whether the fifteen thousand or so troops needed each month to meet the proposed shipping schedule could be found, Hull was obliged to reply that it was doubtful. Later that month, moreover, General Eisenhower endorsed a British request to raise the ultimate American force in North Africa from seven to nine divisions in order to release two British divisions, thus saving shipping by increasing the direct flow of troops from the United States to Africa while reducing the circuitous flow through the British Isles. General Marshall tentatively approved this

arrangement, but pointed out that it would further hold up the movement of American troops to Britain. "At the present rate of increase," noted General Lutes, "it will be two years before the U.K. is built up to the authorized 427,000. Of course, much can happen in that time."[76]

In the combined committees, meanwhile, the British had been fighting another losing battle for BOLERO—in this instance over the amphibious phase of the program. Their contention was that these preparations, at least, should be pushed with full vigor in order to be ready to exploit any German weakening in 1943. U.S. Navy planners (to whom the Army members, on this matter, generally deferred) took their stand on the CCS statement in July that TORCH had made a 1943 ROUND-UP "in all probability" impracticable, and demanded that the original program of American landing craft deliveries to the United Kingdom be cut in order to make more available for operations in the Pacific.[77] Between a fourth and a third of that program, by mid-August 1942, had been completed—about 800 small craft delivered, out of 2,750 of all types scheduled. In the course of the discussions, the Joint Chiefs unilaterally canceled production for 100 LST's, 48 LCI's and 30

---

[75] (1) Msg 62886, Br War Off to Br Army Stf, Washington, 4 Sep 42, ABC 381 BOLERO (3-16-42) Sec 4, Folder 3. (2) Memo cited n. 72(3). (3) Memo, Col Davis for Strategy and Policy Group OPD, 13 Sep 42, sub: Availability of Units for Sp Opn, ABC 381 (7-25-42) Sec 1. (4) Memo, Marshall for Eisenhower, 30 Oct 42, CM-OUT 10217.

[76] (1) Min, 19th mtg BCC(W), 7 Sep 42, ABC 381 BOLERO (3-16-42) Sec 4, Folder 3. (2) Msg, Wansbrough-Jones to Br War Off, 7 Sep 42, BOLERO folder, OCT HB. (3) Related corresp in same file. (4) Msg 325, Eisenhower to WD, 18 Sep 42, Item 9, Exec 5. (5) Msg R-1016, Marshall to Eisenhower, 21 Sep 42, TORCH Radiograms, Logis File, OCMH. (6) Ltr, Lutes to Goodman, 20 Nov 42, Misc Notes, Lutes File.

[77] CCS 94, 24 Jul 42, title: Opns in 1942-43.

LCT's in the interests of more naval warship construction. The debate, which went on with growing acrimony during September and October, produced little result except for an agreement to go ahead with 1942 deliveries, and left a legacy of bitterness caused primarily by the highhanded tactics of the U.S. Navy planners. What to do about 1943 landing craft allocations became part of the bundle of unsettled business passed on to the Casablanca Conference.[78]

In September Prime Minister Churchill personally intervened in the British effort to prevent the BOLERO program from lapsing into suspended animation. The question whether or not to send convoy PQ-19 to the USSR, following the costly experience of its predecessor, raised the problem of what to offer Stalin if it were canceled. Churchill (as Eisenhower wrote Marshall) evidently became aware for the first time of "the inescapable costs of TORCH," and expressed astonishment when told "that TORCH practically eliminates an opportunity for a 1943 ROUNDUP." Eisenhower tried to explain to the Prime Minister "all the additional costs involved in opening a new theater, in establishing a second line of communication, in building new port and base facilities, and in longer turnaround."[79] He spoke of his plans for reducing divisional equipment and using certain British types. But all these details evidently made little impression. Writing immediately to the President, Churchill recited the familiar arithmetic of TORCH's thirteen divisions as against the forty-eight originally planned for ROUNDUP, and made a strong plea for an eight-division build-up of American forces in the British Isles during the next six months. To the President, the Army staff explained again why this could not be done. TORCH was more than a thirteen-division diversion—it was part of a new and expensive strategy that, "envisaging an extensive operation in North Africa and concurrently strengthening our positions in the Pacific and the Middle East, definitely precludes concentrating in the U.K. on the scale previously planned."[80] The President, like Churchill, was an able and frequent exponent of the view that logistical obstacles could usually be overridden by determination and hard work, but he could offer Churchill little encouragement.[81]

In November the Prime Minister, flushed with enthusiasm over the successful North Africa landings, returned to the charge. He protested to the President against what he called a "most grievous decision to abandon ROUNDUP"—which interpretation he had placed upon an order by Eisenhower's deputy in the United Kingdom, Maj. Gen. Russell P. Hartle, to limit base construction there to the needs of an ultimate force of 427,000. Churchill admitted that the original plan for a forty-eight-division ROUNDUP in spring 1943 might have reflected an overoptimistic view of shipping capabilities; it was even possible that, "try as we will, our strength will not reach the necessary levels in 1943."[82] But, he insisted, if an oppor-

---

[78] See CCS 105 series and related papers in ABC 561 (2-19-42) Sec 2.

[79] Ltr, Eisenhower to Marshall, 21 Sep 42, ABC 381 (7-25-42), 4-B, 59.

[80] Draft ltr [by OPD], President to Prime Minister, *circa* 25 Sep 42, marked "not sent," Item 42, Exec 10.

[81] (1) Ltr cited n. 79. (2) Msg 151, Prime Minister to President, 22 Sep 42, ABC 381 (7-25-42), 4-B, 57. (3) Msg 2112, Eisenhower to Marshall, 12 Sep 42, Item 9, Exec 5. (4) Ltr cited n. 80. (5) Msgs, President Roosevelt to Prime Minister, 27 Sep and 5 Oct 42, as quoted in Churchill, *Hinge of Fate*, pp. 573, 576-77. (6) For cancellation of PQ-19, see below, Ch. XXII.

[82] Msg 211, Prime Minister to President, 25 Nov 42, WDCSA 381, 1. Copy, dated 24 Nov 42, is quoted in Churchill, *Hinge of Fate*, pp. 652-53.

TABLE 13—U.S. CONVOYS TO NORTH AFRICA: NOVEMBER 1942–MAY 1943

Convoy	Ports of Departure	Sailing Date	Arrived in North Africa				Losses	
			Date	Ships	Troops	Cargo [a]	Cargo [a]	Ships
UGF–1.....	Hampton Roads.........	25 Oct	7 Nov	22 Troop... 7 Cargo....	}34,000	86,300	(b)	(b)
UGF–2.....	New York.............	2 Nov	18 Nov	9 Troop.... 11 Cargo...	}30,700	161,500	0	0
UGS–2.....	New York.............	13 Nov	1 Dec	32 Cargo... 3 Tanker...	}150	310,200	0	0
UGF–3.....	New York.............	12 Dec	24 Dec	14 Troop... 2 Cargo.... 1 Tanker...	}34,600	41,400	0	0
UGS–3.....	New York.............	12 Dec	30 Dec	30 Cargo... 2 Tanker..	}34	285,000	21,600	2
UGF–4.....	New York.............	14 Jan	25 Jan	12 Troop... 3 Cargo.... 3 Tanker...	}29,100	53,100	0	0
UGS–4.....	New York.............	13 Jan	31 Jan	34 Cargo... 2 Tanker...	}42	316,500	36,700	4
UGF–5.....	New York.............	8 Feb	19 Feb	15 Troop... 3 Cargo.... 1 Tanker...	}34,300	57,500	(c)	(c)
UGS–5.....	New York and Hampton Roads.	7 Feb	25 Feb	36 Cargo... 5 Tanker...	}30	363,500	7,900	1
UGS–5½....	New York, Hampton Roads, and Baltimore.	15 Feb	6 Mar	22 Cargo [d]..	94	222,200	0	0
UGF–6.....	New York.............	5 Mar	18 Mar	16 Troop [e].. 4 Cargo..... 1 Tanker...	}36,400	52,700	0	0
UGS–6.....	New York and Hampton Roads.	4 Mar	21 Mar	34 Cargo... 2 Tanker...	}185	329,500	39,000	5
UGL–1.....	New York.............	23 Feb	28 Mar	10 LST....	0	29,300	.0	0
OT–3.......	(f)	20 Mar	3 Apr	4 Tanker...	0	5,300	0	0
UGS–6½....	New York and Hampton Roads.	19 Mar	11 Apr	18 Cargo... 1 Tanker... 16 LST....	}881	170,500	0	0
UGF–7.....	New York.............	2 Apr	13 Apr	15 Troop [g].. 4 Cargo....	}47,700	48,700	0	0
UGS–7.....	New York, Hampton Roads, Baltimore, and Boston.	1 Apr	19 Apr	31 Cargo... 10 Tanker..	}146	310,600	29,900	3
OT–4.......	(f)	14 Apr	1 May	6 Tanker...	0	19,400	0	0
UGS–7½....	New York, Hampton Roads, Baltimore, and Boston.	14 Apr	4 May	36 Cargo... 9 Tanker... 17 LST....	}2,500	348,600	0	0
UGF–8.....	New York.............	29 Apr	11 May	19 Troop... 2 Cargo.... 1 Tanker...	}57,900	52,200	0	0

[a] Cargo in measurement tons; bulk gasoline and fuel oil are excluded.
[b] Five ships torpedoed after arrival; most of cargo saved.
[c] One transport in collision dropped from convoy at Bermuda. Troops and cargo picked up by UGF–6. Figures included in UGF–6 totals.
[d] One ship, dropped from UGS–5 due to collision, arrived with UGS–5½; cargo included in UGS–5½ totals.

[e] Includes one ship from UGF–5.
[f] Rendezvoused at sea.
[g] Three transports sailed separately (included in figures). Last section of convoy arrived 30 April.

Source: Based on: (1) charts by Statistical Section, OSD, NYPOE, 10 June 1943; (2) ASF Monthly Progress Rpt, Sec 3, Transportation, 31 May 1943; (3) History of 6th Port, OCT HB.

TABLE 14—TYPES OF CARGO IN U.S. CONVOYS TO NORTH AFRICA:
NOVEMBER 1942–MAY 1943 [a]

Convoy	Ammunition	Vehicles (Each)		Gasoline (Thousand Gallons)		Rations (Days of Supply)		Navy	Lend-Lease	Coal (Long Tons)	Consumer Goods
		General Purpose	Special Purpose	Packaged	Bulk	"B"	Emergency				
UGF-1	[b] 11,500	2,061	531	855	0	16.2	3.1	0	0	0	0
UGF-2	8,200	2,174	442	7,010	0	15.6	4.0	4,200	0	0	105
UGS-2	41,400	1,538	817	17,221	9,198	16.6	1.4	2,100	0	5,200	18
UGF-3	700	590	373	0	5,670	0.8	2.8	444	2,300	4,400	0
UGS-3	32,100	3,042	1,544	2,923	8,400	21.9	2.3	18,700	8,100	1,800	5,200
UGF-4	1,700	586	75	0	0	3.0	4.1	1,900	13,800	0	0
UGS-4	22,400	2,448	2,814	804	8,400	30.0	4.6	6,000	27,000	12,500	3,700
UGF-5	354	972	350	0	4,200	4.2	2.6	150	13,500	0	0
UGS-5	18,400	6,047	2,211	92	16,800	38.8	6.1	5,400	56,400	10,000	4,100
UGS-5½	10,300	6,143	655	0	0	11.3	3.2	73	22,800	15,000	246
UGF-6	255	596	115	62	0	1.1	1.2	168	8,800	0	0
UGS-6	8,200	7,358	1,937	59	2,940	23.5	4.9	763	48,600	16,100	420
UGL-1	0	0	123	0	0	0.0	0.1	18,320	0	0	0
OT-3	0	0	0	0	8,232	0.0	0.0	0	0	0	0
UGS-6½	7,800	538	195	0	0	2.1	0.2	505	132,000	1,500	0
UGF-7	856	284	355	473	0	0.0	1.5	668	1,900	0	0
UGS-7	19,100	5,011	1,501	2,974	12,146	2.9	3.6	2	41,500	1,400	390
OT-4	0	0	0	0	8,820	0.0	0.0	0	0	0	0
UGS-7½	24,500	4,625	2,605	7,722	15,162	1.2	0.9	0	45,100	11,700	166
UGF-8	664	177	196	380	5,460	0.0	1.7	0	1,400	0	0

[a] All figures are in ship tons except gasoline, vehicles, coal, and rations.
[b] Estimated.

Source: Based on charts by Statistical Sec, OSD, NYPOE, 10 Jun 43.

tunity should present itself to strike in 1943, the Allies must be ready to grasp it. Churchill's recognition of the possible necessity of deferring the main attack on Germany until 1944 marked a significant change from his position in September. The President now willingly agreed that any opportunity for a cross-Channel attack in 1943 must be exploited, and he reassured Churchill "we shall continue with BOLERO as rapidly as our shipping and other resources permit." How large a force should or could be assembled in 1943 would have to be worked out on the staff level, but for the present North Africa and the Pacific must take precedence over BOLERO.[83]

BOLERO continued to fade. After the sailing of the 29th Division in October, no more divisions were moved to the British Isles for almost a year. Miscellaneous elements, amounting to approximately 37,000 troops, were found to make up shipments during the last three months of 1942, but the sailing schedule set up by the British in September could not be followed. *Queen Mary* was damaged in colli-

[83] Ltr, President to Prime Minister, 26 Nov 42, as quoted in Churchill, *Hinge of Fate,* p. 653. Preliminary drafts are in Item 63a, Exec 10.

sion in October, following her late September voyage, and did not return to the Atlantic run until December. Her absence was partly made good by *Mariposa* late in October, and *Queen Elizabeth,* which gave up a scheduled trip to the Middle East for a North Atlantic crossing on 24 November. During the first four months of 1943 troop movements to the British Isles declined even more more markedly. Cargo shipments at the end of 1942 tumbled from a peak of almost 800,000 ship tons in August to less than 100,000 tons in December; no sizable increase in the flow occurred thereafter until spring.[84]

Meanwhile, American forces in the United Kingdom were being rapidly depleted by the outflow to North Africa. From a peak of 228,000 in October, their strength declined to 135,000 at the end of the year and to 105,000 two months later, by which time 156,000 troops had been withdrawn. In the theater there was a strong disposition to continue construction and administrative preparations on a large scale, looking to an early resumption of heavy troop and supply movements from the States, but these expectations were quashed by the War Department in November. Similarly, the theater's requests for additional service troops merely to operate the existing establishment were generally refused. In November the War Department also ordered the European theater not to stockpile beyond the maintenance needs of the reduced troop basis; authorized supply levels were lowered from ninety to an average of sixty to seventy-five days. At the end of February 1943, when its American establishment had dwindled to 104,510 troops, the European Theater of Operations had become a stand-by theater manned by a skeleton crew.[85]

---

[84] (1) Msg 64942, Br War Off to Br Army Stf, Washington, 12 Sep 42. (2) Msg 70291, Br War Off to Br Army Stf, 6 Oct 42. (3) Msg, Wansbrough-Jones to Br War Off, 9 Oct 42. All in BOLERO folder, OCT HB. (4) Summary, Historical Events and Statistics, New York Port of Embarkation, 1942, in OCT HB. (5) See below, App. E.

[85] See Ruppenthal, *Logistical Support of the Armies,* Chs. II–III.

PART FIVE

THEATERS OF FOREIGN AID

CHAPTER XVIII

The Anglo-American Orbit

Of U.S. munitions production during 1942, approximately 19 percent was exported to Allied nations, either under lend-lease or as a result of foreign contracts negotiated earlier. If computed in terms of assignments rather than actual shipments, this proportion rises to 23 percent. In the general category of automotive vehicles—combat and noncombat—the proportion was higher yet. For example, approximately 42 percent of American production of 23,883 light and medium tanks in 1942 was allocated to other nations. Of the munitions exported, approximately 70 percent went to Great Britain, members of the British Commonwealth, and associated nations; 25 percent to the USSR; and the remainder to China, France, Latin America, and other countries.[1] The United States served as the main reservoir for meeting supply deficiencies the other nations could not meet from their own production. In turn, where U.S. forces operated within the territories of associated powers, they drew as far as possible on local supplies in order to conserve shipping. This was what the common pool meant in the various theaters of war.

Of these theaters, all except the USSR fell within the jurisdiction of the Combined Chiefs of Staff and hence in the Anglo-American orbit, though China represents a sufficiently distinct case to merit separate treatment. By the division of strategic responsibility in March 1942, the Pacific Ocean and China fell to the U.S. Joint Chiefs of Staff, the Middle East and India to the British Chiefs. The Atlantic and Europe formed an area of combined responsibility.[2] Yet this determination of strategic responsibility did not necessarily solve the question of responsibility for supply. Within each broad area, forces of both nations and of their associates operated. While there was usually a supreme Allied commander at the top, channels of supply and administration were distinct. Requests to the Munitions Assignments Boards for material had to be justified by operational need in a theater, but assignments were made on a national basis, and material flowed through national supply channels. The British tenaciously clung to their prerogative to act as agents for those nations they conceived to be within their sphere of influence. In this category they classified all the members of the British Commonwealth, the refugee governments in London, and the various independent nations of the Middle East. Opposition to this British conception grew as American

---

[1] (1) *Report to the 78th Congress on Lend-Lease Operations From the Passage of the Act, March 11, 1941, to December 31, 1942,* pp. 28–37. (2) Hist of Lend-lease Tanks, 11 Mar 41–31 Dec 44, File, ID. (3) Paper, prepared by WPB, no date, sub: Comparison of International Aid Asgmts and Trfs With Pdn of Maj ASP Items, in ID. (4) See below, App. C.

[2] CCS 57/2, 24 Mar 42, title: Strategic Responsibility of U.S. and U.K.

forces, and hence American influence and interest, increased in overseas areas. Each theater came to present certain distinct problems concerning supply channels, as well as the nature and extent of U.S. logistical support to Allied forces. It is with these specific theater problems within the Anglo-American orbit that this chapter will be concerned.[3]

Lend-Lease and Reciprocal Aid in the United Kingdom

The United Kingdom was the nerve center of the war effort of the British Commonwealth. In London, the bulk requirements for Commonwealth forces and for those of other nations the British sponsored were consolidated and deficits that could not be met from production under British control were presented to the MAB in Washington. The assignment of material in Washington was at first made in one bulk allocation to the British and turned over to them at shipside in the United States. The Munitions Assignments Board in London reassigned this bulk allocation along with British munitions production to the various forces and theaters involved. As far as possible, shipment from the United States was made direct to the theater of use, though normally through British channels. American aid flowed directly to all the danger spots around the globe—to the United Kingdom itself, to the Middle East, to Australia and New Zealand, to India, and in smaller quantities to such inactive areas as south and west Africa and the West Indies.

Nevertheless, though the proportion was smaller than in 1941, a larger volume of American military material continued to flow to the United Kingdom than to any other single theater or country. An even greater proportion of the food and industrial and raw materials exported under lend-lease went there.[4] The strengthening of Britain as the most dependable partner in the Allied war effort, and as the principal base for military operations in Europe, continued to be the foundation of American lend-lease policy. England was an industrial center, long accustomed to import food stuffs and raw materials and to export the products of her industry in exchange. With prospects of a continuing flow of American aid, the British, in mid-1940, began to reorganize their whole economy for the long pull ahead. After the passage of the Lend-Lease Act, they were able to virtually abandon their production for the export trade and concentrate their entire industry on production for war. U.S. lend-lease provided the food and raw materials formerly obtained in exchange for British exports and, in addition, machine tools and components necessary to keep British industry operating at full speed. Military materials from the United States provided the marginal quantities British industry was still unable to produce for the Empire and associated forces deployed in various theaters around the globe. This flow of American aid enabled the British to mobilize a far larger proportion of their manpower than they would have been able to had they been totally dependent on their own resources.

During 1942 the British Commonwealth of Nations received 17 percent of its total war supplies from the United States as opposed to only 11.5 percent the previous year. As American war production reached full capacity in early 1943,

---

[3] Supply to British forces in India will be treated separately in Chapter XIX as part of the general story of the CBI theater.

[4] Report to the 78th Congress . . . cited n. 1(1).

this proportion increased considerably. The extent of British reliance on lend-lease for military equipment varied from item to item, American supplies serving both to supplement British production and to fill gaps where little or no British capacity existed. For transport aircraft, amphibious vehicles, tank transporters, 10-ton trucks, jeeps, and self-propelled artillery, the reliance was almost complete since the British did little more than develop experimental models of their own (though in the case of self-propelled artillery, for instance, they got considerable quantities from Canada). Until they began production of the Sten 9-mm. gun in mid-1942 they also depended entirely on the United States for submachine guns (Thompson .45-caliber). In other cases, such as heavy bombers, tractors, and tanks, there was some British production but 40 percent or more of the Commonwealth requirements were met from the United States. For articles such as pursuit aircraft, light and medium bombers, small arms ammunition, and rifles, British dependence on American production was proportionately less, but substantial quantities were still needed to meet vital marginal requirements.[5]

Despite the fact that the United Kingdom was operating with a net deficit that had to be filled by lend-lease, she was still able to make vital contributions to the logistical support of American troops operating in and from the British Isles. It was a matter of using supplies available locally in the most economical manner, of using British installations and services and a supply system that was already operating. This was of particular importance during 1942 when the U.S. Services of Supply in England was still in the development stage. There were, nonetheless, limits beyond which reciprocal aid in the United Kingdom could not be pushed without entailing a corresponding increase in American lend-lease that would, in the end, render the saving in shipping illusory and give the British an undue measure of control over the American supply line. Of these limitations and the dangers inherent in passing beyond them, General Somervell was ever aware.

The largest British contribution was in facilities, installations, and services. American troops in the United Kingdom were housed almost entirely in British installations, many of which had to be specially constructed. During 1942 available British construction labor was almost exclusively absorbed in building for the U.S. Army. The British also furnished the bulk of construction materials and equipment for this effort, though lend-lease contributed to their ability to do so. In the same manner, the British furnished transportation, communication, and housekeeping services essential to the existence of the European Theater of Operations, U.S. Army (ETOUSA) command.

The early build-up of the Eighth Air Force in Britain was achieved only by extensive reliance on British sources of supply. The Eighth used British airdromes, airfields, repair installations, and storage depots. Beyond this it received from the British a large proportion of its supplies. Indeed, its first bombing strikes in July and August 1942 were primarily British-mounted operations though the planes and crews were American. For almost a year afterward the British continued to furnish nearly half the supplies used by the Eighth.

[5] See Hall and Wrigley, Studies of Overseas Supply, first draft, Ch. I, pp. 1–29, Hist Br, Cabinet Off, London.

The dependence of the air force on British sources of supply was greater than that of the ground forces only because of its more rapid build-up. During early 1942 all American forces drew heavily on the British for food, housekeeping and office supplies, and some clothing. When ground units arrived short of equipment, the British frequently made up the deficit out of lend-lease stocks received from the United States or, on rarer occasions, through furnishing British-type substitutes. These emergency issues from British stocks were of particular importance in fitting out the task forces for invasion of North Africa.[6]

Virtually all this British support was furnished as reciprocal aid without money payment and arranged directly by the ETOUSA General Purchasing Board with the proper agencies of the British Government. As far as possible, American demands against British production were presented for advance programming just as British requirements in the United States were presented for inclusion in the Army Supply Program. For assignable items such as guns, ammunition, and vehicles, the Americans had to present bids to the London Munitions Assignments Board, but the bulk of the aid received was in services and nonassignable items such as subsistence, clothing, and construction materials, which were arranged administratively through the British War Office.[7]

This developing pattern of supply to American forces in the United Kingdom through British channels soon aroused General Somervell's fears of British control of the supply line. The British usually asked replacement under lend-lease of articles of equipment furnished American forces, or increased supplies of raw materials and components to enable them to

manufacture these replacements. In the case of food, the British were receiving large quantities under lend-lease at the same time that they were furnishing it to American forces as reciprocal aid. The British espoused the view that their productive facilities could be devoted primarily to supplying all forces in the European theater, while the United States in turn would supply United Nations forces in the so-called Eastern Group of theaters, that is the Middle East, Africa, India, Australia, and New Zealand. But General Somervell was unalterably opposed to this, and relentlessly pushed for a separate American supply system that would rely on the British only for those things they could furnish with no strings attached.

The food issue came to a head first. In June 1942 the British reached an agreement with ETOUSA officers and with Averell Harriman, the lend-lease representative in London, whereby the U.S. Army would import directly only those items not available locally. Staple items such as flour and sugar would be imported by the British in bulk and drawn by the Army from British depots. In addition, the Army would draw some meat and vegetables from British sources, and items such as tea, spices, and coffee, which could thus be imported directly into England without transshipment via the United States. In net effect, the agreement provided for a pool of food largely under British control, though for a separate

[6] (1) For a summary of reciprocal aid in the United Kingdom in more detail, see Ruppenthal, *Logistical Support of the Armies*, Ch. VI. (2) See also, Cheslaw, Quartermaster Operations in the War Against Germany, draft ch., "The Quartermaster Establishment in the United Kingdom." (3) Craven and Cate, *AAF I*, pp. 631-36.
[7] (1) See above, Ch. X. (2) Ruppenthal, *Logistical Support of the Armies*, Ch. VI.

American supply organization that would present its bulk requirements and carry out its distribution through its own channels.[8]

General Somervell registered an immediate and violent dissent. "The whole scheme," he wrote Eisenhower, "in my opinion is one on the part of the British to divert food stuffs to their control and impose their standard of living on our troops."[9] But the problem was far more complex than Somervell presented it, as he himself later acknowledged. It was sound economy to divert local surpluses, which occurred from time to time despite the prevailing food shortage in the United Kingdom, for consumption by American troops, and to use British storage facilities. The SOS ETOUSA showed considerably less fear of British control of the supply line than did Somervell. The War Department in September finally gave ETOUSA instructions that the department thought would be suitable for securing the maximum advantage from local procurement and at the same time would preserve the integrity of the American supply line. The theater was to exploit local resources to the maximum extent possible consistent with furnishing standard equipment and supplies to the U.S. Army in simple direct fashion and under the complete control of the theater commander. Needed items of food were to be procured locally if available and if replacement from the United States were not required. When replacement from the United States was required, procurement from British sources was authorized: (1) where the replacement was to be made in raw materials less bulky than the finished product, (2) when needed in an emergency, (3) where it was desirable to reduce spoilage or loss of British reserves, (4) where special

agreement had been reached between ETOUSA and the War Department. Needed items of clothing, equipment, and other supplies should be procured from British sources if no replacement were required, or if a previous agreement had been reached between ETOUSA and the War Department on each separate case.[10]

The intent of these instructions obviously was to reduce British requests for replacement to a minimum. But meantime the British, at considerable sacrifice, had made large issues from their own stocks to the American forces in TORCH, and clamored for replacement. Maj. Gen. James K. Crain, the U.S. executive on the LMAB, supported them and urged that either ETOUSA or the U.S. staff of LMAB should be empowered to promise replacement for material diverted under such emergency conditions. The Munitions Assignments Committee (Ground) in Washington finally accepted this principle but only subject to many restrictions. As far as possible ETOUSA should make replacement later out of its own stocks, or, if this were impracticable, the War Department should be consulted before any replacement deals were arranged. Where emergency conditions ruled out either possibility, ETOUSA could promise replacements of nonassignable items (foodstuffs, housekeeping supplies, and so forth) and the

---

[8] (1) Msg 3457, John G. Winant to State Dept, 20 Jun 42, Br folder, Hq ASF. (2) Memo, Gen Aurand for USW, 16 Jul 42, sub: Telephone No. 3786 From Harriman to Nelson, Capt Gilmour's Copies Aurand Corresp folder, DAD. (3) Cheslaw chapter cited n. 6(2). (4) Ltr, Maj Gen Sir Harold R. Kerr, Deputy QMG Br Army Stf, to Gen Clay, 22 Oct 42, sub: Procurement of Gen Stores in U.S. for Sup to Br Trs in E Group Theaters of War, AG 400.3295 (10-22-42) (2).

[9] Ltr, Somervell to Eisenhower, 19 Jul 42, ETO (6) 1942–43 folder, Hq ASF.

[10] Cheslaw chapter cited n. 6(2).

U.S. staff of LMAB replacements of assignable items (military equipment) under the priority and at the time requested by the British but subject to final approval by MAC(G) in the light of strategic considerations.

This opposition on the American side soon put an end to British hopes for an extensive system of switch deals whereby the Americans would furnish equipment and supplies to British forces in the Eastern Group of theaters in return for similar British support to the U.S. Army in the United Kingdom. The British finally agreed in December 1942 that the two areas must be treated separately, replacements to the British for supplies furnished ETOUSA as one issue and the supply of British Eastern Group deficiencies as another. Under these dispensations, the pooling of resources in the United Kingdom proceeded. If it did not go to the lengths the British desired, it at least achieved an incalculable saving in shipping space while preserving at the same time the principle of separate national supply lines upon which General Somervell insisted.[11]

The South and Southwest Pacific

In the days of the ABDA Command, the most pressing lend-lease problem in the Pacific was supply to the Netherlands Indies. Dutch requests during 1941 had had to pass virtually unheeded. Their pleas became frantic after the Japanese attack southward began, but little more than a gesture could be made, for the American supply effort had to be concentrated on strengthening American outposts and lines of communication. The Dutch had more cargo space available than the Americans could furnish material to fill, but with the naval situation out of control around the Indies, there was a serious question as to whether any ships could get through. Neither the British nor the Americans were in a position to spare the highly critical materials such as rifles, ammunition, light tanks, and antiaircraft guns that the Dutch requested. Nevertheless, some of these supplies were dispatched at the eleventh hour, but the effort proved as futile as had that to aid Greece and Yugoslavia. The Netherlands Indies fell to the Japanese while most of the material was en route or still in the United States. That en route was diverted to Australia and redistributed by General MacArthur to forces under his command, while supplies still in the United States were purchased back from the Dutch and reassigned by the MAB. Remaining Dutch contracts were either taken over by the United States or canceled. The only Dutch lend-lease program left was for their West Indian forces and those small contingents that made their way from the Netherlands Indies to Australia.[12]

---

[11] (1) Ltr, Gen Crain to Col George A. Rehm, MAB, 29 Oct 42. (2) Memo, Col Franks for ACofS Materiel, Nov 42, sub: Reverse Lend-lease and Loans of Sups to U.S. Forces in U.K. Both in ID 008 Reverse Lend-lease, I. (3) Min 1366, 66th mtg MAC(G), 17 Dec 42. (4) Ltr cited n. 8(4). (5) Ltr, Clay to Kerr, 30 Oct 42. (6) Memo, Gen Clay for Gen Tompkins, MAB, 31 Oct 42. Last two in AG 400.3295 (10-22-42) (2). (7) Ltr, Clay to Venning, 23 Dec 42, AG 400.3295 (9-1-42) (3) Sec 5. (8) Cheslaw chapter cited n. 6(2).

[12] (1) See papers in AG 400.3295 (12-16-41) (1); AG 400.3295 (3-17-41); WPD 4363-21; WPD 4295-4; Netherlands Nov and Dec File, DAD; and Netherlands Corresp Lend-lease 1 and 2 Files, DAD. (2) Ltr, President to J. van den Broek, Netherlands Purch Comm, 19 Dec 41, Auth File of President's Ltrs, DAD. (3) Min 1b, 7th mtg MAB, 18 Mar 42. (4) Ltr, SW to OLLA, 3 Apr 42, G-4/400.3295. (5) Msg 217, AGWAR to CINCSWPA, 12 Jun 42, AG 400.3295 (1-1-42).

As Singapore, the Netherlands Indies, and the Philippines fell in cataclysmic succession, the British Dominions of Australia and New Zealand assumed the pre-eminent place in the pattern of strategic defense in the far Pacific. Australia and New Zealand were primarily agricultural, producing an exportable surplus of foodstuffs and raw materials, which in peacetime they normally exchanged with England for manufactured goods. Though their industry was increasing, and the pace of its development was vastly speeded by the war, it was far from sufficient in 1942 to maintain an essential civilian economy and provide equipment for the armed forces Australia and New Zealand could put into the field. The large American forces sent to the area promised an additional drain on the native economy. These American forces would be operating at the end of one of the longest supply lines in the history of warfare. If they could draw the bulk of their subsistence supplies from local sources, the saving in shipping would be immense. A fairly simple and direct exchange therefore suggested itself whereby Australia and New Zealand would furnish American forces with housing, subsistence, clothing, and miscellaneous supplies and services in return for which the United States would supply the marginal needs of both their military forces and civilian economy.

Such a simple and direct exchange could not be arranged, however, without regard to Australia's and New Zealand's historic ties to the United Kingdom. Dominion forces were armed as part of the empire program. The Americans had previously given no independent consideration to aid to Australia and New Zealand, as their defense was conceived to be a British responsibility and their needs were incorporated in British programs. Their armies were equipped predominantly with British types of matériel not manufactured in the United States. The British considered assignments to Commonwealth nations to be primarily a function of the LMAB. Britain was still counting on receiving foodstuffs and raw materials from Australasia, and if these were entirely diverted to U.S. forces, then the United States would have to make up the deficit in British imports. Even though Australia and New Zealand fell within an area of American strategic responsibility, this established pattern of relationships within the British Commonwealth could not be lightly pushed aside.

The Australians in early 1942 were quite ready to wean themselves from the British connection and establish closer relations with the United States since they felt Britain would offer little support in the Pacific war.[13] They sent a military mission to Washington and established their own procurement agency there. Though less aggressive than the Australians, the New Zealanders generally followed their footsteps. Representatives of both countries presented in Washington requirements separate from those in the British over-all programs, and not necessarily in conformity with them. Among these were urgent requests for construction equipment to build airfields, strategic defense roads, railheads, and other facilities, which they contended were necessary for incoming American troops. By early April 1942 they were also pressing for military equipment for the forces planned by their own Chiefs of Staff, forces somewhat larger than those contemplated by the British in

[13] See the account of the British Prime Minister's difficulties with the Australian Government in Churchill, *Hinge of Fate*, pp. 3–20.

the deployment tables they had presented to CCS.[14]

It was obvious that Australian and New Zealand needs for planes, heavy construction equipment, motor vehicles, tanks, and other equipment must be met by the United States, but the War Department itself was unwilling to assume the burden of supplying their military needs in their entirety, and regarded their stated requirements as excessive. The situation demanded some separate procedure that would permit evaluation of the supply needs and over-all control of the flow of supplies to the area by the Americans, and still allow Australian forces to be supplied partially through British channels. The War Department's solution was to place both determination of requirements and final allocation of supplies in the hands of General MacArthur, and let him split his requisitions between Washington and London in accordance with the normal source of supply of the articles concerned. In May 1942 the Australian Government agreed in principle to this system, and by July procedures had been worked out in detail by the MAB and CCS for putting it into effect. It was easily agreed that naval requirements should be submitted in London and air force requirements in Washington since these were the normal sources of supply in each case. The difficulty arose in determining where requests for ground equipment should be tabled, since part would come from Britain and part from the United States. Both OPD and SOS insisted all ground force requirements should be presented in Washington, on the theory that otherwise the JCS could not exercise proper control over supply to a theater for which they exercised strategic responsibility. They were overruled by MacArthur himself, who

thought such a practice would serve no useful purpose. The CCS finally agreed that all ground force requirements save those for motor vehicles should be tabled in London, with a proviso that the tabling of any item might be changed by mutual agreement.[15]

Under this system, the major portion of ground equipment furnished under lend-lease to Australia was allocated as part of the bulk assignment to the British, and then reallocated by the London board. General Somervell opposed this arrangement from the first and repeatedly sought to change it. He stated the case to General Burns, executive of the MAB, in August 1942:

While the requirements placed before the latter board by the United Kingdom are justified on a theater basis, the bids and allocations are made in a lump sum to the United Kingdom. Frequently these allocations are reassigned by the London Board as it deems desirable. This reassignment may or may not be in accord with the reasons which govern the action of the Washington Board, and may or may not be in harmony with the di-

---

[14] (1) Memo, Col Ralph C. Benner, Chief of Distrib Br DAD, for CofEngrs, 19 Mar 42, sub: Constructional Engineering Equip for Australia and New Zealand, Br Colonies Corresp Lend-lease 1 file, DAD. (2) Min 132, 12th mtg MAC(G), 23 Mar 42; min 150, 13th mtg, 26 Mar 42. (3) Memo, Herbert V. Evatt, Australian Minister for External Affairs, for President, 8 Apr 42, CCS M-I-3, ABC 400 (2-17-42) Sec 1. (4) Min 5, 10th mtg MAB, 8 Apr 42. (5) On British deployment tables, see above, Ch. XI.

[15] (1) Msg 985, AGWAR to Supreme Comdr Australia and Philippines, 30 Mar 42, AG 400.3295 (3-30-42) (1). (2) Curtin-Wasserman-MacArthur Agreement on Proposed Lend-lease Procurement Procedure, 22 May 42. (3) Memo, Gen Burns for Secys CCS, 27 Jun 42, sub: Requests for Mat for SWPA. Last two in OPD 400.3295 Australia, Case 19. (4) Min, 19th mtg CCS, 12 May 42. (5) Memo, OPD for MAB, 20 May 42, sub: Asgmt of Priorities to Requests for Sups for Australia, OPD 400.3295 Australia, Case 7. (6) Min, WD Gen Council mtg, 2 Jun 42. (7) CCS 68/1, MBW 15, 20 Jul 42, title: Alloc of Mun to Australia.

rective from the CCS. Certainly, the United States and the Washington Board have a direct interest in the operational requirements of those theaters where our forces are engaged in joint operations, the success of which must depend on the fulfillment not only of our operational requirements but those of other forces. To insure this, I am of the view that the requirements for the Australian theater should be filed by MacArthur at London or at Washington depending on which place represents the usual source of supply. Moreover, the assignments of the Washington Board should be earmarked and not subject to reallocation in London without the prior approval of the Washington Board.[16]

Somervell's efforts had some effect. The tabling of bids for tractors was transferred to Washington in September 1942. The MAB agreed that assignments made in Washington for Australia and New Zealand should be definitely earmarked and not subject to variation in London without concurrence of the Washington board. Arrangements were made for a fuller interchange of information between the two boards. Nevertheless, the fundamentals of the procedure remained unchanged.[17]

If the procedure was somewhat cumbersome, it worked with a reasonable degree of success. Over-all control quite clearly rested in American hands since General MacArthur's headquarters determined the requirements of the Australian forces and assigned priorities for shipment, whether the material was to come from Britain or from America. The CCS directive in July also gave MacArthur final power to allocate all supplies in his area, and at first lend-lease shipments were consigned to him as commanding general shipments with the provision that he might divert them to whatever purpose he thought best. The Australian Government objected that this conflicted with the existing civilian control of ports, and Mac-

Arthur agreed that he could exercise the necessary control through the Australian machinery. Consequently, after October 1942, shipments of lend-lease to Australia were made entirely through Australian channels. MacArthur exercised his powers of allocation largely through review of requisitions and assignment of shipping priorities rather than by reallocating supplies earmarked for specific forces under his command.[18]

Procedures following the Australian pattern were established in New Zealand, though they did not take final shape until September 1942, when the control of New Zealand land forces finally passed to the American naval commander of the South Pacific Area. The South Pacific commander was also charged with a review of all requirements for his area, with assignments of shipping priorities, and with final allocation of supplies. New Zealand naval requirements, except those for certain bases under development for the U.S. Navy, and all ground force requirements were to be tabled in London, all air force requirements in Washington.[19]

---

[16] Memo, Somervell for Burns, 15 Aug 42, sub: Relationship of WD to MAB and CPRB, MAB folder, Hq ASF.

[17] (1) MBW 15/1, 25 Sep 42, title: Tabling in U.S. of Track-Laying Tractors for Australia. (2) Min 821, 45th mtg MAC(G), 27 Aug 42, with Tab E, Min 880, 48th mtg, 10 Sep 42; Min 936, 51st mtg, 24 Sep 42. (3) Min 6c, 32d mtg MAB, 9 Sep 42. (4) ID Rpt 10, Lend-lease Information, 31 May 43, sec on Australia.

[18] (1) For details of shipment priorities, see Msg AG 88, GHQ SWPA to AGWAR, 27 Jun 42, Australia IN Cables file, Bk. I, ID. (2) Min 272, 23d mtg MAC(G), 27 Apr 42; min 974, 51st mtg, 24 Sep 42. (3) Min, OLLA mtg, 12 Aug 42, ID 337 Confs, I. (4) Ltr, J. Paterson, Australian War Sup Procurement, to ID, 14 Aug 42, ID 008 Shipts, I. (5) Msg C-390, CINCSWPA to AGWAR, 31 Aug 42. (6) Msg C-520, CINCSWPA to AGWAR, 18 Sep 42. Last two in Australia Lend-lease Procurement Cables file, ID.

[19] CCS 115, 25 Sep 42, title: Equip for New Zealand.

While the commanders of the respective theaters could determine the requirements of their areas, the decision on how far they should be met rested with the central machinery in Washington and London. In the directive for assignment of munitions (CCS 50/2), the CCS gave Australia "A" priority for continuous major operations, and New Zealand "A" priority for operations for two months. While of some value to the MAB, these priorities hardly established the most important point, the relative importance of arming Australian and New Zealand forces as opposed to preparations for the invasion of Europe, also assigned an "A" priority in June 1942. In response to the request of the War Department in April, MacArthur drew up a detailed statement of minimum Australian requirements that must be met from either Britain or the United States. But even though these requirements were lower than those presented by the Australians, OPD was reluctant to approve them. "From the point of view of both equipment and shipping," noted one planner, "it is obvious that in the near future we cannot meet the requirements of Bolero and do anything in Australia." [20]

After a detailed study by MAC(G) of the availability of the supplies requested from both British and American sources, the MAB decided in June 1942 that it should accept MacArthur's requirements, but ruled it would be impossible to determine when they could be filled. Assignments would be made "as soon as practicable in accordance with the policies set up in the strategic directive, CCS 50/2." Assignments to New Zealand were placed on the same plane after the troop basis presented by her Chiefs of Staff had been reviewed by the U.S. Joint Staff Planners. [21]

In practice, the flow of supplies to Australia and New Zealand was handled by the Washington and London boards on an individual item basis, geared generally to a situation in which exact theater priorities were indeterminate. Action in Washington to meet MacArthur's and Ghormley's requests for supplies for Australian and New Zealand forces was limited, as was the case with supplies for U.S. forces in their areas, by the shortage of shipping and by the higher priority accorded Operation TORCH. The flow of military lend-lease to Australia and New Zealand during 1942 was large, but second in importance to that to the United Kingdom, the USSR, and the Middle East. The most significant American contributions were planes, trucks, tractors, locomotives, tanks, antiaircraft guns, construction supplies, and specialized jungle equipment. [22]

The supply of military equipment to Australia and New Zealand was but one aspect of coalition supply in the Pacific. American troops had to be supplied in turn from local sources. To furnish these supplies on an adequate scale and to serve as military bases, Australia and New Zealand had to have civilian supplies from the outside. The United States necessarily became the source of these supplies since

---

[20] (1) Memo, Gen Streett for Gen Handy, 3 May 42. (2) Msg 1282, AGWAR to CG USAFIA, 14 Apr 42. (3) Memo, Gen Handy for Theater Group OPD, 26 Apr 42, sub: Australian and Dutch Forces in SWPA. All in ABC 400 (2-17-42) Sec 1. (4) For discussion of CCS 50/2, see above, Ch. XI. (5) Min cited n. 14(4).

[21] (1) Memo, Gen Burns for OPD, 22 Jun 42, sub: Mun for Australia, SW Pac Sup folder, Plng Div ASF. (2) Memo, OPD for Chm MAC(G), 13 May 42, Tab 3 to min, 29th mtg MAC(G), 18 May 42. (3) Min 442, 32d mtg MAC(G), 1 Jun 42; Min 446, 34th mtg, 15 Jun 42; Min 501, 35th mtg, 22 Jun 42. (4) OPD notes on 16th mtg JCS, 25 May 42, ABC 400 (2-17-42) Sec 2. (5) Min, 16th mtg JCS, 25 May 42, Item 3.

[22] (1) See rpt cited n. 17(4). (2) See also above, Ch. XV.

the British were in no position to furnish them. It was of vital importance to the American military command in the area that these imports be of a nature to best serve the war effort and enhance the ability of Australia and New Zealand to support Allied forces in the Pacific and still not absorb too much of the available shipping space. For the Army and the local governments alike, it was essential that American local procurement be carefully planned and co-ordinated with other demands on the Australian and New Zealand economies.

Arrangements along these lines began to take shape after an early period of confusion. In March 1942 an Allied Supply Council was formed in Australia, with Australian, British, American, and Dutch representation, to determine broad supply policy on import requirements and the extent to which all Allied forces in the area could be supported from Australian resources. In response to an Australian request for some single agency with which it could deal on both lend-lease and reciprocal aid matters, the Secretary of State authorized General Roop, whom the War Department had sent out as General Purchasing Agent and chairman of the General Purchasing Board, to act as the American representative on the Allied Supply Council and to speak for the United States on both these questions. Roop was able to make arrangements whereby local procurement for American forces in Australia would be centralized under the supervision of the General Purchasing Board working with Australian Government agencies under broad policies determined by the Allied Supply Council. The Army would as far as possible present its requirements on Australia for advance programming. Except for small emergency purchases by local field

commanders, all Australian supplies transferred to the U.S. military forces would be treated as reverse lend-lease.

The other matter, civilian lend-lease shipments to Australia, was regulated by an agreement signed by MacArthur and William Wasserman, the civilian lend-lease representative in Australia, with the Australian Government in May 1942. Australian civilian requirements would initially be determined in accordance with the plans of the Allied Supply Council, but all lend-lease requisitions would require the final approval of MacArthur's headquarters before being forwarded to Washington. MacArthur would also assign shipping priorities for all materials on approved requisitions. By concurrent arrangements, Wasserman's lend-lease mission was made a part of MacArthur's staff, to work in collaboration with the General Purchasing Agent in reviewing these lend-lease requisitions.[23]

Under this system, MacArthur became the comptroller of all lend-lease to Australia, for civilian as well as military supplies. Every Australian request had to be subjected to the final test of military necessity. A similar system took shape in New Zealand, with the formation of the Joint Purchasing Board there under Colonel Westbrook. The South Pacific commander was entrusted with powers of final review of all lend-lease requisitions, but in practice that power was exercised by the Joint Purchasing Board in co-operation with a civilian lend-lease mission. A supply council was formed in New Zealand to

---

[23] (1) Cable, Secy of State to U.S. Minister, Canberra, for Gen Roop, 14 Mar 42. (2) Memo, Roop for CG SOS, 1 Jul 42, sub: Gen Purch Agent and Gen Purch Bd in Australia: Allied Sup Council. Both in 1-a-1 Jt Sup Prog (SWPA and S Pac Area) IV folder, Plng Div ASF. (3) Curtin-Wasserman-MacArthur Agreement cited n. 15(2).

determine broad supply policy, and American procurement was centralized through New Zealand agencies. Activities of the Joint Purchasing Board extended also to the other scattered islands of the South Pacific Area command.[24]

Within the framework of this system, the pooling of resources was achieved in such manner as to conserve shipping to the utmost degree possible. In no other theater did lend-lease and reciprocal aid serve these ends so well. American troops were fed, housed, and partially clothed from local sources. Some of their petroleum came from British Middle East refineries. Australia and New Zealand provided barracks, airfields, hospitals, repair shops, and numerous other installations for U.S. Army forces, and furnished the construction materials with which to build others. The Australians undertook to supply tires for American vehicles and even to manufacture some American-type ordnance equipment. Another very important contribution was in the manufacture of small boats suited to MacArthur's needs. In turn, critical items of industrial, transportation, and construction equipment furnished from the United States under the careful eye of MacArthur's headquarters and the Joint Purchasing Board made a signal contribution in enabling the native economies to keep moving and furnish the goods and services required. Canning and dehydration equipment enabled the Australians to preserve and distribute food in a more economical manner. Machine tools promoted the expansion of Australian industry in those areas the Americans conceived as best for the war effort. American trucks helped to give the necessary mobility to the economy, and heavy construction equipment enabled the building of the facilities required for

Allied military forces. For many of the boats manufactured in Australia, engines came from the United States.

By the end of 1942 there were sufficient surpluses of certain articles of Australian manufacture to dictate some procedure for allocating supplies outside the country, and an Australian Munitions Assignments Committee was formed. This committee was composed of Australian and British representatives only, for General MacArthur felt that his powers as Commander in Chief gave him the right to divert to the use of forces under his command any munitions produced in Australia, and he limited American representation to a liaison officer.[25]

In an effort to push the pooling principle to the limit and save even more shipping, the combined boards and the Office of Lend-Lease Administration in the fall of 1942 made an intensive effort to eliminate the run from the United Kingdom to Australia and New Zealand entirely. Under their proposal, the United States would meet all Australasian needs for military and industrial equipment, and the Australasian surplus of foodstuffs and raw materials would be used entirely to support Allied forces in the Pacific. The United States would then furnish food to Britain to compensate for her loss from Australian and New Zealand sources. But the necessity of furnishing Australian and New Zealand forces with British-type equipment prevented this goal from ever being fully realized. The United Kingdom-

---

[24] (1) See above, Ch. VII. (2) Memo, Westbrook for CG SOS, 19 Jul 42, sub: Rpt on Orgn and Opn of Jt Purch Bd, S Pac, 2363-1 folder, Asiatic Sec, Theater Br, Plng Div ASF. (3) Rpt, sec on New Zealand, cited n. 17(4).

[25] Msg C-1267, Brisbane to AGWAR, 16 Dec 42, Australia Lend-lease Proced Cables file, ID.

Australasian run was considerably reduced but never entirely eliminated.[26]

The Middle East

The Indian Ocean and Middle East theater, which fell to the British, comprised a vast expanse of territory extending from Libya to Singapore. British forces faced the Germans and Italians on the west, the Japanese on the east. To these outside threats could be added the growing restlessness of native peoples under any form of foreign domination. The constituent countries, almost all under British rule or influence, were ill prepared to furnish many of the sinews of war, or even to serve as adequate bases for support of British armies. The sea lines of communication were long and tenuous, interior supply lines poor and undeveloped. Axis control of both shores of the Mediterranean forced shipping to go around the coast of Africa to ports of entry on the Red Sea, the Nile Delta, the Persian Gulf, and India.

Geography and paucity of transportation and communication facilities divided the area naturally in three separate regions—the eastern basin of the Mediterranean, Iran and Iraq, and India. The bulk of the forces of the British Commonwealth, apart from those in the United Kingdom itself, were deployed throughout these regions, spread thin to cover all the danger points. In the first, one British army was waging an active campaign against Rommel in the Libyan desert, and another was deployed in Syria against a possible German thrust through Turkey. In Iran and Iraq other British forces were preparing to meet a possible German attack southward through Russian Turkestan and were trying to develop a supply line to the USSR. The largest British army

of all, though hardly the most effective, was stationed in India. During 1941 India's role had largely been that of a rear base for the war in the Middle East, but the rapid advance of Japanese armies to the Indian border in early 1942 forced on it a new role as the principal Allied base for the war in Asia.

In 1942 the British were more concerned about protecting their hold on the Middle East and with extending that hold to regain control of the Mediterranean than about pursuing the war against the Japanese from India. In British concern about the Middle East and the Mediterranean lay part of the reason for British reluctance to go ahead with the American plan for an early invasion of Europe. Though the American staff recognized that the Allies could ill afford a setback in this area, bringing as it inevitably would the loss of vital oil fields and communication lines and the threat of a junction of German and Japanese forces, they sought to restrict commitments to the Middle East in the interest of concentrating resources on BOLERO. American opposition to the British plan to base allocation of material on theater deployments was principally motivated by fear that, with British forces deployed throughout the area from Libya to the eastern borders of India, many of them inactive, it would result in commitments of matériel for purposes U.S. Army planners did not conceive to be vital to ultimate

---

[26] (1) Rpts, Com on New Zealand Exports and Imports to Stettinius, 15 Sep and 29 Dec 42, 334.8 S Pac Subcom folder, Plng Div ASF. (2) Memo, Westbrook for CG SOS, 18 Sep 42, Lend-lease folder, Hq ASF. (3) MBW 24, 17 Aug 42, title: Economy of Shipg Through Local Sup Arrangements; MBW 24/1, 20 Aug 42, same title; MBW 24/2, 21 Aug 42, same title; MBW 24/3, 15 Sep 42, title: Economy of Shipg; MBW 24/4, 17 Oct 42, same title. (4) Memo, Franks for Clay, 5 Nov 42, sub: Ltr of E. R. Stettinius . . . , AG 400.3295 (9-1-42) (3) Sec 2.

victory.[27] OPD planners at first took the position that no American troops should be sent to the Middle East, and while they were ready to furnish supplies prerequisite to the success of the British campaign in the desert, they would cut allocations for the inactive areas of Syria, Iran, Iraq, and India to a minimum. While the whole India and Middle East theater got an "A" priority under CCS 50/2, the strategic directive for assignment of munitions, the Americans recognized that priority clearly only in the case of the active operations in Egypt and Libya.

Even this policy promised substantial American support to the British campaign in the Middle East during 1942 and each recurrent crisis forced the Americans to increase their commitment. The flow of American supplies and the commitment of American shipping to the area had begun in 1941. At the ARCADIA Conference it was agreed that shipments to the Middle East (and to the Soviet Union) should have a priority second only to "continuous maintenance of existing overseas Army and Navy garrisons and US fleets."[28] In the crisis of February and March 1942, when General Auchinleck's forces were forced to retreat before Rommel, the President agreed to provide additional troop shipping from the American pool to transport two British divisions to Egypt to replace forces diverted to Australia after the Japanese attack. General Marshall also proposed dispatch of an American air force, but the project was temporarily dropped when Auchinleck stabilized his position.[29]

The dominant note continued to be, as it had been in 1941, supply of matériel for British use. In Washington, assignments to the Middle East were made as part of the bulk allocation to the United Kingdom, though equipment was normally shipped directly from the United States. The main British needs were for planes, tanks, artillery, motor transport, locomotives, communications equipment, and heavy construction material. In general, while the assignments committees could not meet British expectancies in their entirety, they did everything to meet urgent operational needs in the Middle East as far as possible without completely crippling the U.S. Army's training program. By furnishing combat matériel for British use, the Americans sought to avoid commitment of their own troops.

This policy showed very clearly in connection with the military missions under Generals Maxwell and Wheeler, dispatched to Egypt and Iran shortly before Pearl Harbor to aid the British in the development of their lines of communications and in the use and maintenance of American equipment. The services these missions were to perform were essential to the British effort. American observers were generally agreed that the British had inadequate numbers of maintenance troops and installations. The percentage of tanks and vehicles continually laid up for repair, and often lost when they could not be repaired in time, was tremendous, and the wastage contributed to heavy British demands on the United States for new tanks and other vehicles. This was certainly one factor in the reverse suffered by Auchinleck in February and March.[30]

The early blueprints drawn up by the Maxwell and Wheeler missions envisaged

---

[27] (1) See above, Ch. XI. (2) Matloff and Snell, *Strategic Planning: 1941-1942*, pp. 198–202.

[28] Min, ABC-4 JCCSs-10, 12 Jan 42.

[29] Matloff and Snell, *Strategic Planning: 1941-1942*, pp. 198–202.

[30] (1) See above, Ch. IV. (2) Memo, Maj Joseph M. Colby for Chief of U.S. Mil N African Mis, 24 Jan 42, sub: Unserviceable but Repairable Equip, Mis to Middle East (N Africa) file, DAD. (3) Note, DE [Eisenhower] to Gee [Maj Gen Leonard T. Gerow], no date, WPD 4511-28.

a system of depots and construction and maintenance projects serving the entire Middle East, India, the Persian Gulf supply line to the USSR, and possibly China. The larger establishments would be in India or South Africa, with smaller ones located in the base areas serving British armies in Egypt, Syria, Iran, and Iraq, respectively. In Eritrea Maxwell planned facilities for aircraft repair and assembly at Gura, port and naval repair facilities at Massaua, and reconditioning and repair shops for tanks and motor vehicles at Asmara. At Heliopolis, near Cairo, Egypt, and at Tel Litwinsky, near Tel Aviv, Palestine, he would set up generally similar establishments for repair, maintenance, and reconditioning of all types of American equipment. At Umm Qasr or Baghdad in Iraq Wheeler proposed ordnance repair facilities to support the British army in Iraq. In Iran the Americans would undertake to construct and repair roads, rail lines, and port facilities, and to operate truck and aircraft assembly plants to serve both the British and the Russians. The supply and personnel requirements for these projects tended to expand as the mission chiefs became familiar with the difficulties confronting them, and as the British extended their conception of the tasks the missions should perform.[31]

The tasks outlined according to the original conception during the neutral period were to be performed by civilian contractors. Designation of firms, recruiting by them of skilled personnel, and procurement of equipment through War Department lend-lease channels were well under way at the time of Pearl Harbor. American entrance into the war transformed the missions into services of supply for the areas in which they were located and inevitably raised the question of militarization. Even before Pearl Harbor,

General Maxwell had urged that service troops be furnished to perform the work on strictly military installations, and shortly afterward, on 21 December 1941, transmitted a British request for service troops to operate directly in support of the British Army.[32]

There were numerous objections in Washington to both of these proposals. From the practical standpoint, neither an adequate number of service troops nor sufficient troop shipping was available. On the policy side, as General Aurand noted, "The War Plans and G-3 . . . put it very bluntly . . . they will not organize US troops to dog-rob for the foreign countries."[33] Maxwell was informed on 2 January 1942 that no service units would be available for the Middle East at that time, and that he must continue efforts to operate in accordance with the prewar plan.[34] While the proposal to extend American activities to direct support of the British Army was not to be raised again, in Feb-

[31] (1) Original plans submitted by the supply services in November 1941 are in AG 400.3295 (8-9-41) Sec 6. (2) Min of conf in Gen Aurand's off, 1 Feb 42, Item 142, Col Boone's file, DAD; min, 3 Feb 42, Item 150, Col Boone's file, DAD. (3) Memo, Lt Col Noble M. Coe for Col Gross, 4 Feb 42, sub: Proposal To Estab a Depot in the Middle East for Def Aid and Other Mun, Item 151, Col Boone's file, DAD. (4) Memo, Maj Stuart Bullivant, Chief of Home Off U.S. Mil N African Mis, no addressee, 14 Feb 42, sub: Breakdown of Proposed Projects in N Africa Area, N African Mis 330, ID. (5) Memo, Maj Colby for Gen Maxwell, 18 Jan 42, sub: Survey of Proposed Ord Estabs in Iraq, Iran, and India, N African Mis 600.12, ID. (5) Ltr, Gen Wheeler to Gen Moore, 19 Jan 42, Iranian Mis 600.12, ID.
[32] (1) Min, mtg in Aurand's off, 19 Jan 42, Conf Memos file, DAD. (2) Msg 287, Cairo to AGWAR, 2 Dec 41. (3) Msg 384, Cairo to AGWAR, 16 Dec 41. (4) Msg 414, Cairo to AGWAR, 21 Dec 41. Last three in AMSEG IN Cables file, Bk. 1, ID.
[33] Telephone conv, Gen Aurand with Lt Col Holland, OUSW, 12 Jan 42, Misc Corresp Lend-lease 1 file, DAD.
[34] (1) Msg 310, AGWAR to AMSEG, Cairo, 2 Jan 42, AG 400.3295 (8-9-41) Sec 6. (2) Matloff and Snell *Strategic Planning: 1941-1942,* pp. 198-202.

ruary 1942 Robert Patterson, the Under Secretary of War, over the objections of Generals Somervell, Aurand, and Moore that service troops were just not available, decided the missions should be militarized. The War Department on 18 February directed that contract activities overseas, except in the Atlantic bases, should be terminated within six months and taken over by "military organizations and units to be organized in the United States and sent overseas." [35]

In pursuance of the directive for militarization, Generals Maxwell and Wheeler presented their detailed troop requirements for the contemplated projects, mounting to a total of 48,000. While this was reduced in Washington to 40,000, it still represented a commitment that could hardly be fulfilled if service troops were to be readied for BOLERO. Apart from the general shortage of service troops, there were practical difficulties in the organization of troop units to perform fundamentally industrial tasks. No suitable tables of organization existed in many cases; some projects were completely unsuited to military operation; tasks for which the contractors had already laid plans and procured personnel had to be replanned and rescheduled; the construction of the required facilities, the necessary first step, could hardly be completed in the near future if it had to await the arrival of troop units. The War Department soon agreed with Maxwell that construction activities would have to proceed under the contractors and operating activities be initiated under them, and that militarization would have to be gradual. [36]

The truth was that while these elaborate militarization plans for the missions were taking shape, the actual movement of civilian and military personnel and of sup-

plies to the mission areas was alarmingly slow. The absorption of shipping in the initial deployment of U.S. troops overseas in January and February 1942 left mission personnel and cargo stranded at dockside. Given the need for concentration on BOLERO, it was hard to see how more than a trifling amount of shipping could be made available for them in the ensuing months. OPD did not approve the service troop basis of forty thousand for militarization, and the whole matter was left hanging in the air. In these circumstances, SOS decided in early April to curtail temporarily the scope of the mission projects. The original plans were retained as ultimate goals but divided into two objectives. First objective projects in Maxwell's area included the major portion of the work planned for Heliopolis and Eritrea but postponed that in Palestine. All base projects in India and Iraq were similarly postponed and, as the first objective for that area, it was decided to concentrate on development of the ports, roads, and assembly facilities in Iran. Troop requirements for the first objective in North Africa were calculated by SOS at 4,213, for Iran only 654. These were to depart the United States by 1 September 1942 and the first objective projects were to be completed or in operation by the end of the year. The

[35] TAG ltr, 18 Feb 42, sub: Closing Out of Overseas Contracts and Militarization of Contract Activities, Mis to Middle East (N Africa) file, DAD.

[36] (1) Ltr, Col William E. Chickering to Chief of Home Off, U.S. Mil N African Mis, 26 Feb 42, sub: Militarization of Base Projects, N African Mis 330, ID. (2) Memo, Lt Col Maxwell W. Tracy, Chief of Home Off Iranian Mis, for Col John E. Upston, WPD, 24 Feb 42, sub: Militarization of Iranian Mis, with Tabs A–Q, Iranian Mis 370.5, ID. (3) Msg AMSEG 451, Cairo to AGWAR, 20 Feb 42. (4) Msg 673, AGWAR to AMSEG, 25 Feb 42. Last two in AG 400.3295 (8-9-41) Sec 6A. (5) Memo, Melvin Sims for Lt Col Laurence K. Ladue, 31 Mar 42, ID folder, Contl Div ASF.

second objective was to include the rest of the projects set up in the original plans. The new troop requirements were computed at 12,528 men for North Africa and 6,950 for Iran. The reduction of the original troop basis for the projects by almost half was made on the assumption that construction work would be done by the contractors and that native labor would be used to the maximum extent possible.[37]

First priority was thus given to the installations designed to serve the British army in Egypt and Libya, and second to the development of a supply line through Iran to the Soviet Union. Projects to support the inactive British armies in Syria and Iraq were placed in the second objective. The major bases proposed for India were also postponed. While the selection of these objectives came in the guise of a decision merely to postpone certain of the projects originally planned, the postponement in most cases became permanent. The grand scheme of early 1942 for a single system of supply establishments to serve the entire Middle East and India subsequently gave way to regional planning along different lines for three separate areas with separate missions. In North Africa and Palestine, American activities were to be centered on supporting the British armies there, in Iran on developing a supply route to the USSR, and in India on the war with the Japanese. The SOS decision that produced these results was dictated both by the practical difficulties involved in carrying out the earlier plan and by the strategic planners' reluctance to commit resources to the British area of responsibility.

Even the reduced plan for the Middle East missions was so dwarfed by the massive requirements for shipping, troops, and supplies for BOLERO that it was almost lost in the shuffle. OPD remained reluctant to permit diversion of even the most negligible quantities of shipping from BOLERO for the missions. By the end of July most of the civilian contractor personnel had arrived by air ferry, freighter, or troopship, but few military units. Plans were made in late May to dispatch all the first objective troops and part of the second in one large movement in August, but they were soon disrupted by the march of events in the Middle East.[38]

During May, General Auchinleck delayed in launching the attack on Rommel, which Churchill had urged. Then, Rommel struck. By the end of June he had driven the British back into Egypt, and the threat of a German drive to Suez and the Middle East oil fields was ominous. In this crisis, the American staff had to modify its position on commitments to the Middle East. Churchill, in Washington for conferences, received assurances of support from the President. At first General Marshall proposed that an armored task force composed of the 2d Armored Division and supporting units be sent to the Middle East, and plans were hastily drawn up for its shipment to Suez. But they were just as

[37] (1) Msg 516, AGWAR to AMSEG, 10 Apr 42, AG 400.3295 (8-9-41) Sec 6B. (2) Msg 100, AGWAR to AMSIR, Basra, 10 Apr 42, AG 400.3295 (8-9-41) Sec 4. (3) Memo, Home Off U.S. N African Mis for Provost Marshal Gen, SG, CSigO, CofEngrs, and CofOrd, 11 Apr 42, sub: Sv Units for N African Mis. (4) Memo, Maj David Wainhouse, ID, for ACofS OPD, 3 May 42, sub: Activation of Trs for N African and Iranian Mis's. Last two in Mis to Middle East (N Africa) file, DAD.
[38] (1) Memo, Wainhouse for ACofS G-3, 28 Apr 42, sub: Activation of Trs for N Africa and Iran Areas. (2) Memo, Aurand for Somervell, 7 May 42, sub: Trans for N Africa and Iran. Both in Mis to Middle East (N Africa) file, DAD. (3) Msg, AGWAR to AMSEG, 4 Jun 42, CM-OUT 0804. (4) Msg 1031, Cairo to MILID, 10 May 42, AMSEG IN Cables file, Bk. 9, ID.

U.S. TANKS AT HELIOPOLIS, EGYPT, *January 1943, waiting to be repaired.*

hastily abandoned when it was learned that Churchill would not in exchange abandon his plan for an invasion of North Africa. Marshall then proposed shipment of three hundred new-model Sherman tanks and a hundred 105-mm. self-pro-pelled howitzers, and this plan was ac-cepted. Air shipment of tank and antitank ammunition was arranged to counter an imminent shortage in Egypt. To armored force supplies was added emergency action to provide air power in the Middle East, and as part of the Arnold-Slessor-Towers Agreement, six U.S. air groups were slated for that area. In the immediate emergen-cy, bombers en route to India and China were held in Africa and General Brereton was ordered from India to the Middle East

with the bulk of the heavy bombers of the Tenth Air Force. An additional forty light bombers were diverted with Stalin's per-mission from those at Basra in Iraq desig-nated for delivery to the Russians. The first three of the six air groups for the Ninth Air Force were shipped during July.[39]

Though the basic American role of auxiliary to the British in the Middle East remained unchanged, the decision to send air combat troops did alter the functions and status of the North African mission. The principal emphasis in the Middle East after the midsummer crisis was on the

---

[39] (1) This story is told in greater detail in Matloff and Snell, *Strategic Planning: 1941-1942,* Ch. XI, on which this briefer account is based. (2) See also, Churchill, *Hinge of Fate,* pp. 413–31.

WORKSHOP AT HELIOPOLIS. *British soldiers learn to handle American matériel.*

build-up of the Ninth Air Force rather than a services of supply for the British. On 16 June 1942 an overseas command was created called U.S. Army Forces in the Middle East (USAFIME) under General Maxwell at Cairo. Despite the growing differentiation of purpose between the Cairo area and Iran, the Iranian mission was included under the new command. The former mission projects were, in August, assumed by the new SOS USAFIME, which was divided into four service commands, Eritrea, Delta Area, Palestine, and Persian Gulf. The functions of the first three of these commands included support of the Ninth Air Force and the regional activities of the Air Force Ferrying Command, as well as of the British. These

activities extended into Arabia and the Anglo-Egyptian Sudan. The "center of gravity" for air force installations being in Palestine, the projects postponed there had to be revived in August. The old first and second objective priorities ceased to have much meaning, and Maxwell had to redirect the energies of his command toward the new situation facing it.[40]

Despite its new responsibilities, the

---

[40] (1) Memo, Col Franks for CG SOS, 20 Jun 42, sub: Estab of N African and Iran-Iraq Sv Comds, N African Mis 334.8, ID. (2) Msg, AGWAR to AMSEG, 17 Jun 42, CM-OUT 4135. (3) Msg, AGWAR to AMSME, 8 Aug 42, CM-OUT 2451. (4) Msg, AMSME to AGWAR, 19 Jul 42, CM-IN 6872. (5) Msg, AMSME to AGWAR, 29 Jul 42, CM-IN 10115. (6) Msg, AMSME to AGWAR, 4 Aug 42, CM-IN 1123.

A LEND-LEASE 105-MM. HOWITZER *(self-propelled)* in Egypt.

build-up of Maxwell's SOS was slow. The large movement of service troops scheduled for August 1942 had to be canceled to provide shipping for air force personnel and supplies, and was rescheduled as a gradual movement over the following months. The military personnel in the SOS USAFIME totaled only 1,000 in mid-August 1942 and this number had risen to only 2,779 by 2 November. By then approximately 6,000 additional men were en route or scheduled to depart, but most did not arrive until early in 1943. The flow of supplies was similarly delayed, and Maxwell had to improvise as best he could by using native labor and materials. While construction activities in Eritrea were nearing completion by the end of the year, those in Egypt were only half finished and those in Palestine had just begun. Actual maintenance operations were in many cases just beginning in November. Full militarization was not accomplished until 1 January 1943, and even afterward former contractor employees continued to work directly for the Army. The full scale of projects originally contemplated was never realized, as the need for them disappeared with the British victory in the desert campaign in the autumn. Only miscellaneous additional troop commitments were necessary for special projects during 1943. Similarly, the supply of line-of-communications equipment to the British did not measure up to their expectations, and was subordinated to the supply of combat material for the autumn offensive. For instance, of eleven can and drum plants ordered by the British for manufacture of gasoline containers in North Africa, not one was shipped from the United States before March 1943. The importance of these plants was immense for in the asbestos containers in use in the Middle East, loss of gasoline ran as high as 30 percent.[41]

There is no evidence, however, that this failure to provide the maintenance and supply facilities originally contemplated seriously handicapped the British autumn campaign of 1942. The amount of American air and supply support actually furnished proved sufficient and was probably decisive. When the attack on El Alamein was launched, American tanks and American motor transport played a major role in the break-through and its exploitation. The replacements shipped from the United States for one boatload of Sherman tanks that had been lost en route arrived in time to be used in the battle.[42] American automotive equipment and the support of the U.S. Air Forces helped to give the British the superior mobility and superior logistical support to their field army that enabled it to move rapidly across the desert to the borders of Tunisia. If the American supply and maintenance bases were far from complete, they nevertheless played an important role in supplementing the British line of communications. The complete victory scored in Africa by the British Eighth Army and the Anglo-American forces involved in TORCH removed the German menace from North Africa by May 1943, and the Soviet victory at Stalingrad simultaneously removed the threat of a German drive southward from the USSR. The center of gravity for future campaigns moved westward from Egypt and Libya to Tripoli, Tunis, and Algeria. The Middle East remained a rear area base in the Sicilian and Italian campaigns, a way station for troops and supplies en route to the Persian Gulf and Far

East, and a center of ferrying command and air force activities. The critical phase of the logistical problem in the Middle East passed with the victory of General Montgomery at El Alamein, and thereafter the Americans regarded it as a declining theater to which further resources should not be committed.

French Rearmament: The Initial Phase

From the fall of France in June 1940 until the Allied invasion of North Africa in November 1942, only the scattered French possessions in Africa, the Middle East, and the Pacific that threw in their lot with General Charles de Gaulle remained within the Anglo-American orbit.[43] By the arrangements of March 1942, the British assumed responsibility for supplying Free French forces in Africa and the Middle East, the Americans for those in the Pacific islands. Under this dispensation, the British armed a sizable body of French com-

---

[41] (1) Msg, AMSME to AGWAR, 18 Aug 42, CM-IN 6536. (2) Msg, AMSME to AGWAR, 28 Nov 42, CM-IN 12122. (3) Msg, AMSME to AGWAR, 17 Dec 42, CM-IN 7233. (4) Msg, AMSME to AGWAR, 18 Dec 42, CM-IN 3305. (5) Msg, AMSME to AGWAR, 19 Dec 42, CM-IN 8463. (6) Msg, AGWAR to AMSME, 12 Aug 42, CM-OUT 3463. (7) Msg, AGWAR to CG USAFIME, 18 Nov 42, CM-OUT 5676. (8) TAG ltr, 17 Jul 42, sub: Closing Out of Overseas Contracts and Militarization of Contract Activities, AG 160 (2-15-42). (9) See paper, 2 November 1942, listing SOS troops in the Middle East in 370 Mvmt of Trs USAFIME folder, Plng Div ASF. (10) For the long, involved history of the can and drum plants, see Can and Drum Plants Middle East folder, Plng Div ASF.

[42] Ltr, Gen Macready to Gen Somervell, 11 Sep 42, Br folder, Hq ASF.

[43] Except where otherwise indicated, this section is based on a manuscript by Marcel Vigneras, The Rearmament of the French Forces in World War II, Introduction and Chs. I–IV, OCMH.

bat troops and used them as an integral part of their own armies, while the Americans furnished supplies for miscellaneous defense forces on New Caledonia. The American attitude toward de Gaulle was continuously lukewarm, and proposals received from Free French representatives in early 1942 for future large-scale French rearmament under direct American auspices received scant consideration.

The invasion of North Africa in November again brought into the Allied orbit an organized French Army of considerable size. On 13 November the President declared "any French province, colony, protectorate, or mandated territory not under the control of the Axis" eligible for lend-lease, thus clearing the legal path for direct American aid.[44] Before the invasion, in secret conferences with sympathetic French leaders in North Africa, Lt. Gen. Mark W. Clark received from French Général de Brigade Charles Mast a plan for arming eight infantry and two armored divisions, the force Mast said the French could put into the field within a few weeks after the North African landings. The American staff immediately showed an appreciation of the advantages to be gained by rearming such a force. Even if there was a shortage of equipment for training, the greater and more compelling shortage was that of shipping to transport trained troops overseas. In the long run, employment of French troops armed with American equipment in North Africa or Europe would be more economical of shipping than dispatch of both troops and equipment from this country. The Americans thought the British should share the burden by furnishing small arms, the category in which training shortages were most acute, and by accepting proportion-

ate sacrifices in their own allocations under the Weeks-Somervell Agreement. The British, in view of their own strained supply position, objected, suggesting that the French should be rearmed with captured or obsolescent equipment. They argued that taking rifles from their Home Guard (the Enfields sold to them by the United States after Dunkerque) would endanger the security of the British Isles. They insisted that, if the Americans wanted to undertake the program, it should be without interfering with their allocations from American production or with logistical support of agreed combined operations. Undoubtedly there were also political factors in the background. The British did not wish to see American support for a rival political faction to the de Gaulle group, which they themselves were supporting, nor a shift in responsibility for arming the French from London to Washington.

An early clash within the CCS over the issue was soon settled by reference to General Eisenhower, who urged a cautious approach in view of the exigencies of the shipping situation and his doubts about the battleworthiness of French troops. The CCS then agreed that the issue should be postponed, and any assignments and shipments should be governed by Eisenhower's wishes. Thus granted a large measure of control over supplies for the French, the Commander in Chief, Allied Force, in North Africa was soon confronted with a dilemma. He found that he needed French co-operation badly. French troops, armed with obsolescent weapons, soon formed a

---

[44] (1) Ltr, President to Stettinius, 13 Nov 42, ID 008 Lend-lease, II. (2) CCS 50/2, 24 Mar 42, title: Dir for Asgmt of Mun.

vital part of his battle line and quickly dispelled any doubts about their battleworthiness. There was a considerable body of French merchant shipping in northern and western African ports, the major portion of which the French agreed, with some misgivings, to place in the Allied shipping pool. They naturally expected some compensation for their support, and their early co-operation was at least tacitly premised on the expectation of receiving from the United States modern equipment for their North African army and essential supplies for the civilian economy. However much he might wish to meet these expectations, Eisenhower was faced with the limitations on the size of North African convoys and port and overland transport capacity, which left the logistical build-up of his own British-American forces in a tenuous state. The use of the French merchant shipping made available provided no ready solution, for most of the ships were in need of extensive repairs and would not be available for voyages until some months later; even if available, the limitation on the size of convoys would effectively preclude their use.[45]

In these circumstances, Eisenhower's policy was opportunistic. He accepted responsibility for providing the minimum essential supplies for the civilian economy and the principle that the French North African army should be rehabilitated. Meanwhile, he sought to maintain French troops in the line with issues from British-American theater stocks, and asked for token shipments for rearmament. In mid-December 1942 he established a Joint Rearmament Committee as a part of the staff of Allied Force Headquarters, composed of four French and four American officers, to receive and review French requests for military equipment and to develop a long-range program for rehabilitation of French armed forces. In late December, at Eisenhower's recommendation, three ships were added to each UGS convoy to meet his limited commitments for rearmament and civilian supply. Yet by necessity, he had to place rearmament materials in fourth priority for shipment, below materials for the British-American build-up, essential civilian supplies, and supplies for French forces in the field. Rearmament materials, he reasoned, could not be brought to bear on the enemy in the immediate future since French troops to be rearmed would require a period of orientation and training in their use. In short, Eisenhower considered rearming the French to be a long-range problem related to future campaigns in the Mediterranean or Europe and not to the immediate fighting in North Africa. In his cables to Washington in December and January he continually insisted that he could not, in the immediate future, spare any additional shipping space for the purpose; when his build-up was sufficiently advanced, he said, it would be for the CCS to say whether they could, in the light of the world shipping situation, "cope with this new commitment."[46]

Of necessity, War Department policy followed generally along the same line. In late December 1942 Général de Division Marie Emile Béthouart arrived in Washington as head of a military mission dispatched by Général Henri Giraud, new commander in chief of the French North

---

[45] For material on French North African shipping, see French Shipg folder, WSA Douglas File.

[46] Msg 3664, Eisenhower to Marshall, 31 Dec 42, Jt Rearmament Com Cable File, OCMH.

African forces. Béthouart presented a broad program of requirements divided into three priorities. In first priority he placed materials to meet emergency requirements of the French North African army and North Africa's economy and certain materials for the French Air Force; in second, modern equipment for eight infantry and three armored divisions; in third, materials for a services of supply. After reviewing the Béthouart program, the War Department decided the emergency requirements presented, except for air force materials, should be accepted as a charge against American production, but that Eisenhower must continue to control the rate of assignment and shipment. OPD thought that the eleven-division program might well be accepted as a long-range goal, subject to adjustments in the composition of proposed forces, but no one in the War Department was willing to make any rigid commitments in the light of uncertainties as to the availability of shipping and matériel.

A commitment was made, nevertheless, of debatable rigidity, at the Casablanca Conference. Giraud, in conversations with the American political and military leaders, again presented the eleven-division program and added a request for a 1,000-plane air force. Marshall and Somervell gave him assurances that the United States would proceed to equip French troops with the greatest possible speed but, at least in their own minds, made no specific commitments as to the timing or eventual scope of the program. Giraud interpreted the assurances as considerably more. After later conversations with the President, he drew up a memorandum embracing his understanding of the agreements reached. First he stated generally:

". . . it has been agreed between the President and General Giraud that the French Forces are to receive under priority the armament which is absolutely necessary for them to have, and that this material shall be made up of the most modern kind." To this statement the President wrote "Oui" in the margin. Second Giraud stated that in the "ulterior conversations with General Marshall and General Somervell," the total amount of this equipment was specified as sufficient for three armored and eight motorized divisions, and an air force of one thousand planes. Delivery of all this material would be accomplished by summer, enough for three motorized divisions plus armored supporting units and such aviation material as could be delivered by air "in the course of the next few weeks." Shipping would be provided for this purpose and for transport of 65,000 tons of civilian supplies monthly in return for transfer of 165,000 tons of French merchant shipping to the Allied pool. To these specific commitments the President noted "Oui en principe." [47]

General Giraud left the conference jubilant, assuming that the President's "Oui en principe" meant complete acceptance of his views. Undoubtedly the phrase in French meant a great deal more than its literal English translation "Yes in principle," since nobody on the American side interpreted it as an absolute commitment

---

[47] (1) There is no official record of the conversations. The above is based largely on memo, Marshall for McCloy, 4 Feb 43, in ID 475 Equip of Trs France, I. The English text of Giraud's memo and the President's marginal notes are included in Tabs A and B. (2) On the President's use of French, see Vigneras, The Rearmament of the French Forces in World War II, OCMH.

to make materials available on any time schedule. Action immediately following Casablanca, both in North Africa and in Washington, was only aimed at a limited acceleration of the movement of rearmament supplies. On 26 January Eisenhower ruled that 25,000 tons per UGS convoy should be allocated for French rearmament, the priorities on this tonnage to be determined by the Joint Rearmament Committee. At its first meeting in February, MAC(G) began to assign equipment for two French infantry divisions and auxiliary troops in accordance with Eisenhower's requests, but there remained little prospect, under the tonnage limitation, that much of the equipment Giraud had assumed he was promised during the "next few weeks" would actually be delivered for several months.[48]

The French interpretation of the Casablanca agreement could not be so lightly dismissed. In Washington Béthouart pressed for an increase in the shipping allocation from 25,000 to 100,000 tons, insisting that a promise had been made to ship the equipment for three infantry divisions immediately. In North Africa, Eisenhower found his embarrassment growing as the pace of American performance fell so far behind what Giraud publicized as the American promise at Casablanca. There were strong hints that the French might withdraw their co-operation, and Eisenhower became increasingly concerned. While he still felt that he could not spare any more shipping from that regularly allotted him to carry materials for the three French infantry divisions, he asked Marshall in mid-February if 100,-000 tons of additional cargo shipping might not be provided for the purpose either from French ships or other sources.

Marshall asked the SOS to explore the possibilities of getting the ships and at the same time referred Eisenhower's message to the President for some definite policy decision. Roosevelt immediately informed Eisenhower firmly and finally that neither he nor General Marshall had promised equipment for French divisions on any time schedule. Though this placed Marshall and Eisenhower on firmer ground in dealing with Giraud, the situation still seemed to call for some spectacular action to reassure the French of American sincerity. The Navy agreed to furnish escort for a special convoy to sail in March, and on 19 February Somervell asked Lewis Douglas of WSA for an allocation of twenty-five ships. This request came in the midst of a growing squeeze on Atlantic shipping — for the Soviet aid program, for the regular convoys to North Africa, and for the British import program. Douglas characterized it as a "terrifically stiff demand on a very, very tight situation," and at first insisted that it could only be met by diversions from other services.[49] In the end he was able to find nineteen ships without any apparent dislocation elsewhere, and the special convoy (UGS-6½) was arranged to sail in mid-March with 132,000 tons of supplies for the French.[50]

---

[48] (1) Msg 7433, FREEDOM, Algiers, to AGWAR, 26 Jan 43, ID 475 Equip of Trs France, I. (2) Min 1533, 74th mtg MAC(G), 1 Feb 43; Min 1535, 75th mtg, 5 Feb 43; Min 1560, 76th mtg, 9 Feb 43; Min 1590–93, 78th mtg, 16 Feb 43.

[49] Memo, Douglas for Somervell, 19 Mar 43, Shipg folder, Hq ASF.

[50] (1) Memo, Somervell for Douglas, 19 Mar 43, Shipg folder, Hq ASF. (2) Douglas' notes on conf with Somervell, 19 Feb 43, Army Reqmts folder, WSA Douglas File. (3) Memo, Land and Douglas for President, 23 Feb 43, Allocs Gen folder, WSA Douglas File. (4) For British import program, see below, Ch. XXVI.

When the American members of MAC-(G) presented the large requests for assignment of equipment to the French for three infantry divisions, the British objected and the issue was once again brought before the CCS for a policy decision on the ultimate scope of the French program and the priority to be accorded it. The Americans asked that materials be assigned the French up to a limit of eleven divisions and a 450-plane air force at a rate to be determined by their ability to organize units "around a nucleus of trained officers and non-commissioned officers," and to the extent that shipping could be made available for transport of this material.[51] The British countered with objections that rearming the French would interfere with operations agreed on at Casablanca, particularly the build-up in the British Isles and the proposed reconquest of Burma. They thought French rearmament should simply be placed in a strategic priority lower than that of British or American operational needs, and accorded such assignments as this strategic priority merited. When the American staff cited the President's agreement at Casablanca, the British said the Prime Minister had not participated in the decision. In the end the CCS again agreed to disagree on the major questions involved, though they did confirm the assignments for the special convoy, and the British accepted the obligation to furnish rifles for three French divisions. But the British staff still balked at accepting the principle that allocations to the French should come proportionately from their share of American production under the Weeks-Somervell Agreement. In concluding the discussion, they pointed out that the CCS could hardly pursue the matter any further in the face of the President's undertaking

with General Giraud, and suggested that the only recourse was for the Prime Minister to take it up with the President.[52]

Neither the CCS nor the President actually came to grips with the problem again until two months later at the TRIDENT Conference in Washington. There the CCS finally, and with much less friction than before, agreed on a policy. They stipulated that the "rearming and reequipping of the French Forces in North Africa should be proceeded with as rapidly as the availability of equipment will allow, but as a secondary commitment to the requirements of the British and U.S. Forces in the various theaters." At the suggestion of Churchill, the stipulation was added, "The use of captured German equipment for this purpose will be explored."[53] Shortly thereafter, on 10 June 1943, MAC(G) decided, with the British member concurring, that the action of the CCS "made it clear that arming the French Forces in North Africa was now a joint undertaking" and that assignments should be charged to the common pool, that is, partly out of the material earmarked for the British in the Army Supply Program.[54]

The decision at TRIDENT was not a clear confirmation of the ANFA agreement. There was no mention of the eleven-divi-

---

[51] CCS 181, 23 Feb 43, title: Equip of French Forces in N Africa.

[52] (1) *Ibid.* (2) CCS 181/1, 25 Feb 43, title: Equip of French Forces in N Africa. (3) CCS 131/2, 26 Feb 43, same title. (4) CCS 181/3, 2 Mar 43, same title. (5) CCS 181/5, 11 Mar 43, same title. (6) Min, 73d mtg CCS, 26 Feb 43, Item 6; min, 74th mtg, 5 Mar 43, Item 7; suppl to min, 75th mtg, 12 Mar 43.

[53] (1) CCS 242/6, 25 May 43, title: Final Rpt to President and Prime Minister (TRIDENT). (2) Min, 87th mtg CCS, 18 May 43, Item 6. (3) Min, 3d mtg at White House, TRIDENT, 19 May 43, Item 6.

[54] Min 2065, 97th mtg MAC(G), 10 Jun 43.

sion program or the 1,000-plane air force that Giraud had requested. To this extent it represented a compromise with the British. From a practical standpoint, however, it was a ratification of the manner in which the Americans were already carrying out the program and marked the end of British objections to it. As early as March the War Department and JCS had tentatively accepted the eleven-division program and a 450-plane air force as the ultimate goals for rearming the French in North Africa, subject to change in the light of strategic considerations or other material conditions. The priority accorded that program at Trident was approximately the one the Americans were already giving it.[55]

In April both OPD and SOS, accepting the eleven-division commitment, undertook to calculate the impact it would have on equipping U.S. forces. Both concluded that no deferments would be necessary in troop activations, though it would aggravate shortages for troops in training (by 5 percent, the SOS said, on the assumption that shipping would be provided for two-thirds of the program during 1943). The main impact would be absorbed by the reserve pool or cushion in the Army Supply Program for which equipment was being produced, but no specific units had yet been designated in the troop basis. These calculations confirmed what was already apparent, that the more serious impact of the French program was in its competition for shipping, not for material.[56]

Thus the actual rate of fulfillment of the program continued to be governed by the shipping situation. After the special March convoy, shipments reverted to the rate of 25,000 tons a convoy established earlier by General Eisenhower. Despite protests from Béthouart that this rate

should be increased in the light of the French contribution to the Allied shipping pool, Marshall and Somervell refused to raise the allocation. According to War Department figures in mid-April 1943, cargo vessels of 163,000 dead-weight tons had been turned over to the pool by the French. None of these ships had made an outward voyage from the United States at the time, and not all would be available until July. When they became available, allowing for the two-month turnaround involved, there would be a net of 81,500 tons a month. But since 162,000 dead-weight tons of shipping had already been used to transport materials to the French, Marshall told Béthouart that they already had a full *quid pro quo,* though he added the hopeful note that tonnage might be increased in the future if the strategic situation permitted. The 25,000-ton limitation actually meant more in principle than in practice. In April 55,263 tons were shipped and in May 38,359. The average monthly tonnage for the first seven months of 1943 was 21,745, exclusive of the special convoy, UGS-6½. After the heavy shipments of March, the rate slowed perceptibly each month through July, reflecting the absorption of Allied merchant shipping in the build-up and execution of the Sicilian operation (Husky). But the shipments made provided the material for completing the first phase of French rearmament—the equipping of three infantry divisions and a small air force along with numerous supporting armored, anti-

---

[55] See JCS 206/1, Rpt by JPS, 20 Mar 43, title: Equip for French Forces in N Africa.

[56] Memo, Gen Clay for OPD, 27 May 43, sub: Equip for French Forces in N Africa, OPD 400 France, Case 32. (2) Memo, Gen Hull for CofS, 10 Apr 43, sub: French Rearmament Prog, OPD 400 France, Case 35.

aircraft, artillery, and maintenance units.[57]

The system for handling military lend-lease to the French, as it evolved during this period, presented many distinctive features. The United States was undertaking to completely equip a foreign army of considerable size with everything from tanks to shoe laces. The enterprise was to be carried out under the close supervision of an American theater organization. The Army so formed would operate under the strategic direction of the Anglo-American high command. Though the ultimate limits of the program had to be determined by the CCS or at a political level, its composition within those limits was largely a matter for decision by the Joint Rearmament Committee in North Africa. Requirements were not only screened by the Joint Rearmament Committee, they were also formulated by it. In theory, the French were granted full participation, but in practice the U.S. executive staff performed the major portion of the work, leaving control firmly in American hands. In no other theater was this American control over a lend-lease program so extensive or effective.

The system worked generally as follows: The Joint Rearmament Committee drew up, as far in advance of shipping schedules as possible, lists of units to be equipped in order of priority. These lists were cabled to Washington, where SOS agencies under the staff supervision of the International Division spelled out the detailed items necessary according to U.S. Army tables of organization. Bids before MAC(G) for this equipment were sponsored by the International Division, and assignments were made to the commanding general of the Allied forces in North Africa, for delivery to the French, normally at a pace

necessary to insure the maximum utilization of available shipping space and to maintain a small backlog. The assigned material was shipped through U.S. Army channels, consigned to General Eisenhower under the Commanding General shipment system. Eisenhower retained, at least theoretically, the power to divert the material to other uses if he deemed the situation justified it. He retained also sufficient supervision over the subsequent use of material when turned over to the French to insure that it was used for the purposes envisaged by the Joint Rearmament Committee. Materials for French troops in combat in North Africa were requisitioned and handled entirely through American channels, with confirmation of the assignment by the MAB after the transfers were reported. All materials turned over to the French were charged to their lend-lease account in Washington after Eisenhower reported the transfer.

There was a distinction between the rearmament program and supply to other French forces. To enable the whole French North African army to continue to exist, and particularly to supply those units in battle, miscellaneous equipment of various types was supplied largely from theater stocks or from captured equipment. The rearmament equipment was furnished for

[57] (1) Ltr, Béthouart to Marshall, 7 Apr 43, ID 475 Equip of Trs France, II. (2) Ltr, Marshall to Béthouart, 18 Apr 43, OPD 400 France, Case 32. (3) Related papers in same file. (4) Memo, Col Boykin C. Wright, Dir ID, for OCT, 26 Apr 43, sub: Limitation on Mil Tonnage to French Forces in N Africa, ID 400.318 Free French, I. (5) Figures on tonnages shipped taken from Vigneras, The Rearmament of the French Forces in World War II, table at end of Ch. IV, OCMH. (6) French ships placed in the Allied pool were divided 50-50 between the control of WSA and the BMWT. See material in French Shipg folder, WSA Douglas File.

LEND-LEASE MATERIAL FOR THE FRENCH, *North Africa.*

specific troops withdrawn from battle, and the Americans promised at Casablanca that this equipment would be of the most modern kind. This was interpreted by the War Department to mean equipment of the same type available for issue to U.S. troops but not necessarily the latest models. The most significant substitution was of the Enfield (M1917) rifle for the Garand automatic (M1) and the carbine with which U.S. troops were equipped. This substitution brought bitter complaints from General Béthouart, but the shortage of rifles for American troops in training was so great that the War Department refused to change its decision. For the first three divisions, Enfields were furnished by the British out of stocks sold to them by the United States in 1940. There were other substitutions and deletions, particularly of "luxury" items, but in general, equipment for French units was computed by the supply services in accordance with U.S. tables of organization for corresponding units.[58]

Military Supply to Turkey

A competitor, in a sense, with the American program to rearm the French was a British plan to furnish arms to Turkey, the most important of the independent countries lying within the British area of strategic responsibility in the Middle East. Turkey occupied a strategic position athwart the approaches to the Middle East and Winston Churchill assigned her an important place in British plans. As long as the British were hard pressed in North Africa, Churchill hoped only to maintain Turkey as a friendly neutral prepared to defend herself should the Germans attack her. Once the Axis was defeated in North Africa, he envisaged a more ambitious campaign to secure the islands of the eastern Mediterranean and develop air bases in Turkey for raids on southeastern Europe. He regarded Turkish participation in the war on the side of the Allies as a necessary prelude to these later operations. The British Prime Minister proposed to regulate the flow of supplies to Turkey with these purposes in mind. In the defensive phase, Turkey would be given just enough supplies to bolster her defenses and maintain a favorable disposition toward the Allies. When the British were ready to pass to the offensive, he would vastly extend the scope of aid to Turkey as a part of a pressure campaign to induce the Turks to enter the war. In their strategic directive for the assignment of munitions in early 1942 the CCS generally approved Churchill's program for Turkey in the defensive phase, stipulating that "limited amounts of munitions should be allocated to her as a means of influencing her to oppose Germany."[59]

This limited program of aid to Turkey soon became tangled in procedural problems. Like so many other features of the British effort, it was partially dependent upon the flow of supplies from the United States. The Turks showed a definite preference for dealing directly with the United States, rather than receiving American lend-lease aid through British channels. The MAB in June 1942 decided that, in deference to these wishes, assignments should be made directly rather than as a part of the British bulk allocation. The British made no strenuous ob-

[58] (1) See ID, Lend-Lease, II, 1181–1225. (2) Memo, OPD for CG SOS, 15 Mar 43, sub: Equip of French Forces, OPD 400, Case 6. (3) Lengthy correspondence between Béthouart and Col. Wright on the rifle question in ID 475, Equip of Trs France, II.
[59] (1) CCS 50/2 cited n. 44(2). (2) Churchill, Hinge of Fate, pp. 860, 892.

jection at this point, and a procedure was worked out whereby an Anglo-American Coordinating Committee in Ankara would screen all Turkish requirements at their source, the British would decide what portion they should furnish, and the Turks would bid directly in Washington for the remainder. No decision was rendered on the method of shipment and control en route, however, and this was the subject of long and inconclusive negotiations during the latter part of 1942. Just as the British in Washington appeared ready in December to concede that supplies should be shipped from the United States to Turkey consigned to General Maxwell to be turned over by him or the civilian lend-lease authorities in the Middle East, the British Government in London reverted to its original position that Turkey should be entirely a British responsibility.[60]

The British Government evidently feared that the Turkish case would become a precedent for general U.S. control of assignments and shipments to countries within British areas of responsibility. Also, by the end of 1942, Churchill felt the time had come to make a definite bid for Turkish entrance into the war and for planning the operation to secure the eastern Mediterranean, and he thought the entire matter should rest in British hands since it would be primarily a British affair. Churchill and the British staff came to the Casablanca Conference in January 1943 with a complete plan for arming Turkey and for using her armies and territory. They secured the agreement of Roosevelt and General Marshall that Turkey should be treated as a British problem. The CCS ruled:

(a) that Turkey lies within a theater of British responsibility, and that all matters connected with Turkey should be handled by the British in the same way that all matters connected with China are handled by the United States . . . .

(b) that, in particular, under the general direction of the C.C.S., the British should be responsible for framing and presenting to both Assignments Boards all bids for equipment for Turkey. Onward despatch to Turkey from the Middle East of such equipment will be a function of command of the British Commanders in Chief in the Middle East. . . .[61]

After Casablanca Churchill met at Adana with Turkish President Ismet Inönü with a view to preparing the way for Turkish entry into the war in the autumn of 1943. He promised extensive supplies and the development of Turkish airfields. While the results of the conferences were inconclusive, Churchill left with high hopes that the Turks might be persuaded. The British staff, in co-operation with Turkish officials, prepared during the following months an estimate of material to be furnished. The decisions at Casablanca, however, included no indication of the priority Turkish requirements would be given, and British bids for Turkey were often treated in Washington on a level with those for Latin America. At the TRI-DENT Conference in Washington in May 1943, Field Marshal Sir Alan Brooke presented the detailed Turkish requirements and asked for a higher priority for them. On studying the plan, General Somervell reported that out of 700,000 ship tons proposed for 1943 and 1944, about 260,000

---

[60] (1) Min 13, 2d mtg MAC(G), 18 Feb 42; Min 498, 35th mtg, 22 Jun 42; Min 535, 36th mtg, 2 Jul 42. (2) MBW 13/1, 1 Jul 42, title: Proced for Direct Lend-lease Relations Between the U.S. and Turkey, approved by MAB in Min 6, 25th mtg, 22 Jul 42. (3) See voluminous material in ID 008 Lend-lease, I–III; and AG 400.3295 (9-1-42).

[61] (1) Min, 63d mtg CCS, 20 Jan 43, Item 2. (2) CCS 157, memo by Br JPS, 18 Jan 43, title: Allied Plans Relating to Turkey.

must come from the United States with an inevitably serious impact on French rearmament, on training of U.S. troops, and on shipping materials for the build-up in the British Isles. The CCS finally decided that "with due regard to other important commitments" assignments of equipment to Turkey as agreed by them "should be made with the least practicable delay." [62] But General Marshall clearly stipulated that training American troops and French rearmament were "important commitments." [63]

This priority in itself thus gave no assurance of accomplishment of the British program for the Turks. And the whole plan was soon jettisoned because of other developments. The American strategic planners were lukewarm toward Churchill's plans for operations in the eastern Mediterranean and refused to divert materials from the west for that purpose. The failure of the British effort to seize the Dodecanese soon diminished the chances of enlisting Turkey's aid in the war. At the same time, American observers reported the Turks completely unable to make effective use of the material being furnished them. The capacity of Turkish ports also proved too limited to absorb the flow of equipment sent, and in August the British themselves requested a cutback in assignments. As it became apparent that Turkey would probably remain a neutral, the British plan receded into the background. [64]

Control of Lend-Lease by Theater Commanders

Within each of the areas treated in this chapter, the War Department sought to place in the hands of the American military commander a measure of control over the flow of lend-lease. The final decisions as to allocations had necessarily to rest with the central machinery in Washington, but the War Department wished its theater commanders to establish the need for lend-lease, military and civilian, in their areas in much the same manner that they established the need for military supplies for forces under their command, and in some cases to handle the distribution. The elements of this control, if fully exercised, would include initial screening of all lend-lease requirements, dictation of shipping priorities, and supervision of distribution once the material arrived in the theater. This is easily recognizable as the pattern applied in General MacArthur's command in Australia, and somewhat less completely in the South Pacific Area. The War Department accepted the Australian pattern as a model and sought to apply as much of it as possible in other theaters, though it recognized that the system was not readily adaptable to areas where the control of the American theater commander was not so complete. The Lend-Lease Administration, with primary responsibility for civilian lend-lease supply, sent its own representatives abroad, but at first was usually willing to agree that they should either be part of the military commander's staff or else work in close collaboration with it. [65]

---

[62] CCS 242/6 cited n. 53(1).

[63] (1) Min, 91st mtg CCS, 20 May 43, Item 3. (2) Churchill, *Hinge of Fate,* pp. 703–16. (3) CCS 206, memo by Br CsofS, 30 Apr 43, title: Mil Sups for Turkey. (4) Memo, Somervell for Hopkins, 12 May 43, Hopkins folder, Hq ASF.

[64] (1) Min 6, 68th mtg MAB, 26 May 43. (2) Memo, Somervell for Hopkins, 28 Jul 43, Hopkins folder, Hq ASF. (3) Min 2253, 106th mtg MAC(G), 12 Aug 43; Min 2260, 107th mtg, 23 Aug 43. (4) Min, 113th mtg CCS, 20 Aug 43, Item 8.

[65] (1) Ltr, Stettinius to McCloy, 10 Jul 42. (2) Memo, Patterson for OLLA, 18 Jul 42. (3) Memo, Stettinius for McCloy, 2 Sep 42, sub: Relations of Lend-lease Mis's Abroad to U.S. Army. All in ID 008 Lend-lease, I. (4) Cf. memo, Somervell for Lutes, 20 Jul 42, Opns SOS folder, Hq ASF, in which Somervell expressed his more extreme views that the lend-lease representatives should be removed entirely.

Because procedures for lend-lease to the United Kingdom had been long established and because Averell Harriman, the lend-lease representative in England, was in effect a personal representative of the President and Hopkins, very little could ever be done to apply the Australian pattern there. At the instigation of Somervell a Lend-Lease Board of Review was set up in late 1942 composed of representatives of the SOS ETOUSA, the U.S. executive staff of LMAB, and the Harriman mission to screen British requirements in certain fields, but it seems to have accomplished very little. The determination of the lend-lease needs of Britain itself, civilian and military, continued to be made by the combined boards or by negotiations between high officials of the two governments.[66]

It was rather in the outlying areas that the definite attempt was made to establish the Australian pattern, but the British considered it their prerogative to control the flow of supplies to their own areas of responsibility and attempted to prevent the establishment of separate American channels. As early as March 1942, the U.S. members of MAC(G) proposed that shipments of lend-lease to all areas other than the United Kingdom and the USSR be consigned to theater commanders for distribution, but the British would never agree to this practice in India or the Middle East.[67] A War Department proposal in August 1942 that General Maxwell screen civilian lend-lease requirements in the Middle East never came to fruition largely because the British insisted that screening should be accomplished through the established channels of the Middle East Supply Center, an organization they had set up in 1941 to regulate imports to all nations east of Malta. Both Maxwell and Frederick Winant, the lend-lease representative in the Middle East, had membership on this body, and there was a certain logic in the British position, but the result was that the screening procedure established did not follow the Australian pattern of military control. Distribution of lend-lease to independent countries in the Middle East remained in British hands. No serious attempt was made during 1942 to screen British military requirements in the Middle East.[68]

An attempt was also made in August 1942 to have General Wheeler, commander of the American SOS in India, exercise control over lend-lease supply to India, but it met with a similar fate. Wheeler commented on British lend-lease requirements for India on request, but no definite system of screening was established. Wheeler was never even given representation on the Indian Lend-Lease Requirements Committee. On the civilian side, in early 1943 OLLA dispatched to India a mission, headed by Frederick W. Ecker, to screen Indian civilian requirements, study the resources of India, and

[66] (1) See above, Chs. X–XI. (2) Ltr, Gen Somervell to Gen Lee, 5 Oct 42, sub: Screening of Lendlease Reqmts in U.K. (3) Ltr, Lee to Somervell, 16 Dec 42. (4) Ltr, Styer to Lee, 20 Jan 43. Last three in AG 400.3295 (9-1-42) (3) Sec 5.

[67] Min 112, 11th mtg MAC(G), 19 Mar 42; Min 614, 40th mtg, 23 Jul 42.

[68] (1) Msg, AGWAR to AMSME, 18 Aug 42, CM-OUT 5535; paraphrase of Maxwell's reply, 24 Aug 42, is in AG 400.3295 (9-1-42) (3) Sec 1. (2) Memo, Frederick Winant for Dean Acheson, 17 Apr 42, sub: Civilian Sup Reqmts of Near East Countries and Middle East Sup Center, Middle East Corresp Lendlease 1 file, DAD. (3) Ltr, Somervell to Stettinius, 31 Aug 42, ID 008 Lend-lease, I. (4) Msg, AGWAR to AMSME, 3 Sep 42, CM-OUT 1099. (5) Msg, AGWAR to AMSME, 5 Sep 42, CM-OUT 1948. (6) Msg, AGWAR to AMSME, 10 Oct 42, CM-OUT 13336. (7) Msg, AGWAR to AMSME, 29 Nov 42, CM-OUT 9304. (8) Msg, AMSME to AGWAR, 25 Sep 42, CM-IN 10768. (9) Msg, AMSME to AGWAR, 22 Oct 42, CM-IN 91316. (10) Msg, AMSME to AGWAR, 18 Nov 42, CM-IN 7876.

assist in the development of reverse lend-lease procedures. An effort was made to place Ecker on Wheeler's staff following the Australian pattern, but this did not succeed either. In mid-1943 the SOS was still pressing for a much closer supervision over military and civilian lend-lease requirements for India.[69]

In North Africa and in China,[70] where the British had little reason to object, the Americans were able to institute effective control by their theater commanders over lend-lease shipments. As indicated earlier, Eisenhower's control over military supply to the French was virtually complete. Civilian supply in North Africa was a somewhat different problem from that in Australia inasmuch as it was a matter of relief and rehabilitation of an area liberated from German control. Though General Somervell urged application of the Australian pattern of military control there, the President chose to place the planning of civilian supply for liberated areas in the hands of the State Department and of other civilian organizations. In the theater the North African Economic Board, representing most interested American and British civilian and military organizations, was charged with screening civilian requirements and making recommendations to Washington and London on a program of civilian supply. Yet the board operated in effect as a part of Eisenhower's headquarters and the supreme commander controlled the amount of shipping space that could be allocated to civilian supply. Furthermore, the experience in North Africa with divided responsibilities brought a demand for closer military control of the whole matter, and

this was the pattern that emerged in the campaigns in Italy and Sicily.[71]

Thus, as American industrial production rapidly overshadowed British and American military forces spread out over the world, American military leaders came increasingly to assert their control over lend-lease supply lines and to use them as instruments to advance American plans and interests. In Australia and New Zealand, dominions of the British Commonwealth, American commanders exercised almost complete control. After the North African invasion, the French ceased to be protégés of London and became protégés of Washington. In the Middle East and India the British maintained their control over the distribution of American supplies, but the disposition of the Americans to challenge that control was evident by early 1943 despite the concession made regarding Turkey at Casablanca. An attack on the whole British conception of protégé nations and on the powers of reallocation exercised by the London board was soon to follow.

---

[69] (1) Control Division, ASF, Army Service Forces Activities in the Supply of China, Burma, and India, 1942–1943, MS (hereafter cited as ASF in China, Burma, and India), p. 233, OCMH. (2) ID Rpt 10, Lend-lease Information, 31 Oct 43, sec on India. (3) Memo, Franks for Clay, 7 Jan 43, sub: Lend-lease Mis to India, ID 008 Lend-lease, I. (4) Related papers in same file and in ID 008 Lend-lease, III.

[70] On China, see below, Ch. XIX.

[71] (1) See International Division, ASF, Civilian Supply: A History of the Civilian Supply Branch, International Division, ASF, MS, pp. 1–38, OCMH. (2) Memo, Somervell for CofS, 11 Nov 42, sub: Civilian Sup in N Africa, CofS file, Hq ASF.
Treatment of the logistical problems raised by civilian supply in North Africa, Europe, and other areas is reserved for the second volume on global logistics and strategy.

CHAPTER XIX

China, Burma, and India

As far as American plans for the war against Japan had taken shape in early 1942, China occupied an important place in them. The containment of Japanese divisions in China was viewed as of vital importance during the defensive phase of the Pacific war, and it seemed likely that in any ultimate offensive to achieve the final victory over Japan, the Japanese Army would have to be defeated on the Asiatic mainland rather than in the Pacific islands. China also seemed to offer the best possibilities for development of air bases from which massive air attacks against the Japanese homeland could be mounted. Yet most U.S. military and political leaders felt that, at least during the period of concentration on the Atlantic front, the American contribution to the war in Asia should be limited to an air effort and supply support of the Chinese and Anglo-Indian armies. The vast pool of Chinese, Indian, and British manpower, they felt, should be able to carry the burden of the ground war if furnished American supplies; they thought it unreasonable to divert sizable American forces from other theaters, or to commit the large amounts of shipping that would be needed to move them to so distant an area. Supply to China was the principal American problem in this area, ·since American support for the British in India was handled through normal British lend-lease channels as in the Middle East. Arming the Nationalist Army of Chiang

Kai-shek seemed the cheapest and most logical method not only of driving the Japanese from the Asiatic mainland but also of assuring a measure of stability there in the postwar period.

India and Burma fell within the British area of strategic responsibility and both were placed, after the dissolution of Wavell's ABDA Command, under General Headquarters, India. China, on the other hand, occupied a unique place in the Anglo-American command structure. An Allied "China Theater" was created at ARCADIA, simultaneously with Wavell's ABDA Command, and Chiang Kai-shek was named its supreme Allied commander. Chiang was head of a national state and as such did not fit into the chain of command as did other commanders of theaters in the Anglo-American structure. It was much as if the British and Americans had created a Russian Theater and named Marshal Stalin its supreme Allied commander. Chiang could not be held responsible to the CCS, nor expected to concur in a strategy that placed the defeat of Germany foremost.

"China Theater" was really a device by which the President sought to accord Chiang a position due the head of a major Allied state, and still limit his participation in decisions on Allied strategy to those matters involving the war in the Far East. Despite this recognition, China, unlike the USSR, could never make her weight felt because of her own weakness. Chiang's ill-organized, ill-equipped, and weary armies were in no position to wage effective war against the Japanese without extensive outside support. The scope and nature of this support had to be fitted into the Anglo-American plan for global distribution of resources and hence had to be determined by the CCS and MAB. Chiang's effort to secure a place in this machinery failed, and he had to rely on such pressure as he could exert through direct appeals to the President. Within the combined machinery, the British readily conceded strategic and supply responsibility for China to the United States.

Consequently, the real American influence in the determination of military policy in the China Theater derived from control of the all-important supply line. The link between Chinese forces and the CCS lay in the arrangement for exercise of American military responsibility. For some two months after Pearl Harbor, the head of the lend-lease mission, General Magruder, remained the senior American commander in the Orient. To provide for fuller Sino-American collaboration, a new mission was dispatched to China in February 1942 headed by General Stilwell. By agreement between Secretary of War Stimson and Dr. T. V. Soong, Chiang's brother-in-law and Chinese Foreign Minister, Stilwell was to be commander of all U.S. troops in China, Burma, and India, representative of the United States on all international military councils there, and to "supervise and control" all lend-lease affairs relating to China. He was also to be Allied chief of staff to the Supreme Commander, China Theater, Chiang Kai-shek, and to command all Chinese troops Chiang might entrust to him. By agreement with the British, he was charged

with maintaining liaison with the commanders in Burma and India and was granted the right to operate a supply line to China through these countries. The War Department directive to Stilwell specifically assigned him the mission of increasing the effectiveness of American aid to China and assisting in improving the combat effectiveness of the Chinese Army.[1] Around Stilwell's mission the major questions of American policy in China, Burma, and India (CBI) were to revolve for over two and a half years. However, simultaneously with Stilwell's appointment, Claire Chennault, head of the American Volunteer Group in China and air adviser to Chiang Kai-shek, was made an American colonel (in April a brigadier general) and by July his "Flying Tigers" had been transformed into a small American air task force in China. As the principal exponent of the use of American air power in China rather than a laborious effort to spur the Chinese Army to lift itself by its bootstraps, Chennault was also to exercise a powerful influence on both strategy and logistics in CBI.

The Failure of the Prewar Chinese Lend-Lease Program

The objectives of the prewar lend-lease program for China, it will be recalled, included improvement of the Burma Road, construction of a Yunnan-Burma railroad, creation of a Chinese air force, equipping of a ground army of thirty divisions (on a scale considered adequate for war in China), and development of the capacity of the Chinese arsenals. Though only about 70,000 tons of Chinese lend-lease actually left the United States for Ran-

---

[1] Romanus and Sunderland, *Stilwell's Mission to China*, pp. 70–80.

goon in 1941, the prewar production program and assignments schedules for the Chinese promised to make some 50,000 tons of supplies available monthly in early 1942. American entrance into the war in itself necessitated no change in the program, and it continued as a blueprint for aid to China until the Japanese conquest of Burma rendered its fulfillment impossible.[2]

The Chinese regarded the 1941 program as a definite commitment on the part of the U.S. Government, though they had never received any assurance to this effect, and though the whole new theory of munitions assignment belied it. Competent observers with the Magruder mission had already come to regard the program as unrealistic, even before the Japanese conquest of Burma. Transportation experts pointed to the growing stockpiles of Chinese material at Rangoon and Lashio, stockpiles greater than the Burma Road could carry in six months of peak operation, if judged by previous performance. They also found the selection of items for shipment bad. For example, mountains of blankets lay at Rangoon being slowly consumed by white ants while blankets continued to arrive under lend-lease. General Magruder's cables to Washington on priorities clearly reflected the necessity for a program of shipments carefully controlled by the U.S. mission and not by the Chinese in the United States. In a classic message on 13 February 1942, he warned the War Department that the extent of the Chinese war effort was being highly exaggerated by Sinophile propaganda in the United States, and expressed doubts that the Chinese would ever put American supplies to effective use if left to their own devices.[3]

Meantime, the munitions in the cargoes dispatched just before Pearl Harbor became a bone of contention between the British and Chinese. The British impounded some of this material on arrival in Rangoon, and Chiang interpreted this as a seizure. In high dudgeon, he threatened to withdraw all co-operation with the British and to return American lend-lease to its owners. While the matter was satisfactorily adjusted by assurances to Chiang that the War Department would not permit retransfer of Chinese lend-lease to the British without his approval, the crisis had lasting effects. The Chinese were ever after suspicious of British designs on their supplies. To both Magruder and the War Department, on the other hand, the episode proved the need for American control over lend-lease material after its arrival in the theater.[4]

The fall of Rangoon in late February 1942 shut off the supply line through Burma to China and made necessary the development of a new and far more difficult line from Indian ports of entry. There was a convenient hiatus in shipments from the United States from 8 December until mid-January, which made the transition easier. The three ships that departed in January carrying Chinese supplies were diverted to ports on the west coast of India. Some of the supplies at Rangoon were also

---

[2] (1) See above, Ch. III. (2) Memo, Lt W. S. Brewster for Lt Col L. C. Strong, 20 May 42, AMMISCA 319.1, ID. (3) Note, prepared by WPD for Lt Gen Hugh A. Drum, unsigned, Jan 42, Tab B, in App., Stilwell Washington Plng File, to History of China, Burma, India Theater, MS, OPD 314.7 China Theater of Opns. (4) Memo for rcd, unsigned, May 42, ASW 400.336 China.

[3] (1) See Rpt 3, Maj John E. Russell to Gen Magruder, 12 Nov 41, sub: Lend-lease Sup and Trans in Burma, Port of Rangoon folder, CBI Theater Rcds, KCRC. (2) Most of Magruder's messages are conveniently collected in AMMISCA IN Cables file, ID. (3) Msg 256, AMMISCA to AGWAR, 13 Feb 42, AG 400.3295 (4-14-41) Sec 1A.

[4] For a full description of the so-called *Tulsa* crisis, see Romanus and Sunderland, *Stilwell's Mission to China*, pp. 57–60.

evacuated to India. The British had already agreed that General Stilwell might operate a supply line to China through India, and Chiang Kai-shek negotiated an agreement with the Indian Government permitting the use of port, rail, and storage facilities for Chinese supplies. At first an ambitious scheme was considered whereby Bombay would serve as a distributing center for lend-lease for the whole Middle and Far East with materials remaining under U.S. control after their arrival, but the idea was eventually abandoned as impractical, and Karachi, with more limited facilities was chosen as the principal American base. It was not until early 1943 that the situation in the Bay of Bengal permitted a gradual shift to Calcutta, on the eastern coast of India, much closer to China. General Wheeler was already active in Karachi planning projects connected with the Iranian mission, and in February 1942 he was transferred to General Stilwell's new command as head of his Services of Supply. This SOS was to have the dual function of supporting the few U.S. troops in India, largely Army Air Forces, and operating the line of supply through India for China.[5]

The new supply line envisaged for China was formidable to contemplate. It would run from Karachi, already twelve thousand miles by sea from the United States, across the breadth of India to upper Assam on the border of Burma, and thence through or over the north Burma jungle to road and river routes that connected with the Burma Road. In the immediate future only an airlift would be possible, to run from Dinjan, near Sadiya, to Myitkyina in north Burma. It was planned that roads would follow, one to run from Imphal to Mandalay, and another from Ledo, near Sadiya, to Myit-

kyina. Optimists claimed that the Imphal Road could be in operation by the summer of 1942 and the Ledo Road by that November if construction were rushed as a matter of first priority. But even these thin hopes for a supply line via Myitkyina and Mandalay were soon dashed by the crushing defeat of the British and Chinese forces in north Burma. By mid-May, the only remaining access to China was a much longer and more difficult airlift from Dinjan in Assam all the way to Kunming. To avoid the airfield at Myitkyina, now under Japanese control, this airlift had to swing northward over a spur in the Himalayas whose lowest point was fourteen thousand feet, the famous Hump. No road, it proved, could possibly be built over the high and rugged Himalayas to supplement it. *(Map 6)*

While the shorter airlift still seemed possible, arrangements had been made to divert twenty-five commercial transports from airlines in the United States and ten from Pan-American's trans-African line to India, and tentative plans were laid for placing a hundred planes on the airlift by the end of the year, seventy-five to be operated as U.S. Army transports and twenty-five by China National Aviation Corporation. But performance did not

---

[5] (1) Msg 223, Chungking to AGWAR, 27 Jan 42. (2) Msg 233, Chungking to AGWAR, 31 Jan 42. (3) Msg 299, Chungking to AGWAR, 19 Feb 42. (4) Msg 315, Chungking to AGWAR, 27 Feb 42. (5) Msg 333, Chungking to AGWAR, 6 Mar 42. (6) Msg 309, Chungking to AGWAR, 25 Feb 42. (7) Msg 164, AGWAR to AMMISCA, 30 Jan 42. All in AG 400.-3295 (4-14-41) Sec 1A. (8) Min of conf in Gen Aurand's off, 1 Feb 42, Item 142, Col Boone's file, DAD; min, 3 Feb 42, Item 150, Col Boone's file, DAD. (9) Memo, Coe for Gross, 4 Feb 42, sub: Proposal to Estab a Depot in the Middle East for Def Aid and Other Mun, Item 151, Col Boone's file, DAD. (10) Msg 391, AGWAR to AMMISCA, 3 Apr 42, AG 400.3295 (4-3-42). (11) Msg 239, AGWAR to AMMISCA, 4 Mar 42, Stilwell Personal Cable File, DRB AGO.

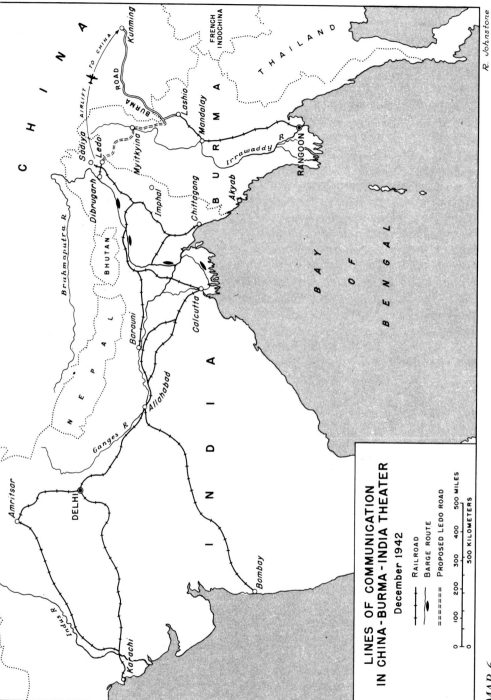

R. Johnstone

LINES OF COMMUNICATION
IN CHINA-BURMA-INDIA THEATER
December 1942

RAILROAD
BARGE ROUTE
PROPOSED LEDO ROAD

0   100 200 300 400 500 MILES

0   300 KILOMETERS

MAP 6

measure up to plans. Transport planes were one of the most critical shortages of 1942. The British had already been promised a sizable number, the Soviet Union was clamoring for an allocation, and the U.S. Army was hard pressed to meet its requirements for other theaters. Even the dispatch of the commercial transports was delayed, none arriving in Karachi until 5 April 1942. The need for air transport across India itself made it impossible to place many of the arriving Army transports on the Hump air line. By July there were still only nine in operation there, and twelve China National Aviation Corporation planes. In addition to the shortage of transports, there were other difficulties. Air supply was a relatively new thing in the logistics of war, and it would take time and experience to develop it under the conditions prevailing in India and China. Lack of spare parts and inadequate maintenance facilities kept many transports on the ground. The construction of additional airfields in Assam, at first a British responsibility, went ahead very slowly because of lack of vital machinery, the unreliability of local labor, and difficult climatic conditions. For all practical purposes, the flow of lend-lease to China stopped with the fall of Burma and was not resumed for some time to come. The small capacity that the airlift did develop during 1942, reaching a peak of 1,600 tons in December, had to be devoted almost entirely to carrying supplies for Chennault's small American air force in China.[6]

The readjustment in Washington to these changed conditions was hesitant and confused. American officials were reluctant to radically reduce a supply program already quite small in relation to those for Britain and the USSR, fearing Chiang Kai-shek might abandon the fight entirely if his hopes for supplies were suddenly dashed. Military and civilian policy makers alike agreed that, as an irreducible minimum, China must be kept in the war. Soong made exaggerated claims as to the capacity of the proposed supply line through India, continued to press for large allocations, and opposed repossession of any of the materials in the United States earmarked for China. There was an inevitable tendency to accept his views and to delay curtailment of the Chinese program, despite continued advice from Magruder and Stilwell that shipment of any sizable quantities of supplies into China would be impossible for many months and that many of Soong's requests were for equipment the Chinese Army could not possibly use.[7]

The Achilles' heel of Soong's effort lay in his inability to secure shipping to transport to India the supplies made available. The average monthly allocation of shipping for Chinese lend-lease continued at around 10,000 tons while supplies earmarked for China normally totaled around 50,000 tons a month. Soong'

[6] (1) Romanus and Sunderland, *Stilwell's Mission* China, pp. 118–48, 163–67, 204–07. (2) Msg 43 AMMISCA to AGWAR, 1 Apr 42, AMMISCA I Cables file, Bk. 4, ID. (3) Msg 201, AMMISCA AGWAR, 19 Jan 42. (4) Msg 252, AMMISCA AGWAR, 5 Feb 42. (5) Ltr, William S. Youngman CDS, to Stettinius, 1 Jan 42. Last three in AG 400 3295 (4-14-41) Sec 1A. (6) Related papers in sam file. (7) Rpt, 24 Aug 42, sub: Visit to China by Lauch lin Currie, OPD 336 China (8-24-42). (8) Craven an Cate, *AAF IV*, pp. 411–15.

[7] (1) See Msg 520, AMMISCA to AGWAR, Apr 42, AMMISCA IN Cables file, Bk. 5, ID. (. Msg 629, AMMISCA to AGWAR, 2 May 42, sam file. In this cable, Magruder, while Stilwell was st absent in the Burma jungles, recommended th Chiang should be asked to designate certain limite organizations of ground and air forces that mig practically be equipped for the war against Japa and that lend-lease should be extended only for th purpose, not for the build-up of national stock Magruder thought Chinese supplies accumulating the United States over and above those necessary f these objectives should be repossessed.

earnest entreaties for an increase failed to move either General Somervell or Admiral Land since the prospects of ultimate delivery of the material to the Chinese were so uncertain. A log jam of Chinese supplies awaiting shipment soon developed. By the end of April there were 1,790 carloads of material at Newport News, where China Defense Supplies, Inc., maintained a special pier, with no shipping in prospect to move them. A rough calculation of material available at factories, depots, and ports and on rail cars revealed a total of 150,000 tons—500,000 if the bulky materials for the Yunnan-Burma Railway were included.[8]

The continuing growth of this log jam in the United States, with no supplies at all moving from India to China, finally forced the Munitions Assignments Board at the end of May 1942 to begin curtailment of the Chinese program. Soong saw he must give ground and presented a new program calling for shipment of 7,500 tons of supplies monthly, basing this on a generous estimate of the Hump airlift when the promised hundred transport planes should be operating on it. He indicated that the Chinese stockpiles in the United States could not be released unless this program were accepted. The Air Forces was simultaneously estimating that only 1,200 tons a month could possibly be transported over the Hump, the availability of a hundred transport planes for many months to come was a doubtful matter, and other estimates of Hump capacity varied in direct ratio to the number of persons making them. The MAB finally decided on a compromise figure of 3,500 tons per month, exclusive of airplane fuel, but directed that this tonnage be shipped to General Stilwell for transfer to China at the time and place he should decide. Based on this figure, a Chi-

nese emergency air transport program was worked out in conferences between China Defense Supplies, Inc. and MAC(G) for the six-month period May through October 1942. The assignments were made firm for May and June, but only tentative for the following four months. With some difficulty, Soong was persuaded to release most of the Chinese stockpile in the United States for this small compensation, and the materials were repossessed and reassigned. Most of the special procurement under way for China was canceled (except 7.92-mm. ammunition), and the remainder of the Chinese military lend-lease production program merely absorbed into the Army Supply Program. Thus by the end of June 1942 only a trickle of 3,500 tons monthly remained earmarked for China out of the ambitious program of 1941.[9]

---

[8] (1) Ltr, Soong to McCloy, 6 Mar 42, ASW 400.-336 China. (2) Memo cited n. 2(4). (3) Ltr, Soong to McCloy, 12 Feb 42. (4) Ltr, McCloy to Soong, 28 Feb 42. Last two in AG 400.3295 (4-14-41) Sec 1A. (5) Memo, Somervell for CofS, 25 Feb 42, sub: Shipg To Move CDS Sups, G-4/32192, Sec 2. (6) Memo for file, Lt Col John E. McCammon, 21 Apr 42, AMMISCA 337, ID. (7) Memo, Col Baird for Gen Aurand, 2 May 42, Tab D, Iranian Mis 563.5, ID. (8) Rpt of MAC(G) subcom, app to min, 29th mtg MAC(G), 18 May 42.

[9] (1) Min 285, 24th mtg MAC(G); 30 Apr 42; Min 327, 342, and 347, 27th mtg, 11 May 42; Min 371 and 373, 29th mtg, 18 May 42; Min 394, 31st mtg, 25 May 42; Min 398, 32d mtg, 1 Jun 42; Min 430, 33d mtg, 8 Jun 42. (2) Min 6, 15th mtg MAB, 13 May 42. (3) 1st Ind, MAB to MAC(G), to min, 27th mtg MAC(G), 11 May 42. (4) Exchange of ltrs, Soong to McCloy, 19–21 May 42. (5) Memo, McCloy for Hopkins, 4 May 42. Last two in ASW 400.336 China. (6) Memo, McCloy for CG SOS, 15 May 42, sub: Relation of Chinese Mats Now Frozen in U.S. (7) Memo, Aurand for Young, 15 May 42, sub: Present Sit With Respect to China. Last two in China Corresp Lend-lease 3 file, DAD. (8) Ltr, Soong to Aurand, 1 Jun 42. (9) Ltr, Aurand to Soong, 5 Jun 42. Last two in Item 376, Col Boone's file, DAD. (10) Ltr, Aurand to Soong, 6 Jun 42. (11) Ltr, Aurand to Soong, 18 Jun 42. (12) Memo, Maj George H. Olmstead, Secy MAC(G), for Chm, 3 Jun 42, sub: Status of Chinese Mun. Last three in ID 400.318 China, I.

Even the 3,500-ton program was threatened in July. There was already in India a stockpile of Chinese supplies estimated at 52,000 tons. The airlift carried only 80 tons in May and 106 in June, almost all for Chennault's air force. Heeding reports that heavy monsoon rains would reduce operations even further in July, General Aurand proposed to MAC(G) that no assignments at all should be made to China for that month. While possibly a realistic proposal in the light of logistical difficulties, it ignored Chinese sensibilities and produced a violent reaction from Soong. General Marshall recognized that the 3,500-ton program was the minimum gesture required to placate the Chinese and, when the case was finally referred by the MAB to CCS, secured a decision to continue the program.[10]

The July crisis marked the last challenge to the 3,500-ton program, though the airlift was not to reach that figure for more than a year afterward. Its adoption marked a definite break in the story of American lend-lease to China. The dominating circumstance conditioning all plans from May 1942 onward was the sheer physical difficulty of getting supplies to the Chinese armies.

Stilwell's Plans and Policies for Supply to China

General Stilwell, from the time of his emergence from the Burma jungle in May 1942 until he left the theater some two and a half years later, saw in the reconquest of Burma the only possible means by which the American policy of support to China could be carried out. He immediately asked for a U.S. corps to participate in such a campaign, but General Marshall could give but scanty consideration to this demand in the light of extensive commitments for the build-up in the British Isles, the Pacific, and the Middle East. American policy envisaged the use of British and Chinese ground forces on the Asiatic mainland with American participation limited to air and supply support. Stilwell had no choice but to frame his plans in terms of this policy. In his role as Allied chief of staff to Chiang, he soon came forward with a plan for retaking Burma in which British and Chinese forces would collaborate, with the possible aid of one U.S. division. While the British would bear the brunt of the campaign—an amphibious attack against Rangoon and an advance from Imphal across central Burma—the Chinese would also play an important part. Chinese forces operating from India, designated the X-RAY Force, would form a junction with another Chinese force operating from Yunnan Province in China, designated the YOKE Force, to drive the Japanese from northern Burma. Marshall had suggested that the stockpile of Chinese lend-lease in India should be turned over to the British, to be used by them in an effort to retake Burma, but Stilwell instead chose to use it to equip a Chinese army in India. Chinese troops who had made their way into India from Burma formed the nucleus of this force but Stilwell got Chiang to agree to supplement them with other troops to be flown in on return trips over the Hump. The British agreed to the establishment of a Chinese training center at Ramgarh in Bihar Province, and by the end of 1942

---

[10] (1) Agenda and Min 4a, 21st mtg MAB, 24 Jun 42; Min 4, 22d mtg, 1 Jul 42; Min 2a, 24th mtg, 15 Jul 42. (2) Min 515, 35th mtg MAC(G), 22 Jun 42; Min 559, 37th mtg, 9 Jul 42. (3) Ltr, Soong to McCloy, 18 Jun 42, ASW 400.336 China. (4) Min, 31st mtg CCS, 16 Jul 42, Item 4. (5) Min, 25th mtg JCS, 14 Jul 42, Item 4.

Stilwell had two full Chinese divisions there.

Any decision on such a major campaign naturally had to rest with the CCS, but pending their approval Stilwell went ahead during the summer and fall of 1942 to shape his plans for Chinese lend-lease around the concept of Chinese participation in an effort to retake Burma. In these plans he incorporated one part of Soong's original blueprint, the thirty-division program, and discarded the rest. American lend-lease to China would be concentrated entirely on the X-RAY and YOKE Forces, the two to make up between them the specified thirty divisions. YOKE Force, by far the larger, would be created by the concentration of understrength Chinese divisions in Yunnan Province and their consolidation into full strength divisions. The airlift would be used to the maximum extent possible to transport YOKE Force supplies, though the major portion of the equipment for YOKE would have to come initially from Chinese sources. Once the supply line through Burma was restored, lend-lease could be used to equip a much larger Chinese force. Even before the first thirty divisions were fully equipped, Stilwell hoped to start a similar program for a second thirty, these to be used in the defense of eastern China and eventually for a drive to open a port on the China coast. The equipment for sixty Chinese divisions was not comparable to that for a similar force of Americans since the Chinese division was smaller and was to receive far less artillery, motor transport, and mechanized equipment.[11]

By the Stimson-Soong agreement of January 1942, Stilwell was given "supervision and control" over lend-lease to China. Though he met with considerable opposition from Chiang Kai-shek (Soong had in fact never informed the Generalissimo of the terms of the agreement), with the support of the War Department and the MAB he was able to make this control reasonably effective by the end of 1942 and to mold the Chinese lend-lease program to his plans. In accepting the 3,500-ton program, the MAB stipulated that shipments should be consigned to General Stilwell and that supplies could be diverted by him to other uses with the approval of the board. Since the Chinese in India had no adequate organization for handling supplies, in August 1942 they agreed that General Wheeler's Services of Supply should take care of the receipt, storage, and transportation of lend-lease material through India. By chartering space on China National Aviation Corporation planes and by insisting that transports be sent for Army operation rather than Chinese, Stilwell was also able, for the most part, to control what moved over the Hump air lines.[12]

In Washington, Stilwell's influence also soon replaced that of CDS in determining Chinese requirements and assignments. While MAC(G) worked out the 3,500-ton program largely on the advice of CDS, its composition conformed to the requirements for the thirty-division program as far as they had been spelled out in June 1942. It was primarily an ordnance program with a sprinkling of signal equipment, medical supplies, and motor transport, part to come from U.S. production

[11] Romanus and Sunderland, *Stilwell's Mission to China*, pp. 135–38, 179–83, 214–21.
[12] (1) *Ibid.*, pp. 211–12. (2) ID, Lend-Lease, II, 1166, 1173. (3) Aide-Memoire, 23 Aug 42, on Chiang's understanding of agreements made with Lauchlin Currie, OPD 400.3295 China, I, Case 29. (4) Msg 1469, Roosevelt to Stilwell for Chiang, 10 Oct 42, Stilwell Personal Cable File, Bk. 1, Item 71, DRB AGO. (5) Craven and Cate, *AAF IV*, p. 413.

CHINESE SOLDIERS AND AN AMERICAN INSTRUCTOR

and part from British or Canadian. When the six-months emergency transport program expired in October, Stilwell took steps to bring assignments in line with the requirements his staff were working out with the Chinese in the theater. Though he recognized that materials were not moving into China, he asked for specific quantities in the following months that would complete equipment for the first thirty divisions, and would provide artillery and other materials for the second thirty and special needs for the Chinese in India. Accordingly, MAC(G) set up a new program of approximately 5,000 tons monthly for the next three months—November through January. As special requests from Stilwell increased, MAC(G)

soon shifted to a policy of meeting these requests instead of setting aside any specified monthly tonnage.[13]

When in late 1942 CDS presented an elaborate program of Chinese requirements for inclusion in the Army Supply Program, it was ruled to be "materially beyond available resources and other requirements" and forwarded to Stilwell for comment.[14] In conferences with Chinese

[13] (1) Tab B to min, 29th mtg MAC(G), 18 May 42. (2) Msg 75, AMMISCA, New Delhi, to AGWAR, 29 Aug 42, AMMISCA IN Cables file, Bk. 1, ID. (3) Msg 1260, AMMISCA to AGWAR, 12 Oct 42, AMMISCA IN Cables file, Bk. 6, ID. (4) Min 1101, 55th mtg MAC(G), 22 Oct 42, and tab to atchd rpt by Asgmts Subcom. (5) ID Rpt 10, Lend-lease Information, 31 Oct 43, Pt. 2, sec on China.

[14] Msg, AGWAR to AMMISCA, 30 Dec 42, CM-OUT 9999.

officials in Chungking, Stilwell pared down these requirements to the essentials for the two thirty-division programs, and further secured an agreement that in the future he should be responsible for presenting Chinese military requirements in Washington. Though CDS was to continue to present civilian requirements, Stilwell was also granted a voice in their determination to the extent his judgment dictated.[15]

In this manner the two thirty-division programs became the basis of the remaining small lend-lease program for China, and the flow of materials came under Stilwell's control subject to decisions on availability by the War Department and the MAB. At Stilwell's recommendation, assignments of planes to China, except for a few transports for the China National Aviation Corporation, were stopped in June 1942 and not resumed until mid-1943. The War Department also tried, in negotiations with the Office of Lend-Lease Administration, to stop shipments of arsenal and other materials procured on CDS requisitions since they only went to increase the stockpile in India. Though the War Department was never entirely successful in this endeavor, these shipments were cut to the bone. And as far as military supplies were concerned, the philosophy of the SOS and of MAC(G) was simply to assign and ship what Stilwell requested if equipment were available for the purpose, in much the same manner that requests were handled for U.S. troops overseas.[16]

Strategic Plans and Logistical Support May–December 1942

Though the Chinese lend-lease program might thus be framed in terms of a pros-

pective reconquest of Burma, there were many barriers in the way of such an operation. None of the three major powers involved—the United States, Great Britain, and China—was ready to commit itself unreservedly to it. The logistical problems were formidable. Active campaigning was considered possible only during the dry season from November through April; from May through October the monsoons made the Burma jungle virtually impassable. For all its vast area and population, India was a poor base. Its disposable resources were few, its climate and hygienic conditions bad, and at least part of its population apathetic or hostile toward the Allied war effort. The supply line from either the United States or United Kingdom was long, running all the way around the coast of Africa. Support of troops in India promised to exact higher shipping costs than in any other Anglo-American theater. While India possessed fine ports of entry in Bombay, Karachi, and Calcutta, interior supply lines were poor and undeveloped. Calcutta, the port nearest the prospective area of operations, could hardly be used at all during 1942 because of the vulnerability of its shipping lanes to Japanese attack. Supplies landed at Bombay or Karachi had to be transported over an inadequate rail net across the vast subcontinent of India. The existing rail net converged on the northwest frontier, the traditional avenue of foreign invasion.

---

[15] (1) Rpt, Pt. 2, cited n. 13(5). (2) Msg, AMMISCA to AGWAR, 16 Jan 43, CM-IN 7220. (3) Msg, AMMISCA to AGWAR, 31 Jan 43, CM-IN 14594.

[16] (1) Msg 904, AMMISCA to AGWAR, 3 Jul 42, Stilwell Personal Cable File, Bk. 1, Item 18, DRB AGO. (2) See voluminous correspondence between WD and OLLA in ID 400.318 Chinese Stockpile in India, I. (3) Rpt, Pt. 2, cited n. 13(5).

THE BENGAL-ASSAM RAILROAD. *American troops operating the single-track meter-gauge line.*

Neither the British nor the Indian Government had ever given much attention to the possibility of military action on the eastern frontier. The line of communications to the eastern frontier was particularly poor and undeveloped and subject to frequent interruptions by floods on the Brahmaputra River. A single-track meter-gauge railway was the only line running east and north into Manipur State and Assam, the jumping off points for an overland invasion of Burma. *(See Map 6.)*

During 1940 and 1941 India's development as a base had been almost exclusively in terms of support of the British effort in the Middle East. The best-trained and equipped Indian divisions had been committed there. The defeat in Burma in the spring of 1942 left India practically denuded of properly trained and equipped defense forces. Though the Indian Army continued to appear formidable on paper—generally estimated at one and a half million men—its real expansion had only begun with the crisis in early 1942 and Indian troops were neither trained, equipped, nor deployed to undertake a major effort against the Japanese on the eastern frontier. A formidable military force had to be continuously maintained along the northwest frontier to keep order among the turbulent tribes there, and other troops of the Indian Army had to be stationed at strategic points to maintain internal security. The British continued during 1942 to use India as a base for the Middle East campaign and a reservoir of reserve forces. In the summer of 1942, hard pressed to maintain even an effective defense of India, they considered a major offensive well beyond their capabilities since it would mean equipping a striking force and maintaining it over an extremely inadequate line of communications.

Under these circumstances, the British showed little enthusiasm for any aggressive policy in Burma. Their own traditional interests inclined them to look toward liberating Singapore and the Netherlands Indies rather than toward opening a supply route to China, the operation on which the Americans placed such emphasis. They made it clear from the beginning that their war effort in India would be heavily dependent upon American support and presented in Washington marginal requirements they could not themselves meet for the whole Indian Army and the Indian civilian economy, requirements well beyond what the Americans wished to accept. As noted earlier, the British at one point asked that the United States assume responsibility for supplying their "Eastern Group of Theaters" in return for British acceptance of similar responsibility for supplying U.S. troops in the European theater. But the Americans shunned this arrangement. To them, India often seemed a huge maw into which vast quantities of supplies might be poured with little appreciable result. American staff opposition to the British theory of equipment allocations in accordance with troop deployments was dictated in no small part by the realization that it would lead to large commitments for a British and Indian Army, only a fragment of which would be engaged in active operations against the Japanese in the foreseeable future. The SOS was also inclined to look askance at the large civilian requirements for India, though it had no direct jurisdiction over them. British opposition to the screening of lend-lease requirements for India by General Wheeler's headquarters was ever a sore point. There was a strong feeling among the Americans that the British wished to use lend-lease to bolster their own position in India rather than to pursue the war against the Japanese, and American policy called for neutrality in the struggle between the British Government of India and the Indian Nationalists. Though the policy was never clearly put in these terms, the American staff really wanted to use lend-lease in India as Stilwell used it for Chinese forces, to equip an army and prepare bases for an assault on Burma; the British felt their responsibilities in India were broader and would never agree that they could concentrate entirely on this end.

These issues, however, were of less significance during 1942 than the fact that the shortage of both supplies and shipping and the higher strategic priorities given by the CCS to the BOLERO build-up, TORCH, the Pacific campaigns, and aid to the USSR prevented any concerted effort to prepare for a major offensive in India. The British placed their principal emphasis on the Middle East and directed the flow of American lend-lease largely in that direction. The defenses of India were bolstered, but little was done in the way of preparations to overcome the logistical obstacles standing in the way of an offensive campaign in Burma.

Similarly, the American planners themselves supported the Burma operation only on the condition that no considerable commitment of American resources would be required. The competition of theaters with higher strategic priority severely limited the build-up even of U.S. air and service forces in India and China, and, as we have seen, of the Hump airlift, the highest priority in CBI. After the fall of the Netherlands Indies, General Brereton moved north to India with the small remnant of his air force to form, with Chennault's command in China, the U.S. Tenth Air Force. But reinforcements came slowly, and with the crisis in the Middle East in June, Brereton was rushed to Egypt with most of the Tenth's bombers and a number of transport planes. In mid-July, Chennault's air task force in China consisted of only fifty-six P-40's and eight B-25's. Wheeler's SOS at the same time contained only slightly more than fifteen hundred men, and until the very end of the year its build-up was not conceived in terms of support of any active ground campaign, although Stilwell had been building his plans around the hope of an offensive in the spring of 1943.[17]

This neglect of CBI combined with the natural caution and defensive psychology of the Chinese to make it very difficult for Stilwell to persuade Chiang Kai-shek that he, Chiang, should prepare his own forces for a Burma campaign. Though Chiang accepted Stilwell's plan and forwarded it to the President as his own, he had no intention of undertaking the Chinese part of the operation without extensive American and British support. There were powerful forces in China working for a policy of inertia. Active campaigning by the Japanese had come to a halt, interrupted only by occasional raids. The Chinese Army, scattered over a broad front, was composed of over three hundred paper divisions, but all were understrength and equipped only with a miscellaneous assortment of arms

of various national origins. Lacking modern transport, it had little mobility and no central system of supply. The war lord commanders of armies and divisions had a vested interest in their organizations from which they derived both prestige and profit. Many were for all practical purposes independent of the control of the Nationalist Government, and they preferred to hoard their men and equipment rather than to use them in the war against the Japanese. Some were engaged in a smuggling trade with Japanese-occupied territory. The individual Chinese soldier in these armies was ill fed, ill clothed, and subject to all sorts of petty graft by his commanders. In the face of Stilwell's urging that he reform and consolidate his armies, Chiang was dilatory. He feared the effects of failure in any effort against the Japanese in Burma, and apparently even those of disturbing the *status quo*. He insisted on greater American air and supply support and thought Stilwell as his Allied chief of staff should support these demands in Washington. Stilwell placed his role as American representative in the theater first and would support only those demands he viewed as realistic in the light of his plans. A thinly veiled hostility between the two was soon evident. Both General Marshall and Secretary Stimson gave their wholehearted support to Stilwell, but Chiang's direct line to the President and the sympathy for Chiang felt by such important presidential advisers as Lauchlin Currie and Harry Hopkins frequently left Stilwell without the crucial

---

[17] (1) ASF in China, Burma, and India, pp. 116, 234–36. (2) Romanus and Sunderland, *Stilwell's Mission to China*, pp. 198–207. (3) ID Rpt 10, Lend-lease Information, 31 May 43, Pt. 2, sec on India. (4) India at War, 1939–1945, MS, prepared by Hist Sec GHQ (India), OCMH. (5) See above, Chs. XI, XVIII.

support he needed at the highest American level.[18]

Disturbed by the curtailment of the Chinese lend-lease program, and particularly incensed by the movement of Brereton's air force without his consent, Chiang in June 1942 presented to the President three demands, which he stated were the minimum requirements for maintenance of the China theater of war. These demands were: (1) three American divisions in India to co-operate with Chinese forces in restoring the line of communications through Burma; (2) an Allied air force in China of 500 planes continuously fighting at the front; (3) monthly transport over the Hump of 5,000 tons of Chinese supplies. He originally set August and September 1942 as the time limits for meeting these demands. In Washington, continuance of China in the war was considered of paramount importance, but no one seriously considered that the Generalissimo's ultimatum could be met if the agreed policy of concentration on the Atlantic front was to survive. The President delayed giving a formal answer to Chiang until October. In the meantime, Lauchlin Currie, as the President's representative, went to China on a special mission in July and in conversations with him Chiang substantially modified his demands by removing the time limit and cutting his requirements for U.S. divisions from three to one. The final answer of the President, generally in accord with the recommendations of General Marshall, rejected entirely the demand for U.S. combat troops because of lack of shipping, but promised to build the air force in China and India as rapidly as possible, and to make transports available for the airline in regular monthly increments until the goal of one hundred in regular operation was reached.

Chiang accepted this response and made no further veiled threats to take China out of the war.[19]

Despite the promises, the build-up of the U.S. air force and of the airlift continued slow and far below the Generalissimo's demands. Roosevelt's answer to the three demands was tacitly premised on acceptance of the Stilwell-Chiang plan for a Burma campaign as a substitute for compliance with them, but when the plan was considered in the councils of the CCS in October, the Combined Staff Planners reported that sufficient trained amphibious troops and landing craft could not be assembled for an operation to recapture all Burma in the dry season of 1942–43. The JCS then fell back on a concept of a limited land offensive, to include Stilwell's plan for an operation to overrun north Burma, and proposed British operations to retake the airfield at Akyab and advance from Imphal to the Chindwin River in central Burma. On 7 December 1942 they accepted this as the basic American strategy for CBI in early 1943.[20]

In the theater Stilwell simultaneously learned in conferences with General Wavell at New Delhi that a limited offensive was the most the British would agree to. On his return to Chungking in November he was able to get Chiang's consent

[18] (1) See Romanus and Sunderland, *Stilwell's Mission to China*, pp. 32–41, 152–57, 173–77, 234–41. (2) See also Joseph W. Stilwell, *The Stilwell Papers*, Theodore H. White, ed. (New York, William Sloane Associates, Inc., 1948), pp. 121, 127, 315–22. (3) See also, rpt cited n. 6(7). (4) For a typical statement of Stilwell's personal view of the Chinese Army, see Msg 204, AMMISCA to AGWAR, 7 Mar 43, Stilwell Personal Cable File, Bk. 1, Item 238, DRB AGO.
[19] See Romanus and Sunderland, *Stilwell's Mission to China*, pp. 169–73, 180–87, 222–25.
[20] (1) CCS 104/3, 30 Oct 42, title: Plan for Retaking Burma. (2) Min, 47th mtg CCS, 6 Nov 42. (3) JCS 162, 7 Dec 42, title: Opn in Burma—March 1943. (4) Min, 45th mtg JCS, 8 Dec 42.

for participation in this limited offensive on condition that the British maintain naval supremacy in the Bay of Bengal and air supremacy over Burma. The target date for the operation was set as 1 March 1943. Wavell assigned Stilwell's Chinese forces to the Hukawng Valley sector north of the British, who would operate along the Imphal–Kalewa line. Wheeler's SOS was assigned responsibility for support of the Chinese from a base at Ledo in Assam. To provide a line of supply for the advancing Chinese forces, the project for a road to run from Ledo to Myitkyina and Lung-ling along the route the Chinese had proposed in the spring was revived, and construction assigned as an American responsibility. If the operation were successful, this road would provide an overland route to China without the restoration of the old line of communications through Burma. In presenting the limited offensive plan to the President, the JCS stressed this road as one of the most important advantages to be derived from the operation.[21]

Acceptance of this plan soon posed a new and unforeseen drain on shipping. On 8 November 1942 Stilwell sent to the War Department a sizable request for men and materials to enable him to operate an SOS in the rear of the Chinese in India and to begin construction of the Ledo Road. He requested that they be in the theater in time for the offensive to begin on 1 March 1943. These requirements were modest by comparison with those of any other major theater of war, including a few engineer, quartermaster, and medical units with their organizational equipment, certain specialized engineering equipment for the Ledo Road, and six months of combat maintenance for the two Chinese divisions at Ramgarh. Stilwell abandoned his earlier request for an infantry division but did ask for one infantry battalion, three anti-aircraft batteries, and one military police battalion. The total troops involved were 10,896 and the cargo came to 109,116 measurement tons.

The War Department was not at all prepared for these requests, having assumed that the Burma offensive would be carried out with resources already in the theater or earmarked for it. The North African campaign, reinforcement of the Pacific theaters, and movement of troops and supplies to the Persian Gulf were currently absorbing all available military troop and cargo shipping. Stilwell was told on 23 November 1942 that "in view of the magnitude of requirements for support of current offensives in other vital theaters," neither troops, materials, nor shipping would be available to meet more than a small part of his requests.[22]

The CBI commander's protest was immediate, strong, and profane. Swayed by this and by the action of the JCS in assigning a priority to the Burma operation second only to that in North Africa, General Marshall asked the SOS to make a diligent effort to meet Stilwell's demands. While troops and materials in most cases had to be diverted from other projects, the really critical issue was shipping. By eliminating all personnel for whom Indian native labor could be substituted, shipping requirements were reduced to 63,000 tons of cargo and 6,375 troop spaces. The Navy transport *Monticello*, currently under consideration for diversion from the North African run to the Pacific, was diverted instead to carry troops to India. Ships to

---

[21] Romanus and Sunderland, *Stilwell's Mission to China*, pp. 225–29, 247.

[22] Msg 1724, AGWAR to AMMISCA, 23 Nov 42, AG 400.3295 (9-1-42) (3) Sec 4.

float the cargo were obtained by diversion from the Pacific and from lend-lease. This first sizable movement of troops and matériel to CBI was carried out in January and February 1943. Efforts were also devoted, following Stilwell's irate protests at delays, to speed the dispatch of twelve transport planes necessary to move essential artillery, ammunition, and gasoline to YOKE Force in Yunnan.[23]

So far as any March 1943 offensive was concerned, these efforts proved to be in vain. Wavell, in India, showed marked reluctance to go ahead with even the limited advance to the Chindwin, and expressed strong doubts to his superiors as to the feasibility of Stilwell's operation. The British attack on Akyab, already launched, ran into serious difficulties. The British could promise neither naval supremacy in the Bay of Bengal nor air supremacy over Burma, the conditions Chiang had made a *sine qua non* to his acceptance of the Chinese role in the limited offensive. In early January 1943, Chiang cabled the President that he could not undertake the operation in March.[24]

This abortive planning for the early 1943 offensive was not entirely without results. It clearly focused attention on the possibilities of a land supply line through north Burma to China as an alternative to restoration of the old line from Rangoon. Construction of the road was begun in December and Chinese troops moved forward to protect it. (*See Map 6.*) The plan for the Ledo Road was soon supplemented by an accessory project for an oil pipeline to run from the Digboi oilfields in India to Kunming. The road and pipeline projects were soon established alongside the airlift as major American logistical responsibilities in CBI.[25] The normal SOS apparatus for planning, procurement, and shipment

of materials was set to work to implement them. Yet, as events were to prove, there were certain dangers in this logistical planning, divorced as it was from any definite strategic commitment for conquest of the territory over which the proposed supply line was to run.

Chennault's Air Plan

While Stilwell had been laboriously developing his plan for building Chinese ground forces, General Chennault, commanding the small American air force in China, was espousing other ideas. Operating on a shoestring and utilizing local supplies and services in China to the utmost, Chennault had accomplished remarkable results in the air war against Japan. Yet since gasoline, ammunition, and spare parts had to be flown over the Hump, his operations were necessarily limited by the supply line and during 1942 remained exceedingly small. Impatient with the long delays necessary in opening an overland supply route, and doubtful of Stilwell's appreciation of the potentialities of an air effort from China, Chennault developed and brought to the attention of the President an alternate plan. He wanted the airlift enlarged and devoted solely to sup-

[23] (1) ASF in China, Burma, and India, pp. 46–50. (2) Msg 181, AMMDEL to AGWAR, 8 Nov 42. (3) Memo, unsigned, no addressee, 1 Dec 42, sub: Sv Trs and Engr Equip for Asiatic Theater. Last two in CBI–31 May 43 folder, Lutes File. (4) Msg 1463, AMMISCA to AGWAR, 28 Nov 42, Stilwell Personal Cable File, Bk. 1, Item 125, DRB AGO. (5) Msg 1500, AMMISCA to AGWAR, 8 Dec 42, Stilwell Personal Cable File, Bk. 1, Item 140, DRB AGO. (6) On the *Monticello* affair, see above, Ch. XV.
[24] (1) Msg COS W 388, Br CsofS to Br Jt Stf Mis, Washington, 9 Dec 42, Item 22, Exec 10. (2) Ltr, Dill to Marshall, 10 Dec 42, WDCSA China. (3) Msg 31, Chiang to Roosevelt, 8 Jan 43, Stilwell Personal Cable File, Bk. 1, Item 140, DRB AGO.
[25] ASF in China, Burma, and India, pp. 50–54.

porting his air force in China. With the small air force that could be supported in this manner, Chennault promised remarkable results. His bombers would conduct devastating raids against Japanese shipping lanes and the Japanese-held coastal cities of China; as a result the Japanese air force would have to fight over China, where Chennault's fighters would destroy it by using proven combat techniques; once the Japanese air force was destroyed, the road would be open for his bombers to attack the vital industrial cities of Japan and destroy them. To accomplish these astounding objectives, Chennault originally said he would need only 105 fighters, 30 medium bombers, 12 heavy bombers, and regular replacements for losses. While these requirements were expanded considerably by mid-1943, the fundamentals of the plan remained unchanged.[26]

Chennault's ambitious proposals cut across the entire fabric of Stilwell's plans. Though both would enlarge the airlift, Chennault would use it almost entirely to support an American air force, while Stilwell would use it predominantly to transport YOKE Force supplies. While Stilwell visualized an eventual air campaign against Japan from China, he thought it would have to await development of an overland supply line to support it and of a Chinese army adequate to protect its bases and airfields. A premature effort, he contended, could not be given sufficient logistical support to succeed, and would only sting the Japanese into a land campaign to overrun the airfields from which it was launched.[27] The logistical implications of these conflicting views are obvious. If Chennault's plan were accepted, resources would be concentrated on furnishing transports, building airfields, and providing the other essentials for operating an air

force in China. Efforts to build the Ledo Road and its accompanying pipeline and to equip sixty Chinese divisions would be slackened or abandoned.

While the War Department continued to support Stilwell, the President was intrigued by this rather brilliant conception of victory at small cost. At the other end of the line, Chiang eagerly grasped at the Chennault thesis as a substitute for Stilwell's plans. In his January message to the President he pointedly suggested expansion of Chennault's force; in the months following he became increasingly dilatory in carrying out Stilwell's plan for a concentration of forces in Yunnan. The British also soon began to show favor for the air alternative and to deprecate the chances of success in a land campaign against Burma. While probably no one accepted Chennault's most extravagant claims, he offered the tempting prospect of more immediate results at small cost.

Casablanca and After

At the Casablanca Conference in January 1943, the CCS provisionally scheduled for November 1943 an operation for the reconquest of all Burma (ANAKIM) generally along the lines of the earlier Stilwell-Chiang plan. The Americans promised to make landing craft available from the Pacific for the British amphibious assault on Rangoon. In the meantime, the British were to continue their thrust at Akyab and initiate the advance toward the Chindwin. If Chinese co-operation could be obtained, advances should also be

---

[26] Claire L. Chennault, *Way of a Fighter* (New York, G. P. Putnam's Sons, 1949), pp. 212-16, 221-22.

[27] For a succinct statement of the opposing views, see records of the TRIDENT Conference in Washington, May 1943.

made in the north along the lines of Stilwell's plan for a junction of X-RAY and YOKE Forces. Then, at the special request of the President, the CCS added a clause on air operations in China, promising additional aircraft for the Hump, build-up of the U.S. air force in China "to the maximum extent that logistical limitations and other important claims will permit," and more sustained air operations beginning in the spring of 1943.[28]

This favorable gesture toward Chennault indicated the President's intense interest in his plan for air operations in China. Immediately following Casablanca, General Arnold went to China (in company with General Somervell and Field Marshal Dill) with a promise from Roosevelt that transports on the Hump run would be rapidly increased from the existing 62 to 137, and that monthly tonnage would be expanded from 1,500 to 4,000 by mid-March. The President stipulated that Chennault should receive a minimum of 1,500 tons out of the proposed 4,000-ton capacity. This time the transports were rushed to India as promised. By 27 March 1943, 133 were either on hand or en route, and a considerable number of older types were replaced by more modern ones. But it took a longer time to build airfields, make other arrangements for support of the increased lift, and develop a smoothly operating air transport organization. The desired goal of 4,000 tons monthly was not to be achieved until July, and in the meantime the struggle between Stilwell and Chennault for the actual capacity was accentuated. The President showed his unmistakable inclination toward Chennault's plan when in March he summarily rejected Stilwell's and Marshall's suggestion that Chiang be required to commit himself definitely to concentrating forces in Yunnan and undertaking the Burma operation as a price for further American support.[29]

The major decision at Casablanca, however, had been on ANAKIM and neither the War Department nor the JCS were so intrigued by Chennault's plan for victory at small cost as was the President. Attention of the Army's logistical agencies in Washington was therefore primarily turned toward meeting the requirements of American, Chinese, and British forces for ANAKIM and toward planning for post-ANAKIM operations. ANAKIM was conceived mainly as a British operation supported by Chinese action. The build-up of Wheeler's SOS in the rear of the Chinese was already being provided for as a follow-up to Stilwell's requests in December and involved relatively small tonnages. Shipments of lend-lease to India for the Chinese were stepped up only slightly, from around 5,000 tons monthly in late 1942 to between 8,000 and 10,000 in early 1943, and most of this material merely went to enlarge the stockpile in India. The major logistical requirements for ANAKIM were British. The British indicated that their participation would depend heavily on American supplies and shipping, particularly since

---

[28] (1) CCS 170/2, 23 Jan 43, title: Final Rpt to President and Prime Minister Summarizing Decisions by CCS. (2) CCS 170, 22 Jan 43, same title. (3) Min, 3d mtg ANFA Conf, 23 Jan 43. (4) For a general discussion of the Casablanca Conference, see below, Ch. XXV.

[29] (1) Henry Harley Arnold, *Global Mission* (New York, Harper & Brothers, 1949), pp. 413–22. (2) Msg SVC 395, Roosevelt to Chiang, 8 Mar 43, Stilwell Personal Cable File, Bk. 2, Item 239, DRB AGO. (3) Craven and Cate, *AAF IV*, p. 441. (4) Romanus and Sunderland, *Stilwell's Mission to China*, pp. 274–292. The authors represent this presidential action as the real turning point of Stilwell's mission in China. Roosevelt wrote of Chiang: ". . . one cannot speak sternly to a man like that or exact commitments from him the way we might do from the Sultan of Morocco." See p. 279.

they had had to reduce their own shipping to India in order to bolster their faltering import program for the United Kingdom itself. They presented requests for material that amounted to 263,000 tons of military cargo and 267,000 tons of civilian supplies, and for American shipping to make 113 trips from either the United States or the United Kingdom to India from April through August, and on a somewhat reduced scale for the rest of the year. Meeting this British shipping request threatened to put a severe drain on cargo shipping available to carry out other military operations, coming as it did in the midst of a crisis created by a far larger British demand for American shipping to support their import program. WSA insisted that if granted it would have to come out of military allocations, and pointed to to the dangers involved in relinquishing control of American shipping for the long period involved in voyages to India. The military authorities agreed that the British requirement for April–August sailings should be reduced from 113 to 90, but in view of the CCS commitment to ANAKIM, General Somervell insisted this reduced scale should be met. As a start twenty additional ships were allocated to sail to India during April, squeezed out of those originally assigned for Panama, Hawaii, the South and Southwest Pacific, and military lend-lease services to Australia and the Middle East. Turnaround time was computed as two and a half times that to the original destinations for these ships, thus meaning a drain equivalent to fifty cargo ships from the pool of shipping available to support other military operations. Allocations for future months were left in abeyance pending, among other things, the opening of the Mediterranean to Allied shipping.[30]

Material was generally made available to fill the twenty ships despite the fact that some of the British requirements had not been previously registered in the Army Supply Program and represented commitments over and above those contemplated in the Weeks-Somervell Agreement. There was, nevertheless, a continuing inclination on the American side to question the scale of British requirements for India, and an open suspicion that much of the material requested was for troops that would not be engaged in ANAKIM. The Operations Division member of MAC(G) tried unsuccessfully to have certain assignments of military matériel earmarked specifically for ANAKIM, to revert to MAB control if the operation were not definitely scheduled in July.[31]

---

[30] (1) On British import program, see below, Ch. XXVI. (2) ASF in China, Burma, and India, pp. 50–57, 236. (3) Rpt cited n. 13(5). (4) Memo, Col Magruder for ACofS Opns ASF, 12 Apr 43, sub: Cargo for ANAKIM. (5) Memo, Gross for Somervell, 29 Apr 43, sub: Shipg for CBI. Last two in CBI-31 May 43 folder, Lutes File. (6) Memo, Somervell for Wedemeyer, 2 Apr 43, sub: ANAKIM Versus BOLERO, Shipg 1942–43 folder, Hq ASF. (7) Ltr, Macready to Somervell, 22 Apr 43, Logis File, OCMH. (8) Douglas' notes on conf at White House, 29 Mar 43, Allocs Gen folder, WSA Douglas File. (9) Memo, Gross for Somervell, 7 Apr 43, sub: Nomination of Twenty Ships for Apr Loading for ANAKIM. (10) Msg, Harriman to Douglas, 20 Apr 43. Last two in Army Reqmts 1 Jan 43 folder, WSA Douglas File.

[31] (1) This move provoked a long series of discussions on the propriety of such earmarking but no final decision was reached by the MAB. The board did rule, however, that the specific assignments in question should proceed. See memo, Gen Tansey for Chm MAC(G), 14 Apr 43, sub: Sp Issue of Equip to U.K. in Support of Sp Opn, Tab G to min, 89th mtg MAC(G), 15 Apr 43; Min 1866, 89th mtg MAC(G), 15 Apr 43; Min 2030–31, 95th mtg, 27 May 43; Min 2042, 96th mtg, 3 Jun 43; Min 2092–97, 98th mtg, 17 Jun 43; Min 3, 63d mtg MAB, 21 Apr 43; Min 4, 65th mtg, 4 May 43; Min 5, 66th mtg, 12 May 43; Min 2a, 70th mtg, 9 Jun 43. (2) For Somervell's views on Indian requirements, see remarks at TRIDENT Conference in min, 90th mtg CCS, 20 May 43, Item 4.

ARRIVING FOR A CONFERENCE IN NEW DELHI, *India, 1943. Left to right: Lt. Gen. B. B. Somervell, Lt. Gen. Allen Hartley, Field Marshal Dill, Lt. Gen. H. H. Arnold, Maj. Gen. Raymond A. Wheeler, Brig. Gen. Clayton L. Bissell, Brig. Gen. William H. Holcombe, Air Commodore J. E. A. Baldwin, Brig. Gen. Benjamin G. Ferris.*

Some of the American staff, General Somervell in particular, favored meeting Stilwell's earlier requests for U.S. troops to take part in the campaigns in Burma and China. On his visit to India in February 1943, Somervell asked General Wheeler for an estimate of requirements for supporting U.S. ground forces of 100,000 and 500,000 men respectively over the supply line into China once it was restored. Wheeler's preliminary plan, submitted on 16 February 1943, was premised less on any such specific manpower goals than on the general requirements for restoring the line of communications through Burma. Wheeler postulated the recapture of Burma by the end of April 1944, development of the supply line during the following monsoon season, May through November, and initiation of further operations in the dry season 1944–45. The Ledo Road would be built in the rear of advancing troops, and continued in use as a secondary supply line after that from Rangoon was restored. He presented material requirements for the pipeline to parallel the Ledo Road, for restoration of the port of Rangoon and the rail and waterways north to Bhamo and Lashio, for petroleum storage and distribution facilities in Burma, and for truck lines on both the Ledo Road and the Burma Road. He asked that 7,500 trucks of seven to ten-ton capacity, 1,500 wooden barges, and 500 towboats arrive in the theater by 1 November 1943, the rest of the required material and necessary service troops by 1 January 1944. On 8 May 1943, at the further request of Somervell, Wheeler presented a more comprehensive plan specifically premised on the support of 100,000 American troops in China. Truck, barge, and pipeline requirements were expanded, but those for the development of Rangoon and of the Burma Railways were omitted on the understanding that the British were requisitioning the necessary material, much of it under lend-lease. As for supplying 500,000 American troops over the route, Wheeler pointed out that it would require an enormous expenditure of manpower and material and could not be achieved at best before June 1946.[32]

Wheeler's plans were studied extensively in the Strategic Logistics Division, SOS, and his stated requirements became the basis for procurement of specialized equipment for CBI. Indeed, the studies were expanded to embrace the whole question of the logistical feasibility of a campaign to defeat Japan through China. While none of the studies was conclusive, they served to point up many of the logistical difficulties involved. It would be difficult to procure the necessary rail cars, locomotives, and cargo trucks. It would require 500,000 tons of cargo shipping for the movement of materials for the line of communications alone. Once the supply line was developed, the bottleneck would be

just where it was before, on the Burma Road. The capacity of the river and rail lines north from Rangoon and the feeder road from Ledo could be increased far more rapidly than could that of the road running northward to Kunming.

Despite these indicated difficulties, Somervell was optimistic about the possibilities of carrying out a major offensive in CBI. In May he had plans drawn up for moving 100,000 American troops to India to permit the opening of an American sector in Assam and north Burma by the end of 1943, accepting all the additional logistical burdens that this would involve.[33]

This logistical planning in the SOS proved premature. At the higher level, everyone from the start had reservations about ANAKIM. Chiang showed as little enthusiasm as before, the British increasing reluctance to go ahead despite the amount of American support they had been promised. The President also was lukewarm and at one point specifically queried the JCS if the shipping needed to support the British effort in India might not be better used to bolster the declining BOLERO program. Since the British were also apparently ready to sacrifice American shipping for ANAKIM if necessary in order to secure a sufficient allotment for their import program, the U.S. military authorities were placed in the peculiar position of defending a British military shipping requirement that the British them-

---

[32] (1) Memo, Wheeler for Somervell, 18 Feb 43, sub: Restoration of Communication Facilities in Burma, CBI-31 May 43 folder, Lutes File. (2) Memo, Wheeler for Somervell, 8 May 43, same sub, in History of the Planning Div, ASF, Vol. III, App. 7-F, OCMH.

[33] (1) ASF in China, Burma, and India, pp. 61–82. (2) History of the Planning Division, ASF, I, 126, OCMH.

selves were unwilling to insist on. Marshall and King told the President that any diminution of preparations in India would be a dangerous invitation to Japanese attack, but they themselves had to recognize that something less than a full-scale assault on Burma might have to suffice. OPD by no means shared Somervell's enthusiasm for sending an American ground army to India.

In the theater itself, meantime, British preparations for ANAKIM fell behind. The thrust at Akyab failed, and Wavell decided against launching the drive on the Chindwin. While the American SOS was optimistically planning for restoration of the supply line through Burma, Wavell was still complaining of insufficient tonnages arriving in India and struggling to develop the line from Calcutta to the bases for the proposed Sino-British drive in Manipur and Assam. In April 1943 the British asked that the review of ANAKIM scheduled for July be held at the TRIDENT Conference in Washington in May. Chiang, now wholly devoted to the air plan, asked Roosevelt to summon Chennault to present it in full. The War Department asked that Stilwell also come, the British sent for Wavell, and when the TRIDENT Conference met, revision of the Casablanca objectives for CBI was to be one of the first orders of business. The decision was almost a foregone conclusion. With the British demurring, ANAKIM for November 1943 was definitely out, and with it went the whole timetable on which the SOS plans were based. Though Stilwell's campaign and a limited British offensive were to remain on the books, Chiang, the President, and Churchill all showed a preference for Chennault's plan, and as a result air operations in China received the highest priority in CBI in the months following TRIDENT.[34]

Reciprocal Aid in India and China

In view of the long supply line from the United States, the growing (though still small) American forces in India and China found it mandatory to rely on local resources to the maximum extent possible. Since most American troops were in India, local procurement there was of greatest importance. By an agreement between General Wheeler and the Government of India in June 1942 it was established that U.S. procurement in India was to be centralized through General Wheeler's headquarters as far as possible and treated as reciprocal aid. Under this agreement, and even earlier by direct purchase, American forces obtained the bulk of their subsistence, clothing, buildings, depot installations, roads, airfields, and labor services from Indian sources. Gasoline until the middle of 1943 came either from Indian refineries or from British-controlled fields in Iran and Iraq. Native labor was utilized to the utmost to replace U.S. service troops in depot installations, at ports, and in the construction of roads and airfields. The installations at Ramgarh, subsistence, and other services for Chinese troops in India were treated as reciprocal aid to the United States and in turn by the United States as lend-lease to China.

The Government of India, reluctant to press for sacrifices from a people whose standard of living was already far too low, found it difficult to meet American expectations. Under the June agreement, the

---

[34] (1) Memo, CofS for President, Apr 43, Item 55, Exec 10. (2) Memo, Wedemeyer for Hull, 25 May 43, ABC 370.5 (2-2-43). (3) Min, 2d mtg at White House, TRIDENT, 14 May 43. (4) CCS 242/6, 25 May 43, title: Final Rpt to President and Prime Minister (TRIDENT). (5) Romanus and Sunderland, *Stilwell's Mission to China*, pp. 302–06, 313–33. (6) See below, Ch. XXVI.

Government of India insisted that supply under reciprocal aid should be limited to the same scales of accommodation as were accorded British troops, and Wheeler found it very difficult to operate under this restriction. Wheeler's lack of representation on the Indian Lend-Lease Requirements Committee, which passed also on reciprocal aid requisitions, handicapped him further. Americans were often forced to purchase in the open market where they were in competition with higher priority orders of the Government of India and therefore had to pay higher prices or go without.[35]

Wheeler was soon airing these grievances in Washington, and his remonstrances produced a pattern that was to become increasingly familiar in connection with American demands on India. British officials in Washington and London, more aware of the necessity for co-operation on a world-wide scale, put pressure on Indian officials. The restriction to British scales was rescinded. The SOS in Washington also took steps to send Wheeler experienced personnel to set up a special section in his headquarters to be concerned with local procurement (though no general purchasing agent or board was created in India). Even more important, the British established in March 1943 an India Munitions Assignments Committee to tie in the disposal of Indian production to that of the rest of the British Empire and the United States in accordance with the accepted principles of distribution on the basis of strategic need. The India Munitions Assignments Committee included representation of the British Commander-in-Chief, India, the British War Office, and the U.S. War Department (General Wheeler). It was a branch of the London Munitions Assignments Board, as

was the committee in Australia. After some controversy, the right of appeal from the Indian committee to the LMAB in all cases was granted, though the British postulated that there were limitations to action the LMAB could take in regard to assignments within the India Command. The British Commander-in-Chief, India, would have to approve assignments made to British and Indian forces in his theater and would have a "close connection" with those made to American and Chinese forces there. But his powers would not extend to assignments made to theaters outside his command, that is, to China, Australia, and the Middle East. After some controversy over assignments of Indian material for Chinese forces in China, it was agreed that long-range requirements on India for outside theaters should be presented in London and planned as part of the empire program while the India Munitions Assignments Committee would consider spot bids on their merits.[36]

These arrangements and continued British pressure for greater co-operation in India smoothed the path of reciprocal aid considerably. By October 1943 the International Division could report:

---

[35] (1) Memo, R. M. Saner, Under Secy of Govt of India, for other govt agencies, 4 Jun 42. (2) Ltr, Gen Wheeler to Lt Gen Vickers, Br QMG, 29 Aug 42, sub: Interpretation of Reverse Lend-lease Proced. (3) Ltr, Wheeler to Clay, 6 Jan 43. All in ID 008 Reverse Lend-lease, I. (4) ASF in China, Burma, and India, pp. 159–60. (5) Romanus and Sunderland, *Stilwell's Mission to China,* Ch. VI. (6) Memo, Wing Comdr T. E. H. Birley for ID ASF, 7 May 43, ID, Lend-Lease, Doc Suppl, V.

[36] (1) Rpt, Pt. 2, sec on India, cited n. 13(5). (2) LMAB (42) 63, Note by War Off Member, 20 Dec 42, title: India Mun Asgmts Com, in ID, Lend-Lease, Doc Suppl, IV. (3) Memo cited n. 35(6). (4) See India Mun Asgmts Com Cables file, ID. (5) ASF in China, Burma, and India, pp. 149–52. (6) Memo, Secy for Chm MAC(G), 13 Jul 43, sub: India Mun Asgmts Com, filed with min. 102d mtg MAC(G).

Although reciprocal aid procurement in India may continue to suffer from lack of public support of the war in India and from Indian concern over the cost of such aid, present indications are that substantial improvement has already been effected and that both the scope and facility of procurement may continue to show improvement.[37]

No formal reverse lend-lease agreement was ever made with China, but U.S. air forces and the small detachments of headquarters, supply, and instructional personnel in China procured most of their subsistence and housekeeping supplies locally by direct purchase. Stilwell continually recommended against use of the reverse lend-lease principle in China, basing his opposition on a realistic appraisal of the Chinese Government's ability to procure supplies with the rapidly depreciating currency at its disposal. Also he did not wish to incur the obligation to the Chinese that would be implied in acceptance of reciprocal aid while China was receiving so little from the United States. In deference to State Department wishes such goods and services as the Chinese offered were accepted in accordance with the terms of Article II of the Master Lend-Lease Agreement Between the United States and China, but the bulk of American procurement continued, as Stilwell wished, by direct purchase.

The amount of this procurement was not large since there were few American troops in China. The greater contribution of the Chinese was really in the construction of airfields, revetments, roads, and other projects of an operational nature that were neither purchased nor treated as reverse lend-lease, but financed by the Chinese Government as Chinese projects. There can be no question that the support given to Chennault's air force in this manner was the only factor that enabled it to operate on a shoestring as it did, and this factor was taken into consideration in determining its very low requirements for logistical support.[38]

Nevertheless, there were definite limits to the local support available in either India or China. As the American air force in China expanded, its proportionate requirements from the outside increased. The paucity of Indian resources and the necessity for heavy importations from the United States for development of the Indian base acted as a continual barrier to the mounting of any major offensive in CBI.

The story of the CBI theater during 1942 and early 1943 was one of constant frustrations and failures. In an area where logistical problems were more formidable than in any other theater of the global war, divergent national interests, conflicting strategic plans, and divided command responsibilities stood in the way of any concerted effort to solve them. The early fall of Burma prevented fulfillment of the initial American plan for supplying a Chinese force that would carry the main burden of the war against the Japanese on the Asiatic mainland. An airlift of exceedingly small capacity became the only remaining line of supply to China, and the basic U.S. strategy one of merely keeping China in the war. General Stilwell insisted with single-minded purpose that the only logi-

[37] Rpt cited n. 13(5).
[38] (1) Msg 988, AMMISCA to AGWAR, 26 Jul 42, AMMISCA IN Cables file, Bk. 6, ID. (2) Msg 1720, AGWAR to AMMISCA, 20 Nov 42, AG 400.3295 (9-1-42) (4). (3) Msg 1461, AMMISCA to AGWAR, 27 Nov 42, Lend-lease (1) folder, Dir of Materiel. (4) Memo, Gen Handy for ASW, 23 Jan 43. (5) Memo, ASW for Handy, 30 Jan 43. Last two in OPD 400.3295, Sec 1, Case 45. (6) A Guide to International Supply, prepared by ID ASF, 31 Dec 45, p. 65. (7) Chennault, *Way of a Fighter, passim.*

cal course of action was to go back and retake Burma, but none of the major governments involved was ever willing to give its full support to the effort. Chiang was reluctant to risk the meager resources at his disposal despite the immense advantages success would bring him. The British in India, with far greater resources and American support, seemed unable or unwilling to use them in an effort to regain Burma, insisting that logistical obstacles would make such an operation unfeasible without more extensive preparations. The American staff in Washington, while continually insisting on the importance of an overland supply route to China, felt that other strategic commitments of higher priority precluded furnishing American ground forces and supporting them over the long supply line involved. The President himself always sought a course of action which would require the least drain of resources from the Atlantic front. Chennault's plan for air operations appealed to Roosevelt as it did to the British and Chinese. With divergent American plans complicating an already difficult situation, both strategic and logistical planning were cast adrift. The postponement of ANAKIM meant that there would be no major land campaign on the Asiatic mainland during 1943 and that, at least temporarily, logistical action would be concentrated on the build-up of the airlift. Supply plans drawn up by the SOS in the light of the ANAKIM plan were left without concrete foundation. The prospects after TRIDENT were that CBI would remain a theater secondary to the Pacific in the war against Japan.

CHAPTER XX

The Long Road to Russia—I

In the sphere of strategy there was little co-ordination of the war effort of the Soviet Union with that of the Western Allies. The Russians fought a separate war on their own front, for different purposes, it later proved, from those that motivated Great Britain and the United States. But while the war was on, there was common agreement on the necessity of defeating Germany in the most expeditious manner possible, and there was little inclination on the part of American leaders to explore the question of differences in postwar aims. Both sides had the same wolf by the ears and neither could afford to let go. American and British leaders had to accept the hard fact that without involvement of the major portion of the German Army on the Eastern Front any realization of the agreed ARCADIA strategy of defeating Germany first would be rendered difficult if not impossible. Since Soviet forces during 1942 and 1943 were carrying the brunt of the land fighting against Germany, and since there seemed to be throughout the period a grave danger that the USSR might be eliminated from the war entirely, the question of how best to aid the Russians was one of the most serious the Allied planners faced. There were two possible means, one by early establishment of a second front in Europe, the other by shipment of supplies. Pursuit of both courses simultaneously was of course desirable, but the Americans and British found it impossible during 1942 and 1943 to establish a second front on the scale the Russians asked. Consequently, the shipment of supplies to the Soviet Union had to be pushed as a matter of utmost urgency by both the President and the Prime Minister. The President was willing to interrupt or curtail supply to the Soviet Union only when sheer physical difficulty made delivery impossible or when it interfered directly with a major Allied project such as the invasion of North Africa. Since policy on aid to the USSR had to be determined at the highest level, the military leaders sometimes regarded it as primarily a political program. The War Department, the JCS, and even the CCS objected on occasion to its interference with Anglo-American operational plans. However, they had little choice but to accept the sacrifices involved, and indeed to recognize the great importance of aid to the USSR in any strategic program aimed at the ultimate defeat of Germany.

These circumstances explain why the program of aid continued to be based on rigid diplomatic commitments and subject to the surveillance of the Munitions Assignments Board only in matters of detail, and why little effort was made to go behind Soviet requests to determine the strategic justification of specific allocations or to secure Soviet co-operation in return for supply aid. Assignments to the USSR were not weighed in the balance of theater priorities, operational necessities, or troop deployments as were those of theaters that fell within the purview of the CCS. Since the Russians were producing results and showed no inclination to permit Americans either to survey their needs or to supervise the use of supplies shipped, there was no alternative during the first part of the war but to accept Soviet requests at their face value, or at least the U.S. Government did not think it wise to pursue any other course. The whole effort to supply the Soviet Union was concentrated simply on meeting a series of annual supply protocols negotiated at the highest governmental level.

Pearl Harbor and the First Protocol

When the bombs fell on Pearl Harbor, shipments to the USSR to meet the First Protocol, signed at Moscow on 2 October 1941, had already fallen far behind monthly schedules of deliveries furnished the Russians at the end of October. An intensive effort was under way to make up the deficit in December. Instead, the suspension of lend-lease shipments following Pearl Harbor and the diversions of material and shipping to meet U.S. needs placed protocol shipments even further in arrears. While General Marshall favored continuation of aid to the USSR to "the maximum extent possible," both he and Secretary Stimson felt the protocol must be revised in the light of the vastly expanded requirements of the U.S. Military Establishment.[1] On 28 December 1941, however, the President directed flatly that "the Soviet Aid Program as provided in the Protocol Agreement be reestablished beginning January 1," with existing deficits to be made up not later than 1 April. He stipulated "specific amendments"

might be made with his approval, but added, "The whole Russian program is so vital to our interest I know that only the gravest consideration will lead you to recommend our withholding longer the munitions our Government has promised to the U.S.S.R."[2]

Stimson replied on 30 December, forwarding a new schedule of deliveries. "While this schedule is not in all cases in accordance with the protocol," he wrote, "there are certain difficulties, including shipping and production difficulties as well as our entry into the war, which have made some departures from the protocol inevitable." None of the 152 90-mm. antiaircraft guns nor the 756 37-mm. antitank guns promised could be shipped before the end of March. Schedules for tanks, trucks, and planes could not be brought up to date by 1 April, though they probably could be by the end of June. The USSR would have to accept limited quantities of ammunition. Schedules for a few chemicals and explosives could not be met before the end of August. Stimson asked that the President approve these departures as specific amendments. He closed with the further warning:

It is also necessary to point out now that we are at war that any substantial failure to produce supplies as scheduled must serve as a basis for readjustment of the amounts to be forwarded . . . . I feel that I must, as a matter of caution, point out that exigencies may arise as a result of our entry into the war which preclude us from making any absolute commitments.[3]

---

[1] (1) Draft memo, Marshall for President, *circa* 13 Dec 41, sub: Aid to Russia, WPD 4557-30. (2) Related papers in same file. (3) See above, Ch. IV.

[2] Ltr, President to SW, 28 Dec 41, AG 400.3295 (8-14-41) Sec 1.

[3] Ltr, SW to President, 30 Dec 41, AG 400.3295 (8-14-41) Sec 1.

The President accepted Stimson's recommendations as "minimum schedules," but reiterated that the objective must remain as before—to re-establish monthly protocol schedules at the earliest practicable time and make up all deficits by 1 April.[4] Restricting the discussion for the moment entirely to the question of availability of materials, even the minimum schedules represented a difficult goal to meet. With production of many critical items still meager, meeting the protocol involved many sacrifices for an Army just entering a major war itself. Whereas British allocations could be adjusted within the assignments machinery on the basis of production rates, actual need, and other factors, the protocol commitments were rigid.

There were additional problems of meeting Soviet specifications on some items, modifications of American standard equipment necessary for use in the USSR on others, and the provision of adequate spare parts and accessories. For some time after the Soviet Government had been formally placed under lend-lease, it continued to regard supplies procured in the United States as purchases and to impose the most critical standards before accepting materials. The military needs of the Red Army were made known in the United States largely through civilian technicians. These Soviet representatives were slow to take any action without the approval of their superiors in Moscow, and at the same time extremely critical of American efforts. They were at first quite reluctant to accept U.S. standards of inspection, packing, and shipping equipment. They changed specifications for items frequently, and were rigorous in their insistence that every change be effected before they would accept the equip-

ment. Since the First Protocol was negotiated before all their needs could crystallize, new demands were constantly presented in keeping with the developing pattern of the war in the USSR and Soviet discovery of desirable items of American production. New requests were submitted in early 1942 for such articles as tractors, rubber floats, transport planes, tarpaulins, webbing, radio equipment, radar, Sten submachine guns, and pyroxylin smokeless powder. The Soviet representatives pressed continually for larger scales of ammunition and spare parts, insisting that even the scales promised were not being met. Though frequently dilatory themselves in submitting detailed specifications, they were implacable in insisting on special efforts to meet their needs, and threw the blame for any delays on the War Department in nearly every instance. Since shipments were far behind schedule, War Department representatives had to be constantly on the defensive.

Despite the difficulty of doing business with Soviet representatives, by utmost exertions the War Department was soon making progress toward reducing or wiping out deficits in nearly every category of equipment for which it was responsible. Allocations for the Soviet Union set up by MAC(G) and MAC(A) in February and March promised that with few exceptions Stimson's revised schedules would be met by the end of June 1942, and these schedules were generally adhered to. Tanks, trucks, and planes were made available in only slightly less than scheduled quantities. This required taking all gas-powered light tanks from U.S. forces in March and canceling the British assignment for

---

[4] Ltr, President to SW, 4 Jan 42, Auth File of President's Ltrs, DAD.

April. The entire U.S. production of field wire in January went to the USSR, 90 percent of it in February and March. The only serious failure to meet protocol commitments, it appeared in mid-April, would be in antiaircraft and antitank guns, where it was decided U.S. Army needs would not permit deliveries.[5]

Of new Soviet requests, some were met immediately, while others, for various reasons, remained the subject of negotiations for a second protocol. Requests for Sten submachine guns were met by offering standard .45-caliber Thompsons, a start was made on deliveries of tractors, rubber boats, tarpaulins, and webbing, and the Russians were granted 10 percent of the powder production of the country to provide for their need for pyroxylin smokeless powder. Initiation of a program for radio equipment was stalled by Soviet failure to present proper specifications, and requests for radar were turned down in the first instance.[6] General Marshall steadfastly refused to allow transport planes to be diverted to the USSR despite pressure from Hopkins, the President, and even the Navy. The MAB went so far as to assign twenty-nine transports in April for delivery in May and June, but its decision was reversed by the CCS on Marshall's insistence. "I can no more agree to the diversion of additional transport plane equipment to Russia," he wrote Admiral King, "while charged with a primary responsibility for the preparation of a major offensive, . . . than you could approve the diversion of ships from naval task forces forming for operations in the immediate future."[7]

Judging from Soviet complaints, the most serious defect in the War Department program lay in the lack of sufficient ammunition, spare parts, and accessories to accompany major items, lack of co-ordination of complementary equipment, and the defective condition of some of the material shipped. Complaints on these matters began with the first shipments and continued long after. The lack of sufficient ammunition could be remedied only by increased production, and so it gradually was. The Soviet allotment in rounds per gun was twice increased between January and June 1942, though it still remained under the stated Soviet requirement. The spare parts situation was less excusable, as was that of shipment of defective equipment. Many of the first tanks and planes shipped via the northern route, the Soviets reported, could not be put into action. The most flagrant case was that of fighter planes shipped from the United States to the USSR on British account. For some time the British and Americans bandied back and forth the responsibility for furnishing spares and accessories for these planes. The spare parts problem in general was gradually ironed out by more aggressive action by the War Department, under Soviet pressure, to see that standard U.S. scales were shipped. But even as these steps were taken, the Russians turned to insist that the U.S. standard scale was inadequate for the in-

---

[5] (1) Correspondence between Soviet representatives and War Department agencies, principally the Defense Aid Division, is in Russia Corresp Lend-lease 1–5 files, and USSR Mis file, ID. (2) Rpts, SW to President, 17 Feb, 17 Mar, and 17 Apr 42, sub: Progress on Soviet Protocol, AG 400.3295 (8-14-41) Sec 1. (3) Min 37, 7th mtg MAC(G), 26 Feb 42.
[6] See lengthy correspondence in Russia Corresp Lend-lease 2–5 files, DAD.
[7] (1) Ltr, Marshall to King, 27 Apr 42, AG 400.3295 (8-9-41) Sec 2. (2) On this incident, see Matloff and Snell, *Strategic Planning: 1941–1942*, pp. 206–10.

tensive combat use required in the Russo-German war.[8]

To prevent shipment of defective equipment, the Soviet Military Mission in Washington insisted that the only remedy was to allow inspection by their agents before the material left factories. Secretary Stimson granted this privilege, very carefully circumscribed, in February 1942. Soviet complaints decreased thereafter, though this probably resulted more from increased War Department care in inspections and shipment than from Soviet inspection at the factories.

Most of the early difficulties, as Stimson informed the Soviet representatives, were due to the hasty manner in which the Soviet aid program had been inaugurated. As production increased, Soviet needs were fitted into existing long-range requirements plans, and difficulties in making equipment available gradually diminished, though meeting the protocols continued to entail certain sacrifices of U.S. Army needs. As procedures were ironed out, difficulties over spares, ammunition, and defective equipment were relegated to the status of administrative problems to be solved by consultation between Soviet representatives and those of the SOS. Though it cannot be said that anything like the co-operation that characterized British-American relations on this level came into being, definite channels were established, and the Soviet representatives agreed to limit their activities to these channels. On the American side, there was an increased understanding of the peculiar needs of the Russians and of the Soviet manner of negotiating. There remained matters of fundamental understanding, of unity of purpose and harmony of ideals that never were and

never could be settled, but given the *raison d'être* of the program, an adequate apparatus for handling mechanical details had evolved before the end of the First Protocol period. In the meantime, the big problem to emerge was that of shipping the supplies made available at such sacrifice.[9]

The First Protocol and the Shipping Problem

The requirement of cargo tonnage for Soviet aid was in constant competition with shipping requirements to execute strategic plans for Anglo-American operations. Even when ships were provided, the routes to the USSR were long, limited in capacity, and subject to enemy interference. To keep them open or to develop them required commitment of other vital military and naval resources.

As recounted earlier, the President and the Prime Minister at ARCADIA refused to accept a 30 percent cut in shipments to the Soviet Union as a condition to sending the POPPY convoy to the Southwest Pacific and ordered Hopkins and Beaverbrook to

[8] (1) See above, Ch. IV. (2) Corresp in Russia Corresp Lend-lease 1–5 files, DAD; Russia (2) file, DAD; and USSR Mis 470.8 and 471, ID. (3) Rpt, 17 Mar 42, cited n. 5(2). (4) Msg 115 [Moscow to State Dept], Brig Gen Philip R. Faymonville to McCabe, 18 Apr 42, Col Boone's file, Item 302, DAD. (5) Memo, ACofS G-2 for CofS, 16 Feb 42, sub: Stf Conf With Soviet Mil Auths, USSR Mis 336, ID. (6) Msg 131, Kuibyshev to MILID, 23 Dec 41, Russian Info Cables file, ID. (7) For details on spare parts question, see ID, Lend-Lease, II, 1078–87.

[9] (1) Memo, Gen Repin, Soviet Mil Mis, to SW, 5 Feb 42. (2) Ltr, Stimson to Repin, 10 Feb 42. Both in AG 400.3295 (8-14-41) Sec 1. (3) Memo, Somervell for Aurand, 23 Apr 42, with atchd copy of memo handed Soviet Ambassador Maxim M. Litvinov, in Russia Corresp Lend-lease 4 file, DAD. (4) Memo, Soviet Purch Comm, 8 May 42, in response to memo, Hq SOS WD, 22 Apr 42, Russia Corresp Lend-lease 5 file, DAD.

"find ships." [10] At ARCADIA consideration was almost solely centered on the northern route, for the Russians insisted that the bulk of material come that way, the Persian Gulf ports were not yet prepared to handle large tonnages, and the Russo-Japanese situation was too uncertain to allow any extensive use of the Pacific. Shipping over the northern route had, during 1941, been virtually unmolested by the Germans, and though ships had to be armed and convoyed by the British Navy from Iceland onward, the problem at ARCADIA and immediately afterward was still primarily one of merchant shipping and not of naval convoy.

To float the cargo scheduled during January 1942, OLLA reported that some fifty ships would be necessary. Despite the presidential fiat, Hopkins found it impossible to find this many. Effective control over the allocation of shipping had yet to be established, and the process of diversion of ships from civilian trades had only begun. There were too few ships degaussed and equipped with antiaircraft guns. Needs for emergency deployment of U.S. troops to hold the line against the Japanese got first priority in practice if not in theory. Only twenty ships sailed from the United States on the northern route to the USSR during January, and four for the Soviet Far East. By mid-January, Roosevelt was "terribly disturbed" about the situation, and wrote Admiral Land: "You simply must find some ships that can be diverted at once . . . ." [11] Despite this admonition, there were even fewer sailings in February. Though the rate was stepped up in March, the progress of shipments continued far behind schedule. On 17 March the President issued a far stronger directive to Land telling him that shipping must be furnished to meet the proto-

col and could be taken from the South American and Caribbean routes "regardless of other considerations." [12] This meant, as Hopkins put it, "the Russian protocol must be completed in preference to any other phase of our war program." [13]

An intensive effort to make up the backlog followed the President's directive. In April some sixty-three ships with material for the Soviet Union departed for the convoy rendezvous off Iceland, six for the Persian Gulf, and ten for the Soviet Far East. The President proposed to place fifty ships monthly in regular service on the northern route between March and November, twenty-five from November through February. WSA began to shape its shipping plans around this schedule, calculating incidentally that it would require a total commitment of 260 ships. [14]

While this massive shipping program was thus taking shape, the Army was struggling with the task of co-ordinating availability of military equipment for Russia with shipping. The necessity of carrying out initial troop and supply movements to overseas bases enormously com-

---

[10] (1) Min, conf at White House, 12 Jan 42, quoted in Sherwood, *Roosevelt and Hopkins,* p. 465. (2) See above, Ch. VI.

[11] (1) Note, President to Adm Land, 16 Jan 42, MS Index to the Hopkins Papers, Bk. V, Aid to Russia, p. 2, Item 10. (2) Ltr, Gen Spalding, OLLA, to Adm Land, 31 Dec 41, Col Boone's file, Item 98, DAD. (3) Report on War Aid to USSR, 28 Nov 45. (4) See above, Ch. VII.

[12] Ltr, President to Adm Land, 17 Mar 42, Def Aid Rpts on Russia to President folder, USSR Mis 319.1, ID. See also, Roosevelt's letters to Stettinius and to Donald Nelson at this time in same file.

[13] (1) Msg, Hopkins to Harriman and Faymonville, 18 Mar 42, MS Index to the Hopkins Papers, Bk. VII, Second Soviet Protocol Agreement, p. 2, Item 10. (2) See below, App. D.

[14] (1) See below, App. D. (2) Memo *re* mtg in Gen Burns' off, 31 Mar 42, *re* Russia, Russian Shipg Matters 17 Mar–31 May 42 folder, WSA Douglas File. (3) Related papers in same file.

plicated the task. Extensive use of the port of New York for the latter purpose forced a shift of cargo for the USSR to Boston, and when it was decided to load troops at Boston also, hasty arrangements had to be made to divert Soviet shipments to Philadelphia, with the overflow to be taken care of at Baltimore. These various shifts created confusion in rail movements to port. In addition, with no central co-ordinating agency to plan Soviet shipments, the multifarious organizations involved found themselves working at cross-purposes. The Soviet representatives continually complained that material they desired to ship was not on hand in time to insure prompt sailing of vessels under their control. They charged that even the low scales of ammunition promised were not being furnished in balance with the guns in which it was to be used. Nevertheless, as the volume of shipments mounted in April, there was considerable improvement in all these matters. A Russian shipping board was formed, composed of members of the Maritime Commission, the Office of the Defense Aid Director and the Lend-Lease Administration, which met weekly with Soviet shipping representatives in the Commercial Traffic Branch of the Office of The Quartermaster General. The airing given problems in these conferences brought beneficial results. The general improvement in handling overseas shipments that followed the confused experiences of early 1942 also was soon reflected in the movement of cargo to the USSR. By the end of April 1942, OLLA could report to the President that "real effectiveness in getting supplies to seaboard had been attained . . . ."[15]

Troubles on the northern route soon eclipsed the successes gained in providing ships and loading them efficiently. In February Hitler began to shift the weight of his naval strength—submarines, surface craft, and planes—to Norway. Ice conditions during the winter were the worst for twenty-five years, forcing many ships to turn back and the rest to follow closely along the Norwegian coast. During the long daylight hours the convoys of slow freighters had to run the gantlet of German attacks. Losses, previously inconsequential, began to mount in March, and each convoy became a serious fleet operation. As the rate of movement of convoys slowed, the growing volume of ships coming from the United States resulted in a log jam of shipping off Iceland. Fearing that if British naval strength were concentrated too heavily in protecting the Murmansk convoys, the Germans would once again shift their strength to the mid-Atlantic, Churchill and the British Admiralty decided in late April that only three convoys of twenty-five to thirty-five ships each could be sent through every two months. Planned loadings in the United States had meantime been going forward on the supposition that 107 ships would move in these convoys during May alone, and the proposed curtailment came as a great disappointment. Roosevelt at first deplored the British decision, but finally acquiesced on 3 May, expressing hope that convoys could be kept at the maximum of thirty-five ships each.[16]

This curtailment of the northern convoys produced a hurried rearrangement

---

[15] (1) Status of the Soviet Aid Program as of April 30, 1942, rpt by OLLA to President. (2) See corresp in Russia Corresp Lend-lease 1–4 files, DAD; and G–4/33388. (3) Min of shipg confs, 27 Feb–2 Apr 42, USSR Mis 337, ID. (4) WSA memo, unsigned, 6 Apr 42, sub: Orgn for Handling Shipts for Russia, Br Contl of Shipg folder, WSA Douglas File.

[16] (1) Churchill, *Hinge of Fate*, pp. 256–66. (2) Min, 16th mtg CCS, 21 Apr 42, Item 4.

of shipping plans in the United States. There was great confusion, to say the least, since so much depended on the actual size of the convoys the British could maintain. After a series of hurried conferences, Harry Hopkins and Lewis Douglas decided in late April that the berthing of additional ships for northern Soviet ports should be halted for the time being, that as many ships as facilities would permit should be diverted to the Persian Gulf, and that all other ships scheduled for the northern route in May should be diverted to Army use except about ten to load high-priority items that might be dispatched in advance of ships involved in the log jam. As a result, only twenty-one ships left the United States for northern ports during May and June. Even these, it proved, were far more than the number for which the British could provide escort. In May they sent through two convoys, PQ-15 and PQ-16, totaling fifty-seven ships, of which nine were lost. In June the ill-fated convoy PQ-17 lost twenty-two out of its thirty-three ships, and the British were forced to suspend convoys entirely during July and August. Twenty-two ships with 129,000 tons of cargo for the Russians were unloaded in the United Kingdom and some of the material diverted to the use of American and British forces there. Others, loaded with cargo of higher priority, remained in Scottish ports awaiting convoy, many not to sail until December, representing perhaps the most flagrant waste of cargo shipping during 1942.[17]

The net effect was to make it impossible for the United States to meet its commitments under the First Protocol, since neither the Persian Gulf nor the Pacific route was yet ready to handle tonnages that would substantially compensate.

Since all the material made available could not be shipped, mounting backlogs appeared in the United States. The increasing delicacy of relations with Stalin prevented any move to modify the protocol commitments, and the War Department had to continue to make most articles available on schedule as before. The 45-day Rule[18] was not generally applied to protocol materials, and the adjustment of backlogs became a matter of negotiation with the Russians in each individual instance. The most serious problem was that of military trucks. The protocol stipulated 10,000 trucks monthly, and by April the War Department was finally ready to meet this schedule and make up most previous deficits. But for some time the Russians placed a lower shipping priority on trucks than on munitions, and by 1 April 1942 there was a backlog of 28,-000 assigned and unshipped, with an additional 20,000 scheduled for assignment in April. Since the Russians shipped standard U.S. Army trucks in preference to nonstandard ones ordered especially for them, the backlog was a particularly serious one, for the Army could not use nonstandard trucks. It was only with great difficulty that the Soviet representatives were finally persuaded to agree to

---

[17] (1) Churchill, *Hinge of Fate*, pp. 262-71. (2) Memo, Aurand for Somervell, 30 Apr 42, sub: Conf *re* Shipts to Russia. (3) Memo, Burns for Hopkins, 1 May 42, sub: Steps for Relieving Log Jam of Ships for Russia. (4) Memo, Burns for Hopkins, 4 May 42, sub: Conf *re* Log Jam of Ships to Russia. Last three in USSR Mis 337, ID. (5) Douglas' notes on conf with Gen Burns, 27 Apr 42, Russian Shipg Matters 17 Mar–31 May 42 folder, WSA Douglas File. (6) Related papers in same file. (7) Memo, Douglas for Hugh Fulton, 9 Apr 43, Russian Shipg 1 Jan 43 folder, WSA Douglas File. (8) Morison, *Battle of the Atlantic*, pp. 169–92. (9) See below, App. D. (10) For effects of this release of shipping to the Army on the Bolero program, see above, Ch. XIV.

[18] See above, Ch. X.

TABLE 15—WAR DEPARTMENT PERFORMANCE UNDER THE FIRST SOVIET PROTOCOL

Item	Protocol Commitment	Made Available	Exported
Protocol			
Planes	1,800	1,727	1,285
Tanks	2,250	2,289	2,249
90-mm. antiaircraft guns	152	4	4
37-mm. antitank guns	756	63	63
Jeeps	5,000	7,001	6,823
Cargo trucks	85,000	71,584	36,865
Field telephones	108,000	81,510	56,445
Field telephone wire (miles)	562,000	505,000	381,431
Armor plate (tons)	9,000	8,945	8,321
Toluol and TNT (pounds)	59,600,000	73,691,566	59,455,620
Assorted chemicals (pounds)	30,738,586	37,339,082	30,134,653
Machine tools	Maximum possible	(*)	3,253
Forging and pressing equipment (items)	627	(*)	167
Army shoes (pairs)	1,600,000	1,810,909	1,681,515
Army cloth (yards)	1,000,000	1,822,744	1,769,591
Military Items in Addition to Protocol			
Scout cars		624	400
Personnel carriers		308	219
Thompson submachine guns		98,220	81,287
Rubber floats (6-ton)		2,421	2,421
Tractors		887	392
Battery charging sets		2,024	0

*Information not supplied in source.

Source: Ltr, SW to President, 18 Aug 42, transmitting final rpt on mil items included in First (Moscow) Protocol, AG 400.3295 (8-14-41) Sec 1.

ship trucks in an over-all ratio corresponding to the ratio of types in production for them. Despite the urgent recommendations of General Aurand, there was little curtailment in truck assignments.[19]

While trucks were the outstanding backlog problem, there were many others. By the end of the First Protocol period shipping rather than availability of supplies had become the principal bottleneck and was to remain so. Table 15 shows clearly both the extent to which the War Department was successful in meeting availability schedules and the extent to which lack of shipping prevented the de-

livery of materials made available. Only in the cases of antiaircraft and antitank guns were there any signal failures to furnish materials promised; while there were other instances where availability did not meet protocol commitments, the amount furnished in each case was always

[19] (1) Memo, Capt H. W. Coon for Chief of Opns Br Trans Div SOS, no date. (2) Telephone convs, Aurand with Schley and McCabe of OLLA, 7 Apr 42. Both in ID 451 Russia, I. (3) Ltr, McCabe to Lukashev, 11 Apr 42. (4) Ltr, Lukashev to McCabe, 17 Apr 42. (5) Ltr, I. I. Karzov, Soviet Purch Comm, to Col Taylor, DAD, 14 Apr 42. Last three in Russia Corresp Lend-lease 4 file, DAD. (6) Memo cited n. 17(2).

greater than the Russians could ship. For other items, the War Department went beyond official promises, supplying, for instance, more shoes, cloth, jeeps, and explosives than the Russians had originally asked. It must be kept in mind, nevertheless, that much of the material shipped did not reach the USSR, but was unloaded or immobilized in England, or sent to the bottom.

Formulation of the Second Protocol

The difficulties encountered in meeting the First Protocol posed a serious question as to the future course of the Soviet aid program. As the cost of continuing shipments over the northern route mounted there was an unmistakable competition with the shipping requirements for BOLERO, and the opening of a second front after all promised far greater relief to the Russians than the shipment of supplies. War Department supply agencies, in negotiations with the Soviet Purchasing Commission on a multiplicity of new items, were reluctant to make any promises as to future schedules of delivery. Army strategic planners viewed aid to the USSR as essential but subordinate to the main objective of invasion of Europe. The CCS in their strategic directive for assignment of munitions asked that the First Protocol be re-examined as soon as possible, revised, and extended to the end of 1942, the revised protocol to be "based upon giving maximum aid to Russia within the transportation capabilities to the ultimate destination, provided essential United States and British operations will not be unduly handicapped." [20] However, the President settled the whole issue when he wrote the Secretaries of War and the Navy on 24 March 1942:

I understand that, from a strategical point of view, the Army and Navy feel that aid to Russia should be continued and expanded to the maximum extent possible, consistent with shipping possibilities and the vital needs of the United States, the British Commonwealth of Nations and other of the United Nations. I share such a view.

In the near future, I expect to discuss this question with the U.S.S.R. I desire that you submit to me by April 6th next the monthly assignment schedules of major items pertaining to your department which you recommend be offered the U.S.S.R. during the period July 1, 1942–June 30, 1943. It is appreciated that Soviet needs may not be known, but, when necessary, assumptions should be made which are based on your estimate of the Soviet situation. [21]

Roosevelt designated Hopkins as his agent to consolidate and co-ordinate recommendations of the various departments and agencies, and each was asked to name someone to represent its view in the formulation of the new protocol. Stimson designated General Somervell to represent the War Department. An informal interdepartmental committee came into being that was to be formally constituted in October 1942 as the President's Soviet Protocol Committee, responsible for formulation and administration of the Soviet aid program including co-ordination of shipping therefor. [22] Though it had, at least on its military side, virtually an interlocking directorate with the MAB (Hopkins was chairman and General Burns was executive officer of both organizations), it was not under the CCS.

---

[20] (1) CCS 50/2, 24 Mar 42, title: Dir for Asgmt of Mun. (2) Memo, Aurand for Stettinius, 11 Mar 42, sub: Negotiations With Respect to Continuance of Russian Protocol, Russia Corresp Lend-lease 3 file, DAD. (3) Related papers in same file. (4) Matloff and Snell, *Strategic Planning: 1941-1942*, pp. 174–83.

[21] Ltr, President to SW, 24 Mar 42, AG 400.3295 (8-14-41) Sec 1.

[22] Ltr, President to SW, 30 Oct 42, ID 031.1, IV.

War Department recommendations were ready by 11 April 1942, and they generally met the President's directive that "aid to Russia should be continued and expanded to the maximum extent possible." For instance, proposed tank deliveries from the United States were increased from 2,250 over the nine-month period of the First Protocol to 7,500 over the twelve-month period of the second. Truck schedules continued at ten thousand monthly despite the shipping experiences of the preceding months. Radio equipment and other new material, which had been a subject of interim negotiations, were added. Only in the case of planes were the new schedules definitely disappointing to the Russians. Stimson accepted AAF contentions and told the President that only the existing rate—100 pursuits, 100 light bombers, and 12 heavy bombers monthly—would be possible without seriously disrupting the development of an AAF equal to its responsibilities. Stimson also proposed that, to clear up backlogs and to permit sufficient flexibility to meet variations in production and shipping availability, unfloated material offered under the First Protocol should apply on the second, and that only accumulated totals for the first and second six months, not monthly schedules, should be met.[23]

The War Department's offerings were consolidated with those of other agencies by the informal protocol committee, and the total came to some 7.2 million short tons of supplies—1.1 million tons of military and naval equipment, 1.8 million tons of raw materials, machinery, and industrial equipment, and 4.3 million tons of food products. With a British offering of one million short tons, this made a grand total of eight million tons on the joint account of the two countries—several times the amount offered on the First Protocol and, as events were proving, much more than could possibly be shipped. The Combined Shipping Adjustment Board reported that three million tons could be carried over the northern route, one million via the Persian Gulf, and estimated that shipping could be found to float this four million short tons on the assumption that losses would not exceed 10 percent. The current British estimate for the northern route was three convoys every two months, an average of forty-five ships per month. Figuring 6,000 tons to a ship, the CSAB calculated convoy limitations would still permit 3,240,000 short tons to be carried over the northern route during the twelve-month period, substantially in accord with the port clearance capacities in the USSR and with the shipping to be available. No estimate was made for the Vladivostok route because of the continuing uncertainty of Russo-Japanese relations. The informal protocol committee therefore decided to offer the Russians 8 million short tons of material, from which they would select the 4.4 million tons they desired most.[24]

This seemingly careful estimate was highly optimistic and concealed a competition for shipping with BOLERO and other operations contemplated by the CCS. The rate of loss on the convoy route during March, April, and May had been 18 per-

---

[23] (1) Ltr, SW to President, 11 Apr 42, Def Aid Rpts on Russia to President folder, USSR Mis 319.1, ID. (2) Ltr, SW to President, 23 Apr 42, AG 400.3295 (8-14-41) Sec 2. (3) For British offerings under the Second Protocol, see Russia Corresp Lend-lease 5 file, DAD. These offers were a continuation of rates under the First Protocol. Much of the material promised by the British, planes in particular, was to come from the United States under lend-lease to Britain.

[24] Memo, Gen Burns for JCS, 12 May 42, sub: Status of Proposed 2d Russian Protocol, ABC 400.-3295 Russia (4-19-42) Sec 1.

cent instead of 10 percent and prospects were that losses would increase. The CSAB had actually made its estimates on the northern route before the convoy crisis, and there is every indication that they were based more on the estimated capacity of northern Soviet ports than on shipping or convoy limitations. The estimate of one million tons via the Persian Gulf, as will be shown later, was not based on any realistic appraisal of the situation there. In justice to Lewis Douglas, the American representative on the CSAB, it should be noted that he first placed Persian Gulf capacity at 600,000 short tons and accepted the one million figure, apparently under pressure, with some skepticism. He wrote General Burns that it was "in excess of anything that has so far been lifted and handled with reasonable dispatch through Persian Gulf ports for Russian account." [25] The figures on availability of shipping were the most questionable of all since the military planners continually foresaw a deficit. On 4 May 1942 Admiral King called some of these matters to the attention of the JCS, pointing out the general shortage of shipping, the great difficulties encountered in getting convoys into northern Soviet ports, and the requirements incident to manning a second front in Europe, and suggested the protocol be revised. He thought the BOLERO preparations ought to be a convincing argument toward agreement on a reduction by the Russians themselves.

As a result of King's representations, the Joint Staff Planners undertook a study and on 21 May came up with quite different conclusions from those of the Combined Shipping Adjustment Board. They noted the loss rate on the northern route and the fact that additional escort could only be furnished by robbing convoys in other areas. They also noted that the Combined Military Transportation Committee was currently reporting an over-all shortage of three million tons of shipping to support Anglo-American operations planned for 1942 and 1943 and that there seemed no way of reconciling the CSAB figures with these estimates. "In view of the general shortage of shipping," they concluded, ". . . the allocation of this shipping to transport 4.4 millions tons of munitions to Russia will, of necessity, curtail some other war effort." [26]

Admiral King and General Marshall brought the matter to the personal attention of the President on 31 May, shortly after the arrival of Vyacheslav M. Molotov, the Soviet Foreign Minister, on a mission to the United States and, in fact, after Roosevelt had presented Molotov with the draft protocol. The next day the President did propose to Molotov that shipment of general supplies during the next year be curtailed from 2,300,000 tons to 700,000 in the interests of getting more shipping for the second front, though he assured Molotov that shipment of military supplies would continue as planned. As Hopkins reported part of the interview:

The President repeated that we expected to set up a second front in 1942, but that every ship we could shift to the English run

[25] (1) Memo, Douglas for Burns, 18 Apr 42, Russian Shipg Matters 17 Mar–31 May 42 folder, WSA Douglas File. (2) Related papers in same file.

[26] (1) JPS 28/1, 21 May 42, title: Russian Mun Protocol. (2) Memo cited n. 25(1). General Burns at the request of the JCS presented the informal protocol committee's estimates to them at the meeting on 12 May 1942 and informed them that the proposed protocol was already at the White House for final approval by the President. (3) OPD notes on 17th mtg JPS, 20 May 42. (4) Memo, Adm King for JCS, 1 May 42. Last two in ABC 400.3295 Russia (4-19-42) Sec 1. (5) Min, 13th mtg JCS, 4 May 42; 14th mtg, 11 May 42, Item 11; 15th mtg, 18 May 42, Item 5. (6) Min, 17th mtg JPS, 20 May 42, Item 6.

meant that the second front was so much closer to being realized. After all, ships could not be in two places at once, and hence, every ton we could save out of the total of 4,100,000 tons would be so much to the good. The Soviets could not have their cake and eat it too.[27]

Molotov's replies were very guarded, and he showed both a reluctance to give up essential industrial supplies and some doubt of American sincerity on the question of the second front. He even submitted a counterproposal for an American naval convoy to Archangel. Since in fact the prospects of the second front began to fade shortly afterward, the President never pushed his proposal for reduction any further. As a consequence, there was little the Joint Staff Planners could do but ignore the results of their own study. On 10 June 1942 they noted that the proposed protocol was already in the hands of the Russians and that "further study of this subject with a view to revision would serve no useful purpose at this time."[28]

Though the Second Protocol was not formally signed until October, it was accepted by Soviet Ambassador Maxim M. Litvinov on 7 July 1942 and really went into effect on 1 July with the expiration of the first agreement. As Stimson asked, materials resting available and unshipped against the First Protocol were applied against the second, lessening the burden of assignment on items such as military trucks, and taking care, at least momentarily, of the most serious backlog problems. The Second Protocol also contained a safeguarding clause, somewhat stronger than that in the first but still not as strong as General Marshall had recommended. The clause read, "It is understood that any program of this sort must be tentative in character and must be subject to unforeseen changes which the progress of

the war may require from the standpoint of stores as well as from the standpoint of shipping."[29]

General Marshall also tried to get a clause inserted in the Second Protocol providing for a possible reduction in aircraft deliveries. He proposed that:

Airplanes . . . be delivered up to August 15th to complete the Protocol Agreement for 30 June 1942. Thereafter the monthly rate of 100 pursuit, 100 light bombardment, and 12 medium bombardment planes will be supplied provided the rate of attrition suffered in the British-American air offensive over the European continent permits; but in any event a monthly minimum of 50 pursuits, 50 light bombardment, and 12 medium bombardment planes will be guaranteed by the United States.[30]

The President would not accept this condition and insisted that the minimum commitment be set at 212 monthly until October and afterward adjusted "on the basis of developments incident to the progress of the war."[31] In accepting the protocol in July, Litvinov expressed the hope that the aircraft schedules might be increased in October, and in the intervening period the Russians exerted heavy pressure for such an increase.[32]

---

[27] Sherwood, *Roosevelt and Hopkins*, pp. 570–75. Cf. official figure of 4,400,000 tons.

[28] (1) Min, 19th mtg JPS, 10 Jun 42, Item 3. (2) Sherwood, *Roosevelt and Hopkins*, pp. 574–76.

[29] (1) Ltr, Litvinov to Cordell Hull, 7 Jul 42. (2) Memo, Burns for Hopkins, 20 Jun 42. (3) Ltr, Burns to Maj Gen Alexander I. Belyaev, 23 Jun 42. (4) Ltr, Belyaev to Burns, 23 Jun 42. All in ID 031.1, I. (5) For official text of Second Protocol as adopted, see U.S. Dept of State, *Soviet Supply Protocols*, Pub 2759. For earlier drafts, see OPD 400.3295 Russia. (6) For Marshall's suggestions on a safeguarding clause, see min, 15th mtg JCS, 18 May 42, Item 5.

[30] Min cited n. 29(6).

[31] U.S. Dept of State, *Soviet Supply Protocols*, Pub, 2759.

[32] (1) Notes on War Council mtg, 18 May 42, SW Confs file, Vol. II, WDCSA. (2) Ltr cited n. 29(1).

The Search for Alternate Routes

No sooner had the Second Protocol been formulated and accepted than the heavy losses on PQ-17 and the consequent British decision to suspend the northern convoys during July and August revealed the tenuous character of the shipping estimates on which it was based. Shortly afterward came the President's and Prime Minister's decision on the invasion of North Africa, a step that meant there would certainly be no second front in Europe in 1942 and probably not in 1943. A period of acute embarrassment for both Churchill and Roosevelt *vis-à-vis* Stalin ensued. There were serious doubts that the convoys, even if resumed in September, could be continued during the execution of TORCH. In this situation, the U.S. Government turned to an intensive effort to develop alternate routes for forwarding supplies to the USSR.

The Pacific offered one obvious avenue of approach. Ships flying the Soviet flag had been carrying supplies to Vladivostok from U.S. west coast ports since the inauguration of the Soviet aid program in 1941. During the summer months of 1942 these were supplemented by a limited program of shipments to Siberian arctic ports. But Soviet flag shipping in the Pacific was very limited, and American flag ships could not use the route to Vladivostok because it ran directly through waters close to the Japanese homeland. Even the Soviet ships carried only civilian-type supplies. In early July 1942 the Office of Lend-Lease Administration suggested opening a route through the Bering Strait and Arctic Ocean around the northern fringe of Siberia to Murmansk and Archangel, pointing out that the Russians claimed they were using this route during the sum-

mer months. Pursuing this idea, WSA found some cargo vessels it considered suited to arctic service, and in August turned over seven of them and one tanker to the Russians. But even the Russians apparently found this arctic route too formidable and instead placed the ships on the regular run to Vladivostok. Since these ships were able to proceed under the Soviet flag unmolested by the Japanese, further transfers were soon under consideration.[33]

In July and August 1942, however, as the Germans pushed relentlessly forward in the Caucasus, the Russians were insisting on shipment of finished munitions and minimizing the need for civilian supplies. In selecting material from the Second Protocol list, they specified that all items except foodstuffs would be taken at the full rates offered.[34] It was doubtful that the Pacific route could ever serve for shipment of planes, tanks, guns, and ammunition since it was so vulnerable to interruption by the Japanese. Vladivostok also was a long way from the critical Soviet front in the southern Caucasus. Americans had but meager knowledge of Siberian port facilities or of the ability of the Trans-Siberian Railway to transport supplies to the European front. Operations in the Pacific were already placing a strain on shipping available there and transfers to the

---

[33] (1) Status of the Soviet Aid Program as of July 31, 1942, and Status of the Soviet . . . as of August 31, 1942, rpts by OLLA to President. (2) Ltr, John N. Hazard, OLLA, to Maj Goodman, ID, 20 Jun 42, USSR Mis 400.3295, ID. (3) Ltr, McCabe to Adm Land, 2 Jul 42. (4) Memo, David Scoll for Lewis Douglas, 15 Jul 42, sub: Resume of Russian Negotiations . . . . Last two in Russian Shipg 1 Jun–31 Dec 42 folder, WSA Douglas File. (5) Memo, Land and Douglas for President, 12 Oct 42, Russia–Rpts to President folder, WSA Douglas File.
[34] Status of the Soviet Aid Program as of November 30, 1942, rpt by OLLA to President.

Soviet flag could only be made at considerable sacrifice.

There was always the possibility of flight delivery of planes. There were two possible ferry routes—one via Brazil, the South Atlantic, central Africa, and the Persian Gulf; the other via Alaska to Siberia. The former route was the longer, involving single flights possible only for bombers, and dependent on availability of American pilots and development of airfields in Iran. The latter route could accommodate all types of planes, but presented problems of winterization, navigation under difficult climatic conditions, and proper facilities in Siberia for receipt of planes. The United States first suggested the Alaskan ferry route in December 1941, but found the Russians singularly unreceptive and suspicious since they did not want to give information on their airfields in Siberia. The AAF thought a survey of these facilities was necessary to proper operation of the route.[35] After Pearl Harbor, American military interest was dual, for the Siberian air bases might eventually be used for an air assault against Japan. American insistence on linking this consideration with that of operation of the ferry routes made Soviet officials even more uncommunicative.

Finally, in May 1942, the USSR did agree to consider taking plane deliveries in Alaska if Soviet pilots flew them to Siberia and if there were no question of American operations in Soviet territory. Taking advantage of this small opening, the President proposed conversations in Moscow, and a special air mission under Maj. Gen. Follett Bradley was constituted and sent to the USSR in July. Bradley encountered the usual frustrations to which American missions in Moscow were subject, but was finally permitted by Stalin to send a small survey party by Soviet bomber over the ferry route. The survey party agreed that the route was a feasible one. Negotiations both in Washington and in Moscow then began to take some curious turns. First the Russians, evidently on the assumption that the full protocol commitment of 212 planes monthly would be flown over the route, demanded 43 transport planes to ferry Soviet crews back and forth from Alaska. The War Department, still facing a critical shortage of transports and wishing to test both the route and Soviet intentions before committing itself completely, offered only ten. The Soviet Government first agreed on this basis that ferrying operations should commence on a reduced scale in September, and then suddenly on 21 September, after the AAF had started the movement of planes to Fairbanks, Alaska, Maj. Gen. Alexander I. Belyaev, head of the Russian military mission in Washington, announced that only the planes then at Fairbanks would be delivered by the ferry. The War Department, quite irritated, decided the route was closed, and refused to turn the ten transports over to the Russians. Just as suddenly on 6 October 1942, Belyaev again reversed his position and said the USSR was ready to go ahead with the program.[36]

There seems little explanation for these turnabouts beyond some mysterious policy

---

[35] (1) State Dept Msg 2066, Kuibyshev and Faymonville to Spalding, 16 Dec 41, Cables From Russia file, ID. (2) Matloff and Snell, *Strategic Planning: 1941–1942*, Ch. XV.

[36] (1) Matloff and Snell, *Strategic Planning: 1941–1942*, Ch. XV. (2) For more detailed account, see Edwin M. Snell, The USSR in U.S.-British Plans and Operations in 1942, research draft MS, OCMH. (3) OPD Diary, 9, 12, 15, 21, 27, 28 Aug, 24, 27 Sep, and 5–7 Oct 42 entries, OPD Hist Unit File. (4) Msg 135, Marshall to Bradley, 6 Sep 42, AG 400.3295 (9-6-42) (1).

decisions in the inner councils of the Polit-
buro. Be this as it may, there was no further Soviet opposition to delivery of planes
by the Alaskan route as long as Soviet
pilots and crews took delivery in Alaska.
Bradley proposed, and the JCS agreed,
that the route be developed by May 1943
so that it could handle all the planes assigned to the Soviet Union, and about half
the monthly assignment in the meantime.
Immediate results were disappointing.
There were insufficient transport planes to
ferry the Soviet pilots and crews. Delays
developed in providing proper winterization equipment and navigational apparatus for flights over the Bering Sea. Deliveries continued meager during the fall and
winter of 1942–43 and failed to take the
major burden off the Atlantic route. Only
eighty-five planes were actually delivered
via Alaska through the end of 1942. Nor
could the South Atlantic ferry route carry
more than a small number of light and
medium bombers. The rest had still to be
transported by water to the Persian Gulf
or over the northern convoy route if they
were to be delivered at all.[37]

Thus, the Persian Gulf remained the
only alternative to the northern route for
all types of war material. By August 1942
the Persian Gulf had come to occupy the
most important place in Anglo-American
plans for continuing supply to the USSR.
In September the CCS agreed that the
U.S. Army should assume responsibility
for development of port and transportation facilities there, and it is necessary to
pause briefly here to review the background for this decision.

Development of the Persian Gulf
January–July 1942

The Persian Gulf lay within the British
area of strategic responsibility and the ini-

tial American conception was that the
British should develop and operate the
supply line there with American material
aid and the technical assistance of General
Wheeler's Iranian mission. But the British
had only limited means available, and
were concerned with supplying their own
forces in Iran and Iraq as well as with developing a supply line to the Soviet Union.
Pursuit of the two objectives together was
not always compatible. Beyond this, the
Russians themselves were difficult to deal
with and slow to accept the necessity for
deliveries via the Persian Gulf rather than
over the exposed northern convoy route.

When the British took over southern
Iran in August 1941, they faced a formidable task in developing the line of communications. The only port in the area
with any considerable capacity (outside
that on Abadan Island, reserved almost
exclusively for handling the products of
the large oil refinery there) was Basra in
Iraq. The British needed nearly all Basra's
capacity for their own military use. The
Iranian ports proper—Khorramshahr,
Bandar Shahpur, Tanuma, Bushire, and
Ahwaz—lacked dock and handling facilities. The Iranian State Railway, which
ran northward from Bandar Shahpur to
the Caspian Sea, was constructed on modern lines, but lacked rolling stock and was
capable of carrying only 6,000 tons
monthly. Motor roads northward from the
ports were poor and undeveloped. *(See
Map 7.)* The capacity of the British truck
assembly plant at Bushire and plane assembly facilities at Shubaiba near Basra
were little more than sufficient to meet

---

[37] (1) Snell MS cited n. 36(2). (2) OLLA rpt cited
n. 34. (3) Rpt, SW to President, 9 Dec 42, sub:
Progress on Soviet Protocol, AG 400.3295 (9-1-42) (3)
Sec 12. (4) Rpt, SW to President, 10 Feb 42, ID 031.1,
II.

requirements of the British Army.

By an aggressive program of development, the British proposed to increase facilities in the Persian Gulf so that by the spring of 1942 some 60,000 to 100,000 tons of material could be forwarded to the USSR monthly. The achievement of this goal was predicated on extensive American aid, plans for which were submitted in Washington by General Wheeler in December 1941 and January 1942. It will be recalled that in these plans the larger assembly and distributing centers were to be in Karachi, India. These centers were not only to serve the British in India but also as points for storage and transshipment of lend-lease supplies for both the British and the Russians via the Persian Gulf, and as a direct point of supply for a secondary route to the USSR running from Karachi via Zahidan and Meshed to Ashkhabad on a rail line within the Soviet Union. At the head of the Persian Gulf itself, the Americans would undertake improvement of port facilities at Umm Qasr in Iraq and at Khorramshahr and Bandar Shahpur in Iran, and adjacent road and rail connections; they would operate a plane assembly plant at Abadan, two TUP truck assembly plants at Andimeshk, Iran, and ordnance repair and assembly centers at Umm Qasr. It was also seriously proposed that the Americans operate the Iranian State Railway in the British zone.[38]

The failure of the War Department to provide either the personnel or supplies required for Wheeler's projects in the period immediately following Pearl Harbor and the reasons therefor have already been noted.[39] First priority within the limited resources available went to projects designated for support of the British. The reason lay not only in the fact of Brit-

ish control in the Persian Gulf, but also in Soviet insistence on the use of the northern route. In late December, the Soviet ambassador in Iran informed Wheeler that only 2,000 trucks and 100 light bombers should be delivered monthly through the Persian Gulf, all other war supplies by the northern ports. The USSR objected to the Zahidan route, claiming that it would provide supplies too far from the combat zone, and that it was too poorly developed for use in the near future. This insistence on limited use of the Persian Gulf route seemed to justify postponement of projects for Soviet aid save for truck and plane assembly plants. The first American personnel to arrive were assigned the task of developing the port of Umm Qasr in Iraq. The suggestion that the Americans take over the Iranian State Railway was dropped. General Wheeler centered most of his attention on Karachi in India and in February was given additional duties as head of General Stilwell's SOS.[40]

Shipments of material via the Persian Gulf during the early months of 1942 were accordingly very limited and were cut back from the December 1941 schedule, when some seven fully loaded and five

---

[38] (1) For a fuller story of project planning, see Motter, *Persian Corridor*, pp. 44–59, 63, 143–45, 124–27. (2) See also above, Ch. XVIII. (3) Brig R. Micklem, *Army: Transportation*, THE SECOND WORLD WAR, 1939–1945 (London, His Majesty's Stationery Office, 1950), pp. 73–92. (4) Ltr, Gen Spalding to Gen Greely, 28 Nov 42, USSR Mis 617, ID. (5) Ltr, Wheeler to Moore, 19 Jan 42, Iranian Mis 600.12, ID.

[39] See above, Ch. XVIII.

[40] (1) Motter, *Persian Corridor*, pp. 56–57, 63–64, 335–37. (2) Msg MASTA NOSSY 1295, London to Salter, 4 Dec 41. (3) Msg MASTA NOSSY 1307, London to Salter, 4 Dec 41. (4) Msg VVY/802/Q, ARMINDIA to War Off, London, 14 Jan 42. Last three in USSR Mis 635, ID. (5) Msg VVY/757/Q, Wheeler to Moore [via Br channels], 13 Jan 42, Iranian Mis 600.12, ID.

partially loaded ships sailed from the United States carrying mainly trucks and planes. During January 1942 the only cargo for the Russians dispatched to the Persian Gulf was some deck-loaded planes; during February the total, on two fully loaded and twelve partially loaded ships, was only 6,000 tons. In accordance with Soviet wishes, plans were laid on the basis of maximum shipments of 2,000 trucks, one hundred planes, and perhaps 400 tons of miscellaneous cargo monthly. Pending the development of American facilities at Andimeshk and Abadan, the British had to assemble the trucks at Bushire and the planes at Basra. Port facilities at Basra had to carry the bulk of the load. Native drivers operating under the United Kingdom Commercial Corporation (UKCC), a government sponsored transportation agency, delivered the assembled trucks over rough roads to the Russians at Tehran. The RAF handled the planes. The Russians complained of slow deliveries and of defects in the trucks and planes when they arrived. Soviet inspectors would accept nothing less than perfection, and the British were obviously unable to deliver equipment in perfect condition. The Americans, who had a measure of responsibility for these deliveries, found themselves without the power to substantially affect them since they could dictate to neither the British nor the Russians.[41]

The existence of a second American mission in the area specifically charged with expediting the flow of materials to the USSR further complicated the picture. The U.S. Military Mission to the USSR under General Greely had originally expected to enter the Soviet Union and there render technical advice and assistance to the Russians on the use of American lend-lease, but the Russians showed no inclination to accept such assistance. General Greely and his small party arrived in Basra in mid-February 1942 and then moved to Tehran, but were unable to obtain visas from the Soviet Government to permit them to enter the USSR. At Tehran, Greely inevitably became involved in expediting the flow of supplies through Iran.[42]

The effects of this early confusion and neglect were increasingly felt as the need for routing shipments via the Persian Gulf mounted during March, April, and May 1942. The Russians agreed that some general supplies might be sent that way in addition to trucks and planes; the tonnage shipped in March mounted to eighteen thousand and to twenty-one thousand in April.[43]

When the SOS decided in early April to limit the objectives of the Middle East missions to realizable projects, first priority was shifted from the projects for the British in Iraq to the Soviet aid projects in Iran. The Americans moved their small construction force from Umm Qasr to Khorramshahr. Simultaneously, General

---

[41] (1) Report on War Aid to USSR, 28 Nov 45. (2) Ltr, Gen Moore to Brig W. E. R. Blood, Br Army Stf, 22 Jan 42, sub: Deliveries to Russia via Persian Gulf and India, G-4/33388. (3) State Dept Msg 82, Faymonville to McCabe, 24 Mar 42, ID 451 Russia, I. (4) Msg 16, Tehran to AGWAR, 27 Mar 42, AG 400.-3295 (8-14-41) Sec 1. (5) Msg 100, AMSIR to AGWAR, 31 Mar 42, AG 400.3295 (8-9-41) Sec 4. (6) For fuller account of early assembly and delivery problems, see Motter, *Persian Corridor*, pp. 124–55.

[42] (1) For formation of Greely mission, see above, Ch. IV. (2) For full account of Greely mission, see Motter, *Persian Corridor*, pp. 65–81.

[43] (1) Report on War Aid to USSR, 28 Nov 45. (2) Ltr, L. A. Razin, Soviet Purch Comm, to W. C. Armstrong, OLLA, 12 Mar 42. (3) Ltr, Armstrong to Razin, 17 Mar 42. (4) Ltr, William O. Hart, WSA, to Armstrong, 21 Mar 42. Last three in USSR Mis 635, ID. (5) See below, App. D.

Wheeler was assigned exclusively as commanding general of Stilwell's SOS in India, and his deputy, Col. Don G. Shingler, was appointed chief of the Iranian mission. In addition, the Greely mission was dissolved in early May, General Greely reassigned as military adviser to the Iranian Government, and his duties with regard to Soviet lend-lease transferred to Shingler. These steps at least made the forwarding of supplies to the USSR the primary mission of the Americans in Iran, though the original conception that they should only aid the British and not assume responsibility for these deliveries themselves remained unchanged. Also, Shingler was not yet assured of any considerable number of service troops or quantities of supplies to carry out his mission.[44]

There was a certain lack of realism, therefore, in the decision at the end of April, when the convoys over the northern route were curtailed, to divert large tonnages to the Persian Gulf. In a conference held by Harry Hopkins and General Burns with WSA and SOS officials, it was decided that twelve ships should be dispatched there in May and twelve in June. Then, at the instigation of the Russians, who now reversed their previous position, Hopkins proposed that eight more should be allocated monthly if the Persian Gulf could handle them. Previous restrictions on types of cargo were lifted, and May shipments included all sorts of munitions and some civilian supplies in addition to trucks and planes. Actual tonnages shipped zoomed upward from 21,000 in April to 87,000 in May and 91,000 in June. As noted earlier, plans for the Second Protocol were shaped on the basis of forwarding one million short tons of cargo via the Persian Gulf over a twelve-month period.[45]

These decisions were hastily made in an atmosphere of sudden crisis, and not based on any studied conclusions of what port and inland clearance capacities in the Persian Gulf actually were. Hopes that twenty ships might be accommodated in any one month in the near future were soon dashed. Shingler reported that Iranian ports could not possibly handle twenty ships (120,000 tons of Soviet cargo) until the end of October 1942, when planned improvements were scheduled for completion. Even then inland clearance would be limited to 78,000 tons monthly, and there would be insufficient storage to take care of the excess pending improvement in clearance capacity. American and British shipping authorities agreed that maximum capacity for Soviet lend-lease in July and August, when the heavy May–June shipments would start to arrive, would be much less. The British Ministry of War Transport tended to be somewhat more pessimistic than Shingler about the possible pace of development.[46]

Authorities in Washington were reluctant, nevertheless, to curtail the rate of

---

[44] (1) For the story of the early plan for militarization of the Middle East missions and the cutback in personnel in April, see above, Ch. XVIII. (2) See also, Motter, *Persian Corridor*, pp. 63–64, 79–81. (3) Msg 100, AGWAR to AMSIR, 10 Apr 42, AG 400.3295 (8-9-41) Sec 4.

[45] (1) Memo, Col Baird for Gen Aurand, 8 May 42, sub: Russian Shipts in May and June, Iranian Mis 563.5, ID. (2) Report on War Aid to USSR, 28 Nov 45. (3) Msg, AGWAR to AMSIR, 20 May 42, CM-OUT 4018. (4) Msg, Basrah to IMMEDIATE AMSIR, 26 May 42, CM-IN 7325. (5) Ltr, McCabe to Land, 5 May 42, Russian Shipg Matters 17 Mar–31 May 42 folder, WSA Douglas File.

[46] (1) Msg, AMSIR, Basra, to AMSIR, Washington, 17 May 42, CM-IN 4571. (2) Msg, AMSIR, Basra, to AMSIR, Washington, 7 Jun 42, CM-IN 2226. (3) Msg, Seaholm, WSA Basra, to Wilcox, WSA Washington, 6 May 42. (4) Msg MAST 14188 SABLO 7, BMWT, London, to BMWT, Washington, 10 May 42. Last two in Iranian Mis 563.5, ID.

TRUCKING SUPPLIES TO TEHRAN *through the Persian Corridor. The mountainous terrain necessitated the construction of many switchbacks on this highway.*

shipment, and there was only a moderate cutback in July and August 1942 (to 63,000 and 66,000 gross long tons, respectively). Meanwhile, there was an inevitable time lag in applying the other possible remedy—acceleration in the pace of development of facilities. The main result was heavily increased pressure for accomplishment, but there was no over-all plan and divided responsibilities in the Persian Gulf area continued to cause confusion. Shipments of necessary transportation, construction, and port equipment, both to the British and to Shingler's command, were expedited, but the effects of earlier neglect could not be erased by this belated action. Also, too frequently delays developed in shipping the most critical items—

for example, port cranes, rail equipment, and heavy construction supplies. In no particular did progress during the three months following the May decision justify optimism about the capacity of the Persian Gulf, and the heavy shipments to the Gulf ports inevitably brought an increasing threat of port congestion.

Shingler's predictions proved highly optimistic. Development of the ports lagged behind the schedule on which these predictions were based. Inland clearance, which as Shingler pointed out was the biggest bottleneck, lagged even further. The Iranian State Railway, necessarily the primary reliance, had to fulfill certain normal obligations for the Iranian civilian economy and for hauling supplies for the

TRAIN LOADED WITH TANKS FOR THE USSR *winds through the hills in Iran.*

British Army in Iran, Polish forces the British were evacuating from the USSR through Iran, and oil from coastal refineries, as well as material from the United States for the USSR. Shipment of rolling stock and rails from the United States, promised in 1941, was not well under way until July 1942; operation by native labor under British supervision was far from satisfactory; construction of line extensions fell behind schedule. As late as August 1942, the Iranian State Railway carried only 35,770 long tons of supplies for all purposes, of which only 12,440 were Soviet lend-lease. The trucking operations of the United Kingdom Commercial Corporation were but a poor supplement. UKCC operations were handicapped by bad roads or lack of roads,

insufficient trucks, poor handling by native drivers, and inefficiency in management. Both Somervell and Shingler suggested, as early as May 1942, that an American trucking fleet be sent to supplement that of the UKCC, but the proposal received little immediate consideration. In fact, since road construction lagged further behind than any other single activity (for lack of heavy construction equipment), the supplementary trucking fleet could have had little appreciable effect without a concomitant program of road development. While the two U.S. truck assembly plants at Andimeshk and Bandar Shahpur and the plane assembly plant at Abadan were in operation by the end of April, it took time to develop efficient operation, and truck assembly was further

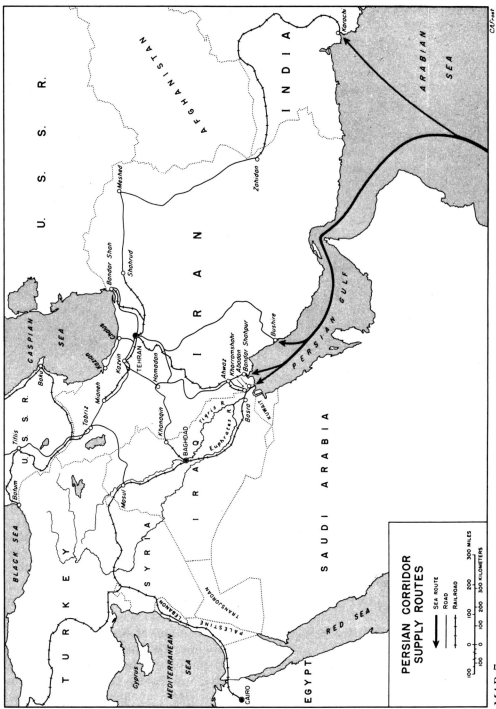

PERSIAN CORRIDOR
SUPPLY ROUTES

SEA ROUTE
ROAD
RAILROAD

| 100 | 0 | 100 | 200 | 300 MILES |
| 100 | 0 | 100 | 200 | 300 KILOMETERS |

MAP 7

limited by the lack of port and inland clearance capacity.[47]

Such was the situation in the Persian Corridor when the cancellation of the northern convoys in July 1942 convinced the highest authorities in Washington and London that it would have to serve as the only dependable route for forwarding military supplies to the USSR. This new urgency meant that the May target of one million short tons over the Second Protocol year would have to be pushed upward before there was any assurance, in the light of the actual state of facilities in the Persian Gulf, that this one-million-ton figure could be met. The only possible answer lay in the development of a co-ordinated plan for improvement of Iranian facilities and the commitment of additional resources to the task. In the opinion of all concerned, only the Americans were capable of accomplishing this feat. *(Map 7)*

---

[47] (1) Report on War Aid to USSR, 28 Nov 45. (2) Motter, *Persian Corridor*, pp. 101–55 and App. A, Table 5. (3) Micklem, *Army: Transportation*, pp. 74, 81–88. (4) Msg, AGWAR to AMSIR, 9 May 42, CM-OUT 1887. (5) Msg, Basrah to AMSIR, Washington, 18 May 42, CM-IN 4957. (6) Msg, Basrah to AMSIR, Washington, 7 Jun 42, CM-IN 2226. (7) Msg, AGWAR to AMSIR, 9 Jun 42, CM-OUT 1957. (8) Msg, Basrah to AMSIR, Washington, 1 Jul 42, CM-IN 0483. (9) Msg, AGWAR to AMSIR, 4 Jul 42, CM-OUT 1005. (10) Msg, Basrah to AMSIR, Washington [Spalding to Burns], 1 Aug 42, CM-IN 0028. (11) Msg, Somervell to Spalding, 10 Aug 42, CM-OUT 2907.

CHAPTER XXI

The Long Road to Russia—II

The Persian Gulf
Decision on U.S. Responsibility

In anticipation of the British decision to suspend the northern convoys during July and August 1942, Averell Harriman suggested to Harry Hopkins on 13 July that to increase the flow of supplies through the Persian Gulf the Americans should offer to take over the Iranian State Railway. In replying on 16 July to Churchill's formal notification of the suspension, the President endorsed Harriman's proposal. Meanwhile, Brig. Gen. Sidney P. Spalding, General Burns' assistant on the MAB executive staff, had been dispatched to the Persian Gulf to report at first hand on means of improving operations. Though initially concerned with the goals set up in May, Spalding soon turned his attention to projects for a much greater increase in the capacity of the supply line through Iran. Brig. Gen. Philip R. Faymonville flew down from Moscow to lend his advice, and both Churchill and Harriman came to Cairo and Tehran after their visit to Stalin in August. All except Faymonville assembled in Cairo in late August, and Shingler came over from Basra to join the conclave. The result of their studies, estimates, and consultations was a recommendation from Maj. Gen. Russell L. Maxwell to the War Department on 22 August 1942 that the United States take over responsibility not only for

the Iranian State Railway but also for the Iranian ports and operate a truck fleet to supplement that of the UKCC. A day later, Churchill formally proposed this solution to the President. "Only in this way," he said, "can we insure an expanding flow of supplies to Russia while building up the military forces which we must move into Northern Persia to meet a possible German advance." [1]

On 25 August the President directed the War Department to prepare a plan, and the detailed task was assigned the SOS. The SOS Plan, prepared by the Strategic Logistics Division, was ready by 4 September. General Somervell himself dictated the conclusions and recommendations. [2] The task of the SOS was to formulate definite and realistic goals for performance, calculate the manpower, materials, and shipping necessary to accomplish them, and evaluate the possibilities of furnishing these resources in relation to other approved programs and plans. The recommendations drawn up at Cairo formed the foundation on which the SOS Plan

[1] Msg, Churchill to Roosevelt, 22 Aug 42, quoted in Motter, *Persian Corridor,* p. 190; see also, pp. 175-91. (2) Msg AMSME 857, to AGWAR, 23 Aug 42, CM-IN 9806.
[2] Plan for the Operation of Certain Iranian Communications Facilities Between Persian Gulf Ports and Teheran by U.S. Army Forces, 3 Sep 42, Persian Gulf 235 folder, OCMH. Papers relating to the formulation of the plan are in Control Division, ASF, folder of same title (hereafter cited as SOS Plan folder, Contl Div ASF).

was built. These recommendations were based on a minimum goal of 200,000 tons of Soviet aid monthly via the Persian Gulf, more than twice the amount contemplated in May. Maxwell proposed U.S. operation of Iranian rail facilities south of Tehran, dock facilities at Bandar Shahpur, Khorramshahr, Tanuma, and Bushire, and the establishment of an American trucking organization to operate out of these ports. The British would remain responsible for the ports of Basra in Iraq, Abadan and Ahwaz in Iran, and for continuing their existing truck lines. *(See Map 7.)* The conferees agreed on the target for the four U.S.-operated ports as 261,000 tons monthly, for the railroad as 180,000 tons monthly north of Andimeshk, and for combined American, British, and Russian trucking operations as 172,000 tons monthly. Accomplishment of these objectives would provide capacity for 200,000 tons of Soviet aid monthly in addition to tonnages necessary to supply British and Polish forces and the Iranian civilian economy, with some reserve capacity remaining.[3]

The troop requirements calculated at Cairo to meet these objectives were three port battalions, two railway operating battalions, one engineer battalion, and two truck regiments—a total of approximately 8,365. Material requirements in addition to organizational equipment for the service troops were set at 75 additional steam locomotives, 2,200 20-ton freight cars or their equivalent in 40-ton cars for the railway, and 7,200 trucks, averaging seven tons in capacity, for the trucking fleet.[4]

SOS planners accepted the proposed division of responsibility, the tonnage targets, and material requirements agreed at Cairo, but found it necessary to expand the troop basis to nearly three times that of the Maxwell estimates to provide for a balanced service command. The final troop requirement was set at 23,876, though 4,515 road maintenance personnel were placed in a contingent category to be shipped only if experience in the field proved them necessary. Meeting these troop and matériel requirements posed serious problems. The pool of service troops available was small and production of heavy transportation equipment limited. A large proportion of the service troops activated had either been earmarked for BOLERO, or would be necessary for TORCH. Outside of domestic requirements, the major portion of heavy transportation equipment under production had been earmarked for the British. And shipping to transport both troops and matériel was the most critical factor of all. As the SOS Plan noted, "all troops and cargo ships have been assigned missions, any new operation must be at the expense of other projects." Only because the invasion of the Continent had been postponed was the project to develop the Persian Gulf feasible.

The SOS Plan proposed that of the minimum essential troops, 8,969 could be made available by diversion from BOLERO, 8,002 from other troop units already activated, and 1,501 from new activations. It was thought that one port battalion of 889 men might be diverted from Karachi, where, Maxwell claimed, it was not doing

---

[3] (1) Msg cited n. 1(2). (2) Detailed calculations made at Cairo included estimates that an additional 50,000 tons of Soviet aid might be handled monthly at Basra and 30,000 at Karachi for forwarding over the Zahidan–Meshed route. See memo, Spalding for Somervell, 4 Sep 42, sub: Target Ests of Persian Gulf Routes, SOS Plan folder, Contl Div ASF.
[4] (1) Msg cited n. 1(2). (2) Msg AMSME 924, Spalding and Maxwell to Burns and Somervell, 28 Aug 42, SOS Plan folder, Contl Div ASF.

port work. Of the matériel, it appeared that trucks would be the most difficult to provide. While ultimate production of locomotives and rail cars would have to be increased to meet over-all requirements, it appeared that 50 locomotives could be procured in the near future by diversion from domestic use and from the British in Egypt, and 1,200 freight cars, originally destined for British use in Iraq, could be obtained from Karachi. There was also a possibility of repossession of 500 10-ton trucks from the British and diversion of 600 of unknown capacity from Chinese lend-lease material at Karachi, but it would be necessary to substitute 2½-ton cargo trucks for the rest of the requirement of 7,200 of 7-ton capacity. Scheduled production of heavy trucks was totally inadequate.

Shipping requirements for men and materials, according to Transportation Corps estimates, amounted to 471,000 ship tons. The SOS Plan provided for movement of 11,000 men on the *West Point* or *Wakefield* in late October, the rest on British troopships in January 1943 after they had completed movement of the Ninth Air Force to the Middle East. Cargo shipments would begin on 1 October and continue through January at the rate of 110,000 tons monthly, approximately ten ships. Both troop and cargo shipping would in effect be a diversion from BOLERO, though the pool of cargo shipping would be increased by releases from the northern convoy route.[5]

The most critical issue was timing, for the need of a secure route to the USSR was immediate and urgent. At Cairo, Colonel Shingler presented estimates worked out with American and British transportation experts, and set the date for meeting the final port and inland clearance targets as June 1943. The British were not convinced that even this deadline could be met. But both General Spalding and Averell Harriman insisted that the target date could be moved forward to February 1943, and Spalding presented estimates on this basis to Somervell on his return. The SOS planners refused to commit themselves definitely, but postulated a "material advancement" of the June target date set by Shingler.[6]

The whole SOS Plan was geared to this "material advancement." Proposed priorities were: rail operations first, ports second, and road operations third. The troops required for the railroad and ports could be taken care of in the first movement scheduled in October. Equipment could be made available and shipped in co-ordination with the troops, which should be in the theater and ready to take over operation of the ports and railroads by the end of the year. The truck regiments, in third priority, would follow in January and should be in the theater at least by early March. Either heavy trucks or smaller substitutes could probably be made available by this time. General Somervell concluded that the Persian Gulf could be developed to meet the goal of 200,000 tons of Soviet aid monthly if high enough priority were given to the movement of troops and supplies.

---

[5] See memo, Gross for Somervell, 30 Aug 42, sub: Trans Sv For Persian Gulf, SOS Plan folder, Contl Div ASF, on which SOS transportation plan was based.

[6] (1) Plan, par. 4, cited n. 2. (2) Memo cited n. 3(2). (3) Memo, Gen Spalding for Col Dabney O. Elliott, 5 Sep 42, with incl comments by Lt. Col W. E. V. Abraham, Br Middle East Comd, SOS Plan folder, Contl Div ASF. (4) For Shingler's detailed calculations on port and inland clearance capacities, somewhat broader than those included in Maxwell's cable, see Bykofsky and Larson, Trans III, Ch. VI.

As it was a matter of combined concern, General Marshall referred the SOS Plan to the CCS for consideration and approval. Before CCS approval was given on 22 September, the Combined Staff Planners added Ahwaz to the list of Iranian ports to be operated by the Americans and modified the movement plan to provide that five cargo ships monthly rather than ten should be accepted as the maximum rate at the outset, to be increased progressively as port and rail facilities were developed. This latter change was made at the behest of the British members of the Combined Military Transportation Committee, who insisted that the discharge capacity at the Persian ports would not be sufficient to accommodate 110,000 tons of U.S. military cargo monthly (for development of Iranian facilities) without cutting into Soviet lend-lease or other essential shipments. The CPS noted that on the assumption that 44 cargo sailings would be required to complete the move, the cost to BOLERO would be a total of 110 sailings, since turnaround time to the Persian Gulf was two and a half times that to England. The CCS was willing to accept this sacrifice, recognizing that "if shipping losses continue at their present excessive rate along the Northern Russian route, it may become necessary to use the Persian Gulf entirely." [7]

In proposing American operation of ports and rail facilities in the Persian Gulf, Churchill stipulated that the British should continue to exercise strategic responsibility for the defense of the area against attack and for internal security. Consequently, he said, the British must retain control of movement priorities. OPD strategic planners, never very enthusiastic about this diversion of American resources from the primary objective of a cross-Channel invasion, were reluctant to ac-

cept the American mission under this condition, but in the end a compromise was worked out. The British Commander-in-Chief, Persia-Iraq Command, was granted control of "priority of traffic and allocation of freight," but in recognition of the primary American objective of supplying the Soviet Union, it was "definitely understood that the British control . . . must not be permitted to militate against the attainment of such objective, subject always to the requirements for preparing to meet a threat to the vital Persian Gulf oil areas." [8] The U.S. commanding general in the Persian Gulf was granted the right of appeal through the JCS to the CCS on any British decision that he thought would prejudice the flow of supplies to the Soviet Union. Under normal circumstances, those supplies would have highest priority once the relatively static British requirements for forces deployed in Iran and essential civilian needs were met. [9]

The Persian Gulf: Plans Versus Accomplishments

An entire new command headquarters was formed to be sent to the Persian Gulf to carry out the SOS Plan. On 1 October 1942 Brig. Gen. Donald H. Connolly was chosen to head this new Persian Gulf

---

[7] (1) CCS 109/1, rpt by CPS, 22 Sep 42, title: Development of Persian Trans Facilities. (2) CMT 27/1, 12 Sep 42, same title. (3) CMT 27/2, 15 Sep 42, same title.

[8] CCS 109/1 cited n. 7(1).

[9] (1) CCS 109, 2 Sep 42, title: Development of Persian Trans Facilities. (2) Memo, Col Elliott for Gen Lutes, 4 Sep 42, OPD 334.8 CCS, Case 16. (3) Snell, The USSR in U.S.-British Plans and Operations in 1942, OCMH. (4) For discussion of the practical workings of the arrangement, see Motter, *Persian Corridor*, pp. 233–39.

Service Command, and told his primary mission would be to "insure the uninterrupted flow of an expanding volume of supplies to Russia." He was to be permitted "wide latitude" in carrying out this mission, but was to be subject to "the administrative supervision" of the Commanding General, USAFIME (then General Maxwell).[10] On 2 October 1942 the President directed that "the project for the operation and enlargement of the Persian Corridor be given sufficient priority and support in the form of men, equipment and ships to insure its early and effective accomplishment."[11] This was essentially the priority General Somervell had postulated as necessary for the fulfillment of the SOS Plan. Yet only after numerous vicissitudes and delays, and long after the February 1943 deadline, was the SOS to find it possible to achieve the goals set for itself in that plan.

To provide a center for co-ordination of planning, Somervell activated Headquarters 1616 in Washington with Col. Stanley L. Scott as chief of staff, even before Connolly was appointed commander of the Persian Gulf Service Command. Headquarters 1616 remained in Washington until March 1943, acting as a home office for Persian Gulf activities. Connolly and Scott, before departing for Iran, worked out a more detailed analysis of requirements and priorities. They asked for an increase in the troop basis to twenty-nine thousand through the addition of miscellaneous service units, but when this was refused they tentatively dropped some of the units scheduled for late shipment. Connolly also juggled the order of shipment so that, in general, troops and material for port operations were given first priority and those for the railroad second, leaving the motor transport service, as before, in

third. However, he shifted three engineer truck companies, set up originally in the contingent group for road maintenance, into first priority.[12]

The movement of men and materials was generally carried out in the order prescribed by Connolly, but encountered a series of delays. On 4 October the Transportation Corps submitted a new shipping plan in keeping with the modifications made by the CMTC and by the interim developments in the shipping situation. Personnel would be moved in four groups: 5,500 about 1 November, 4,000 about 14 November, 6,000 about 15 December, and the remainder in January 1943. Cargo shipments would proceed at the rate of five or six ships per month, beginning on 15 October. This would provide 15,500 men and 160,000 tons of cargo in the Persian Gulf by 18 February 1943. But this plan, premised on the availability of one of the British *Queens* for a December sailing to India (troops for the Persian Gulf would be transshipped by smaller boats to Khorramshahr) and on cargo shipments from the United States' east coast, had to be redrafted on 17 October because of the

---

[10] Ltr, CofS to Gen Connolly, 1 Oct 42, sub: Ltr of Instns, 12a Persian Gulf folder, Plng Div ASF. The arrangement for placing Connolly's command under USAFIME, viewed by many as undesirable at the start, never proved satisfactory. Maxwell and his successors at Cairo were primarily concerned with matters other than aid to the USSR, and Cairo was one thousand miles from the Persian Gulf. Communications were as difficult as with Washington. But despite Connolly's continuing complaints, his command was not completely separated from USAFIME until December 1943. See Motter, *Persian Corridor*, pp. 226–33.

[11] Memo, President for SW, 2 Oct 42, AG 400.3295 (9-1-42) Sec 12.

[12] (1) Memos, Scott for Somervell, 5 and 6 Oct 42, subs: Mvmt of Trs, Equip, and Sups to Persan Gulf Sv Comd, Abstracts, Persian Gulf 262 file, OCMH. (2) Plng Div SOS Diary, 19 Oct 42 entry, Plng Div ASF.

submarine threat off the Cape of Good Hope. The British were forced to cancel the sailing of one of the *Queens,* and many cargo shipments had to be shifted from the east to the west coast. While the new schedule, providing for three troop shipments instead of four, still promised to put 15,500 men and 150,000 tons of cargo in the Persian Gulf by the end of February 1943, the effects of cumulative delays were becoming evident even in the planning phase.[13]

Meantime troops and material were readied to meet this schedule, but here too there were unforeseen difficulties. Most of the service units listed in the SOS Plan were neither at full strength nor had they completed their training. Maj. Gen. Raymond A. Wheeler refused to permit even the temporary loan of the port battalion at Karachi. More new activations were required than originally planned, and in many cases untrained or semitrained units had to be shipped. It proved impossible, as in the case of the port battalion, to extract the material the SOS planners had thought would be available in the Middle East and India from the tenacious grip of commanders in those areas. Also, the British had already shipped most of the 500 10-ton trucks proposed for repossession. But with the cargo shipment schedule cut back by the CMTC, it proved possible to furnish material to meet it from U.S. sources. The rolling stock requirements were met by diversion of 1,000 20-ton freight cars and gondolas and 650 40-ton cars, originally set up in the Army Supply Program for BOLERO. At the suggestion of Harriman, himself once a railroad executive, 57 high-powered diesel locomotives from U.S. railroads were substituted for the 75 steam locomotives requested. MAC(G) on 24 September assigned 150 10-ton trucks, 656 2½-ton tractors with 7-ton trailers, and 2,600 2½-ton cargo trucks to the Persian Gulf Service Command, the heavier types by repossession from the British. On 19 October 1942 supply service representatives reported that with the exception of a few items, the required supplies or adequate substitutes would be available in accordance with the shipping schedule.[14]

In the end it proved impossible to find shipping to meet the troop and cargo schedules. Approximately 5,500 troops, including part of those for port operations, departed on 1 November 1942 from New York on the *West Point* and arrived in Khorramshahr in mid-December. The second shipment was carried out on the *Île de France* from San Francisco on 8 December, and the third on the *Mauretania* from the same port in mid-January. All these vessels carried troops for India as well as those for the Persian Gulf. There were about 11,000 troops in the Persian Gulf by the end of February instead of the 15,000 planned, but those from the *Mauretania,* about 6,500, arrived in mid-March. There were no troop shipments in February, and in the meantime Connolly had increased his requirement again to around 28,500. The remainder went out in small shipments in March, May, and June. Assigned strength in the theater reached 25,-

---

[13] (1) Memo, Gross for Somervell, 4 Oct 42, sub: Proposal for Mvmt to Persian Gulf. (2) Memo, Gross for Somervell, 17 Oct 42, sub: Revision of Mvmt to Persian Gulf. Both in OCT 370.5 Persian Gulf.

[14] (1) Ltrs, Scott to Connolly, 20 and 28 Oct 42, extracts in Persian Gulf notes, Logis File, OCMH. (2) Diary, 27 Sep, 4 and 19 Oct 42 entries, cited n. 12(2). (3) Papers in SOS Plan folder, Contl Div ASF. (4) Harold H. Dunham, U.S. Army Transportation in the Persian Corridor, 1941-1945, Monograph 25, pp. 51-56, 66-67, OCT HB. (5) Min 941 and 942, 51st mtg MAC(G), 24 Sep 42.

423 by the end of June, and 28,584 by the end of August 1943.[15]

Meantime, the delay in cargo shipments was far more serious. Whereas at least five vessels per month had been scheduled, none sailed in October, only two in November, three in December, and three in January 1943. WSA proved unable to allocate the required vessels, primarily because of the cumulative effects of submarine sinkings and the expansion of demands from North Africa and the Pacific. There was the added and somewhat ironical fact that delays in unloading in the Persian Gulf caused by congestion of ships carrying Soviet aid discouraged the allocation of ships to carry materials for the very purpose of clearing up that backlog. Some additional space for Army cargo was provided on vessels carrying lend-lease, but by the end of January movements were far behind, and no vessels were provided to remedy the situation in February. Shipments were finally stepped up during March and April, but at the end of April some 54,000 measurement tons of cargo remained on hand for shipment.[16]

These delays in the movement of men and materials to the Persian Gulf were the principal cause of corresponding delays in expanding the flow of supplies to the USSR. Brig. Gen. Stanley L. Scott wrote in June 1943, "The rate at which the capacity of the Corridor is developed and has been is governed by the rate the War Department furnishes us men and equipment."[17] Yet there were other factors that must not be entirely ignored. Even had the movement of men and materials lived up to the SOS Plan, it does not seem likely that the target of two hundred thousand tons to the Soviet Union could have been met before mid-1943. It took time for the

Americans to become accustomed to their tasks and to iron out difficulties in operating ports, railroads, and truck lines. Many of the troop units, dispatched with little specialized training, had to learn while on the job in the theater. They also had to adjust themselves to climate and other local conditions. Then Maj. Gen. Donald H. Connolly's planning in Washington proved faulty in that first priority was given port development while inland clearance was actually the worst bottleneck. Connolly wrote to General Gross on 1 December 1942:

> My biggest mistake in estimating the situation before I left Washington was in thinking the ports were the bottleneck. I find that at present the rate of removing cargo from shipside determines the rate of unloading . . . . If I had known the above before leaving Washington I would have arranged my priorities of men and equipment differently."[18]

This miscalculation is not entirely understandable in view of the fact that as early as May 1942 Shingler had pointed out

---

[15] (1) Monograph, pp. 44–45, cited n. 14(4). Figures given by Dunham here are erroneous, however, in that they include the full load of each ship and not just those troops destined for the Persian Gulf. (2) Memos, OPD for CG SOS, 10, 20, 30 Oct, and 9 Nov 42, subs: Priorities for . . . Shipt of Trs to India and Middle East, OCT 370.5 Persian Gulf. (3) Rpts, SW to President, 10 Mar and 9 Apr 43, subs: Progress on Soviet Protocol, ID 031.1, III, Pt. 2. (4) Rpt, SW to President, 8 May 43, same sub, ID 031.1, IV. (5) Operational Summary, Persian Gulf Sv Comd, 1 Jun 43, 12a Persian Gulf folder, Plng Div ASF. (6) Motter, *Persian Corridor*, App. A, Table 12.

[16] (1) Operational Summary cited n . 15(5). (2) Monograph, pp. 45–47, cited n. 14(4). (3) Ltr, Col Vissering to Maj Gokay, 28 Dec 42, sub: Shipg to Persian Gulf, OCT 563.5 Persian Gulf. (4) Rpt, 8 May 43, cited n. 15(4). (5) Ltr, Col Raymond M. Hicks, Water Div OCT, to WSA, 2 Apr 43, Persian Gulf Comd Plng folder, OCT HB.

[17] Ltr, Gen Scott to Col John B. Luscombe, Persian Gulf Sv Comd Plans Br Opns Div ASF, 19 Jun 43, 12a Persian Gulf folder, Plng Div ASF.

[18] Ltr, Connolly to Gross, 1 Dec 42, Gross Day File, Middle East.

LIBERTY SHIPS UNLOADING *at the port of Khorramshahr.*

that inland clearance would lag far behind port capacity.[19]

The low priority given trucks and motor transport personnel also proved unfortunate. The rail line offered the best possibilities for developing inland clearance in the long run and required proportionately less expenditure of men and material, but the increase in rail capacity was bound to be gradual. The ideal solution would have been an emergency trucking fleet, as both Shingler and Somervell had proposed in May 1942. By the end of October, Colonel Scott had recognized this: "The development of railroad tonnage will lag behind the development of port tonnage with the result that there will be great need for movement away from port by trucks in order to prevent congestion." [20] But there were obstacles in the way of emergency

trucking operations that could hardly have been overcome, even if Connolly and Scott had recognized the need earlier. Heavy trucks of the type needed in Iran were just not available, and production had to be hurriedly boosted in the fall of 1942. Connolly did not look with favor on the smaller 2½-ton cargo trucks the SOS Plan proposed as a substitute. They would require more drivers, maintenance, gas, and tires; convoys over the dusty roads in Iran had to be held to a minimum length to permit adequate intervals between trucks. The shipping situation being what it was, the 2½-ton trucks assigned in September were held back for several months

---

[19] See above, Ch. XX.
[20] Ltr, Col Scott, no addressee, 28 Oct 42, Persian Gulf notes, Logis File, OCMH.

in favor of higher priority cargo. The 150 10-ton trucks and some of the 656 7-ton tractor-trailers were shipped, but a competing demand for the latter came from the Alcan Highway. Attempts to secure further allocations of 10-ton trucks were blocked by the British, who had prior requirements. There was no new production of tractor-trailers until January 1943, and total production of 10-ton trucks reached only 320 in that month. It was not until after the Casablanca Conference that the British would agree to release 828 tractor-trailers that in August 1942 had been assigned to the UKCC for use in Iraq and Iran. Assignments were finally made in the early months of 1943 that would give Connolly a trucking fleet capable of moving 40,000 tons monthly, but at the end of April many of these were still to be floated.

The movement of trucking personnel was equally slow. The U.S. Motor Transport Service in the Persian Gulf began operations in March 1943 with one of the dump truck companies that came on the first troopship, a Negro trucking battalion that came on the second, and another provisional company organized from other personnel in the command. The rest of the two trucking regiments promised did not arrive until May and July, respectively. Though Connolly had recognized the importance of the roads by advancing the priority of road maintenance personnel, it was difficult to make up the previous delays in road construction. The net result was that movement of cargo through Iran by truck, like that by rail, expanded but slowly during the critical months from August 1942 to March 1943, the period of greatest need for emergency means of inland clearance. By the time the truck fleet was in full operation, the Iranian State Railway was also reaching its peak, and

no attempt was ever made to expand the Motor Transport Service to meet the goals originally set up in August 1942.[21]

Other errors and miscalculations were made. Wharves built at Bandar Shahpur and Khorramshahr were too narrow; insufficient attention was given to dockside storage; heavy equipment that had to be discharged first at Abadan, the only port in 1942 with sufficient heavy lift, was often stowed below other cargo; the proportion of unassembled trucks and aircraft shipped was much less than expected.[22] Difficulties of this sort were almost inevitable, given the haste with which the project was conceived. The truth was that in their anxiety to provide some immediate substitute for the northern route, the Allied leaders allowed themselves to be overoptimistic about the rate at which the Persian Gulf could be developed. The transition from British to American operation took longer than planned, and the Americans also took longer to make their operation effective. Under British operation,

---

[21] (1) Monograph, pp. 187–88, cited n. 14(4). (2) Motter, *Persian Corridor*, pp. 309–17. (3) Cables exchanged between the War Department and General Connolly on truck requirements are conveniently collected in Trucks for Persian Gulf Sv Comd Cable file, ID. (4) Min 1040, 53d mtg MAC(G), 8 Oct 42; Min 1059, 54th mtg, 15 Oct 42; Min 1103D, 55th mtg, 22 Oct 42; Min 1114, 56th mtg, 29 Oct 42; Min 1359, 66th mtg, 17 Dec 42; Min 1367, 68th mtg, 31 Dec 42; Min 1422, 69th mtg, 7 Jan 43; Min 1653, 81st mtg, 27 Feb 43; Min 1696, 83d mtg, 11 Mar 43; Min 1726, 84th mtg, 18 Mar 43; Min 1770, 86th mtg, 24 Mar 43; Min 2158, 101st mtg, 6 Jul 43, with Ord Tab 7 to agenda. (5) Diary, 7, 26 Oct, and 22 Dec 42 entries, cited n. 12(2). (6) Rpt, 8 May 43, cited n. 15(4). (7) Min of Highway Div OCT conf, Pentagon, 9 Nov 43, p. 1, Persian Gulf Motor Trans Sv folder, OCT HB.

[22] Report on Transportation at Persian Gulf Ports by Lt Col Benjamin C. Allin and Capt Robert G. Stone, no date, with accompanying memo for Gen Gross, 10 Jul 43, Persian Gulf Comd Plng folder, OCT HB.

improvement was slow during the latter half of 1942. Approximately 40,000 long tons of Soviet aid were delivered through the Corridor in September 1942, only 51,000 in January 1943. Total tonnage on the Iranian State Railway expanded only from 36,000 in August 1942 to 52,000 in January 1943. Between January and May, the Americans assumed operation step by step, and the turnover was generally complete by 1 May. During this transition period, total tonnage delivered to the Russians expanded to 101,000 in April, while the railroad carried 65,000 tons in March. Under complete American operation, the figure for tonnage delivered to the USSR had nearly doubled by September 1943 to 199,000, and the railroad achieved a capacity of 175,000 tons in October. This achievement of the target loads came six months after the date predicted by Harriman and Spalding and three months after that proposed by Shingler in August 1942.[23]

Meantime, overoptimism both in the theater and in Washington led to the dispatch of more vessels during the latter part of 1942 than Persian Gulf facilities could unload and clear. In October eleven vessels reached the Gulf ports and only seven left them; in November ten arrived and only nine departed; in December sixteen arrived and only five departed. Discharge time per vessel averaged fifty-five days, and the number awaiting discharge reached thirty-two by mid-January. Some 19,000 tons of steel had to be diverted to Karachi to make way for unloading higher priority cargoes, a diversion the Russians vigorously protested. The unloading bottleneck in the Persian Gulf ports represented a serious waste of the most critical resource in the whole Anglo-American war effort—ships.[24]

Second Protocol Deliveries Fall Behind

At the same time that the performance of the Persian Gulf was most disappointing, the Germans continued to make the operation of the convoys over the northern route so expensive that they could not be maintained. After two months during which no convoys sailed, the British tried again in September 1942 using a very heavy escort, only to lose some thirteen cargo vessels out of forty. Neither this rate of loss nor this scale of convoy escort could be sustained during the early stages of TORCH and therefore convoys had to be canceled again during October and November. This decision, though inevitable, was an extremely embarrassing one for the President and Prime Minister, for Stalin felt that the Western Allies had already reneged on their promise of a second front in 1942. As Churchill told Roosevelt on 22 September, it was a "formidable moment in Anglo-American-Soviet relations." "My persisting anxiety is Russia," he said, "and I do not see how we can reconcile it with our consciences or with our interests to have no more PQ's till 1943, no offer to make joint plans for Jupiter [the invasion of Norway], no signs of a spring, summer or even autumn offensive in Europe."[25]

The President proved willing, on this

---

[23] Estimate for August 1942 is based on msg, AMSIR to AGWAR, 12 Oct 42, CM-IN 05027. All other figures are from Motter, *Persian Corridor*, App. A, Tables, 4–5.

[24] (1) Status of the Soviet Aid Program as of November 30, 1942, rpt by OLLA to President. (2) JCS 191, 11 Jan 43, title: Soviet Sup Progs. (3) Memo, Adm Land for JCS, 30 Jan 43, sub: Shipg Prog of Aid to Russia, ABC 400.3295 Russia (4-19-42) Sec 1. (4) CCS 162/2, 27 Feb 43, title: U.S. Aid to Russia.

[25] (1) Msg 151, Prime Minister to President, 22 Sep 42, ABC 381 (7-25-42), 4-B. (2) Morison, *Battle of the Atlantic*, pp. 360–65.

occasion, to accept some sacrifice to the protocol shipping program in order to put American troops in active combat against the Germans, and to gamble that Stalin would not make a separate peace because of Allied failure to fulfill supply commitments on time. He showed some confidence that the Battle of Stalingrad, then mounting to its full fury, would be won by the Russians. In laying down policy for the War Department, he informed Stimson on 2 October:

> Because of enemy action on convoys to North Russia, it has not and may not be feasible to send the full tonnage of supplies contemplated in this protocol. It is therefore of importance that every effort be made to utilize to the maximum the supply routes that may be available to us.[26]

He directed that ships be made available for such convoys as might sail the northern route, and for lifting all cargo that could be cleared through the Persian Corridor; that cargoes be furnished to load such ships as might be dispatched to the USSR by all routes; that planes be delivered in accordance with protocol schedules; and, as noted earlier, that the Persian Gulf project be given sufficient priority to insure its early accomplishment. Meantime, in replying to the Prime Minister, he suggested that the project, then under consideration, for placing an Anglo-American air force in the Caucasus be pushed and that single vessels be sent over the northern route without convoy escort. He thought Stalin should not be informed of the cancellation of the October convoys until the last minute.

The real reaction of Stalin to these developments can only be conjectured. His reply to Churchill's cable informing him of the cancellation of the northern convoys was only a curt "Thank you," followed by an ominous silence. Yet some days earlier he cabled Roosevelt that the Soviet Union "in order to relieve the tonnage situation" would be willing to agree to some curtailment of delivery of war matériel—tanks, artillery, munitions, pistols—in return for shipment of 500 "pursuit planes of a modern type," 8,000 to 10,000 trucks, 5,000 tons of aluminum, 4,000 to 5,000 tons of explosives monthly, and 2 million tons of grain within twelve months. He suggested that the foodstuffs could be imported via Vladivostok if the Americans would agree to turn over twenty or thirty ships to reinforce the Soviet merchant marine in the Pacific.[27] In the end this message proved more significant than the ominous silence that followed the cable to Churchill, for it presaged the change in the Soviet situation that was to follow the decisive victory at Stalingrad.

Except for the planes, the materials Stalin requested were already part of the Second Protocol schedules, though trucks and grain had previously had a low priority compared with tanks, guns, and ammunition. Yet Stalin regarded the planes as most vital, and it was this part of his request that the Americans were most reluctant to meet. Soviet requests for an increase in plane deliveries had been pending with the MAB and JCS since July, while the existing rate of 212 monthly had been continued. The request from Stalin, with American-Soviet relations at such a critical point, naturally generated a terrific additional pressure. Hopkins wrote Marshall that although he realized it was impossible to furnish the requested 500

---

[26] (1) Memo cited n. 11. (2) Sherwood, *Roosevelt and Hopkins*, pp. 638–41.

[27] Msg, Stalin to Roosevelt, 7 Oct 42, quoted in Sherwood, *Roosevelt and Hopkins*, pp. 639–40.

SOVIET AND AMERICAN OFFICIALS *at Qaleh Morgeh airport, Iran, 1943. Left to right: Brig. Gen. Stanley L. Scott, Chief of Staff, Persian Gulf Service Command; Col. Leonid I. Zorin, Chief, Iran-Soviet Transportation; Maj. Gen. Donald H. Connolly, Commanding General, Persian Gulf Service Command; Maj. Gen. Ivan V. Kargin, Chief of Soviet Transportation Department in Iran; Brig. Gen. Philip R. Faymonville, Office of Lend-Lease Administration representative in the USSR; Donald M. Nelson, Chairman, U.S. War Production Board; Vasili P. Migunoff, Chief Commercial Representative, USSR; Mikhail A. Maximov, acting Soviet Ambassador to Iran.*

planes monthly, he thought the United States ought to send at least 100 additional fighters monthly over the next three months. On this point the JCS were adamant. They felt they could not permit any additional diversions of aircraft without crippling the development of the AAF, and argued that the dispatch of an Anglo-American air force to the Caucasus would be of greater value than any slight increase. The President this time accepted the advice of his military chiefs, and put the main emphasis on furnishing the air force in the Caucasus, a solution generally along the lines of that adopted in the mid-summer agreement with the British on air allocations. After long and fruitless negotiations, Stalin ended any possibility of this step in January 1943, saying that the Russians too had more pilots than they had planes to fly. There was continued Soviet pressure for more planes and in January 1943 the JCS did finally give in to the extent of promising the Russians that 200 transport planes would definitely be allocated them during 1943, and an additional 100 if production schedules would permit.[28]

Stalin's request for additional shipping in the Pacific brought a more ready response. The President promised the Soviet leader that the United States would transfer to the Soviet flag five cargo ships a month beginning 1 November 1942. By the end of October, General Belyaev was asking that all twenty be transferred immediately, but with concurrent demands for shipping from the South and Southwest Pacific mounting to a crisis in November, even Harry Hopkins was forced to admit it could not be done. Nonetheless, with presidential pressure behind them, the transfers were made on an accelerated schedule. In December Lewis Douglas deliberately accepted the risk of failure to meet the Navy's stated requirements in order to provide nine ships for the Vladivostok run. Before the transfer of the original twenty, all old steamers, was completed in February 1943, an additional commitment to deliver five new Liberty ships had been accepted. The whole program, however essential, inevitably weighed heavily on the shipping shortage to meet military requirements in the Pacific. Diversions from the Alaskan run brought bitter complaints from General De Witt.[29]

These transfers and the high priority that the Russians now placed on foodstuffs and petroleum products made the Pacific route of equal or greater importance than the Persian Gulf. Yet there were delays in the Pacific also as Soviet-operated vessels took a longer turnaround time than anticipated and were unable to meet shipment schedules. Together these two alternate routes gave promise of eventually fully compensating for failure to maintain the northern convoys, but neither was ready for full operation during the autumn months of 1942. While the great Battle of Stalingrad hung in the balance, the shipment of supplies from the United States fell far behind Second Protocol schedules. As of the end of November 1942, only 840,000 short tons had been shipped against a scheduled 1,608,000.

In December 1942 the prospects brightened somewhat as the British resumed convoy service on the northern route. The interim diversion of German naval and air strength to North Africa gave some hope of success. While the single December convoy of eighteen vessels, PQ-19, was composed principally of ships loaded earlier, loading in the United States for future convoys over the northern route began again in December. The problem shifted once again to the matter of finding cargo vessels and escort craft to maintain these convoys.[30]

---

[28] (1) Ltr, Hopkins to Marshall, 10 Oct 42, MS Index to the Hopkins Papers, Bk. V, Aid to Russia, p. 24, Item 72(q). See also, p. 27, Item 84, and p. 32, Item 95. (2) For more detailed treatment of these negotiations, see Matloff and Snell, *Strategic Planning: 1941-1942*, Ch. XV. (3) On aircraft agreement with the British, see above, Ch. XI.

[29] (1) Ltr, Hopkins to Douglas, 13 Oct 42. (2) Ltr, Douglas to Hopkins, 26 Nov 42. Both in Russian Shipg 1 Jun–31 Dec 42 folder, WSA Douglas File. (3) Memo, Cushing for Douglas, 5 Jan 43, sub: Pac Coast Lend-lease Ship Deliveries, Russian Shipg 1 Jan 43 folder, WSA Douglas File. (4) Douglas' notes on conf with President, Hopkins, and Land, 21 Oct 42, and on conf with Hopkins, 7 Dec 42, Hopkins folder, WSA Douglas File. (5) Memos, Douglas and Land for President, 11 Jan and 10 Feb 43, Russia-Rpts to President folder, WSA Douglas File. (6) Memo, Burns for Hopkins, 28 Oct 42. (7) Memo, Hopkins for Burns, 29 Oct 42. Last two in MS Index to Hopkins Papers, Bk. VII, Lend-lease Aid to Russia (1942), p. 4, Item 38. (8) Ltr, Gen De Witt to CofS, 1 Dec 42, OCT 565.4 Alaska. (9) Related papers in same file. (10) On Pacific shipping situation at the time, see above, Ch. XV.

[30] (1) Rpt cited n. 24(1). (2) Status of the Soviet Aid Program as of December 31, 1942, rpt by OLLA to President.

The Casablanca Decisions

In early January 1943 the President turned his attention once again to the problem of getting Soviet aid shipments back on schedule. On 6 January he wrote Stimson:

> I understand both the Army·and Navy are definitely of the opinion that Russian continuance as a major factor in the war is of cardinal importance, and therefore it must be a basic factor in our strategy to provide her with the maximum amount of supplies that can be delivered to her ports. I fully endorse this concept . . . in executing the Second Protocol and in planning the overall program to the end of the fiscal year 1944, the necessity of meeting Soviet needs in accordance with the above strategical viewpoint must be regarded as a matter of paramount importance.[31]

As a follow-up to this directive, the President on the 9th forwarded to the JCS a report from the Lend-Lease Administration pointing out that Second Protocol shipments were only 55 percent of schedule at the end of 1942 and that with the reopening of the northern route, "opportunity arises for reinstituting delivery at Protocol rates." [32]

The implication that protocol shipments must be brought up to schedule in the months following was as embarrassing to the Army in January 1943 as it had been a year earlier. Military estimates made in December 1942 on the availability of shipping and the possibility of moving troops, naval forces, supplies, and equipment during 1943 allowed for no ships for the northern route, and a total of 276 sailings during the first six months of 1943 over the Pacific and Persian Gulf routes (15 per month to the Persian Gulf, 31 per month to Vladivostok). Even this program, General Gross calculated in late December, would result in cutting the number of troops whose equipment could be moved to Europe by some 375,000. As a result of the President's directive, the Combined Military Transportation Committee made a further study and reported that fulfilling the requirements of the Second Protocol within the capacity of all routes would require 432 sailings during the first six months of 1943. This was 156 more than the Army and Navy had allowed in their calculations, 120 on the northern route and 36 to the Persian Gulf. To fulfill this additional requirement would divert 105 cargo ships from their military employment for six months, reducing the number of troops whose equipment and maintenance could be carried to the European and North African theaters by an additional 176,000.[33]

This dilemma presented by the Soviet aid program was one of the major problems confronting the grand conference at Casablanca in mid-January. With the decision made there to invade Sicily (Operation HUSKY) in the summer of 1943, there was little further possibility of a cross-Channel invasion in 1943. The Soviet Union in Admiral King's words remained the "main reliance in Europe." [34] There was little the conference could do

---

[31] Memo, President for SW, 6 Jan 43, ID 031.1, II.
[32] JCS 191 cited n. 24(2), with note by Secys incl rpt by OLLA to President and referred by President to JCS.
[33] (1) Memo, Gross for CG SOS, 31 Dec 42, sub: Effect of Increase in Russian Shipts on Current Opns, NATOUSA TORCH Plng folder, OCT HB. Gross' estimates·were based on 300 sailings rather than 276. (2) CCS 162, 19 Jan 43, title: U.S. Aid to Russia. (3) CCS 143, rpt by CMTC, 11 Jan 43, title: U.S. Aid to Russia—Implications of Shipg Prog.
[34] Min, 56th mtg JCS, 20 Jan 43. The question, King said, was not one of "placating Stalin," as many were prone to represent it, but of "implementing the Russians to our own interest."

but agree that Soviet aid should have a priority second only to the antisubmarine campaign.[35] Nevertheless, both General Marshall and Admiral of the Fleet Sir Dudley Pound of the British Navy opposed continuance of Soviet aid at "prohibitive cost" to Anglo-American operations and suggested that running the northern convoys might prove as expensive in 1943 as it had in 1942.[36] The British Navy reported that the best it could do with destroyer escort at its disposal was one convoy of twenty-eight ships every forty-two days, and naval officers doubted that this rate could be maintained during the invasion of Sicily. A study by the CPS revealed it would be impossible for the U.S. Navy to supplement the British escort without curtailing other convoy services. So, accepting the forty-two-day convoy cycle, General Somervell produced a shipping schedule, which he and Lord Leathers presented to the conference on 20 January. Under Somervell's proposal, protocol shipments would be brought up to schedule not by the end of June 1943, but by spreading the deficit over the rest of the year, on the assumption that Third Protocol commitments would be the same as those for the second. A total of 376 sailings during the first half of 1943 would leave a deficit of 56 sailings at the end of June 1943 to be more than compensated for by an increase from 288 to 346 during the second half of the year.

Adherence to this schedule, Somervell thought, would reduce troop deployments by 128,000 during the first half of 1943 and 187,000 for the whole year, if the monthly shipping loss was 2.6 percent. But if that rate could be brought down even to 2.4 percent, the Soviet aid program could be carried out without lessening troop movements; if the rate were re-

duced yet lower, movements might actually be increased.[37]

In the discussion of Somervell's proposal, Marshall contended that if the 2.6 percent loss rate were accepted then the whole problem must be re-examined to consider its effect on the troop lift, and Sir Dudley Pound challenged the assumption that the northern convoys could be run throughout the year. Finally, both accepted Somervell's assurances on the one hand that a loss rate of 2.4 percent could be expected with reasonable certainty, and on the other that the Persian Gulf could easily compensate by July for any interruption of the northern convoys. The CCS finally approved the schedule, though with the distinct understanding that the northern convoys might have to

---

[35] CCS 170/2, 23 Jan 42, title: Final Rpt to President and Prime Minister Summarizing Decisions by CCS.

[36] Min, 63d mtg CCS, 20 Jan 43, Item 1.

[37] (1) CCS 160, Rpt by CPS, 19 Jan 43, title: Minimum Escort Reqmts To Maintain Sea Communications of the United Nations. (2) CCS 162 cited n. 33(2). Since the report was primarily concerned with U.S. shipping, Leathers' participation was only perfunctory. In the 63d meeting of CCS, 20 January 1943, he said he was not in full agreement. The revision that was approved, CCS 162/1, 20 January 1943, contained only a minor change. The detailed schedule was as follows:

	Total	Northern Route	Persian Gulf Route	Pacific Route
1943	722	128	222	372
1st 6 months	376	64	126	186
January	62	16	16	31
February	65	16	18	31
March	51	0	20	31
April	69	16	22	31
May	71	16	24	31
June	57	0	26	31
2d 6 months	346	64	96	186
July	63	16	16	31
August	63	16	16	31
September	47	0	16	31
October	63	16	16	31
November	63	16	16	31
December	47	0	16	31

be interrupted. In the final report to the President and Prime Minister, they said:

We have examined the extent of shipments to Russia required to fulfill the United States and British obligations throughout 1943 with a view to estimating the effect of these shipments on other commitments. Our conclusion is that, providing a shipping loss rate of not more than 2.4% per month can be relied on, it will be possible to meet full commitments by the end of the calendar year 1943; and we have approved a program of shipments on this basis subject to the proviso that supplies to Russia shall not be continued at prohibitive cost to the United Nations effort.[38]

New Disappointments

The War Shipping Administration, the organization actually responsible for allocating shipping for the Soviet aid program, was not represented at Casablanca and in the meantime had been doing its own planning in Washington. While the Joint Chiefs themselves were absent, their representatives in Washington considered the earlier CMTC report on shipping requirements for the Second Protocol, were unable to resolve the conflict with requirements for military operations, and consequently asked WSA to investigate the feasibility of getting ships from other than U.S. military allocations. Admiral Land replied on 30 January that WSA had included the necessary sailings to meet arrears in protocol shipments in its program since early January, and considered they could be accomplished, but that shipments over the northern route would depend on convoys and those to the Persian Gulf on capacity of facilities there. He understood the WSA obligation in regard to the Persian Gulf to be only "to keep the route full with respect to ability to discharge the cargo with reasonable dispatch," and

called attention to the "serious congestion in the Persian ports since last autumn. . . . caused principally by the dispatch of more ships for Russian and Army account . . . than these ports have been able to handle." [39]

When the Casablanca schedule was referred to WSA, these doubts were reiterated and expanded. WSA contended the schedule for the first half of 1943 could not be met because of congestion in the Persian Gulf and slow turnaround time in the Pacific. Its own estimates of the maximum sailings possible during the first half of 1943 were 63 on the northern route, 94 to the Persian Gulf, and 152 to Vladivostok, a total of 309 instead of the 376 proposed by Somervell. This would increase the deficit at the end of the Second Protocol period to 123, and require 411 sailings during the second half of the year to make it up.[40] WSA pointed to the 175,000 tons of cargo on ships tied up in the Persian Gulf at the end of January, as opposed to the discharge of only 90,000 tons in that month—a record high. While the civilian shipping officials admitted that conditions would improve with U.S. Army operation, they did not think this improvement would be rapid enough to clear up the backlog and permit sailings at the rate proposed. Accordingly, they cut back shipments in February to the Persian Gulf to seven sailings in contrast to the eighteen proposed in the Casablanca schedule, and insisted that March sailings be limited to fourteen.

Somervell, on the other hand, continued to be optimistic, even after his return

---

[38] (1) CCS 170/2 cited n. 35. (2) See min cited n. 36. (3) See also discussion in min, 3d mtg ANFA Conf, 23 Jan 43.

[39] (1) Memo cited n. 24(3). (2) Min, 50th mtg JCS, 13 Jan 43, Item 1.

[40] CCS 162/2 cited n. 24(4).

from a personal visit to the Persian Gulf after Casablanca. He thought the estimate of the combined Anglo-American capacity committee in Iran that twenty-one ships could safely be dispatched in March was if anything too modest, and told the JCS that if necessary twenty-nine ships could be sent in that month for June discharge in the Persian Gulf. Somervell's contention was generally supported by a study made in the Strategic Logistics Division, SOS, in mid-February. The CMTC also reported to the CCS that the theater estimate of twenty-one ships should be accepted. WSA gave in, and nineteen ships actually sailed for the Persian Gulf during March.[41]

Thus, as the situation stood at the end of February, fulfillment of the Casablanca schedule for the first half of 1943 depended on maintaining the northern convoys, cleaning up the congestion in the Persian Gulf, and expanding the volume of shipments in the Pacific. Hopes for maintaining the northern convoys were soon dashed. On 18 March 1943 Churchill informed Roosevelt that the renewed German naval concentration at Narvik presented a danger so great that he deemed it inadvisable to risk further convoys to Murmansk. Roosevelt again acquiesced, and it soon became apparent that no more would sail until autumn because the invasion of Sicily would absorb all available escort during the summer. On 30 March Churchill informed Stalin of the decision, stressing the compensation that the Persian Gulf and Pacific routes would offer. Stalin was unimpressed, calling the action a "catastrophic diminution of supplies," which could not fail to affect the position of Soviet troops. He thought the Pacific and Persian Gulf routes could in no measure compensate because of lack of shipping in the Pacific and "small transit capacity" through Iran.[42]

Despite Stalin's critical reaction, no other decision was possible without jeopardizing the whole naval position in the Atlantic, and no more convoys were to sail over the northern route until September 1943. In contrast to the proposed sixty-four vessels from the United States for the northern route during the first half of 1943, only thirty-six sailed, and of these twenty-nine were unloaded in the United Kingdom. In the light of the waste that the retention of loaded ships in England during 1942 had caused, this time Lewis Douglas of WSA insisted that the ships be unloaded. Vigorous Soviet protests were to no avail. The Russians then turned to demand compensating shipments via the Persian Gulf and Pacific. Unfortunately, developments in the Persian Gulf were bearing out WSA's pessimism as to clearance capacity. In response to Somervell's request on 27 February for an "all-out effort . . . to unload and release ships," Connolly bent every resource to the task, but as shown earlier, the obstacles were too great.[43] At the end of April a survey made by SOS officers confirmed the need for cutting shipments drastically in order to clear up the backlog, and the SOS had to accept the inevitable. Only four fully

---

[41] (1) *Ibid.* (2) See below, App. D. (3) Memo, Col Elliott for ACofS Opns SOS, 11 Feb 43, sub: Communications in Iran, 12a Persian Gulf folder, Plng Div ASF. (4) Min, 64th mtg JCS, 2 Mar 42, Item 2. (5) Memo, Land and Douglas for President, 10 Mar 43, Russian-Rpts to President folder, WSA Douglas File.

[42] (1) Msg, Premier Stalin to Prime Minister, 2 Apr 43, as quoted in Churchill, *Hinge of Fate*, p. 755. See also, pp. 752-57. (2) Msg, Churchill to Roosevelt, 18 Mar 43, MS Index to the Hopkins Papers, Bk. V, Aid to Russia, p. 38, Item 107.

[43] Msg AMPSC 309, AGWAR to CG Persian Gulf Sv Comd, 27 Feb 43, Persian Gulf 26-A File, OCMH.

TABLE 16—SOVIET AID SHIPMENTS TO PERSIAN GULF VERSUS CASABLANCA PROGRAM:
JANUARY–JUNE 1943

Month	Casablanca Schedule (CCS 162/1)	Number of Ships Sailed		Cargo (Long Tons)
		Fully Loaded	Partially Loaded	
Total..	126	75	15	553,000
January..	16	12	4	87,000
February...	18	7	0	40,000
March..	20	19	1	131,000
April..	22	18	3	145,000
May..	24	15	4	121,000
June...	26	4	3	29,000

Source: (1) CCS 162/1, 20 Jan 43, title: U.S. Aid to Russia.   (2) Report on War Aid to USSR, 28 Nov 45.

loaded Soviet ships were dispatched in June. Total shipments to the Persian Gulf between January and June 1943 were far below the Casablanca schedule and even below WSA's February estimates.[44] (Table 16)

There remained the Pacific route. Soviet representatives at first proposed that the United States transfer to the USSR vessels in the Pacific in equal tonnages to those unloaded in England. Though the Americans would not accept this proposition, they did agree to transfer twenty more Liberty ships to the Russians in the Pacific during April, May, and June, and added several tankers in response to Soviet representations that aviation fuel was urgently needed. The total transfers to the Soviet flag in the Pacific reached fifty-three cargo vessels and six tankers by the end of June 1943. With this additional fleet, performance in the Pacific (including shipments to Soviet arctic ports) was considerably above the Casablanca schedule and even the WSA estimates, but it was still far from sufficient to make up for cancellation of the northern

shipments and the disappointing performance of the southern route.[45] (Table 17)

The net tonnage deficit for all routes at the end of the Second Protocol period, June 1943, was nearly a million long tons, not including cargoes unloaded in England, a considerably greater deficit than either the SOS or WSA had estimated. This does not mean, however, that the Casablanca planning for protocol ship-

[44] (1) Ltr, Gen Belyaev to Hopkins, 17 Apr 43, MS Index to the Hopkins Papers, Bk. VII, Lend-lease Aid to Russia (1942–43) p. 4, Item 40. (2) Ltr, Hopkins to Belyaev, 20 Apr 43, MS Index to the Hopkins Papers, Bk. VII, Lend-lease Aid to Russia (1942–43) p. 5, Item 42. (3) For Soviet complaints, see also MS Index to the Hopkins Papers, Bk. V, Aid to Russia, pp. 41–43, Items 113–114, 116, and 120. (4) Memo, Douglas for Hopkins, 25 Mar 43, Russian Shipg 1 Jan 43 folder, WSA Douglas File. (5) Allin-Stone rpt cited n. 22. (6) For a fuller discussion of the Allin-Stone mission, see Motter, Persian Corridor, pp. 400–408. (7) Ltr, Gen Wylie, Asst CofTrans, to W. S. MacPherson, WSA, 16 May 43, OCT 333.1 Persian Gulf.

[45] (1) See above, n. 44(1)–(4). (2) Memo, Douglas and Land for President, 10 Apr 43, Russia-Rpts to President folder, WSA Douglas File. (3) Status of the Soviet Aid Program as of March 31, 1943, rpt by OLLA to President; Status . . . as of April 30, 1943; Status . . . as of May 31, 1943; and Status . . . as of June 30, 1943.

TABLE 17—SOVIET AID SHIPMENTS VIA PACIFIC VERSUS CASABLANCA PROGRAM: JANUARY–JUNE 1943

Month	Casablanca Schedule (CCS 162/1)	Number of Ships Sailed		Cargo (Long Tons)
		Fully Loaded	Partially Loaded	
Total..	186	211	10	1,017,000
January...............................	31	22	0	97,000
February..............................	31	28	1	129,000
March................................	31	26	0	123,000
April.................................	31	37	0	193,000
May..................................	31	48	1	228,000
June..................................	31	50	8	247,000

Source: (1) CCS 162/1, 20 Jan 43, title: U.S. Aid to Russia. (2) Report on War Aid to USSR, 28 Nov 45.

ments must be dismissed as totally visionary. By June 1943 the Persian Gulf and the Pacific were finally ready to carry the necessary load. The shipping loss rate had fallen considerably below the 2.4 percent monthly figure stipulated at Casablanca. While much of the excess thus made available was absorbed by increased British and American needs, shipments to the USSR were to be brought up to schedule by the end of 1943.

War Department Supply Agencies and the Second Protocol

During the Second Protocol period, the shipping problem held the center of the stage. The difficulties the War Department had encountered earlier in making materials available for the Soviet aid program became less and less serious. The very fact that shipping was limited reduced the pressure for production, although the full commitment under the protocol had to be accepted as the production goal. The President directed that ma-

terials should be made available in the exact priorities the Russians desired for loading the ships sailing by any and all routes. The SOS, with the task of procuring and delivering the supplies for which the War Department was responsible, geared its actions to this end.[46]

Measured against its total commitments under the Second Protocol, the War Department could report, by November 1942, that it was on or ahead of schedule in furnishing 70 percent of the items involved, and behind on 30 percent. The principal shortages were tanks, antiaircraft guns, submachine guns, scout cars, field repair shops, trucks, armor plate, toluol, communications equipment, webbing, leather, and medical supplies. Production officials in SOS regarded few of these shortages as serious for there were unshipped backlogs of many of these very items, and they felt that if shipping were made available, production deficits could, in most cases, be made good by the end of

---

[46] (1) MS Index to the Hopkins Papers, Bk. V, Aid to Russia, p. 17, Item 65. (2) Memo cited n. 11.

the protocol year. Many of the shortages were due only to delays in delivery of complementary equipment and did not affect major items. The most serious shortages resulted from delays on the part of the Russians in furnishing specifications and a continuing obdurate Soviet insistence that the War Department meet these specifications to the letter regardless of the difficulty involved.[47]

The largest continuing problem was signal communications equipment. It was of utmost concern to the USSR, for the evidence indicates that it was the area in which Soviet production and technical knowledge were weakest. In January 1943 General Belyaev registered strong complaints with the War Department regarding delays in the delivery of radio equipment, complaints reminiscent of the early period of the First Protocol when they were an everyday affair. In the SOS view, however, the major fault lay with the Russians themselves. They had changed completely the distribution of radios by types as computed for them by the Signal Corps; they demanded metal radio tubes requiring special production facilities at a time when the total American usage was of glass tubes; they failed to present timely specifications for radio components, measuring and testing equipment, and direction finders (radar). Nevertheless, SOS agreed to make a strenuous effort to meet their needs and, as a result of certain Soviet compromises on types, it was able to solve the problem of radio sets and tubes, though production of direction finders, measuring and testing equipment, and radio components continued to lag. Radar equipment presented a distinct problem. In addition to specification troubles there was also a serious question of release for reasons of military secrecy and of heavy

competing demands from the U.S. services and the British.[48]

Despite these continuing difficulties on signal equipment, by late 1942 SOS was far more concerned with the obverse of the coin, the accumulation of unshipped material on protocol account. Though available shipping was little more than half that anticipated during the last six months of 1942, factory deliveries continued to be based on total protocol quantities. A much higher proportion of shipping than expected moved over the Pacific route where munitions could not be carried, and, beginning in September 1942, the Russians began to shift their priorities from ground munitions to foodstuffs and petroleum products. Stalin's message to the President in October confirmed this shift. Of military materials, only planes, trucks, and communications equipment continued in the highest priority, and the lack of means of delivery seriously curtailed the number of trucks that could be shipped. These factors combined to make a backlog of immobilized equipment in idle storage inevitable. Yet in the autumn of 1942 the Soviet representatives in Washington showed little inclination to accept curtailment of delivery of items placed in low priority and insisted that the

---

[47] (1) Rpt, SW to President, 9 Nov 42, sub: Progress on Soviet Protocol, AG 400.3295 (9-1-42) (3) Sec 12. (2) Memo, Col Franks for Dir of Procurement, 31 Oct 42, sub: Shortages on 2d Russian Protocol. (3) Memo, Gen Harrison for Col Franks, 9 Nov 42, same sub. Last two in ID 031.1, I. (4) Memo, Somervell for President's Soviet Protocol Com, 16 Nov 42, sub: Rpt of WD Concerning Status of Russian Protocol, ID 031.1, II.

[48] (1) Memo, Clay for Somervell, 22 Feb 43, sub: Rpt to President's Soviet Protocol Com, ID 031.1, III, Pt. 1. (2) Ltr, Gen Belyaev to Maj Gen Dawson Olmstead, CSigO SOS, 12 Jan 43. Ltr, Belyaev to Burns, 13 Jan 43. Last two in ID 031.1, II. (4) Other detailed corresp in same file.

total protocol commitment be readied for shipment.[49]

From July to November 1942, while the shipping situation was at its worst, both the War Department and the MAB followed the policy of allowing military items on the protocol to accumulate. The embarrassing protocol shortages in early 1942 were of too recent memory to permit of any other course, and the main emphasis continued to be on making the materials available. The MAB and its ground committee did make some adjustments in assignments in view of the shipping situation, and did enforce the 45-day rule when there was no strenuous objection from the Russians. Assignments of trucks, for instance, were held well below the 10,-000 monthly scheduled since average monthly shipments were only 2,520, and at the end of October there was an unshipped backlog of 26,000. Also, assignments of medium tanks to the Soviet Union were cut back, with Soviet permission, to permit meeting certain British and American needs in the light of a general shortfall in production. There was inevitably some slackening of pressure on and within the supply services on protocol items because of a general feeling that the Russians could not ship what was being made available.[50]

These mild palliatives were insufficient to avert the threat of a very large backlog of immobilized material by the end of 1942. In a mid-November report to the President's Soviet Protocol Committee, General Somervell boldly recommended that "unshipped accumulations of any War Department item be limited to one and one-half times the monthly Protocol commitment, and that no obligation be assumed to make available any materials

withheld in accordance with this policy."[51] The protocol committee agreed to application of this forty-five-day backlog principle in certain cases, but it would never accept the stipulation that there was no obligation to replace materials so withheld. To have done so would have been tantamount to conceding the War Department the power to cut back protocol commitments in the categories of articles not shipped. The protocol committee preferred to tread more lightly on Soviet toes, proceeding by negotiation rather than by unilateral action.[52]

The one and a half months' backlog policy was applied with the sanction of the MAB to the supply of trucks and proved an adequate solution, but no satisfactory remedy was found for perhaps the most troublesome accumulation, that of chemicals. There was still a backlog of four

[49] (1) Rpts cited n. 24(1) and n. 30(2); Status of the Soviet Aid Program as of September 30, 1942, rpt by OLLA to President; Status . . . as of October 31, 1942; and Status . . . as of January 31, 1943. (2) MS Index to the Hopkins Papers, Bk. V, Aid to Russia, p. 21, Item 72(e). (3) Memo, Somervell for Clay, 28 Oct 42, AG 400.3295 (10-28-42) (2).
The problem was by no means confined to military items. The greatest accumulations were of carbon steels.
[50] (1) Memo cited n. 47(4). (2) Min 10, 41st mtg MAB, 11 Nov 42. (3) For a case history in leniency, see corresp in ID 319.1 Rpts Storage. (4) Memo, OQMG for ID, 16 Jan 43, sub: 2d Russian Protocol. (5) Memo, Franks for Clay, 26 Jan 43, sub: 2d Russian Protocol–Weekly Rpt on . . . Deficiencies . . . . Last two in ID 031.1, II. (6) For tanks, see above, Ch. XI.
[51] Memo cited n. 47(4).
[52] (1) Min, mtgs of President's Soviet Protocol Com Subcom on Sups, 10 and 26 Dec 42. (2) Memo, Clay for Chm President's Soviet Protocol Com Subcom on Sups, 12 Dec 42, sub: Rpt on Accumulated Chemicals and Proposed Solution. (3) Memo, Somervell for Chm President's Soviet Protocol Com, 5 Jan 43, sub: Rpt of WD Concerning Status of Russian Protocol. All in ID 031.1, II.

months' supply in July 1943.[53] On other items the International Division pressed Soviet representatives for a clear statement of what they did and did not want to ship in view of the impossibility of floating all the material promised. Such a clear statement was never forthcoming, but the Soviet representatives did show a measure of co-operation by canceling from time to time items they no longer desired. By the end of April they had canceled in whole or in part their Second Protocol requirements for light and medium tanks, 57-mm. antitank guns, scout cars, armor plate, 37-mm. and 90-mm. antiaircraft guns, and Thompson submachine guns. These cancellations reflected clearly the shift in Soviet needs and the effects of the victory at Stalingrad. The most surprising cancellation was that of light and medium tanks, for the Russians had placed such emphasis on them in 1941 and 1942 as to seriously interfere with the British and American armored programs. There was an accumulated backlog of 2,583 tanks unshipped by February 1943 and the cancellation was welcome indeed to the War Department. With the cancellation of tank and gun requirements went as a corollary reduction in Soviet requirements for ammunition of American caliber. The cancellations considerably eased the production problem and made possible the repossession of sizable backlogs. Suspension of tank shipments made additional shipping space available for trucks.[54]

There was thus no real policy solution to the backlog crisis, but the improvement in the shipping situation, Soviet cancellations, partial application of the 45-day backlog principle, and various pressures on the Soviet reresentatives to release materials at least alleviated it. The final record of the War Department on the Second Protocol reveals a reasonable degree of success in meeting Soviet needs and also in regulating the flow of material to avoid undue accumulations. Of the fifty-four items for which it was responsible, eight were canceled. Of the forty-six outstanding, the full commitment was made available on twenty-nine, and on six more supply was in accord with reduced Soviet requirements (dry cells and various chemicals). Of the remaining eleven where commitments were not met, on five it was because material had to be withheld in accordance with the 45-day backlog policy (other chemicals, field repair shops, army cloth, and webbing). Also 94,047 cargo trucks were made available out of the total commitment of 120,000, the shortage being solely due to the slow rate of shipment during 1942. Leather deliveries were delayed and only 74 percent complete because of the shortage of shipping to bring it from South American sources. On the other four items, all signal equipment, delays in obtaining specifications were in large measure responsible. The only flat

---

[53] (1) Memo, Franks for Clay, 12 Jan 43, sub: Status of Motor Vehicles . . . Under 2d Protocol, ID 031.1, II. (2) See succeeding reports of the same nature in ID 031.1, II–V. (3) Min 1319, 65th mtg MAC(G), 10 Dec 42; Min 1472, 70th mtg, 14 Jan 43; Min 1524, 73d mtg, 28 Jan 43. (4) On the chemical problem, see min cited n. 52(1), and min, mtg of President's Soviet Protocol Com Subcom on Sups, 6 Jul 43, ID 031.1, V. (5) Ltr, Gen Wesson to Gen Belyaev, 6 Apr 43, ID 031.1, III, Pt. 2.

[54] (1) Ltr, Col Willet J. Baird to Gen Belyaev, 30 Jan 43, ID 031.1, III, Pt. 1. (2) Related papers in same file. (3) Ltr, Molchanov to Franks, 12 Jan 43, ID 031.1, IV. (4) Memo, Burns for Hopkins, 23 Feb 43, MS Index to the Hopkins Papers, Bk. VII, Lend-lease Aid to Russia (1942–43), p. 2, Item 19. (5) Ltr, Belyaev to Spalding, 17 Apr 43. (6) Ltr, Hazard to Baird, 19 May 43. Last two in ID 031.1, IV. (7) Rpt, SW to President, 6 Jul 43, sub: Progress on Soviet Protocol, ID 031.1, V.

SOVIET FREIGHTER *docked at Portland, Oregon, 1943.*

failure was in the case of radar, where deliveries were only 12 percent complete. The Combined Communications Board finally decided to release radar to the Russians, but U.S. and British demands plus specification difficulties continued to prevent deliveries of any sizable quantities. In all, the War Department made available some 783,000 short tons of supplies out of its commitment of 1,100,000. Of this some 127,363 short tons of armament and a considerable but undetermined tonnage of miscellaneous supplies remained unshipped at the end of June 1943.

A word must be added with regard to aircraft, for the USSR put the utmost emphasis upon them. Aircraft were not furnished in the quantities the USSR desired, but were furnished to the full extent of commitments both for American account and for British as far as they were a charge against U.S. production. In addition 80 transports, 30 trainers, and one heavy bomber were delivered over and above these protocol promises. Of these, all but 141 on U.S. account and 135 on British account had departed the United States by the end of June. Some 1,151 went via the Alaskan ferry, 375 via the South Atlantic ferry, and 2,071 by water to northern Soviet ports or the Persian Gulf. In truth the planes shipped seem to have been, as in the case of other materials, about all that the available delivery routes could handle.[55]

During the first two protocol periods, the United States proved unable, despite the tremendous effort exerted, to deliver supplies to the Soviet Union on the scale promised. *(See Appendix C.)* Shipments over the northern route, the main reliance in the beginning, could not be continuously maintained at the heavy cost in merchant shipping and naval convoy involved. Alternate routes—the Pacific and the Persian Gulf—were not ready to assume the burden. In the Pacific only civilian-type supplies could be carried and these in ships flying the Soviet flag. Soviet flag shipping was scarce during 1942 and the Russians placed primary emphasis on munitions of war rather than civilian materials. The Persian Gulf area lacked the port and transport facilities necessary for any extensive supply program. The tremendous political pressure behind the Soviet aid program, however, resulted in a concentration of American effort on the development of facilities in the Persian Gulf and in transfer of a sizable fleet of American vessels to the Soviet flag in the Pacific. Improvement in the Soviet military situation after the Stalingrad victory brought about a shift of emphasis from munitions of war to foodstuffs, petroleum products, and raw and industrial materials, all of which could be shipped over the Pacific route. By mid-1943 capacities of the Persian Gulf and Pacific routes alone appeared adequate to meet commitments during the following year on the scale of those of the Second Protocol, and the relative decline of German naval and air power presaged a period when the northern route also might again be used without excessive losses. The fall in the shipping loss rate to well below the 2.4 percent monthly figure stipulated at Casablanca and the booming American ship production promised that in the foreseeable future ships could be furnished for carrying supplies to the USSR without impinging on Anglo-American plans for major operations. In short, by the end of the Second Protocol period the problems of delivering supplies over the long hard route to Russia seemed to be well on their way to solution.

---

[55] (1) Rpt cited n. 54(7). (2) Memo, Somervell for President's Soviet Protocol Com, 23 Jul 43, sub: Rpt of WD Concerning Status of Russian Protocol, ID 031.1, V.

PART SIX

THE CASABLANCA PERIOD
STRATEGIC PLANS
AND LOGISTICAL METHOD

CHAPTER XXII

War Production and Shipping: Year's End Outlook

The logistical war, from the Army's vantage point, entered an unmistakably new phase late in 1942 and early in 1943. This phase had many characteristics not easily described by a single adjective or as a single trend. The magnitudes were greater, of course—in numbers of troops to be supplied, transported, and serviced, in quantities of material and shipping available, in the range of operations to be supported. There was somewhat less improvisation, less wasteful haste, less misdirected effort, and somewhat more action planned in detail, co-ordinated with other concurrent action, reduced to standardized methods, and made routine. Efforts were made in such fields as the joint and combined committees and interservice coordination overseas to rationalize logistical organization and methods—though with but limited success. There was considerable talk of and some real striving for economy. The general trend seemed to be toward more economy of force, the accomplishing of more for each unit of effort.

These trends in logistics coincided with the basic change that was occurring in the military position of the Anglo-American coalition—the regaining of the strategic initiative. The shift was heralded by the limited offensives launched in the Pacific and North Africa, and by the meeting of

military and political leaders at Casablanca in January 1943 to chart the future course of offensive strategy. To a large degree the improvement in the military situation was a result of the huge outpouring of munitions from American factories and of ships from American yards. The new strategic outlook and the vast output of the implements of war were, at the end of 1942, the two massive and overriding facts of the situation.

But between strategy and the logistical plans and systems that made it possible to implement strategy, there was scarcely more harmony or direct correlation than there had been during the tumultuous first half of 1942. With the shelving of plans for an early attack on German-dominated Europe across the English Channel, Allied strategy had embarked upon a more diffuse effort, involving major operations in several widely separated theaters, thus enormously complicating the problems of co-ordinating deployment and distributing shipping. This new course of action, moreover, had been launched without any clear agreement between the major Allies or even among their respective staffs as to its ultimate objectives. At Casablanca the leaders tried without success to draw up a master plan for winning the war with which their current projects could be harmonized. It was only with difficulty, indeed, that they reached agreement upon the next concrete steps on the strategic agenda, for which it was imperative to inaugurate detailed planning and preparations immediately. All this uncertainty, both before and after Casablanca, as to goals lying beyond the immediate future, forced the logistical planners to proceed blindly in drawing up deployment, production, and distribution programs, without any guidance other than their own independent assumptions and speculations.

From late 1942 until mid-1943, in fact, the planning of war production was shaped in broad outline, not by strategic goals but by the estimated limits of national productivity. The cuts in supply programs these limitations dictated, weeks before the strategic planners met at Casablanca, had already predetermined to an important degree the volume of overseas deployment and the relative weight of land, sea, and air power to be employed in the great offensives of 1943 and 1944.

The Cutback in Military Supply

War production in 1942, as Donald Nelson reported to the President, "forged ahead mightily."[1] Its aggregate dollar value (munitions, construction, and non-munitions for war purposes) was $58.7 billion, as compared with only $16.5 billion in 1941, and it engrossed about 31 percent of the total national production, as against only 9 percent in 1941. In the last quarter of the year war production amounted to almost 40 percent of the national product. But the advance had been uneven. In April munitions output increased 19 percent over that of the previous month, but September registered a gain of only 10 percent over August, and October only 4

percent over September. Not until the very end of the year did output rise again sharply. Only in naval and merchant ship construction, including landing craft, did the "hump" occur during the middle months, from early spring through the summer. Only a few of the President's spectacular end-item goals had been attained—notably tanks (but not all tank-type units) and certain antiaircraft guns. Aircraft, the largest single item, had fallen far behind early schedules and machine guns for ground forces had also lagged. Merchant ship construction, despite ample yard capacity and spectacular speed records in output of mass-produced types such as the Liberty, had been held back by a shortage of steel.[2]

It was becoming apparent by the end of 1942 that strenuous and generally ill-co-ordinated pushing toward maximum production in all categories was causing serious imbalance. The armed services placed the blame upon faulty control of the flow of materials to the producers of end-items; production officials insisted that the shortage of materials had not been sufficiently acute to account for the leveling off of output in September and October, and that the fault lay in defective scheduling of components and end-items by the services. Before the end of the year, however, arrangements were concluded between the WPB and the services that held out good prospects of remedying these difficulties. WPB had adopted and was soon to put into effect the Controlled Materials Plan, a "vertical" system of allocating key materials to claimant agencies, which the services had favored over the "horizontal" method of allocating di-

---

[1] CPA, *Industrial Mobilization for War*, p. 533.
[2] (1) *Ibid.*, Pt. III, Ch. XV. (2) See also below, App. B.

rectly to producers that was embodied in the Production Requirements Plan in effect during most of 1942. On the other hand **WPB, through its new Production Executive Committee** headed by Charles E. Wilson, had succeeded in securing closer control over production scheduling, though this remained within the procurement function of the services. In the next few months scheduling and materials control were to be the foremost production problems.[3]

Production plans and objectives during the first half of 1942 had reflected a widespread adherence to the theory of "incentive" goals; no real effort had been made to bring programs within the limits of productive capacity, and the experts differed widely among themselves as to where those limits actually lay. Studies of the feasibility of the early programs for 1942 and 1943 were undertaken as early as February 1942 by the Planning Committee of the War Production Board. The President was not overly impressed by the committee's recommendations for reductions, submitted to him by Mr. Nelson. In May he even raised some of his "must" objectives and also gave a general endorsement to the complementary supply programs of the military services. Nelson thereupon allowed the question of feasibility to lapse.[4]

Through the spring and summer the gap between actual production and quotas necessary to meet 1942 objectives steadily widened. In August Simon Kuznets of the WPB Planning Committee completed and Nelson approved a detailed analysis indicating that war production in 1942 would probably fall short of objectives by about $15 billion (a remarkably accurate prediction), and that the goals for 1943 were even less attainable. This report brought

from General Somervell (to whom, among others, it had been forwarded for comment) an explosion of wrath and the retort that it ought to be "carefully hidden from the eyes of thoughtful men."[5] The whole issue came at once to a head since the WPB experts had warned that an immediate cutback of existing goals was imperative to avert serious dislocation among the various programs and misdirection of effort that might make impossible even the objectives they thought feasible.

Somervell vigorously disputed the WPB's specific findings and in particular scoffed at the technique of measuring productive capacity in dollars. He argued that even if the goals should prove to be excessive, this would mean only that they would be postponed; to reduce them at the outset would relax the pressure that in an economy geared to war was essential in order to achieve maximum effort.[6]

On this matter his own civilian superior, Under Secretary Patterson, thought otherwise. "Production objectives," Patterson told him, "ought not to be far in front of estimated maximum production . . . otherwise our scheduling of production cannot represent reality, and . . . without realistic scheduling we will continue to suffer from maldistribution of materials, thus cutting down the actual output of finished weapons."[7] In his mind, the important point was that reduction of objec-

---

[3] CPA, *Industrial Mobilization for War*, Chs. XII–XIII, XV.

[4] (1) See Com on Pub Admin Cases, Feasibility Dispute, Ch. III. (2) See also above, Ch. VIII.

[5] Memo, Somervell for Robert R. Nathan, Chm Plng Com WPB, 12 Sep 42, WPD 1942(2) folder, Hq ASF.

[6] (1) See Com on Pub Admin Cases, Feasibility Dispute, Chs. IV–V. (2) See also, Millett, *ASF*, Chs. XIII–XV.

[7] Memo, Patterson for Somervell, 7 Oct 42, quoted in Com on Pub Admin Cases, Feasibility Dispute, pp. 102–03.

tives should be made by the Joint Chiefs, who alone were qualified to evaluate the pertinent strategic considerations. Most WPB officials were willing to concede this point.[8]

Somervell backed down, and it was on his suggestion that Nelson, on 19 October, referred the problem to the Joint Chiefs, asking them for guidance "in deciding which part of the program can be extended to 1944 with least damage to the war effort." [9] Existing objectives, for munitions, facilities, and war construction, had been estimated at a total value of $92.9 billion for 1943, to which was added an estimated deficit from the 1942 program (excluding aircraft) of another $5 billion, bringing the whole to almost $98 billion. The national economy, Nelson stated, would be unable to produce in these categories more than a total of $75 billion. Twenty-three billion, evidently, would have to be eliminated or postponed.[10]

This attack upon the military supply programs coincided with an equally determined one upon military demands for manpower. By late summer of 1942 labor shortages throughout the country, while still local or regional rather than general, had become a serious embarrassment to production, and the pool of unemployed, which heretofore had served to cushion the impact of military and industrial expansion upon the nation's manpower, had for practical purposes disappeared. Talk of national service legislation was in the air, criticism of manpower waste in the armed services mounted in volume, and investigating committees in both the Senate and the House were examining the whole manpower problem. As the largest military user of the nation's manpower, the Army naturally was the principal target of the critics. During the first eight months of

1942 the Army's estimates of its ultimate manpower needs had remained indefinite. Only the mobilization Troop Basis for 1942 had the stamp of presidential approval; the larger and rather theoretical Victory Program goals for 1943 and beyond served primarily as guides for supply planning. Rumors of these latter formidable figures filtered down to the public, and in September a statement by Maj. Gen. Lewis B. Hershey, Director of Selective Service, that the armed services might eventually have to mobilize 13 million men was widely misinterpreted to mean that the Army alone had its eye on that number. Like the WPB, the civilian manpower agencies were becoming impatient with both the vastness and the vagueness of the armed services' long-range objectives. In mid-September Paul V. McNutt, Chairman of the War Manpower Commission, asked the Joint Chiefs to join with the commission and WPB in settling upon the ultimate manpower needs of industry, agriculture, and the armed services.[11]

---

[8] *Ibid.* and pp. 100–104.

[9] Memo, Nelson for JCS, 19 Oct 42, sub: U.S. War Pdn Objective 1943, circulated as JCS 134, in CCS 400.17 (7-6-42) Sec 3.

[10] (1) *Ibid.* (2) Com on Pub Admin Cases, Feasibility Dispute, pp. 104–05. (3) CPA, *Industrial Mobilization for War*, pp. 284–89.
The $75 billion maximum was the Planning Committee's estimate. Nelson believed the maximum lay somewhere between $75 and $85 billion. Nonmunitions expenditures were expected to add another $18 billion to existing objectives, making a total war production goal for 1943 of $115 billion—about 75 percent of the estimated national product.

[11] (1) Maj William P. Moody, "Manpower Becomes a Problem: Conflict Between the JCS and Civilian War Agencies, September–December 1942," Ch. VI, Sec II-C of Mobilization and Demobilization of Military Manpower, JCS study, pp. 1–12, JCS Hist Sec. (2) Jonathan Grossman, Industrial Relations and Labor Problems, a volume in preparation for the series UNITED STATES ARMY IN WORLD WAR II, draft chapter, "Size of the Army."

Under these pressures the Army and Navy in September rushed to completion their detailed troop requirements for 1943. The Army's needs were set at 8,208,000 officers and enlisted men, in a grand total for all the armed services of 10.9 million. Requirements for 1944 and beyond remained under study. To the 1943 troop bases, as submitted by the JCS, the President promptly gave provisional approval on 30 September, holding out the possibility of later increases if needed.[12]

These objectives, particularly the Army's strength goals, immediately came under bitter attack from the civilian production and manpower agencies. These officials challenged both the feasibility and the need for mobilization of ground forces on such a scale. They argued that the national economy, including both civilian and war production, would be seriously weakened by the drain of men from factories and farms, and questioned whether the Army could in fact transport its forces overseas in numbers sufficient to prevent the accumulation at home, as the WPB Planning Committee put it, of "a stagnant pool of manpower, contributing neither to the defense of the country in a military sense nor to its productive output."[13] Manpower ceilings for the armed forces were suggested that would hold the size of the Army in 1943 to a limit as low as 6.5 million.

In the midst of the controversy the President himself, late in October, startled his military advisers by suggesting, with overtones of command, a new set of military strength objectives which, as General Marshall and his staff interpreted the somewhat devious wording, would limit the Army by mid-1944 to the 7,533,000 enlisted men and 675,000 officers already approved on 30 September as the goal for the *end of 1943*. A little later the President further muddied the water by commenting that the Army would be "lucky if it gets over 7,000,000 [enlisted men] by December 31, 1943."[14] But before the end of November, after "much correspondence and many conferences," as General McNarney described it, the President was persuaded to reaffirm his earlier approval of a 7.5-million-man Army for 1943 (8.2 million including officers), though this time with the warning that in all probability there would be no further expansion after 1943.[15] "We should stop talking," observed Brig. Gen. Idwal H. Edwards, the Assistant Chief of Staff, G-3, "about increasing beyond this figure."[16] A few days later the Joint Chiefs decided that a subcommittee report setting the Army's ultimate personnel requirements at 13,594,000 men and women (in a total of 17,497,145 for all services) had better be kept discreetly under cover.[17]

For the now solidly approved 1943 objectives military spokesmen made no apologies. If those objectives had not been pared down to the bone of every precisely calculable need, it was argued, neither were they hastily contrived or heavily padded guesses, and there was no convinc-

---

[12] Memo, Adm Leahy for President, 30 Sep 42, with ind by President, CCS 320.2 (7-25-42) Sec 1.

[13] Moody chapter, pp. 13–14, cited n. 11(1).

[14] Memo, President for Marshall, 10 Nov 42, WDCSA 320.2 (11-10-42) Sec 1942–43.

[15] Min, WD Gen Council mtg, 23 Nov 42.

[16] *Ibid.*

[17] (1) Memo, President for Dir of the Budget, 29 Oct 42, quoted in E. Roosevelt, ed., *F. D. R.: His Personal Letters, 1928-1945*, II, 1358. (2) Ltr, Dir of the Budget to SW, 4 Nov 42, WDCSA 020 (11-7-42) SW Open Files. (3) Memo cited n. 14. (4) Min cited n. 15. (5) JPS 57/6, 22 Oct 42, title: Tr Bases for All Svs . . . . (6) Min, 44th mtg JCS, 1 Dec 42.

Part of the confusion over approved Army goals in October grew out of the President's reference to average strengths for fiscal years 1943 and 1944, instead of to terminal strengths for calendar year 1943.

ing evidence that the national economy could not support them. The Joint Chiefs in November sharply challenged the charge by WPB that the planned expansion of the armed forces would cripple the war economy by siphoning off too much labor from industry. The estimates, General Marshall publicly declared in December, were the fruit of exhaustive study over a period of six months, and no factor had been more carefully studied than the prospects of overseas deployment. In any case, he boldly asserted, the risks of overexpansion were trivial as compared to those of underexpansion.

It would be far better to have more trained men than we could ship than to have empty bottoms for which there were no trained troops, to support commanders whose forces might be wiped out for lack of them . . . . It would be utterly impossible to improvise troops on short notice. A year or more is required to build fighting divisions.[18]

Army officials, on the whole, were not unduly concerned over the limitation placed upon the Army's growth. The year 1944 was far in the future, and even if no further numerical expansion were permitted after 1943, the Army would continue to develop its fighting power—by plowing overhead personnel back into the ranks as training programs shrank, and by squeezing out the residual fat, "of which," as General McNarney privately admitted, "we have plenty."[19]

The armed services were less successful in weathering the assault upon their supply programs for 1943. The Joint Chiefs, indeed, seemed little inclined to dispute the findings set forth in Nelson's letter of 19 October 1942, although Somervell continued to insist that the dollar yardstick was not a valid measure of productive capacity and to argue that the proper function of the War Production

Board was not to question military requirements but to help meet them by providing raw materials and expediting production—duties he felt the WPB was not performing satisfactorily. The Joint Strategic Committee was put to work to review the whole military program and recommend possible cuts. On 24 November its recommendations, only slightly amended, were approved by the JCS and forwarded to Nelson. The total objective of the 1943 program was reduced, by elimination or deferment of various items, from $92 billion to $80.15 billion, presumably including the expected $5 billion carry-over from 1942. The WPB Planning Committee decided that this program was "within the realms of possible accomplishment."[20] (Table 18)

Almost seven weeks earlier Judge Patterson had predicted:

If a cut in military production objectives is to be made, it will be borne by the Army and the Navy. It is safe to say that with the shipping situation what it is, the program of the Maritime Commission will not be touched, and it is also plain enough that the program for expansion of production of raw materials will not be cut below its present size. . . . I should suppose, in the light of the most recent military developments, that no reduction in the aircraft program would be considered by the Joint Chiefs of Staff.[21]

Patterson was a good prophet, his only major error being the anticipation that

---

[18] (1) Statement by Marshall quoted in *Time* (December 21, 1942), p. 83. (2) Ltr, Leahy to Nelson, 24 Nov 42, CCS 400.17 (7-6-42) Sec 4.

[19] Min cited n. 15.

[20] (1) Memo, Nathan to Charles E. Wilson, 11 Dec 42, quoted in CPA, *Industrial Mobilization for War*, pp. 289–90; quote is from p. 290. (2) Memo, Somervell for CofS, 30 Oct 42, filed with JPS 74/2, 29 Oct 42, title: Price Levels in Connection With Pdn Prog, in CCS 400.17 (7-6-42) Sec 3. (3) Ltr, JCS to Nelson, 24 Nov 42, same file. (4) Related papers in same file. (5) JPS 74/10, 21 Nov 42, title: U.S. War Pdn Objective for 1943. (6) Min, 43d mtg JCS, 24 Nov 42.

[21] Memo cited n. 7.

TABLE 18—REVISED 1943 MILITARY PROGRAM
(MILLIONS OF DOLLARS)

Program	Original Estimate	Reduction		Revised Program
		Amount	Percent	
Total	92,900	12,750	14	80,150
President's "must" and related items	48,800	3,200	7	45,600
Aircraft program	37,000	3,730	10	33,270
Merchant shipbuilding program	3,600	+800	+22	4,400
Minor combat vessels (antisubmarine types)	4,000	270	7	3,730
Soviet protocol	2,700	0	0	2,700
Materials plants	1,500	0	0	1,500
Other programs	44,100	9,550	22	34,550
Army ground program	18,800	3,950	21	14,850
Navy (including Navy lend-lease, but excluding minor combat vessels)	10,400	2,300	22	8,100
Lend-lease (excluding Soviet protocol and Navy lend-lease)	7,800	1,900	24	5,900
Army	6,000	1,900	32	4,100
Treasury	1,800	0	0	1,800
Military construction and war housing (excluding airfields and bases)	5,100	1,050	21	4,050
Army	3,200	1,000	31	2,200
Navy	1,200	50	4	1,150
War housing	700	0	0	700
Industrial facilities (excluding aircraft, merchant ships, and materials)	2,000	350	18	1,650
Army and Army-sponsored	960	0	0	960
Navy and Navy-sponsored	1,030	350	34	680
Maritime Commission	10	0	0	10

Source: JPS 74/10, 21 Nov 42, title: U.S. War Pdn Objective for 1943.

the aircraft program would be left intact. Before Mr. Nelson demanded the over-all reduction, in fact, the Joint Chiefs had agreed to curtail the AAF program for 1943. The approved total program represented slashes in major categories as follows:[22]

	Percent
Aircraft program	10
Army ground program	21
Navy program	17.8
Lend-lease	24.3

Under these reduced programs, the Joint Chiefs hoped to be able to provide some 109,000 aircraft, munitions for an army

[22] The 17.8 percent of Navy program includes naval lend-lease procurement, a relatively small item. Percentages for both Army ground and Navy programs exclude military construction and facilities expansion; if these are included, the percentage reductions are 21.5 and 20.6 for Army ground and Navy, respectively. Lend-lease excludes Russian protocol and Navy lend-lease. For merchant shipping program, see below, pp. 624–31.

of 7,500,000 enlisted men (with 50 percent allowances for troops in training), naval ship construction of 227 major combat vessels and many minor types, and supplies and construction for the Navy's shore and base establishment.

Evidently the old problem of balance was far from being solved. The items in the revised program, according to the JCS, were "balanced within themselves and against each other." [23] But the "must" items, formerly 52 percent of the whole military program, now engrossed 57 percent of it. The emphasis, more than ever, was upon air power, ocean transportation, and aid to the USSR, at the expense of ground and naval power (in major combat vessels) and lend-lease to countries other than the Soviet Union. The aircraft objective alone had risen relatively, despite its absolute reduction, from 40 to almost 42 percent, while the ground army program had dropped from 20 to about 18 percent. The augmented merchant ship and antisubmarine vessel programs did represent balance in the sense that they were expected to enable overseas deployment to keep pace with the expansion of the Army in the United States. Otherwise the new program, even more than the old, was selective rather than balanced.

The crux of the debate on balance was air power. More than any other group, its partisans argued for a concentrated—that is, unbalanced—effort in production and strategy alike, as against a balanced one among all arms. Their blueprint for victory, presented in September 1942 and centering upon the strategic bombing offensive against Germany, recognized the need for support by other arms (including naval air), for shipping, and for maintaining the civil economy. But it proposed to place air power at the center of the na-

tional war effort. General Arnold candidly denied, as inconsistent with any scheme of selective emphasis, the principle advanced by the Joint Planners that all the major parts of the military program should be considered "of equal importance." [24] The exponents of air power held, in effect, that aircraft should be given precedence over other items whenever a conflict arose over materials or facilities; at the same time, they insisted that this arrangement would not cripple the other programs. Whether it would or would not, unfortunately, only the event would demonstrate, and the production experts, military and civilian, could not agree. The Joint Chiefs, in any case, faced the inconvenient fact that the President had laid down, as objectives that "must" be fulfilled, not only the aircraft program but several others as well. Even with a reduced aircraft program, Nelson told them late in October, only about 70 percent of the "nonmust" programs probably could be completed in 1943. Hoping to persuade the President to modify his "must" objectives, the JCS had directed the planners to disregard these and to draw up a "balanced" program. But somewhere in the process this aim was abandoned. The cuts, in the end, were made almost entirely in the "nonmust" categories. [25]

In October the Air Forces shifted the battle for air power from the question of objectives to that of priorities, demanding an overriding and exclusive rating for aircraft alone. This demand the Navy met head on, proposing instead to place in

---

[23] JCS 134/3, 26 Nov 42, title: U.S. War Pdn Objectives 1943.

[24] Min, 41st mtg JCS, 10 Nov 42.

[25] (1) Craven and Cate, *AAF II,* pp. 288–95. (2) Memo, Nelson for JCS, 20 Oct 42, CCS 452 (8-27-42) Sec 1. (3) Min, 38th mtg JCS, 20 Oct 42. (4) JPS 74/D, 21 Oct 42, title: U.S. War Pdn Objective 1943.

what the working committees called the first order of "emphasis" not merely aircraft but a large part of the naval and some of the maritime construction as well. Other claimants clamored for equal attention. Unable to agree, the Joint Chiefs, on 25 November, took the problem to the White House. There, the President settled it in his own fashion. Making a few changes in some notes Admiral King had brought along, he handed it back as a new "must" list, now labeled "Number One Group":

(a) 82,000 combat aircraft, 25,000 training aircraft—with necessary accessories and related equipment, sufficient for active operations during next six months.
(b) Munitions and miscellaneous expendable ground supplies (Sections I and III of Army Supply Program)—sufficient for active operations during next six months.
(c) Naval construction program for 1943, together with sufficient additional construction to ensure completion of scheduled units in 1944.
(d) Maritime Commission construction scheduled for 1943.

The President directed the Joint Chiefs to ask Mr. Nelson if this program could be accomplished.[26] Mr. Nelson's verdict, which he rendered on 3 December, seemed to the JCS "somewhat noncommittal,"[27] and a second report at the end of the month was little more illuminating. As Nelson pointed out, the "Number One Group" could hardly stand alone. The critical raw materials expansion program at least would have to be included—synthetic rubber, aluminum, alloy steel—along with aviation gasoline, and with all these the total came to over $50 billion, more than the original "must" list. Most of Nelson's experts were dubious, but Nelson himself and his vice chairman, Charles Wilson, were inclined to think that the ob-

jectives might be "well within feasible limits."[28]

In general the military leaders could not view the prospects for production in 1943 with any great confidence. "We are entering into 1943," reported General Somervell and Admiral Horne, "with our procurement and production objectives ill-defined, and with an immediate need for a clarification in the priority ratings to be assigned to the several production programs." Production was going ahead, in fact, under interim priority directives, which generally favored aircraft but which, Somervell and Horne warned, "may not be in accord with important strategical considerations."[29] Mr. Bernard Baruch had recently issued an alarming report on the rubber situation indicating a need for rapid expansion of synthetic rubber plants in 1943, which would probably have a serious effect upon high-octane gasoline and naval escort production. Production during the first quarter of 1943 was to lag in many lines, most seriously in aircraft, and there were a number of cutbacks in these and other objectives. No solution had been found for the overloading of top priorities. The

---

[26] (1) Min, 44th mtg JPS, 4 Nov 42; 45th mtg, 11 Nov 42. (2) Min, 41st mtg JCS, 10 Nov 42; 43d mtg, 24 Nov 42. (3) JPS 51/3, 13 Nov 42, title: Priorities in Pdn of Mun . . . . (4) See JCS 146 series and related correspondence in CCS 400.17 (2-20-42) Sec 2. (5) Notes on JCS mtg in exec off of President, 25 Nov 42, filed with JCS min, JCS Hist Sec.
[27] JCS 146/6, 5 Dec 42, title: Priorities in Pdn of Mun . . . .
[28] (1) Ltr, Nelson to Leahy, 3 Dec 42, CCS 400.17 (2-20-42) Sec 2. (2) CPA, Industrial Mobilization for War, pp. 290–92. (3) JCS 146/5, 31 Nov 42, title: Priorities in Pdn of Mun . . . . (4) JCS 146/6 cited n. 27. (5) Ltr, Nelson to Leahy, 31 Dec 42, circulated as JCS 151/10, in CCS 561.4 (11-12-42) Sec 2.
[29] Memo, Horne and Somervell for JCS, 4 Jan 43, sub: Pdn Priorities, circulated as JCS 186, in CCS 400.17 (2-20-42) Sec 2.

President's "Number One Group" had proved to be, not a smaller and more feasible "must" list, but only one of a number of programs that, for practical purposes, had to be considered as of equal importance. Somervell and Horne felt no assurance that all of them could be completed in 1943, and warned, "if any program, or parts thereof, are placed ahead of other programs, the latter will necessarily be delayed." [30]

Finally, war production evidently would have to continue in 1943, as it had done in 1942, without a solid basis in strategy. Military requirements were not correlated closely with strategic plans, which indeed were still not projected far enough ahead to permit a firm and detailed calculation of requirements. Among the working committees, the absence of fixed strategic plans was as vexing as it was to the civilian production officials. In November 1942 the JUSSC, laboring to draw up a program of requirements that would be both balanced and feasible, tried again, as it had tried the preceding spring, to bring home to the Joint Chiefs the difficulties they faced:

The lack of an overall strategic plan upon which to base production planning is deplored. Production programs are now geared to the equipment and employment of forces for which no general strategic plan has been enunciated. The size and general composition of the forces which will result may not be adequate or suitable for successful conduct of the war.

In the early part of the war, such production planning was justified. However, the time has now arrived when this type of planning is dangerous and unsound. It is vital that broad strategic plans be developed which will determine objectives, troop strength, shipping, and advanced bases necessary. Until such plans are developed and promulgated, our production planning is on an unsound basis. [31]

The Joint Planners deleted these passages from their report to the JCS.

Even if the chiefs had been able to give their logistical staffs a firm over-all strategic plan, it may be doubted whether the production program would have been much affected. The American method of mobilizing war resources was by this time fixed. It aimed at providing not a collection of special tools each designed for a specific purpose, but a balanced "kit" of components and general-purpose tools— trained manpower and finished munitions. The interpretations of "balance" were many, and the committee system had produced inevitable compromises among the advocates of various strategies, at times almost to the point of precluding any kind of emphasis. Yet the production and manpower programs that emerged late in 1942 had a definite emphasis and a definite shape. The most obvious emphasis was upon air power. This was in part a recognition of the danger that, despite the phenomenal expansion of shipbuilding, the enemy might still be able to prevent the deployment of massive ground armies overseas. This possibility, together with practical limitations upon the manpower available to the armed forces, necessitated a continued emphasis upon foreign aid to arm the trained manpower of other anti-Axis nations, above all the massive armies of the Soviet Union.

The attacks upon the military production and manpower goals were accompanied by renewed demands from many quarters for a more thoroughgoing "arsenal of democracy" strategy, in which

[30] (1) *Ibid.* (2) CPA, *Industrial Mobilization for War*, pp. 599–606. (3) Craven and Cate, *AAF II*, p. 295. (4) See below, App. B.

[31] JPS 134/2, 23 Nov 42, title: U.S. War Pdn Objective 1943, with rough draft prepared by JUSSC, in CCS 400.17 (7-6-42) Sec 3.

the United States would drastically curtail its contribution of ground forces to the anti-Axis war. The WPB Planning Committee, for example, expressed the opinion,

. . . the United States could contribute more toward a successful termination of the war by producing and shipping to our Allies the great quantities of munitions needed, than by shipping and supplying large numbers of American troops, which would interfere with our munitions production. . . . Although foreign labor cannot be brought in to relieve our industrial manpower shortage, foreign soldiers can be substituted for American soldiers in many of the theaters of war. A true combined strategy of the United Nations would free shipping and rationalize the use of manpower.[32]

General Marshall suspected that this "fallacious and humiliating proposition," as his staff immediately styled it, lay behind the President's perplexing oscillations during October and November on the matter of the 1943 troop basis. Marshall now vigorously reasserted, in words reminiscent of those he had used in September 1941 when the same issue had been raised, the Army's insistence upon a major American contribution in ground armies as well as in weapons. "The morale of the hostile world must be broken," he declared, "not only by aggressive fighting but, as in 1918, by the vision of an overwhelming force of fresh young Americans being *rapidly* developed in this country."[33] Before many weeks had passed, however, the Army was to launch a substantial program for rearming French troops that would carry it well along the path the WPB committee desired. At this juncture of the war, with British manpower mobilized to the hilt, there were in fact no other foreign troops available who might be substituted for American soldiers in overseas theaters.

These concepts of emphasis and balance, shaped largely by the estimated limits of the country's capacity to produce for war while preserving its economic health, went far to mark out the broad channels strategy would have to follow in 1943. The military leaders at Casablanca and later could only maneuver within them.

Shipping and the New Drift of Deployment

One immediate consequence of the shift of logistical effort that accompanied the Allied offensive in North Africa was the temporary disappearance of the shipping shortage in the Atlantic area. Shipping in the Atlantic as a whole was now called on to support a smaller aggregate deployment, both of troops and of matériel, than would have been required had the BOLERO program continued at an ascending tempo as originally planned. August was the great month of BOLERO deployment. One hundred and two thousand troops and 773,000 ship tons of cargo were then launched across the North Atlantic; another 80,000 tons of cargo were sent to the Middle East. Nothing like this volume of deployment was attained, during any of the four months following, to the three principal areas—the British Isles, North Africa, and the Middle East—that Atlantic shipping had to serve. The amount of shipping actually in Army service in this region declined, as a result, from a peak of 3,991,500 dead-weight tons in September to 3,621,500 tons in November.[34]

---

[32] Min, WPB Plng Com mtg, 5 Nov 42, p. 99.

[33] (1) Draft memo, Marshall for President, 7 Nov 42, marked "not sent." (2) Memo, Marshall for President, 9 Nov 42, WDCSA 320.2 (11-10-42) Sec 1942–43. (3) See above, Ch. V.

[34] (1) See below, Charts 15–19 in Ch. XXVII. (2) ASF Monthly Progress Report, Transportation, Feb 43, Sec 3.

What limited deployment during these months, as has been shown in earlier chapters, was not an over-all shortage of shipping but a combination of impediments to its effective employment. Convoy restrictions limited the number of ships that could be used, long turnarounds lengthened the time required to deliver a given amount of cargo or a given number of troops, some of the ports in North Africa could not have accommodated more ships even if convoys had been run more frequently, ports in the Persian Gulf could not handle as much cargo as they received. In August, because of the change in strategic plans, the Army found itself unable to use all the cargo tonnage assigned to the North Atlantic run. Troop and cargo movements to the British Isles dropped sharply in the months following, held back partly by lack of escorts, partly by lack of ready troop units, the latter shortage serving automatically to curtail the movement of accompanying cargo. In September and October shipping was immobilized in the convoys assembling for North Africa. These did not get under way until late in October. Also, the last three months of the year saw a marked upswing in troop and cargo shipments around the Cape, principally to the Persian Gulf, removing a large block of tonnage for many weeks from Atlantic service altogether.

In all this deloyment, moreover, shipping performance was far from efficient. The sudden shift in strategy disrupted and complicated the flow of troops and material, preventing careful scheduling of movements and levying a heavy toll in delays, last-minute changes, and uneconomical improvisation. Ships were held idle in harbor while being refitted, waiting for convoys to be assembled, or waiting for an open berth. Time was consumed in combat loading and in reloading ships that had been improperly loaded. Ships had to be completely discharged, on the eve of sailing, because a plan had changed or troops had failed to arrive at port. Ships sailed partly loaded; a few returned only partly unloaded. Supply moved circuitously from the United States to England and thence, after being discharged, warehoused, and loaded once more, to North Africa. TORCH was a brilliant achievement in overriding logistical obstacles, but it also provided a classic object lesson in the costs of improvisation and hasty planning. Much of the cost was reflected in the uneconomical use of shipping. Some suggestion of this cost is conveyed by the downward trend in the volume of cargo moved by each deadweight ton of cargo shipping in the Atlantic area. (Table 19)

The Atlantic pool of shipping was thus fully employed, or almost so, in supporting even the relatively small deployment of the last four months of 1942. To the planners, expecting losses of 20 to 30 percent in the North African convoys and an enemy attempt to cut communications through the Strait, an acute shortage seemed both imminent and inevitable. Since midyear, shipping losses had fluctuated erratically, belying predictions from week to week. Allied losses of dry cargo shipping declined from 936,000 dead-weight tons in June to 597,000 in August and, after a rise in September, to 519,000 tons in October. But in particular sectors the toll was heavy. In July the northern convoy route to the USSR became so costly that movements there were suspended. August saw the beginning of U-boat "wolf-pack" tactics in the central Atlantic, where the convoys lacked air cover, and in September submarine at-

TABLE 19—MEASUREMENT TONS OF CARGO MOVED PER DEAD-WEIGHT TON OF SHIPPING: JUNE–DECEMBER 1942

Period	Atlantic & Middle East	Pacific & Far East
Average, June–December	0.39	0.42
Average, June–August [a]	.45	.44
June	.44	.37
July	.41	.49
August	.51	.47
Average, September–December [b]	.35	.41
September	.33	.33
October	.29	.47
November	[c].47	.38
December	.31	.44

[a] In these months eastward cargo shipments moved mainly to the British Isles.

[b] In these months eastward cargo shipments moved in considerable volume to North Africa and the Middle East as well as to the British Isles.

[c] The relatively high efficiency shown here is misleading in that it reflects in part the movement of convoys to North Africa that had been loading during the two preceding months. It also reflects the dispatch of over 100,000 ship tons of cargo to the Middle East.

Source: ASF Monthly Progress Report, Sec 3, Transportation, Jun 42–Jan 43.

tacks were stepped up in the South Atlantic, where cargo vessels were not then sailing in convoy. During September, also, the undersea craft penetrated into the Gulf of St. Lawrence with deadly effect, and the large convoy (PQ-18) to northern Soviet ports suffered losses out of proportion to its heavy escort. New enemy submarines were coming into action in growing numbers during the autumn, and new techniques, such as the use of large supply submarines ("milch cows"), promised to become more effective with practice. In November losses from all causes swung upward to an appalling total of 1,202,000 dead-weight tons; sinkings on the North Atlantic route during October and November occurred at a rate of almost one ship a day. Toward the end of the year, too, submarines began to operate just east of the Brazilian bulge. The North African convoys, surprisingly, escaped with fairly light punishment; the slow convoys from the United States, through March, suffered only 3.4 percent losses by enemy action. On the other hand, British shipping was hard hit, as an indirect result of the North African operation, on the routes where convoying had to be abandoned. Sinkings averaged 10 percent, and one group of ships lost seventeen out of forty-four. The experiment proved too costly and was shortly terminated.[35]

In the Pacific, losses of merchant shipping were relatively inconsequential. On the other hand, tonnage available in that

[35] (1) Morison, *Battle of the Atlantic*, Ch. XIV. (2) See below, App. H. (3) For losses in UG convoys, see above, Ch. XVII. (4) Min, 55th mtg CCS, 14 Jan 43.

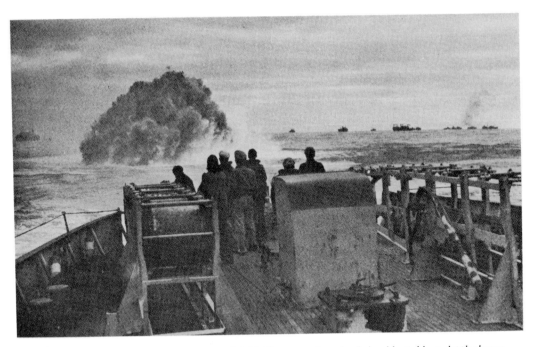

THE WAR AGAINST THE U-BOAT. *German submarine being blasted by a depth charge from a Coast Guard cutter on escort duty. Convoy is visible in background.*

area had to carry a heavier burden proportionately than shipping in the Atlantic. Distances were vast, and most of the routes were entirely over water, involving repeated transshipment. Shipping thus had to carry part of the load which, on the Atlantic side, was passed on to the roads and railroads. Interisland and coastal shipping played a vastly larger role than in the Atlantic area. Above all, the lack of adequate port facilities in Alaska and west of Hawaii, except for the New Zealand and southeast Australia ports far from the front, reduced immeasurably the effectiveness of shipping performance. Forces throughout the Pacific had to depend for support largely on the tonnage there available, supplemented by some new construction from the west coast yards—transfers from the Atlantic area, except for fast troop transports, were seldom practicable and always exorbitantly expensive in voyage time. Supply of garrisons in relatively quiet areas, moreover, absorbed relatively more of the available shipping in the Pacific than in the Atlantic. Many of these forces, to be sure, were in the comparatively accessible Alaska-Hawaii-Panama triangle, a circumstance that helps to explain the fact that the volume of cargo moved by each dead-weight ton of shipping compared favorably with that in the Atlantic area. *(See Table 19.)* But the forces fighting Japan were far less generously supported by shipping than were those on the other side of the world. At the end of 1942 each American soldier deployed against the European Axis was backed up by 5.9 dead-weight tons of shipping (troop and cargo), while each soldier against

Japan was supported by only 3.3 dead-weight tons.[36]

Before the end of 1942 the shipping shortage in the Pacific was serious, considering the area as a whole, and was becoming more so. The limited offensives launched there in the latter half of the year were more or less impromptu reactions to enemy moves, undertaken without adequate advance preparation. By the end of the year American forces were deeply committed in both South and Southwest Pacific areas, and the operations had proved far more costly than anticipated. In the Southwest Pacific the shortage of shipping was acute. In the South Pacific, to which more had been allotted, huge tonnages clogged the harbor at Nouméa and some of the smaller bases, held up by inadequate discharge facilities. In both areas the need for construction materials was still unsatisfied, and the increased volume of troop deployment had brought with it additional heavy demands for maintenance supplies and special equipment.[37] Congestion in Persian Gulf ports, meanwhile, was immobilizing shipping that might otherwise have helped to relieve the worsening situation in the Pacific.

From a year's end vantage point, the world-wide shipping situation showed some improvement. During the last six months of 1942, new construction more than balanced total losses of Allied shipping, and there was even an absolute decline in the total volume of losses as compared with the first half of the year. Dry cargo shipping losses were somewhat heavier, tanker losses considerably lighter in the second half than in the first half of the year. The average monthly loss for the entire year (percentage of tonnage in use) was slightly over 2.16 percent for all types, 2.39 percent for dry cargo shipping and

1.98 for tankers. Considerably more ship tonnage had been placed at the disposal of the Army than its planners had expected early in the year. In contrast to General Somervell's "bold" estimate in January 1942 that about 300 cargo vessels would be made available to support Army deployment in 1942, the number actually in Army service at the end of August was 432. At the end of the year, despite reduced allocations, the Army still had at its disposal 391 cargo vessels aggregating 3.1 million dead-weight tons.[38]

One source of shipping for military use was drying up. Late in October War Shipping Administration warned "the end has about been reached in the process of diverting WSA ships from less to more essential services."[39] Some of the essential import services, in fact, had been expanded—bauxite, for example—as had most of the lend-lease services, canceling out some of the gains from compression. In the aggregate, U.S. tonnage employed for the war economy and lend-lease had declined from about 4.5 million to 4.1 million, but by mid-October lend-lease shipments alone were employing 1,986,000 dead-weight tons of shipping, as against 1,219,000 the preceding March, while shipping in the import services as a whole had been pared down from 1,991,000 to 1,063,000 dead-weight tons. Army planners were now resigned to the probability that foreign aid shipments were to be a permanent burden upon U.S. merchant

---

[36] (1) See below, Charts 18 and 19. (2) For comparison of maintenance tonnages, see below, App. A-3.
[37] See above, Chs. XV, XXI.
[38] (1) CCS 174, rpt by CMTC, 4 Feb 43, title: Loss Rate for 1943. (2) Contl Div, ASF, *Statistical Review, World War II.* (3) Rpt cited n. 34(2).
[39] Memo, Land and Douglas for President, 27 Oct '42, sub: Reqmts for Additional Tonnage, Shipg 1941–43 folder, Hq ASF.

shipping. Even with the diminution of deployment during the last four months of 1942, they were alarmed by the extent to which allocations of shipping for Army use dwindled. In November, especially, as the Battle of the Atlantic reached its climax, the Army had only 216 vessels to carry its cargo in that area, 46 fewer than the month before. "Any strategic concepts," an OPD officer noted in that bleak month, "that envisage new movements of major forces overseas must necessarily face the fact that there are available neither the transports to handle personnel, cargo vessels to maintain them, nor tankers to supply fuel to their tanks, trucks and planes." [40] Late in October, even before losses had reached their peak, WSA warned that there was "no surplus of shipping in the Atlantic," and that there were "not enough ships to sustain two major military operations simultaneously in widely separated theatres." [41]

The Pressure for Economy in Ship Operations

Since spring of 1942 the War Shipping Administration, while conscripting merchant tonnage for war uses, had also been energetically seeking economies in ship employment. Ship repair operations were accelerated, U.S. shipping laid up in American yards declining from over 14 percent in April to less than 8 percent in September. Imports of nonessential goods were rigidly restricted, routings were more carefully planned. WSA improved its own loading operations in U.S. ports to a point where ships were being loaded to within 2 percent of their full weight capacity, and broken stowage (unused space) was reduced from a normal peacetime average of 25 percent to about 16 percent. Overseas the WSA organization was shaken up

and expanded during the latter part of 1942 in an effort to speed American shipping operations in foreign ports. Through continuous collaboration with the British Ministry of War Transport, the merchant tonnage of the two countries was pooled to a growing degree, routes and sources of supply were rearranged in the interests of shipping economy—for example, meat was imported by the United Kingdom from the United States instead of from Australia and New Zealand. Ships loaded mixed American and British freight in order to balance their cargoes—for example, U.S. Army equipment and British lend-lease steel. WSA even exerted pressure upon British shipping authorities to improve their own operations—for example, to reduce congestion in Indian Ocean ports. [42]

After mid-1942 WSA became increasingly critical of the operating practices of the military services, particularly during the period of administrative confusion attendant upon the new operations in North Africa and the Pacific. In his joint report with Harriman to the President and Prime Minister on 2 August, following a study of the flagging BOLERO program, Douglas set forth his main objective: to program and co-ordinate all cargo movements, freely mixing and interchanging cargoes, so that available shipping space might be utilized to the maximum. The movement of military cargo lay at the heart of the problem.

---

[40] Shipg Sit tab, with OPD Weekly Strategic Resume, 14–28 Nov 42, ABC 381 (9-25-41) Sec 6.

[41] (1) Memo cited n. 39. (2) Shipg Sit tab cited n. 40. (3) Ltr, Douglas to Leahy, 28 Oct 42, filed with JCS 143 in ABC 570 (2-14-42) Sec 3.

[42] (1) Memo cited n. 39. (2) Memos, Douglas for Hopkins, 18 and 25 May 42. (3) Ltr, Douglas to Hopkins, 15 Jul 42. Last two in Hopkins folder, WSA Douglas File. (4) Corresp in Anglo-American Mis folder and WSA Gen folder, WSA Douglas File. (5) See above, Ch. XVII.

Military cargo, at best, was wasteful of space because of its many irregular shapes and its high proportion of bulk to weight. The demands of military supply (the right item, in the right amount, at the right time, at the right place) were not easily reconciled with the demands of economy, and the services were prone to construe broadly the claims of military necessity. Under the agreements reached with WSA in May and June, finally, the independent pools of shipping and the large port facilities controlled by the two services virtually defied assimilation into any integrated system of cargo pooling and ship utilization.[43]

On 9 October Douglas wrote to Somervell citing evidences of inefficient performance in the Army's ship operations and urged that the Army co-ordinate its loading operations with those of WSA and British agencies in the United States. In the plan he set forth, all Army cargo except that of the ships under its permanent control and that involved in amphibious expeditions and other special combat operations would be pooled with other export cargo in a "bank" distributed among all the ports. Shipments would be scheduled and cargo loaded with a view to maximum utilization of space, short routings, and efficient discharge at destination. Loading ports would be assigned, irrespective of agency, in the light of the destinations of each voyage; most voyages would have multiple destinations. The keynote of the proposal was co-ordinated planning and programing, among all the agencies concerned. Douglas suggested that a co-ordinating group be appointed, under WSA chairmanship, representing the three principal agencies.[44]

Somervell and Gross immediately scented danger. Douglas' plan, on the face of it, was merely an extension of the ar-

rangements already in force for mixing Army cargo and lend-lease steel on the North Atlantic run. Nevertheless, while proposing no more than informal interagency co-ordination to bring about desired economies, Douglas' plan obviously pointed in the direction of the kind of rational management and planning of all overseas cargo movements that Britain had achieved through centralized civilian control. The mere suggestion of emulating British methods roused Somervell to derision. Moreover, Douglas had ventured to suggest, as a "natural corollary" of cargo pooling, "that vessels should load their entire cargo at one berth and under the same continuous supervision"—which sounded to Somervell and Gross like a move to abrogate the Army's control of its own loadings, a central feature of the June 1942 *modus operandi* with WSA.[45] Somervell waited ten days before sending a singularly offhand, almost flippant reply. Noting that he had given his "best efforts to discovering some advantage that might be gained" from the measures suggested, he called Douglas' conclusions "non sequiturs," implied that his statistics bore "no relation to actualities," reminded him that commercial standards of stowage could not be expected in emergency shipments and combat loadings (explicitly exempted from Douglas' proposals), devoted a disparaging paragraph to alleged

---

[43] (1) For Army-Navy logistical co-ordination, see above, Ch. XV, and below, Ch. XXIV. (2) For the Douglas-Harriman report, see above, Ch. XIV. (3) See also, Rpt by WSA and BMWT to CSAB, 17 Aug 42, in OCT 565.2 England. (4) For comparison of space requirements of various types of cargo, see below, App. A-1.

[44] (1) Ltr, Douglas to Somervell, 9 Oct 42, with atchd memo, unsigned, no addressee, 8 Oct 42. (2) Ltr, Douglas to Somervell, 22 Oct 42. All in Shipg 1941–43 folder, Hq ASF.

[45] Memo, 8 Oct 42, cited n. 44(1).

waste in Britain's ship operations, opined that the hoped-for savings (estimated by Douglas at over half a million tons of shipping) would be "a small business," objected to "forming any more committees"—and finished by inviting Douglas to lunch.[46]

Douglas came to lunch, and the meeting—after Somervell's blast—proved both anticlimactic and inconclusive. Both principals jovially agreed they had been "silly" and "cantankerous" and that they would be well advised in future to write no more letters. Somervell hinted that their chief subordinates were really responsible for the friction—General Gross in his own establishment, and Capt. Granville Conway, the WSA official at the New York port—which suspicion, as far as Conway was concerned, Douglas politely rejected. The specific WSA proposals, it was decided, would be approached "very slowly" and put into effect only to the extent that experience on the operating level proved them to be practicable.[47]

This was the first round. At New York, where outbound traffic was heaviest, Army port officials showed during subsequent weeks that they were conscious of being under WSA's critical eye. Emphasis on "full and down" loadings from the east coast during that autumn and winter was carried to the point where shipments to the United Kingdom and North Africa finally became badly unbalanced. The results of combining Army with nonmilitary cargo at New York during November were, from WSA's point of view, most promising—"an extraordinary loading performance," Douglas told Hopkins.[48] But WSA officials, rightly or wrongly, were convinced that this performance had been achieved largely at their own piers, not the Army's. Meanwhile, the worsen-

ing congestion at Nouméa and other Pacific ports, along with the general turmoil of initial movements to North Africa, did little to inspire confidence in the efficiency of the Army's ship operations. By December, in fact, WSA was ready to intervene in the Nouméa crisis. In general, the huge volume of ship losses during November, together with upward climbing requirements, seemed to herald a new and general shipping crisis.[49]

At the beginning of December General Gross, without warning, terminated the policy of mixed loading at New York, indicating that henceforth the Army would load with its own cargo the ships assigned to it. Whatever the reasons for this decision (Army officials in the theater had complained that packages in commercially loaded cargoes could not be identified), Douglas regarded it as the last straw. To Hopkins he declared, "I am about at the end of my rope" in the effort to secure economies through persuasion. Hopkins expressed full accord and advised him to go to the President. "These fellows," Hopkins commented, "will not be persuaded."[50]

Douglas acted swiftly. On the 16th he sought an audience with the President and two days later appeared at the White House, armed with a draft presidential order reaffirming the authority of WSA,

<hr>

[46] (1) Ltr, Somervell to Douglas, 19 Oct 42. (2) Memo, Gross for Somervell, 21 Oct 42, sub: Memo From Mr. L. Douglas. Both in Shipg 1941–43 folder, Hq ASF. (3) Ltr cited n. 44(2).

[47] This account is based on Douglas' notes, dated 27 October 1942, in Loading of Ships folder, WSA Douglas File.

[48] Douglas' notes on conf with Hopkins, 7 Dec 42, Hopkins folder, WSA Douglas File.

[49] (1) For the Nouméa crisis and WSA's intervention, see above, Ch. XV. (2) See below, App. H-1.

[50] (1) Douglas' notes cited n. 48. (2) Douglas' notes on conf, 16 Dec 42, WSA Dir 12-18-42 folder, WSA Douglas File.

under its original charter, to control the "operations, including loading" of all merchant vessels other than those used in special task and assault forces and those that could "truly be classed as fleet auxiliaries." Roosevelt listened approvingly to Douglas' exposition of the problem, read the directive, and wondered whether it should not first be shown to the Army and Navy. Douglas vehemently objected, arguing that such a step would produce only "violent dissent," that the services were bent on taking over control of the merchant fleet, and that the directive merely made more explicit the authority already vested in the WSA—authority the services had "refused to obey." Apparently convinced, the President signed the directive, remarking only, "If this doesn't work you will catch hell." [51]

As expected, the directive brought an explosion of wrath from the services. Secretary Stimson flatly refused to put the order into effect until its implications had been studied since the War Department had not been consulted in advance. Considered by itself, the directive seemed unequivocally to assert the authority of WSA to control, as part of the "operations" of merchant shipping, the loading of all military cargo except that in combat loaded and similar tactical shipping. Even the loading of regular Army and Navy transports, for lack of explicit exemption, would appear to fall under WSA jurisdiction. So construed, the directive abrogated at a stroke the basic division of functions between WSA and the services as embodied in the agreements of May and June 1942. [52]

Douglas did not so construe the directive. In a clarifying statement issued less than a week after the President had signed the order he took a far more moderate position, and on the 28th, when Douglas

and Admiral Land appeared before the Joint Chiefs (Somervell and Rear Adm. Robert M. Griffin, head of the Naval Transportation Service, also attended) to discuss the directive, Douglas explained his stand in full. The wording, he confessed, was perhaps unfortunate, though in a literal sense accurate. He reassured the JCS on two points: first, that the directive was not intended to go beyond the terms of WSA's charter—the executive order of February 1942, which exempted the military transport fleets from WSA's control—and second, that WSA had no desire to take over any of the actual loading functions of the military transport services. "Operations," he continued to insist, did include loading, and in a broad sense WSA claimed the power under its charter to co-ordinate the loading of military along with other cargo in merchant-type shipping—including that permanently controlled by the Army and Navy. But the primary aim of WSA was economy in the use of shipping and shipping facilities, which meant, among other things, making maximum use of the military transport services in their accustomed spheres. WSA wanted merely to participate with the services in the over-all planning of military cargo movements in order to ensure that, as far as was consistent with strategic necessity, all merchant shipping would be operated in a liquid pool and all

[51] (1) Douglas' notes on conf with President, 18 Dec 42, WSA Dir 12-18-42 folder, WSA Douglas File. (2) Memo, President for Chm Maritime Comm and WSA, 18 Dec 42, ABC 570 (12-21-42). (3) Related papers in same file. (4) For concurrent pressure on the Navy, see Ballantine, Shipping in Naval Logistics, pp. 103–05, Naval Hist Div, OCNO.

[52] (1) Ltr, Stimson to Land, 23 Dec 42, Shipg 1941–43 folder, Hq ASF. (2) Other corresp in WSA Dir 12-18-42 folder and Reading File Dec 42–Jan 43 folder, WSA Douglas File; and MS Index to the Hopkins Papers, Bk. V, Orgn of WSA, pp. 1–2, Items 6–7.

cargo movements of a "nontactical" character brought under a single co-ordinated program. The aim would be to consolidate shipments destined for a single area, use the most direct routes, bank cargo at loading ports, and mix heavy with bulky cargo to achieve maximum utilization of space. The military services could continue as before to load all combatant vessels, all vessels carrying cargo and personnel in initial movements, all vessels under their permanent control, and, in addition, other vessels carrying military cargo "in conformity with satisfactory stowage and loading plans arrived at through intimate cooperation" with WSA.[53]

The military leaders were not mollified. While Admiral Leahy maintained a judicious, if frosty, calm, King's comments were sharp, and even General Marshall was obviously unhappy. All pointedly stressed the discrepancy between what the directive stated and what Douglas now said he construed it to mean. There must have been some reason for issuing it, Somervell remarked, and he bluntly demanded why, if the directive added nothing to the executive order of February 1942, it should not be rescinded forthwith. All, including Marshall, were outspokenly resentful because Douglas and Land had appealed to the President. The atmosphere of the meeting was charged with hostility, and a supplementary proposal that Douglas later sent to Somervell and Griffin was instantly rejected "with some heat."[54]

One reason, at least, for the resistance to Douglas' proposals was a strong feeling that economy should not be made an overriding consideration in military supply. The point of departure in Douglas' economy program was that only a small part of military supply, that flowing directly to the scene of operations (as in an amphibious assault) rather than through a graded system of stocks and transshipment points (Douglas lumped this category loosely under the term "maintenance") really required emergency handling and strict adherence to strategic priorities without consideration of economy in shipping. Even to this principle he admitted exceptions, but argued that "reasonable men" should be able to reach agreement in specific instances.[55] Somervell rejected—indeed, ignored—this whole conception. Against it he advanced the theory of the integrity of all military supply. The movement of supply from factory to troops, he insisted, was an unbroken chain subject at every point to the guiding impulse of strategic need. Economy must be sought within this conception, never in defiance of it. Commercial methods of loading and mixing military and nonmilitary cargo often resulted in intolerable delays in delivery of needed items; banking of all types of cargo in port areas might congest military terminal facilities, and make it difficult to find particular items for prompt shipment; programing of cargo movements by destination might make it impossible for theater commanders to divert shipments at the last moment to another port of entry. Commercial terminal operators could not follow swiftly

[53] (1) Proposal Submitted to Gen Somervell and Adm Griffin, 28 Dec 42. (2) Memorandum re the President's Directive . . . , 23 Dec 42. (3) Min of mtg in Adm Leahy's off, 28 Dec 42. All in WSA Dir 12-18-42 folder, WSA Douglas File. (4) The official transcript of this meeting and Douglas' notes (both in same file) are in substantial agreement. (5) Memo, Douglas for Hopkins, 23 Dec 42, MS Index to the Hopkins Papers, Bk. V, Orgn of WSA, p. 6, Item 36.
[54] (1) Min cited n. 53(3). (2) Douglas' notes cited n. 53(4). (3) Other corresp in WSA Dir 12-18-42 folder and Reading File Dec 42–Jan 43 folder, WSA Douglas File.
[55] Min cited n. 53(3).

changing military priorities, and were unfamiliar with the technicalities of military supply and loading. In any case, Somervell argued, the contention that civilian control would necessarily bring greater economy and efficiency would not bear examination. The military services would have to maintain large standby port establishments in the States, under any system, to handle emergency situations; overseas ports would have to remain under military control; and the personnel making up the military transportation organization were as experienced and competent as those employed by WSA.[56]

The integrity and effectiveness of military supply, Somervell concluded, depended upon military control over the whole process—an assumption he derived from the principle that authority must be commensurate with responsibility. That WSA might indeed meet military needs, as the President's order stated, "in accordance with the detailed requirements and priorities . . . established and presented by the Army and Navy," Somervell was unwilling to concede. If the President's order were enforced, he declared, it would "cause a violent dislocation of our supply system" and perhaps "jeopardize the success of our overseas operations."

In effect, it destroys the authority of the armed services over the movement of supplies essential to their success and substitutes for an existing extensive and effective system . . . a complicated arrangement controlled by an agency unfamiliar with military requirements and equipment and one with which the services have found mounting dissatisfaction. It injects into the chain of supply . . . another agency having no direct responsibility for that supply or for the military success of those forces. Such a break can only result in confusion and failure . . . . The Joint Chiefs cannot escape, nor would they

wish to, the full responsibility for active operations overseas. They must therefore have the necessary authority, including full control of the flow of their supplies.[57]

The controversy had thus become laden with all the emotional overtones of the classic issue of civilian versus military control. Admiral King, at the meeting on the 28th, objected to Douglas' direct appeal to the President on the ground, as he put it, that the JCS had "authority" in the matter—to which Douglas tartly retorted that WSA derived its authority from the President, not the JCS. He further rejected King's proposal to refer the matter to the Joint Strategic Survey Committee, since this would simply mean allowing the military to judge its own case. Admiral Griffin ran into a sharp verbal bout with Admiral Land, on the same occasion, when he asserted that the military services should not have to submit their shipping requirements to WSA. On both sides the animosity threatened almost to prevent discussion of the substantive issues. Douglas complained bitterly to Leahy and Marshall of the rebuffs he had received from Army and Navy officers—"even personal insults"—and at first refused to talk with Somervell and Griffin unless they were formally designated to represent their civilian superiors, the two service secretaries, to whom the President's directive had been sent originally. Somervell sought to make repeal of the directive a prior condition to any discussions, but finally, at Admiral Leahy's insistence and under

---

[56] (1) Min cited n. 53(3). (2) Draft memo for President, [for Adm Leahy's signature], 6 Jan 43, JCS 1942–44 folder, Hq ASF. This draft, prepared by Somervell, was not approved. See corresp between Somervell and Hopkins in MS Index to the Hopkins Papers, Bk. V, Orgn of WSA, p. 7, Item 38.

[57] Draft memo cited n. 56(2).

protest, yielded. Admiral Griffin contin-ued vehemently to argue that the two services should be allowed complete free-dom to handle all military cargo move-ments, without interference by any "third party."[58]

Gradually the air cleared. In private talks with Admiral Leahy and General Marshall, neither of whom had been fully briefed before the stormy meeting of 28 December, Douglas succeeded in allaying their suspicions and in persuading them that an effort should be made on the oper-ating level to carry out WSA's economy program. While declining to ask the Presi-dent to modify his directive, Douglas agreed to rephrase his supplementary pro-posals to remove any implication that the loading of military cargo by the two serv-ices was done on sufferance of WSA. On the other hand he firmly rejected a move by the military to create a joint Army-Navy-WSA inspection service that might have given to the military services much of the influence over the utilization of mer-chant shipping that WSA, under its char-ter, exercised as its exclusive prerogative. Douglas was also able, through his con-tacts with Hopkins, Wayne Coy, Harold D. Smith, Oscar S. Cox, and others close to the President, to prevent any weaken-ing in that quarter. Within the service de-partments, Secretaries Stimson and Knox do not appear to have taken an active hand in the matter, and Assistant Secretary of War McCloy supported Douglas. In the end, indeed, the intransigent opponents of WSA in both services stood isolated from their own superiors and the issue was a foregone conclusion.[59]

In effect, Douglas had maneuvered his opponents into a position where accept-ance of his rather moderate proposal for a joint exploration on the operating level

of the possibilities of shipping economies—under stipulations by the services that he was willing to accept—could be regarded as a face-saving escape from an awkward situation. On 9 January Douglas received word from Coy that the President stood firm on his executive order, but wanted Douglas, Gross, and Griffin to sit down to-gether "every day for the next three weeks" and reach an agreement on the basis of day-to-day operating experi-ence.[60] Apparently similar instructions had already gone to Somervell, for when Douglas met the latter at lunch later that same day (Gross, Styer, and McCloy were also present), he found him in a genial mood. Somervell playfully chided Douglas and Gross as "cantankerous" characters and urged them to see more of each other; Douglas replied that he would be de-lighted to hobnob with Gross, but doubted whether Gross could stand it. With the ice thus broken, Douglas pressed his desire for a joint loading program, though conced-ing the necessity for deviations in accord-ance with changing military needs, and alluded to the promising joint planning already under way at San Francisco be-tween General Gilbreath and the WSA representative, Frazer Bailey. Somervell agreed there should be more co-operation of this kind.[61]

---

[58] (1) Min cited n. 53(3). (2) Douglas' notes on tele-phone conv with Somervell, 28 Dec 42. (3) Douglas' notes on conf with Leahy, 31 Dec 42. (4) Douglas' notes on conf with Marshall, 4 Jan 43. (5) Douglas' notes on conf in Adm Horne's off, 16 Jan 43. Last four in WSA Dir 12-18-42 folder, WSA Douglas File.

[59] Corresp in WSA Dir 12-18-42 folder and Read-ing File Dec 42–Jan 43 folder, WSA Douglas File.

[60] Douglas' notes on telephone conv with Wayne Coy, 9 Jan 43, WSA Dir 12-18-42 folder, WSA Douglas File.

[61] (1) Douglas' notes on lunch conf in Somervell's off, 9 Jan 43, WSA Dir 12-18-42 folder, WSA Douglas File. (2) See above, Ch. XV, and below, Ch. XXIV.

Somervell thereupon departed for the Casablanca Conference, and during the week following WSA and Army representatives quickly reached agreement on an operating procedure. The Navy held out longer. As late as 15 January McCloy told Douglas "the admirals had dropped anchor and had concluded to be very firm" (in demanding modification of the President's directive).[62] But on the next day Douglas, at a meeting in the office of the Vice Chief of Naval Operations, Admiral Horne (with Under Secretary Forrestal and several admirals present), received a promise of complete co-operation from Horne, who courteously but firmly quashed every objection raised by the still obdurate Admiral Griffin. (Griffin, in fact, was forthwith replaced as chief of the Naval Transportation Service by Rear Adm. William W. Smith.) On the 18th Douglas was able to report to the President that WSA and the military services had agreed upon a comprehensive plan for the programing of cargo movements. Under this plan, the Army and WSA at San Francisco and all Atlantic ports were jointly to work out on a continuous basis "a consolidated loading program embracing all cargo moving to identical destinations," subject, of course, to modification in the light of overriding military needs.[63] Whether the actual loading was to be done by WSA or Army agencies would be determined in each case on the basis of the most effective use of terminal facilities. It was further stipulated that the local joint committees carrying out this programing were not to constitute an echelon in the chain of command. At San Francisco, by a separate agreement with the Navy, the joint committee was to include naval representatives as well and work out a cargo loading program along tripartite lines.[64]

Douglas' victory was more form than substance. The directive of 18 December, still on the books, gave WSA a more solid basis than that provided by its charter for the power to exercise over-all co-ordination of all merchant shipping operations, including the loading of military cargo. But in view of Douglas' repeated disclaimers of any design to encroach upon the accustomed operations of the military transport services, this power remained largely theoretical as far as the actual loading of most military cargo was concerned. Whether the joint committees at the ports, with purely advisory functions, could succeed in working out effective cargo movement programs, pooling all types of cargo as extensively as Douglas desired, depended in the main on the degree to which Army and Navy officials were willing to co-operate in the endeavor. There was more pooling of cargo from January 1943 on than before, mainly because the logistical support of military operations overseas from the United States took on a more routine character that lent itself more readily to fairly stable programs. The military may have also been influenced by the thought that WSA might at any time reinvoke the formidable 18 December directive, and the President had left little doubt as to his views on the issues involved. To instill such a thought may well have been Douglas' whole purpose.

---

[62] Douglas' notes on telephone conv with McCloy, 15 Jan 43, WSA Dir 12-18-42 folder, WSA Douglas File.

[63] (1) WSA Progress Report to the President, 18 Jan 43, WSA Dir 12-18-42 folder, WSA Douglas File. (2) Douglas' notes cited n. 58(5).

[64] (1) Rpt cited n. 63(1). (2) Memo, Frazer Bailey for Douglas, 12 Jan 43, WSA Dir 12-18-42 folder, WSA Douglas File. (3) See papers in ABC 570. (12-21-42).

*Enlarging and Balancing
the Merchant Fleet*

Parallel with the drive by WSA for economy in ship utilization, the Maritime Commission had been working tirelessly to reverse the President's decision of July 1942 cutting back ship construction goals to less than indicated yard capacity. The commission asserted that at least 2.8 million more dead-weight tons, perhaps 4 million, could be built if the necessary steel were forthcoming. Admiral Land took his case first to Mr. Nelson and then, through Hopkins, to the President. In August and again in September the British also supported the plea for more construction, and in the latter month the Combined Shipping Adjustment Board, of which Admiral Land was chairman, strongly urged upon the Joint Chiefs the military advantages to be gained by adding four million tons to the 1943 program. "Every extra ship built," declared the board, "or made available by recommended economies, may be rightly regarded as meaning as much more military equipment in the sphere of combat as that ship can transport, and therefore a corresponding addition to U.S. troops in action." [65] The 3,400 tons of steel that went into a freighter, it pointed out, would thereby make it possible, in the course of a year, to transport overseas seven times that weight of military stores. In mid-October Land and Douglas appealed directly to the President. They rested their case on the argument that shipping was the limiting factor in the war effort.

The intricate chain of war activities is as weak as its weakest links. The two weakest links are merchant shipping and escorts. Many of the services demanding steel and other facilities will be unable to bring their forces to bear on the enemy unless the shipping shortage is relieved. Increased shipping tonnage will make our army more mobile, and increase the strength that can be concentrated against the enemy. Accordingly, the additional merchant shipping and escort vessels that can be produced in existing shipyard facilities should be, with a few other critical items such as a considered airplane program, the *constants in relation to which other factors in war production should be adjusted.* [66]

They urged a 2,856,000-ton increase in the 1943 merchant ship program and immediate construction of seventy corvette-type escort vessels. [67]

The escort vessel program by now had widespread support. Escort construction had suffered hitherto in competition with the landing craft program, which in July had been first on the Navy's precedence list, while escorts had been only tenth. By September escorts had moved up to third place, and the Joint Chiefs formally supported the Navy's contention that more must be built, even if at the expense of merchant ship construction. Merchant ships were being destroyed faster than they could be built, Admiral Leahy wrote the President in October, and enemy submarines were being built faster than they could be destroyed. Increased protection for shipping, Leahy pointed out, would not only reduce attrition but shorten turnaround (through more efficient scheduling), thus bringing more cargoes safely to their destinations. The President agreed and on 23 October added seventy more

[65] Memo, Land and Salter for CPRB, 28 Sep 42, with incls, filed with JPS 66/1/D, 1 Oct 42, title: Steel Alloc for Merchant Shipg, in ABC 411.5 (10-4-42) Sec 1.
[66] Memo, Land and Douglas for President, 16 Oct 42, ABC 411.5 (10-4-42) Sec 1. Italics are the authors'.
[67] (1) *Ibid.* (2) JCS 121, 4 Oct 42, title: Steel Alloc for Merchant Shipg. (3) William Chaikin and Charles H. Coleman, Shipbuilding Policies of the War Production Board, WPB Sp Study 26, pp. 43–45.

escort vessels to the Maritime Commission's program.[68]

There were other contenders for the role of "constant" in the mobilization program, and the common denominators of steel and facilities brought merchant shipping into competition with practically all of them. The Navy above all, fighting a rear guard action in defense of its program for major combat vessels, had to yield to the President's determination that air power must be favored, but strenuously resisted any addition to the merchant shipping program. Not merely steel, but many components—propulsion units, instruments, valves, turbines, gears—were involved in this conflict. Other programs became critical toward the end of the year—a proposed emergency "big inch" oil pipeline to run from Illinois to the East Coast, extending the existing line from the Texas oilfields, and synthetic rubber and high-octane gasoline plants. Naturally enough, the champions of any of these programs were ill disposed to accept the proposition that any other should be regarded as the "constant" to which their own should be adjusted. Army officials, for example, otherwise favorable to more merchant ship construction as likely to permit a larger troop deployment, lost some of their enthusiasm when it appeared that the necessary steel plate probably would have to come from the Army's allotment.[69]

There was no meeting of minds among the experts as to the precise extent to which additional merchant ship construction would conflict with other programs. Opinions differed, above all, as to whether the steel shortage would continue into the second quarter of 1943. When the emergency pipeline was approved in October, Nelson informed the JCS that

the military programs would necessarily be affected. Meanwhile, the decision on over-all production, demanded by WPB's verdict that existing programs exceeded the country's capacity to produce, could not wait. In the slimmed-down war production program that the Joint Chiefs approved on 24 November, $4.4 billion was tentatively included, pending later confirmation, for the Maritime Commission's several programs; the cost of the original two-year program of 24 million deadweight tons of construction had been only $3.6 billion. The larger figure was expected to provide in 1943 about 18.8 million dead-weight tons of merchant shipping, 50 to 70 escort vessels, and 50 light aircraft carriers. This was the only item of the military program representing an increase in goals.[70]

The military shipping experts, meanwhile, had been studying the implications of the proposed increase in terms of deployment. On 12 November the Joint Military Transportation Committee submitted to the Joint Chiefs a study revealing that, if the increased construction were

---

[68] (1) JCS 121/1, 24 Oct 42, title: Steel Alloc for Merchant Shipbuilding. (2) Memo, CofS for Army members JPS, 23 Oct 42, CofS WDGS Oct–Dec 42 (3A) folder, Hq ASF. (3) Memo, Leahy for President, 16 Oct 42, JCS 1942–44 folder, Hq ASF. (4) WPB Sp Study 26, pp. 18–20, 85–86, cited n. 67(3). (5) Mowry, Landing Craft and the War Production Board, WPB Sp Study 11, p. 74. (6) Corresp in ABC 570 (2-14-42) Sec 2.

[69] (1) Corresp in CCS 400.17 (7-6-42) Sec 3; CCS 452 (8-27-42) Sec 2; CCS 679 (10-22-42); and CCS 561.4 (9-29-42). (2) Memo, Somervell for Gross, 23 Sep 42. (3) Memo, Plng Div OCT for Gross, 7 Oct 42, with charts. Last two in Plng Div Studies folder, OCT HB. (4) Memo, Somervell for Marshall, 24 Sep 42, CofS WDGS 1942 (2) folder, Hq ASF.

[70] (1) Ltr, Nelson to JCS, 30 Oct 42. (2) Memo, Secy JPS for Secy JCS, 24 Oct 42. Both in CCS 679 (10-22-42). (3) JCS 121/1 cited n. 68(1). (4) JCS 121/2, 26 Oct 42, title: Steel Alloc for Merchant Shipbuilding. (5) Related corresp in CCS 561.4 (9-29-42). (6) JPS 74/10 cited n. 20(5). (7) Ltr cited n. 20(3).

given entirely to dry cargo shipping, much of this shipping would be left idle for lack of balancing troop-carrying capacity.[71] In any case, there were other categories of shipping in which additional tonnage was badly needed. One of these was small interisland freighters, needed primarily in the Southwest Pacific but also in the Alaskan area, the South Pacific, the Caribbean, and Iceland. Aggregate requirements, in November, were estimated at 135 vessels.[72]

There was also an indicated need for more tankers, despite the favorable trend of losses and construction during the second half of 1942. More than 3 million dead-weight tons, out of the 16 million set in July as the goal for 1943, represented tanker tonnage. In August OPD noted that tanker losses were still running at a rate which, if continued, would reduce the Allied tanker fleet by the following June by 16 percent. If Middle East oil were lost, the necessary changes in routing might require 140 more tankers than were now available. In October the British also were worried over their shrinking domestic stocks of petroleum products. The "big inch" pipeline was expected to bring economies after mid-1943 equivalent to a hundred or more tankers, largely for the benefit of United Kingdom imports. Even so, the Joint Military Transportation Committee predicted a deficit of about 82 "notional" tankers, equivalent to more than 900,000 dead-weight tons, by the end of 1942. Somervell told the Secretary of War at the end of October that "the shortage of tanker construction is more serious than in all other types of ships."[73]

The Joint Military Transportation Committee proposed, therefore, to divide the 2.8 million tons of additional construction among several types of vessels—troop transports, tankers, small and large cargo vessels—besides the authorizations already given for escorts and auxiliary aircraft carriers:

(a) 10 troop transports per month, by conversion of EC-2 (Liberty) hulls;
(b) about 100 "notional" tankers, mostly by conversion of EC-2 hulls;
(c) 80 small cargo ships, about 400 dead-weight tons each, diesel powered; new construction;
(d) EC-2 freighters up to the remaining capacity of yards, steel allocations, and auxiliary components.

Through the remainder of November and all of December the Joint Chiefs vainly sought to pry from the experts a clear "yes" or "no" to the question: Could the additional merchant shipping be built without interfering with other primary programs? On 3 December Mr. Nelson said that all the top-priority programs "would appear to fall within feasible limits," but that bottlenecks had to be overcome in raw materials, machine tools, and common components; much depend-

---

[71] JCS 151, rpt by JMTC, 13 Nov 42, title: Modification of 1943 Shipbuilding Prog `. . . .`

[72] See above, Ch. XV.

[73] (1) Memo, Col R. H. Givens for Brig Gen Albert C. Wedemeyer, 27 Aug 42, sub: Tanker Capacity of United Nations, ABC 570 (2-14-42) Sec 2. (2) Msg 3869, London to AGWAR, 21 Oct 42, OCT 565.3-900 England. (3) Memo, Somervell for SW, 30 Oct 42, Shipg 1941–43 folder, Hq ASF. (4) Memo, unsigned, no addressee, no date, sub: World-Wide Tanker-Borne Petroleum Reqmts, Incl C to JPS 74/9, 19 Nov 42, title: Tanker Needs To Meet Reqmts of Our Armed Forces. (5) JCS 151 cited n. 71.

Tanker estimates at this time varied widely, with respect to availability as well as to requirements. The tanker situation, therefore, is difficult to describe in terms of precise figures. The "notional" tanker was a fictitious stereotype used in planning, having 11,000 dead-weight tons, a speed of 10 knots, and operating for 320 days out of the year (the British allowed only 300 days). Tanker statistics, when actual vessels are meant, are difficult to reconcile owing to differences in categories.

ed on proper scheduling and expediting.[74] On the 23d he wrote Admiral Leahy that the additional shipping could be built without "unduly clashing" with other programs.[75] On the 31st he thought that completion of the augmented shipping program was "a reasonably safe expectancy."[76] None of these answers satisfied the military leaders, but nothing more definite was to be had. Meanwhile, Admiral Land late in November again came out strongly for additional construction, not of 2.8 million, but of 4 million deadweight tons over the original 16 million tons authorized for 1943. On 5 January, finally, the Joint Chiefs conditionally approved the 18,890,000-ton modified program—"provided it does not conflict with or delay the accomplishment of the 'Number 1 Group Program.'"[77]

The President was not troubled by any of these doubts. On 21 October Land and Douglas had discussed with him and Hopkins their recommendation for an increase in merchant shipbuilding, along with the question of naval escorts. The President expressed confidence that there would be plenty of steel to go around—if necessary, more could be taken from the public works program—and, after reading the Douglas-Land paper of 16 October, said that it "made sense" and should be approved.[78] Hopkins favored referring the matter to the JCS. Douglas objected that if this were done the proposal "would soon sink from sight in a swamp of military procedure."[79] The thing to do, he urged, was to summon the Joint Chiefs and tell them that the shipbuilding program had been decided upon. At the close of the meeting the President seemed to have decided to follow this course. Evidently one of the first to learn of the decision to expand the building program was Churchill, who

cabled back his congratulations to the President within a few days after the White House meeting of the 21st. With the Joint Chiefs the President apparently was not quite so forthright. On the 28th Admiral Leahy, on behalf of the JCS, advised him to withhold decision on the building program until it could be studied in conjunction with the other war production programs. To this the President blandly replied, two days later, that he was "very glad that it appears likely that the steel will be available for the increased merchant shipping" since this program was the "most important unfinished business we have from a production point of view." "Every day's delay in getting it started," he pointedly added, "means that the ships will come out at a later date on the other end."[80] Almost simultaneously Douglas was able to report that the British had offered to waive some 300,000 tons of their allocation of American steel during the next five months "on the understanding that this steel will be used to augment the shipbuilding program here."[81] More steel

---

[74] Ltr cited n. 28(1).

[75] Ltr, Nelson to Leahy, 23 Dec 42, CCS 561.4 (11-12-42) Sec 2.

[76] Ltr cited n. 28(5).

[77] (1) Min, 49th mtg JCS, 5 Jan 43. (2) Ltr, JCS to Nelson, 6 Jan 43, CCS 561.4 (11-12-42) Sec 2. (3) Other corresp in same file and in CCS 561.4 (11-12-42) Sec 1. (4) On 3 March 1943 the JCS told Adm Land it was thought inadvisable to construct more than the 2.8 million tons additional. Ltr, Leahy to Land, 3 Mar 43, ABC 411.5 (10-4-42) Sec 1. Actual maritime construction in 1943 came to 19,209,991 tons, including 632,293 tons of military types. See Lane, *Ships for Victory*, p. 343.

[78] Douglas' notes on conf with President, Hopkins, and Land, 21 Oct 42, Hopkins folder, WSA Douglas File.

[79] *Ibid.*

[80] (1) Memo, President for Leahy, 30 Oct 42. (2) Memo, Leahy for President, 28 Oct 42. Both in CCS 561.4 (9-29-42).

[81] Ltr, Douglas to Isador Lubin, 2 Nov 42, Construction folder, WSA Douglas File.

ARMY, NAVY, AND CIVILIAN CHIEFS *at lunch, 8 December 1942. Left to right: General Arnold, Admiral Land, Harry Hopkins, Admiral William D. Leahy, Paul V. McNutt, Admiral King, Donald Nelson, Elmer Davis, and Brig. Gen. John R. Deane.*

also seemed likely to be forthcoming from other programs held up by other shortages. And on 30 November, following the decision on the total war production program for 1943, the President wrote Churchill:

. . . we are moving aggressively here to increase [merchant shipping] . . . and have given [it] . . . the highest priority for matériel and machine tools . . . . we have, after reexamination of our steel plate problem and other facilities, determined to increase it to 18,800,000 deadweight tons in 1943. I intend to raise this to 20 million if . . . it should prove possible.[82]

Finally, early in December, the President wrote Land authorizing him "to make plans at once and to obtain approval from the Bureau of the Budget to build an additional 2,889,000 tons of merchant shipping." Curiously enough, in view of his earlier actions, he sent this memorandum first to Admiral Leahy with a covering note, "I am going to send this to Land unless the Joint Board [*sic*] protests. Let me know."[83] Leahy received the letter on the 8th. This apparently was the first unequivocal intimation to the military chiefs that the President had decided to go ahead with the augmented shipping program. As recently as the 5th, Brig. Gen.

[82] (1) Ltr, President to Prime Minister, 30 Nov 42, ABC 400 (11-19-42). (2) Douglas' notes cited n. 78. (3) Corresp in Construction folder, WSA Douglas File. (4) Lane, *Ships for Victory,* p. 339.

[83] Memo, President for Land, no date, cited in WPB Sp Study 26, p. 16, n. 42, cited above n. 67(3), and in Lane, *Ships for Victory,* p. 340, n. 19. The WPB study gives the two dates of transmission of this memo. Lane dates it before 24 November, on the assumption that the JCS action on that date on the over-all production program constituted final approval of the Maritime Commission program. It seems more likely (to the present author) that it was written early in December, shortly before its actual delivery.

John R. Deane, the secretary of the JCS, had noted that the 18.8 million tons of shipping had not yet been approved by the JCS nor, to his knowledge, by the President. At any rate, the Joint Chiefs bowed at once to the President's desires, and on the 14th Leahy forwarded the President's letter to Land with the added comment: "Joint Chiefs of Staff approve." In the light of this sequence of events, their conditional approval of the program three weeks later, on 6 January, seems somewhat anticlimactic.[84]

The Fever Chart of Deployment Forecasting

Approximately 1,060,000 Army troops were overseas at the end of 1942. In August of that year Somervell's staff, heartened by the decline in shipping losses and not anticipating the costs of TORCH and its affiliated enterprises in longer sea voyages and less efficient use of shipping, had hoped to have 1,200,000 troops overseas by the end of the year and 2,900,000 at the end of 1943. But in September, as losses took an upward turn and these costs began to manifest themselves, the staff lowered its estimates for both 1942 and 1943. Under various assumptions, the staff produced forecasts for end-1943 overseas strength ranging from 1,560,000 to 2,470,000—all based on the estimated sustaining capacity of cargo shipping. A deficit was expected in troop-carrying capacity, but it was hoped that borrowed British transports would make up the difference.[85]

In November the planners took a new reading to determine the probable effects of the proposed augmentation of merchant ship construction in 1943. In the light of the earlier studies, the elaborate calculations of the Joint Military Transportation Committee (submitted to the JCS on 12 November) were scarcely needed to show that little would be gained by building more cargo shipping unless it were balanced by additional troop-carrying tonnage. The proposed augmentation, if it were to consist entirely of new dry cargo shipping, would build up a tremendous sustaining capacity in 1943, sufficient to support a troop population of over 2.8 million overseas—which was almost 400,000 more than could be built up by all the troop transport in sight.[86] The committee recommended that part of the increased construction be used to build troop-carrying capacity so that, with expected British assistance, it would approximately balance the sustaining capacity of cargo shipping. Under the most favorable assumptions, it appeared that troop strength overseas might now be brought up to 2.7 million.

Even as these studies were being prepared and debated, enemy submarines and the drift of strategic plans were demolishing their basic assumptions. When the staffs looked anew into the crystal ball in December and January, they had to

---

[84] (1) *Ibid.* (2) Memo, Deane for Leahy, King, Marshall, and Arnold, 5 Dec 42, CCS 400.17 (2-20-42) Sec 2. (3) On 26 December the Joint Chiefs saw for the first time a copy of the President's 30 November letter to Churchill, revealed to them "very unofficially and confidentially" by the British military representatives. Memo, Deane for Marshall, King, and Arnold, 26 Dec 42, CCS 400 (11-30-42). At Sir John Dill's suggestion to Hopkins, the President finally sent them a copy formally two weeks later. Memo, President for Marshall, 8 Jan 43, same file.

[85] (1) Memo, Somervell for G-3, 26 Aug 42, Plng Div Studies folder, OCT HB. (2) Related papers in same file. (3) Memo cited n. 69(2). (4) JPS 57/4, 23 Sep 42, title: Availability of United Nations Shipg for Mil Trans.

[86] JCS 151 cited n. 71.

start from a lower base figure for existing tonnage and to assume a higher rate of losses for 1943 than they had in their previous calculations. Campaigns in the Mediterranean could be expected to bring heavy attrition, and expanding operations in the Pacific meant a longer average turnaround. These pessimistic assumptions, mainly affecting cargo shipping, tipped the balance again. It now appeared that cargo shipping in 1943 might be barely sufficient to support two million troops overseas, while troop shipping, even with heavier losses and longer turnarounds than assumed in November, would have the capacity to build up overseas strength to 2.6 million.[87]

Deployment forecasting had come full circle. Once again, as in late summer 1942, cargo shipping loomed as the limiting factor. But it was not until 5 January that the Joint Chiefs finally decided to approve the modified building program that in November had appeared necessary to preserve balance in the merchant fleet. By this time the modification seemed likely to throw it completely out of balance. This was only one of many matters hurriedly disposed of on the eve of the Casablanca Conference. During January deployment planning floundered or remained in abeyance, awaiting the firm decisions on grand strategy that it was hoped would emerge from the conference. A subcommittee of the Joint Planners, given the task of matching deployment requirements against available shipping during the first half of 1943, confirmed the general impression given by the December studies that cargo shipping would be the bottleneck in overseas deployment, particularly during the first half of the year, even though there would be local shortages in troop shipping. On 10 February, accord-

ingly, the Joint Chiefs wrote Admiral Land that they thought a "more flexible viewpoint" was now in order and that they desired to suspend the program for converting freighter hulls to troop transports.[88]

But events would not stand still. At Casablanca it had been decided to adopt common shipping loss factors in all British and American deployment planning. Early in February the Combined Military Transportation Committee recommended separate loss rate factors for the first and second half of 1943, broken down in percentages by type as follows: [89]

	Dry Cargo	Tankers
Average	2.15	1.58
1st half 1943	2.39	1.78
2d half 1943	1.91	1.38

These figures, which the CCS accepted forthwith, were well under the actual loss rates of 1942 (weighted average 2.16 percent).[90] Cargo shipping forecasts for 1943

[87] (1) Capabilities of Dry Cargo Shipg . . . 4 Jan 43 tab, 18 Shipg file, II, Case 36, Plng Div ASF, Job A46-371. (2) Shipg Implications of Certain Proposed Opns 8 Jan 43 tab, Incl IX in Proposed Opns in Certain Theaters, 4 Dec 42, study prepared by Strategic Logis Div SOS, in Plng Div ASF, Job A47-147. (3) Plng Div OCT paper, 12 Jan 43, sub: Basic Data for Possible Growth of U.S. Forces Overseas 1943 and 1944. (4) Plng Div OCT paper, 12 Jan 43, sub: U.S. Dry Cargo Shipg Employment and Availability 1943 and 1944. Last two in Plng Div Studies folder, OCT HB.

[88] (1) Ltr, JCS to Land, 10 Feb 43, ABC 570 (2-14-42) Sec 4. (2) Related papers in same file. (3) JPS 92/2, rpt by JPS subcom, 2 Feb 43, title: Trans Reqmts to 1 Jul 43. (4) Min, 60th mtg JCS, 2 Feb 43; 61st mtg, 9 Feb 43. (5) Memo, Col Vissering for Plng Div OCT, 26 Jan 43, sub: Availability of Shipg, 18 Shipg file, II, Case 46, Plng Div ASF. (6) For Casablanca Conference, see below, Ch. XXV.

[89] The dry cargo category included all cargo vessels other than tankers and other than nontankers permanently controlled by the fighting services. Tankers, however, included those controlled by the fighting services (for example, Navy oilers).

[90] (1) CCS 174 cited n. 38(1). (2) Min, 55th mtg CCS, 14 Jan 43; 70th mtg, 5 Feb 43.

accordingly climbed upward again. Using an average loss rate of 2 percent, instead of the 2.6 percent used in the studies that influenced the Joint Chiefs to adopt their "more flexible viewpoint," the SOS staff produced estimates early in February (even before the JCS decision on the 10th) indicating that cargo shipping in 1943 would be able to support almost 300,000 more troops overseas than troop shipping could transport. Moreover, OPD was working out plans for reducing overseas garrisons and shifting troops from static to active areas; the troops thus moved would engage passenger tonnage, but relatively little cargo tonnage, without adding to total strength overseas. Late in February Gross informed Somervell that, on the basis of all these considerations, he expected an increase of less than 1.1 million in the overseas troop population during 1943, though cargo shipping would support many more. He suggested that it might be advisable to resume the conversion of cargo vessels to troop transports in order to restore the balance. Precisely sixteen days earlier the Joint Chiefs had hoped to achieve balance by suspending conversion.[91]

The logistical planners might reasonably have concluded after this experience that the effort to keep up with the bewildering oscillation of the factors on which their planning had to rest was not worth the candle, and that long-range logistical planning was an art better forgotten. Nevertheless their long-range estimates of deployment capabilities were the most up-to-date and best-informed predictions available, and certainly afforded a more reliable guide than some of the wishful estimates then being produced by the strategic planners. It was perhaps no coincidence that the whole function of logistical planning was at this time undergoing critical re-examination in the JCS committee system, with a view to enabling it to contribute more effectively to the formulation of strategy.

---

[91] (1) On the reduction of overseas garrisons, see corresp in ABC 320.2 (3-14-43) Sec 1, and in ABC 370.5 (2-2-43). (2) Memo, Col Marcus B. Stokes, Jr., for Col Chamberlain, 2 Feb 43, Plng Div Studies folder, OCT HB. (3) Memo, Gross for Somervell, 26 Feb 43, sub: Deployment of U.S. Army Forces in 1943, Item 16, Exec 1. (4) Eventually more than 400 freighters—Libertys and standard types—were fitted with temporary or permanent accommodations for troop service. See Wardlow, *Trans I*, Ch. VIII.

CHAPTER XXIII

Economy and Stabilization

Economy and system could hardly be called the keynotes of the Army's logistical operations during 1942. But to recognize this is not to disparage the significance of the trend that became evident toward the end of that year. By the following spring the trend had become more positive. Administrative reform, especially in the development of routine procedures, was marching forward on a broad front and there was much talk of economy and conservation, accompanied by some effective action. Most significant, the probable limits of war production had been authoritatively defined, and the scale of military mobilization had been compressed to fit within those limits. The trend was far from orderly, however, and was accompanied by much misdirected effort and interagency friction. In the spring of 1943 the economy drive, at least, could show few tangible results. Not until late 1943 and 1944 was the whole movement toward economy and system to reach full tide, as the period of mobilization yielded to one of stabilized and more carefully regulated effort.

The Reduced Army Supply Program

The great cutback in military supply finally ordered in November 1942 was reflected in two revisions of the Army Supply Program: that of 12 November 1942 (already in preparation while the committees were working out the Joint Chiefs' reply to Mr. Nelson's letter of 19 October), and

that of 1 February 1943. The two may conveniently be analyzed together. (*See Table 20.*)

In the main, the reduction in requirements was accomplished by reducing the size of forces to be supplied and equipped, especially the heavily accoutered elements. Late in August the SOS staff was computing Army supply requirements for 1943 on the basis of a terminal strength of 8.2 million enlisted men. For the 1 September revision of the equipment program this figure was reduced for procurement of critical items to 7.8 million enlisted men, and for procurement of essential items to 7.5 million. Reductions were also ordered in the troop bases used for computation of the 1944 program, bringing these figures down from 9.8 million enlisted men to less than 9.5 million. The 1 September Army Supply Program formed part of the total war production program for 1943 which, despite these reductions, the WPB attacked in October as too large for the national economy to support. Accordingly, procurement goals for critical items of equipment were reduced to the amounts required for 7.5 million enlisted men, conforming to the level already ordered with respect to essential items, and the presidential "must" items in this category, wherever they exceeded computed requirements for the troop basis, were cut back to this level. The Army Supply Program that emerged from this ordeal of purgation in November had thus been shrunk to the general proportions indicated by the 1943 troop mobilization program of 8.2 million officers and men finally approved by the President in the same month.[1]

The composition of the 1943 Army was also a subject of lively debate. As late as August 1942 it had been intended to mobilize 143 divisions by the end of 1943, and 192 by 1944, heavily weighted with armored, motorized, and airborne elements. By the end of 1942 the objective had been lowered to a hundred divisions for 1943, the deepest cuts having been made in armored, motorized, and mountain divisions, and in nondivisional tank-destroyer, tank, artillery, and infantry units. Earlier goals of 1.2 million service troops were reduced to about a million. The Air Forces' planned strength of over 2 million remained untouched. Of the total 7.5 million enlisted men planned for 1943, .5 million were to be set aside as an unassigned pool for unexpected contingencies; for these personnel, therefore, no organizational equipment requirements were included in the supply program.[2]

The supply program was not held in its entirety to the level of computed requirements for a 7.5-million-man army. In the February 1943 supply program were included sixteen additional divisional sets of initial equipment for 1943, and forty-eight additional sets for 1943–44, along with similar requirements for a number of other additional nondivisional units. In effect, these additional requirements added a 20 percent surplus or strategic reserve to the supply program, part of which was expected to be used to outfit troops of Allied and liberated countries, notably the Fighting French.[3]

Nevertheless, the new supply programs marked a turning point of no little signifi-cance in the development of the war economy, for they represented the first attempt to use the yardstick of productive capacity to limit the aggregate volume of military supply. After requirements had been computed, they were checked by major categories both against the capacity of industrial facilities and against the amounts of critical raw materials expected to be available, and necessary reductions were made. Lend-lease requirements, other than those of the Soviet protocol, were drastically cut, and the 50 percent allowances of critical items of equipment (other than rifles) already applied to troops in training in 1942 were extended to the bulk of the forces expected to be in training during 1943; some twenty divisions, thirty-two tank-destroyer battalions, fourteen tank battalions, and seventy assorted artillery units, besides other components, were so affected.[4]

The computation of maintenance allow-

---

[1] (1) Frank, Army Supply Requirements, pp. 34–36 and Docs 40, 42, OCMH. (2) See above, Ch. XXII.

[2] Greenfield, Palmer, and Wiley, *AGF I,* pp. 214–17.

Actually, the unassigned pool was absorbed before the end of 1942 by allocations to AAF, the Women's Army Auxiliary Corps, and the Army Specialized Training Program.

[3] (1) Frank, Army Supply Requirements, Doc 72, OCMH. (2) See also, Robert R. Palmer, "Ground Forces in the Army, December 1941–April 1945: A Statistical Study," in Greenfield, Palmer, and Wiley, *AGF I.*

In order to provide a statistical basis for computing this strategic reserve, the 1944 Troop Basis, for supply purposes, was assumed to total over 9 million enlisted men, even though there was no expectation that more than 7.5 million would actually be mobilized. Equipment actually assigned to French and other Allied forces in 1943 naturally would have to come from existing stocks and current production. The strategic reserve in the supply program merely provided for eventual absorption of these and similar requirements. For French rearmament, see above, Ch. XVIII.

[4] (1) Frank, Army Supply Requirements, pp. 35–36, 52–55, and Docs 47, 51, 73, OCMH. (2) For effect on assignments to the British, see above, Ch. XI.

ances in the new supply program was also more economical in some particulars than in previous programs. Allowances for combat maintenance not only were based on estimated average instead of year-end overseas strengths but also were applied only to active theatres. Hawaii and overseas areas in the Western Hemisphere— since subject only to "sporadic raids"— were considered to be part of the zone of interior. By this last expedient some 400,000 troops per year were lopped off the total number for which combat maintenance would otherwise have been provided. Calculations of maintenance were also based upon an expectation that the troop population overseas would reach about 2.5 million by the end of 1943 and 4 million by the end of 1944—more realistic figures than those used in the September and earlier programs. Rates of combat maintenance remained generally unchanged—averaging about 4 percent per month for all types of equipment.

As in earlier programs, allowances for maintenance actually included some for filling the pipeline and making good losses incurred in the process of distribution, over and above a separate distribution or "pipeline" allowance labeled as such. The latter was a flat percentage of total initial equipment requirements (applied to the 7.5-million and 9-million troop bases). In addition, provision was made for four and a half months of reserve stocks in all overseas theaters, based on terminal overseas strength in 1943 and 1944, besides the regular flow of maintenance. Finally, to absorb shipping losses, an allowance of 2 percent of all material expected to be shipped overseas was added. This 2 percent was roughly equivalent to the planning factors established early in 1943 by agreement with the British.

The whole theory of distribution allowances had been for some time under critical examination. The most significant result of this study was the development, by the requirements staff of the Office of The Quartermaster General, of the so-called carry-over method of computing distribution allowances. Under this method the Quartermaster staff proposed to change the current system of computing distribution allowances as flat percentages of initial allowances. Pointing to the obvious fact that distribution allowances actually served to set up stocks throughout the pipeline during one period to meet maintenance needs that would emerge in the period following, the staff suggested that distribution allowances be merged with maintenance allowances, and that both be expressed in terms of numbers of days or months of use or consumption. Under the same assumption, the allowances would be computed on the basis of the troop strength during the period when the stocks were actually to be used. As proposed by the Office of The Quartermaster General in September 1942, this method would actually have provided more generous distribution allowances than those currently embodied in the supply program, but it was combined with certain economies in the computation of maintenance allowances. Whether the net result of applying this plan would have been more or less economical than the current methods is uncertain. At all events, the September and November revisions of the supply program carried forward the old system of distribution and maintenance allowances. In the February revision, however, the Office of The Quartermaster General was permitted to compute its own supply requirements by a method that embodied the carry-over principle, merging distribution with maintenance allowances. In the computations for the next revision, scheduled for August 1943, distribution allowances, as such, were abandoned for the whole program.[5]

The February revision also marked the first attempt to determine total assets of material on hand—that is, in the pipeline and in the possession of troops—in order to arrive at net requirements for production. The effort was not very successful. Inventory records were fragmentary, inaccurate, or nonexistent, especially at levels below the depots, and there was no practicable means of inventorying material in the hands of troops or in the distribution system overseas. The only reasonably accurate relevant data for 1942 were the amounts of material produced, number of troops inducted, and certain known losses such as ship sinkings. It was necessary therefore to combine these data with estimates of aggregate "wastage" during 1942 and with what few reliable inventory records existed to produce a hypothetical "on hand" figure as of 1 January 1943. A simpler method by which "on hand" amounts would have been defined solely in terms of quantities available for issue in depots in the United States (arbitrarily assuming that the remaining quantities in the pipeline and in the hands of troops were adequate for purposes of distribution) was rejected because it was believed desirable to have a statement of total (gross) requirements in the supply program. Only in the case of ammunition were "on hand" quantities defined as stocks available for issue in the United States. Computed requirements for ammunition accordingly omitted allowances for reserves for the one-million-odd troops already overseas at the end of 1942. The deplorable state of stock records revealed

in the course of the effort to determine "on hand" assets was one of the factors leading, in the spring of 1943, to a wholesale reform of the stock control system.[6]

Subsistence requirements were based on the mobilization troop basis of 7.5 million for 1943 and 1944, but with the addition of several other categories of personnel that would have to be fed: officers, Army nurses, Women's Army Auxiliary Corps, and prisoners of war. The total strength, for both 1943 and 1944, came to about 8.7 million. Allowances were also provided for clothing and individual equipment to be sold to officers and to be issued to prisoners of war, and an additional allowance of 18 percent ("attrition" factor) was provided to absorb losses through severance of personnel from the service.[7] *(Table 20)*

The Attack on Waste

The slashes made in the great military supply programs late in 1942 were the most conspicuous products of a growing pressure, evident within the Military Establishment as well as exerted upon it from without, to abate the extravagance attendant upon mobilization and deployment pushed at full speed. This economy drive had many facets. In one important respect it was merely a continuation of the unending effort to maximize the effectiveness of shipping—through more efficient administration of ship operations and rigorous subordination of less to more essential de-

---

[5] (1) Donald F. Bradford, *Methods of Forecasting War Requirements for Quartermaster Supplies*, QMC Hist Study 14 (Washington, 1946), pp. 100–109. (2) Erna Risch, *The Quartermaster Corps: I, Organization, Supply, and Services*, UNITED STATES ARMY IN WORLD WAR II (Washington, 1953), pp. 224–25.

[6] Frank, Army Supply Requirements, pp. 42–44, 57–58, and Doc 75, OCMH.

[7] *Ibid.*, pp. 58–60, and Docs 77–78.

TABLE 20—REDUCTION OF 1943 ARMY SUPPLY PROGRAM: NOVEMBER 1942
(MILLIONS OF DOLLARS)

Program	September 1942	12 November 1942	Reduction
Total Army Supply Program [a]	$40,660	$35,360	$5,300
Section I	25,160	18,910	6,250
II	4,460	5,410	+950
III	2,900	3,300	+400
IV	920	1,700	+780
V	6,220	5,040	1,180
VI	1,000	1,000	0
Aircraft program	8,140	9,750	+1,610
ASP Section I	1,360	760	600
II	3,860	5,410	+1,550
IV	920	1,700	+780
V	2,000	1,880	120
Lend-lease and Soviet protocol (excluding Navy lend-lease)	8,700	6,800	1,900
ASP Section I	7,500	5,800	1,700
II	200	0	200
VI	1,000	1,000	0
Army ground program	18,800	14,850	3,950
ASP Section I	15,500	11,550	3,950
II	400	0	400
III	2,900	3,300	+400
Navy program (including Navy lend-lease, but excluding minor combat vessels)	800	800	0
ASP Section I	800	800	0
Military construction and war housing (excluding airfields and bases)	3,260	2,200	1,060
ASP Section V	3,260	2,200	1,060
Industrial facilities (excluding those for aircraft, merchant ships, and critical materials)	960	960	0
ASP Section V	960	960	0

[a] For revision of the total war production program, see table 18. The figures shown for the specific programs listed represent only those portions of the programs covered by the Army Supply Program. The Army ground program was the only one entirely covered by the ASP, and must be narrowly defined in order to be so covered. Construed somewhat more broadly, as it is on page 000, the Army ground program was cut back by about 23.6 percent; the reduction indicated in the table above is about 21 percent.

Source: Adapted from Doc 44 in Frank, Army Supply Requirements, OCMH.

mands upon shipping. The ramifications of this last line of endeavor were virtually boundless, since it implied a critical scrutiny of the essentiality of every item of military equipment and supply that might ever have to be shipped overseas. Moreover, economy of supply was coming to be regarded by spring of 1943 as an end in

TABLE 21—SHIPPING SPACE REQUIRED FOR MOVING A DIVISION OVERSEAS: LATE 1942

Item	Infantry Division			Armored Division		
	Ship Tons	Percent of Total		Ship Tons	Percent of Total	
		With Vehicles on Wheels	With Vehicles Boxed		With Vehicles on Wheels	With Vehicles Boxed
Total:						
With vehicles on wheels.....................	144, 704	100. 0	—	239, 919	100. 0	—
With vehicles boxed........................	106, 135	—	100. 0	194, 179	—	100. 0
Organizational equipment, fuel and lubricants [a]						
With vehicles on wheels.....................	63, 857	44. 1	—	139, 049	57. 9	—
With vehicles boxed........................	25, 288	—	23. 8	93, 309	—	48. 1
Personnel, with individual equipment [b]...........	58, 200	40. 2	54. 8	55, 000	22. 9	28. 3
Ammunition (10 units of fire)....................	5, 582	3. 8	5. 2	9, 763	4. 1	5. 0
30 days of maintenance [c].......................	17, 065	11. 9	16. 2	36, 107	15. 1	18. 6

Dash equals inapplicable.

[a] Includes thirty days' gasoline and oil. Gasoline requirements based on 1.2 gallons per man per day for infantry, about 4.1 gallons for armored elements.

[b] These figures based on 3.75 ship tons per man (FM 101-10, 1941 edition, par. 116).

[c] Maintenance on a basis of 1.1 ship tons per man per month, excluding ammunition, gasoline, and oil; armored elements include 25 percent replacement of vehicles per month besides normal maintenance.

Infantry Division: 15,514 personnel, 2,322 vehicles.

Armored Division: 14,643 personnel, 3,698 vehicles.

Source: Miscellaneous Shipping Data, Logis File, OCMH.

itself, apart from its impact upon the specific problem of shipping; there was a growing feeling that waste, whether or not the item wasted was plentiful, could no longer be tolerated.

The most direct road to economy in shipping was by reduction of the tonnages that were to be shipped. Since Army cargo tended to be bulky in proportion to its weight, two approaches were involved— reduction of items and quantities required and compression of bulky items, through efficient stowage, packing, and crating, into smaller space. The main hope for economy, ironically enough, lay in reducing the very element by which the modern army had striven to make itself mobile—motor transport—since the human body was an irreducible item, and the soldier's individual equipment and supply, even his weapons and ammunition, while more elaborate than at any other time in history, still represented a relatively small part of the Army's total paraphernalia. The great bulk of it was made up of vehicles and the fuel that they consumed. (*Table 21*)

Since early in 1942 the necessity of reducing organic allowances of equipment, especially of vehicles, in order to permit maximum troop deployment with available shipping had been apparent to everyone. There were even those, such as General McNair, the AGF commander, who believed that judicious pruning of motor transport, if accompanied by rigorous pooling, reductions in unessential equipment, and abandonment of the effort to make the division completely self-sufficient, would not merely reduce weight and bulk but would actually make American ground forces, unit for unit, more mobile and effective in combat. Looming shortages of rubber, in spring of 1942, indicated that motor transport would have to be reduced in any case, and the first attempts to draw up shipping schedules for BOLERO revealed in concrete terms the extent to which capacity to deploy forces overseas on a large scale and over a long period could be defined in terms of the capacity to move cargo. In June 1942 the Chief of Staff ordered Army Ground Forces to make the "maximum practicable reduction of motor transport and of administrative overhead in all types of units to save cargo space." [8]

But each truck and each weapon, in the existing tables, had its vehement defenders who were convinced it was indispensable. In March 1942 the infantry division, following months of study, was actually enlarged, receiving additional personnel, weapons, and 219 more motor vehicles than in earlier tables. In April and May AGF made certain reductions in organic motor transport for infantry and artillery units, substituting light vehicles for some heavy ones and eliminating others. By agreement with SOS, moreover, AGF succeeded in reducing somewhat the scale of maintenance vehicles assigned to the infantry regiment. But the mountainous backlog of equipment left behind by the Western Task Force for lack of shipping to move it vividly demonstrated the inadequacy of the economies thus far achieved. On 2 October the War Department ordered the three major commands to review their tables of organization with a view to

eliminating 20 percent of the motor transport and 15 percent of the personnel. This order, as G-3 admitted, remained essentially an exhortation, since no machinery of enforcement—no board of "No-Men," as General McNair had urged—was provided to overrule pleas to retain or augment equipment allowances. Each command, in effect, was told to provide its own "No-Men." When the War Department a little later reduced the troop basis, notably in armored, mobile, and heavily equipped components, it confessed in effect that the Army was still equipped on a scale too lavish to permit its full deployment overseas in available shipping. The trend, it was announced, must be "toward light, easily transportable units." [9]

Pressure to add armament to units was heavy and continuous. A proposal by General Somervell in spring of 1943, for example, would have quadrupled the number of truck-mounted .50-caliber machine guns and provided many 3-inch antitank cannon for protecting motor convoys and advanced depots. There were other demands to assign heavier weapons organically to divisions, which meant adding more organic transport as well. Partly because of the growing emphasis on air power, partly because of the temperament and convictions of General McNair, the task of making units light and transportable fell mainly upon the Army Ground Forces. An AGF Reduction Board early in 1943 proposed sweeping

---

[8] (1) Greenfield, Palmer, and Wiley, *AGF I*, pp. 281–82. (2) JAdC 7, 15 May 43, title: Measures for Effecting Economies in Cargo Shipg. (3) JCS 339, 26 May 43, same title.

[9] (1) Memo, G-3 for AGF and SOS, 25 Oct 42, sub: Tr Basis 1943, WDGCT 320.2 Gen (10-25-42). (2) AG ltr to maj comds, 2 Oct 42, sub: Revision of Orgn and Equip Reqmts, AG 400 (9-30-42). (3) Greenfield, Palmer, and Wiley, *AGF I,* pp. 286–89.

alterations in the organization tables of virtually all ground combat units, involving a reduction of the infantry division's vehicles, for example, from 2,149 to 1,640, its antitank and field artillery pieces from 181 to 129. These reforms were accepted only in part. In revised tables issued in July 1943, the infantry division emerged with 2,012 vehicles and 123 artillery pieces. The armored division, however, which in March 1942 had 490 tanks and 3,630 wheeled noncombat vehicles, was pared down drastically in 1943 to 263 tanks and 2,653 noncombat vehicles.[10]

In the service establishment, economy came even more slowly. Service support in most overseas theaters was inadequate throughout 1942, and the SOS fought persistently to build it up. Economies were sought primarily by elimination of units of regimental and brigade size (too large for most overseas areas) and by creating general purpose, composite organizations with interchangeable parts rather than specialized units. But this program was hardly more than well under way in spring of 1943.[11]

Standardization of equipment and supplies and of the quantities in which they were issued was itself a potential source of wasted shipping space whenever the planners failed to give adequate consideration to the peculiar local conditions under which the material was to be used. The problem was not as simple, perhaps, as the more flagrant mistakes—stockpiling of antifreeze fluid and wool shirts in Puerto Rico, for example—would indicate. Specialization to fit local conditions could be carried too far—as commanders in the Pacific found when they equipped their troops lightly in the Japanese manner— and it might require more, not less shipping. Nevertheless, it seemed difficult to justify the shipping of full allowances of trucks to Pacific islands that were devoid of roads, or full allowances of ground radio equipment to air squadrons in the United Kingdom where the British communications net was at their disposal. And the overburdening of the individual soldier going overseas (a composite evil resulting both from overspecialization and overstandardization) remained generally unremedied in the spring of 1943. Officers as highly placed as General McNair considered it scandalous, but were apparently unable to do anything about it. In general, the War Department had to depend on overseas commanders to request whatever departures from standard equipment tables they considered appropriate for their particular areas, but overseas commanders, while quick to ask for additional equipment and supplies, both standard and special, seldom bothered to specify which items troops coming into their areas might leave behind. In April 1943 the War Department was still admonishing them to do so. "The issue of equipment to individuals and units," an investigating committee observed later in the summer, "simply because the documentary tables call for it, is sheer waste." [12]

---

[10] (1) Greenfield, Palmer, and Wiley, *AGF I*, pp. 290ff and tables on pp. 274–75, 320–21.
All these changes involved changes in personnel strength as well. (2) See below, Apps. A-4, A-5.

[11] (1) See above, Ch. XIII. (2) Memo, Marshall for McNair, Somervell, and Edwards, 29 Dec 42. (3) Memo, Somervell for CofS, 31 Dec 42, sub: Orgn of Sv Trs. Last two in CofS WDGS (3A) folder, Hq ASF. (4) Memo, Lutes for CofS ASF, 5 May 43, sub: Proposed Orgn of Sv Activities, Sv Trs 1942–43 folder, Case 55, Lutes File. (5) Memo, G-3 for CG SOS, 12 Jan 43, sub: Reorgn of Sv Units, WDGCT 320 (1-12-43).

[12] (1) Report of WD Procurement Review Board, p. 54. (2) JCS 339 cited n. 8(3). (3) WD ltr to overseas comdrs, 5 Apr 43, sub: Equip and Sup To Accommodate Overseas Tr Mvmts, AG 400 (3-4-43).

Economy through packing and crating, especially of motor vehicles, was energetically pursued and loudly debated through 1942. Early British estimates for the BOLERO program looked forward to massive savings by shipping vehicles completely knocked down (CKD) in crates, but the problem of assembling the vehicles at the receiving end created difficulties. Before the end of 1942 some vehicles were being shipped CKD to the British Isles, though in limited numbers because of the shortage of labor, and also to India, Australia, and New Zealand; plans to set up CKD assembly facilities in the Red Sea area did not materialize. The more widely used method of shipment was the more easily assembled twin-unit pack (TUP), or medium knocked down pack (MKD), which by the end of 1942 had been developed to the point where it occupied only about a third of the space occupied by a fully erected truck. This technique, by which two vehicles were broken down sufficiently to be crated in from two to five separate packs, superseded earlier variants, such as the single-unit pack (SUP), and was used to ship large numbers of standard vehicles to practically all the theaters, except where adequate CKD facilities existed and in combat-loaded movements. TUP shipments offered the advantage that they could be erected by comparatively inexperienced personnel without heavy tools; two mechanics with eight unskilled helpers performed satisfactorily in one test. At the beginning of 1943 plans envisaged crating of 80 percent of all vehicles to be sent overseas in that year, a goal that in fact was almost attained.

Economy in the shipment of vehicles was also sought through the provision of sufficient spare parts to ensure maximum use of all vehicles sent overseas. The major problem here was in maintaining the large number of old-model nonstandard vehicles overseas that were used by British forces. A General Motors representative returning from the Middle East in February 1943 reported that out of 120,000 (largely American-type) vehicles in that whole area, 20,000 were laid up for repairs. American forces in the Pacific were also plagued by the "old-model" problem.[13]

Improvements in stowage and packing were sought in many other ways. By mid-1943, for example, the Ordnance Department reported an 8 percent saving in space through better-designed ammunition containers. A new "V"-type fiber box had allegedly brought about a 16 percent saving in the packing of subsistence. By removing one wheel of motorcycles and rearranging other parts in packing, shipping space had been reduced by a third, and a similar saving had been made in packing the Browning .50-caliber machine gun. Savings in shipping space by such means were reported in June 1943 to have amounted to 10 percent of the total tonnage of Army supplies shipped overseas.[14]

Construction materials, an important category of military cargo, were used in

---

[13] (1) Min, 3d mtg U.S.-Br Planners, 12 Apr 42, ABC 381 BOLERO (3-16-42) Sec 5. (2) Memo, Somervell for Marshall, 20 Oct 42, CofS WDGS 1942 (3A) folder, Hq ASF. (3) Memo, Somervell for Marshall, 24 Sep 42, CofS WDGS 1942 (2) folder, Hq ASF. (4) CCS 110/4, 22 Oct 42, title: Shipt of Motor Vehicles. (5) See other papers in the CCS 110 series. (6) See 451 Vehicles Misc 1943 folder, Plng Div ASF. (7) Plng Div SOS Diary, 19 Feb 43 entry, Plng Div ASF. (8) Wardlow, Trans II, Ch. V, table on p. 91, showing 76 percent of 1943 vehicle shipments made in boxes. (9) MBW 29, 14 Sep 42, title: Shipg Reqmts for Automotive Equip. (10) See other papers in the MBW 29 series.

[14] *Annual Report of the Army Service Forces, 1943*, pp. 78–79. Basis for figures is not given.

enormous quantities in the development of outposts in the Western Hemisphere and along lines of communications during 1942. By the end of the year, the course of the war had left a backwash of tens of thousands of troops, elaborately housed and fortified in areas far from combat. Merely to maintain these forces was a heavy drain on shipping, a cost that had to be weighed against the tonnages required to redeploy them elsewhere; redeployment did not really get under way until early 1943. It also proved difficult to curb lavish construction in static areas, despite repeated orders from the War Department to abandon unessential projects and to employ only "theater of operations" types of building. As late as March 1943, The Inspector General, after touring the Caribbean Defense Command, found that planned construction for the coming year in that area had been reduced by only about $11 million out of a total outlay of $162 million, a result, it appeared, of General Brett's uncertainty as to the strategic role of his command. "No nation," an investigating committee declared severely in summer of 1943, referring to this persistent problem, "is rich enough or productive enough to supply and maintain battle-fronts where there is no longer a battle." [15]

After more than a year of war the effort to build up reserve and operating stocks overseas, "filling the pipeline," was bearing fruit. The pipeline, to be sure, was in no literal sense full. There were shortages of specific critical items, such as signal equipment, in most theaters, and general shortages in some theaters. But there were also huge and embarrassing accumulations—subsistence and small arms ammunition in North Africa, aircraft bombs in the United Kingdom. Admiral King wrote indignantly in February 1943 of the

stagnation of supplies in theater reservoirs, both Army and Navy, and of the excessive stockages resulting from overindulgence in Washington and the greed of theater commanders.[16] Inordinately high authorized levels of supply were partly responsible for this condition, but few reductions were made before mid-1943. Imbalance, however, was a result of many causes—fluctuating expenditures, emergency shipments and issues, lax control over the more plentiful categories of supply, and rudimentary stock control methods. Indeed, as far as stock control was concerned, it was not until spring of 1943 that the War Department put its own house in order and began to institute effective controls overseas. Of all the overseas theaters, only the United Kingdom and Australia, before the end of 1942, had reasonably efficient supply systems. A War Department letter late in February 1943, confessing that supply had been "relatively uncontrolled," directed theater commanders to survey their establishments and to "seek out overstockage and stagnation." [17]

The winter and spring of 1943 saw the beginning of an organized movement for economy and conservation in the Army,

---

[15] (1) Report of WD Procurement Review Board, pp. 56–58. (2) WD ltr to various comdrs, 16 Apr 42, sub: WD Construction and Real Estate Policy, AG 600.12 (4-15-42). (3) Other ltrs in same series. (4) WD Memo W100-3-42, 14 Oct 42, sub: Jt Use of Construction Mats . . . . (5) WD Memo W100-11-43, 27 Apr 43, sub: Rpts on Overseas Construction. (6) JCS 339, App. A, cited n. 8(3).
[16] (1) Report of WD Procurement Review Board, pp. 35–36, 41–44, 50. (2) Memo, Lutes for Gross, 27 Mar 43. (3) Ltr, Magruder to Lutes, 28 Mar 43. Last two in Misc Notes, Lutes File. (4) Memo, COMINCH for CINC's Pac and Atlantic Fleets, and Vice CNO, 11 Feb 43, G-4/400.
[17] (1) WD Memo W700-11-43, 24 Feb 43. (2) WD ltr, 1 Oct 42, sub: Excess Issues of Equip, AG 400 (9-25-42).

coinciding with the considerable public attention then being focused upon proposals to remove military procurement from the control of the armed services. Assistant Secretary McCloy's tour of some of the battle fronts in the spring focused public and governmental attention upon waste and overstockage in overseas theaters. In ASF there was some discussion of creating an "economy" officer with wide authority similar to the highly placed British Comptroller General of Economy. This British official was responsible not merely for maintenance policies, salvage, and conservation through use of substitutes—activities supervised in the United States by separate ASF agencies—but more broadly for making the British Army economy-minded. General Lee wrote Somervell that American troops coming to the European theater had been guilty of shocking "wastefulness and wanton destruction of property, equipment and supplies," and suggested that the British Comptroller General of Economy, Maj. Gen. J. Buckley, be invited to tour Army installations in the United States in order to indoctrinate American troops in British economy measures.[18] This suggestion aroused no enthusiasm in Somervell's headquarters, where it was argued that the American system of making economy a function of command would not lend itself to the British method of supervision. It was felt that the gospel of economy had made more headway in the States than overseas, and that the first place to attack waste should be on the battlefield. Lee's suggestion was tactfully rejected, and General Marshall addressed new and strongly worded orders to theater commanders to instill supply discipline in their troops. Greater pressure was also applied to have scrap metal and other salvage in overseas

theaters collected and returned to the United States. In ASF a poster display program was launched to make troops in the zone of interior more economy-minded, and the editing of requisitions at ports of embarkation became noticeably "tougher." [19]

Administrative Improvements in Overseas Supply and Deployment

A parallel effort, the development of standing operating procedures, probably yielded more substantial economies than the measures directly aimed at economy. The late winter and spring of 1943 saw a general stabilization of the procedures of overseas supply and deployment, rounding off the improvements and experimentation of the year preceding.[20] The most significant development was the abandonment of unregulated automatic supply. In May 1943 subsistence and fuel joined the controlled list on a status report basis. Three reports were prescribed: the monthly Materiel Status Report, now shorn of its ammunition items; a monthly Automatic Supply Report for subsistence, some medical supplies, and fuel; and an Ammunition Supply Report submitted every ten days. The job of preparing them was assigned primarily to the ports (except for certain data inserted in the Materiel Status

---

[18] Ltr, Lee to Somervell, 11 May 43, ETO (6) 1942–43 folder, Hq ASF.

[19] (1) Corresp in ETO (6) 1942 folder, Hq ASF. (2) Memo, G. H. Chambers for Gen Clay, 18 Mar 43, Misc Notes, Lutes File. (3) ASF Circular S850-19-43, 1 Apr 43, sub: Conservation Indoctrination Through Medium of Display Posters. (4) *Annual Report of the Army Service Forces, 1943*, pp. 106–07. (5) Leighton, Overseas Supply Policies and Procedures, pp. 210–13, OCMH.

[20] See above, Ch. XIII.

Report at technical service headquarters), and overseas commanders were finally required to forward to the ports, under a prescribed schedule, the necessary information relating to supply status in their commands. OPD similarly was required to provide the ports with timely troop basis data. The new reports, finally, were to serve not merely as instruments of statistical control but as a basis for automatic supply action as well. Thus ended the experiment launched the preceding October, though some time passed before the procedures of status report supply were fully clarified. Control of these items was still lodged in OPD, which had the allocating power, and in AAF and ASF headquarters and the technical services, which administered their distribution; petroleum products were controlled through the machinery of the Army-Navy Petroleum Board. But control of all these commodities, as well as of those which the ports shipped independently, depended absolutely on the supply status information that now funneled into the ports. With the shutting off of unregulated shipments to North Africa in the spring, the bulk of all overseas supply came under the requisition method, and most automatic shipments, whether of scarce or plentiful categories, were based on the new periodic status reports. Unregulated automatic supply was reserved for the critical early stages of new operations.[21]

Procedures of ammunition supply underwent other changes. Early in 1943 theater ammunition levels, like other categories, were redefined in terms of days of supply; the unit of fire was retained only for tactical computations within a theater, and theater commanders were permitted to adjust its content to suit their own operating conditions. The War De-

partment prescribed a uniform ammunition day of supply, applying to all theaters, for each category. Later in the spring a reporting system was instituted designed to amass expenditure data from each theater in order to provide a basis for eventually establishing separate days of supply for each theater. Before midyear the War Department was acting upon theater recommendations to change prescribed levels, the number of rounds in the day of supply, and percentages by types, though separate days of supply for each theater were not developed. In the spring, too, arrangements were made to send overseas teams of trained officers, familiar with the mysteries of the Army Supply Program and the uses of statistics, to study conditions affecting expenditure of ammunition and wear and attrition of equipment. In June these teams were placed at the disposal of theater commanders, who were made responsible for collecting and forwarding expenditure and maintenance data of all kinds.[22]

Prescribed levels of all overseas reserves underwent wholesale revision in July 1943. (See Appendix F-1.) Reductions were modest, but operating levels (working stocks) over and above minimum reserves were now restricted to subsistence (Class I supply), noncontrolled equipment (Class II), and fuel (Class III), and were not normally to exceed ninety days of supply.

---

[21] (1) See WD ltr, 5 May 43, sub: Materiel Status Rpt, Automatic Sup Rpt, Am Sup Rpt, AG 400 (4-25-43). (2) See also, History of the Planning Division, ASF, Vol. II, Ch. X, OCMH. (3) Leighton, Overseas Supply Policies and Procedures, pp. 198–201, OCMH.

[22] (1) WD ltr, 16 Feb 43, sub: Am Sup Policy, AG 400 (2-13-43). (2) Report of WD Procurement Review Board, p. 49. (3) FM 101-10, Staff Officers' Field Manual: Organizational, Technical and Logistical Data, Oct 43, par. 321. (4) See above, Chs. XII–XIII.

Their determination was left to the port, by agreement with the theater.[23]

Port reserves, another cushion against emergency, were also acquiring new uses. By 1943 the expanding system of filler depots backing up the ports was fulfilling most of the purposes of port reserves, even the provision of filler cargo on short notice. During March and April an experiment was run at San Francisco, using the stock at the port essentially as a filler depot during normal and slack periods and drawing upon other filler depots when the workload became heavier. A regular flow of replenishment shipments into the port stocks was maintained and, through careful scheduling, part of the work of marking and packing for overseas shipment was shifted to the filler depots. Port stocks of this kind were generally authorized in July, quantities being left to the discretion of the port commanders. In effect, a backwash was eliminated from the flow of supply—the concept of the flowing pipeline was replacing that of reserves stocked in echelon.[24]

During the first half of 1943 the marking system for overseas shipments finally approached a point of refinement that permitted theater officials to identify the item shipped with the item requested. The theaters in 1942 had been given the task of developing their own marking codes, and it was the European theater that developed the basic elements of the system finally adopted. The essence of the plan was the use of a single code symbol in all shipping papers and correspondence pertaining to shipments based on a single requisition. The common denominator was the symbol identifying the originating requisition. Thus, "A007" might be the seventh in the series "A" of Quartermaster requisitions (assigned the block of numbers 001 to 099). In front of the requisition symbol was placed the four-letter symbol of the overseas base, together with the abbreviations of the procuring service and the class of supply—"BOBO-QMII-A007." Further letter and number symbols might be added to the requisition symbol to designate a partial shipment on a requisition, or a specific depot in the theater to which it was destined—highly important refinements from the theater's point of view. To the supply organization in the European theater this system promised to remedy the chronic delays and other defects in the current procedures by which the theater was notified of the status of its requests and of the movement of incoming shipments. It would permit prompt notification by cable of all items in a shipment before it left New York, without danger of confusion over nomenclature. It would also permit the routing of incoming shipments promptly to their users.

The system encountered strong opposition in the Transportation Corps, which placed its trust in improving the existing manifest procedures and feared that the new method would require complete reindoctrination of supply and shipping personnel with resulting disruption of operations. General Lutes, while more favorably inclined, objected that the theater wanted the ASF to "go into the retail business" by documenting its shipments

---

[23] (1) See WD ltr, 10 Jul 43, sub: Levels of Sup . . . , AG 400 (7-8-43). (2) See also, History of the Planning Division, ASF, Vol. II, Ch. XI, OCMH. (3) Leighton, Overseas Supply Policies and Procedures, pp. 201–02, OCMH.

[24] (1) Memo, Lutes for Gross, 21 Jul 43, SPDDI 323.91 POE file, OCT. (2) Leighton, Overseas Supply Policies and Procedures, pp. 144–47, OCMH. (3) Larson, Role of the Transportation Corps in Oversea Supply, pp. 46–52, OCT HB.

for direct delivery to a specific depot.[25] The whole system of overseas supply, of course, rested on the principle of wholesale distribution from the United States to the theater, which in turn implied a system of graded distribution in the theater. In Australia such a system had been developed, but in the United Kingdom short distances, crowded facilities, and other factors made it necessary to rely more heavily on direct movement of shipments from the ports to the interior depots.

The European theater pressed its case with vigor, however, and in May the new marking system was formally offered to overseas commanders and shortly thereafter put into effect. Under this system, it was explained, "separate shipments may be identified by container and . . . shipping papers may be dispatched and connected with the shipments concerned."[26] In July, as a corollary of standardization in marking shipments, the War Department put into tentative operation a single standardized shipping document, prepared in multiple copies at the depot originating a shipment and replacing most of the multitude of shipping papers formerly used at various stages of the journey. About the same time, finally, a significant distinction was established between supply and transportation channels in the flow of information connected with shipments. As the official instructions stated:

The limitation of information flowing along the transportation channels . . . will simplify tremendously the processing and preparation of shipping papers. It is apparent that transportation agencies should be basically interested only in packages, and become interested in contents or identification by article only when such information is necessary to identify shipments.[27]

"Marking is a step child of many War Department agencies," General Lutes wryly commented in May 1943 in the midst of these administrative reforms. "It is considered so simple that it is everybody's business, until the real work of developing policies begins, at which time these agencies begin to drop out."[28] By the middle of the year, happily, the process had been virtually completed.

The general movement toward administrative stabilization brought two important improvements in the procedures for equipping troops going overseas. The first was a change in the procedures for transferring equipment from units in training to alerted units. Until September 1942 an alerted unit, after exhausting normal local sources of supply at and near the home station, drew first upon units near at hand and then upon more distant ones. This involved complex administrative channels, and alternating action by supply and tactical agencies—the station supply officer, after drawing upon local sources, reported shortages to the unit commander, who relayed them to the major command to which the unit belonged, which filled them as far as possible from other units under control of the major command before reporting the remaining shortages (back into supply channels) to the supply services. Thus units in training had to give up equipment before the supply services had the opportunity to draw upon depot

---

[25] Ltr, Lutes to Lee, 6 Mar 43, ETO folder, Lutes File.

[26] WD ltr, 26 May 43, sub: Identification of Separate Shipts to Overseas Destinations, AG 400.161 (5-22-43).

[27] (1) Quoted in Leighton, The Problem of Troop and Cargo Flow in Preparing the European Invasion, pp. 75–76, OCMH. (2) Papers in AG 400.161 (3-19-43). (3) Ruppenthal, *Logistical Support of the Armies*, Ch. III.

[28] Ltr, Gen Lutes to Maj Gen Everett S. Hughes, 9 May 43, Misc Notes, Lutes File.

stocks beyond the immediate orbit of the alerted unit. A revision of standard instructions (Inclosure No. 1 to movement orders) issued on 1 September 1942 established a new sequence of action: station supply officers reported shortages directly to the supply services immediately after exhausting local station and depot stocks, and the supply services tapped all their depot resources before referring remaining shortages to SOS headquarters, which in turn referred them to the major commands to fill by transfers from other units. The new procedure, happily, went into effect before the turmoil of troop movements for North Africa began.[29]

Largely as a reaction to that turmoil, the system of status reporting on readiness of alerted units was tightened in November 1942 to include specific reports on readiness in terms of equipment. Commanders making the reports were admonished to be precise ("remarks such as 25 per cent equipment shortages; so and so has fulfilled responsibilities; and lists of shortages have been submitted to proper agencies, will *not* be used since they fail to indicate the true status of equipment.")[30] A whole system of supporting reports soon grew up within the SOS establishment with a view to providing an up-to-date picture of the equipment status of high-priority units and of sources available for filling shortages. Early in January 1943 inspections of alerted units by The Inspector General, formerly made sporadically or on request, became regular procedure.[31]

This last measure was part of the whole effort to establish an orderly and synchronized process of organization, training, and equipping for troops in the United States, in order that deployment plans might be based upon reasonably reliable knowledge of the forces that would be ready for overseas service at a given date. Basic to the whole system was the War Department's Six Months' List, a periodic forecast of units expected to move overseas within that period, based upon a balancing of requirements laid down by OPD and the major commands' expectations of meeting them. The procedural monument of the system was "POM" (Preparation for Overseas Movement), a thirty-four-page pamphlet of instructions setting forth in detail the duties of all agencies concerned in overseas movement. A composite product of many hands in the three major commands and the General Staff (the provisions dealing with equipment and transportation naturally originated mainly in SOS), the first edition appeared on 1 February 1943. POM was widely distributed, unlike the classified Inclosure No. 1 to movement orders which it replaced, and was placed in the hands of unit and station commanders well in advance of the date when preparations were to begin. (*Chart 10*) Those preparations, as far as completion of equipment was concerned, normally could now be expected to begin at least three months before the unit sailed, when its commander, or the station commander, was notified of its assignment to an A-4 priority for equipment. This inaugurated the process of equipment inspections and

---

[29] (1) Incl No. 1, 1 Sep 42, AG 370.5. (2) See Charts 8, 9.

[30] Ltr, SOS, 26 Nov 42, sub: Shortage Rpts, SPX 400 (11-25-42).

[31] (1) Memo, OPD for AGF, AAF, and SOS, 29 Nov 42, sub: Status Rpts for Units Scheduled for Overseas Mvmt, and revision of 4 Feb 43, OPD 370.5. (2) WD ltr, 5 Jan 43, sub: Orgn, Tng, and Equipg of Units for Overseas Sv, AG 320.2 (1-2-43). (3) Distrib Div, ASF, History of Supply in the Zone of Interior, Ch. IV, OCMH.

CHART 10—PROCEDURE FOR EQUIPPING A TYPICAL AGF UNIT FOR OVERSEAS MOVEMENT (POM): FEBRUARY 1943

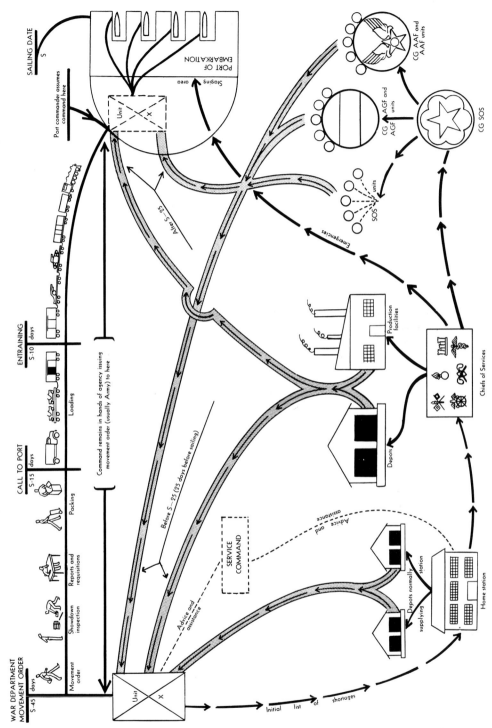

progressive filling of shortages leading up to final readiness.[32]

All this was only a beginning; sterner measures were over the horizon. The cumulative net effect of all efforts to reduce the continuing logistical overhead of war can scarcely be measured since so much of it consisted of immeasurable administrative economies and more efficient performance of routine functions. By spring of 1943 some effect could be seen in the reduced cargo space required for the complex apparatus of weapons, equipment, and supplies accompanying troops moving overseas; these were now estimated to occupy, together with the space needed by the troops themselves, an average of seven measurement tons per man, which was probably somewhat less than that needed a year earlier.[33] This was a net result of reductions in equipment allowances and economies in packing and stowage, largely counteracted by the remorseless advance of the technology of war, especially in the demand for more mobility and fire power. The principal hope, indeed, for further increasing the amount of effective fighting power that each ship could deliver overseas lay in the trend of deployment itself to become more routine, involving a growing proportion of troops and matériel ferried, in mass and in bulk, to established bases overseas, with fewer combat-loaded and task force movements from the United States. Only a wholesale type of deployment offered much scope for compressing the bulk of military cargo by improvements in packing and stowage and other economies in cargo space utilization. Moreover, the

support of a growing troop population overseas imposed a mounting overhead cost in shipping that was far more difficult to curtail. Despite all efforts to economize, the American soldier overseas in spring of 1943 still required for his support an average of 1.3 ship tons of cargo each month, slightly more than he had needed a year earlier. Eventually, of course, reductions in initial requirements would be reflected in maintenance requirements, but only to a limited degree since food was a well-nigh irreducible item and the expenditure of fuel and ammunition in 1943 was on the increase. On the whole, the demand for economy had not yet become a pervasive pressure in the military organization by spring of 1943. In May the Joint Administrative Committee (JAdC), reporting on steps taken by both services to curtail overseas construction, reduce organically assigned equipment to "bare essentials," and lower prescribed levels of overseas reserves, gave a long "corrective-measures-are-being-taken" review of the progress made, and concluded with the recommendation that "no action by the JCS appears necessary."[34]

---

[32] (1) See Palmer, Wiley, and Keast, *AGF II*, pp. 581–91. (2) Preparation for Overseas Movement (POM), 1 Feb 43, AG 370.5 (1-16-43). (3) Troop Movements in World War II, 31 Oct 45, OCMH. (4) Distrib Div, ASF, History of Supply in the Zone of Interior, Ch. IV, OCMH. (5) Memo, Gen Lutes for OPD, 3 Dec 42, in Frierson, Preparations for "Torch," App. I, OCMH. (6) See Chart 10.

[33] (1) In 1949 (the most recent published data) Army planners assumed that only four measurement tons of initial equipment were needed by a soldier going overseas. See FM 101-10, Staff Officers' Field Manual: Organizational, Technical and Logistical Data, Aug 49, par. 287c. (2) See also below, App. A-5.

[34] (1) JCS 339, App. A, cited n. 8(3). (2) See below, Apps. A-2, A-3, A-4, A-5.

CHAPTER XXIV

Joint Logistical Planning and Co-ordination

By the end of 1942 the JCS committee system was solidly established, but it still offered no assured method for securing swift and decisive action in the face of interservice disagreement. In most such cases the Joint Chiefs chose the outlet of compromise, however unsatisfactory to both services, rather than brave the President's annoyance by appealing to him to break a deadlock. To each service (and to the Army Air Forces as well), the committee method offered insurance against undue domination or coercion by the other. Any reform aimed at unification, therefore—whether by departmental merger or merely by creation of some form of joint general staff under a single commander—stood very little chance of acceptance, at least as a wartime measure. Most efforts at reform, in fact, were designed to improve the existing machinery of planning, rather than at developing a unified system of central command. In the field, by contrast, operations involving forces of both services normally were carried out under unified command arrangements; this lesson of Pearl Harbor had been taken to heart. Unity of command in the field, however, had not been extended into administration, especially supply and transportation, which remained sacrosanct preserves of service prerogative.

Logistics in Joint Strategic Planning

Since the central U.S. committee system represented a partnership rather than a merger of the services, it was not surprising that strategic planning at that level was largely a process of reconciling fully formed points of view and objectives rather than integrated thinking based on an approach free from service-rooted preconceptions. As a practical matter, the Army ground, Army air, and Navy members of the lower committees assumed that their proper business was to see to it that joint plans reflected, as faithfully as possible, the desires of their respective chiefs. To the extent that these desires were generalized and flexible, there was room for compromise, and when a paper, with or without accompanying minority reports, finally reached the Joint Staff Planners, it was often possible for the latter, after individually consulting their chiefs, to reach agreement. But this system was scarcely calculated to achieve a dispassionate balancing of ends against means. In the combined committees, the American members usually managed to present at least the semblance of a united front to their British allies. In their own house, the U.S. committees more often than not debated questions of logistical capabilities in terms of the clashing interests of the Army and the Navy. The dispute during November and December 1942 over assignment of the *Monticello* and the Navy combat loaders used in the Casablanca landings was one of many such instances, and the following March and April the effort of the JMTC and JPS to cut down projected overseas deployment for 1943 to the indicated capacity of shipping dissolved in a virtual anarchy of fruitless interservice recriminations over the apportionment of the cuts. As the JCS Secretariat, analyzing the working of the joint committee system early in 1943, cautiously observed with respect to the Joint Planners:

> At times they have become factional regarding the interests of their respective services as a cumulative result of attempting to compose disagreements.
> They have sometimes entered on their deliberations with instructions from higher authority or with fixed and preconceived ideas.[1]

Factionalism, of course, could infest any type of organizational structure. The JCS Secretariat put its finger on another problem of the joint committee system which, to its critics from late 1942 on, seemed to call for structural change:

> Their [referring to the JPS] studies and recommendations have, perhaps, not always represented the best and most expert thought on the subject at hand.[2]

In the early development of the JCS system the claims of the expert—and especially the logistical expert, since his province was so broad—to a voice in the final stages of strategic planning had been stubbornly resisted.[3] The strategic planners held generally to the doctrine that while the expert's knowledge was indispensable, his conclusions were likely to be too narrow and inflexible to be useful in framing a bold and imaginative strategy. Yet the

widening gulf between military supply programs and the estimated limits of national productivity, and the strong tendency of the planning staffs to overreach logistical capabilities, shed a glaring light during the latter half of 1942 upon the difficulties, under the existing system, of producing logistically feasible strategy.

Production officials were increasingly concerned over the lack of machinery for keeping strategic planning in line with logistical limitations. One of the proposals advanced by the WPB Planning Committee in August 1942, in connection with its analysis of production possibilities for the coming year, was to set up a supreme war production council consisting of representatives responsible for "military strategy, production strategy, and social and political strategy," on a higher plane of authority than the Joint Chiefs themselves.[4] This plan General Somervell denounced as an "inchoate mass of words."[5] "What good," he demanded, "would be a board composed of an economist, a politician, and a soldier who does not know production?"[6] The military services similarly resisted suggestions that civilian production officials should "sit in" when strategy was being formulated. At a stormy meeting between military and WPB offi-

---

[1] (1) JCS 202, 16 Jan 43, title: War Plng Agencies, Annex B, title: Draft Proposal Prepared by JCS Secy Suggesting That It Be Referred to JCS by CofS, U.S. Army, 16 Jan 43. (2) See discussion in Cline, *Washington Command Post*, pp. 234ff. (3) For the *Monticello* affair, see above, Chs. XV, XIX. (4) For deployment discussion of March–April 1943, see below, Ch. XXVI.

[2] Annex B to JCS 202 cited n. 1(1).

[3] See above, Ch. IX.

[4] Com on Pub Admin Cases, Feasibility Dispute, p. 71.

[5] Memo, Somervell for Nathan, 12 Sep 42, WPB 1942 (2) folder, Hq ASF.

[6] Com on Pub Admin Cases, Feasibility Dispute, p. 93.

cials on 6 October, General Somervell appeared as the War Department's designated representative "for the interpretation of strategy to the War Production Board"[7]—a note of condescension that perhaps helps to explain Leon Henderson's bitter remark on that occasion that "maybe if we can't wage a war on 90 billions, we ought to get rid of our present Joint Chiefs, and find some who can," and the violent personal attack that he then launched against Somervell himself.[8] A few days later the WPB Planning Committee considered the advisability of attempting to force Somervell to demonstrate the specific strategic need for this or that requirement. "The minute these questions really get discussed in the War Production Board," a member predicted, "you will find the Chiefs of Staff appearing and not General Somervell."[9] But the attempt was not made, and the plan for a supreme strategy-production board was quietly dropped.[10]

Somervell's stand in this matter did not grow out of unawareness of the need for a more informed consideration of logistical factors on the top planning levels. On 9 September he urged General Marshall to support a proposal that the Joint Chiefs create a standing supply committee composed of himself and the top Navy supply officer, Admiral Horne, to which they would refer all matters specifically pertaining to logistics; General Macready of the British Army Staff would join the group when combined matters were discussed. Somervell bluntly declared that the JPS and CPS were not competent to appraise logistical capabilities. "There is no one among the Staff planners who knows much about supply, and the views they express must therefore be those of others, with consequent delay . . . or else their own opinions which are predicated neither on knowledge or experience."[11] Somervell's blast naturally brought a strong reaction from OPD, which provided the Army members of the JPS and JUSSC. General Handy thought that any logistics committee that reported directly to the JCS would inevitably usurp the functions of the JPS, "since supply matters have a definite bearing on all subjects dealing with strategy."[12] Wedemeyer argued, "our planning must still be based on operations, and not on logistical factors alone. Otherwise we will have the tail wagging the dog."[13]

Meanwhile Harry Hopkins had come up with a proposal that the powers of the U.S. members of the Munitions Assignments Board be broadened to include determination of requirements, and that each service add a director of requirements as an *ex officio* member of that board, these directors also to attend meetings of the JPS and JCS in an advisory capacity. Under this plan the MAB would have become the principal joint and combined logistical plans agency, and the directors of requirements the top logistical authorities in each service. OPD endorsed the plan as preferable to Somervell's, but it was a greatly watered down version of this scheme that the JCS finally adopted. Four requirements representatives from each service were appointed to serve as liaison officers with the civilian produc-

---

[7] *Ibid.*, p. 91.
[8] *Ibid.*, p. 95.
[9] *Ibid.*, p. 96.
[10] (1) *Ibid.*, pp. 70–104. (2) See above, Ch. XXII.
[11] Memo, Somervell for Marshall, 9 Sep 42, WDCSA 400 (1942).
[12] Memo, ACofS OPD for CofS, 27 Sep 42, sub: Standing Com . . . , OPD 334.8 JCS, 17.
[13] Memo, Wedemeyer for Handy, 14 Sep 42, OPD 334.8 JCS, 17.

tion agencies and to sit in JPS meetings in an advisory capacity. Representation on the Army side was from SOS, AAF, G-1, and OPD's Logistics Group. Somervell thus gained a nonvoting representative on the JPS, but the system still lacked a joint supply planning agency. With the requirements representatives and other *ad hoc* members, moreover, the JPS was becoming an unwieldy body.[14]

By the end of 1942 the joint planning machinery was badly in need of being tightened. The Americans found themselves at a serious disadvantage in working with the smoothly functioning British organization, especially at Casablanca in January 1943, where the British operated with steam-roller efficiency. In that month, at the instigation of Lt. Gen. Joseph T. McNarney, a special committee of the Joint Deputy Chiefs of Staff (which had been created late in 1942 to relieve the JCS of decisions on administrative and routine matters) and the JCS Secretariat was appointed to study the workings of the entire joint committee system. The committee submitted to the JCS at the end of March new draft charters of all existing JCS agencies, including the JCS itself, the Joint Deputy Chiefs, the secretariat, the JPS, JMTC, Joint Strategic Survey Committee (an "elder statesmen" long-range planning group created late in 1942), Joint Intelligence Committee, Joint Communications Board, Joint Committee on New Weapons and Equipment, Joint Meteorological Committee, ANPB, and the U.S. representatives, MAB. To these the committee proposed to add a Joint War Plans Committee to replace the JUSSC as a working committee for the JPS, and a Joint Administrative Committee. To this last group were assigned, rather vaguely, all matters "not primarily

concerned with war plans," and it was to serve, with the Joint Deputy Chiefs, to relieve the JCS and the Joint Planners of the burden of "problems of production, and administrative and miscellaneous planning."[15] The JPS and their working committee could thus devote their exclusive attention to strategic plans, though this would evidently continue to include whatever aspects of logistical planning that pertained thereto.[16] Clearly, the JAdC was not to be the kind of agency Somervell had recommended in September. (*Chart 11*)

SOS membership, in the committee's plan, was limited to the specialized logistical agencies—the JMTC, ANPB, and MAB. The JAdC was to be composed of one Army, one Navy, and one AAF representative, the Army member to come from OPD. Even on the JMTC, SOS membership was to be limited to General Gross, Chief of Transportation—omitting General Somervell—and a member from G-4 was added. To Somervell the whole reorganization plan appeared as an OPD move to have its Logistics Group drive SOS out of the logistical planning field. He protested bitterly to General Marshall:

Owing to our exceptionally long supply lines, the location of our theaters of operation around the entire globe, and critical shortages in shipping, logistics are, in most cases, the final governing factors in decisions involving action in the field. If this war has demonstrated anything, it has shown that

---

[14] (1) Papers in JCS 98 series. (2) Min, 31st mtg JCS, 1 Sep 42; 32d mtg, 8 Sep 42; 33d mtg, 15 Sep 42. (3) Min, 36th mtg JPS, 23 Sep 42; 37th mtg, 30 Sep 42; 38th mtg, 7 Oct 42. (4) Memo, Secy JCS for Clay and Tompkins, 31 Aug 42, sub: Determination of Reqmts. (5) Ltr, JCS to Nelson, Hopkins, Richard, Stettinius, McNutt, Land, and Hershey, 16 Oct 42. Last two in CCS 334 JR and MAB (8-31-42).
[15] JCS 202/2, 25 Mar 43, title: War Plng Agencies.
[16] JCS 202 cited n. 1(1).

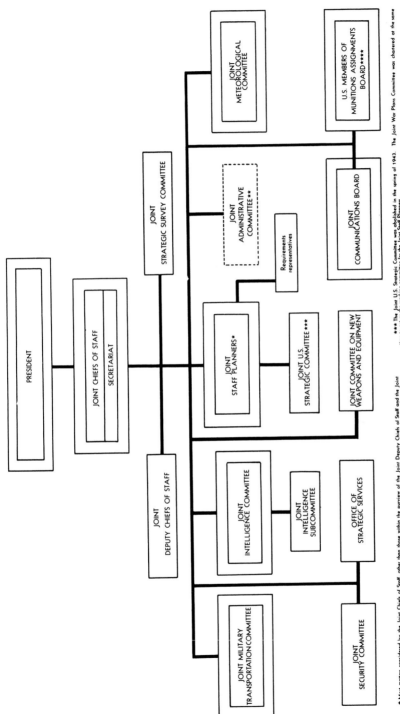

CHART 11—THE JOINT COMMITTEE SYSTEM: DECEMBER 1942

our efforts to launch attacks on the enemy have, in every case, been governed by logistics—transportation and supply. When these factors have not been given due weight, confusion, delay and disaster have come only too rapidly . . . . Unless you are represented on the Planners by an able officer who KNOWS supply, its ramifications, requirements, adaptability, production, availability, etc. and our capabilities in transportation, and moreover by one who has intimate touch with all sources of information, you will be badly served, the Army will suffer, the war will suffer, and America will suffer.[17]

Somervell also lashed out at the proposed structure of the JAdC and at the assignment of matters of production and administration to the Joint Deputy Chiefs, and he complained of being "thrown off" the JMTC. Finally, he recommended that instead of the proposed JAdC a Joint Logistics Committee be constituted with membership from the Navy, the AAF, and the SOS.[18]

Somervell's attack did not shake the insistence of the OPD staff that the proper function of the SOS was to provide technical advice to the planners, not share in the making of policy and strategy. With some acerbity General Wedemeyer pointed out that if logistical planning in the past had been based on inadequate knowledge, the SOS, which had been consulted in every case, must be to blame. Representation of OPD on the JAdC and of G-4 on the JMTC, he insisted, was both "competent and proper." He rejected the implication that no other agency in the Army except the SOS recognized the importance of logistics or was capable of intelligent logistical planning.[19]

In the end a compromise was reached. The proposed charters for supporting agencies of the JCS were all approved early in May 1943, but with only the number of Army and Navy members on each committee specified, not the particular agencies to be represented. General Marshall later granted the SOS a member on the JAdC, and returned Somervell to his place on the JMTC. But only OPD and AAF officers were placed on the JPS and the Joint War Plans Committee. Somervell had won half a loaf.[20]

Strategic planning thus remained an integrated rather than a compartmented function, in which logistical specialists did not take part. The reorganization of spring 1943 reduced the process of strategic planning in its final stages to an orderly and graded system, as far as the committee method of operation permitted; strategic plans passed through a series of stages in which the JPS, Joint War Plans Committee, and Joint Strategic Survey Committee had fairly well-defined responsibilities and the JCS Secretariat played an increasingly important guiding role. This machinery was to remain intact for the remainder of the war.

The process of logistical planning, which in its specialized aspects remained outside this sphere, was not similarly regularized by the reorganization. The JAdC, in its charter, was responsible for matters "which do not come under the jurisdiction of one

---

[17] Memo, Somervell for CofS, 27 Mar 43, sub: Reorgn of Supporting Agencies of JCS—JCS 202/2, CofS (Jt and Combined) folder, Hq ASF.

[18] Ibid.

[19] Memo, Wedemeyer for CofS, 5 Apr 43, sub: Comments on Gen Somervell's Memo to CofS . . . , WDCSA 334 JCS, II.

[20] (1) JCS 202 series, May 1943. (2) Min, 77th mtg JCS, 4 May 43; 79th mtg, 10 May 43. (3) Memo, McNarney for Secy JCS, 5 May 43, ABC 334.8 JAdC (5-5-43). (4) Memo, McNarney for Secy JCS, 13 May 43, sub: Army Reps on JCS Coms, WDCSA 334 JCS. (5) Papers in ABC 381 (12-19-42) Secs 1–3. (6) For a detailed study of the reorganization of the JCS committees at this time, see Vernon E. Davis, Development of the JCS Committee Structure, Vol. II of History of the Joint Chiefs of Staff Organizational Developments, pp. 590–683, JCS Hist Sec.

of the other committees." [21] Other logistical functions were assigned variously to the JMTC, the U.S. representatives on the MAB, the ANPB, and other committees. The JAdC did not gain control of the activities of these committees, and despite Somervell's efforts it did not become the principal logistical planning group for the JCS. While the language of the charters implied a relationship of equality between the JPS and the JAdC, both reporting directly to the JCS, the JAdC was never able, in fact, to function on that plane because the planners had become indispensable as the group that filtered plans and problems for final decision by the Joint Chiefs, and this function spread over the whole field of strategic-logistical planning. At the level at which both JPS and JCS considered problems, functional demarcation had proved to be impracticable. As an OPD study expressed this philosophy:

Sound planning requires that strategy and logistics be integrated in the preparation of plans. There exists an obvious weakness when the two essential factors of planning are considered separately on a lower echelon and suddenly find themselves vis-a-vis on a higher level. Thus, it is essential that strategy and logistics be integrated as the plan progresses, and that when a plan reaches the JCS level, the factors should be completely married. [22]

To this principle Somervell might have shouted a loud "Amen," but he saw no hope for a happy marriage between strategy and logistics, progressive or otherwise, as long as the latter was relegated to the role of an obedient housewife, with no voice in the running of the business.

The Army-Navy Basic Logistical Plan

To a large degree the difficulties of joint strategic planning in the JCS committees had their origin in the field. Even in the system of unified commands under which the bulk of American forces overseas were organized in 1942, the lines of administrative control and support for Army and Navy forces remained separate. Thus all the data on requirements, available resources, and projected movements and operational plans, on which central strategic planning had to be based, flowed into the JCS system from overseas through separate channels. "No joint procedure exists," complained a joint subcommittee in February 1943, "for determination of the relative needs of various areas, nor is there available any coordinated statement of future plans for troop movements." [23] As a minimum prerequisite to orderly long-range planning, the committee urged, there should be a joint priority list of troop movements for each overseas area, together with co-ordinated joint data on resources controlled by each service in the various areas. [24]

In April 1942, when both services had flirted briefly with the idea of a joint supply line in the Pacific, it was Army opposition that had killed the proposal, then favored by the Navy. By the time the issue came up again at the end of the year, the two services had each undergone a change of heart, reversing their respective former positions. [25] The phenomenon can be explained, in large part, by the organizational development of the services. The Army's Services of Supply, emerging uncertainly in April from the War Depart-

[21] JCS 202/10/D, 5 May 43, title: Charter JAdC.
[22] (1) OPD study, no date, title: Proposed Integration of a Jt Logis Com into JCS Orgn, ABC 334.8 JAdC (5-5-43) Sec 1A. (2) Cline, *Washington Command Post*, p. 238.
[23] JPS 92/2, 2 Feb 43, title: Trans Reqmts to 1 Jul 43.
[24] Notes on 58th mtg JPS, 4 Feb 43, ABC 570 (2-14-42) Sec 4.
[25] See above, Ch. VII.

ment reorganization, by the end of the year was far surer of its powers and interests. The Navy's supply organization, by contrast, had undergone no fundamental reorganization; the bureaus remained relatively more independent than their Army counterparts, the supply arms and services, while the Naval Transportation Service, created shortly after Pearl Harbor, was weaker and more circumscribed in its functions than the Army's rapidly expanding Transportation Corps. The Naval Transportation Service was a port and shipping agency only; movements into port were controlled by the Bureau of Supplies and Accounts, while within the ports Naval Transportation Service shared control with the several bureaus. The whole system was decentralized, and it developed in 1942 less by plan than for lack of one. It reflected, above all, the peculiar nature of the Navy's supply problem. For the Navy, logistics involved mainly support of mobile fleet units that operated in task forces of fluctuating size, moving rapidly over immense distances; supply requirements for such operations were almost impossible to calculate far in advance. Naval supply had to be flexible in the highest degree, and was best served by decentralizing authority and dispersing the means of logistical support. Navy leaders, probably with justice, felt that a union with the more centralized, massive, and relatively inflexible Army system would require too drastic a readjustment of their own system.[26]

A new impetus to unified supply came late in 1942 from the demonstrated waste and confusion attendant on operation of separate supply lines to the South Pacific. General Lutes, no apostle of unification before making his trip to the Pacific in October 1942, returned to Washington an ardent convert. He recommended to Somervell

. . . that a unified Services of Supply be organized in all theaters for the supply of Army, Navy and Marine forces ashore, and that a unified control of cargo shipping, exclusive of those vessels normally under the fleet commander for supply of vessels afloat, be established for the supply of both fleet and shore forces.[27]

In each theater Lutes envisaged a unified theater SOS under a single commander with a mixed Army-Navy staff, and a joint organization at the stateside ports for forwarding supplies. The theater commander would determine the total requirements for his area and establish priorities within total allocations of shipping; the joint port commander would be responsible for meeting the theater's requests. Lutes proposed to assign the Army primary responsibility for overland transportation and port operations both in the United States and overseas, with the Navy to control all military shipping. His plan presupposed that WSA would allocate shipping permanently to the military services, not for single voyages as it was then doing.[28]

General Gross objected to turning over the Army's transport fleet to the Navy. His plan, drawn up at Somervell's request, called instead for the Coast Guard to man all military shipping, the Army Transport Service to control and operate it, the Navy's role to be confined to routing and escort. Col. J. H. Graham, a close adviser of Somervell, also warned against the loss

---

[26] Ballantine, *Naval Logistics*, pp. 45–54, 76–93, 126–28, 162–66.

[27] (1) Memo, Lutes for CG SOS, 12 Nov 42, sub: Recommendations for a Jt SOS in the Pac Theater, Unified Sup: Army-Navy 1942–43 folder, Lutes File. (2) See above, Ch. XV.

[28] Memo cited n. 27(1).

of "independence of action" that might result from turning over Army shipping to the Navy. The SOS, he declared, should not "trade its birthright for a mess of pottage." [29]

Evidently Somervell overruled Gross, for the latter drew up another plan that in general followed Lutes' thinking. This plan became the basis for discussion with the Navy.[30] Meanwhile, the Navy had been studying the matter independently. In October 1942, at the invitation of Secretary Knox, Walter Franklin, vice president of the Pennsylvania Railroad, undertook a survey of naval transportation. Franklin's recommendations, submitted on 13 November, became the basis for a Navy counterproposal. Franklin recognized the need for unified supply arrangements in the theaters, determination of shipping priorities by theater commanders, and a single channel for the flow of requisitions and supplies. He suggested turning over to the Army the loading of shipments for overseas shore establishments, and to the Navy operation of all military shipping. Rail movement of naval freight to port would remain under Navy jurisdiction.[31]

Gross felt that if the Navy would not surrender control over movement of supplies, the Army should certainly not surrender control over shipping. He returned forthwith to his original position:

Nothing less than the full control over the use of all transports and dry cargo ships by the Army to move all troops and cargo in accordance with theater priorities and within allocations set from time to time by the Joint Chiefs of Staff would do the job effectively. Conflicting decisions as to the use of ships cannot be satisfactory to the Army in view of its supply responsibility.[32]

Gross recommended that the agreement with the Navy be limited to the question of priorities and staff organization in the Pacific and necessary co-operation in supply arrangements at the ports. Lutes, evidently seeing no use in further argument on the matter of shipping, agreed.[33]

Somervell still had hopes of agreement on a broader basis. On 13 December 1942 he proposed to Admiral Horne that the two services go beyond the Navy plan and consolidate the two ocean transportation services. The constituent agencies would continue to perform separately those functions peculiar to each, and supply of the fleet would be totally excepted. The Navy would handle the manning and repair of vessels, control of vessels in port, routing, and escorting; the Army (through SOS) movement of supplies to port, storage, and loading. The all-important control of shipping would be vested in the joint service

---

[29] (1) Memo, JHG [Col J. H. Graham] for Somervell, 20 Nov 42. (2) Memo marked in Gross' handwriting "To Gen Somervell, Gross 11/9." Both in Trans 1941–43 folder, Hq ASF.

[30] (1) The documentary evidence on this point is incomplete. In Trans 1941–43 folder, Hq ASF, immediately following Gross' 9 November memo, is a second plan of unidentified authorship dated 12 Nov 42 providing for manning of ships by the Coast Guard or the Navy and for operation by the Navy. This memo bears Somervell's initials, and is similar to the later, more detailed outline plan. (2) In the same file is an undated draft plan for "Army-Navy Unified System of Supply," which also appears in the Gross Day File, 16 November 1942, indicating Gross' authorship. (3) For evidence that Gross was accepting the whole scheme reluctantly, see his undated handwritten memo for Somervell, subject: Conference With Navy on Plan for Overseas Supply, in Trans 1941–43 folder, Hq ASF. Also, Gen Lutes in an interview on 13 September 1949 stated his opinion that Gross at this conference ruined for a year the chances of unifying Army-Navy supply by insisting on Army control of all military shipping.

[31] (1) Ballantine, *Naval Logistics,* pp. 124–25. (2) Digest of Navy counterproposal, atchd to memo, Gross for Somervell, 23 Nov 42, Gross Day File.

[32] Memo cited n. 31(2).

[33] (1) *Ibid.* (2) Memo, Lutes for Somervell, 22 Nov 42, sub: Unified Supply . . . , Unified Sup: Army-Navy 1942–43 folder, Lutes File.

commander. And Somervell thought that since 75 to 90 percent of all forces overseas would belong to the Army, the consolidated service should be headed by an Army officer (presumably Gross), responsible to him. Somervell, in turn, would have a dual responsibility, as Gross' superior, to the Chief of Staff and the Chief of Naval Operations.[34]

On 30 December General Styer forwarded a detailed draft to the Navy. In theaters of joint operations, under the plan, theater commanders would institute unified logistical planning, determine joint requirements of Army and Navy forces under their command, and establish shipping priorities. In the United States a unified transportation service would be set up along the lines of Somervell's suggestion to Horne, except that its chief (not necessarily an Army officer) would be directly responsible jointly to the Chief of Staff and the Chief of Naval Operations, with the JCS reconciling any differences in directives sent to him individually by the two service chiefs. Movement of supplies to port would continue under separate auspices as before, but the joint service would plan all overseas movements. The JMTC would be supplanted by a planning and allocation committee of which the chief of the Army-Navy transportation service would be chairman. This committee would advise the JCS on shipping allocations among the various theaters.[35]

Despite the modifications of Somervell's first proposals, the joint organization as outlined still closely resembled the Army's supply system, and would require drastic readjustments of the Navy's logistical organization. The Franklin plan itself had many enemies within the Navy, as had Lutes' earlier proposals within the Army. Both plans had been based at first on the assumption that WSA would make permanent allocations of shipping to the military services, but all hopes for such allocations had been dashed by the end of December. To most Navy officials the SOS plan looked like a thinly disguised formula for Army control of naval overseas supply.

On 7 January 1943, Rear Adm. Oscar C. Badger came back with another counterproposal, stressing co-ordination rather than unification. He suggested "closely coordinated, possibly unified" supply systems in theaters of joint operation, "full and complete coordination of effort" between Army and Navy supply and shipping agencies in the United States, "cooperation and mutual understanding" between these military agencies and WSA.[36] He would create a chief co-ordinator of Army-Navy overseas transportation to act as agent of the JCS and head up a transportation control board on which there would be, for each service, a deputy co-ordinator and four other members. District co-ordinators reporting to the board would be stationed at domestic and overseas ports.[37]

Somervell's Control Division, after studying the Navy's proposals, concluded that they were drawn in "such general terms that it is impossible to determine what the Navy's detailed intentions

---

[34] Memo, Somervell for Horne, 13 Dec 42, Trans 1941–43 folder, Hq ASF. This was evidently based on a draft by Gross, 10 Dec 42, in Gross Day File.

[35] (1) Contl Div ASF, Rpt 34, Unified Supply Service and Unified Transportation Service for Army and Navy, 30 Dec 42. (2) Memo, CofS SOS for Rear Adm Oscar C. Badger, 30 Dec 42, sub: Unified Sup Sv for A&N, Unified Sup: Army-Navy 1942–43 folder, Lutes File.

[36] Ltr, Asst CNO to Vice CNO for Logis Plans, 7 Jan 43, sub: Plan for Co-ord . . . , Jt A&N Logis folder, OCT HB.

[37] (1) Ibid. (2) Ballantine, Naval Logistics, pp. 125–28.

are." [38] It also thought that the JMTC could co-ordinate better than a cumbersome control board. Perceiving that the Navy was not ready to accept a unified transportation system, SOS fell back on the more limited plan for unified supply systems overseas (when joint operations were involved) and co-operative arrangements at ports of embarkation. [39]

A "Basic Logistical Plan" along these lines was formally published early in March 1943, over the signatures of Admiral King and General Marshall. It began with the statement:

The key idea of this plan is to insure co-ordinated logistical effort and procedure in each command area . . . involving joint Army-Navy operations in which unity of command and responsibility has been established to the end that combined personnel, equipment, supplies, facilities, shipping and other services of the Army and Navy are most effectively utilized and adequately provided. [40]

Each theater commander was to determine joint requirements for personnel and matériel and prepare a single consolidated priority list. Either through organization of a joint logistical staff or by providing for joint staff planning by Army and Navy staffs, he was to set up a unified supply system in the theater, details to be left to his discretion. Existing Army and Navy seaboard shipping agencies were expected to co-ordinate their actions in loading and scheduling ships to meet fully the combined theater requirements.

The Basic Logistical Plan was intended mainly as a blueprint for the South and Central Pacific, where the problem of joint operations was most acute. In the Atlantic theaters naval operations were largely confined to the fleet at sea and its supply was necessarily separate. In the Southwest Pacific General MacArthur

had already established a tight control over priorities for all forces in his area and his system remained relatively intact. And even in the South and Central Pacific the immediate effects of the plan were not impressive. Both Admiral Halsey and Admiral Nimitz chose at first to set up joint logistical boards rather than joint staffs. In neither area was a unified SOS command established. The joint priority lists developed slowly and uncertainly. In general, co-ordination moved along the lines on which it was already proceeding. In the South Pacific, where the confusion of 1942 had amply demonstrated the necessity, an effective degree of co-ordination was achieved at the working level despite the lack of any genuine joint logistical staff. [41] In the Central Pacific, the forces of inertia were far stronger. The Army and Navy had long maintained separate supply facilities in Hawaii, and there were as yet no active joint operations to jolt commanders into a realization of the necessity for joint supply. Until these active operations began in the fall of 1943, the establishment of the joint logistical board provided more the form than the substance of co-ordination. [42]

The plan, nevertheless, did provide a framework within which a unified logistical system could take shape in the theaters. Its real defect lay in the failure to

[38] Memo, Contl Div SOS and Contl Div TC for CofS SOS, 13 Jan 43, sub: Navy Dept Paper of 7 Jan . . . , Unified Sup: Army-Navy 1942–43 folder, Lutes File.

[39] (1) Ibid. (2) Memo, Styer for Badger, 16 Jan 43, sub: Plans for Co-ord of A&N Logis, Unified Sup: Army-Navy 1942–43 folder, Lutes File.

[40] TAG ltr to all comds, 7 Mar 43, sub: Bsc Logis Plan for Comd Areas Involving Jt A&N Opns, AG 381 (3-5-43).

[41] See above, Ch. XV.

[42] (1) Ballantine, *Naval Logistics*, pp. 129–31. (2) Bykofsky and Larson, Trans III, Ch. VII.

provide for anything beyond the most elementary co-ordination in the operation of the supply system in the United States. Immediately following the issuance of the plan in March 1943, the Chief of Transportation directed all port commanders to take the initiative in establishing committees representing the Army, Navy, and WSA "with the mission of the discussion of common problems in the employment of shipping."[43] As noted earlier, such a committee had already been formed in San Francisco in January, and indeed arrangements made by the military services with WSA at that time provided for similar committees in the other ports. The Basic Logistical Plan made no fundamental change in these arrangements, though the committees were now charged more specifically with assuring Army-Navy co-ordination. The committee at San Francisco achieved considerable success in pooling shipping space and in joint scheduling of shipping to Pacific destinations, but in itself could not provide the genuine unified supply line to the Pacific that Lutes and others had envisaged since separate channels for routine supply requisitions for Army and Navy continued to be used. The degree of co-ordination at the other ports varied with the situation. Back of the ports, there was no provision at all

in the plan for co-ordination in storage or internal movement of supplies. With the Navy depot system almost entirely concentrated in port areas, and with a very loose system of Navy requisitioning, Army port authorities thought there was an inevitable tendency for Navy shipping requirements to be shaped in terms of cargo available for shipment rather than theater requirements or priorities. In addition, no provision was made, except in the high-level decisions of the Joint Military Transportation Committee and the JCS, for allocation of shipping and supplies among the several theaters of the Pacific war. It was the conviction of General Lutes and many other Army officers that only with the unification of all Pacific theaters under one joint command could a satisfactory system of unified logistics for that area be developed.[44]

---

[43] Ltr, Gen Wylie to POE's, 24 Mar 43, sub: Army-Navy-WSA Com, Jt A&N Logis folder, OCT HB.

[44] (1) Ballantine, Shipping in Naval Logistics, pp. 174–75, Naval Hist Div, OCNO. (2) Ltr, Wylie to CG SFPOE, 7 Mar 43. (3) Ltr, Lt Col Richard D. Meyer to C. C. Wardlow, 21 Jul 49. Last two in Jt A&N Logis folder, OCT HB. (4) Memo, Gen Lutes for Maj Gen Walter A. Wood, Jr., 31 Oct 44, sub: Contl of Dry Cargo Shipg in POA, 10a Shipg-Central Pac folder, Plng Div ASF, Job A46-371. (5) For Army-Navy co-ordination in procurement, see Millett, *ASF*, Ch. XVIII.

CHAPTER XXV

Casablanca and the Strategic-Logistical Debate

TORCH not only failed to settle, but further unsettled, the fundamental issue of Anglo-American strategy—the division of effort between the European and the Pacific-Asiatic wars—as well as the subsidiary division among the theaters of each of those wars. This was essentially a logistical problem, belonging to the realm of planning where final evaluations of logistical assets and liabilities enter into the formulation of strategy—what Somervell's planners aptly referred to as "strategic logistics." The issue became more urgent as 1942 drew to an end, because the material means—munitions, merchant shipping, naval escorts, and landing craft—appeared likely to be more abundant in the months to come, offering the Allies their long-awaited opportunity to seize the initiative. But the prospect of relative plenty, while widening the range of alternatives, also complicated the problem of selection. The initiative could not be grasped and held without a long-range strategic program on the order of the short-lived BOLERO-ROUNDUP plan of the preceding spring. The staffs were no more able than they had been then to foresee with assurance the availability of critical resources a year or more in advance, and the uncertainty of their long-range estimates operated fully as effectively as the natural clash of competing views on strategy to prevent agreement on a single long-range program. Through the last four months of 1942 the effort to chart the course of coalition strategy for 1943 dragged on. At Casablanca, where the Allied political and military leaders met in January 1943, it reached a climax but not an end. Disagreeing not only on the basic division of effort but also on the sequence and timing of specific operations, the Allied chiefs were able to make no concrete decisions except those necessary to maintain the momentum that by now had been gained in all major theaters. Beyond these next steps, a broad pattern of strategy was outlined and certain operations were tentatively scheduled, but definite decisions were postponed.

Apart from the basic issue of over-all division of effort, three subsidiary logistical problems were involved in this long debate on strategy. The first grew out of the threat to the sea communications into and through the Mediterranean, which decisively influenced American views on proposed operations in that region. A second problem centered in the now familiar competition for shipping and escorts between the great build-up and "war economy" programs (BOLERO, the Soviet aid program, and British imports) and the demands of current or imminent operations. Finally, with amphibious operations being contemplated in the Mediterranean and the Atlantic, Indian, and Pacific Oceans, landing craft again loomed as a potential limitation.

The Two Wars

The Japan-first alternative to concentration in northwestern Europe remained very much alive in the thinking of Army planner's for more than three months following the decision on TORCH. As the great battle raged over Stalingrad and German armies pushed into the Caucasus, the planners faced the possibility that the alternative of an Allied invasion of Europe might soon disappear altogether, leaving no choice except to seek a decision in the Pacific. Meanwhile, the bloody struggles in the southern Solomons and New Guinea, "going" operations that must be sustained and followed up, threatened also to suck in American forces and drain off the substance of TORCH. Then, during late October and November, the tide turned in all three critical areas—the USSR, North Africa, and the Solomons—and the urgent question became one not of whether, but of how the war in Europe should be pressed forward. Primacy between the two wars was no longer a serious issue, but there remained the important question of degree. During December the Joint Chiefs of Staff approved a program of action that called for further limited offensives in the Solomons-Bismarck Archipelago-eastern New Guinea area and reconquest of Burma and the land bridge to China.[1]

Measured against the goals of the BOLERO-ROUNDUP plans of the preceding spring, the effort poured into the war against Japan during 1942 was already impressive. Admiral King asserted, on the eve of Casablanca, that only 15 percent of American military strength was then marshaled against Japan. The facts scarcely bore him out. Army forces deployed against Japan at the end of the year numbered about 464,000, as against only about 378,000 against Germany and Italy. The latter figure was well below the 435,000 set the preceding March as the goal of deployment to the European area, and the forces deployed against Japan exceeded by some 200,000 the number earlier planned. It was now intended to build up these forces to about 635,000 in 1943. Since July, to be sure, the preponderant movement of Army forces overseas had been into the theaters of the European war, but the balance had not yet tipped in this direction. Army-controlled shipping was already heavily concentrated in the Atlantic area, though by no means in an 85-15 ratio; about 61 percent of all merchant tonnage, and 63 percent of the cargo tonnage used by the Army was operating in the theaters of the European war. To these theaters had been sent 59 percent of the Army's cargo shipments during the last four months of the year. To be sure, the bulk of the Navy's whole effort went into the war against Japan. On the other hand, lend-lease shipments, an important

---

[1] (1) JSSC 1, 11 Dec 42, title: Bsc Strategic Concept for 1943. (2) JCS 167, 11 Dec 42, same title. (3) JCS 167/1, 20 Dec 42, same title. (4) JCS 167/2, 23 Dec 42, same title, circulated as CCS 135 on 26 Dec 42. (5) Matloff and Snell, *Strategic Planning: 1941–1942*, Chs. XVI–XVII. (6) See above, Ch. XV. (7) John Miller, jr., CARTWHEEL: The Reduction of Rabaul, a volume in preparation for the series UNITED STATES ARMY IN WORLD WAR II.

part of the total American war effort, flowed primarily into the European war.[2]

The feeling of American military leaders that the war against the European Axis was absorbing too much of the total Allied effort, while reflecting a change in perspective since the preceding spring, did not signify (least of all, for Marshall and Arnold) an abandonment of their belief that the major effort should be made against Germany. They held, rather, that the war against Germany had been diverted into a peripheral, encircling line of action that would long delay the decisive attack upon the German citadel. The strategy of concentration that had been accepted in April 1942, only to be rejected a few weeks later, might have justified taking certain risks in the war against Japan, but the American chiefs were unwilling to take these same risks to further the current indecisive course of action, as they regarded it, in the Mediterranean. Beyond this, the situation in the Pacific had changed. Operations of considerable scope were in progress and would have to be pressed forward; these would lead inevitably to other operations. Japan was trying with some success to consolidate her gains, and this process must be arrested before it was too late.

The Joint Chiefs were worried, moreover, by what they regarded as a dangerous drift toward complacency in the British attitude toward this "other" war. The full extent of the drift became clear early in January when the British presented a paper setting forth a startlingly optimistic analysis of the present status and future prospects of the war against Japan. They were confident that Japan's offensive power had been blunted, and they warned that Germany might soon become unbeatable if allowed to crush the Soviet Union, whereas Japan's downfall would be ensured by defeat of Germany. Offensive pressure on Japan now would give the Russians no comfort and might require so much naval strength that the Germans might drive Allied shipping from the Atlantic altogether. To rescue China would not contribute to the defeat of Germany, whereas Soviet help might be decisive in defeating Japan. Operations against Japan in 1943, the British therefore thought, should be "on a scale sufficient only to contain the bulk of Japanese forces" in the Pacific; an invasion of Burma should be attempted only "as soon as resources permit." In Europe the Allies should bring their full strength to bear—"we must now agree on a plan that will lead to victory, quickly and decisively."[3]

The American staff found this analysis disturbing. It grossly underestimated Japan's capabilities, they thought, for organizing outposts, communications, and defenses in depth, exploiting conquered territories, and otherwise entrenching herself during the coming year. A current intelligence report estimated:

---

[2] (1) Min, 39th mtg JCS, 5 Jan 43. (2) Strength of the Army Report, STM-30, 1 Jan 48. (3) Matloff and Snell, *Strategic Planning: 1941-1942,* Ch. XVI. About half the ground divisions overseas and about one third of the combat air groups overseas were arrayed against Japan. (4) Shipping figures are from ASF Monthly Progress Report, Transportation, Feb 43, Sec 3. (5) For cargo shipments, see below, App. E-1. (6) Statisticians near the end of the war estimated that only slightly more than half of American production of combat munitions, in the period 1938-44, had gone into the European war. See *World Production of Munitions at the End of the War in Europe,* WPB Doc 25 (Washington, June 15, 1945), p. 8. (7) For division of effort, see below, Charts 15–19.

[3] CCS 135/2, 3 Jan 43, title: American-Br Strategy in 1943.

Japan's only urgent need is time. Greater East Asia's as yet undeveloped resources and as yet untrained manpower are sufficient for creation and maintenance of a far greater and more dangerous military and industrial power. . . . During 1943 Japan cannot hope to grow in strength as we will grow, but she may well intrench herself so that effective action against her will become very much more difficult and costly. She will beyond all doubt do so, unless the rate of attrition imposed on her is sufficient to absorb in current operations all her industrial capacity.[4]

The Joint Chiefs accordingly reaffirmed their strong statement of late December on the necessity for more aggressive action against Japan in 1943.[5]

The British, meanwhile, had taken the offensive in the debate on European strategy. Fired by the success of Allied arms in Egypt, Morocco, and Algeria, the Prime Minister in November toyed joyously with all sorts of Mediterranean projects to follow the expected victory in Tunisia. On the 18th he wrapped up all of them in an eloquent message to the President urging that the Allies "strike at the underbelly of the Axis . . . in the shortest time."[6] Descents on Sardinia and/or Sicily seemed to be obvious first steps, to be followed by intensified air attacks on Italy and, if necessary, a land invasion, to knock her out of the war. Churchill also thought it was time to bring Turkey into the war, as a base for attacks on the Balkans and to gain access to the Black Sea. This ambitious program, Churchill himself insisted, need not rule out a cross-Channel invasion in the late summer of 1943 under the conditions he imposed for attempting it, namely a marked deterioration in German morale and capacity for resistance. Churchill declared he would not abandon this hope "without a massive presentation of facts and figures which

prove physical impossibility."[7] Up to the end of November he put strong pressure on the President to accelerate the waning BOLERO program, intermittently pleaded for American help in a diversionary landing in Norway, and persistently needled his own staff for its "unduly negative"[8] view of the opportunities for a blow across the Channel in 1943. "We have pulled in our horns," he complained "to an almost extraordinary extent."[9] By early December he was convinced that Germany could spare no more troops from the East to meet an attack in the West. Even after the Tunisia Campaign bogged down later that month, the British still contended that their Mediterranean program, together with an intensified air bombardment of Germany and an amphibious campaign in Burma late in the year, could all be carried out without interfering with the assembling of twenty-one British and American divisions in time for an opportunistic attack across the Channel in August or September.[10]

There were plenty of American champions of further action in the Mediterranean. Some Navy strategists favored it as a course less likely than a rapid build-

[4] Est by Off of Strategic Sv, in JPS 106, 7 Jan 43, title: Bsc Strategic Concept for 1943.

[5] (1) Memo, JSSC for JCS, sub: Bsc Strategic Concept for 1943, in JCS 167/3, 5 Jan 43, title: Bsc Strategic Concept for 1943—The European Theater. (2) Min, 49th mtg JCS, 5 Jan 43. (3) Papers in ABC 381 (9-25-41) Sec 4.

[6] Msg 195, Prime Minister to President, 18 Nov 42, circulated as JCS 153, 18 Nov 42, title: Plans and Opns in Mediterranean, Middle East, and Near East.

[7] Churchill's comments to Br CsofS, 18 Nov 42, as quoted in Churchill, *Hinge of Fate*, p. 651.

[8] Churchill, *Hinge of Fate*, p. 649.

[9] Churchill's comments, p. 650, cited n. 7.

[10] (1) Msg cited n. 6. (2) Churchill, *Hinge of Fate*, Bk. II, Ch. 13. (3) CCS 135/1, 2 Jan 43, title: Bsc Strategic Concept for 1943—The European Theater. (4) See above, Ch. XVII.

up in the British Isles to interfere with an expanding effort against Japan. Most of General Marshall's own staff were resigned to at least a limited campaign in the western Mediterranean in order to maintain pressure on Germany and possibly to knock out Italy, though not to undertaking an invasion of the peninsula. Above all, they regarded as imperative the protection of sea communications to North African ports. It might even be possible to reopen a passage through the Mediterranean to Suez. But they took a dim view of any undertaking in the Balkans, fearing that Turkish belligerency at this juncture would cost more than it was worth, and they flatly disagreed with the British contention that an offensive could be mounted in Burma late in 1943 if major operations were in progress in the West during the summer and autumn. The airmen and some of Marshall's other advisers opposed any post-Tunisia amphibious operations in the Mediterranean or retention of ground forces there beyond the minimum needs of security, and urged that the build-up of invasion forces in the British Isles be resumed with all speed. This group looked to co-ordinated strategic bombardment, from the northwest, south, and southeast, to soften Germany for the kill; General Arnold asserted the job could be done within six months.[11]

The Joint Chiefs themselves, on the eve of the Casablanca Conference, opposed further amphibious ventures in the Mediterranean as probably incompatible with a cross-Channel invasion in 1943 and dangerous to one early in 1944. The Joint Strategic Survey Committee declared further that any attempt to seize Sardinia or Sicily would be "unwarranted, uneco-

nomical and possibly a disastrous venture."[12] As Marshall presented the case, the basic problem was still, as it had been the preceding spring, one of logistics. Troops were relatively plentiful; shipping was not. Therefore, the strongest attack that could be mounted would be one based on the British Isles. Shipping losses in such an attack would probably be acceptable, whereas in a Mediterranean operation they might be crippling. "To state it cruelly," Marshall told the President, "we could replace troops, whereas a heavy loss in shipping . . . might completely destroy any opportunity for successful operations against the enemy in the near future."[13]

Marshall, King, and Arnold reached something like agreement on a "party line" to follow at Casablanca. Marshall and Arnold would help King in insisting on a larger effort against Japan in 1943, particularly on an invasion of Burma in order to enlist British participation. King would support Marshall and Arnold in urging full resumption of the invasion build-up in the British Isles and in resisting the British Mediterranean program. Arnold's strategic air program would also be supported. This agreement was shaky at best, and did not extend to details. Among the staffs there was wide disagreement. The President, moreover, did not dictate

---

[11] (1) For Navy views, see min, 26th mtg JCS, 28 Jul 42; 28th mtg, 11 Aug 42; min, 24th mtg JPS, 22 Jul 42; and memo, Wood for Somervell, 5 Dec 42, sub: Opns Subsequent to TORCH, 20 Sup Gen Security folder, Case 19, Plng Div ASF, Job A46-371. (2) For AAF views, see Craven and Cate, AAF II, pp. 277–88. (3) JCS 167/3 cited n. 5(1). (4) JPS 106 cited n. 4. (5) Matloff and Snell, Strategic Planning: 1941-1942, pp. 365–66, 379–80.

[12] JCS 167/3 cited n. 5(1).

[13] Min of mtg at White House, 7 Jan 43, Item 45, Exec 10.

AT CASABLANCA, JANUARY 1943. *Seated left to right: General Marshall, President Roosevelt, Admiral King; standing left to right: Harry Hopkins, General Arnold, General Somervell, Averell Harriman.*

an agreed strategy, nor did he even promise to support the principle of concentration in northwestern Europe, toward which his chief advisers seemed to be leaning. The American chiefs had to go to Casablanca, therefore, with only the thin shell of a united front.[14]

At Casablanca the British exploited the initiative they had already seized in the debate on European strategy. By midconference the Americans had agreed to push on in the Mediterranean by invading Sicily. This decision rendered almost inevitable the postponement of a cross-

Channel invasion to 1944—late 1944, many American planners thought—although all agreed that if a good opportunity offered in 1943 it should be grasped. The Allied leaders also agreed to begin at once a heavy bombing offensive against Germany by combined British and U.S.

[14] (1) JCS 167/3 cited n. 5(1). (2) JCS 167/5, rpt by JSSC, 10 Jan 43, title: Bsc Strategic Concept for 1943—The European Theater. (3) Min of mtg at White House, 10 Dec 42, Tab 42, Item 2, Exec 5. (4) Min cited n. 13. (5) For discussions at Casablanca concerning the war in southeast Asia and aid to the USSR, see above, Chs. XIX and XXI, respectively.

strategic air forces in order to disrupt her economy and undermine her morale.[15]

For the war against Japan in 1943, the Americans presented a program that called for seizure of the Rabaul area (Tasks Two and Three of the July 1942 plan), occupation of Kiska and Agattu in the Aleutians, and, after Rabaul, a drive through the Central Pacific to occupy the Gilberts, Marshalls, and Carolines, together with an extension of New Guinea operations westward to the Dutch border. Of this program, only the Rabaul operation had been agreed to by the Army and Navy before the conference, and even there the line of approach and command arrangements were still in dispute. The Americans also wanted the British, in conjunction with the Chinese, to undertake a major invasion of Burma late in 1943, to which currently planned limited operations in the spring were to serve as a prelude.[16]

Over the division of resources among these operations, and between them and those of the European war, the American and British representatives staged a lively debate. General Marshall proved a tower of strength in supporting the Pacific program and, more generally, Admiral King's effort to play up the war against Japan in Allied strategy; none of the real disagreement between them came out into the open. Though he was mildly skeptical of King's "85-15" arithmetic, it was Marshall who proposed, at the opening meeting of the conference, that the 15 percent "effort" ought to be at least doubled. He reminded the British that during the preceding year a hand-to-mouth strategy in the Pacific had brought the Americans to the brink of disaster and, in turn, through emergency diversions to save the situation, had jeopardized Allied strategy in Europe.

To risk further disasters in the Pacific, Marshall warned, might lead to a "huge diversion of U.S. effort" to that theater.[17] The United States "could not stand another Bataan." [18]

The discussion moved in a kind of a vacuum, for no one could predict at this point what would be needed or what would be available to carry out the program. The British feared, in general, that the proposed line of action in the Pacific would interfere with the conquest of Burma, and that both together would drain away too many resources from the war in Europe. In reply, the Americans argued that in the Pacific, owing to long lines of communications, shipping already committed was a fixed overhead that could scarcely be reduced even if no further offensives were undertaken. Enemy submarines, on the other hand, were a minor threat. Therefore, few escorts were needed, movements could be scheduled efficiently, and shipping could run on direct routes. In the Atlantic, until the submarine menace abated, it was doubtful whether deployment could be accelerated much with any amount of shipping; no real improvement could be expected there before October. The Americans also agreed to underwrite the Burma opera-

---

[15] (1) CCS 116/1/D, 21 Jan 43, title: Bombing Offensive From U.K. (2) Harrison, *Cross-Channel Attack*, pp. 38–45. (3) Craven and Cate, *AAF II*, pp. 300–307.
[16] (1) CCS 153 (revised), 17 Jan 43, title: Sit To Be Created in E Theater (Pac and Burma) in 1943. (2) Min, 56th mtg CCS, 14 Jan 43. (3) See above, Ch. XV.
[17] Min, 60th mtg CCS, 18 Jan 43.
[18] (1) Min, 59th mtg CCS, 17 Jan 43; 55th mtg, 14 Jan 43; 56th mtg, 14 Jan 43; 60th mtg, 18 Jan 43. (2) Min, JCS mtg with President, 16 Jan 43. (3) CCS 153/1, memo fr Br JPS, 17 Jan 43, title: Sit To Be Created in E Theater (Pac and Burma) in 1943. (4) See Churchill's shrewd comment on the Marshall-King co-operation at Casablanca in *Hinge of Fate*, p. 676.

tion, as far as landing craft requirements were concerned.[19]

The British remained stubbornly dubious to the end, and agreed to the American program only with reservations underlining the primacy of the war against Germany. They undertook to push their limited drive in Burma, and tentatively scheduled the full-scale offensive there for November 1943, after the monsoon season, but final decision was to be withheld until summer. The Americans agreed, despite some grumbling from Admiral King, that after Rabaul further operations in the Pacific would be undertaken only "with the resources available in the theater" and only "if time and resources allow."[20] The Aleutians were to be made "as secure as may be"; how, was not specified.[21] There was also some discussion of possible attacks on the Japanese homeland by the "very-long-range" B-29 and B-32 bombers, not yet in mass production, and Roosevelt and Churchill admonished the military chiefs to build up Chennault's air forces in China more rapidly in order to intensify attrition of Japanese shipping (already pared down, it was estimated, by a sixth during the past year). These hopeful allusions to air power reflected British misgivings, shared by the President, over the costs of an island-hopping strategy.[22]

The Americans probably succeeded, at any rate, in convincing the British of their determination to press the war against Japan more aggressively. Brig. Gen. Albert C. Wedemeyer, in an otherwise pessimistic summary, credited Admiral King with this achievement. Churchill, with a keen eye to American sensibilities, declared in midconference his willingness to sign a pact that the British Empire would throw all its resources into the struggle with Japan once Germany had been defeated. Becomingly, the President refused, re-

marking, "the American people accept the word of a great English gentleman."[23]

The Mediterranean Life Line

In November and December jubilation among the Army planning staffs over the enemy's failure to maul the early convoys to North Africa was tempered by uneasiness. Up to this point Allied efforts to move shipping within range of enemy shore-based power had been invariably expensive and often disastrous. Convoys to northern USSR ports had been suspended, resumed, and suspended again; Malta had been kept alive, but at fearful cost. In the discussions following Churchill's "underbelly" proposals of November, even those of the Army staff who believed that some further post-Tunisia operations in the Mediterranean would be necessary thought of them primarily as measures to secure the line of communications.[24]

---

[19] (1) CCS 153 cited n. 16(1). (2) CCS 153/1 cited n. 18(3). (3) Min, 54th mtg JCS, 18 Jan 43. (4) Min, 59th mtg CCS, 17 Jan 43; 60th mtg, 18 Jan 43. (4) For landing craft, see below, pp. 61–73.

[20] Min cited n. 17.

[21] CCS 168, 22 Jan 43, title: Conduct of the War in Pac Theater in 1943.

[22] (1) CCS 153 cited n. 16(1). (2) Min, 60th mtg CCS, 18 Jan 43; 61st mtg, 19 Jan 43; 67th mtg, 22 Jan 43. (3) CCS 155/1, 19 Jan 43, title: Conduct of the War in 1943. (4) CCS 168 cited n. 21. (5) CCS 170/2, 23 Jan 43, title: Final Rpt to President and Prime Minister Summarizing Decisions by CCS. (6) Min, final mtg ANFA Conf, 22 Jan 43. (7) See John Miller, jr., "The Casablanca Conference and Pacific Strategy," *Military Affairs*, Vol. XIIII, No. 4 (Winter 1949), pp. 209–15.

[23] (1) Roosevelt's remark on 12 Feb 43, quoted in Sherwood, *Roosevelt and Hopkins*, p. 702. (2) Min, 2d mtg ANFA Conf, 18 Jan 43. (3) Msg, Prime Minister to Deputy Prime Minister and War Cabinet, 20 Jan 43, as quoted in Churchill, *Hinge of Fate*, pp. 683–84. (4) Ltr, Wedemeyer to Handy, 22 Jan 43, Item 1a, Exec 3.

[24] (1) CPS 49/1, 27 Nov 42, title: Plng for Opns Subsequent to TORCH. (2) Related papers in ABC 381 (11-17-42). (3) Min, 39th mtg CPS, 20 Nov 42; 41st mtg, 4 Dec 42. (4) Papers in Item 10a, Exec 1.

The staff already had a large bundle of outline projects addressed to this problem. A prerequisite would be the amassing of larger forces in North Africa itself, after the enemy's expulsion from Tunisia—as many as 1.25 million, according to one estimate—with ten divisions to be poised along the Spanish Moroccan frontier alone, others to watch Sicily, and 200,000 service troops to man ports and overland communication lines. Other projects envisaged major onslaughts and minor forays into Spain, descents upon the Canaries, the Cape Verdes, the Azores, the Balearics, and Madeira, and, of course, an occupation of Sicily and/or Sardinia. These schemes lacked reality, for shipping studies in early December indicated that only about three hundred thousand troops, over and above current plans, could be deployed to the Mediterranean in 1943, primarily after midyear. It was assumed, too, that shipping used in the Mediterranean would be sunk at the rate of 15 to 20 percent each month.[25]

The implications of an effective closure of the Strait, for example by a sudden enemy occupation of Spain, were grim to contemplate. Allied forces in North Africa, from Tunisia westward, would then have to depend on the long overland route from the Atlantic coast across the Atlas Mountains. *(See Map 6.)* East of Petitjean the trunk rail line had a smaller capacity than to the west, and, since use of the tramontane highway for continuous supply would require more motor transport than the staffs then thought it feasible to bring into the theater, the capacity of this long eastern span of the railroad determined the size of the forces that could be sustained east of the mountains. Indeed most of the capacity of the western span as well would be absorbed in this task, throwing upon the highways of Morocco most of the burden of supporting forces west of the mountains. The staff estimated that more than 3,000 trucks and trailers (2½-ton) would be needed solely to sustain five divisions assigned to occupy Spanish Morocco.[26] *(Table 22)*

According to deployment schedules current in December 1942, Allied forces in Northwest Africa were expected to reach a total of 750,000 by July 1943, with 678,000 disposed forward in Algeria and Tunisia (including 300,000 British and 150,000 French, but not the British Eighth Army or Fighting French troops). If the Strait was closed, 568,000 troops would evidently have to be evacuated across the mountains to the eastern seaboard, and from 270,000 to 366,000 (assuming the 150,000 French were self-sustaining) evacuated from the theater altogether. This would be a costly and dangerous operation, requiring full utilization of all avail-

---

[25] (1) See outline plans in SYMBOL: Casablanca Bk., Vol. I, Tab F, Exec 6. (2) Memo, ACW [Wedemeyer] for Handy, 1 Dec 42. (3) Memo, Lt Gen Stanley D. Embick for Gen Marshall, 1 Dec 42, sub: Minority Rpt on Future Action in Mediterranean. (4) CPS 49 series. Last three in ABC 381 (11-17-42). (5) Memo, Chief of Strategy and Policy Group OPD, no addressee, 16 Nov 42, sub: Consideration of Offensive Opns in Mediterranean . . . , ABC 381 (7-25-42) Sec 4-B, 80. (6) Memo, Gross for Somervell, 7 Dec 42, sub: Shipg Implications of Certain Proposed Opns, with atchd study, Baumer file, Item 20, OPD Hist Unit File. (7) Related papers in same file. (8) Strategic Logis Div study, 4 Dec 42 (revised to 7 Jan 43), title: Proposed Opns in Certain Theaters, Plng Div ASF, Job A47-147.

[26] (1) Memo, Lutes for Strategic Logis Div, 8 Jan 43, sub: Communications in N Africa . . . , 20 Sup Gen Security folder, Case 51, Plng Div ASF, Job A46-371. (2) Strategic Logis Div study, 9 Feb 43, title: Sup of United Nations Forces in N Africa by Overland Routes from Atlantic Ports, same file. Both the assumptions and the basic data used in this study differ in many respects from those in the September and October studies mentioned in Ch. XVII, above; for example, the planners now assumed 20 percent curtailment of port and rail operations by enemy bombardment.

TABLE 22—ESTIMATED CAPACITY TO SUPPORT FORCES IN NORTH AFRICA THROUGH MOROCCO: JANUARY–FEBRUARY 1943

Capacity	Troops Supported	
Port:		
Deep water ports only [a]		334,000
All ports		430,000
Overland:		
West of Atlas Mountains only (by rail and road)		in excess of 430,000
East of Atlas Mountains only (by rail only) [b]		110,000

	Using Deep Water Ports	Using All Ports
Maximum number of troops supported	334,000	430,000
West of Atlas Mountains (limited by port capacity) [c]	224,000	320,000
East of Atlas Mountains (limited by rail capacity) [b]	110,000	110,000

[a] Casablanca, Safi, and Fedala.

[b] Truck requirements for road transport over so great a distance were considered prohibitive. See table 12.

[c] Using residual rail capacity not employed in supporting forces east of the mountains, supplemented by road capacity west of the mountains, up to limits of port intake capacity.

Source: (1) Strategic Logis Div Study, 9 Feb 43, title: Sup of United Nations Forces in N Africa by Overland Routes from Atlantic Ports, and (2) Memo, Lutes for Strategic Logis Div, 8 Jan 43, sub: Communications in N Africa . . ., both in 20 Sup Gen Security folder, Case 51, Plng Div ASF.

able road and rail transport strung out along a thirteen-hundred-mile defile, exposed throughout its length to enemy air power. The overland movement, it was estimated, would require about a month and a half; to outload the troops at Atlantic ports from four to five and a half months. In short, if these calculations had any validity, it appeared that the enemy, merely by sealing the Strait passage, could win the battle for Tunisia, drive the Allies out of most of Algeria as well, if not back into Morocco, and force them to carry out a difficult and costly logistical operation that, however successful, could produce only the negative result of salvaging the bulk of Allied forces committed to North Africa. The Allied timetable would be set back a year or more.

While the logistical staffs were oppressed by these gloomy forebodings, the President, catching Churchill's mood, was buoyantly urging his military advisers to give thought to Allied operations in the eastern Mediterranean and suggesting that, while the Tunisia Campaign was being wound up, large additional American forces should be assembled simultaneously in North Africa and the British Isles in readiness for whatever enterprise might seem profitable a few months hence. Marshall's staff produced figures showing that, under existing convoy restrictions, a double build-up was virtually out of the question. Only about 180,000 more troops, they pointed out, could be shipped to North Africa alone during the next four months, but considerably larger forces could be deployed to the British Isles within the same period if movements to

North Africa were suspended. During December and early January Marshall soberly warned the President against further wasteful "dabbling" in the Mediterranean.[27] To keep open communications in the western Mediterranean would be costly enough. All forces not needed there, Marshall wanted to pour into the British Isles with a view to being ready, by March or April, for a quick assault on Brest or Boulogne if the Germans showed signs of weakening, or, as seemed more likely, if they should invade Spain. Concentration in the British Isles, he thought, could thus help to provide security in the western Mediterranean. The President evidently was not impressed. On the eve of Casablanca he still talked of massing strong forces in both England and North Africa, postponing the decision as to where to strike.[28]

The staffs, for their part, had failed to find in any purely defensive line of action real insurance against a cutting of the Mediterranean life line. Indeed, a bold course seemed scarcely more dangerous, and possibly more profitable than any other. The situation resembled that in the Pacific, where the only means of offsetting the enormous disadvantage of exterior lines was to seize and hold the strategic initiative. The British, after a long history of defending exposed sea communications, had learned to live with the problem. At Casablanca, as five months earlier, they were convinced that aggressive action by the Allies would strengthen Spain's resistance to any German incursion. Even if the enemy should gain the northern shore of the Strait, British naval representatives thought that, with airfields in Spanish Morocco and Majorca in Allied hands, convoys could get through without prohibitive losses. German coastal guns on the Pas-de-Calais, Sir Dudley Pound reminded the Americans, had failed to sink a single ship. On the positive side, there was the lure of opening a passage through the whole length of the Mediterranean. The British planned, as soon as the tip of Tunisia was won, to begin running thirty-ship cargo convoys through to Suez every ten days, counting on the shorter turnaround (as compared with the Cape route) to offset losses. Over a period of five months perhaps 225 sailings, the equivalent of about 1,825,000 tons of shipping, might be saved by using the shorter route. Personnel and tanker movements would have to wait until cover could be provided from the north shore, but troop movements to the Middle East were on the wane in any case. Access to Middle East oil, on the other hand, through the pipeline terminus at Haifa, would be a great prize.[29]

Enemy air power based on Sicily and Sardinia posed the most dangerous threat to Allied shipping movements through the Mediterranean, and the discussion of "next steps" in the Mediterranean centered mainly upon these two objectives.[30]

---

[27] Min cited n. 14(3).

[28] (1) *Ibid.* (2) Min cited n. 13. (3) Memo, Dill for Prime Minister, 14 Dec 42, as quoted in Churchill, *Hinge of Fate*, pp. 658–59. (4) Memo, Handy for Marshall, 18 Dec 42, sub: Shipt of Trs to U.K., ETO folder, Lutes File. (5) OPD draft memo, CofS for President, no date, Item 54, Exec 10.

[29] (1) Min, 50th mtg JCS, 13 Jan 43; 51st mtg, 14 Jan 43; 52d mtg, 16 Jan 43. (2) Min, 55th mtg CCS, 14 Jan 43; 57th mtg, 15 Jan 43; 58th mtg, 16 Jan 43; 60th mtg, 18 Jan 43. (3) Min, 1st mtg ANFA Conf, 15 Jan 43.

[30] War Department and SOS staffs had not studied these operations carefully as planning for Mediterranean operations was the responsibility of the theater staff. Since General Eisenhower himself did not bring a large staff or much planning data with him to the conference, the Army representatives found themselves at a disadvantage. General Somervell, the only

The Sardinia operation (BRIMSTONE) seemed likely to be a smaller undertaking than an attack on Sicily (HUSKY)—four divisions as against seven or more, by British reckoning—and it probably could be mounted earlier. Either operation would probably require diversion of Navy combat loaders from the Pacific. As a ferrying operation, either was theoretically within the capacity of cargo shipping in 1943, though the margin was slim. Shipping time would be lost, as it had been lost in TORCH, in assembling the large initial convoys; convoying would have to be curtailed all over the world; and the problems of transshipping from bases in North Africa were still unexplored. Limited port capacity on both islands promised to restrict the build-up in the early stages; much supply would have to flow over the beaches. In general, the logistical problems were similar, though looming somewhat larger for HUSKY. On the other hand, better air cover could be provided for an attack on Sicily than for one on Sardinia. Even if taken, Sardinia might turn out to be a dangerous salient, which the Germans could isolate by sea and air while invading Spain. To hold Sardinia, it would probably be necessary to go on to Corsica and

Sicily. Most important, possession of Sardinia would offer little protection to the Mediterranean convoy route as long as the enemy held Sicily. And, as General Marshall put it, to strike at "the softest spot before turning to the hardest spot" was likely merely to "make the hard spot harder." [31]

The British wanted Sardinia, in fact, less as a flanking guardpost for the Mediterranean convoy route than as a stepping-stone to Italy. From Sardinia, Italy could be bombed and harried by amphibious forays, and, conceivably, driven to surrender without an invasion. Sicily offered some of these advantages, but at greater cost. From this point of view, BRIMSTONE seemed the quicker and cheaper alternative, a means of maintaining momentum and of gaining results early. It left open the possibility of a sudden leap across the English Channel in midsummer, if the opportunity offered, while it could also provide a springboard for a major effort against Italy. "BRIMSTONE in June," Air Marshall Portal remarked, "would be better than HUSKY in September." [32]

To the Americans this seemed a perverted strategy. To knock out Italy, Marshall bluntly told the British, was less important than to open the Mediterranean to shipping, and to this BRIMSTONE would contribute little. Allied possession of Sicily,

---

American logistical expert accompanying Marshall, was not permitted to bring any staff officers with him and had to borrow two of Eisenhower's staff to help him. The logistical studies and data available to the Army representatives at Casablanca are contained in one of three black loose-leaf notebooks made up by the OPD staff. Somervell's copies are filed in Planning Division, ASF, files. Somervell's correspondence and work papers for the Casablanca Conference are filed in Ltrs, Memos, and Msgs Between Somervell and Styer folder, Planning Division, ASF. Lack of prepared logistical studies and data on the American side was probably one of the considerations that lay behind General Wedemeyer's rueful remark that the British "swarmed down on us like locusts with a plentiful supply of planners and various other assistants with prepared plans . . . ." Ltr, Wedemeyer to Handy, 22 Jan 43, Item 1a, Exec 3.

[31] (1) Min, 66th mtg, CCS, 22 Jan 43. (2) Outline plans in SYMBOL: Casablanca Bk., Vol. I, Tabs F-1, F-2, Exec 6. (3) Study cited n. 25(8). (4) Strategic Logis Div study (11-17-42), Sec 1-B. (5) Min, 50th mtg JCS, 13 Jan 43; 52d mtg, 16 Jan 43; 54th mtg, 18 Jan 43; 57th mtg, 21 Jan 43. (6) Min, 57th mtg CCS, 15 Jan 43; 58th mtg, 16 Jan 43. (7) JPS 106 cited n. 4.
[32] (1) Min cited n. 31(1). (2) Min, 52d mtg JCS, 16 Jan 43. (3) Min cited n. 18(2). (4) Min, 64th mtg CCS, 20 Jan 43; 66th mtg, 22 Jan 43. (5) Min, 3d mtg ANFA Conf, 23 Jan 43. (6) CCS 135/2, Annex III, cited n. 3. (7) CCS 161, 20 Jan 43, title: Opn HUSKY. (8) CCS 161/1, 21 Jan 43, same title.

on the other hand, might reduce the losses of convoys moving through the narrows by as much as a third. The British themselves were divided on the question, and Churchill had always favored HUSKY. Their chief objection to this operation was that it would require too long to mount. In the first plan presented by the British staff, the assault date was set for late in September on the assumption that training and the assembling of forces and shipping could not begin until ports and base facilities in Tunisia were available. The alternative, considered too dangerous, was to send most of the assault forces from the United Kingdom, passing a large convoy through the Sicilian narrows on D Day. Instructed to re-examine their figures, the planners came back a day later with a 30 August assault date, which the chiefs still considered too late. The chiefs pushed the planners; the President and Prime Minister pushed the chiefs. In the end the date for the assault was set, more or less by fiat, in the period of the favorable July moon, with the stipulation that strenuous efforts would be made by "contrivance and ingenuity" to advance the date to June.[33] HUSKY was on; it remained to work out a plan.

Bolero Renewed

Agreement on Sicily did not mean agreement on European strategy. Sicily undeniably would be a substantial prize; its capture would free the passage through the narrows and perhaps jolt Italy out of the war. But the American chiefs were worried about what was to follow. Recently the Joint Strategic Survey Committee had characterized an operation against Sicily as one "of major magnitude" that would absorb "all available means through a large part of 1943"—possibly an exaggerated estimate, but an ominous one nonetheless.[34] Even while accepting HUSKY, the Americans wondered, as General Marshall said, whether the British regarded it "as a part of an integrated plan to win the war or simply taking advantage of an opportunity." What was the "main plot"? How was HUSKY to be prevented from becoming a "suction pump," draining Allied strength away from the main effort?[35] That effort was against Germany, not her satellites, and must eventually be made from the northwest, not the south.[36]

Agreeing with this general proposition, the British nevertheless painted vistas beyond the capture of Sicily that the Americans found disturbing. The British saw Sicily, like Sardinia, as a steppingstone to Italy; Italy must be knocked out at whatever cost in effort and time. They estimated the cost to Germany of Italy's defection at fifty-four divisions and 2,250 first-line aircraft. If Turkey could be drawn into the war, there would be a further diversion of German forces. Meanwhile, Germany could be pounded from the air on all sides. In this way, the British argued, the Allies could create in 1943 the second front they lacked the strength to mount in northwestern Europe. Germany's main logistical strength lay in her east-west communications. In two weeks, the British asserted, she could move seven divisions across the Continent to any threatened point in the West, as against only one to the Mediterranean over a route exposed to Allied air attack. In any case, the Germans already

[33] (1) CCS 171/2/D, 23 Jan 43, title: Dir to CINC Allied Exped Forces in N Africa. (2) Min cited n. 31(1). (3) See above, n. 32. (4) Churchill, *Hinge of Fate*, pp. 654–55, 678.
[34] Memo, JSSC for JCS, 31 Dec 42, sub: Opns Subsequent to TORCH, SYMBOL: Casablanca Bk., Vol. II, Tab F, Exec 6.
[35] Min, 58th mtg CCS, 16 Jan 43.
[36] (1) Min cited n. 23(2). (2) Min cited n. 17.

10, Downing Street,
Whitehall.

Anfa Camp.

January 18, 1943

My dear General Somervell,

Thank you so much for your figures of the monthly loss rates of dry cargo ships available to the United Nations in 1942.

It must be remembered that the last six months of 1942 include the exceptional losses of TORCH. Since then only six weeks have passed and I agree with you that this is too small a basis for calculation. However I hazard the forecast that for the four months including December and January a rate of 2% or less will rule.

I cannot risk my reputation as a Prophet by probing ahead further.

Yours sincerely,

Winston S. Churchill

Lieut.-General B. B. Somervell,
    Anfa Camp,
        CASABLANCA.

P.S. Write to me if I am wrong on April 1.

CHURCHILL ON SHIPPING LOSSES. *At the Casablanca Conference Churchill followed closely the discussion by the staffs of the problem of shipping losses, which decisively influenced Mediterranean and European strategy.*

had forty-four divisions in the West. Any bridgehead that the Allies could win there in 1943 would be hemmed in "with wire and concrete" during the winter while the Germans built up their power.[37] Only internal disintegration in Germany would offer any chance of success to an Allied invasion from the northwest in 1943, but such a condition might yet be produced, the British still felt, by their program in the Mediterranean and by continued German setbacks in the USSR. To the skeptical Americans, this looked like postponing the invasion to the Greek Kalends.[38]

But what was the alternative? For weeks before the conference, the American staffs had been exploring the possibilities of various "modified" cross-Channel operations that might be undertaken in 1943 as a prelude to a major invasion in 1944. The limitations upon build-up of forces were discouraging enough, apart from the difficulties to be overcome in the operation itself. Even if movements to North Africa were stopped in January 1943, convoy restrictions would permit no more than half a million American troops to be assembled in the United Kingdom and made ready to cross the Channel by July—about eight divisions with supporting troops (assuming a 4-to-1 ratio of ground to air). If convoy restrictions were lifted, eleven divisions in a force of about 680,000 might be assembled, cargo shipping constituting the limiting factor. After midyear, cargo-carrying capacity was expected to overbalance passenger capacity. For a September 1943 operation, perhaps twelve American divisions could be ferried to Britain, to join some thirteen British divisions—a force not likely to shatter Germany's fixed defenses and forty-four divisions in western Europe.[39]

At Casablanca General Somervell and

the British shipping expert, Lord Leathers, were asked to take a fresh look at the whole problem of building up an invasion force in the British Isles. The most uncertain assumptions that had to be made related to the ability of the navies to protect ocean movements. Shipping losses had declined somewhat in December from their November peak, but the U.S. Navy, currently engaged in a bitter dispute with the Army Air Forces over policies and division of responsibility in combating enemy attacks on shipping, anticipated no early relief. The Combined Planners reported that "minimum acceptable requirements" for convoying would not be met by new construction until August or September 1943, and that the battle against the submarine could not be expected to take a favorable turn until the end of the year.[40] Meanwhile, the convoy system in the Atlantic was still suffering from disruption caused by TORCH, and the British import program faced a crisis. There was every reason to believe that the Sicily operation would similarly disrupt convoy service. If, as the experts predicted, escorts were engaged in that operation for four months, the Murmansk convoys, re-

---

[37] Min, 58th mtg CCS, 16 Jan 43.
[38] (1) Min, 55th mtg CCS, 14 Jan 43; 58th mtg, 16 Jan 43; 60th mtg, 18 Jan 43. (2) Min, 52d mtg JCS, 16 Jan 43. (3) Min cited n. 18(2).
[39] (1) Memo, Lutes for Somervell, 22 Dec 42, sub: Summary of ROUNDUP 1943, Opns SOS 1942–43 folder, Hq ASF. (2) Memo cited n. 28(4). (3) OPD draft memo, CofS for President, 15 Dec 42, Item 54, Exec 10. (4) JPS 106 cited n. 4. (5) Outline Plan, title: Modified ROUNDUP, in SYMBOL: Casablanca Bk., Vol. I, Tab F-5a, Exec 6. (6) Paper, no date, sub: Gen Concept of Opns, T-1 Trs folder, Plng Div ASF, Job A47-147. (7) CCS 135/1 cited n. 10(3).
As usual, the figures are difficult to reconcile, but the conclusions regarding the September operation seem to be supported by all the estimates.
[40] CCS 160, rpt by CPS, 19 Jan 43, title: Minimum Escort Reqmts To Maintain Sea Communications of the United Nations.

sumed in December, would have to be suspended again. In making this proposal the military leaders drew upon their heads the displeasure of the President and Prime Minister, who were determined to increase rather than diminish shipments to the Soviet Union. Sharp words were exchanged, and General Marshall bluntly declared that it was folly to accept prohibitive losses on the northern route "simply to keep Mr. Stalin placated." [41]

Somervell and Leathers could do no more than note this problem and assume that convoy arrangements would be worked out to permit full use of available shipping. On this basis, and on the additional assumption that considerable British assistance in troop and cargo shipping would be provided, Somervell drew up a schedule of U.S. Army deployment in 1943—allowing for the movement of close to a million troops to the British Isles. (Table 23) The chiefs accepted it as a starting point for more detailed deployment planning. [42]

The BOLERO deployment in this schedule represented the estimated maximum capacity of cargo shipping during the first half of 1943, and of troop shipping during the second half. It assumed, further, a continuous inflow of cargo to British ports at a rate of 150 ships per month, a rate that, Lord Leathers warned, could not be sustained during the late fall and winter months and to maintain which American dock labor and locomotives would be needed even in the summer.

Shelved for the present, this problem was to cause trouble later. Allowing as it did for a substantial deployment to the Mediterranean and for an accelerated deployment of air forces to the United Kingdom for the combined bomber offensive, Somervell's schedule anticipated that only seven or eight ground divisions would be

ready in the British Isles by mid-September instead of the twelve divisions predicted in preconference estimates. This brought the total force that might be available for a late-summer cross-Channel operation well under even the twenty-one divisions that the British had estimated in conjunction with their earlier four-division Sardinia project. It was, in fact, no more than a fair beginning in a build-up for a 1944 invasion. [43]

---

[41] (1) Min cited n. 23(2). (2) CCS 160 cited n. 40. (3) Related papers in ABC 560 Atlantic (1-19-43) Sec 1. (4) Min, 56th mtg JCS, 20 Jan 43. (5) Min, 55th mtg CCS, 14 Jan 43; 63d mtg, 20 Jan 43. (6) Min cited n. 32(5). (7) Craven and Cate, AAF I, Ch. XV; AAF II, Ch. VIII. (8) Morison, Battle of the Atlantic. (9) For shipping losses, see above, Ch. XXII, and below, Apps. J, K. (10) For the Soviet aid program, see above, Ch. XXI.

[42] CCS 172, note by Somervell, 22 Jan 43, title: Shipg Capabilities for BOLERO Build-up. For other currrent deployment estimates, see above, Ch. XXII. The following were the principal assumptions in this estimate:

(a) British aid to BOLERO: 345,000 personnel lift, mainly during spring and summer; 1,600,000 ship tons cargo lift, mainly in last quarter.

(b) Conversion of Liberty hulls to troop transports to be suspended, but some conversion to tankers. Total new U.S. construction in 1943, 18,562,000 tons. Five cargo vessels to be converted to Navy combat loaders each month through April 1943.

(c) Initial movement requirements: 8 ship tons per man; maintenance, 1.3 ship tons per man per month (but 1 ton per man in U.K.).

(d) Navy use of dry cargo shipping increased by 300,000 dead-weight tons each quarter, reaching 2,360,000 tons in last quarter 1943.

(e) 4,000,000 dead-weight tons shipping reserved for war economy and defense aid, and 170 sailings additional in 1943 for Soviet aid.

(f) No shipping to be withdrawn from British import program.

(g) Average cargo ship turnaround, 2½ months.

(h) 12½ percent of dry cargo fleet constantly under repair.

(i) Average losses, 2.6 percent.

[43] This estimate was based on a "division slice" of from 40,000 to 50,000 ground troops, declining to the former figure as the build-up proceeded. It also reflected an allowance of forty-five days between sailing and final readiness of troops. See (1) Min cited n. 32(5); (2) Min, 68th mtg CCS, 23 Jan 43; and (3) CCS 170/2 cited n. 22(5). (4) Msg, Leathers to Somervell, 21 Jan 43, Ltrs, Memos, and Msgs Between Somervell and Styer folder, Plng Div ASF.

TABLE 23—PROPOSED U.S. ARMY DEPLOYMENT FOR 1943: JANUARY 1943

| Area | Overseas [a] 31 Dec 42 | Proposed Deployment for 1943 | | | | | Overseas 31 Dec 43 |
		Total 1943	1st Qtr	2d Qtr	3d Qtr	4th Qtr	
Total.....................	1,060,000	1,325,600	208,000	327,000	418,500	371,900	2,385,600
South and Southwest Pacific.......	224,000	111,200	48,700	30,500	24,500	7,500	335,200
Burma.........................	31,000	30,000	7,500	7,500	15,000	0	61,000
North Africa....................	216,000	184,000	68,000	[b] 116,000	0	0	400,000
Bases.........................	454,000	[c] 17,400	4,000	4,000	4,000	5,400	471,400
United Kingdom.................	135,000	983,000	80,000	169,000	375,000	359,000	1,118,000

[a] Includes troops en route.
[b] One division (16,000) combat loaded from United States for HUSKY.
[c] Movements to bases during 1943 to be limited to 17,400 to Persian Corridor.

Source: CCS 172, note by Somervell, 22 Jan 43, title: Shipg Capabilities for BOLERO Build-up.

British Imports
The Six-Million-Ton Misunderstanding

Even so, Somervell's whittled-down BOLERO program was more optimistic than he knew. It depended heavily upon expectations of British assistance in shipping during 1943, and these in turn were bound up with assumptions concerning the British import program that were startlingly at variance with the facts.

In March 1942, at a dark hour in the battle for shipping, Churchill had written to Roosevelt, "When I reflect how I have longed and prayed for the entry of the United States into the war, I find it difficult to realise how gravely our British affairs have deteriorated by what has happened since December 7." [44] Throughout that year Britain continued to suffer heavier proportionate losses in shipping than her ally, and far more than in the year preceding when she had been fighting the war at sea alone. The organizing of American antisubmarine defenses owed much to British help, which involved a thinning-out of Britain's own escort cover-

age and a lengthening of convoy cycles with consequent reductions in the flow of imports. During the latter half of 1942, while the American shipping situation was gradually improving, the British merchant fleet, operating in more exposed areas and possessing only a limited replacement capacity, continued to dwindle. By the end of April 1943 Britain's dry cargo tonnage had fallen from 16.2 million gross tons in November 1941 to about 14 million. [45]

The effort to meet the growing demands of military operations upon Britain's shipping resulted in a steady encroachment during 1942 upon the flow of her imports. These had declined from a prewar average of over 50 million dead-weight tons to 42 million in 1940 and 31 million in 1941; in 1942 they fell to 23 million. Desperate efforts were made in this year to arrest the decline. Shipping space was

---

[44] Msg, Former Naval Person to President Roosevelt, 5 Mar 42, as quoted in Churchill, *Hinge of Fate*, p. 191.
[45] (1) Hancock and Gowing, *British War Economy*, pp. 412–14, 416–17. (2) See above, Chs. VIII, XVII.

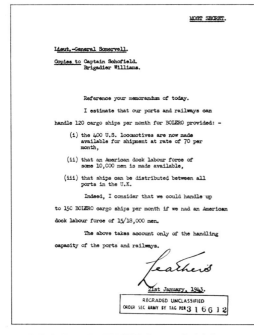

MOST SECRET.

Lieut.-General Somervell.

Copies to Captain Schofield.
         Brigadier Williams.

Reference your memorandum of today.

I estimate that our ports and railways can

handle 120 cargo ships per month for BOLERO provided: -

(i) the 400 U.S. locomotives are now made
    available for shipment at rate of 70 per
    month,

(ii) that an American dock labour force of
     some 10,000 men is made available,

(iii) that ships can be distributed between all
      ports in the U.K.

Indeed, I consider that we could handle up

to 150 BOLERO cargo ships per month if we had an American

dock labour force of 15/18,000 men.

The above takes account only of the handling

capacity of the ports and railways.

Leathers

21st January, 1943.

RECRADED UNCLASSIFIED
ORDER SEC ARMY BY TAG PER 3 1 6 6 1 2

LORD LEATHERS *on British port capacity.*

saved by crating vehicles, improvements in spare parts supply, reduction in military vehicle allowances, more efficient stowage and cargo handling. Ship routings were carefully arranged with a view to drawing upon near sources of supply. At the same time, the needs that imports filled were curtailed. A new milling ratio, adopted in March 1942, promised to save 400,000 tons of imported grain per year. Domestic food production was increased by an estimated 50 percent over prewar. Imported materials for nonmilitary production and services were cut to low levels—newsprint by 80 percent, for example. Production of munitions was stepped up (though this required more raw materials), so that imported finished munitions in 1942 amounted to less than 10 percent of the total volume of imports.[46]

These expedients failed to close the gap.

Britain had to eat into her stocks, which by the end of 1942 had fallen an estimated 2.5 million tons, to a level dangerously near what the War Cabinet had decided must be regarded as irreducible. Relatively little help was given by American shipping during 1942. New construction in the United States did not appreciably outpace losses until midyear, conversion of merchant shipping to essential war services was slow, and British import needs were subordinated, both in British and American policy, to those of military lend-lease and military services. By late summer American officials as well as British were growing uneasy over the trend. Lewis Douglas, deputy administrator of WSA, visited London in July and he and Averell Harriman, the President's lend-lease representative there, submitted a special report to the President on 2 August, supplementing a more comprehensive one by the two Combined Shipping Adjustment Boards (Washington and London), warning that substantial American aid in shipping would be needed if Britain were to continue her war effort on its present scale. Early in October the United States, through the CSAB, formally accepted the principle that, as the merchant shipbuilder for the United Nations, it would undertake to assign an "appropriate portion" of the surplus tonnage (over losses) being produced by American yards "to relieve the burden on the war services of each of the other United Nations."[47] Before the end of that month

[46] (1) Hancock and Gowing, *British War Economy*, pp. 418–23. (2) Memorandum on U.K. Import Requirements Submitted to CSAB by Joint Economic Analysts, 8 Feb 43, U.K. Imports folder, WSA Douglas File. (3) CCS 183/3, 18 Mar 43, title: Note . . . on Br Import Prog.

[47] WSA paper, 6 Oct 42, sub: Employment of U.S. Tonnage . . . , Employment of Shipg Corresp folder, WSA Douglas File.

the President had decided to expand the merchant shipbuilding program for 1943. But the British Government, while reasonably confident that Britain would be the largest foreign beneficiary of this expansion, felt that the clear drift of the national economy toward disaster called for more specific assurance and concrete action. It decided to seek from its ally "a solemn compact, almost a treaty," setting forth the amount of shipping Britain could expect.[48]

In November Sir Oliver Lyttelton, British Minister of Production, came to Washington to negotiate such a settlement in the whole field of munitions and shipping. Depletion of domestic stocks, he pointed out, had gone so far that imports had little or no margin left for fluctuation; henceforth the flow must keep pace with consumption. Lyttelton requested that the United States guarantee enough shipping in 1943 to enable Britain to bring her dry cargo imports up to 27 million tons, a figure that would not, indeed, restore depleted stocks but would suffice to keep them just above the danger level—involving further depletion by 1.6 million tons during 1943—while providing raw materials for an expanded output of munitions. The proposal envisaged an actual transfer of U.S. shipping to the British flag equivalent to an average carrying capacity throughout the year of 2.5 million tons.[49]

The President's response was prompt and sympathetic. "In all probability," he wrote to Admiral Land, "the British are going to lose again in 1943 more ships than they can build. If we are going to keep England in the war at anything like this maximum capacity, we must consider the supplementing of their merchant fleet as one of the top military necessities of the war."[50] His principal civilian advisers concurred, and there is no indication that

the military were consulted on the matter. Replying formally to the Prime Minister on 30 November, Roosevelt noted that the U.S. shipbuilding program was being augmented to at least 18.8 million deadweight tons in 1943, possibly 20 million. The British goal of 27 million tons of imports in 1943 he thought "substantially correct," and he promised that the War Shipping Administration would make available (though not by transfer of flag) sufficient ship tonnage to meet this goal, along with requirements for military supply and essential war services, to the extent that British shipping proved inadequate.[51] Since the British estimated their own carrying capacity for imports in 1943 at about 20 million tons, the President thus committed American shipping to carry some 7 million tons of imports to the United Kingdom during 1943. This requirement the experts estimated would mean turning over each month, and leaving in continuous service thereafter, an average of 300,000 dead-weight tons of shipping—in all, perhaps 30 percent of the expected net increase in the American merchant fleet. The President warned that transfers would lag during the next three months because of current commitments in the Mediterranean, and expressed the hope that

---

[48] (1) Hancock and Gowing, *British War Economy*, pp. 423–26. (2) Msg, Harriman and Douglas to President, 2 Aug 42. (3) Douglas' notes on conf with President, Hopkins, and Land, 21 Oct 42. Last two in Hopkins folder, WSA Douglas File. (4) Paper cited n. 47. (5) Memo, Sir Arthur Salter, no addressee, 26 Oct 42, Br Merchant Shipg Mis Misc folder, WSA Douglas File. (6) Corresp in U.K. Imports folder, WSA Douglas File. (7) See above, Chs. XIV, XXII.

[49] (1) Hancock and Gowing, *British War Economy*, pp. 421, 428–29. (2) Memorandum on U.K. Import Requirements . . . , cited n. 46(2) For agreement on munitions allocation, see above, Ch. XI.

[50] Memo, FDR for Land, 30 Nov 42, MS Index to the Hopkins Papers, Bk. VII, Shipg, p. 4, Item 3(f).

[51] Ltr, President to Churchill, 30 Nov 42, ABC 400 (11-19-42).

smaller tonnages would be sufficient to maintain the flow of imports after the Mediterranean passage had been cleared. He also made the reservation that in an emergency it might be necessary to divert tonnage temporarily from British imports, and that other cases might arise "in which we shall wish jointly to confer." But he assured Churchill "that any important diversions of tonnages will be made only with my personal approval." [52]

The President's warning of a probable lag in early deliveries was immediately borne out. The first schedules worked up by WSA envisaged that most of the movement would be postponed to the second half of 1943, with only 1.8 million tons of imports to be delivered by American shipping during the first half. Shipments during December 1942 were hardly more than token in character, and in January Douglas, confronted by multiplying military demands for shipping in all theaters, suggested that the scheduled 1.8 million tons of imports might have to be reduced to about 1,150,000 tons, leaving over 6 million to be carried after June. But the British, meanwhile, were also running into difficulties. Their military requirements in the Mediterranean proved "more onerous and more prolonged" than expected, with a resulting additional drain upon import-carrying tonnage that made it necessary to revise downward by some 2.7 million tons the previous estimate of 20 million tons of imports to be carried in British shipping during 1943.[53] Fearing new military demands and uneasy over the lag in American aid, the British Government began to doubt the wisdom of permitting domestic stocks to drop a full four million tons below their end-1941 level. In January Churchill took the drastic step of shifting fifty-two out of the ninety-two vessels engaged in supporting British forces in the

Indian Ocean area back to the Atlantic to carry import cargoes from nearer sources of supply in order, as he put it, not to make Britain "live from hand to mouth, absolutely dependent on the fulfillment of American promises in the last six months of the year." [54] The British argued that the savings from this rerouting of shipping must be used to retard the depletion of their stocks rather than to lighten the burden upon American tonnage. American officials in London, studying the situation, not merely agreed with this position but recommended that, far from reducing the American contribution of shipping during the first six months of 1943, it would be prudent to increase it to some three million tons. If too large a portion of the total import burden were pushed forward past midyear, British ports and railroads might prove unable to carry the load.[55]

The Casablanca Conference took place in the midst of these negotiations. Among the military problems that made up the agenda of the conference, the British import program, a "civil" matter, had no place, and the military leaders merely reaffirmed the maintenance of Britain's war

---

[52] (1) *Ibid.* (2) Memo, Nelson, Wickard, and Harriman for FDR, 10 Nov 42, MS Index to the Hopkins Papers, Bk. VII, Shipg, p. 4, Item 3(d). (3) Memo, Nelson, Wickard, and Harriman for FDR, 19 Nov 42, U.K. Imports folder, WSA Douglas File. (4) Paper, 19 Nov 42, sub: Allocs Needed To Maintain Br Sv, with notes, Allocs Gen folder, WSA Douglas File. (5) Memo, Land, Douglas, and Harriman for FDR, 20 Nov 42, Reading file, WSA Douglas File.

[53] Memo, Salter for Douglas, 25 Feb 43, Allocs Gen folder, WSA Douglas File.

[54] Ltr, Prime Minister to Gen Ismay, 5 Jan 43, as quoted in Churchill, *Hinge of Fate,* p. 926.

[55] (1) Memorandum on U.K. Import Requirements . . . , cited n. 46(2). (3) Memo cited n. 53. (4) Ltr, Nathan to Douglas, 16 Feb 43, U.K. Imports folder, WSA Douglas File. (5) Related corresp, Douglas with Lubin, same file. (6) Memo, Douglas for Salter, 11 Feb 43, Reading file, WSA Douglas File. (7) Corresp in Salter Memoranda folder, WSA Douglas File. (8) Hancock and Gowing, *British War Economy,* pp. 429-30.

economy as one of the "first charges" upon the Allied war effort. On the American side, the Joint Chiefs had not even learned of the President's commitment until late in December, when a copy of his letter of 30 November was shown to them "very unofficially and confidentially" by the British military representatives.[56] Presumably this tardy intelligence was passed on to General Somervell, but that officer displayed at Casablanca a degree of confusion over the precise terms of the President's letter and of the program set up to implement it that Lord Leathers, representing British shipping interests at the conference, must have found puzzling. And, unfortunately, the WSA officials who alone could have spoken with authority on the matter were not present.[57]

The result was one of the most curious misunderstandings in the whole course of Anglo-American wartime collaboration. Somervell's first, and more general, misconception was in regarding the American commitment as being aimed at replacing British net shipping losses (a conception dating back to the Victory Program of 1941) rather than at meeting British marginal requirements for shipping. The difference could mean much or little, in actual tonnages, depending on the course of ship losses in 1943. Somervell's second misconception, however, was both more specific and more fundamental: he interpreted the implied ceiling of 300,000 tons upon the monthly American contribution of shipping for British use, stated in the President's letter, in terms of equivalent single-voyage sailings, rather than a tonnage that would remain in British service. The carriage of British imports in American bottoms during 1943, he thus calculated, would amount at most to only 3.6 million tons, not 7 million. Somervell was optimistic, moreover, on the basis of

current loss trends, that the total might be far less. "If there is a reduction in the number of sinkings," his final deployment paper (CCS 172) noted, "the assistance required will be reduced. As a reduction is expected, in some measure there will be a credit on this account."[58]

The substantial movement of American troops and matériel to Britain that Somervell held out as a possibility for 1943 rested not merely upon this optimistic assumption, but also upon an alleged promise by the British to help out to the extent of some 1,600,000 measurement tons of cargo shipping. Somervell did indeed elicit from Lord Leathers a tentative undertaking to contribute shipping to the BOLERO program, but it was heavily qualified to protect both Britain's import program and her major operational needs from encroachment. It was, in fact, conditional upon Britain having a surplus of shipping over and above her needs—a wholly unreal condition, as Leathers subsequently pointed out, since, as he understood the President's commitment of 30 November, Britain was to receive only enough American shipping to fill whatever marginal requirements her own shipping proved insufficient to fill. There could, therefore, be no "surplus" to give back to the Americans. In any case, the figure of 1,600,000 was a rapid estimate "subject to check." Somervell, Leathers asserted, "fully understood this and repeatedly acknowledged his understanding." As Sir Arthur Salter, Leathers'

[56] Memo, Deane for Marshall, King, and Arnold, 26 Dec 42, CCS 400 (11-30-42).

[57] Ibid.

[58] (1) CCS 172 cited n. 42. Curiously enough, CCS 172 omitted any reference to the 300,000-ton ceiling, and thus might be interpreted (as the British later pointed out) to commit the U.S. to unlimited replacement of British losses. (2) CCS 162, 19 Jan 43, title: U.S. Aid to Russia. (3) CCS 162/1, 20 Jan 43, same title. (4) CCS 160 cited n. 40.

representative in the United States, summed it up:

Lord Leathers gave an overoptimistic estimate (safeguarded because slated to be checked) on an unreal assumption given by General Somervell. It was in any case a provisional estimate (even on that unreal basis) and not a commitment, and it was all on the repeatedly stated, and acknowledged, basis that it was only an estimate of what, on a given assumption, might be available after British import requirements had been met.[59]

The shipping discussions at Casablanca must repeatedly have come within a hair's breadth of revealing to both sides how far apart their fundamental assumptions were. The British counted on American shipping to carry over 7 million tons of their imports in 1943, whereas, in Somervell's expectations, considerably less than half, perhaps only a third, of this amount was to be carried and the British themselves were to turn back, for BOLERO shipments, enough tonnage to offset a large part of the American import contribution. Between the two sets of expectations stretched a gap roughly equivalent to almost 6 million dead-weight tons of carrying capacity over the span of the coming year, or almost a fourth of the entire tonnage of cargo that was actually to be shipped overseas to the U.S. Army in that year.[60] So gigantic a misunderstanding could not long endure, and the longer its duration the more explosive must be the effects of terminating it. The revelation, when it came, was to nearly upset the whole Casablanca strategy.

Limitations on Amphibious Assault

Technological change in amphibious warfare had kept well ahead of operations during 1942. As Rear Adm. Charles M. Cooke, Jr., remarked early in the Casa-

blanca Conference, it would be unwise to look back to the experience of the past year in weighing capabilities in the year to come. General Somervell expatiated with enthusiasm on the new means for attacking an enemy-held shore with the large types of landing vessels, especially the tank landing ship (LST), the large personnel carrier (LCI(L)), and the tank landing craft (LCT(5)). Using these vessels, an assaulting force could move directly from nearby base ports to the target area and there land troops and heavy equipment over the beaches rapidly and in large numbers. By June 1943, Somervell thought, it would be possible to assemble enough large landing ships and craft in the Mediterranean to shuttle almost 90,-000 troops ashore with heavy equipment in the first wave. Combat loaders, brought in wherever protection could be provided, could land additional troops in small boats. So large an effort, of course, would require absolute priority over every other operation. A survey by OPD late in January indicated a reasonable possibility of concentrating enough British and American amphibious shipping in the Atlantic-Mediterranean area to land about 63,000

---

[59] (1) Memo cited n. 53. (2) CCS 172 cited n. 42. (3) Msg, Harriman to Douglas, 23 Feb 43, Allocs Gen folder, WSA Douglas File. (4) Br JPS paper, 22 Jan 43, sub: BOLERO Build-up, Ltrs, Memos, and Msgs Between Somervell and Styer folder, Plng Div ASF.

[60] Precisely how much shipping aid Somervell expected would have to be provided is not clear; Gross, on separate later occasions, mentioned 3 million and 2.4 million tons of imports. See memo, Gross for Marshall, 17 Mar 43; and handwritten notes on msg, Douglas to Harriman, 9 Mar 43. Both are in Shipg 1941–43 folder, Hq ASF. The 1,600,000 measurement tons of cargo shipping allegedly promised by Leathers (and therefore to be deducted from the above figures) were perhaps equivalent to about 1,120,000 dead-weight tons of imports, assuming single voyages and not cumulative employment. Army cargo shipped overseas in 1943 was about 28.5 million measurement tons, or about 24 million dead-weight tons. For conversion factors, see below, App. A-1.

troops and 2,300 tanks in a single wave.[61]

Behind these estimates lay a substantial production achievement. Between August and December 1942 production had been lifted from its summer doldrums and accelerated at a rate unprecedented in the history of naval construction. LST's had begun to emerge from U.S. yards in October; 43 were completed in December, 46 in January, and production was to reach a peak of 61 in February 1943. Of the large infantry craft (LCI(L)), over 150 had been completed by the end of 1942, and a peak of 70 was reached in January 1943. Production of the tank lighters (LCT(5)'s) had attained a high volume in September and before the end of the year the July 1942 program of 470 had been substantially completed. About 90 of these craft were already in the United Kingdom. Completion of the LST and LCI(L) programs was expected during the spring. Small personnel and vehicle craft (LCP's and LCV's) were available in large numbers; production of the slightly larger LCM(3) was lagging. Amphibious vehicles and tractors were coming into production. Total tonnages delivered rose from 24,443 in September to 57,863 in November and 85,000 in December; production in the last half of 1942 was twenty times that in the first half. Before the end of the year the diminishing urgency of the landing craft program was reflected in its decline on the Navy's Shipbuilding Precedence List from first to third place. In December a large part of the LST program, already reduced from 490 to 390 units, was removed from the category of programs demanding expediting, and in January landing craft disappeared from the President's "Number One" list.[62]

Two of the newer types of craft deserve mention. The landing craft, assault (LCA), was a small armored vessel, about forty feet long, equipped with a ramp and capable of rapidly discharging thirty-six men onto a beach. Developed by the British, and as yet without an American counterpart, it was considered by British experts as indispensable to any attack on a well-defended beach. Its range was limited—fifty miles at the most—making it primarily an instrument of ship-to-shore assault, requiring combat loaders to transport it to the scene of action. The Americans had developed a new vessel, the landing craft, vehicle and personnel (LCVP), combining the functions of the small personnel and vehicle craft. It had the additional feature that it could be completely knocked down for shipment overseas and assembled with light tools by inexperienced personnel. As many as five hundred LCVP's could be loaded on one Liberty ship. The range of the LCVP was short, however, and while it was seaworthy enough, its passengers in a choppy sea would soon be unfit for combat. It had been designed primarily with an eye to operations in the Pacific, where shipping space was at a premium and small boats were needed in large numbers, and at Casablanca was not considered suitable for the forthcoming Mediterranean operations.[63]

[61] (1) Min cited n. 32(2). (2) Min cited n. 35. (3) Memo for file, Capt Warren, 16 Dec 42, sub: Availability of Landing Craft, 18 Shipg file, I, Case 95, Plng Div ASF, Job A46-371. (4) Memo, Col Maddocks for ACofS OPD, 24 Jan 43, sub: Availability of Landing Craft . . . , Case 6, Item 1a, Exec 3. (5) See below, App. A-7.
[62] Mowry, Landing Craft and the War Production Board, WPB Sp Study 11, pp. 12–22 and App. C.
[63] (1) CCS 161 cited n. 32(7). (2) Min, 53d mtg JCS, 17 Jan 43; 57th mtg, 21 Jan 43. (3) Min cited n. 31(1). (4) Memo, Capt Warren for Col Appleman, 18 Dec 42, sub: Landing Craft, OCT 370.5 Mvmt Bolero. (5) Coll and Rosenthal, Engr I, draft ch., "The Engineer Amphibian Command," OCMH. (6) See below, App. A-7. (7) Harrison, Cross-Channel Attack, pp. 60–61.
The original model of the LCA dated back to 1938.

Abundance, as always, was relative. The offensives contemplated for 1943 would almost all have to be launched from or across the water—in the Pacific, the Mediterranean, the English Channel, and the Bay of Bengal. At Casablanca it was too early to fix requirements for all these proposed operations, but certain limitations became clearly evident. British plans for HUSKY indicated a need for over 1,000 craft of various sizes, including 100 LST's, 120 LCI(L)'s, and 72 LCT's, besides 26 combat loaders and several more specialized vessels. The requirement for LST's, at least, seemed likely to conflict with the U.S. Navy's plans in the Pacific and with training in the United Kingdom. The British promised to produce ample numbers of LCA's (30 to 40 per month) to meet any Mediterranean requirements by summer, but engines would have to come from the United States— about 400 during the next four months, a stiff demand. A major bottleneck, of uncertain dimensions, was looming in crew-training, largely because of dislocations in the United Kingdom during the mounting of TORCH. In the States, the Navy was unwilling for the Army engineers to continue to train boat crews, but was unable to give an unequivocal commitment to meet the requirements for impending operations in the Mediterranean. All these problems were discussed at Casablanca; none was settled. Landing craft stood near the top of the headache list passed on to the HUSKY planners.[64]

A 1943 ROUNDUP or SLEDGEHAMMER was an even more uncertain, and certainly a bigger, proposition. At Casablanca General Eisenhower indicated his belief, based mainly on the experience of TORCH, that a cross-Channel assault would have to be twice as strong as earlier planned, and that most of the craft used in the first wave probably would be lost. The strong commando forces maintained by the British in home waters would be inadequate for such an effort, and their even larger mobile amphibious forces were earmarked for operations in the Mediterranean during the summer. If a cross-Channel operation was to be mounted in late summer, following amphibious operations in the Mediterranean, it evidently would be necessary to shift most of the landing vessels used in the Mediterranean back to the British Isles and refit them. Lord Louis Mountbatten was sure this task would consume three months. The problem of timing thus posed would be baffling enough if only a relatively modest undertaking such as the attack on Sardinia were in view. With the decision to attempt Sicily instead, the problems became virtually insoluble—at any rate, Casablanca produced no solution. Three types of cross-Channel operations, it was agreed, were hypothetically possible in 1943—hit-and-run raids, an opportunistic attack with whatever forces were available, and the seizure of a bridgehead on the Cotentin peninsula preliminary to a major invasion the following spring. The U.S. Joint Chiefs recorded that they saw no prospect of finding or manning the landing vessels needed for the two larger types of operations, if HUSKY were to be carried out. Cross-Channel attacks in 1943 receded far back into the realm of the improbable.[65]

[64] (1) Min, 52d mtg JCS, 16 Jan 43; 53d mtg, 17 Jan 43. (2) Min, 58th mtg CCS, 16 Jan 43; 67th mtg with annex, 22 Jan 43; 68th mtg, 23 Jan 43. (3) CCS 161 cited n. 32(7). (4) CCS 161/1 cited n. 32(8). (5) Coll and Rosenthal, Engr I, draft ch., "The Engineer Amphibian Command," OCMH.

[65] (1) Memo cited n. 28(4). (2) Memo cited n. 39(1). (3) Outline plan cited n. 39(5). (4) CCS 135/1 cited n. 10(3). (5) JPS 106 cited n. 4. (6) Min, 52d mtg JCS, 16 Jan 43; 59th mtg, 23 Jan 43. (7) Min, 58th mtg CCS, 16 Jan 43; 67th mtg, 22 Jan 43. (8) Min cited n. 23(2). (9) CCS 167, 22 Jan 43, title: Continental Opns in 1943.

TABLE 24—TENTATIVE ALLOCATIONS OF AMERICAN LANDING CRAFT AT CASABLANCA CONFERENCE

Allocations	LST			LCI(L)	LCT(5)
	1 Apr 43	1 Aug 43	1 Mar 44	1 Apr 43	1 Apr 43
Total expected production	216	285	390	300	470
Allocations:					
Pacific	80	117	174	96	180
Atlantic (U.S.)	68	84	96	54	101
British	68	84	120	150	150

British allocations included those for India. Allocations for 1944 were highly tentative. The British had requested, by August 1943, 150 LST's, 194 LCI's, 150 LCT's, and 646 LCM(3)'s, as well as smaller types. Note that not all of production of LCT (5)'s was allocated.

Source: (1) Min, 67th mtg CCS, with annex, 22 Jan 43. (2) Memo, Somervell for Styer, no date, Annex 2, JCS 1942–44 folder, Hq ASF.

The amphibious operations in Burma, tentatively scheduled for November, posed an even more difficult problem of timing in the movement of amphibious shipping and landing craft to the Bay of Bengal from the Atlantic and Mediterranean. Before Casablanca the American staffs doubted whether the transfer could be made in time, if either a cross-Channel operation or further campaigns in the Mediterranean were undertaken in 1943. But since the JCS made an issue of the Burma offensive, as part of their insistence upon a stronger effort against Japan, they were driven into the position of having to underwrite ANAKIM, the Burma operation, with respect to those requirements the British could not themselves meet—notably landing craft. Estimated requirements included thirty LST's, ten LCT(5)'s, and twenty LCM(3)'s. The British, indeed, sought concrete assurances on this score, and expressed pointed fears lest the proposed American operations in the Pacific following Rabaul might compete with ANAKIM. The Americans were confident that output would meet all requirements

by the end of 1943. Pressed further, they promised to divert vessels from the Pacific to Burma if necessary. The British persisted: would the United States, Sir Alan Brooke asked, provide all the craft "over and above those needed in all other operations under consideration, including Roundup?" [66] Admiral Cooke assured him that they would be provided.[67] (Table 24)

To the world in general the Allied leaders at Casablanca proclaimed their hope that Germany would be defeated in 1943. But their program of action scarcely supported this aim. It was agreed that the assembling of an invasion force in the British Isles was to proceed as rapidly as possible, but subject to the prior claims of operations in the Mediterranean, the Pacific,

[66] Min, 65th mtg CCS, 21 Jan 43.
[67] (1) Outline Plan, title: Retaking Burma, in SYMBOL: Casablanca Bk., Vol. I, Tab F-8, Exec 6. (2) Min, 53d mtg JCS, 17 Jan 43; 54th mtg, 18 Jan 43. (3) Min, 58th mtg CCS, 16 Jan 43; 59th mtg, 17 Jan 43; 60th mtg, 18 Jan 43; 65th mtg, 21 Jan 43. (4) CCS 145, rpt by Br JPS, 17 Jan 43, title: Opns in Burma. (5) CCS 164, 20 Jan 43, title: Opn ANAKIM, Provision of Forces. (6) CCS 164/1, 21 Jan 43, same title.

and the Far East and an enlarged program of aid to the Soviet Union. The necessity of protecting and exploiting the sea route in the Mediterranean and the conquests in North Africa demanded further operations in that region, with a further investment of forces, shipping, and landing craft. This the American chiefs recognized, despite their misgivings over being drawn more deeply into a theater they regarded as "neither vital nor final," by agreeing to the attack upon Sicily as the next step in that region.[68] Fearing, moreover, that Japan, if given a respite, might be able in the coming year to make her new conquests impregnable, the JCS were determined to press the war in the Pacific and the Far East more vigorously than had been done in 1942, even at the risk of prolonging the war in Europe. They succeeded in winning from the British a tentative commitment to contribute to this effort by an offensive in Burma.

This program for 1943, even though its requirements could not yet be precisely measured, promised to spread Allied resources at least as widely as they had been spread in 1942, and, in effect, to carry forward both wars on several fronts rather than seek an overwhelming concentration of effort upon either one—or, still less, upon a single front of one war. The final decision in Europe, the Americans expected, would be sought only in 1944 through an invasion across the English Channel, after Germany had been weakened by more than a year of heavy bombing, blockade, campaigns of attrition in the Mediterranean, perhaps the loss of her chief satellite, Italy, and the enormous drain of the war in the USSR. Somervell's tentative schedule for deploying U.S. Army forces, approved as a basis for the development of detailed schedules, envisaged that by the end of 1943 the build-up of American strategic air forces in the United Kingdom would be substantially completed, the administrative establishment for U.S. forces there greatly expanded, and the amassing of an invasion force well advanced by the shipment (mainly during the last three or four months of the year) of as many as nineteen U.S. ground divisions.

Casablanca thus foreshadowed, if it did not clearly delineate, a compromise strategy for the European war, blending the British concept of attrition and peripheral attacks with the American concept of frontal assault in overwhelming force. Some of the American planners lamented this compromise as a surrender to British views. As General Wedemeyer remarked: "We lost our shirts . . . we came, we listened and we were conquered." [69] But given the American insistence upon an augmented effort in the Pacific, the implication that a decisive cross-Channel invasion could have been mounted in 1943 under any reasonable allotment of resources to other theaters was not borne out by the best available estimates. In early 1943 it was all too easy to forget how flimsy had been the logistical basis of the original BOLERO-ROUNDUP plans of March and April 1942. The logistical estimates of the Casablanca planners, it almost immediately appeared, were just as flimsy.

---

[68] Min cited n. 32(2).
[69] Ltr cited n. 30.

CHAPTER XXVI

After Casablanca

In the weeks immediately following the Casablanca Conference, the strategic program there laid down—build-up in the British Isles, overwhelming air bombardment of Germany, relentless offensive against the submarine, aggressive advance in the western Mediterranean, preparation for an offensive in Burma, a rapid close-in upon Rabaul, and a push into the Central Pacific—seemed to be faltering. In the Pacific, the Guadalcanal and Buna-Gona operations came to a successful conclusion early in the year, and in February forces from Guadalcanal occupied the Russell Islands, next step up the Solomons ladder on the way to Rabaul, without opposition. But the theater commanders' estimates of the forces required to push rapidly on and take Rabaul, largely glossed over in the optimistic timetable drawn up at Casablanca, now demanded attention. The whole Pacific program remained in suspense, early in March, awaiting the verdict of a conference in Washington (the Pacific Military Conference) between Army and Navy planners there and representatives from the theaters. In Burma, meanwhile, the British drive toward Akyab, down the coast from the Indian border, had made no progress, Field Marshal Sir Archibald Wavell was becoming more and more reluctant to undertake the planned offensive in the Chindwin valley, and the feud between Stilwell and Chennault was reaching a critical stage. On the other side of the world plans were maturing for the attack on Sicily, but the campaign in Tunisia during February and March held small promise of the early termination upon which those plans hinged. In the Kasserine-Feriana area in mid-February, the 1st Armored Division suffered severe reverses and the enemy held the initiative throughout that month and well into March. The British Eighth Army, meanwhile, was halted before the formidable Mareth Line defenses in the south. With troops and shipping being diverted to this theater, the build-up of American forces in the British Isles slowed almost to a standstill.[1]

Deployment Planning Adrift

With operations thus going awry, the deployment schedule approved at Casablanca began to break down. Troop movements during the first three months of 1943 flowed in different directions from those planned, and, in the aggregate, lagged behind the Casablanca forecast. *(Chart 12)* Late in February a committee of Army planners under OPD's direction drew up a new schedule, purportedly in consonance with changing requirements

---

[1] (1) Memo, Wedemeyer for Marshall, 16 Mar 43, sub: Conf on Opns in Pac, ABC 370.26 (7-8-43), 4. (2) Churchill, *Hinge of Fate*, Bk. II, Ch. 19. (3) Howe, Operations in Northwest Africa. (4) Miller, CARTWHEEL: The Reduction of Rabaul, Ch. II. (5) See above, Chs. XV, XIX.

CHART 12—DISSOLUTION OF THE CASABLANCA DEPLOYMENT PROGRAM: FIRST QUARTER 1943

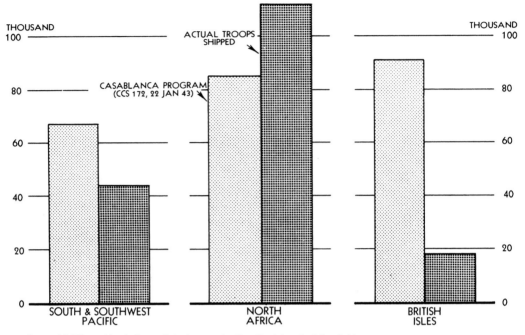

Source: (1) CCS 172, Note by Somervell, 22 Jan 43, title: Ship¢ Capabilities for Bolero Build-up.
(2) Contl Div, ASF, Statistical Review, World War II, App. G, pp. 121–22.

and with recent slashes of about 137,000 troops in authorized garrison strengths in various areas. It provided for a somewhat heavier deployment to the Mediterranean and for an enormous increase in strength in the South and Southwest Pacific Areas, while in the European theater it sought to meet the expanded strategic bombardment program of the Army Air Forces (involving an increase in AAF deployment from the 172,000 troops estimated at Casablanca to about 500,000) without wrecking the movement of balanced ground forces to the British Isles.[2] *(Chart 13)*

Somervell's characterization of the new schedule was outspoken. "This deployment," he told OPD, "was obviously made without regard to shipping."[3] Admittedly the committee's aim had been to make up

a schedule "to implement the plans agreed on at Casablanca," and its examination of current shipping estimates had been somewhat cursory.[4] The result was a deployment curve that ran diametrically counter to the curve of indicated shipping capabilities. It provided for an enormous volume of movements—over 600,000—during the second quarter, when all shipping certainly would be tight, and a diminishing volume during the second half of the year, when

[2] Memo, OPD for listed offs, 23 Feb 43, sub: Deployment of U.S. Army Forces in 1943, with atchd Apps. A and C, ABC 320.2 (3-14-43) Sec 1.
[3] Memo, Somervell for Handy, 3 Mar 43, sub: Scheme of Deployment for U.S. Army Forces in 1943, ACofS OPD 1942–44 folder, Hq ASF.
[4] Memo, unsigned, no addressee, 6 Mar 43, sub: Comments on Recommendations of SOS and AAF, Item 16, Exec 1.

CHART 13—THE EFFORT TO FORMULATE A DEPLOYMENT PROGRAM: FEBRUARY–MARCH 1943
OPD VERSUS SOS ESTIMATES

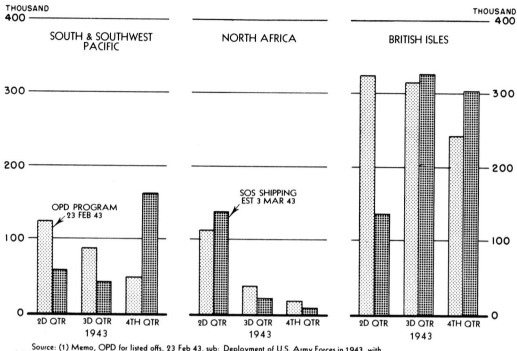

Source: (1) Memo, OPD for listed offs, 23 Feb 43, sub: Deployment of U.S. Army Forces in 1943, with atchd Apps. A and C, ABC 320.2 (3–14–43) Sec. 1.   (2) Memo, Somervell for Handy, 3 Mar 43, sub: Scheme of Deployment for U.S. Army Forces in 1943, ACofS OPD 1942–44 folder, Hq ASF.

cargo shipping almost certainly would become increasingly abundant. In an effort to maintain the flow of ground forces to the United Kingdom, the committee hoped to ship 325,000 troops there in the second quarter alone and almost as many in the third quarter, taking advantage of more ample port capacity during the spring and summer months. These second-quarter objectives were astronomical, and the scheduling of heavy movements during the third quarter, as well, nullified any chance of spreading a deficit. The SOS staff calculated that in the second quarter, even with reduced shipments to static areas, there would be a deficit in troop-carrying capacity of 250,000, with a proportionate dearth

of cargo space. In the last quarter a surplus loomed. The new program thus meant waste at both ends—troops and equipment waiting for transport early in the schedule, unused space going begging late in the schedule.[5]

In his counterplan Somervell tried to set up a schedule more in conformity with shipping expectations. (Chart 13) He drastically pared down the planned deployment to the Pacific in the second and third quarters in order to augment that to the Mediterranean and to salvage part of the

[5] (1) Memo cited n. 3. (2) Memo, Gross for Somervell, 26 Feb 43, sub: Deployment of U.S. Army Forces in 1943, Item 16, Exec 1.

larger ground force objective in the United Kingdom. This would require a transfer of shipping from the Pacific to the Atlantic. Convinced of the necessity for a larger American contribution to the war in Burma, he urged that U.S. troops be transferred there from the Pacific. By the end of March, he pointed out, there would be in the South and Southwest Pacific 340,000 U.S. troops, including marines, not to mention four Australian and New Zealand divisions, available for unlimited service, and seven militia divisions, for home defense. The scale of the proposed effort in the Pacific seemed to him out of all proportion to the ends in view. It appeared that the Navy intended to move 250,000 more of its own forces into the Pacific during 1943. "It is impossible for me to understand," Somervell bluntly declared, "how they can possibly use this number." [6]

Somervell's suggestions were not kindly received in OPD. The charge that the committee had ignored obvious shipping limitations provoked evident resentment, and his views on strategy were dismissed with the curt comment: "This was not provided for in the Casablanca Conference." [7] But the shipping problem could not be so cavalierly dismissed. Since November, when losses had reached a catastrophic level, the main trend had been downward during December, January, and part of February. But late in February the wolf packs struck with deadly effect in the North Atlantic, and in March losses shot upward beyond the one-million-ton mark. While this, as it proved, was the expiring gasp of the U-boat, so much could hardly be known at the time. At this juncture, when shipping losses were soaring, the whole question of shipping assistance to Britain came unexpectedly to a head. [8]

British Imports: The "Bombshell"

For almost seven weeks after the Casablanca Conference, the monumental misunderstanding concerning the scale of American shipping aid to Britain in 1943 remained undisturbed. Somervell left the conference on a tour of North Africa, the Middle East, and India still under the impression that the United States was committed to carry only about 2.5 million dead-weight tons of British imports, instead of the 7.2 million tons that War Shipping Administration, under the President's instructions, had actually undertaken to carry. Somervell's deployment schedule for U.S. Army forces in 1943, and therefore, in considerable measure, the whole Casablanca strategic program, rested upon this erroneous assumption. [9]

The awakening came in stages and almost by accident. On 19 February Lewis Douglas of WSA had a talk with Somervell, just returned from his trip. Somervell wanted to set up a special convoy of twenty-five ships to carry matériel and supplies to the French in North Africa. Douglas was dubious—if the demand were met in full, he said, ships would probably have to be taken from British imports, and this, under the arrangement Somervell no doubt knew of, could only be done with the President's consent. Somervell looked blank, asked "What arrangement?" and, when reminded of the President's letter of 30 November, suggested that this had now been superseded by his agreement at Casablanca with Lord Leathers. [10] He showed

---

[6] (1) Memo cited n. 3. (2) See above, Ch. XIX.
[7] Memo cited n. 4.
[8] (1) *Ibid.* (2) For shipping losses, see below, App. H.
[9] See above, Ch. XXV.
[10] Douglas' notes on conf with Somervell, 19 Feb 43, Army Reqmts folder, WSA Douglas File.

Douglas a copy of CCS 172, his Casablanca deployment paper, containing the heavily qualified British offer to contribute 1.6 million measurement tons of cargo shipping to the BOLERO program. Douglas discreetly refrained from argument, promised to do what he could to find ships for the North Africa convoy, and, after some desultory talk about Somervell's trip, hurried back to his office.[11]

Within a few days, after a quick check with Sir Arthur Salter in Washington and an exchange of cables with Harriman in London, Douglas had the British version of the Casablanca bargain—namely, that any British assistance to the BOLERO program would depend on their having a surplus of shipping after meeting all their own needs. This, as Douglas himself well knew, was a somewhat unreal condition, since those needs could not be met without the loan of American shipping—though Douglas may have wondered why Lord Leathers, who now stressed its unreality, had been persuaded at Casablanca to agree to it. Meanwhile, faced by an alarming lag in the flow of British imports, WSA was drawing up new schedules greatly increasing the amount of American tonnage to be diverted to British use during the critical first half of the year.[12]

Yet almost two more weeks passed before Somervell and Gross realized what had happened. Douglas had told Somervell enough on the 19th to indicate the actual scope of the American commitment to maintain British imports; he may have assumed that Somervell now understood the situation. As for the special convoy, with most of the needed vessels in sight, Douglas was anxious to avoid asking the President to invoke the escape clause of the 30 November commitment in order to take the remainder from the British import

> OFFICE OF THE CHIEF OF TRANSPORTATION
>
> To: General Somervell   3/10
>
> REMARKS:
>
> Lord Leathers made his promise to you with US help to the extent of lifting 7,000,000 tons in mind.
>
> You accepted it with that help reduced to 30 sailings a month in mind or about 2,400,000 tons left.
>
> The whole matter of US help in the UK import program must come out in open
>
> DATE: for decision by CCS.   Gross
>
> MAJOR GENERAL C. P. GROSS
> CHIEF OF TRANSPORTATION
> 4-E-678 PENTAGON BUILDING
> W. D., EXTENSION 4512

program. While this matter was still pending, Gross notified Douglas on the 27th that the Army would appreciate WSA pressure upon the British to make good their "commitments" of BOLERO assistance. Douglas replied that the latest messages from Harriman offered little hope on this score in the light of the current deterioration of the British import program. Still later Douglas (according to his own account) again explained the British position to Somervell, and Somervell, on 9 March, approved a cable Douglas sent to Harriman noting his (Somervell's) understanding of that position. But what neither Gross nor even Somervell (despite his discussions with Douglas on 19 February and subse-

---

[11] (1) *Ibid.* (2) For the North African convoy (UGS-6½), see above, Chs. XVII–XVIII.

[12] (1) Douglas' notes on conf with Salter, 19 Feb 43, Army Reqmts folder, WSA Douglas File. (2) Msg, Harriman to Douglas, 23 Feb 43. (3) Memo, Salter for Douglas, 25 Feb 43. Last two in Allocs Gen folder, WSA Douglas File.

quently) understood up to this point, apparently, was the extent of the gap, in terms of actual tonnages, between the amount of American shipping they, and the amount that the British, expected would have to be loaned to meet Britain's full import requirements. Precisely what caused the light suddenly to dawn is not clear, but on the 10th Gross scribbled a startled notation to Somervell:

Lord Leathers made his promise to you with U.S. help to the extent of lifting 7,000,000 tons in mind. You accepted it with that help reduced to 30 sailings a month in mind, or about 2,400,000 tons lift. The whole matter of U.S. help in the U.K. import program must come out in open for decision by the CCS.[13]

The British, meanwhile, were growing worried. Late in February Eisenhower sent in a request for still another special convoy (UGF-7½) of from thirty to thirty-eight ships to sail in April. This made a decision on the import program unavoidable at a time when other decisions for combined allocations of shipping were pressing for attention—for the ANAKIM and HUSKY build-up movements, which must shortly begin, and for reviving the flagging BOLERO program. Finally, there was a growing feeling in British Government circles that a new and definitive division of shipping resources between the two countries was imperative. A War Cabinet paper stated about this time:

Our tonnage constantly dwindles, the American increases. We have undertaken arduous and essential operations encouraged by the belief that we could rely on American shipbuilding to see us through. But we must know where we stand. We cannot live from hand to mouth on promises limited by provisos. This . . . may in the long run even imperil good relations. Unless we can get a satisfactory long-term settlement, British ships will have to be withdrawn from their present military service even though our agreed operations are crippled or prejudiced.[14]

On 12 March Foreign Secretary Anthony Eden arrived in Washington to discuss this and other matters, and on the same day the British brought before the Combined Chiefs their estimated shipping requirements for carrying out their share of the Casablanca strategic program for 1943. Their presentation was masterly. Its point of departure was that the import program of 27 million tons was above discussion, and there was no allusion to current estimates, then under discussion with WSA, that up to 9 million of the 27 million tons of imports might have to be carried in American shipping. The paper emphasized that the maintenance of Britain's domestic war economy had always been recognized by the leaders of both countries as a first charge on coalition resources, and it warned that the current rate of imports held out little prospect of meeting even a 12-million-ton total by midyear, which the British considered imperative if the quota for the entire year were to be met. Over and above import assistance and

---

[13] (1) Note dated 10 Mar 43 on msg, Douglas to Harriman, 9 Mar 43, Shipg 1941-43 folder, Hq ASF. (2) Douglas' notes on telephone conv with Hopkins, 19 Feb 43. (3) Douglas' notes on conf with Gross, 1 Mar 43. Last two in Army Reqmts folder, WSA Douglas File. (4) Douglas' notes on telephone conv with Hopkins, 22 Feb 43, Hopkins folder, WSA Douglas File. (5) Memo, Land and Douglas for President, 23 Feb 43. (6) Ltr, Gross to Douglas, 27 Feb 43. (7) Msg, Douglas to Harriman, 3 Mar 43. (8) Msg, Harriman to Douglas, no date. Last four in Allocs Gen folder, WSA Douglas File.

[14] (1) Douglas' notes cited n. 13(3). (2) Douglas' notes on telephone conv with Somervell, 5 Mar 43, Army Reqmts folder, WSA Douglas File. (3) Memo, Salter for Douglas, 3 Mar 43, Allocs Gen folder, WSA Douglas File. (4) Msg cited n. 13(8). (5) Cabinet paper quoted in Hancock and Gowing, *British War Economy*, p. 430.

other current commitments of American aid in the Indian Ocean, Africa, and Australasia, the British listed the following additional requirements for American shipping:

(a) Fourteen sailings per month to the eastern Mediterranean in April, May, and June for maintenance of HUSKY in its early stages;
(b) twenty-five sailings per month in April, May, and June, and nineteen per month in July and August, to the Indian Ocean for ANAKIM build-up.[15]

Moreover, no British cargo shipping would be forthcoming for BOLERO. Without the requested American aid, it was stated, Britain would be able only to carry out her share of the attack on Sicily (but not sustain it), maintain her forces in the Mediterranean and elsewhere on the current meager scale, and continue through May only her present contribution of ten ships a month to the Murmansk convoys. The war in southeast Asia would come to a standstill. As for the implications of carrying out the planned major operations in the Mediterranean and Burma without the requested American aid and regardless of the cost, the British regarded this as an academic question since it would mean, they said, abandoning the Murmansk convoys immediately and putting their forces in North Africa (other than those to be used in Sicily) on half rations of everything throughout the spring and summer.[16]

To the American staffs, hurriedly calculating the probable effects upon the American part of the Casablanca program if the British demands were met, the implications seemed equally disastrous. The Casablanca deployment schedule had contemplated that some 1.4 million Army troops would go overseas in 1943, and recent tentative cuts in planned Navy deployment promised to add another 150,000 to

this figure—or, alternatively, to permit raising British import assistance to about five million tons. To divert American cargo shipping to carry a further 2 million tons of imports would reduce the Army's deployment by 225,000; to grant the tonnage requested for building up British forces in the Mediterranean and India would reduce it by 375,000. Taken together, the British proposals thus threatened to cut a potential American deployment of over 1.5 million in 1943 down to .8 million, or by almost half. Moreover, the cut would be made primarily in the critical spring months, when shipping would be at its tightest and when, according to present plans, the battle in Tunisia was to reach its climax, preparations for HUSKY were to be completed, and the build-up of air forces in Britain was to hit full stride. During these months, if British demands were met in full, the movement of American forces overseas would virtually cease.[17]

The American reaction to the British proposals, therefore, was violent. Subcommittee members referred to them as "the British bombshell."[18] In CCS conclave the Americans held that the irreducible minimum of British imports was not a question to be determined unilaterally by the Brit-

---

[15] CCS 183/1, memo by Br CsofS, 12 Mar 43, title: Review of Availability of United Nations Shipg.
[16] (1) Suppl to min, 75th mtg CCS, 12 Mar 43. (2) CCS 183/1 cited n. 15. (3) Incl B to CCS 183/2, rpt by JMTC, 18 Mar 43, title: Review of Availability of United Nations Shipg. (4) For Eden's mission, see Sherwood, *Roosevelt and Hopkins*, pp. 707ff.
The proposal also included the use of thirty U.S. vessels in the Indian Ocean-Red Sea area for the British build-up for HUSKY, in exchange for an equivalent number of sailings to be deducted from U.S.-to-U.K. movements; and an indeterminate number of sailings for supply shipments to Turkey.
[17] (1) Memo, Gross for Marshall, 17 Mar 43, sub: CCS 183/1 . . . , ABC 560 (2-26-43) Sec 1A. (2) CCS 183/2 cited n. 16(3).
[18] Notes on 66th mtg JPS, 24 Mar 43, ABC 560 (2-26-43) Sec 1A.

ish, but should be weighed in the light of other demands. Admiral King even challenged the premise that maintenance of the British economy at a given level was a first charge on Allied resources. Somervell's view was that American shipping for British imports should be provided only "to the extent that the United States thinks is necessary,"[19] and the staffs, in presenting their estimates, pointedly noted that if American shipping assistance to Britain were held to current commitments, U.S. Army deployment in 1943 might reach two million. General Gross, according to Douglas who saw him immediately after the British submitted their proposals, was "very much disturbed and upset,"[20] and in a meeting of the Combined Military Transportation Committee three days later his complaints against the British (in the presence of their representatives), for having concealed at Casablanca the extent of their dependence on American shipping, were couched in language so blunt that the committee decided to consider most of the discussion off the record. Gross saw no reason why the British import program should be sacrosanct. "If they were to exert their utmost endeavors," he wrote to Marshall, pointing to the 4-million-ton gap between 1942 imports and the 1943 goal, "the call upon us would be equal to . . . shipping to lift 3,400,000 tons of imports," not seven or nine million.[21] A sacrifice of even three million tons of imports, according to staff estimates, would free enough shipping to meet Britain's military needs in full.[22]

General Marshall showed Gross' suggestion to Sir John Dill. The latter remarked, with exquisite tact, that it was "a good straightforward and objective review of this baffling problem" and merely reminded Marshall that the War Cabinet decision on a 27-million-ton import quota

for 1943 was his "Bible," and that the program imposed deep cuts upon civilian production in Britain in order to build up the production of munitions by some 50 percent. "I am most anxious," Dill concluded, "that all our cards should be put on the table. The shipping problem is terribly serious and time is rushing by."[23]

Military Operations Versus War Economy

American military leaders needed no such reminder. The Casablanca strategic program for 1943 seemed, in mid-March, to be going up in smoke. While the staffs were working out their estimates, the Pacific Military Conference in Washington was struggling with General MacArthur's new plan for the reduction of Rabaul (ELKTON). This called for a series of five operations in which forces from Southwest Pacific and South Pacific were to converge on New Britain, Bougainville, and New Ireland, and finally take Rabaul on New Britain. The plan lacked a timetable, but listed the ground and air forces needed and stipulated that they must all be assembled in the theater in advance—22⅔ Allied ground divisions and 45 Allied air groups, which was 7 more divisions and 30 more air groups than were then in the two areas.[24]

---

[19] Suppl cited n. 16(1).
[20] Douglas' notes on conf with Gross, 12 Mar 43, Army Reqmts folder, WSA Douglas File.
[21] Memo cited n. 17(1).
[22] (1) Suppl cited n. 16(1). (2) Douglas' notes cited n. 20. (3) Memo, Keating for Douglas, 30 Mar 43, CMTC folder, WSA Douglas File. (4) Memo cited n. 17(1). (5) Notes cited n. 18. (6) CCS 183/2 cited n. 16(3). (7) Rpt by JSSC, 23 Mar 43, sub: Review of Availability of United Nations Shipg, ABC 560 (2-26-43) Sec 1A.
[23] Note, Dill to Marshall, 18 Mar 43, Shipg 1941–43 folder, Hq ASF.
[24] (1) See min, 76th mtg CCS, 19 Mar 43. (2) See also notes cited n. 18. (3) ELKTON Plan for Seizure and Occupation of New Britain-New Ireland-New Guinea Area, 28 Feb 43, Item 1H, Exec 2. (4) Miller, CARTWHEEL: The Reduction of Rabaul, Ch. II.

The Army planners regarded this formidable list with dismay. Sufficient ground troops could be provided, but to meet the air requirements seemed out of the question; in any case, shipping was not available to move and supply all these combat forces and the elaborate supporting establishment that would have to go with them. Landing craft and combat shipping could not be released from the Mediterranean until after the Sicily operation; to do so even then would interfere with further operations there, in northwestern Europe, and in Burma. After re-examining the shipping situation the JPS concluded that by skimping and careful scheduling it might be possible either to send one additional division to the South Pacific and two to the Southwest, along with a few additional aircraft, or to build up air strength in the South Pacific at the expense of the additional division. There was also a faint possibility, under the second alternative, of building up air strength somewhat in both areas with no more than the existing scale of service support. Preferring the second alternative, the Joint Chiefs asked the Pacific representatives what they could accomplish with these resources. The latter replied that they would only be able to gain a lodgment on southeastern Bougainville, occupy the eastern part of New Guinea as far as Madang, push on to Woodlark and Kiriwina in the Trobriand Islands, and advance to Cape Gloucester in western New Britain. This program (in essence, Task Two of the July 1942 directive) was embodied in a JCS directive to MacArthur and Halsey on 28 March, and became the strategic agenda for 1943 in the South and Southwest Pacific. MacArthur was given strategic direction of the whole operation, leaving Halsey in direct command of forces operating in the South Pacific. Admiral

Nimitz was to retain control of all naval forces in the Pacific except those assigned by JCS for these operations. Rabaul evidently had become an objective for 1944, not the spring of 1943, and the Navy's plans for an advance into the Central Pacific remained undefined. Preparations for the more limited task, laid down at Casablanca, of making the Aleutians "as secure as may be," meanwhile moved forward the impending attack on Attu.[25]

With the Pacific timetable thus stretching into the indefinite future, American interest in Burma now became more pointed. But, despite Somervell's optimism regarding the possibility of creating an American ground sector in that theater, all studies of the problem of moving forces there emphasized the enormous logistical costs of even a modest undertaking and, by contrast, the far greater forces that could be built up either in the British Isles or in the Mediterranean by a comparable logistical effort.[26] The war against the European Axis, meanwhile, seemed to have settled down to a localized effort against Germany's satellite, Italy. BOLERO clearly was faltering. By March the flow of American troops across the North Atlantic had dwindled almost to the vanishing point for lack of the escorts diverted to North African convoys, and the promise of British assistance in cargo shipping starting in April had now evaporated. In view of the magnitude of Britain's shipping needs, and the expanding demands of the strategic air

[25] (1) CCS 168, 22 Jan 43, title: Conduct of the War in Pac Theater in 1943. (2) Miller, CARTWHEEL: The Reduction of Rabaul, Ch. II. (3) Memo, Col Blizzard for Gen Wedemeyer, 19 Mar 43, sub: Est of Sit in Pac 1943–44, ABC 381 Strategy Sec Papers (1-7-43), 2–95. (4) Min cited n. 24(1). (5) Craven and Cate, AAF IV, pp. 129–35, 151–53, 207–09. (6) JCS 238/5/D, 28 Mar 43, title: Plan for Opns for the Seizure of the Solomon Islands-New Guinea-New Britain-New Ireland Area.

[26] See above, Ch. XIX.

offensive, BOLERO seemed likely to remain in virtual suspense until late in the year. On 17 March the OPD planners concluded that a six-division balanced force was probably the maximum expectation for the build-up of American ground troops in Britain by the end of the year, and that only two or three divisions could be ready for an August 1943 operation.[27]

The Joint Strategic Survey Committee, reviewing the whole situation late in March, listed eight developments that had upset the Casablanca strategic program: the alarming increase in shipping losses, the stubborn resistance of the enemy in Tunisia, the mounting costs of HUSKY, the revived German offensive in the USSR, the collapse of plans for an early capture of Rabaul, the consequent retarding of the Pacific timetable, the British slow-down in Burma, and the delay in amassing American air forces in the British Isles. "The overall strategic situation," the committee observed, "or more exactly the capabilities of the Allies to control that situation have considerably deteriorated since Casablanca," largely because the planners at that time had "overestimated prospective resources, particularly shipping, and underestimated the demands on them."[28]

In this perspective, many of the American military began to feel that the time had come to challenge the sacrosanct character of the "war economy" programs. Unless these could be made to yield up some of the shipping frozen in their service, the Casablanca strategic program seemed likely to be crippled. The temper of this feeling in the Army staff was revealed in the outburst that greeted a proposal by the Joint Strategic Survey Committee late in March to distinguish between what it called "commitments" and "undertakings." In "commitments" the committee

included such "first charges" as the battle against the submarine, maintenance of forces overseas, Soviet aid, and the war economy programs. The committee suggested that "strategic undertakings"—that is, military operations—be limited to what could be supported by residual shipping not needed for "strategic commitments."[29] To some members of OPD this was "indicative of a state of mind which is highly dangerous to the successful prosecution of the war"—it smacked of "hoisting a white flag" and "fleeing the battlefield."[30] General Handy, conceding the difficulties raised by shipping losses and the recent British demands, insisted nevertheless that strenuous efforts must be made to find shipping to carry out the Casablanca military program, if necessary by imposing "severe cuts" on the nonmilitary programs.[31]

In the Combined Chiefs of Staff, the Americans were pressing the same point. In a wrangle over strategic priorities, they sharply dissented from the British interpretation of the "first charge" label attached at Casablanca to the British war economy and Soviet aid programs—though they concentrated their attack upon the former. These programs, they argued with some heat, should not be allowed to become irreducible fixed charges but, like military requirements, should be subject to adjustment. Strategy must not be made the residuary legatee of "war economy" arbitrarily sustained at a

[27] OPD Strategy Sec paper, 17 Mar 43, sub: Study of Effects . . . , ABC 381 (9-25-41) Sec 6.
[28] JSSC 11, memo by JSSC for JCS, 22 Mar 43, sub: Survey of Present Sit, ABC 381 (9-25-41) Sec 4.
[29] JSSC 11 cited n. 28.
[30] Notes atchd to memo, Handy for Marshall, 28 Mar 43, Case 55, Item 1A, Exec 3.
[31] (1) Memo cited n. 30. (2) Related papers in Case 55, Item 1A, Exec 3.

level that, in a deteriorating military situation, might seem relatively luxurious.[32]

The American military leaders, however, were conscious that they were fighting a losing battle. In the argument over priorities the British refused to budge. The Americans secured only a devious amendment to the effect that the "first charge" programs were somehow to be supported "concurrently" with the other military operations. At this juncture the problem was snatched from them. Before the Joint Chiefs could get their teeth into the substance of the new British shipping requirements, they were informed the President had appointed a "special board" headed by Harry Hopkins to look into the matter, and there was nothing to do but await the decision. Since, as Admiral King glumly remarked, "shipping [is] at the root of everything," it seemed not unlikely that the new board would "reorientate strategic policy" and "in effect supersede the Combined Chiefs." [33]

As it happened, the JCS were granted one more move. Hopkins asked Somervell to draw up a scheme of shipping allocations along the lines that the military thought the situation demanded. Somervell proved a faithful spokesman for the Joint Chiefs. His first plan, completed in three days, offered little aid to the British import program, and that little mainly at the expense of the Soviet aid program. Military operations, both American and British, were to receive full support. This scheme would leave only enough American shipping to move about 3.9 million tons of British imports during 1943, almost all in the final quarter of the year—or, if the requested aid for ANAKIM were eliminated, about 5.4 million tons. It was not pointed out that in the latter case, presumably, the British would then have to divert some of their own shipping to India at the expense of domestic imports.[34]

This plan Somervell replaced almost immediately by a second one, dealing still more harshly with British imports but more tenderly with Soviet aid shipments. Probably this was done in response to hints from above that, in view of the recent decision to suspend the northern convoys, the President was not likely to be receptive to suggestions that, if adopted, would further exacerbate the Russians. Somervell's second plan therefore provided a handsome *quid pro quo* for Stalin by raising the quota of sailings to the Persian Gulf during the second half of 1943 well above even the earlier estimates of the maximum capacity of that route. He proposed to find some of the shipping for this program and for planned military operations by paring down or eliminating various Western Hemisphere services, lopping off twenty-three sailings from the British ANAKIM build-up in expectation of savings from the opening of the Mediterranean, and reducing military shipments to Alaska and areas of passive defense. The deepest cut would be made in the allotment of American tonnage to carry British imports. These were to be reduced to about 2.3 million tons during the last three quarters of 1943, possibly supplemented by another 1.7 million tons sandwiched in with Army

---

[32] (1) See min cited n. 24(1). (2) See also, notes cited n. 18.

[33] Min cited n. 24(1).

[34] (1) Memo, Somervell for Hopkins, 22 Mar 43. (2) Memo, Somervell for CofS, 23 Mar 43. (3) Chart, "Demands on U.S. Cargo Shipping . . . ," 22 Mar 43. All in ABC 560 (2-26-43) Sec 1A. The import figures included 800,000 tons allegedly delivered by American shipping in the first quarter; Hancock and Gowing, *British War Economy*, pp. 429–30, indicate only 366,000 tons were delivered. (4) Memo, Maj Gen Lucius D. Clay for Gen Styer, 20 Mar 43, sub: Conf With Hopkins, Shipg 1941–43 folder, Hq ASF.

cargoes to the United Kingdom—making an estimated grand total, with first quarter shipments, of 4.8 million tons. As in the first plan, the bulk of the shipments would be made in the last quarter of the year.[35]

These recommendations were forwarded through the Chief of Staff, whom Somervell also urged, in vigorous language, to assert the primacy of military over war economy needs:

> To divert shipping in excess of that required to meet the bare necessities of living is indefensible on any ground. To do so will jeopardize the success of the campaigns approved by the President at Casablanca, devitalize our offensive spirit, unnecessarily prolong the death and destruction of the war, and may well weaken the will of the Russians to continue the struggle. We must strike in 1943 and 1944 and with all the force at our command. Our troops must meet the Germans and Japanese on the battlefield and in such numbers as to deliver telling and decisive blows. Shipping must be provided, provided now and throughout the year, if this is to be done.

The shipping recommended, Somervell insisted, was the bare minimum needed for planned military operations. "If we are in this war to win, [the shipping] must be provided. It is recommended that we press for Presidential approval."[36]

The Joint Chiefs found Somervell's plan wholly to their liking, but were uncertain as to how to put the case to the President. Admiral Leahy, who had consulted Hopkins, believed it would be tactless to recommend specific reductions in lend-lease shipments or in British imports, since the allocation of shipping belonged to WSA jurisdiction; better merely to spell out military requirements, leaving it to the President to make the obvious inference that nonmilitary programs must be cut. King and Marshall, however, thought it

their duty to advise the President on the whole problem, and their view prevailed. Admiral Leahy accordingly wrote to the President on 10 April that "drastic curtailment of civilian commitments as well as reductions in U.S. shipping allocations to the British import program" would be necessary if the Casablanca decisions were to be carried out.[37] He appended Somervell's recommended scheme of allocations.[38]

The President Disposes

The military chiefs' plea came almost two weeks late. The President, characteristically, had already made up his mind, and the influences that shaped his decision did not stem from the military. Soon after the British *démarche* of 12 March, Lewis Douglas had set quietly to work to find a solution that would not force the President to void his original commitment to Churchill. Douglas had strong convictions on the matter. He was worried by the rebellious mood developing among the military and by the recrudescence of latent anti-British feeling that he had noted as long ago as March 1942. The drying up of the British import program, the reality of which competent American observers in England had confirmed beyond any doubt, in his opinion menaced the entire Allied war effort. He was determined, therefore, as he wrote Harriman, to do what he could "to prevent our mili-

---

[35] (1) Table, "Proposed Allocation of U.S. Cargo Shipping . . . ," atchd to memo, Somervell for CofS, 25 Mar 43, ABC 560 (2-26-43) Sec 1A. (2) For Soviet shipments, see above, Ch. XXI.

[36] Memo cited n. 35(1).

[37] Memo, Leahy for President, 10 Apr 43, Incl A in JCS 251/2, 10 Apr 43, title: Alloc of Allied Shipg.

[38] (1) Notes on 72d mtg JCS, 6 Apr 43. (2) Notes on 73d mtg JCS, 9 Apr 43. (3) Memo, Secy JCS for JPS, 20 Mar 43, sub: Alloc of Allied Shipg. All in ABC 560 (2-26-43) Sec 1A. (4) Memo cited n. 37.

tary from successfully pressing home their claims . . . . They do not seem to realize . . . that the U.K. import program is as important to the military success of our armies as is, for example, the bauxite movement to the United States."[39] He also suspected that the vehement opposition of the military to further loans of shipping to bolster British imports portended a new challenge to civilian control over the allocation of American shipping. His representative sitting in the CMTC had reported to him, on the 15th, an imprudent remark by General Gross that WSA should have consulted the Joint Chiefs before complying with the President's instructions on shipping allocations—and Douglas promptly passed the remark on to Hopkins.[40]

It was evidently Douglas' warning that a concerted attack by the military upon the British import program was in the making that led Hopkins on the 19th to take personal charge of the negotiations over the British proposals. There was no "special board." Hopkins merely consulted the various individuals who could give him the essential information bearing on the question—Douglas, Somervell, Sir Arthur Salter, and others. Douglas, standing at the very center of the shipping picture and enjoying close personal relations with Hopkins, held the key. During the last week of March he evidently succeeded in convincing Hopkins, first, that "the President had already made a commitment and that we had to look at the matter in that light," and, second, that since the military were unlikely to concede this as a valid point of departure, nothing would be gained by drawing them into the negotiations.[41] Meanwhile, the President was being pressed by Anthony Eden not merely to fulfill the original commit-

ment of assistance to the British import program, but to expand it.[42]

On 29 March Hopkins, Douglas, and Eden met with the President at the White House. No military representatives were present and Douglas, with occasional promptings from Hopkins, held the floor. He presented two main arguments—that the British import program must be sustained, and that this, the warnings of the military notwithstanding, could in fact be done without crippling the Casablanca strategic program. Douglas explained that the present rate of importation would bring only 16 million tons to the United Kingdom by the end of the year, and that even if American commitments were met in full the decline in British carrying capacity would result in a year's total almost two million tons less than the 27 million tons upon which both governments had agreed in November. The program, he argued, was an "essential part of the productive processes" of the United Nations, and any serious shortfall "would at last come back to us" in the form of a weakening of the total Allied war effort. Douglas stressed further the dangers, inherent in the Army's proposed allocations, of accumulating a deficit in the spring and summer that might be too heavy to handle in the autumn.[43]

Speaking to his second point, Douglas

[39] Ltr, Douglas to Harriman, 27 Mar 43, Reading file, WSA Douglas File.

[40] (1) *Ibid.* (2) For Douglas' earlier views, see memo of 19 March 1942, in Contl of Trans folder, WSA Douglas File; and reference to "the isolationist crowd here in the military establishment" in his notes on conference with Radner *et al.,* in WSA Gen folder, WSA Douglas File. (3) Douglas' notes on lunch conf with Hopkins, 19 Mar 43, Hopkins folder, WSA Douglas File. (4) Memo cited n. 22(3).

[41] Douglas' notes cited n. 40(3).

[42] Memo cited n. 34(4).

[43] Douglas' notes on conf at White House, 29 Mar 43, Allocs Gen folder, WSA Douglas File.

remarked that the Navy had not even submitted its requirements beyond the second quarter, and that the Army had never allowed WSA to see the "inner guts" of its cargo requirements. In practice, Douglas bluntly charged, the military services' stated requirements had always turned out to be inflated. He thought they probably were inflated now. Beyond midyear, he was certain, both military and nonmilitary programs could be carried out, if shipping were carefully budgeted. The problem was really localized in the second quarter—April, especially, was "very, very tight." Douglas believed, nevertheless, that if military needs were discounted somewhat, particularly in their regular maintenance services, it would be possible not merely to accelerate the British import program, but also to carry forward all the planned military operations and programs, including requested military assistance to the British, with the exception of the ANAKIM build-up. The latter, he said, hinged largely on the opening of the Mediterranean and, in any case, probably would have to be delayed at least a month.[44]

The President apparently needed little convincing, for, before Douglas had got well into his discussion of capabilities for carrying out military operations, he abruptly announced, "Well, we can consider the import program settled." Turning to Eden, he added, "You can tell the Prime Minister it's a settled matter and we will . . . make good our commitment." Neither Douglas nor even Eden (who had said virtually nothing during the meeting) pressed the demand for an enlargement of the American commitment beyond seven million tons—evidently, as Hopkins later telephoned Douglas, Eden had been "educated."[45]

It remained, as the President remarked at the end of the meeting, "to settle it with the military."[46] With the agreement to fulfill British import commitments now fixed as a point of departure, and in the light of Douglas' analysis of the shipping situation, the question centered upon the build-up for ANAKIM. Paradoxically, the American military leaders now stood virtually alone in insisting that this operation, almost wholly a British undertaking, be carried forward. British enthusiasm for it had waned almost to the vanishing point, and the President (probably after his briefing by Douglas on the 29th) went so far as to attempt to persuade his military advisers to abandon it and to divert the shipping to BOLERO. Marshall and King stood their ground, arguing that it was imperative to maintain heavy pressure on the Japanese in southeast Asia, and the President was unwilling to overrule them. Douglas' own analysis of the shipping problem, on the 29th, tended to support the thesis that it was usually possible to scrape together a few more ships by skimping here and there. Presently, therefore, Douglas received instructions from Hopkins to try to meet at least the April requirement for ANAKIM, which the military thought could be reduced to twenty sailings; by May, perhaps, the Mediterranean would be open and more shipping might be available. Douglas doubted the wisdom of making a heavy commitment of American tonnage to the other side of the world where it could not be promptly retrieved in an emergency, at least until the outcome of the impend-

---

[44] *Ibid.*

[45] (1) *Ibid.* (2) Sherwood, *Roosevelt and Hopkins,* pp. 716–17. (3) Ltr, Douglas to Harriman, 30 Mar 43, Reading file, WSA Douglas File.

[46] Douglas' notes cited n. 43.

TABLE 25—PROPOSED VERSUS SCHEDULED U.S. SHIPPING ASSISTANCE TO BRITISH IMPORTS

Plan	Cargo Ship Sailings: 1943				Total Imports To Be Carried (Million Tons) [a]
	2d Qtr	3d Qtr	4th Qtr	Total	
Somervell's first plan:					
Alternative A	0	95	320	415	3.9
Alternative B	79	198	344	621	5.4
Somervell's second plan	10	61	235	306	4.8
Douglas' recommendations	240	300	300	840	7.0
Scheduled sailings, as of early May 1943	200	270	300	770	(b)

[a] Estimated tonnage to be carried in U.S. shipping, including 800,000 tons allegedly delivered during first quarter.
[b] Information not supplied in source.

Source: (1) Memo, Somervell for Hopkins, 22 Mar 43, ABC 560 (2-26-43) Sec 1A. (2) Table, "Proposed Allocation of U.S. Cargo Shipping . . . ," atchd to memo, Somervell for CofS, 25 Mar 43, same file. (3) Douglas' notes on conf at White House, 29 Mar 43, Allocs Gen folder, WSA Douglas File. (4) Table, 28 Mar 43, same file. (5) Table I, 6 May 43, atchd to Notes on Statements of Dry Cargo Shipping Position, 10 May 43, signed by Salter and Douglas, Shipg 1941–43 folder, Hq ASF.

ing Mediterranean operations could be foreseen. On the other hand, he saw the value of sweetening the bitter pill—the decision on British imports—that the military had been made to swallow. To this end, in assembling the ANAKIM ships, he not merely contrived to spare the principal military operational programs, squeezing instead the military and civilian maintenance services, but also persuaded the British to share the burden by contributing nine sailings, for five of which they were to be compensated by equivalent space in American tonnage added to British services in the North Atlantic and Anzac areas. Thus the twenty sailings for April were found.[47]

Undeniably, the whole action taken on the British "bombshell" of 12 March constituted a serious rebuff—comparable in significance to that in the dispute over war production programs the preceding autumn—to the American military leaders' views on the proper distribution of American merchant tonnage. With respect to American assistance to the British import

program, the rebuff can be measured in terms of the gap between what the Joint Chiefs had recommended and what the President decided should be given. (Table 25)

Nor could American military leaders take much comfort in the decision to proceed with the ANAKIM build-up since, according to their own staff calculations, the shipping for it, and that requested for British forces in the Sicily operation, would now have to be taken from American military operations. Somervell and Gross, at least, did not disguise their chagrin over the President's decisions. Douglas, conferring with them on the final arrangements for the April ANAKIM shipments, found them both in a disgruntled mood, Somervell grumbling that the British "were getting off very light," [48] Gross still insisting that Britain could manage very well in

[47] (1) See above, Ch. XIX. (2) Corresp in Allocs Gen folder and Army Reqmts folder, WSA Douglas File.
[48] Douglas' notes on conf with Adm Smith, Gens Somervell, Gross, and Wiley, 7 Apr 43, Army Reqmts folder, WSA Douglas File.

1943 with only sixteen million tons of imports. A few days later Somervell made a final appeal to the President, complaining that the shipping allocations made by WSA, contrary to Douglas' claims, would not provide the shipping needed for American military operations.[49]

The President held to his course. The British import program, spurred by American aid, rapidly revived during the spring. Imports rose from their low point of 4.5 million tons in the first quarter to 7.2 million tons in the second quarter, making a total only 300,000 tons short of the 12 million that had seemed so unattainable in March. On the eve of the TRIDENT Conference in May, when the Army's logistical staffs were darkly predicting huge shipping deficits after midyear, shipping schedules envisaged not only undiminished support of British imports but also 107 more cargo sailings to British forces assigned to the Sicily and Burma operations—not far short of the 116 originally requested for May through August. And later in May the President took a more far-reaching step, directing WSA to transfer to Britain, under bareboat charter for the duration of the war, fifteen to twenty cargo vessels a month over the next ten months. This placed the capstone on the series of measures, flowing from the policy enunciated on 6 October 1942, by which the United States had progressively assumed the role of merchant shipbuilder for the anti-Axis coalition.[50]

"For Planning Purposes Only"

This whole massive shift of American shipping into British services, decided upon during a crisis in the war at sea, was admittedly a gamble—one the American military leaders naturally resisted, since their operations stood to lose if the gamble did not pay off. Under the circumstances, it was hardly to be expected that they would shave their estimated needs as close as WSA officials demanded they should. The Army's logistical planners, indeed, found themselves pulled in opposite directions—by the civilian shipping authorities, who insisted upon the closest possible calculation of military requirements, and by their own strategic planners, who were projecting a deployment of Army forces overseas far beyond the most optimistic estimates of shipping capabilities. Deployment planning fluctuated erratically during March while the crisis precipitated by the British proposals of the 12th was at its height. A subcommittee of the Joint Staff Planners submitted two proposed deployment schedules during that month, each of which became obsolete before it could be discussed by the Joint Chiefs. In general these schedules followed the pattern of the one prepared by OPD at the end of February, with a great second-quarter "hump" followed by a steep decline in movements during the second half of the year—the very features Somervell and Gross had criticized so sharply. Yet the JCS were reluctant to make the necessary cuts and adjustments to bring the schedules into conformity with indicated ship-

---

[49] (1) For British import sailings, see table, 28 Mar 43, Allocs Gen folder, WSA Douglas File; Douglas' notes cited n. 43; and Table I, 6 May 43, atchd to Notes on Statements of Dry Cargo Shipping Position, 10 May 43, signed by Salter and Douglas, Shipg 1941-43 folder, Hq ASF. (2) Douglas' notes cited n. 48. (3) Memo, Douglas for Hopkins, 13 Apr 43, Army Reqmts folder, WSA Douglas File. (4) Draft memo for signature of President, Somervell for Hopkins, 12 Apr 43, Reading file [under "H"], Hq ASF.

[50] (1) Table I cited n. 49(1). (2) Hancock and Gowing, *British War Economy*, table on p. 357; see also p. 431. (3) Ltr, President to Prime Minister, 28 May 43, MS Index to the Hopkins Papers, Bk. VII, The TRIDENT Conf, p. 4, Item 23. (4) Corresp in Br Merchant Shipg Mis Misc folder, WSA Douglas File.

CHART 14—COMPARISON OF "AGREED DEPLOYMENT" PROGRAM WITH ACTUAL ARMY
DEPLOYMENT: APRIL–DECEMBER 1943

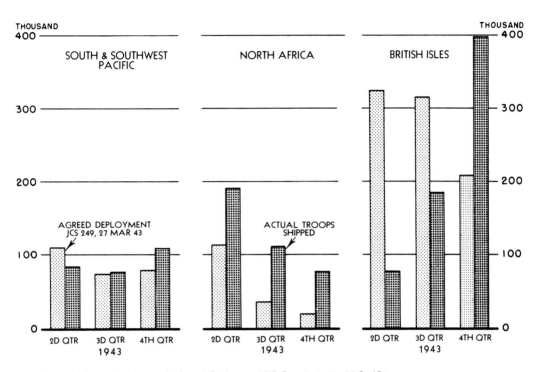

Source: (1) JCS 249, 27 Mar 43, title: Strategic Deployment of U.S. Forces for 1943.   (2) Contl Div,
ASF, Statistical Review, World War II, App. G, pp. 121–22.

ping capacity, desiring, for one thing, to retain some margin against the across-the-board cuts in deployment they anticipated would be dictated by the British request for shipping. In the planning committees the attempt to "integrate" deployment schedules with shipping capacity bogged down amid charges and countercharges between representatives of the two services that each was seeking to shift the burden of reductions to the other.[51]

At the end of March the JCS finally decided to accept the latest deployment schedule provisionally as an "agreed deployment," pending completion of the shipping studies by the JMTC that would show whether it could be carried out. (Chart 14) When these studies, as pre-

dicted by the SOS staff, indicated a large probable deficit of shipping capacity in the second quarter and surpluses late in the year, the Joint Planners after a fruitless debate referred both the JMTC studies and the "agreed deployment" to the Joint Chiefs without change. It was argued that deployment plans would continue to fluctuate and could be used, anyhow, "for planning purposes only."[52] The JCS had no better solution. Their "agreed

---

[51] (1) Notes on 66th mtg JCS, 24 Mar 43. (2) Notes on 71st mtg JCS, 30 Mar 43. Both in ABC 320.2 (3-14-43) Sec 1. (3) CCS 183/2, cited n. 16(3). (4) Notes on 69th mtg JPS, 14 Apr 43, ABC 560 (5-8-43).

[52] JPS 142/1, approved "for planning purposes" as JCS 249, 27 Mar 43, title: Strategic Deployment of U.S. Forces for 1943.

deployment" remained "unintegrated" with shipping capacity and the revised joint schedules early in May merely reflected cumulative additions made by both services since March.[53]

Against the counsel of its own logistical experts, the Army's "planned" deployment for 1943 thus came to reflect hopes rather than expectations. By contrast WSA, focusing its attention for the present upon the immediate problem of meeting current requirements, had real ships in view—those to be saved when the Mediterranean was opened and those its officials felt the Army could easily do without in some of the military maintenance services. After a canvass of the situation in March Douglas told the President and Hopkins bluntly that, with 80 to 90 percent of the merchant fleet engaged in military services, little or no tonnage remained to be squeezed from the commercial trades, which were mainly employing "old crocks" anyway.[54] Of the thirty-odd ships finally earmarked to make up the twenty ANAKIM sailings in April, almost two thirds were to be taken from military maintenance services. Douglas was further determined to press vigorously his drive for greater economy in the utilization of shipping generally by the armed services, the issue that had lain behind the crisis precipitated by the President's directive of 18 December 1942. And in April, when Somervell and Gross complained to the President that WSA was not meeting the Army's current requirements, Douglas retorted that these requirements, as stated, were purely "theoretical"—that WSA was in fact providing enough shipping space to move all the cargo the Army had to move, even though the number of ships provided fell short of the Army's demands.[55]

The actual course of Army deployment during April, May, and June, while falling far short of the strategic planners' schedules, did in fact belie the gloomy predictions of the SOS staff. *(See Chart 14.)* What brought this about, however, was not the squeezing of military services and the economies in military ship operations that WSA had hoped for. Beginning in April the war against enemy submarines took a sudden and decisive turn. Ship losses dipped to less than half those in March, and in June reached a level (182,000 tons) that by comparison with the whole experience since Pearl Harbor seemed insignificant. New construction, meanwhile, continued to climb, in May and June making net gains over losses of more than 1.5 million tons a month in all types of merchant shipping. The military shipping staffs continued to shake their heads—the trend would not last. Early in May they still foresaw huge deficits of cargo shipping. As late as July the Combined Military Transportation Committee, analyzing monthly average losses during the first five months of 1943, which had fallen well below the agreed planning factors set up in February, were suspicious as to the meaning of "the present lull in Axis submarine action."[56] They recom-

[53] (1) *Ibid.* (2) Plng Div OCT table, "Comparison of Proposed U.S. Army Deployment . . . ," 29 Mar 43, Plng Div Studies folder, OCT HB. (3) JCS 249 (revised), 12 May 43. (4) JMT 13/2, rpt by JMTC, 7 May 43, title: Shipg Necessary for Tr and Cargo Lift 1943. (5) JPS 160/1, 8 May 43, same title. (6) JCS 266 (revised), 11 May 43, same title.

[54] Douglas' notes cited n. 43.

[55] (1) Memo cited n. 49(3). (2) Ltr, Douglas to Hopkins, 26 Mar 43, Hopkins folder, WSA Douglas File. (3) Douglas' notes cited n. 43. (4) Memo, Douglas for President, 7 Apr 43, Army Reqmts folder, WSA Douglas File.

[56] CCS 174/1, rpt by CMTC, 2 Jul 43, title: Loss Rate for 1943.

mended the planning factors be reduced now but another reading of the situation be taken the following September.[57]

The whole experience of the planning staffs since Casablanca had been of such a character as to discourage excursions in long-range planning. The civilian shipping experts, indeed, had always been skeptical of predictions of shipping availability farther than six months in the future—approximately the length of the longest turnaround—and on the eve of the TRIDENT Conference Douglas and Salter sounded a general note of caution to the strategic planners:

All estimates of available shipping and requirements . . . covering a long period extending into the future are necessarily unprecise and subject to all the changing fortunes of war. Shipping availabilities fluctuate with the progress of submarine warfare, routing, loss of shipping in assault operations, and a variety of additional factors. Military requirements vary in accordance with developments in the theaters of war and modified strategic plans.

The alarming deficits of shipping currently predicted by the military staffs, they thought, were "within the margin of error inherent in a forward projection" and "may well prove to be manageable." [58]

Evidently the strategic planners had been acting upon a similar assumption, though with less caution, ever since Casablanca, for in their deployment planning they had cast adrift of logistical calcula-tions to a degree not equaled in 1942 when the outlook had been even more obscure. Strategy for 1943 still had not been mapped—Allied leaders were to have another go at this task at TRIDENT—but "agreed deployment" schedules on the eve of the conference envisaged a lavish provision of forces in every theater, far beyond any indicated capabilities of shipping. Despite the favorable turn of the war at sea, deployment during April and early May lagged well behind the planners' goals, piling a deficit upon the already grandiose objectives of the second half of the year. But in the long run the gamble paid off. The phenomenal decline in shipping losses during the spring proved to be a permanent victory, releasing the flood of American munitions and troops that poured into the major overseas theaters after mid-1943.

---

[57] (1) *Ibid.* (2) Notes on Statements of Dry Cargo Shipping Position, 10 May 43, signed by Salter and Douglas, Shipg 1941–43 folder, Hq ASF. (3) See below, Apps. J, K. The following table illustrates the relation between planning factors and actual losses in percentages:

	Nontankers	Tankers
Agreed Factors (Feb 43)		
1st half 1943	2.4	1.8
2d half 1943	1.9	1.4
Losses Jan–May 43 (monthly average)	1.6	1.0
Recommended Factors (Jul 43)		
2d half 1943	1.7	1.2
1st half 1944	1.5	1.1

Source: CCS 174/1, rpt by CMTC, 2 Jul 43, title: Loss Rate for 1943.

[58] Notes on . . . Cargo Shipping Position, cited n. 57(2).

PART SEVEN

CONCLUSION

CHAPTER XXVII

Logistical Planning and Its End Products

However diluted by improvisation, logistics is essentially a planned and organized activity. Every armed soldier placed and sustained on the firing line is an end product of many months of logistical preparation—the long process of designing, manufacturing, and distributing his weapons and supply, the somewhat shorter one of training him and moving him to the scene of action. The need for the soldier and his weapons and supply at a particular time and place, therefore, must be anticipated.

From this circumstance grows a fundamental dilemma. During the period dealt with in this volume, the length of logistical "lead time," covering the process of logistical preparation, varied widely according to circumstances, types of matériel, and character of training; the industrial processes alone were usually estimated to require eighteen months to two years. The specific military operations that this preparation made possible could, of course, seldom be even dimly envisaged so far ahead; to foresee their material requirements in detail was out of the question. The process of fashioning, mobilizing, and distributing the tools of war had to begin, therefore, and invariably was well advanced, long before the specific purposes for which the tools were to be used could be known. Had it been necessary to perform the entire process of logistical preparation after the initial decision was made, the North African operation, which was decided upon in July 1942, might have been carried out some time in 1944 instead of November 1942. "Lead time," in other words, was far longer than planning time.

How, then, could the logistical process itself be planned in advance of that late stage when specific objectives finally were determined? The Army's answer to this problem was the system, described at length in some of the foregoing chapters, by which it shaped its long-range requirements. These estimates, compiled in the Army Supply Program and the War Department Troop Basis, for the most part did not attempt the probably impossible task of anticipating far in advance the needs of specific military operations. The aim was rather to create a general fund or pool of ingredients—finished munitions, supplies, organized and equipped manpower—along with the capacity for replenishing or enlarging the fund, from which specific needs might be met as they arose. The ingredients were varied and represented a judicious balance between general-purpose items, such as the infantry division or the 2½-ton cargo truck, and such specialized ones as the mountain division or the ambulance, thus covering a wide range of possible uses. In its distribution system, the Army similarly sought to complete as much as possible of the logistical process before specific objectives were finally determined. Except for equipment and supplies that troops took overseas with them, matériel was distributed wholesale to the established overseas bases to be stocked in areas immediately behind the combat zones and at intervals along lines of communications. For the bulk of their needs, troops at the front could thus be supplied retail from stocks near at hand, these in turn being replenished wholesale from stocks farther to the rear. Relatively few needs, under this system, had to be filled directly by the time-consuming process of sending special requisitions back to the supply organization in the States.

Such a system of requirements, procurement, and distribution involved a penalty. A large part of the logistical process had to be carried through without knowledge of the specific purposes it was to serve. Broad assumptions had to be made, therefore, and large, general objectives laid down, based upon what little guidance was afforded by the general orientation of strategy. Inevitably, assumptions and objectives often proved to be wide of the mark; unforeseen needs arose that could not be met from the general fund of ingredients. Much of the haste and waste of logistical preparations in 1942 was caused by last-minute efforts to improvise from insufficient or unsuitable materials the means for carrying out military operations. The only defense against such waste was another kind of waste—the calculated oversupply produced by general estimates of maintenance and resupply require-

ments and other "cushions" built into the Army Supply Program. In the distribution pipeline overseas, stagnant backwaters of supply were left behind by the advance of the fighting fronts and the shifting of supply routes.

Whether any other logistical system, based on a more specific prediction of future requirements, would have worked better can only be conjectured. The most likely alternative in 1942, and seemingly the only method by which concrete requirements could be projected at long range in the absence of a fully formed strategic program, was the one employed by the British. They calculated their requirements theater by theater on the basis of projected deployment and predicted intensity of combat in each area. From 1941 onward, they tried to persuade their American allies to adopt this method, as part of a combined requirements program based on present and projected theater deployments, which would provide a firm guide to the allocation of both American and British munitions, administered as a pool. For the British the system worked well enough, since their theater establishments were well developed and they had few forces remaining at home that could be shipped overseas. Major redistribution of their forces already overseas seemed unlikely. The bulk of the U.S. Army in 1942 was still in training, with millions of soldiers still to be mobilized. Any predictions as to the timing, scale, and direction of its eventual overseas deployment might run counter to strategic plans yet unborn. Beyond this consideration, the Americans feared that a combined program of theater requirements, if tied in as the British wished with the actual allocation of munitions by Anglo-American agencies, might syphon off the bulk of American munitions production into overseas theaters still manned predominantly by British forces, starve the great American army mobilizing at home, and tie the United States to British concepts of strategy.

This danger weighed more heavily with some influential American planners than the defects of the method *per se*. General Patrick Tansey, chief of the OPD Logistics Group during a large part of the war, concluded in 1945 that the British system of calculating requirements was superior to the American, but that it could not have been adopted by the U.S. Army in 1942 because of the "existence of the present form of munitions assignments machinery." [1] Army programs, from the start, did reflect in a general way the broad expectations of overseas deployment based upon rather generous estimates of future shipping capacity. There was some sentiment among Army logistical planners, too, that supply programs should include allowances calculated in detail from specific, even though hypothetical, operational plans. In 1943 the programs began to show some of this kind of leavening in the form of bills of requirements for specific construction projects for which theater commanders anticipated a need. The dominant feeling among the logistical staffs, however, was that individual theater requirements could take form only within the framework of a settled long-range strategy and detailed operational plans. Failing these, the over-all troop basis combined with rough predictions of total overseas deployment over a given period of time seemed to offer the most solid foundation for calculating long-range supply requirements.

The British plan for combined requirements, one facet of their effort to place their expectations from American produc-tion on a stable and predictable basis, thus broke down, as did other attempts to peer into an uncertain future. Each country computed its own requirements by its own methods, and British and other foreign claims upon American military production, insofar as they were accepted, were included in the American military supply programs. But these long-range foreign requirements provided only an upper limit for actual allocations of finished munitions. The combined assignments committees had to make their decisions from month to month according to the relative urgency of the demands that came before them. Even the Soviet aid program, embodied in protocols that rendered it immune to adjustments on administrative levels, sometimes had to yield to the exigencies of the shipping situation. Disappointed in the operation of this system, the British were able, late in 1942, to secure a long-range allocation agreement—almost a "British Protocol"—embodying specific allotments of American munitions to be made under a definite schedule during the coming year. These allotments reflected the British staff's own long-range calculations, though adjusted downward in the course of negotiations. The new policy moved definitely in the direction of binding the distribution of lend-lease material to a firm long-range program, even though not a specifically strategic one. Among some of the American planners, however, the agreement inspired misgiving, precisely because the stability it promised might preclude later adjustments to a changing military situation and new strategic plans. As 1943 wore on, the Army's planners in OPD generally in-

---

[1] Memo, prepared by Tansey, no addressee, no date, sub: Alloc of Mun for Logis Support of Global Strategy, ABC 400 (2-17-42) Sec 6.

sisted that assignments of military matériel, even under the above agreement,
must be justified by destined use on the
battlefield under specific operational
plans that fitted into the evolving pattern
of Allied strategy. Since plans of this sort
were seldom crystallized far in advance,
allocation policy continued, as in 1942, to
be shaped primarily by short-term considerations, and the prospect of developing a system in which requirements and
distribution would flow harmoniously out
of a firm long-range strategic program
seemed as remote as ever.

Forced to proceed more or less blindly,
as far as specific objectives were concerned,
the logistical process was also hampered
by its own uncertainties. The war economy was a growing and changing thing,
and while the volume of output in 1942—
both in munitions and in shipping—was
phenomenal, it surged forward too jerkily
to permit accurate predictions of deliveries far in advance. *(See Appendixes B, H.)*
To a very considerable degree, of course,
performance actually exceeded expectations—the spectacular rise in output of
Liberty ships in spring of 1942 was a notable example. In sharp contrast, production programs for the less standardized
items of matériel tended to be both erratic
and sluggish—as witness the landing craft
program, launched belatedly in spring of
1942 and plagued thereafter by chronic
disagreements over types, objectives, and
priorities.

Yet the most unstable element in the
logistical process was not the capacity to
produce, but the capacity to deliver fighting power to the firing line. Through 1942
and into spring of 1943 the war at sea was
a continuous crisis, and in mid-1942 no
great effort of the imagination was needed

to foresee a day when German submarines
might succeed in sealing off the eastward
flow of American deployment altogether.
From the latter part of 1942 on, to be sure,
the attrition of shipping failed to match
the swelling output of American shipyards,
but the drain of ships and cargoes could
not be sustained indefinitely. Surface and
air protection had to be provided for the
sea routes, to some degree at the expense
of new ship construction, and the whole
system of convoying, scheduling, and eva-
sive and circuitous routing, developed to
meet the submarine menace, constituted
in effect a bottleneck to overseas deployment more restrictive than the shortage of
shipping itself.

Had ocean transport been a predictable
bottleneck, its limitations might at least
have provided strategy with a solid basis
of expectation. But because its capabilities
were shaped so largely by the course of the
fighting war itself—the war at sea—it remained perhaps the most baffling single
question mark in the whole logistical equa-
tion, though numerous others—reception
and clearance capacity of overseas ports
and beaches, capacity of overland communications, rates of expenditure, wear and
loss of matériel—were elusive enough. For
a year and a half following Pearl Harbor,
the most basic expectation upon which
any plan of operations had to rest—the
number of troops and the amount of armament that could be made available at the
time and place needed—could never be
much more than a wishful estimate.

Uncertainty and instability during 1942
were largely inherent in the general situation, and thus beyond remedy. The
logistical staffs did make a determined
attack, however, upon disorder that grew
out of purely administrative causes. There
was much shifting and buckling in the

organizational structure throughout 1942 and early 1943, but from it emerged a more efficient division of labor and clearer jurisdictional relationships, notably in the allocation of U.S. merchant shipping, the assignment of munitions, supply and transportation for U.S. Army forces, and logistical planning in the JCS committees. Logistical method was improved and standardized—a many-sided endeavor involving such disparate measures as the refinement of procedures for drawing up the Army Supply Program, the application of workload measurement techniques in the Military Establishment, the use of tested stock-control procedures in depot operations, and the development of space-saving methods of crating military vehicles for shipment. The underlying purpose here was to standardize method in those large areas of the logistical process where operations were routine and repetitive, applying to each operation the procedures and techniques that scientific analysis showed to be most efficient. By spring of 1943 the Army had made substantial improvements in these areas of logistical administration, particularly in the procedures of overseas supply and control of military traffic. Yet the tendency of logistical operations to become more stable about this time undoubtedly owed less to procedural and organizational improvements than to larger developments—the gradual levelling-off of war production, crystallization of the ultimate goals of production and troop mobilization, and the providential absence of major shifts in strategy and of large, hastily prepared undertakings like the invasion of North Africa. In spring of 1943 the routine shipments of troops and supplies overseas to support operations already in progress was the principal business of the Army's logistical staffs.

The major obstacle to effective logistical planning and preparations lay outside the logistical process itself and beyond the jurisdiction of the logistical agencies: specific strategic objectives could not be fixed far in advance. Throughout 1942 the civilian production, shipping, and manpower authorities and the military logistical staffs themselves pleaded repeatedly for a longer projection and greater stability in strategic and operational planning—not, indeed, for a projection equivalent in length to the whole span of logistical "lead time," but rather for a settled strategic program of perhaps a year's duration, fixed in its general orientation and the sequence of major operations, with operational plans worked out in some detail for several months ahead. Unfortunately, as long as the enemy held the strategic initiative all planning was necessarily highly provisional; the Allies could only counter enemy moves as they were made. The program of amassing forces for an invasion of northwestern Europe in spring 1943, which American and British leaders adopted as their major course of action in April 1942 during a lull in the war in the Pacific and the Middle East, met some of the specifications laid down by the logistical planners. But this program, of doubtful logistical feasibility from the beginning, was soon elbowed from the top rank of Allied undertakings and the date for its consummation was postponed indefinitely. Operations during the remainder of the year—limited offensives in the Pacific and the Mediterranean which spelled no irrevocable commitment to any specific course of action beyond—were planned at short range and preparations for them, rushed to completion amid a flurry of eleventh-hour changes of plan, were largely extemporized from resources at hand.

As the end of 1942 drew near, many pressures came into play seeking to replace this hand-to-mouth strategy by a more stable long-range program. The year to come held out the promise of vast resources for offensive action. It was imperative to decide upon the direction and nature of that action. The ultimate limits of war resources had been fixed, in October and November 1942, in terms of the country's estimated capacity to produce. Within these limits, the military supply and construction programs now had to compete with one another and with nonmilitary programs for materials, facilities, and manpower. The probable limits of mobilization of military manpower were also in sight. Hence the urge for balance among the tools of war, and balance could only be defined in terms of the strategic purposes for which those tools were to be used. Adequate logistical preparations depended on early answers to many questions. Was the deployment of forces to be oriented primarily to one theater, or was it to be more widely dispersed? Would it be directed to near or to distant theaters? Would it take the form primarily of ferrying massive and balanced land and air forces to large overseas bases, or would it involve a high incidence of amphibious operations by relatively small, special-purpose task forces? To what extent would strategic bombardment be employed as a substitute for land campaigns against an enemy still greatly preponderant in land power? What specific operations were to be undertaken? What forces would be required? When?

What emerged from the Casablanca Conference of January 1943 could hardly be called a long-range strategic program, and its answers to the above questions were both incomplete and tentative. Be-

yond certain immediate "next steps" such as the attack on Sicily, for which the timing and specific arrangements were still unsettled, the leaders could agree only on strategic concepts too broad and generalized to give much help in logistical planning. Almost immediately the whole program began to dissolve as undertakings proved larger and available means smaller than anticipated. March 1943 brought a new shipping crisis. Strategy, deployment plans, and logistical calculations all drifted in separate orbits during the late winter and early spring of 1943—strategy almost at a standstill, awaiting new decisions, deployment planning conjuring up bright and patently unattainable visions, logistical planning producing sober predictions which the strategic planners chose generally to ignore and which the course of the war at sea soon began to demolish. At the TRIDENT Conference in May Allied leaders were to attempt again to fill in and sharpen the blurred lineaments of the strategic outlook. But few felt any confidence, on the eve of that conference, that the recent setbacks to the German submarine offensive would prove to be a permanent and crushing victory offering a relatively stable basis for long-range planning in the most critical segment of the long logistical process.

At the beginning of May 1943 the Army had 1,399,643 troops in position overseas or on the way. This was almost entirely an achievement of the seventeen months following Pearl Harbor.[2] Compared with the achievement of 1918—the Army's only previous experience in overseas deployment on a massive scale—the numbers were not in themselves overly impressive.

[2] Less than 200,000 troops were overseas at the time of Pearl Harbor.

The magnitude of the performance must be measured, of course, in the light of the immense distances, wide dispersion, and other factors that held down the volume of movement.

Whatever the point of view, this deployment constituted a spectacular reversal of the "Arsenal of Democracy" theory of limited, mainly air and naval participation in the anti-Axis war, toward which military policy, on the eve of Pearl Harbor, had appeared to be drifting. Allied forces had, indeed, been supplied on a generous scale. Lend-lease material was enabling the British, as Churchill later acknowledged, to fight as though they were a nation of 58 million instead of 48 million.[3] British victories in the Middle East owed much to this aid, and by mid-1943 the French in North Africa were ready to put three divisions in the field, equipped with American matériel, for the impending campaigns in the Mediterranean and northwestern Europe. American matériel had also contributed substantially, if not decisively, to the Soviet victory at Stalingrad and promised in the future to provide Soviet armies with increased mobility, larger reserves, and better communications. Two large American establishments overseas, in the Persian Corridor and in China-Burma-India, had as their major tasks the forwarding of war matériel, over long and difficult routes, to the Soviet Union and to China. During the first year of American participation in the war, approximately 20 to 25 percent of the matériel procured by the Army had been assigned to or earmarked for the armies of Allied nations.

The Army's almost 1.5 million troops overseas in May 1943 were scattered far and wide—among six major active theaters and many rear and intervening areas. Through June 1942, the movement of

forces and matériel, and the assignment of shipping to move them, had been preponderantly into the theaters of the Japanese war, broadening out from the limited build-up in the Philippines inaugurated in September 1941. The decision in April 1942 to begin preparations for an invasion of northwestern Europe had scarcely affected this trend. Not until July did the tide begin to flow more strongly toward the theaters of the European war. Only briefly, during July and August, was it concentrated heavily on the amassing of invasion forces in Britain, and from October on the North African theater absorbed the bulk of the Army's eastbound shipments of troops and cargo. Army forces arrayed against Japan meanwhile were being steadily augmented, and, if major areas alone are considered, were not outnumbered by those in the major theaters of the European war until May 1943. The balance in shipping, however, as well as in forces present in all overseas areas of each war (and also in air power), had tipped in this direction considerably earlier. (*See Charts 15–19.*)

In the extent of its dispersion and the multiplicity and length of its lines of communications, this deployment was a far cry from the relatively cautious conceptions of ABC-1 and RAINBOW 5. Two major supply lines extended to the Antipodes—the route around the Cape of Good Hope to the Persian Gulf and Indian Ocean, and the route through the South Pacific to Australia and the New Guinea and Solomons battle fronts. (*See Map 8.*) Along these routes, as well as in the North Atlantic, the Caribbean, and the North Pacific, thousands of troops were scattered

---

[3] (1) Churchill, *Their Finest Hour*, pp. 7–8. (2) Strength figures are from Strength of the Army Report, STM-30, 1 Jan 48.

in small outposts which, to a large extent, could be kept alive only by the costly logistical method of transshipping supplies and replacements from ocean-going vessels plying the main routes into other carriers—smaller ships, transport planes, barges, and rail and road transport.

These logistical commitments had not been assumed as a matter of choice. They were a legacy of Japan's attack and the partnership with Britain, which, in conjunction, had drawn the United States into a global rather than merely a North Atlantic war. American troops in spring of 1943 were fighting in the Solomons and New Guinea largely because of the decisions, in 1941, to develop the Philippines

as the American bastion of the Far East and, immediately after Pearl Harbor, to attempt to support the bastion, now beleaguered, through a base in Australia. Since then the Pacific war, on the American side, had been primarily an effort to develop and make secure the Australian base and the long lines of communications leading to it, an investment too heavy to abandon even after the Philippines fell. The other globe-girdling route, around the Cape, was Britain's main imperial supply line before the opening of the Mediterranean in mid-1943. By the Americans it was used primarily to ship military equipment and supplies to British, Soviet, and Chinese forces, only secondarily to support the

CHART 15—THE TWO WARS
THE DIVISION OF EFFORT: JANUARY 1942–MARCH 1943

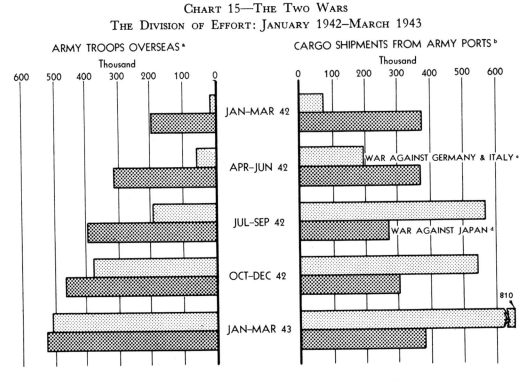

* Assigned strength at the end of the last month in each quarter.
ᵇ Monthly average number of measurement tons in each quarter.
ᶜ European, African, and Middle Eastern areas.
ᵈ Pacific and Asiatic areas, including Alaska.

CHART 16—THE TWO WARS
THE FLOW OF ARMY TROOPS OVERSEAS: DECEMBER 1941–APRIL 1943★

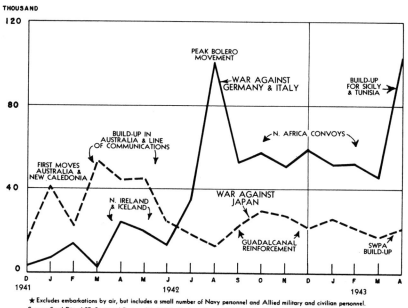

THOUSAND

★ Excludes embarkations by air, but includes a small number of Navy personnel and Allied military and civilian personnel.
Source: Contl Div, ASF, Statistical Review, World War II, App. G, pp. 121–22.

CHART 17—THE TWO WARS
THE FLOW OF ARMY CARGO OVERSEAS: DECEMBER 1941–APRIL 1943

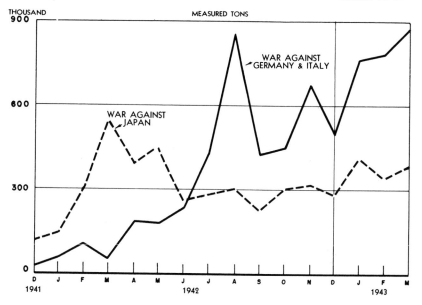

THOUSAND

Source: Contl Div, ASF, Statistical Review, World War II, App. G, pp. 131–32.

CHART 18—THE TWO WARS
BUILD-UP OF ARMY STRENGTH OVERSEAS: 31 DECEMBER 1941–30 APRIL 1943

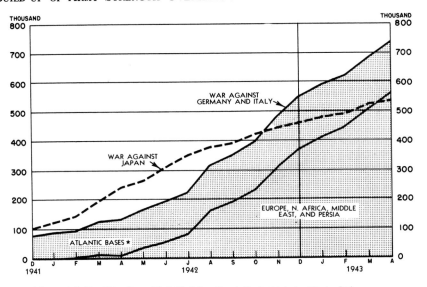

★ Troops in the Caribbean Defense Command, South Atlantic bases, Bermuda, Greenland, Iceland, and Newfoundland.

Source: Strength of the Army Report, STM–30, 1 Jan 48.

CHART 19—THE TWO WARS
BUILD-UP OF ARMY ASSIGNED SHIPPING: MARCH 1942–MARCH 1943

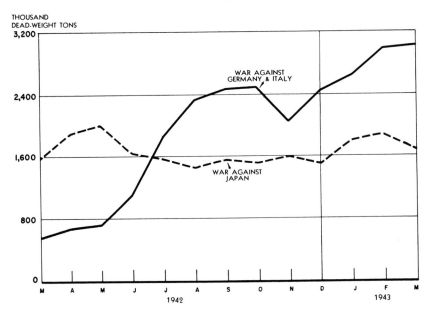

Source: ASF Monthly Progress Report, Transportation, 28 Feb 43, Sec 3.

small U.S. Army contingents in China, India, and the Persian Gulf. Army logisticians chafed under the necessity of operating these long and costly routes, and seldom missed an opportunity to emphasize to their superiors how much more powerful a punch could be delivered over the short and direct routes across the North Atlantic. For one circumstance, at least, they could be grateful. The costs of the long routes grew chiefly out of the time required for ships to reach their destinations and to return, rather than out of the number of ships sunk en route. After mid-1942, losses on the Cape route, except for a short time at the very end of the year, were not severe, and in the Pacific shipping was virtually unmolested.

The Army's main logistical effort, in any case, was in the relatively accessible Atlantic-western Mediterranean area. To a very large extent the debate over the strategy of the war against Germany had revolved about the problem of lines of communications. The champions of the strategy of an early large-scale invasion of northwestern Europe from the British Isles, toward which Allied preparations were briefly directed in the spring and summer of 1942, had argued persuasively that no other course offered supply routes so short, direct, or potentially secure, so firmly based upon the major industrial centers of both countries and accessible to the vital heart of German power. These arguments remained generally valid, but by summer of 1942 continued heavy shipping losses in the North Atlantic and the draining away of Allied strength to the Pacific and Middle East had made it patently impossible to achieve at any early date the necessary ratio of superiority over the forces Germany could mass to oppose a cross-Channel attack. For these and

other reasons it was decided to postpone the invasion. Still, the British Isles remained the most favorably situated and most richly endowed base for decisive operations against the Continent.

When the decision was made at the end of July 1942 to launch a major coalition effort in the Mediterranean—inevitably at the expense of the concentration of forces in the British Isles—the line-of-communication factor again decisively shaped the specific character that American strategists imposed upon the new venture. The center of gravity in the North African landings was placed in the west, covering both eastward and westward approaches to the vital Strait of Gibraltar, and securing the communications inland from the Atlantic Moroccan coast over which, if worst came to worst, the invading forces might have to retreat. For these advantages the Americans were willing to jeopardize, indeed virtually to abandon, the opportunity of gaining an early lodgment in Tunisia. At Casablanca the following January, security of sea communications was again a paramount consideration, on the American side, in the selection of Sicily rather than Sardinia as the next target for Allied attack, and in the resolute American opposition to more ambitious undertakings against Italy or in the eastern Mediterranean. Without the lure of a possible opening of the whole inland sea to Allied traffic, indeed, the Americans might have rejected further Mediterranean offensives in any form.

The Army's logistical effort in the European war, by spring of 1943, thus had been neither concentrated nor economical. Two great bases for operations against Europe had been developed and manned. They were supported by separate lines of communications, and the main effort had gone into the less favorably situated of those bases—more distant, less developed, with more hazardous sea and land communications. Elaborate amphibious operations had been required to gain the North African base, massive ferrying operations to develop it. Further amphibious landings in the Mediterranean were to follow. In an effort to compensate for postponement of the cross-Channel invasion, American air power was being built up at maximum speed in the British Isles in order to intensify the strategic air offensive against Germany. But in spring of 1943 this program had hardly more than begun. Throughout the Atlantic region, dispersion of effort and abrupt changes in basic plans had disrupted production and training programs and necessitated immobilizing and rerouting of shipping. Escort protection had been concentrated on certain routes, resulting in higher losses on others. Supply had flowed along circuitous routes, retarded by transshipment and rehandling. Inadequate planning and hurried preparations had caused confusion and waste.

Army forces arrayed against Germany, as a net result, were still relatively few in number and widely dispersed. Against the original goal of more than a million American troops to be massed against Germany by April 1943 (a goal the planners too readily assumed to have been realizable from the beginning), only 508,000 had been deployed by that date to the areas of the European war, including troops scattered along communication lines and in rear areas in Africa and the Middle East. About 110,000 were in the British Isles, about 334,000 in North Africa. The American military leaders in resisting this "scatterization" had succeeded only in orienting part of the total deployment in

another direction, into the theaters of the war against Japan where, by April 1943, some 525,000 Army troops were still deployed.[4]

In two fundamental respects the logistical basis of Anglo-American power, by spring of 1943, had been solidly laid. The enemy's hold on the most vital segment in Britain's historic life line, the Mediterranean, had finally been broken, and May saw the arrival at Suez of the first through cargo convoy from Gibraltar since early in the war. (See Map 8.) With the lopping off of some eight thousand miles from the longest line of communications, the Allies gained the equivalent of many hundreds of thousands of tons of shipping for the planned offensives in Burma and the central Mediterranean and for the flow of American supplies to the Soviet Union and to the Middle and Far East. And after more than two years of close collaboration, the two economic centers of gravity on each side of the North Atlantic basin—the British Isles and the eastern seaboard of Canada and the United States—had been firmly knit together by an unprecedented concentration of maritime shipping plying the North Atlantic routes, protected by an effective combination of naval and air power. The North Atlantic had become, as faintly foreshadowed in the ABC-1 conversations of February 1941, securely an Anglo-American lake, and both the war production and the shipping resources of the two countries had been co-ordinated in the common cause to a degree that, at many points, amounted to a genuine pooling of effort. The military power generated by this North Atlantic merger was to prove

---

[4] Strength figures are from Strength of the Army cited n. 3(2).

sufficient, before long, to profit fully by the mobility inherent in control of the sea and to overcome the handicaps of distance—permitting the two countries the luxury of fighting an aggressive two-front war on opposite side of the globe. *(Map 8)*

By spring of 1943 the deployment of the U.S. Army was perceptibly moving toward this phase. April and May saw the quickening of tempo, the spectacular increase in delivery of men and matériel at the overseas end of the distribution pipeline, that had been heralded somewhat prematurely at Casablanca. War material continued to flow in growing volume into the Pacific and Asiatic theaters, and shipments into the theaters of the European war swelled suddenly, and for the first time, beyond even the record amounts shipped the preceding August. This upsurge in cargo movements at first went mainly to the Mediterranean, but the British Isles received some of it. Troop deployment also leaped spectacularly upward in these months, mainly to the Mediterranean but substantially also to the Pacific areas. *(See Appendix E.)* These movements of troops and matériel in April and May were the real beginning of a new period of build-up in both wars—for the converging operations against Rabaul and the drive into the Central Pacific, for the descent on Sicily and Italy, and, over the horizon, for the invasion of northwestern Europe.

Appendix A

SHIPPING TERMINOLOGY AND PLANNING DATA: 1942–43

APPENDIX A-1—WEIGHT AND SPACE

Weight Measurements

Type	Pounds	Short Tons	Long Tons	Metric Tons
1 Short Ton...	2,000	1.0000	0.8929	0.9072
1 Long Ton...	2,240	1.1200	1.0000	1.0160
1 Metric Ton...	2,204.6	1.1023	0.9842	1.0000

1 nautical mile....................................	1.1516 statute or land miles.
1 knot..	A speed of 1 nautical mile per hour.
1 ship ton or measurement ton (M/T).............	40 cubic feet of cargo or ship's cargo space.
1 register ton....................................	100 cubic feet of ship's space.
Gross tonnage....................................	Entire enclosed space on a ship expressed in register tons
Net tonnage......................................	Entire *useful* cargo capacity of a ship expressed in register tons.
Dead-weight tonnage..............................	Ship's total carrying capacity, including ship's gear, supplies, and personnel, expressed in long tons.
Dead-weight effective lift........................	Effective cargo lift of a ship expressed in long tons; approximately 80 percent of the dead-weight tonnage.
1,000 gross tons.................................	Approximately 1,500 dead-weight tons, or approximately 1,200 dead-weight effective lift, or 1,775 measurement tons.

Approximate Shipping Space Required for One Long Ton of Various Types of Cargo

Type of Cargo	Cubic Feet	Measurement Tons
Average military cargo*...	102.4	2.56
Coal..	53.6	1.34
Gasoline in bulk...	47.6	1.19
Gasoline in 55-gallon drums..	62.4	1.56
Oil in bulk..	40.0	1.00
Oil in 55-gallon drums...	54.8	1.37
Average lend-lease cargo...	57.6	1.44

*No valid corresponding figure can be given for commercial cargo because of the extremely wide variation in its composition from one area to another. In general, commercial cargo had a considerably lower cubic content in relation to its weight, as compared to military cargo.

Source: Strategic Logis Div rpt, 1 Oct 42, sub: Logis Implications of Opns of Sp Task Force, Plng Div ASF.

Selected Cargo Ship Capacities: 1941–42

Type	Speed in Knots	Dead-Weight Tonnage	Cargo Capacity
Cargo:			
C–1[a]...	14.0	9,075	11,236 M/T
C–2[a]...	15.5	8,794	13,421 M/T
C–3[a]...	16.5	12,500	18,404 M/T
EC–2 (Liberty)[b].................................	11.0	10,800	12,506 M/T
Tankers:			
T–2...	14.5	16,735	141,000 bbls
ZET–1 (Liberty)...................................	11.5	10,800	65,000 bbls

[a] The C-type cargo vessels were standard types developed by the Maritime Commission, not specifically for wartime use.

[b] The EC–2 (Emergency Cargo, popularly called Liberty ship) was considered, for military planning purposes, to be the "average" or "notional" type of dry cargo vessel. This term had no statistical significance, since the Liberty, whether measured by cargo capacity, displacement tonnage, or any other standard, was far from being the arithmetical average vessel in the U. S. merchant fleet. In 1941–42 it was not even the most commonly employed carrier of Army cargo, and was far outnumbered by the older, mostly smaller vessels. Moreover, the planning yardstick contained no allowance for the shortfalls from maximum capacity that were normal rather than exceptional in the loading of military cargo because of the bulky character of most such cargo, haste in loading, sailing of vessels before loading was completed, and similar circumstances. As a result, actual performance repeatedly fell short of advance estimates. The present authors have noted some cases, within the period covered by this volume, where planners discounted their estimates to allow for the above factors, but the practice does not appear to have been general. For long-range estimates, projected into 1943 and beyond, the Liberty-ship yardstick had somewhat more validity.

APPENDIX A-2—MAINTENANCE REQUIREMENTS FOR OVERSEAS FORCES: 1942–43

Supplies	Pounds Per Man Per Day	Per Man Per Month			
		Short Tons	Conversion Factors [a]	Ship Tons	Ship Tons With 15 Per- cent Stowage
Total......	45.04	0.6755	—	1.1189	1.2886
Class I					
Rations......	6.22	0.0933	1.3	0.1213	0.1395
Class II					
Total......	3.11	0.0466	—	0.1258	0.1441
Clothing and equipage......	0.84	0.0126	2.0	0.0252	0.0290
General supplies......	0.32	0.0048	2.0	0.0096	0.0110
Replacement vehicles......	0.62	0.0093	5.0	0.0465	0.0530
Other......	1.33	0.0199	2.24	0.0445	0.0511
Class III					
Total......	10.67	0.1600	—	0.3037	0.3493
Ground force gasoline, oil, and grease [b]......	0.83	0.0124	1.5	0.0186	0.0214
Air force fuel and lubricants [b]......	1.34	0.0201	1.5	0.0301	0.0346
Solid fuel for temperate zone [c]......	8.50	0.1275	2.0	0.2550	0.2933
Class IV					
Total......	15.46	0.2320	—	0.4610	0.5326
Medical......	0.27	0.0041	2.9	0.0119	0.0137
Motor maintenance......	0.18	0.0027	1.0	0.0027	0.0031
Quartermaster sales items......	0.27	0.0041	2.0	0.0082	0.0094
Air force supply and replacement......	2.84	0.0426	4.0	0.1704	0.1994
Engineer construction material......	11.90	0.1785	1.5	0.2678	0.3070
Class V					
Total......	9.58	0.1436	—	0.1071	0.1231
Ground ammunition......	5.17	0.0775	0.81	0.0628	0.0722
Air force ammunition......	4.41	0.0661	0.67	0.0443	0.0509

[a] Based on average cubage for each item. Ship tons (40 cu. ft.) of any one item can be found by multiplying its short-ton (2,000 lbs.) weight by that item's conversion factor.

[b] These figures represent only 10 percent of total liquid fuel and lubricant requirements; the remaining 90 percent normally was shipped by tanker, and was calculated separately.

[c] Arctic requirements for solid fuel were twice as great as those for the Temperate Zone. Solid fuel was shipped 50 percent coal and 50 percent coke by volume.

Source: FM 101-10, Staff Officers' Field Manual: Organization, Technical and Logistical Data, 10 Oct 43, par. 312. A number of obvious errors in the source have been corrected in the above table. The corrected table eventually appeared, substantially as shown above, in the 21 December 1944 edition of FM 101-10.

APPENDIX A-3—TONNAGE REQUIREMENT FACTORS FOR OVERSEAS SHIPMENTS: JULY 1941– JUNE 1943

(SHIP TONS PER SOLDIER) [a]

Destination	Jul–Dec 41		Jan–Jun 42		Jul–Dec 42		Jan–Jun 43	
	Initial	Mainte- nance [b]	Initial	Mainte- nance	Initial	Mainte- nance	Initial	Mainte- nance
Iceland......	8.75	1.7	8.0	1.5	—	0.97	6.0	1.0
United Kingdom......	8.75	1.3	8.0	1.5	6.8	1.5	7.0	1.3
Mediterranean......	—	—	—	—	7.5	1.3	7.0	1.0
Central Africa and South Atlantic......	8.75	1.3	7.0	1.0	—	—	8.0	1.0
Persian Gulf and Middle East......	—	—	7.0	1.0	—	—	8.0	1.0
China, Burma, India......	—	—	7.0	1.0	—	—	6.0	1.0
Southwest Pacific......	—	—	7.0	1.0	5.8	1.0	8.0	0.9
South Pacific......	8.75	0.97	7.0	1.0	—	—	6.0	0.8
Central Pacific......	8.75	1.3	7.0	1.0	—	0.8	6.0	0.8
Caribbean Defense Command......	8.75	1.3	7.0	1.0	—	—	6.0	1.0
Alaska......	8.75	1.7	9.5	2.0	—	1.5	6.0	1.8
Greenland......	8.75	1.7	9.5	2.0	—	—	6.0	1.5
Over-all......	8.75	1.0	8.0	1.5	9.0	1.0	7.0	1.3

—Data not available.

[a] In general, initial requirements factors include allowances for the individual soldier and his personal equipment, for average requirements in organizational equipment, and for 60 days accompanying maintenance supplies. Maintenance requirements factors represent allowances of subsistence, ammunition, and fuel normally sufficient to support one soldier for one month.

[b] 1941 factors for specific areas were used in early RAINBOW 5 calculations. Over-all factors for 1941 were those agreed upon by the Army and Navy in March 1941.

Source: These estimated factors have been compiled from numerous sources and represent, in many cases, only the factors used at a particular time for a particular calculation. No significance, therefore, should be attached to differences of one and two decimal points. Source documents include FM 101-10, Staff Officers' Field Manual: Organization, Technical and Logistical Data, Jun 41 and Oct 43; ASF Manual M-409, Logistical Planning and Reference Data, Dec 43.

APPENDIX A-4—INITIAL CARGO SHIPPING REQUIREMENTS FOR SELECTED UNITS: LATE 1942

Unit		Ship Tons With 15 Percent Stowage						
	Total Per Man [a]	Organizational Equipment		60 Days Mainte- nance [b]	10 Units of Fire	60 Days Gas and Oil [c]	Strength	Number of Vehicles and Wheeled Guns
		With Vehicles Boxed	With Vehicles On Wheels					
Infantry Div.....................	6.8	21,898	60,469	34,130	5,582	6,780	15,514	2,322
Armored Div....................	17.9	82,309	128,049	72,214	9,763	22,000	14,643	3,698
Medium Tank Bn................	18.1	5,118	6,984	3,024	756	3,198	768	167
Light Tank Bn...................	15.4	3,938	5,376	2,292	470	1,614	631	156
Field Artillery Regt (155-mm. how- itzer).........................	11.1	4,097	10,601	3,014	1,009	598	1,370	388
Field Artillery Bn (105-mm. how- itzer).........................	11.3	1,389	4,316	1,304	826	260	593	160
Antiaircraft Gun Bn (Mobile).....	14.0	4,420	8,321	1,758	717	348	799	176
Engineer Regt (Combat)..........	8.5	5,519	8,314	3,224	253	640	1,465	299
Engineer Regt (Gen Sv).........	6.7	3,372	5,479	2,906	80	576	1,321	161
Engineer Bn (Aviation)..........	11.7	5,949	7,219	1,776	119	352	807	200
Ordnance Bn (Auto Maint).......	12.3	3,414	4,650	1,048	12	206	476	106
Ordnance Bn (Ammunition).......	4.2	533	1,978	2,576	30	510	1,171	67
Medical Regt....................	8.0	2,688	6,205	2,546	0	504	1,157	206
Quartermaster Truck Regt........	30.7	9,885	45,924	3,598	66	712	1,635	1,343

APPENDIX A-5—INITIAL CARGO SHIPPING REQUIREMENTS FOR SELECTED UNITS: LATE 1943

Unit		Ship Tons With 15 Percent Stowage						
	Total Per Man [d]	Organizational Equipment		60 Days Mainte- nance [b]	10 Units of Fire	60 Days Gas and Oil [c]	Strength	Number of Vehicles and Wheeled Guns
		With Vehicles Boxed	With Vehicles On Wheels					
Infantry Div.....................	4.4	18,003	48,488	31,365	6,340	6,220	14,253	2,144
Armored Div....................	13.1	82,479	125,834	72,590	9,766	22,044	14,250	3,703
Medium Tank Bn................	15.7	5,118	6,984	3,024	756	3,198	768	167
Light Tank Bn..................	13.1	3,938	5,376	2,296	470	1,614	631	156
Field Artillery Regt (155-mm. how- itzer).........................	6.3	4,094	10,546	3,036	1,009	602	1,380	340
Field Artillery Bn (105-mm. how- itzer).........................	6.7	1,300	3,443	1,146	850	228	521	134
Antiaircraft Gun Bn (Mobile).....	5.9	2,080	6,740	1,702	445	338	774	205
Engineer Regt (Combat)..........	6.6	5,607	9,577	3,224	253	640	1,465	336
Engineer Regt (Gen Sv).........	5.2	3,390	5,495	2,906	80	576	1,321	169
Engineer Bn (Aviation)..........	10.1	5,967	6,930	1,776	119	352	807	202
Ordnance Bn (Auto Maint).......	10.8	3,667	4,818	984	11	194	447	102
Ordnance Bn (Ammunition).......	2.9	533	1,987	2,576	30	310	1,171	67
Medical Regt....................	5.0	2,688	6,205	2,546	0	504	1,157	206
Quartermaster Truck Regt........	8.7	9,885	45,924	3,598	66	712	1,635	1,343

[a] With all vehicles on wheels.
[b] Computed on a basis of 1.1 ship tons per man per month, excluding ammunition and gasoline and oil. Armored elements have an added allowance of 25 percent replacement of vehicles monthly.
[c] Computed on a basis of 1.2 gallons per man per day for ground troops. Armored elements use based on armored force data.
[d] With all general purpose vehicles boxed. During 1943 most of the general purpose vehicles were shipped in this manner.

Source: (1) For 1942, Misc Shipg Data, Logis File, OCMH. (2) For 1943, ASF Manual M-409, Logistical Planning and Reference Data, 14 Dec 43.

APPENDIX A-6—CARGO VESSEL TURNAROUND TIME IN DAYS: 1943 [a]

Voyage	Transports		Cargo Ships	
	Planning [b]	Actual [c]	Planning [b]	Actual [c]
Boston to:				
Newfoundland..	30	26.0	40	40.3
Greenland...	45	68.0	60	102.3
New York to:				
United Kingdom...	50	40.0	75	59.8
Iceland...	45	48.5	60	(d)
Mediterranean theater..................................	45	53.5	75	78.1
Near East via Cape of Good Hope.......................	120	(d)	160	210.0
Near East via Mediterranean...........................	(d)	(d)	(d)	e 109.0
New Orleans to:				
Puerto Rico...	20	(d)	30	44.2
Trinidad..	25	56.0	30	65.0
Panama...	20	43.2	30	40.2
San Francisco to:				
Hawaii..	30	32.2	45	41.6
South Pacific theater...................................	60	77.9	100	133.6
Southwest Pacific theater..............................	90	69.4	120	115.3
Charleston to:				
India...	120	(d)	150	185.1
Seattle to:				
Alaska..	30	55.8	30	42.1

a Turnaround time is a cycle of days; time in U.S. port plus outbound sailing time plus time in foreign port plus inbound sailing time.

b For planning purposes sailing time was based on a speed of 15 knots, or 360 nautical miles per day, for transports and 10 knots, or 240 nautical miles per day, for cargo vessels. Ten percent was added to chart distances for zigzagging, weather, and other delaying circumstances. A total of 20 days (10 days at each end) was allowed cargo ships for loading and unloading. The theoretical character of the planning figures is indicated by a comparison with the actual time involved. The differences were mainly due to varying port capacities and facilities.

c The average turnaround is given. These figures are based upon all ships that ended their return voyage during the period 1 Jan 43–30 Jun 43. Time spent at intermediate points of call and time spent awaiting convoys at points other than the home and end ports is included.

d Data not available.

e Average turnaround during first half of 1944, by which time regular traffic had been resumed through the Mediterranean.

Source: (1) Planning factors are from ASF Manual M-409, Logistical Planning and Reference Data, 14 Dec 43, p. 26. (2) Actual turnaround figures are from ASF Monthly Progress Report, Sec 3, Transportation, 30 Jun 43 and 31 Jul 44.

APPENDIX A-7—SELECTED TYPES OF LANDING CRAFT AVAILABLE IN 1941–42

	Nomenclature	Early Designation	Length (Feet)
LCA	Landing Craft, Assault [a] [b]	ALC	40
LCI(L)	Landing Craft, Infantry (Large)	APY; Giant Y; GRC Mark II	159
LCI(S)	Landing Craft, Infantry (Small)[a]	GRC Mark I	120
LCM(2)	Landing Craft, Mechanized (Mark II)[c]	WL; TLL	45
LCM(3)	Landing Craft, Mechanized (Mark III)	WM; TLHM	50
LCP(L)	Landing Craft, Personnel (Large)[d]	Eureka; Y; T; LBP; RC	36
LCP(R)	Landing Craft, Personnel (Ramp)[d]	TP; LBP	36
LCP(S)	Landing Craft, Personnel (Small)[a]	R. C.	28
LCT(1)	Landing Craft, Tank, Mark I [a]	TLC, Mk I	152
LCT(2)	Landing Craft, Tank, Mark II [a]	TLC, Mk II	160
LCT(3)	Landing Craft, Tank, Mark III [a]	TLC, Mk III	190
LCT(4)	Landing Craft, Tank, Mark IV [a]	TLC, Mk IV	186
LCT(5)	Landing Craft, Tank, Mark V [e]	YTL; TLC	108
LCV	Landing Craft, Vehicle [f]	TR; YR; LBV; VLC	36
LCVP	Landing Craft, Vehicle, Personnel [g]		36
LSD	Landing Ship, Dock	APM; TCS	458
LSI(C)	Landing Ship, Infantry (Converted)[a] [h]	IAS, Class III	500
LSI(H)	Landing Ship, Infantry (Hand-hoisted boats)[a] [i]	Butterflies	291–357
LSI(L)	Landing Ship, Infantry (Large)[a] [j]	ISA, Class I	468
LSI(M)	Landing Ship, Infantry (Medium)[a] [k]	IAS, Class I	380
LSI(S)	Landing Ship, Infantry (Small)[a] [l]	IAS, Class II	360
LST	Landing Ship, Tank	ATL; TLS	328
LVT(1)	Landing Vehicle, Tracked, Mark I [m]	Z	21
LVW	Landing Vehicle, Wheeled (DUKW)		31

[a] British types.
[b] British assault craft with ramp and armor.
[c] The 1941 tank lighter.
[d] A modification of the LCP(L) to provide narrow bow ramps.
[e] Bow ramps only.
[f] Companion to the LCP(L).
[g] First appeared in November 1942 to replace the LCP(L) and the LCV as the standard United States small assault craft.
[h] British equivalent to the assault troop ship (APA).
[i] Small cross-Channel vessels.
[j] Infantry assault ships, converted "Glen" class vessels.
[k] Ex-Dutch cross-Channel vessels.
[l] Ex-Belgian cross-Channel vessels.
[m] The original Roebling "Alligator."

Source: Chart prepared by JCS Hist Sec.

Appendix A-8—Principal U.S. and British Convoys: Autumn 1939–Spring 1943

Terminal Points	Designation Outbound	Designation Inbound	Type [a]	Escort Responsibility	Days En Route	Speed in Knots	Normal Interval Sep 39–May 43	Normal Interval 1 May 43 [b]
Transoceanic convoys:								
Halifax-U.K.	HX	ON	Cargo	US-C-Br (e)	17	10	e 8-10	(d)
New York-U.K.d	HX	ON	Cargo	US-C-Br (e)	16	10	f 7-10	5
Sydney, Cape Breton I.-U.K.	g SC	ONS	Cargo	US-C-Br (e)	20	8	e 8-10	(d)
Halifax-U.K.d	g SC	ONS	Cargo	US-C-Br (e)	20	8	f 7-10	8
Halifax-U.K.	NA	AN	Troop	US-C-Br	13.6	12.5	25 (approx.)	Discontinued Sep 42
New York-U.K.	AT	TA	Troop	US-C-Br	13.6	12.5	32 (approx.)	Discontinued Sep 42
Curaçao-U.K.h	CU	UC	Tanker	U.S.	14	14.5	32	54
Iceland-Murmansk	PQ	QP	Cargo	Br	11	9	42	Discontinued
Scotland-Murmansk	JW	QP(RA)	Cargo	Br	11	9	42	42
Scotland-Iceland	UR	RU	Mixed	Br	4	8	Not in operation	7
Sydney-Greenland	SG	GS	Mixed	U.S.	5	8	18	18
New York-Gibraltar	UGF	GUF	Troop	U.S.	13	14.5	25	25
New York-Gibraltar	UGS	GUS	Cargo	U.S.	16.5	9.5	25	25
U.K.-Gibraltar	KMF	MKF	Troop	Br	7	15	14	30
U.K.-Gibraltar	KMS	MKS	Cargo	Br	12	9	14	20
U.K.-Gibraltar	OG	HG	Cargo	Br	13	7.5	(i)	30
Trinidad-Gibraltar h	OT	TO	Tanker	U.S.	13	14.5	32	28
U.K.-Freetown-Far East.	WS	(i)	Troop	Br	14	15	30 (approx.)	Joined KMF/MKF
U.K.-Freetown-Far East.	OS	SL	Cargo	Br	16.5	9.5	(i)	Joined KMS/MKS
U.S. East Coast-West Africa.	AS	SA	Troop	U.S.	(i)	(i)	(i)	Discontinued
San Francisco-Australia.	(i)	(i)	Mixed	U.S.	(i)	(i)	30	Discontinued
San Francisco-Hawaii.	SP	PS	Mixed	U.S.	(i)	(i)	6	6
							Depart Outbound	**Depart Inbound**
Interlocking coastal convoys: [k]								
Boston-Halifax	BX	XB	Cargo	US-C-Br e	2.5	7.5	5 days	5 days · 4
New York-Guantanamo, Cuba.	NG	GN	Cargo	U.S.	7.5	8	Sun & Thurs	Tues & Sat · 5
New York-Key West	NK	KN	Cargo	U.S.	6.3	8	Fri	Tues · 5
Guantanamo-Aruba-Trinidad.	GAT	TAG	Tanker	U.S.	5.9	8	Mon & Thurs	Tues & Sat · 5
Guantanamo-Panama.	GZ	ZG	Cargo	U.S.	3.8	8	Sun	Mon · 10
Key West-Guantanamo.	KG	GK	Cargo	U.S.	3	8	Tues & Fri	Mon & Thurs · 10
Key West-Galveston, Texas.	KH	HK	Cargo	U.S.	3	8	Thurs	Fri · 5
Key West-Pilottown, Louisiana.	KP	PK	Cargo	U.S.	(i)	(i)	Tues	Sat · Joined KH/HK
Trinidad-Bahia, Brazil l.	TB	BT	Mixed	US-Brazil	14	8	(i)	(i) · 10

a Most cargo convoys included some tankers. Mixed convoys included tankers, troopers, and cargo vessels. UGF/GUF and KMF/MKF included a few fast cargo vessels.

b As set up by the Atlantic Convoy Conference 2/1, App. A.

c Until March 1942 the average interval was 8 days; thereafter it was increased to 10.

d Beginning in August 1942, HX convoys sailed in two sections, the major one leaving New York, the other leaving Halifax, and rendezvousing at sea. SC convoys also sailed in two sections, the major one leaving Halifax, the other leaving Sydney and rendezvousing at sea.

e On 1 May 43 escort responsibility passed to British-Canadian control.

f From August 1942 to October 1942 the interval was 10 days; thereafter it was 7.

g Odd-numbered SC convoys took ships bound for Iceland.

h Established in February 1943.

i Data not available.

j Variable.

k The Interlocking Coastal Convoy System was set up in August 1942 and was tied to the terminal point of New York. The key convoys of this system were the GN and KN, scheduled to arrive in New York one to two days before the departure of the HX and SC convoys. The local convoys in this system were scheduled to arrive at the terminal points of Guantanamo and Key West in time to catch the northbound GN and KN convoys. Other smaller convoys are not mentioned here.

l The TB/BT convoy was inaugurated on 15 Dec 42 and was under U.S. control as far as Belem, Brazil, and then passed to Brazilian control. Ships bound for South Africa, Suez, and the Far East traveled with this convoy to Bahia (with the inception of the Trinidad-Rio de Janeiro (TJ/JT) convoys in July 1943 to Rio de Janeiro) and then sailed independently for Capetown.

Source: (1) Metcalf draft study, May 45, title: Hist of Convoy and Routing, Off of Naval Hist. (2) Min, Atlantic Convoy Conf, 1 Mar 43–12 Mar 43, Convoy and Routing folder, Misc file, OCT HB.

Appendix B

PROCUREMENT: 1940–43

APPENDIX B-1—DELIVERIES OF SELECTED ITEMS OF MUNITIONS TO THE ARMY: 1940–43

Item	1940 Jul–Dec	1941 Jan–Jun	1941 Jul–Dec	1942 Jan–Jun	1942 Jul–Dec	1943 Jan–Jun
Aircraft:						
Fighter, bomber, reconnaissance	1,473	2,267	4,889	8,220	11,010	15,438
Transport, trainer, communications	1,656	3,243	5,461	9,840	12,022	15,474
Artillery:						
Heavy field, towed, and self-propelled [a]	3	17	45	185	462	915
Light field, tank, towed, self-propelled, and antitank [a]	1,141	2,416	7,935	24,578	47,440	37,471
105-mm. towed howitzers	0	61	536	2,070	1,255	2,040
75-mm. tank guns	0	50	1,166	6,431	12,454	12,175
57-mm. antitank guns	0	0	0	517	3,660	4,708
37-mm. antitank guns	340	174	2,078	4,937	9,392	4,517
Other types	801	2,131	4,155	10,623	20,679	14,031
Antiaircraft	170	295	210	2,410	12,099	13,273
Mortars, Ordnance types [a]	1,173	3,679	4,666	4,561	5,599	11,157
Rocket launchers, 2.36-inch	0	0	0	5,000	62,428	47,036
Small Arms:						
Rifles, .30- and .303-cal	56,782	106,750	191,964	518,473	907,453	1,205,595
Carbines, .30-cal	0	0	5	382	115,411	663,998
Ground machine guns	707	768	17,636	75,111	195,145	177,338
.50-cal	707	215	2,234	15,650	56,565	60,488
.30-cal	0	553	15,402	59,461	138,580	116,850
Aircraft machine guns	4,525	7,505	45,145	142,497	210,403	239,671
Antiaircraft machine guns	624	1,842	4,255	17,242	21,933	14,815
Ammunition (thousand rounds):						
Heavy field artillery [a]	29	352	500	2,663	3,536	3,568
Light field, tank, antitank artillery [a]	317	423	1,473	23,674	47,098	43,715
105-mm. howitzer	0	62	291	4,378	6,109	5,253
75-mm. gun and howitzer	310	132	645	8,294	10,498	10,182
57-mm. antitank gun	0	0	0	0	426	1,749
37-mm. tank and antitank gun	7	221	531	10,822	27,070	23,077
Other types	0	8	6	180	2,995	3,454
Antiaircraft artillery [a]	53	38	1,702	6,882	10,104	11,735
Rocket, 2.36-inch	0	0	0	0	155	1,109
Mortar, Ordnance types [a]	12	136	526	5,932	5,581	13,125
Small arms: [b]						
.50-cal	10,130	29,719	44,633	375,531	1,256,614	2,081,043
.45-cal	8,300	97,100	166,100	356,100	498,100	1,313,300
.30-cal	97,696	267,642	441,193	2,214,145	4,158,503	5,429,353
.303-cal	0	0	0	261,000	266,000	252,000
Aircraft bombs, general purpose, demolition, armor-piercing, fragmentation (thousands) [a]	18	58	231	1,305	1,945	2,796
Tanks	286	677	3,375	7,921	17,076	16,508
Heavy	0	0	0	0	1	9
Medium	6	77	1,384	4,568	9,481	11,916
Light	280	600	1,991	3,353	7,594	4,583
Motor carriages for medium field-artillery and antitank guns	0	0	86	4,323	6,321	6,182
Trucks	20,577	72,396	111,218	286,219	333,516	293,113
Under 2½-ton	13,307	49,480	62,173	198,714	215,658	176,542
¼-ton command 4 x 4 (jeep)	70	3,123	12,278	83,195	89,531	80,914
½-ton and ¾-ton weapons carriers 4 x 4	2,972	12,724	8,075	16,238	34,375	28,381
1½-ton cargo 4 x 4	5,288	7,552	12,489	15,960	18,631	9,437
Other types	4,977	26,081	29,331	83,321	73,121	57,810
2½-ton	6,698	20,397	41,726	78,059	103,990	99,042
2½-ton cargo 6 x 6	6,046	17,916	36,157	52,849	62,187	65,109
Other types	652	2,481	5,569	25,210	41,803	33,933
Over 2½-ton	572	2,519	7,319	9,446	13,868	17,529
4-ton cargo 6 x 6	374	1,360	1,449	1,287	1,232	1,476
6-ton cargo and prime mover 6 x 6	108	392	215	627	980	1,807
10-ton general service 6 x 4	0	0	199	482	1,375	2,035
Other types	90	767	5,456	7,050	10,281	12,211
Tractors, crawler-type, diesel (Engineer-procured) [a]	(c)	(c)	(c)	3,407	8,527	9,265
Tractors, high-speed, gasoline [a]	0		d 111	1,227	1,715	2,648
Bailey bridge panels	(c)	(c)	(c)	0	33	182
Men's service shoes (thousand pair)	1,387	6,180	6,849	11,913	14,994	13,387
Jungle boots (thousand pair)	0	0	0	0	538	616
Socks, cotton, tan (thousand pair)	5,652	13,357	11,045	5,660	24,351	29,214
Tents, shelter half (thousands)	0	0	203	1,683	9,616	3,032
Portable ground radios, short-range	1,258	d 7,497		17,510	12,487	20,579
SCR 536 (handy-talky)	0	d 385		8,683	5,905	10,835
Other types	1,258	d 7,112		8,827	6,582	9,744

[a] Includes all types listed under this heading in Whiting, Statistics, and comprises the great bulk of the types produced in this category.

[b] The four types listed here comprise the bulk of small arms ammunition production; production of the other types was relatively insignificant and the data are uncertain.

[c] Data not available.

[d] Totals for 1941; half-year totals not available.

Source: Data in the above table were obtained from a variety of sources. The most recent official Department of the Army figures on World War II procurement by the Army have been published tentatively in Statistics, Procurement Section, 9 April 1952 draft. This draft was prepared by Richard H. Crawford and Lindsley F. Cook under the direction of Theodore Whiting. Since, with certain exceptions, it does not contain item totals for periods shorter than a year, the data in the above table, except those for aircraft, were obtained from other sources. These include various supporting work papers to the Crawford and Cook draft, and an unpublished report, "Procurement Issues and Stock," prepared in 1945 by Headquarters, ASF, copies filed in Office of the Comptroller of the Army; "Official Munitions Production of the United States, By Months, July 1-1940-August 31, 1945," prepared by Civilian Production Administration, May 1, 1947; the "Monthly Progress Reports," Section 1-A, Procurement, prepared by Headquarters, ASF. See also Bibliographical Note.

Appendix B-2—Estimated Value of War Department Procurement Deliveries: January 1942–30 June 1943 [a]

(In Thousands of Dollars)

Category	Total	1942				1943 (First Half)	
		1st Qtr	2d Qtr	3d Qtr	4th Qtr	1st Qtr	2d Qtr
Total......................	$33,251,574	$2,517,195	$3,816,534	$5,455,110	$6,702,474	$6,991,751	$7,768,510
Army Service Forces...............	22,364,574	1,611,195	2,566,534	3,796,110	4,760,474	4,706,751	4,923,510
Ordnance Department............	12,144,932	955,899	1,436,331	1,994,417	2,428,894	2,543,827	2,785,564
Heavy field artillery...........	56,833	4,893	4,667	8,670	10,482	10,128	17,993
Light and medium artillery......	1,410,589	61,940	134,226	235,622	316,954	335,407	326,440
Small arms....................	745,381	53,069	88,363	120,410	144,807	158,562	180,170
Ammunition:							
Heavy artillery...............	332,137	34,280	53,943	67,161	66,757	75,904	34,092
Light and medium artillery....	1,593,457	147,570	232,207	289,113	287,371	306,881	330,315
Small arms..................	1,028,173	44,135	101,878	162,611	190,306	236,503	292,740
Bombs.......................	577,645	37,117	47,651	73,833	107,937	138,038	173,069
Tanks.......................	2,481,104	179,256	262,537	415,257	584,420	491,699	547,935
Self-propelled weapons.........	627,657	6,525	17,572	61,982	148,344	190,940	202,294
Trucks:							
Under 2½-tons...............	1,090,664	150,269	198,203	216,364	209,400	141,477	174,951
2½-tons....................	993,050	120,486	158,921	173,481	167,898	171,492	200,772
Over 2½-tons...............	461,308	49,845	65,746	71,771	69,460	91,649	112,837
Other Ordnance items..........	746,934	66,514	70,417	98,142	124,758	195,147	191,956
Corps of Engineers..............	1,262,547	72,228	114,569	222,501	241,325	274,336	337,588
Boats and bridging............	66,269	3,147	2,012	6,376	13,489	19,563	21,682
Tractors, crawler-type.........	216,279	13,620	22,687	37,744	47,837	43,601	50,790
Construction equipment........	282,023	11,655	30,127	41,371	49,195	60,707	88,968
Other Engineer items..........	697,976	43,806	59,743	137,010	130,804	150,465	176,148
Quartermaster Corps.............	6,929,572	500,917	844,578	1,322,822	1,654,637	1,399,146	1,207,472
Clothing.....................	2,303,987	215,553	304,254	417,601	482,643	481,714	402,222
Equipage....................	1,415,454	100,016	174,210	314,488	351,393	283,237	192,110
Subsistence...................	2,563,389	151,512	316,949	474,840	627,661	506,070	486,357
Other Quartermaster items.......	646,742	33,836	49,165	115,893	192,940	128,125	126,783
Medical Department.............	299,794	10,581	18,458	37,972	60,931	74,519	97,333
Chemical Warfare Service........	397,008	22,406	47,564	56,045	81,194	97,425	92,374
Signal Corps....................	921,809	36,242	76,853	129,672	198,043	231,649	249,350
Radio equipment..............	277,687	5,649	17,629	46,687	65,709	74,294	67,719
Radar equipment.............	169,267	3,958	6,846	16,916	38,308	54,270	48,969
Telegraph and telephone equip...	62,184	5,495	4,943	6,147	8,505	14,249	22,845
Wire and cable................	114,298	8,601	17,135	16,635	22,381	23,920	25,626
Other Signal items.............	298,373	12,539	30,300	43,287	63,140	64,916	84,191
Transportation Corps.............	408,912	12,922	28,181	32,681	95,450	85,849	153,829
Railway equipment............	193,433	776	13,404	14,678	36,371	48,874	79,330
Marine equipment.............	213,312	12,146	14,777	18,003	59,079	36,069	73,238
Other Transportation items......	2,167	0	0	0	0	906	1,261
Army Air Forces....	10,887,000	906,000	1,250,000	1,659,000	1,942,000	2,285,000	2,845,000
Aircraft......................	8,876,000	774,000	1,040,000	1,302,000	1,533,000	1,859,000	2,368,000
Signal equipment..............	852,000	34,000	72,000	172,000	201,000	184,000	189,000
Other........................	1,159,000	98,000	138,000	185,000	208,000	242,000	288,000

[a] The estimated total value of War Department deliveries for the period 1 July 1940 through 31 December 1943 was $56,835,734 thousand. This amount includes the following estimates for 1940 and 1941 (in thousands of dollars): 1940, third quarter, $390,000; fourth quarter, $566,000; 1941, first quarter, $773,000; second quarter, $1,032,000; third quarter, $1,378,000; and fourth quarter, $1,735,000. These dollar amounts were computed from physical quantities delivered and unit costs as of 1945; they do not take into consideration price changes or contract renegotiations, and do not measure exact cost to the government.

Source: Whiting, Statistics, Procurement Sec, 9 Apr 52 draft, pp. 14–20.

Appendix C

Lend-Lease Transfers

Appendix C-1—War Department Procurement Deliveries and Lend-Lease Shipments: January 1942–June 1943

(Thousands of Dollars)

Agency	Procurement Deliveries	Lend-Lease Shipments [a]						
		Total [b]	Amount			Percent of Total		
			United Kingdom	USSR	Others	United Kingdom	USSR	Others
Total War Department...	[c] 30, 688, 000	5, 835, 662	3, 897, 010	1, 461, 070	477, 582	67	25	8
Army Air Forces..............	[c] 10, 887, 000	1, 557, 579	1, 016, 741	428, 710	112, 128	65	28	7
Army Service Forces..........	[d] 19, 801, 185	4, 278, 083	2, 880, 269	1, 032, 360	365, 454	67	24	9
Chemical Warfare Service...	397, 008	71, 272	46, 326	18, 854	6, 092	65	26	9
Engineer Corps	1, 262, 547	113, 816	102, 307	5, 315	6, 194	90	5	5
Medical Department.	299, 794	21, 320	8, 635	7, 144	5, 541	41	33	26
Quartermaster Corps.	[d] 4, 366, 183	182, 338	60, 196	104, 676	17, 466	33	57	10
Signal Corps.	921, 809	129, 270	70, 846	50, 314	8, 110	55	39	6
Transportation Corps.	408, 912	46, 852	46, 852	0	0	100	0	0
Ordnance Department.	12, 144, 932	3, 712, 963	2, 544, 886	846, 057	322, 020	69	23	8
Finance Department.	0	252	221	0	31	88	0	12

[a] Actual shipments (not the total scheduled in the period for lend-lease beneficiaries) do not include transfers by theater of operation commanders.

[b] Includes $189,216,000 of shipments made between 11 March and 31 December 1941, for which distribution by agency by recipient country is not available.

[c] Rounded figure.

[d] Excludes subsistence.

Source: Whiting, Statistics, Procurement and Lend-Lease secs, 9 Apr 42 draft.

Appendix C–2—Lend-Lease Shipments Compared With War Department Procurement Deliveries: 1 January 1941–30 June 1943★

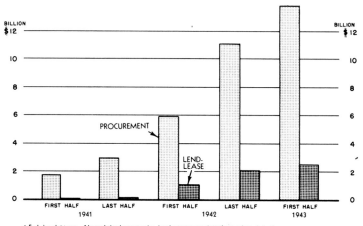

★ Excludes subsistence. Also excludes theater transfers, but these were not of significant volume during these years.
Source: Whiting, Statistics, Procurement and Lend-Lease secs, 9 Apr 52 draft.

Appendix D

NUMBER OF VESSELS AND CARGO TONNAGE SHIPPED FROM UNITED STATES TO USSR: 22 JUNE 1941–30 JUNE 1943

(CARGO IN THOUSANDS OF LONG TONS)

Date	Total Shipped		Destination								USSR Cargo Undelivered	
			North Russia		Persian Gulf		Soviet Far East		Soviet Arctic		Un-loaded in U.K.	Lost at Sea
	Ships	Cargo	Ships	Cargo	Ships	Cargo	Ships	Cargo	Ships	Cargo		
Total...............	838	4,640	242	1,359	*168	1,272	*396	1,916	32	93	343	388
First Protocol												
1941												
Jun..................	1	3	0	0	0	0	1	3	0	0	0	0
Jul...................	5	28	0	0	0	0	5	28	0	0	0	0
Aug..................	16	97	1	4	0	0	15	93	0	0	0	0
Sep..................	7	38	3	11	0	0	4	27	0	0	0	0
Oct..................	15	65	10	48	0	0	5	17	0	0	0	3
Nov..................	13	58	9	41	1	3	3	14	0	0	0	3
Dec..................	25	71	14	50	7	10	4	11	0	0	0	8
1942												
Jan..................	24	89	20	63	0	0	4	26	0	0	3	16
Feb..................	19	93	13	65	2	6	4	22	0	0	0	14
Mar..................	43	214	31	170	6	18	6	26	0	0	28	40
Apr..................	79	441	63	382	6	21	10	38	0	0	84	118
May..................	30	195	13	75	10	87	7	33	0	0	14	49
Jun..................	34	194	8	55	11	91	9	30	6	18	0	56
Second Protocol												
Jul...................	35	183	2	13	5	63	12	63	16	44	0	9
Aug..................	36	216	11	69	5	66	19	79	1	2	0	23
Sep..................	29	180	4	28	8	72	17	80	0	0	0	0
Oct..................	32	229	0	0	13	121	19	108	0	0	0	0
Nov..................	34	177	0	0	8	70	26	107	0	0	0	12
Dec..................	39	243	4	29	11	91	24	123	0	0	7	0
1943												
Jan..................	46	258	12	74	12	87	22	97	0	0	48	0
Feb..................	58	342	23	173	7	40	28	129	0	0	150	14
Mar..................	46	263	1	9	19	131	26	123	0	0	9	8
Apr...................	55	338	0	0	18	145	37	193	0	0	0	7
May..................	63	349	0	0	15	121	44	216	4	12	0	8
Jun..................	54	276	0	0	4	29	45	230	5	17	0	0

*In addition, 74 vessels sailed for the Persian Gulf and 15 for the Soviet Far East carrying cargo, a minor portion of which was consigned to the USSR.

Source: Report on War Aid to USSR, 28 Nov 45.

Appendix E

Overseas Deployment

Appendix E-1—Personnel Movement Overseas in Army-Controlled Shipping by Theater: December 1941–June 1943*

Month and Year	Total	European	North African	Central Africa-Middle East	North, South, and Latin America	Alaska	Central Pacific	South Pacific	Southwest Pacific	China-Burma-India
Total	1,673,221	386,309	407,231	68,909	129,572	131,741	164,313	133,214	221,904	30,028
1941										
Dec	29,839	2,046	0	327	10,314	2,068	15,084	0	0	0
1942										
Jan	61,206	6,902	0	28	9,048	4,114	3,082	3,850	34,182	0
Feb	47,379	13,034	0	431	8,813	3,605	1,363	0	20,133	0
Mar	67,556	15	0	2,022	8,071	4,400	16,354	182	32,374	4,138
Apr	87,988	23,495	0	440	10,912	8,967	10,085	10,986	23,100	3
May	80,419	18,711	0	1,259	7,379	8,438	14,609	14,496	7,982	7,545
Jun	54,609	12,069	0	327	1,279	17,066	16,362	1,899	5,582	25
Jul	70,850	29,569	0	5,233	9,170	8,228	8,573	3,415	6,653	9
Aug	121,785	102,298	0	174	582	6,028	10,595	2,043	31	34
Sep	87,701	45,263	0	7,026	8,078	4,805	10,145	7,262	5,105	17
Oct	100,587	16,057	33,584	6,759	10,242	4,372	4,524	22,628	2,411	10
Nov	80,321	10,742	31,693	8,398	5,171	6,634	10,774	6,121	783	5
Dec	94,847	10,990	37,583	9,697	10,069	5,397	2,834	5,054	11,158	2,065
1943										
Jan	82,527	14,443	29,548	7,102	2,624	3,197	1,869	10,586	6,348	6,810
Feb	88,543	2,921	43,692	5,351	8,168	6,185	2,482	3,671	13,258	2,815
Mar	73,630	680	38,576	6,024	4,539	6,749	6,081	6,741	3,847	393
Apr	155,629	3,362	108,108	746	3,598	17,811	7,042	9,410	5,100	92
May	148,320	40,627	32,570	7,366	6,353	4,300	11,168	12,279	27,664	5,993
Jun	139,485	33,085	51,877	199	5,162	9,377	10,927	12,591	16,193	74

*Includes 1,601,228 Army troops, approximately 40,000 Navy personnel, and 32,000 civilian and Allied military personnel. The distribution by theater of these totals is not available.

Source: Contl Div, ASF, *Statistical Review, World War II,* pp. 121–22.

APPENDIX E-2—CARGO MOVEMENT OVERSEAS IN ARMY-CONTROLLED SHIPPING BY THEATER: DECEMBER 1941–JUNE 1943

(MEASUREMENT TONS)

Month and Year	Total	European	North African	Central Africa-Middle East	North, South, and Latin America	Alaska	Central Pacific	South Pacific	Southwest Pacific	China-Burma-India
Total	23,828,344	3,716,326	6,007,307	1,294,882	2,833,797	3,375,948	2,280,018	1,446,665	2,272,415	600,986
1941										
Dec	284,023	18,456	0	2,848	101,798	45,978	77,756	0	37,187	0
1942										
Jan	479,075	35,134	0	24,595	128,054	72,528	89,342	14,277	114,705	440
Feb	630,335	56,874	1	45,360	101,516	62,447	152,211	309	211,617	0
Mar	882,689	28,909	0	23,355	206,039	74,819	207,750	22,449	299,796	19,572
Apr	810,651	144,975	15	44,602	155,080	69,406	149,697	71,007	144,316	31,553
May	938,620	119,647	11	53,385	203,081	109,308	177,816	91,125	147,352	36,895
Jun	815,146	188,429	0	45,354	155,788	166,403	103,879	63,931	69,363	21,999
Jul	1,095,284	338,506	0	88,693	178,188	203,567	126,659	49,450	92,969	17,252
Aug	1,559,780	772,805	0	80,591	165,944	238,131	120,484	81,778	63,930	36,117
Sep	1,078,999	312,208	0	115,407	258,098	164,128	100,314	67,841	33,602	27,401
Oct	1,147,731	170,832	239,855	38,193	159,184	231,689	98,871	123,996	65,201	19,910
Nov	1,286,301	135,760	428,033	108,620	153,148	140,965	131,236	118,486	57,917	12,136
Dec	1,110,384	97,793	351,892	57,504	106,445	208,976	98,304	97,928	84,529	7,013
1943										
Jan	1,512,086	129,694	465,762	170,839	150,800	175,422	105,744	135,525	121,091	57,209
Feb	1,507,016	92,948	653,300	36,202	151,558	226,209	129,042	96,281	87,629	33,847
Mar	1,598,839	115,856	643,541	120,417	101,854	232,272	86,284	120,695	144,487	33,433
Apr	2,325,879	134,950	1,263,565	95,371	116,694	310,053	133,080	101,501	118,822	51,843
May	2,300,773	257,067	1,063,742	83,073	119,839	292,622	114,362	88,828	171,514	109,726
Jun	2,464,733	565,483	897,590	60,473	120,689	351,025	77,187	101,258	206,388	84,640

Source: Contl Div, ASF, *Statistical Review, World War II*, pp. 131–32.

Appendix F

Appendix F-1—Authorized Levels of

Class I, II, III, and IV Days of Supply [a]

Area [b]	Class I [c]		Class II		Class III		Class IV	
	1942	1943	1942	1943	1942	1943	1942	1943
United Kingdom............................	60	60	60	60	60	45	60	45
Iceland...................................	120	90	120	90	180	90	120	90
North Africa..............................	(d)	45	(d)	45	(d)	45	(d)	45
Central Africa............................	e 120	e 120	120	120	120	120	120	120
Middle East (including Persian Gulf)............	120	g 120	120	g 120	120	g 120	120	g 120
Southwest Pacific..........................	h 120	90	90	90	90	90	90	90
South Pacific..............................	e h 120	e 90	90	90	90	90	90	90
Hawaiian Department........................	e 90	e 75	90	75	90	75	90	75
China....................................	j 450	180	j 450	180	j 450	180	j 450	180
Burma and India..........................	180	180	180	150	180	180	180	150
Bermuda..................................	e 45	e 40	45	30	45	45	45	30
Panama, Guatemala, Ecuador, Peru, and the Galapagos Islands............................	45	30	45	30	45	30	45	30
Puerto Rican Sector [l]......................	e 45	e 30	45	30	45	30	45	30
Trinidad Sector [m].........................	e 60	e 45	60	45	60	45	60	45
Brazil....................................	(d)	e 60	(d)	60	(d)	60	(d)	60
Ascension Island...........................	e 150	e 120	90	120	150	120	150	120
Alaska...................................	180	180	180	180	180	180	180	180
Western Canada............................	(d)	60	(d)	60	(d)	60	(d)	60
Eastern Canada [n].........................	(d)	300	(d)	300	(d)	300	(d)	300
Newfoundland.............................	90	90	90	90	150	90	90	90
Greenland................................	180	120	180	120	180	120	180	120

[a] Minimum levels. Maximum levels determined as follows: *Class I* (subsistence and forage) Maximum levels defined as minimum level plus quantity (operating level or working stock), determined by port commander in collaboration with overseas commander, required for normal consumption until expected arrival of next supply shipment. July 1943 instructions stipulated that operating levels might be authorized by the War Department when shipping or tactical situation demanded. Exceptions similarly permitted for icebound stations. *Class II* (items of supply issued under Allowance Tables) Maximum level defined as minimum level plus 90 days of supply. July 1942 instructions permitted higher operating levels, with approval of CG SOS, when shipping or tactical situation demanded. July 1943 instructions stipulated War Department approval in such cases, and made provisions for icebound stations as under Class I. *Class III* (fuels and lubricants) Maximum level determined by port commander and overseas commander, as for Class I, with reference to shipping or tactical situation and also to available storage capacity in the theater. *Class IV* (items of supply not issued under Allowance Tables, other than Classes I, III, and V, such as construction equipment) Requirements to be based on mission and tactical situation; no provision for operating level. July 1943 instructions emphasized the importance of early submission of requirements to permit procurement and stockpiling. *Class V* (ammunition) as released by the War Department.

[b] For the area in general, but see notes g, h, and j.

[c] Emergency rations included in Class I level of supply.

SUPPLY

OVERSEAS SUPPLIES: JULY 1942 AND JULY 1943 [a]

Class V Months of Supply (M/S) or Units of Fire (U/F) [a]

Aircraft		Antiaircraft		Artillery		Mortar		Small Arms		Area [b]
M/S	M/S	U/F	M/S	U/F	M/S	U/F	M/S	U/F	M/S	
1942	1943	1942	1943	1942	1943	1942	1943	1942	1943	
5	8	10	4	10	4	10	4	10	4	United Kingdom
5	5	18	4	12	4	12	4	12	4	Iceland
(d)	8	(d)	6	(d)	4	(d)	4	(d)	4	North Africa
5	5	f 5	4	f 5	4	f 5	4	f 5	4	Central Africa
5	8	f 5	2	f 5	2	f 5	2	f 5	2	Middle East (including Persian Gulf)
5	8	20	4	10	4	15	6	10	i 6	Southwest Pacific
5	8	20	6	10	2	15	6	10	4	South Pacific
5	8	20	(d)	10	(d)	15	(d)	10	(d)	Hawaiian Department
5	8	15	6	10	6	10	6	10	k 6	China
5	8	15	6	10	6	10	6	10	6	Burma and India
5	5	10	3	5	2	5	2	5	2	Bermuda
5	5	20	6	10	3	5½	2	5½	3	Panama, Guatemala, Ecuador, Peru, and the Galapagos Islands
5	5	10	6	5	3	5	2	5	3	Puerto Rican Sector l
5	5	10	6	5	3	5	2	5	3	Trinidad Sector m
(d)	(d)	(d)	(d)	(d)	(d)	(d)	(d)	(d)	(d)	Brazil
5	5	15	(d)	10	(d)	10	(d)	10	(d)	Ascension Island
5	5	15	(d)	10	(d)	15	(d)	10	(d)	Alaska
(d)	(d)	(d)	(d)	(d)	(d)	(d)	(d)	(d)	(d)	Western Canada
(d)	(d)	(d)	1	(d)	1	(d)	1	(d)	1	Eastern Canada n
5	5	10	3	5	2	5	2	5	2	Newfoundland
5	5	10	3	10	3	10	3	10	3	Greenland

d Not indicated in source document.

e Overseas commanders were authorized to recommend to the War Department the number of civilians for whom an equivalent level of supply should be established.

f For SOS troops only. Movement orders would establish the levels for all other troops within this area.

g Zone of interior maintenance levels only in the Persian Gulf Command.

h 90 days of supply only for Australia and New Zealand.

i 8 months of supply for the 30-caliber rifle only.

j 270 days of supply only in China, the balance to be held in reserve in India.

k 10 months of supply for the 30-caliber rifle only.

l Puerto Rico, Antigua, Cuba, Jamaica, St. Croix, St. Thomas.

m Trinidad, Aruba, British Guiana, Dutch Guiana (Surinam), Curaçao, and St. Lucia.

n Fort Chimo, Frobisher Bay, Goose Bay, and Mingan (all weather stations).

Source: (1) WD ltr, 19 Jul 42, sub: Levels of Sup . . . , AG 400 (7-11-42). (2) WD ltr, 10 Jul 43, same sub, AG 400 (7-8-43).

APPENDIX F-2—AMMUNITION: THE UNIT OF FIRE

(In

Ammunition Type	Unit of Fire (Per Weapon)*	Day of Supply (Per Weapon)	Infantry Division (T/O 7, 1 Aug 42)		Infantry Regiment (T/O 7-11, 1 Apr 42)		Armored Division (T/O 17, 1 Mar 42)	
			Unit of Fire	30 Days of Supply	Unit of Fire	30 Days of Supply	Unit of Fire	30 Days of Supply
Carbine, .30-caliber	60	2	389, 520	389, 520	67, 680	67, 680	274, 620	274, 620
.30-caliber	—	—	1, 783, 200	2, 446, 900	520, 200	714, 600	4, 813, 080	10, 049, 500
Rifle	150	5	934, 950	934, 950	270, 450	270, 450	400, 000	375, 000
Automatic rifle (BAR)	750	45	425, 250	765, 450	141, 750	255, 150	0	0
Light machine gun	2, 000	150	150, 000	337, 500	36, 000	81, 000	4, 126, 080	9, 121, 500
Heavy machine gun	3, 000	150	273, 000	409, 000	72, 000	108, 000	287, 000	553, 000
.45-caliber	—	—	26, 002	68, 232	1, 491	2, 556	580, 420	1, 727, 040
Pistol	7	0.4	7, 602	13, 032	1, 491	2, 556	42, 210	48, 240
Submachine gun	200	20	18, 400	55, 200	0	0	538, 210	1, 678, 800
.50-caliber machine gun	—	—	127, 800	426, 000	9, 000	30, 000	203, 720	1, 986, 000
Ground	900	100	127, 800	426, 000	9, 000	30, 000	203, 720	1, 986, 000
Antiaircraft	1, 200	90	0	0	0	0	0	0
2.36-inch rocket	—	—	0	0	0	0	0	0
60-mm. mortar	100	7.5	8, 100	18, 225	2, 700	6, 075	11, 400	12, 825
81-mm. mortar	100	5	5, 700	8, 550	1, 800	2, 700	3, 402	4, 050
37-mm. gun	100	10	10, 900	32, 700	2, 400	7, 200	40, 397	129, 300
57-mm. gun	—	—	0	0	0	0	0	0
75-mm. gun	—	—	0	0	0	0	11, 600	69, 600
75-mm. howitzer	300	40	5, 400	21, 600	1, 800	7, 200	12, 600	50, 400
90-mm. gun	125	10	0	0	0	0	0	0
105-mm. howitzer	225	30	9, 450	37, 800	450	1, 800	12, 150	48, 600
155-mm. howitzer	150	20	1, 800	7, 200	0	0	0	0

*Does not apply to the armored division or the medium tank battalion. In 1942 the Armored Force had a separate Unit of Fire, adjusted to the number of rounds carried in vehicles of the Armored Force units, and therefore on a per-vehicle rather than a per-weapon basis. The Day of Supply was the same for all elements.

APPENDIX F 737

AND THE MONTH OF SUPPLY, OCTOBER 1942

ROUNDS)

Medium Tank Battalion (T/O 17-25, 1 Mar 42)		Antiaircraft Regiment (Mobile) (T/O 4-11, 1 Apr 42)		Engineer Regiment (General Service) (T/O 5-21, 1 Apr 42)		Unit of Fire (Per Weapon)*	Day of Supply (Per Weapon)	Ammunition Type
Unit of Fire	30 Days of Supply	Unit of Fire	30 Days of Supply	Unit of Fire	30 Days of Supply			
9,000	9,000	16,200	16,200	11,340	11,340	60	2	Carbine, .30-caliber
281,440	285,600	294,600	294,600	176,800	211,800	—	—	.30-caliber
5,440	5,100	294,600	294,600	148,800	148,800	150	5	Rifle
0	0	0	0	0	0	750	45	Automatic rifle (BAR)
276,000	280,500	0	0	28,000	63,000	2,000	150	Light machine gun
0	0	0	0	0	0	3,000	150	Heavy machine gun
42,245	59,868	70	120	665	1,140	—	—	.45-caliber
3,560	4,068	70	120	665	1,140	7	0.4	Pistol
38,685	55,800	0	0	0	0	200	20	Submachine gun
5,250	42,000	81,600	183,600	6,300	21,000	—	—	.50-caliber machine gun
5,250	42,000	0	0	6,300	21,000	900	100	Ground
0	0	81,600	183,600	0	0	1,200	90	Antiaircraft
0	0	0	0	0	0	—	—	2.36-inch rocket
0	0	0	0	0	0	100	7.5	60-mm. mortar
378	450	0	0	0	0	100	5	81-mm. mortar
600	1,200	0	0	0	0	100	10	37-mm. gun
0	0	0	0	0	0	—	—	57-mm. gun
1,350	16,200	0	0	0	0	—	—	75-mm. gun
900	3,600	0	0	0	0	300	40	75-mm. howitzer
0	0	2,000	4,800	0	0	125	40	90-mm. gun
0	0	0	0	0	0	225	30	105-mm. howitzer
0	0	0	0	0	0	150	20	155-mm. howitzer

Source: (1) Armored Force Units of Fire based on FM 101-10, Staff Officers' Field Manual: Organizational, Technical and Logistical Data, 15 June 41, par. 127; Tables of Basic Allowances No. 7, 1 Oct 42, No. 5, 1 Dec 42, and No. 11, 1 Aug 42. (2) Units of Fire for other units, and Days of Supply for all units, are based on data in Misc Shipg folder, Logis File, OCMH, and on the Tables of Organization cited.

APPENDIX F-3—AMMUNITION: THE UNIT OF FIRE

(IN

Ammunition Type	Unit of Fire (Per Weapon)*	Day of Supply (Per Weapon)	Infantry Division (T/O & E 7, 15 Jul 43)		Infantry Regiment (T/O & E 7-11, 15 Jul 43)		Armored Division (T/O & E 17, 15 Sep 43)	
			Unit of Fire	30 Days of Supply	Unit of Fire	30 Days of Supply	Unit of Fire	30 Days of Supply
Carbine, .30-caliber	60	2	315,720	315,720	51,180	51,180	317,160	317,160
.30-caliber	—	—	1,499,950	2,070,050	431,100	593,700	2,589,450	5,358,450
Rifle	150	5	977,700	977,700	286,350	286,350	309,450	309,450
Automatic rifle (BAR)	750	45	182,250	328,050	60,750	109,350	0	0
Light machine gun	2,000	150	160,000	360,000	36,000	90,000	1,986,000	4,468,500
Heavy machine gun	2,000	150	180,000	405,000	48,000	108,000	258,000	580,500
.45-caliber	—	—	29,570	67,884	2,750	3,390	561,470	1,682,844
Pistol	10	0.4	11,570	13,884	2,750	3,300	870	1,044
Submachine gun	200	20	18,000	54,000	0	0	560,600	1,681,800
.50-caliber machine gun	—	—	118,000	647,000	17,500	94,500	339,500	1,833,300
Ground	500	90	118,000	647,000	17,500	95,500	339,500	1,833,300
Antiaircraft	1,200	100	0	0	0	0	0	0
2.36-inch rocket	6	0.25	3,336	4,170	672	840	3,642	4,553
60-mm. mortar	100	7.5	9,000	20,250	2,700	6,075	6,300	14,275
81-mm. mortar	100	5	5,400	8,300	1,800	2,700	4,800	7,200
37-mm. gun	100	10	1,300	3,900	0	0	13,100	39,300
57-mm. gun	100	10	5,700	17,100	1,800	5,400	3,000	9,000
75-mm. gun	100	10	0	0	0	0	16,800	50,400
75-mm. howitzer	300	40	0	0	0	0	5,100	20,400
90-mm. gun	125	10	0	0	0	0	0	0
105-mm. howitzer	200	30	10,800	48,600	1,200	5,400	14,400	64,800
155-mm. howitzer	150	20	1,800	7,200	0	0	0	0

*In 1943 the Unit of Fire was standard for Armored Force and other elements on a per-weapon basis.

and The Day of Supply, October 1943

Rounds)

Medium Tank Battalion (T/O & E 17-25, 15 Sep 43)		Antiaircraft Battalion (Mobile) (T/O & E 44-15, 18 Mar 43)		Engineer Regiment (General Service) (T/O & E 5-21, 1 Apr 42)		Unit of Fire (Per Weapon)*	Day of Supply (Per Weapon)	Ammunition Type
Unit of Fire	30 Days of Supply	Unit of Fire	30 Days of Supply	Unit of Fire	30 Days of Supply			
15,420	15,420	4,620	4,620	11,340	11,340	60	2	Carbine, .30-caliber
377,000	844,500	79,950	79,950	163,000	198,000	—	—	.30-caliber
3,000	3,000	79,950	79,950	135,000	135,000	150	5	Rifle
0	0	0	0	0	0	750	45	Automatic rifle (BAR)
374,000	841,500	0	0	28,000	63,000	2,000	150	Light machine gun
0	0	0	0	0	0	2,000	150	Heavy machine gun
89,830	269,436	22,620	67,824	950	1,140	—	—	.45-caliber
30	36	20	24	950	1,140	10	0.4	Pistol
89,800	269,400	22,600	67,800	0	0	200	20	Submachine gun
42,500	205,500	28,700	99,300	0	0	—	—	.50-caliber machine gun
42,500	205,500	9,500	51,300	0	0	500	90	Ground
0	0	19,200	48,000	0	0	1,200	100	Antiaircraft
210	263	0	0	0	0	6	0.25	2.36-inch rocket
0	0	0	0	0	0	100	7.5	60-mm. mortar
900	1,350	0	0	0	0	100	5	81-mm. mortar
1,700	5,100	0	0	0	0	100	10	37-mm. gun
0	0	0	0	0	0	100	10	57-mm. gun
5,300	15,900	0	0	0	0	100	10	75-mm. gun
0	0	0	0	0	0	300	40	75-mm. howitzer
0	0	2,000	4,800	0	0	125	10	90-mm. gun
1,200	5,400	0	0	0	0	200	30	105-mm. howitzer
0	0	0	0	0	0	150	20	155-mm. howitzer

Source: (1) Days of Supply and Units of Fire for individual weapons cited in FM 101-10, Staff Officers' Field Manual: Organizational, Technical and Logistical Data, 10 Oct 43, par. 322. (2) Days of Supply and Units of Fire for selected units are computed from cited Tables of Organization and Equipment, using the applicable per-weapon Days of Supply and Units of Fire. (3) Tables, similar to those shown here, in ASF Manual M-409, Logistical Planning and Reference Data, Dec 43, contain numerous errors, and therefore have not been used.

Appendix G

SUPPLY RESPONSIBILITIES OF THE PORTS OF EMBARKATION

Port	July 1942	July 1943
Boston..............	Greenland Iceland Newfoundland Several North Atlantic weather stations	Greenland Iceland Newfoundland Several North Atlantic weather stations
Charleston...........	Ascension Island Bermuda (after 1 Sep 42 asgd to Hampton Roads) China India Central Africa	Bahama Islands Central Africa French West Africa and Senegal Middle East (including Persian Gulf SvC)
Hampton Roads.......	Bermuda (after 1 Sep 42) Middle East	Bermuda
New Orleans.........	Latin America Puerto Rican Sector Antigua Jamaica Puerto Rico Trinidad Sector Aruba British Guiana Dutch Guiana Curaçao St. Lucia Trinidad South American Ferry Command Panama	Latin America Antigua Jamaica Puerto Rico Cuba St. Croix St. Thomas Guatemala Ecuador Galapagos Peru Aruba British Guiana Surinam (Dutch Guiana) Curaçao St. Lucia Trinidad Panama Brazil Ascension Island
San Francisco........	Australia Bora Bora New Caledonia Efate Espiritu Santo Fiji New Zealand Tonga Tabu Hawaiian Department Christmas Island Canton Island Fanning Island	Australia South Pacific Aitutaki Bora Bora New Caledonia Efate Espiritu Santo Fiji Solomon Islands New Zealand Tongareva Hawaiian Department Christmas Island Canton Island Fanning Island
Seattle..............	Alaska	Alaska
New York...........	United Kingdom	United Kingdom North Africa (Algeria, Morocco, Tunisia)
Los Angeles..........	Subport under San Francisco; partly supplied Panama	Independent port; supplied China, Burma, & India

Appendix H

SHIPPING LOSSES AND GAINS

APPENDIX H–1—CONSTRUCTION AND LOSSES OF DRY CARGO SHIPS, UNITED STATES, ALLIED, AND NEUTRAL: SEPTEMBER 1939–JUNE 1943★

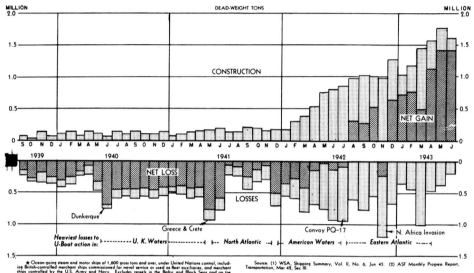

★ Ocean-going steam and motor ships of 1,600 gross tons and over, under United Nations control, including British-controlled merchant ships commissioned for naval service or used as fleet auxiliaries, and merchant ships controlled by the U.S. Army and Navy. Excludes vessels in the Baltic and Black Seas and on the Great Lakes.

Source: (1) WSA, Shipping Summary, Vol. II, No. 6, Jun 45. (2) ASF Monthly Progress Report, Transportation, Mar 43, Sec III.

APPENDIX H–2—CONSTRUCTION AND LOSSES OF TANKERS, UNITED STATES, ALLIED, AND NEUTRAL: FOURTH QUARTER 1939–JUNE 1943★

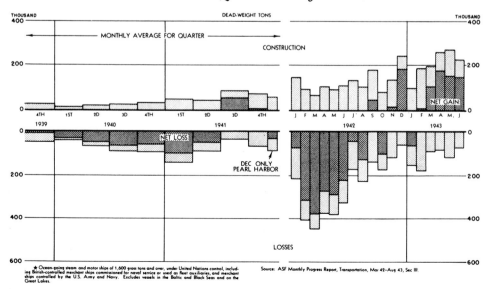

★ Ocean-going steam and motor ships of 1,600 gross tons and over, under United Nations control, including British-controlled merchant ships commissioned for naval service or used as fleet auxiliaries, and merchant ships controlled by the U.S. Army and Navy. Excludes vessels in the Baltic and Black Seas and on the Great Lakes.

Source: ASF Monthly Progress Report, Transportation, Mar 42–Aug 43, Sec III.

Appendix I

GROWTH OF THE SERVICE ESTABLISHMENT: 1942

Branch	31 December 1941		31 December 1942		
	Strength	Percent of Total	Strength	Percent of Total	Percent Increase Over 1941
Total Army Strength......................	1, 686, 403	100. 0	5, 397, 674	100. 0	220
Service Branches............................	443, 213	26. 3	1, 857, 042	34. 4	319
Adjutant General..........................	996	0. 1	4, 418	0. 1	344
Engineers.................................	93, 109	5. 5	333, 209	6. 2	258
Signal....................................	51, 463	3. 0	241, 227	4. 5	369
Medical (incl Army Nurses).................	131, 060	7. 8	469, 981	8. 7	259
Ordnance.................................	35, 518	2. 1	235, 350	4. 4	563
Quartermaster............................	124, 483	7. 4	327, 794	6. 1	163
Chemical.................................	6, 584	0. 4	46, 182	0. 8	601
Military Police............................	0	0. 0	147, 840	2. 7	—
Transportation............................	0	0. 0	51, 041	0. 9	—
Ground Arms (Infantry, Cavalry, Tank Destroyer, Armored, and Field, Coast, and Antiaircraft Artillery).....................................	885, 624	52. 5	1, 937, 917	35. 9	118
Air Corps..................................	275, 889	16. 4	1, 270, 677	23. 5	361
All Others*	81, 677	4. 8	332, 038	6. 2	306

—Inapplicable.

*General officers, General Staff Corps, Inspector General's Department, Military Intelligence Division, USMA professors, warrant and flight officers; plus all WAAC's, Corps of Chaplains, Finance Department, Judge Advocate General's Department, Detached Lists, and miscellaneous personnel.

Source: Whiting, Statistics, Military Personnel sec, 9 Apr 52 draft.

Bibliographical Note
and Guide to Footnotes

Global Logistics and Strategy, like the previous volumes published in the series UNITED STATES ARMY IN WORLD WAR II, is based largely, though far from exclusively, upon records of various agencies of the War Department, most of them at present in the physical custody of the Departmental Records Branch, Adjutant General's Office, Department of the Army (DRB AGO). These records are generally described in *Federal Records of World War II,* Vol. II, Military Agencies, prepared by the General Services Administration, Archives and Records Service, The National Archives (Washington, 1951). The range of records consulted has necessarily been broad, ranging from those of the joint and combined agencies for strategic planning at the top to the lower agencies in the War Department charged with logistical operations. The enormous volume of logistical business in which the War Department was involved is reflected in the bulky and generally amorphous bodies of records of this business that have been preserved. In sifting this mass of records, the authors have been aided to a limited degree by the monographic studies prepared during the war and afterward under the supervision of the Office, Chief of Military History, or other staff agencies, and by the researches of their colleagues on various volumes in UNITED STATES ARMY IN WORLD WAR II, published and unpublished.

Information in the footnote citations of documents and manuscript histories is designed to identify each sufficiently for the needs of researchers having a passing familiarity with Army files. File references have not been given in cases where documents can be readily located in certain master serial files. In this category fall the minutes and papers of the Joint Board (JB), Joint Chiefs of Staff (JCS), Combined Chiefs of Staff (CCS), and other joint and combined committees, the Munitions Assignments Board (MAB) and the Munitions Assignments Committee (Ground) (MAC (G)); certain letters and directives issued by The Adjutant General's Office; general orders and memoranda of various Army headquarters. Messages identified only by CM-IN and CM-OUT numbers with date may be located in the Classified Message Center serial file. In general, file references at present can be located through the Historical Records Section, DRB AGO, and manuscript drafts prepared by Army agencies through the General Reference Section, Office of the Chief of Military History (OCMH). If, as is anticipated, these materials are eventually retired to National Archives, the fundamental arrangement of files will in all probability remain the same.

The files of the various staff agencies of Headquarters, Army Service Forces (ASF), make up the most important single group of records used in preparation of this volume (see *Federal Records,* pp. 252–

302). These files were retired to DRB AGO at various times during and after the war, and the process of indexing and cataloguing them is still far from complete. There is no central ASF file. The file identified in the footnotes as the Hq ASF file consists of a collection of official and personal papers of General Somervell, extremely valuable when used in connection with other materials but seldom providing by itself a complete story of action on any given problem. The Chief of Staff, ASF, file consists largely of stayback copies of Maj. Gen. Wilhelm D. Styer's correspondence and memoranda. The Hq ASF staff conferences fall into a separate group filed serially in DRB AGO.

The files of the various staff divisions under the supervision of Maj. Gen. LeRoy Lutes, wartime Director of Operations, ASF, provide the most important materials for a detailed story of ASF logistical planning and operations. These are described in *Federal Records* under the headings Plans and Operations, Planning Division, Mobilization Division, and Requirements and Stock Control Division, in accordance with the way in which these records are grouped in DRB AGO. Of these, the most important for purposes of this volume are those of the Planning Division, including as they do records of its predecessor organizations, the General Planning Branch and the Strategic Logistics Division. General Lutes' own personal files, identified in the footnotes as Lutes File, have not been retired to DRB AGO but remain in his personal custody. General Lutes kindly granted access to them at various times during the war and afterward. Footnote references to folders in this file follow the arrangement at the time they were consulted. The classification "Misc Notes, Lutes File" covers certain

notes taken by researchers during the war from these files for which no folder reference could be given.

Of the records of the Office of the Director of Materiel, the central files of Maj. Gen. Lucius D. Clay's office (Director of Materiel file) and those of the International Division have been most useful. The International Division (ID) files are the most important source for any study of War Department lend-lease activities. The International Division inherited the files of its predecessor organizations, the Office of the Defense Aid Director, the Defense Aid Division of the Office of the Under Secretary of War (DAD), the Clearance Committee of the Army and Navy Munitions Board (CC ANMB), the Defense Aid Section, G-4 (DAS, G-4) as well as those of the home offices of the various overseas lend-lease missions. The files of the Defense Aid Division and those of the Office of the Defense Aid Director are completely consolidated and form one file identified in the footnotes by the symbol DAD. Each home office for the overseas lend-lease missions maintained its own files and these have been identified separately in the footnotes, for instance, "N African Mis" for the files of the U.S. Military Mission to North Africa. Also among the records of the International Division are the minutes and papers of the Munitions Assignments Committee (Ground) and a virtually complete file of those of the Munitions Assignments Board. Though the minutes of the board have been identified with the standard abbreviation MAB, the serial papers have been listed, as originally designated, by the symbol MBW.

The files of the Distribution Division, ASF, have also been of value, as have those of the Control Division. In addition to studies made of various ASF activities during the war, Control Division files also contain various materials collected as a result of that agency's responsibility during the war for administering the ASF historical program. An additional group of notes taken from various sources by this historical unit of the Control Division during and immediately after the war has fallen into the custody of the authors and where the original sources of these notes have not been identifiable they have been cited as part of the Logistics File, OCMH. These notes will eventually be deposited in the custody of the General Reference Section, OCMH.

As a part of this ASF historical program a number of histories of staff agencies and monographs on various subjects were prepared. Several contain elaborate documentary supplements. Though most of these studies were hastily done and vary greatly in both accuracy and extent of coverage, many have proved useful. The following are particularly worthy of note:

History of the Planning Division, Army Service Forces (2 volumes text and 10 volumes appendixes), prepared by the Planning Division, Office of the Director of Plans and Operations, ASF.

The Determination of Army Requirements (1 volume text and 4 volumes documentary supplement), prepared by Lt. Col. S. M. Frank, Requirements and Stock Control Division, Office of the Director of Plans and Operations, ASF.

History of the Movements Branch, Mobilization Division, Army Service Forces, 20 volumes, prepared by the Movements Branch, Mobilization Division, Office of the Director of Plans and Operations, ASF.

Troop Units Activated by the Army Service Forces for Overseas Use, prepared by the Troop Unit Branch, Mobilization

Division, Office of the Director of Plans and Operations, ASF.

Lend-Lease as of September 30, 1945 (2 volumes text and 10 volumes documentary supplement); History of Reciprocal Aid, 9 May 1941–31 December 1945 (1 volume text and 1 volume documentary supplement); and Civilian Supply: A History of the Civilian Supply Branch, International Division, Army Service Forces, all prepared by the International Division, Office of the Director of Materiel, ASF.

History of Preshipment; History of Supply in the Zone of Interior; and History of Stock Control in the Army Service Forces, all prepared by the Distribution Division, Office of the Director of Supply, ASF.

History of the Control Division, Army Service Forces (1 volume text and 1 volume appendix); and Development of Overseas Supply Policy and Procedures, both prepared by Richard M. Leighton, Control Division, ASF.

Organizational Problems of the ASF, 1942–45 (1 volume text and 4 volumes documentary supplement); and Overseas Movement of the 1st Infantry and 1st Armored Divisions, both prepared by John D. Millett, Control Division, ASF.

Preparations for "Torch," prepared by William Frierson, Control Division, ASF.

Army Service Forces Activities in the Supply of China, Burma, and India; and The United States Supply Echelon in Australia, both prepared by Mrs. Elizabeth Bingham, Control Division, ASF.

Development of the United States Supply Base in Australia, prepared by Mrs. Elizabeth Bingham and Richard M. Leighton, Control Division, ASF.

Movement of U.S. Army Troops and Supplies to the South Pacific Theater of Operations, prepared by Mrs. Jesse Roach, Control Division, ASF.

In addition to these wartime and immediate postwar studies, two more finished monographs by Mrs. Susan Frost Parrish, Logistical Support of the Pacific Campaign: Early Task Force Deployment to the Line of Communications; and Growth of a Pacific Supply Structure, have served as a primary basis for Chapter VII and part of Chapter VI.

Of the records of the various technical services of the ASF, most are too voluminous and of too technical a nature to warrant extensive consultation in a broad study of logistics. The records of the Transportation Corps are an exception, since transportation was the most important single facet òf logistics during World War II. Extensive use has been made of the various collections of Transportation Corps records made by its Historical Branch and identified in the footnotes as OCT HB files. Other material from regular files of the Office of the Chief of Transportation deposited in DRB AGO are identified by the symbol OCT. The OCT HB files contain a number of historical monographs prepared during the war and immediately afterward that have also been quite useful. All these Transportation Corps records and studies are further identified in the "Bibliographical Note" and "Guide to Footnotes" in Chester Wardlow, *The Transportation Corps: Responsibilities, Organization, and Operations* (Washington, 1951), pp. 426–31. Wardlow's published volume and the drafts of the two succeeding volumes of the Transportation Corps history provide extensive information on transportation operations both in the United States and in overseas theaters. A broader view of wartime transportation in the United States, in both its military and civilian aspects, is given in Joseph R. Rose, *American Wartime Transportation* (New York, Thomas Crowell Co., 1953). Some use has also been made of published volumes, special studies, and selected draft chapters of histories of the Quartermaster Corps and the Corps of Engineers.

For the period preceding the War Department reorganization of March 1942, supervision and staff planning of logistical matters rested with the Supply Division of the War Department General Staff, G-4, and with the Office of the Under Secretary of War. Records of the Under Secretary's office deal largely with procurement matters and are fragmentary. (See *Federal Records,* pp. 70–74.) G-4 records, on the other hand, are relatively complete, well arranged and indexed in accordance with the prewar General Staff system of filing by serial numbers. G-4 records for the period following March 1942, filed according to the Dewey decimal system, are of considerably less value since with the reorganization of the War Department, the ASF absorbed most of G-4's functions.

The records of the Adjutant General's Office (*Federal Records,* pp. 63–67), the central office of record for the War Department, are another important group. These records are filed and carefully cross-indexed by subject according to the Dewey decimal system. They are most valuable for the period 1940–41 and the early part of 1942. Afterward a far smaller proportion of records of the various agencies and commands was forwarded to The Adjutant General for central filing. As far as possible, documents in The Adjutant General files have been identified by the folder in which they are actually to be found rather than by the formal classification at the head of the letter, memorandum, or directive.

For matters involving strategy, high policy, and the relation of logistics thereto, main reliance has been placed on the records maintained by the Operations Division, War Department General Staff, and its predecessor, the War Plans Division, and secondarily on those of the Office of the Chief of Staff (WDCSA or OCofS) and of the Secretary of War (SW). Five different groups of the OPD files may be distinguished: (1) the official central file of the War Plans Division, identified by the symbol WPD; (2) the official central file of the Operations Division, identified by the symbol OPD; (3) the WPD and OPD Message Center file; (4) the plans file of the Strategy and Policy Group, OPD, identified by the symbol ABC; (5) the informal policy file of the Executive Office, OPD, identified by the symbol Exec. All these files, with the exception of the Executive Office files (still in the custody of the G-3 division of the General Staff) are located in DRB AGO, though access to them is controlled by G-3. No separate file of the records of the Logistics Group, OPD, exists; some of its papers may be found scattered among the various groups outlined above. Several detailed monographs prepared by the OPD History Unit, OCMH, based on material in these files have been of considerable value. Both the files and the monographs are further described in Ray S. Cline, *Washington Command Post: The Operations Division* (Washington, 1951) and in Maurice Matloff and Edwin M. Snell, *Strategic Planning for Coalition Warfare: 1941–1942* (Washington, 1953). These two works, in themselves, have obviated the necessity for much detailed research on strictly strategic matters. Mark S. Watson, *Chief of Staff: Prewar Plans and Preparations* (Washington, 1950) is similarly important as a source of information for the period preceding Pearl Harbor.

The ABC files contain virtually a complete set of JCS and CCS papers, those of the various subordinate parts of the JCS and CCS organization such as the Joint Staff Planners (JPS) and Combined Staff Planners (CPS), the Joint Strategic Survey Committee (JSSC), and the Joint and Combined Military Transportation Committees (JMTC and CMTC), and records of the major Anglo-American wartime conferences. Except in isolated instances, use of the official files of the joint and combined organizations, in the custody of the JCS, has not been necessary. Some use has been made, however, of the various studies under preparation in the Joint Chiefs Historical Section, notably those on logistical matters prepared by Lt. Col. S. E. Otto, Maj. Edward Katzenbach, 1st Lt. Bernard Weisberger, and the study on amphibious craft prepared by Col. A. T. Mason.

The War Shipping Administration (WSA), operating agency for the Maritime Commission, controlled the allocation and operation of the bulk of the U.S. merchant shipping during World War II. WSA records, under the jurisdiction of the Commerce Department, are at present housed in the Federal Records Center at Lawrence Avenue N.E., Washington, D.C. The segments of these files used most extensively in the preparation of this volume are the letters, papers, and other documents of Lewis Douglas, who was Admiral Land's deputy administrator for the WSA during the period covered. For the work of the Maritime Commission itself, Frederic C. Lane, *Ships for Victory: A History of Shipbuilding Under the U.S. Maritime Commission in World War II* (Baltimore, Md., The Johns Hopkins Press, 1951) is a detailed and important study.

In supplementing the documentary record of wartime decisions, some of the memoir literature has been of great assistance, notably three volumes of Winston S. Churchill's series, THE SECOND WORLD WAR—*Their Finest Hour* (Boston, Houghton Mifflin Company, 1949), *The Grand Alliance* (Boston, Houghton Mifflin Company, 1950), and *The Hinge of Fate* (Boston, Houghton Mifflin Company, 1950)—and Robert E. Sherwood, *Roosevelt and Hopkins: An Intimate History* (New York, Harper & Brothers, 1950). The Manuscript Index to the Hopkins Papers, loaned to the Office of the Chief of Military History by Robert E. Sherwood, has provided additional information on material in Hopkins' papers (located in the Roosevelt Library at Hyde Park) beyond that to be found in the printed biography.

The main reliance for material particularly relating to overseas theaters of operations has been on the theater volumes (or drafts thereof) of the series UNITED STATES ARMY IN WORLD WAR II and on various manuscript histories prepared in the theaters under the wartime history program. Particularly useful have been T. H. Vail Motter, *The Persian Corridor and Aid to Russia* (Washington, 1952), Charles F. Romanus and Riley Sunderland, *The China-Burma-India Theater: Stilwell's Mission to China* (Washington, 1953), and Roland G. Ruppenthal, *Logistical Support of the Armies* (Washington, 1953), the last in the European theater subseries. Another special study in the European theater subseries, Marcel Vigneras, The Rearmament of the French Forces, has been the primary source for the account of French lend-lease in this volume. The first volume of the Western Hemisphere subseries under preparation by Stetson Conn and Byron Fairchild, The Framework of Hemisphere Defense, has been valuable not only for its treatment of development of adjacent Atlantic and Pacific bases but also for that of strategy and high policy in 1940-41.

The various volumes of THE ARMY AIR FORCES IN WORLD WAR II, edited by Wesley Frank Craven and James Lea Cate, have served as the main source of information on Air Forces operations and incidentally on Air Forces logistics. The most recent publication in this series, Volume VI, *Men and Planes* (Chicago, University of Chicago Press, 1955), surveys part of the latter field, and a more detailed treatment of the AAF procurement program is being written for the present series, by Dr. Irving Holley, under the title Buying Air Power: Procurement of Matériel. Similarly, information on naval operations has been largely drawn from the series of volumes written by Samuel Eliot Morison. For naval logistics, the volume by Duncan S. Ballantine, *U.S. Naval Logistics in the Second World War* (Princeton, N.J., Princeton University Press, 1947) is the best summary. Certain of the more detailed studies on this subject prepared as part of the Navy's history program during and after World War II have also been useful, notably Ballantine's Shipping in Naval Logistics: The History of the Naval Transportation Service, Monograph 5 in the series U.S. NAVAL ADMINISTRATION IN WORLD WAR II, and Building the Navy's Bases in World War II: History of the Bureau of Yards and Docks and the Civil Engineer Corps, 1940-1946 (Washington, 1947), prepared by the Bureau of Yards and Docks.

The story of Army procurement will be the subject of a separate volume in this series, Army Procurement and Economic Mobilization, by R. Elberton Smith. Some of the material on production problems and priorities has been drawn from draft chapters of this volume. However, more extensive use has been made of the War Production Board study prepared by the Civilian Production Administration, *Industrial Mobilization for War: Program and Administration* (Washington, 1947), and of various unpublished War Production Board historical monographs. On the subject of production priorities, a special debt is due to Colonel Otto's study, 1942 Production Priorities for 1943, a monograph prepared as part of the JCS historical program.

Information on British problems and the British point of view has been gleaned from records of the combined organizations, from British papers included in U.S. Army records, from Churchill's memoirs, and from published volumes in the British series HISTORY OF THE SECOND WORLD WAR. In the last, there is as yet no study dealing specifically with military logistics, but the histories in the United Kingdom Civil Series have been of inestimable value. Two published works, W. K. Hancock and M. M. Gowing, *British War Economy* (London, His Majesty's Stationery Office, 1949) and M. M. Postan, *British War Production* (London, Her Majesty's Stationery Office, 1952), particularly the former, throw much light on both British and combined economic problems that had to enter into every calculation of the military logisticians. In addition, the British have kindly permitted us to see two of their works as yet unpublished, H. Duncan Hall, North American Supply, in galley proof, and H. Duncan Hall and C. C. Wrigley, Studies of Overseas Supply, in typescript draft, both of which are excellent studies dealing primarily with American supply to Britain as seen from the vantage point of the British themselves. Unfortunately these studies were not available until the manuscript of this book was undergoing final revision and therefore were not used as extensively as they might have been. Footnote references to North American Supply are to the galleys, the form in which the study was used. Another recent publication in the British official series, Capt. S. W. Roskill's, *The War at Sea: 1939–45*, Volume I, *The Defensive* (London, Her Majesty's Stationery

Office, 1954), covering the period 1939–41, also appeared too late to be used to full advantage.

While the present volume contains its share of statistics, it is concerned in the main with broad trends of war activity that can be demonstrated without detailed statistical analysis. Consequently, there has been no need for the kind of systematic study of original raw data that would call into play the skills of the professional statistician. For the most part, standard recent official compilations have been relied upon. The best and most important of these is the collection prepared under the direction of Theodore E. Whiting, of the Office of the Comptroller of the Army, and released in draft form in 1952 for eventual publication in the UNITED STATES ARMY IN WORLD WAR II series. It is cited in this volume as Whiting, Statistics. The sections on procurement and lend-lease have been used most extensively herein. Other major sources include Strength of the Army (STM-30), published by The Adjutant General, Department of the Army; the War Shipping Administration *Shipping Summary; Statistical Review, World War II* (Control Division, ASF, 1946); and *Official Munitions Production of the United States By Months, July 1, 1940–August 31, 1945* (Civilian Production Administration, May 1, 1947). Less generally used sources, cited primarily for detail not shown in the larger compilations, include the Army Service Forces Monthly Progress Reports for the years 1942–44, especially Section 1-A, Procurement, and Section 3, Transportation; the President's *Reports to Congress on Lend-Lease Operations;* Summary Report of Acceptances, Tank-Automotive Materiel, 1940–45 (ASF, Office, Chief of Ordnance, Detroit Engineering-Manufacturing Division, December 1945); and various statistical progress reports prepared in 1941 and 1942 by the

Statistics Branch of the War Department General Staff, by the several supply services, and by Headquarters, Services of Supply. These and other sources less frequently used are cited in footnotes in the text and in notes on sources appended to each statistical table.

Even in the limited kind of statistical analysis attempted in the present volume, certain problems have been encountered against which the reader should be forewarned, particularly the reader who may himself expect to work with the statistics of this period. Even the best and most recently compiled data, which in the case of the major sources cited above reflect years of painstaking research by trained statisticians, cannot pretend to absolute and literal accuracy, and for the historian the choice between conflicting figures not infrequently becomes a question of judgment based on inconclusive, though voluminous, evidence. Part of the difficulty can be laid to the shortcomings of wartime reporting caused by a lack of sufficient trained statisticians to record accurately so huge a volume and variety of activity. Wartime figures were also shaped by the enormous administrative pressure put on lower echelons during the war to "come up with a figure" on short notice, the result being a heavy admixture of what one statistician has called "midnight estimates." But beyond these factors, the historian encounters discrepancies and contradictions in the statistical record arising solely from the sheer complexity of the materials, processes, and events recorded. He finds it difficult, for example, to combine data on merchant ship losses within a given period, since some losses were reported on a notification basis and some on an occurrence basis; in addition, the various kinds of weight and space tonnage used in the data cannot all be converted accurately to a common unit of measure. The multiplicity of types in the weapons of modern war in itself poses innumerable variants of the classic problem of adding together apples and potatoes, and this is further complicated by the intricate processes of design change and modification, which sometimes caused a single item of equipment to migrate through a whole series of reporting categories, repeatedly changing its nomenclature and generating duplicating statistics as it went. For soldiers and troop units the statistical record is equally complex.

The historian is fortunate indeed if the standard official compilations meet his needs, for in them all these problems are concealed behind a solid facade of totals, representing the end products of many more manhours of more highly skilled labor than he can hope to bring to bear on the subject. When the official compilations disagree (as they occasionally do), or when they lack the specific details of item and time coverage that the historian requires, he must either revise his requirements or "go behind the totals" into a morass of case histories of individual items or categories. In the latter instance, he faces the probability that he will be unable to trace back through the entire course of research by which his predecessors arrived at their final figures, and will merely uncover fragmentary data that further complicate his problem. Fortunately, the areas of statistical doubt are only marginal and do not affect the massive facts and trends of war activity that emerge from a study of the synthesized data in readily available secondary sources. In the end, though perhaps agreeing with Mark Twain's views on statistics, the historian will probably find these sources sufficient for his needs, round off the discrepant figures, and leave the last three digits to the statisticians.

List of Abbreviations

AAF	Army Air Forces
ABC	American-British Conversations (Jan–Mar 41)
ABDA (Comd)	Australian-British-Dutch-American (Command)
ACofS	Assistant Chief of Staff
Actg	Acting
Admin	Administration, administrative, administrator
AFHQ	Allied Force Headquarters
AG	Adjutant General
AGF	Army Ground Forces
AGWAR	Adjutant General, War Department
AKA	Cargo ship, attack
Alloc (s)	Allocation (s)
Am	Ammunition
AMMDEL	American Military Mission, Delhi. Designation for American headquarters at New Delhi, India
AMMISCA	American Military Mission to China. Designation for American headquarters at Chungking, China
AMSEG	Cable designation for Cairo messages
AMSIR	American Military Mission, Iran, and its home office in Washington
AMSME	American Military Mission, Middle East
A&N	Army and Navy
ANMB	Army and Navy Munitions Board
ANPB	Army-Navy Petroleum Board
APA	Transport, attack
App. (s)	Appendix (es)
AR	Army Regulations
ASF	Army Service Forces
Asgmt (s)	Assignment (s)
ASN	Assistant Secretary of the Navy
ASP	Army Supply Program
Asst	Assistant
ASW	Assistant Secretary of War
Atchd	Attached
Atchmt (s)	Attachment (s)
Auth	Authority
BCC(L)	BOLERO Combined Committee, London
BCC(W)	BOLERO Combined Committee, Washington
Bd (s)	Board (s)
BMWT	British Ministry of War Transport
Br	British, branch
Bsc	Basic
C ('s)	Chief (s) (in combination)

CBI	China-Burma-India
CC ANMB	Clearance Committee, Army and Navy Munitions Board
CCS	Combined Chiefs of Staff
CDS	China Defense Supplies, Inc.
CG ('s)	Commanding General (s)
Chm	Chairman
CINC	Commander in Chief
CM-IN	Classified message, incoming
CM-OUT	Classified message, outgoing
CMTC	Combined Military Transportation Committee
CNO	Chief of Naval Operations
CO	Commanding Officer
C(s)ofS	Chief (s) of Staff
Com (s)	Committee (s)
Comd (s)	Command (s)
Comdr (s)	Commander (s)
COMINCH	Commander in Chief, U.S. Fleet
Comm	Commission
Conf (s)	Conference (s)
Cong	Congress
Contl	Control
Conv (s)	Conversation (s)
Co-ord	Co-ordination, co-ordinated
Corresp	Correspondence
CPA	Civilian Production Administration
CPOE	Charleston Port of Embarkation
CPRB	Combined Production and Resources Board
CPS	Combined Staff Planners
CSAB	Combined Shipping Adjustment Board
CWS	Chemical Warfare Service
DAD	Defense Aid Division (to 1 Oct 41), Defense Aid Director (1 Oct 41–Mar 42)
DAS	Defense Aid Section, G-4
DCofS	Deputy Chief of Staff
DDAR	Division of Defense Aid Reports
Def (s)	Defense (s)
Deleg	Delegation
Dir (s)	Directive (s), director
Distrib	Distribution
Div (s)	Division (s)
DRB AGO	Departmental Records Branch, Adjutant General's Office
Engr (s)	Engineer (s)
EO	Executive Order
Equip (g)	Equipment (equipping)
Est (d)	Estimate (d)
Estab	Establish, establishment, establishing

ETO	European Theater of Operations
ETOUSA	European Theater of Operations, U.S. Army
Exch	Exchange
Exec	Executive
Exped (s)	Expedition (s), expeditionary
FM	Field Manual
G-1	Personnel division of the War Department General Staff
G-2	Intelligence division of the War Department General Staff
G-3	Operations division of the War Department General Staff
G-4	Supply division of the War Department General Staff
GHQ	General Headquarters
GO	General Orders
Gt Brit	Great Britain
HD	Hawaiian Department
Hist	History, historical
HR	House of Representatives
HRPOE	Hampton Roads Port of Embarkation
ID	International Division, Army Service Forces
Incl (s)	Inclosure (s), inclosed, inclosing
Ind (s)	Indorsement (s)
Info	Information
Instn (s)	Instruction (s)
ISC	International Supply Committee
JAdC	Joint Administrative Committee
JB	Joint Board
JCS	Joint Chiefs of Staff
JMTC	Joint Military Transportation Committee
JPC	Joint Planning Committee
JPS	Joint Staff Planners
JSSC	Joint Strategic Survey Committee
Jt	Joint
JUSSC	Joint U.S. Strategic Committee
KCRC	Kansas City Records Center
LMAB	Munitions Assignments Board, London
Ln	Liaison
Logis	Logistics, logistical
MAB	Munitions Assignments Board, Washington
MAC(A)	Munitions Assignments Committee (Air)
MAC(G)	Munitions Assignments Committee (Ground)
MAC(N)	Munitions Assignments Committee (Navy)
Mat (s)	Material (s)
MBW	Alternate abbreviation for MAB
Mil	Military
MILID	Military Intelligence Division
Min	Minutes
Mis ('s)	Mission (s)

MS	Manuscript
Msg (s)	Message (s)
Mtg	Meeting
Mun	Munitions
Mvmt (s)	Movement (s)
Natl	National
NATOUSA	North African Theater of Operations, U.S. Army
NDAC	Advisory Commission to the Council of National Defense
NYPOE	New York Port of Embarkation
O	Office, officer (in combination)
OCMH	Office of the Chief of Military History
OCT	Office of the Chief of Transportation
OCT HB	Historical Branch, Office of the Chief of Transportation
Off (s)	Office (s), officer (s)
OLLA	Office of Lend-Lease Administration
OPD	Operations Division
Opn (s)	Operation (s)
Ord	Ordnance
Orgn	Organization
Pac	Pacific
Pdn	Production
PL	Public Law
Plng	Planning
PMP	Protective Mobilization Plan
POA	Pacific Ocean Area
POE ('s)	Port (s) of embarkation
Prob (s)	Problem (s)
Proced	Procedure, procedural
Prog (s)	Program (s)
PTO	Pacific Theater of Operations
Pub	Public, publication
Purch	Purchasing
QMC	Quartermaster Corps
QMG	Quartermaster General
RAF	Royal Air Force
Rcd (s)	Record (s)
Regt (s)	Regiment (s)
Reinf (s)	Reinforcement (s), reinforce
Reorgn	Reorganization
Rep (s)	Representative (s)
Reqmt (s)	Requirement (s)
Ret	Retired
Rpt (s)	Report (s)
SAS	Supply Arms and Services
Sec (s)	Section (s)
Secy	Secretary, secretariat

Ser	Serial, series
SFPOE	San Francisco Port of Embarkation
SG	Surgeon General
SGS	Secretary of the General Staff
Shipg	Shipping
Shipt (s)	Shipment (s)
Sig	Signal
Sit	Situation
SN	Secretary of the Navy
SOS	Services of Supply
Sp	Special
Stf	Staff
Sub (s)	Subject (s)
Sup (s)	Supply (supplies)
Suppl	Supplement
Sv (s)	Service (s)
SW	Secretary of War
SWPA	Southwest Pacific Area
TAG	The Adjutant General
TC	Transportation Corps
TIG	The Inspector General
Tng	Training
TQMG	The Quartermaster General
Tr (s)	Troop (s)
Trans	Transport, transportation
Trf (s)	Transfer (s)
Trfd	Transferred
U.K.	United Kingdom
UKCC	United Kingdom Commercial Corporation
Ult	Ultimate
USAFBI	U.S. Army Forces in the British Isles
USAFFE	U.S. Army Forces in the Far East
USAFIA	U.S. Army Forces in Australia
USAFIME	U.S. Army Forces in the Middle East
USAFISPA	U.S. Army Forces in the South Pacific Area
USFOR	U.S. Forces in London
USN	Under Secretary of the Navy
USNR	U.S. Naval Reserve
USW	Under Secretary of War
Vic	Victory
WD	War Department
WDCSA	Chief of Staff, U.S. Army
WDGS	War Department General Staff
WPB	War Production Board
WPD	War Plans Division
WSA	War Shipping Administration

Glossary of Code Names

ANAKIM	Plan for recapture of Burma.
ANFA	Sometimes used by OPD officers as a code name for the Casablanca Conference of January 1943.
ARCADIA	U.S.-British conference in Washington, December 1941–January 1942.
BOBCAT	Bora Bora.
BOLERO	Build-up of U.S. forces and supplies in United Kingdom for cross-Channel attack.
BRIMSTONE	Plan for capture of Sardinia.
ELKTON	MacArthur's 12 February 1943 plan for recapture of Rabaul.
FREEDOM	Cable designation for Algiers messages.
GRAY	Plan for capture and occupation of the Azores.
GYMNAST	Early plan for invasion of North Africa, referring to either the American plan for landing at Casablanca or the British plan for landing farther eastward on the Mediterranean coast. (See SUPER-GYMNAST.)
HUSKY	Allied invasion of Sicily in July 1943.
INDIGO	Plan for movement of troops to Iceland.
MAGNET	Movement of first U.S. forces to Northern Ireland.
POPPY	New Caledonia.
RAINBOW	Various plans prepared between 1939 and 1941 to meet Axis aggression.
ROUNDUP	Plan for major U.S.-British attack across the Channel in 1943.
SLEDGEHAMMER	Plan for limited cross-Channel attack in 1942.
SUPER-GYMNAST	Plan for Anglo-American invasion of French North Africa, combining U.S. and British plans and often used interchangeably with GYMNAST.
SYMBOL	Casablanca Conference, 14–23 January 1943.
TORCH	Allied invasion of North and Northwest Africa, November 1942.
TRIDENT	International conference at Washington, 12–25 May 1943.
"X"	Australia.
X-RAY	Chinese Army in India.
YOKE	American sponsored Chinese force in Yunnan Province.

UNITED STATES ARMY IN WORLD WAR II

The following volumes have been published:

Index

British War Cabinet, 38, 678, 692
British War Office, 494
Brooke, Field Marshal Sir Alan, 521, 685
Brown, Douglas, 111
Buckley, Maj. Gen. J., 642
Budge, Alexander, 163n
Buna, 389, 407, 408
Buna-Gona operations, 687
Bundy, Lt. Col. Charles W., 132
Bureau of Supplies and Accounts, USN, 656
Burma, 53, 397, 525, 541, 544, 545, 695
    British offensive in, 539, 541, 542, 543, 547, 687,
       693, 696, 700, 701
    Japanese successes in, 527, 528, 536, 549
    planning for offensive in, 532–33, 535, 537–38,
       539–40, 541, 542–43, 547, 662, 667, 668,
       685, 686, 687, 720
    supply route to China through, 527, 533, 540,
       545–46, 547
Burma Road, 86–87, 108, 108n, 109, 526, 527, 546
Burns, Maj. Gen. James H., 78, 95, 95n, 97n, 109,
    131n, 253, 562n
Bushire, 566, 568, 575

Cairns, 168
Cairo, 574
Calcutta, 528, 535
Calvert, 444
Campion, Brigadier Donald, 249n, 254n, 271
Canada, 254, 273
Canadian Munitions Assignments Committee, 254–
    55
Canary Islands, 75, 152, 669
Canton Island, 124, 150, 151, 161, 178, 186, 187,
    334
Cape Gloucester, 695
Cape of Good Hope, 16, 47, 54, 120, 579, 715, 716
Cape Verde Islands, 74, 152, 669
Cargo, 369, 370, 371
    discharge, 182–83, 218, 398, 402, 449–52, 583
    loading, 157, 181–82, 218, 236, 404, 441–45, 616
Cargo manifest, 331, 332
Cargo shipping. *See* Shipping, cargo.
Carib Plan, 66
Caribbean, 143, 715
Caribbean Defense Command, 641
Caroline Islands, 56, 667
Casablanca, 153, 386n, 387, 417, 419, 420, 423,
    468. *See also* GYMNAST; TORCH; Western
    Task Force.
Casablanca Conference, 285, 414, 474, 484, 514,
    515, 521, 542, 582, 587, 588, 591, 680, 682,
    684, 687, 690, 693
    strategic planning at, 601–02, 661, 666, 685–86,
       687, 692, 694, 696, 699, 714, 719
Caucasus, 662
Cavalry Division, 6th, 71n

Cavalry Regiment, 101st, 308
CCS. *See* Combined Chiefs of Staff.
CCS 5/2, 353n
CCS 19/1, 253n, 278n, 285n
CCS 39/1, 207n, 357n
CCS 50, 272n
CCS 50/2, 273, 273n, 274, 275, 276, 278, 279, 280,
    284, 285, 291, 296n, 500, 500n, 504, 512n,
    520n, 560n
CCS 50/3, 275n
CCS 57/2, 175n, 491n
CCS 58/2, 362n
CCS 68/1, 498n
CCS 69, 363n
CCS 72, 364n
CCS 72/1, 365n
CCS 78, 380n
CCS 82, 279n
CCS 82/1, 279n
CCS 82/2, 281n
CCS 84, 365n
CCS 87, 373n, 457n
CCS 87/4, 458n
CCS 91, 280, 280n
CCS 94, 387n, 392n, 483n
CCS 100/1, 457n
CCS 102, 280n
CCS 102/1, 281n
CCS 103, 421n, 422
CCS 103/10, 466n
CCS 104/3, 539n
CCS 105, 484n
CCS 109/1, 577n
CCS 110, 640n
CCS 110/4, 640n
CCS 115, 499n
CCS 116/1/D, 667n
CCS 117, 281n
CCS 135, 662n
CCS 135/1, 664n, 675n, 684n
CCS 135/2, 663n, 672n
CCS 143, 587n
CCS 145, 685n
CCS 153, 668n
CCS 153/1, 667n, 668n
CCS 157, 521n
CCS 160, 675n, 676n, 681n
CCS 161, 672n, 683n, 684n
CCS 161/1, 672n, 684n
CCS 162, 587n, 588n, 681n
CCS 162/1, 588n, 591n, 681n
CCS 162/2, 583n, 589n
CCS 164, 685n
CCS 164/1, 685n
CCS 167, 684n
CCS 168, 668n, 695n
CCS 170/2, 543n, 588n, 589n, 668n, 676n
CCS 171/2/D, 673n

☆ U.S. GOVERNMENT PRINTING OFFICE: 1995   382–686

PIN : 038755–000